THE
LITTLE OXFORD
DICTIONARY

THE
LITTLE OXFORD
DICTIONARY
OF CURRENT ENGLISH

First edited by
George Ostler

SIXTH EDITION
EDITED BY JULIA SWANNELL

OXFORD
AT THE CLARENDON PRESS

Oxford University Press, Walton Street, Oxford OX2 6DP

Oxford New York Toronto
Delhi Bombay Calcutta Madras Karachi
Petaling Jaya Singapore Hong Kong Tokyo
Nairobi Dar es Salaam Cape Town
Melbourne Auckland

and associated companies in
Berlin Ibadan

Oxford is a trade mark of Oxford University Press

First edition 1930
Second edition 1937   Third edition 1941
Fourth edition 1969   Fifth edition 1980
Sixth edition 1986

Reprinted 1986, 1987 (twice), 1988 (twice)

British Library Cataloguing in Publication Data
The little Oxford dictionary of current English—6th ed.
I. English Language—Dictionaries
I. Ostler, George.   II. Swannell, Julia
423 PE1625

ISBN 0-19-861188-9

Library of Congress Cataloging in Publication Data
The Little Oxford dictionary of current English.
1. English language—Dictionaries.
I. Ostler, George, d. 1919.   II. Swannell, Julia.
III. Oxford University Press.
PE1628.L54 1986   423   86-8365
ISBN 0-19-861188-9

Printed in Great Britain by
Richard Clay (The Chaucer Press) Ltd.
Bungay, Suffolk

Contents

Preface to the Sixth Edition

The Little Oxford Dictionary was first compiled by Mr George Ostler, who was for many years a member of the composing and reading staff of the Oxford University Press. After his death in 1929, Mrs Jessie Coulson, a member of the editorial staff of the *Oxford English Dictionary*, took the work over and saw it through the final stages to its publication in 1930. Mrs Coulson prepared the subsequent three editions of the dictionary and remained its editor until I succeeded her to prepare the fifth edition.

In preparing this sixth edition I have again been helped in large measure by members of the Oxford English Dictionary department, and I am particularly grateful to Dr Robert Allen, editor of the *Concise* and *Pocket Oxford Dictionaries*, for his friendly guidance and support. The work of setting and producing the dictionary on the Oxford Text System could not have been achieved without the tireless assistance of Mr G. Roberts of OUP's Information Systems Division, and I am deeply indebted also to Mrs A. Whear for her help in this task. Dr D.J. Thompson, Dr M.A. Cooper, Mr M.A. Mabe, and Mrs J.H. Harker read the proofs and to them also I extend my thanks.

August 1985   J.C.S

Introduction

throw /θrəʊ/ 1 *v.* (*past* **threw**; *p.p.* **thrown**) release (thing) after imparting motion, propel through space, send forth or dismiss esp. with some violence; compel to in specified condition; project (rays, light, etc.); cast (shadow); bring to the ground; *colloq.* disconcert; put (clothes etc.) carelessly or hastily *on* or *off* etc.; cause (dice) to fall on table etc., obtain (specified number) thus; cause to pass or extend suddenly to another state or position; move (switch or lever) to on position; shape (pottery) on wheel; have (fit, tantrum, etc.); *colloq.* give (a party). 2 *n.* act of throwing; distance a missile is or may be thrown; being thrown in wrestling.

3 **throw away** part with as unwanted, lose by neglect, waste, fail to make use of; **throw-away** (thing) to be thrown away after (one) use, deliberately under-emphasized; **throw back** (usu. in *pass.*) compel to rely *on*; **throw-back** reversion to ancestral character, instance of this; **throw in** add as makeweight, interpose (word, remark), throw (football) from edge of pitch where it has gone out of play; **throw off** discard, contrive to get rid of, write or utter in offhand manner; **throw out** put out forcibly or suddenly, reject, confuse or distract; **throw over** desert, abandon; **throw up** abandon, resign from, vomit, erect, bring to notice.

1. The headword appears in bold: **throw**.

2. A guide to pronunciation is given, when necessary, in IPA (see page xi): /θrəʊ/.

3. The part of speech is given in italics: *v.* (and later *n.*). It is preceded by a bold number (**1, 2**) if the headword exists as more than one part of speech.

4. Inflexional forms such as irregularly-formed past tenses are given in bold: (*past* **threw**; *p.p.* **thrown**). Irregularly-formed present participles (for example **lying** at the entry for **lie**[1]) and comparatives and superlatives of adjectives and adverbs (for example **better** and **best** at the entry for **good**) are given in the same way.

5. Labels to indicate that a word or sense is restricted to a particular level of formality or to a particular subject are given in italics: *colloq.*, *sl.*, *Law*, *Crick.*, etc.

6. Round brackets () are used to enclose words that are explanatory or optional; for example 'release (thing) after imparting motion', or 'project (rays, light, etc.)', indicating the type of noun that often appears as the object of this verb; '**throw-away** (thing) to be thrown away', indicating that 'throw-away' can be an adjective meaning 'to be thrown away' *or* a noun meaning 'a thing to be thrown away'.

7. Words such as prepositions or adverbs which are commonly used with the headword in any particular sense are given in italic. For example 'put (clothes etc.) hastily *on* or *off* etc.' indicates that the usual construction would be 'to throw one's clothes on' or 'to throw one's clothes off' or any similar phrase.

8. Phrases and combinations involving the headword are listed together in strict alphabetical order, followed by any derivatives of obvious meaning, which are included without definition:

> **hole 1** *n.* cavity in solid body; opening
> through or sunken place on surface;
> burrow; *colloq.* small or gloomy place;
> *sl.* awkward situation; cavity into
> which ball must be got in some games,
> *Golf* section of course from tee to hole.
> **2** *v.* make hole(s) in; hit golf-ball into
> hole. **3 hole-and-corner** underhand;
> **hole up** *sl.* hide oneself. **4 holey** *a.*

9. When a word normally written with a lower-case initial letter also has a sense in which it is written with a capital letter, or vice versa, this is indicated by the word being repeated with the capital (or lower case) initial letter:

> **Apostle** /ə'pɒs(ə)l/ *n.* any of twelve
> sent forth by Christ to preach gospel;
> **apostle** leader of reform.

10. Headwords which are foreign and not fully naturalized in English are given in bold italics, and an indication of the language or origin is given in square brackets at the end of the entry:

> **métier** /'metjeɪ/ *n.* one's trade or profession; one's forte. [F]

11. Space has been saved by not listing obvious and regularly-formed derivatives such as agent-nouns in *-er* (for example *player*), nouns in *-ness* (for example *kindness*), or adverbs in *-ly* (for example *bravely*).

The Appendix of Some Points of English Usage

On page 665 there is a new Appendix which aims to give guidance on some matters of pronunciation, spelling, and usage, etc. It is a selective list, concentrating on errors which cause particular offence and areas where confusion is particularly common. Many of the items contained in it are also marked in the main text by □ and a direction to the page in the Appendix where the relevant information can be found.

Pronunciation

Guidance on pronunciation follows the system of the International Phonetic Alphabet (IPA). Only the pronunciation standard in southern England is given. Where more than one permissible pronunciation exists, constraints of space have often compelled the omission of any but the preferred form.

International Phonetic Alphabet

Consonants

The following consonants have their usual English sound-values: b, d, f, h, k, l, m, n, p, r, s, t, v, w, z.

g as in go	ʃ as in ship	tʃ as in chin
ŋ as in sing	ʒ as in vision	dʒ as in jam
θ as in thin	j as in yet	
ð as in then	x (Scots etc.) as in loch	

Vowels

æ as in fat	ʊ as in book	eɪ as in fate
ɑ: as in cart	u: as in boot	eə(r) as in fare
e as in met	ɜ: as in fur	ɪə(r) as in fear
ɪ as in bit	ə as in ago, taker	ɔɪ as in boil
i: as in meet	aɪ as in bite	ʊə(r) as in tour
ɒ as in got	aʊ as in brow	əʊ as in goat
ɔ: as in port	aɪə(r) as in fire	
ʌ as in dug	aʊə(r) as in sour	

Stress is indicated by ' preceding the relevant syllable.

˜ over a vowel indicates nasalization as in French *ancien régime* (ãsɪæ̃ reɪ'ʒim)

Abbreviations used in the Dictionary

Abbreviations that are in general use appear in the dictionary itself.

a.	adjective	compar.	comparative
abbr(s).	abbreviation(s)	conj.	conjunction
abs.	absolute	Crick.	cricket
adj(s).	adjective(s)	derog.	derogatory
adv(s).	adverb(s)	dial.	dialect
Aeron.	aeronautics	Eccl.	ecclesiastical
Afr.	African	Econ.	economics
Alg.	algebra	Electr.	electricity
Amer.	America(n)	emphat.	emphatic
Anat.	anatomy	Engl.	English
ant.	antiquities	erron.	erroneous
approx.	approximately	esp.	especially
arch.	archaic	euphem.	euphemistic
Archit.	architecture	Eur.	Europe(an)
Astrol.	astrology	exc.	except
Astron.	astronomy	expr.	expressing
attrib.	attributive(ly)	F	French
Aus.	Australian	fem.	feminine
aux.	auxiliary	fig.	figurative
Bibl.	biblical	Footb.	football
Biol.	biology	freq.	frequently
Bot.	botany	fut.	future
c.	century	G	German
C.Amer.	Central America(n)	Geog.	geography
		Geol.	geology
Can.	Canadian	Geom.	geometry
cc.	centuries	Gk	Greek
Ch.	Church	Gmc	Germanic
Chem.	chemistry	Gram.	grammar
Cinemat.	cinematography	Her.	heraldry
collect.	collective(ly)	Hist.	history
colloq.	colloquial	imper.	imperative
comb.	combination	impers.	impersonal
Commerc.	commercial	Ind.	Indian

inf.	infinitive	poet.	poetical
int.	interjection	Polit.	political
interrog.	interrogative	pop.	popularly, not technically
intr.	intransitive		
Ir.	Irish	poss.	possessive (case)
iron.	ironical	p.p.	past participle
It.	Italian	pr.	pronounced
joc.	jocular	pred.	predicative
L	Latin	pref.	prefix
Math.	mathematics	prep.	preposition
Mech.	mechanics	pres.	present (tense)
Med.	medicine	Print.	printing
Metaphys.	metaphysics	pron(s).	pronoun(s)
Meteor.	meteorology	Psych.	psychology
Mil.	military	refl.	reflexive
Mus.	music	rel.	relative
Myth.	mythology	Rom.	Roman
n.	noun	Sc.	Scottish
Naut.	nautical	sing.	singular
neg.	negative	sl.	slang
ns.	nouns	Sp.	Spanish
obj.	objective (case)	St. Exch.	Stock Exchange
occas.	occasionally	subj.	subjective (case)
opp.	opposed to	superl.	superlative
orig.	originally	Theatr.	theatre
P	proprietary term (see below)	Theol.	theology
		trans.	transitive
Parl.	parliament(ary)	transf.	transferred
partic.	(esp. present) participle	univ.	university
		usu.	usually
pass.	passive	v.	verb
pers.	person(al)	vbl.	verbal
Philos.	philosophical	vbs.	verbs
Phon.	phonetics	v.i.	verb intransitive
Photog.	photography	v.t.	verb transitive
Phys.	physics	vulg.	vulgar
Physiol.	physiology	Zool.	zoology
pl.	plural		

Note on proprietary terms

This dictionary includes some words which are, or are asserted to be, proprietary names or trade marks. Their inclusion does not imply that they have acquired for legal purposes a non-proprietary or general significance, nor is any other judgement implied concerning their legal status. In cases where the editor has some evidence that a word is used as a proprietary name or trade mark this is indicated by the letter **P**, but no judgement concerning the legal status of such words is made or implied thereby.

A

a, an, /ə, ən; *emphat.* eɪ, æn/ *a.* one, some, any, to or for each.

A *abbr.* ampere(s).

AA *abbr.* anti-aircraft; Automobile Association; Alcoholics Anonymous.

aback /ə'bæk/ *adv.* backwards, behind; **taken aback** disconcerted, surprised.

abacus /'æbəkəs/ *n. (pl.* **-cuses**) frame with wires along which beads are slid for calculating.

abaft /ə'bɑːft/ **1** *adv. Naut.* in or towards stern of ship. **2** *prep.* behind.

abandon /ə'bænd(ə)n/ **1** *v.t.* give up, forsake. **2** *n.* reckless freedom.

abandoned *a.* forsaken; profligate.

abandonment *n.* reckless freedom.

abase /ə'beɪs/ *v.t.* humiliate; degrade. **abasement** *n.*

abashed /ə'bæʃt/ *a.* embarrassed; disconcerted.

abate /ə'beɪt/ *v.* make or become less; diminish. **abatement** *n.*

abattoir /'æbətwɑː(r)/ *n.* slaughterhouse.

abbess /'æbes/ *n.* female head of abbey of nuns.

abbey /'æbɪ/ *n.* building occupied by community of monks or nuns; such community; church or house that was formerly abbey.

abbot /'æbət/ *n.* head of abbey of monks.

abbreviate /ə'briːvɪeɪt/ *v.t.* shorten. **abbreviation** *n.*

ABC /eɪbiː'siː/ *n.* alphabet; rudiments of subject; alphabetical guide.

abdicate /'æbdɪkeɪt/ *v.* renounce or resign from (throne etc.); renounce throne. **abdication** *n.*

abdomen /'æbdəmən/ *n.* belly; hinder part of insect etc. **abdominal** /-'dɒm-/ *a.*

abduct /æb'dʌkt/ *v.t.* carry off (person) illegally by force or fraud. **abduction** *n.*; **abductor** *n.*

aberrant /æ'berənt/ *a.* showing aberration. **aberrance** *n.*

aberration /æbə'reɪʃ(ə)n/ *n.* departure from normal type or accepted standard; deviation from biological type; distortion.

abet /ə'bet/ *v.t.* encourage or assist (offender or offence). **abetter**, (in *Law*) **abettor**, *n.*

abeyance /ə'beɪəns/ *n.* temporary disuse; suspension.

abhor /əb'hɔː(r)/ *v.t.* regard with disgust and hatred.

abhorrence /əb'hɒrəns/ *n.* disgust, hatred.

abhorrent *a.* disgusting *to.*

abide /ə'baɪd/ *v.* (*past & p.p.* **abode** or **abided**) tolerate; *arch.* remain, continue. **abide by** act upon, remain faithful to.

abiding *a.* permanent.

ability /ə'bɪlɪtɪ/ *n.* sufficient power or being able (*to do*); cleverness; talent.

abject /'æbdʒekt/ *a.* degraded; craven. **abjection** *n.*

abjure /əb'dʒʊə(r)/ *v.t.* renounce on oath. **abjuration** *n.*

ablaze /ə'bleɪz/ *pred.a.* on fire; glittering; excited.

able /'eɪb(ə)l/ *a.* having power (*to do*); talented. **able-bodied** healthy, fit; **able rating, seaman,** one fit for all duties. **ably** *adv.*

ablution /ə'bluːʃ(ə)n/ *n.* usu. in *pl.* ceremonial washing of hands etc.; *colloq.* washing onself, place for this.

ably: see **able.**

abnegate /'æbnɪgeɪt/ *v.t.* give up, renounce. **abnegation** *n.*

abnormal /æb'nɔːm(ə)l/ *a.* exceptional; deviating from its type. **abnormality** *n.*

aboard /ə'bɔːd/ *adv. & prep.* on board.

abode[1] *n. arch.* dwelling-place.

abode[2] *past & p.p.* of **abide.**

abolish /ə'bɒlɪʃ/ *v.t.* end existence of. **abolition** /æbə'lɪʃ(ə)n/ *n.*

abolitionist /æbə'lɪʃənɪst/ *n.* person who favours abolition (esp. of capital punishment).

A-bomb /'eɪbɒm/ *n.* atomic bomb.

abominable /ə'bɒmɪnəb(ə)l/ *a.* detestable, loathsome. **Abominable Snowman** yeti.

abominate /ə'bɒmɪneɪt/ *v.t.* detest, loathe.

abomination /əbɒmɪ'neɪʃ(ə)n/ *n.*

loathing or disgust; object etc. deserving this.

aboriginal /æbə'rɪdʒɪn(ə)l/ **1** a. indigenous; of the Australian Aborigines. **2** n. aboriginal inhabitant, esp. (**Aboriginal**) of Australia.

aborigines /æbə'rɪdʒɪniːz/ n.pl. aboriginal inhabitants, esp. (**Aborigines**) of Australia. □ See page 666.

abort /ə'bɔːt/ v. cause or undergo abortion; (cause to) remain undeveloped; bring or come to premature end.

abortion /ə'bɔːʃ(ə)n/ n. natural or (esp.) induced premature expulsion of foetus, esp. in first 28 weeks of pregnancy; stunted or misshapen creature. **abortionist** n.

abortive /ə'bɔːtɪv/ a. producing abortion; unsuccessful.

abound /ə'baʊnd/ v.i. be plentiful; be rich in; teem with.

about /ə'baʊt/ **1** prep. pertaining to; in connection with; on subject of; surrounding; somewhere near; here and there. **2** adv. approximately; here and there; on the move, in action; all around; facing in opposite direction. **3 about turn** turn made so as to face in opposite direction, reversal of policy etc.; **be about to** intend to (do something).

above /ə'bʌv/ **1** prep. over, higher than; more than; of higher rank, importance, etc. than; out of reach of, too good for. **2** adv. at or to higher point; overhead; in addition; further back in book etc. **3 above-board** without concealment.

abracadabra /æbrəkə'dæbrə/ n. magic formula, spell; gibberish.

abrade /ə'breɪd/ v.t. scrape or wear away by rubbing.

abrasion /ə'breɪʒ(ə)n/ n. rubbing or scraping away; area of damage made thus.

abrasive /ə'breɪsɪv/ **1** a. capable of rubbing or grinding down; harsh and offensive in manner. **2** n. abrasive substance.

abreast /ə'brest/ adv. side by side and facing same way. **abreast of** up to date with.

abridge /ə'brɪdʒ/ v.t. condense, shorten. **abridgement** n.

abroad /ə'brɔːd/ adv. in or to a foreign country; at large, over a wide area.

abrogate /'æbrəgeɪt/ v.t. repeal, cancel. **abrogation** n.

abrupt /ə'brʌpt/ a. sudden, hasty; disjointed; steep.

abscess /'æbsɪs/ n. swollen area of body in which pus gathers.

abscond /æb'skɒnd/ v.i. go away secretly; flee from law.

abseil /'æbseɪl/ **1** n. descent of rockface by using doubled rope fixed at higher point. **2** v.i. make abseil.

absence /'æbsəns/ n. being away; nonexistence or lack of. **absence of mind** inattentiveness.

absent 1 /'æbsənt/ a. not present, not existing. **2** /æb'sent/ v.refl. **absent oneself** go or keep away. **3 absent-minded** forgetful, inattentive.

absentee /æbsən'tiː/ n. person not present, esp. at work or on his property.

absenteeism /æbsən'tiːɪz(ə)m/ n. practice of absenting oneself from work esp. illicitly.

absinthe /'æbsɪnθ/ n. liqueur orig. flavoured with wormwood.

absolute /'æbsəluːt/ a. complete, perfect; unrestricted; independent; despotic; not relative; out of (ordinary) grammatical relation. **absolute majority** one over all rivals combined; **absolute temperature** one measured from absolute zero; **absolute zero** lowest possible temperature (-273˚C).

absolutely adv. completely, without restrictions; colloq. quite so, yes.

absolution /æbsə'luːʃ(ə)n/ n. formal forgiveness of sins.

absolutism /'æbsəluːtɪz(ə)m/ n. principle of government with unlimited powers. **absolutist** n. & a.

absolve /əb'zɒlv/ v.t. set or pronounce free of blame or obligation.

absorb /əb'sɔːb/ v.t. swallow up; assimilate; suck in; deal with easily, reduce intensity of; engross attention or interest of.

absorbent /əb'sɔːbənt/ a. having tendency to absorb. **absorbency** n.

absorption /əb'sɔːpʃ(ə)n/ n. absorbing, being absorbed. **absorptive** a.

abstain /əb'steɪn/ v.i. refrain, esp. from alcohol; decline to use one's vote.

abstemious /æb'stiːmɪəs/ a. sparing or moderate, esp. in eating and drinking.

abstention /əb'stenʃ(ə)n/ n. abstaining, esp. not using one's vote.

abstinence /'æbstɪnəns/ n. abstaining from an indulgence, esp. food or alcohol. **abstinent** a.

abstract 1 /'æbstrækt/ a. to do with or existing in theory rather than practice, not concrete; (of painting etc.) not representational. **2** /əb'strækt/ v.t. remove; summarize. **3** /'æbstrækt/ n. summary; abstract idea or painting etc. **4 abstraction** n.

abstracted a. inattentive.

abstruse /æb'stru:s/ a. hard to understand; profound.

absurd /əb'sɜ:d/ a. wildly inappropriate; ridiculous. **absurdity** n.

abundance /ə'bʌnd(ə)ns/ n. quantity more than enough; plenty; wealth.

abundant a. plentiful; rich.

abuse 1 /ə'bju:z/ v.t. make bad use of; maltreat; attack verbally. **2** /ə'bju:s/ n. misuse; corrupt practice; offensive language.

abusive /ə'bju:sɪv/ a. using insulting language; insulting.

abut /ə'bʌt/ v. adjoin, border *on*; touch or lean *on* or *against*.

abysmal /ə'bɪzm(ə)l/ a. very bad.

abyss /ə'bɪs/ n. bottomless or deep chasm.

AC abbr. alternating current.

a/c abbr. account.

acacia /ə'keɪʃə/ n. tree with yellow or white flowers.

academic /ækə'demɪk/ **1** a. scholarly; to do with learning; not of practical relevance. **2** n. member of scholarly institution. **3 academically** adv.

academician /əkædə'mɪʃ(ə)n/ n. member of an Academy.

academy /ə'kædəmɪ/ n. place of study; place of special training; Sc. secondary school; **Academy** society for cultivating art and learning etc.

acanthus /ə'kænθəs/ n. herbaceous plant with prickly leaves.

ACAS abbr. Advisory, Conciliation, and Arbitration Service.

accede /æk'si:d/ v.i. take office; come *to* throne; join party; assent *to*.

accelerate /ək'seləreɪt/ v. make or become quicker; (cause to) happen earlier. **acceleration** n.

accelerator /ək'seləreɪtə(r)/ n. device for increasing speed, esp. pedal that controls speed of motor vehicle; *Phys.* apparatus for producing fast charged particles.

accent 1 /'æksənt/ n. prominence given to syllable by stress or pitch; local or national mode of pronunciation; mark indicating stress, vowel quality, etc.; emphasis. **2** /æk'sent/ v.t. pronounce with accent; write accents on; emphasize.

accentuate /æk'sentjʊeɪt/ v.t. emphasize, make prominent. **accentuation** n.

accept /ək'sept/ v. consent to receive; answer affirmatively (invitation etc.); regard with favour; receive as valid or suitable. **acceptance** n.

acceptable /ək'septəb(ə)l/ a. worth accepting; welcome; tolerable. **acceptability** n.

access /'ækses/ **1** n. means of admission, approach; attack, outburst, esp. *of* emotion. **2** v.t. obtain (data) from computer etc.

accessible /ək'sesɪb(ə)l/ a. able to be reached or obtained or understood. **accessibility** n.

accession /æk'seʃ(ə)n/ n. acceding esp. *to* throne; thing added.

accessory /æk'sesərɪ/ **1** n. additional or extra thing, (esp. in *pl.*) thing serving as accompaniment; person who helps in or is privy *to* illegal act. **2** a. additional, extra.

accidence /'æksɪd(ə)ns/ n. part of grammar dealing with inflexions.

accident /'æksɪd(ə)nt/ n. event without apparent cause; unexpected event; unintentional act; unfortunate esp. harmful event.

accidental /æksɪ'dent(ə)l/ **1** a. happening or done by accident. **2** n. *Mus.* sharp, flat, or natural attached to single note and not in key signature.

acclaim /ə'kleɪm/ **1** v.t. welcome loudly; hail. **2** n. shout of applause, welcome, etc.

acclamation /æklə'meɪʃ(ə)n/ n. loud and eager assent.

acclimatize /ə'klaɪmətaɪz/ v. accustom or become accustomed to new climate or conditions. **acclimatization** n.

acclivity /ə'klɪvɪtɪ/ n. upward slope.

accolade /'ækəleɪd/ n. bestowal of praise; sign at bestowal of knighthood.

accommodate /əˈkɒmədeɪt/ v.t. provide lodging for; do favour to; supply with; adapt, harmonize, reconcile.

accommodating a. obliging.

accommodation /əkɒməˈdeɪʃ(ə)n/ n. lodging; adaptation, adjustment; convenient arrangement. **accommodation address** one used on letters to person without permanent address.

accompaniment /əˈkʌmpənɪmənt/ n. instrumental or orchestral part supporting singer(s) or solo instrument etc.; accompanying thing.

accompanist /əˈkʌmpənɪst/ n. Mus. person who plays accompaniment.

accompany /əˈkʌmpənɪ/ v.t. go with, escort, attend; be done or found with; supplement; Mus. play accompaniment for.

accomplice /əˈkʌmplɪs/ n. partner in crime.

accomplish /əˈkʌmplɪʃ/ v.t. perform, carry out; succeed in doing.

accomplished a. clever; skilled.

accomplishment n. skill; socially useful ability; completion; thing achieved.

accord /əˈkɔːd/ 1 v. be consistent with; grant, give. 2 n. harmony; consent. 3 **of one's own accord** without being requested.

accordance /əˈkɔːd(ə)ns/ n. harmony, agreement. **accordant** a.

according adv. **according as** in proportion as; **according to** in manner consistent with, as stated by.

accordingly adv. as the (stated) circumstances suggest; therefore.

accordion /əˈkɔːdɪən/ n. portable musical instrument with bellows, metal reeds, and keyboard.

accost /əˈkɒst/ v.t. approach and speak to; (of prostitute) solicit.

account /əˈkaʊnt/ 1 n. statement of money etc. received and expended; business relationship esp. with bank or firm granting credit; narration; explanation; importance; reckoning. 2 v. regard as. 3 **account for** give reckoning of, answer for, explain; **on account** to be paid for later, in part payment; **on account of** because of.

accountable a. responsible; explicable. **accountability** n.

accountant /əˈkaʊnt(ə)nt/ n. person who keeps or inspects accounts. **accountancy** n.

accoutrements /əˈkuːtrəmənts/ n.pl. equipment, trappings.

accredit /əˈkredɪt/ v.t. attribute (to); credit (with); send (ambassador etc.) with credentials to person etc.; gain belief or influence for.

accredited a. holding credentials.

accretion /əˈkriːʃ(ə)n/ n. growth by accumulation or organic enlargement; the resulting whole; (adhesion of) extraneous matter added.

accrue /əˈkruː/ v.i. come as natural increase or advantage, esp. financial.

accumulate /əˈkjuːmjʊleɪt/ v. heap up, bring together; get more and more of; produce or acquire thus; become numerous, go on increasing. **accumulation** n.; **accumulative** a.

accumulator /əˈkjuːmjʊleɪtə(r)/ n. rechargeable electric cell; storage register in computer.

accurate /ˈækjʊrət/ a. precise, exact, correct. **accuracy** n.

accursed /əˈkɜːsɪd/ a. lying under a curse; colloq. detestable, annoying.

accusative /əˈkjuːzətɪv/ Gram. 1 n. case expressing object of action. 2 a. of or in accusative.

accuse /əˈkjuːz/ v.t. indict, charge; lay blame on. **accusation** /ækjʊˈzeɪʃən/ n.; **accusatory** /əˈkjuːzətərɪ/ a.

accustom /əˈkʌstəm/ v.t. make used to.

accustomed a. used to; customary.

ace n. playing-card with single spot; person who excels at something; Tennis service that opponent cannot return.

acerbic /əˈsɜːbɪk/ a. harsh and sharp, esp. of speech, temper, etc. **acerbity** n.

acetate /ˈæsɪteɪt/ n. compound of acetic acid, esp. cellulose acetate used for textile fibre etc.

acetic /əˈsiːtɪk/ a. of vinegar. **acetic acid** essential ingredient of vinegar.

acetone /ˈæsɪtəʊn/ n. colourless volatile solvent of organic compounds.

acetylene /əˈsetɪliːn/ n. colourless gas burning with bright flame.

ache /eɪk/ 1 n. continuous or prolonged pain or longing. 2 v.i. suffer ache.

achieve /əˈtʃiːv/ v.t. reach or attain by effort; accomplish, perform. **achievement** n.

Achilles /əˈkɪliːz/ *n.* **Achilles' heel** vulnerable point; **Achilles' tendon** tendon attaching calf muscles to heel.

achromatic /ækrəʊˈmætɪk/ *a.* free from colour; transmitting light without separating it into constituent colours. **achromatically** *adv.*

achy /ˈeɪkɪ/ *a.* suffering aches.

acid /ˈæsɪd/ **1** *n. Chem.* any of a class of substances that neutralize alkalis, and of which most contain hydrogen and are sour; *sl.* drug LSD. **2** *a.* sour; biting, severe. **3 acid drop** sharp-tasting boiled sweet; **acid rain** rain containing acid formed from industrial waste in atmosphere; **acid test** severe or conclusive test. **4 acidic** /-ˈsɪd-/*a.*; **acidify** /-ˈsɪd-/ *v.t.*; **acidity** /-ˈsɪd-/ *n.*

acidulate /əˈsɪdjʊleɪt/ *v.t.* make acidulous.

acidulous /əˈsɪdjʊləs/ *a.* somewhat acid.

acknowledge /əkˈnɒlɪdʒ/ *v.t.* agree to truth of; admit; report receipt of (letter etc.); express appreciation of (service etc.); show that one has noticed.

acknowledgement *n.* acknowledging; thing given or done in return for service etc.

acme /ˈækmɪ/ *n.* highest point.

acne /ˈæknɪ/ *n.* skin eruption with red pimples esp. on face.

acolyte /ˈækəlaɪt/ *n.* person assisting priest in service etc.; assistant.

aconite /ˈækənaɪt/ *n.* poisonous plant with yellow or blue flowers.

acorn /ˈeɪkɔːn/ *n.* fruit of oak.

acoustic /əˈkuːstɪk/ *a.* of sound or sense of hearing; (of guitar etc.) not electric.

acoustics *n.pl.* acoustical properties (of room etc.); (as *sing.*) science of sound. **acoustical** *a.*; **acoustically** *adv.*

acquaint /əˈkweɪnt/ *v.t.* make aware or familiar. **be acquainted with** know.

acquaintance /əˈkweɪnt(ə)ns/ *n.* being acquainted (with); person one knows slightly. **acquaintanceship** *n.*

acquiesce /ækwɪˈes/ *v.i.* agree, esp. tacitly; not object. **acquiescence** *n.*; **acquiescent** *a.*

acquire /əˈkwaɪə(r)/ *v.t.* gain, come to have. **acquirement** *n.*

acquisition /ækwɪˈzɪʃ(ə)n/ *n.* (esp. useful) thing acquired.

acquisitive /əˈkwɪzɪtɪv/ *a.* keen to acquire things.

acquit /əˈkwɪt/ *v.t.* declare not guilty, clear of blame etc. **acquit oneself** perform, conduct oneself.

acquittal /əˈkwɪt(ə)l/ *n.* deliverance from charge by verdict etc.

acre /ˈeɪkə(r)/ *n.* measure of land, 4840 sq. yards, 0.405 ha.; piece of land, field.

acreage /ˈeɪkərɪdʒ/ *n.* number of acres.

acrid /ˈækrɪd/ *a.* bitterly pungent; bitter in temper etc. **acridity** /-ˈkrɪd-/*n.*

acrimonious /ækrɪˈməʊnɪəs/ *a.* bitter in manner or temper. **acrimony** /ˈækrɪmənɪ/.

acrobat /ˈækrəbæt/ *n.* performer of acrobatics. **acrobatic** *a.*

acrobatics /ækrəˈbætɪks/ *n.pl.* spectacular gymnastic feats.

acronym /ˈækrənɪm/ *n.* word made from initial letters of other words.

acropolis /əˈkrɒpəlɪs/ *n.* citadel of elevated part of ancient Greek city, esp. Athens.

across /əˈkrɒs/ **1** *prep.* from side to side of; to or on other side of; forming a cross with. **2** *adv.* from side to side; to or on other side. **3 across the board** applying to all.

acrostic /əˈkrɒstɪk/ *n.* poem etc. in which first or first and last letters of lines form word(s).

acrylic /əˈkrɪlɪk/ **1** *a.* of material made with synthetic substance derived from acrylic acid. **2** *n.* acrylic fibre or paint etc. **3 acrylic acid** colourless organic acid.

act 1 *n.* thing done, deed; process of doing; performance; pretence; item in variety etc. performance; main division of play; decree of legislative body. **2** *v.* perform functions or actions, behave; be actor; play part of; serve *as*.

actinism /ˈæktɪnɪz(ə)m/ *n.* property of short-wave radiation that produces chemical changes, as in photography. **actinic** /æk'tɪnɪk/ *a.*

action /ˈækʃ(ə)n/ *n.* process of doing or performing; exertion of energy or influence; thing done; series of events in drama; battle; mechanism of instrument; mode or style of movement of horse or player etc.; legal process.

action replay immediate repeat of section of broadcast sports event.

actionable *a.* providing grounds for legal action.

activate /ˈæktɪveɪt/ *v.t.* make active; make radioactive. **activation** *n.*

active /ˈæktɪv/ *a.* consisting in or marked by action; energetic, diligent; working, operative. **active voice** *Gram.* all forms of verbs attributing action of verb to person etc. whence it proceeds.

activism /ˈæktɪvɪz(ə)m/ *n.* policy of vigorous action in politics etc. **activist** *n.*

activity /ækˈtɪvɪtɪ/ *n.* being active; sphere or kind of operation.

actor /ˈæktə(r)/ *n.* performer in play or film etc. **actress** *n.*

actual /ˈæktʃʊəl/ *a.* existing, real; present, current. **actuality** /-ˈæl-/ *n.*

actually *adv.* in actual fact, really.

actuary /ˈæktʃʊərɪ/ *n.* person who calculates insurance risks and premiums. **actuarial** /-ˈeər-/ *a.*

actuate /ˈæktʃʊeɪt/ *v.t.* communicate motion to; cause to function or act. **actuation** *n.*

acuity /əˈkjuːɪtɪ/ *n.* acuteness.

acumen /ˈækjʊmen/ *n.* keen perception, insight.

acupuncture /ˈækjʊpʌŋktʃə(r)/ *n.* pricking of body tissues with needles as medical treatment.

acute /əˈkjuːt/ *a.* keen, penetrating; clever, perceptive; (of disease) coming sharply to crisis, not chronic; (of difficulty etc.) serious, critical; (of angle) less than right angle. **acute accent** accent (´) over vowels.

ad *n. colloq.* advertisement.

AD *abbr.* of the Christian era (*Anno Domini*).

adage /ˈædɪdʒ/ *n.* proverb, maxim.

adagio /əˈdɑːʒɪəʊ/ *Mus.* 1 *adv.* in slow time. 2 *n.* (*pl.* **-ios**) passage to be played thus.

adamant /ˈædəmənt/ *a.* stubbornly resolute.

Adam's apple /ˈædəm/ cartilaginous projection at front of neck.

adapt /əˈdæpt/ *v.t.* fit, adjust; make suitable; modify, alter. **adaptation** *n.*

adaptable /əˈdæptəb(ə)l/*a.* able to be adapted; able to adapt oneself to new surroundings etc. **adaptability** *n.*

adaptor /əˈdæptə(r)/ *n.* device for making things compatible; *Electr.* device for connecting several plugs to one socket.

add *v.* join as increase or supplement; unite numbers to get their total; say further. **add up** find sum of, amount *to.*

addendum /əˈdendəm/ *n.* (*pl.* **-da**) thing to be added; in *pl.* appendix to book etc.

adder /ˈædə(r)/ *n.* small venomous snake.

addict /ˈædɪkt/ *n.* person addicted to drug etc.; enthusiastic devotee.

addicted /əˈdɪktɪd/ *a.* given over habitually *to* (drug etc.); devoted *to.*

addiction /əˈdɪkʃ(ə)n/ *n.* condition of being addicted.

addictive /əˈdɪktɪv/ *a.* causing addiction.

addition /əˈdɪʃ(ə)n/ *n.* adding; thing added. **in addition** as something added (*to*).

additional /əˈdɪʃən(ə)l/ *a.* added, extra.

additive /ˈædɪtɪv/ *n.* substance added to another to impart specific qualities.

addle /ˈæd(ə)l/ *v.t.* muddle, confuse.

addled /ˈæd(ə)ld/ *a.* (of egg) rotten, producing no chick; muddled, confused.

address /əˈdres/ 1 *n.* place where person lives or firm etc. is situated; particulars of this esp. for postal purposes; speech delivered to an audience. 2 *v.t.* write postal directions on (envelope etc.); direct in speech or writing; speak or write to; apply (*oneself*).

addressee /ædreˈsiː/ *n.* person to whom letter etc. is addressed.

adduce /əˈdjuːs/ *v.t.* cite as proof or instance. **adducible** *a.*

adenoids /ˈædɪnɔɪds/ *n.pl.* enlarged tissue at back of nose, often hindering breathing.

adept /ˈædept/ 1 *a.* thoroughly proficient. 2 *n.* adept person.

adequate /ˈædɪkwət/ *a.* satisfactory in quantity or quality (*to* need). **adequacy** *n.*

adhere /ədˈhɪə(r)/ *v.i.* stick fast; give support or allegiance *to.* **adherence** *n.*; **adherent** *n.* & *a.*

adhesion /ədˈhiːʒ(ə)n/ *n.* adhering, sticking.

adhesive /əd'hiːsɪv/ **1** *a*. sticking, sticky. **2** *n*. adhesive substance.

ad hoc /æd ˈhɒk/ for this purpose. [L]

adieu /əˈdjuː/ *int*. & *n*. (*pl*. **adieus**) goodbye.

ad infinitum /æd ɪnfɪˈnaɪtəm/ for ever. [L]

adipose /ˈædɪpəʊz/ *a*. of fat, fatty. **adiposity** /-ˈpɒs-/ *n*.

adjacent /əˈdʒeɪsənt/ *a*. lying near; next (*to*). **adjacency** *n*.

adjective /ˈædʒɪktɪv/ *n*. word indicating attribute, added to noun to describe thing etc. **adjectival** /-ˈtaɪv-/ *a*.

adjoin /əˈdʒɔɪn/ *v.t*. be next to and joined with.

adjourn /əˈdʒɜːn/ *v*. postpone, break off; suspend proceedings; move *to* another place. **adjournment** *n*.

adjudge /əˈdʒʌdʒ/ *v*. pronounce judgement on; pronounce or award judicially. **adjudgement** *n*.

adjudicate /əˈdʒuːdɪkeɪt/ *v*. act as judge and give decision; adjudge. **adjudication** *n*.; **adjudicator** *n*.

adjunct /ˈædʒʌŋkt/ *n*. thing subordinate or incidental to another.

adjure /əˈdʒʊə(r)/ *v.t*. charge or request solemnly or earnestly. **adjuration** *n*.

adjust /əˈdʒʌst/ *v*. arrange, put in order; regulate; harmonize; adapt. **adjustment** *n*.

adjutant /ˈædʒʊt(ə)nt/ *n*. army officer assisting in administrative duties.

ad lib /æd ˈlɪb/ to desired extent; *colloq*. improvise(d).

administer /ədˈmɪnɪstə(r)/ *v.t*. manage (affairs etc.); formally give out; apply, give.

administrate /ədˈmɪnɪstreɪt/ *v*. act as administrator (of).

administration /ədmɪnɪˈstreɪʃ(ə)n/ *n*. administering; esp. of public affairs; the Government.

administrative /ədˈmɪnɪstrətɪv/ *a*. of management of affairs.

administrator /ədˈmɪnɪstreɪtə(r)/ *n*. person who manages affairs of organization, institution, etc.

admirable /ˈædmərəb(ə)l/ *a*. worthy of admiration; excellent.

admiral /ˈædmər(ə)l/ *n*. commander-in-chief of navy; naval officer commanding fleet or squadron. **red, white, admiral,** kinds of butterfly.

Admiralty /ˈædmərəltɪ/ *n*. (*also* **Admiralty Board**) department formerly administering Royal Navy.

admire /ədˈmaɪə(r)/ *v.t*. regard with approval, respect, or satisfaction; express admiration of. **admiration** *n*.

admirer *n*. woman's suitor; devotee of able or famous person.

admissible /ədˈmɪsɪb(ə)l/ *a*. worthy of being accepted or considered. **admissibility** *n*.

admission /ədˈmɪʃ(ə)n/ *n*. acknowledgement (*of* error etc.); admitting, being admitted.

admit /ədˈmɪt/ *v*. recognize as true; acknowledge, confess *to*; let in, allow entrance of; have room for. **admit of** allow as possible. **admittance** *n*.

admittedly /ədˈmɪtɪdlɪ/ *adv*. as acknowledged fact.

admixture /ædˈmɪkstʃə(r)/ *n*. thing added, esp. minor ingredient; adding of this.

admonish /ədˈmɒnɪʃ/ *v.t*. reprove; urge, warn, remind.

admonition /ædməˈnɪʃ(ə)n/ *n*. reproof; warning. **admonitory** /-ˈmɒn-/ *a*.

ad nauseam /æd ˈnɔːzɪæm/ to sickening extent. [L]

ado /əˈduː/ *n*. fuss; difficulty.

adobe /əˈdəʊbɪ or əˈdəʊb/ *n*. unburnt sun-dried brick.

adolescent /ædəˈlesənt/ **1** *a*. between childhood and adulthood. **2** *n*. adolescent person. **3 adolescence** *n*.

adopt /əˈdɒpt/ *v.t*. take into relationship, esp. as one's own child; take over; accept; take up, choose. **adoption** *n*.

adoptive /əˈdɒptɪv/ *a*. due to adoption.

adorable /əˈdɔːrəb(ə)l/ *a*. worthy of love; *colloq*. charming, delightful.

adore /əˈdɔː(r)/ *v.t*. regard with deep respect and affection; worship; *colloq*. like very much. **adoration** *n*.

adorn /əˈdɔːn/ *v.t*. add beauty to, be ornament to; furnish with ornaments. **adornment** *n*.

adrenal /əˈdriːn(ə)l/ *a*. close to kidneys. **adrenal gland** each of two ductless glands above the kidneys.

adrenalin /əˈdrenəlɪn/ *n*. hormone secreted by adrenal glands, stimulating circulation and muscular activity.

adrift /ə'drɪft/ *adv.* & *pred.a.* drifting; at mercy of circumstances; *colloq.* unfastened.

adroit /ə'drɔɪt/ *a.* dextrous, skilful.

adulation /ædjʊ'leɪʃ(ə)n/ *n.* obsequious flattery. **adulatory** *a.*

adult /'ædʌlt/ 1 *a.* grown up, mature. 2 *n.* adult person. 3 **adulthood** *n.*

adulterate /ə'dʌltəreɪt/ *v.t.* debase (esp. food) by admixture of other substances. **adulteration** *n.*

adultery /ə'dʌltərɪ/ *n.* voluntary sexual intercourse of married person other than with spouse. **adulterer** *n.*; **adulteress** *n.*; **adulterous** *a.*

adumbrate /'ædʌmbreɪt/ *v.t.* indicate faintly; represent in outline; foreshadow. **adumbration** *n.*

advance /əd'vɑːns/ 1 *v.* come or go forward; progress; put forward; help on; make (claim etc.); bring (event) to earlier date; lend (money); raise (price). 2 *n.* going forward; progress; loan; payment beforehand; in *pl.* amorous approaches; rise in price. 3 *a.* done etc. beforehand. 4 **in advance** ahead, beforehand. 5 **advancement** *n.*

advanced *a.* ahead of times, others, etc.; far on in progress. **advanced level** higher level in GCE examination.

advantage /əd'vɑːntɪdʒ/ 1 *n.* favourable circumstance; superiority; *Tennis* next point won after deuce. 2 *v.t.* be advantage to; help, profit. 3 **take advantage of** use or exploit for personal benefit. 4 **advantageous** /-'teɪdʒ-/ *a.*

Advent /'ædvent/ *n.* season before Christmas; coming of Christ; **advent** important arrival.

Adventist *n.* member of sect believing in imminent second coming of Christ.

adventitious /ædven'tɪʃəs/ *a.* accidental, casual.

adventure /əd'ventʃə(r)/ 1 *n.* unusual and exciting experience; daring enterprise. 2 *v.i.* dare, venture.

adventurer *n.* person who seeks adventures; person ready to take risks for personal gain. **adventuress** *n.*

adventurous /əd'ventʃərəs/ *a.* venturesome, enterprising.

adverb /'ædvɜːb/ *n.* word expressing manner or degree or circumstance etc. and used to modify adjective or verb or other adverb. **adverbial** *a.*

adversary /'ædvəsərɪ/ *n.* opponent; enemy. **adversarial** /-'seərɪ(ə)l/ *a.*

adverse /'ædvɜːs/ *a.* unfavourable; harmful.

adversity /əd'vɜːsɪtɪ/ *n.* trouble; misfortune.

advert¹ /'ædvɜːt/ *n.* *colloq.* advertisement.

advert² /æd'vɜːt/ *v.i.* refer or allude *to.*

advertise /'ædvətaɪz/ *v.* proclaim merits of, esp. to encourage sales; make generally or publicly known; ask *for* by notice in newspaper etc. **advertisement** /əd'vɜːtɪsmənt/ *n.*

advice /əd'vaɪs/ *n.* opinion given as to action; information; notice of transaction.

advisable /əd'vaɪzəb(ə)l/ *a.* to be recommended; expedient. **advisability** *n.*

advise /əd'vaɪz/ *v.* give advice (to); recommend; inform.

advisedly /əd'vaɪzɪdlɪ/ *adv.* deliberately.

adviser /əd'vaɪzə(r)/ *n.* person who advises, esp. officially.

advisory /əd'vaɪzərɪ/ *a.* giving advice.

advocacy /'ædvəkəsɪ/ *n.* pleading in support *of*; advocate's function.

advocate 1 /'ædvəkət/ *n.* person who speaks in favour of policy etc.; person who pleads for another, esp. in law courts. 2 /'ædvəkeɪt/ *v.t.* support or plead for (policy etc.).

adze /ædz/ *n.* kind of axe with arched blade at right angles to handle.

aegis /'iːdʒɪs/ *n.* (*pl.* **-ises**) protection; sponsorship.

aeolian /iː'əʊlɪən/ *a.* wind-borne. **aeolian harp** stringed instrument producing musical sounds on exposure to wind.

aeon /'iːɒn/ *n.* long or indefinite period of time; an age.

aerate /'eəreɪt/ *v.t.* charge with carbon dioxide; expose to action of air. **aeration** *n.*

aerial /'eərɪəl/ 1 *n.* wire or rod transmitting or receiving radio waves. 2 *a.* from the air; existing in the air; like air.

aerie var. of **eyrie.**

aero- in comb. of air or aircraft.

aerobatics /eərə'bætɪks/ *n.pl.* feats of expert and spectacular flying.

aerobics /eə'rəʊbɪks/ *n.pl.* vigorous exercises designed to increase oxygen intake.

aerodrome /ˈeərədrəʊm/ n. airfield.

aerodynamics /ˈeərəʊdaɪˈnæmɪks/ n.pl. usu. treated as sing. dynamics of solid bodies moving through air. **aerodynamic** a.

aerofoil /ˈeərəfɔɪl/ n. aircraft wing, fin, or tailplane, designed to give lift in flight.

aeronautics /eərəʊˈnɔːtɪks/ n.pl. usu. treated as sing. science or practice of aerial navigation. **aeronautical** a.

aeroplane /ˈeərəpleɪn/ n. mechanically driven heavier-than-air aircraft with wings.

aerosol /ˈeərəsɒl/ n. system of minute particles suspended in gas; device for producing fine spray of substance packed under pressure.

aerospace /ˈeərəʊspeɪs/ n. technology of aviation in earth's atmosphere and outer space.

aesthete /ˈiːsθiːt/ n. appreciator of beauty in art etc.

aesthetic /iːsˈθetɪk/ a. concerned with or capable of appreciation of beauty. **aestheticism** n.

aetiology /iːtɪˈɒlədʒɪ/ n. study of causation or of causes of disease. **aetiological** a.

afar /əˈfɑː(r)/ adv. at or to a distance. **from afar** from a distance.

affable /ˈæfəb(ə)l/ a. easy to approach and talk to; courteous. **affability** n.

affair /əˈfeə(r)/ n. matter, concern; love-affair; colloq. thing or event; in pl. business.

affect /əˈfekt/ v.t. produce effect on; (of disease) attack; move, touch; pretend to have or feel or to do.

affectation /æfekˈteɪʃ(ə)n/ n. artificial manner; pretentious display.

affected a. full of affectation.

affection /əˈfekʃ(ə)n/ n. goodwill, fond feeling; disease.

affectionate /əˈfekʃənət/ a. loving.

affiance /əˈfaɪəns/ v.t. promise in marriage.

affidavit /æfɪˈdeɪvɪt/ n. written statement on oath.

affiliate /əˈfɪlɪeɪt/ v. adopt or attach or connect as member or branch (to or with).

affiliation n. affiliating or being affiliated. **affiliation order** one compelling putative father of illegitimate child to help support it.

affinity /əˈfɪnɪtɪ/ n. attraction; relationship, resemblance; Chem. tendency of substances to combine with others.

affirm /əˈfɜːm/ v. state as fact; make affirmation.

affirmation /æfəˈmeɪʃ(ə)n/ n. affirming; solemn declaration in place of oath.

affirmative /əˈfɜːmətɪv/ 1 a. affirming, answering that a thing is so. 2 n. that which affirms.

affix 1 /əˈfɪks/ v.t. attach, fasten; add in writing. 2 /ˈæfɪks/ n. thing affixed; prefix or suffix.

afflict /əˈflɪkt/ v.t. distress physically or mentally.

affliction n. distress, suffering; cause of this.

affluence /ˈæflʊəns/ n. wealth, abundance.

affluent /ˈæflʊənt/ 1 a. rich; abundant. 2 n. tributary stream.

afford /əˈfɔːd/ v.t. have enough money for; manage to spare (time etc.); provide; be in a position to.

afforest /əˈfɒrɪst/ v.t. convert into forest; plant with trees. **afforestation** n.

affray /əˈfreɪ/ n. breach of peace by fighting or rioting in public.

affront /əˈfrʌnt/ 1 n. open insult. 2 v.t. insult openly.

Afghan /ˈæfgæn/ 1 n. native or language of Afghanistan. 2 a. of Afghanistan. 3 **Afghan hound** large dog with long silky hair.

afield /əˈfiːld/ adv. away from home; at or to a distance.

afire /əˈfaɪə(r)/ adv. & pred.a. on fire.

aflame /əˈfleɪm/ adv. & pred.a. in flames; very excited.

afloat adv. & pred.a. floating; at sea; out of debt.

afoot /əˈfʊt/ adv. & pred.a. progressing; in operation.

afore /əˈfɔː(r)/ adv. & prep. before. **aforementioned, -said,** previously mentioned; **aforethought** premeditated.

a fortiori /eɪ fɔːtɪˈɔːraɪ/ with stronger reason. [L]

afraid /əˈfreɪd/ pred.a. frightened, alarmed; colloq. politely regretful.

afresh /əˈfreʃ/ adv. with fresh start.

African /ˈæfrɪkən/ 1 n. native (esp.

dark-skinned) or inhabitant of Africa.
2 *a.* of Africa.

Afrikaans /æfrɪˈkɑːns/ *n.* language derived from Dutch, used in S. Africa.

Afrikaner /æfrɪˈkɑːnə(r)/ *n.* Afrikaans-speaking white person in S. Africa.

Afro /ˈæfrəʊ/ *a.* (of hair) long and bushy, as grown by some Blacks.

aft /ɑːft/ *adv.* in, near to, or towards, stern of ship or tail of aircraft.

after /ˈɑːftə(r)/ **1** *prep.* following in time; behind; in pursuit or quest of; about, concerning; according to; in allusion to or imitation of; despite. **2** *conj.* after time when. **3** *adv.* later; behind. **4** *a.* later, hinder. **5** **afterbirth** placenta etc. discharged after childbirth; **aftercare** attention after leaving hospital, prison, etc; **after-effect** effect after interval or after primary effect; **afterlife** life after death; **aftershave** lotion applied after shaving; **afterthought** thing thought of or added later.

aftermath /ˈɑːftəmæθ or -mɑːθ/ *n.* consequences; after-effects.

aftermost /ˈɑːftəməʊst/ *a.* furthest aft.

afternoon /ɑːftəˈnuːn/ *n.* time between midday and evening.

afterwards /ˈɑːftəwədz/ *adv.* later, subsequently.

again /əˈɡeɪn or əˈɡen/ *adv.* another time, once more; further, besides; on the other hand.

against /əˈɡeɪnst or əˈɡenst/ *prep.* in opposition to; into collision or in contact with; in contrast to; in anticipation of; as compensating factor to, in return for.

agape /əˈɡeɪp/ *adv.* & *pred.a.* gaping.

agate /ˈæɡət/ *n.* kind of hard semi-precious stone with streaked colouring.

agave /əˈɡeɪvɪ/ *n.* a spiny-leaved plant.

age **1** *n.* length of past life or existence; *colloq.* (esp. in *pl.*) a long time; historical period; old age. **2** *v.* (*partic.* **ageing**) (cause to) grow old or show signs of age. **3** **come of age** reach legal majority.

aged *a.* /ˈeɪdʒd/ of the age of; /ˈeɪdʒɪd/ old.

ageism /ˈeɪdʒɪz(ə)m/ *n.* prejudice or discrimination against people because of their age.

ageless /ˈeɪdʒlɪs/ *a.* never growing or appearing old.

agency /ˈeɪdʒənsɪ/ *n.* business or establishment of agent; active operation, action; intervening action.

agenda /əˈdʒendə/ *n.* (*pl.* **-das**) list of items of business to be considered at meeting.

agent /ˈeɪdʒənt/ *n.* person acting for another in business, politics, etc.; person or thing producing effect.

agent provocateur /ɑːʒɑ̃ prəvɒkəˈtɜː/ (*pl.* **-ts -rs** *pr.* same) person employed to detect suspected offenders by tempting them to overt action. [F]

agglomerate /əˈɡlɒmərət/ *v.* collect into mass. **agglomeration** *n.*

agglutinate /əˈɡluːtɪneɪt/ *v.* stick together as with glue; join (words) into compounds. **agglutination** *n.*; **agglutinative** *a.*

aggrandize /əˈɡrændaɪz/ *v.t.* increase power, rank, or wealth of; make seem greater. **aggrandizement** /-dɪz-/ *n.*

aggravate /ˈæɡrəveɪt/ *v.t.* increase seriousness of; *colloq.* annoy. **aggravation** *n.*

aggregate **1** /ˈæɡrɪɡət/ *n.* sum total; gravel, broken stone, etc., used in making concrete. **2** /ˈæɡrɪɡət/ *a.* collected, total. **3** /ˈæɡrɪɡeɪt/ *v.* collect together, unite; *colloq.* amount to. **4** **aggregation** *n.*

aggression /əˈɡreʃ(ə)n/ *n.* unprovoked attack; hostile act or feeling. **aggressor** *n.*

aggressive /əˈɡresɪv/ *a.* given to aggression; forceful, self-assertive; hostile.

aggrieved /əˈɡriːvd/ *a.* having grievance.

aggro /ˈæɡrəʊ/ *n.* *sl.* deliberate trouble-making.

aghast /əˈɡɑːst/ *a.* amazed and horrified.

agile /ˈædʒaɪl/ *a.* quick-moving; nimble. **agility** /əˈdʒɪlɪtɪ/ *n.*

agitate /ˈædʒɪteɪt/ *v.* disturb, excite; stir up disquiet and unrest; shake about. **agitation** *n.*; **agitator** *n.*

AGM *abbr.* annual general meeting.

agnail /ˈæɡneɪl/ *n.* torn skin at root of finger-nail; resulting soreness.

agnostic /æɡˈnɒstɪk/ *n.* person who believes that nothing is or can be known of existence of God or any but material phenomena. **agnosticism** *n.*

ago /ə'gəʊ/ *adv.* in the past.

agog /ə'gɒg/ *adv.* & *pred.a.* eager, expectant.

agonize /'ægənaɪz/ *v.* undergo mental anguish; suffer agony; cause agony to.

agony /'ægənɪ/ *n.* intense physical or mental suffering; severe struggle. **agony aunt** *colloq.* writer answering personal problems in magazine etc.; **agony column** *colloq.* personal column.

agoraphobia /ægərə'fəʊbɪə/ *n.* morbid dread of open spaces.

agrarian /ə'greərɪən/ 1 *a.* relating to land or its cultivation. 2 *n.* advocate of redistribution of landed property. 3 **agrarianism** *n.*

agree /ə'griː/ *v.* hold similar opinion; consent; be or become in harmony (*with*); approve as correct; reach agreement about. **agree with** be compatible with.

agreeable *a.* pleasing; willing to agree.

agreement *n.* sharing of opinion; mutual understanding; contract, promise.

agriculture /'ægrɪkʌltʃə(r)/ *n.* cultivation of the soil and rearing of animals. **agricultural** *a.*; **agriculturalist** *n.*

agronomy /ə'grɒnəmɪ/ *n.* soil management and crop production.

aground /ə'graʊnd/ *adv.* on or to bottom of shallow water.

ague /'eɪgjuː/ *n.* malarial fever with cold, hot, and sweating stages; fit of shivering.

ah /ɑː/ *int.* expr. surprise, admiration, sorrow, entreaty, etc.

aha /ə'hɑː/ *int.* expr. surprise, triumph, mockery, irony, etc.

ahead /ə'hed/ *adv.* in advance, in front; forward.

ahoy /ə'hɔɪ/ *int. Naut.* used in hailing.

aid 1 *n.* help; person who or that which helps. 2 *v.* help, assist, promote. 3 **in aid of** in support of, *colloq.* for purpose of.

aide /eɪd/ *n.* aide-de-camp; assistant.

aide-de-camp /eɪd də 'kɑ̃/ *n.* (*pl.* **aides-** *pr.* same) officer assisting senior officer.

AIDS *abbr.* acquired immune deficiency syndrome.

aikido /aɪ'kiːdəʊ/ *n.* Japanese form of self-defence.

ail *v.* trouble or afflict in body or mind; be in poor condition.

aileron /'eɪlərɒn/ *n.* hinged flap on aircraft wing controlling lateral balance.

ailment /'eɪlmənt/ *n.* illness, esp. minor one.

aim 1 *v.* direct or point (*at*); take aim; direct one's ambition etc. 2 *n.* object aimed at, purpose; aiming; directing of weapon, missile, etc. at object. 3 **take aim** direct weapon at object.

aimless /'eɪmlɪs/ *a.* purposeless.

air 1 *n.* gaseous mixture, chiefly of oxygen and nitrogen, enveloping earth; atmosphere; open space; atmosphere as place where aircraft operate; appearance, manner; in *pl.* affected manner; melody. 2 *v.t.* expose to air, ventilate; make known, show off. 3 **air-bed** inflated mattress; **airborne** transported by air, (of aircraft) in the air after taking off; **air-brick** brick perforated for ventilation; **airbus** short-range aircraft operating like bus; **air commodore** RAF officer next below Air Vice-Marshal; **air-conditioning** regulation of humidity and temperature in building, apparatus for this; **airfield** area with runway(s) for aircraft; **air force** branch of armed forces fighting in the air; **airgun** gun using compressed air as propelling force; **air-hostess** stewardess in aircraft; **airlift** *n.* transport of supplies etc. by air esp. in emergency, (*v.t.*) transport thus; **airline** public air transport system or company; **airliner** large passenger aircraft; **airlock** stoppage of flow by air-bubble in pipe etc., compartment providing access to pressurized chamber; **airmail** mail carried by air; **airman** pilot or member of crew of aircraft; **Air (Chief-, Vice-) Marshal** high ranks in RAF; **airplane** *US* aeroplane; **airport** airfield with facilities for passengers and goods; **air raid** attack by aircraft; **airship** flying machine lighter than air; **airspace** air above country and subject to its jurisdiction; **air speed** aircraft's speed relative to air through which it is moving; **airstrip** strip of ground for take-off and landing of aircraft; **air terminal** place in town with transport to and from airport; **airway** regular route of aircraft; **by air** in or by aircraft; **on the air** (being) broadcast.

aircraft /ˈeəkrɑːft/ n. (pl. same) aeroplane, helicopter. **aircraft-carrier** ship that carries and acts as base for aircraft; **aircraftman, -woman,** lowest rank in RAF.

Airedale /ˈeədeɪl/ n. terrier of large rough-coated breed.

airless /ˈeəlɪs/ a. stuffy; still, calm.

airtight a. impermeable to air.

airworthy a. (of aircraft) fit to fly. **airworthiness** n.

airy /ˈeərɪ/ a. well-ventilated; light as air; insubstantial; flippant.

aisle /aɪl/ n. side part of church divided by pillars from nave; passage between rows of pews, seats in theatre, etc.

aitchbone /ˈeɪtʃbəʊn/ n. rump-bone of animal; cut of beef lying over this.

ajar /əˈdʒɑː(r)/ adv. (of door etc.) slightly open.

akimbo /əˈkɪmbəʊ/ adv. (of arms) with hands on hips and elbows out.

akin /əˈkɪn/ pred.a. similar; related.

alabaster /ˈæləbɑːstə(r)/ 1 n. translucent usu. white form of gypsum. 2 a. of alabaster; resembling it in whiteness or smoothness.

à la carte /ɑː lɑː ˈkɑːt/ ordered as separate items from menu.

alacrity /əˈlækrɪtɪ/ n. briskness, readiness.

à la mode /ɑː lɑː ˈməʊd/ in the fashion, fashionable.

alarm /əˈlɑːm/ 1 n. warning, warning sound or device; frightened expectation of danger etc.; alarm clock. 2 v.t. disturb, frighten; arouse to sense of danger etc. 3 **alarm clock** clock with device that rings at set time.

alarmist /əˈlɑːmɪst/ n. person spreading unnecessary alarm.

alas /əˈlæs/ int. expr. grief.

alb n. white vestment reaching to feet, worn by priests etc.

albacore /ˈælbəkɔː(r)/ n. large kind of tunny.

albatross /ˈælbətrɒs/ n. long-winged sea bird related to petrel.

albeit /ɔːlˈbiːɪt/ conj. although.

albino /ælˈbiːnəʊ/ n. (pl.-nos) person or animal lacking colouring pigment in skin and hair. **albinism** /ˈæl-/ n.

album /ˈælbəm/ n. blank book for photographs etc.; long-playing gramophone record with several items.

albumen /ˈælbjʊmɪn/ n. white of egg.

albumin /ˈælbjʊmɪn/ n. water-soluble protein found in egg-white, milk, blood, etc.

alchemy /ˈælkəmɪ/ n. medieval chemistry, esp. seeking transmutation of base metals into gold. **alchemical** /-ˈkem-/ a.; **alchemist** n.

alcohol /ˈælkəhɒl/ n. colourless volatile liquid, intoxicant present in wine, beer, spirits, etc., also used as solvent and fuel; liquor containing this; Chem. compound of this type.

alcoholic /ælkəˈhɒlɪk/ 1 a. of or like or containing or caused by alcohol. 2 n. person suffering from alcoholism.

alcoholism /ˈælkəhɒlɪz(ə)m/ n. continual heavy drinking of alcohol; diseased condition resulting from this.

alcove /ˈælkəʊv/ n. recess in wall of room, garden, etc.

alder /ˈɔːldə(r)/ n. tree related to birch.

alderman /ˈɔːldəmən/ n. (pl. -men) chiefly hist. civic dignitary next in rank to mayor. **aldermanic** /-ˈmæn-/ a.

ale n. beer.

alert /əˈlɜːt/ 1 a. watchful. 2 n. alarmcall; state or period of special vigilance. 3 v.t. make alert to; warn. 4 **on the alert** watchful, looking out for danger etc.

A level advanced level in GCE examination.

alfalfa /ælˈfælfə/ n. clover-like plant used for fodder.

alfresco /ælˈfreskəʊ/ a. & adv. in the open air.

alga /ˈælgə/ n. (pl. **-gae** /-dʒiː/) nonflowering stemless plant, e.g. seaweed or plankton.

algebra /ˈældʒɪbrə/ n. study of the properties of numbers using general symbols. **algebraic** /-ˈbreɪk/ a.

ALGOL n. mathematically-based computer language.

algorithm /ˈælgərɪðəm/ n. process or rules for (esp. machine) calculation etc.

alias /ˈeɪlɪəs/ 1 adv. called at other times. 2 n. assumed name.

alibi /ˈælɪbaɪ/ n. (pl. **-bis**) plea that one was elsewhere. □ See page 666.

alien /ˈeɪlɪən/ 1 n. non-naturalized foreigner; a being from another world.

2 *a.* foreign; not one's own; of a different kind; unfamiliar.

alienate /'eɪlɪəneɪt/ *v.t.* estrange; transfer ownership of. **alienation** *n.*

alight[1] /ə'laɪt/ *pred.a.* on fire; lighted up.

alight[2] /ə'laɪt/ *v.i.* get down or off *from*; settle, come to earth.

align /ə'laɪn/ *v.t.* place in or bring into line; ally (country, *oneself*, etc.) with party or cause. **alignment** *n.*

alike /ə'laɪk/ **1** *pred.a.* similar, like. **2** *adv.* in like manner.

alimentary /ælɪ'mentərɪ/ *a.* concerning nutrition; nourishing. **alimentary canal** channel through which food passes during digestion.

alimony /'ælɪmənɪ/ *n.* allowance paid by man to his divorced or separated wife, maintenance.

alive *pred.a.* living; lively, active; responsive *to*; abounding in.

alkali /'ælkəlaɪ/ *n.* (*pl.* **-lis**) any of a class of compounds that neutralize acids and form caustic or corrosive solutions in water. **alkaline** *a.*; **alkalinity** /-'lɪn-/ *n.*

alkaloid /'ælkələɪd/ *n.* any of a class of vegetable bases often used as drugs.

all /ɔːl/ **1** *a.* whole amount, number, or extent of. **2** *n.* all persons concerned; everything; the whole *of*. **3** *adv.* entirely, quite. **4 all along** from the beginning; **all but** very nearly; **all-clear** signal that danger or difficulty is over; **all fours** hands and knees; **all in** exhausted; **all-in** *attrib.* inclusive of all; **all in all** everything considered; **all out** involving all one's strength etc.; **all over** completely finished, over one's whole body; **all right** satisfactory, safe and sound, in good condition, satisfactorily, as desired, I consent; **all round** in all respects, for each person; **all-round** (of person) versatile; **all-rounder** versatile person; **All Saints Day** 1 Nov.; **all the same** nevertheless; **all there** *colloq.* mentally alert; **in all** in total, altogether.

Allah /'ælə/ *n.* Muslim name of God.

allay /ə'leɪ/ *v.t.* (*past & p.p.* **allayed**) alleviate, lessen.

allege /ə'ledʒ/ *v.t.* state as fact, esp. without proof. **allegation** /-'geɪʃ-/ *n.*; **allegedly** /ə'ledʒɪdlɪ/ *adv.*

allegiance /ə'liːdʒəns/ *n.* duty of subject to sovereign or government; loyalty.

allegorize /'ælɪgəraɪz/ *v.t.* treat as or by means of an allegory. **allegorist** *n.*

allegory /'ælɪgərɪ/ *n.* narrative symbolizing another esp. abstract meaning. **allegorical** /-'gɒr-/ *a.*

allegro /ə'legrəʊ/ *Mus.* **1** *adv.* in lively tempo. **2** *n.* (*pl.* **-os**) passage to be played this way.

alleluia /ælɪ'luːjə/ **1** *int.* God be praised. **2** *n.* (*pl.* **-as**) song of praise to God.

allergenic /ælə'dʒenɪk/ *a.* causing allergic reaction.

allergic /ə'lɜːdʒɪk/ *a.* having an allergy *to*; caused by allergy.

allergy /'ælədʒɪ/ *n.* condition of reacting adversely to certain foods or pollen etc.; *colloq.* antipathy.

alleviate /ə'liːvɪeɪt/ *v.t.* lessen or make less severe (pain, evil). **alleviation** *n.*; **alleviatory** /ə'liːv-/ *a.*

alley /'ælɪ/ *n.* narrow passage or street; channel for balls skittles etc.

alliance /ə'laɪəns/ *n.* union or agreement to co-operate, esp of States by treaty or families by marriage.

allied /'ælaɪd/ *a.* having similar origin or character to.

alligator /'ælɪgeɪtə(r)/ *n.* Amer. or Chinese reptile of crocodile family.

alliteration /əlɪtə'reɪʃ(ə)n/ *n.* recurrence of same initial letter or sound in several words of a phrase. **alliterate** *v.*; **alliterative** *a.*

allocate /'æləkeɪt/ *v.t.* assign (*to*). **allocation.** *n.*

allot /ə'lɒt/ *v.t.* distribute officially; apportion (*to*).

allotment /ə'lɒtmənt/ *n.* small plot of land let out for cultivation; something allotted.

allow /ə'laʊ/ *v.* permit; let happen; assign fixed sum to, esp. regularly; provide or set aside for a purpose. **allow for** take into consideration.

allowance /ə'laʊəns/ *n.* sum or quantity allowed; deduction or discount. **make allowances for** judge leniently.

alloy 1 /'ælɔɪ/ *n.* mixture of metals; inferior metal mixed esp. with gold or silver. **2** /ə'lɔɪ/ *v.t.* mix (metals); debase by admixture; spoil (pleasure).

allspice /'ɔːlspaɪs/ *n.* aromatic spice

got from dried berry of pimento tree;
this berry.

allude /ə'lu:d/ *v.i.* make indirect or
passing reference *to*.

allure /ə'ljʊə(r)/ **1** *v.t.* entice, tempt,
charm. **2** *n.* charm, attractiveness. **3**
allurement *n.*

allusion /ə'lu:ʒ(ə)n/ *n.* indirect or
passing reference. **allusive** /-sɪv/ *a.*

alluvium /ə'lu:vɪəm/ *n.* (*pl.* **-via**) deposit left by flood, esp. in river valley.
alluvial *a.*

ally 1 /'ælaɪ/ *n.* State or person formally co-operating or united with another for special purpose. **2** /ə'laɪ/ *v.t.*
combine or unite in alliance.

almanac /'ɔ:lmənæk/ *n.* calendar of
months and days, usu with astronomical data.

almighty /ɔ:l'maɪtɪ/ *a.* infinitely
powerful; *colloq.* very great. **the Almighty** God.

almond /'ɑ:mənd/ *n.* edible kernel of
fruit related to plum; tree bearing it.

almoner /'ɑ:mənə(r)/ *n.* social worker
attached to a hospital.

almost /'ɔ:lməʊst/ *adv.* very nearly, all
but.

alms /ɑ:mz/ *n.* donation of money or
food given to the poor. **almshouse**
house founded by charity for the poor.

aloe /'æləʊ/ *n.* plant with erect spikes of
flowers and bitter juice; in *pl.* purgative
drug from aloe juice.

aloft *adv.* high up, overhead.

alone 1 *pred.a.* by oneself or itself;
without company, assistance, or
addition. **2** *adv.* only, exclusively.

along 1 *adv.* onward, into more advanced state; in company, in addition;
beside or through part or whole of
thing's length. **2** *prep.* beside or
through part or whole of the length of.
3 alongside close to side (of); **along
with** in addition to.

aloof /ə'lu:f/ **1** *a.* unconcerned, lacking
in sympathy. **2** *adv.* away, apart.

aloud /ə'laʊd/ *adv.* in a normal voice
so as to be audible.

alp *n.* mountain-peak, esp. in *pl.* (**the
Alps**) those in Switzerland and adjacent countries.

alpaca /æl'pækə/ *n.* (*pl.* **-as**) llama with
long wool; its wool; fabric made from
it.

alpha /'ælfə/ *n.* (*pl.* **-as**) first letter of

Greek alphabet (*A*, α). **Alpha and
Omega** beginning and end; **alpha particle** helium nucleus emitted by radioactive substance.

alphabet /'ælfəbet/ *n.* set of letters
used in a language; symbols or signs
for this. **alphabetical** /-'bet-/ *a.*

alphanumeric /ælfənju:'merɪk/ *a.* of
or denoting or using the set of symbols
consisting of the letters of the alphabet
and the digits 0–9.

Alpine /'ælpaɪn/ **1** *a.* of the Alps or
other high mountains. **2** *n.* plant suited
to mountain regions.

already /ɔ:l'redɪ/ *adv.* before the time
in question; as early as this.

alright *incorrect* □See page 665.and **all**.

Alsatian /æl'seɪʃ(ə)n/ *n.* large dog of a
breed of wolfhound.

also /'ɔ:lsəʊ/ *adv.* in addition, besides.
also-ran loser in race, undistinguished
person.

altar /'ɔ:ltə(r)/ *n.* flat-topped block for
offerings to deity; table used for Communion service.

alter /'ɔ:ltə(r)/ *v.* change in character,
position, size, shape, etc. **alteration** *n.*

altercation /ɔ:ltə'keɪʃ(ə)n/ *n.* dispute,
wrangle. **altercate** *v.i.*

alternate 1 /ɔ:l'tɜ:nət/ *a.* (of things of
two kinds) occurring each after one of
the other kind; (with *pl.*, of one class of
thing) every other. □ See page 666. **2**
/'ɔ:ltəneɪt/ *v.* arrange or occur alternately; consist of alternate things. **3**
alternating current electric current
reversing direction at regular intervals. **4 alternation** *n.*

alternative /ɔ:l'tɜ:nətɪv/ **1** *a.* available
in place of something else. **2** *n.* choice
available in place of another; one of two
or more possibilities. □ See page 666.

alternator /'ɔ:ltəneɪtə(r)/ *n.* dynamo
producing alternating current.

although /ɔ:l'ðəʊ/ *conj.* though.

altimeter /'æltɪmi:tə(r)/ *n.* instrument
measuring altitude.

altitude /'æltɪtju:d/ *n.* height, esp. of
object above sea-level or star above
horizon.

alto /'æltəʊ/ *n.* (*pl.* **-os**) low singing
voice of woman or boy; highest adult
male singing voice; singer with alto
voice; music for alto voice.

altogether /ɔ:ltə'geðə(r)/ *adv.* totally;
on the whole.

altruism /'æltruɪz(ə)m/ *n.* regard for others as principle of action. **altruist** *n.*; **altruistic** *a.*

alum /'æləm/ *n.* double sulphate of aluminium and another element, esp. potassium.

alumina /ə'lu:mɪnə/ *n.* aluminium oxide, e.g. corundum.

aluminium /ælju'mɪnɪəm/ *n.* a light silvery metallic element.

alumnus /ə'lʌmnəs/ *n.* (*pl.* **-ni** /-naɪ/) esp. *US* former pupil or student of a school or university etc.

always /'ɔ:lweɪz/ *adv.* at all times; on all occasions; whatever the circumstances.

am 1st person sing. of **be**.

a.m. *abbr.* before noon (*ante meridiem*).

amalgam /ə'mælgəm/ *n.* mixture, blend; alloy of any metal with mercury.

amalgamate /ə'mælgəmeɪt/ *v.* mix; unite, combine. **amalgamation** *n.*

amanuensis /əmænju'ensɪs/ *n.* (*pl.* **-ses** /-si:z/) person who writes from dictation.

amaranth /'æmərænθ/ *n.* kind of plant with coloured foliage; imaginary unfading flower. **amaranthine** /-θaɪn/ *a.*

amaryllis /æmə'rɪlɪs/ *n.* plant with lily-like flowers.

amass /ə'mæs/ *v.t.* heap together, accumulate.

amateur /'æmətə(r)/ *n.* one who engages in a sport or interest etc. as a pastime not a profession.

amateurish /æmə'tɜ:rɪʃ/ *a.* suggestive of an amateur, unskilled.

amatory /'æmətərɪ/ *a.* of or showing (esp. sexual) love.

amaze *v.t.* fill with surprise or wonder. **amazement** *n.*

amazon /'æməzən/ *n.* strong or athletic woman; (**Amazon**) one of a mythical race of female warriors. **amazonian** /-'zəʊn-/ *a.*

ambassador /æm'bæsədə(r)/ *n.* diplomat sent by sovereign or State as permanent representative or on mission to another; official messenger. **ambassadorial** /-'dɔ:r-/ *a.*

amber 1 *n.* yellow translucent fossil resin; colour of this; yellow traffic-light denoting caution. 2 *a.* made of or coloured like amber.

ambergris /'æmbəgrɪs/ *n.* waxlike substance from intestines of sperm whale, used in perfumery.

ambidextrous /æmbɪ'dekstrəs/ *a.* able to use either hand equally well.

ambience /'æmbɪəns/ *n.* surroundings.

ambient /'æmbɪənt/ *a.* surrounding.

ambiguous /æm'bɪgjʊəs/ *a.* having more than one possible meaning; doubtful, uncertain. **ambiguity** /-'gju:-/ *n.*

ambit *n.* scope, bounds.

ambition /æm'bɪʃ(ə)n/ *n.* desire for advancement; desire for specific attainment; object of this.

ambitious /æm'bɪʃəs/ *a.* full of ambition; of high aspiration.

ambivalent /æm'bɪvələnt/ *a.* having mixed feelings towards person or thing. **ambivalence** *n.*

amble /'æmb(ə)l/ 1 *v.i.* walk at a leisurely pace. 2 *n.* leisurely pace.

ambrosia /æm'brəʊzjə/ *n.* food of the gods in classical myth; thing delicious to taste or smell. **ambrosial** *a.*

ambulance /'æmbjʊləns/ *n.* vehicle for conveying sick or injured to hospital; mobile hospital serving army.

ambulatory /'æmbjʊlətərɪ/ *a.* of or for walking.

ambuscade /æmbəs'keɪd/ *n.* & *v.t.* ambush.

ambush /'æmbʊʃ/ 1 *n.* surprise attack by persons lying concealed; act or place of concealment for this. 2 *v.t.* attack from ambush; lie in wait for.

ameliorate /ə'mi:lɪəreɪt/ *v.* make or become better. **amelioration** *n.*

amen /ɑ:'men or eɪ-/ *int.* so be it (esp. at end of prayer).

amenable /ə'mi:nəb(ə)l/ *a.* willing to be influenced or persuaded; answerable (*to* law etc.).

amend /ə'mend/ *v.t.* correct error in; make minor alterations in.

amendment *n.* minor alteration or addition in document etc.; article added to US constitution.

amends *n.* **make amends** give compensation *for*.

amenity /ə'mi:nɪtɪ/ *n.* pleasant or useful feature or facility; pleasantness of a place.

American /ə'merɪkən/ 1 *a.* of America, esp. the United States. 2 *n.* citizen of US; native of America; English as spoken in US. **3 Americanize** *v.t.*

Americanism /ə'merɪkənɪz(ə)m/ *n.* word or phrase peculiar to or originating in US.

amethyst /'æməθɪst/ *n.* a precious stone, purple or violet quartz.

amiable /'eɪmɪəb(ə)l/ *a.* friendly and pleasant in temperament, likeable. **amiability** *n.*

amicable /'æmɪkəb(ə)l/ *a.* friendly. **amicability** *n.*

amid /ə'mɪd/ *prep.* in the middle of.

amidships /ə'mɪdʃɪps/ *adv.* in or to the middle of ship.

amidst var. of **amid**.

amino /ə'mi:nəʊ/ *a.* **amino acid** organic acid found in proteins.

amiss 1 *pred.a.* out of order, wrong. **2** *adv.* wrongly, inappropriately. **3 take amiss** be offended by.

amity /'æmɪtɪ/ *n.* friendship.

ammeter /'æmɪtə(r)/ *n.* instrument for measuring electric current.

ammo /'æməʊ/ *n. sl.* ammunition.

ammonia /ə'məʊnɪə/ *n.* pungent gas with strong alkaline reaction; solution of this in water. **ammoniac** *a.*

ammonite /'æmənaɪt/ *n.* coil-shaped fossil shell.

ammunition /æmjʊ'nɪʃ(ə)n/ *n.* military projectiles (bullets, shells, etc.) and propellants; points used to advantage in argument.

amnesia /æm'ni:zjə/ *n.* loss of memory. **amnesiac** *a. & n.*

amnesty /'æmnɪstɪ/ *n.* general pardon, esp. for political offences.

amnion /'æmnɪɒn/ *n. (pl.* **-nia)** membrane enclosing foetus. **amniotic** *a.*

amoeba /ə'mi:bə/ *n. (pl.* **-bas)** microscopic one-celled aquatic organism.

amok /ə'mɒk/ *adv.* **run amok** run about wildly in violent rage.

among /ə'mʌŋ/ *prep.* (also **amongst**) surrounded by; in the category or number of; from the joint resources of; between.

amoral /eɪ'mɒr(ə)l/ *a.* not based on moral standards; having no moral principles.

amorous /'æmərəs/ *a.* showing or feeling sexual love.

amorphous /ə'mɔ:fəs/ *a.* shapeless; ill organized; *Min.* & *Chem.* uncrystallized.

amount 1 *n.* total number, size, extent, etc. **2** *v.i.* be equivalent in number, size, etc. *to.*

amour /ə'mʊə(r)/ *n.* love-affair, esp. secret one.

amour propre /æmʊə 'prɒpr/ self-respect. [F]

amp *n.* ampere; *colloq.* amplifier.

ampere /'æmpeə(r)/ *n.* unit of electric current.

ampersand /'æmpəsænd/ *n.* the sign & (= 'and').

amphetamine /æm'fetəmɪn/ *n.* synthetic stimulant drug.

amphibian /æm'fɪbɪən/ *n.* amphibious animal or vehicle.

amphibious /æm'fɪbɪəs/ *a.* able to live on land and in water; (of vehicle etc.) able to operate on land and on water; involving military forces landed from the sea.

amphitheatre /'æmfɪθɪətə(r)/ *n.* unroofed oval or circular building with tiers of seats surrounding central space.

amphora /'æmfərə/ *n. (pl.* **-rae** /-ri:/) Greek or Roman two-handled jar.

ample /'æmp(ə)l/ *a.* abundant, extensive; enough or more than enough. **amply** *adv.*

amplifier /'æmplɪfaɪə(r)/ *n.* apparatus for amplifying sounds or electrical signals.

amplify /'æmplɪfaɪ/ *v.t.* increase strength of (sound or electrical signal); add details to (story etc.). **amplification** *n.*

amplitude /'æmplɪtju:d/ *n.* spaciousness; maximum departure from average of oscillation, alternating current, etc.

ampoule /'æmpu:l/ *n.* small sealed vessel holding solution for injection.

amputate /'æmpjʊteɪt/ *v.t.* cut off (diseased or injured limb). **amputation** *n.*

amuck var. of **amok**.

amulet /'æmjʊlɪt/ *n.* thing worn as charm against evil.

amuse /ə'mju:z/ *v.t.* cause (person) to laugh or smile; interest or occupy. **amusing** *a.*

amusement *n.* being amused; thing that amuses.

an see **a**.

anachronism /ə'nækrənɪz(ə)m/ *n.* attribution of thing to period to which it does not belong; thing thus attributed; person or thing not suited to the period. **anachronistic** a.

anaconda /ænəˈkɒndə/ n. large tropical S. Amer. snake.

anaemia /əˈniːmɪə/ n. deficiency of red cells or their haemoglobin in the blood.

anaemic /əˈniːmɪk/ a. suffering from anaemia; pale, lacking vitality.

anaesthesia /ænɪsˈθiːzjə/ n. artificially induced insensibility to pain.

anaesthetic /ænɪsˈθetɪk/ 1 n. drug, gas, etc., producing anaesthesia. 2 a. producing anaesthesia.

anaesthetist /əˈniːsθətɪst/ n. one who administers anaesthetics.

anaesthetize /əˈniːsθətaɪz/ v.t. administer anaesthetics to.

anagram /ˈænəgræm/ n. word or phrase formed by transposing letters of another. **anagrammatic** /-ˈmæt-/ a.

anal /ˈeɪn(ə)l/ a. of the anus.

analgesia /ænælˈdʒiːzjə/ n. absence or relief of pain.

analgesic /ænælˈdʒiːsɪk/ 1 n. painkilling drug. 2 a. pain-killing.

analogous /əˈnæləgəs/ a. partially similar or parallel to.

analogue /ˈænəlɒg/ n. analogous thing. **analogue computer** one that uses physical quantities e.g. length or voltage to represent numbers.

analogy /əˈnælədʒɪ/ n. correspondence, similarity; reasoning from parallel cases. **analogical** /-ˈlɒdʒ-/ a.

analyse /ˈænəlaɪz/ v.t. perform analysis on.

analysis /əˈnæləsɪs/ n. (pl. -ses /-siːz/) detailed examination; ascertaining elements or structure of substance etc.; psychoanalysis.

analyst /ˈænəlɪst/ n. one who analyses.

analytical /ænəˈlɪtɪk(ə)l/ a. of or using analysis.

anarchism /ˈænəkɪz(ə)m/ n. belief that government and law should be abolished. **anarchist** n.; **anarchistic** a.

anarchy /ˈænəkɪ/ n. disorder, esp. political; lack of government. **anarchic** /əˈnɑːkɪk/ a.

anathema /əˈnæθəmə/ n. detested thing; curse of God or Church.

anathematize /əˈnæθəmətaɪz/ v.t. curse.

anatomy /əˈnætəmɪ/ n. science of bodily structure; structure of animal or plant. **anatomical** /ænəˈtɒmɪk(ə)l/ a.

ancestor /ˈænsestə(r)/ n. any person from whom one's father or mother is descended. **ancestress** n.

ancestral /ænˈsestr(ə)l/ a. inherited from ancestors.

ancestry /ˈænsestrɪ/ n. one's ancestors; ancient descent.

anchor /ˈæŋkə(r)/ 1 n. heavy metal structure used to moor ship to sea-bottom etc. or balloon etc. to ground. 2 v. secure (ship) with anchor; fix firmly; cast anchor. 3 **anchor man** person who co-ordinates activities, esp. compère in broadcast.

anchorage /ˈæŋkərɪdʒ/ n. place for anchoring; lying at anchor.

anchorite /ˈæŋkəraɪt/ n. hermit, recluse.

anchovy /ˈæntʃəvɪ/ n. small pungent-flavoured fish of herring family.

ancien régime /ɑ̃sjæ̃ reɪˈʒiːm/ political and social system formerly in being, esp. in France before Revolution.

ancient /ˈeɪnʃənt/ a. of times long past; old.

ancillary /ænˈsɪlərɪ/ a. susidiary, auxiliary.

and conj. connecting words, clauses, and sentences.

andante /ænˈdæntɪ/ Mus. 1 adv. in moderately slow time. 2 n. passage to be played thus.

andiron /ˈændaɪən/ n. stand for supporting logs in hearth.

androgynous /ænˈdrɒdʒɪnəs/ a. hermaphrodite.

anecdote /ˈænɪkdəʊt/ n. narrative of amusing or interesting incident. **anecdotal** a.

anemometer /ænɪˈmɒmɪtə(r)/ n. instrument for measuring force of wind.

anemone /əˈnemənɪ/ n. plant akin to buttercup. **sea amemone** polyp with petal-like tentacles.

aneroid /ˈænərɔɪd/ a. (of barometer) that measures air-pressure by its action on lid of metal box containing vacuum.

aneurysm /ˈænjʊərɪz(ə)m/ (also **aneurism**) n. excessive enlargement of artery.

anew /ə'nju:/ *adv.* again; in a different way.

angel /'eɪndʒ(ə)l/ *n.* attendant or messenger of God; kind or innocent person. **angel cake** very light sponge cake. **angelic** /æn'dʒelɪk/ *a.*

angelica /æn'dʒelɪkə/ *n.* an aromatic plant; its candied stalks.

angelus /'ændʒɪləs/ *n. RC Ch.* devotional exercise said at morning, noon, and sunset; bell rung for this.

anger /'æŋgə(r)/ **1** *n.* extreme displeasure. **2** *v.t.* make angry.

angina /æn'dʒaɪnə/ *n.* (in full **angina pectoris**) pain in chest brought on by exertion, owing to poor blood supply to heart.

angle¹ /'æŋg(ə)l/ **1** *n.* space between two meeting lines or surfaces; inclination of two lines to each other; corner; *colloq.* point of view. **2** *v.t.* move or place obliquely; *colloq.* present (news etc.) from particular point of view.

angle² /'æŋg(ə)l/ *v.i.* fish with line and hook. **angler** *n.*

Anglican /'æŋglɪkən/ **1** *a.* of Church of England. **2** *n.* member of Anglican Church. **3 Anglicanism** *n.*

Anglicism /'æŋglɪsɪz(ə)m/ *n.* English idiom.

Anglicize /'æŋglɪsaɪz/ *v.t.* make English in form or character.

Anglo- /'æŋgləʊ/ *in comb.* English, British.

Anglo-Catholic 1 *a.* of section of Church of England that insists on its accordance with Catholic doctrine. **2** *n.* adherent of Anglo-Catholic belief.

Anglo-Indian 1 *a.* of England and India; of British descent but having lived long in India. **2** *n.* Anglo-Indian person.

Anglophile /'æŋgləʊfaɪl/ *n.* person well-disposed towards the English.

Anglo-Saxon 1 *a.* of English Saxons before Norman Conquest. **2** *n.* Anglo-Saxon person or language.

angora /æŋ'gɔːrə/ *n.* fabric made from hair of angora goat or rabbit. **angora cat, goat, rabbit,** long-haired varieties.

angostura /æŋgə'stjʊərə/ *n.* aromatic bitter bark of S. Amer tree.

angry /'æŋgrɪ/ *a.* feeling or showing anger; (of wound etc.) inflamed, painful.

angstrom /'æŋstrəm/ *n.* unit of wavelength measurement.

anguish /'æŋgwɪʃ/ *n.* severe mental or bodily pain. **anguished** *a.*

angular /'æŋgjʊlə(r)/ *a.* having sharp corners; lacking plumpness or smoothness. **angular distance** distance between two points in terms of the angle they make with a third. **angularity** /-'lær-/ *n.*

anhydrous /æn'haɪdrəs/ *a. Chem.* without water of crystallization.

aniline /'ænɪliːn/ *n.* oily liquid got from coal tar and used in dye-making.

animadvert /ænɪmæd'vɜːt/ *v.i.* pass criticism or censure (on). **animadversion** *n.*

animal /'ænɪm(ə)l/ **1** *n.* living being having sensation and usu. ability to move; (esp.) other than man. **2** *a.* of or like animal; carnal.

animalcule /ænɪ'mælkjuːl/ *n.* microscopic animal.

animality /ænɪ'mælɪtɪ/ *n.* the animal world; animal behaviour.

animate 1 /'ænɪmət/ *a.* having life; lively. **2** /'ænɪmeɪt/ *v.t.* enliven; give life to.

animated *a.* spirited, lively; (of film) characterized by animation.

animation /ænɪ'meɪʃ(ə)n/ *n.* liveliness, ardour; being alive; technique of film-making by photographing successive drawings or positions of puppets etc. to create illusion of movement.

animator /'ænɪmeɪtə(r)/ *n.* artist who prepares animated films.

animism /'ænɪmɪz(ə)m/ *n.* attribution of soul to inanimate objects and natural phenomena. **animist** *n.*; **animistic** *a.*

animosity /ænɪ'mɒsɪtɪ/ *n.* hostility.

animus /'ænɪməs/ *n.* animosity shown in speech or action.

anion /'ænaɪən/ *n.* negatively charged ion. **anionic** /ænaɪ'ɒnɪk/ *a.*

anise /'ænɪs/ *n.* plant with aromatic seeds.

aniseed /'ænɪsiːd/ *n.* seed of anise.

ankle /'æŋk(ə)l/ *n.* joint connecting foot with leg.

anklet /'æŋklɪt/ *n.* ornament worn round ankle.

ankylosis /æŋkɪ'ləʊsɪs/ *n.* stiffening of joint by uniting of bones.

annals /'æn(ə)lz/ *n.pl.* narrative of events year by year; historical records. **annalist** *n.*

anneal /əˈniːl/ *v.t.* heat (metal, glass) and allow to cool slowly, esp. to toughen.

annelid /ˈænɪlɪd/ *n.* worm made of segments, e.g. earth-worm.

annex /æˈneks/ *v.t.* add or append as subordinate part; take possession of. **annexation** *n.*

annexe /ˈæneks/ *n.* supplementary building.

annihilate /əˈnaɪəleɪt/ *v.t.* destroy utterly. **annihilation** *n.*

anniversary /ˌænɪˈvɜːsərɪ/ *n.* yearly return of date; celebration of this.

Anno Domini /ˈænəʊ ˈdɒmɪnaɪ/ in the year of the Christian era; *colloq.* advancing age.

annotate /ˈænəʊteɪt/ *v.t.* add explanatory notes to (book etc.). **annotation** *n.*

announce /əˈnaʊns/ *v.t.* make publicly known; make known the approach of. **announcement** *n.*

announcer /əˈnaʊnsə(r)/ *n.* person who announces, esp. in broadcasting.

annoy /əˈnɔɪ/ *v.t.* cause slight anger or mental distress to; molest. **annoyance** *n.*

annual /ˈænjʊəl/ 1 *a.* reckoned by year; recurring yearly. 2 *n.* book etc. published yearly; plant living only one year.

annuity /əˈnjuːɪtɪ/ *n.* yearly grant or allowance; investment entitling one to fixed annual sum.

annul /əˈnʌl/ *v.t.* declare invalid; abolish, cancel. **annulment** *n.*

annular /ˈænjʊlə(r)/ *a.* ring-shaped.

annulate /ˈænjʊlət/ *a.* marked with or formed of rings.

annunciation /əˌnʌnsɪˈeɪʃ(ə)n/ *n.* announcement, esp. (**Annunciation**) that of the Incarnation made by Gabriel to Mary.

anode /ˈænəʊd/ *n.* positive electrode or terminal.

anodyne /ˈænəʊdaɪn/ 1 *a.* pain-killing; soothing. 2 *n.* anodyne drug, circumstance, etc.

anoint /əˈnɔɪnt/ *v.t.* apply ointment or oil to esp. as religious ceremony.

anomalous /əˈnɒmələs/ *a.* irregular, abnormal.

anomaly /əˈnɒməlɪ/ *n.* anomalous thing.

anon /əˈnɒn/ *adv.* *arch.* soon, presently.

anon. *abbr.* anonymous.

anonymous /əˈnɒnɪməs/ *a.* of unknown name or authorship; featureless. **anonymity** (/-ˈnɪm-/) *n.*

anorak /ˈænəræk/ *n.* weatherproof jacket usu. with hood.

anorexia /ˌænəˈreksɪə/ *n.* lack of appetite for food, esp. (in full **anorexia nervosa**) as chronic illness.

another /əˈnʌðə(r)/ 1 *a.* additional; one more; a different. 2 *n.* an additional or other or different person or thing.

answer /ˈɑːnsə(r)/ 1 *n.* thing said, written, or done to deal with question, accusation, etc.; solution to problem. 2 *v.* make an answer (to); act in response to; be satisfactory (*for*); be responsible *for* or *to*; correspond *to* description.

answerable /ˈɑːnsərəb(ə)l/ *a.* responsible (*for*, *to*); that can be answered.

ant *n.* small usu. wingless insect living in complex social group. **ant-eater** mammal living on ants; **anthill** mound over ants' nest.

antacid /ænˈtæsɪd/ *n.* & *a.* preventive or corrective of acidity.

antagonism /ænˈtæɡənɪz(ə)m/ active opposition. **antagonistic** *a.*

antagonist /ænˈtæɡənɪst/ *n.* opponent.

antagonize /ænˈtæɡənaɪz/ *v.t.* evoke hostility in.

Antarctic /ænˈtɑːktɪk/ *a.* of south polar region.

ante /ˈæntɪ/ *n.* stake put up by poker player before drawing new cards.

ante- /ˈæntɪ/ *in comb.* before.

antecedent /ˌæntɪˈsiːd(ə)nt/ 1 *n.* preceding event or circumstance; *Gram.* noun, clause, etc., to which following adverb or pronoun refers; in *pl.* person's past history. 2 *a.* previous (*to*). 3 **antecedence** *n.*

antechamber /ˈæntɪtʃeɪmbə(r)/ *n.* ante-room.

antedate /ˈæntɪdeɪt/ *v.t.* precede in time; give earlier than true date to.

antediluvian /ˌæntɪdɪˈluːvɪən/ *a.* before the Flood; *colloq.* very old.

antelope /ˈæntɪləʊp/ *n.* swift-running deer-like animal.

antenatal /ˌæntɪˈneɪtəl/ a. before birth; relating to pregnancy.

antenna /ænˈtenə/ n. (pl. **-tennae** /-ˈteniː/) one of pair of sensory organs on head of insect or crustacean; feeler; (pl. **-tennas**) radio aerial.

anterior /ænˈtɪərɪə(r)/ a. nearer the front; prior (to).

ante-room /ˈæntɪruːm/ n. small room leading to more important one.

anthem /ˈænθəm/ n. choral composition for church use; song of praise, esp. for nation.

anther /ˈænθə(r)/ n. part of stamen containing pollen.

anthology /ænˈθɒlədʒɪ/ n. collection of passages from literature, esp. poems.

anthracite /ˈænθrəsaɪt/ n. hard kind of coal. **anthracitic** /-ˈsɪt-/ a.

anthrax /ˈænθræks/ n. disease of sheep and cattle, transmissible to humans.

anthropoid /ˈænθrəpɔɪd/ 1 a. manlike in form. 2 n. anthropoid ape.

anthropology /ænθrəˈpɒlədʒɪ/ n. study of mankind, esp. societies and customs. **anthropological** a.; **anthropologist** n.

anthropomorphism /ænθrəpə-ˈmɔːfɪz(ə)m/ n. attributing of human form or personality to god, animal, or thing. **anthropomorphic** a.

anthropomorphous /ænθrəpə-ˈmɔːfəs/ a. of human form.

anti- in comb. opposed to; retarding or preventing; of opposing kind.

anti-aircraft a. for defence against hostile aircraft.

antibiotic /æntɪbaɪˈɒtɪk/ 1 n. substance capable of destroying or injuring bacteria etc. 2 a. functioning as antibiotic.

antibody /ˈæntɪbɒdɪ/ n. protein produced in reaction to antigens in body.

antic n. (usu. in pl.) foolish behaviour.

anticipate /ænˈtɪsɪpeɪt/ v.t. deal with or use before due time; forestall. □ See page 666. **anticipation** n.; **anticipatory** a.

anticlimax /-ˈklaɪmæks/ n. lame conclusion to anything promising climax.

anticlockwise /-ˈklɒkwaɪz/ adv. & a. moving in curve opposite in direction to hands of clock.

anticyclone /-ˈsaɪkləʊn/ n. system of winds rotating outwards from area of high barometric pressure, producing fine weather.

antidote /ˈæntɪdəʊt/ n. medicine used to counteract poison.

antifreeze /ˈæntɪfriːz/ n. substance added to water (esp. in radiator of motor vehicle) to lower its freezing-point.

antigen /ˈæntɪdʒ(ə)n/ n. foreign substance that causes body to produce antibodies.

anti-hero n. (pl. **-oes**) central character in story etc. who lacks conventional heroic qualities.

antihistamine /-ˈhɪstəmɪn/ n. substance that counteracts effect of histamine.

antimacassar /-məˈkæsə(r)/ n. protective covering for chair-back.

antimony /ˈæntɪmənɪ/ n. brittle bluish-white metallic element.

antipathy /ænˈtɪpəθɪ/ n. strong or deep-seated aversion. **antipathetic** /-ˈθet-/ a.

antiperspirant /-ˈpɜːspɪrənt/ a. substance that inhibits perspiration.

antiphon /ˈæntɪf(ə)n/ n. hymn sung antiphonally.

antiphonal /ænˈtrɪfən(ə)l/ a. sung alternately by two bodies of singers.

antipodes /ænˈtɪpədiːz/ n.pl. places diametrically opposite each other on the earth, esp. Australasia in relation to Europe. **antipodean** /-ˈdiːən/ a. & n.

antipyretic /-paɪˈretɪk/ 1 a. that counteracts fever. 2 n. antipyretic drug.

antiquarian /æntɪˈkweərɪən/ 1 a. of or dealing in rare books. 2 n. antiquary.

antiquary /ˈæntɪkwərɪ/ n. student or collector of antiques or antiquities.

antiquated /ˈæntɪkweɪtɪd/ a. old-fashioned, out of date.

antique /ænˈtiːk/ 1 n. object, esp. furniture etc., of considerable age. 2 a. of or existing since old times; old-fashioned.

antiquity /ænˈtɪkwɪtɪ/ n. ancient times, esp. before Middle Ages; in pl. remains from ancient times.

antirrhinum /æntɪˈraɪnəm/ n. snap-dragon.

antiscorbutic /-skɔːˈbjuːtɪk/ a. that prevents or cures scurvy.

anti-Semitic /-sɪˈmɪtɪk/ a. hostile to Jews. **anti-Semite** /-ˈsiːmaɪt/ n.; **anti-Semitism** /-ˈsem-/ n.

antiseptic /-'septɪk/ 1 *a.* that counteracts sepsis by destroying bacteria. 2 *n.* antiseptic substance.

antisocial /-'səʊʃ(ə)l/ *a.* not sociable; opposed or harmful to existing social order.

antistatic /-'stætɪk/ *a.* that counteracts effect of static electricity.

antithesis /æn'tɪθəsɪs/ *n.* (*pl.* **-ses** /-siːz/) direct opposite; contrast; contrast of ideas marked by parallelism of contrasted words. **antithetical** /-'θet-/ *a.*

antitoxin /-'tɒksɪn/ *n.* antibody that counteracts a toxin.

antitrades /-'treɪdz/ *n.* winds blowing above and in opposite direction to trade winds.

antler /'æntlə(r)/ *n.* branched horn of deer.

antonym /'æntənɪm/ *n.* word opposite in meaning to another.

anus /'eɪnəs/ *n.* excretory opening at end of alimentary canal in mammals.

anvil *n.* block on which smith works metal.

anxiety /æŋ'zaɪətɪ/ *n.* troubled state of mind; eagerness.

anxious /'æŋkʃəs/ *a.* troubled; uneasy in mind; eagerly wanting *to* do.

any /'enɪ/ 1 *a.* one or some, no matter which. 2 *pron.* any one; any number or amount. 3 *adv.* at all, in some degree. 4 **anybody** any person, person of importance; **anyhow** anyway, at random; **anyone** anybody; **anything** any thing, a thing of any kind; **anyway** in any way, in any case; **anywhere** (in or to) any place.

Anzac /'ænzæk/ *n.* soldier in Aus. and NZ Army Corps (1914-18).

aorist /'eərɪst/ *n. Gram.* past tense denoting occurrence without reference to continuance, completion, etc.

aorta /eɪ'ɔːtə/ *n.* main artery carrying blood from left ventricle of heart.

apace /ə'peɪs/ *adv.* swiftly.

apart /ə'pɑːt/ *adv.* separately; into pieces; at or to a distance.

apartheid /ə'pɑːtheɪt/ *n.* racial segregation, esp. in S. Africa.

apartment /ə'pɑːtmənt/ *n.* flat (*US*); in *pl.* set of rooms; single room.

apathy /'æpəθɪ/ *n.* lack of interest, indifference; insensibility. **apathetic** /-'θet-/ *a.*

ape 1 *n.* tailless monkey; imitator. 2 *v.t.* imitate.

aperient /ə'pɪərɪənt/ *a. & n.* laxative.

aperitif /əperɪ'tiːf/ *n.* alcoholic drink as appetizer before meal.

aperture /'æpətjʊə(r)/ *n.* opening, gap.

apex /'eɪpeks/ *n.* (*pl.* **apexes**) highest point, pointed end.

aphasia /ə'feɪʒə/ *n.* loss of ability to speak or of understanding of speech. **aphasic** *a.*

aphelion /æ'fiːlɪən/ *n.* (*pl.* **-lia**) point of orbit farthest from sun.

aphid /'eɪfɪd/ *n.* insect infesting plants.

aphis /'eɪfɪs/ *n.* (*pl.* **aphides** /'eɪfɪdiːz/) aphid.

aphorism /'æfərɪz(ə)m/ *n.* short pithy maxim. **aphoristic** *a.*

aphrodisiac /æfrə'dɪzɪæk/ 1 *a.* arousing sexual desire. 2 *n.* aphrodisiac substance.

apiary /'eɪpɪərɪ/ *n.* place where bees are kept. **apiarist** *n.*

apiculture /'eɪpɪkʌltʃə(r)/ *n.* bee-keeping.

apiece /ə'piːs/ *adv.* for each one.

aplomb /ə'plɒm/ *n.* self-confidence.

apocalypse /ə'pɒkəlɪps/ *n.* revelation, esp. of the future of the world. **apocalyptic** *a.*

Apocrypha /ə'pɒkrɪfə/ *n.pl.* OT books not in Hebrew Bible and not considered genuine.

apocryphal /ə'pɒkrɪf(ə)l/ *a.* of doubtful authenticity.

apogee /'æpədʒiː/ *n.* highest point; point in orbit of moon farthest from earth.

apologetic /əpɒlə'dʒetɪk/ *a.* making apology, expressing regret; of nature of apology.

apologia /æpə'ləʊdʒə/ *n.* written defence of conduct or opinions.

apologist /ə'pɒlədʒɪst/ *n.* one who defends by argument.

apologize /ə'pɒlədʒaɪz/ *v.i.* make apology.

apology /ə'pɒlədʒɪ/ *n.* regretful acknowledgement of offence; explanation.

apophthegm /'æpəθem/ *n.* terse or pithy saying.

apoplexy /'æpəpleksɪ/ *n.* sudden inability to feel and move, caused by blockage or rupture of artery in brain. **apoplectic** *a.*

apostasy /ə'pɒstəsɪ/ n. abandonment of belief or religious faith etc.

apostate n. person who renounces former belief. **apostatize** /-'pɒs-/ v.i.

a posteriori /eɪ pɒsterɪ'ɔːraɪ/ from effects to causes; involving reasoning thus.

Apostle /ə'pɒs(ə)l/ n. any of twelve sent forth by Christ to preach gospel; **apostle** leader of reform.

apostolic æpəs'tɒlɪk/ a. of Apostles; of the Pope.

apostrophe /ə'pɒstrəfɪ/ n. sign (') showing omission of letter(s) or number(s), or denoting possessive case.

apostrophize /ə'pɒstrəfaɪz/ v.t. address (esp. absent person or thing.)

apothecary /ə'pɒθəkərɪ/ n. arch. druggist.

apotheosis /əpɒθɪ'əʊsɪs/ n. (pl. **-ses** /-siːz/) deification; deified ideal; highest development of a thing.

appal /ə'pɔːl/ v.t. dismay, shock.

apparatus /æpə'reɪtəs/ n. equipment for scientific or other work.

apparel /ə'pær(ə)l/ n. arch. clothing. **apparelled** a.

apparent /ə'pærənt/ a. readily visible or perceivable; seeming.

apparition /æpə'rɪʃ(ə)n/ n. appearance, esp. of startling kind; ghost.

appeal /ə'piːl/ 1 v.i. make earnest request; be attractive or good; call attention to as support; apply to higher court, tribunal, etc., for revision of lower court's decision; Crick. ask umpire to declare batsman out. 2 n. act or right of appealing; request for aid; feature or quality that appeals.

appear /ə'pɪə(r)/ v.i. become or be visible; give certain impression, seem; present oneself; be published.

appearance /ə'pɪərəns/ n. appearing, outward aspect; in pl. outward show of prosperity or good behaviour etc.

appease /ə'piːz/ v.t. make calm or quiet, esp. conciliate (aggressor) with concessions; satisfy. **appeasement** n.

appellant /ə'pelənt/ n. person who appeals to higher court.

appellate /ə'pelət/ a. Law (of court) concerned with appeals.

appellation /æpə'leɪʃ(ə)n/ n. name, title.

append /ə'pend/ v.t. attach, affix; add.

appendage /ə'pendɪdʒ/ n. thing attached; addition.

appendectomy /əpen'dektəmɪ/ n. (also **appendicectomy** /-dɪ'sek-/) surgical removal of appendix.

appendicitis /əpendɪ'saɪtɪs/ n. inflammation of the appendix.

appendix /ə'pendɪks/ n. (pl. **-dices** /-dɪsiːz/ or **-dixes**) subsidiary matter at end of book etc.; outgrowth of tissue attached to intestine.

appertain /æpə'teɪn/ v.i. belong or relate to.

appetite /'æpɪtaɪt/ n. desire, inclination (for food, pleasure, etc.); one's relish for food.

appetizer /'æpɪtaɪzə(r)/ n. thing eaten or drunk to stimulate appetite.

appetizing /'æpɪtaɪzɪŋ/ a. (esp. of food) stimulating appetite.

applaud /ə'plɔːd/ v. express approval (of), esp. by clapping; commend.

applause /ə'plɔːz/ n. loud approbation, esp.by clapping.

apple /'æp(ə)l/ n. rounded firm fleshy fruit. **apple of one's eye** cherished person or thing; **apple-pie bed** bed with sheets so folded that one cannot stretch out one's legs; **apple-pie order** extreme neatness.

appliance /ə'plaɪəns/ n. device or equipment for specific task.

applicable /'æplɪkəb(ə)l/ a. that may be applied (to). **applicability** n.

applicant /'æplɪkənt/ n. person who applies for job etc.

application /æplɪ'keɪʃ(ə)n/ n. applying; thing applied; request; diligence; relevance.

applicator /'æplɪkeɪtə(r)/ n. device for applying substance etc.

appliqué /æ'pliːkeɪ/ 1 n. ornamental work in which fabric is cut out and attached to surface of other fabric. 2 v.t. (past & p.p. **-quéd**; partic. **-quéing**) decorate with appliqué.

apply /ə'plaɪ/ v. make formal request; put close (to) or in contact; administer (remedy); devote or direct to; be relevant or use as relevant (to).

appoint /ə'pɔɪnt/ v.t. assign job or office to; fix (time etc.); equip, furnish.

appointment n. appointing, esp. of time and place for meeting; job or office assigned to person; in pl. equipment or fittings.

apportion /əˈpɔːʃ(ə)n/ v.t. portion out; assign as share. **apportionment** n.

apposite /ˈæpəzɪt/ a. well-expressed, appropriate.

apposition /æpəˈzɪʃ(ə)n/ n. juxtaposition, esp. Gram. placing of word etc. syntactically parallel to another.

appraise /əˈpreɪz/ v.t. estimate value or quality of. **appraisal** n.

appreciable /əˈpriːʃəb(ə)l/ a. significant; considerable.

appreciate /əˈpriːʃɪeɪt/ v. set high value on; be grateful for; estimate rightly; rise in value. **appreciation** n.; **appreciative** /-ˈʃɪ-/ a.

apprehend /æprɪˈhend/ v.t. seize, arrest; understand.

apprehension /æprɪˈhenʃ(ə)n/ n. fearful anticipation; arrest; understanding.

apprehensive /æprɪˈhensɪv/ a. uneasy, anticipating with fear.

apprentice /əˈprentɪs/ 1 n. learner of craft bound to employer for specified term. 2 v.t. bind as apprentice. 3 **apprenticeship** n.

apprise /əˈpraɪz/ v.t. inform of.

approach /əˈprəʊtʃ/ 1 v. come nearer (to) in space or time; be similar to; approximate to; set about. 2 n. act or means of approaching; approximation; final part of aircraft's flight before landing.

approachable /əˈprəʊtʃəb(ə)l/ a. that can be approached; friendly.

approbation /æprəˈbeɪʃ(ə)n/ n. approval, consent. **approbatory** a.

appropriate 1 /əˈprəʊprɪət/ a. suitable, proper. 2 /əˈprəʊprɪeɪt/ v.t. take possession of; devote (fund etc. to purpose). 3 **appropriation** n.; **appropriator** n.

approval /əˈpruːv(ə)l/ n. approving; **on approval** returnable to supplier if not satisfactory.

approve /əˈpruːv/ v. confirm, give assent to; pronounce good, have favourable opinion of.

approximate 1 /əˈprɒksɪmət/ a. fairly correct; near to the actual. 2 /əˈprɒksɪmeɪt/ v. be or make near (to). 3 **approximation** n.

appurtenances /əˈpɜːtɪnənsɪz/ n.pl. accessories; belongings.

Apr. abbr. April.

après-ski /æpreɪˈskiː/ done or worn after day's skiing at resort. [F]

apricot /ˈeɪprɪkɒt/ n. orange-pink stone-fruit.

April /ˈeɪprɪl/ n. fourth month of year. **April fool** victim of hoax on 1 April (**April Fools' Day**).

a priori /eɪ prɑɪˈɔːraɪ/ from cause to effect; involving reasoning thus; assumed without investigation.

apron /ˈeɪprən/ n. garment worn in front of body to protect clothes; area on airfield used for manœuvring and loading aircraft; extension of stage in front of curtain.

apropos /ˈæprəpəʊ/ 1 a. to the point or purpose. 2 adv. incidentally. 3 **apropos of** in connection with.

apse /æps/ n. arched or domed recess esp. at end of church.

apsidal /ˈæpsɪd(ə)l/ a. of the form or shape of an apse; of apsides.

apsis n. (pl. **apsides** /æpˈsaɪdiːz/) aphelion or perihelion of planet, apogee or perigee of moon.

apt a. suitable, appropriate; having a tendency (to); quick-witted.

apteryx /ˈæptərɪks/ n. kiwi.

aptitude /ˈæptɪtjuːd/ n. talent; ability, esp. in particular skill.

aqualung /ˈækwəlʌŋ/ n. portable underwater breathing apparatus.

aquamarine /ˌækwəməˈriːn/ n. bluish-green beryl; colour of this.

aquaplane /ˈækwəpleɪn/ 1 n. board for riding on water, pulled by speed-boat. 2 v.i. ride on aquaplane; (of vehicle) glide uncontrollably on wet surface of road.

aquarelle /ækwəˈrel/ n. painting in transparent water-colours.

aquarium /əˈkweərɪəm/ n. (pl. **-iums**) tank for keeping fish and other aquatic life; building with such tanks.

Aquarius /əˈkweərɪəs/ n. eleventh sign of zodiac.

aquatic /əˈkwætɪk/ a. living in or near water; done in or on water.

aquatint /ˈækwətɪnt/ n. print produced from copper plate engraved with nitric acid.

aqueduct /ˈækwɪdʌkt/ n. artificial channel, esp. raised structure across valley for conveying water.

aqueous /ˈeɪkwɪəs/ a. of or like water; produced by action of water.

aquiline /'ækwɪlaɪn/ *a.* of or like an eagle; (of nose) hooked like eagle's beak.

Arab /'ærəb/ 1 *n.* member of Semitic people orig. inhabiting Saudi Arabia, now Middle East generally. 2 *a.* of Arabia or Arabs.

arabesque /ærə'besk/ *n.* decoration with intertwined leaves, scrollwork, etc.; ballet dancer's pose on one foot with other leg extended behind.

Arabian /ə'reɪbɪən/ 1 *a.* of Arabia. 2 *n.* an Arab.

Arabic /'ærəbɪk/ 1 *n.* language of Arabs. 2 *a.* of the Arabs or their language. **3 Arabic numerals** 1, 2, 3, etc., (opp. Roman numerals).

arable *a.* fit for ploughing and growing crops.

arachnid /ə'ræknɪd/ *n.* any of class comprising spiders, scorpions, etc.

Aramaic /ærə'meɪɪk/ 1 *n.* language of Syria at time of Christ. 2 *a.* of or in Aramaic.

arbiter /'ɑːbɪtə(r)/ *n.* judge; person with influence over or control *of.*

arbitrary /'ɑːbɪtrərɪ/ *a.* based on random choice or whim; capricious, despotic.

arbitrate /'ɑːbɪtreɪt/ *v.* determine; settle dispute. **arbitration** *n.*

arbitrator /'ɑːbɪtreɪtə(r)/ *n.* person appointed by parties involved to settle dispute.

arboreal /ɑː'bɔːrɪəl/ *a.* of or living in trees.

arborescent /ɑːbə'resənt/ *a.* tree-like in growth or form. **arborescence** *n.*

arboretum /ɑːbə'riːtəm/ *n.* (*pl.* -ta) tree-garden.

arboriculture /'ɑːbərɪkʌltʃə(r)/ *n.* cultivation of trees or shrubs. **arboricultural** *a.*

arbour /'ɑːbə(r)/ *n.* shady retreat enclosed by trees or climbing plants.

arc *n.* part of circumference of circle or other curve; large luminous flow of electric current through gas. **arc lamp** one using electric arc.

arcade /ɑː'keɪd/ *n.* covered walk esp. lined with shops; series of arches supporting or along wall.

Arcadian /ɑː'keɪdɪən/ *a.* ideally rustic.

arcane /ɑː'keɪn/ *a.* mysterious, secret.

arch¹ 1 *n.* curved structure supporting bridge, floor, etc.; archlike curvature. 2

v. form arch; provide with or form into arch.

arch² *a.* consciously or affectedly playful.

archaeology /ɑːkɪ'ɒlədʒɪ/ *n.* study of ancient peoples esp. by excavation of physical remains. **archaeological** *a.*; **archaeologist** *n.*

archaic /ɑː'keɪɪk/ *a.* of early period in culture; antiquated; (of word) no longer in ordinary use.

archaism /'ɑːkeɪɪz(ə)m/ *n.* archaic word etc.; use of the archaic. **archaistic** *a.*

archangel /'ɑːkeɪndʒ(ə)l/ *n.* angel of highest rank. **archangelic** /-'dʒel-/ *a.*

archbishop /ɑːtʃ'bɪʃəp/ *n.* chief bishop.

archbishopric *n.* office or diocese of archbishop.

archdeacon /ɑːtʃ'diːkən/ *n.* church dignitary next below bishop.

archdeaconry *n.* office or residence of archdeacon.

archdiocese /ɑːtʃ'daɪəsɪs/ *n.* archbishop's diocese. **archdiocesan** /-daɪ'ɒsɪz(ə)n/ *a.*

archduke /ɑːtʃ'djuːk/ *n.* *hist.* title of son of Emperor of Austria.

archer /'ɑːtʃə(r)/ *n.* person who shoots with bow and arrows.

archery /'ɑːtʃərɪ/ *n.* use of bow and arrows.

archetype /'ɑːkɪtaɪp/ *n.* original model, typical specimen. **archetypal** *a.*

archipelago /ɑːkɪ'peləgəʊ/ *n.* (*pl.* -gos) sea with many islands; group of islands.

architect /'ɑːkɪtekt/ *n.* designer of buildings, ships, etc.

architectonic /ɑːkɪtek'tɒnɪk/ *a.* of architecture; of systematization of knowledge.

architecture /'ɑːkɪtektʃə(r)/ *n.* art or science of building; style of building. **architectural** *a.*

architrave /'ɑːkɪtreɪv/ *n.* moulded frame round doorway or window.

archive /'ɑːkaɪv/ *n.* (freq. in *pl.*) collection of documents or records; place where these are kept. **archival** *a.*

archivist /'ɑːkɪvɪst/ *n.* keeper of archives.

archway /'ɑːtʃweɪ/ *n.* arched entrance or passage.

Arctic /'ɑːktɪk/ *a.* of north polar regions.

ardent /'ɑːd(ə)nt/ *a.* eager, zealous, fervent; burning. **ardency** *n.*

ardour /'ɑːdə(r)/ *n.* zeal, enthusiasm.

arduous /'ɑːdjʊəs/ *a.* hard to accomplish; strenuous.

are¹: see **be.**

are² /ɑː(r)/ *n.* metric unit of measure, 100 square metres.

area /'eərɪə/ *n.* region; space set aside for a purpose; extent or measure of surface; scope, range; space in front of house basement.

areca /'ærɪkə/ *n.* kind of palm-tree. **areca nut** astringent seed of areca.

arena /ə'riːnə/ *n.* centre of amphitheatre; scene of conflict; sphere of action.

aren't: see **be.**

arête /æ'reɪt/ *n.* sharp mountain ridge.

argon /'ɑːgɒn/ *n.* inert gaseous element.

argosy /'ɑːgəsɪ/ *n.* *hist.* large merchant-ship.

argot /'ɑːgəʊ/ *n.* jargon, orig. esp. of thieves.

argue /'ɑːgjuː/ *v.* exchange views, esp. heatedly; maintain by reasoning (*that*); reason; prove, indicate. **arguable** *a.*

argument /'ɑːgjʊm(ə)nt/ *n.* (esp. heated) exchange of views; reason advanced; reasoning; summary in book etc. **argumentation** *n.*

argumentative /ɑːgjʊ'mentətɪv/ *a.* fond of arguing.

aria /'ɑːrɪə/ *n.* song for one voice in opera, oratorio, etc.

arid /'ærɪd/ *n.* dry, parched. **aridity** *n.*

Aries /'eəriːz/ *n.* first sign of zodiac.

aright /ə'raɪt/ *adv.* rightly.

arise /ə'raɪz/ *v.i.* (*past* **arose**; *p.p.* **arisen** /ə'rɪz(ə)n/) originate, result; present itself; rise.

aristocracy /ærɪs'tɒkrəsɪ/ *n.* supremacy of privileged order; *the* nobility.

aristocrat /'ærɪstəkræt/ *n.* member of aristocracy.

aristocratic /ærɪstə'krætɪk/ *a.* of the aristocracy; grand, distinguished.

Aristotelian /ærɪstə'tiːlɪən/ *a.* of Aristotle.

arithmetic 1 /ə'rɪθmətɪk/ *n.* science of numbers; computation, use of numbers. **2** /ærɪθ'metɪk/ *a.* of arithmetic. **3 arithmetical** /-'met-/ *a.*; **arithmetician** /-'tɪʃ-/ *n.*

ark *n.* covered floating wooden vessel in which Noah was saved in Flood; **Ark of the Covenant** wooden chest containing tables of Jewish law.

arm¹ *n.* upper limb of human body; sleeve; raised side part of chair; branch; armlike thing. **arm-chair** chair with arms; **armpit** hollow under arm at shoulder.

arm² **1** *n.* (usu. in *pl.*) weapon; branch of military forces; in *pl.* heraldic devices. **2** *v.* equip with arms; equip oneself with arms; provide *with.*

Armada /ɑː'mɑːdə/ *n.* Spanish fleet sent against England in 1588.

armadillo /ɑːmə'dɪləʊ/ *n.* (*pl.* **-os**) S. Amer. burrowing mammal with body cased in bony plates.

Armageddon /ɑːmə'ged(ə)n/ *n.* scene of supreme battle at end of world.

armament /'ɑːməmənt/ *n.* military weapon etc.; equipping for war.

armature /'ɑːmətʃə(r)/ *n.* wire-wound core of dynamo or electric motor; bar of soft iron placed in contact with poles of magnet; internal framework on which sculpture is constructed.

armistice /'ɑːmɪstɪs/ *n.* stopping of hostilities; short truce.

armlet /'ɑːmlɪt/ *n.* band worn round arm.

armorial /ɑː'mɔːrɪəl/ *a.* of heraldic arms.

armour /'ɑːmə(r)/ *n.* defensive covering formerly worn in fighting; metal plates etc. protecting ship, car, tank, etc.; armoured vehicles etc.

armoured /'ɑːməd/ *a.* furnished with armour; equipped with armoured vehicles.

armourer /'ɑːmərə(r)/ *n.* maker of arms or armour; official in charge of arms.

armoury /'ɑːmərɪ/ *n.* arsenal.

army /'ɑːmɪ/ *n.* organized force armed for fighting on land; vast number; organized body.

arnica /'ɑːnɪkə/ *n.* kind of plant with yellow flowers; medicine made from it.

aroma /ə'rəʊmə/ *n.* fragrance, sweet smell; subtle quality. **aromatic** /ærə'mætɪk/ *a.*

arose *past* of **arise.**

around /ə'raʊnd/ **1** *adv.* on every side;

all round; *colloq.* near at hand. **2** *prep.* on or along the circuit of; on every side of; about.

arouse /əˈraʊz/ *v.t.* awake from sleep; stir into activity.

arpeggio /ɑːˈpedʒɪəʊ/ *n.* (*pl.* -os) sounding of notes of chord in rapid succession; chord so sounded.

arrack /ˈærək/ *n.* alcoholic spirit made esp. from rice.

arraign /əˈreɪn/ *v.t.* indict, accuse; find fault with. **arraignment** *n.*

arrange /əˈreɪndʒ/ *v.* put in order; plan or provide for; give instructions; agree (*with* person) about procedure for; *Mus.* adapt (composition). **arrangement** *n.*

arrant /ˈærənt/ *a.* downright, unmitigated.

arras /ˈærəs/ *n.* tapestry wall hanging.

array /əˈreɪ/ **1** *n.* imposing series; ordered arrangement, esp. of troops; *Math.* an arrangement of numbers in rows and columns; arrangement of data in computer such that program can access items by means of a key. **2** *v.t.* set in order; marshal (forces).

arrears /əˈrɪəz/ *n.pl.* outstanding debts; what remains not done; **in arrears** behindhand.

arrest /əˈrest/ **1** *v.t.* seize by authority; stop; catch attention of. **2** *n.* legal arresting of offender; stoppage.

arrive /əˈraɪv/ *v.i.* come to destination; establish one's position; *colloq.* be born, come. **arrival** *n.*

arrogant /ˈærəgənt/ *a.* aggressively haughty; presumptuous. **arrogance** *n.*

arrogate /ˈærəgeɪt/ *v.t.* claim without right. **arrogation** *n.*

arrow /ˈærəʊ/ *n.* pointed missile shot from bow; representation of (head of) arrow, esp. to show direction.

arrowroot /ˈærəʊruːt/ *n.* nutritious starch got from W. Ind. plant.

arse /ɑːs/ *n.* *vulg.* buttocks.

arsenal /ˈɑːsən(ə)l/ *n.* place for storage or manufacture of weapons and ammunition.

arsenic /ˈɑːsənɪk/ *n.* brittle steel-grey chemical element; its violently poisonous trioxide. **arsenical** /-ˈsen-/ *a.*

arson /ˈɑːsən/ *n.* criminal and deliberate act of setting on fire house or other property. **arsonist** *n.*

art *n.* human creative skill or its ap-

plication; branch of creative activity concerned with imitative and imaginative designs, e.g. painting; fine arts; thing in which skill can be exercised; in *pl.*, certain branches of learning (esp. languages, literature, history, etc.) as distinct from sciences; knack; cunning.

artefact /ˈɑːtɪfækt/ *n.* man-made object.

arterial /ɑːˈtɪərɪəl/ *a.* of or like an artery. **arterial road** important main road.

arteriosclerosis /ɑːtɪərɪəʊsklɪəˈrəʊsɪs/ *n.* hardening of walls of arteries.

artery /ˈɑːtərɪ/ *n.* muscular-walled blood-vessel conveying blood from heart; important channel of supplies etc.

artesian well /ɑːˈtiːʒ(ə)n/ well in which water rises to surface by natural pressure through vertically-drilled hole.

artful /ˈɑːtfʊl/ *a.* sly, crafty.

arthritis /ɑːˈθraɪtɪs/ *n.* inflammation of joint. **arthritic** /-ˈrɪt-/ *a.*

arthropod /ˈɑːθrəpɒd/ *n.* animal with segmented body and jointed limbs, e.g. insect or crustacean.

artichoke /ˈɑːtɪtʃəʊk/ *n.* plant allied to thistle with partly edible flowers; Jerusalem artichoke.

article /ˈɑːtɪk(ə)l/ **1** *n.* particular item or commodity; short self-contained piece of writing in newspaper etc.; clause of agreement etc. **2** *v.t.* bind by articles of apprenticeship. **3 definite article** 'the'; **indefinite article** 'a, an'.

articular /ɑːˈtɪkjʊlə(r)/ *a.* of joints.

articulate 1 /ɑːˈtɪkjʊlət/ *a.* expressing oneself fluently and coherently; (of speech) in which separate sounds and words are clear; having joints. **2** /ɑːˈtɪkjʊleɪt/ *v.* speak distinctly; express clearly; connect with joints. **3 articulated lorry** one with sections connected by flexible joint. **4 articulation** *n.*

artifice /ˈɑːtɪfɪs/ *n.* trick; cunning; skill.

artificer /ɑːˈtɪfɪsə(r)/ *n.* craftsman.

artificial /ɑːtɪˈfɪʃ(ə)l/ *a.* produced by art, man-made; not natural or real. **artificial insemination** injection of semen into uterus other than by sexual intercourse; **artificial respiration**

manual or mechanical stimulation of breathing. **artificiality** *n.*

artillery /ɑːˈtɪlərɪ/ *n.* large guns used in fighting on land; branch of army using these. **artilleryman** *n.*

artisan /ɑːtɪˈzæn/ *n.* skilled workman or craftsman.

artist /ˈɑːtɪst/ *n.* person who practises fine art, esp. painting; highly gifted practiser of any craft; artiste. **artistic** *a.*; **artistry** *n.*

artiste /ɑːˈtiːst/ *n.* professional singer, dancer, etc.

artless /ˈɑːtlɪs/ *a.* guileless, ingenuous; not resulting from art; clumsy.

arty /ˈɑːtɪ/ *a.* pretentiously or quaintly artistic.

arum /ˈeərəm/ *n.* kind of plant with small flowers enclosed in bracts.

Aryan /ˈeərɪən/ **1** *n.* speaker of parent language of Indo-European family; *incorrect* (esp. in Nazi Germany) non-Jewish Caucasian. **2** *a.* of Indo-European family of languages.

as /æz/ **1** *adv. & conj.* in the same degree; in the manner in which; in the form or function of; while, when; since, seeing that. **2** *rel. pron.* that, who, which. □ See page 667.

asafoetida /æsəˈfiːtɪdə/ *n.* resinous gum with strong smell.

asbestos /æsˈbestɒs/ *n.* a fibrous silicate mineral; fire-resistant substance made from this.

asbestosis /æsbesˈtəʊsɪs/ *n.* lung disease caused by inhaling asbestos particles.

ascend /əˈsend/ *v.* go or come up; rise, mount, climb.

ascendancy /əˈsendənsɪ/ *n.* dominant control *over.*

ascendant /əˈsend(ə)nt/ *a.* rising; gaining favour or control; rising towards zenith; *Astrol.* (of sign) just above eastern horizon. **in the ascendant** at or near peak of one's fortunes.

ascension /əˈsenʃ(ə)n/ *n.* ascent, esp. (**Ascension**) of Christ into Heaven.

ascent /əˈsent/ *n.* ascending, rising; upward path or slope.

ascertain /æsəˈteɪn/ *v.t.* find out. **ascertainment** *n.*

ascetic /əˈsetɪk/ **1** *a.* severely abstinent, severe in self-discipline. **2** *n.* ascetic person. **3** **asceticism** *n.*

ascorbic acid /əˈskɔːbɪk/ vitamin C.

ascribe /əˈskraɪb/ *v.t.* regard (thing or circumstance) as belonging *to;* attribute. **ascription** *n.*

asdic /ˈæzdɪk/ *n.* earlier form of sonar.

asepsis /eɪˈsepsɪs/ *n.* absence of sepsis or harmful bacteria; aseptic method in surgery.

aseptic /eɪˈseptɪk/ *a.* free from sepsis; surgically sterile; securing absence of septic matter; sterilized.

asexual /eɪˈseksjʊəl/ *a.* without sex; without sexuality; (of reproduction) not involving fusion of gametes.

ash[1] *n.* (freq. in *pl.*) powdery residue left after combustion of a substance; in *pl.* remains of human body after cremation; **the Ashes** symbol of victory in Anglo-Australian test cricket; **Ash Wednesday** first day of Lent.

ash[2] *n.* forest tree with silver-grey bark; its wood.

ashamed /əˈʃeɪmd/ *a.* feeling or affected by shame.

ashen /ˈæʃ(ə)n/ *a.* of ashes; pale.

ashlar /ˈæʃlə(r)/ *n.* (masonry made of) square-cut stones.

ashore /əˈʃɔː(r)/ *adv.* to or on shore.

ashram /ˈæʃræm/ *n.* orig. in India, retreat for religious meditation.

ashy /ˈæʃɪ/ *a.* ashen; covered with ash.

Asian /ˈeɪʃ(ə)n/ **1** *a.* of Asia or its peoples or languages. **2** *n.* native of Asia.

Asiatic /eɪzɪˈætɪk/ *a. & n.* Asian (usu. with geogr. reference).

aside /əˈsaɪd/ **1** *adv.* to or on one side, away, apart. **2** *n.* words spoken aside, esp. by actors.

asinine /ˈæsɪnaɪn/ *a.* like an ass; stupid.

ask /ɑːsk/ *v.* call for answer to or about; seek to obtain from another person; make request (for); invite.

askance /əˈskæns/ *adv.* sideways; **look askance at** view suspiciously.

askew /əˈskjuː/ *adv.* crookedly; out of true position.

aslant /əˈslɑːnt/ **1** *adv.* on a slant. **2** *prep.* obliquely across.

asleep /əˈsliːp/ **1** *pred.a.* sleeping; *colloq.* inattentive; (of limb) numb. **2** *adv.* into state of sleep.

asp *n.* small venomous snake.

asparagus /əsˈpærəgəs/ *n.* plant with

feathery leaves; its edible young shoots.

aspect /'æspekt/ n. way thing presents itself to eye or mind; direction in which thing faces; side facing in specified direction; *Astrol.* relative position of planets.

aspen /'æspən/ n. kind of poplar with fluttering leaves.

asperity /æs'perɪtɪ/ n. harshness; roughness.

aspersion /əs'pɜːʃ(ə)n/ n. damaging or derogatory remark; **cast aspersions on** defame.

asphalt /'æsfælt/ 1 n. tarlike bitumen made from petroleum; mixture of this with sand etc. for surfacing roads etc. 2 v.t. surface with asphalt.

asphodel /'æsfədel/ n. kind of lily; *poet.* immortal flower in Elysium.

asphyxia /æs'fɪksɪə/ n. condition caused by lack of oxygen in blood; suffocation.

asphyxiate /əs'fɪksɪeɪt/ v.t. suffocate. **asphyxiation** n.

aspic /'æspɪk/ n. clear meat jelly.

aspidistra /æspɪ'dɪstrə/ n. houseplant with broad tapering leaves.

aspirant /'æspɪrənt/ 1 n. person who aspires. 2 a. aspiring.

aspirate 1 /'æspɪreɪt/ v.t. pronounce with h. 2 /'æspɪrət/ n. sound of h; consonant blended with this.

aspiration /æspɪ'reɪʃ(ə)n/ n. desire, ambition; aspirating.

aspire /ə'spaɪə(r)/ v.i. feel earnest desire or ambition; seek *after*.

aspirin /'æsprɪn/ n. white powder used to relieve pain and reduce fever; tablet of this.

ass n. four-legged animal with long ears, related to horse; stupid person.

assail /ə'seɪl/ v.t. attack; pester. **assailant** n.

assassin /ə'sæsɪn/ n. killer, esp. of important person for political motives.

assassinate /ə'sæsɪneɪt/ v.t. kill (esp. political etc. leader) by treacherous violence. **assassination** n.

assault /ə'sɔːlt/ 1 n. sudden violent attack; *euphem.* rape; unlawful personal attack. 2 v.t. make assault upon. 3 **assault course** series of obstacles to be climbed over or under etc. as part of military training.

assay /ə'seɪ/ 1 n. test of metal or ore

for quality. 2 v.t. make assay of; *arch.* attempt.

assegai /'æsɪɡaɪ/ n. throwing-spear of S. Afr. peoples.

assemblage /ə'semblɪdʒ/ n. collection, group.

assemble /ə'semb(ə)l/ v. fit together parts of (machine etc.); bring or come together.

assembly /ə'semblɪ/ n. assembling; collection of persons, esp. of deliberative body; fitting together of components. **assembly line** sequence of machines, workers, etc., assembling product.

assent /ə'sent/ 1 n. consent, approval. 2 v.i. agree *to*.

assert /ə'sɜːt/ v.t. declare; maintain claim to. **assert oneself** insist on one's rights.

assertion /ə'sɜːʃ(ə)n/ n. declaration; forthright statement.

assertive /ə'sɜːtɪv/ a. asserting oneself; forthright, positive.

assess /ə'ses/ v.t. estimate magnitude or value or quality of; fix amount of (fine, tax, etc.). **assessment** n.

assessor n. one who assesses taxes etc.; adviser to judge in court.

asset /'æset/ n. possession having value; (often in *pl.*) property available to meet debts; useful quality or person.

asseverate /ə'sevəreɪt/ v.t. declare solemnly. **asseveration** n.

assiduous /ə'sɪdjʊəs/ a. persevering, diligent. **assiduity** /æsɪ'djuːɪtɪ/ n.

assign /ə'saɪn/ v.t. allot; appoint, ascribe; make over formally.

assignation /æsɪɡ'neɪʃ(ə)n/ n. appointment, esp. of lovers; assigning.

assignee /əsaɪ'niː/ n. person to whom property or right is legally transferred.

assignment /ə'saɪnmənt/ n. task assigned.

assimilate /ə'sɪmɪleɪt/ v. absorb, be absorbed, into system; make or become like. **assimilable** a.; **assimilation** n.; **assimilative** a.

assist /ə'sɪst/ v. help; take part *in*; be present *at*. **assistance** n.

assistant /ə'sɪst(ə)nt/ n. helper; subordinate worker, esp. serving customers in shop.

assizes /ə'saɪzɪz/ n. hist. periodical session for administration of civil and criminal justice.

Assoc. *abbr.* Association.

associate 1 /əˈsəʊʃɪeɪt/ *v.* connect; join, combine; have frequent dealings (*with*). **2** /əˈsəʊʃɪət/ *n.* subordinate member of society etc.; partner or colleague. **3** /əˈsəʊʃɪət/ *a.* joined, allied.

association /əsəʊsɪˈeɪʃ(ə)n/ *n.* body of persons organized for joint purpose; connection of ideas; companionship. **Association football** kind played with round ball which may be handled only by goalkeeper.

assonance /ˈæsənəns/ *n.* resemblance of sound between two syllables; rhyme depending on similarity of vowel-sounds only. **assonant** *a.*

assort /əˈsɔːt/ *v.* arrange in sorts; suit, harmonize (*with*).

assorted *a.* of various sorts put together.

assortment *n.* set composed of several sorts.

assuage /əˈsweɪdʒ/ *v.t.* soothe, allay.

assume /əˈsjuːm/ *v.t.* take to be true; take upon oneself; simulate.

assumption /əˈsʌmpʃ(ə)n/ *n.* assuming, thing assumed. **the Assumption** taking of Virgin Mary bodily into heaven.

assurance /əˈʃʊərəns/ *n.* declaration; self-confidence; impudence; insurance, esp. of life.

assure /əˈʃʊə(r)/ *v.t.* make (person) sure (*of*); tell (person) confidently; ensure happening etc. of; insure (esp. life).

assuredly /əˈʃʊərɪdlɪ/ *adv.* certainly.

aster /ˈæstə(r)/ *n.* garden plant with bright daisy-like flowers.

asterisk /ˈæstərɪsk/ *n.* star-shaped symbol (*) used esp. as mark of reference.

astern /əˈstɜːn/ *adv.* in or to rear of ship or aircraft; behind; backwards.

asteroid /ˈæstərɔɪd/ *n.* any of numerous small planets between orbits of Mars and Jupiter.

asthma /ˈæsmə/ *n.* disorder marked by difficulty in breathing. **asthmatic** /-ˈmæt-/ *a.* & *n.*

astigmatism /əˈstɪɡmətɪz(ə)m/ *n.* defect in eye or lens in which light rays from a point produce a line image. **astigmatic** /-ˈmæt-/ *a.*

astir /əˈstɜː(r)/ *adv.* & *pred.a.* in motion; out of bed.

astonish /əˈstɒnɪʃ/ *v.t.* amaze, surprise. **astonishment** *n.*

astound /əˈstaʊnd/ *v.t.* shock with surprise.

astrakhan /æstrəˈkæn/ *n.* dark curly fleece of Astrakhan lamb; imitation of this.

astral /ˈæstr(ə)l/ *a.* of or connected with stars.

astray /əˈstreɪ/ *adv.* out of right way.

astride /əˈstraɪd/ **1** *adv.* with one leg on each side (*of*). **2** *prep.* astride of.

astringent /əˈstrɪndʒ(ə)nt/ **1** *a.* that causes contraction of body tissue; austere, severe. **2** *n.* astringent substance. **3 astringency** *n.*

astrolabe /ˈæstrəleɪb/ *n.* instrument for measuring altitudes of stars etc.

astrologer /əˈstrɒlədʒə(r)/ *n.* person who practises astrology.

astrology /əˈstrɒlədʒɪ/ *n.* study of influence of movements of stars etc. on human affairs. **astrological** *a.*

astronaut /ˈæstrənɔːt/ *n.* space traveller. **astronautical** *a.*

astronautics /æstrəˈnɔːtɪks/ *n.pl.* usu. treated as *sing.* science of space travel.

astronomer /əˈstrɒnəmə(r)/ *n.* person who practises astronomy.

astronomical /æstrəˈnɒmɪk(ə)l/ *a.* (of number etc.) very big or high; of or concerned with astronomy.

astronomy /əˈstrɒnəmɪ/ *n.* science of heavenly bodies.

astrophysics /æstrəʊˈfɪzɪks/ *n.* study of physics and chemistry of heavenly bodies. **astrophysical** *a.*; **astrophysicist** *n.*

astute /əˈstjuːt/ *a.* shrewd; crafty.

asunder /əˈsʌndə(r)/ *adv.* apart, in pieces.

asylum /əˈsaɪləm/ *n.* place of refuge or safety; (in full **political asylum**) protection given by State to political refugee from another country; *hist.* mental institution.

asymmetry /æˈsɪmətrɪ/ *n.* lack of symmetry. **asymmetrical** /æsɪˈmet-/ *a.*

at /æt/ *prep.* expr. position or state of activity or point in time or on a scale, or motion or aim towards. **at all** in any way, to any extent; **at that** moreover.

atavism /ˈætəvɪz(ə)m/ *n.* resemblance to remote ancestors; reversion to earlier type. **atavistic** *a.*

ate *past* of eat.

atelier /ə'teljeı/ *n.* workshop; artist's studio.

atheism /'eıθıız(ə)m/ *n.* belief that no God exists. **atheist** *n.*; **atheistic** *a.*

atherosclerosis /æθərəʊsklıə'rəʊsıs/ *n.* formation of fatty deposits in the arteries.

athlete /'æθliːt/ *n.* person who competes or excels in physical exercises. **athlete's foot** fungous disease of foot.

athletic /æθ'letık/ *a.* of athletes; physically powerful. **athleticism** *n.*

athletics *n.pl.* (occas. treated as *sing.*) sports such as running, jumping, etc.

atlas /'ætləs/ *n.* book of maps.

atmosphere /'ætməsfıə(r)/ *n.* mixture of gases surrounding earth or heavenly body; mental or moral environment; tone, mood, etc., conveyed by place, book, etc.; air in room etc. **atmospheric** /-'fer-/ *a.*

atmospherics /ætməs'ferıks/ *n.pl.* electrical disturbance in atmosphere; interference with telecommunications caused by this.

atoll /'ætɒl/ *n.* ring-shaped coral reef enclosing lagoon.

atom /'ætəm/ *n.* smallest particle of chemical element that can take part in chemical reaction; this as source of atomic energy; minute portion or thing. **atom bomb** atomic bomb.

atomic /ə'tɒmık/ *a.* of atom(s); using or concerned with atomic energy or atomic bombs. **atomic bomb** bomb whose power comes from release of nuclear energy; **atomic energy** nuclear energy; **atomic number** number of unit positive charges carried by nucleus of atom; **atomic weight** ratio between mass of one atom of element and 1/12 weight of atom of isotope carbon 12.

atomize /'ætəmaız/ *v.t.* reduce to atoms; reduce (liquid) to fine spray. **atomization** *n.*; **atomizer** *n.*

atonal /eı'təʊn(ə)l/ *a. Mus.* not written in any key. **atonality** /-'næl-/ *n.*

atone /ə'təʊn/ *v.t.* make amends (*for* wrong). **atonement** *n.*

atrium /'eıtrıəm/ *n.* (*pl.* **-tria** or **-triums**) either of two upper cavities of heart.

atrocious /ə'trəʊʃəs/ *a.* very bad; extremely wicked.

atrocity /ə'trɒsıtı/ *n.* wicked or cruel act.

atrophy /'ætrəfı/ **1** *n.* wasting away for lack of nourishment or use. **2** *v.* cause atrophy in; suffer atrophy.

atropine /'ætrəpın/ *n.* poisonous alkaloid got from deadly nightshade.

attach /ə'tætʃ/ *v.* fasten, join; accompany, form part of; attribute or be attributable *to*; seize by legal authority.

attaché /ə'tæʃeı/ *n.* person attached to ambassador's staff. **attaché case** small rectangular case for carrying documents etc.

attachment /ə'tætʃmənt/ *n.* attaching, thing attached, esp. device; affection, devotion.

attack /ə'tæk/ **1** *v.* make attack (on); act harmfully on; (in sport) try to score against. **2** *n.* violent attempt to hurt or defeat; adverse criticism; onset.

attain /ə'teın/ *v.* gain, accomplish; reach; come to (goal etc.).

attainment *n.* attaining; (usu. in *pl.*) skills, achievements.

attar /'ætɑː(r)/ *n.* fragrant oil esp. made from rose-petals.

attempt /ə'tempt/ **1** *v.t.* try; try to accomplish or conquer. **2** *n.* attempting; endeavour.

attend /ə'tend/ *v.* be present at; go regularly to; apply mind or oneself (*to*); accompany, wait on.

attendance /ə'tend(ə)ns/ *n.* attending; number of persons present.

attendant /ə'tend(ə)nt/ **1** *n.* person attending, esp. to provide service. **2** *a.* waiting *on*; accompanying.

attention /ə'tenʃ(ə)n/ *n.* act or faculty of applying one's mind; consideration, care; *Mil.* erect attitude of readiness; in *pl.* formal courtesies.

attentive /ə'tentıv/ *a.* giving or paying attention (*to*).

attenuate /ə'tenjʊeıt/ *v.t.* make slender or thin; reduce in force or value. **attenuation** *n.*

attest /ə'test/ *v.* act as evidence of; certify validity of; bear witness *to*. **attestation** *n.*

attested *a.* (of cattle or milk) officially certified free from disease.

attic[1] /'ætık/ *n.* room or space in storey immediately under roof.

Attic[2] /'ætık/ *a.* of Athens or Attica.

attire /əˈtaɪə(r)/ n. dress, esp. formal.

attitude /ˈætɪtjuːd/ n. way of regarding things; disposition or reaction (to person or thing); posture of body.

attitudinize /ætɪˈtjuːdɪnaɪz/ v.i. adopt attitudes; show affectation.

attorney /əˈtɜːnɪ/ n. person appointed to act for another in business or legal affairs; US qualified lawyer. **Attorney-General** chief legal officer of government.

attract /əˈtrækt/ v.t. draw to itself or oneself; arouse interest or pleasure in.

attraction /əˈtrækʃ(ə)n/ n. attracting, thing that attracts; charm, inducement.

attractive /əˈtræktɪv/ a. inviting, pleasing.

attribute 1 /əˈtrɪbjuːt/ v.t. regard as belonging or appropriate to. 2 /ˈætrɪbjuːt/ n. quality ascribed to person or thing; characteristic quality; object regularly associated with person etc. 3 **attribute to** consider to be caused by. 4 **attribution** /ætrɪˈbjuːʃ(ə)n/ n.

attributive /əˈtrɪbjʊtɪv/ a. expressing an attribute; (of adj.) coming before noun it qualifies.

attrition /əˈtrɪʃ(ə)n/ n. gradual wearing down; friction; abrasion.

attune /əˈtjuːn/ v.t. adapt; tune; bring into musical accord.

atypical /eɪˈtɪpɪk(ə)l/ a. not belonging to any type.

aubergine /ˈəʊbədʒiːn/ n. plant with oval usu. purple fruit; this fruit, used as vegetable.

aubrietia /ɔːˈbriːʃə/ n. spring-flowering dwarf perennial rock-plant.

auburn /ˈɔːbən/ a. reddish-brown.

auction /ˈɔːkʃ(ə)n/ 1 n. sale in which each article is sold to highest bidder. 2 v.t. sell by auction.

auctioneer /ɔːkʃəˈnɪə(r)/ n. person who conducts auctions.

audacious /ɔːˈdeɪʃəs/ a. daring, bold; impudent. **audacity** /-ˈdæs-/ n.

audible /ˈɔːdɪb(ə)l/ a. that can be heard. **audibility** n.

audience /ˈɔːdɪəns/ n. group of listeners or spectators; formal interview.

audio /ˈɔːdɪəʊ/ n. (reproduction of) sound. **audio typist** one who types directly from recording; **audio-visual** using both sight and sound.

audit /ˈɔːdɪt/ 1 n. official examination of accounts. 2 v.t. conduct audit of.

audition /ɔːˈdɪʃ(ə)n/ 1 n. trial hearing of actor, singer, etc. 2 v. give audition to; hold auditions; be auditioned.

auditor /ˈɔːdɪtə(r)/ n. person who audits accounts.

auditorium /ɔːdɪˈtɔːrɪəm/ n. (pl. -iums) part of theatre etc. occupied by audience.

auditory /ˈɔːdɪtərɪ/ a. of hearing.

au fait /əʊ ˈfeɪ/ well acquainted with. [F]

Aug. abbr. August.

auger /ˈɔːgə(r)/ n. tool for boring holes in wood.

aught /ɔːt/ n. arch. anything.

augment /ɔːgˈment/ v.t. make greater, increase. **augmentation** n.

augmented a. Mus. (of interval) increased by semitone.

augur /ˈɔːgə(r)/ 1 n. Roman religious official who foretold events by observing omens; soothsayer. 2 v. portend; serve as omen for.

augury /ˈɔːgjʊrɪ/ n. divination; omen.

august¹ /ɔːˈgʌst/ a. venerable, imposing.

August² /ˈɔːgəst/ n. eighth month of year.

auk /ɔːk/ n. Northern sea-bird with small narrow wings.

aunt /ɑːnt/ n. parent's sister or sister-in-law. **Aunt Sally** (figure used as target in) throwing game, target of general abuse.

aunty /ˈɑːntɪ/ n. (also **auntie**) colloq. aunt.

au pair /əʊ ˈpeə(r)/ young woman usu. from abroad who helps with housework in return for room and board.

aura /ˈɔːrə/ n. atmosphere diffused by or attending person etc.; subtle emanation.

aural /ˈɔːr(ə)l/ a. of ear or hearing.

aureola /ɔːˈrɪəʊlə/ n. (also **aureole**) halo.

au revoir /əʊ rəˈvwɑː(r)/ (good-bye) till we meet again. [F]

auricle /ˈɔːrɪk(ə)l/ n. external part of ear; atrium of heart.

auricular /ɔːˈrɪkjʊlə(r)/ a. pertaining to ear. **auricular confession** confession made privately to priest.

auriferous /ɔːˈrɪfərəs/ a. yielding gold.

aurora /ɔːˈrɔːrə/ n. luminous electrical radiation from northern (**aurora borealis** /bɔːrɪˈeɪlɪs/) or southern (**aurora australis** /ɔːˈstreɪlɪs/) magnetic pole.

auscultation /ɔːskəlˈteɪʃ(ə)n/ n. listening to sound of heart etc. for diagnosis.

auspice /ˈɔːspɪs/ n. omen; in pl. patronage.

auspicious /ɔːˈspɪʃəs/ a. promising; favourable.

Aussie /ˈɒzɪ/ n. & a. colloq. Australian.

austere /ɔːˈstɪə(r)/ a. severely simple; stern; morally strict. **austerity** /-ˈter-/ n.

austral /ˈɔːstr(ə)l/ a. southern.

Australasian /ɒstrəˈleɪʒ(ə)n/ a. of Australia and S.W. Pacific Islands.

Australian /ɒsˈtreɪlɪən/ 1 a. of Australia. 2 n. native or inhabitant of Australia.

autarchy /ˈɔːtɑːkɪ/ n. absolute sovereignty.

autarky /ˈɔːtɑːkɪ/ n. self-sufficiency.

authentic /ɔːˈθentɪk/ a. of undisputed origin, genuine; trustworthy. **authentically** adv.; **authenticity** /-ˈtɪs-/ n.

authenticate /ɔːˈθentɪkeɪt/ v.t. establish truth, authorship, or validity of. **authentication** n.

author /ˈɔːθə(r)/ n. writer of book etc.; originator. **authoress** n.; **authorship** n.

authoritarian /ɔːθɒrɪˈteərɪən/ 1 a. favouring unqualified obedience to authority. 2 n. authoritarian person.

authoritative /ɔːˈθɒrɪtətɪv/ a. having or claiming authority.

authority /ɔːˈθɒrɪtɪ/ n. power or right to enforce obedience; person or body having this; delegated power; personal influence; (book etc. referred to for) conclusive opinion or statement; expert.

authorize /ˈɔːθəraɪz/ v.t. give authority to; recognize officially. **Authorized Version** English translation (1611) of Bible. **authorization** n.

autism /ˈɔːtɪz(ə)m/ n. mental condition esp. in children preventing proper response to environment. **autistic** a.

autobiography /ɔːtəʊbaɪˈɒɡrəfɪ/ n. story of one's own life. **autobiographer** n.; **autobiographical** a.

autochthonous /ɔːˈtɒkθənəs/ a. indigenous; aboriginal.

autocracy /ɔːˈtɒkrəsɪ/ n. absolute government by one person.

autocrat /ˈɔːtəkræt/ n. absolute ruler. **autocratic** a.

autocross /ˈɔːtəʊkrɒs/ n. motor-racing across country or on unmade roads.

autograph /ˈɔːtəɡrɑːf/ 1 n. person's own handwriting, esp. signature. 2 v.t. sign or write on in one's own hand.

automate /ˈɔːtəmeɪt/ v.t. subject to or operate by automation.

automatic /ɔːtəˈmætɪk/ 1 a. working of itself, without direct human involvement; done without thought or from habit; occurring as a necessary consequence; (of firearm) having mechanism for continuous loading and firing. 2 n. automatic gun etc.; vehicle with automatic transmission. 3 **automatic transmission** system in motor vehicle for automatic change of gears. 4 **automatically** adv.

automation /ɔːtəˈmeɪʃ(ə)n/ n. use of automatic equipment to save mental or manual labour.

automaton /ɔːˈtɒmət(ə)n/ n. (pl. **-ta** or **-tons**) machine responding to automatic control.

automobile /ˈɔːtəməbiːl/ n. US motor car.

automotive /ɔːtəˈməʊtɪv/ a. concerned with motor vehicles.

autonomous /ɔːˈtɒnəməs/ a. self-governing. **autonomy** n.

autopsy /ˈɔːtɒpsɪ/ n. post-mortem examination.

auto-suggestion /ɔːtəʊsəˈdʒestʃ(ə)n/ n. hypnotic or subconscious suggestion proceeding from subject himself.

autumn /ˈɔːtəm/ n. season of year between summer and winter. **autumnal** /-ˈtʌmn(ə)l/ a.

auxiliary /ɔːkˈzɪlɪərɪ/ 1 a. giving help, additional, subsidiary. 2 n. auxiliary person or thing; in pl. foreign or allied troops in service of nation at war; verb used in forming tenses etc. of other verbs.

avail /əˈveɪl/ 1 v. be of use or help (to). 2 n. use, profit. 3 **avail oneself of** use, profit by.

available /əˈveɪləb(ə)l/ a. capable of being used; at one's disposal. **availability** n.

avalanche /ˈævəlɑːnʃ/ n. mass of snow, earth, and ice falling down mountain; sudden onrush.

avant-garde /ævɑ̃ˈgɑːd/ 1 n. group of innovators in art and music and literature. 2 a. new, progressive.

avarice /ˈævərɪs/ n. greed for gain. **avaricious** a.

avatar /ˈævətɑː(r)/ n. Hindu Myth. descent of god to earth in bodily form.

avenge /əˈvendʒ/ v.t. inflict retribution on behalf of; exact retribution for.

avenue /ˈævənjuː/ n. road or path, usu. bordered by trees etc.; way of approach.

aver /əˈvɜː(r)/ v.t. assert, affirm.

average /ˈævərɪdʒ/ 1 n. usual amount or extent or rate; number obtained by dividing total of given numbers by how many there are. 2 a. usual, ordinary; estimated by average. 3 v. amount on average to; do etc. on average; estimate average of. 4 **on average** as an average rate etc.

averse /əˈvɜːs/ a. opposed, disinclined, unwilling.

aversion /əˈvɜːʃ(ə)n/ n. dislike or antipathy; object of dislike.

avert /əˈvɜːt/ v.t. prevent; turn away.

aviary /ˈeɪvɪərɪ/ n. large cage or building for keeping birds.

aviation /eɪvɪˈeɪʃ(ə)n/ n. flying in aircraft.

aviator /ˈeɪvɪeɪtə(r)/ n. person who flies aircraft.

avid /ˈævɪd/ a. eager; greedy. **avidity** n.

avocado /ævəˈkɑːdəʊ/ n. (pl. **-dos**) pear-shaped tropical fruit.

avocation /ævəˈkeɪʃ(ə)n/ n. secondary activity; colloq. one's occupation.

avocet /ˈævəset/ n. wading bird with long upturned bill.

avoid /əˈvɔɪd/ v.t. keep away or refrain from; escape from. **avoidance** n.

avoirdupois /ævədjuˈpɔɪz/ n. system of weights based on pound of 16 ounces.

avow /əˈvaʊ/ v.t. declare; confess. **avowal** n.; **avowedly** adv.

avuncular /əˈvʌŋkjʊlə(r)/ a. of or like an uncle.

await /əˈweɪt/ v.t. wait for.

awake /əˈweɪk/ 1 v. (past **awoke**; p.p. **awoken**) rouse from sleep; cease to sleep; become active. 2 pred.a. not asleep; alert.

awaken /əˈweɪk(ə)n/ v. awake, draw attention of (person to).

award /əˈwɔːd/ 1 v.t. order to be given as payment, penalty, or prize. 2 n. judicial decision; thing awarded.

aware /əˈweə(r)/ a. conscious, having knowledge (of).

awash /əˈwɒʃ/ pred.a. at or near surface of water; covered or flooded by water.

away 1 adv. to or at distance; into nonexistence; constantly, continuously. 2 a. (of match etc.) played on opponent's ground.

awe /ɔː/ 1 n. admiration mixed with reverential fear. 2 v.t. inspire with awe. 3 **awestruck** struck with awe.

aweigh /əˈweɪ/ adv. (of anchor) just lifted from sea bottom.

awesome /ˈɔːsəm/ a. inspiring awe.

awful /ˈɔːfʊl/ a. inspiring awe; colloq. very bad; notable in its kind.

awfully adv. colloq. very.

awhile /əˈwaɪl/ adv. for a short time.

awkward /ˈɔːkwəd/ a. difficult to use; clumsy; embarrassing, embarrassed; hard to deal with.

awl /ɔːl/ n. small tool for pricking holes, esp.in leather.

awning /ˈɔːnɪŋ/ n. fabric roof, shelter.

awoke(n) past & p.p. of **awake**.

AWOL /ˈeɪwɒl/ abbr. absent without leave.

awry /əˈraɪ/ adv. crookedly; amiss.

axe /æks/ 1 n. chopping-tool. 2 v.t. cut down (costs, services, etc.); remove.

axial /ˈæksɪəl/ a. of, forming, or placed around axis.

axiom /ˈæksɪəm/ n. established principle; self-evident truth. **axiomatic** a.

axis /ˈæksɪs/ n. (pl. **axes** /-iːz/) imaginary line about which object rotates; line dividing regular figure symmetrically; reference line for measurement of coordinates etc.

axle /ˈæks(ə)l/ n. spindle on or with which wheel revolves; rod connecting pair of wheels.

ayatollah /aɪəˈtɒlə/ n. religious leader in Iran.

aye¹ /aɪ/ 1 adv. arch. yes. 2 n. affirmative answer or vote.

aye² /aɪ/ adv. arch. always.

azalea /əˈzeɪlɪə/ *n.* flowering shrubby plant.

azimuth /ˈæzɪməθ/ *n.* arc along horizon from N. or S. meridian to meridian through given point.

azure /ˈæʒə(r)/ **1** *a.* sky-blue. **2** *n.* sky-blue colour; clear sky.

B

B *abbr.* black (pencil lead).

b. *abbr.* born.

BA *abbr.* Bachelor of Arts.

baa /bɑː/ *n. & v.i.* (*past & p.p.* **baaed** or **baa'd**) bleat.

baba /ˈbɑːbɑː/ *n.* (*pl.* **babas**) sponge-cake soaked in rum syrup.

babble /ˈbæb(ə)l/ 1 *v.* make incoherent sounds, talk inarticulately, say incoherently, divulge foolishly; (of stream) murmur. 2 *n.* idle talk; murmur of water etc.

babe *n.* baby.

babel /ˈbeɪb(ə)l/ *n.* confused noise esp. of voices; scene of confusion.

baboon /bəˈbuːn/ *n.* large kind of monkey.

baby /ˈbeɪbɪ/ *n.* very young child; childish person; youngest member of family etc.; thing small of its kind; young or small animal. **baby grand** small grand piano; **baby-sit** act as **baby-sitter**, person looking after child while parents are out.

baccarat /ˈbækərɑː/ *n.* gambling card-game.

Bacchanalia /bækəˈneɪlɪə/ *n.pl.* festival of Bacchus, Roman god of wine. **Bacchanalian** *a.*

bachelor /ˈbætʃələ(r)/ *n.* unmarried man; person who has taken university first degree. **bachelor girl** *colloq.* young unmarried woman living independently.

bacillus /bəˈsɪləs/ *n.* (*pl.* **-illi** /-ˈɪlaɪ/) rod-shaped bacterium. **bacillary** *a.*

back 1 *n.* rear surface of human body from shoulders to hips; upper surface of animal's body; side or part at rear or normally away from spectator or direction of motion; part of garment covering back; defensive player in football etc. 2 *a.* situated behind or away from front; overdue; reversed. 3 *adv.* to rear; away from front; in or into the past or an earlier or normal position or condition; in return; at a distance. 4 *v.* help with money or moral support; cause to move backwards; go backwards; bet on; provide with or serve as back or support or backing to. 5 **back-bencher** MP without senior office; **backbite** speak badly of; **back-boiler** one behind domestic fire etc.; **back-bone** spine, main support, firmness of character; **backchat** impudent repartee; **backcloth** painted cloth at back of stage or scene; **backdate** put earlier date to, make retrospectively valid; **back door** *fig.* secret or ingenious means of gaining objective; **back down** abandon claim etc.; **backdrop** backcloth; **backfire** (of engine or vehicle) undergo premature explosion in cylinder or exhaust-pipe, (of plan etc.) have opposite of intended effect; **backhand** stroke esp. in tennis with back of hand towards opponent; **back-handed** indirect, ambiguous; **back-hander** blow with back of hand, *sl.* bribe; **backlash** excessive or violent reaction; **backlog** arrears (of work etc.); **back number** old issue of magazine etc., *sl.* out-of-date person or thing; **back out** withdraw; **backpack** rucksack; **back-pedal** *fig.* reverse previous action or opinion; **back room** *fig.* place where (esp. secret) work goes on; **back seat** *fig.* inferior position or status; **backside** *colloq.* buttocks; **backslide** relapse into error or bad ways; **backstage** behind the scenes; **backstairs** *fig.* =**back door**; **backstroke** stroke made by swimmer lying on back; **backtrack** find way back by route by which one came, *fig.* =**back-pedal**; **back up** support by subordinate action; **back-up** support; **backwash** motion of receding wave, repercussions; **backwater** place remote from centre of activity or thought, stagnant water fed from stream; **back-woods** remote uncleared forest land.

backgammon /ˈbækgæmən/ *n.* game played on double board with draughts moved according to throw of dice.

background /ˈbækgraʊnd/ *n.* back part of scene etc.; inconspicuous or obscure position; person's education or social circumstances etc.; explanatory information etc.

backing *n.* help or support; material used to form thing's back or support; musical accompaniment.

backward *a.* directed backwards; slow in learning; shy.

backwards *adv.* away from one's

front; back foremost; in reverse of usual way; back towards starting-point.

bacon /'beɪk(ə)n/ *n.* cured meat from back and sides of pig.

bacteriology /bæktɪərɪ'ɒlədʒɪ/ *n.* science of bacteria. **bacteriological** *a.*

bacterium /bæk'tɪərɪəm/ *n.* (*pl.* **-ria** □ See page 666.) single-celled micro-organism. **bacterial** *a.*

bad *a.* (*compar.* **worse**; *superl.* **worst**) inferior; defective; unpleasant; harmful; serious, severe; wicked; naughty; decayed; ill, injured; incorrect, not valid.

bade *past* of **bid**.

badge *n.* small flat emblem fixed to clothing etc. as sign of office, membership, etc. or bearing slogan etc.

badger /'bædʒə(r)/ 1 *n.* nocturnal burrowing mammal with black and white stripes along muzzle. 2 *v.t.* pester.

badinage /'bædɪnɑ:ʒ/ *n.* banter. [F]

badly *adv.* (*compar.* **worse**; *superl.* **worst**) in a bad manner; very much; severely.

badminton /'bædmɪnt(ə)n/ *n.* game played with rackets and shuttlecocks.

baffle /'bæf(ə)l/ 1 *v.t.* perplex, frustrate. 2 *n.* plate etc. hindering or regulating passage of fluid or sound. 3 **bafflement** *n.*

bag 1 *n.* receptacle of flexible material with opening usu. at top; in *pl. colloq.* large amount; sac in animal body; amount of game shot by sportsman. 2 *v.* secure, take possession of; bulge, hang loosely; put in bag.

bagatelle /bægə'tel/ *n.* game like billiards played with small balls on inclined board; a mere trifle.

baggage /'bægɪdʒ/ *n.* luggage; portable equipment of army.

baggy *a.* hanging loosely.

bagpipes /'bægpaɪps/ *n.pl.* musical instrument with wind-bag for pumping air through set of reed-pipes. **bagpiper** *n.*

bail¹ 1 *n.* security given for released prisoner's return for trial; person(s) pledging thus. 2 *v.t.* (often with *out*) give bail for (person in prison) and secure release of.

bail² *n. Crick.* one of two cross-pieces resting on stumps.

bail³ *v.* scoop water out of (boat etc.).

bail out make emergency parachute jump from aircraft.

bailey /'beɪlɪ/ *n.* outer wall of castle; court enclosed by this.

bailie /'beɪlɪ/ *n.* Scottish municipal councillor serving as magistrate.

bailiff /'beɪlɪf/ *n.* sheriff's officer who executes writs, performs distraints, etc.; landlord's agent or steward.

bailiwick /'beɪlɪwɪk/ *n.* district of bailie.

bairn /beən/ *n. Sc.* child.

bait 1 *v.t.* torment (chained animal); harrass (person); put bait on or in (fish-hook, trap, etc.). 2 *n.* food to entice prey; allurement.

baize /beɪz/ *n.* coarse woollen usu. green fabric used for coverings etc.

bake *v.* cook by dry heat esp. in oven; harden by heat; be or become baked; *colloq.* be hot. **baking-powder**, mixture of chemicals used as raising agent in cooking.

bakelite /'beɪkəlaɪt/ *n.* kind of plastic.

baker /'beɪkə(r)/ *n.* professional bread-maker. **baker's dozen** thirteen.

bakery /'beɪkərɪ/ *n.* place where bread is made or sold.

baksheesh /bæk'ʃiːʃ/ *n.* gratuity, tip; alms.

Balaclava /bælə'klɑ:və/ *n.* (in full **balaclava helmet**) woollen covering for head and neck.

balalaika /bælə'laɪkə/ *n.* Russian triangular-bodied guitar-like musical instrument.

balance /'bæləns/ 1 *n.* weighing apparatus; regulating gear of clock etc.; even distribution of weight or amount, stability of body or mind; preponderating weight or amount; difference between credits and debits; remainder. 2 *v.* offset or compare; bring or come into or keep in equilibrium; equalize debits and credits of account, have debits and credits equal. 3 **balance of payments** difference between payments into and out of a country; **balance of power** position in which no country, party, etc., predominates, power held by small group when larger groups are of equal strength; **balance of trade** difference between exports and imports; **balance-sheet** statement of assets and liabilities.

balcony /'bælkənɪ/ *n.* outside balustraded or railed platform with access from upper-floor window; upper tier of seats in public building, theatre, cinema, etc.

bald /bɔːld/ *a.* with scalp wholly or partly hairless; without fur, feathers, etc.; with surface worn away; direct; dull.

balderdash /'bɔːldədæʃ/ *n.* nonsense.

balding /'bɔːldɪŋ/ *a.* becoming bald.

bale[1] 1 *n.* bundle or package of merchandise, hay, etc. 2 *v.t.* make up into bales.

bale[2] var. of **bail**[3].

baleful /'beɪlfʊl/ *a.* pernicious, destructive; malignant.

balk /bɔːlk/ 1 *v.* thwart, hinder, disappoint; refuse, hesitate (*at*). 2 *n.* hindrance, stumbling-block.

ball[1] /bɔːl/ *n.* solid or hollow sphere, esp. one used in games; material gathered or wound into round mass; rounded part of foot or hand at base of big toe or thumb; missile for cannon etc.; delivery of ball in a game; in *pl.*, *vulg.* testicles; nonsense, muddle. **ball-bearing** bearing using small metal balls to avoid friction, one such ball; **ballcock** valve in cistern etc. opened or shut by falling or rising of floating ball; **ballpoint** (**pen**) pen whose writing-point is a small ball.

ball[2] /bɔːl/ *n.* formal social gathering for dancing; *sl.* enjoyable time.

ballad /'bæləd/ *n.* simple or sentimental song; (esp. traditional) narrative poem in short stanzas. **balladry** *n.*

ballast /'bæləst/ 1 *n.* heavy material carried in ship's hold for stability or in balloon for control of height; coarse stone etc. as bed of road or railway. 2 *v.t.* furnish with ballast.

ballerina /bælə'riːnə/ *n.* female ballet-dancer esp. taking leading role.

ballet /'bæleɪ/ *n.* theatrical performance of dancing and mime to music.

ballistic /bə'lɪstɪk/ *a.* of projectiles. **ballistic missile** one that moves under gravity after being initially powered and guided.

ballistics *n.pl.* (usu. treated as *sing.*) science of projectiles and firearms.

balloon /bə'luːn/ *n.* small inflated rubber bag as toy; large round bag inflated with gas or hot air so as to rise in air, esp. one with basket etc. below for carrying persons; outline containing words or thoughts of character in strip cartoon. **balloonist** *n.*

ballot /'bælət/ 1 *n.* voting in writing and usu. secret; votes recorded in ballot. 2 *v.* hold ballot among; vote by ballot. 3 **ballot-box** container for **ballot-papers**, slips for marking votes.

ballroom /'bɔːlrʊm/ large room for dancing. **ballroom dancing** formal kind done in pairs.

bally /'bælɪ/ *a. & adv. sl.* mild or joc. euphem. for **bloody**.

ballyhoo /bælɪ'huː/ *n. sl.* vulgar or misleading publicity.

balm /bɑːm/ *n.* fragrant exudation from some trees; ointment; healing or soothing influence; kind of aromatic herb.

balmy /'bɑːmɪ/ *a.* fragrant, mild, soothing; *sl.* crazy.

balsa /'bɒlsə/ *n.* lightweight wood from tropical Amer. tree, used for making models.

balsam /'bɔːlsəm/ *n.* balm from trees; ointment; tree yielding balsam; a flowering plant.

baluster /'bæləstə(r)/ *n.* one of series of short pillars, usu. with curving outline; rail.

balustrade /bælə'streɪd/ *n.* railing supported by balusters esp. on balcony etc.

bamboo /bæm'buː/ *n.* tropical giant grass; its hollow jointed stem(s).

bamboozle /bæm'buːz(ə)l/ *v.t.* hoax, mystify; cheat.

ban 1 *v.t.* prohibit, forbid, esp. formally. 2 *n.* formal or authoritative prohibition.

banal /bə'nɑːl/ *a.* commonplace, trite. **banality** /-'næl-/ *n.*

banana /bə'nɑːnə/ *n.* long curved yellow tropical fruit; tree bearing it.

band 1 *n.* flat strip of thin material; hoop of iron, rubber, etc.; stripe of colour etc.; body of musicians; group of persons; range of wavelengths; division of gramophone record. 2 *v.t.* unite, form into league; put band on; in *p.p.* striped. 3 **bandbox** box for hats etc.; **bandmaster** conductor of musical band; **bandsman** member of musical band; **bandstand** platform for musicians, esp. outdoors.

bandage /'bændɪdʒ/ **1** n. strip of material for binding up wound etc. **2** v.t. tie up with bandage.

bandanna /bæn'dænə/ n. large handkerchief with spots or other pattern.

bandeau /'bændəʊ/ n. (pl. -deaux /-dəʊz/) band worn round head.

bandit /'bændɪt/ n. outlaw; brigand. **banditry** n.

bandoleer /bændə'lɪə(r)/ (also **bandolier**) n. shoulder-belt with loops for ammunition.

bandwagon /'bændwægən/ n. wagon carrying musical band esp. in parade; **climb** etc. **on the bandwagon** join in popular or successful cause.

bandy[1] /'bændɪ/ v.t. exchange (words etc. with).

bandy[2] /'bændɪ/ a. (of legs) curved wide apart at knees. **bandy-legged** a.

bane n. cause of ruin or trouble. **baneful** a.

bang 1 v. strike or shut noisily; make or cause to make sound as of blow or explosion. **2** n. sound of blow or explosion; sharp blow. **3** adv. with bang, abruptly; colloq. exactly. **4 bang on** sl. exactly right.

banger /'bæŋə(r)/ n. firework made to explode with bang; sl. sausage, old car.

bangle /'bæŋg(ə)l/ n. rigid ring as bracelet or anklet.

banian /'bænɪən/ n. Indian fig-tree whose branches take root in ground.

banish /'bænɪʃ/ v.t. condemn to exile; dismiss from one's presence or mind. **banishment** n.

banister /'bænɪstə(r)/ n. (usu. in pl.) stair rail and supporting uprights; these uprights.

banjo /'bændʒəʊ/ n. (pl. -jos) musical instrument like guitar with circular body. **banjoist** /-dʒəʊɪst/ n.

bank[1] **1** n. establishment where money is deposited in accounts, lent, etc.; storage place; pool of money in gambling-game. **2** v. deposit (money) at bank; keep money at or with bank; count or rely on. **bank card** cheque card; **bank holiday** public holiday when banks are closed; **banknote** promissory note from central bank payable on demand, serving as money.

bank[2] **1** n. sloping ground on each side of river; raised shelf of ground, esp. in sea; mass of cloud etc. **2** v. provide with or form with bank or slope; (freq. with up) heap or rise in banks, pack (fire) tightly for slow burning; incline (aircraft) laterally for turning; (of aircraft) incline thus.

bank[3] n. row of lights, switches, organ keys, etc.; tier (of oars).

banker n. owner or manager of bank; keeper of bank in gambling-game. **banker's card** cheque card.

bankrupt /'bæŋkrʌpt/ **1** a. insolvent; bereft (of quality etc.). **2** n. insolvent person. **3** v.t. make bankrupt. **4 bankruptcy** n.

banner /'bænə(r)/ n. cloth, board, etc., carrying design or slogan, held high at rallies etc.; flag.

bannister var. of **banister**.

bannock /'bænək/ n. Sc. & N. Engl. round flat usu. unleavened loaf.

banns n.pl. public announcement of intended marriage read in church.

banquet /'bæŋkwɪt/ **1** n. elaborate formal dinner. **2** v. give banquet for; attend banquet.

banquette /bæŋ'ket/ n. long upholstered seat attached to wall.

banshee /'bænʃiː/ n. spirit whose wail is said to portend death in a house.

bantam /'bæntəm/ n. small variety of fowl; small but assertive person. **bantamweight** boxing-weight (up to 54 kg.).

banter /'bæntə(r)/ **1** n. gentle ridicule. **2** v. make good-humoured fun of; jest.

banyan var. of **banian**.

baobab /'beɪəbæb/ n. African tree with extremely thick stem and edible fruit.

bap n. round flat soft bread roll.

baptism /'bæptɪz(ə)m/ n. religious rite of immersing in or sprinkling with water in sign of admission to Christian Church, usu. with name-giving; giving of name. **baptismal** a.

Baptist /'bæptɪst/ n. member of non-conformist Church practising adult baptism by immersion.

baptize /bæp'taɪz/ v.t. administer baptism to, christen; give name to.

bar[1] **1** n. long piece of rigid material, esp. used to confine or obstruct; oblong piece (of chocolate, soap, etc.); (room containing) counter at which alcoholic drinks are served; counter for particular service; barrier; place where prisoner stands in lawcourt; (**the bar**) barristers, their profession; *Mus.* vertical line dividing piece into sections of equal time value, such section; broad line or band; strip of silver below clasp of medal as extra distinction. 2 *v.t.* fasten with bars; keep *in* or *out* thus; obstruct, prevent; exclude. 3 *prep.* except, excluding. 4 **barmaid, -man, -tender**, attendant at bar in public house etc.

bar² *n.* unit of atmospheric pressure.

barathea /ˌbærəˈθiːə/ *n.* fine wool cloth.

barb 1 *n.* back-curved point of arrow, fish-hook, etc.; *fig.* wounding remark. 2 *v.t.* furnish with barb. 3 **barbed wire** wire with twisted wire spikes along length, for fences.

barbarian /bɑːˈbeərɪən/ 1 *a.* primitive; uncultured; very coarse or cruel. 2 *n.* such person.

barbaric /bɑːˈbærɪk/ *a.* primitive; very coarse or cruel.

barbarism /ˈbɑːbərɪz(ə)m/ *n.* coarse or uncultured state; (use of) unacceptable word or expression in language.

barbarity /bɑːˈbærɪtɪ/ *n.* savage cruelty.

barbarous /ˈbɑːbərəs/ *a.* uncivilized, cruel.

barbecue /ˈbɑːbɪkjuː/ □ See page 665. 1 *n.* metal frame for cooking meat esp. above open fire; meat thus cooked; open-air party at which such food is served. 2 *v.t.* cook on barbecue.

barber /ˈbɑːbə(r)/ *n.* person who cuts men's hair and shaves or trims beards.

barbican /ˈbɑːbɪk(ə)n/ *n.* outer defence to city or castle, esp. double tower over gate or bridge.

barbiturate /bɑːˈbɪtjʊrət/ *n.* sedative derived from an organic (**barbituric**) acid.

bard *n.* poet; Celtic poet. **bardic** *a.*

bare /beə(r)/ 1 *a.* unclothed, uncovered; exposed; unadorned, plain; scanty; only just sufficient. 2 *v.t.* uncover, reveal. **bareback** on unsaddled horse; **barefaced** shameless, impudent; **barefoot** with bare feet; **bareheaded** without a hat.

barely /ˈbeəlɪ/ *adv.* scarcely, only just.

bargain /ˈbɑːgɪn/ 1 *n.* agreement on terms of transaction; thing acquired on terms advantageous to the buyer. 2 *v.i.* discuss terms of transaction; be prepared *for.*

barge /bɑːdʒ/ 1 *n.* flat-bottomed freight-boat for canal or river; ornamental vessel for state occasions. 2 *v.i.* lurch or rush heavily. 3 **barge in** interrupt.

bargee /bɑːˈdʒiː/ *n.* person in charge of barge.

baritone /ˈbærɪtəʊn/ *n.* adult male voice between tenor and bass; singer with baritone voice; music for baritone voice.

barium /ˈbeərɪəm/ *n.* white metallic element. **barium meal** barium compound swallowed before radiography of digestive tract.

bark¹ 1 *n.* tough outer skin of tree trunk and branches. 2 *v.t.* graze (shin etc.); strip bark from.

bark² 1 *v.* (of dog etc.) utter sharp explosive cry; speak or utter petulantly or imperiously. 2 *n.* sound of barking.

barker *n.* tout at auction or side-show.

barley /ˈbɑːlɪ/ *n.* cereal used as food and in preparation of malt; (also **barleycorn**) its grain. **barley-sugar** hard sweet made of boiled sugar; **barley-water** drink made from water and boiled barley.

barm *n.* froth on fermenting malt liquor, yeast.

bar mitzvah /bɑː ˈmɪtsvə/ religious initiation for Jewish boy of 13.

barmy /ˈbɑːmɪ/ *a. sl.* crazy.

barn *n.* roofed building for storing grain etc. **barn dance** social gathering for country dancing **barn owl** brown and white kind of owl.

barnacle /ˈbɑːnək(ə)l/ *n.* marine shellfish which clings to rocks and ships' bottoms etc. **barnacle goose** kind of Arctic goose.

barometer /bəˈrɒmɪtə(r)/ *n.* instrument measuring atmospheric pressure and used to forecast weather. **barometric** *a.*

baron /ˈbærən/ *n.* member of lowest order of British or foreign nobility; powerful or influential person.

baroness /ˈbærənɪs/ *n.* baron's wife or widow; woman holding own rank of baron.

baronet /ˈbærənɪt/ *n.* member of lowest British hereditary titled order. **baronetcy** n.

baronial /bə'rəʊnɪəl/ a. of or befitting a baron.

barony /'bærənɪ/ n. baron's rank or domain.

baroque /bə'rɒk/ 1 a. ornate and exuberant in style, esp. of 17th-18th-c. European architecture and music. 2 n. baroque style.

barrack[1] /'bærək/ n. usu. in pl. permanent building for housing soldiers; large building of severely plain appearance.

barrack[2] /'bærək/ v. shout or jeer (at).

barracuda /bærə'ku:də/ n. large voracious W. Ind. sea-fish.

barrage /'bærɑ:ʒ/ n. artillery bombardment to keep enemy pinned down; rapid succession of questions etc.; artificial barrier in river etc.

barrel /'bær(ə)l/ 1 n. cylindrical wooden or metal vessel; contents or capacity of this; tube forming part of thing, esp. gun or pen. 2 v.t. (past & p.p. **barrelled**) put in barrels. 3 **barrel-organ** musical instrument with pin-studded cylinder acting on pipes or keys.

barren /'bær(ə)n/ a. unable to bear young; unable to produce fruit or vegetation; unprofitable, dull. **barrenness** n.

barricade /'bærɪkeɪd/ 1 n. barrier, esp. hastily improvised one across street. 2 v.t. block or defend with barricade.

barrier /'bærɪə(r)/ n. fence or other obstacle barring advance or access; obstacle or circumstance etc. that keeps apart. **barrier cream** cream used to protect skin from damage or infection; **barrier reef** coral reef separated from land by channel.

barrister /'bærɪstə(r)/ n. lawyer entitled to practise as advocate in higher courts.

barrow[1] /'bærəʊ/ n. two-wheeled hand-cart; wheelbarrow.

barrow[2] /'bærəʊ/ n. mound over prehistoric burial-place.

barter /'bɑ:tə(r)/ 1 v. exchange goods, rights, etc., for something other than money. 2 n. trade by exchange.

basal /'beɪs(ə)l/ a. of, at, or forming base; fundamental.

basalt /'bæsɔ:lt/ n. dark-coloured rock of volcanic origin. **basaltic** a.

base[1] 1 n. what a thing rests or depends on, foundation; principle, starting-point; place from which operation or activity is directed; main ingredient; *Math.* number in terms of which other numbers are expressed; *Chem.* substance capable of combining with acid to form salt. 2 v.t. found or rest on; establish.

base[2] a. lacking moral worth, cowardly; despicable; menial; debased, not pure; of low value.

baseball /'beɪsbɔ:l/ n. game played esp. in US with bat and ball and circuit of four bases.

baseless /'beɪslɪs/ a. unfounded; groundless.

basement /'beɪsmənt/ n. lowest floor of building, usu. below ground level.

bash 1 v.t. strike bluntly and with great force. 2 n. heavy blow; *sl.* attempt.

bashful /'bæʃfʊl/ a. shy; self-conscious.

basic /'beɪsɪk/ a. serving as base; fundamental; simplest, lowest in level; of a chemical base. **basically** adv.

basil /'bæzɪl/ n. an aromatic herb.

basilica /bə'sɪlɪkə/ n. oblong hall with double colonnade and apse; such building used as church.

basilisk /'bæzɪlɪsk/ n. mythical reptile with lethal breath or look; tropical crested lizard.

basin /'beɪs(ə)n/ n. round vessel with sloping or curving sides for holding water etc.; hollow depression; tract drained by river; land-locked harbour.

basis /'beɪsɪs/ n. (pl. **bases** /-si:z/) foundation; main ingredient or principle; starting-point for discussion etc.

bask /bɑ:sk/ v.i. lie or sit etc. comfortably warming oneself (in sun, firelight, popularity).

basket /'bɑ:skɪt/ n. container made of plaited or woven canes or wire etc.; amount held by basket. **basket-ball** team game in which goals are scored by tossing ball into net fixed high at opponent's end.

bas-relief /'bæsrɪli:f/ n. carving or sculpture projecting only slightly from background.

bass[1] /beɪs/ 1 n. lowest adult male voice; singer with bass voice; music for bass voice; *colloq.* double bass, bass guitar. **2** *a.* lowest in pitch; deep-sounding.

bass² /bæs/ *n.* kind of fish of perch family, including common perch.

bass³ /bæs/ *n.* inner bark of lime tree; other similar fibre.

basset /'bæsɪt/ *n.* (in full **basset-hound**) short-legged hunting-dog.

bassoon /bə'su:n/ *n.* bass woodwind instrument of oboe family.

bast /bæst/ var. of **bass³**.

bastard /'bɑːstəd/ **1** *n.* person born of unmarried parents; *colloq.* person regarded with dislike or pity. **2** *a.* illegitimate by birth; spurious; hybrid. **3** **bastardy** *n.*

bastardize /'bæstədaɪz/ *v.t.* declare bastard.

baste¹ /beɪst/ *v.t.* sew together with long loose stitches, tack.

baste² /beɪst/ *v.t.* moisten (roasting meat etc.) with fat etc.; beat, thrash.

bastinado /bæstɪ'neɪdəʊ/ **1** *n.* (*pl.* **-dos**) caning on soles of feet. **2** *v.t.* cane thus.

bastion /'bæstɪən/ *n.* a projection from fortification; *fig.* thing regarded as protecting.

bat¹ **1** *n.* implement with handle for striking ball in various games; batsman. **2** *v.* use bat; strike (as) with bat; have turn at batting. **3** **batsman** person who bats, esp. at cricket.

bat² *n.* small nocturnal mouselike winged mammal.

bat³ *v.t.* **not bat an eyelid** *colloq.* show no reaction.

batch *n.* group or collection or set; loaves baked at one time.

bated /'beɪtɪd/ *a.* **with bated breath** anxiously.

bath¹ /bɑːθ/ **1** *n.* immersion in water etc. for cleansing; water etc. or vessel for bathing in; (usu. in *pl.*) building for bathing or swimming. **2** *v.* wash in bath. **3** **bath salts** additive for scenting and softening bath water.

bath² /bɑːθ/ *n.* **bath bun** kind with sugar on top; **bath chair** invalid's wheelchair.

bathe /beɪð/ **1** *v.* immerse in or treat with liquid; lie immersed in water etc., esp. to swim or wash; (of sunlight etc.) envelop. **2** *n.* instance of bathing. **3**

bathing-suit garment worn for swimming.

bathos /'beɪθɒs/ *n.* fall from sublime to commonplace; anticlimax. **bathetic** /bə'θetɪk/ *a.*

bathyscaphe /'bæθɪskeɪf/, **bathysphere** /-sfɪə(r)/ *ns.* vessel for deep-sea diving and observation.

batik /bə'tiːk/ *n.* method of printing coloured designs on textiles by waxing parts not to be dyed.

batiste /bə'tiːst/ *n.* fine light cotton or linen fabric.

batman /'bætmən/ *n.* (*pl.* **-men**) member of army etc. acting as officer's servant.

baton /'bæt(ə)n/ *n.* thin stick used by conductor for beating time; short stick carried in relay race; staff of office.

batrachian /bə'treɪkɪən/ **1** *a.* of amphibians that discard gills and tail, e.g. frog and toad. **2** *n.* such animal.

battalion /bə'tælɪən/ *n.* large body of men in battle array; infantry unit forming part of regiment or brigade.

batten¹ /'bæt(ə)n/ **1** *n.* long narrow piece of squared timber used in joining and fixing; strip of wood esp. to secure hatchway tarpaulin. **2** *v.t.* strengthen or fasten with battens.

batten² /'bæt(ə)n/ *v.i.* feed, grow fat, *on.*

batter /'bætə(r)/ **1** *v.* strike repeatedly so as to bruise or break. **2** *n.* mixture of flour and eggs beaten up with liquid for cooking. **3** **battering-ram** swinging beam for breaching walls.

battery /'bætərɪ/ *n.* portable container of cell or cells for supplying electricity; series of cages etc. for poultry or cattle; set of connected or similar instruments etc.; *Mil.* emplacement for heavy guns; *Law* physical violence inflicted on person.

battle /'bæt(ə)l/ **1** *n.* combat, esp. of organized forces; contest. **2** *v.i.* struggle *with, for,* etc. **3** **battleaxe** medieval weapon, *colloq.* domineering middle-aged woman; **battle-cruiser** heavy-gunned ship of higher speed and lighter armour than battleship; **battledress** soldier's etc. everyday uniform; **battlefield** scene of battle; **battleship** most heavily armed and armoured warship.

battlement /'bæt(ə)lmənt/ *n.* usu. in

pl. parapet with gaps at intervals at top of wall.

bauble /'bɔːb(ə)l/ *n.* showy trinket.

baulk var. of **balk**.

bauxite /'bɔːksaɪt/ *n.* earthy mineral, chief source of aluminium.

bawd *n.* woman keeper of brothel.

bawdy /'bɔːdɪ/ *a.* humorously indecent. **2** *n.* bawdy talk or writing. **3 bawdy-house** brothel.

bawl *v.* shout or weep noisily. **bawl out** *colloq.* reprimand severely.

bay¹ *n.* broad inlet of sea where land curves inward.

bay² *n.* section of wall between buttresses etc.; recess; projecting window-space; compartment, allotted area. **bay window** window projecting from line of wall.

bay³ **1** *v.* bark loudly (at). **2** *n.* bark of large dog, esp. chorus of pursuing hounds. **3 at bay** unable to escape; **keep at bay** ward off.

bay⁴ *n.* kind of laurel with deep-green leaves; in *pl.* conqueror's or poet's bay wreath, fame. **bay-leaf** leaf of bay tree used for flavouring.

bay⁵ **1** *a.* reddish-brown (esp. of horse). **2** *n.* bay horse.

bayonet /'beɪənet/ **1** *n.* stabbing-blade attachable to rifle. **2** *v.t.* stab with bayonet. **3 bayonet fitting** connecting-part engaged by pushing and twisting.

bazaar /bə'zɑː(r)/ *n.* Oriental market; sale of fancy goods etc. esp. for charity.

BBC *abbr.* British Broadcasting Corporation.

BC *abbr.* before Christ; British Columbia.

be *v.i.* (*pres.* **am**, **are**, **is**, *pl.* **are**; *past* **was**, **were**, **was**, *pl.* **were**; *part.* **being**; *p.p.* **been**) exist, live; occur; remain, continue; have specified state or quality. **2** *v.aux.* with *p.p.* of *v.t.* forming passive, with *pres. part.* forming continuous tenses, with *inf.* expr. duty, intention, possibility, etc.

beach /biːtʃ/ **1** *n.* sandy or pebbly shore of sea, lake, etc. **2** *v.t.* run or haul up on shore. **3 beachcomber** /-kəʊmə(r)/ vagrant living by beach; **beach-head** fortified position set up on beach by landing forces.

beacon /'biːkən/ *n.* signal-fire on hill or pole; signal; signal-station; Belisha beacon.

bead 1 *n.* small ball pierced for threading with others; drop of liquid; small knob in front sight of gun; narrow moulding. **2** *v.t.* furnish or ornament with bead(s) or beading; string together.

beading /'biːdɪŋ/ *n.* bead moulding.

beadle /'biːd(ə)l/ *n.* ceremonial officer of church, college, etc.

beady /'biːdɪ/ *a.* (of eyes) small and bright.

beagle /'biːg(ə)l/ *n.* small hound used for hunting hares.

beak *n.* bird's horny projecting jaws; hooked nose; *hist.* prow of warship; *sl.* magistrate.

beaker /'biːkə(r)/ *n.* small relatively tall cup for drinking; lipped glass for scientific experiments.

beam 1 *n.* long piece of squared timber used in house-building etc.; ray of light or radiation; this as guide to aircraft or missile; radiance; bright smile; cross-bar of balance; in *pl.* horizontal cross-timbers of ship. **2** *v.* emit (light, radio waves, etc.); shine; smile radiantly.

bean *n.* leguminous plant with kidney-shaped seeds in long pods; seed of this or of coffee or other plant.

beano /'biːnəʊ/ *n.* (*pl.* **-nos**) *sl.* party, celebration.

bear¹ /beə(r)/ *n.* heavy thick-furred mammal; rough surly person; *Stock Exch.* person who sells for future delivery hoping to buy cheaper before then. **bear-garden** noisy or rowdy scene; **bear-hug** powerful embrace; **bearskin** guardsman's tall furry cap.

bear² /beə(r)/ *v.* (*past* **bore**; *p.p.* **borne** or **born**) carry; show; produce, yield; give birth to; sustain; endure, tolerate.

bearable /'beərəb(ə)l/ *a.* endurable.

beard /bɪəd/ **1** *n.* hair growing on lower part of face; part on animal (esp. goat) resembling beard. **2** *v.t.* oppose, defy. **3 bearded** *a.*

bearer /'beərə(r)/ *n.* carrier of message, cheque, etc.; carrier of coffin, or of equipment on safari.

bearing /'beərɪŋ/ *n.* outward behaviour, posture; relation, relevance; part of machine supporting rotating part; direction; in *pl.* relative position; heraldic device or design.

beast /biːst/ *n.* animal, usu. four-footed

and wild; brutal person; disliked person or thing.

beastly /'bi:stlɪ/ a. like a beast; colloq. unpleasant.

beat 1 v. ((past **beat**; p.p. **beaten**) strike repeatedly or persistently; inflict blows on; overcome, surpass; exhaust, perplex; forestall; drive or alter or shape by blows; stir vigorously; pulsate; move up and down; mark (time of music) with baton, foot, etc. **2** n. main accent in music or verse; strongly marked rhythm of popular music etc.; stroke on drum; movement of conductor's baton; throbbing; policeman's etc. appointed course; one's habitual round.

beater /'bi:tə(r)/ n. whisk; implement for beating carpet; person who rouses game at a shoot.

beatific /bɪə'tɪfɪk/ a. making blessed; colloq. blissful.

beatify /bɪ'ætɪfaɪ/ v.t. make happy; RC Ch. pronounce to be in heaven as first step to canonization. **beatification** n.

beatitude /bɪ'ætɪtjuːd/ n. blessedness; in pl. the blessings in Matt. 5: 3–11.

beau /bəʊ/ n. (pl. **beaux** /bəʊz/) dandy; ladies' man; suitor.

Beaufort scale /'bəʊfət/ scale of wind speeds.

Beaujolais /'bəʊʒəleɪ/ n. red or white wine from Beaujolais district of France.

beauteous /'bju:tɪəs/ a. poet. beautiful.

beautician /bju:'tɪʃ(ə)n/ n. specialist in beauty treatment.

beautiful /'bju:tɪfəl/ a. having beauty; excellent.

beautify /'bju:tɪfaɪ/ v.t. make beautiful, adorn. **beautification** n.

beauty /'bju:tɪ/ n. combination of qualities that delights the sight or other senses or the mind; person or thing having this. **beauty queen** woman judged most beautiful in contest; **beauty spot** beautiful locality.

beaver 1 n. amphibious broad-tailed soft-furred rodent; its fur; hat of this; **Beaver** member of most junior branch of Scout Association. **2** v. **beaver away** work hard at.

becalm /bɪ'kɑːm/ v.t. deprive (ship etc.) of wind.

because /bɪ'kɒz/ conj. for the reason that. **because of** by reason of.

beck¹ n. **at person's beck and call** subject to his constant orders.

beck² n. brook, mountain stream.

beckon /'bek(ə)n/ v. summon by mute signal; signal thus.

become /bɪ'kʌm/ v. (past **became**; p.p. **become**) come to be, begin to be; suit, look well on. **become of** happen to.

bed 1 n. thing to sleep or rest on, esp. piece of furniture with mattress and coverings; garden plot for plants; bottom of sea, river, etc.; flat base on which thing rests; stratum. **2** v.t. put or go to bed; plant in bed; fix firmly. **3 bedclothes** sheets, blankets, etc.; **bedpan** pan for use as toilet by invalid in bed; **bedridden** confined to bed by infirmity; **bedrock** solid rock under alluvial deposits etc., fig. foundation, bottom; **bedroom** room for sleeping in; **bed-sitting-room, bed-sitter,** combined bedroom and sitting-room; **bedsore** one developed by lying in bed; **bedspread** coverlet; **bedstead** framework of bed; **bed-time** hour for going to bed.

bedaub /bɪ'dɔːb/ v.t. smear with paint etc.

bedding /'bedɪŋ/ n. mattress and bedclothes; litter for cattle etc.

bedeck /bɪ'dek/ v.t. adorn, decorate.

bedevil /bɪ'dev(ə)l/ v.t. (**bedevilled**) trouble, confuse, torment. **bedevilment** n.

bedlam /'bedləm/ n. scene of confusion or uproar.

bedouin /'beduːɪn/ n. (pl. same) nomadic Arab of the desert.

bedraggled /bɪ'dræg(ə)ld/ a. dishevelled, untidy.

bee n. four-winged stinging social insect producing wax and honey; busy worker; meeting for combined work or amusement. **beehive** hive; **beeline** straight line between two places; **beeswax** wax secreted by bees for honeycomb.

Beeb n. sl. the BBC.

beech /bi:tʃ/ n. smooth-barked glossyleaved tree; its wood. **beechmast** fruit of beech.

beef 1 n. meat of ox, bull, or cow; (pl. **beeves**) beef animal; sl. (pl. **beefs**) protest. **2** v.i. sl. complain. **3 beefburger** hamburger; **beef-eater** warder in

Tower of London; **beef tea** stewed beef juice for invalids.

beefy /'biːfɪ/ a. like beef; solid, muscular.

been p.p. of **be**.

beep 1 n. short high-pitched sound. **2** v.i. emit beep.

beer /bɪə(r)/ n. alcoholic liquor made from fermented malt etc. flavoured esp. with hops.

beery /'bɪərɪ/ a. of beer; showing influence of beer.

beeswing /'biːzwɪŋ/ n. filmy scales of tartar on old port wine etc.

beet n. kind of plant with succulent root used for salads etc. and sugar-making.

beetle[1] /'biːt(ə)l/ n. insect with hard outer wings.

beetle[2] /'biːt(ə)l/ n. heavy-headed tool for ramming or crushing etc.

beetle[3] /'biːt(ə)l/ **1** a. projecting, shaggy, scowling. **2** v.i. overhang.

beetroot /'biːtruːt/ n. crimson root of garden beet, used as vegetable.

befall /bɪ'fɔːl/ v. (past **befell**; p.p. **befallen** /-'fɔːlən/) happen, happen to.

befit /bɪ'fɪt/ v.t. be suited to.

befog /bɪ'fɒg/ v.t. envelop in fog; obscure.

before /bɪ'fɔː(r)/ **1** prep. in front of, ahead of; in presence of; earlier than. **2** adv. ahead, in front; previously, already; in the past. **3** conj. sooner than; rather than.

beforehand /bɪ'fɔːhænd/ adv. in anticipation, in readiness, before time.

befriend /bɪ'frend/ v.t. act as friend to; help.

befuddle /bɪ'fʌd(ə)l/ v.t. make drunk; confuse.

beg v. ask for as gift; ask earnestly, entreat; live by seeking charity; ask formally. **beg the question** assume truth of thing to be proved; **go begging** be unwanted.

began past of **begin**.

beget /bɪ'get/ v.t. (past **begot**, arch. **begat**; p.p. **begotten**) be the father of; give rise to.

beggar /'begə(r)/ **1** n. person who begs or lives by begging; poor person; colloq. person, fellow. **2** v.t. reduce to poverty. **3 beggary** n.

beggarly /'begəlɪ/ a. poor, needy; mean.

begin /bɪ'gɪn/ v. (past **began**; p.p. **be-**

gun) perform first part of; come *to do* thing; take first step; start, come into being.

beginner n. learner.

beginning n. first part; time at which thing begins; source, origin.

begone /bɪ'gɒn/ int. go away at once!

begonia /bɪ'gəʊnɪə/ n. plant with ornamental foliage and bright flowers.

begot past of **beget**.

begotten p.p. of **beget**.

begrudge /bɪ'grʌdʒ/ v.t. grudge; feel or show resentment at or envy of.

beguile /bɪ'gaɪl/ v.t. (partic. **beguiling**) charm or divert; delude, cheat. **beguilement** n.

beguine /bɪ'giːn/ n. a W. Ind. dance; its music or rhythm.

begum /'beɪgəm/ n. title of married woman in India and Pakistan.

begun p.p. of **begin**.

behalf /bɪ'hɑːf/ n. **on behalf of**, **on one's behalf**, in the interests of, as representative of.

behave /bɪ'heɪv/ v. conduct *oneself* or act in specified manner; show good manners; work well (or in specified manner).

behaviour /bɪ'heɪvjə(r)/ n. manners, conduct, way of behaving. **behavioural** a.

behaviourism /bɪ'heɪvjərɪz(ə)m/ n. study of human actions by analysis of stimulus and response. **behaviourist** n. & a.

behead /bɪ'hed/ v.t. cut head from; execute thus.

beheld past & p.p. of **behold**.

behest /bɪ'hest/ n. command, request.

behind /bɪ'haɪnd/ **1** adv. & prep. in or to rear of; hidden by, on farther side (of); in arrears (*with*); in support of. **2** n. colloq. buttocks. **3 behindhand** in arrears, behind time, too late; **behind time** unpunctual.

behold /bɪ'həʊld/ v.t. (past & p.p. **beheld**) look at; take notice, observe.

beholden /bɪ'həʊld(ə)n/ pred.a. under obligation (*to*).

behove /bɪ'həʊv/ v.t. be incumbent on; befit.

beige /beɪʒ/ **1** a. of sandy fawn colour. **2** n. this colour.

being /'biːɪŋ/ n. existence; constitution, nature; existing person etc.

belabour /bɪˈleɪbə(r)/ v.t. attack physically or verbally.

belated /bɪˈleɪtɪd/ a. coming late or too late.

bel canto /bel ˈkæntəʊ/ singing marked by full rich tone.

belch /beltʃ/ 1 v. emit wind from stomach through mouth; (of volcano, gun, etc.) emit (fire, smoke, etc.) 2 n. act of belching.

beleaguer /bɪˈliːgə(r)/ v.t. besiege.

belfry /ˈbelfrɪ/ n. bell-tower; space for bells in church tower.

belie /bɪˈlaɪ/ v.t. fail to confirm, fulfil, or justify; give false notion of.

belief /bɪˈliːf/ n. act of believing; what one believes; trust, confidence; acceptance as true.

believe /bɪˈliːv/ v. accept as true; think; have faith or confidence in; trust word of; have religious faith. **believer** n.

Belisha beacon /bəˈliːʃə/ flashing orange ball on striped post, marking pedestrian crossing.

belittle /bɪˈlɪt(ə)l/ v.t. disparage.

bell 1 n. hollow esp. cup-shaped metal body emitting musical sound when struck; sound of bell; bell-shaped thing. 2 v.t. provide with bell. 3 **bell-bottomed** (of trousers) widening below knee; **bell-pull** cord attached to wire to sound bell; **bell-push** button to operate electric bell; **bell-tent** conical tent; **bell-wether** leading sheep of flock.

belladonna /beləˈdɒnə/ n. deadly nightshade; drug obtained from this.

belle /bel/ n. handsome woman; reigning beauty.

belles-lettres /bel ˈletr/ n.pl. writings or studies of purely literary kind. [F]

bellicose /ˈbelɪkəʊs/ a. eager to fight. **bellicosity** /-ˈkɒs-/ n.

belligerent /bɪˈlɪdʒər(ə)nt/ 1 a. engaged in war; given to constant fighting; pugnacious. 2 n. belligerent person or nation. **belligerency** n.

bellow /ˈbeləʊ/ 1 v. roar like bull. 2 n. bellowing sound.

bellows /ˈbeləʊz/ n.pl. device for driving air into fire, organ, etc.; expandable part of camera etc.

belly /ˈbelɪ/ 1 n. cavity of body containing stomach, bowels, etc.; stomach; front of body from waist to groin; cavity or bulging part of anything. 2 v. swell

out. 3 **belly-dance** dance by woman with voluptuous movements of belly; **belly-laugh** loud unrestrained laugh.

belong /bɪˈlɒŋ/ v.i. be proper to or connected with; be rightly placed or classified. **belong to** be property of or member of.

belongings /bɪˈlɒŋɪŋz/ n.pl. person's movable property or luggage.

beloved /bɪˈlʌvɪd/ 1 a. loved. 2 n. beloved person.

below /bɪˈləʊ/ 1 prep. under; lower than; less than; of lower rank or importance etc. than; unworthy of. 2 adv. at or to lower point or level; further on in book etc.

belt 1 n. strip of leather etc. worn round waist or across chest; encircling strip of colour etc.; zone or district; looped strip connecting pulleys etc. 2 v. put belt round; thrash; sl. move rapidly.

bemoan /bɪˈməʊn/ v.t. lament, complain of.

bemuse /bɪˈmjuːz/ v.t. stupefy; make (person) confused.

bench n. long seat of stone or wood; carpenter's or laboratory table; lawcourt; judge's or magistrate's seat; seat for particular group in Parliament. **bench-mark** standard or point of reference; surveyor's mark at point in line of levels.

bend 1 v. (past & p.p. **bent**) force into curve or angle; be altered in this way; incline from vertical; bow, stoop; (force to) submit. 2 n. bending, curve; bent part of thing; in pl. symptoms due to too rapid decompression under water.

beneath /bɪˈniːθ/ adv. & prep. below, under; not worthy of.

Benedictine /benɪˈdɪktiːn/ 1 n. monk or nun of Order of St Benedict; (P) kind of liqueur. 2 a. of St Benedict or his order.

benediction /benɪˈdɪkʃ(ə)n/ n. utterance of blessing. **benedictory** a.

benefaction /benɪˈfækʃ(ə)n/ n. charitable gift; doing good.

benefactor /ˈbenɪfæktə(r)/ n. person who has given financial or other help. **benefactress** n.

benefice /ˈbenɪfɪs/ n. living from a church office.

beneficent /bɪˈnefɪs(ə)nt/ a. doing good; actively kind. **beneficence** n.

beneficial /benɪ'fɪʃ(ə)l/ *a.* advantageous.

beneficiary /benɪ'fɪʃərɪ/ *n.* receiver of benefits; holder of church living.

benefit /'benɪfɪt/ **1** *n.* advantage, profit; payment made under insurance or social security; performance or game etc. of which proceeds go to particular player or charity. **2** *v.* do good to; receive benefit. **3 benefit of the doubt** assumption of innocence rather than guilt.

benevolent /bɪ'nevəl(ə)nt/ *a.* wishing to do good; charitable; kind and helpful. **benevolence** *n.*

Bengali /beŋ'gɔːlɪ/ **1** *a.* of Bengal. **2** *n.* native or language of Bengal.

benighted /bɪ'naɪtɪd/ *a.* in darkness; intellectually or morally ignorant.

benign /bɪ'naɪn/ *a.* kindly, gentle; favourable; salutary; *Med.* mild, not malignant. **benignity** /-'nɪg-/ *n.*

benignant /bɪ'nɪgnənt/ *a.* kindly; beneficial. **benignancy** *n.*

bent **1** *past* & *p.p.* of **bend**. **2** *a.* curved or having angle; *sl.* dishonest, illicit. **3** *n.* inclination, bias. **4 bent on** determined on.

benthos /'benθɒs/ *n.* flora and fauna of sea bottom. **benthic** *a.*

benumb /bɪ'nʌm/ *v.t.* make numb; deaden; paralyse.

benzene /'benziːn/ *n.* substance got from coal tar and used as solvent.

benzine /'benziːn/ *n.* spirit obtained from petroleum and used as cleaning agent.

benzoin /'benzəʊɪn/ *n.* aromatic resin of E. Asian tree. **benzoic** *a.*

bequeath /bɪ'kwiːð/ *v.t.* leave by will; transmit to posterity.

bequest /bɪ'kwest/ *n.* thing bequeathed.

berate /bɪ'reɪt/ *v.t.* scold.

bereave /bɪ'riːv/ *v.t.* leave desolate; deprive *of* near relative. **bereavement** *n.*

bereft /bɪ'reft/ *a.* deprived (*of*).

beret /'bereɪ/ *n.* round flat felt or cloth cap.

berg *n.* iceberg.

bergamot /'bɜːgəmɒt/ *n.* a citrus tree; perfume from its fruit; an aromatic herb.

beriberi /berɪ'berɪ/ *n.* disease caused by deficiency of vitamin B.

Bermuda shorts /bə'mjuːdə/ knee-length shorts.

berry /'berɪ/ *n.* any small round juicy stoneless fruit. **berried** *a.*

berserk /bə'sɜːk/ *pred.a.* wild, frenzied.

berth /bɑːθ/ **1** *n.* sleeping-place; ship's place at wharf; sea-room; situation, appointment. **2** *v.t.* moor (ship) in berth; provide sleeping-berth for.

beryl /'ber(ə)l/ *n.* kind of (esp. green) precious stone; mineral species including this and emerald.

beryllium /bə'rɪlɪəm/ *n.* very light white metallic element.

beseech /bɪ'siːtʃ/ *v.t.* (*past* & *p.p.* -**sought** /-'sɔːt/) entreat; ask earnestly for.

beset /bɪ'set/ *v.t.* (*past* & *p.p.* **beset**) attack or harass persistently.

beside /bɪ'saɪd/ *prep.* at side of, close to; compared with; irrelevant to. **beside oneself** frantic with anger or worry etc.

besides /bɪ'saɪdz/ **1** *prep.* in addition to; apart from. **2** *adv.* also, as well.

besiege /bɪ'siːdʒ/ *v.t.* lay siege to; crowd round; assail with requests.

besmirch /bɪ'smɜːtʃ/ *v.t.* soil, dishonour.

besom /'biːz(ə)m/ *n.* long-handled broom made of twigs.

besot /bɪ'sɒt/ *v.t.* (*past* & *p.p.* **besotted**) stupefy; infatuate.

besought *past* & *p.p.* of **beseech**.

bespatter /bɪ'spætə(r)/ *v.t.* spatter all over; cover with abuse.

bespeak /bɪ'spiːk/ *v.t.* (*past* -**spoke**; *p.p.* -**spoken**) engaged beforehand; order (goods); be evidence of.

bespoke /bɪ'spəʊk/ *a.* ordered in advance; made to measure.

best **1** *a.* (*superl.* of **good**) of most excellent kind. **2** *adv.* (*superl.* of **well**) in best manner; to greatest degree. **3** *n.* that which is best. **4** *v.t. colloq.* defeat, outwit. **5 best man** bridegroom's chief attendant at wedding; **best-seller** book with large sale, author of such book.

bestial /'bestɪəl/ *a.* of or like beasts; brutish. **bestiality** *n.*; **bestially** *adv.*

bestiary /'bestɪərɪ/ *n.* medieval treatise on beasts.

bestir /bɪ'stɜː(r)/ *v.t.* exert or rouse (*oneself*).

bestow /bɪˈstəʊ/ v.t. confer as gift. **bestowal** n.

bestrew /bɪˈstruː/ v.t. (p.p. **-strewed** or **-strewn**) strew; lie scattered over.

bestride /bɪˈstraɪd/ v.t. (past **-strode**; p.p. **-stridden**) sit astride on; stand astride over.

bet 1 v. (past & p.p. **bet** or **betted**) risk one's money etc. against another's on result of event. 2 n. such arrangement; sum of money bet.

beta /ˈbiːtə/ n. second letter of Greek alphabet (B, β). **beta particle** fast-moving electron emitted by radioactive substance.

betake /bɪˈteɪk/ v.refl. (past **-took**; p.p. **-taken**) go (to).

betatron /ˈbiːtətrɒn/ n. apparatus for accelerating electrons.

betel /ˈbiːt(ə)l/ n. tropical Asian plant whose leaf is chewed with betel-nut. **betel-nut** areca nut.

bête noire /bet ˈnwɑː(r)/ n. particularly disliked person or thing. [F]

bethink /bɪˈθɪŋk/ v.refl. (past & p.p. **-thought** /-ˈθɔːt/) reflect, stop to think; be reminded.

betide /bɪˈtaɪd/ v. happen; happen to.

betimes /bɪˈtaɪmz/ adv. in good time, early.

betoken /bɪˈtəʊkən/ v.t. be sign of.

betook past of **betake**.

betray /bɪˈtreɪ/ v.t. be disloyal to; give up or reveal treacherously; reveal involuntarily; be evidence of. **betrayal** n.

betroth /bɪˈtrəʊð/ v.t. bind with promise to marry. **betrothal** n.

better /ˈbetə(r)/ 1 a. (compar. of **good**) having good qualities in higher degree; partly or fully recovered from illness. 2 adv. (compar. of **well**) in better manner; to greater degree. 3 n. better thing or person. 4 v. improve (upon); surpass. 5 **get the better of** defeat, outwit.

betterment /ˈbetəmənt/ n. improvement.

between /bɪˈtwiːn/ 1 prep. in or into space or interval; to and from; in shares among; (choose etc.) one or other of. 2 adv. between two or more points; between two extremes. 3 **in between** intermediately in position.

betwixt /bɪˈtwɪkst/ prep. & adv. between.

bevel /ˈbev(ə)l/ 1 n. tool for making angles in carpentry and stonework; slope from horizontal or vertical; sloping edge or surface. 2 v. (past & p.p. **bevelled**) impart bevel to, slant.

beverage /ˈbevərɪdʒ/ n. drink.

bevy /ˈbevi/ n. company or flock.

bewail /bɪˈweɪl/ v.t. wail over; mourn for.

beware /bɪˈweə(r)/ v. take heed, be cautious (of).

bewilder /bɪˈwɪldə(r)/ v.t. perplex, confuse. **bewilderment** n.

bewitch /bɪˈwɪtʃ/ v.t. enchant, greatly delight; cast spell on.

beyond /bɪˈjɒnd/ 1 adv. at or to further side, further on. 2 prep. at or to further side of; outside the range of; more than; further on. 3 n. the future life. 4 **back of beyond** very remote place.

bezel /ˈbez(ə)l/ n. sloped edge of chisel etc.; oblique face of cut gem; groove holding watch-glass or gem.

bezique /bɪˈziːk/ n. card-game for two.

biannual /baɪˈænjʊəl/ a. occurring etc. twice a year.

bias /ˈbaɪəs/ 1 n. predisposition, prejudice; distortion of statistical results; (in bowls) bowl's curved course due to its lopsided form; diagonal across fabric. 2 v.t. (past & p.p. **biased**) give bias to; prejudice.

bib n. cloth put under child's chin while eating; apron top.

Bible /ˈbaɪb(ə)l/ n. Christian sciptures; copy of these; any authoritative book. **biblical** /ˈbɪb-/ a.

bibliography /bɪblɪˈɒɡrəfi/ n. list of books of any author, subject, etc.; history of books, their editions, etc. **bibliographer** n.; **bibliographic(al)** a.

bibliophile /ˈbɪblɪəʊfaɪl/ n. collector of books, book-lover.

bibulous /ˈbɪbjʊləs/ a. fond of or addicted to alcoholic drink.

bicameral /baɪˈkæmər(ə)l/ a. having two legislative chambers.

bicarbonate /baɪˈkɑːbəneɪt/ n. carbonate containing double proportion of carbon dioxide. **bicarbonate of soda** compound used in cooking and medicine.

bicentenary /baɪsenˈtiːnəri/ n. 200th anniversary.

bicentennial /baɪsenˈteniəl/ 1 a. lasting or occurring every 200 years. 2 n. bicentenary.

biceps /'baɪseps/ n. muscle with double head or attachment, esp. that at front of upper arm.

bicker /'bɪkə(r)/ v.i. quarrel, wrangle.

bicuspid /baɪ'kʌspɪd/ 1 a. having two cusps. 2 n. bicuspid tooth.

bicycle /'baɪsɪk(ə)l/ 1 n. two-wheeled pedal-driven vehicle. 2 v.i. ride bicycle. 3 **bicyclist** n.

bid 1 v. (past & p.p. **bid**) offer (price); make bid; (also with past **bade** /bæd/; p.p. **bidden**) command, invite; salute with welcome etc. 2 n. offer of price; Bridge statement of number of tricks player hopes to make.

biddable /'bɪdəb(ə)l/ a. obedient, docile.

bidding /'bɪdɪŋ/ n. command, invitation.

bide v.t. await (one's time).

bidet /'bi:deɪ/ n. low washbasin that one can sit astride on.

biennial /baɪ'enɪəl/ 1 a. lasting or recurring every two years. 2 n. plant that flowers, fruits, and dies in second year.

bier /bɪə(r)/ n. movable stand on which coffin or corpse rests.

biff sl. 1 n. smart blow. 2 v.t. strike.

bifid /'baɪfɪd/ a. divided by cleft into two parts.

bifocal /baɪ'fəʊk(ə)l/ 1 a. (of spectacle-lenses) with two segments of different focal lengths. 2 n. in pl. bifocal spectacles.

bifurcate /'baɪfəkeɪt/ v. divide into two branches; fork. **bifurcation** n.

big 1 a. large; grown up; important; boastful; colloq. ambitious. 2 adv. colloq. in a big manner; with great effect. 3 **Big Brother** seemingly benevolent dictator; **big business** large-scale commerce; **big end** end of connecting-rod in engine encircling crank-pin; **big-head** colloq. conceited person; **big shot** colloq. important person; **big time** sl. highest rank among entertainers; **big top** main tent at circus; **bigwig** important person.

bigamy /'bɪgəmɪ/ n. crime of making second marriage while first is still valid. **bigamist** n.; **bigamous** a.

bight /baɪt/ n. loop of rope; recess of coast, bay.

bigot /'bɪgət/ n. obstinate and intolerant adherent of creed or view. **bigoted** a.; **bigotry** n.

bijou /'bi:ʒu:/ 1 n. (pl. **-oux** pr. same) jewel, trinket. 2 a. small and elegant.

bike /baɪk/ n. colloq. bicycle; motor cycle.

bikini /bɪ'ki:nɪ/ n. woman's brief two-piece bathing-suit.

bilateral /baɪ'lætər(ə)l/ a. of or on or with two sides; between two parties.

bilberry /'bɪlbərɪ/ n. N. European heathland shrub; its small dark-blue berry.

bile n. bitter fluid secreted by liver to aid digestion; bad temper, peevishness.

bilge /bɪldʒ/ n. nearly flat part of ship's bottom; (also **bilge-water**) foul water in bilge; sl. nonsense, rubbish.

bilharzia /bɪl'hɑ:tsɪə/ n. disease caused by tropical parasitic flatworm.

biliary /'bɪlɪərɪ/ a. of bile.

bilingual /baɪ'lɪŋgw(ə)l/ a. of or in or speaking two languages.

bilious /'bɪlɪəs/ a. affected by disorder of the bile; bad-tempered.

bilk v.t. evade payment of, cheat.

bill[1] 1 n. statement of charges for goods, work done, etc.; draft of proposed law; poster; Law written statement of case; programme of entertainment; US banknote. 2 v.t. anounce, put in programme; advertise as; send statement of charges to. 3 **bill of exchange** written order to pay sum on given date; **bill of fare** menu; **bill of health** certificate regarding infectious disease on ship or in port at time of sailing; **billposter**, **billsticker**, person who pastes up advertisements on hoardings etc.

bill[2] 1 n. beak (of bird); narrow promontory. 2 v.i. (of doves etc.) stroke bill with bill. 3 **bill and coo** exchange caresses.

bill[3] n. hist. weapon with hook-shaped blade.

billabong /'bɪləbɒŋ/ n. Aus. branch of river forming backwater.

billboard /'bɪlbɔ:d/ n. large outdoor board for advertisements.

billet[1] 1 n. place where soldier etc. is lodged; appointment, job. 2 v.t. allocate lodging to by billet.

billet[2] /'bɪlɪt/ n. thick piece of firewood; small metal bar.

billet-doux /bɪleɪ'du:/ n. (pl. **billets-doux** /bɪleɪ'du:z/) love-letter.

billhook /'bɪlhʊk/ concave-edged pruning-instrument.

billiards /'bɪlɪədz/ *n.* game played with cues and 3 balls on cloth-covered table.

billion /'bɪlɪən/ *n.* million millions; (esp. *US*) thousand millions.

billow /'bɪləʊ/ **1** *n.* large wave. **2** *v.i.* rise or move in billows. **3 billowy** *a.*

billy /'bɪlɪ/ *n.* (in full **billycan**) tin can serving as kettle etc. in camping.

billy-goat *n.* male goat.

bin *n.* large box-shaped container for storage; receptacle for refuse.

binary /'baɪnərɪ/ *a.* consisting of two parts, dual; of arithmetical system using 2 as base. **binary digit** either of two used in binary system.

bind /baɪnd/ *v.t.* (*past & p.p.* **bound** /baʊnd/) tie or fasten or hold together; restrain; fasten *round* etc.; fasten (sheets or more) into cover; be obligatory on; impose constraint or duty on; edge with braid etc.

binder /'baɪndə(r)/ *n.* loose cover for papers; bookbinder; sheaf-binding machine.

bindery /'baɪndərɪ/ *n* bookbinder's workshop.

binding /'baɪndɪŋ/ **1** *n.* book-cover; braid etc. for edging. **2** *a.* obligatory (*on*).

bindweed /'baɪndwiːd/ *n.* convolvulus.

bine *n.* stem of climbing plant, esp. hop; flexible shoot.

binge /bɪndʒ/ *n. sl.* drinking-bout, spree.

bingo /'bɪŋɡəʊ/ *n.* gambling game similar to lotto.

binnacle /'bɪnək(ə)l/ *n.* case for ship's compass.

binocular /bɪ'nɒkjʊlə(r)/ **1** *n.* in *pl.* instrument with lens for each eye, for viewing distant objects. **2** *a.* for two eyes.

binomial /baɪ'nəʊmɪəl/ **1** *n.* algebraic expression of sum or difference of two terms. **2** *a.* consisting of two terms.

biochemistry /baɪəʊ'kemɪstrɪ/ *n.* chemistry of living organisms.

biodegradable /baɪəʊdɪ'ɡreɪdəb(ə)l/ *a.* capable of being decomposed by bacteria.

biography /baɪ'ɒɡrəfɪ/ *n.* written life of person. **biographer** *n.*; **biographical** /-'ɡræf-/ *a.*

biological /baɪə'lɒdʒɪk(ə)l/ *a.* of bi-

ology; of plants and animals. **biological warfare** use of bacteria etc. to spread disease among enemy.

biology /baɪ'ɒlədʒɪ/ *n.* science dealing with origin, forms, and behaviour of plants and animals. **biologist** *n.*

bionic /baɪ'ɒnɪk/ *a.* having electronically-operated body-parts.

bipartite /baɪ'pɑːtaɪt/ *a.* consisting of two parts; in which two parties are concerned.

biped /'baɪped/ **1** *n.* two-footed animal. **2** *a.* two-footed.

biplane /'baɪpleɪn/ *n.* aeroplane with two pairs of wings one above the other.

birch /bɜːtʃ/ **1** *n.* smooth-barked forest tree; bundle of birch twigs used for flogging. **2** *v.t.* flog with birch.

bird /bɜːd/ *n.* feathered vertebrate with two wings and two feet; *sl.* young woman. **birdlime** sticky stuff spread to catch birds; **bird of passage** migratory bird, person who travels habitually; **birdseed** seeds as food for caged birds; **bird's-eye view** general view from above; **bird table** platform on which food for wild birds is placed.

biretta /bɪ'retə/ *n.* square cap of (esp. RC) priest.

Biro /'baɪərəʊ/ *n.* (**P**) (*pl.* **-ros**) kind of ball-point pen.

birth /bɜːθ/ *n.* emergence of young from mother's body; origin, beginning; inherited position. **birth-control** prevention of undesired pregnancy; **birthday** anniversary of birth; **birthmark** unusual mark on body from birth; **birth-rate** number of births per thousand of population per year; **birthright** rights belonging to one by birth; **give birth to** produce (young).

biscuit /'bɪskɪt/ *n.* flat thin unleavened cake, usu. dry and crisp and often sweetened; porcelain etc. after first firing and before glazing; light-brown colour.

bisect /baɪ'sekt/ *v.t.* divide into two (usu. equal) parts. **bisection** *n.*; **bisector** *n.*

bisexual /baɪ'seksjʊəl/ *a.* sexually attracted to members of both sexes; having both sexes in one individual. **bisexuality** *n.*

bishop /'bɪʃəp/ *n.* senior clergyman in charge of diocese; mitre-shaped piece in chess.

bishopric /'bɪʃəprɪk/ n. office or diocese of bishop.

bismuth /'bɪzməθ/ n. reddish-white brittle metallic element; compound of it used medicinally.

bison /'baɪs(ə)n/ n. wild ox; buffalo.

bisque[1] /bɪsk/ n. advantage of one free point or stroke awarded to player in certain games.

bisque[2] /bɪsk/ n. unglazed white china for statuettes.

bistre /'bɪstə(r)/ n. brown pigment made from soot; colour of this.

bistro /'bɪstrəʊ/ n. (pl. **-os**) small bar or restaurant.

bit[1] n. small piece or amount; short time or distance; mouthpiece of bridle; cutting part of tool etc.

bit[2] n. *Computers* unit of information expressed as choice between two possibilities, binary digit.

bit[3] *past of* **bite**.

bitch /bɪtʃ/ 1 n. female dog, fox, or wolf; abusive term for woman. 2 v. be spiteful; grumble. 3 **bitchy** a.

bite 1 v. (*past* **bit**; *p.p.* **bitten**) nip or cut into or off with teeth; sting; penetrate, grip; have desired effect; be sharp; accept bait. 2 n. act of biting; wound so made; small amount to eat; incisiveness.

bitten *p.p. of* **bite**.

bitter /'bɪtə(r)/ 1 a. having sharp pungent taste, not sweet; showing or feeling resentment; harsh, biting, virulent. 2 n. bitter beer, strongly flavoured with hops; in *pl.* liquor with bitter flavour, esp. of wormwood.

bittern /'bɪt(ə)n/ n. marsh bird allied to heron.

bitumen /'bɪtjʊmɪn/ n. mixture of tarlike substances derived from petroleum. **bituminous** /-'tjuːmɪn-/ a.

bivalve /'baɪvælv/ 1 a. having two valves or (of shellfish) a hinged double shell. 2 n. bivalve shellfish.

bivouac /'bɪvʊæk/ 1 n. temporary encampment without tents. 2 v.i. make open camp.

bizarre /bɪ'zɑː(r)/ a. strange in appearance or effect; grotesque.

blab v. talk or tell foolishly or indiscreetly.

black 1 a. colourless from absence or complete absorption of light; very dark-coloured; dark-skinned; **Black** of

Negroes; dusky, gloomy; sinister, wicked; sullen; declared untouchable by workers in dispute. 2 n. black colour, paint, clothes, etc.; (player using) darker pieces in chess etc.; credit side of account; **Black** Negro. 3 v.t. make black; polish with blacking; declare (goods etc.) 'black'. 3 **black and blue** badly bruised; **black and white** not in colour, comprising only opposite extremes, *in* print; **black art** magic; **blackball** exclude from club, society, etc.; **blackbeetle** common cockroach; **black belt** (holder of) badge of proficiency in judo; **black box** flight-recorder in aircraft; **blackcock** male black grouse; **black coffee** coffee without milk or cream; **black comedy** comedy presenting tragedy in comic terms; **black eye** bruised skin round eye; **blackfly** kind of aphid; **black grouse** British species of grouse; **blackhead** black-topped pimple; **black hole** *Astron.* region from which matter and radiation cannot escape; **black ice** thin hard transparent ice; **blackjack** *US* short heavy club with pliable shaft; **blacklead** graphite; **blackleg** person who refuses to join strike or trade union; **black magic** magic involving invocation of devils; **Black Maria** police vehicle for transporting prisoners; **black market** illicit traffic in officially controlled or scarce commodities; **black mass** travesty of mass in worship of Satan; **black out** obscure (windows etc.) to prevent light entering or escaping, undergo blackout; **black-out** being blacked out, temporary esp. sudden or momentary loss of vision or consciousness; **black pudding** sausage of blood, suet, etc.; **Black Rod** chief usher of House of Lords; **black sheep** scoundrel, disreputable member *of*; **blackshirt** Fascist; **black spot** place of danger or difficulty; **blackthorn** thorny shrub bearing white flowers and sloes; **black velvet** mixture of stout and champagne; **black widow** Amer. spider of which female devours mate.

blackberry /'blækbərɪ/ n. dark edible fruit of bramble.

blackbird /'blækbɜːd/ n. European song-bird.

blackboard /'blækbɔːd/ n. board for chalking on in classroom etc.

blackcurrant /blæk'karənt/ n. small black fruit; shrub on which it grows.

blacken /'blækən/ v. make or become black; slander.

blackguard /'blægɑːd/ 1 n. villain, scoundrel. 2 v.t. abuse scurrilously. 3 **blackguardly** a.

blacking /'blækɪŋ/ n. black polish for boots.

blacklist /'blæklɪst/ 1 n. list of persons etc. in disfavour. 2 v.t. put on blacklist.

blackmail /'blækmeɪl/ 1 n. extortion by threats or pressure. 2 v.t. extort money from thus.

blacksmith /'blæksmɪθ/ n. smith working in iron.

bladder /'blædə(r)/ n. sac in human or other animal body, esp. that holding urine; inflated thing.

blade n. cutting-part of knife etc.; flat part of oar or spade or propeller etc.; flat narrow leaf of grass and cereals; flat bone of shoulder.

blain n. inflamed sore.

blame 1 v.t. find fault with; fix blame on. 2 n. censure; responsibility for bad result. 3 **blameworthy** deserving blame.

blameless /'bleɪmlɪs/ a. innocent.

blanch /blɑːntʃ/ v. make white by peeling or by depriving (plant) of light; immerse briefly in boiling water; make or grow pale.

blancmange /blə'mɒnʒ/ n. opaque jelly of sweet flavoured cornflour and milk.

bland a. insipid, tasteless; mild, gentle, suave.

blandishment /'blændɪʃmənt/ n. usu. in pl. flattering attention; cajolery.

blank 1 a. not written or printed on; (of form etc.) not filled in; without interest, result, or expression etc. 2 n. space to be filled up in document etc.; empty surface; dash written in place of word; blank cartridge. 3 **blank cartridge** one without bullet; **blank cheque** one with amount left for payee to fill in; **blank verse** unrhymed verse, esp. iambic pentameters.

blanket /'blæŋkɪt/ 1 n. large woollen sheet as bed-covering etc.; thick covering layer. 2 a. general, covering all cases or classes. 3 v.t. (past & p.p. **blanketed**) cover (as) with blanket.

blare /bleə(r)/ 1 v. make sound of trumpet; utter or sound loudly. 2 n. blaring sound.

blarney /'blɑːnɪ/ 1 n. empty or flattering talk. 2 v. flatter, use blarney.

blasé /'blɑːzeɪ/ a. bored or indifferent, esp. through familiarity.

blaspheme /blæs'fiːm/ v. speak profanely of; talk impiously.

blasphemy /'blæsfəmɪ/ n. impious speech, profanity. **blasphemous** a.

blast /blɑːst/ 1 n. explosion; destructive wave of air from this; strong gust; sound of wind instrument or car horn or whistle etc.; severe criticism or reprimand. 2 v.t. blow up with explosive; make explosive sound; blight; colloq. criticise forcibly. 3 int. damn. 4 **blast-furnace** one for smelting with compressed hot air driven in; **blast off** (of rocket) take off from launching-pad; **blast-off** n.

blatant /'bleɪt(ə)nt/ a. flagrant, unashamed.

blather /'blæðə(r)/ 1 v.i. chatter foolishly. 2 n. foolish talk.

blaze[1] 1 n. bright flame or fire; violent outburst of passion; bright display or light. 2 v.i. flame; burn with excitement etc.

blaze[2] 1 n. white mark on face of horse or chipped in bark of tree. 2 v.t. mark (tree, path) with blaze(s).

blaze[3] v.t. proclaim (abroad, forth).

blazer /'bleɪzə(r)/ n. light jacket esp. with colours of a school, team, etc.

blazon /'bleɪz(ə)n/ 1 n. heraldic shield, coat of arms, etc. 2 v.t. proclaim; inscribe ornamentally; describe or paint (coat of arms). 3 **blazonry** n.

bleach /bliːtʃ/ 1 v. make or become white or pale in sunlight or by chemical process. 2 n. bleaching process or substance.

bleak a. dreary; bare; chilly.

bleary /'blɪərɪ/ a. dim-sighted, blurred.

bleat 1 v. utter cry of sheep or goat etc.; speak foolishly or plaintively. 2 n. bleating cry.

bleed v. (past & p.p. **bled**) emit blood; draw blood from; emit or draw off other fluid; colloq. extort money from.

bleep 1 v. emit intermittent high-pitched sound; summon by bleep. **2** *n.* such sound.

blemish /'blemɪʃ/ **1** *v.t.* spoil beauty of, mar. **2** *n.* flaw, defect, stain.

blench /blentʃ/ *v.i.* flinch, quail.

blend 1 *v.* mix (various sorts) into required sort; mingle intimately; become one. **2** *n.* blending, mixture.

blende /blend/ *n.* native zinc sulphide.

blenny /'blenɪ/ *n.* spiny-finned sea-fish.

bless *v.t.* invoke divine favour on; consecrate; thank; make happy.

blessed /'blesɪd/ *attrib.a.* holy; *RC Ch.* beatified; *euphem.* cursed.

blessing /'blesɪŋ/ *n.* invocation of divine favour; grace at meals; benefit or advantage.

blether var. of **blather**.

blew *past* of **blow**.

blight /blaɪt/ **1** *n.* disease of plants caused esp. by insects; such insect; obscure malignant influence. **2** *v.t.* affect with blight, destroy; spoil.

blighter /'blaɪtə(r)/ *n. sl.* annoying person.

blimey /'blaɪmɪ/ *int.* expr. surprise.

blimp *n.* small non-rigid airship; **Blimp** diehard reactionary.

blind /blaɪnd/ **1** *a.* without sight; without adequate knowledge or information or foresight; reckless; not governed by purpose; concealed; closed at one end. **2** *v.* deprive of sight or judgement; deceive. **3** *n.* obstruction to sight or light; screen for window; misleading thing. **4 blind date** social engagement between man and woman who have not met before; **blind-man's buff** game in which blindfold player tries to catch others; **blind spot** spot on retina insensitive to light, area where vision or judgement fails; **blindworm** slow-worm; **turn a blind eye to** pretend not to notice.

blindfold /'blaɪndfəʊld/ **1** *a. & adv.* with eyes covered; without care and attention. **2** *n.* covering for eyes to prevent person seeing. **3** *v.t.* cover eyes of (person) with blindfold.

blink 1 *v.* move eyelids; look with eyes opening and shutting; shut eyes for a moment; cast sudden or momentary light; ignore or shirk (facts). **2** *n.* blinking movement; momentary gleam. **3 on**

the **blink** *sl.* (of machine etc.) out of order.

blinker /'blɪŋkə(r)/ *n.* usu. in *pl.* screen on bridle preventing horse from seeing sideways.

blinking /'blɪŋkɪŋ/ *a. & adv. sl.* expr. mild annoyance.

blip *n.* small spot or image on radar-screen.

bliss *n.* perfect joy; being in heaven. **blissful** *a.*; **blissfully** *adv.*

blister /'blɪstə(r)/ **1** *n.* small bubble on skin filled with watery fluid; any swelling resembling this. **2** *v.* raise blister on; become covered with blisters.

blithe /blaɪð/ *a.* joyous, gay; carefree, casual.

blithering /'blɪðərɪŋ/ *a. colloq.* utter, hopeless; talking senselessly.

blitz /blɪts/ **1** *n.* intensive (esp. aerial) attack. **2** *v.t.* damage or destroy in blitz.

blizzard /'blɪzəd/ *n.* severe snowstorm.

bloat *v.* inflate, swell.

bloater /'bləʊtə(r)/ *n.* herring cured by salting and smoking.

blob *n.* small drop or spot.

bloc *n.* combination of countries, parties, or groups sharing some common purpose.

block 1 *n.* large solid piece of hard material; large building, esp. when subdivided; group of buildings surrounded by usu. four streets; obstruction; large quantity as a unit; piece of wood or metal engraved for printing. **2** *v.t.* obstruct; stop (cricket ball) with bat. **3 blockhead** stupid person; **block letter** separate capital letter; **block vote** vote proportional in size to number of persons voter represents; **mental block** mental inability due to sub-conscious factors.

blockade /blɒ'keɪd/ **1** *n.* surrounding or blocking of place by hostile forces. **2** *v.t.* subject to blockade.

blockage /'blɒkɪdʒ/ *n.* obstruction; blocked-up state.

bloke *n. sl.* man, fellow.

blond (of woman usu. **blonde**) **1** *a.* fair-haired; (of hair) light-coloured. **2** *n.* fair-haired person.

blood /blʌd/ **1** *n.* liquid, usu. red, circulating in arteries and veins of animals; murder, bloodshed; race, descent; relationship. **2** *v.t.* give first taste of blood to (hound); initiate (person). **3 blood bank** reserve of blood for transfusion; **blood-bath** massacre; **blood count** count of red corpuscles in blood; **blood-curdling** horrifying; **blood donor** giver of blood for transfusion; **blood group** any of types of human blood; **bloodhound** large keen-scented dog used for tracking; **blood-letting** surgical removal of blood; **blood orange** one with red-streaked pulp; **blood-poisoning** poisoning due to harmful bacteria in blood; **blood pressure** force exerted by blood in arteries; **blood-relation** one related by common descent; **bloodshed** killing or wounding of people; **bloodshot** (of eyeball) tinged with blood; **blood sport** one involving killing of animals; **bloodstream** circulating blood; **bloodsucker** leech, extortioner; **bloodthirsty** eager for bloodshed; **blood-vessel** vein, artery, or capillary conveying blood.

bloodless /'blʌdlɪs/ a. without blood or bloodshed; unemotional; pale.

bloody /'blʌdɪ/ 1 a. of or like blood; blood-stained, running with blood; involving bloodshed, cruel; sl. expr. annoyance. 2 adv. sl. extremely. 3 v.t. make bloody. 4 **bloody-minded** colloq. deliberately unco-operative.

bloom /bluːm/ 1 n. flower; flowering state; prime; freshness; powdery deposit on fruit etc. 2 v.i. bear blooms; be in flower; flourish.

bloomer /'bluːmə(r)/ n. sl. blunder.

bloomers /'bluːməz/ n.pl. loose knee-length trousers formerly worn by women; colloq. knickers.

blooming /'bluːmɪŋ/ a. & adv. in bloom; sl. expr. mild annoyance.

blossom /'blɒsəm/ 1 n. flower; mass of flowers on tree. 2 v.i. open into flower; thrive.

blot 1 n. spot of ink etc.; blemish; disgraceful act. 2 v.t. make blot on; stain; dry with blotting-paper. 3 **blot out** obliterate.

blotch n. inflamed patch on skin; dab of ink etc. **blotchy** a.

blotter /'blɒtə(r)/ n. device for holding blotting-paper.

blotting-paper /'blɒtɪŋ/ n. absorbent paper for drying wet ink.

blouse /blaʊz/ n. garment like shirt,

worn by women; jacket forming part of military uniform.

blow[1] /bləʊ/ 1 v. (past **blew**; p.p. **blown**) send directed air-current from mouth; move as wind does; puff, pant; sound (wind instrument); clear (nose) by sudden forceful breath; make or shape or work by blowing; break or burst suddenly; cause (fuse) to break; sl. (p.p. **blowed**) curse, confound, squander. 2 n. blowing; inhaling of fresh air. 3 **blow-dry** use hand-held drier on (washed) hair; **blowfly** bluebottle; **blow in** break or drive inwards by explosion; **blowlamp** apparatus for directing intensely hot flame on limited area; **blow out** extinguish by blowing, send outwards by blowing; **blow-out** burst in pneumatic tyre, sl. large meal; **blowpipe** tube from which dart or arrow is projected by blowing; **blow up** shatter or be shattered by explosion, inflate, enlarge (photograph), colloq. reprove.

blow[2] /bləʊ/ n. hard stroke with fist or weapon; disaster, shock.

blower /'bləʊə(r)/ n. device for blowing; colloq. telephone.

blowy /'bləʊɪ/ a. windy.

blowzy /'blaʊzɪ/ a. coarse-looking, red-faced; dishevelled.

blub v.i. sl. weep.

blubber /'blʌbə(r)/ 1 n. whale fat. 2 v.i. sob, weep noisily. 3 a. swollen, protruding.

bludgeon /'blʌdʒ(ə)n/ 1 n. heavy stick. 2 v.t. beat with bludgeon; coerce.

blue /bluː/ 1 a. coloured like clear sky or deep sea; sad, depressed; indecent. 2 n. blue colour, paint, clothes, etc.; person who has represented Oxford or Cambridge university at sport; in pl. melancholy, kind of melancholy music of Amer. Black origin. 3 v.t. make blue; sl. squander. 4 **blue baby** one with congenital heart defect; **bluebell** wild hyacinth, harebell; **blue blood** noble birth; **blue book** Parliamentary or Privy Council report; **bluebottle** large buzzing fly; **blue cheese** cheese with veins of blue fungus; **blue-collar** of manual work; **blue-eyed boy** colloq. favourite; **blue-pencil** correct or edit, censor; **Blue Peter** blue flag with central white square hoisted before sailing; **blueprint** photographic print on blue paper of plans for building etc., *fig.* detailed plan; **blue ribbon** high honour; **blue-stocking** intellectual woman; **blue tit** small bird with blue and yellow plumage.

bluff[2] 1 *v.* make pretence of strength to gain advantage etc.; deceive thus. 2 *n.* act of bluffing.

bluff[2] 1 *a.* with steep or vertical broad front; blunt, frank, hearty. 2 *n.* bluff headland.

blunder /ˈblʌndə(r)/ 1 *v.i.* make serious mistake; move about clumsily. 2 *n.* stupid or careless mistake.

blunderbuss /ˈblʌndəbʌs/ *n.* disused kind of short gun with large bore.

blunt 1 *a.* without sharp edge or point; dull, not sensitive; plain-spoken. 2 *v.t.* make blunt.

blur 1 *v.t.* make or become less distinct; smear. 2 *n.* thing seen or heard indistinctly.

blurb *n.* publisher's commendation of book, printed on its jacket etc.

blurt *v.t.* (usu. with *out*) utter abruptly or tactlessly.

blush 1 *v.i.* be or become red (as) with shame or other emotion; be ashamed. 2 *n.* blushing; pink tinge.

bluster /ˈblʌstə(r)/ 1 *v.* storm boisterously. 2 *n.* noisy self-assertive talk, threats. 3 **blustery** *a.*

BMA *abbr.* British Medical Association.

BO *abbr.* body odour.

boa /ˈbəʊə/ *n.* large S. Amer. snake that kills its prey by crushing it; woman's long throat-wrap of fur or feather. **boa constrictor** Brazilian boa, python.

boar /bɔː(r)/ *n.* male wild pig; uncastrated male pig.

board /bɔːd/ 1 *n.* thin piece of sawn timber; material resembling this; wooden or cardboard etc. slab used in games or for posting notices etc.; thick stiff card; provision of meals; directors of company; council-table; committee; in *pl. the* stage. 2 *v.* go on board (ship etc.); cover with boards; provide or receive meals at fixed rate. 3 **boarding-house** house providing board and lodging; **boarding-school** one providing board and lodging for pupils; **boardroom** meeting-place of board of directors; **on board** on or into ship or train or aircraft etc.

boarder /ˈbɔːdə(r)/ *n.* pupil who boards at boarding-school.

boast 1 *v.* declare one's achievements etc. with pride; own with pride. 2 *n.* excessively proud statement; thing one is proud of. 3 **boastful** *a.*

boat 1 *n.* small open oared or engined or sailing vessel; (small) ship; boat-shaped utensil for sauce etc. 2 *v.i.* go in boat esp. for pleasure. 3 **boat-hook** long pole with hook and spike; **boat-house** shed at water's edge for boats; **boatman** one who hires out or provides transport by boats; **boat-train** train timed to connect with ship.

boater /ˈbəʊtə(r)/ *n.* hard flat straw hat.

boatswain /ˈbəʊs(ə)n/ *n.* ship's officer in charge of crew and sails etc.

bob[1] 1 *v.* move up and down, rebound; cut (hair) short. 2 *n.* bobbing movement, curtsy; bobbed hair; horse's docked tail; weight on pendulum etc. 3 **bobtail** docked tail, horse or dog with this.

bob[2] *n.* (*pl.* same) *sl.* former shilling, 5p.

bobbin /ˈbɒbɪn/ *n.* cylinder for holding thread etc., reel, spool.

bobble /ˈbɒb(ə)l/ *n.* small woolly ball as ornament or trimming.

bobby /ˈbɒbɪ/ *n. sl.* uniformed policeman.

bob-sled /ˈbɒbsled/ (also **bob-sleigh**) *n.* sledge with two sets of runners.

bode *v.* portend, foretell.

bodice /ˈbɒdɪs/ *n.* upper part of woman's dress down to waist; undergarment for same part of body.

bodiless /ˈbɒdɪlɪs/ *a.* lacking (a) body.

bodily /ˈbɒdɪlɪ/ 1 *a.* of or affecting human body. 2 *adv.* as a whole, in a body.

bodkin /ˈbɒdkɪn/ *n.* blunt thick needle for drawing tape etc. through hem.

body /ˈbɒdɪ/ *n.* material part of man or animal alive or dead; trunk apart from head and limbs; main part; group of persons regarded as a unit; *colloq.* person; piece of matter; solidity, substantial characteristic or flavour. **bodyguard** escort or personal guard; **body politic** State; **body stocking** woman's undergarment covering trunk and legs; **bodywork** structure of vehicle body.

Boer /ˈbəʊə(r)/ *n.* Dutch-descended S. African.

boffin /'bɒfɪn/ n. colloq. person engaged in scientific or technical research.

bog 1 n. wet spongy ground, morass; sl. lavatory. 2 v.t. trap or submerge in bog. 3 **bogged down** unable to move or make progress.

bogey /'bəʊgɪ/ n. par or one more than par on a hole in golf.

boggle /'bɒg(ə)l/ v.i. be startled or baffled; hesitate, demur (at).

boggy /'bɒgɪ/ a. marshy, spongy.

bogie /'bəʊgɪ/ n. wheeled undercarriage pivoted below locomotive etc.

bogus /'bəʊgəs/ a. sham, spurious.

bogy /'bəʊgɪ/ n. evil spirit, goblin; awkward thing or circumstance.

Bohemian /bə'hi:mɪən/ 1 a. socially unconventional; of Bohemia. 2 n. such person, esp. artist or writer. 3 **Bohemianism** n.

boil¹ v. (of liquid or its vessel) bubble up with heat, reach temperature at which liquid turns to vapour; bring to boiling-point; subject to heat of boiling water, cook thus; be agitated like boiling water. 2 n. boiling heat. 3 **boiled sweet** one made of boiled sugar; **boiling (hot)** colloq. very hot; **boiling-point** temperature at which liquid boils.

boil² n. inflamed pus-filled swelling under skin.

boiler /'bɔɪlə(r)/ n. fuel-burning apparatus for heating hot-water supply; tank for heating water or turning it into steam; vessel for boiling things in. **boiler suit** one-piece garment combining overalls and shirt.

boisterous /'bɔɪstərəs/ a. noisily cheerful; violent, rough.

bold /bəʊld/ a. confident; adventurous; courageous; impudent; distinct or vivid.

bole n. stem or trunk of tree.

bolero /bə'leərəʊ/ n. (pl. **-ros**) a Spanish dance; (also /'bɒlərəʊ/) woman's short jacket without fastenings.

boll /bəʊl/ n. round seed-vessel of cotton, flax, etc.

bollard /'bɒləd/ n. short thick post in street etc.; post on ship or quay for securing ropes to.

boloney /bə'ləʊnɪ/ n. sl. nonsense.

Bolshie /'bɒlʃɪ/ sl. 1 a. rebellious or unco-operative. 2 n. such person.

bolster /'bəʊlstə(r)/ 1 n. long stuffed pillow. 2 v. support with bolster, prop up.

bolt¹ /bəʊlt/ n. door-fastening of metal bar and socket; headed metal pin secured with rivet or nut; act of bolting; discharge of lightning; short heavy crossbow arrow. 2 v. fasten with bolt; gulp down unchewed; dart off, run away; (of horse) escape from control; run to seed. 3 **bolt-hole** means of escape; **bolt upright** erect.

bolt² /bəʊlt/ v.t. sift.

bomb /bɒm/ 1 n. high explosive or incendiary material or smoke etc. in container for release on impact or by time mechanism; the atomic bomb; sl. large amount of money. 2 v.t. attack with bombs; throw or drop bombs on; sl. travel fast. 3 **bombshell** cause of great surprise or disappointment.

bombard /bɒm'bɑːd/ v.t. attack with heavy guns; assail with abuse etc.; subject to stream of high-speed particles. **bombardment** n.

bombardier /bɒmbə'dɪə(r)/ n. artillery NCO below sergeant; US airman who releases bombs from aircraft.

bombast /'bɒmbæst/ n. pompous or extravagant language. **bombastic** a.

Bombay duck /'bɒmbeɪ/ dried fish eaten as relish esp. with curry.

bombazine /'bɒmbəziːn/ n. twilled worsted dress-material.

bomber /'bɒmə(r)/ n. aircraft used for bombing; person who throws or plants bombs.

bona fide /bəʊnə 'faɪdɪ/ in good faith, genuine.

bonanza /bə'nænzə/ n. source of great wealth; rich mine.

bon-bon n. sweet.

bond¹ 1 n. thing or force that unites or (usu. in pl.) restrains; binding agreement; document binding person to pay or repay money; adhesion; Chem. linkage of atoms in molecule. 2 v.t. bind or connect together; put in bond. 3 **bond paper** high-quality writing-paper; **in bond** stored by Customs until duty is paid.

bondage /'bɒndɪdʒ/ n. slavery; confinement, subjection to constraint.

bondman /'bɒndmən/ (also **bondsman**) n. serf or slave.

bone 1 n. any of separate parts of vertebrate skeleton; in pl. skeleton, mortal remains; substance of which these consist; thing made of this. **2** *v.t.* remove bones from. **3 bone china** fine semi-translucent earthenware; **bone-dry** quite dry; **bonehead** *sl.* stupid person; **bone idle** completely idle; **bone-meal** crushed bone as fertilizer; **boneshaker** jolting vehicle.

bonfire /'bɒnfaɪə(r)/ *n.* open-air fire. **Bonfire Night** 5 Nov.

bongo /'bɒŋgəʊ/ *n.* (*pl.* **-gos** or **-goes**) one of pair of small drums played with fingers.

bonhomie /bɒnɒ'mi/ *n.* geniality. [F]

bonnet /'bɒnɪt/ *n.* woman's or child's outdoor head-dress with strings; *Sc.* man's round cap; hinged cover over engine of motor vehicle.

bonny /'bɒnɪ/ *a.* comely, healthy-looking.

bonsai /'bɒnsaɪ/ *n.* dwarf tree or shrub; art of growing these.

bonus /'bəʊnəs/ *n.* something extra, esp. addition to dividends or wages.

bony /'bəʊnɪ/ *a.* of or like bone; thin with prominent bones.

boo 1 *int.* expr. disapproval or contempt. **2** *n.* the sound *boo.* **3** *v.* utter boos (at).

boob *sl.* **1** *n.* silly mistake; woman's breast. **2** *v.i.* make mistake.

booby /'bu:bɪ/ *n.* silly or awkward person. **booby prize** small prize for last competitor in contest; **booby trap** disguised exploding device triggered by unknowing victim, device to trick unsuspecting person, (*v.t.*) set booby trap in.

book /bʊk/ **1** *n.* sheets of paper, written or printed on or blank, fastened together usu. hingewise in cover; literary composition that would fill such sheets; set of tickets, stamps, matches, cheques, etc., bound up together; main division of literary work or Bible; in *pl.* society's records, trader's accounts; *colloq.* magazine; record of bets made; libretto. **2** *v.* enter in book or list; bring charge against; secure (seat etc.) in advance; obtain ticket for journey etc.; make reservation. **3 bookcase** cabinet containing shelves for books; **book-ends** pair of props to support row of books; **bookkeeper** person who keeps accounts of business etc.; **bookmaker** person whose business is taking bets;

bookmark strip of card or leather etc. for marking place in book; **book-plate** label in book with owner's name; **book token** voucher exchangeable for books of given value; **bookworm** person devoted to reading, larva that eats through books.

bookie /'bʊkɪ/ *n. colloq.* bookmaker.

bookish /'bʊkɪʃ/ *a.* fond of reading; getting knowledge from books only.

booklet /'bʊklɪt/ *n.* small usu. paper-covered book.

boom[1] /bu:m/ **1** *n.* deep resonant sound. **2** *v.* emit or utter with boom.

boom[2] /bu:m/ **1** *n.* sudden activity in commerce etc. **2** *v.i.* be prosperous or very successful.

boom[3] /bu:m/ *n.* long pole with one fixed end to support sail-foot, camera, microphone, etc.; barrier across harbour etc.

boomerang /'bu:məræŋ/ **1** *n.* Australian missile of curved wood that can be so thrown as to return to thrower. **2** *v.i.* (of scheme) recoil on originator.

boon[1] /bu:n/ *n.* advantage or benefit; blessing.

boon[2] /bu:n/ *a.* convivial, jolly.

boor /bʊə(r)/ *n.* uncouth or ill-mannered person. **boorish** *a.*

boost /bu:st/ **1** *v.t.* increase strength or reputation of; *colloq.* push from below, increase, assist. **2** *n.* act or effect of boosting.

booster *n.* device for increasing power or signal; auxiliary engine or rocket for initial acceleration; dose increasing effect of earlier one.

boot /bu:t/ **1** *n.* outer foot-covering reaching above ankle; luggage compartment of motor car etc.; *sl.* dismissal. **2** *v.t.* kick; *Computers* bootstrap.

bootee /bu:'ti:/ *n.* infant's woollen boot; woman's short lined boot.

booth /bu:ð/ *n.* temporary structure of canvas or wood; enclosure for public telephone etc. or for voting.

bootleg /'bu:tleg/ *a.* smuggled, illicit. **bootlegger** *n.*

bootstrap /'bu:tstræp/ **1** *n.* in *pl.* unaided effort. **2** *v.t.* load operating system etc. into (computer), esp. from disc etc.

booty /'bu:tɪ/ *n.* plunder gained esp. in war; prize.

booze /buːz/ *colloq.* **1** *n.* alcoholic drink; drinking of it. **2** *v.i.* drink liquor, esp. excessively. **3 boozy** *a.*

boozer /ˈbuːzə(r)/ *n. colloq.* hard drinker; public house.

boracic /bəˈræsɪk/ *a.* of borax. **boracic acid** boric acid.

borage /ˈbɒrɪdʒ/ *n.* blue-flowered plant used in salads etc.

borax /ˈbɔːræks/ *n.* salt of boric acid used as antiseptic.

border /ˈbɔːdə(r)/ **1** *n.* side, edge, boundary, or part near it; frontier; distinct edging round anything. **2** *v.* put or be border to; adjoin. **3 borderline** boundary between areas or classes, (*a.*) on borderline.

bore[1] **1** *v.* make (hole), esp. with revolving tool; drill (shaft of well); make hole (in) thus. **2** *n.* hollow of gun-barrel or cylinder; diameter of this; deep narrow hole made to find water etc.

bore[2] **1** *v.t.* weary by tedious talk or dullness. **2** *n.* tiresome person or thing; nuisance.

bore[3] *n.* tide-wave of exceptional height rushing up estuary.

bore[4] *past* of **bear**[1].

boredom /ˈbɔːdəm/ *n.* being bored (**bore**[2]).

boric acid /ˈbɔːrɪk/ acid used as mild antiseptic.

born *a.* existing as a result of birth; being (specified thing) by nature; destined *to be.*

boron /ˈbɔːrɒn/ *n.* a non-metallic element.

borough /ˈbʌrə/ *n.* administrative area esp. of Greater London; *hist.* town with municipal corporation.

borrow /ˈbɒrəʊ/ *v.* get temporary use of (something to be returned); adopt or use as one's own (idea, word, etc.).

Borstal /ˈbɔːst(ə)l/ *n.* institution to which young offenders were formerly sent for reformative training.

bortsch /bɔːtʃ/ *n.* Russian beetroot soup.

borzoi /ˈbɔːzɔɪ/ *n.* Russian wolf-hound.

bosh *n.* nonsense, rubbish.

bosom /ˈbuz(ə)m/ *n.* person's breast; enclosure formed by breast and arms; enfolding relationship; part of dress covering breast. **bosom friend** intimate friend.

boss[1] **1** *n.* employer or manager, super-

visor. **2** *v.t.* be boss of, control. **boss about** continually give orders to.

boss[2] *n.* protuberance, round knob or stud.

boss[3] *a. sl.* **boss-eyed** cross-eyed, crooked; **boss shot** failure, bungle.

bossy /ˈbɒsɪ/ *a.* domineering. **bossiness** *n.*

bo'sun /ˈbəʊs(ə)n/ *n.* boatswain.

botany /ˈbɒtənɪ/ *n.* science of plants. **botanical** (/-ˈtæn-/) *a.*; **botanist** *n.*

botch **1** *v.t.* bungle; patch clumsily. **2** *n.* botched work, bungle.

both /bəʊθ/ **1** *a. & pron.* the two (not only one). **2** *adv.* with equal truth in two cases.

bother /ˈbɒðə(r)/ **1** *v.* give trouble to, worry; take trouble. **2** *n.* person or thing that bothers; nuisance. **3** *int.* of impatience. **4 bothersome** *a.*

bottle /ˈbɒt(ə)l/ **1** *n.* narrow-necked usu. glass vessel for storing liquid; liquid in bottle; *sl.* courage. **2** *v.t.* put into bottles; preserve (fruit etc.) in jars. **3 bottle-green** dark green; **bottleneck** point at which flow of traffic or production etc. is constricted, narrow place; **bottle-party** one to which each guest contributes a bottle of drink; **bottle up** restrain (feelings etc.).

bottom /ˈbɒtəm/ **1** *n.* lowest point or part; buttocks; less honourable end of table, class, etc.; ground under water of sea etc.; bottom of ship's hull, ship; basis; essential nature. **2** *a.* lowest, last. **3** *v.* provide with bottom; touch bottom (of); find extent of.

bottomless /ˈbɒtəmlɪs/ *a.* without bottom; inexhaustible.

botulism /ˈbɒtjʊlɪz(ə)m/ *n.* food-poisoning caused by bacillus in inadequately preserved food.

bouclé /ˈbuːkleɪ/ *n.* yarn with looped or curled strands.

boudoir /ˈbuːdwɑː(r)/ *n.* woman's private room.

bougainvillaea /buːgənˈvɪlɪə/ *n.* tropical plant with large coloured bracts.

bough /baʊ/ *n.* branch of tree.

bought /bɔːt/ *past & p.p.* of **buy**.

bouillon /ˈbuːjõ/ *n.* broth. [F]

boulder /ˈbəʊldə(r)/ *n.* large stone worn smooth by weather or water.

boulevard /ˈbuːləvɑːd/ *n.* broad tree-lined street.

boult var. of **bolt**[2].

bounce /baʊns/ 1 v. rebound; cause to rebound; *sl.* (of cheque) be returned by bank when there are no funds to meet it; rush noisily. 2 n. rebound; boast, swagger; *colloq.* energy. 3 **bouncy** a.

bouncer /n. sl./ person employed to eject troublesome people from night-club etc.

bouncing a. big and healthy.

bound¹ /baʊnd/ 1 v.i. spring, leap; (of ball etc.) recoil from wall or ground. 2 n. springy upward or forward movement; recoil of ball etc.

bound² /baʊnd/ 1 n. usu. in *pl.* limit of territory, limitation, restriction. 2 v.t. set bounds to; be boundary of. 3 **out of bounds** beyond permitted area.

bound³ /baʊnd/ a. ready to start or having started (*for*).

bound⁴ /baʊnd/ a. (*past* & *p.p.* of **bind**) required by duty; certain *to* do. **bound up** closely associated *with*.

boundary /ˈbaʊndərɪ/ n. line etc. indicating bounds or limits; *Crick.* hit to limit of field, runs scored for this.

bounder /ˈbaʊndə(r)/ n. sl. cheerfully ill-mannered person.

bounteous /ˈbaʊntɪəs/ a. freely bestowed.

bountiful /ˈbaʊntɪfʊl/ a. generous.

bounty /ˈbaʊntɪ/ n. generosity in giving; gift; official reward.

bouquet /boˈkeɪ/ n. bunch of flowers; perfume of wine; *fig.* praise. **bouquet garni** (/ˈgɑːnɪ/) bunch of herbs for flavouring.

bourbon /ˈbɜːbən/ n. US whisky distilled from maize and rye.

bourgeois /ˈbʊəʒwɑː/ 1 a. of middle class; conventional; materialist. 2 n. bourgeois person.

bourgeoisie /bʊəʒwɑːˈziː/ n. bourgeois class.

bourn /bʊən/ n. stream.

bourse /bʊəs/ n. money-market, esp. **Bourse** stock exchange in Paris.

bout /baʊt/ n. spell or turn of fit of work, illness, etc.; match at wrestling or boxing.

boutique /buːˈtiːk/ n. small shop selling fashionable clothes etc.

bouzouki /bʊˈzuːkɪ/ n. Greek instrument like mandolin.

bovine /ˈbəʊvaɪn/ a. of oxen; dull, inert.

bow¹ /bəʊ/ 1 n. shallow curve or bend; weapon for shooting arrows; rod with horsehair stretched from end to end for playing violin etc.; ornamental knot with two loops, ribbon etc. so tied. 2 v.t. use bow on (violin etc.). 3 **bow-legged** having bandy legs; **bow-tie** necktie for tying in double loop; **bow-window** curved bay window.

bow² /baʊ/ 1 v. bend or kneel in sign of submission or reverence or greeting or assent; incline head in salutation. 2 n. bowing of head or body.

bow³ /baʊ/ n. fore-end of boat or ship; rower nearest bow.

bowdlerize /ˈbaʊdləraɪz/ v.t. expurgate. **bowdlerization** n.

bowel /ˈbaʊəl/ n. intestine; in *pl.* innermost parts.

bower /ˈbaʊə(r)/ n. arbour, summerhouse, leafy nook. **bower-bird** Australian bird that adorns its run with shells etc. **bowery** a.

bowie knife /ˈbəʊɪ/ hunting-knife with long curved blade.

bowl¹ /bəʊl/ n. hollow dish esp. for food or liquid; hollow part of tobacco-pipe, spoon, etc.

bowl² /bəʊl/ 1 n. hard heavy ball made with bias to run in curve; in *pl.* game with these on grass. 2 v. play bowls; roll (ball); *Crick.* deliver ball, put (batsman) out by knocking off bails with bowled ball; go along by rolling or on wheels. 3 **bowling-alley** long enclosure for playing skittles or bowling; **bowling-green** lawn for playing bowls.

bowler¹ /ˈbəʊlə(r)/ n. *Crick.* player who bowls.

bowler² /ˈbəʊlə(r)/ n. hard felt hat with rounded crown.

bowsprit /ˈbaʊsprɪt/ n. spar running forward from ship's bow.

box¹ n. container, usu. with flat sides and of firm material; quantity contained in this; separate compartment in theatre or stable etc.; enclosed area or space; witness-box; telephone-box; receptacle at newspaper office for replies to advertisement; *colloq. the* television; coachman's seat. 2 v. put in or provide with box. 3 **box girder** girder with square cross-section; **box junction** yellow-striped road area which vehicle may only enter if exit is clear; **box-office** office for booking seats at theatre

box 59 **brandy**

etc.; **box-pleat** two parallel pleats forming raised band.

box² 1 v. fight with fists, usu. in padded gloves, as sport; slap (person's ears). 2 n. slap on ear.

box³ n. kind of evergreen shrub with small dark-green leaves; its wood.

boxer n. fighter using fists; smooth-coated dog of bulldog type.

boxing n. fighting with fists. **boxing-glove** padded kind worn in this.

Boxing Day first weekday after Christmas Day.

boy n. male child, young man; male servant, attendant, etc. **boy-friend** girl's or woman's regular male companion. **boyhood** n.; **boyish** a.

boycott /ˈbɔɪkɒt/ 1 v.t. refuse social or commercial relations with by common consent; refuse to handle (goods). 2 n. such refusal.

bra /brɑː/ n. brassière.

brace 1 n. thing that clamps or fastens tightly; in pl. straps supporting trousers from shoulders; wire device for straightening teeth; pair. 2 v.t. fasten tightly; strengthen, make taut; invigorate.

bracelet /ˈbreɪslɪt/ n. ornamental band or chain worn on arm or wrist; in pl., sl. handcuffs.

bracken /ˈbrækən/ n. fern abundant on heaths; mass of this.

bracket /ˈbrækɪt/ 1 n. projection from wall serving as support; angular support for something fastened to wall; mark used in pairs (), [], {}, for enclosing words or figures; group classified as similar or falling between limits. 2 v.t. enclose in brackets; group in same category.

brackish /ˈbrækɪʃ/ a. (of water) slightly salt.

bract n. Bot. leaf or scale below calyx.

brad n. thin flat nail.

bradawl /ˈbrædɔːl/ n. small boring-tool.

brae /breɪ/ n. Sc. hillside.

brag 1 v. talk boastfully, boast. 2 n. boastful statement or talk; card-game like poker.

braggart /ˈbrægət/ n. person given to bragging.

Brahma /ˈbrɑːmə/ n. supreme Hindu deity.

brahmin /ˈbrɑːmɪn/ n. member of Hindu priestly caste.

braid 1 n. silk, thread, wire, etc. woven into band for trimming etc; plaited tress of hair. 2 v.t. trim with braid; form into braid.

Braille /breɪl/ n. system of writing or printing for the blind formed by raised points interpreted by touch.

brain n. organ of convoluted nervous tissue in skull of vertebrates; centre of sensation or thought; in sing. or pl. (source of) intellectual power. 2 v.t. dash out brains of. 3 **brain-child** colloq. product of thought; **brain-storm** violent mental disturbance; **brains trust** group of experts giving impromptu answers to questions; **brain-wash** systematically replace established ideas in person's mind by new ones; **brainwave** bright idea.

brainy /ˈbreɪnɪ/ a. intellectually clever.

braise /breɪz/ v.t. stew (esp. meat) slowly in closed container with small amount of liquid.

brake¹ 1 n. apparatus for checking motion of wheel or vehicle. 2 v. apply brake; retard with brake.

brake² n. thicket, brushwood.

brake³ n. estate car.

bramble /ˈbræmb(ə)l/ n. wild prickly shrub with long trailing shoots, blackberry.

bran n. husks separated from flour after grinding. **bran-tub** lucky dip with prizes hidden in bran.

branch /brɑːntʃ/ 1 n. limb growing from stem or bough of tree; lateral extension or subdivision of river, railway, family, etc.; local establishment of business etc. 2 v.i. put out branches; divide, diverge, strike off, out, etc. in new path.

brand 1 n. goods of particular name or trade mark; permanent mark deliberately made with hot iron, iron stamp for this; stigma; piece of burning or smouldering wood; torch. 2 v.t. label with trade mark; stigmatize; stamp with hot iron; impress indelibly. 3 **brand-new** completely or obviously new.

brandish /ˈbrændɪʃ/ v.t. wave or flourish.

brandy /ˈbrændɪ/ n. strong spirit distilled from wine or fermented fruit-juice. **brandy-snap** crisp usu. rolled-up gingerbread wafer.

brash *a.* vulgarly assertive; impudent.

brass /brɑːs/ 1 *n.* dark yellow alloy of copper and zinc; brass objects; brass wind-instruments; memorial tablet of brass; brass ornament worn by horse; *colloq.* effrontery; *sl.* money. 2 *a.* made of brass. 3 **brass band** band of musicians with brass instruments; **brass hat** *colloq.* high-ranking officer; **brass-rubbing** reproducing design from sepulchral brass on paper by rubbing with heelball; **brass tacks** *sl.* actual details.

brasserie /ˈbræsəri/ *n.* restaurant, orig. one serving beer with food.

brassica /ˈbræsɪkə/ *n.* plant of family including cabbage.

brassière /ˈbræsɪeə(r)/ *n.* undergarment worn by women to support breasts.

brassy /ˈbrɑːsɪ/ *a.* impudent; showy; loud and blaring; of or like brass.

brat *n. derog.* child.

bravado /brəˈvɑːdəʊ/ *n.* show of boldness.

brave 1 *a.* able to face and endure danger or pain; splendid, spectacular. 2 *v.* defy, encounter bravely. 3 *n.* N. Amer. Indian warrior. 4 **bravery** *n.*

bravo[1] /ˈbrɑːvəʊ/ *int.* & *n.* (*pl.* **-vos**) cry of approval.

bravo[2] /ˈbrɑːvəʊ/ *n.* (*pl.* **-voes**) hired ruffian or killer.

bravura /brəˈvjʊərə/ *n.* brilliant or ambitious performance; music requiring brilliant technique.

brawl 1 *n.* noisy quarrel. 2 *v.i.* engage in brawl; (of stream) flow noisily.

brawn *n.* muscle, muscular strength; pressed jellied meat made esp. from pig's head.

brawny /ˈbrɔːnɪ/ *a.* muscular.

bray 1 *n.* loud strident cry of donkey; harsh sound. 2 *v.* emit bray; utter harshly.

braze *v.t.* solder with alloy of brass.

brazen /ˈbreɪz(ə)n/ 1 *a.* shameless; of or like brass. 2 *v.t.* **brazen out** face or undergo shamelessly.

brazier /ˈbreɪzɪə(r)/ *n.* portable pan or stand for holding burning coals.

Brazil nut /brəˈzɪl/ large three-sided nut from S. Amer. tree.

breach /briːtʃ/ 1 *n.* breaking or neglect of rule, duty, promise, etc.; breaking off of relations, quarrel; gap. 2 *v.t.* break, make gap in.

bread /bred/ *n.* food of baked dough of flour usu. leavened with yeast; *sl.* money. **breadcrumbs** bread crumbled for use in cooking; **breadline** subsistence level; **bread-winner** person whose work supports a family.

breadth /bredθ/ *n.* broadness, distance from side to side; freedom from mental limitations or prejudices.

break /breɪk/ 1 *v.* (*past* **broke**; *p.p.* **broken**) divide or split or separate otherwise than by cutting; make or become inoperative; fall to pieces, shatter; break bone in (limb etc.); interrupt, pause; fail to observe or keep; make or become weak, destroy; tame, subdue; reveal or be revealed; come, produce, change, etc., with suddenness or violence; (of voice) change in quality at manhood or with emotion; escape, emerge from; (of ball) change direction after touching ground. 2 *n.* breaking; point where thing is broken; gap; pause in work etc.; sudden dash; a chance; points scored in one sequence at billiards etc. 3 **break away** make or become free or separate; **break down** fail or collapse, itemize, analyse; **breakdown** collapse, failure of health or mental power or mechanical action, analysis; **break even** emerge with neither gain nor loss; **break in** intrude forcibly esp. as thief, interrupt, accustom to habit; **breakneck** (of speed) dangerously fast; **break off** detach by breaking, bring to an end, cease talking etc.; **break open** open forcibly; **break out** escape, exclaim, become covered *in* (rash etc.); **breakthrough** major advance in knowledge etc.; **break up** break into pieces, disband, part; **breakup** disintegration, collapse; **breakwater** object breaking force of waves; **break wind** emit wind through anus.

breakable /ˈbreɪkəb(ə)l/ *a.* easily broken.

breakage /ˈbreɪkɪdʒ/ *n.* breaking, broken thing.

breaker /ˈbreɪkə(r)/ *n.* heavy wave breaking on coast or over reef.

breakfast /'brekfəst/ 1 *n*. first meal of day. 2 *v.i.* have breakfast.

bream *n*. yellowish freshwater fish; similar sea-fish.

breast /brest/ 1 *n*. either of two milk-secreting organs on upper front of woman's body; upper front of body; seat of emotions. 2 *v.t.* face up to; contend with; reach top of (hill). 3 **breastbone** that connecting ribs in front; **breastfeed** feed (baby) from breast, not from bottle; **breastplate** armour covering breast; **breast-stroke** stroke made while swimming on breast by extending arms forward and sweeping them back.

breath /breθ/ *n*. air as used by lungs; breathing; breath as perceived by senses; one respiration; slight movement of air. **breathtaking** spectacular, very exciting; **breath test** test of breath to determine level of alcohol in blood.

breathalyser /'breθəlaɪzə(r)/ *n*. device for measuring alcohol in breath.

breathe /briːð/ *v*. take air into lungs and send it out again; perform comparable function; live; take breath, pause; send out or take in (as) with breathed air; utter or speak softly. **breathing-space** time to breathe, pause.

breather /'briːðə(r)/ *n*. short spell of rest.

breathless /'breθlɪs/ *a*. panting, out of breath; unstirred by wind.

bred *past* & *p.p.* of **breed**.

breech /briːtʃ/ *n*. back part of gun or gun-barrel; in *pl*. short trousers fastened below knee. **breech birth** birth in which baby's buttocks emerge first.

breed 1 *v*. (*past* & *p.p.* **bred**) produce offspring; propagate; raise (cattle etc.); yield, result in; train, bring up; arise, spread; *Phys*. create (fissile material) by nuclear reaction. 2 *n*. stock of animals within species; race, lineage; sort, kind. 3 **breeder reactor** nuclear reactor that can create more fissile material than it consumes.

breeding *n*. result or qualities of upbringing.

breeze¹ 1 *n*. gentle wind. 2 *v.i. colloq.* move in lively or offhand manner.

breeze² *n*. small cinders used to make **breeze blocks**, lightweight building blocks.

breezy /'briːzɪ/ *a*. pleasantly windy.

Bren *n*. lightweight quick-firing machine-gun.

brent *n*. smallest kind of wild goose.

brethren /'breðrən/ *n.pl. arch.* brothers, esp. (fellow-)members of religious order etc.

Breton /'bret(ə)n/ 1 *n*. native or language of Brittany. 2 *a*. of Brittany.

breve /briːv/ *n*. mark (˘) over short or unstressed vowel; *Mus*. note equal to two semibreves.

breviary /'briːvɪərɪ/ *n*. book containing RC Divine Office for each day.

brevity /'brevɪtɪ/ *n*. conciseness, shortness.

brew 1 *v*. make (beer etc.) by infusion, boiling, and fermenting; make (tea etc.) by infusion or mixture; undergo these processes; *fig*. be forming. 2 *n*. amount brewed; liquor brewed.

brewery /'bruːərɪ/ *n*. place where beer is brewed commercially.

briar¹,² var. of **brier**¹,².

bribe 1 *n*. inducement offered to procure esp. dishonest or illegal service to giver. 2 *v.t.* persuade by offering bribe. 3 **bribery** *n*.

bric-à-brac /'brɪkəbræk/ *n*. miscellaneous old ornaments, furniture, etc.

brick 1 *n*. small rectangular block of baked clay, used in building; toy building-block; brick-shaped block of anything; *sl*. generous or loyal person. 2 *a*. made of bricks. 3 *v.t.* block *up* with brickwork. 4 **brickbat** piece of brick esp. as missile; **bricklayer** person who builds with bricks; **brickwork** structure or building in brick.

bridal /'braɪd(ə)l/ *a*. of bride or wedding.

bride *n*. woman on her wedding day or shortly before or after it. **bridegroom** man on wedding day or shortly before or after it; **bridesmaid** unmarried woman or girl attending bride.

bridge¹ *n*. structure carrying way over road, railway, river, etc.; upper bony part of nose; prop under strings of violin etc.; raised platform from which ship is directed; false tooth or teeth connected to real teeth on each side. 2 *v.t.* be or make bridge over; join, connect. 3 **bridgehead** position held on far side of river etc. facing enemy; **bridging**

loan loan to cover interval between buying one house and selling another.

bridge² *n.* card-game developed from whist.

bridle /'braɪd(ə)l/ **1** *n.* gear to control horse etc.; restraint. **2** *v.* put bridle on, control, curb; express resentment, esp. by throwing up head and drawing in chin. **3** **bridle-path** path suitable for horse-riding.

brief /briːf/ **1** *a.* of short duration; concise. **2** *n.* solicitor's summary of case for guidance of barrister; in *pl.* very short knickers or pants. **3** *v.t.* give instructions, necessary information, etc. to; give legal brief to (counsel).

briefcase /'briːfkeɪs/ *n.* flat case for documents etc.

brier¹ /braɪə(r)/ *n.* wild-rose bush. **brier-rose** wild rose.

brier² /braɪə(r)/ *n.* shrub with root used for tobacco-pipes; pipe made from this.

brig¹ *n.* Sc. bridge.

brig² *n.* two-masted square-rigged vessel.

brigade /brɪ'geɪd/ *n.* military sub-unit of division; organized band of workers etc.

brigadier /brɪgə'dɪə(r)/ *n.* Army officer next below major-general.

brigand /'brɪgənd/ *n.* member of robber gang. **brigandage** *n.*

bright /braɪt/ *a.* emitting or reflecting much light, shining; vivid, conspicuous; intelligent, talented; cheerful, vivacious.

brighten /'braɪt(ə)n/ *v.* make or become bright.

brill *n.* flat-fish resembling turbot.

brilliant /'brɪlɪənt/ **1** *a.* bright, sparkling; highly talented; distinguished. **2** *n.* diamond of finest quality. **3** **brilliance** *n.*

brilliantine /'brɪlɪəntiːn/ *n.* cosmetic for making hair glossy.

brim **1** *n.* edge of cup, hollow, channel, etc.; projecting edge of hat. **2** *v.* fill or be full to brim.

brimstone /'brɪmstəʊn/ *n.* *arch.* sulphur.

brindled /'brɪnd(ə)ld/ *a.* brown with streaks of other colour.

brine **1** *n.* salt water; sea-water. **2** *v.t.* soak in brine.

bring *v.t.* (*past* & *p.p.* **brought** /brɔːt/)

come with or convey; cause to be present; cause, result in; be sold for; prefer (charge); initiate (legal action). **bring about** cause to happen; **bring down** cause to fall; **bring forward** draw attention to, move to earlier time or date; **bring in** introduce, produce as profit, pronounce (verdict); **bring off** succeed in; **bring round** restore to consciousness, win over; **bring to bear** apply; **bring up** educate, rear, draw attention to, vomit.

brink *n.* edge of precipice etc.; furthest point before something dangerous etc. is encountered. **brinkmanship** policy of pursuing dangerous course to brink of catastrophe.

briny /'braɪnɪ/ *a.* of brine or sea, salt. **the briny** *sl.* the sea.

briquette /brɪ'ket/ *n.* block of compressed coal-dust.

brisk *a.* active, lively, quick.

brisket /'brɪskɪt/ *n.* animal's breast, esp. that of beef animal as joint of meat.

brisling /'brɪzlɪŋ/ *n.* small herring or sprat.

bristle /'brɪs(ə)l/ **1** *n.* short stiff hair; bristle of pig etc. used in brushes etc. **2** *v.* show temper; (of hair etc.) stand up; cause to bristle; be thickly set (*with* obstacles etc.).

Britannia /brɪ'tænɪə/ *n.* Britain personified. **Britannia metal** silvery alloy.

Britannic /brɪ'tænɪk/ *a.* of Britain.

British /'brɪtɪʃ/ **1** *a.* of Britain. **2** *n.pl.* *the* British people.

Briton /'brɪt(ə)n/ *n.* one of people in S. Britain before Roman conquest; native of Great Britain.

brittle /'brɪt(ə)l/ *a.* apt to break, fragile.

broach /brəʊtʃ/ *v.t.* raise (subject) for discussion; pierce or begin drawing liquor from (cask); open and start using.

broad /brɔːd/ **1** *a.* large across, extensive; of specified breadth; (of accent) marked; strong; tolerant; comprehensive; coarse; full, clear. **2** *n.* broad part; expanse of water formed by widening of river; *US sl.* woman. **3** **broad bean** variety of bean with large flat seeds, one of these seeds; **broadcloth** fine twilled or plain-woven cloth; **broadloom** (carpet) woven in broad width; **broadsheet** large sheet of paper printed on one side only.

broadcast /ˈbrɔːdkɑːst/ 1 v. (past & p.p. **-cast**) transmit (news, musical performance, etc.) by radio or television; speak or perform thus; disseminate widely; sow (seed) by scattering freely. 2 n. transmission by radio or television. 3 a. transmitted by broadcasting; scattered widely.

broaden /ˈbrɔːd(ə)n/ v. make or become broader.

broadside /ˈbrɔːdsaɪd/ n. firing of all guns on one side of ship; fierce verbal attack; ship's side above water. **broadside on** sideways on.

brocade /brəˈkeɪd/ n. kind of fabric with raised patterns woven in.

broccoli /ˈbrɒkəlɪ/ n. hardy variety of cauliflower with greenish flower-head.

brochure /ˈbrəʊʃə(r)/ n. booklet, pamphlet, esp. containing information etc.

broderie anglaise /brəʊdərɪ ˈɑ̃gleɪz/ openwork embroidery on fine cotton etc. fabric.

brogue /brəʊg/ n. strong shoe for sports and country wear; rough shoe of untanned leather; marked local esp. Irish accent.

broil v. cook on fire or gridiron; make or be very hot.

broiler /ˈbrɔɪlə(r)/ n. young chicken raised for broiling.

broke 1 past of **break**. 2 a. colloq. having no money, bankrupt.

broken /ˈbrəʊkən/ 1 p.p. of **break**. 2 a. that has been broken; (of language) spoken imperfectly; interrupted. 3 **broken-hearted** crushed by grief; **broken home** one where parents are separated or divorced.

broker /ˈbrəʊkə(r)/ n. middleman, agent; pawnbroker; stockbroker; appraiser and seller of distrained goods. **broking** n.

brokerage /ˈbrəʊkərɪdʒ/ n. broker's fee or commission.

brolly /ˈbrɒlɪ/ n. colloq. umbrella.

bromide /ˈbrəʊmaɪd/ n. compound of bromine esp. used as sedative; trite remark.

bromine /ˈbrəʊmiːn/ n. poisonous liquid non-metallic element with rank smell.

bronchial /ˈbrɒŋkɪəl/ a. of two main divisions of windpipe or smaller tubes into which they divide.

bronchitis /brɒŋˈkaɪtɪs/ n. inflammation of bronchial mucous membrane.

bronco /ˈbrɒŋkəʊ/ n. (pl.-cos) wild or half-tamed horse of western US

brontosaurus /brɒntəˈsɔːrəs/ n. large plant-eating dinosaur.

bronze /brɒnz/ 1 n. brown alloy of copper and tin; its colour; work of art or medal in it. 2 a. made of or coloured like bronze. 3 v. give bronzelike surface to; make or grow brown; tan. 4 **Bronze Age** stage of culture when tools were of bronze; **bronze medal** medal given usu. as third prize.

brooch /brəʊtʃ/ n. ornamental hinged pin.

brood /bruːd/ 1 n. bird's or other animal's young produced at one hatch or birth; joc. children of a family. 2 v. worry or ponder resentfully; (of hen) sit on eggs.

broody /ˈbruːdɪ/ a. (of hen) wanting to incubate eggs; fig. depressed.

brook[1] /brʊk/ n. small stream.

brook[2] /brʊk/ v.t. tolerate; allow.

broom /bruːm/ n. long-handled sweeping-brush; yellow-flowered shrub. **broomstick** broom-handle.

Bros. abbr. Brothers.

broth /brɒθ/ n. thin meat or fish soup.

brothel /ˈbrɒθ(ə)l/ n. house of prostitution.

brother /ˈbrʌðə(r)/ n. son of same parents; close man friend, equal; member of religious order, esp. monk; (pl. **brethren**) man who is fellow member of religious society etc. **brother-in-law** wife's or husband's brother, sister's husband. **brotherly** a.

brotherhood /ˈbrʌðəhʊd/ n. relationship (as) between brothers; (members of) association for mutual help etc.

brought past & p.p. of **bring**.

brow /braʊ/ n. eyebrow (usu. in pl.); forehead; summit of pass or hill; edge of cliff etc.

browbeat /ˈbraʊbiːt/ v.t. bully with looks and words.

brown /braʊn/ 1 a. of colour produced by mixing red, yellow, and black pigments; dark-skinned; tanned. 2 n. brown colour, paint, clothes, etc. 3 v.

make or become brown. **4 brown bread** bread made of wholemeal flour or resembling such bread; **browned off** sl. bored, fed up; **brown sugar** partially refined kind.

Brownie /ˈbraʊnɪ/ n. junior Guide; **brownie** benevolent sprite in folklore, haunting house.

browse /braʊz/ **1** v. read or look around desultorily; feed on leaves and young shoots. **2** n. browsing.

bruise /bruːz/ **1** n. injury caused by blow or pressure and discolouring but not breaking skin. **2** v. inflict bruise on; be susceptible to bruises.

bruiser /ˈbruːzə(r)/ n. tough brutal person.

bruit /bruːt/ v.t. arch. spread about, abroad.

brunette /bruːˈnet/ n. woman with dark hair.

brunt n. chief impact of attack etc.

brush 1 n. cleaning or hairdressing or painting implement of bristles etc. set in holder; application of brush; skirmish; fox's tail; brushlike carbon or metal piece serving as electrical contact. **2** v. use brush on; touch lightly, graze in passing. **3 brush-off** dismissal, rebuff; **brush up** clean up or smarten, renew acquaintance with (subject); **brushwood** cut or broken twigs etc., undergrowth, thicket; **brushwork** painter's way of using brush.

brusque /brʊsk/ a. blunt, off-hand.

Brussels sprouts /ˈbrʌs(ə)lz/ edible buds of kind of cabbage.

brutal /ˈbruːt(ə)l/ a. savagely cruel; coarse; mercilessly frank. **brutality** /-ˈtæl-/ n.; **brutalize** v.t.

brute 1 n. animal other than man; cruel person; colloq. unpleasant person. **2** a. unable to reason; stupid; unthinking. **3 brutish** a.

bryony /ˈbraɪənɪ/ n. climbing hedge plant.

B.Sc. abbr. Bachelor of Science.

BST abbr. British Summer Time.

BT abbr. British Telecom.

Bt. abbr. Baronet.

bubble /ˈbʌb(ə)l/ **1** n. globular film of liquid enclosing air or gas; air-filled cavity in glass etc.; transparent domed cavity; visionary project. **2** v.i. send up or rise in bubbles, boil; make sound of bubbles. **3 bubble-and-squeak** cooked potatoes and cabbage fried together; **bubble bath** additive to make bathwater bubbly; **bubble car** small car with transparent dome; **bubble gum** chewing-gum that can be blown into large bubbles.

bubbly /ˈbʌblɪ/ **1** a. full of bubbles. **2** n. sl. champagne.

bubonic /bjuːˈbɒnɪk/ a. (of plague) marked by swellings esp. in groin and armpits.

buccaneer /bʌkəˈnɪə(r)/ n. pirate, adventurer. **buccaneering** a. & n.

buck[1] n. male deer, hare, or rabbit; attrib. sl. male. **2** v. (of horse) jump vertically with back arched, throw (rider) thus. **3 buckshot** coarse shot; **bucktooth** projecting tooth; **buck up** hurry up, cheer up.

buck[2] n. small object placed before dealer at poker. **pass the buck** shift responsibility (to).

buck[3] n. US & Aus. sl. dollar.

bucket /ˈbʌkɪt/ **1** n. round open container with handle, for carrying or holding water etc.; amount contained in this; compartment in water-wheel or dredger or grain-elevator. **2** v.i. move jerkily or bumpily. **3 bucket seat** one with rounded back, to fit one person; **bucket-shop** agency dealing in cheap airline tickets, unregistered broking agency; **kick the bucket** die.

buckle /ˈbʌk(ə)l/ **1** n. metal rim with usu. hinged pin for securing strap or belt etc. **2** v. fasten with buckle; (cause to) crumple under pressure. **3 buckle down** make determined start.

buckler /ˈbʌklə(r)/ n. small round shield.

buckram /ˈbʌkrəm/ n. coarse linen or cloth stiffened with paste etc.

buckshee /bʌkˈʃiː/ a. & adv. sl. free, gratis.

buckwheat /ˈbʌkwiːt/ n. a cereal plant.

bucolic /bjuːˈkɒlɪk/ a. of shepherds, rustic, pastoral.

bud 1 n. projection from which branch or leaf-cluster or flower develops; flower or leaf not fully open; asexual growth separating from organism as new animal. **2** v. put forth buds, sprout as bud; begin to grow or develop; graft bud of (plant) on another plant.

Buddhism /'bʊdɪz(ə)m/ n. Asian religion founded by Gautama Buddha. **Buddhist** a. & n.

buddleia /'bʌdlɪə/ n. shrub with usu. purple or yellow flowers.

buddy /'bʌdɪ/ n. colloq. friend; mate.

budge v. move in slightest degree.

budgerigar /'bʌdʒərɪgɑ:(r)/ n. kind of Australian parakeet often kept as caged bird.

budget /'bʌdʒɪt/ 1 n. annual estimate of country's revenue and expenditure; similar estimate for person or group; amount of money required or available. 2 v. allow or arrange for in budget. 3 **budgetary** a.

buff 1 n. velvety dull-yellow leather; colour of this; sl. the skin; colloq. enthusiast. 2 a. buff-coloured. 3 v.t. polish; make velvety like buff.

buffalo /'bʌfələʊ/ n. (pl. **-loes**) any of various kinds of ox; Amer. bison.

buffer[1] /'bʌfə(r)/ n. apparatus for deadening impact esp. of railway vehicles. **buffer state** minor one between two great ones, regarded as reducing danger of quarrels.

buffer[2] /'bʌfə(r)/ n. sl. old or incompetent fellow.

buffet[1] /'bʊfeɪ/ n. place where light meals may be bought and eaten; provision of food where guests serve themselves; sideboard. **buffet car** railway coach in which refreshments are served.

buffet[2] /'bʌfɪt/ 1 n. blow with hand; shock. 2 v.t. deal blows to, knock about.

buffoon /bə'fu:n/ n. silly or ludicrous person; jester. **buffoonery** n.

bug 1 n. flat evil-smelling blood-sucking insect infesting beds etc.; US any small insect; colloq. virus, infection; concealed microphone; defect in machine or computer program etc. 2 v.t. conceal microphone in; sl. annoy.

bugbear /'bʌgbeə(r)/ n. cause of annoyance; object of baseless fear.

bugger /'bʌgə(r)/ 1 n. sodomite; vulg. unpleasant person or thing. 2 v. commit sodomy with; vulg. damn, mess about or up, clear off. 3 **buggery** n.

buggy /'bʌgɪ/ n. light horse-drawn vehicle for one or two persons; small sturdy motor vehicle.

bugle[1] /'bju:g(ə)l/ 1 n. brass instrument like small trumpet. 2 v.i. sound bugle. 3 **bugler** n.

bugle[2] /'bju:g(ə)l/ n. creeping plant with usu. blue flowers.

build /bɪld/ 1 v. (past & p.p. **built**) construct by putting parts or material together; develop or establish. 2 n. style of construction; proportions of human body. 3 **build up** gradually establish or be established; **build-up** favourable description in advance, gradual approach to climax.

builder /'bɪldə(r)/ n. contractor who builds houses etc.

building /'bɪldɪŋ/ n. house or other structure with roof and walls. **building society** society of investors that lends money on mortgage to those buying houses.

built past & p.p. of **build**. **built-in** forming integral part of structure etc.; **built-up** increased in height or thickness etc., covered with buildings.

bulb n. globular base of stem of some plants; electric lamp filament, its glass container; object or part shaped like bulb.

bulbous /'bʌlbəs/ a. bulb-shaped, having bulb or bulbs; swollen.

bulge /bʌldʒ/ 1 n. irregular swelling-out of surface or line; colloq temporary increase in numbers or volume. 2 v.i. form or show bulge. 3 **bulgy** a.

bulk 1 n. size, magnitude, esp. when great; the greater part of; large quantity. 2 v. increase size or thickness of; seem in terms of size or importance. 3 **bulk buying** buying in large amounts; **bulkhead** upright partition between compartments in ship, aircraft, vehicle, etc.

bulky /'bʌlkɪ/ a. large, unwieldy.

bull[1] /bʊl/ n. uncastrated male ox; male whale or elephant etc.; bull's-eye of target; Stock Exch. person who buys hoping to sell at higher price later. **bulldog** dog of sturdy powerful large-headed breed, tenacious and courageous person. **bulldog clip** strong sprung clip for papers etc. **bulldoze** clear with bulldozer, colloq. make one's way forcibly, intimidate; **bulldozer** powerful tractor with broad vertical blade for clearing ground; **bullfight** Spanish etc. sport of baiting bulls as public spectacle; **bullfinch** small song-bird with strong beak and fine plumage; **bullfrog** large Amer. frog with loud bellow; **bullring** arena for bullfight; **bull's-eye** centre of target; **bull-terrier** cross between bulldog and terrier.

bull² /bʊl/ *n.* Papal edict.

bull³ /bʊl/ *n.* absurdly illogical statement; *sl.* unnecessary routine tasks.

bullet /'bʊlɪt/ *n.* missile, usu. round or cylindrical with pointed end, fired from rifle or revolver, etc.

bulletin /'bʊlɪtɪn/ *n.* short official statement or broadcast report of news etc.

bullion /'bʊlɪən/ *n.* gold or silver in lump or valued by weight.

bullock /'bʊlək/ *n.* castrated bull.

bully¹ /'bʊlɪ/ 1 *n.* person using strength or power to coerce others by fear. 2 *v.* persecute or oppress by force or threats. 3 *int. sl.* very good.

bully² /'bʊlɪ/ 1 *n.* putting ball into play in hockey. 2 *v.i.* **bully off** start play thus.

bully³ /'bʊlɪ/ *n.* (in full **bully beef**) corned beef.

bulrush /'bʊlrʌʃ/ *n.* tall rush, esp. reed-mace; *Bibl.* papyrus.

bulwark /'bʊlwək/ *n.* earthwork or other material defence; person or principle that protects; usu. in *pl.* ship's side above deck.

bum¹ *n. sl.* buttocks.

bum² *colloq.* 1 *v.* loaf, wander *around*; cadge. 2 *n.* loafer, dissolute person. 3 *a.* worthless, of poor quality.

bumble /'bʌmb(ə)l/ *v.i.* blunder; act ineptly; make buzz. **bumble-bee** large loud-humming bee.

bump 1 *n.* dull-sounding blow or collision; swelling caused by it; rounded swelling or lump on a surface; uneven patch on road etc.; prominence on skull, thought to indicate mental faculty. 2 *v.* come or strike with a bump against; hurt thus; move *along* etc. with bumps. 3 **bump into** *colloq.* meet by chance; **bump off** *sl.* murder. 4 **bumpily** *adv.* **bumpy** *a.*

bumper /'bʌmpə(r)/ 1 *n.* unusually large or fine example; metal etc. bar on motor vehicle to reduce damage in collisions; brim-full glass. 2 *a.* unusually large or abundant.

bumpkin /'bʌmpkɪn/ *n.* rustic or awkward person.

bumptious /'bʌmpʃəs/ *a.* self-assertive, conceited.

bun *n.* small soft sweet cake often with dried fruit; small coil of hair at back of head.

bunch 1 *n.* cluster of things growing or fastened together; lot; *sl.* gang, group. 2 *v.i.* arrange in bunch(es); gather in folds; cling or crowd together. 3 **bunchy** *a.*

bundle /'bʌnd(ə)l/ 1 *n.* collection of things tied or fastened together; *sl.* large amount of money. 2 *v.* tie in bundle; throw confusedly *in(to)* receptacle; go or send unceremoniously *away* or *out* etc.

bung 1 *n.* stopper, esp. large cork stopping hole in cask. 2 *v.t.* stop with bung; stop *up*; *sl.* throw.

bungalow /'bʌngələʊ/ *n.* one-storeyed house.

bungle /'bʌng(ə)l/ *v.* mismanage, fail to accomplish; work awkwardly. 2 *n.* bungled work or attempt.

bunion /'bʌnɪən/ *n.* swelling on side of big toe.

bunk¹ *n.* shelflike bed against wall. **bunk-bed** two or more bunks one above the other.

bunk² *sl.* **do a bunk** run away.

bunk³ *n. sl.* nonsense, humbug.

bunker /'bʌnkə(r)/ 1 *n.* container for fuel; reinforced underground shelter; sand-pit or hollow as hazard on golf-course. 2 *v.* fill fuel bunkers of (ship etc.).

bunkum /'bʌnkəm/ *n.* nonsense, humbug.

bunny /'bʌnɪ/ *n.* childish name for rabbit.

Bunsen burner /'bʌns(ə)n/ gas-burner burning mixed air and gas, giving great heat.

bunting¹ /'bʌntɪŋ/ *n.* flags and other decorations; loosely-woven fabric used for these.

bunting² /'bʌntɪŋ/ *n.* small bird related to finch.

buoy /bɔɪ/ 1 *n.* anchored float as navigational mark etc.; lifebuoy. 2 *v.t.* mark with buoy(s). 3 **buoy up** keep afloat, sustain.

buoyant /'bɔɪənt/ *a.* apt to float, light; cheeful. **buoyancy** *n.*

bur *n.* clinging seed-vessel or other part of plant, plant producing burs; person hard to shake off.

burble /'bɜːb(ə)l/ *v.i.* make murmuring noise; speak lengthily.

burden /'bɜːd(ə)n/ 1 *n.* thing carried, load; weight of duty or sorrow etc.; obligatory expense; ship's carrying-capacity; refrain of song; theme. 2 *v.t.* load, encumber, oppress. 3 **beast of burden** animal used for carrying or pulling loads; **burden of proof** obligation to prove one's case. 4 **burdensome** *a.*

burdock /'bɜːdɒk/ *n.* plant with prickly flowers and docklike leaves.

bureau /'bjʊərəʊ/ *n.* (*pl.* **-reaux** or **-reaus** /-rəʊz/) writing-desk with drawers; *US* chest of drawers; office or department for transacting specific business; government department.

bureaucracy /bjʊə'rɒkrəsɪ/ *n.* government by central administration; officialism; set of dominant officials.

bureaucrat /'bjʊərəkræt/ *n.* official in bureaucracy. **bureaucratic** *a.*

burgeon /'bɜːdʒən/ *v.i.* begin to grow rapidly, flourish.

burger /'bɜːgə(r)/ *n. colloq.* hamburger; food resembling hamburger.

burgess /'bɜːdʒɪs/ *n.* citizen of borough.

burgh /'bʌrə/ *n.* Scottish borough.

burgher /'bɜːgə(r)/ *n.* citizen esp. of foreign town.

burglar /'bɜːglə(r)/ *n.* person who commits burglary. **burglarious** /-'gleər-/ *a.*

burglary /'bɜːglərɪ/ *n.* illegal entry into building to commit theft.

burgle /'bɜːg(ə)l/ *v.* commit burglary (on).

burgomaster /'bɜːgəmɑːstə(r)/ *n.* Dutch or Flemish mayor.

burgundy /'bɜːgəndɪ/ *n.* red or white wine produced in Burgundy; similar wine from elsewhere.

burial /'berɪəl/ *n.* burying, esp. of dead body; funeral.

burlesque /bɜː'lesk/ 1 *n.* dramatic or literary parody; *US* broadly humorous variety show. 2 *a.* of derisively imitative kind. 3 *v.t.* make or give burlesque of, travesty.

burly /'bɜːlɪ/ *a.* of stout sturdy build.

burn¹ 1 *v.* (*past & p.p.* **burnt** or

burned) (cause to) be consumed by fire; blaze or glow with fire; (cause to) be injured or damaged by fire, sun, or great heat; brand; give or feel sensation or pain (as) of heat. 2 *n.* sore or mark made by burning. 3 **burnt offering** sacrifice offered by burning.

burn² *n. Sc.* brook, stream.

burner /'bɜːnə(r)/ *n.* part of lamp or cooker etc. that emits and shapes flame.

burnish /'bɜːnɪʃ/ *v.t.* polish by rubbing.

burnous /bɜː'nuːs/ *n.* Arab or Moorish hooded cloak.

burnt *past & p.p.* of **burn**.

burp *n. & v.i. colloq.* belch.

burr¹ *n.* rough sounding of *r*; rough edge left by cutting metal etc.

burr² var. of **bur**.

burrow /'bʌrəʊ/ 1 *n.* hole excavated by animal as dwelling. 2 *v.* make or live in burrow; excavate; investigate or search *into*.

bursar /'bɜːsə(r)/ *n.* treasurer of college etc.; holder of bursary. **bursarial** /-'seər-/ *a.*

bursary /'bɜːsərɪ/ *n.* scholarship or grant awarded to student; bursar's office.

burst 1 *v.* (*past & p.p.* **burst**) fly violently apart or give way suddenly, explode; rush, move, speak, be spoken, etc. suddenly or violently. 2 *n.* bursting, explosion, outbreak; spurt.

burton /'bɜːt(ə)n/ *n. sl.* **go for a burton** be lost, destroyed, or killed.

bury /'berɪ/ *v.t.* place (dead body) in the earth or tomb or sea, celebrate burial rites over; put underground, hide in earth; consign to obscurity; involve (oneself) deeply.

bus /bʌs/ 1 *n.* (*pl.* **buses**, *US* **busses**) large public passenger-carrying vehicle usu. plying on fixed route. 2 *v.* (*past & p.p.* **bused**, *US* **bussed**) go by bus; *US* transport by bus (esp. to counteract racial segregation). 3 **busman** bus-driver; **busman's holiday** leisure spent in same occupation as working hours; **bus-shelter** roadside shelter for persons awaiting bus; **bus-stop** regular stopping-place of bus.

busby /'bʌzbɪ/ *n.* tall fur cap worn by hussars, guardsmen, etc.

bush¹ /bʊʃ/ *n.* shrub, clump of shrubs; clump of hair or fur; *Aus.* etc. wood-

land, untilled land; **bush-baby** small
Afr. tree-climbing lemur; **Bushman**
aboriginal or language of a S.Afr. people; **bushman** dweller or traveller in
Aus. bush; **bush telegraph** rapid
spreading of information, rumour, etc.
bush² /buʃ/ *n.* metal lining of axle-hole
etc.; electrically insulating sleeve.
bushel /ˈbuʃ(ə)l/ *n.* measure of capacity for corn, fruit, etc. (8 gals., c.
36.4l.)
bushy /ˈbuʃɪ/ *a.* growing thickly or like
bush; having many bushes.
business /ˈbɪznɪs/ *n.* one's occupation
or affairs; one's province or duty; serious work; thing(s) needing dealing
with; buying and selling, trade; commercial firm; action on theatre stage.
business-like practical, systematic;
business man (or **woman**) man (or
woman) engaged in trade or commerce.
busker /ˈbʌskə(r)/ *n.* street musician;
itinerant entertainer.
bust¹ *colloq.* 1 *v.* (*past* & *p.p.* **bust** or
busted) burst, break; arrest. 2 *a.* burst,
broken; bankrupt. 3 *n.* sudden failure,
drinking-bout; arrest. 4 **bust-up** quarrel; explosion; collapse.
bust² *n.* sculptural representation of
head, shoulders, and chest; upper front
or circumference of (woman's) body.
bustard /ˈbʌstəd/ *n.* large swift-
running bird.
bustle¹ /ˈbʌs(ə)l/ 1 *v.* make show of activity, hurry *about*; make (person)
hurry. 2 *n.* excited activity.
bustle² /ˈbʌs(ə)l/ *n. hist.* pad or framework used to puff out back of woman's
skirt.
busy /ˈbɪzɪ/ 1 *a.* working with concentrated attention, fully employed;
full of activity; fussy, meddlesome. 2
v.t. occupy, keep busy. 3 **busybody**
meddlesome person.
but 1 *conj.* however; on the other hand;
otherwise than. 2 *prep.* except, apart
from. 3 *adv.* only. 4 *pron.* who not.
butane /ˈbjuːteɪn/ *n.* hydrocarbon of
paraffin series used in liquefied form as
fuel.
butch /butʃ/ *a. sl.* masculine,
tough-looking.
butcher /ˈbutʃə(r)/ 1 *n.* person who
sells meat; slaughterer of animals for
food; person who causes people to be
killed needlessly or brutally. 2 *v.*

slaughter or cut up (animal); kill or destroy wantonly or cruelly; make a mess
of. 3 **butchery** *n.*
butler /ˈbʌtlə(r)/ *n.* chief manservant
of household in charge of wine-cellar
and plate.
butt¹ 1 *v.* push with head; meet end to
end; 2 *n.* (violent) push or blow with
head or horns. 3 **butt in** intervene,
meddle.
butt² *n.* object of ridicule etc., person
habitually ridiculed or teased; mound
behind target; in *pl.* shooting-range.
butt³ *n.* thicker end esp. of tool or weapon; remnant of smoked cigarette etc.
butt⁴ *n.* large cask.
butter /ˈbʌtə(r)/ *n.* yellow fatty food-
substance made from cream; substance
of similar texture. 2 *v.t.* spread, cook,
etc., with butter. 3 **butter bean** dried
large flat white kind; **buttercup** a
yellow-flowered plant; **butter-fingers**
person likely to drop things; **but-
termilk** liquid left after butter-
making; **butter muslin** thin
loosely-woven cloth; **butterscotch**
sweet made of butter and sugar; **butter
up** flatter.
butterfly /ˈbʌtəflaɪ/ *n.* insect with
large often showy wings, active by day;
in *pl.* nervous sensation in stomach.
butterfly nut *Mech.* nut with projections turned with finger and thumb;
butterfly stroke method of swimming
with both arms lifted at same time.
buttery¹ /ˈbʌtərɪ/ *a.* like or containing
butter.
buttery² /ˈbʌtərɪ/ *n.* place in college
etc. where provisions are kept.
buttock /ˈbʌtək/ *n.* either protuberance on lower rear part of human
body; corresponding part of animal.
button /ˈbʌt(ə)n/ 1 *n.* disc or knob
sewn to garment etc. as fastening or for
ornament; small rounded object; knob
etc. pressed to operate electrical
device. 2 *v.* fasten with buttons. 3 **button mushroom** small unopened
mushroom.
buttonhole /ˈbʌtənhəʊl/ 1 *n.* slit to receive fastening button, flower(s) worn
in coat-lapel buttonhole. 2 *v.* seize or
detain (reluctant listener).
buttress /ˈbʌtrɪs/ 1 *n.* support built
against wall etc. 2 *v.t.* support or
strengthen.

buxom /'bʌksəm/ *a.* plump, large and shapely.

buy /baɪ/ 1 *v.t.* (*past & p.p.* **bought** /bɔːt/) obtain in exchange for money or other consideration; gain (over) by bribery; *sl.* accept, believe. 2 *n.* purchase.

buyer /'baɪə(r)/ *n.* person who buys, esp. stock for large shop etc. **buyer's market** time when goods are plentiful and prices low.

buzz 1 *v.* make humming sound of bee; be filled with activity etc.; interfere with (aircraft) by flying close. 2 *n.* humming sound; confused low sound; sound of buzzer.

buzzard /'bʌzəd/ *n.* kind of predatory hawk.

buzzer /'bʌzə(r)/ *n.* electric machine producing buzzing sound as signal.

by /baɪ/ 1 *adv.* near at hand; aside, in reserve; past. 2 *prep.* near, beside, along, via, past; through action, agency, means, or instrumentality of; as soon as, not later than; in accordance with; to extent of. 3 **by and by** before long, *the* future; **by-election** election of MP in single constituency; **bypath** secluded path; **by-play** subsidiary action in play; **by-product** substance etc. produced incidentally in making of something else; **by-road** minor road; **by the by, by the way**, incidentally; **byway** by-road or bypath; **byword** person or thing cited as notable example, proverb.

bye /baɪ/ *n. Crick.* run made from ball that passes batsman without being hit; (in tournament) position of competitor left without opponent in round.

bye-bye *int. colloq.* goodbye.

bygone /'baɪgɒn/ 1 *a.* past, departed. 2 *n.* in *pl.* past offences.

by-law /'baɪlɔː/ *n.* regulation made by local authority etc.

byline /'baɪlaɪn/ *n.* line in newspaper etc. naming writer of article etc.

bypass /'baɪpɑːs/ 1 *n.* road round town or its centre as alternative route for through traffic. 2 *v.* (*past & p.p.* **-passed**) avoid; provide with bypass.

byre /baɪə(r)/ *n.* cow-shed.

bystander /'baɪstændə(r)/ *n.* person who stands by but does not take part.

Byzantine /baɪ'zæntaɪn/ *a.* of Byzantium or E. Roman Empire; of architectural etc. style developed in Eastern Empire; complicated, underhand.

C

C, c, Roman numeral 100.

C *abbr.* centigrade; Celsius.

c. *abbr.* cent; century; chapter.

c. *abbr.* circa.

cab *n.* taxi, *hist.* hackney carriage; compartment for driver of train, lorry, crane, etc.

cabal /kə'bæl/ *n.* secret intrigue; political clique.

cabaret /'kæbəreɪ/ *n.* entertainment in restaurant etc. while guests are at table; such restaurant etc.

cabbage /'kæbɪdʒ/ *n.* green vegetable with leaves forming round heart or head; *colloq.* person without ambition or interests. **cabbage white** white butterfly.

cabby /'kæbɪ/ *n.* *colloq.* taxi-driver.

caber /'keɪbə(r)/ *n.* tree-trunk used in Sc. sport of **tossing the caber**.

cabin /'kæbɪn/ *n.* small dwelling or shelter esp. of wood; room or compartment in ship, aircraft, etc. **cabin-boy** ship's waiter; **cabin cruiser** large motor-boat with cabin.

cabinet /'kæbɪnɪt/ *n.* case or cupboard with drawers, shelves, or compartments; wooden etc. container for radio, television, etc.; **Cabinet** group of ministers controlling Government policy. **cabinet-maker** skilled joiner.

cable /'keɪb(ə)l/ **1** *n.* encased group of insulated wires for transmitting electricity or telegraph messages; anchor chain of ship; thick rope of wire or hemp; cablegram. **2** *v.* send (message), communicate, by undersea cable. **3 cable-car** car mounted on endless cable and drawn up and down mountainside etc.; **cablegram** message sent by undersea cable; **cable-stitch** knitting stitch resembling twisted rope; **cable television** transmission of television programmes by cable to subscribers.

caboodle /kə'buːd(ə)l/ *n. sl.* **the whole caboodle** the whole lot.

caboose /kə'buːs/ *n.* kitchen on ship's deck; *US* guard's van on goods train.

cacao /kə'kɑːəʊ/ *n.* seed from which cocoa and chocolate are made; tree producing it.

cachalot /'kæʃəlɒt/ *n.* sperm-whale.

cache /kæʃ/ **1** *n.* place for hiding or storing treasure or supplies; things so hidden. **2** *v.t.* place in cache.

cachet /'kæʃeɪ/ *n.* distinctive stamp; mark of authenticity; prestige; flat capsule for medicine.

cack-handed *a. colloq.* clumsy, awkward; left-handed.

cackle /'kæk(ə)l/ **1** *n.* clucking of hen; noisy inconsequential talk; loud silly laughter. **2** *v.* emit cackle; utter or express with cackle.

cacophony /kə'kɒfənɪ/ *n.* harsh discordant sound. **cacophonous** *a.*

cactus /'kæktəs/ *n.* (*pl.* **-ti** /-taɪ/ or **-tuses**) plant with thick fleshy stem, usu. with spines but no leaves.

cad *n.* person (esp. man) who behaves dishonourably. **caddish** *a.*

cadaver /kə'deɪvə(r)/ *n.* corpse. **cadaverous** /-'dæv-/ *a.*

caddie /'kædɪ/ **1** *n.* golfer's attendant carrying clubs etc. **2** *v.i.* act as caddie.

caddis /'kædɪs/ *n.* **caddis-fly** four-winged insect living near water; **caddis-worm** larva of caddis-fly.

caddy[1] /'kædɪ/ *n.* small box for holding tea.

caddy[2] var. of **caddie**.

cadence /'keɪd(ə)ns/ *n.* fall of the voice, esp. at end of phrase; tonal inflexion; movement of sound; close of musical phrase.

cadenza /kə'denzə/ *n. Mus.* elaborate improvisation by soloist near end of concerto movement.

cadet /kə'det/ *n.* young trainee in armed services or police force.

cadge *v.* get or seek by begging; be beggar.

cadi /'kɑːdɪ/ *n.* judge in Muslim country.

cadmium /'kædmɪəm/ *n.* soft bluish-white metallic element.

cadre /'kɑːdə(r)/ *n.* basic unit, esp. of servicemen; politically active group in Communist countries.

caecum /'siːkəm/ *n.* (*pl.* **-ca**) *Biol.* tube with closed end forming first part of large intestine.

Caerphilly /keə'fɪlɪ/ *n.* kind of mild pale cheese.

Caesarean /sɪ'zeərɪən/ *a.* (of birth) effected by cutting into womb through wall of abdomen.

caesura /sɪ'zjʊərə/ n. pause in verse line.

café /'kæfeɪ/ n. coffee-house or restaurant.

cafeteria /kæfə'tɪərɪə/ n. self-service restaurant.

caffeine /'kæfi:n/ n. alkaloid stimulant found in coffee and tea plants.

caftan /'kæftæn/ n. long usu. belted tunic worn by men in Near East; woman's long loose dress.

cage 1 n. structure of wire or bars, esp. for confining animals; open framework, mineshaft lift-frame, etc. 2 v.t. confine in cage.

cagey /'keɪdʒɪ/ a. sl. cautious and uncommunicative; wary.

cagoule /kə'gu:l/ n. light hooded waterproof jacket.

cahoots /kə'hu:ts/ n. sl. **in cahoots** in league or partnership.

caiman var. of **cayman.**

cairn /keən/ n. pyramid of rough stones. **cairn terrier** small short-legged shaggy-haired terrier.

cairngorm /'keəŋɡɔ:m/ n. yellow or wine-coloured gem-stone.

caisson /'keɪsɒn/ n. watertight chamber in which underwater construction work can be done.

cajole /kə'dʒəʊl/ v.t. persuade or soothe by flattery or deceit. **cajolery** n.

cake 1 n. mixture of flour, butter, eggs, sugar, etc., baked in oven; flattish compact mass. 2 v. form into cohesive mass, harden.

calabash /'kæləbæʃ/ n. gourd or hard-shelled fruit of tropical Amer. tree; bowl or pipe made from gourd.

calamine /'kæləmaɪn/ n. pink powder, chiefly zinc carbonate or oxide, used esp. in skin lotion.

calamity /kə'læmɪtɪ/ n. grave disaster. **calamitous** a.

calcareous /kæl'keərɪəs/ a. of or containing limestone.

calceolaria /kælsɪə'leərɪə/ n. plant with slipper-shaped flower.

calcify /'kælsɪfaɪ/ v. harden by deposit of calcium salts. **calcification** n.

calcine /'kælsaɪn/ v. reduce or be reduced to quicklime or powder by burning or roasting. **calcination** n.

calcium /'kælsɪəm/ n. light silver-white malleable metallic element.

calculate /'kælkjʊleɪt/ v. compute by

figures, ascertain by exact reckoning; plan deliberately; US colloq. suppose, believe. **calculation** n.

calculated a. done with awareness of likely consequences; designed to do.

calculator n. device, esp. small electronic one, used for making calculations.

calculus /'kælkjʊləs/ n. (pl. **-li** /-laɪ/ or **-luses**) Math. particular method of calculation; Med. stone or concretion in some part of body.

caldron var. of **cauldron.**

Caledonian /kælɪ'dəʊnɪən/ 1 a. of Scotland. 2 n. Scotsman or Scotswoman.

calendar /'kælɪndə(r)/ n. system fixing year's beginning, length, etc.; chart showing days, weeks, and months of particular year; adjustable device showing day's date etc.; list of special dates or events.

calends /'kælɪndz/ n.pl. first month in ancient Roman calendar.

calf¹ /kɑ:f/ n. (pl. **calves** /kɑ:vz/) young of cow, elephant, whale, etc.; calf-leather. **calf-love** immature romantic affection.

calf² /kɑ:f/ n. (pl. **calves** /kɑ:vz/) fleshy hind part of human leg below knee.

calibrate /'kælɪbreɪt/ v.t. determine or correct graduations of (gauge); find calibre of. **calibration** n.

calibre /'kælɪbə(r)/ n. internal diameter of gun or tube; diameter of bullet or shell; degree of merit or importance.

calico /'kælɪkəʊ/ 1 n. (pl. **-oes**) cotton cloth, esp. plain white kind; US printed cotton cloth. 2 a. of calico; US multi-coloured.

caliph /'keɪlɪf/ n. chief civil and religious ruler in Muslim countries.

calk US var. of **caulk.**

call /kɔ:l/ 1 v. cry, shout, speak loudly; summon; order to take place; invite; name, describe, or regard as; communicate (with) by radio or telephone; make brief visit; utter characteristic sound. 2 n. shout; summons; telephone conversation; signal on bugle etc.; short visit; need, occasion; bird's cry. 3 **call-box** telephone-box; **call-girl** prostitute who accepts appointments by telephone; **call in** withdraw from circulation, seek advice or help from, make brief visit; **call off** cancel, abandon; **call-sign** one which indicates identity of radio transmitter; **call up** summon (esp. to do military service), ring up; **call-up** summons to do military service. **4 caller** *n.*

calligraphy /kə'lıgrəfı/ *n.* handwriting; art of fine handwriting. **calligraphic** /kælı'græfık/ *a.*

calling /'kɔːlıŋ/ *n.* profession, occupation.

calliper /'kælıpə(r)/ *n.* **calliper compasses** or **callipers** pair of hinged arms for measuring diameters; metal support for weak or injured leg.

callisthenics /kælıs'θenıks/ *n.pl.* exercises to develop strength and grace.

callosity /kə'lɒsıtı/ *n.* hardness of skin, callus.

callous /'kæləs/ *a.* unfeeling, unsympathetic; (of skin) hardened.

callow /'kæləʊ/ *a.* raw, inexperienced.

callus /'kæləs/ *n.* thickened part of skin or soft tissue.

calm /kɑːm/ **1** *a.* tranquil, windless, not agitated; confident. **2** *n.* calm condition or period. **3** *v.* make or become calm, pacify.

calomel /'kæləmel/ *n.* a purgative compound of mercury.

Calor gas /'kælə(r)/ **(P)** liquefied butane etc. under pressure in containers for use as domestic fuel.

calorie /'kælərı/ *n.* unit of heat, amount required to raise temperature of one kg. (**large calorie**) or one g. (**small calorie**) of water 1°C; large calorie as unit of energy value of foods.

calorific /kælə'rıfık/ *a.* heat-producing.

calumniate /kə'lʌmnıeıt/ *v.t.* slander. **calumniation** *n.*

calumny /'kæləmnı/ *n.* malicious misrepresentation, slander. **calumnious** /-'lʌm-/ *a.*

Calvary /'kælvərı/ *n.* place or representation of Crucifixion.

calve /kɑːv/ *v.i.* give birth to calf.

calves *pl.* of **calf**[1],[2].

Calvinism /'kælvınız(ə)m/ *n.* Calvin's theology, esp. his doctrine of predestination. **Calvinist** *n.*; **Calvinistic** *a.*

calx *n.* (*pl.* **calces** /'kælsiːz/) friable residue left after burning of metal or mineral.

calypso /kə'lıpsəʊ/ *n.* (*pl.* **-sos**) W. Ind song, usus. with improvised topical words.

calyx /'keılıks/ *n.* (*pl.* **-lyces** /-lısıːz/ or **-lyxes**) whorl of leaves forming outer case of bud.

cam *n.* projecting part of wheel etc. in machinery, shaped to convert circular into reciprocal or variable motion.

camaraderie /kæmə'rɑːdərı/ *n.* comradeship; mutual trust and friendship.

camber /'kæmbə(r)/ **1** *n.* convex or arched shape of road or deck etc. **2** *v.t.* construct with camber.

cambric /'kæmbrık/ *n.* fine linen or cotton cloth.

came *past of* **come**.

camel /'kæm(ə)l/ *n.* large four-legged animal with one hump or two, used as beast of burden in arid regions; fawn colour.

camellia /kə'miːlıə/ *n.* evergreen flowering shrub.

Camembert /'kæməmbeə(r)/ *n.* a kind of rich soft white cheese.

cameo /'kæmıəʊ/ *n.* (*pl.* **-os**) onyx or similar stone carved in relief; short literary sketch or acted scene.

camera /'kæmərə/ *n.* apparatus for taking photographs or film or television pictures. **cameraman** operator of esp. film or television camera; **in camera** in private.

camisole /'kæmısəʊl/ *n.* under-bodice; blouse with straight top and broad shoulder-straps.

camomile /'kæməmaıl/ *n.* aromatic herb with flowers used to make medicinal tea.

camouflage /'kæməflɑːʒ/ **1** *n.* disguising of guns, ships, etc., by obscuring with splashes of various colours, foliage, etc.; means of disguise or evasion. **2** *v.t.* hide (as) by camouflage.

camp[1] **1** *n.* place where troops etc. are lodged or trained; fortified site; accommodation of tents, huts, etc. for temporary holiday-makers, nomads, explorers, etc. **2** *v.* live in camp; make camp. **3 camp-bed** portable folding bed; **camp-follower** civilian worker in military camp; **camp out** lodge in open air or in temporary quarters; **camp-site** place for camping.

camp[2] **1** *a.* affected; effeminate; homosexual; exaggerated for effect. **2** *n.* camp behaviour. **3** *v.* behave or do in camp way.

campaign /kæm'peɪn/ **1** *n.* organized course of action in politics etc.; series of military operations. **2** *v.i.* take part in campaign.

campanile /kæmpə'niːlɪ/ *n.* detached bell-tower.

campanology /kæmpə'nɒlədʒɪ/ *n.* study of bells; bell-ringing. **campanologist** *n.*

campanula /kæm'pænjʊlə/ *n.* plant with bell-shaped flowers.

camphor /'kæmfə(r)/ *n.* crystalline bitter substance used in medicine and to repel insects.

camphorate /'kæmfəreɪt/ *v.t.* impregnate with camphor.

campion /'kæmpɪən/ *n.* wild plant with white or pink notched flowers.

campus /'kæmpəs/ *n.* grounds of university or college.

camshaft /'kæmʃɑːft/ *n.* shaft carrying cams.

can¹ *v.aux.* (*neg.* **cannot, can't** /kɑːnt/; *past* **could** /kʊd/, *neg.* **could not, couldn't** /'kʊd(ə)nt/) be able to; have the right to; *colloq.* be permitted to.

can² **1** *n.* metal vessel for liquids; tin plate container in which food etc. is sealed for preserving. **2** *v.t.* preserve (food etc.) in can. **3 canned music** music recorded for reproduction; **carry the can** bear responsibility.

Canadian /kə'neɪdɪən/ **1** *a.* of Canada. **2** *n.* native or inhabitant of Canada.

canal /kə'næl/ *n.* artificial waterway for inland navigation or irrigation; duct; tubular passage in plant or animal.

canalize /'kænəlaɪz/ *v.t.* convert (river) into canal; give desired direction to.

canapé /'kænəpeɪ/ *n.* piece of bread, toast, etc., with small savoury on top.

canard /'kænɑːd/ *n.* unfounded rumour.

canary /kə'neərɪ/ *n.* small songbird with yellow plumage.

canasta /kə'næstə/ *n.* card-game resembling rummy.

cancan /'kænkæn/ *n.* high-kicking dance.

cancel /'kæns(ə)l/ *v.* (*past & p.p.* **cancelled**) withdraw, revoke, discontinue;

obliterate, delete; mark (ticket, stamp, etc.) to invalidate it; annul; neutralize, counterbalance; *Math.* strike out (equal factor) on each side of equation etc. **cancel out** neutralize (each other). **cancellation** *n.*

cancer /'kænsə(r)/ *n.* malignant tumour, disease featuring this; *fig.* corruption; **Cancer** fourth sign of zodiac. **cancerous** *a.*

candelabrum /kændɪ'lɑːbrəm/ *n.* (*pl.* **-bra**) large usu. branched candlestick.

candid /'kændɪd/ *a.* frank, not hiding one's thoughts; informal, of photograph taken usu. without subject's knowledge.

candidate /'kændɪdeɪt/ *n.* person who seeks, or is nominated for, election, office, position, etc.; person who sits examination etc. **candidacy** *n.*; **candidature** *n.*

candle /'kænd(ə)l/ *n.* cylinder of wax, tallow, etc. enclosing wick, for burning to give light. **candlepower** unit of luminous intensity; **candlestick** holder for candle(s); **candlewick** thick soft yarn, material with raised tufted pattern in this.

candour /'kændə(r)/ *n.* candidness.

candy /'kændɪ/ **1** *n.* sugar crystallized by repeated boiling and evaporation; *US* sweets, a sweet. **2** *v.* preserve (fruit etc.) by impregnating with sugar. **3 candy-floss** mass of fluffy spun sugar; **candy-striped** patterned in alternate white and esp. pink stripes

candytuft /'kændɪtʌft/ *n.* garden plant with flowers in flat clusters.

cane 1 *n.* hollow jointed stem of giant reed or grass, or of slender palm, used for wickerwork or as walking-stick, instrument of punishment, etc.; sugarcane; stem of raspberry etc. **2** *v.t.* beat with cane; weave cane into (chair etc.).

canine /'keɪnaɪn/ **1** *a.* of a dog or dogs. **2** *n.* dog; canine tooth. **3 canine tooth** tooth between incisors and molars.

canister /'kænɪstə(r)/ *n.* small usu. metal box for tea etc.; cylinder of shot or tear-gas.

canker /'kæŋkə(r)/ **1** *n.* disease of plants and trees; ulcerous disease of animals; *fig.* corrupting influence. **2** *v.t.* consume with canker; corrupt. **3 cankerous** *a.*

cannabis /'kænəbɪs/ *n.* hemp plant;

preparation of parts of it used as intoxicant. **cannabis resin** sticky product of this plant.

cannibal /'kænɪb(ə)l/ 1 *n.* person or animal that eats its own species. 2 *a.* of or having this habit. 3 **cannibalism** *n.*; **cannibalistic** *a.*

cannibalize /'kænɪbəlaɪz/ *v.t.* use (machine etc.) as source of spare parts for others.

cannon /'kænən/ 1 *n. hist.* large gun; *Billiards* hitting of two balls successively by player's ball. 2 *v.i.* make cannon at billiards; collide heavily *against, into,* etc. 3 **cannon-ball** large metal ball fired by cannon.

cannonade /kænə'neɪd/ 1 *n.* continuous gunfire. 2 *v.* bombard with cannon.

cannot see **can**[1].

canny /'kænɪ/ *a.* shrewd, thrifty, circumspect.

canoe /kə'nu:/ 1 *n.* light boat propelled with paddle(s). 2 *v.i. (partic.* canoeing) go in or paddle canoe. 3 **canoeist** *n.*

canon /'kænən/ *n.* general law, rule, or principle; criterion; church decree; member of cathedral chapter; body of (esp. sacred) writings etc. accepted as genuine; *Mus.* piece with different parts taking up same theme successively.

canonical /kə'nɒnɪk(ə)l/ *a.* according to or ordered by canon law; included in canon of Scripture; authoritative or accepted; of cathedral canon or chapter.

canonize /'kænənaɪz/ *v.t.* declare officially to be a saint. **canonization** *n.*

canopy /'kænəpɪ/ 1 *n.* covering hung or held up over throne, bed, person, etc.; *fig.* sky or overhanging shelter; rooflike projection. 2 *v.t.* supply or be canopy to.

cant[1] 1 *n.* insincere pious or moral talk; language peculiar to one class of people; jargon. 2 *v.i.* use cant.

cant[2] 1 *n.* slanting surface, bevel; oblique push or jerk; tilted position. 2 *v.* push or jerk or hold out of level.

can't see **can**[1].

cantaloup /'kæntəlu:p/ *n.* small round ribbed melon.

cantankerous /kæn'tæŋkərəs/ *a.* bad-tempered, quarrelsome.

cantata /kæn'tɑ:tə/ *n.* choral work like oratorio but usu. shorter.

canteen /kæn'ti:n/ *n.* restaurant for employees in factory, office, etc.; shop for provisions or liquor in barracks or camp; case or chest containing set of cutlery; soldier's or camper's water-flask.

canter /'kæntə(r)/ 1 *n.* easy gallop. 2 *v.* go at a canter.

canticle /'kæntɪk(ə)l/ *n.* song or chant on biblical text.

cantilever /'kæntɪli:və(r)/ *n.* beam, bracket, etc., projecting from wall to support balcony etc.; beam or girder fixed at one end only. **cantilever bridge** one in which cantilevers project from piers and are connected by girders.

canto /'kæntəʊ/ *n.* (*pl.* -**tos**) division of long poem.

canton 1 /'kæntɒn/ *n.* subdivision of country, esp. Switzerland. 2 /kæn'tu:n/ *v.t.* put (troops) in their quarters.

cantonment /kæn'tu:nmənt/ *n.* lodgings of troops.

cantor /'kæntɔ:(r)/ *n.* precentor in synagogue.

canvas /'kænvəs/ *n.* strong coarse cloth used for sails and tents and as surface for oil-painting, etc.; a painting.

canvass /'kænvəs/ 1 *v.* solicit votes (from), ascertain opinions of; solicit custom of; propose (idea etc.). 2 *n.* canvassing.

canyon /'kænjən/ *n.* deep gorge cut by river.

cap 1 *n.* soft brimless head-covering, freq. with peak; nurse's or woman servant's indoor head-dress; cap awarded as sign of membership of sports team; academic mortar-board; cover resembling cap, or designed to close, seal or protect something; explosive device esp. of paper for toy pistol; contraceptive diaphragm. 2 *v.t.* put cap on; cover top or end of; award sports cap to; lie on top of, surpass.

CAP *abbr.* Common Agricultural Policy (of EEC).

capable /'keɪpəb(ə)l/ *a.* able, competent. **capable of** having ability, fitness, or necessary quality for, susceptible or admitting of. **capability** *n.*; **capably** *adv.*

capacious /kə'peɪʃəs/ a. roomy, able to hold much.

capacitance /kə'pæsɪt(ə)ns/ n. ability of apparatus to store electric charge.

capacitor /kə'pæsɪtə(r)/ n. Electr. device able to store electric charge.

capacity /kə'pæsɪtɪ/ n. power of containing, producing, etc.; maximum amount that can be contained, produced, etc.; mental power; function or character.

caparison /kə'pærɪs(ə)n/ 1 n. harness, trappings; finery. 2 v.t. adorn.

cape[1] n. sleeveless cloak.

cape[2] n. headland, promontory; **the Cape** Cape of Good Hope.

caper[1] /'keɪpə(r)/ 1 v.i. move playfully. 2 n. playful jump or leap; sl. activity, occupation.

caper[2] /'keɪpə(r)/ n. bramble-like shrub; in pl. its pickled flower-buds.

capercaillie /kæpə'keɪlɪ/ n. (also **capercailzie**) largest kind of grouse.

capillary /kə'pɪlərɪ/ 1 a. of hair; of hairlike fineness. 2 n. capillary tube, blood-vessel, etc. 3 **capillary attraction** tendency of liquid to be drawn up in capillary tube.

capital /'kæpɪt(ə)l/ 1 n. most important town or city of a country or region; money etc. with which company starts business; accumulated wealth; capital letter; head of column or pillar. 2 a. most important; colloq. excellent; involving punishment by death; (of letters of alphabet) large in size and form, such as begin sentence and name. 3 **capital gain** profit from sale of investments or property; **capital transfer tax** tax levied on transfer of capital, e.g. by gift or bequest.

capitalism /'kæpɪtəlɪz(ə)m/ n. economic system with ownership and control of capital in private hands.

capitalist /'kæpɪtəlɪst/ 1 n. person using or possessing capital. 2 a. of or favouring capitalism. 3 **capitalistic** a.

capitalize /'kæpɪtəlaɪz/ v. convert into or provide with capital; write (letter of alphabet) as capital, begin (word) with capital letter. **capitalize on** use to one's advantage. **capitalization** n.

capitulate /kə'pɪtjʊleɪt/ v.i. surrender esp. on stated conditions. **capitulation** n.

capon /'keɪpən/ n. castrated cock.

caprice /kə'priːs/ n. unaccountable change of mind or conduct; work of lively fancy.

capricious /kə'prɪʃəs/ a. liable to caprice, unpredictable.

Capricorn /'kæprɪkɔːn/ n. tenth sign of zodiac.

capsicum /'kæpsɪkəm/ n. tropical plant with hot-flavoured seeds; its edible fleshy seed-pod.

capsize /kæp'saɪz/ v. overturn, esp. on water.

capstan /'kæpst(ə)n/ n. thick revolving cylinder round which cable or rope is wound; revolving spindle carrying spool on tape recorder. **capstan lathe** one with tools mounted on capstan-like holder.

capsule /'kæpsjuːl/ n. small soluble case enclosing dose of medicine; detachable nose-cone of rocket etc. or compartment of spacecraft; enclosing membrane; plant's seed-case.

captain /'kæptɪn/ 1 n. chief, leader; naval officer next below commodore; master of merchant ship; army officer next below major; pilot of civil aircraft; leader of side at games. 2 v.t. be captain of. 3 **captaincy** n.

caption /'kæpʃ(ə)n/ 1 n. heading of chapter, article, etc.; wording on cinema or televison screen, or appended to illustration or cartoon. 2 v.t. provide with caption.

captious /'kæpʃəs/ a. fond of finding fault, quibbling, etc.

captivate /'kæptɪveɪt/ v.t. fascinate, charm. **captivation** n.

captive /'kæptɪv/ 1 n. person or animal taken prisoner or confined. 2 a. taken prisoner; in confinement; unable to escape. 3 **captivity** n.

captor /'kæptə(r)/ n. one who captures.

capture /'kæptʃə(r)/ 1 v.t. take prisoner; seize; portray in permanent form. 2 n. act of capturing; thing or person captured.

Capuchin /'kæpjʊtʃɪn/ n. friar of branch of Franciscans; **capuchin** Amer. monkey with hair like black hood.

car n. wheeled vehicle; motor car; railway carriage of specified type; US any railway carriage or van. **car-park** area for parking cars; **carport** roofed open-sided shelter for car; **car-sick** affected by nausea through motion of car.

caracul var. of **karakul**.

carafe /kəˈræf/ n. glass container for water or wine.

caramel /ˈkærəmel/ n. brown substance got by heating sugar or syrup; soft toffee made with this.

carapace /ˈkærəpeɪs/ n. upper shell of tortoise or crustacean.

carat /ˈkærət/ n. unit of weight for precious stones; unit of purity of gold.

caravan /ˈkærəvæn/ n. vehicle equipped for living in and usu. towed by motor vehicle; company travelling together esp. across desert.

caravanserai /kærəˈvænsəraɪ/ n. Eastern inn with central courtyard.

caravel /ˈkærəvel/ n. hist. small light fast ship.

caraway /ˈkærəweɪ/ n. plant with small aromatic fruit (**caraway-seed**) used in cakes etc.

carbide /ˈkɑːbaɪd/ n. compound of carbon with metal.

carbine /ˈkɑːbaɪn/ n. kind of short rifle.

carbohydrate /kɑːbəʊˈhaɪdreɪt/ n. energy-producing compound of carbon, hydrogen, and oxygen.

carbolic /kɑːˈbɒlɪk/ n. (in full **carbolic acid**) kind of disinfectant and antiseptic; **carbolic soap** soap containing this.

carbon /ˈkɑːbən/ n. non-metallic element occurring as diamond, graphite, charcoal, etc. and in all organic compounds; carbon paper, carbon copy; carbon rod used in arc-lamp. **carbon copy** copy made with carbon paper; **carbon dating** determination of age of object etc. from decay of radio-carbon in it; **carbon dioxide** gas formed by burning carbon or by breathing; **carbon monoxide** poisonous gas formed by burning carbon incompletely; **carbon paper** thin carbon-coated paper for making copy as thing is typed or written.

carbonate /ˈkɑːbəneɪt/ 1 n. salt of carbonic acid. 2 v.t. impregnate with carbon dioxide.

carbonic /kɑːˈbɒnɪk/ a. of carbon. **carbonic acid** weak acid formed from carbon dioxide and water.

carboniferous /kɑːbəˈnɪfərəs/ a. producing coal.

carbonize /ˈkɑːbənaɪz/ v.t. reduce to charcoal or coke by burning; coat with carbon. **carbonization** n.

carborundum /kɑːbəˈrʌndəm/ n. compound of carbon and silicon used as abrasive etc.

carboy /ˈkɑːbɔɪ/ n. large globular glass bottle.

carbuncle /ˈkɑːbʌŋk(ə)l/ n. severe abscess in the skin; bright red jewel.

carburettor /kɑːbjʊˈretə(r)/ n. apparatus mixing air with petrol vapour in internal-combustion engine.

carcass /ˈkɑːkəs/ n. (also **carcase**) n. dead body of animal or bird or (derog.) person; framework, worthless remains.

carcinogen /ˈkɑːsɪnədʒ(ə)n/ n. substance that produces cancer. **carcinogenic** /-ˈdʒen-/ a.

card¹ n. thick paper or thin pasteboard; piece of this for writing or printing on, esp. to send greetings, to identify person, or to record information; playing-card; in pl. card-playing; in pl. colloq. employee's documents; sl. eccentric person. **card-carrying** having valid membership (esp. of political party); **card index** one with each item on separate card; **card-sharp** swindler at card-games; **card vote** block vote.

card² 1 n. toothed instrument or wire brush etc. for combing wool etc. 2 v.t. treat with card.

cardamom /ˈkɑːdəməm/ n. E. Ind. spice from seeds of aromatic plant.

cardboard /ˈkɑːdbɔːd/ n. stiff paper or pasteboard.

cardiac /ˈkɑːdɪæk/ a. of the heart.

cardigan /ˈkɑːdɪgən/ n. knitted jacket with buttons down front.

cardinal /ˈkɑːdɪn(ə)l/ 1 a. chief, fundamental; of deep scarlet. 2 n. one of leading officials of RC Church, who elect Pope. 3 **cardinal numbers** those representing quantity 1, 2, 3, etc. (cf. **ordinal**).

cardiogram /ˈkɑːdɪəgræm/ n. record of heart movements.

cardio-vascular /kɑːdɪəʊˈvæskjʊlə(r)/ a. of heart and blood-vessels.

care /keə(r)/ 1 n. anxiety, worry; serious attention; caution; task, charge, protection. 2 v.i. feel concern or interest or affection. 3 **in care** (of child) under supervision of local authority etc.

careen /kə'ri:n/ v. turn (ship) on side for repair; tilt, lean over.

career /kə'rɪə(r)/ 1 n. course through life, esp. in a profession; profession or occupation; swift course. 2 v.i. move or swerve about wildly.

careerist /kə'rɪərɪst/ n. person predominantly concerned with personal advancement.

carefree /'keəfri:/ a. free from anxiety or responsibility.

careful /'keəfʊl/ a. painstaking; cautious; done with care and attention.

careless /'keəlɪs/ a. lacking care or attention; unthinking, insensitive; light-hearted.

caress /kə'res/ 1 v.t. touch lovingly, kiss. 2 n. loving touch, kiss.

caret /'kærɪt/ n. omission-mark.

caretaker /'keəteɪkə(r)/ n. person in charge of maintenance etc. of house, building, etc.; attrib. taking temporary control.

careworn /'keəwɔ:n/ a. fatigued by trouble and anxiety.

cargo /'kɑ:gəʊ/ n. (pl. -goes) goods carried by ship, aircraft, etc.

Caribbean /kærɪ'bi:ən/ a. of the West Indies.

caribou /'kærɪbu:/ n. N. Amer. reindeer.

caricature /'kærɪkətjʊə(r)/ 1 n. grotesque or ludicrously exaggerated representation. 2 v.t. make or give caricature of. 3 **caricaturist** n.

caries /'keəri:z/ n. (pl. same) decay of tooth or bone.

carillon /'kærɪljən/ n. set of bells sounded mechanically or from keyboard; tune played on this.

Carmelite /'kɑ:məlaɪt/ 1 n. member of ascetic order of friars or of nuns. 2 a. of Carmelites.

carminative /'kɑ:mɪnətɪv/ 1 a. curing flatulence. 2 n. carminative drug.

carmine /'kɑ:maɪn/ 1 a. of vivid crimson colour. 2 n. this colour.

carnage /'kɑ:nɪdʒ/ n. great slaughter.

carnal /'kɑ:n(ə)l/ a. worldly; sensual; sexual. **carnality** n.

carnation /kɑ:'neɪʃ(ə)n/ 1 n. cultivated clove-scented pink; rosy pink colour. 2 a. of this colour.

carnelian var. of **cornelian²**.

carnival /'kɑ:nɪv(ə)l/ n. festival or festivities, esp. preceding Lent; riotous revelry.

carnivore /'kɑ:nɪvɔ:(r)/ n. animal or plant that feeds on flesh. **carnivorous** /-'nɪv-/ a.

carol /'kær(ə)l/ 1 n. joyous song, esp. Christmas hymn. 2 v.i. (past & p.p. **carolled**) sing joyfully.

carotid /kə'rɒtɪd/ 1 a. of two main arteries carrying blood to head. 2 n. carotid artery.

carouse /kə'raʊz/ 1 v.i. have noisy drinking-party. 2 n. such party. 3 **carousal** n.

carp¹ n. freshwater fish freq. bred in ponds.

carp² v.i. find fault, complain.

carpal /'kɑ:p(ə)l/ a. of the wrist-bone.

carpel /'kɑ:p(ə)l/ n. Bot. unit of compound pistil.

carpenter /'kɑ:pəntə(r)/ 1 n. craftsman in woodwork. 2 v. do, make by, carpenter's work. 3 **carpentry** n.

carpet /'kɑ:pɪt/ 1 n. textile fabric for covering floors etc.; ground covering of grass, flowers, etc. 2 v.t. cover (as) with carpet. 3 **carpet-bag** travelling-bag orig. made of carpet material; **carpet-bagger** political candidate etc. without local connections; **carpet slipper** one of kind with uppers made orig. of carpet-like material.

carpus /'kɑ:pəs/ n. (pl. **-pi** /-paɪ/) one of small bones connecting hand and forearm.

carriage /'kærɪdʒ/ n. wheeled passenger vehicle esp. drawn by horse(s); railway coach; conveying of goods etc.; cost of this; carrying; bearing, deportment; sliding etc. part of machine shifting position of other parts; guncarriage. **carriageway** part of road used by vehicles.

carrier /'kærɪə(r)/ n. person or thing that carries; person or company conveying goods or pasengers for payment; carrier-bag; part of bicycle etc. for carrying luggage etc.; person or animal that transmits disease without suffering from it; aircraft-carrier. **carrier bag** large paper or plastic bag with handles; **carrier pigeon** homing pigeon used for carrying messages etc.; **carrier wave** high-frequency electromagnetic wave used to convey signal.

carrion /ˈkærɪən/ n. dead flesh; garbage, filth. **carrion crow** black crow living on carrion.

carrot /ˈkærət/ n. plant with tapering orange-red sweet fleshy edible root; this root; *fig.* means of enticement. **carroty** a.

carry /ˈkærɪ/ v. support or hold up, esp. while moving; convey; have with one, possess; take (process etc.) to specified point; involve, imply; transfer (figure) to column of higher value; (of sound) be heard at a distance; win victory or acceptance for; capture. **carry away** remove, inspire, deprive of self-control; **carry-cot** portable cot for baby; **carry forward** transfer (figure) to new page or account; **carry off** remove by force, win, render acceptable or passable; **carry on** continue, *colloq.* behave excitedly, flirt; **carry out** put into practice; **carry through** complete, bring safely out of difficulties.

cart 1 n. strong two- or four-wheeled vehicle for carrying heavy goods etc.; light vehicle for pulling or pushing by hand. 2 v.t. carry in cart; *sl.* carry (esp. cumbersome thing) with difficulty. 3 **cart-horse** horse of heavy build; **cart-wheel** wheel of cart, sideways somersault with arms and legs extended.

carte blanche /kɑːt ˈblɑ̃ʃ/ full discretionary power. [F]

cartel /kɑːˈtel/ n. manufacturers' or producers' union to control prices etc.

Carthusian /kɑːˈθjuːzjən/ 1 n. monk of comtemplative order founded by St Bruno. 2 a. of the Carthusians.

cartilage /ˈkɑːtɪlɪdʒ/ n. tough flexible tissue in vertebrates; structure of this. **cartilaginous** /-ˈlædʒ-/ a.

cartography /kɑːˈtɒgrəfɪ/ n. mapdrawing. **cartographer** n.; **cartographic** a.

carton /ˈkɑːt(ə)n/ n. light cardboard etc. box for goods.

cartoon /kɑːˈtuːn/ n. humorous esp. topical drawing in newspaper etc., sequence of these; film made by photographing series of drawings; full-size drawing as sketch for work of art. **cartoonist** n.

cartouche /kɑːˈtuːʃ/ n. scroll-like or-

nament; oval enclosing name of ancient Egyptian king.

cartridge /ˈkɑːtrɪdʒ/ n. case containing charge of explosive, with bullet or shot if for small arms; spool of film, magnetic tape, etc., in container; removable pick-up head of record-player; ink-container for insertion in pen. **cartridge paper** thick rough kind for drawing etc.

carve v. cut, make by cutting; cover or adorn with carved figures etc.; cut up meat at or for table. **carve out** take from larger whole; **carve up** subdivide. **carver** n.

carvel /ˈkɑːv(ə)l/ var. of **caravel**. **carvel-built** (of boat) with planks flush with side.

carving /ˈkɑːvɪŋ/ n. carved object, esp. as work of art.

cascade /kæsˈkeɪd/ 1 n. waterfall esp. one in series. 2 v.i. fall in or like cascade.

case¹ /keɪs/ n. instance of thing's occurring; hypothetical or actual situation; instance or condition of person receiving medical treatment; person being treated; crime etc. investigated by detective or police; *Law* suit or cause for trial; sum of arguments presented on one side; *Gram.* (relation expressed by) inflected form of noun etc. **case-law** law as settled by decided cases; **casework** social work concerned with individual cases; **in any case** whatever the fact is; **in case** in event (of); **is (not) the case** is (not) so.

case² /keɪs/ 1 n. container or covering serving to enclose or contain something. 2 v.t. enclose in case; surround (*with*); *sl.* inspect or examine closely, esp. for criminal purpose. 3 **case-harden** harden surface of (esp. steel), *fig.* make callous.

casement /ˈkeɪsmənt/ n. part of window hinged to open like door.

cash 1 n. money in form of coin or bank-notes; money paid in full at time of purchase. 2 v.t. give or obtain cash for. 3 **cash and carry** store selling goods which are paid for in cash and removed by buyer, this method of trading; **cash crop** crop produced for sale; **cash flow** movement of money into and out of a business etc.; **cash in** ob-

cashew /'kæʃuː/ *n.* kidney-shaped edible nut; tropical tree bearing it.

cashier[1] /kæˈʃɪə(r)/ *n.* person in charge of cash in bank or other business firm.

cashier[2] /kæˈʃɪə(r)/ *v.t.* dismiss from service.

cashmere /kæʃˈmɪə(r)/ *n.* fine soft material of wool of goats of Kashmir etc.

casing /'keɪsɪŋ/ *n.* enclosing material or framework etc.

casino /kəˈsiːnəʊ/ *n.* (*pl.* **-nos**) public building for gambling etc.

cask /kɑːsk/ *n.* barrel, esp. for alcoholic liquor.

casket /'kɑːskɪt/ *n.* small box for holding valuables; *US* coffin.

cassava /kəˈsɑːvə/ *n.* W. Ind. plant; starch or flour obtained from its roots.

casserole /'kæsərəʊl/ **1** *n.* covered dish in which food is cooked and served; food thus prepared. **2** *v.t.* cook in casserole.

cassette /kəˈset/ *n.* small sealed case containing magnetic tape or film, ready for insertion.

cassia /'kæsɪə/ *n.* kind of cinnamon; plant yielding senna.

cassock /'kæsək/ *n.* long close usu. black tunic worn by clergy and choristers etc.

cassowary /'kæsəweərɪ/ *n.* large flightless bird related to emu.

cast /kɑːst/ **1** *v.* (*past & p.p.* **cast**) throw, emit; cause to fall, direct; shed or lose; record or register (vote); shape (molten metal or plastic material) in mould; make (product) thus; assign (actor) *as* character; allocate roles in (play, film, etc.); add *up*; calculate (horoscope). **2** *n.* throwing of missile, dice, fishing-line, etc.; (thing made in) mould for molten metal etc.; moulded mass of solidified material; set of actors in play etc.; tinge of colour; slight squint; form, type, or quality; worm-cast. **3 cast about, around, for** try to find or think of; **cast down** depress; **cast iron** hard alloy of iron, carbon, and silicon, cast in mould; **cast-iron** of cast iron, *fig.* hard, unshakeable; **cast off** abandon, *Knitting* pass (stitch) over next and drop from needle, cast off stitches of; **cast-off** *a. & n.* abandoned or discarded (thing, esp.

garment); **cast on** *Knitting* make first row of loops on needle.

castanet /kæstəˈnet/ *n.* one of pair of small concave wooden or ivory shells held in palm of hand and clicked or rattled in time with dancing.

castaway /'kɑːstəweɪ/ **1** *n.* shipwrecked person. **2** *a.* shipwrecked.

caste /kɑːst/ *n.* Hindu hereditary class with members having no social contact with other classes; exclusive social class.

castellated /'kæstəleɪtɪd/ *a.* built with battlements.

caster var. of **castor**[1].

castigate /'kæstɪgeɪt/ *v.t.* punish, chastise. **castigation** *n.*

castle /'kɑːs(ə)l/ **1** *n.* building designed to serve as both residence and fortress; *Chess* rook. **2** *v.i. Chess* make combined move of king and rook.

castor[1] /'kɑːstə(r)/ *n.* small swivelled wheel enabling heavy furniture to be moved; vessel with perforated top for sprinkling sugar etc. **castor sugar** finely granulated white sugar.

castor[2] /'kɑːstə(r)/ *n.* substance from beaver used in perfumery etc.

castor oil /'kɑːstə(r)/ vegetable oil used as purgative and lubricant.

castrate /kæsˈtreɪt/ *v.t.* remove testicles of, geld. **castration** *n.*

casual /'kæʒjʊəl/ **1** *a.* due to chance; not regular or permanent; careless, unconcerned; not ceremonious; (of clothes etc.) informal. **2** *n.* casual worker; in *pl.* casual clothes or shoes.

casualty /'kæʒjʊəltɪ/ *n.* person killed or injured in war, accident, etc.; casualty ward; accident. **casualty department, ward**, one for treatment of accidental injuries etc.

casuist /'kæzjʊɪst/ *n.* theologian etc. who studies and resolves cases of conscience etc.; sophist, quibbler. **casuistic** *a.*; **casuistry** *n.*

cat *n.* small furry domestic quadruped; any wild feline or catlike animal; spiteful or malicious woman; *sl.* person, esp. jazz fan; cat-o'-nine-tails. **cat burglar** one who enters by climbing wall to upper storey; **catcall** (make) shrill whistle of disapproval; **catfish** fish with whisker-like filaments round mouth; **catnap** (have) short sleep; **cat-o'-nine-tails** whip of nine knotted cords; **cat's-cradle** child's game with string; **Cat's-eye** (P) reflector stud on road etc.; **cat's-paw** person used as tool by another; **catsuit** close-fitting garment with trouser legs, that covers body from neck to feet; **catwalk** narrow footway.

catachresis /ˌkætəˈkriːsɪs/ n. (pl -ses /-siːz/) incorrect use of words. **catachrestic** (/-ˈkriːs-/).

cataclysm /ˈkætəklɪz(ə)m/ n. violent event; political or social upheaval. **cataclysmic** a.

catacomb /ˈkætəkuːm/ n. underground gallery for burials.

catafalque /ˈkætəfælk/ n. structure for display or conveying of coffin at funeral.

catalepsy /ˈkætəlepsɪ/ n. seizure or trance with rigidity of body. **cataleptic** a. & n.

catalogue /ˈkætəlɒg/ 1 n. complete list, usu. in alphabetical or other systematic order. 2 v.t. make catalogue of; enter in catalogue.

catalysis /kəˈtæləsɪs/ n. (pl. -ses /-siːz/) n. Chem. effect of substance that aids chemical change without itself changing.

catalyst /ˈkætəlɪst/ n. substance causing catalysis; person or thing that precipitates a change. **catalytic** (/-ˈlɪt-/) a.

catamaran /ˌkætəməˈræn/ n. boat or raft with two hulls side by side.

catamite /ˈkætəmaɪt/ n. passive partner in male homosexual practices, esp. boy.

catapult /ˈkætəpʌlt/ 1 n. forked stick with elastic for shooting stones; hist. military machine for hurling stones etc.; mechanical device for launching glider etc. 2 v. launch with catapult; fling forcibly; leap or be hurled forcibly.

cataract /ˈkætərækt/ n. waterfall; downpour; progressive opacity of eye-lens.

catarrh /kəˈtɑː(r)/ n. inflammation of mucous membrane; watery discharge in nose or throat due to this. **catarrhal** a.

catastrophe /kəˈtæstrəfɪ/ n. great usu. sudden disaster; disastrous event. **catastrophic** /-ˈstrɒf-/ a.

catch /kætʃ/ 1 v. (past & p.p. **caught** /kɔːt/) capture, lay hold of, seize; detect or surprise; trick; receive and hold (moving thing) in hand etc.; Crick. dismiss (batsman) by catching ball directly from bat; get by infection etc.; apprehend; be in time for (train etc.); reach or overtake; check or be checked suddenly; become entangled. 2 n. act of catching; Crick. chance or act of catching ball; thing or person caught or worth catching; question etc. intended to trick; unexpected difficulty or disadvantage; device for fastening door or window etc.; musical round. 3 **catch crop** one grown between two staple crops; **catch fire** begin to burn; **catch on** colloq. become popular, understand what is meant; **catch out** detect in mistake etc., Crick. catch; **catchpenny** intended merely to sell quickly; **catch-phrase** one in frequent current use; **catch up** reach (person etc. ahead), make up arrears; **catchword** word or phrase in frequent current use, word so placed as to draw attention.

catching /ˈkætʃɪŋ/ a. colloq. infectious.

catchment area /ˈkætʃmənt/ area from which rainfall flows into river etc., area served by school or hospital etc.

catchy /ˈkætʃɪ/ a. (of tune) easily remembered, attractive.

catechism /ˈkætəkɪz(ə)m/ n. summary of principles of a religion in form of questions and answers; series of questions.

catechize /ˈkætəkaɪz/ v.t. instruct by question and answer; put questions to.

catechumen /ˌkætəˈkjuːmən/ n. person being instructed before baptism.

categorical /ˌkætɪˈgɒrɪk(ə)l/ a. unconditional, absolute, explicit. **categorically** adv.

categorize /ˈkætɪgəraɪz/ v.t. place in category. **categorization** n.

category /ˈkætɪgərɪ/ n. class or division (of ideas or things).

cater /ˈkeɪtə(r)/ v.i. supply food; provide what is required for.

caterpillar /ˈkætəpɪlə(r)/ n. larva of butterfly or moth; **Caterpillar track** (P) articulated steel band with treads passing round wheels of vehicle to be used on rough ground.

caterwaul /ˈkætəwɔːl/ v.i. scream like cat.

catgut /ˈkætɡʌt/ n. thread made from dried intestines of sheep etc. used for strings of musical instruments etc.

catharsis /kəˈθɑːsɪs/ n. (pl. **-ses** /-siːz/) purgation; emotional release in drama or art.

cathartic /kəˈθɑːtɪk/ 1 a. effecting catharsis; purgative. 2 n. cathartic drug.

cathedral /kəˈθiːdr(ə)l/ n. principal church of diocese.

Catherine wheel /ˈkæθərɪn/ rotating firework.

catheter /ˈkæθɪtə(r)/ n. tube inserted into body-cavity (esp. bladder) to drain fluid. **catheterize** v.t.

cathode /ˈkæθəʊd/ n. negative electrode or terminal. **cathode ray** beam of electrons from cathode of high-vacuum tube; **cathode-ray tube** vacuum tube in which cathode rays produce luminous image on fluorescent screen.

catholic /ˈkæθəlɪk/ 1 a. universal, all-embracing; broad-minded; Roman Catholic; **Catholic** including all Christians or all of Western Church. 2 n. **Catholic** Roman Catholic. 3 **catholicism** /-ˈθɒl-/ n. **catholicity** /-ˈlɪs-/ n.

cation /ˈkætaɪən/ n. positively charged ion. **cationic** a.

catkin /ˈkætkɪn/ n. hanging flower of willow, hazel, etc.

catmint /ˈkætmɪnt/ n. aromatic plant with blue flowers.

catnip /ˈkætnɪp/ n. catmint.

cattle /ˈkæt(ə)l/ n.pl. livestock, esp. oxen. **cattle-grid** grid covering ditch, allowing vehicles to pass over but not livestock.

catty /ˈkætɪ/ a. catlike; spiteful.

caucus /ˈkɔːkəs/ n. local political party committee.

caudal /ˈkɔːd(ə)l/ a. of or at or like tail.

caudate /ˈkɔːdeɪt/ a. tailed.

caught past & p.p. of **catch**.

caul /kɔːl/ n. membrane enclosing foetus; part of this sometimes found on child's head at birth.

cauldron /ˈkɔːldrən/ n. large vessel for boiling things in.

cauliflower /ˈkɒlɪflaʊə(r)/ n. kind of cabbage with edible white flower-head.

caulk /kɔːk/ v.t. stop up (ship's seams) with oakum and pitch.

causal /ˈkɔːz(ə)l/ a. relating to cause and effect. **causality** n.

causation /kɔːˈzeɪʃ(ə)n/ n. causing, causality.

cause /kɔːz/ 1 n. what produces effect; reason or motive for action; justification; principle or belief advocated or upheld; matter about which person goes to law. 2 v.t. be cause of; produce, make (to do etc.).

cause célèbre /kəʊz seˈlebr/ (pl. **causes célèbres** pr. same) lawsuit that excites much interest. [F]

causeway /ˈkɔːzweɪ/ n. raised road across low or wet ground; raised footway at side of road.

caustic /ˈkɔːstɪk/ 1 a. that burns or corrodes; sarcastic, biting. 2 n. caustic substance. 3 **caustic soda** sodium hydroxide. 4 **causticity** n.

cauterize /ˈkɔːtəraɪz/ v.t. burn (tissue) with caustic substance or hot iron, esp. to destroy infection. **cauterization** n.

caution /ˈkɔːʃ(ə)n/ 1 n. avoidance of rashness, attention to safety; warning; sl. surprising or amusing person or thing. 2 v.t. warn, admonish.

cautionary /ˈkɔːʃənərɪ/ a. that warns.

cautious /ˈkɔːʃəs/ a. having or showing caution.

cavalcade /kævəlˈkeɪd/ n. company of riders, cars, etc.

cavalier /kævəˈlɪə(r)/ 1 n. courtly gentleman or soldier; arch. horseman; **Cavalier** hist. supporter of Charles I in English Civil War. 2 a. offhand, curt, discourteous.

cavalry /ˈkævəlrɪ/ n. (usu. treated as pl.) soldiers on horseback or in armoured vehicles.

cave 1 n. large hollow in side of hill, cliff, etc. or underground. 2 v. explore caves. 3 **cave in** (cause to) subside or fall in, yield to pressure, submit.

caveat /ˈkævɪæt/ n. warning, proviso.

cavern /ˈkæv(ə)n/ n. cave, esp. large or dark one.

cavernous /ˈkævənəs/ a. full of caverns; huge or deep as cavern.

caviare /ˈkævɪɑː(r)/ n. pickled sturgeon-roe.

cavil /ˈkævɪl/ 1 v.i. take exception at, find fault. 2 n. petty objection.

cavity /ˈkævɪtɪ/ n. hollow within solid body. **cavity wall** double wall with internal cavity.

cavort /kə'vɔːt/ v.i. prance.

caw 1 n. cry of rook etc. 2 v.i. utter caw.

cayenne /ker'en/ n. (in full **cayenne pepper**) hot red pepper from capsicum.

cayman /'keɪmən/ n. S. Amer. alligator.

CBE abbr. Commander of the Order of the British Empire.

CBI abbr. Confederation of British Industry.

cc abbr. cubic centimetre(s).

CD abbr. Corps Diplomatique; compact disc.

cease /siːs/ 1 v. end; stop; come or bring to an end. 2 **without cease** not ceasing. 3 **cease-fire** halt in hostilities.

ceaseless /'siːslɪs/ a. without end.

cedar /'siːdə(r)/ n. evergreen coniferous tree; its fragrant fine-grained wood.

cede /siːd/ v.t. give up one's rights to or possession of.

cedilla /sə'dɪlə/ n. mark written under c (ç) to show that it is sibilant.

ceilidh /'keɪlɪ/ n. esp. Sc. & Ir. informal gathering for music, dancing, etc.

ceiling /'siːlɪŋ/ n. upper interior surface of room or other compartment; material forming this; upper limit; maximum altitude of aircraft.

celandine /'selandaɪn/ n. a yellow-flowered wild plant.

celebrant /'selɪbrənt/ n. officiating priest at Eucharist.

celebrate /'selɪbreɪt/ v. mark (event or festival) with festivities; perform (rite or ceremony); honour or praise publicly; engage in festivities after success etc. **celebration** n.

celebrated /'selɪbreɪtɪd/ a. famous.

celebrity /sə'lebrɪtɪ/ n. well-known person; fame.

celeriac /sɪ'lerɪæk/ n. variety of celery with edible turnip-like root.

celerity /sɪ'lerɪtɪ/ n. arch. swiftness.

celery /'selərɪ/ n. plant of which stems are used as salad and vegetable.

celesta /sɪ'lestə/ n. keyboard musical instrument with metal plates struck with hammers.

celestial /sɪ'lestɪəl/ a. of sky or heavenly bodies; heavenly, divinely good or beautiful etc.

celibate /'selɪbət/ 1 a. unmarried, esp. for religious reasons; abstaining from sexual relations. 2 n. unmarried person. 3 **celibacy** n.

cell /sel/ n. small room esp. in monastery or prison; cavity or compartment in honeycomb etc.; Biol. unit of structure of organic matter; portion of protoplasm usu. enclosed in membrane; group as nucleus of political activity; vessel containing electrodes for current-generation or electrolysis.

cellar /'selə(r)/ n. underground room for storage etc.; wine-cellar, stock of wines.

cello /'tʃeləʊ/ n. (pl. -os) bass instrument like large violin, held upright on floor by seated player. **cellist** n.

Cellophane /'seləfeɪn/ n. (P) tough glossy transparent wrapping-material.

cellular /'seljʊlə(r)/ a. of or having or consisting of cells; porous, of open texture. **cellularity** n.

celluloid /'seljʊlɔɪd/ n. plastic made from cellulose nitrate and camphor.

cellulose /'seljʊləʊs/ n. main chief constituent of cell-walls of plants; derivative of this used in making rayon, plastics, glossy paints, etc.

Celsius /'selsɪəs/ a. Centigrade.

Celt /kelt/ n. member of one of ancient peoples of W. Europe or of peoples speaking languages related to those of ancient Gauls.

Celtic /'keltɪk/ 1 a. of the Celts. 2 n. group of languages spoken by Celtic peoples.

cement /sɪ'ment/ 1 n. substance of lime and clay that sets like stone after mixing with water; substance for filling cavities in teeth; adhesive material. 2 v.t. apply cement to; unite firmly.

cemetery /'semɪtərɪ/ n. burial ground, esp. one not in churchyard.

cenotaph /'senətɑːf/ n. monument to person(s) whose remains are elsewhere.

censer /'sensə(r)/ n. incense-burning vessel.

censor /'sensə(r)/ 1 n. official with power to suppress whole or parts of books, plays, films, news, letters, etc. on grounds of obscenity, threat to security, etc. 2 v.t. act as censor of; make deletions or changes in. 3 **censorial** a.; **censorship** n.

censorious /sen'sɔːrɪəs/ a. severely critical.

censure /'senʃə(r)/ 1 *n.* expression of disapproval or blame. 2 *v.t.* criticize harshly; reprove.

census /'sensəs/ *n.* official count of population.

cent /sent/ *n.* hundredth part of dollar or other metric unit of currency.

centaur /'sentɔ:(r)/ *n. Gk. Myth.* creature with head, arms, and trunk of man joined to body and legs of horse.

centenarian /sentɪ'neərɪən/ 1 *n.* person 100 or more years old. 2 *a.* of 100 years.

centenary /sen'ti:nərɪ/ 1 *n.* 100th anniversary. 2 *a.* of 100 years; of a centenary.

centennial /sen'tenɪəl/ 1 *a.* lasting for or occurring every 100 years. 2 *n.* centenary.

centigrade /'sentɪɡreɪd/ *a.* pertaining to scale of temperature on which water freezes at 0° and boils at 100°.

centigram /'sentɪɡræm/ *n.* hundredth part of gram.

centilitre /'sentɪli:tə(r)/ *n.* hundredth part of litre.

centime /'sɑ:ti:m/ *n.* hundreth part of franc.

centimetre /'sentɪmi:tə(r)/ *n.* hundredth part of metre.

centipede /'sentɪpi:d/ *n.* small crawling creature with long body and many legs.

central /'sentr(ə)l/ *a.* of, in, at, etc. centre; leading, principal. **central bank** national bank issuing currency etc.; **central heating** heating of building from central source. **centrally** *adv.*

centralize /'sentrəlaɪz/ *v.t.* concentrate (administration etc.) at single centre; subject (State etc.) to this system. **centralization** *n.*

centre /'sentə(r)/ 1 *n.* middle point or part; place or group of buildings forming central point in district etc. or main area for activity etc.; point of concentration or dispersion; political party holding moderate opinions. 2 *v.* concentrate or be concentrated *in, on, at,* etc.; place in centre. 3 **centre-forward, centre-half,** *Footb.* etc. middle player in forward, half-back, line; **centre of gravity** point about which the mass of an object is evenly distributed; **centre-piece** ornament for middle of table, main item; **centre spread** two facing middle pages of magazine etc.

centrifugal /sen'trɪfjʊɡ(ə)l/ *a.* moving or tending to move from centre. **centrifugal force** force with which body revolving round centre seems to tend from it. **centrifugally** *adv.*

centrifuge /'sentrɪfju:dʒ/ *n.* machine using centrifugal force for separating e.g. cream from milk.

centripetal /sen'trɪpɪt(ə)l/ *a.* moving or tending to move towards centre.

centrist /'sentrɪst/ *n.* person, party, etc. holding moderate views. **centrism** *n.*

centurion /sen'tjʊərɪən/ *n.* commander of century in ancient Roman army.

century /'sentjʊrɪ/ *n.* 100 years; *Crick.* 100 runs in one batsman's innings; company in ancient Roman army.

cephalic /sɪ'fælɪk/ *a.* of or in head.

cephalopod /'sefələpɒd/ *n.* mollusc with tentacles attached to head, e.g. octopus.

ceramic /sə'ræmɪk/ 1 *a.* of pottery, porcelain or other items of baked clay. 2 *n.* pottery etc. article.

ceramics *n.pl.* pottery collectively; (usu. treated as *sing.*) ceramic art.

cereal /'sɪərɪəl/ 1 *a.* of edible grain. 2 *n.* any kind of grain used as food; breakfast food made from cereal.

cerebellum /serɪ'beləm/ *n.* smaller part of brain.

cerebral /'serɪbr(ə)l/ *a.* of brain; intellectual.

cerebration /serɪ'breɪʃ(ə)n/ *n.* working of brain.

cerebro-spinal /serɪbrəʊ'spaɪn(ə)l/ *a.* of brain and spinal cord.

cerebrum /'serɪbrəm/ *n.* principal part of brain.

ceremonial /serɪ'məʊnɪəl/ 1 *a.* with or of ceremony, formal. 2 *n.* system of rites or ceremonies.

ceremonious /serɪ'məʊnɪəs/ *a.* fond of or characterized by ceremony, formal.

ceremony /'serɪmənɪ/ *n.* piece of formal procedure; religious rite; observance of formalities; punctilious behaviour; **stand (up)on ceremony** insist on formalities.

cerise /sə'ri:z/ *n.* & *a.* light clear red.

cert /sɜːt/ *n. sl.* event or result certain to happen; horse sure to win.

certain /'sɜːt(ə)n/ *a.* settled, unfailing; unerring; reliable; indisputable; convinced, sure; particular but not named; some.

certainly /'sɜːtənlɪ/ *adv.* no doubt, yes, I admit it.

certainty /'sɜːtəntɪ/ *n.* undoubted fact; absolute conviction.

certificate /sə'tɪfɪkət/ *n.* document formally attesting fact. **2** /sə'tɪfɪkeɪt/ *v.t.* furnish with certificate. **3 certification** *n.*

certify /'sɜːtɪfaɪ/ *v.t.* declare by certificate, make formal statement of; officially declare insane. **certifiable** *a.*

certitude /'sɜːtɪtjuːd/ *n.* feeling certain.

cerulean /sə'ruːlɪən/ *a.* sky-blue.

cervical /sə'vaɪk(ə)l/ *a.* of cervix. **cervical smear** smear taken from cervix to test for cancer.

cervix /'sɜːvɪks/ *n.* (*pl.* -**vices** /-vɪsiːz/) *Anat.* neck; neck-like structure, esp. neck of womb.

cessation /se'seɪʃ(ə)n/ *n.* ceasing.

cession /'seʃ(ə)n/ *n.* ceding.

cesspit /'sespɪt/ *n.* pit for liquid waste or sewage.

cesspool /'sespuːl/ *n.* cesspit.

cetacean /sɪ'teɪʃ(ə)n/ **1** *n.* member of order of mammals including whales. **2** *a.* of cetaceans.

cf. *abbr.* compare.

cg. *abbr.* centigram(s).

CH *abbr.* Companion of Honour.

Chablis /'ʃæbliː/ *n.* kind of dry white wine.

chaconne /ʃæ'kɒn/ *n.* piece of music on ground bass; dance to this.

chafe /tʃeɪf/ **1** *v.* rub (skin etc.) to restore warmth; make or become sore by rubbing; irritate; show irritation, fret. **2** *n.* sore caused by rubbing.

chafer /'tʃeɪfə(r)/ *n.* large slow-moving beetle.

chaff /tʃɑːf/ **1** *n.* separated grain-husks; chopped hay or straw; worthless stuff; good-humoured teasing. **2** *v.t.* banter, tease.

chaffer /'tʃæfə(r)/ *v.i.* bargain, haggle.

chaffinch /'tʃæfɪntʃ/ *n.* a common European finch.

chafing-dish /'tʃeɪfɪŋ/ *n.* vessel in which food is cooked or kept warm at table.

chagrin /'ʃægrɪn/ **1** *n.* acute vexation or mortification. **2** *v.t.* affect with this.

chain 1 *n.* series of links; sequence, connected series (*of* proof, events, mountains, etc.); in *pl.* fetters, restraining force; measure of length (66 ft.). **2** *v.t.* secure with chain. **3 chain-gang** convicts chained together at work etc.; **chain-mail** armour made from interlaced rings; **chain reaction** reaction forming products which themselves cause further reactions, *fig.* series of events each due to previous one; **chain-saw** one with teeth on loop of chain; **chain-smoke** smoke continuously, esp. by lighting next cigarette etc. from previous one; **chain store** one of series of shops owned by one firm and selling same class of goods.

chair 1 *n.* movable backed seat for one; seat of authority; (office of) chairman; professorship; sedan-chair. **2** *v.t.* install in chair of authority; conduct (meeting) as chairman; carry aloft in honour. **3 chair-lift** series of chairs on loop of cable for carrying passengers up mountain etc.; **chairman, chairperson, chairwoman**, person who presides over meeting or board or committee.

chaise /ʃeɪz/ *n.* light open carriage for one or two persons.

chaise longue /ʃeɪz 'lɒŋg/ kind of chair with seat long enough to support sitter's legs.

chalcedony /tʃæl'sedənɪ/ *n.* precious stone of quartz kind.

chalet /'ʃæleɪ/ *n.* Swiss hut or cottage; small villa; small cabin in holiday camp etc.

chalice /'tʃælɪs/ *n.* goblet; cup used in Eucharist.

chalk /tʃɔːk/ **1** *n.* white soft limestone; this or similar white or coloured substance used for drawing, writing on blackboard, etc. **2** *v.* mark, draw, write, rub, etc. with chalk. **3 chalky** *a.*

challenge /'tʃælɪndʒ/ **1** *n.* call to take part in contest etc. or to prove or justify something; demanding or difficult task; calling to respond; *esp.* sentry's call for password etc. **2** *v.t.* call to respond; take exception to; dispute; summon to contest.

chamber /'tʃeɪmbə(r)/ n. assembly hall, the council etc. that meets in it; one of the houses of a parliament or its debating-room; in pl. set of rooms esp. in Inns of Court; judge's room for hearing cases not needing to be taken in court; cavity or compartment in body, machinery, etc., esp. part of gun that contains charge; room, esp. bedroom. **chambermaid** woman employed to clean bedrooms in hotel etc.; **chamber music** music for small group of instruments; **chamber-pot** vessel for urine etc. used in bedroom.

chamberlain /'tʃeɪmbəlɪn/ n. officer managing royal or noble household; treasurer of corporation etc.

chameleon /kə'miːlɪən/ n. lizard able to change colour to suit surroundings.

chamfer /'tʃæmfə(r)/ 1 v.t. bevel symmetrically. 2 n. surface so made.

chamois /'ʃæmwɑː/ n. small mountain antelope; (/'ʃæmɪ/) soft leather from sheep, goats, etc.

champ[1] 1 v. munch or bite noisily or vigorously. 2 n. noise of champing. 3 **champ at the bit** fig. show impatience.

champ[2] n. sl. champion.

champagne /ʃæm'peɪn/ n. white sparkling wine from Champagne in France.

champion /'tʃæmpɪən/ 1 n. person or thing that has defeated all competitors; person who fights for another or for cause. 2 a. that is a champion; colloq. first-class. 3 v.t. support cause of, defend.

championship n. contest to decide champion in sport etc.; position of this.

chance /tʃɑːns/ 1 n. way things happen; absence of design or discoverable cause; opportunity, possibility. 2 a. due to chance. 3 v. happen; risk.

chancel /'tʃɑːns(ə)l/ n. part of church near altar.

chancellery /'tʃɑːnsələrɪ/ n. chancellor's department or staff or residence; office attached to embassy.

chancellor /'tʃɑːnsələ(r)/ n. State or law official; non-resident head of university; **Lord Chancellor** highest officer of the Crown, presiding over House of Lords; **Chancellor of the Exchequer** British finance minister who prepares budget.

Chancery /'tʃɑːnsərɪ/ n. Lord Chancellor's division of High Court of Justice.

chancy /'tʃɑːnsɪ/ a. risky.

chandelier /ˌʃændə'lɪə(r)/ n. branched hanging support for lights.

chandler /'tʃɑːndlə(r)/ n. dealer in supplies for ships; dealer in candles. **chandlery** n.

change /tʃeɪndʒ/ 1 n. making or becoming different; substitution of one for another; variation; money in small coins; money returned as balance of that tendered in payment; one of different orders in which bells can be rung. 2 v. make or become different, alter; take or use another instead of; interchange, exchange; put on other clothes; give or get money change for; put fresh clothes, coverings, etc., on. 3 **change hands** pass to different owner. 4 **changeful** a.; **changeless** a.

changeable /'tʃeɪndʒəb(ə)l/ a. liable to change; inconstant. **changeability** n.

changeling /'tʃeɪndʒlɪŋ/ n. child believed to have been substituted for another child.

channel /'tʃæn(ə)l/ 1 n. bed in which water runs; navigable part of waterway; piece of water connecting two seas; passage for liquid; groove; medium of communication, agency; narrow band of frequencies used for radio and esp. television transmission; path for transmitted electrical signal or data. 2 v. form channels in; guide, direct.

chant /tʃɑːnt/ 1 n. song; melody for reciting unmetrical texts. 2 v. sing; intone, sing to chant; utter rhythmically.

chanter /'tʃɑːntə(r)/ n. melody-pipe of bagpipes.

chantry /'tʃɑːntrɪ/ n. endowment for singing of masses for founder's soul; chapel or priests so endowed.

chaos /'keɪɒs/ n. utter confusion; formless primordial matter. **chaotic** /keɪ'ɒtɪk/ a.

chap[1] n. colloq. fellow; boy.

chap[2] 1 v. (of skin etc.) develop cracks or soreness; (of wind etc.) cause this. 2 n. crack in skin etc.

chap[3] n. lower jaw or half of cheek, esp. of pig as food.

chaparral /ʃæpə'ræl/ n. US dense tangled brushwood.

chapatti /tʃə'pætɪ/ *n.* small flat cake of unleavened bread.

chapel /'tʃæp(ə)l/ *n.* place of worship attached to institution or private house; separate part of cathedral or church with its own altar; place of worship of Nonconformist bodies; association or meeting of workers in printing-office.

chaperon /'ʃæpərəʊn/ **1** *n.* older woman in charge of young unmarried woman on certain social occasions. **2** *v.t.* act as chaperon to. **3 chaperonage** *n.*

chaplain /'tʃæplɪn/ *n.* clergyman of institution, private chapel, ship, regiment, etc. **chaplaincy** *n.*

chaplet /'tʃæplɪt/ *n.* wreath or circlet for head; string of beads, short rosary.

chapter /'tʃæptə(r)/ *n.* division of book; period of time; canons of cathedral etc.; meeting of these.

char[1] *v.* scorch or blacken with fire; burn to charcoal.

char[2] **1** *n.* charwoman. **2** *v.t.* work as charwoman.

char[3] *n.* fish of trout kind.

charabanc /'ʃærəbæŋ/ *n.* early form of motor coach.

character /'kærɪktə(r)/ *n.* distinguishing quality or qualities; mental or moral qualities; reputation; odd or eccentric person; person in novel, play, etc.; letter, sign; testimonial.

characteristic /kærɪktə'rɪstɪk/ **1** *a.* typical or distinctive. **2** *n.* characteristic feature or quality.

characterize /'kærɪktəraɪz/ *v.t.* describe *as*; be characteristic of. **characterization** *n.*

charade /ʃə'rɑːd/ *n.* game of guessing word from acted clues; absurd pretence.

charcoal /'tʃɑːkəʊl/ *n.* black porous residue of partly burnt wood etc.

chard *n.* kind of beet with edible leaves and stalks.

charge **1** *n.* price; expense; accusation; exhortation; task, duty; care, custody; thing or person entrusted; appropriate quantity of material to put into receptacle, mechanism, etc. at one time, esp. of explosive for gun; quantity of electricity carried by body. **2** *v.* ask (amount) as price; ask (person) for amount as price; debit cost of *to*; make ac-

cusation *that*; instruct or urge; entrust *with*; attack or rush impetuously; load or fill with charge of explosive etc.; fill (*with*). **3 charge-sheet** record of charges made at police station; **charge with** accuse of; **in charge** having command.

chargeable /'tʃɑːdʒəb(ə)l/ *a.* capable of being charged *to* particular account.

chargé d'affaires /ʃɑːʒeɪ dæ'feə/ (*pl.* **-gés** *pr.* same) ambassador's deputy; ambassador to minor government.

charger /'tʃɑːdʒə(r)/ *n.* cavalry-horse; apparatus for charging battery.

chariot /'tʃærɪət/ *n. hist.* two-wheeled vehicle used in ancient fighting and racing.

charioteer /tʃærɪə'tɪə(r)/ *n.* chariot-driver.

charisma /kə'rɪzmə/ *n.* capacity to inspire followers or disciples with devotion and enthusiasm; divine gift or talent. **charismatic** /kærɪz'mætɪk/ *a.*

charitable /'tʃærɪtəb(ə)l/ *a.* having or marked by charity; of or connected with charity.

charity /'tʃærɪtɪ/ *n.* giving voluntarily to those in need or distress; leniency in judging others; institution or organization for helping those in need, help so given; love of fellow men.

charlatan /'ʃɑːlət(ə)n/ *n.* person falsely claiming knowledge or skill. **charlatanism** *n.*

charlock /'tʃɑːlɒk/ *n.* field mustard.

charlotte /'ʃɑːlɒt/ *n.* pudding of cooked fruit under bread-crumbs etc.

charm **1** *n.* power of giving delight; usu. in *pl.* quality or feature that arouses admiration; fascination, attractiveness; speech or action or object supposedly having occult power. **2** *v.t.* delight, captivate; influence or protect by magic.

charming /'tʃɑːmɪŋ/ *a.* delightful.

charnel-house /'tʃɑːn(ə)l/ *n.* place containing corpses or bones.

chart **1** *n.* map esp. for sea or air navigation or showing weather conditions etc.; sheet of information in form of tables or diagrams; list of currently most popular gramophone records. **2** *v.t.* make chart of.

charter /'tʃɑːtə(r)/ **1** *n.* written grant of rights esp. by sovereign or legislature; written description of organization's functions etc. **2** *v.t.* grant charter to; hire (aircraft etc.) for one's own use. **3 charter flight** flight by chartered aircraft.

chartered *a.* having royal charter; belonging to chartered body.

Chartism /'tʃɑːtɪz(ə)m/ *n.* working-class reform movement of 1837-48. **Chartist** *n.*

chartreuse /ʃɑː'trɜːz/ *n.* green or yellow brandy liqueur.

charwoman /'tʃɑːwʊmən/ *n.* (*pl.* **-women** /-wɪmɪn/) woman hired by day or hour for housework.

chary /'tʃeərɪ/ *a.* cautious; sparing *of.*

chase[1] /tʃeɪs/ **1** *v.* pursue, hunt; hurry; *colloq.* try to attain. **2** *n.* pursuit; unenclosed parkland.

chase[2] /tʃeɪs/ *v.t.* emboss or engrave (metal).

chaser *n.* horse for steeplechasing; *colloq.* drink taken after another of different kind.

chasm /kæz(ə)m/ *n.* deep cleft, gulf, fissure; wide difference.

chassis /'ʃæsɪ/ *n.* base-frame of motor-car, carriage, etc.

chaste /tʃeɪst/ *a.* abstaining from extramarital or from all sexual intercourse; pure in taste or style, unadorned.

chasten /'tʃeɪs(ə)n/ *v.t.* discipline by inflicting suffering, restrain.

chastise /tʃæs'taɪz/ *v.t.* punish, beat. **chastisement** *n.*

chastity /'tʃæstɪtɪ/ *n.* being chaste.

chasuble /'tʃæzjʊb(ə)l/ *n.* sleeveless vestment worn by celebrant of Mass or Eucharist.

chat 1 *v.i.* talk in light familiar way. **2** *n.* informal talk.

chateau /'ʃætəʊ/ *n.* (*pl.* **-teaux** /-təʊz/) large French country-house.

chatelaine /ʃætəleɪn/ *n.* mistress of country house; *hist.* appendage to woman's belt for carrying keys etc.

chattel /'tʃæt(ə)l/ *n.* usu. in *pl.* movable possession.

chatter /'tʃætə(r)/ **1** *v.* talk fast, incessantly, or foolishly. **2** *n.* such talk.

chatty /'tʃætɪ/ *a.* fond of or resembling chat.

chauffeur /'ʃəʊfə(r)/ *n.* person employed to drive private or hired car.

chauvinism /'ʃəʊvɪnɪz(ə)m/ *n.* exaggerated patriotism; excessive or prejudiced support or loyalty for something. **chauvinist** *n.*; **chauvinistic** *a.*

cheap *a.* low in price; charging low prices; easily got; of little account.

cheapen /'tʃiːpən/ *v.* make or become cheap; degrade.

cheapjack /'tʃiːpdʒæk/ **1** *n.* seller of inferior cheap goods. **2** *a.* shoddy.

cheat 1 *v.* trick, deceive; deprive *of* by deceit; act fraudulently. **2** *n.* swindler; unfair player; deception.

check 1 *n.* sudden stopping or slowing of motion; pause; rebuff; restraint; means of testing or ensuring accuracy etc.; pattern of cross-lines forming squares; fabric so patterned; *US* cheque; *US* counter used in games; token of identification; (announcement of) exposure of chess king to attack. **2** *v.* stop or slow motion of, restrain; test, examine, verify; *US* agree on comparison; threaten (opponent's king) at chess. **3 check** in register at hotel or airport or workplace etc.; **check out** leave hotel or airport etc. with formalities; **check-out** pay-desk in supermarket etc.; **check-up** careful (esp. medical) examination.

checked *a.* having a check pattern.

checker var. of **chequer**.

checkmate /'tʃekmeɪt/ **1** *n.* check at chess from which there is no escape; final defeat. **2** *v.t.* put into checkmate; frustrate.

cheddar /'tʃedə(r)/ *n.* kind of firm smooth cheese.

cheek 1 *n.* side of face below eye; impertinent speech, effrontery; *sl.* buttocks. **2** *v.t.* address impudently.

cheeky /'tʃiːkɪ/ *a.* impertinent, saucy.

cheep 1 *n.* shrill feeble note as of young bird. **2** *v.i.* make such cry.

cheer 1 *n.* shout of encouragement or applause; *arch.* mood, disposition. **2** *v.* urge *on* by shouts etc.; applaud; shout for joy; comfort, gladden. **3 cheer up** make or become happier.

cheerful /'tʃɪəfʊl/ *a.* in good spirits; bright, pleasant; not reluctant. **cheerfully** *adv.*

cheerless /'tʃɪəlɪs/ *a.* gloomy, dreary.

cheery /'tʃɪərɪ/ *a.* lively, genial.

cheese /tʃiːz/ *n.* food made from pressed curds; cake etc. of this within rind; thick conserve of fruit. **cheeseburger** hamburger with cheese in or on it; **cheesecake** tart filled with sweetened curds, *sl.* display of shapely female body in advertisement etc.; **cheesecloth** loosely-woven cotton fabric; **cheesed off** *sl.* bored, fed up; **cheese-paring** stingy, stinginess. **cheesy** *a.*

cheetah /ˈtʃiːtə/ *n.* swift-running spotted feline resembling leopard.

chef /ʃef/ *n.* cook, esp. head cook, in hotel etc.

Chelsea /ˈtʃelsɪ/ *n.* **Chelsea bun** kind of spiral-shaped currant bun; **Chelsea pensioner** inmate of Chelsea Royal Hospital for old or disabled soldiers.

chemical /ˈkemɪk(ə)l/ 1 *a.* of, made by, or employing chemistry. 2 *n.* substance obtained by or used in chemistry. 3 **chemical warfare** warfare involving use of poison gas or other chemicals. 4 **chemically** *adv.*

chemise /ʃəˈmiːz/ *n.* woman's loose-fitting undergarment or dress.

chemist /ˈkemɪst/ *n.* dealer in medical drugs; person skilled in chemistry.

chemistry /ˈkemɪstrɪ/ *n.* science of elements and their laws of combination and change.

chenille /ʃəˈniːl/ *n.* tufted velvety yarn; fabric made of this.

cheque /tʃek/ *n.* written order to bank to pay sum of money; printed form for this. **cheque-book** book of forms for writing cheques; **cheque card** card issued by bank to guarantee honouring of cheques up to stated value.

chequer /ˈtʃekə(r)/ 1 *n.* (often in *pl.*) pattern of squares often alternately coloured; *US* in *pl.* game of draughts. 2 *v.t.* mark with chequers, variegate; break uniformity of; (in *p.p.*) with varied fortunes.

cherish /ˈtʃerɪʃ/ *v.t.* tend lovingly; hold dear; cling to.

cheroot /ʃəˈruːt/ *n.* kind of cigar made with both ends open.

cherry /ˈtʃerɪ/ 1 *n.* small stone-fruit, tree bearing it, wood of this; light red. 2 *a.* of light red colour.

cherub /ˈtʃerəb/ *n.* (*pl.* **cherubim** or **cherubs**) angelic being; beautiful child. **cherubic** /-ˈruːb-/ *a.*

chervil /ˈtʃɜːvɪl/ *n.* garden herb with aniseed flavour.

chess *n.* game for two players with 32

chessmen on chequered **chessboard** of 64 squares.

chest *n.* large box, esp. for storage or transport; part of body enclosed by ribs, front surface of body from neck to waist; small cabinet for medicines etc. **chest of drawers** piece of furniture with set of drawers in frame.

chesterfield /ˈtʃestəfiːld/ *n.* sofa with padded seat, back, and ends.

chestnut /ˈtʃesnʌt/ 1 *n.* glossy hard brown edible nut (**sweet chestnut**); horse-chestnut; deep reddish-brown; horse of this colour; stale anecdote. 2 *a.* chestnut-coloured.

chesty /ˈtʃestɪ/ *a. colloq.* inclined to or symptomatic of chest disease. **chestily** *adv.* **chestiness** *n.*

cheval-glass /ʃəˈvælglɑːs/ *n.* tall mirror swung on upright frame.

chevalier /ʃevəˈlɪə(r)/ *n.* member of certain orders of knighthood etc.

cheviot /ˈtʃevɪət/ *n.* sheep of breed with short thick wool; wool or cloth from it.

chevron /ˈʃevrən/ *n.* V-shaped mark of rank or long service on uniform sleeve.

chew 1 *v.* work (food etc.) between teeth; crush or indent thus; meditate *on*; ruminate *over*. 2 *n.* act of chewing; thing for chewing. 3 **chewing-gum** flavoured gum for prolonged chewing.

chewy /ˈtʃuːɪ/ *a.* suitable for or requiring chewing.

chez /ʃeɪ/ *prep.* at the house or home of. [F]

Chianti /kɪˈæntɪ/ *n.* dry usu. red Italian wine.

chiaroscuro /kɪɑːrəˈskʊərəʊ/ *n.* treatment of light and shade in painting; use of contrast in literature etc.

chic /ʃiːk/ 1 *n.* stylishness, elegance, in dress. 2 *a.* stylish, elegant.

chicane /ʃɪˈkeɪn/ 1 *v.* use chicanery, cheat. 2 *n.* chicanery; artificial barrier or obstacle on motor-racing course.

chicanery /ʃɪˈkeɪnərɪ/ *n.* trickery; clever but misleading talk; deception.

chick *n.* young bird; *sl.* young woman.

chicken /ˈtʃɪkɪn/ 1 *n.* young bird, esp. of domestic fowl; flesh of domestic fowl as food; youthful person. 2 *a.* cowardly. 3 *v.i.* (usu. with *out*) *sl.* withdraw through cowardice. 4 **chicken-feed** food for poultry, *colloq.* insignificant amount esp. of money. **chicken-pox**

infectious disease with rash of small blisters.

chick-pea /'tʃɪkpiː/ n. dwarf pea with knobby yellow seeds.

chickweed /'tʃɪkwiːd/ n. a small weed.

chicle /'tʃɪk(ə)l/ n. juice of tropical S. Amer. tree, chiefly used in chewing-gum.

chicory /'tʃɪkərɪ/ n. salad plant; its root, roasted and ground and used with or instead of coffee.

chide v. (past **chid** or **chided**; p.p. **chidden** or **chid**) rebuke, scold.

chief /tʃiːf/ 1 n. leader or ruler; head of tribe or clan; head of department etc. 2 a. first in importance or influence; prominent, leading.

chiefly /'tʃiːflɪ/ adv. above all; mainly but not exclusively.

chieftain /'tʃiːft(ə)n/ n. chief of clan, tribe, or other group. **chieftaincy** n.

chiff-chaff n. bird of warbler kind.

chiffon /'ʃɪfɒn/ n. diaphanous silky fabric.

chigger /'tʃɪɡə(r)/ var. of **chigoe**.

chignon /'ʃiːnjɒ/ n. large coil or plait etc. of hair at back of head.

chigoe /'tʃɪɡəʊ/ n. tropical flea that burrows into skin.

chihuahua /tʃɪ'wɑːwə/ n. tiny short-haired orig. Mexican dog.

chilblain /'tʃɪlbleɪn/ n. itching swelling on hand or foot etc. caused by exposure to cold.

child /tʃaɪld/ n. (pl. **children** /'tʃɪldrən/) young human being; one's son or daughter; descendant, follower, or product (of). **child benefit** regular payment by State to parents of child up to certain age; **childbirth** process of giving birth to child; **child's play** easy task.

childhood /'tʃaɪldhʊd/ n. state or period of being a child.

childish /'tʃaɪldɪʃ/ a. of or like child; immature, silly.

childlike /'tʃaɪldlaɪk/ a. innocent, frank, etc., like child.

chili var. of **chilli**.

chill 1 n. cold sensation; feverish cold; unpleasant coldness of air etc.; depressing influence. 2 a. chilly. 3 v. make or become cold; depress, dispirit; preserve (food) at low temperature without freezing.

chilli /'tʃɪlɪ/ n. hot-tasting pod of kind of capsicum.

chilly /'tʃɪlɪ/ a. rather cold; sensitive to cold; cold-mannered.

chime 1 n. set of attuned bells; sounds made by this. 2 v. (of bells) ring; show (hour) by chiming; be in agreement; join in.

chimera /kaɪ'mɪərə/ n. bogy; wild impossible scheme or fancy. **chimerical** /kɪ'merɪk(ə)l/ a.

chimney /'tʃɪmnɪ/ n. structure by which smoke or steam is carried off; part of this above roof; glass tube protecting lamp-flame. **chimney-breast** projecting wall round chimney; **chimney-piece** mantelpiece; **chimney-pot** pipe at top of chimney; **chimney-sweep** person who clears chimneys of soot.

chimpanzee /tʃɪmpæn'ziː/ n. manlike African ape.

chin n. front of lower jaw. **chin-wag** n. & v.i. sl. talk.

china /'tʃaɪnə/ n. fine semi-transparent or white earthenware, porcelain; things made of this. **china clay** kaolin.

Chinaman /'tʃaɪnəmən/ n. (pl. -**men**) arch. a Chinese.

chinchilla /tʃɪn'tʃɪlə/ n. small S. Amer. rodent; its soft grey fur; breed of domestic cat or rabbit.

chine[1] /tʃaɪn/ v.t. cut or slit along or across chine. 2 n. backbone; joint of meat from backbone; hill-ridge.

chine[2] n. deep narrow ravine.

Chinese /tʃaɪ'niːz/ 1 n. native or language of China; person of Chinese descent. 2 a. of China. 3 **Chinese lantern** collapsible lantern of coloured paper, plant with inflated orange calyx.

chink[1] n. narrow opening.

chink[2] 1 n. sound as of glasses or coins striking together. 2 v. (cause to) make chink.

chintz n. colour-printed usu. glazed cotton cloth.

chip 1 v. cut or break (off) at surface or edge; shape thus; suffer chipping; cut (potato) into chips. 2 n. piece chipped off; chipped place; long slender piece of potato fried; US in pl. potato crisps; counter used in game of chance; microchip. 3 **chipboard** board made of compressed wood chips.

chipmunk /'tʃɪpmʌŋk/ n. N. Amer. striped animal like squirrel.

chipolata /tʃɪpə'lɑːtə/ n. kind of thin sausage.

Chippendale /'tʃɪpəndeɪl/ n. 18th-c. elegant style of furniture.

chiropody /kɪ'rɒpədɪ/ n. treatment of feet and their ailments. **chiropodist** n.

chiropractic /kaɪərə'præktɪk/ n. treatment of physical disorders by manipulation of spinal column. **chiropractor** n.

chirp 1 n. short sharp thin note as of small bird. 2 v. emit chirp(s); express thus; talk merrily.

chirpy /'tʃɜːpɪ/ a. cheerful.

chirrup /'tʃɪrəp/ 1 n. series of chirps. 2 v.i. emit chirrup.

chisel /'tʃɪz(ə)l/ 1 n. tool with bevelled sharp end for shaping wood, stone, or metal. 2 v.t. (past & p.p. **chiselled**) cut or shape with chisel; sl. defraud.

chit[1] n. young child, little woman.

chit[2] n. written note.

chit-chat n. light conversation, gossip.

chitterlings /'tʃɪtəlɪŋz/ n.pl. smaller intestines of pig etc. as food.

chivalry /'ʃɪvəlrɪ/ n. courtesy and honour, esp. shown to those weaker; medieval knightly system. **chivalrous** a.

chive n. herb related to onion.

chivvy /'tʃɪvɪ/ v.t. colloq. chase, harry.

chloral /'klɔːr(ə)l/ n. compound used as sedative and analgesic.

chloride /'klɔːraɪd/ n. compound of chlorine with metal.

chlorinate /'klɔːrɪneɪt/ v.t. impregnate or disinfect (water etc.) with chlorine. **chlorination** n.

chlorine /'klɔːriːn/ n. heavy yellowish-green gas with irritating smell and powerful bleaching and disinfecting properties.

chloroform /'klɒrəfɔːm/ 1 n. thin colourless liquid whose inhaled vapour produces unconsciousness. 2 v.t. render unconscious with this.

chlorophyll /'klɒrəfɪl/ n. colouring matter of green parts of plants.

choc n. colloq. chocolate. **choc-ice** bar of ice cream enclosed in chocolate.

chock 1 n. block of wood, wedge. 2 v.t. make fast or wedge with chocks. 3 **chock-a-block** jammed together,

crammed with; **chock-full** crammed full (of).

chocolate /'tʃɒkələt/ 1 n. edible substance made as paste or powder or solid block etc., from ground cacao seeds; sweet shape of or covered with this; hot drink made from chocolate; dark brown colour. 2 a. flavoured with chocolate; chocolate-coloured.

choice 1 n. act or power of choosing; variety to choose from; thing or person chosen. 2 a. of special quality.

choir /kwaɪə(r)/ n. group of trained singers; chancel in large church. **choirboy** boy singer in church choir.

choke 1 v. stop breath of, suffocate; suffer such stoppage; block up. 2 n. valve in petrol engine controlling inflow of air; Electr. device for smoothing variations of current.

choker /'tʃəʊkə(r)/ n. high collar; close-fitting necklace.

choler /'kɒlə(r)/ n. arch. anger, irascibility.

cholera /'kɒlərə/ n. infectious, often fatal, bacterial disease with severe intestinal symptoms.

choleric /'kɒlərɪk/ a. easily angered.

cholesterol /kə'lestərɒl/ n. steroid alcohol present in human tissues.

choose /tʃuːz/ v. (past chose; p.p. chosen) select out of greater number; decide or think fit to do; make choice (between or from).

chop[1] 1 v. cut with axe or heavy edge-tool; mince; make chopping blow (at); strike (ball) with heavy edgewise blow. 2 n. chopping stroke; thick slice of meat usu. including rib. 3 **chop up** cut into small pieces.

chop[2] n. usu. in pl. jaw of animal or person.

chop[3] v.i. **chop and change** vacillate.

chopper /'tʃɒpə(r)/ n. large-bladed short axe; cleaver; colloq. helicopter.

choppy /'tʃɒpɪ/ a. (of water) breaking in short waves.

chopstick /'tʃɒpstɪk/ n. one of pair of sticks held in one hand used in some Asian countries to lift food to mouth.

chop-suey /tʃɒp'suːɪ/ n. Chinese dish of meat or fish fried with various vegetables.

choral /'kɔːr(ə)l/ a. of or for or sung by choir; of or with chorus.

chorale /kə'rɑːl/ n. simple tune or

hymn usu. sung in unison; group of singers.

chord¹ /kɔːd/ n. Mus. combination of notes sounded together.

chord² /kɔːd/ n. Math. straight line joining ends of arc; string of harp etc.

chore n. routine or tedious task; odd job.

choreography /kɒrɪˈɒɡrəfɪ/ n. design or arrangement of ballet or stage-dance. **choreograph** /ˈkɒr-/ v.; **choreographer** n.; **choreographic** /-ˈɡræf-/ a.

chorister /ˈkɒrɪstə(r)/ n. member of choir; choir-boy.

chortle /ˈtʃɔːt(ə)l/ v.i. sl. chuckle loudly.

chorus /ˈkɔːrəs/ 1 n. group of singers, choir; such group singing and dancing in opera, musical comedy, etc.; refrain of song; thing sung or said by several people at once; group of dancers and singers in ancient Greek plays and religious rites, any of its utterances. 2 v. speak or say or sing in chorus. 3 **in chorus** with all singing or speaking in unison.

chose past of **choose**.

chosen p.p. of **choose**.

chough /tʃʌf/ n. red-legged crow.

chow n. Chinese breed of dog; sl. food.

chowder /ˈtʃaʊdə(r)/ n. soup or stew esp. of fish with bacon and onions etc.

chow mein /tʃaʊ ˈmeɪn/ n. Chinese dish of fried noodles usu. with shredded meat and vegetables.

chrism /ˈkrɪz(ə)m/ n. consecrated oil.

christen /ˈkrɪsən/ v.t. baptize and give name to; name.

Christendom /ˈkrɪstʃ(ə)dəm/ n. Christians, Christian countries.

Christian /ˈkrɪstʃ(ə)n/ 1 a. of Christ or his teaching; believing in or professing or belonging to Christian religion; charitable, kind. 2 n. adherent of Christianity. 3 **Christian era** counted from birth of Christ; **Christian name** name given at christening, personal name; **Christian Science** system by which Christian faith is alleged to overcome disease without medical treatment; **Christian Scientist** adherent of this.

Christianity /krɪstɪˈænɪtɪ/ n. Christian faith or quality or character.

Christmas /ˈkrɪsməs/ n. festival of

Christ's birth celebrated on 25 Dec. **Christmas-box** small present or tip given at Christmas; **Christmas card** card sent as Christmas greeting; **Christmas Day** 25 Dec.; **Christmas Eve** 24 Dec.; **Christmas pudding** rich boiled pudding with dried fruit; **Christmas rose** white-flowered winter-flowering hellebore; **Christmas tree** evergreen tree decorated with lights etc. at Christmas. **Christmassy** a.

chromatic /krəˈmætɪk/ a. of colour, in colours; Mus. of or having notes not belonging to prevailing key. **chromatic scale** one that proceeds by semitones. **chromatically** adv.

chrome /krəʊm/ n. chromium; yellow pigment got from compound of chromium.

chromium /ˈkrəʊmɪəm/ n. metallic element used esp. in electroplating and making of stainless steel alloys.

chromosome /ˈkrəʊməsəʊm/ n. Biol. structure occurring in pairs in cell-nucleus, carrying genes.

chronic /ˈkrɒnɪk/ a. (of disease) lingering, long-lasting; (of patient) having chronic illness; colloq. bad, intense, severe.

chronicle /ˈkrɒnɪk(ə)l/ 1 n. record of events in order of occurrence. 2 v.t. enter or record in chronicle.

chronological /krɒnəˈlɒdʒɪk(ə)l/ a. according to order of occurrence.

chronology /krəˈnɒlədʒɪ/ n. science of computing dates; arrangement of events with dates.

chronometer /krəˈnɒmɪtə(r)/ n. time-measuring instrument, esp. one unaffected by temperature changes.

chrysalis /ˈkrɪsəlɪs/ n. pupa, esp. quiescent one of butterfly or moth; case enclosing it.

chrysanthemum /krɪˈsænθəməm/ n. garden plant flowering in autumn.

chub n. river fish of carp family.

chubby /ˈtʃʌbɪ/ a. plump, round-faced.

chuck¹ 1 v. fling or throw in careless manner. 2 n. act of chucking. 3 the **chuck** sl. dismissal; **chuck it** sl. stop; **chuck out** expel; **chuck person under the chin** give him playful or affectionate touch there; **chuck up** abandon.

chuck² 1 n. part of lathe holding work;

cut of beef from neck to ribs. **2** *v.t.* fix in chuck.

chuckle /ˈtʃʌk(ə)l/ **1** *n.* quiet or suppressed laugh. **2** *v.i.* emit chuckle.

chuffed /tʃʌft/ *a. sl.* pleased; displeased.

chug *v.i.* make intermittent explosive sound; progress with this.

chukker /ˈtʃʌkə(r)/ *n.* period of play in game of polo.

chum 1 *n. colloq.* close friend. **2** *v.i.* strike *up* friendship. **3 chummy** *a.*

chump *n.* lump of wood; thick end of loin of lamb or mutton; *colloq.* foolish person.

chunk *n.* lump cut or broken off.

chunky /ˈtʃʌŋkɪ/ *a.* consisting of or resembling chunks; small and sturdy.

chunter /ˈtʃʌntə(r)/ *v.i. colloq.* mutter, talk at length.

chupatty var. of **chapatti**.

church *n.* building for public Christian worship; public worship; **Church** collective body of Christians, organized Christian society; *the* clerical profession. **churchgoer** person who goes to church; **churchman** member of clergy or church; **churchwarden** elected lay representative of parish, long clay pipe; **churchyard** enclosed ground round church, esp. used for burials.

churl *n.* bad-mannered, surly, or stingy person. **churlish** *a.*

churn 1 *n.* butter-making vessel; large milk can. **2** *v.* agitate (milk) in churn; make (butter) in churn; stir *up* or agitate violently. **3 churn out** produce in quantity without quality.

chute /ʃuːt/ *n.* slide for conveying things to lower level; *colloq.* parachute.

chutney /ˈtʃʌtnɪ/ *n.* relish made of fruits and vinegar and spices etc.

chyle /tʃaɪl/ *n.* milky fluid into which chyme is converted.

chyme /tʃaɪm/ *n.* pulp into which gastric secretion converts food.

ciao /tʃaʊ/ *int. colloq.* goodbye; hello.

cicada /sɪˈkɑːdə/ *n.* winged chirping insect.

cicatrice /ˈsɪkətrɪs/ *n.* scar of healed wound.

cicely /ˈsɪsəlɪ/ *n.* flowering plant related to parsley and chervil.

CID *abbr.* Criminal Investigation Department.

cider /ˈsaɪdə(r)/ *n.* drink made from fermented apple-juice.

cigar /sɪˈgɑː(r)/ *n.* roll of tobacco-leaf for smoking.

cigarette /sɪɡəˈret/ *n.* finely-cut tobacco etc. rolled in paper for smoking.

cilium /ˈsɪlɪəm/ *n.* (*pl.* **-lia**) eyelash; similar fringe on leaf or insect's wing etc.; hairlike vibrating organ on animal or vegetable tissue. **ciliary** *a.*

cinch /sɪntʃ/ *n. sl.* sure or easy thing; certainty.

cinchona /sɪŋˈkəʊnə/ *n.* S. Amer. evergreen tree; its bark which yields quinine.

cincture /ˈsɪŋktʃə(r)/ *n.* girdle, belt, border.

cinder /ˈsɪndə(r)/ *n.* residue of coal etc. after burning.

Cinderella /sɪndəˈrelə/ *n.* neglected or despised member of group etc.

cine- /sɪnɪ/ *in comb.* cinematographic.

cine-camera *n.* motion-picture camera.

cinema /ˈsɪnəmə/ *n.* theatre where motion-picture films are shown; production of these as art or industry. **cinematic** *a.*

cinematograph /sɪnəˈmætəgrɑːf/ *n.* apparatus for making or projecting motion-picture films. **cinematographic** *a.*; **cinematography** *n.*

cineraria /sɪnəˈreərɪə/ *n.* kind of flowering plant with downy leaves.

cinerary /ˈsɪnərərɪ/ *a.* of ashes (esp. of urn holding cremated ashes).

cinnabar /ˈsɪnəbɑː(r)/ *n.* red mercuric sulphide; vermilion.

cinnamon /ˈsɪnəmən/ *n.* spice from aromatic inner bark of SE Asian tree; this tree; yellowish-brown.

cinquefoil /ˈsɪŋkfɔɪl/ *n.* plant with compound leaf of 5 leaflets.

Cinque Ports /sɪŋk/ group of ports (orig. 5) in SE England, with ancient privileges.

cipher /ˈsaɪfə(r)/ **1** *n.* secret or disguised writing, key to this; arithmetical symbol 0; person or thing of no importance; monogram. **2** *v.t.* write in cipher.

circa /ˈsɜːkə/ *prep.* about. [L]

circle /ˈsɜːk(ə)l/ **1** *n.* perfectly round plane figure; roundish enclosure, ring; curved upper tier of seats in theatre etc.; set or restricted group of people;

persons grouped round centre of interest; period or cycle. 2 v. move in circle (round).

circlet /'sɜːklɪt/ n. small circle; circular band esp. as ornament.

circuit /'sɜːkɪt/ n. line or course or distance enclosing an area; path of electric current, apparatus through which current passes; judge's itinerary through district, such a district; chain of theatres or cinemas etc. under single management; motor-racing track; sequence of sporting events.

circuitous /sə'kjuːɪtəs/ a. roundabout, indirect.

circuitry /'sɜːkɪtrɪ/ n. system of electric circuits.

circular /'sɜːkjʊlə(r)/ 1 a. having form of or moving in circle; (of letter, notice) addressed to circle of persons, customers, etc. 2 n. circular letter or notice. 3 **circular saw** rotating toothed disc for sawing wood etc. 4 **circularity** n.

circularize /'sɜːkjʊləraɪz/ v.t. send circular to.

circulate /'sɜːkjʊleɪt/ v. be or put in circulation; send particulars to (several people).

circulation /sɜːkjʊ'leɪʃ(ə)n/ n. movement from and back to starting-point, esp. movement of blood from and back to heart; transmission, distribution; number of copies of newspaper etc. sold. **circulatory** a.

circumcise /'sɜːkəmsaɪz/ v.t. cut off foreskin of (male person) as religious rite or surgical operation. **circumcision** /-'sɪʒ(ə)n/ n.

circumference /sə'kʌmfərəns/ n. line enclosing circle; distance round thing.

circumflex /'sɜːkəmfleks/ n. (in full **circumflex accent**) mark (ˆ) over vowel to indicate contraction or length etc.

circumlocution /sɜːkəmlə'kjuːʃ(ə)n/ n. use of many words where a few would do; evasive speech. **circumlocutory** a.

circumnavigate /sɜːkəm'nævɪgeɪt/ v.t. sail round. **circumnavigation** n.; **circumnavigator** n.

circumscribe /'sɜːkəmskraɪb/ v.t. enclose or outline; mark or lay down limits of; confine, restrict. **circumscription** n.

circumspect /'sɜːkəmspekt/ a. wary, taking everything into account. **circumspection** n.

circumstance /'sɜːkəmst(ə)ns/ n. occurrence, fact, detail, esp. in pl. connected with or affecting an event etc.; in pl. financial condition; ceremony, fuss.

circumstantial /sɜːkəm'stænʃ(ə)l/ a. (of account, story) detailed; (of evidence) tending to establish a conclusion by reasonable inference.

circumvent /sɜːkəm'vent/ v.t. evade, outwit.

circus /'sɜːkəs/ n. travelling show of performing animals and acrobats and clowns etc.; group of persons performing in sports etc.; open space in town with streets converging on it; hist. arena for sports and games.

cirrhosis /sɪ'rəʊsɪs/ n. chronic progressive disease of liver.

cirriped /'sɪrɪped/ n. marine crustacean in valved shell, e.g. barnacle.

cirrus /'sɪrəs/ n. (pl. cirri /-raɪ/) white wispy cloud.

Cistercian /sɪs'tɜːʃ(ə)n/ 1 n. monk or nun of strict Benedictine order. 2 a. of the Cistercians.

cistern /'sɪst(ə)n/ n. tank for water esp. supplying taps or as part of flushing lavatory; underground reservoir.

cistus /'sɪstəs/ n. flowering shrub with white or red flowers.

citadel /'sɪtəd(ə)l/ n. fortress protecting or dominating city.

citation /saɪ'teɪʃ(ə)n/ n. citing or passage cited; description of reasons for award.

cite v.t. adduce as instance; quote in support; summon at law.

citizen /'sɪtɪz(ə)n/ n. native or inhabitant of State; inhabitant of a city. **citizen's band** system of local intercommunication by radio. **citizenship** n.

citrate /'sɪtreɪt/ n. salt of citric acid.

citric /'sɪtrɪk/ a. **citric acid** sharptasting acid found in juice of lemon, orange, etc.

citron /'sɪtrən/ n. fruit of lemon kind but larger; tree bearing it.

citronella /sɪtrə'nelə/ n. a fragrant oil; grass from S. Asia yielding it.

citrus /'sɪtrəs/ n. tree of group including orange, lemon, etc.; fruit of such tree.

city /'sɪtɪ/ n. important town; town created city by charter, esp. as containing cathedral; **the City** part of London governed by Lord Mayor and Corporation, business quarter of this, commercial circles.

civet /'sɪvɪt/ n. strong musky perfume got from **civet cat** a catlike animal of Central Africa.

civic /'sɪvɪk/ a. of city or citizenship.

civics n.pl. treated as sing. study of civic rights and duties.

civil /'sɪv(ə)l/ a. of or belonging to citizens; non-military; polite, obliging; Law concerning private rights and not criminal offences. **civil defence** organization for protecting civilians in case of enemy action; **civil engineer** one who designs or maintains works of public utility; **civil list** annual allowance by Parliament for sovereign's household expenses etc.; **civil marriage** one solemnized without religious ceremony; **Civil Servant** member of **Civil Service**, all non-military branches of State administration; **civil war** one between sections of one State.

civilian /sɪ'vɪlɪən/ 1 n. person not in or of armed forces. 2 a. of or for civilians

civility /sɪ'vɪlɪtɪ/ n. politeness; act of politeness.

civilization /sɪvɪlaɪ'zeɪʃ(ə)n/ n. advanced stage of social development; civilized conditions or society; making or becoming civilized.

civilize /'sɪvɪlaɪz/ v.t. bring out of barbarism; enlighten, refine.

cl. abbr. centilitre(s).

clack 1 v.i. make sharp sound as of boards struck together. 2 n. such sound; chatter.

clad a. clothed; provided with cladding.

cladding /'klædɪŋ/ n. protective covering or coating.

claim 1 v.t. demand as one's due; represent oneself as having; assert; deserve. 2 n. demand; right or title (to); assertion; thing (esp. land) claimed.

claimant /'kleɪmənt/ n. person making claim, esp. in lawsuit.

clairvoyance /kleə'vɔɪəns/ n. supposed faculty of seeing mentally things or events in the future or out of sight. **clairvoyant** n. & a.

clam 1 n. edible bivalve mollusc. 2 v.i. **clam up** become reticent.

clamber /'klæmbə(r)/ v.i. climb with help of hands or with difficulty.

clammy /'klæmɪ/ a. damp and sticky.

clamour /'klæmə(r)/ 1 n. shouting, confused noise; loud protest or demand. 2 v. make clamour, shout or assert. 3 **clamorous** a.

clamp¹ 1 n. device, esp. brace or band of iron etc., for strengthening or holding things together. 2 v.t. strengthen or fasten with clamp. 3 **clamp down on** become stricter about.

clamp² n. mound of potatoes etc. stored under straw and earth.

clan n. group of families with common ancestor, esp. in Scotland; family holding together; group with common interest. **clannish** a.; **clansman** n.

clandestine /klæn'destɪn/ a. surreptitious, secret.

clang 1 n. loud resonant metallic sound. 2 v.i. make clang.

clangour /'klæŋgə(r)/ n. continued clanging. **clangorous** a.

clank 1 n. sound as of heavy pieces of metal struck together. 2 v. (cause to) make clank.

clap¹ 1 v. strike palms of hands loudly together, applaud; put or place with vigour or determination; flap (wings) audibly. 2 n. sound or act of clapping; explosive noise, esp. of thunder; slap. 3 **clap eyes on** colloq. see.

clap² n. vulg. gonorrhoea.

clapper /'klæpə(r)/ n. tongue or striker of bell. **clapper-board** device in film-making for making sharp noise for synchronization of picture and sound.

claptrap /'klæptræp/ n. insincere or pretentious language; nonsense.

claque /klæk/ n. hired group of applauders in theatre.

claret /'klærɪt/ n. red Bordeaux wine.

clarify /'klærɪfaɪ/ v. make or become clear; free from obscurity or impurities. **clarification** n.

clarinet /klærɪ'net/ n. wood-wind musical instrument with single reed.

clarion /'klærɪən/ n. rousing sound, call to action.

clarity /'klærɪtɪ/ n. clearness.

clash 1 n. loud jarring sound as of metal objects being struck together; collision, conflict; discord of colours etc. 2 v. (cause to) make clash; coincide awkwardly; be at variance with.

clasp /klɑːsp/ **1** *n.* device with interlocking parts for fastening; grip of arms or hand, embrace, handshake; bar on medal-ribbon. **2** *v.* fasten with clasp; grasp, embrace. **3 clasp-knife** large folding knife.

class /klɑːs/ **1** *n.* division or order of society; any set of persons or things grouped together or differentiated from others; set of students taught together; their time of meeting; their course of instruction. **2** *v.t.* place in a class. **3 classroom** room where class of students is taught.

classic /ˈklæsɪk/ **1** *a.* of acknowledged excellence; important; typical; of ancient Greek or Latin culture etc.; resembling this esp. in restraint and harmony; having historic associations. **2** *n.* classic writer, work, example, etc.; in *pl.* study of ancient Greek and Latin.

classical /ˈklæsɪk(ə)l/ *a.* of ancient Greek and Latin literature etc.; (of language) having form used by standard authors; (of music) serious or conventional.

classicism /ˈklæsɪsɪz(ə)m/ *n.* following of classic style; classical scholarship. **classicist** *n.*

classify /ˈklæsɪfaɪ/ *v.t.* arrange in classes; class; designate as officially secret. **classification** *n.*; **classificatory** *a.*

classy /ˈklɑːsɪ/ *a. sl.* superior. **classiness** *n.*

clatter /ˈklætə(r)/ **1** *n.* sound as of hard objects struck together or falling; noisy talk. **2** *v.* make clatter; fall etc. with clatter.

clause /klɔːz/ *n.* single statement in treaty or law or contract etc.; *Gram.* distinct part of sentence, including subject and predicate.

claustrophobia /klɔːstrəˈfəʊbɪə/ *n.* morbid dread of confined places.

claustrophobic /klɔːstrəˈfəʊbɪk/ *a.* suffering from or inducing claustrophobia.

clavichord /ˈklævɪkɔːd/ *n.* earliest stringed keyboard instrument.

clavicle /ˈklævɪk(ə)l/ *n.* collarbone.

claw 1 *n.* pointed nail of animal's or bird's foot; foot armed with claws; pincers of shellfish; device for grappling, holding, etc. **2** *v.* scratch or maul or pull with claws or fingernails.

clay *n.* stiff sticky earth, used esp. for bricks, pottery, etc. **clay pigeon** breakable disc thrown into air as target for shooting. **clayey** *a.*

claymore /ˈkleɪmɔː(r)/ *n. hist.* Sc. two-edged broad-sword.

clean 1 *a.* free from dirt; unsoiled; preserving what is regarded as original state; free from obscenity or indecency; clear-cut; attentive to cleanness. **2** *adv.* completely; simply; in a clean manner. **3** *v.* make or become clean. **4** *n.* process of cleaning. **5 clean-cut** sharply outlined; **clean out** clean thoroughly, empty or deprive (esp. *sl.* of money); **clean-shaven** without beard or moustache; **clean up** *sl.* acquire as profit, make profit.

cleanly[1] /ˈkliːnlɪ/ *adv.* in clean manner.

cleanly[2] /ˈklenlɪ/ *a.* habitually clean; attentive to cleanness. **cleanliness** *n.*

cleanse /klenz/ *v.t.* make clean or pure.

clear 1 *a.* not clouded; transparent; readily perceived or understood; able to discern readily; unobstructed, open; net, complete; unhampered, free (*of*). **2** *adv.* clearly; completely; apart. **3** *v.* make or become clear; free from or *of* obstruction, suspicion, etc.; show or declare innocent *of*; pass over or by without touching; make (sum) as net gain; pass (cheque) through clearing-house. **4 clear-cut** sharply defined; **clear off** get rid off, *colloq.* go away; **clear out** empty, remove, *colloq.* go away; **clearway** *n.* road where vehicles may not stop on carriageway.

clearance /ˈklɪərəns/ *n.* removal of obstructions etc.; space allowed for passing of two objects; permission to proceed; clearing (esp. of cheques etc.). **clearance sale** sale to dispose of surplus stock.

clearing /ˈklɪərɪŋ/ *n.* piece of land in forest cleared esp. for cultivation. **clearing bank** member of clearing-house; **clearing-house** bankers' institution where cheques etc. are exchanged, agency for collecting and distributing information etc.

cleat *n.* projecting piece to provide footing or for fastening ropes to.

cleavage /ˈkliːvɪdʒ/ *n.* hollow between

woman's breasts; way in which thing tends to split.

cleave[1] v. (past **clove** or **cleft**; p.p. **cloven** or **cleft**) split, divide; break or come apart.

cleave[2] v.i. (past & p.p. **cleaved**) stick fast; adhere to.

cleaver /ˈkliːvə(r)/ n. heavy chopping-tool used by butchers etc.

clef n. Mus. symbol showing pitch of staff.

cleft[1] past & p.p. of **cleave**[1]. **cleft palate** congential split in roof of mouth; **in a cleft stick** in a difficult position.

cleft[2] n. fissure, split.

clematis /ˈklemətɪs/ n. cultivated climbing flowering plant.

clement /ˈklemənt/ a. mild, merciful. **clemency** n.

clementine /ˈkleməntaɪn/ n. kind of small orange.

clench 1 v. close tightly, grasp firmly; clinch (nail, rivet). 2 n. clenching or clenched state.

clergy /ˈklɜːdʒɪ/ n. (usu. treated as pl.) all persons ordained as priests or ministers.

clergyman /ˈklɜːdʒɪmən/ n. (pl -**men**) member of clergy.

cleric /ˈklerɪk/ n. clergyman.

clerical /ˈklerɪk(ə)l/ a. of clergy or clergyman; of or done by clerks.

clerihew /ˈklerɪhjuː/ n. witty or humorous 4-line verse on (usu.) biographical subject.

clerk /klɑːk/ 1 n. person employed to keep records, accounts etc., attend to correspondence etc.; record-keeper or agent of council, court, etc.; lay officer of parish church etc. 2 v.i. work as clerk.

clever /ˈklevə(r)/ a. skilful, talented, quick to learn and understand; ingenious.

clew 1 n. lower corner of sail; arch. ball of thread or yarn. 2 v.t. Naut. haul up or let down (sail).

cliché /ˈkliːʃeɪ/ n. hackneyed phrase or opinion.

click 1 n. slight sharp sound as of switch being operated. 2 v. make click; sl. be successful or understood, become friendly with person.

client /ˈklaɪənt/ n. person using services of lawyer or other professional person; customer.

clientele /kliːɒnˈtel/ n. clients collectively; customers.

cliff n. steep rock-face, esp. on coast. **cliff-hanger** story etc. with strong element of suspense.

climacteric /klaɪˈmæktərɪk/ n. period of life when physical powers being to decline.

climate /ˈklaɪmət/ n. prevailing weather conditons of an area; region with certain weather conditions; prevailing trend of opinion etc. **climatic** /-ˈmæt-/ a.; **climatically** adv.

climax /ˈklaɪmæks/ 1 n. event or point of greatest intensity or interest, culmination. 2 v. reach or bring to a climax.

climb /klaɪm/ 1 v. ascend, mount, go up; (of plant) grow up wall etc. by clinging etc.; rise in social rank. 2 n. action of climbing; place to be climbed.

climber /ˈklaɪmə(r)/ n. mountaineer; climbing plant; person climbing socially.

clime n. region; climate.

clinch v. confirm or settle; settle conclusively; (of boxer) come too close to opponent for full-arm blow; secure (nail or rivet) by driving point sideways when through. 2 n. clinching, resulting state or position; colloq. embrace.

cling v.i. (past & p.p. **clung**) maintain grasp, keep hold, adhere closely.

clinic /ˈklɪnɪk/ n. private or specialized hospital; place or occasion for giving medical treatment or advice; teaching of medicine at hospital bedside.

clinical /ˈklɪnɪk(ə)l/ a. of or for the treatment of patients; fig. objective, coldly detached.

clink[1] 1 n. sharp ringing sound. 2 v. (cause to) make clink.

clink[2] n. sl. prison.

clinker /ˈklɪŋkə(r)/ n. mass of slag or lava; stony residue from burnt coal.

clinker-built a. (of boat) with external planks overlapping downwards.

clip[1] n. device for attaching something or holding things together; set of cartridges for firearm, held together at base. 2 v.t. fix with clip; grip tightly. 3 **clipboard** board with spring clip for holding papers etc.

clip[2] 1 v. cut with shears or scissors; colloq. hit sharply; remove small piece from (bus etc. ticket) to show it has been used; cut short. **2** *n.* clipping; *colloq.* sharp blow; yield of wool; extract from motion-picture film.

clipper /'klɪpə(r)/ *n.* fast sailing-ship; usu. in *pl.*, instrument for clipping.

clipping /'klɪpɪŋ/ *n.* piece clipped off; newspaper cutting.

clique /kliːk/ *n.* exclusive set of associates. **cliquish** *a.*; **cliquy** *a.*

clitoris /'klɪtərɪs/ *n.* small erectile part of female genitals.

cloak 1 *n.* loose usu. sleeveless outdoor garment; covering; pretext. **2** *v.* cover with cloak; conceal, disguise. **3 cloak-room** room for temporary deposit of clothes or luggage, *euphem.* lavatory.

clobber[1] /'klɒbə(r)/ *sl. n.* clothing, personal belongings.

clobber[2] /'klɒbə(r)/ *v.t. sl.* hit repeatedly; defeat; criticize severely.

cloche /klɒʃ/ *n.* small translucent cover for outdoor plants; woman's close-fitting bell-shaped hat.

clock[1] **1** *n.* instrument measuring time and indicating it on dial or by displayed figures; clocklike device showing readings on dial; seed-head of dandelion. **2** *v.t.* time (race etc.) by stop-watch. **3 clock in** or **on**, or **out** or **off**, register time of arrival or departure by automatic clock; **clock (up)** attain or register (time, speed, distance, etc.); **clockwise** moving in a curve corresponding in direction to hands of clock; **clockwork** mechanism with coiled springs etc. on clock principle (**like clockwork** with mechanical precision).

clock[2] *n.* ornamental pattern on side of stocking or sock.

clod *n.* lump of earth or clay.

clog 1 *n.* wooden-soled shoe; *arch.* encumbrance. **2** *v.* impede; (cause to) become obstructed; choke *up*.

cloister /'klɔɪstə(r)/ **1** *n.* covered walk esp. in convent, college, or cathedral; monastic house or life. **2** *v.t.* seclude in convent.

clone 1 *n.* group of organisms produced asexually from one ancestor; one such organism. **2** *v.* propagate as clone.

close[1] /kləʊs/ **1** *a.* near together; dense, compact; nearly equal; rigorous; shut; secret; niggardly; stifling. **2** *adv.* closely. **3** *n.* enclosed place; street

closed at one end; precinct of cathedral. **4 close harmony** singing of parts within an octave or a twelfth; **close season** time when killing of game etc is illegal; **close shave** narrow escape; **close-up** photograph etc. taken at short range.

close[2] /kləʊz/ **1** *v.* shut, block up; bring or come to an end; end day's business; bring or come closer or into contact etc; make (electric circuit) continuous. **2** *n.* conclusion, end. **3 closed-circuit** (of television) transmitted by wires for restricted number of receivers; **closed shop** business etc. where employees must belong to agreed trade union.

closet /'klɒzɪt/ **1** *n.* small cupboard or room; water-closet. **2** *v.t.* shut away esp. in private consultation etc.

closure /'kləʊʒə(r)/ **1** *n.* closing, closed state; closing of debate. **2** *v.t.* apply closure to.

clot 1 *n.* semi-solid lump formed from liquid, esp. blood; *sl.* stupid person. **2** *v.* form into clots. **3 clotted cream** thick cream formed by slow scalding.

cloth /klɒθ/ *n.* woven or felted material; piece of this; *the* clergy.

clothe /kləʊð/ *v.t.* (*past & p.p.* **clothed** or **clad**) put clothes upon; provide with clothes; cover as with clothes.

clothes /kləʊðz/ *n.pl.* things worn to cover body and limbs; bedclothes.

clothier /'kləʊðɪə(r)/ *n.* dealer in cloth and men's clothes.

clothing /'kləʊðɪŋ/ *n.* clothes.

cloud /klaʊd/ **1** *n.* visible mass of condensed watery vapour floating in air; mass of dust, smoke, etc.; great number (*of* birds, insects, etc.) moving together; state of gloom, trouble or suspicion. **2** *v.* cover or darken with clouds; become overcast or gloomy. **3 cloudburst** sudden violent rainstorm.

cloudy /'klaʊdɪ/ *a.* covered with clouds; not transparent, unclear.

clout /klaʊt/ **1** *n.* heavy blow; *colloq.* power of effective action; influence; piece of cloth or clothing. **2** *v.t.* hit hard.

clove[1] *n.* dried bud of tropical tree, used as spice.

clove[2] *n.* segment of bulb of garlic etc.

clove[3] *past* of **cleave**[1].

clove hitch knot for fastening rope round pole etc.

cloven /'kləʊv(ə)n/ *p.p.* of **cleave**[1].

cloven hoof one that is divided, as of oxen or sheep.

clover /ˈkləʊvə(r)/ n. kind of trefoil used as fodder; **in clover** in ease and luxury.

clown /klaʊn/ 1 n. comic entertainer esp. in circus; person acting like clown. 2 v.i. behave like clown. 3 **clownish** a.

cloy v.t. satiate or weary by richness, sweetness, etc.

club 1 n. heavy stick used as weapon; stick with head, used in golf etc.; playing-card of suit marked with black trefoils; body of persons associated for social, sporting, etc. purposes; premises of this. 2 v. strike with club; combine *together* or *with* esp. in making up sum of money. 3 **club-foot** congenitally deformed foot; **clubhouse** premises used by club; **club-root** disease of cabbages etc.; **club sandwich** one with two layers of filling between three slices of bread or toast.

cluck 1 n. guttural cry like that of hen. 2 v.i. make clucks.

clue 1 n. guiding or suggestive fact; piece of evidence used in detection of crime; word(s) used to indicate word(s) for insertion in crossword. 2 v. **clue in** or **up** sl. inform.

clump 1 n. cluster *of* trees or plants etc. 2 v. form clump; arrange in clump; tread heavily.

clumsy /ˈklʌmzɪ/ a. awkward in movement or shape; difficult to handle or use; tactless.

clung past & p.p. of cling.

cluster /ˈklʌstə(r)/ 1 n. close group or bunch of similar things. 2 v. be in or form into cluster; gather *round*.

clutch[1] 1 v. seize eagerly; grasp tightly; snatch *at*. 2 n. tight or (in pl.) cruel grasp; (in motor vehicle) device for connecting engine to transmission, pedal operating this.

clutch[2] n. set of eggs; brood of chickens.

clutter /ˈklʌtə(r)/ 1 n. crowded untidy collection of things. 2 v.t. fill with clutter, crowd untidily.

cm abbr. centimetre(s).

CND abbr. Campaign for Nuclear Disarmament.

c/o abbr. care of.

CO abbr. Commanding Officer.

Co. abbr. company; county.

coach 1 n. single-decker bus usu. for longer journeys; railway carriage; closed horse-drawn carriage; tutor or trainer. 2 v.t. instruct or train. 3 **coachman** driver of horse-carriage; **coachwork** bodywork of road or railway vehicle.

coagulant /kəʊˈægjʊlənt/ n. substance that causes coagulation.

coagulate /kəʊˈægjʊleɪt/ v. change from liquid to semisolid state; clot, curdle. **coagulation** n.

coal n. hard black mineral used as fuel etc.; piece of this. **coal-face** exposed surface of coal in mine; **coalfield** area yielding coal; **coal gas** mixed gases extracted from coal and used for heating, cooking, etc.; **coal-scuttle** receptacle for coal to supply domestic fire; **coal tar** tar extracted from coal; **coal-tit** small bird with grey plumage.

coalesce /kəʊəˈles/ v.i. come together and form one mass etc. **coalescence** n.; **coalescent** a.

coalition /kəʊəˈlɪʃ(ə)n/ n. fusion into one whole; temporary alliance of political parties.

coaming /ˈkəʊmɪŋ/ n. raised border round ship's hatches etc.

coarse /kɔːs/ a. rough, loose, or large in texture etc.; lacking delicacy, unrefined; inferior, common; vulgar, obscene. **coarse fish** freshwater fish other than salmon or trout.

coarsen /ˈkɔːs(ə)n/ v. make or become coarse.

coast 1 n. border of land near sea; seashore. 2 v.i. ride or move (usu. downhill) without use of power; sail along coast; *fig.* make progress without exertion. 3 **coastguard** (one of) body of men employed to keep watch on coasts, prevent smuggling, etc.; **coastline** line of sea-shore esp. with regard to its shape. 4 **coastal** a.

coaster /ˈkəʊstə(r)/ n. coasting vessel; tray or mat for bottle or glass.

coat 1 n. sleeved outer garment, overcoat, jacket; animal's hair or fur; layer of paint etc. 2 v.t. cover *with* coat or layer, form covering to. 3 **coat of arms** heraldic bearings or shield; **coathanger** shaped piece of wood, wire, etc. from which clothes may be hung in normal shape.

coating /'kəʊtɪŋ/ n. covering of paint, chocolate, etc; cloth for coats.

coax v.t. persuade gradually or by flattery; manipulate gently.

coaxial /kəʊ'æksɪəl/ a. having common axis; (of electric cable etc.) transmitting by means of two concentric conductors separated by insulator.

cob n. roundish lump; corn-cob; stout short-legged riding-horse; male swan; large hazel nut; roundish loaf.

cobalt /'kəʊbɔ:lt/ n. silvery-white metallic element; deep-blue pigment made from it.

cobber /'kɒbə(r)/ n. Aus. & NZ colloq. companion, friend.

cobble[1] /'kɒb(ə)l/ 1 n. rounded stone used for paving. 2 v.t. pave with cobbles.

cobble[2] /'kɒb(ə)l/ v.t. mend or patch (esp. shoes); put together roughly.

cobbler /'kɒblə(r)/ n. mender of shoes.

COBOL /'kəʊbɒl/ n. computer language designed for use in business operations.

cobra /'kəʊbrə/ n. venomous hooded snake.

cobweb /'kɒbweb/ n. spider's network or thread. **cobwebby** a.

coca /'kəʊkə/ n. S. Amer. shrub; its leaves chewed as stimulant.

cocaine /kəʊ'keɪn/ n. drug from coca used as local anaesthetic and as stimulant.

coccyx /'kɒksɪks/ n. bone at base of spinal column.

cochineal /kɒtʃɪ'nɪəl/ n. scarlet dye; insects whose dried bodies yield this.

cock[1] 1 n. male bird, esp. of domestic fowl; vulg. penis; lever in gun raised to be released by trigger; tap or valve controlling flow. 2 v.t. put in noticeably upright position; turn or move (eye or ear) attentively, knowingly, etc.; raise cock of (gun). 3 **cock-a-hoop** exultant; **cock-a-leekie** Scottish soup of chicken broth with leeks; **cock-crow** dawn; **cocked hat** triangular brimless hat pointed at front, back, and top; **cock-eyed** sl. crooked, askew, absurd.

cock[2] n. small conical heap of hay.

cockade /kə'keɪd/ n. rosette etc. worn in hat.

cockatoo /kɒkə'tu:/ n. crested parrot.

cockchafer /'kɒktʃeɪfə(r)/ n. large pale-brown beetle.

cocker /'kɒkə(r)/ n. breed of spaniel.

cockerel /'kɒkər(ə)l/ n. young cock.

cockle /'kɒk(ə)l/1 n. edible bivalve shellfish; its shell; pucker or wrinkle. 2 v. make or become puckered. 3 **cockles of the heart** innermost feelings.

cockney /'kɒknɪ/ 1 n. native of London, esp. East End; cockney dialect. 2 a. of cockneys.

cockpit /'kɒkpɪt/ n. site of battle(s); place for pilot etc. in aircraft or space-craft or for driver in racing car; arena of war etc.

cockroach /'kɒkrəʊtʃ/ n. dark-brown insect infesting esp. kitchens.

cockscomb /'kɒkskəʊm/ n. cock's crest.

cocksure /kɒk'ʃʊə(r)/ a. quite convinced; dogmatic, confident.

cocktail /'kɒkteɪl/ n. drink of spirits with bitters etc.; appetizer containing shellfish etc.; finely-chopped fruit salad. **cocktail stick** small pointed stick.

cocky /'kɒkɪ/ a. conceited, arrogant.

coco /'kəʊkəʊ/ n. (pl. **-cos**) a tropical palm-tree.

cocoa /'kəʊkəʊ/ n. powder of crushed cacao seeds, drink made from this.

coconut /'kəʊkənʌt/ n. large brown seed of coco, with edible white lining enclosing whitish liquid (**coconut milk**). **coconut matting** matting made from fibre of coconut husks; **coconut shy** fairground side-show where balls are thrown to dislodge coconuts.

cocoon /kə'ku:n/ 1 n. silky case spun by larva (esp. of silkworm) to protect it as pupa; protective covering. 2 v.t. wrap (as) in cocoon.

cocotte /kə'kɒt/ n. small fireproof dish for cooking and serving food.

cod[1] n. large sea fish. **cod-liver oil** medicinal oil rich in vitamins.

cod[2] n. & v. hoax, parody.

COD abbr. cash on delivery.

coddle /'kɒd(ə)l/ v. treat as an invalid; pamper; cook gently in water just below boiling-point.

code 1 n. system of signals or of symbols etc. used for brevity, secrecy, or machine processing of information; systematic set of laws etc.; standard of moral behaviour. 2 v.t. put into code.

codeine /'kəʊdi:n/ n. alkaloid got from

opium, used as pain-killer and sedative.

codex /'kəʊdeks/ n. (pl. **codices** /'kəʊdisiːz/) manuscript volume esp. of ancient texts.

codger /'kɒdʒə(r)/ n. sl. fellow.

codicil /'kəʊdisil/ n. supplement modifying or revoking will etc.

codify /'kəʊdifaɪ/ v.t. arrange (laws etc.) into code. **codification** n.

codling[1] /'kɒdlɪŋ/ n. (also **codlin**) variety of apple; moth whose larva feeds on apples.

codling[2] /'kɒdlɪŋ/ n. small cod.

coeducation /ˌkəʊedjʊ'keɪʃ(ə)n/ n. education of both sexes together. **coeducational** a.

coefficient /ˌkəʊi'fiʃ(ə)nt/ n. Math. quantity placed before and multiplying another; Phys. multiplier or factor by which a property is measured.

coequal /kəʊ'iːkw(ə)l/ n. & a. equal.

coerce /kəʊ'ɜːs/ v.t. impel or force into obedience. **coercive** a.; **coercion** n.

coeval /kəʊ'iːv(ə)l/ 1 a. having same age, existing at same epoch. 2 n. coeval person.

coexist /ˌkəʊɪg'zɪst/ v.i. exist together (with).

coexistence /ˌkəʊɪg'zɪst(ə)ns/ n. coexisting, esp. peaceful existence with nations professing different ideologies etc. **coexistent** a.

coextensive /ˌkəʊɪks'tensɪv/ a. extending over same space or time.

C. of E. abbr. Church of England.

coffee /'kɒfiː/ n. drink made from roasted and ground seeds of a tropical shrub; a cup of this; the seeds or shrub; pale brown colour. **coffee-bar** café selling coffee and other refreshments; **coffee-bean** seed of coffee; **coffee-grounds** sediment of coffee after infusion; **coffee-mill** small machine for grinding coffee-beans; **coffee-table** small low table; **coffee-table book** large illustrated book.

coffer /'kɒfə(r)/ n. box esp. for valuables; in pl. funds or treasury; sunk panel in ceiling etc.

coffin /'kɒfɪn/ n. chest in which corpse is buried or cremated.

cog n. one of series of projections on wheel etc. transferring motion by engaging with another series.

cogent /'kəʊdʒ(ə)nt/ a. convincing, compelling. **cogency** n.

cogitate /'kɒdʒɪteɪt/ v. ponder, meditate. **cogitation** n.

cognac /'kɒnjæk/ n. French brandy.

cognate /'kɒgneɪt/ 1 a. descended from same ancestor or root or origin. 2 n. cognate word or person.

cognition /kɒg'nɪʃ(ə)n/ n. knowing or perceiving or conceiving; notion. **cognitive** a.

cognizance /'kɒgnɪz(ə)ns/ n. being aware, notice; distinctive device or mark.

cognizant /'kɒgnɪz(ə)nt/ a. having knowledge or taking note of.

cognomen /kɒg'nəʊmən/ n. nickname, surname.

cohabit /kəʊ'hæbɪt/ v.i. live together as husband and wife. **cohabitation** n.

cohere /kəʊ'hɪə(r)/ v.i. stick together, remain united; be logical or consistent.

coherent /kəʊ'hɪərənt/ a. sticking together; consistent, easily understood. **coherence** n.

cohesion /kəʊ'hiːʒ(ə)n/ n. force with which parts cohere; tendency to cohere. **cohesive** a.

cohort /'kəʊhɔːt/ n. tenth part of Roman legion; persons banded together.

coif /kɔɪf/ n. hist. kind of close-fitting cap.

coiffeur /kwæ'fɜː(r)/ n. (fem. **coiffeuse** /-'fɜːz/) n. hairdresser. [F]

coiffure /kwæ'fjʊə(r)/ n. hair style. [F]

coign /kɔɪn/ n. **coign of vantage** place affording good view.

coil 1 v. arrange or be arranged in concentric rings; move sinuously. 2 n. coiled length of rope etc.; coiled arrangement; flexible loop as contraceptive device in womb; coiled wire for passage of electric current.

coin 1 n. piece of stamped metal money; coins collectively. 2 v.t. make (money) by stamping metal; make (metal) into money; invent (new word etc.).

coinage /'kɔɪnɪdʒ/ n. coining; coins; system of coins in use; invention of new word, word so invented.

coincide /ˌkəʊɪn'saɪd/ v.i. occur at same time; agree or be identical with.

coincidence /kəʊ'ɪnsɪd(ə)ns/ n. remarkable concurrence of events without apparent causal connection. **coincident** a.

coincidental /kəʊɪnsɪ'dent(ə)l/ *a.* occurring by or in the nature of a coincidence.

coir /'kɔɪə(r)/ *n.* fibre of coconut husk used for ropes and matting etc.

coition /kəʊ'ɪʃ(ə)n/ *n.* sexual intercourse.

coitus /'kəʊɪtəs/ *n.* coition.

coke[1] 1 *n.* solid substance left after gases have been extracted from coal. 2 *v.* convert into coke.

coke[2] *n. sl.* cocaine.

col *n.* depression in summit-line of mountain-chain.

cola /'kəʊlə/ *n.* W. Afr. tree with seed producing extract used as tonic etc.; carbonated drink flavoured with this.

colander /'kʌləndə(r)/ *n.* perforated vessel used as strainer in cookery.

cold /kəʊld/ 1 *a.* of or at low temperature; not heated; having lost heat; feeling or suggesting cold; *sl.* unconscious; lacking ardour or affection or geniality; depressing, dispiriting; (of hunting-scent) faint. 2 *n.* prevalence of low temperature; cold condition; catarrh of nose or throat or both. 3 **cold-blooded** having blood temperature varying with that of environment, *fig.* callous; **cold cream** ointment for cleansing and softening the skin; **cold feet** fear, reluctance; **cold shoulder** deliberately unfriendly treatment; **cold storage** storage in refrigerator, *fig.* state of abeyance; **cold war** hostility between nations without actual fighting.

coleopterous /kɒlɪ'ɒptərəs/ *a.* of the order of insects with front wings forming hard sheaths for hind pair.

coleslaw /'kəʊlslɔː/ *n.* salad of sliced raw white cabbage etc.

coley /'kəʊlɪ/ *n.* fish akin to cod.

colic /'kɒlɪk/ *n.* griping belly-pain.

colitis /kə'laɪtɪs/ *n.* inflammation of colon.

collaborate /kə'læbəreɪt/ *v.i.* work jointly (*with*). **collaboration** *n.*; **collaborator** *n.*

collage /'kɒlɑːʒ/ *n.* picture made by gluing pieces of paper or other items on to backing; art of making these.

collapse /kə'læps/ 1 *n.* tumbling down or falling to ruin; physical or mental breakdown. 2 *v.* (cause to) suffer collapse; fold up. 3 **collapsible** *a.*

collar /'kɒlə(r)/ 1 *n.* neckband, upright or turned over, of coat, shirt, dress, etc.; leather band round animal's neck; collar-shaped piece in machine etc. 2 *v.t.* seize by collar; lay hold of; *sl.* take, esp. without permission. 3 **collarbone** bone joining breastbone and shoulder-blade.

collate /kə'leɪt/ *v.* compare in detail; collect and put in order. **collator** *n.*

collateral /kə'lætər(ə)l/ *a.* side by side; additional but subordinate; connected but aside from main subject; descended from same stock but by different line. 2 *n.* collateral person or security. 3 **collateral security** property pledged as guarantee for repayment of money.

collation /kə'leɪʃ(ə)n/ *n.* collating; light meal.

colleague /'kɒliːg/ *n.* associate in office etc.; member of same profession etc.

collect[1] /kə'lekt/ *v.* bring or come together; assemble, accumulate; seek and obtain (books, stamps, etc.) for addition to others; get (contributions, taxes, etc.) from a number of people; call for, fetch; concentrate (one's thoughts etc.).

collect[2] /'kɒlɪkt/ *n.* short prayer of Anglican or RC Church.

collected *a.* not perturbed or distracted.

collection /kə'lekʃ(ə)n/ *n.* collecting; things collected; money collected, esp. in meeting or church service etc.

collective /kə'lektɪv/ 1 *a.* representing or including many; taken as a whole, aggregate, common; owned or worked in common. 2 *n.* collective farm or other enterprise; collective noun. 3 **collective bargaining** negotiation of wages etc. by organized body of employees; **collective farm** jointly-operated amalgamation of several smallholdings; **collective noun** singular noun denoting group of individuals. 4 **collectivize** *v.t.*

collectivism /kə'lektɪvɪz(ə)m/ *n.* theory or practise of collective ownership of land and means of production. **collectivist** *n. & a.*

collector /kə'lektə(r)/ *n.* person who collects things of interest; person who collects money due.

colleen /'kɒliːn/ *n. Ir.* girl.

college /'kɒlɪdʒ/ *n.* establishment for

higher or professional education; body of teachers and students within a university, their premises; small university, school; organized body of persons with shared functions and privileges.

collegian /kəˈliːdʒ(ə)n/ n. member of college.

collegiate /kəˈliːdʒət/ a. of or constituted as a college, corporate.

collide /kəˈlaɪd/ v.i. come into collision.

collie /ˈkɒlɪ/ n. sheep-dog of orig. Scottish breed.

collier /ˈkɒlɪə(r)/ n. coal-miner; coal-ship, member of its crew.

colliery /ˈkɒlɪərɪ/ n. coal-mine.

collision /kəˈlɪʒ(ə)n/ n. violent striking of moving body against another or against fixed object; clashing of opposed interests etc.

collocate /ˈkɒləkeɪt/ v.t. place (esp. words) together; arrange. **collocation** n.

colloid /ˈkɒlɔɪd/ n. gluey substance; substance in non-crystalline state, with very large molecules. **colloidal** a.

colloquial /kəˈləʊkwɪəl/ a. belonging or proper to ordinary conversation, not formal or literary.

colloquialism /kəˈləʊkwɪəlɪz(ə)m/ n. colloquial word or phrase; use of these.

colloquy /ˈkɒləkwɪ/ n. talk, dialogue.

collusion /kəˈluːʒ(ə)n/ n. secret agreement or co-operation esp. for fraud or deceit.

collywobbles /ˈkɒlɪwɒb(ə)lz/ n.pl. colloq. ache or rumbling in stomach; apprehensive feeling.

cologne /kəˈləʊn/ n. eau-de-Cologne.

colon[1] /ˈkəʊlən/ n. punctuation-mark (:).

colon[2] /ˈkəʊlən/ n. lower and greater part of large intestine. **colonic** /-ˈlɒn-/ a.

colonel /ˈkɜːn(ə)l/ n. officer commanding regiment next in rank below brigadier. **colonelcy** n.

colonial /kəˈləʊnɪəl/ 1 a. of a colony or colonies. 2 n. inhabitant of colony.

colonialism /kəˈləʊnɪəlɪz(ə)m/ n. policy of having colonies.

colonist /ˈkɒlənɪst/ n. settler in or inhabitant of colony.

colonize /ˈkɒlənaɪz/ v. establish colony (in); join colony. **colonization** n.

colonnade /kɒləˈneɪd/ n. row of columns supporting entablature or roof.

colony /ˈkɒlənɪ/ n. settlement or settlers in new territory remaining subject to parent State; persons of one nationality or occupation etc. forming community in town etc.; group of animals that live close together; organized group of Beavers.

colophon /ˈkɒləf(ə)n/ n. tail-piece in book.

Colorado beetle /kɒləˈrɑːdəʊ/ small beetle with larva destructive to potato.

coloration /kʌləˈreɪʃ(ə)n/ n. colouring, arrangement of colours.

coloratura /kɒlərəˈtjʊərə/ n. elaborate ornamentation in vocal music; soprano singer of such music.

colossal /kəˈlɒs(ə)l/ a. gigantic, huge; colloq. splendid, glorious.

colossus /kəˈlɒsəs/ n. (pl. -lossi /-ˈlɒsaɪ/ or -lossuses) statue of more than life size; gigantic person or personified empire.

colour /ˈkʌlə(r)/ 1 n. one, or any mixture, of the constituents into which light can be separated as in spectrum or rainbow; use of all colours as in photography; colouring substance, esp. paint; skin pigmentation, esp. when dark; ruddiness of face; appearance or aspect; flag of regiment or ship etc.; coloured ribbon, rosette, dress, etc. worn as symbol of school or club or party etc. 2 v. give colour to, paint, stain, dye; blush. 3 **colour-blind** unable to distinguish certain colours; **colour-fast** dyed in colours that will not fade or run.

coloured /ˈkʌləd/ 1 a. having colour; wholly or partly of non-white descent; **Coloured** S. Afr. of mixed white and non-white descent. 2 n. coloured person.

colourful /ˈkʌləfʊl/ a. full of colour or interest.

colouring /ˈkʌlərɪŋ/ n. arrangement of colours; substance giving colour; facial complexion.

colourless /ˈkʌləlɪs/ a. lacking colour or vividness.

colt /kəʊlt/ n. young male horse; inexperienced person.

coltsfoot /ˈkəʊltsfʊt/ n. weed with large leaves and yellow flowers.

columbine /ˈkɒləmbaɪn/ n. garden

flower with pointed projections on its petals.

column /'kɒləm/ n. round pillar, esp. one with base and capital; column-shaped thing; vertical division of printed page; part of newspaper devoted to particular subject or by one writer; narrow-fronted deep arrangement of troops, vehicles, etc.

columnist /'kɒləmnɪst/ n. journalist who contributes regularly to a newspaper.

coma /'kəʊmə/ n. prolonged deep unconsciousness.

comatose /'kəʊmətəʊz/ a. in coma; very sleepy.

comb /kəʊm/ 1 n. toothed strip of rigid material for tidying and arranging hair; thing of similar shape or function, esp. for dressing wool; red fleshy crest of cock etc.; honeycomb. 2 v.t. draw comb through (hair), dress (wool etc.) with comb; search thoroughly.

combat /'kɒmbæt/ 1 n. fight, struggle. 2 v. do battle; contend with, oppose.

combatant /'kɒmbət(ə)nt/ 1 a. fighting. 2 n. fighter.

combative /'kɒmbətɪv/ a. pugnacious.

combe var. of **coomb**.

combination /kɒmbɪ'neɪʃ(ə)n/ n. combining; combined state; combined set of persons or things; sequence of numbers etc. used to open **combination lock**; motor cycle with sidecar attached; in pl. single undergarment for body and legs.

combine 1 /kəm'baɪn/ v. join together; unite; form into chemical compound; co-operate. 2 /'kɒmbaɪn/ n. combination of persons or firms acting together in business. 3 **combine harvester** combined reaping and threshing machine.

combustible /kəm'bʌstɪb(ə)l/ 1 a. capable of or used for burning. 2 n. combustible thing. 3 **combustibility** n.

combustion /kəm'bʌstʃ(ə)n/ n. burning; consumption by fire.

come /kʌm/ v.i. (past **came**; p.p. **come**) move or be brought towards, or reach, a place, time, situation, or result; be available; occur; become; traverse; colloq. behave like. **come about** happen; **come across** meet or find; **come-back** colloq. retort or retaliation; **come by** obtain; **come clean** colloq. confess;

come-down downfall, degradation; **come down with** begin to suffer from (disease); **come in for** receive; **come of** be result of, be descended from; **come off** succeed, occur, fare; **come out** appear, go on strike, be satisfactorily visible in photograph, be solved, make début; **come round** recover normal state, esp. of consciousness; **come to** revive, recover; **come true** be realized in fact; **come up** be mentioned or discussed; **come up against** be faced with or opposed to; **come up to** reach, be equal to; **come-uppance** US sl. one's deserts (for misbehaviour etc.); **come up with** produce (idea etc.); **come what may** whatever happens.

comedian /kə'miːdɪən/ n. humorous performer; actor in comedy.

comedienne /kəmiːdɪ'en/ n. woman comedian.

comedy /'kɒmədɪ/ n. stage-play or film of light amusing character; humorous genre of drama etc.; humour; amusing aspects of life.

comely /'kʌmlɪ/ a. pleasant to look at.

comestibles /kə'mestɪb(ə)lz/ n.pl. things to eat.

comet /'kɒmɪt/ n. heavenly body with starlike nucleus and luminous 'tail', moving in path about sun.

comfit /'kʌmfɪt/ n. sweet consisting of nut etc. in sugar.

comfort /'kʌmfət/ 1 n. physical or mental well-being; relief from trouble or hardship; consolation; in pl. things that make life comfortable. 2 v. bring comfort to; make comfortable.

comfortable /'kʌmfətəb(ə)l/ a. at ease in body or mind; promoting comfort.

comforter /'kʌmfətə(r)/ n. person who comforts; baby's dummy; woollen scarf.

comfrey /'kʌmfrɪ/ n. tall bell-flowered plant growing in damp places.

comfy /'kʌmfɪ/ a. colloq. comfortable.

comic /'kɒmɪk/ 1 a. of or like comedy; designed to amuse; funny. 2 n. comedian; comic paper, esp. periodical with narrative mainly in pictures. 3 **comic strip** sequence of drawings telling comic or serial story in newspaper etc.

comical /'kɒmɪk(ə)l/ a. laughable. **comicality** n.

comity /'kɒmɪtɪ/ n. courtesy. **comity**

of nations friendly recognition of each other's law and customs.

comma /'kɒmə/ *n.* punctuation-mark (,).

command /kə'mɑːnd/ 1 *v.* order, issue orders; have authority over or control of; have at one's disposal; deserve and get; look down over, dominate. 2 *n.* order given; description of, or signal initiating, operation in computer; exercise or tenure of authority; control, mastery; forces or district under commander. 3 **command performance** one given by royal command.

commandant /kɒmən'dænt/ *n.* commander of military force.

commandeer /kɒmən'dɪə(r)/ *v.t.* seize for military purposes; take arbitrarily.

commander /kə'mɑːndə(r)/ *n.* person who commands, esp. naval officer ranking next below captain. **commander-in-chief** supreme commander esp. of nation's forces.

commanding /kə'mɑːndɪŋ/ *a.* in command; exalted or impressive; dominant.

commandment /kə'mɑːndmənt/ *n.* divine command.

commando /kə'mɑːndəʊ/ *n.* (*pl.* **-dos**) body of specially-trained shock troops; member of this.

commemorate /kə'meməreɪt/ *v.t.* keep in memory by celebration or ceremony; be memorial of. **commemoration** *n.*; **commemorative** *a.*

commence /kə'mens/ *v.* begin, start.

commencement /kə'mensmənt/ *n.* beginning; *US* graduation ceremony.

commend /kə'mend/ *v.t.* praise; recommend; entrust. **commendation** *n.*

commendable /kə'mendəb(ə)l/ *a.* praiseworthy.

commensurable /kə'menʃərəb(ə)l/ *a.* measurable by same standard. **commensurability** *n.*

commensurate /kə'menʃərət/ *a.* co-extensive; proportionate.

comment /'kɒment/ 1 *n.* explanatory note; remark, opinion. 2 *v.* make comment(s) *on, upon, that.*

commentary /'kɒməntərɪ/ *n.* series of comments on book or performance etc.

commentator /'kɒmənteɪtə(r)/ *n.* writer or speaker of commentary; person who comments on current events. **commentate** *v.*

commerce /'kɒmɜːs/ *n.* buying and selling; all forms of trading.

commercial /kə'mɜːʃ(ə)l/ 1 *a.* of, in, or for, commerce; done primarily for financial profit; (of broadcasting) financed by revenue from advertising. 2 *n.* broadcast advertisement. 3 **commercial traveller** representative sent out to obtain orders for firm's products.

commingle /kə'mɪŋg(ə)l/ *v.* mix, unite.

comminute /'kɒmɪnjuːt/ *v.t.* reduce to small fragments or portions. **comminution** *n.*

commiserate /kə'mɪzəreɪt/ *v.* have or express sympathy *with.* **commiseration** *n.*; **commiserative** *a.*

commissar /'kɒmɪsɑː(r)/ *n. hist.* head of government department in USSR.

commissariat /kɒmɪ'seərɪət/ *n.* department responsible for supply of food etc. for army; food supplied.

commissary /'kɒmɪsərɪ/ *n.* deputy, delegate. **commissarial** /-'seər-/ *a.*

commission /kə'mɪʃ(ə)n/ 1 *n.* task given to person to perform; body of persons constituted to perform certain duties; warrant conferring authority, esp. that of officer in armed forces above a certain rank; pay or percentage received by agent; committing. 2 *v.t.* empower by commission; commit task to (person); give (officer) command of ship; prepare (ship) for active service. 3 **in commission** (of warship) ready for active service; **out of commission** not in service, not in working order.

commissionaire /kəmɪʃə'neə(r)/ *n.* uniformed attendant at door of theatre, office, etc.

commissioner /kə'mɪʃənə(r)/ *n.* member of commission; official representing government in a district etc.; person who has been commissioned.

commit /kə'mɪt/ *v.t.* be doer of (crime etc.); entrust, consign; send (person) to prison; involve in course of action; pledge or dedicate one*self.*

commitment /kə'mɪtmənt/ *n.* undertaking or pledge that restricts freedom of action; dedication to or involvement with a particular action, cause, etc.

committal /kə'mɪt(ə)l/ *n.* action of committing.

committee /kə'mɪtiː/ *n.* group of persons appointed usu. out of larger body to attend to particular business.

commode /kə'məʊd/ *n.* chamber-pot mounted in chair or box with cover; chest of drawers.

commodious /kə'məʊdɪəs/ *a.* roomy.

commodity /kə'mɒdɪtɪ/ *n.* article of trade esp. product as opp. service.

commodore /'kɒmədɔː(r)/ *n.* naval officer next below rear-admiral; commander of squadron or other division of fleet; president of yacht-club.

common /'kɒmən/ **1** *a.* shared by all; of or belonging to the whole community; occurring often; ordinary, the most familiar or numerous kind; of inferior quality, vulgar; *Gram.* (of noun) applicable to any one of a class, (of gender) applicable to individuals of either sex. **2** *n.* land belonging to community, esp. unenclosed waste land. **3** **common ground** basis for argument accepted by both sides; **common law** unwritten law of England based on custom and precedent; **common-law husband, wife,** one recognized by common law without formal marriage; **Common Market** European Economic Community; **common or garden** *colloq.* ordinary; **common-room** room for social use of students or teachers at college etc.; **common sense** good practical sense esp. in everyday matters; **common time** *Mus.* four crotchets in a bar; **in common** shared by several, in joint use.

commonalty /'kɒmənltɪ/ *n.* general community, common people.

commoner /'kɒmənə(r)/ *n.* person below rank of peer.

commonly /'kɒmənlɪ/ *adv.* usually, frequently.

commonplace /'kɒmənpleɪs/ **1** *n.* event, topic, etc. that is ordinary or usual; trite remark. **2** *a.* lacking originality or individuality.

commons /'kɒmənz/ *n.pl.* common people; **(House of) Commons** lower house of Parliament; provisions shared in common. **short commons** not enough food.

commonwealth /'kɒmənwelθ/ *n.* independent community. **the Commonwealth** republican government of Britain 1649–1660; **the (British) Commonwealth** association of UK with various independent States and dependencies.

commotion /kə'məʊʃ(ə)n/ *n.* noisy disturbance.

communal /'kɒmjʊn(ə)l/ *a.* shared between members of group or community. **communally** *adv.*

commune[1] /'kɒmjuːn/ *n.* group of people, not all of one family, sharing living accommodation and goods; small territorial administrative district.

commune[2] /kə'mjuːn/ *v.i.* communicate spiritually or feel in close touch (*with*).

communicant /kə'mjuːnɪkənt/ *n.* receiver of Holy Communion; person who imparts information.

communicate /kə'mjuːnɪkeɪt/ *v.* impart *to*, have social dealings *with*; convey information; receive Holy Communion.

communication /kəmjuːnɪ'keɪʃ(ə)n/ *n.* imparting or exchange of information; letter, message, etc.; social dealings; connection or means of access; in *pl.* science and practice of transmitting information. **communication cord** cord or chain for pulling by passenger to stop train in emergency.

communicative /kə'mjuːnɪkətɪv/ *a.* ready and willing to talk.

communion /kə'mjuːnɪən/ *n.* communing; fellowship; body of Christians of same denomination; **(Holy) Communion** Eucharist.

communiqué /kə'mjuːnɪkeɪ/ *n.* official communication, esp. report.

communism /'kɒmjʊnɪz(ə)m/ *n.* social system based on common ownership of property, means of production, etc.; **Communism** movement or political party advocating communism. **communist** *n. & a.*; **communistic** *a.*

community /kə'mjuːnɪtɪ/ *n.* group of people etc. living in same locality or having same religion, race, profession, interests, etc.; commune; joint ownership. **community centre** place providing social, recreational, and educational facilities for a neighbourhood; **community home** institution for housing young offenders; **community singing** singing in chorus by large gathering of people.

commute /kə'mju:t/ v. travel regularly by train or bus or car to work at a distance from home; exchange, interchange; change (punishment *to* another less severe).

commuter n. person who commutes to and from work.

compact[1] 1 /kəm'pækt/ a. closely or neatly packed together; occupying small space. 2 /kəm'pækt/ v.t. make compact. 3 /'kɒmpækt/ n. small flat case for face-powder etc. **4 compact disc** small disc from which sound is reproduced by laser action.

compact[2] /'kɒmpækt/ n. agreement or contract.

companion /kəm'pænjən/ n. one who accompanies or associates with another; woman paid to live with another; handbook or reference-book; thing that matches another; member of some orders of distinction. **companion-way** staircase from deck of ship to cabins etc.

companionable /kəm'pænjənəb(ə)l/ a. sociable, agreeable as companion.

companionship /kəm'pænjənʃɪp/ n. state of being companions.

company /'kʌmpəni/ n. being with another or others; number of people assembled; guests; body of persons combined for commercial or other purpose; group of actors etc.; subdivision of infantry battalion. **ship's company** entire crew.

comparable /'kɒmpərəb(ə)l/ a. that can be compared (*with*, *to*). □ See page 665.

comparative /kəm'pærətɪv/ 1 a. of or involving comparison; perceptible or estimated by comparison; considered in relation to each other; *Gram.* expressing a higher degree of a quality. 2 n. *Gram.* comparative degree or form.

compare /kəm'peə(r)/ 1 v. estimate similarity of; liken *to*; bear comparison (*with*). 2 n. comparison. **3 compare notes** exchange information or ideas.

comparison /kəm'pærɪs(ə)n/ n. comparing. **bear comparison** be able to be compared favourably *with*; **degrees of comparison** *Gram.* positive, comparative, and superlative of adjectives and adverbs.

compartment /kəm'pɑːtmənt/ n. division or space partitioned off, esp. in railway-carriage.

compass /'kʌmpəs/ n. instrument showing direction of magnetic north and bearings from it; (usu. in *pl.*) V-shaped hinged instrument for drawing circles and taking measurements; circumference, area, extent, scope, range.

compassion /kəm'pæʃ(ə)n/ n. pity.

compassionate /kəm'pæʃənət/ a. sympathetic, showing compassion; granted out of compassion.

compatible /kəm'pætɪb(ə)l/ a. able to coexist (*with*); (of equipment) able to be used in combination. **compatibility** n.

compatriot /kəm'pætrɪət/ n. person from same country.

compeer /kəm'pɪə(r)/ n. equal; comrade.

compel /kəm'pel/ v.t. force or constrain; bring about irresistibly.

compelling /kəm'pelɪŋ/ a. rousing strong interest.

compendious /kəm'pendɪəs/ a. comprehensive but brief.

compendium /kəm'pendɪəm/ n. (*pl.* **-dia** or **-diums**) abridgement, summary; collection of table-games etc.

compensate /'kɒmpənseɪt/ v. recompense, make amends for; counterbalance.

compensation /kɒmpen'seɪʃ(ə)n/ n. compensating, thing (esp. money) that compensates. **compensatory** a.

compère /'kɒmpeə(r)/ 1 n. person who introduces performers in variety entertainment etc. 2 v.t. act as compère to.

compete /kəm'piːt/ v. take part in contest, race, examination, etc.; strive *with* or *against* others.

competence /'kɒmpɪt(ə)ns/ n. being competent; ability; comfortably adequate income.

competent /'kɒmpɪt(ə)nt/ a. having adequate ability, knowledge, or authority; adequate, effective.

competition /kɒmpə'tɪʃ(ə)n/ n. event in which persons compete; competing; those competing with one.

competitive /kəm'petɪtɪv/ a. of, enjoying, or involving competition; (of prices etc.) comparable with those of rivals.

competitor /kəm'petɪtə(r)/ n. one who competes; rival, esp. in trade.

compile /kəm'paɪl/ v.t. collect together (facts, quotations, etc.); make (book) thus. **compilation** /-pɪl-/n.

complacent /kəm'pleɪs(ə)nt/ a. self-satisfied; calmly content. **complacency** n.

complain /kəm'pleɪn/ v.i. express dissatisfaction. **complain of** say that one is suffering from.

complaint /kəm'pleɪnt/ n. statement that one is aggrieved or dissatisfied; formal protest; illness.

complaisant /kəm'pleɪz(ə)nt/ a. inclined to please or defer to others; acquiescent. **complaisance** n.

complement 1 /'kɒmplɪmənt/ n. something which completes whole; full number, complete set or provision; *Gram.* word(s) added to verb to complete predicate; deficiency of angle from 90°. 2 /'kɒmplɪment/ v.t. complete; form complement to. 3 **complementary** a.

complete /kəm'pli:t/ 1 a. having all its parts; finished; total. 2 v.t. make complete, finish; fill in (form etc.) 3 **completion** n.

complex /'kɒmpleks/ 1 a. consisting of several parts; complicated. 2 n. complex whole; group of usu. repressed ideas etc. causing abnormal mental state. 3 **complexity** n.

complexion /kəm'plekʃ(ə)n/ n. natural colour and texture of skin, esp. of face; character.

compliance /kəm'plaɪəns/ n. acting in accordance with request or command etc.

compliant /kəm'plaɪənt/ a. ready to comply.

complicate /'kɒmplɪkeɪt/ v.t. (esp. in *p.p.*) make complex, confused, or difficult.

complication /kɒmplɪ'keɪʃ(ə)n/ n. complicated state; complicating circumstance.

complicity /kəm'plɪsɪtɪ/ n. involvement in wrongdoing.

compliment 1 /'kɒmplɪmənt/ n. expression or implication of praise; in *pl.* formal greetings. 2 /'kɒmplɪment/ v.t. pay compliment to.

complimentary /kɒmplɪ'mentərɪ/ a. expressing or conveying compliment; given free of charge.

comply /kəm'plaɪ/ v.i. act in accordance (*with*).

component /kəˈpəʊnənt/ 1 a. being one of the parts of a whole. 2 n. component part.

comport /kəm'pɔ:t/ v. behave or conduct (one*self*); agree or accord *with*.

compose /kəm'pəʊz/ v.t. create in music or writing; make up, constitute; set up (type); set in type; arrange artistically or for specified purpose; make calm. □ See page 666.

composed /kəm'pəʊzd/ a. calm, self-possessed

composer /kəm'pəʊzə(r)/ n. person who composes, esp. music.

composite /'kɒmpəzɪt/ 1 a. made up of various parts or materials; (of plant) having head of many flowers forming one bloom. 2 n. composite thing or plant.

composition /kɒmpə'zɪʃ(ə)n/ n. composing; thing composed; constitution of substance; compound artificial substance.

compositor /kəm'pɒzɪtə(r)/ n. person who sets up type for printing.

compost /'kɒmpɒst/ n. prepared mixture, esp. of rotted organic matter, for horticultural use.

composure /kəm'pəʊʒə(r)/ n. calmness.

compote /'kɒmpəʊt/ n. fruit in syrup.

compound[1] 1 /'kɒmpaʊnd/ n. thing made up of two or more parts or ingredients; substance consisting of two or more elements chemically united. 2 /kəm'paʊnd/ v. mix or combine (ingredients etc.), make up (whole); complicate; condone (offence etc.) for personal gain; settle (matter) by mutual concession; come to terms. 3 /'kɒmpaʊnd/ a. made up of two or more parts or ingredients; combined, collective. 4 **compound fracture** one complicated by skin wound; **compound interest** interest paid on principal and accumulated interest.

compound[2] /'kɒmpaʊnd/ n. enclosure, fenced-in space.

comprehend /kɒmprɪ'hend/ v.t. grasp mentally; include.

comprehensible /kɒmprɪ'hensɪb(ə)l/ a. that can be understood.

comprehension /kɒmprɪ'henʃ(ə)n/ n. understanding; inclusion.

comprehensive /kɒmprɪˈhensɪv/ **1** *a.* including much or all; of wide scope; (of secondary school) providing education for children of all abilities. **2** *n.* comprehensive school.

compress 1 /kəmˈpres/ *v.* squeeze together, bring into smaller space. **2** /ˈkɒmpres/ *n.* pad or cloth pressed on to part of body to stop bleeding or relieve inflammation etc.

compression /kəmˈpreʃ(ə)n/ *n.* compressing; reduction in volume of fuel mixture in internal-combustion engine before ignition.

compressor /kəmˈpresə(r)/ *n.* machine for compressing air or other gases.

comprise /kəmˈpraɪz/ *v.t.* have or include as constituent parts; consist of. □ See page 666.

compromise /ˈkɒmprəmaɪz/ **1** *n.* agreement reached by mutual concession. **2** *v.* settle (dispute) or modify (principles etc.) by compromise; bring under suspicion or into danger; make compromise.

comptroller /kənˈtrəʊlə(r)/ *n.* controller.

compulsion /kəmˈpʌlʃ(ə)n/ *n.* act of compelling; irresistible urge. **under compulsion** because one is compelled.

compulsive /kəmˈpʌlsɪv/ *a.* resulting or acting (as if) from compulsion; irresistible.

compulsory /kəmˈpʌlsərɪ/ *a.* that must be done; required by the rules etc. **compulsorily** *adv.*

compunction /kəmˈpʌŋkʃ(ə)n/ *n.* pricking of conscience.

compute /kəmˈpjuːt/ *v.* reckon, calculate; use computer. **computation** *n.*

computer /kəmˈpjuːtə(r)/ *n.* electronic apparatus for analysing or storing data, making calculations, or controlling operations.

computerize /kəmˈpjuːtəraɪz/ *v.t.* equip with or perform by or produce by computer. **computerization** *n.*

comrade /ˈkɒmreɪd/ *n.* associate or companion in some activity; fellow socialist or communist, =etc. **comradeship** *n.*

con¹ *sl.* **1** *v.t.* persuade, swindle. **2** *n.* confidence trick.

con² *v.t. arch.* study, learn by heart.

con³ *v.t.* direct steering of (ship).

concatenate /kɒnˈkætɪneɪt/ *v.t.* link together; form sequence of. **concatenation** *n.*

concave /kɒnˈkeɪv/ *a.* curved like interior of circle or sphere. **concavity** /-ˈkæv-/ *n.*

conceal /kənˈsiːl/ *v.t.* hide or keep secret. **concealment** *n.*

concede /kənˈsiːd/ *v.t.* admit to be true; grant; admit defeat in (contest etc.).

conceit /kənˈsiːt/ *n.* personal vanity; fanciful notion, far-fetched comparison.

conceited /kənˈsiːtɪd/ *a.* having too high an opinion of oneself.

conceive /kənˈsiːv/ *v.* become pregnant; form in mind; imagine, think (*of*). **conceivable** *a.*

concentrate /ˈkɒnsəntreɪt/ **1** *v.* employ one's full thoughts or efforts (*on*); bring together at or on one point; increase strength of (liquid etc.) by removing water. **2** *n.* concentrated substance.

concentration /kɒnsənˈtreɪʃ(ə)n/ *n.* concentrating or being concentrated; amount or strength of substance in mixture; mental faculty of exclusive attention. **concentration camp** place for detention of political prisoners etc.

concentric /kənˈsentrɪk/ *a.* having the same centre. **concentricity** *n.*

concept /ˈkɒnsept/ *n.* generalized idea or notion.

conception /kənˈsepʃ(ə)n/ *n.* conceiving, being conceived; thing conceived; idea.

conceptual /kənˈseptjʊal/ *a.* of mental concepts. **conceptually** *adv.*

conceptualize /kənˈseptjʊalaɪz/ *v.t.* form concept or idea of.

concern /kənˈsɜːn/ **1** *v.t.* be relevant or important to; affect; relate to; interest (oneself). **2** *n.* thing of interest or importance to one; solicitude, anxiety; firm or enterprise; in *pl.* one's affairs.

concerned /kənˈsɜːnd/ *a.* anxious or troubled; involved or interested.

concerning /kənˈsɜːnɪŋ/ *prep.* about.

concert /ˈkɒnsət/ *n.* live musical entertainment; combination of voices etc.; agreement, union.

concerted /kənˈsɜːtɪd/ *a.* effected by mutual agreement; done in co-operation.

concertina /kɒnsəˈtiːnə/ **1** *n.* portable

musical instrument consisting of reeds sounded by bellows worked by the player's hands. **2** *v.* compress or collapse in folds like those of concertina.

concerto /kənˈtʃeatəʊ/ *n.* (*pl.* **-tos**) musical piece for solo instrument and orchestra.

concession /kənˈseʃ(ə)n/ *n.* conceding, thing conceded; right to use land, sell goods, etc.; reduction in price for certain category of person.

concessionaire /kənseʃəˈneə(r)/ *n.* holder of concession.

concessive /kənˈsesɪv/ *a. Gram.* expressing concession.

conch /kɒntʃ/ *n.* spiral shell of certain shellfish; such shellfish, esp. large gastropod.

conchology /kɒŋˈkɒlədʒɪ/ *n.* study of shells and shellfish.

conciliate /kənˈsɪlɪeɪt/ *v.t.* win over from anger or hostility; reconcile. **conciliation** *n.*; **conciliatory** *a.*

concise /kənˈsaɪs/ *a.* brief, condensed.

conclave /ˈkɒŋkleɪv/ *n.* private meeting; assembly or meeting-place of cardinals for papal election.

conclude /kənˈkluːd/ *v.* bring or come to end; settle finally; draw conclusion.

conclusion /kənˈkluːʒ(ə)n/ *n.* ending; judgement reached by reasoning; settling *of* peace etc.

conclusive /kənˈkluːsɪv/ *a.* decisive, convincing.

concoct /kənˈkɒkt/ *v.t.* prepare, esp. by mixing; invent or devise. **concoction** *n.*

concomitant /kənˈkɒmɪt(ə)nt/ **1** *a.* accompanying. **2** *n.* accompanying thing. **3 concomitance** *n.*

concord /ˈkɒŋkɔːd/ *n.* agreement, harmony; *Mus.* chord satisfactory in itself; *Gram.* agreement between words in gender, number, etc. **concordant** *a.*

concordance /kənˈkɔːd(ə)ns/ *n.* agreement; index of words used by author in book, esp. Bible.

concordat /kənˈkɔːdæt/ *n.* official agreement between Church and State.

concourse /ˈkɒŋkɔːs/ *n.* crowd; open central area in large public building, railway station, etc.

concrete /ˈkɒŋkriːt/ **1** *n.* mixture of cement and gravel etc., used in building etc. **2** *a.* existing in material form, real, definite; not abstract; made of concrete.

3 *v.* cover with or embed in concrete; /kənˈkriːt/ form into mass, solidify.

concretion /kənˈkriːʃ(ə)n/ *n.* hard solid mass; forming of this by coalescence.

concubine /ˈkɒŋkjʊbaɪn/ *n.* woman who cohabits with man without marriage; (among polygamous peoples) secondary wife. **concubinage** /-ˈkjuː-bɪnɪdʒ/ *n.*

concupiscence /kənˈkjuːpɪs(ə)ns/ *n.* sexual desire. **concupiscent** *a.*

concur /kənˈkɜː(r)/ *v.i.* (*past* & *p.p.* **concurred**) agree; coincide.

concurrent /kənˈkʌrənt/ *a.* existing or acting together or at the same time. **concurrence** *n.*

concuss /kənˈkʌs/ *v.t.* subject to concussion.

concussion /kənˈkʌʃ(ə)n/ *n.* temporary unconsciousness or incapacity due to injury to head; violent shaking.

condemn /kənˈdem/ *v.t.* give judicial decision against; sentence (*to*); doom *to*; pronounce unfit for use etc. **condemnation** *n.*; **condemnatory** *a.*

condensation /kɒndenˈseɪʃ(ə)n/ *n.* condensing; condensed material.

condense /kənˈdens/ *v.* make denser or briefer; compress; change or be changed from gas or vapour to liquid.

condescend /kɒndɪˈsend/ *v.i.* consent *to* do something less dignified than is fitting or customary.

condescending /kɒndɪˈsendɪŋ/ *a.* patronizing.

condescension /kɒndɪˈsenʃ(ə)n/ *n.* condescending manner or act.

condign /kənˈdaɪn/ *a.* adequate, fitting.

condiment /ˈkɒndɪmənt/ *n.* seasoning or relish for use with food.

condition /kənˈdɪʃ(ə)n/ **1** *n.* thing necessary for something else to be possible; state of being, state of physical fitness or fitness for use; ailment or abnormality; in *pl.* circumstances. **2** *v.t.* bring into desired condition; teach, accustom; govern, determine; be essential to.

conditional /kənˈdɪʃən(ə)l/ *a.* dependent (*on*), not absolute; *Gram.* expressing condition.

condole /kənˈdəʊl/ *v.i.* express sympathy in sorrow. **condolence** *n.*

condom /ˈkɒndəm/ n. contraceptive sheath.

condominium /kɒndəˈmɪnɪəm/ n. joint control of State by other States; *US* building in which flats are individually owned.

condone /kənˈdəʊn/ v.t. forgive, overlook. **condonation** n.

condor /ˈkɒndɔː(r)/ n. large S. Amer. vulture.

conduce /kənˈdjuːs/ v.i. lead or contribute *to*. **conducive** a.

conduct 1 /ˈkɒndʌkt/ n. behaviour, manner of conducting oneself, business, etc. **2** /kənˈdʌkt/ v.t. lead, escort; control, manage; be conductor of (orchestra etc.); behave one*self*; transmit (heat) by contact.

conduction /kənˈdʌkʃ(ə)n/ n. conducting of heat, electricity, etc.

conductive /kənˈdʌktɪv/ a. having property of conducting heat or electricity. **conductivity** /-ˈtɪv-/ n.

conductor /kənˈdʌktə(r)/ n. director of orchestra, choir, etc.; person who collects fares on bus etc.; substance that conducts heat or electricity. **conductress** n.

conduit /ˈkɒndɪt/ n. channel or pipe for conveying liquid or protecting insulated cable.

cone n. solid figure with usu. circular base and tapering to a point; cone-shaped object; dry fruit of pine or fir; ice-cream cornet.

coney var. of **cony**.

confab /ˈkɒnfæb/ n. colloq. confabulation.

confabulate /kənˈfæbjʊleɪt/ v.i. talk together. **confabulation** n.

confection /kənˈfekʃ(ə)n/ n. mixture; delicacy, esp. made of sweet ingredients.

confectioner /kənˈfekʃənə(r)/ n. dealer in sweets or pastries etc. **confectionery** n.

confederacy /kənˈfedərəsɪ/ n. alliance or league esp. of confederate States.

confederate 1 /kənˈfedərət/ a. allied. **2** /kənˈfedərət/ n. ally; accomplice. **3** /kənˈfedəreɪt/ v.t. bring or come into alliance. **4 Confederate States** those which seceded from US in 1860-1.

confederation /kənˈfedəˈreɪʃ(ə)n/ n. union or alliance of States or organizations.

confer /kənˈfɜː(r)/ v. (*past & p.p.* **conferred**) bestow; meet for discussion.

conference /ˈkɒnfər(ə)ns/ n. consultation; meeting (esp. regular) for discussion etc.

conferment /kənˈfɜːmənt/ n. conferring *of* honour etc.

confess /kənˈfes/ v. acknowledge, admit; declare one's sins, esp. to priest; (of priest) hear confession of.

confessedly /kənˈfesɪdlɪ/ adv. by personal or general admission.

confession /kənˈfeʃ(ə)n/ n. confessing; thing confessed; statement of principles etc.

confessional /kənˈfeʃən(ə)l/ **1** n. enclosed place where priest hears confession. **2** a. of confession.

confessor /kənˈfesə(r)/ n. priest who hears confession.

confetti /kənˈfetɪ/ n. small bits of coloured paper thrown by wedding guests at bride and bridegroom.

confidant /ˈkɒnfɪdænt/ n. (fem. **confidante** pr. same) person to whom one confides knowledge of one's private affairs.

confide /kənˈfaɪd/ v. tell (secret) or entrust (task) *to*. **confide in** talk confidentially to.

confidence /ˈkɒnfɪd(ə)ns/ n. firm trust; assured expectation; self-reliance; boldness; something told confidentially. **confidence trick** swindle in which victim is persuaded to trust swindler in some way; **in confidence** as a secret; **in person's confidence** trusted with his secrets.

confident /ˈkɒnfɪd(ə)nt/ a. feeling or showing confidence.

confidential /kɒnfɪˈdenʃ(ə)l/ a. spoken or written in confidence; entrusted with secrets; inclined to confide. **confidentially** a.; **confidentiality** n.

configuration /kənfɪgəˈreɪʃ(ə)n/ n. manner of arrangement, shape, outline.

confine 1 /kənˈfaɪn/ v.t. keep or restrict within certain limits; imprison. **2** /ˈkɒnfaɪn/ n. (usu. in *pl.*) boundary. **3 be confined** be in childbirth.

confinement /kənˈfaɪnmənt/ n. confining, being confined; childbirth.

confirm /kənˈfɜːm/ v.t. provide support for truth or correctness of; es-

tablish more firmly; formally make definite; administer confirmation to.

confirmation /kɒnfəˈmeɪʃ(ə)n/ n. corroborative circumstance or statement; rite confirming baptized person as member of Christian Church.

confiscate /ˈkɒnfɪskeɪt/ v.t. take or seize by authority. **confiscation** n.

conflagration /kɒnfləˈgreɪʃ(ə)n/ n. great and destructive fire.

conflate /kənˈfleɪt/ v.t. fuse together, blend.

conflict 1 /ˈkɒnflɪkt/ n. fight, struggle; opposition; clashing. 2 /kənˈflɪkt/ v.i. struggle; clash, be incompatible with.

confluent /ˈkɒnfluənt/ 1 a. merging into one. 2 n. one of confluent streams etc. 3 **confluence** n.

conform /kənˈfɔːm/ v. (cause to) fit or be suitable; comply with rules or general custom.

conformable /kənˈfɔːməb(ə)l/ a. adapted or corresponding (to), consistent with.

conformation /kɒnfɔːˈmeɪʃ(ə)n/ n. thing's structure.

conformist /kənˈfɔːmɪst/ n. person who conforms to an established practice. **conformism** n.

conformity /kənˈfɔːmɪtɪ/ n. conforming with established practice; suitability.

confound /kənˈfaʊnd/ v.t. baffle; confuse; overthrow or defeat; (as mild oath) damn.

confront /kənˈfrʌnt/ v.t. meet or stand facing, esp. in hostility or defiance; (of problem etc.) present itself to; bring face to face with. **confrontation** n.

confuse /kənˈfjuːz/ v.t. throw into disorder; bewilder; mix up; make obscure. **confusion** n.

confute /kənˈfjuːt/ v.t. prove to be false or wrong. **confutation** n.

conga /ˈkɒŋgə/ n. Latin-Amer. dance usu. performed in single file.

congeal /kənˈdʒiːl/ v. solidify by cooling; stiffen, coagulate. **congelation** n.

congenial /kənˈdʒiːnɪəl/ a. having sympathetic nature, similar interests, etc.; suited or agreeable to. **congeniality** a.

congenital /kənˈdʒenɪt(ə)l/ a. existing or as such from birth.

conger /ˈkɒŋgə(r)/ n. large sea eel.

congeries /kɒnˈdʒɪəriːz/ n. (pl. same) disorderly collection; mass, heap.

congest /kənˈdʒest/ v.t. affect with congestion.

congestion /kənˈdʒestʃ(ə)n/ n. abnormal accumulation or obstruction, esp. of traffic etc. or mucus in nose etc.

conglomerate 1 /kənˈglɒmərət/ a. gathered into a rounded mass. 2 /kənˈglɒmərət/ n. conglomerate mass; business etc. corporation formed by merging separate firms. 3 /kənˈglɒməreɪt/ v. collect into coherent mass. 4 **conglomeration** n.

congratulate /kənˈgrætjʊleɪt/ v.t. express pleasure at happiness or excellence or good fortune of. **congratulatory** a.

congratulation /kəngrætjʊˈleɪʃ(ə)n/ n. congratulating, (usu. in pl.) expression of this.

congregate /ˈkɒŋgrɪgeɪt/ v. collect or gather in crowd.

congregation /kɒŋgrɪˈgeɪʃ(ə)n/ n. assembly of people, esp. for religious worship; group of persons regularly attending at particular church etc.

congregational /kɒŋgrɪˈgeɪʃən(ə)l/ a. of congregation; **Congregational** of or adhering to Congregationalism.

Congregationalism /kɒŋgrɪˈgeɪʃənəlɪz(ə)m/ n. system of ecclesiastical organization whereby individual churches are self-governing. **Congregationalist** n.

congress /ˈkɒŋgres/ n. formal meeting of delegates for discussion; **Congress** national legislative body of US etc. **congressional** a.

congruent /ˈkɒŋgrʊənt/ a. suitable, agreeing (with); (of geometrical figures) coinciding exactly when superimposed. **congruence** n.

conic /ˈkɒnɪk/ a. of cone. **conic section** Math. figure formed by intersection of cone and plane.

conical /ˈkɒnɪk(ə)l/ a. cone-shaped.

conifer /ˈkɒnɪfə(r)/ n. cone-bearing tree. **coniferous** /kəˈnɪfərəs/ a.

conjectural /kənˈdʒektjʊər(ə)l/ a. involving conjecture.

conjecture /kənˈdʒektʃə(r)/ 1 n. guessing, guess. 2 v. make conjecture, guess.

conjoin /kənˈdʒɔɪn/ v. join, combine.

conjoint /kən'dʒɔɪnt/ a. associated, conjoined.

conjugal /'kɒndʒʊg(ə)l/ a. of marriage; between husband and wife.

conjugate 1 /'kɒndʒʊgeɪt/ v. give the different forms of (verb); unite, become fused. **2** /'kɒndʒʊgət/ a. joined together; coupled, fused.

conjugation /kɒndʒʊ'geɪʃ(ə)n/ n. Gram. (system of) verbal inflexion.

conjunct /kən'dʒʌŋkt/ a. joined, combined, associated.

conjunction /kən'dʒʌŋkʃ(ə)n/ n. joining, connection; Gram. word used to connect clauses, phrases, words, etc.; combination of events or circumstances.

conjunctiva /kɒndʒʌŋk'taɪvə/ n. mucous membrane lining inner eyelid.

conjunctive /kən'dʒʌŋktɪv/ a. joining, uniting; Gram. of nature of a conjunction.

conjunctivitis /kəndʒʌŋktɪ'vaɪtɪs/ n. inflammation of conjunctiva.

conjuncture /kən'dʒʌŋktʃə(r)/ n. position of affairs at particular moment.

conjure /'kʌndʒə(r)/ v. perform deceptive tricks esp. by movement of hands; produce as if from nothing. **conjure up** evoke.

conjuror /'kʌndʒərə(r)/ n. (also **conjurer**) skilled performer of conjuring tricks.

conk[1] n. sl. nose.

conk[2] v.i. sl. **conk out** break down.

conker /'kɒŋkə(r)/ n. horse-chestnut fruit; in pl. children's game played with these threaded on strings.

connect /kə'nekt/ v. join, be joined; associate mentally or practically (with); (of train, boat, etc.) arrive in time for passengers to catch another conveyance; put into communication by telephone; (usu. in pass.) unite or associate with others in relationship etc. **connecting-rod** rod between piston and crankpin etc. in engine. **connector** n.

connection /kə'nekʃ(ə)n/ n. being connected or related; association of ideas; connecting part; close associate, group of associates etc.; connecting train etc.

connective /kə'nektɪv/ a. serving to connect.

conning-tower /'kɒnɪŋtaʊə(r)/ n.

raised structure of submarine containing periscope; pilot-house of warship.

connive /kə'naɪv/ v.i. **connive at** disregard or tacitly consent to (wrongdoing). **connivance** n.

connoisseur /kɒnə'sɜː(r)/ n. person with good taste and judgement (of, in).

connote /kə'nəʊt/ v.t. imply; include in its meaning. **connotation** /kɒnə'teɪʃ(ə)n/ n.; **connotative** a.

connubial /kə'njuːbɪəl/ a. connected with marriage.

conquer /'kɒŋkə(r)/ v. overcome, defeat; be victor; subjugate. **conqueror** n.

conquest /'kɒŋkwest/ n. conquering, what is won by it; person whose affections have been won.

consanguineous /kɒnsæŋ'gwɪnɪəs/ a. descended from same ancestor; akin. **consanguinity** n.

conscience /'kɒnʃ(ə)ns/ n. moral sense of right and wrong, esp. as affecting person's behaviour. **conscience money** money paid to relieve conscience, esp. in respect of evaded payment etc.; **conscience-stricken** made uneasy by bad conscience.

conscientious /kɒnʃɪ'enʃəs/ a. obedient to conscience; scrupulous; assiduous. **conscientious objector** person who refuses to do military service on grounds of conscience.

conscious /'kɒnʃəs/ **1** a. awake and aware of one's surroundings etc.; aware (of), knowing; consciously performed or felt etc. **2** n. the conscious mind.

consciousness n. awareness; person's conscious thoughts and feelings as a whole.

conscript 1 /kən'skrɪpt/ v. summon for compulsory State (esp. military) service. **2** /'kɒnskrɪpt/ n. conscripted person. **3 conscription** n.

consecrate /'kɒnsɪkreɪt/ v.t. make or declare sacred (to); dedicate formally to religious purpose; devote to. **consecration** n.

consecutive /kən'sekjʊtɪv/ a. following continuously; proceeding in logical sequence.

consensus /kən'sensəs/ n. agreement in opinion; majority view.

consent /kən'sent/ **1** v.i. express willingness, give permission; agree *to*. **2** *n*. agreement, compliance; permission.

consequence /ˈkɒnsɪkwəns/ *n*. that which follows from any cause or condition; importance.

consequent /ˈkɒnsɪkwənt/ *a*. that results; following as consequence.

consequential /kɒnsɪˈkwenʃ(ə)l/ *a*. following as result or inference; self-important. **consequentiality** *n*.

conservancy /kənˈsɜːvənsɪ/ *n*. board controlling river, port, etc. or concerned with conservation.

conservation /kɒnsəˈveɪʃ(ə)n/ *n*. preservation, esp. of natural environment. **conservation of energy** *Phys*. principle that quantity of energy etc. of any closed system of bodies remains constant.

conservationist /kɒnsəˈveɪʃənɪst/ *n*. supporter or advocate of conservation.

conservative /kənˈsɜːvətɪv/ **1** *a*. tending to conserve; averse to rapid change; (of estimate) purposely low. **2** *n*. conservative person; **Conservative** member or supporter of Conservative Party. **3 Conservative Party** political party disposed to promote private enterprise. **4 conservatism** *n*.

conservatoire /kənˈsɜːvətwɑː(r)/ *n*. (usu. Continental) school of music or other arts. [F]

conservatory /kənˈsɜːvətərɪ/ *n*. greenhouse for tender plants; (US) *conservatoire*.

conserve /kənˈsɜːv/ **1** *v.t*. preserve, keep from harm, decay, or loss. **2** *n*. fruit etc. preserved in sugar; jam.

consider /kənˈsɪdə(r)/ *v*. contemplate; deliberate thoughtfully; make allowance for, take into account; have the opinion *that*; show consideration for.

considerable /kənˈsɪdərəb(ə)l/ *a*. not negligible; of some importance or size.

considerate /kənˈsɪdərət/ *a*. thoughtful for feelings or rights of others.

consideration /kənsɪdəˈreɪʃ(ə)n/ *n*. careful thought; being considerate; fact or thing regarded as a reason; compensation.

considering /kənˈsɪdərɪŋ/ *prep*. in view of.

consign /kənˈsaɪn/ *v.t*. commit or deliver *to*; send (goods etc.) *to*.

consignee /kɒnsaɪˈniː/ *n*. person to whom goods are sent.

consignor /kənˈsaɪnə(r)/ *n*. person by whom goods are sent.

consignment /kənˈsaɪnmənt/ *n*. consigning, goods consigned.

consist /kənˈsɪst/ *v.i*. be composed *of*; have its essential features *in*; be consistent *with*.

consistency /kənˈsɪstənsɪ/ *n*. degree of density, esp. of thick liquids; being consistent.

consistent /kənˈsɪst(ə)nt/ *a*. compatible; constant to same principles.

consistory /kənˈsɪstərɪ/ *n*. council of cardinals.

consolation /kɒnsəˈleɪʃ(ə)n/ *n*. alleviation of grief or disappointment. **consolation prize** given to competitor just failing to win main prizes. **consolatory** /kənˈsɒlətərɪ/ *a*.

console[1] /kənˈsəʊl/ *v.t*. bring consolation to.

console[2] /ˈkɒnsəʊl/ *n*. bracket supporting a shelf etc.; cabinet with keys and stops of organ; panel for controls of electronic or mechanical equipment; cabinet for radio etc. equipment.

consolidate /kənˈsɒlɪdeɪt/ *v*. make or become strong or solid; combine (territories, companies, debts, etc.) into one whole. **consolidation** *n*.

consols /ˈkɒnsɒlz/ *n.pl*. Government securities.

consommé /kənˈsɒmeɪ/ *n*. clear soup.

consonance /ˈkɒnsənəns/ *n*. agreement or harmony.

consonant /ˈkɒnsənənt/ **1** *n*. speech sound that forms a syllable only in combination with vowel, letter representing this. **2** *a*. in agreement or harmony *with*; agreeable *to*. **3 consonantal** /-ˈnænt-/ *a*.

consort[1] **1** /ˈkɒnsɔːt/ *n*. wife or husband; ship sailing with another. **2** /kənˈsɔːt/ *v.i*. associate or keep company (*with*); be in harmony.

consort[2] /ˈkɒnsɔːt/ *n*. *Mus*. group of players or instruments.

consortium /kənˈsɔːtɪəm/ *n*. (*pl*. **-tia**) association esp. of several business companies.

conspectus /kənˈspektəs/ *n*. general view; synopsis.

conspicuous /kənˈspɪkjʊəs/ *a*. clearly visible; attracting attention.

conspiracy /kən'spɪrəsɪ/ n. act of conspiring; unlawful combination or plot.

conspirator /kən'spɪrətə(r)/ n. person who takes part in conspiracy. **conspiratorial** /-'tɔːr-/ a.

conspire /kən'spaɪə(r)/ v.i. combine secretly for unlawful or harmful purpose; agree together.

constable /'kʌnstəb(ə)l/ n. policeman; policeman or policewoman of lowest rank; hist. principal officer of royal household. **Chief Constable** head of police force of county etc.

constabulary /kən'stæbjʊlərɪ/ n. police force.

constancy /'kɒnstənsɪ/ n. quality of being unchanging and dependable.

constant /'kɒnst(ə)nt/ 1 a. continuous; frequently occurring; having constancy. 2 n. Math. & Phys. unvarying quantity.

constellation /kɒnstə'leɪʃ(ə)n/ n. group of fixed stars.

consternation /kɒnstə'neɪʃ(ə)n/ n. amazement or dismay.

constipate /'kɒnstɪpeɪt/ v.t. affect with constipation.

constipation /kɒnstɪ'peɪʃ(ə)n/ n. difficulty in evacuating bowels.

constituency /kən'stɪtjʊənsɪ/ n. body electing representative; area represented.

constituent /kən'stɪtjʊənt/ 1 a. making part of whole; appointing, electing. 2 n. constituent part; member of constituency.

constitute /'kɒnstɪtjuːt/ v.t. be essence or components of; appoint, make into; establish.

constitution /kɒnstɪ'tjuːʃ(ə)n/ n. composition; form in which State is organized; body of fundamental principles according to which State etc. is governed; condition of person's body as regards health, strength, etc.

constitutional /kɒnstɪ'tjuːʃən(ə)l/ 1 a. of or in harmony with or limited by the constitution. 2 n. walk taken as healthy exercise. 3 **constitutionality** n.

constitutive /'kɒnstɪtjuːtɪv/ a. able to form or appoint; constituent.

constrain /kən'streɪn/ v.t. compel, force; confine; in p.p. forced, embarrassed.

constraint /kən'streɪnt/ n. compulsion; restriction; emotional etc. self-control.

constrict /kən'strɪkt/ v.t. compress, make narrow or tight. **constriction** n.; **constrictive** a.

constrictor /kən'strɪktə(r)/ n. muscle that draws together a part; snake that kills by compressing.

construct 1 /kən'strʌkt/ v.t. fit together, frame, build; Geom. draw. 2 /'kɒnstrʌkt/ n. thing constructed, esp. by the mind. 3 **constructor** n.

construction /kən'strʌkʃ(ə)n/ n. constructing or thing constructed; syntactical connection; interpretation or explanation. **constructional** a.

constructive /kən'strʌktɪv/ a. of construction; positive, helpful.

construe /kən'struː/ v.t. interpret; combine grammatically with; translate word for word.

consubstantial /kɒnsəb'stænʃ(ə)l/ a. of one substance.

consubstantiation /kɒnsəbstænʃɪ'eɪʃ(ə)n/ n. doctrine of presence of body and blood of Christ together with bread and wine of Eucharist.

consul /'kɒns(ə)l/ n. official appointed by State to live in foreign town and protect subjects there and assist commerce; hist. either of two annually-elected magistrates in ancient Rome. **consular** a.

consulate /'kɒnsjʊlət/ n. position of consul; consul's official residence.

consult /kən'sʌlt/ v. seek information or advice from; take counsel (with); take into consideration.

consultant /kən'sʌlt(ə)nt/ n. person who gives expert advice in medicine, business, etc. **consultancy** n.

consultation /kɒnsəl'teɪʃ(ə)n/ n. consulting; meeting for consulting.

consultative /kən'sʌltətɪv/ a. of or for consultation.

consume /kən'sjuːm/ v.t. eat or drink; use up; destroy.

consumer /kən'sjuːmə(r)/ n. user of product or service.

consumerism /kən'sjuːmərɪz(ə)m/ n. protection or promotion of consumers' interests.

consummate 1 /kən'sʌmɪt/ a. complete, perfect; supremely skilled. 2 /'kɒnsəmeɪt/ v.t. complete (esp. marriage by sexual intercourse). **3 consummation** n.

consumption /kən'sʌmpʃ(ə)n/ n. consuming; purchase and use of goods etc.; wasting disease, esp. pulmonary tuberculosis.

consumptive /kən'sʌmptɪv/ **1** a. tending to or affected with tuberculosis. **2** n. consumptive person.

contact /'kɒntækt/ **1** n. condition or state of touching, meeting, or communicating; person who is, or may be, contacted for information etc.; *Med.* person likely to carry contagion through being near infected person; *Electr.* connection for passage of current. **2** v.t. get in touch with. **3 contact lens** small lens placed against eyeball to correct faulty vision.

contagion /kən'teɪdʒ(ə)n/ n. spreading of disease by contact; corrupting influence. **contagious** a.

contain /kən'teɪn/ v.t. have or hold or have the capacity for holding within itself; include; comprise; enclose, prevent from moving or extending; control, restrain.

container /kən'teɪnə(r)/ n. vessel, box, etc. designed to contain particular things; large boxlike receptacle of standard design for transport of goods.

containerize /kən'teɪnəraɪz/ v.t. pack in or transport by container. **containerization** n.

containment /kən'teɪnmənt/ n. action or policy of preventing expansion of hostile nation etc.

contaminate /kən'tæmɪneɪt/ v.t. pollute, infect. **contamination** n.

contemn /kən'tem/ v.t. poet. despise; disregard.

contemplate /'kɒntəmpleɪt/ v.t. survey with eyes or mind; regard as possible; intend. **contemplation** n.

contemplative /kən'templətɪv/ a. of or given to (esp.) religious contemplation and prayer.

contemporaneous /kəntempə'reɪnɪəs/ a. existing or occurring at same time.

contemporary /kən'tempərərɪ/ **1** a. belonging to same time or of same age; modern in style or design. **2** n. contemporary person etc.

contempt /kən'tempt/ n. feeling that person or thing is inferior or worthless;

condition of being held in contempt; disobedience, disrespect.

contemptible /kən'temptɪb(ə)l/ a. deserving contempt.

contemptuous /kən'temptjʊəs/ a. feeling or showing contempt.

contend /kən'tend/ v.i. strive, struggle; compete; argue (*with*), maintain (*that*).

content[1] /'kɒntent/ n. what is contained, esp. in vessel or house or book etc. (usu. in *pl.*); capacity (of vessel); amount contained in thing; substance of book etc. as opposed to *form*.

content[2] /kən'tent/ **1** *pred.a.* satisifed (*with*); willing (*to* do). **2** v.t. make content; satisfy. **3** n. contented state, satisfaction. **4 contentment** n.

contention /kən'tenʃ(ə)n/ n. strife, controversy, rivalry; point etc. contended for in argument etc.

contentious /kən'tenʃəs/ a. quarrelsome, likely to cause argument.

contest 1 /'kɒntest/ n. contending; a competition. **2** v.t. /kən'test/ dispute; contend or compete for.

contestant /kən'test(ə)nt/ n. person who takes part in contest.

context /'kɒntekst/ n. what precedes and follows word or passage. **contextual** a.

contiguous /kən'tɪgjʊəs/ a. next to; touching; in contact (*with*). **contiguity** /kɒntɪ'gjuːɪtɪ/ n.

continent /'kɒntɪnənt/ **1** n. one of the main continuous bodies of land of the earth. **2** a. exercising self-restraint; able to control one's excretions. **3 the Continent** mainland of Europe. **4 continence** n.

continental /kɒntɪ'nent(ə)l/ a. of or characteristic of continent; **Continental** characteristic of the Continent. **Continental breakfast** light breakfast of coffee and rolls etc.; **Continental quilt** duvet.

contingency /kən'tɪndʒənsɪ/ n. event that may or may not occur; unknown or unforeseen circumstance.

contingent /kən'tɪndʒ(ə)nt/ **1** a. conditional or dependent (*on*); that may or may not occur; incidental. **2** n. body of troops or ships etc. forming part of larger group.

continual /kən'tɪnjʊəl/ a. frequently recurring; always happening.

continuance /kən'tɪnjʊəns/ n. continuing in existence or operation; duration.

continuation /kəntɪnjʊ'eɪʃ(ə)n/ n. act of continuing; thing that continues something else.

continue /kən'tɪnju:/ v. maintain; keep up; resume; prolong, remain.

continuity /kɒntɪ'nju:ɪtɪ/ n. being continuous; logical sequence; detailed scenario of film; linkage between broadcast items.

continuo /kən'tɪnjʊəʊ/ n. (pl. -nuos) Mus. continuous bass accompaniment played usu. on keyboard instrument.

continuous /kən'tɪnjʊəs/ a. connected without break; uninterrupted.

continuum /kən'tɪnjʊəm/ n. (pl. -nua) thing of continuous structure.

contort /kən'tɔ:t/ v.t. twist or force out of normal shape. **contortion** n.

contortionist /kən'tɔ:ʃənɪst/ n. performer who can twist his body into unusual positions.

contour /'kɒntʊə(r)/ n. outline; line on map joining points at same altitude; line separating differently-coloured parts of design.

contraband /'kɒntrəbænd/ 1 n. smuggled goods; smuggling. 2 a. forbidden to be imported or exported.

contraception /kɒntrə'sepʃ(ə)n/ n. use of contraceptives.

contraceptive /kɒntrə'septɪv/ 1 a. preventive of pregnancy. 2 n. contraceptive device or drug.

contract 1 /'kɒntrækt/ n. written or spoken agreement esp. one enforceable by law; document recording it. 2 /kən'trækt/ v. make or become smaller; make contract; incur (disease, debt); form (habit etc.); draw together; shorten. 3 **contract bridge** type of bridge in which only tricks bid and won count towards game; **contract in, out**, elect to enter, not to enter, scheme etc.

contractile /kən'træktaɪl/ a. capable of or producing contraction.

contraction /kən'trækʃ(ə)n/ n. contracting; shrinking; diminution; shortened word.

contractor /kən'træktə(r)/ n. person who undertakes contract, esp. in building, engineering, etc.

contractual /kən'træktjʊəl/ a. of or in the nature of a contract.

contradict /kɒntrə'dɪkt/ v. deny; oppose verbally; be at variance with. **contradiction** n.; **contradictory** a.

contradistinction /kɒntrədɪs'tɪŋkʃ(ə)n/ n. distinction by contrast.

contralto /kən'træltəʊ/ n. (pl. -tos) lowest female voice; singer with contralto voice; music for contralto voice.

contraption /kən'træpʃ(ə)n/ n. machine or device, esp. strange one.

contrapuntal /kɒntrə'pʌnt(ə)l/ a. of or in counterpoint.

contrariwise /kən'treərɪwaɪz/ adv. on the other hand; in the opposite way.

contrary /'kɒntrərɪ/ 1 a. opposed in nature or tendency or direction; colloq. /kən'treərɪ/ perverse, self-willed. 2 n. the opposite. 3 adv. in opposition (to).

contrast 1 /'kɒntrɑːst/ n. comparison showing striking differences; difference so revealed; thing or person having noticeably different qualities (to); degree of difference between tones in photograph or television picture. 2 /kən'trɑːst/ v. make or show contrast between.

contravene /kɒntrə'vi:n/ v.t. infringe, conflict with. **contravention** n.

contretemps /kɒntrətɑ̃/ n. unlucky accident; embarrassing occurrence.

contribute /kən'trɪbju:t/ □ See page 665. v. give jointly with others (to common fund etc.); supply (article etc.) for publication with others. **contribute** help to bring about. **contributor** n.

contribution /kɒntrɪ'bju:ʃ(ə)n/ n. contributing; thing contributed.

contributory /kən'trɪbjʊtərɪ/ a. that contributes, using contributions.

contrite /kən'traɪt/ a. penitent for one's sin. **contrition** /kən'trɪʃ(ə)n/ n.

contrivance /kən'traɪv(ə)ns/ n. something contrived, esp. a device or plan; act of contriving.

contrive /kən'traɪv/ v. devise, think out; plan, manage.

control /kən'trəʊl/ 1 n. power of directing or restraining; self-restraint; means of restraining or regulating; (usu. in pl.) device to operate machine, esp. car or aircraft etc.; place where something is controlled or verified; standard of comparison for checking results of experiment; personality said to direct actions etc. of spiritualist medium. 2 v.t. have control of; regulate;

serve as control to; verify. **3 in control** in charge (*of*); **out of control** unrestrained.

controller *n.* person or thing that controls; officer controlling expenditure.

controversial /kɒntrə'vɜːʃ(ə)l/ *a.* causing or subject to controversy.

controversy /'kɒntrəvɜːsɪ/ □ See page 666. *n.* dispute, argument.

controvert /kɒntrə'vɜːt/ *v.t.* dispute truth of.

contumacy /'kɒntjʊməsɪ/ *n.* stubborn disobedience. **contumacious** /-'meɪ-/ *a.*

contumely /'kɒntjuːmlɪ/ *n.* insulting language or treatment. **contumelious** /-'miː-/ *a.*

contuse /kən'tjuːz/ *v.t.* bruise. **contusion** *n.*

conundrum /kə'nʌndrəm/ *n.* riddle.

conurbation /kɒnɜː'beɪʃ(ə)n/ *n.* group of towns and suburbs united by expansion.

convalesce /kɒnvə'les/ *v.i.* recover health after illness.

convalescent /kɒnvə'les(ə)nt/ *a.* **1** *a.* recovering from sickness. **2** *n.* convalescent person. **3 convalescence** *n.*

convection /kən'vekʃ(ə)n/ *n.* transmission of heat by movement of heated substance.

convector /kən'vektə(r)/ *n.* heating appliance that circulates warm air.

convene /kən'viːn/ *v.* summon, assemble.

convenience /kən'viːnɪəns/ *n.* quality of being convenient; freedom from difficulty or trouble; advantage; useful thing; public lavatory. **convenience food** manufactured food needing little further preparation.

convenient /kən'viːnɪənt/ *a.* serving one's comfort or interests; available or occurring at suitable time or place; *colloq.* well situated for access.

convent /'kɒnv(ə)nt/ *n.* religious community, esp. of nuns; its house.

convention /kən'venʃ(ə)n/ *n.* assembly or conference; agreement or treaty; general agreement on social behaviour etc. by implicit consent of the majority; customary practice.

conventional /kən'venʃ(ə)n(ə)l/ *a.* depending on or according with convention; attentive to social conventions; not spontaneous or sincere; (of weapon,

power source, etc.) other than nuclear.

conventionalism *n.*; **conventionality** *n.*

converge /kən'vɜːdʒ/ *v.i.* come together or towards the same point. **converge on** approach from different directions. **convergence** *n.*; **convergent** *a.*

conversant /kən'vɜːs(ə)nt/ *a.* well acquainted (*with* subject etc.).

conversation /kɒnvə'seɪʃ(ə)n/ *n.* informal exchange of ideas etc. by spoken words; instance of this.

conversational /kɒnvə'seɪʃ(ə)n(ə)l/ *a.* of or in conversation; colloquial.

conversationalist /kɒnvə'seɪʃənəlɪst/ *n.* person fond of or good at conversation.

converse¹ **1** /kən'vɜːs/ *v.i.* have conversation. **2** /'kɒnvɜːs/ *n. arch.* conversation.

converse² /'kɒnvɜːs/ **1** *a.* opposite, contrary, reversed. **2** *n.* converse statement or proposition.

conversion /kən'vɜːʃ(ə)n/ *n.* converting or being converted.

convert **1** /kən'vɜːt/ *v.t.* change (*into*); cause (person) to change beliefs or party etc.; change (money etc.) into different form or currency etc.; *Rugby footb.* kick goal from (try). **2** /'kɒnvɜːt/ *n.* person converted esp. to religious faith.

convertible /kən'vɜːtɪb(ə)l/ **1** *a.* that may be converted. **2** *n.* motor car with folding or detachable roof.

convex /'kɒnveks/ *a.* curved like outside of sphere or circle. **convexity** *n.*

convey /kən'veɪ/ *v.t.* transport, carry; communicate (meaning etc.); transfer by deed or legal process; transmit.

conveyance /kən'veɪəns/ *n.* conveying; vehicle, carriage; legal transfer of property, deed effecting this.

conveyancing /kən'veɪənsɪŋ/ *n.* branch of law dealing with transfer of property.

convict **1** /kən'vɪkt/ *v.t.* prove or declare guilty. **2** /'kɒnvɪkt/ *n.* sentenced criminal.

conviction /kən'vɪkʃ(ə)n/ *n.* convicting or being convicted; firm belief.

convince /kən'vɪns/ *v.t.* firmly persuade.

convivial /kən'vɪvɪəl/ *a.* fond of company; sociable, lively. **conviviality** *n.*

convocation /kɒnvəˈkeɪʃ(ə)n/ *n.* convoking; provincial synod of Anglican clergy; legislative assembly of university.

convoke /kənˈvəʊk/ *v.t.* call together; summon to assembly.

convoluted /kɒnvəˈljuːtɪd/ *a.* coiled, twisted; complex.

convolution /kɒnvəˈljuːʃ(ə)n/ *n.* coiling, coil, twist.

convolvulus /kənˈvɒlvjʊləs/ *n.* twining plant, esp. bindweed.

convoy /ˈkɒnvɔɪ/ 1 *v.t.* escort as protection. 2 *n.* convoying; group of ships, vehicles, etc., travelling together.

convulse /kənˈvʌls/ *v.t.* affect with convulsions.

convulsion /kənˈvʌlʃ(ə)n/ *n.* violent irregular motions of limbs or body caused by momentary contraction of muscles; violent disturbance; in *pl.* uncontrollable laughter. **convulsive** *a.*

cony /ˈkəʊnɪ/ *n.* rabbit.

coo 1 *n.* soft murmuring sound as of doves. 2 *v.i.* emit coo.

cooee /ˈkuːiː/ 1 *n.* & *int.* sound used to attract attention esp. at a distance. 2 *v.i.* emit cooee.

cook /kʊk/ 1 *v.* prepare food; prepare (food) by heating; undergo cooking; *colloq.* falsify (accounts etc.). 2 *n.* person who cooks esp. professionally or in specified way.

cooker /ˈkʊkə(r)/ *n.* appliance or vessel for cooking food; fruit etc. suitable for cooking.

cookery /ˈkʊkərɪ/ *n.* art of cooking. **cookery-book** book of recipes and instructions in cookery.

cookie /ˈkʊkɪ/ *n. US* sweet biscuit.

cool /kuːl/ 1 *a.* of or at fairly low temperature; suggesting or achieving coolness; unperturbed, self-possessed; lacking zeal or cordiality. 2 *n.* coolness; cool place; *sl.* composure. 3 *v.* make or become cool. 4 **cool one's heels** be kept waiting. 5 **coolly** *adv.*

coolant /ˈkuːlənt/ *n.* cooling agent esp. fluid to remove heat from engine.

cooler /ˈkuːlə(r)/ *n.* vessel in which thing is cooled; *sl.* prison cell.

coolie /ˈkuːlɪ/ *n.* unskilled native labourer in Eastern countries.

coomb /kuːm/ *n.* valley on side of hill; steep valley.

coon /kuːn/ *n.* racoon.

coop /kuːp/ 1 *n.* cage for keeping poultry. 2 *v.t.* keep (fowl) in coop; confine.

co-op /ˈkəʊɒp/ *n. colloq.* co-operative society or shop; co-operative.

cooper /ˈkuːpə(r)/ *n.* maker or repairer of casks and barrels.

co-operate /kəʊˈɒpəreɪt/ *v.i.* work or act together. **co-operation** *n.*

co-operative /kəʊˈɒpərətɪv/ 1 *a.* co-operating, willing to co-operate; jointly owned by and managed for use and profit of members of organized group. 2 *n.* co-operative association or enterprise. 3 **co-operative society** trading etc. organization in which profits are shared among members esp. as dividend on purchases.

co-opt /kəʊˈɒpt/ *v.t.* elect into body by votes of existing members. **co-option** *n.*; **co-optive** *a.*

co-ordinate 1 /kəʊˈɔːdɪnət/ *a.* equal in status. 2 /kəʊˈɔːdɪnət/ *n.* each of set of quantities used to fix position of point, line, or plane; in *pl.* items of women's clothing that can be worn together harmoniously. 3 /kəʊˈɔːdɪneɪt/ *v.t.* make co-ordinate; bring into proper relation; cause to function together or in proper order. 4 **co-ordination** *n.*; **co-ordinative** *a.*; **co-ordinator** *n.*

coot /kuːt/ *n.* a water-bird.

cop *sl.* 1 *n.* policeman; capture. 2 *v.t.* catch. 3 **cop-out** cowardly evasion.

copal /ˈkəʊp(ə)l/ *n.* kind of resin used for varnish.

copartner /kəʊˈpɑːtnə(r)/ *n.* partner, associate. **copartnership** *n.*

cope[1] *v.i.* deal effectively or contend *with*; *colloq.* manage successfully.

cope[2] *n.* long cloak worn by priest in processions etc. 2 *v.t.* furnish with cope or coping.

copeck /ˈkəʊpek/ *n.* hundredth of rouble.

copier /ˈkɒpɪə(r)/ *n.* person or machine that copies (esp. documents).

coping /ˈkəʊpɪŋ/ *n.* top course of masonry or brickwork, usu. sloping. **coping-stone** stone used in coping.

copious /ˈkəʊpɪəs/ *a.* abundant, plentiful; producing much.

copper[1] /ˈkɒpə(r)/ 1 *n.* metal of brownish-pink colour; bronze coin. 2 *a.* made of or coloured like copper. 3 *v.t.* cover with copper. 4 **copperplate** copper plate for engraving or etching, print taken from it, sloping rounded cursive handwriting.

copper² /'kɒpə(r)/ *n. sl.* policeman.

coppice /'kɒpɪs/ *n.* small wood of undergrowth and small trees.

copula /'kɒpjʊlə/ *n.* part of verb *be* connecting subject with predicate.

copulate /'kɒpjʊleɪt/ *v.i.* have sexual intercourse. **copulation** *n.*

copy /'kɒpɪ/ **1** *n.* thing made to look like another; specimen of book etc.; matter to be printed; material of newspaper article; text of advertisement. **2** *v.* make copy (of); imitate. **3 copy-book** book containing models of handwriting etc. for learners to imitate; **copy-typist** typist working from copy; **copy-writer** writer of copy esp. for advertisements.

copyist /'kɒpɪɪst/ *n.* person who makes copies; imitator.

copyright /'kɒpɪraɪt/ **1** *n.* exclusive right to print, publish, perform, etc., a work. **2** *a.* protected by copyright. **3** *v.t.* secure copyright for.

coquette /kɒ'ket/ **1** *n.* woman who flirts. **2** *v.i.* flirt. **3 coquettish** *a.*; **coquetry** *n.*

coracle /'kɒrək(ə)l/ *n.* small boat made of wicker covered with waterproof material.

coral /'kɒr(ə)l/ **1** *n.* hard substance built up by marine polyps. **2** *a.* of coral, of red colour of coral. **3 coral island** one formed by growth of coral. **4 coralline** /-laɪn/ *a.*

cor anglais /kɔːr 'ɑ̃gleɪ/ *n.* wood-wind instrument like oboe but lower in pitch.

corbel /'kɔːb(ə)l/ *n.* stone or timber projection from wall, acting as supporting bracket.

cord **1** *n.* thick string; piece of this; similar structure in body; ribbed cloth, esp. corduroy; in *pl.* corduroy trousers; electric flex or telephone wire. **2** *v.t.* secure with cords.

cordial /'kɔːdɪəl/ **1** *a.* heartfelt, sincere; warm, friendly. **2** *n.* fruit-flavoured drink. **3 cordiality** *n.*

cordite /'kɔːdaɪt/ *n.* smokeless explosive.

cordon /'kɔːd(ə)n/ **1** *n.* line or circle of police etc.; ornamental cord or braid; fruit-tree trained to grow as single stem. **2** *v.t.* enclose or separate *off* with cordon of police etc.

cordon bleu /kɔːdɔ̃ 'blɜː/ first-class cook.

corduroy /'kɔːdərɔɪ/ *n.* fabric with velvety ribs; in *pl.* corduroy trousers.

core **1** *n.* horny central part of certain fruits, containing seeds; centre or most important part of anything; region of fissile material in nuclear reactor; unit of structure in computer, storing one bit of data; inner strand of electric cable; piece of soft iron forming centre of magnet etc. **2** *v.t.* remove core from.

coreopsis /kɒrɪ'ɒpsɪs/ *n.* plant with daisy-like usu. yellow flowers.

co-respondent /kəʊrɪ'spɒnd(ə)nt/ *n.* person charged with committing adultery with respondent in divorce case.

corgi /'kɔːgɪ/ *n.* small Welsh breed of dog.

coriander /kɒrɪ'ændə(r)/ *n.* aromatic plant with fruit (**coriander seed**) used as flavouring.

cork **1** *n.* thick light tough elastic bark of cork-oak; piece of this as bottle-stopper, float, etc. **2** *v.t.* stop (*up*) (as) with cork; bottle *up* (feelings etc.).

corkage /'kɔːkɪdʒ/ *n.* charge made by restaurant etc. for serving wine etc.

corked /kɔːkt/ *a.* (of wine) spoiled by defective cork.

corkscrew /'kɔːkskruː/ **1** *n.* spiral steel device for extracting corks from bottles. **2** *v.* move spirally.

corm *n.* swollen underground stem in certain plants, e.g. crocus.

cormorant /'kɔːmərənt/ *n.* large voracious sea-bird.

corn¹ *n.* cereal before or after harvesting, esp. wheat or maize; grain or seed of cereal plant; *colloq.* something corny. **corn-cob** cylindrical centre of ear of maize (**corn on the cob** maize eaten in this form); **corncrake** bird with harsh grating cry; **corn dolly** figure made of plaited straw; **cornflakes** breakfast cereal of toasted flakes made from maize flour; **cornflour** fine-ground maize flour; **cornflower** blue-flowered plant growing in cornfields.

corn² *n.* horny tender place with hard centre, esp. on foot.

cornea /'kɔːnɪə/ *n.* transparent membrane covering iris and pupil of eyeball.

corned /kɔːnd/ a. preserved in salt or brine.

cornel /ˈkɔːn(ə)l/ n. a hard-wooded tree; cornelian cherry.

cornelian /kɔːˈniːliən/ n. red dull variety of chalcedony.

cornelian cherry /kɔːˈniːliən/ European berry-bearing tree.

corner /ˈkɔːnə(r)/ 1 n. place where converging sides, edges, streets, etc. meet; recess formed by meeting of two internal sides of room, box, etc.; difficult or inescapable position; remote or secluded place; action or result of buying whole available stock of a commodity. 2 v. force into difficult or inescapable position; establish corner in (commodity); move round corner. 3 **corner-stone** stone in projecting angle of wall, indispensable part or basis.

cornet /ˈkɔːnɪt/ n. brass musical instrument resembling trumpet; conical wafer for holding ice cream.

cornice /ˈkɔːnɪs/ n. horizontal moulding in relief, esp. along top of internal wall.

Cornish /ˈkɔːnɪʃ/ 1 a. of Cornwall. 2 n. Celtic language of Cornwall. 3 **Cornish pasty** seasoned meat and vegetables baked in pastry.

cornucopia /kɔːnjʊˈkəʊpiə/ n. symbol of plenty.

corny /ˈkɔːnɪ/ a. colloq. old-fashioned, trite, sentimental.

corolla /kəˈrɒlə/ n. whorl of petals forming inner envelope of flower.

corollary /kəˈrɒlərɪ/ n. proposition that follows from one proved; natural consequence.

corona /kəˈrəʊnə/ n. (pl. -nae /-niː/) small circle of light round sun or moon, esp. that seen in total eclipse of sun.

coronary /ˈkɒrənərɪ/ 1 a. of the arteries supplying blood to the heart. 2 n. coronary artery or thrombosis. 3 **coronary thrombosis** blockage of coronary artery by blood-clot.

coronation /kɒrəˈneɪʃ(ə)n/ n. ceremony of crowning sovereign.

coroner /ˈkɒrənə(r)/ n. officer holding inquest on deaths thought to be violent or accidental.

coronet /ˈkɒrənɪt/ n. small crown.

corpora pl. of **corpus**.

corporal[1] /ˈkɔːpər(ə)l/ n. non-

commissioned army or RAF officer next below sergeant.

corporal[2] /ˈkɔːpər(ə)l/ a. of human body. **corporal punishment** punishment by flogging etc. **corporality** n.

corporate /ˈkɔːpərət/ a. of or being or belonging to a corporation or group.

corporation /kɔːpəˈreɪʃ(ə)n/ n. body of persons authorized to act as individual; civic authorities.

corporative /ˈkɔːpərətɪv/ a. of corporation; (of State) organized in professional, industrial, etc. corporations.

corporeal /kɔːˈpɔːrɪəl/ a. having body; material, tangible. **corporeality** n.

corps /kɔː(r)/ n. (pl. same /kɔːz/) military force; organized body.

corpse /kɔːps/ n. dead (usu. human) body.

corpulent /ˈkɔːpjʊlənt/ a. fleshy, bulky. **corpulence** n.

corpus /ˈkɔːpəs/ n. (pl. **corpora** /ˈkɔːpərə/) body of writings of particular kind; collection.

corpuscle /ˈkɔːpʌs(ə)l/ n. minute body or cell in organism, esp. (in pl.) red and white cells in blood of vertebrates. **corpuscular** /-ˈpʌs-/ a.

corral /kəˈrɑːl/ US 1 n. pen for horses, cattle, etc., or for capturing wild animals. 2 v.t. (past & p.p. **corralled**) put or keep in corral.

correct /kəˈrekt/ 1 a. true, accurate; proper, in accordance with taste, standards, etc. 2 v.t. set right; mark errors in; admonish; counteract; bring into accordance with standard. 3 **corrector** n.

correction /kəˈrekʃ(ə)n/ n. correcting; thing substituted for what is wrong; arch. punishment.

correctitude /kəˈrektɪtjuːd/ n. consciously correct behaviour.

corrective /kəˈrektɪv/ 1 a. serving to correct. 2 n. corrective measure or thing.

correlate /ˈkɒrɪleɪt/ 1 v. have or bring into mutual relation (with, to). 2 n. each of two related or complementary things. 3 **correlation** n.

correlative /kəˈrelətɪv/ 1 a. having a mutual relation; Gram. corresponding and regularly used together. 2 n. correlative thing or word.

correspond /kɒrɪˈspɒnd/ v.i. be analogous (to) or in agreement (with); communicate by interchange of letters.

correspondence /kɒrɪ'spɒnd(ə)ns/ n. agreement or similarity; communication by letters; letters sent or received. **correspondence course** course of study conducted by post.

correspondent /kɒrɪ'spɒnd(ə)nt/ n. person who writes letters to another; person employed by newspaper etc. to write regularly on particular subject.

corridor /'kɒrɪdɔː(r)/ n. passage or gallery with doors leading into many rooms etc.; passage in railway coach giving access along its length; strip of territory etc. running through or over territory of another state etc.

corrigendum /kɒrɪ'dʒendəm/ n. (pl. -da) thing to be corrected, esp. in book.

corrigible /'kɒrɪdʒɪb(ə)l/ a. that can be corrected.

corroborate /kə'rɒbəreɪt/ v.t. give support to, confirm. **corroboration** n.; **corroborative** a.; **corroboratory** a.

corrode /kə'rəʊd/ v. wear away, esp. by chemical action; destroy gradually; decay.

corrosion /kə'rəʊʒ(ə)n/ n. corroding; corroded part or substance. **corrosive** a. & n.

corrugate /'kɒrəgeɪt/ v. bend into wavy ridges. **corrugation** n.

corrupt /kə'rʌpt/ 1 a. morally depraved; influenced by or using bribery. 2 v. make or become corrupt. 3 **corruptible** a.; **corruption** n.

corsage /kɔː'sɑːʒ/ n. US small bouquet worn by woman.

corsair /'kɔː'seə(r)/ n. pirate ship; pirate.

corset /'kɔːsɪt/ n. tight-fitting supporting undergarment worn esp. by women.

corslet /'kɔːslɪt/ n. garment covering body; hist. coat of armour.

cortège /kɔː'teɪʒ/ n. procession, esp. for funeral.

cortex /'kɔːteks/ n. outer covering of some organs; outer grey matter of brain. **cortical** a.

cortisone /'kɔːtɪzəʊn/ n. hormone used medicinally against inflammation and allergy.

corundum /kə'rʌndəm/ n. crystallized native alumina used as abrasive.

coruscate /'kɒrəskeɪt/ v.i. sparkle, flash. **coruscation** n.

corvette /kɔː'vet/ n. small naval escort-vessel.

cos¹ /kɒs/ n. crisp long-leaved lettuce.

cos² /kɒs/ abbr. cosine.

cosh colloq. 1 n. short heavy stick. 2 v.t. hit with cosh.

cosine /'kəʊsaɪn/ n. sine of complement of given angle.

cosmetic /kɒz'metɪk/ 1 a. designed to beautify hair or skin etc.; intended (only) to improve appearances. 2 n. cosmetic preparation. 3 **cosmetic surgery** undertaken to correct defects or alter features etc. 4 **cosmetically** adv.

cosmic /'kɒzmɪk/ a. of the cosmos. **cosmic rays** high-energy radiations originating in outer space.

cosmogony /kɒz'mɒgənɪ/ n. origin of universe; theory about this.

cosmology /kɒz'mɒlədʒɪ/ n. science or theory of the universe. **cosmological** a.; **cosmologist** n.

cosmonaut /'kɒzmənɔːt/ n. Russian astronaut.

cosmopolitan /kɒzmə'pɒlɪt(ə)n/ 1 a. of all parts of world; free from national limitations. 2 n. cosmopolitan person. 3 **cosmopolitanism** n.

cosmos /'kɒzmɒs/ n. universe as a well-ordered whole.

Cossack /'kɒsæk/ n. member of S. Russian people famous as horsemen.

cosset /'kɒsɪt/ v.t. pamper, pet.

cost 1 v.t. (past & p.p. cost) have as price; involve payment or sacrifice of; (past & p.p. costed) fix or estimate cost of. 2 n. what thing costs; in pl. legal expenses. 3 **cost-effective** effective in relation to its cost; **cost of living** cost of basic necessities of life.

costal /'kɒst(ə)l/ a. of ribs.

coster(monger) /'kɒstəmʌŋgə(r)/ n. person who sells fruit etc. from barrow.

costive /'kɒstɪv/ a. constipated.

costly /'kɒstlɪ/ a. costing much, expensive. **costliness** n.

costume /'kɒstjuːm/ n. style of dress; set of outer clothes; garment(s) for particular activity; matching jacket and skirt; actor's clothes for part. **costume jewellery** jewellery made from artificial materials.

costumier /kɒs'tjuːmɪə(r)/ n. person who deals in or makes costumes.

cosy /'kəʊzɪ/ 1 a. snug, comfortable. 2

n. cloth etc. cover to retain warmth in teapot or boiled egg.

cot[1] *n.* small tall-sided bed for child etc.; small or light bed. **cot-death** unexplained death of sleeping baby.

cot[2] *n. poet.* small shelter, cote; small cottage.

cote *n.* shelter esp. for birds or animals.

coterie /'kəʊtərɪ/ *n.* set of persons with exclusive interests; select circle.

cotoneaster /kətəʊnɪ'æstə(r)/ *n.* shrub or small tree bearing red or orange berries.

cottage /'kɒtɪdʒ/ *n.* small house, esp. in the country. **cottage cheese** soft white cheese; **cottage hospital** one without resident medical staff; **cottage industry** one carried on at home; **cottage loaf** one with smaller mass of bread on top of larger; **cottage pie** shepherd's pie.

cottager /'kɒtɪdʒə(r)/ *n.* person who lives in cottage.

cotter pin /'kɒtə(r)/ bolt or wedge for securing parts of machinery.

cotton /'kɒt(ə)n/ 1 *n.* white downy fibrous substance covering seeds of certain plants; such a plant; thread or cloth made from this. 2 *v.i.* be drawn *to*. 3 **cotton on (to)** *sl.* understand; **cotton wool** raw cotton, wadding made from this.

cotyledon /kɒtɪ'liːd(ə)n/ *n.* first leaf produced by plant embryo.

couch /kaʊtʃ/ 1 *n.* piece of furniture made for reclining on; sofa; *arch.* bed. 2 *v.* express *in* specified terms; place (as) on couch; (of animal) lie, esp. in lair.

couchette /kuː'ʃet/ *n.* railway carriage etc. with seats convertible into sleeping-berths; berth in this.

couch-grass /'kɒtʃgrɑːs/ *n.* kind of grass with long creeping roots.

cougar /'kuːgə(r)/ *n. US* puma.

cough /kɒf/ 1 *v.* expel air from lungs violently and with characteristic noise. 2 *n.* act or sound of coughing; condition of respiratory organs causing coughing. 3 **cough mixture** medicine to relieve cough; **cough-sweet** medicated sweet to relieve cough; **cough up** *sl.* bring out or provide (money, information, etc.) reluctantly.

could *past* of **can**[1].

coulomb /'kuːlɒm/ *n.* unit of electric charge.

coulter /'kəʊltə(r)/ *n.* vertical blade in front of ploughshare.

council /'kaʊns(ə)l/ *n.* advisory, deliberative, or administrative body; local administrative body of county, city, town, etc. **council house** house owned and let by local council.

councillor /'kaʊnsələ(r)/ *n.* member of council.

counsel /'kaʊns(ə)l/ 1 *n.* advice; consultation; legal adviser, esp. barrister; a group of these. 2 *v.t.* advise.

counsellor /'kaʊnsələ(r)/ *n.* adviser.

count[1] /kaʊnt/ 1 *v.* find number of esp. by assigning successive numerals; repeat numerals in order; include or be included in reckoning or consideration; consider to be. 2 *n.* counting, reckoning; total; *Law* each charge in an indictment. 3 **countdown** counting numbers backwards to zero, esp. before launching rocket etc.; **count on** rely on for help etc.; **count out** exclude; complete count of 10 seconds over (fallen boxer etc.).

count[2] /kaʊnt/ *n.* foreign nobleman equivalent in rank to earl.

countenance /'kaʊntɪnəns/ 1 *n.* face, esp. with respect to its expression; composure of face; moral support. 2 *v.t.* give approval to; connive at.

counter[1] /'kaʊntə(r)/ *n.* flat-topped fitment in bank or shop etc., at which customer is served or business transacted; similar structure in cafeteria etc.; small disc etc. used in scoring at cards etc.; token representing coin; device for counting things.

counter[2] /'kaʊntə(r)/ 1 *v.* oppose, contradict; meet or baffle by answering move etc. 2 *adv.* in opposite direction 3 *a.* opposite. 4 *n.* return blow, countermove; curved part of ship's stern.

counteract /kaʊntə'rækt/ *v.t.* neutralize or hinder by contrary action. **counteraction** *n.*

counter-attack /kaʊntərə'tæk/ *v.* & *n.* attack in reply to enemy's attack.

counterbalance /kaʊntə'bæləns/ 1 *n.* weight balancing another. 2 *v.t.* neutralize by contrary force or influence.

counter-clockwise /kaʊntə-'klɒkwaɪz/ *adv.* & *a.* anticlockwise.

counter-espionage /ˈkaʊntər-ˈespɪənaːʒ/ n. action against an enemy's spy system.

counterfeit /ˈkaʊntəfɪt/ 1 a. made in imitation; forged; not genuine. 2 n. counterfeit thing. 3 v.t. imitate; forge; simulate.

counterfoil /ˈkaʊntəfɔɪl/ n. part of cheque, receipt, etc. retained as record.

counter-intelligence /ˈkaʊntər-ɪnˈtelɪdʒ(ə)ns/ n. counter-espionage.

countermand /ˈkaʊntəˈmaːnd/ v.t. revoke (order), recall by contrary order; cancel order for.

countermarch /ˈkaʊntəmaːtʃ/ 1 n. march in opposite direction. 2 v. (cause to) march back.

counterpane /ˈkaʊntəpeɪn/ n. bedspread.

counterpart /ˈkaʊntəpaːt/ n. duplicate; person or thing naturally complementary to another.

counterpoint /ˈkaʊntəpɔɪnt/ n. Mus. harmonious combination of simultaneous parts or voices in music; one part or voice added to another.

counterpoise /ˈkaʊntəpɔɪz/ 1 n. balancing of each other by two weights or forces; counterbalancing weight or force. 2 v.t. counterbalance; compensate for.

counter-productive /ˈkaʊntəprəˈdʌktɪv/ a. having the opposite of the desired effect.

counter-revolution /ˈkaʊntərevəˈluːʃ(ə)n/ n. revolution opposed to former one or reversing its effects.

countersign /ˈkaʊntəsaɪn/ 1 v. add confirming signature to. 2 n. word to be given in answer to sentry's challenge.

countersink /ˈkaʊntəsɪŋk/ v.t. (past & p.p. -sunk) shape (screw-hole) so that screw-head lies level with surface; provide (screw) with countersunk hole.

counter-tenor /ˈkaʊntətenə(r)/ n. male alto.

countervail /ˈkaʊntəveɪl/ v. counterbalance; avail against.

countess /ˈkaʊntɪs/ n. earl's or count's wife or widow; woman with own rank of earl or count.

countless /ˈkaʊntlɪs/ a. too many to count.

countrified /ˈkʌntrɪfaɪd/ a. rustic.

country /ˈkʌntrɪ/ n. nation's territory; State of which one is a member; land of a region with regard to its aspect etc.; open regions of fields etc. as opp. town; country-and-western. **country-and-western** rural or cowboy songs to guitar etc.; **country dance** rural or traditional dance; **countryman**, **countrywoman**, member of same State or district as oneself, person living in rural parts; **country seat** country house with park; **countryside** rural areas generally.

county /ˈkaʊntɪ/ n. territorial division of country, forming chief unit of local administration and justice; political and administrative division of State of US etc.; people, esp. gentry, of county. **county council** elective governing body of county; **county court** local judicial court (in England for civil actions); **county town** town that is centre of county administration.

coup /kuː/ n. successful stroke or move; coup d'état.

coup de grâce /kuː də ˈgraːs/ finishing stroke. [F]

coup d'état /kuː deɪˈtaː/ sudden overthrow of government esp. by force. [F]

coupé /ˈkuːpeɪ/ n. closed 2-door car with sloping back.

couple /ˈkʌp(ə)l/ 1 n. man and woman together, esp. married etc.; pair of partners in dance etc.; two things or a few. 2 v. link or fasten or associate together; copulate.

couplet /ˈkʌplɪt/ n. pair of successive lines of rhyming verse.

coupling /ˈkʌplɪŋ/ n. link connecting railway-carriages or parts of machine.

coupon /ˈkuːpɒn/ n. detachable ticket or form entitling holder to something.

courage /ˈkʌrɪdʒ/ n. readiness to face and capacity to endure danger; courageous mood. **courageous** /kəˈreɪdʒəs/ a.

courgette /kʊəˈʒet/ n. small vegetable marrow.

courier /ˈkʊrɪə(r)/ n. special messenger; person employed to guide and assist group of tourists.

course /kɔːs/ 1 n. onward movement in space or time; direction of going; line of conduct or action; series or sequence; series of lectures or lessons etc.; each of successive parts of meal; golf-course, race-course, etc.; continuous line of masonry or bricks at one level of building. **2** *v.* use hounds in coursing; move or flow freely.

courser /'kɔːsə(r)/ *n.* swift horse.

court /kɔːt/ **1** *n.* space enclosed by wall or buildings; number of houses enclosing a yard; area within walls or marked boundaries used for some games; sovereign's residence, his establishment and retinue; body with judicial powers, tribunal; place in which court sits. **2** *v.t.* treat with flattering or amorous attention; seek favour or love of; unwisely invite. **3** **court-card** playing-card that is king or queen or jack; **court martial** (*pl.* **courts martial**) judicial court of military officers; **court-martial** try by court martial; **court shoe** woman's light shoe with low-cut upper; **courtyard** space enclosed by walls or buildings; **pay court to** court (person) to win favour.

courteous /'kɜːtɪəs/ *a.* polite, considerate.

courtesan /kɔːtɪ'zæn/ *n.* prostitute, esp. one whose clients are wealthy or upper-class.

courtesy /'kɜːtəsɪ/ *n.* courteous behaviour or act. **courtesy light** light in car switched on when door is opened.

courtier /'kɔːtɪə(r)/ *n.* companion of sovereign at court.

courtly /'kɔːtlɪ/ *a.* polished or refined in manners. **courtliness** *n.*

courtship /'kɔːtʃɪp/ *n.* courting esp. of intended spouse or mate.

cousin /'kʌz(ə)n/ *n.* child of one's uncle or aunt. **cousinly** *a.*

couture /kuː'tjʊə(r)/ *n.* design and making of fashionable garments.

cove 1 *n.* small bay or inlet of coast; sheltered recess; curved moulding at junction of ceiling and walls. **2** *v.t.* provide (room etc.) with cove.

coven /'kʌv(ə)n/ *n.* assembly of witches.

covenant /'kʌvənənt/ **1** *n.* agreement, *Law* sealed contract. **2** *v.* agree, esp. by legal covenant.

Coventry /'kɒvəntrɪ/ *n.* **send to Coventry** refuse to associate with.

cover /'kʌvə/ **1** *v.t.* be over whole top or front of; lie over or above; conceal or shield; enclose or include; (of sum) be large enough to meet (expense); protect by insurance; investigate or describe as reporter; have within range

(of gun etc.). **2** *n.* thing that covers, wrapper; screen or pretence; shelter, protection; funds to meet liability or contingent loss; place laid for one person at meal. **3** **cover charge** service charge per person in restaurant; **cover-point** *Crick.* fielder standing behind point.

coverage /'kʌvərɪdʒ/ *n.* area or amount covered or reached; reporting of events in newspaper etc.

coverlet /'kʌvəlɪt/ *n.* cover lying over other bedclothes.

covert /'kʌvət/ **1** *a.* secret, disguised; not open or explicit. **2** *n.* wood or thicket affording cover for game; in *pl.* feathers covering base of wing and tail feathers.

covet /'kʌvɪt/ *v.t.* envy another the possession of; long to possess.

covetous /'kʌvɪtəs/ *a.* avaricious, grasping.

covey /'kʌvɪ/ *n.* brood of partridges etc.; family, set.

cow[1] /kaʊ/ *n.* fully-grown female of any bovine animal, esp. of domestic kind; female of elephant or rhinoceros or whale or seal etc. **cowboy** *US* man in charge of grazing cattle on ranch, *colloq.* unscrupulous or reckless business man or workman; **cowherd** person who looks after cattle at pasture; **cowhide** cow's hide, leather or whip made of this; **cow-pat** roundish flat piece of cow-dung; **cowpox** disease of cows, source of smallpox vaccine.

cow[2] /kaʊ/ *v.t.* intimidate.

coward /'kaʊəd/ *n.* person having little or no bravery.

cowardice /'kaʊədɪs/ *n.* cowardly conduct.

cowardly /'kaʊədlɪ/ *a.* of or like a coward.

cower /'kaʊə(r)/ *v.i.* crouch or shrink with fear or with cold.

cowl /kaʊl/ *n.* monk's hooded cloak; its hood; hood-shaped top of chimney or shaft. **cowl neck** wide loose roll neck on garment.

cowrie /'kaʊrɪ/ *n.* tropical mollusc with bright shell; its shell, used as money in some parts of Asia etc.

cowslip /'kaʊslɪp/ *n.* yellow-flowered plant growing in pastures etc.

cox 1 *n.* coxswain. **2** *v.* act as cox (of).

coxcomb /'kɒkskəʊm/ *n.* conceited

showy person; *hist.* medieval jester's cap.

coxswain /ˈkɒks(ə)n or ˈkɒksweɪn/ *n.* steersman of (esp. rowing-)boat.

coy *a.* (affectedly) modest, shy.

coyote /ˈkɔɪˈəʊtɪ/ *n.* N. Amer. prairie-wolf.

coypu /ˈkɔɪpuː/ *n.* aquatic beaver-like rodent orig. from S. Amer.

cozen /ˈkʌz(ə)n/ *v.* cheat; defraud.

crab 1 *n.* shellfish with ten legs; flesh of edible species of this; crab-apple; crab-louse. **2** *v. colloq.* criticize adversely; act so as to spoil. **3 catch a crab** get oar jammed under water by faulty stroke; **crab-apple** wild apple-tree, sour fruit of this; **crab-louse** parasite infesting human body.

crabbed /ˈkræbd/ *a.* crabby; (of hand-writing) ill-formed and hard to decipher.

crabby /ˈkræbɪ/ *a.* perverse, morose, irritable.

crack 1 *n.* sudden sharp noise; sharp blow; narrow opening; split or rift not extending far enough to break thing; *sl.* cutting or witty remark. **2** *v.* (cause to) make crack; suffer crack or partial break; (of voice) become dissonant as effect of emotion or age; tell (joke); open (bottle of wine etc.); break into (safe); find solution to (problem); give way, yield. **3 crack-brained** crazy; **crack down on** take severe measures against; **crack of dawn** daybreak; **crackpot** *colloq.* eccentric or impractical person; **crack up** *colloq.* collapse under strain.

cracked /krækt/ *a. colloq.* crazy.

cracker /ˈkrækə(r)/ *n.* explosive firework; small paper cylinder containing paper hat, etc., and exploding with crack when ends are pulled; thin crisp savoury biscuit.

crackers /ˈkrækəz/ *pred.a. colloq.* crazy.

crackle /ˈkræk(ə)l/ **1** *n.* sound of repeated slight cracking. **2** *v.i.* emit crackle.

crackling /ˈkræklɪŋ/ *n.* crisp skin of roast pork.

cracknel /ˈkrækn(ə)l/ *n.* light crisp biscuit.

cradle /ˈkreɪd(ə)l/ **1** *n.* infant's bed esp. on rockers; place regarded as origin of something; supporting framework or

structure. **2** *v.t.* place in cradle; contain or shelter as in cradle.

craft /krɑːft/ *n.* skill, cunning; branch of skilled handiwork; (*pl.* same) boat, vessel, aircraft, or spacecraft.

craftsman /ˈkrɑːftsmən/ *n.* (*pl.* **-men**) person who practises a craft; private soldier in REME. **craftsmanship** *n.*

crafty /ˈkrɑːftɪ/ *a.* cunning, artful; ingenious.

crag *n.* steep rugged rock. **craggy** *a.*

cram *v.* fill to excess; force (thing) *into*; study intensively for examination.

cramp 1 *n.* sudden painful contraction of muscles from chill or strain etc. **2** *v.t.* affect with cramp; restrict, enclose too narrowly.

cramped /kræmpt/ *a.* (of space) too narrow; (of handwriting) small and difficult to read.

crampon /ˈkræmpɒn/ *n.* spiked iron plate fixed to boot for climbing etc. on ice.

cranberry /ˈkrænbərɪ/ *n.* small dark-red acid berry; shrub bearing it.

crane 1 *n.* machine for moving heavy weights; large wading bird. **2** *v.* stretch (one's neck) in order to see something. **3 crane-fly** two-winged long-legged fly; **crane's-bill** kind of wild geranium.

cranium /ˈkreɪnɪəm/ *n.* (*pl.* **-nia**) bones enclosing brain, skull. **cranial** *a.*

crank 1 *n.* part of axis bent at right angles for converting rotary into reciprocal motion and vice versa; eccentric person. **2** *v.t.* turn with crank. **3 crankpin** pin attaching connecting-rod to crank; **crankshaft** shaft driven by crank; **crank up** start (motor engine) by turning crank.

cranky /ˈkræŋkɪ/ *a.* shaky; eccentric; ill-tempered.

cranny /ˈkrænɪ/ *n.* chink, crevice.

crap *vulg.* **1** *n.* faeces; nonsense; rubbish. **2** *v.i.* defecate. **3 crappy** *a.*

crape *n.* crêpe, usu. of black silk, esp. for mourning-dress.

craps *n. US* game of chance played with dice.

crapulence /ˈkræpjʊləns/ *n.* state following intemperate drinking or eating. **crapulent** *a.*; **crapulous** *a.*

crash 1 *n.* sudden violent noise; violent fall or impact esp. with loud noise; sudden downfall or collapse; *attrib.* done rapidly or urgently. **2** *v.* (cause to) fall or collide with crash; make crash; (of aircraft or pilot) fall violently to land or sea; fail, esp. financially; gatecrash. **3 crash barrier** barrier against car leaving road etc.; **crash-dive** (of submarine) dive hastily and steeply, (of aircraft) dive and crash; **crash-helmet** helmet worn to protect head in case of crash; **crash-land** (of aircraft or pilot) make emergency landing.

crass *a.* grossly stupid; insensitive.

crate 1 *n.* open-work case of wooden bars or basket-work etc. **2** *v.t.* pack in crate.

crater /ˈkreɪtə(r)/ *n.* mouth of volcano; bowl-shaped cavity.

cravat /krəˈvæt/ *n.* scarf, neck-tie.

crave *v.t.* greatly desire, long for; *arch.* ask for

craven /ˈkreɪv(ə)n/ **1** *a.* cowardly, abject. **2** *n.* craven person.

craving /ˈkreɪvɪŋ/ *n.* strong desire, longing.

craw *n.* crop of bird or insect.

crawfish /ˈkrɔːfɪʃ/ *n.* large spiny sea-lobster.

crawl 1 *v.i.* move slowly with body on or close to ground, or on hands and knees; go slowly; *colloq.* behave ingratiatingly *to.* **2** *n.* crawling motion; slow rate of motion; fast swimming-stroke.

crayfish /ˈkreɪfɪʃ/ *n.* lobster-like freshwater crustacean; crawfish.

crayon /ˈkreɪən/ **1** *n.* stick or pencil of coloured wax or material for drawing. **2** *v.t.* draw or colour with crayons.

craze 1 *n.* great but usu. temporary enthusiasm; object of this. **2** *v.t.* drive crazy.

crazy /ˈkreɪzɪ/ *a.* insane; outrageously foolish; madly eager; unsound, shaky. **crazy paving** paving made of irregular pieces.

creak 1 *n.* harsh grating noise as of un-oiled hinge. **2** *v.i.* emit creak. **3 creaky** *a.*

cream 1 *n.* part of milk with high content of fat; yellowish-white colour of this; food or drink like or made with cream; creamlike preparation or ointment; *the* best part or pick *of.* **2** *v.* take cream from; work to creamy consistency; treat with cosmetic cream;

form cream or scum. **3 cream cheese** soft rich cheese made of cream and unskimmed milk; **cream cracker** crisp unsweetened biscuit; **cream off** remove best part of; **cream of tartar** purified tartar used in medicine and cookery. **4 creamy** *a.*

creamer /ˈkriːmə(r)/ *n.* jug for cream.

creamery /ˈkriːmərɪ/ *n.* place where dairy products are produced or sold.

crease /kriːs/ **1** *n.* line made by folding; wrinkle; *Crick.* line defining position of bowler or batsman. **2** *v.* make creases in, develop creases; *sl.* tire out.

create /kriːˈeɪt/ *v.* bring into existence; originate; invest with rank; *sl.* make fuss.

creation /kriːˈeɪʃ(ə)n/ *n.* creating; all created things; production of human mind.

creative /kriːˈeɪtɪv/ *a.* inventive, imaginative. **creativity** *n.*

creator /kriːˈeɪtə(r)/ *n.* one who creates; **the Creator** God.

creature /ˈkriːtʃə(r)/ *n.* created being, esp. animal; person, esp. one in subservient position.

crèche /kreʃ/ *n.* day-nursery for babies and young children.

credence /ˈkriːd(ə)ns/ *n.* belief, credit.

credentials /krɪˈdenʃ(ə)lz/ *n.pl.* letters of recommendation (also *fig.*).

credible /ˈkredɪb(ə)l/ *a.* believable; worthy of belief. **credibility** *n.*

credit /ˈkredɪt/ **1** *n.* belief, trust; good reputation; acknowledgement of merit or (usu. in *pl.*) of contributor's services to film or book etc.; allowing customers to take goods and defer payment; acknowledgement of payment by entry in account; sum at person's disposal in bank etc. or entered on credit side of account; *US* certificate of completion of course by student. **2** *v.t.* believe; enter on credit side of account; attribute (*to*). **3 credit card** card authorizing obtaining of goods on credit; **credit person with** ascribe to him; **give person credit for** acknowledge that he may have; **to one's credit** in one's favour.

creditable /ˈkredɪtəb(ə)l/ *a.* praiseworthy.

creditor /ˈkredɪtə(r)/ *n.* person or body to whom debt is owing.

credo /ˈkriːdəʊ/ *n.* (*pl.* **-dos**) creed.

credulous /ˈkredjʊləs/ a. too ready to believe. **credulity** n.

creed n. system of (esp. religious) belief; formal summary of Christian doctrine.

creek n. inlet on sea-coast or arm of river; small stream.

creel n. angler's fishing-basket.

creep 1 v.i. (past & p.p. **crept**) crawl; move stealthily or timidly or slowly; (of plant) grow along ground or up wall etc.; experience nervous shivering sensation; develop gradually. 2 n. spell of creeping; sl. unpleasant person; gradual change in shape of metal under stress. 3 **the creeps** colloq. creeping sensation.

creeper /ˈkriːpə(r)/ n. creeping or climbing plant.

creepy /ˈkriːpɪ/ a. causing nervous revulsion or fear; having this feeling. **creepy-crawly** small creeping insect etc.

cremate /krɪˈmeɪt/ v.t. burn (corpse) to ashes. **cremation** n.

crematorium /kreməˈtɔːrɪəm/ n. (pl. **-ria** or **-riums**) place where corpses are cremated.

crematory /ˈkremətərɪ/ 1 a. of cremation. 2 n. US crematorium.

crenellated /ˈkrenəleɪtɪd/ a. having battlements. **crenellation** n.

Creole /ˈkriːəʊl/ 1 n. descendant of European settlers in W. Indies or Central or S. America, or of French settlers in southern US; person of mixed European and Negro descent; language spoken by Creoles. 2 a. that is a Creole; **creole** of local origin or production.

creosote /ˈkriːəsəʊt/ n. oily wood-preservative distilled from wood-tar.

crêpe /kreɪp/ n. textile fabric with wrinkled surface; wrinkled sheet rubber used for shoe-soles etc.; **crêpe de Chine** /də ˈʃiːn/ fine silk crêpe; **crêpe paper** thin crinkled paper.

crepitate /ˈkrepɪteɪt/ v.i. make crackling sound. **crepitation** n.

crept past & p.p. of **creep**.

crepuscular /krɪˈpʌskjʊlə(r)/ a. of twilight; (of animal) active etc. at twilight.

crescendo /krɪˈʃendəʊ/ Mus. 1 adv. with gradually increasing volume. 2 n. (pl. **-dos**) passage to be performed thus.

crescent /ˈkres(ə)nt/ 1 n. waxing moon; figure with this outline esp. as emblem of Turkey or Islam; street of houses on curve. 2 a. increasing; crescent-shaped.

cress n. plant with pungent edible leaves.

crest 1 n. comb or tuft on animal's head; plume of helmet; top esp. of mountain; curl of foam on wave; heraldic device above shield or used separately. 2 v.t. reach top of; crown; serve as crest to. 3 **crestfallen** mortified, dejected.

cretaceous /krɪˈteɪʃəs/ a. chalky.

cretin /ˈkretɪn/ n. person with deformity and mental retardation caused by thyroid deficiency; colloq. stupid person. **cretinism** n.; **cretinous** a.

cretonne /kreˈtɒn/ n. unglazed colour-printed cotton cloth.

crevasse /krɪˈvæs/ n. deep open crack in ice of glacier.

crevice /ˈkrevɪs/ n. narrow opening, fissure.

crew[1] 1 n. body of persons engaged in particular piece of work, esp. manning ship or aircraft or spacecraft etc.; these other than the officers. 2 v. supply or act as (member of) crew (for). 3 **crew cut** man's hair cut short all over; **crew neck** round close-fitting neckline.

crew[2] arch. past of **crow**.

crewel /ˈkruːəl/ n. thin worsted yarn for embroidery. **crewel needle** blunt-ended embroidery needle.

crib 1 n. wooden framework for fodder; child's bed; model representing nativity scene at Bethlehem; colloq. cribbage; colloq. plagiarism; translation. 2 v. confine in small space; plagiarize, copy.

cribbage /ˈkrɪbɪdʒ/ n. a card-game.

crick 1 n. sudden painful stiffness in neck or back. 2 v.t. cause crick in.

cricket[1] /ˈkrɪkɪt/ n. open-air game played with ball, bats, and wickets between two teams of 11. **not cricket** colloq. unfair, infringing code of fair play. **cricketer** n.

cricket[2] /ˈkrɪkɪt/ n. jumping chirping insect.

cried past & p.p. of **cry**.

crier /ˈkraɪə(r)/ n. officer who makes public announcements in judicial court or in streets of town etc.

crikey /ˈkraɪkɪ/ int. sl. expressing astonishment.

crime *n.* act punishable by law; wicked act; such acts collectively.

criminal /ˈkrɪmɪn(ə)l/ **1** *n.* person guilty of crime. **2** *a.* of or involving or concerning crime. **3 criminality** *n.*

criminology /krɪmɪˈnɒlədʒɪ/ *n.* study of crime. **criminologist** *n.*

crimp *v.t.* press into small folds; frill, corrugate.

crimson /ˈkrɪmz(ə)n/ *a.* & *n.* rich deep red.

cringe *v.i.* cower; behave obsequiously.

crinkle /ˈkrɪŋk(ə)l/ *n.* & *v.* wrinkle. **crinkly** *a.*

crinoline /ˈkrɪnəlɪn/ *n.* hooped petticoat used to make long skirt stand out; stiff fabric of horsehair etc.

cripple /ˈkrɪp(ə)l/ **1** *n.* lame person. **2** *v.t.* lame, disable; impair.

crisis /ˈkraɪsɪs/ *n.* (*pl.* **-ses** /-siːz/) decisive moment; time of acute danger or difficulty.

crisp 1 *a.* hard but brittle; bracing; brisk; clear-cut; decisive; crackling; curly. **2** *n.* very thin slice of potato fried crisp. **3** *v.* make or become crisp. **4 crispy** *a.*

criss-cross 1 *n.* pattern of crossing lines etc. **2** *a.* crossing, in crossing lines. **3** *adv.* crosswise. **4** *v.t.* mark with criss-cross lines.

criterion /kraɪˈtɪərɪən/ *n.* (*pl.* **-ria** □ See page 667.) principle taken as standard in judging.

critic /ˈkrɪtɪk/ *n.* person who censures; person who reviews or judges merit of artistic etc. work.

critical /ˈkrɪtɪk(ə)l/ *a.* fault-finding; expressing criticism; of the nature of a crisis, decisive; marking transition from one state to another.

criticism /ˈkrɪtɪsɪz(ə)m/ *n.* finding fault, censure; work of a critic; critical article or remark etc.

criticize /ˈkrɪtɪsaɪz/ *v.* find fault (with); discuss critically.

critique /krɪˈtiːk/ *n.* critical essay.

croak 1 *n.* deep hoarse note as of frog or raven. **2** *v.* utter or speak with croak; *sl.* kill, die.

crochet /ˈkrəʊʃeɪ/ **1** *n.* kind of handiwork done with thread and single hooked needle. **2** *v.* (*past* & *p.p.* **crocheted** /ˈkrəʊʃeɪd/) do crochet; make by crochet.

crock[1] *n.* worn-out or disabled or inefficient person or thing.

crock[2] *n.* earthenware jar; broken piece of earthenware.

crockery /ˈkrɒkərɪ/ *n.* earthenware etc. vessels and plates.

crocodile /ˈkrɒkədaɪl/ *n.* large amphibious reptile; *colloq.* line of schoolchildren etc. walking in pairs. **crocodile tears** insincere grief.

crocus /ˈkrəʊkəs/ *n.* (*pl.* **-cuses**) dwarf plant with corm and yellow or purple or white flowers.

croft 1 *n.* small piece of arable land close to house; small agricultural holding esp. of crofter. **2** *v.i.* farm croft.

crofter /ˈkrɒftə(r)/ *n.* person who rents a smallholding, esp. joint tenant of divided farm in Scotland.

croissant /ˈkrwæsɑ̃/ *n.* rich crescent-shaped bread roll.

cromlech /ˈkrɒmlek/ *n.* dolmen; circle of upright stones.

crone *n.* withered old woman.

crony /ˈkrəʊnɪ/ *n.* close friend.

crook /krʊk/ **1** *n.* hooked staff, esp. of shepherd or bishop; bend, curve; *colloq.* swindler, criminal. **2** *v.* bend, curve.

crooked /ˈkrʊkɪd/ *a.* not straight; bent, twisted; dishonest.

croon /kruːn/ **1** *v.* hum or sing in low subdued voice. **2** *n.* such singing.

crop 1 *n.* produce of any cultivated plant or of land; group or amount produced at one time; thick end of whip; hair cut very short; pouch in bird's gullet as preliminary digesting-place. **2** *v.* cut off; (of animal) bite off or eat down; cut short; raise crop on; bear crop. **3 crop up** occur unexpectedly or by chance.

cropper /ˈkrɒpə(r)/ *n. sl.* **come a cropper** fall heavily.

croquet /ˈkrəʊkeɪ/ **1** *n.* lawn game with hoops, wooden balls, and mallets; croqueting. **2** *v.t.* drive away (player's ball) by striking one's own ball placed in contact with it.

croquette /krəˈket/ *n.* fried breaded ball of meat, potato, etc.

crosier /ˈkrəʊzɪə(r)/ *n.* hooked staff carried by bishop as symbol of office.

cross 1 *n.* stake used for crucifixion usu. with transverse bar; representation of this as emblem of

Christianity; cross-shaped thing; figure or mark etc. of two roughly equal lines etc. crossing near their centres; decoration indicating rank in some orders of knighthood or awarded for personal valour; intermixture of breeds, hybrid; mixture or compromise *between*; trial or annoyance. 2 *v.* go across (road, sea, etc.); cross road etc.; place crosswise; draw line(s) across; make sign of cross on or over; meet and pass; thwart; (cause) to interbreed; cross-fertilize (plants). 3 *a.* transverse; reaching from side to side; intersecting; reciprocal; out of temper, angry *with*. 4 **be at cross purposes** talk without either party realizing that the other is talking of a different thing; **crossbar** horizontal bar esp. between uprights; **crossbench** bench in Parliament for members not belonging to Government or official opposition party; **crossbow** bow fixed across wooden stock, with mechanism working string; **crossbred** hybrid; **cross-breed** (produce) hybrid animal or plant; **cross-check** check by alternative method of verification; **cross-country** across fields etc., not following roads; **cross-examine** examine (esp. witness in lawcourt) minutely to check or extend previous testimony; **cross-examination** *n.*; **cross-eyed** having one or both eyes turned inwards; **cross-fertilize** fertilize (animal or plant) from a different individual; **crossfire** firing of guns in two crossing directions; **cross-grained** (of wood) with grain running irregularly, (of person) perverse, intractable; **cross-legged** with ankles crossed and knees apart; **cross off, out**, cancel, expunge; **cross-patch** *colloq.* bad-tempered person; **cross-ply** (of tyre) having fabric layers with cords lying crosswise; **cross-pollinate** pollinate (plant) from another; **cross-question** cross-examine; **cross-reference** reference to another passage in same book; **crossroad** (often in *pl.*) intersection of roads; **cross-section** transverse section, diagram etc. of thing as if cut through, representative sample; **cross-stitch** one formed of two stitches that cross; **crossword** puzzle in which words crossing each other vertically

and horizontally have to be filled in from clues; **on the cross** diagonally.

crossing /'krɒsɪŋ/ *n.* place where things (esp. roads) meet; part of street marked for pedestrians to cross by; travel across water.

crosswise /'krɒswaɪz/ *adv.* in shape or manner of cross.

crotch *n.* fork, esp. of human body where legs join trunk.

crotchet /'krɒtʃɪt/ *n. Mus.* black-headed note with stem, equal to half minim.

crotchety /'krɒtʃətɪ/ *a.* peevish.

crouch /kraʊtʃ/ 1 *v.i.* stand or lie with legs bent close to body. 2 *n.* this position.

croup /kru:p/ *n.* laryngitis in children, with sharp cough.

croup [2] /kru:p/ *n.* rump, esp. of horse.

croupier /'kru:pɪə(r)/ *n.* person in charge of gaming-table.

croûton /'kru:tɒn/ *n.* small piece of fried or toasted bread. [F]

crow /krəʊ/ 1 *n.* any of various kinds of large black-plumaged bird; cock's cry; infant's crowing; crowbar. 2 *v.i.* (*past* **crowed**, *arch.* **crew**) utter cock's cry; (of infants) utter joyful sounds; exult. 3 **crow's-foot** wrinkle at outer corner of eye; **crow's nest** barrel fixed at masthead as shelter for look-out man.

crowbar /'krəʊbɑ:(r)/ *n.* bar of iron used as lever.

crowd /kraʊd/ 1 *n.* number of people or animals standing or moving close together without order; *colloq.* set, gang, large number of things. 2 *v.* collect in crowd; fill or cram (*with*); force way *into* or *through* etc. confined space etc. 3 **crowd out** exclude by crowding.

crown /kraʊn/ 1 *n.* monarch's head-covering or circlet; *the* supreme governing power in monarchy; wreath for head, esp. as emblem of victory; top part of thing, esp. of head or hat etc.; visible part of tooth, artificial replacement for (part of) this; British coin worth 25p; perfection, completion. 2 *v.t.* put crown on; make king or queen; be consummation or reward or finishing touch to; *sl.* hit on head. 3 **Crown Court** court of criminal jurisdiction in England and Wales; **crown green** bowling green with raised middle part; **crown jewels** sovereign's regalia;

Crown Prince male heir to throne; **Crown Princess** wife of Crown Prince, female heir to throne.

crozier var. of **crosier**.

CRT *abbr.* cathode-ray tube.

cruces *pl.* of **crux**.

crucial /ˈkruːʃ(ə)l/ *a.* decisive between two hypotheses; very important. □ See page 666.

crucible /ˈkruːsɪb(ə)l/ *n.* melting-pot for metals.

cruciferous /kruːˈsɪfərəs/ *a.* with four equal petals arranged crosswise.

crucifix /ˈkruːsɪfɪks/ *n.* image of Christ on Cross.

crucifixion /kruːsɪˈfɪkʃ(ə)n/ *n.* crucifying, esp. of Christ.

cruciform /ˈkruːsɪfɔːm/ *a.* cross-shaped.

crucify /ˈkruːsɪfaɪ/ *v.t.* put to death by fastening to a cross; persecute, torment.

crude 1 *a.* in natural or raw state; lacking finish, unpolished; rude, blunt. 2 *n.* natural mineral oil. 3 **crudity** *n.*

cruel /kruːəl/ *a.* indifferent to or taking pleasure in another's suffering; causing pain or suffering. **cruelty** *n.*

cruet /ˈkruːɪt/ *n.* small stoppered bottle for condiments at table; stand holding cruets and mustard pot etc.

cruise /kruːz/ 1 *v.i.* sail about without precise destination, or calling at series of places; travel at **cruising speed**, economical travelling speed. 2 *n.* cruising voyage. 3 **cruise missile** one able to fly at low altitudes and guide itself by reference to features of region traversed.

cruiser *n.* warship faster and less heavily armoured than battleship. **cruiser-weight** light heavyweight.

crumb /krʌm/ 1 *n.* small fragment of bread or *of* food etc.; soft inner part of loaf. 2 *v.t.* coat with breadcrumbs; crumble (bread). 3 **crumby** *a.*

crumble /ˈkrʌmb(ə)l/ 1 *v.* break or fall into crumbs or fragments. 2 *n.* dish, esp. of cooked fruit, with crumbly topping. 3 **crumbly** *a.*

crummy /ˈkrʌmɪ/ *a. sl.* squalid, inferior.

crumpet /ˈkrʌmpɪt/ *n.* flat soft battercake eaten toasted; *sl.* sexually attractive woman or women.

crumple /ˈkrʌmp(ə)l/ *v.* crush or become crushed into creases; give way, collapse.

crunch 1 *v.* crush with teeth, esp. noisily; make or emit crunch. 2 *n.* crunching sound; *sl.* decisive event. 3 **crunchy** *a.*

crupper /ˈkrʌpə(r)/ *n.* strap looped under horse's tail from back of saddle.

crusade /kruːˈseɪd/ 1 *n.* campaign or movement against recognized evil; **Crusade** medieval Christian military expedition to recover Holy Land from Muslims. 2 *v.* take part in crusade.

cruse /kruːz/ *n. arch.* earthenware jar.

crush 1 *v.* compress with violence so as to break or bruise or crumple; be liable to crumple; defeat utterly; discomfit. 2 *n.* act of crushing; crowded mass of people; drink made of juice of crushed fruit; *sl.* infatuation.

crust 1 *n.* hard outer part of bread etc.; pastry covering pie; rocky outer part of earth; deposit on sides of wine-bottle. 2 *v.* cover with or form into crust; become covered with crust.

crustacean /krʌsˈteɪʃ(ə)n/ 1 *n.* member of group of hard-shelled mainly aquatic animals. 2 *a.* of crustacea.

crusty /ˈkrʌstɪ/ *a.* having a crisp crust; irritable, surly.

crutch *n.* support for lame person usu. with cross-piece fitting under armpit; support; crotch.

crux *n.* (*pl.* **cruces** /ˈkruːsiːz/) decisive point, crucial element of problem.

cry /kraɪ/ 1 *v.* (*past* & *p.p.* **cried** /kraɪd/) make loud or shrill sound, esp. to express pain or grief or joy etc.; weep; utter loudly, exclaim. 2 *n.* loud inarticulate utterance of grief or fear or joy etc.; loud excited utterance; appeal; fit of weeping; watchword; call esp. of birds; yelping of hounds. 3 **crybaby** person who weeps easily or without good reason; **cry down** disparage; **cry off** abandon undertaking; **cry up** praise; **a far cry** a long way; **in full cry** in full pursuit.

crying /ˈkraɪɪŋ/ *a.* (of injustice etc.) flagrant, demanding redress.

cryogenics /kraɪəʊˈdʒenɪks/ *n.* branch of physics dealing with very low temperatures.

crypt /krɪpt/ *n.* vault, esp. one below church used as burial-place.

cryptic /'krɪptɪk/ *a.* secret, mysterious; obscure in meaning.

cryptogam /'krɪptəgæm/ *n.* plant with no true flowers or seeds, e.g. fern or fungus. **cryptogamous** /-'tɒg-/ *a.*

cryptogram /'krɪptəgræm/ *n.* thing written in cipher.

crystal /'krɪst(ə)l/ **1** *n.* clear transparent colourless mineral; highly transparent glass; substance solidified in definite geometrical form. **2** *a.* made of or as clear as crystal.

crystalline /'krɪstəlaɪn/ *a.* of or like or clear as crystal.

crystallize /'krɪstəlaɪz/ *v.* form into crystals; become definite; preserve (fruit) in sugar. **crystallization** *n.*

CSE *abbr.* Certificate of Secondary Education.

cu. *abbr.* cubic.

cub *n.* young of fox or bear or lion etc.; ill-mannered child or youth; *colloq.* inexperienced newspaper reporter; **Cub (Scout)** junior Scout.

cubby-hole /'kʌbɪhəʊl/ *n.* very small confined room, cupboard, etc.

cube /kjuːb/ **1** *n.* solid contained by six equal squares; cube-shaped block; product of a number multiplied by its square. **2** *v.t.* find cube of; cut into small cubes. **3 cube root** number which produces given number when cubed.

cubic /'kjuːbɪk/ *a.* of three dimensions; involving cube of a quantity. **cubic metre** etc. volume of cube whose edge is one metre etc.

cubical /'kjuːbɪk(ə)l/ *a.* cube-shaped.

cubicle /'kjuːbɪk(ə)l/ *n.* small separate sleeping-compartment; enclosed space screened for privacy.

cubism /'kjuːbɪz(ə)m/ *n.* style in art in which objects are represented by juxtaposed geometrical figures. **cubist** *a.* & *n.*

cubit /'kjuːbɪt/ *n.* ancient measure of length, equal to length of forearm.

cuboid /'kjuːbɔɪd/ **1** *a.* like a cube; cube-shaped. **2** *n.* rectangular parallelepiped.

cuckold /'kʌkəʊld/ **1** *n.* husband of adulterous wife. **2** *v.t.* make cuckold of.

cuckoo /'kʊkuː/ **1** *n.* migratory bird with characteristic cry. **2** *a. sl.* crazy. **3 cuckoo-pint** wild arum; **cuckoo-spit** froth exuded by larvae of certain insects.

cucumber /'kjuːkʌmbə(r)/ *n.* long green fleshy fruit used in salads etc.; plant producing this.

cud *n.* half-digested food chewed by ruminant.

cuddle /'kʌd(ə)l/ **1** *v.* hug; lie close and snug; nestle. **2** *n.* hug, embrace.

cudgel /'kʌdʒ(ə)l/ **1** *n.* thick stick used as weapon. **2** *v.t.* beat with cudgel.

cue[1] /kjuː/ **1** *n.* last words of actor's speech as signal for another to begin; signal, hint. **2** *v.t.* give cue to. **3 cue in** insert cue for.

cue[2] /kjuː/ **1** *n.* long tapered rod for striking ball in billiards etc. **2** *v.t.* strike with cue.

cuff[1] *n.* thicker end part of sleeve; separate band of material worn round wrist; in *pl. colloq.* handcuffs; **cuff-link** one of pair of fasteners for shirt cuffs; **off the cuff** extempore, without preparation.

cuff[2] **1** *v.t.* strike with open hand. **2** *n.* cuffing blow.

cuisine /kwɪ'ziːn/ *n.* style of cooking.

cul-de-sac /'kʌldəsæk/ *n.* street, passage, etc., closed at one end.

culinary /'kʌlɪnərɪ/ *a.* of or for cooking.

cull 1 *v.t.* pick (flowers); select; select and kill (surplus animals etc.). **2** *n.* culling; what is culled.

culminate /'kʌlmɪneɪt/ *v.i.* reach highest point of development. **culmination** *n.*

culpable /'kʌlpəb(ə)l/ *a.* deserving blame. **culpability** *n.*

culprit /'kʌlprɪt/ *n.* person accused of or guilty of offence.

cult *n.* system of religious worship; devotion or homage to person or thing.

cultivar /'kʌltɪvɑː(r)/ *n.* variety of plant produced by cultivation.

cultivate /'kʌltɪveɪt/ *v.t.* prepare and use (soil) for crops; raise, produce (plant etc.); improve, develop; pay attention to, cherish. **cultivation** *n.*

cultivator /'kʌltɪveɪtə(r)/ *n.* agricultural implement for breaking up ground etc.

culture /'kʌltʃə(r)/ **1** *n.* refined understanding of the arts and other intellectual achievement; customs and civilization of a particular time or people; improvement by care and training; cultivation of plants, rearing of bees or silkworms etc.; quantity of bacteria grown for study. 2 *v.t.* grow (bacteria) for study. 3 **cultural** *a.*

cultured /ˈkʌltʃəd/ *a.* exhibiting culture. **cultured pearl** one formed by oyster after insertion of foreign body into its shell.

culvert /ˈkʌlvət/ *n.* underground channel or conduit for water crossing road etc.

cumber /ˈkʌmbə(r)/ *v.t.* hamper, hinder; burden.

cumbersome /ˈkʌmbəsəm/ *a.* hampering; inconveniently large or heavy.

cumin /ˈkʌmɪn/ *n.* plant with aromatic seed.

cummerbund /ˈkʌməbʌnd/ *n.* waist-sash.

cumulative /ˈkjuːmjʊlətɪv/ *a.* increasing in force etc. by successive additions.

cumulus /ˈkjuːmjʊləs/ *n.* (*pl.* **-li** /-laɪ/) cloud in heaped-up rounded masses.

cuneiform /ˈkjuːnɪfɔːm/ 1 *a.* of or using writing composed of wedge-shaped marks. 2 *n.* cuneiform writing.

cunning /ˈkʌnɪŋ/ 1 *a.* skilled in ingenuity or deceit; ingenious. 2 *n.* skill in deceit; craftiness.

cup 1 *n.* drinking-vessel, usu. with one side-handle; cupful; cup-shaped thing; wine or cider etc. with various flavourings; ornamental vessel as prize. 2 *v.t.* make cup-shaped. 3 **Cup Final** *Footb.* etc. final match in competition for cup; **cup-tie** match in such competition.

cupboard /ˈkʌbəd/ *n.* recess or piece of furniture with door and (usu.) shelves, in which things may be stored.

Cupid /ˈkjuːpɪd/ *n.* Roman god of love pictured as winged boy with bow.

cupidity /kjuːˈpɪdɪtɪ/ *n.* greed for gain.

cupola /ˈkjuːpələ/ *n.* small dome; kind of furnace; ship's or fort's revolving gun-turret.

cur *n.* worthless or snappish dog; contemptible person.

curaçao /ˈkjʊərəsəʊ/ *n.* liqueur flavoured with orange-peel.

curacy /ˈkjʊərəsɪ/ *n.* curate's office.

curare /kjʊˈrɑːrɪ/ *n.* vegetable poison that paralyses motor nerves.

curate /ˈkjʊərət/ *n.* assistant to parish priest.

curative /ˈkjʊərətɪv/ 1 *a.* tending to cure. 2 *n.* curative drug or measure.

curator /kjʊəˈreɪtə(r)/ *n.* person in charge esp. of museum or library.

curb 1 *n.* check, restraint; chain or strap passing under horse's lower jaw; kerb. 2 *v.t.* restrain; apply curb to.

curd *n.* coagulated substance formed by action of acids on milk, made into cheese or eaten as food.

curdle /ˈkɜːd(ə)l/ *v.* coagulate, form into curd.

cure /kjʊə(r)/ 1 *n.* thing that cures; restoration to health; course of treatment. 2 *v.t.* restore to health; remedy; relieve *of* disease etc.; preserve (meat etc. or skins).

curé /ˈkjʊəreɪ/ *n.* parish priest in France etc. [F]

curette /kjʊəˈret/ 1 *n.* surgeon's scraping-instrument. 2 *v.t* scrape with this. 3 **curettage** *n.*

curfew /ˈkɜːfjuː/ *n.* prohibition of being out of doors during specified hours.

curie /ˈkjʊərɪ/ *n.* unit of radioactivity.

curio /ˈkjʊərɪəʊ/ *n.* (*pl.* **-rios**) object prized for its rarity etc.

curiosity /kjʊərɪˈɒsɪtɪ/ *n.* desire to know; tendency to pry; strange or rare thing.

curious /ˈkjʊərɪəs/ *a.* eager to learn; inquisitive; strange, surprising.

curl 1 *v.* bend or coil into spiral shape; move in curve; play at curling. 2 *n.* curled lock of hair; anything spiral or curved inwards. 3 **curly** *a.*

curler /ˈkɜːlə(r)/ *n.* pin or clip etc. for curling the hair.

curlew /ˈkɜːljuː/ *n.* long-billed wading bird with musical cry.

curling /ˈkɜːlɪŋ/ *n.* game like bowls played on ice with large flattish stones.

curmudgeon /kɜːˈmʌdʒ(ə)n/ *n.* churlish or miserly person.

currant /ˈkʌrənt/ *n.* dried fruit of small seedless grape; any of various shrubs producing red or black or white berries; such a berry.

currency /ˈkʌrənsɪ/ *n.* money in use in a country; being current; prevalent.

current /ˈkʌrənt/ 1 *a.* belonging to present time; happening now; in general circulation or use. 2 *n.* body of water or air etc., moving in definite direction; general tendency or course; movement of electrically charged particles. 3 **cur-**

rent account bank account that may be drawn on by cheque.

curriculum /kə'rɪkjʊləm/ n. (pl. -la) course (of study). **curriculum vitae** /'viːtaɪ/ brief account of one's life.

curry¹ /'kʌrɪ/ 1 n. dish of meat etc. cooked with various spices and usu. served with rice. 2 v.t. make into or flavour like curry. 3 **curry paste**, **powder**, preparation of spices suitable for flavouring curry.

curry² /'kʌrɪ/ v.t. rub down or dress (horse etc.) with curry-comb; dress (leather). **curry-comb** metal brush for horses etc.

curse /kɜːs/ 1 n. invocation of destruction or punishment; profane oath; great evil, bane. 2 v. utter curse against; afflict with; utter curses. 3 **the curse** colloq. menstruation.

cursed /'kɜːsɪd/ a. damned.

cursive /'kɜːsɪv/ 1 a. (of writing) done with joined characters. 2 n. cursive writing.

cursor /'kɜːsə(r)/ n. indicator on VDU screen showing particular position in displayed matter; transparent slide on slide-rule.

cursory /'kɜːsərɪ/ a. without attention to details; rapid, desultory.

curt a. noticeably or rudely brief.

curtail /kɜː'teɪl/ v.t. cut down, shorten, reduce. **curtailment** n.

curtain /'kɜːt(ə)n/ 1 n. piece of cloth etc. hung up as screen esp. at window or between stage and auditorium; rise or fall of curtain in theatre; curtain-call; in pl. sl. the end. 2 v.t. provide or shut off with curtains. 3 **curtain-call** audience's summons to actor(s) to take bow after fall of curtain; **curtain-raiser** short opening theatre-piece, preliminary event.

curtsy /'kɜːtsɪ/ 1 n. woman's or girl's salutation made by bending knees. 2 v.i. make curtsy.

curvaceous /kɜː'veɪʃəs/ a. colloq. having many curves (esp. of shapely female figure).

curvature /'kɜːvətʃə(r)/ n. curving; curved form.

curve 1 n. line or surface of which no part is straight; line showing diagrammatically a continuous variation of quantity or force etc. 2 v. bend or shape so as to form a curve.

curvet /kɜː'vet/ 1 n. horse's frisky leap. 2 v.i. perform curvet.

curvilinear /kɜːvɪ'lɪnɪə(r)/ a. of curved lines.

cushion /'kʊʃ(ə)n/ 1 n. bag filled with mass of soft material or air; means of protection against shock; elastic lining of billiard table's sides; body of air supporting hovercraft. 2 v.t. provide or protect with cushions; mitigate effects of.

cushy /'kʊʃɪ/ a. colloq. (of job etc.) easy, pleasant.

cusp n. point at which two curves meet.

cuss colloq. 1 n. curse; awkward person. 2 v. curse.

cussed /'kʌsɪd/ a. awkward and stubborn.

custard /'kʌstəd/ n. dish or sauce made with milk and beaten eggs, usu. sweetened; sweet sauce made of milk and flavoured cornflour etc.

custodian /kʌs'təʊdɪən/ n. curator, guardian.

custody /'kʌstədɪ/ n. keeping, guardianship; imprisonment.

custom /'kʌstəm/ n. usual way of behaving or acting; established usage; business patronage; customers; in pl. duty levied on imports, government department dealing with this. **custom-house** office at which customs duties are levied; **custom-made** etc., made etc. to customer's order.

customary /'kʌstəmərɪ/ a. in accordance with custom; usual.

customer /'kʌstəmə(r)/ n. person entering shop etc. to buy; person who buys; colloq. person one has to deal with.

cut 1 v. (past & p.p. cut) divide or wound or penetrate with edged instrument; detach or trim or shape by cutting; cause pain to; reduce (prices, services, etc.); cross, intersect; divide (pack of cards); Cinemat. edit (film), stop cameras; end the acquaintance or ignore presence of; avoid or absent oneself from; hit (ball) with chopping motion; switch off (engine etc.); pass through etc. as shorter route; US dilute; have (tooth) come through gum. 2 n. act of cutting; wound made by cutting; stroke with sword or whip or cane etc.; reduction (in price, wages, services, etc.); cessation (of power supply etc.);

excision of part of play, film, book, etc.; *sl.* commission, share of profits, etc.; way thing is cut; joint or piece of meat; cutting of ball; cutting of acquaintance. **3 a cut above** noticeably superior to; **cut and dried** completely decided, inflexible; **cut back** reduce (expenditure), prune; **cut-back** *n.*; **cut both ways** serve both sides; **cut a dash** make brilliant show; **cut in** interpose in talk or action, obstruct path of vehicle one has just overtaken; **cut no ice** *sl.* achieve nothing; **cut off** bring to abrupt end, intercept, shut off, exclude *from* access etc.; **cut out** shape by cutting, (cause to) cease functioning, stop doing or using (something); **cutthroat** murderer, murderous, (of competition) intense and merciless; **cutthroat razor** one with long blade set in handle; **cut up** cut in pieces, (esp. in *p.p.*) keenly distress; **cut up rough** show resentment.

cutaneous /kjuːˈteɪnɪəs/ *a.* of the skin.

cute /kjuːt/ *a. colloq.* clever, ingenious; *US* attractive.

cuticle /ˈkjuːtɪk(ə)l/ *n.* skin at base of finger-nail or toe-nail.

cutlass /ˈkʌtləs/ *n.* short broad-bladed curved sword.

cutlery /ˈkʌtlərɪ/ *n.* knives, forks, and spoons, for use at table.

cutlet /ˈkʌtlɪt/ *n.* neck-chop of mutton or lamb; small piece of veal etc. for frying; flat cake of minced meat etc.

cutter /ˈkʌtə(r)/ *n.* tailor etc. who cuts cloth; small fast sailing-ship; small boat carried by large ship.

cutting /ˈkʌtɪŋ/ **1** *n.* piece cut from newspaper etc.; piece cut from plant for replanting; excavation of high ground for railway, road, etc. **2** *a.* that cuts; wounding to feelings.

cuttlefish /ˈkʌtəlfɪʃ/ *n.* ten-armed sea mollusc that ejects black fluid when pursued.

cutwater /ˈkʌtwɔːtə(r)/ *n.* forward edge of ship's prow; wedge-shaped projection from bridge-pier.

cwm /kuːm/ *n.* Welsh coomb.

cwt. *abbr.* hundredweight.

cyanide /ˈsaɪənaɪd/ *n.* highly poisonous substance used in extraction of gold and silver.

cyanosis /saɪəˈnəʊsɪs/ *n.* blue discoloration of skin.

cybernetics /saɪbəˈnetɪks/ *n.* science of control and communications in animals and machines.

cyclamate /ˈsɪkləmeɪt/ *n.* artificial sweetening agent.

cyclamen /ˈsɪkləmən/ *n.* plant with pinkish-purple or white flowers with reflexed petals.

cycle /ˈsaɪk(ə)l/ **1** *n.* recurrent period; period of thing's completion; recurring series; complete set or series; bicycle, tricycle, etc.; hertz. **2** *v.i.* ride bicycle etc.; move in cycles.

cyclic /ˈsaɪklɪk/ *a.* recurring in cycles; of or forming cycle or circle.

cyclist /ˈsaɪklɪst/ *n.* person who rides bicycle etc.

cyclone /ˈsaɪkləʊn/ *n.* system of winds rotating around low-pressure region; violent destructive form of this. **cyclonic** /-ˈklɒn-/ *a.*

cyclostyle /ˈsaɪkləstaɪl/ **1** *n.* apparatus for making copies of written document from stencil-plate. **2** *v.* reproduce thus.

cyclotron /ˈsaɪklətrɒn/ *n. Phys.* apparatus for acceleration of charged atomic particles revolving in magnetic field.

cygnet /ˈsɪgnɪt/ *n.* young swan.

cylinder /ˈsɪlɪndə(r)/ *n.* solid or hollow roller-shaped body; container for liquefied gas etc.; cylindrical part of machine, e.g. piston-chamber in engine. **cylindrical** /-lɪn-/ *a.*

cymbal /ˈsɪmb(ə)l/ *n.* concave brass etc. plate struck with another or with stick etc. to make ringing sound.

cynic /ˈsɪnɪk/ *n.* person who has little faith in human sincerity and merit; **Cynic** philosopher of ancient Greek sect showing contempt for sophistication and luxury. **cynical** *a.*; **cynicism** /-sɪz(ə)m/ *n.*

cynosure /ˈsaɪnəzjʊə(r)/ *n.* centre of attention or admiration.

cypress /ˈsaɪprəs/ *n.* coniferous tree with dark foliage, symbolic of mourning.

cyst /sɪst/ *n.* sac formed in body, containing morbid matter.

cystic /ˈsɪstɪk/ *a.* of the bladder; like a cyst.

cystitis /sɪsˈtaɪtɪs/ *n.* inflammation of the bladder.

czar var. of **tsar**.

D

D, d, Roman numeral 500.

d. *abbr.* daughter; departs; died; (former) pence or penny.

dab¹ 1 *v.* press (surface) briefly with sponge etc. without rubbing; press (sponge etc. or colour) on surface thus; aim feeble blow (*at*); strike lightly. 2 *n.* dabbing or light blow; smear of paint etc.; in *pl. sl.* fingerprints.

dab² *n.* & *a. colloq.* adept. **dab hand** expert.

dab³ *n.* kind of small flat-fish.

dabble /ˈdæb(ə)l/ *v.* take casual interest or part (*in*); wet slightly or partly; soil, splash; move (hand, foot, object) about in shallow water, mud, etc.

dabchick /ˈdæbtʃɪk/ *n.* little grebe.

dace *n.* (*pl.* same) small freshwater fish.

dacha /ˈdætʃə/ *n.* Russian country cottage.

dachshund /ˈdækshʊnd/ *n.* small short-legged long-bodied dog.

dad *n. colloq.* father.

daddy /ˈdædɪ/ *n. colloq.* & *childish* father. **daddy-long-legs** crane-fly.

dado /ˈdeɪdəʊ/ *n.* (*pl.* -dos) lower part of interior wall when of different material or colour.

daffodil /ˈdæfədɪl/ *n.* bulbous plant with trumpet-shaped yellow flowers.

daft /dɑːft/ *a.* foolish, wild, crazy.

dagger /ˈdægə(r)/ *n.* short stabbing-weapon; obelus.

daguerreotype /dəˈgerəʊtaɪp/ *n.* early kind of photograph.

dahlia /ˈdeɪlɪə/ *n.* garden plant with large brightly-coloured flowers.

Dáil (Eireann) /dɔɪl ˈeɪrən/ *n.* lower house of Parliament in Republic of Ireland.

daily /ˈdeɪlɪ/ 1 *a.* done or produced or occurring every (week)day. 2 *adv.* every day; constantly. 3 *n.* daily newspaper; *colloq.* charwoman.

dainty /ˈdeɪntɪ/ 1 *a.* delicately pretty; choice; fastidious. 2 *n.* choice morsel, delicacy.

daiquiri /ˈdækərɪ/ *n.* cocktail of light rum and lime-juice etc.

dairy /ˈdeərɪ/ *n.* place for keeping, processing, or selling milk and milk products. **dairy farm** one producing chiefly milk etc.; **dairymaid** woman employed in dairy; **dairyman** dealer in milk etc.

dais /ˈdeɪɪs/ *n.* low platform, esp. at end of room or hall.

daisy /ˈdeɪzɪ/ *n.* wild or garden flower with yellow centre and usu. white rays. **daisy-chain** string of field daisies threaded together; **daisy-wheel** printing-head in form of spokes radiating from centre, with characters at ends, printer having this.

dale *n.* valley, esp. in N. England.

dally /ˈdælɪ/ *v.i.* delay; waste time; flirt (*with*). **dalliance** *n.*

Dalmatian /dælˈmeɪʃ(ə)n/ *n.* large white dark-spotted dog.

dam¹ 1 *n.* barrier restraining flow of water in stream etc. 2 *v.t.* confine, block (*up*), or restrain (as) with dam.

dam² *n.* mother (usu. of animal).

damage /ˈdæmɪdʒ/ 1 *n.* harm; injury; loss; in *pl.* sum claimed or adjudged in compensation for loss or injury. 2 *v.t.* do harm to, injure.

damask /ˈdæməsk/ 1 *n.* fabric woven with pattern visible on both sides. 2 *a.* made of damask; velvety pink. 3 **damask rose** old sweet-scented variety.

dame *n.* (title of) woman who has received order of knighthood (**Dame**); comic female pantomime character played by man; *arch.* or *US sl.* woman.

damn /dæm/ 1 *v.t.* curse; condemn, censure; condemn to hell. 2 *n.* uttered curse. 3 **damn all** *sl.* nothing.

damnable /ˈdæmnəb(ə)l/ *a.* hateful; annoying.

damnation /dæmˈneɪʃ(ə)n/ 1 *n.* eternal punishment in hell. 2 *int.* of annoyance.

damned /dæmd/ 1 *a.* damnable. 2 *adv.* extremely.

damp 1 *n.* moisture in air or on surface or diffused through solid. 2 *a.* slightly wet, moist. 3 *v.t.* make damp; stifle, dull, extinguish; discourage, depress; *Mus.* stop vibration of (string etc.). 4 **damp course** layer of damp-proof material in wall to keep damp from rising.

dampen /ˈdæmpən/ *v.* make or become damp.

damper /ˈdæmpə(r)/ *n.* device that reduces shock or noise; small pad to stop vibration of piano string; metal plate in flue controlling combustion.

damsel /'dæmz(ə)l/ *n. arch.* young unmarried woman.

damson /'dæmz(ə)n/ *n.* small darkpurple plum; tree bearing it.

dance /dɑːns/ 1 *v.* move with rhythmical steps and gestures etc., usu. to music; jump about, move in a lively way. 2 *n.* piece of dancing; special form of this; dancing-party. 3 **dance attendance** wait (*on*) with assiduous attention.

dandelion /'dændɪlaɪən/ *n.* yellowflowered wild plant.

dander /'dændə(r)/ *n. colloq.* temper, indignation.

dandle /'dænd(ə)l/ *v.t.* dance (child) on knee or in arms.

dandruff /'dændrʌf/ *n.* dead skin in small scales among hair.

dandy /'dændɪ/ 1 *n.* man paying excessive attention to smartness in his dress etc. 2 *a. colloq.* splendid. 3 **dandy-brush** stiff brush for cleaning horses. 4 **dandyism** *n.*

Dane *n.* native of Denmark; *hist.* Norse invader of England in Anglo-Saxon period. **great dane** large powerful short-haired dog.

danger /'deɪndʒə(r)/ *n.* liability or exposure to harm; thing that causes peril. **danger-money** extra payment for dangerous work.

dangerous /'deɪndʒərəs/ *a.* involving or causing danger, unsafe.

dangle /'dæŋg(ə)l/ *v.* hang loosely; hold or carry swaying loosely; hold as temptation (*before*).

Danish /'deɪnɪʃ/ 1 *a.* of Denmark. 2 *n.* language of Denmark. 3 **Danish blue** white cheese with blue veins; **Danish pastry** kind of yeast cake with icing and nuts etc..

dank *a.* damp and cold.

daphne /'dæfnɪ/ *n.* a flowering shrub.

dapper /'dæpə(r)/ *a.* neat, smart in appearance.

dapple /'dæp(ə)l/ *v.t.* mark with rounded spots or patches of colour or shadow. **dapple-grey** (of horse) grey with darker spots.

Darby and Joan devoted old married couple. **Darby and Joan club** social club for elderly people.

dare /deə(r)/ 1 *v.* venture, have cour-

age or impudence, (to); defy, challenge. 2 *n.* challenge. 3 **daredevil** reckless (person); **I dare say** very likely, I am prepared to believe.

daring /'deərɪŋ/ 1 *n.* adventurous courage. 2 *a.* bold, fearless.

dariole /'dærɪəʊl/ *n.* savoury or sweet dish cooked and served in individual mould.

dark 1 *a.* with little or no light; of deep or sombre colour; browncomplexioned or dark-haired; gloomy; secret, mysterious. 2 *n.* absence of light; lack of knowledge; dark place. 3 **after dark** after nightfall; **Dark Ages** Middle Ages, esp. 5th-10th-c., *fig.* unenlightened period; **dark horse** littleknown person who is unexpectedly successful; **dark-room** room with daylight excluded for photographic work; **in the dark** without information.

darken /'dɑːkən/ *v.* make or become dark.

darkness /'dɑːknɪs/ *n.* state of being dark.

darling /'dɑːlɪŋ/ 1 *n.* beloved person or animal. 2 *a.* loved, lovable.

darn[1] 1 *v.t.* mend (esp. knitted fabric) by interweaving yarn across hole. 2 *n.* place so mended.

darn[2] *n. & v.t. sl.* mild form of **damn**.

darnel /'dɑːn(ə)l/ *n.* grass growing as weed among corn.

dart 1 *n.* small pointed missile esp. used as weapon; in *pl.* treated as *sing.*, indoor game in which darts are thrown at target; sudden rapid movement; tapering stitched tuck in garment. 2 *v.* throw (missile); direct suddenly (glance, flash); move with sudden rapid motion. 3 **dartboard** circular target in game of darts.

Darwinian /dɑː'wɪnɪən/ *a.* of Darwin's doctrine of evolution of species. **Darwinism** *n.*; **Darwinist** *n.*

dash 1 *v.* go with great haste or force; strike with violence so as to shatter; fling (*against* etc.); knock, drive, throw, thrust, (*away*, *off*, etc.); frustrate; daunt, dispirit; *sl.* (mild form of) damn. 2 *n.* rush, onset; (capacity for) vigorous action; showy appearance or behaviour; horizontal stroke in writing or printing; longer signal of two in Morse code; slight admixture; dashboard. 3 **dashboard** surface beneath windscreen of motor vehicle, containing instruments and controls; **dash off** write (letter etc.) hurriedly.

dashing /'dæʃɪŋ/ a. spirited, showy.

dastardly /'dæstədlı/ a. malicious and cowardly.

data /'deɪtə/ n.pl. □ See page 667. and **datum**. known facts or things used as basis for inference or reckoning; facts, information; material (to be) processed or stored etc. by computer. **data bank** large store of computer-processed information; **database** organized store of data held on computer; **data processing** performance of operations on data by computer.

date¹ 1 n. day of month; statement in document etc. of time of composition or publication; period to which work of art etc. belongs; time at which thing happens or is to happen; colloq. social appointment; US colloq. person of opposite sex with whom one has social engagement. 2 v. mark with date; refer to its time; bear date; have origin from; be recognizable as of particular date; colloq. be or become out of date; colloq. make social appointment with. 3 **dateline** line partly along meridian 180° from Greenwich east and west of which date differs, line in newspaper at top of dispatch etc. to show date and place of writing; **out of date** old-fashioned, obsolete; **to date** until now; **up to date** in accordance with modern standards or latest knowledge.

date² n. oblong stone-fruit; tree (**datepalm**) bearing this.

dative /'deɪtɪv/ 1 n. Gram. case expressing indirect object of action of verb. 2 a. of or in the dative.

datum /'deɪtəm/ n. (pl. **data**) fixed starting-point of scale etc.

daub 1 v. coat or smear with clay etc.; paint crudely or unskilfully. 2 n. material for daubing walls etc.; smear of grease etc.; crude painting.

daughter /'dɔːtə(r)/ n. female child in relation to her parents; female descendant; female member of family etc. **daughter-in-law** son's wife.

daunt v.t. discourage, intimidate.

dauntless /'dɔːntlɪs/ a. not to be daunted, intrepid.

dauphin /'dɔːfɪn/ n. hist. title of eldest son of king of France.

davenport /'dævənpɔːt/ n. kind of writing-desk; US large sofa.

davit /'dævɪt/ n. one of pair of curved uprights for suspending or lowering ship's boat.

daw n. jackdaw.

dawdle /'dɔːd(ə)l/ v.i. loiter, be sluggish, idle.

dawn 1 n. first light, daybreak; incipient gleam; beginning. 2 v.i. begin to be day, grow light, become evident. 3 **dawn chorus** early-morning birdsong.

day n. time during which sun is above horizon; daylight; part of day allotted for work; period of 24 hours as unit of time; period; lifetime, period of prosperity; specified or appointed day. **day-dream** (indulge in) fancy or reverie while awake; **daylight** light of day, dawn, visible interval (between); **daylight robbery** colloq. excessive charge or expense; **daylight saving** obtaining longer evening daylight in summer by making clocks show later time; **day nursery** one for children in daytime esp. while mothers work; **day release** system of allowing employees days off work for education; **day-return** ticket at reduced rate for journey both ways in one day; **day-school** one attended by pupils living at home; **daytime** time of daylight.

daze 1 v.t. stupefy, bewilder. 2 n. dazed state.

dazzle /'dæz(ə)l/ 1 v.t. confuse sight of by excess of light or intricate motion etc.; impress or overpower (person) by brilliant display. 2 n. bright blinding light.

dB abbr. decibel(s).

DC abbr. direct current; District of Columbia.

DDT abbr. white chlorinated hydrocarbon used as an insecticide.

deacon /'diːkən/ n. clergyman of order below priest; layman dealing with secular affairs of church. **deaconess** n. fem.

deactivate /dɪ'æktɪveɪt/ v.t. render inactive or less reactive.

dead /ded/ 1 a. no longer alive; numb; insensitive (to); not effective; extinct; inactive; inanimate; dull; not resonant; lacking activity; not transmitting sounds; out of play; abrupt; complete; exact; unqualified. 2 adv. absolutely, completely. **3** *n.* dead person(s); inactive or silent time. **4 dead-and-alive** dull, spiritless; **dead beat** *a.* utterly exhausted; **dead-beat** penniless person; **dead end** closed end of passage etc.; **dead-end** having no prospects; **dead heat** race etc. in which winners finish exactly even; **dead letter** law etc. no longer observed, undelivered or unclaimed letter; **deadline** time-limit; **deadlock** state of affairs from which no progress is possible; **dead loss** useless person or thing; **dead man's handle** controlling handle on electric train etc. disconnecting power supply if released; **dead march** funeral march; **dead-pan** expressionless; **dead reckoning** estimation of position of ship etc. without taking observations; **dead shot** unerring marksman; **dead weight** inert mass; **dead wood** *fig.* useless person(s) or thing(s).

deaden /'ded(ə)n/ *v.* deprive of or lose vitality, force, etc.; make insensible (to).

deadly /'dedlɪ/ **1** *a.* causing fatal injury or serious damage; intense; accurate; deathlike. **2** *adv.* as if dead; extremely. **3 deadly nightshade** woody plant with poisonous black berries.

deaf /def/ *a.* wholly or partly without hearing; unresponsive (to). **deaf-aid** hearing aid; **deaf-and-dumb alphabet** manual signs for communication with the deaf; **deaf mute** deaf and dumb person.

deafen /'def(ə)n/ *v.t.* be so loud as to deprive of hearing.

deal[1] *v.* (*past* & *p.p.* **dealt** /delt/) distribute among several; distribute (cards) to players; assign as share; deliver (blow); behave in specified way (*with*). **2** *n.* dealing, turn to deal; business transaction, bargain; *colloq.* a large amount. **3 deal in** be seller of; **deal with** do business with, take measures regarding, treat (subject).

deal[2] *n.* sawn fir or pine wood.

dealer /'di:lə(r)/ *n.* player dealing at cards; trader.

dealings /'di:lɪŋz/ *n.pl.* conduct or transactions.

dean *n.* head of cathedral chapter; fellow of college with disciplinary functions; head of university faculty; (also

rural dean) head of clergy in division of archdeaconry.

deanery /'di:nərɪ/ *n.* dean's house or office; group of parishes presided over by rural dean.

dear 1 *a.* beloved (often *iron.* or as polite form esp. at beginning of letters); precious *to*; high-priced. **2** *n.* dear person. **3** *adv.* at high price. **4** *int.* (usu. **oh dear!** or **dear me!**) expressing surprise or distress etc.

dearth /dɜːθ/ *n.* scarcity or lack, esp. of food.

death /deθ/ *n.* dying, end of life; being dead; cause of death; ceasing to be; destruction. **death duty** tax levied on property after owner's death; **death-mask** cast taken from dead person's face; **death penalty** capital punishment; **death rate** yearly number of deaths per 1000 of population; **death toll** number of people killed in war or disaster etc.; **death-trap** unsafe place or vehicle etc.; **death-warrant** order for execution (also *fig.*); **death-watch (beetle)** small beetle whose larvae bore into wood with ticking sound.

deathless /'deθlɪs/ *a.* immortal.

deathly /'deθlɪ/ *a.* & *adv.* deadly; like death.

deb *n. colloq.* débutante.

débâcle /deɪ'bɑːk(ə)l/ *n.* utter collapse or downfall.

debar /dɪ'bɑː(r)/ *v.t.* exclude *from*.

debark /dɪ'bɑːk/ *v.* disembark. **debarkation** *n.*

debase /dɪ'beɪs/ *v.t.* lower in character, quality, or value; depreciate (coin) by alloying etc.

debatable /dɪ'beɪtəb(ə)l/ *a.* open to dispute.

debate /dɪ'beɪt/ **1** *v.* discuss; hold formal argument esp. in legislature or public meeting; consider, ponder. **2** *n.* formal discussion; public argument.

debauch /dɪ'bɔːtʃ/ **1** *v.t.* corrupt morally; deprave or debase; in *p.p.* dissolute. **2** *n.* bout of sensual indulgence.

debauchery /dɪ'bɔːtʃərɪ/ *n.* excessive sensual indulgence.

debenture /dɪ'bentʃə(r)/ *n.* bond of company etc. acknowledging sum on which interest is due, esp. as prior charge on assets.

debilitate /dɪ'bɪlɪteɪt/ *v.t.* enfeeble.

debility /dɪˈbɪlɪtɪ/ n. feebleness, weakness.

debit /ˈdebɪt/ 1 n. entry in account for sum owing. 2 v.t. enter (sum) on debit side of account *against* or *to*.

debonair /debəˈneə(r)/ a. carefree, self-assured.

debouch /dɪˈbaʊtʃ/ v.i. issue from ravine or woods etc. into open ground.

debrief /diːˈbriːf/ v.t. obtain report from, after completion of mission etc.

debris /ˈdebriː/ n. scattered fragments; wreckage.

debt /det/ n. money etc. owing; obligation; state of owing something.

debtor /ˈdetə(r)/ n. person in debt.

debug /diːˈbʌg/ v.t. remove hidden microphones from; correct operational defects in.

debunk /diːˈbʌŋk/ v.t. *colloq.* expose false claims or pretensions of.

début /ˈdeɪbjuː/ n. first appearance as performer or in society etc.

débutante /ˈdebjuːtɑːnt/ n. young woman making her social début.

Dec. *abbr.* December.

deca- /ˈdekə/ *in comb.* ten.

decade /ˈdekeɪd/ n. 10 years; set or series of 10.

decadence /ˈdekəd(ə)ns/ n. period of decline esp. of art or literature; decadent attitude or behaviour.

decadent a. declining; belonging to decadent age; self-indulgent.

decaffeinate /diːˈkæfɪneɪt/ v.t. remove caffeine from.

decagon /ˈdekəgən/ n. plane figure with 10 sides and angles. **decagonal** /-ˈkæg-/ a.

decagram /ˈdekəgræm/ n. 10 grams.

decalitre /ˈdekəliːtə(r)/ n. 10 litres.

Decalogue /ˈdekəlɒg/ n. the Ten Commandments.

decametre /ˈdekəmiːtə(r)/ n. 10 metres.

decamp /diːˈkæmp/ v.i. break up or leave camp; take oneself off, go away suddenly.

decanal /dɪˈkeɪn(ə)l/ a. of dean; of south (dean's) side of choir.

decant /dɪˈkænt/ v.t. pour off (wine etc.) leaving sediment behind; move or transfer as if by pouring.

decanter /dɪˈkæntə(r)/ n. stoppered bottle into which wine or spirit is decanted.

decapitate /dɪˈkæpɪteɪt/ v.t. behead. **decapitation** n.

decarbonize /diːˈkɑːbənaɪz/ v.t. remove carbon deposit from (engine of car etc.).

decathlon /dɪˈkæθlən/ n. composite athletic contest of 10 events.

decay /dɪˈkeɪ/ 1 v. (cause to) rot, decompose; decline in quality or power or energy etc. 2 n. ruinous state; decline, loss of quality; decomposition.

decease /dɪˈsiːs/ n. esp. *Law* death.

deceased /dɪˈsiːst/ 1 a. dead. 2 n. person who has died.

deceit /dɪˈsiːt/ n. concealing of truth in order to mislead; trick. **deceitful** a.

deceive /dɪˈsiːv/ v.t. persuade of what is false; mislead; use deceit.

decelerate /diːˈseləreɪt/ v. decrease speed (of). **deceleration** n.

December /dɪˈsembə(r)/ n. twelfth month of year.

decency /ˈdiːsənsɪ/ n. decent behaviour; recognized code of propriety; in *pl.* requirements of respectable behaviour.

decennial /dɪˈsenɪəl/ a. lasting 10 years; recurring every 10 years.

decent /ˈdiːs(ə)nt/ a. seemly; not immodest or obscene; respectable; passable; good enough; *colloq.* kind, obliging.

decentralize /diːˈsentrəlaɪz/ v.t. transfer from central to local authority; distribute among local centres.

deception /dɪˈsepʃ(ə)n/ n. deceiving or being deceived; thing that deceives.

deceptive /dɪˈseptɪv/ a. apt to mislead.

deci- /ˈdesɪ/ *in comb.* one-tenth.

decibel /ˈdesɪbel/ n. unit used in comparison of intensities of sound.

decide /dɪˈsaɪd/ v. bring or come to resolution or decision; settle by giving victory to one side; give judgement.

decided a. definite, unquestionable; positive in judgement.

deciduous /dɪˈsɪdjʊəs/ a. (of plant) shedding leaves annually; periodically or normally shed.

decigram /ˈdesɪgræm/ n. one-tenth of a gram.

decilitre /ˈdesɪliːtə(r)/ n. one-tenth of a litre.

decimal /ˈdesɪm(ə)l/ 1 a. of tenths or 10; proceeding by tens; of decimal coinage. 2 n. decimal fraction. 3 decimal

coinage one using decimal system; **decimal fraction** one with power of 10 as denominator, esp. expressed as figures after decimal point; **decimal point** dot placed after unit figure in decimal notation; **decimal system** that in which each denomination or weight or measure etc. is worth 10 times the value of the one immediately below it.

decimalize /ˈdesɪməlaɪz/ v.t. express as decimal; convert to decimal system. **decimalization** n.

decimate /ˈdesɪmeɪt/ v.t. kill tenth or large proportion of. □ See page 666. **decimation** n.

decimetre /ˈdesɪmiːtə(r)/ n. one-tenth of a metre.

decipher /dɪˈsaɪfə(r)/ v.t. convert (text written in cipher or unfamiliar script) into understandable form; make out meaning of. **decipherment** n.

decision /dɪˈsɪʒ(ə)n/ n. act of deciding; settlement; conclusion; resolve; tendency to decide firmly.

decisive /dɪˈsaɪsɪv/ a. that decides issue; conclusive; positive.

deck 1 n. platform extending from side to side of (part of) ship or boat; floor of bus etc.; part of record player or tape recorder which moves or plays etc. record or tape; *US* pack (of cards). 2 v.t. array, adorn. 3 **deck-chair** outdoor folding chair.

declaim /dɪˈkleɪm/ v. speak or utter rhetorically; recite; deliver impassioned speech. **declamation** n.; **declamatory** a.

declaration /dekləreɪʃ(ə)n/ n. declaring; emphatic, deliberate, or formal statement. **declaratory** /-ˈklær-/ a.

declare /dɪˈkleə(r)/ v. announce openly or formally; pronounce (person, thing) to be (something); acknowledge possession of (dutiable goods, income, etc.); *Crick.* choose to end one's side's innings before all wickets have fallen; *Cards* name trump suit.

declassify /diːˈklæsɪfaɪ/ v.t. cease to designate as secret.

declension /dɪˈklenʃ(ə)n/ n. *Gram.* list of inflexions for noun, adjective, etc.; class according to which noun etc. is declined; decline, deterioration.

declination /deklɪˈneɪʃ(ə)n/ n. downward bend; angular distance N. or S. of

celestial equator; deviation of compass needle from true N.

decline /dɪˈklaɪn/ 1 v. deteriorate, lose strength or vigour; decrease; refuse; show downward tendency; *Gram.* inflect, state case forms of (noun etc.). 2 n. deterioration; decay.

declivity /dɪˈklɪvɪtɪ/ n. downward slope.

declutch /diːˈklʌtʃ/ v.i. disengage clutch of motor vehicle.

decoction /dɪˈkɒkʃ(ə)n/ n. extraction by boiling; liquid obtained thus.

decode /diːˈkəʊd/ v.t. convert (coded message) into understandable language.

decoke /diːˈkəʊk/ v.t. *colloq.* decarbonize.

décolletage /deɪkɒlˈtɑːʒ/ n. low-cut neckline of woman's dress. [F]

décolleté /deɪˈkɒlteɪ/ a. having low neckline. [F]

decompose /diːkəmˈpəʊz/ v. rot; separate into elements. **decomposition** n.

decompress /diːkəmˈpres/ v.t. relieve pressure on (person etc.) by means of an air-lock. **decompression** n.

decongestant /diːkənˈdʒest(ə)nt/ n. drug etc. that relieves congestion.

decontaminate /diːkənˈtæmɪneɪt/ v.t. remove (esp. radioactive) contamination from. **decontamination** n.

décor /ˈdeɪkɔː(r)/ n. furnishings and decoration of room, stage, etc.

decorate /ˈdekəreɪt/ v.t. adorn; paint and paper etc. (room etc.); invest with order or medal etc.

decoration /dekəˈreɪʃ(ə)n/ n. decorating; thing serving to decorate; medal etc.; in *pl.* flags etc. put up on festive occasion.

decorative /ˈdekərətɪv/ a. serving to decorate; *colloq.* pleasing to look at.

decorator /ˈdekəreɪtə(r)/ n. person who decorates houses etc. esp. professionally.

decorous /ˈdekərəs/ a. not offending against decency or seemliness.

decorum /dɪˈkɔːrəm/ n. seemliness, propriety; etiquette.

decoy 1 /ˈdiːkɔɪ/ n. thing or person used to lure animal or other person into trap; bait, enticement. 2 /dɪˈkɔɪ/ v. lure by means of decoy.

decrease 1 /dɪˈkriːs/ v. make or become smaller or fewer. 2 /ˈdiːkriːs/ n.

decreasing; amount by which thing decreases.

decree /dɪˈkriː/ 1 *n.* authoritative order; judicial decision. 2 *v.* ordain by decree. 3 **decree nisi** /ˈnaɪsaɪ/ order for divorce, remaining conditional for period.

decrepit /dɪˈkrepɪt/ *a.* weakened by age or hard use; dilapidated. **decrepitude** *n.*

decretal /dɪˈkriːt(ə)l/ *n.* papal decree.

decry /dɪˈkraɪ/ *v.t.* disparage.

dedicate /ˈdedɪkeɪt/ *v.t.* devote or give up (*to* God, person, purpose, etc.); put words in (book etc.) as compliment to friend or patron etc.; in *p.p.* devoted, having single-minded loyalty. **dedicatory** *a.*

dedication /dedɪˈkeɪʃ(ə)n/ *n.* dedicating or being dedicated; words with which book is dedicated.

deduce /dɪˈdjuːs/ *v.t.* draw as logical conclusion. **deducible** *a.*

deduct /dɪˈdʌkt/ *v.t.* take away; put aside; withhold.

deductible /dɪˈdʌktɪb(ə)l/ *a.* that may be deducted esp. from one's tax or taxable income.

deduction /dɪˈdʌkʃ(ə)n/ *n.* deducting; amount deducted; inference from general to particular; thing deduced.

deductive /dɪˈdʌktɪv/ *a.* of or reasoning by deduction.

deed *n.* thing consciously done; actual fact; performance; legal document. **deed poll** deed made and executed by one party only.

deem *v.t.* regard or consider or judge to be.

deep 1 *a.* going or situated far down or in; to or at specified depth; low-pitched; intense; profound, heartfelt; fully absorbed *in*. 2 *adv.* far down or in. 3 *n.* deep place; *the* sea. 4 **deep-freeze** freezer; **deep fry** fry with fat covering food; **deep-laid** secret and elaborate.

deepen /ˈdiːpən/ *v.* make or become deep or deeper.

deer *n.* (*pl.* same) four-footed ruminant animal of which the male usu. has antlers. **deerstalker** cloth cap with peak in front and at back.

deface /dɪˈfeɪs/ *v.t.* spoil appearance of; make illegible. **defacement** *n.*

de facto /deɪ ˈfæktəʊ/ existing in fact, whether by right or not. [L]

defalcate /ˈdiːfælkeɪt/ *v.i.* misappropriate money.

defalcation /diːfælˈkeɪʃ(ə)n/ *n.* misappropriation of money; shortcoming.

defame /dɪˈfeɪm/ *v.t.* attack good name of. **defamation** /def-/ *n.*; **defamatory** /-ˈfæm-/ *a.*

default /dɪˈfɔːlt/ 1 *n.* failure to act or appear or pay; option selected by computer program etc. unless given alternative instruction. 2 *v.i.* fail to meet obligations.

defaulter *n.* person who defaults, esp. soldier guilty of military offence.

defeat /dɪˈfiːt/ 1 *v.t.* overcome in battle or other contest; frustrate, baffle. 2 *n.* defeating; being defeated.

defeatism /dɪˈfiːtɪz(ə)m/ *n.* tendency to expect defeat. **defeatist** *n.* & *a.*

defecate /ˈdiːfɪkeɪt/ *v.i.* discharge faeces from bowels. **defecation** *n.*

defect 1 /ˈdiːfekt/ *n.* failing, shortcoming; blemish. 2 /dɪˈfekt/ *v.i.* desert, transfer allegiance to another country, party, etc. 3 **defection** *n.*; **defector** *n.*

defective /dɪˈfektɪv/ *a.* incomplete; faulty; lacking, deficient.

defence /dɪˈfens/ *n.* defending; means of resisting attack; justification; defendant's case or counsel; players in defending position in game; in *pl.* fortifications. **defenceless** *a.*

defend /dɪˈfend/ *v.* ward off attack made on; protect; uphold by argument; *Law* conduct defence (of).

defendant /dɪˈfend(ə)nt/ *n.* person accused or sued in court of law.

defensible /dɪˈfensəb(ə)l/ *a.* able to be defended or justified.

defensive /dɪˈfensɪv/ *a.* done or intended for defence. **on the defensive** in attitude or position of defence.

defer[1] /dɪˈfɜː(r)/ *v.t.* put off, postpone. **deferment** *n.*

defer[2] /dɪˈfɜː(r)/ *v.i.* yield or make concessions *to*.

deference /ˈdefərəns/ *n.* respectful conduct; compliance with advice etc. of another. **in deference to** out of respect for.

deferential /defəˈrenʃ(ə)l/ *a.* showing deference.

defiance /dɪˈfaɪəns/ *n.* defying; open disobedience or disregard. **defiant** *a.*

deficiency /dɪˈfɪʃənsɪ/ *n.* lack or shortage; thing lacking; deficit. **deficiency**

disease one caused by lack of essential element in diet.

deficient /dɪˈfɪʃ(ə)nt/ a. incomplete or insufficient in some essential respect.

deficit /ˈdefɪsɪt/ n. amount by which total falls short of what is required; excess of liabilities over assets.

defile¹ /dɪˈfaɪl/ v.t. make dirty; pollute; profane. **defilement** n.

defile² /dɪˈfaɪl/ 1 n. narrow gorge or pass. 2 v.i. march in file.

define /dɪˈfaɪn/ v.t. state precise meaning of; describe scope of; outline; mark out (limits, boundary).

definite /ˈdefɪnɪt/ a. with exact limits; determinate, distinct, precise.

definition /defɪˈnɪʃ(ə)n/ n. defining; statement of precise meaning; degree of distinctness.

definitive /dɪˈfɪnɪtɪv/ a. final, decisive, unconditional; most authoritative.

deflate /dɪˈfleɪt/ v. let air out of (tyre etc.); (cause to) lose confidence; apply deflation to (economy); pursue policy of deflation.

deflation /dɪˈfleɪʃ(ə)n/ n. deflating; reduction of amount of money in circulation to increase its value. **deflationary** a.

deflect /dɪˈflekt/ v. bend or turn aside from straight course. **deflexion** n.

deflower /diːˈflaʊə(r)/ v.t. deprive of virginity; ravage; strip of flowers.

defoliate /diːˈfəʊlɪeɪt/ v.t. remove leaves from. **defoliant** n.; **defoliation** n.

deform /dɪˈfɔːm/ v.t. spoil appearance or shape of; put out of shape. **deformation** n.

deformity /dɪˈfɔːmɪtɪ/ n. deformed state; malformation.

defraud /dɪˈfrɔːd/ v.t. cheat by fraud.

defray /dɪˈfreɪ/ v.t. provide money to pay.

defrost /diːˈfrɒst/ v.t. remove frost or ice from; unfreeze.

deft a. dextrous, skilful.

defunct /dɪˈfʌŋkt/ a. no longer existing or in use; dead.

defuse /diːˈfjuːz/ v.t. remove fuse from (bomb etc.); reduce danger in (crisis etc.).

defy /dɪˈfaɪ/ v.t. resist openly; present insuperable obstacles to; challenge to do or prove something.

degenerate 1 /dɪˈdʒenərət/ a. having lost qualities proper to race or kind, debased. 2 /dɪˈdʒenərət/ n. degenerate person etc. 3 /dɪˈdʒenəreɪt/ v.i. become degenerate. 4 **degeneracy** n.; **degeneration** n.

degrade /dɪˈgreɪd/ v.t. reduce to lower rank or simpler structure; bring into dishonour or contempt. **degradation** /deg-/ n.

degrading a. humiliating; lowering one's self-respect.

degree /dɪˈgriː/ n. stage in ascending or descending scale; unit of angular measurement or in scale of temperature; academic rank conferred by university etc. for proficiency in specified subject(s).

dehumanize /diːˈhjuːmənaɪz/ v.t. remove human qualities from.

dehydrate /diːˈhaɪdreɪt/ v. remove water from; make dry; lose water. **dehydration** n.

de-ice /diːˈaɪs/ v.t. remove ice from; prevent formation of ice on.

deify /ˈdiːɪfaɪ/ v.t. make a god of, worship as a god. **deification** n.

deign /deɪn/ v.i. condescend to.

deism /ˈdiːɪz(ə)m/ n. belief in existence of a god without accepting revelation. **deist** n.; **deistic** a.

deity /ˈdiːɪtɪ/ □ See page 665. n. divine status or nature; god.

déjà vu /deɪʒɑː ˈvuː/ illusion of having already experienced present situation. [F]

deject /dɪˈdʒekt/ v.t. make sad or gloomy.

dejection /dɪˈdʒekʃ(ə)n/ n. dejected mood.

de jure /diː ˈdʒʊərɪ/ rightful, by right. [L]

delay /dɪˈleɪ/ 1 v. make or be late; hinder; postpone. 2 n. act or process of delaying; hindrance, time lost by delaying.

delectable /dɪˈlektəb(ə)l/ a. delightful.

delectation /diːlekˈteɪʃ(ə)n/ n. enjoyment.

delegacy /ˈdelɪgəsɪ/ n. body of delegates.

delegate 1 /ˈdelɪgət/ n. person appointed as representative; member of deputation. 2 /ˈdelɪgeɪt/ v.t. appoint or send as representative; entrust (task) to representative.

delegation /delɪ'geɪʃ(ə)n/ *n.* delegating, delegacy.

delete /dɪ'liːt/ *v.t.* strike out (word, passage, etc.). **deletion** *n.*

deleterious /delɪ'tɪərɪəs/ *a.* harmful.

delft *n.* kind of glazed earthenware.

deliberate 1 /dɪ'lɪbərət/ *a.* intentional, fully considered. 2 /dɪ'lɪbəreɪt/ *v.* think carefully (about); take counsel.

deliberation /dɪlɪbə'reɪʃ(ə)n/ *n.* careful consideration; careful slowness.

deliberative /dɪ'lɪbərətɪv/ *a.* of or for deliberation.

delicacy /'delɪkəsɪ/ *n.* delicateness; sensitiveness; choice kind of food.

delicate /'delɪkət/ *a.* fine in texture or construction; subtle, hard to discern; tender, easily harmed; requiring deftness or tact.

delicatessen /delɪkə'tes(ə)n/ *n.* shop selling prepared foods and delicacies; such food.

delicious /dɪ'lɪʃəs/ *a.* highly delightful esp. to taste or smell.

delight /dɪ'laɪt/ 1 *v.* please greatly; take great pleasure *in.* 2 *n.* great pleasure; source of this. 3 **delightful** *a.*

delimit /dɪ'lɪmɪt/ *v.t.* determine limits or boundaries of. **delimitation** *n.*

delineate /dɪ'lɪnɪeɪt/ *v.t.* portray by drawing or description. **delineation** *n.*; **delineator** *n.*

delinquent /dɪ'lɪŋkwənt/ 1 *a.* committing an offence; failing in a duty. 2 *n.* offender. 3 **delinquency** *n.*

deliquesce /delɪ'kwes/ *v.i.* become liquid; dissolve in moisture from the air. **deliquescence** *n.*; **deliquescent** *a.*

delirious /dɪ'lɪrɪəs/ *a.* affected with delirium; raving; wildly excited.

delirium /dɪ'lɪrɪəm/ *n.* disordered state of mind; wildly excited mood. **delirium tremens** /'triːmenz/ form of delirium with terrifying delusions due to prolonged drunkenness.

deliver /dɪ'lɪvə(r)/ *v.t.* convey (letters, goods) to destination; transfer or hand over; utter (speech); launch, aim, (blow, ball, attack); rescue, save, set free; assist in giving birth or at birth of. **be delivered of** give birth to.

deliverance /dɪ'lɪvərəns/ *n.* rescue, setting free.

delivery /dɪ'lɪvərɪ/ *n.* delivering or being delivered; periodical distribution of letters or goods; manner of delivering.

dell *n.* small wooded hollow.

delphinium /del'fɪnɪəm/ *n.* garden plant with usu. blue flowers; larkspur.

delta /'deltə/ *n.* fourth letter of Greek alphabet (*Δ, δ*); triangular alluvial tract at mouth of river. **delta wing** triangular swept-back wing of aircraft.

delude /dɪ'luːd/ *v.t.* fool, deceive.

deluge /'deljuːdʒ/ 1 *n.* flood; downpour; overwhelming rush. 2 *v.t.* flood, overwhelm.

delusion /dɪ'luːʒ(ə)n/ *n.* false belief or impression; false hope. **delusive** *a.*

de luxe /də 'lʌks/ of superior kind; sumptuous.

delve *v.* make laborious research; search *in* or *among*; *arch.* dig.

demagogue /'deməgɒg/ *n.* political agitator appealing to emotions of mob. **demagogic** /-'gɒgɪk/ *a.*; **demagogy** /-gɒgɪ/) *n.*

demand /dɪ'mɑːnd/ 1 *n.* request made as of right or peremptorily; urgent claim; desire of would-be purchasers for commodity. 2 *v.t.* make demand for; require.

demarcation /diːmɑː'keɪʃ(ə)n/ *n.* marking of boundary or limits of anything.

demean /dɪ'miːn/ *v.t.* lower dignity of.

demeanour /dɪ'miːnə(r)/ *n.* bearing; outward behaviour.

demented /dɪ'mentɪd/ *a.* driven mad, crazy.

dementia /dɪ'menʃə/ *n.* insanity with loss of intellectual power; **dementia praecox** /'priːkɒks/ schizophrenia.

demerara /demə'reərə/ *n.* yellowish-brown raw cane sugar.

demerit /diː'merɪt/ *n.* fault, defect.

demesne /dɪ'miːn/ *n.* landed property, estate; possession (of land) as one's own.

demigod /'demɪgɒd/ *n.* partly divine being; *fig.* godlike person.

demijohn /'demɪdʒɒn/ *n.* large wicker-cased bottle.

demilitarize /diː'mɪlɪtəraɪz/ *v.t.* remove military forces from.

demi-monde /'demɪmɒnd/ *n.* women of doubtful repute in society; group behaving with doubtful legality etc. [F]

demise /dɪ'maɪz/ *n.* death (*lit.* or *fig.*).

demisemiquaver /demɪ'semɪkweɪvə(r)/ *n. Mus.* note equal to half semiquaver.

demist /diːˈmɪst/ *v.* clear mist from (windscreen etc.).

demo /ˈdeməʊ/ *n.* (*pl.* -mos) *colloq.* political etc. demonstration.

demobilize /diːˈməʊbɪlaɪz/ *v.t.* release from military service. **demobilization** *n.*

democracy /dɪˈmɒkrəsɪ/ *n.* government by all the people, usu. through elected representatives; equality of rights in society, group, etc.

democrat /ˈdeməkræt/ *n.* advocate of democracy; **Democrat** member of US Democratic Party.

democratic /deməˈkrætɪk/ *a.* of or practising etc. democracy. **democratically** *adv.*; **democratize** /-ˈmɒk-/ *v.t.*

demography /dɪˈmɒgrəfɪ/ *n.* statistical study of life in human communities. **demographic** *a.*

demolish /dɪˈmɒlɪʃ/ *v.t.* pull or throw down (building); destroy; refute. **demolition** /deməˈlɪʃ(ə)n/ *n.*

demon /ˈdiːmən/ *n.* devil; evil spirit; malignant or energetic person. **demonic** /-ˈmɒn-/ *n.*

demoniac /dɪˈməʊnɪæk/ **1** *a.* possessed by evil spirit; of or like demon; frenzied. **2** *n.* demoniac person.

demonology /diːməˈnɒlədʒɪ/ *n.* study of beliefs about demons.

demonstrable /ˈdemənstrəb(ə)l/ *a.* capable of being shown or proved.

demonstrate /ˈdemənstreɪt/ *v.* show evidence of; describe and explain by help of specimens or experiments; prove truth or existence of; take part in public demonstration.

demonstration /demənˈstreɪʃ(ə)n/ *n.* demonstrating; show of feeling; collective expression of opinion e.g. by public meeting; show of armed force.

demonstrative /dɪˈmɒnstrətɪv/ *a.* showing or proving; given to or marked by open expression of feelings; *Gram.* indicating person or thing referred to.

demonstrator /ˈdemənstreɪtə(r)/ *n.* person making or taking part in demonstration.

demoralize /diːˈmɒrəlaɪz/ *v.t.* weaken morale of. **demoralization** *n.*

demote /diːˈməʊt/ *v.t.* reduce to lower rank or grade.

demur /dɪˈmɜː(r)/ **1** *v.i.* raise objection; be unwilling. **2** *n.* raising of objection.

demure /dɪˈmjʊə(r)/ *a.* quiet and serious or affectedly so.

den *n.* wild beast's lair; resort of criminals etc.; person's small private room.

denarius /dɪˈneərɪəs/ *n.* (*pl.* -rii /-rɪaɪ/) ancient Roman silver coin.

denary /ˈdiːnərɪ/ *a.* of 10; decimal.

denationalize /diːˈnæʃənəlaɪz/ *v.t.* transfer (industry etc.) from national to private ownership. **denationalization** *n.*

denature /diːˈneɪtʃə(r)/ *v.t.* change properties of; make (alcohol) unfit for drinking.

denial /dɪˈnaɪəl/ *n.* denying or refusing; contradiction.

denier /ˈdenɪə(r)/ *n.* unit of weight for estimating fineness of yarn.

denigrate /ˈdenɪgreɪt/ *v.t.* blacken, defame.

denim /ˈdenɪm/ *n.* twilled cotton fabric; in *pl.* garment made of this.

denizen /ˈdenɪz(ə)n/ *n.* inhabitant or occupant (*of* place).

denominate /dɪˈnɒmɪneɪt/ *v.t.* give name to, describe as, call.

denomination /dɪnɒmɪˈneɪʃ(ə)n/ *n.* name, designation; Church or religious sect; class of units in numbers, money, etc.

denominational /dɪnɒmɪˈneɪʃən(ə)l/ *a.* of a particular religious denomination.

denominator /dɪˈnɒmɪneɪtə(r)/ *n.* number below line in vulgar fraction; divisor.

denote /dɪˈnəʊt/ *v.t.* be name for; be sign of; indicate; signify. **denotation** *n.*

dénouement /deɪˈnuːmɔ̃/ *n.* final resolution in play, novel, etc.

denounce /dɪˈnaʊns/ *v.t.* inform against; accuse publicly; speak violently against.

dense /dens/ *a.* closely compacted; crowded together; stupid. **density** *n.*

dent 1 *n.* depression in surface (as) from blow. **2** *v.t.* make dent in.

dental /ˈdent(ə)l/ *a.* of tooth or teeth or dentistry; (of sound) made with tongue-tip against front teeth. **dental floss** fine strong thread used to clean between teeth; **dental surgeon** dentist.

dentate /ˈdenteɪt/ *a.* toothed, notched.

dentifrice /'dentɪfrɪs/ n. powder or paste etc. for cleaning teeth.

dentine /'denti:n/ n. hard dense tissue forming main part of tooth.

dentist /'dentɪst/ n. person who treats diseases etc. of teeth. **dentistry** n.

dentition /den'tɪʃ(ə)n/ n. characteristic arrangement of teeth in species; teething.

denture /'dentʃə(r)/ n. set of artificial teeth.

denude /dɪ'nju:d/ v.t. make naked or bare; strip of. **denudation** n.

denunciation /dɪnʌnsɪ'eɪʃ(ə)n/ n. denouncing; invective. **denunciatory** a.

deny /dɪ'naɪ/ v.t. declare untrue or non-existent; disavow; refuse. **deny oneself** be abstinent.

deodorant /dɪ'əʊdərənt/ 1 a. that removes or conceals odours. 2 n. deodorant substance.

deodorize /dɪ'əʊdəraɪz/ v.t. destroy odour of. **deodorization** n.

deoxyribonucleic acid /dɪɒksɪraɪbəʊnju:'kli:ɪk/ substance in chromosomes storing genetic information.

depart /dɪ'pɑ:t/ v. go away, leave; set out; diverge or deviate. **depart this life** die.

departed a. bygone, deceased.

department /dɪ'pɑ:tmənt/ n. separate part of complex whole, esp. of business or of municipal or State administration; French administrative district. **department store** large shop selling variety of goods. **departmental** a.

departure /dɪ'pɑ:tʃə(r)/ n. departing.

depend /dɪ'pend/ v.i. (usu. with on or upon) be controlled or determined by; be unable to do without.

dependable /dɪ'pendəb(ə)l/ a. that may be depended on.

dependant /dɪ'pend(ə)nt/ n. person who depends on another for support.

dependence /dɪ'pend(ə)ns/ n. depending, being dependent; reliance.

dependency /dɪ'pendənsɪ/ n. country etc. controlled by another.

dependent /dɪ'pend(ə)nt/ a. depending (on); unable to do without something; maintained at another's cost; *Gram.* in subordinate relation to another word.

depict /dɪ'pɪkt/ v.t. represent in picture or words. **depiction** n.

depilate /'depɪleɪt/ v.t. remove hair from. **depilation** n.

depilatory /dɪ'pɪlətərɪ/ 1 a. that removes unwanted hair. 2 n. depilatory substance.

deplete /dɪ'pli:t/ v.t. empty out; reduce numbers or quantity of. **depletion** n.

deplorable /dɪ'plɔ:rəb(ə)l/ a. lamentable; to be regretted; exceedingly bad.

deplore /dɪ'plɔ:(r)/ v.t. find or call deplorable.

deploy /dɪ'plɔɪ/ v. spread out, put into or take up position, for most effective action etc. **deployment** n.

deponent /dɪ'pəʊnənt/ n. maker of legal deposition.

depopulate /di:'pɒpjʊleɪt/ v.t. reduce population of. **depopulation** n.

deport /dɪ'pɔ:t/ v.t. remove into exile; send out of the country; behave or conduct *oneself*. **deportation** n.

deportment /dɪ'pɔ:tmənt/ n. behaviour, bearing.

depose /dɪ'pəʊz/ v. remove from office; dethrone; state *that*; testify *to*.

deposit /dɪ'pɒzɪt/ 1 n. thing stored for safe keeping; sum placed in bank; sum paid as pledge or first instalment; layer of accumulated matter. 2 v.t. entrust for keeping; pay as pledge; lay or set down; leave as deposit.

depositary /dɪ'pɒzɪtərɪ/ n. person to whom thing is entrusted.

deposition /di:pə'zɪʃ(ə)n/ n. deposing; sworn evidence; giving of this.

depositor /dɪ'pɒzɪtə(r)/ n. person who deposits money or property etc.

depository /dɪ'pɒzɪtərɪ/ n. storehouse.

depot /'depəʊ/ n. storehouse, esp. for military supplies; headquarters of regiment; place from which goods or vehicles etc. are dispatched.

deprave /dɪ'preɪv/ v.t. corrupt morally; in *p.p.* wicked, dissolute.

depravity /dɪ'prævɪtɪ/ n. wickedness; moral corruption.

deprecate /'deprɪkeɪt/ v. express disapproval of. **deprecation** n.; **deprecatory** a. □ See page 666.

depreciate /dɪ'pri:ʃɪeɪt/ v. lower in value; disparage. □ See page 666.

depreciation /dɪpri:ʃɪ'eɪʃ(ə)n/ n. depreciating; fall in value.

depreciatory /dɪ'pri:ʃətərɪ/ a. disparaging.

depredation /depri'deiʃ(ə)n/ n. (usu. in pl.) plundering, destruction.

depress /di'pres/ v.t. make despondent, deject; lower or reduce; affect with economic depression; push down.

depressant /di'pres(ə)nt/ 1 a. causing depression. 2 n. depressant agent or influence.

depression /di'preʃ(ə)n/ n. state of extreme dejection; long period of financial and industrial slump; lowering of barometric pressure; sunken area in surface.

depressive /di'presiv/ 1 a. characterized by or tending to depression. 2 n. person suffering from depression.

deprivation /depri'veiʃ(ə)n/ n. depriving, being deprived; loss.

deprive /di'praiv/ v.t. prevent from use or enjoyment of; strip of; in p.p., (esp. of child) lacking normal home life etc.

dept. abbr. department.

depth n. deepness or measure of it; (usu. in pl.) deep or lowest or inmost part, middle (of night, winter, etc.). **depth-charge** bomb exploding under water; **in depth** thoroughly.

deputation /depju'teiʃ(ə)n/ n. body of persons sent to represent others.

depute /di'pju:t/ v.t. commit (task, authority) to another; appoint as substitute.

deputize /'depjotaiz/ v.i. act as deputy (for).

deputy /'depjoti/ n. person appointed to act for another; parliamentary representative in some countries.

derail /di'reil/ v.t. cause (train etc.) to leave rails. **derailment** n.

derange /di'reindʒ/ v.t. throw into confusion, disrupt; make insane. **derangement** n.

Derby /'da:bi/ n. annual horse-race at Epsom; similar race elsewhere; important sporting event.

derelict /'derilikt/ 1 a. left ownerless (esp. of ship at sea or decrepit property); abandoned by society. 2 n. derelict property; socially forsaken person.

dereliction /deri'likʃ(ə)n/ n. neglect (of duty etc.); shortcoming.

deride /di'raid/ v.t. scoff at. **derision** /-'riʒ-/ n.

derisive /di'raisiv/ a. mocking, ironical. □ See page 666.

derisory /di'raisəri/ a. showing derision; deserving derision. □ See page 666.

derivation /deri'veiʃ(ə)n/ n. deriving; formation of word from its origin; tracing of this.

derivative /di'rivətiv/ 1 a. derived, from a source, not original. 2 n. derivative word or substance.

derive /di'raiv/ v. get or obtain (from source); have origin from; trace or assert origin and formation of (word etc.).

dermatitis /dɜ:mə'taitis/ n. inflammation of skin.

dermatology /dɜ:mə'tɒlədʒi/ n. study of skin and its diseases. **dermatological** a.; **dermatologist** n.

derogate /'derəgeit/ v.i. detract from. **derogation** n.

derogatory /di'rɒgətəri/ a. involving discredit or disparagement to.

derrick /'derik/ n. kind of hoisting apparatus; framework over deep borehole, esp. oil-well.

derris /'deris/ n. insecticide made from powdered root of tropical plant.

derv n. diesel fuel used in heavy road vehicles.

dervish /'dɜ:viʃ/ n. member of Muslim religious order vowed to poverty and austerity.

descant 1 /'deskænt/ n. melodic treble accompaniment to hymn-tune etc. 2 /di'skænt/ v.i. talk lengthily upon. 3 **descant recorder** highest-pitched of standard kinds of recorder.

descend /di'send/ v. come or go down; make sudden attack or unexpected visit on; sink; stoop (to unworthy act); be derived or transmitted from.

descendant /di'send(ə)nt/ n. person etc. descended from another.

descended /di'sendid/ a. having origin from.

descent /di'sent/ n. act or way of descending; downward slope; lineage; sudden attack; decline, fall.

describe /di'skraib/ v.t. set forth in words; list characteristics of; mark out, draw, or move in (specified line or curve etc.).

description /di'skripʃ(ə)n/ n. describing; verbal portrait; sort, kind, class.

descriptive /dɪˈskrɪptɪv/ a. serving or seeking to describe.

descry /dɪˈskraɪ/ v.t. catch sight of; succeed in discerning.

desecrate /ˈdesɪkreɪt/ v.t. violate sanctity of. **desecration** n.; **desecrator** n.

desegregate /diːˈsegrɪgeɪt/ v.t. abolish racial segregation in.

desert[1] /dɪˈzɜːt/ v. abandon, forsake; cease to frequent; leave military service unlawfully. **desertion** n.

desert[2] /ˈdezət/ 1 n. uninhabited and barren esp. waterless region. 2 a. uninhabited, barren.

desert[3] /dɪˈzɜːt/ n. deserving, being worthy of reward or punishment; in pl. deserved recompense.

deserve /dɪˈzɜːv/ v. be entitled to, esp. by conduct or qualities.

deservedly /dɪˈzɜːvɪdlɪ/ adv. as deserved.

deserving /dɪˈzɜːvɪŋ/ a. worthy (of); worth rewarding or supporting.

desiccate /ˈdesɪkeɪt/ v.t. remove moisture, dry. **desiccation** n.

desideratum /dɪzɪdəˈrɑːtəm/ n. (pl. -ta) something required or desired.

design /dɪˈzaɪn/ 1 n. sketch or plan etc. for future product; art of making these; scheme of lines or shapes forming a decoration; layout; established form of product; mental plan; purpose. 2 v. make design for; be designer; intend.

designate 1 v. /ˈdezɪgneɪt/ v. specify; indicate as having some function; describe as; appoint to office. 2 a. /ˈdezɪgnət/ (placed after n.) appointed but not installed.

designation /dezɪgˈneɪʃ(ə)n/ n. designating; name or title.

designedly /dɪˈzaɪnɪdlɪ/ adv. intentionally.

designer /dɪˈzaɪnə(r)/ n. person who makes designs for products, clothes, stage sets, etc.

designing /dɪˈzaɪnɪŋ/ a. crafty, scheming.

desirable /dɪˈzaɪərəb(ə)l/ a. worth having or wishing for; causing desire. **desirability** n.

desire /dɪˈzaɪə(r)/ 1 n. unsatisfied longing; feeling of potential pleasure in something; expression of this; request; thing desired; lust. 2 v.t. have desire for; ask for.

desirous /dɪˈzaɪərəs/ a. having desire; wishful.

desist /dɪˈzɪst/ v.i. cease (from).

desk n. piece of furniture with flat or sloping top for reading or writing etc. at; compartment for cashier or receptionist etc.; subdivision of (esp. newspaper) office.

desolate 1 /ˈdesələt/ a. left alone; uninhabited; dreary, forlorn. 2 /ˈdesəleɪt/ v.t. depopulate; devastate; make wretched. 3 **desolation** n.

despair /dɪˈspeə(r)/ 1 n. loss or absence of hope; thing that causes this. 2 v.i. lose all hope (of).

despatch var. of **dispatch**.

desperado /despəˈrɑːdəʊ/ n. (pl. -does) desperate or reckless criminal.

desperate /ˈdespərət/ a. leaving little or no room for hope; extremely dangerous or serious; reckless from despair.

desperation /despəˈreɪʃ(ə)n/ n. despair; reckless state of mind.

despicable /dɪˈspɪkəb(ə)l/ a. deserving to be despised; contemptible.

despise /dɪˈspaɪz/ v.t. regard with contempt.

despite /dɪˈspaɪt/ prep. in spite of.

despoil /dɪˈspɔɪl/ v.t. plunder, strip. **despoliation** n.

despondent /dɪˈspɒnd(ə)nt/ a. in low spirits, dejected. **despondency** n.

despot /ˈdespɒt/ n. absolute ruler; tyrant.

despotic /dɪˈspɒtɪk/ a. having unrestricted power, tyrannous.

despotism /ˈdespətɪz(ə)m/ n. rule by despot; country ruled by despot.

dessert /dɪˈzɜːt/ n. sweet course ending meal. **dessertspoon** spoon between teaspoon and tablespoon in size.

destination /destɪˈneɪʃ(ə)n/ n. place to which person or thing is going.

destine /ˈdestɪn/ v.t. settle or determine future of; set apart for purpose.

destiny /ˈdestɪnɪ/ n. what is destined to happen; fate; power that foreordains.

destitute /ˈdestɪtjuːt/ a. in great need, esp. of food or shelter etc.; devoid of. **destitution** n.

destroy /dɪˈstrɔɪ/ v.t. pull or break down; make useless; kill.

destroyer /dɪˈstrɔɪə(r)/ n. small fast warship.

destruct /dɪˈstrʌkt/ v.t. US bring about

deliberate destruction of (one's own equipment etc.). **destructible** a.

destruction /dɪˈstrʌkʃ(ə)n/ n. destroying or being destroyed.

destructive /dɪˈstrʌktɪv/ a. causing destruction; tending to destroy; criticizing without amending.

desuetude /dɪˈsjuːɪtjuːd/ n. state of disuse.

desultory /ˈdezəltrɪ/ a. going constantly from one thing to another, unmethodical.

detach /dɪˈtætʃ/ v.t. unfasten and remove (from); send off on separate mission.

detached /dɪˈtætʃt/ a. standing apart; separate, not joined to another; unemotional, impartial.

detachment /dɪˈtætʃmənt/ n. detaching or being detached; lack of emotion or concern; party of soldiers etc. detached for special duty.

detail /ˈdiːteɪl/ 1 n. item, small or subordinate particular; dealing with things item by item; small detachment for special duty. 2 v.t. give particulars of, relate in detail; assign for special duty etc.

detain /dɪˈteɪn/ v.t. keep in custody or under restraint; keep waiting, delay.

detainee /diːteɪˈniː/ n. person detained in custody usu. on political grounds.

detect /dɪˈtekt/ v.t. discover, find out. **detection** n.; **detector** n.

detective /dɪˈtektɪv/ n. person, esp. policeman, employed in investigating crime.

détente /deɪˈtɑːt/ n. relaxing of strained diplomatic relations. [F]

detention /dɪˈtenʃ(ə)n/ n. detaining; being detained. **detention centre** institution for brief detention of young offenders.

deter /dɪˈtɜː(r)/ v.t. discourage, hinder.

detergent /dɪˈtɜːdʒ(ə)nt/ 1 n. cleansing agent, esp. substance used with water for removing dirt etc. 2 a. cleansing.

deteriorate /dɪˈtɪərɪəreɪt/ v.i. become worse. **deterioration** n.

determinant /dɪˈtɜːmɪnənt/ n. decisive factor.

determinate /dɪˈtɜːmɪnət/ a. limited; of definite scope or nature.

determination /dɪtɜːmɪˈneɪʃ(ə)n/ n. resolute purpose or conduct; determining; fixing of intention.

determine /dɪˈtɜːmɪn/ v. ascertain or fix with precision; settle, decide; be decisive factor in.

determined a. resolute.

determinism /dɪˈtɜːmɪnɪz(ə)m/ n. theory that action is determined by forces independent of will. **determinist** n.; **deterministic** a.

deterrent /dɪˈterənt/ 1 a. serving to deter. 2 n. thing that deters, esp. nuclear weapon deterring attack by enemy country.

detest /dɪˈtest/ v.t. hate, loathe. **detestation** n.

detestable /dɪˈtestəb(ə)l/ a. hated, loathed.

dethrone /diːˈθrəʊn/ v.t. remove (ruler) from throne. **dethronement** n.

detonate /ˈdetəneɪt/ v. (cause to) explode with loud report. **detonation** n.

detonator /ˈdetəneɪtə(r)/ n. device for detonating explosive.

detour /ˈdiːtʊə(r)/ n. divergence from direct or intended route; roundabout way.

detract /dɪˈtrækt/ v. take away from. **detract from** reduce credit due to, depreciate. **detraction** n.; **detractor** n.

detriment /ˈdetrɪmənt/ n. damage, harm; thing causing this. **detrimental** a.

detritus /dɪˈtraɪtəs/ n. Geol. matter produced by erosion, e.g. gravel or rock debris.

de trop /də trəʊ/ not wanted; in the way. [F]

deuce[1] /djuːs/ n. two on dice or cards; Tennis state of score at which either side must gain two successive points or games to win.

deuce[2] /djuːs/ n. the Devil.

deuterium /djuːˈtɪərɪəm/ n. heavy isotope of hydrogen with mass about twice that of ordinary hydrogen.

Deutschmark /ˈdɔɪtʃmɑːk/ n. currency unit of Federal Republic of Germany.

devalue /diːˈvæljuː/ v.t. reduce value of, esp. currency relative to that of other currencies or gold. **devaluation** n.

devastate /ˈdevəsteɪt/ v.t. lay waste; cause great destruction to. **devastation** n.

develop /dɪˈveləp/ v. make or become fuller or bigger or more elaborate or systematic; bring or come to active or visible state or to maturity; reveal or be revealed; begin to exhibit or suffer from; build on or make fuller use of (land); treat (photographic material) to make picture visible. **developing country** poor or primitive country developing better social and economic conditions.

development /dɪ'veləpmənt/ n. developing or being developed; growth or evolution; stage of advancement, product; area of developed land. **developmental** a.

deviant /'di:vɪənt/ 1 a. that deviates from normal behaviour. 2 n. deviant person or thing.

deviate /'di:vɪeɪt/ v.i. turn aside (from); digress; diverge.

deviation /di:vɪ'eɪʃ(ə)n/ n. deviating, esp. divergence from standard or normal position etc.

device /dɪ'vaɪs/ n. thing made or adapted for particular purpose; scheme, trick; emblematic or heraldic design. **left to one's own devices** without supervision or help.

devil /'dev(ə)l/ 1 n. personified spirit of evil, esp. *the* Devil supreme spirit of evil; cruel or malignant being; mischievously energetic or clever person. 2 v. cook with hot condiments. 3 **devil-may-care** cheerful and reckless; **devil's advocate** person who tests proposition by arguing against it.

devilish /'devəlɪʃ/ 1 a. of or like a devil; mischievous. 2 adv. colloq. very.

devilment /'devəlmənt/ n. mischief; wild spirits.

devilry /'devəlrɪ/ n. wickedness; reckless mischief; black magic.

devious /'di:vɪəs/ a. winding, circuitous; unscrupulous, insincere.

devise /dɪ'vaɪz/ v.t. plan or think out; leave (real estate) by will.

devoid /dɪ'vɔɪd/ a. **devoid of** quite lacking or free from.

devolution /di:və'lu:ʃ(ə)n/ n. delegation of power esp. from central to local or regional government.

devolve /dɪ'vɒlv/ v. (of duties etc.) pass or be passed on to another; (of property) descend in succession.

devote /dɪ'vəʊt/ v.t. apply or give over *to* particular activity or purpose.

devoted /dɪ'vəʊtɪd/ a. showing devotion; very loyal or loving.

devotee /devəʊ'ti:/ n. person devoted to something, enthusiast; very pious person.

devotion /dɪ'vəʊʃ(ə)n/ n. great love or loyalty; enthusiastic zeal; in *pl.* worship, prayers. **devotional** a.

devour /dɪ'vaʊə(r)/ v.t. eat greedily or quickly; destroy or consume; take in greedily with eyes or ears.

devout /dɪ'vaʊt/ a. earnestly religious; reverent; sincere.

dew n. atmospheric vapour condensed in droplets during night; beaded moisture resembling it. **dewberry** fruit like blackberry; **dew-claw** rudimentary inner toe of some dogs; **dewdrop** drop of dew; **dew-point** temperature at which dew forms. **dewy** a.

dewlap /'dju:læp/ n. fold of loose skin hanging from throat esp. in cattle.

dexterity /dek'sterɪtɪ/ n. dextrousness.

dextrous /'dekstrəs/ a. handling things neatly; skilful, clever.

dg. abbr. decigram.

dharma /'dɑ:mə/ n. right behaviour; Buddhist truth; Hindu moral law.

dhoti /'dəʊtɪ/ n. loin-cloth worn by male Hindus.

dhow /daʊ/ n. Arabian-Sea ship.

DHSS abbr. Department of Health and Social Security.

diabetes /daɪə'bi:ti:z/ n. disease in which sugar and starch are not properly absorbed by the body.

diabetic /daɪə'betɪk/1 a. of or having diabetes; for diabetics. 2 n. diabetic person.

diabolic /daɪə'bɒlɪk/ a. (also **diabolical**) of the Devil; inhumanly cruel or wicked.

diabolism /daɪ'æbəlɪz(ə)m/ n. devil-worship; sorcery.

diaconal /daɪ'ækən(ə)l/ a. of a deacon.

diaconate /daɪ'ækənət/ n. office of a deacon; body of deacons.

diacritical /daɪə'krɪtɪk(ə)l/ a. distinguishing; (of mark) indicating that written letter has particular sound.

diadem /'daɪədem/ n. crown.

diaeresis /daɪ'ɪərəsɪs/ n. (pl. -reses /-rəsi:z/ mark (¨) placed over vowel to show it is sounded separately.

diagnose /daɪəg'nəʊz/ v.t. determine

nature of or deduce presence of (disease).

diagnosis /daɪəg'nəʊsɪs/ n. (pl. -noses /-'nəʊsiːz/) identification of disease by means of symptoms etc.

diagnostic /daɪəg'nɒstɪk/1 a. of or assisting diagnosis. 2 n. symptom.

diagonal /daɪ'ægən(ə)l/ 1 a. crossing a straight sided figure from corner to corner, oblique. 2 n. straight line joining opposite corners of a thing.

diagram /'daɪəgræm/ n. drawing done to explain or illustrate statement or process etc. **diagrammatic** /-'mæ-/ a.

dial /'daɪəl/ 1 n. face of clock or watch; plate on which measurement is registered by pointer; numbered plate on telephone with movable disc for making call to selected number; device for selecting radio wavelength or television channel. 2 v. make telephone call by using dial; call (number) thus.

dialect /'daɪəlekt/ n. form of speech peculiar to particular region etc. **dialectal** a.

dialectic /daɪə'lektɪk/ n. (often in pl.) art of investigating truth by logical discussion etc. **dialectical** a.

dialogue /'daɪəlɒg/ n. conversation, esp. as represented in play, novel, etc.; discussion between representatives of two groups.

dialysis /daɪ'æləsɪs/ n. (pl. -ses /-siːz/) separation of particles by difference in their ability to pass through suitable membrane; purification of blood thus.

diamanté /dɪə'mâteɪ/ a. sparkling with powdered crystal etc.

diameter /daɪ'æmɪtə(r)/ n. straight line passing from side to side through centre of circle or sphere; transverse measurement.

diametrical /daɪə'metrɪk(ə)l/ a. of or along diameter; (of opposition etc.) direct, complete.

diamond /'daɪəmənd/ n. transparent usu. colourless very hard brilliant precious stone; rhombus; playing-card of suit marked with red rhombuses. **diamond wedding** 60th or 75th anniversary of wedding.

diapason /daɪə'peɪz(ə)n/ n. entire compass of musical instrument or voice; organ-stop extending through whole compass.

diaper /'daɪəpə(r)/ n. linen or cotton

fabric with small diamond pattern; baby's nappy.

diaphanous /daɪ'æfənəs/ a. (of fabric etc.) light and almost transparent.

diaphragm /'daɪəfræm/ n. muscular partition between thorax and abdomen in mammals; vibrating membrane etc. in acoustic instrument; device for varying aperture of camera lens; contraceptive cap fitting over cervix.

diarist /'daɪərɪst/ n. keeper of diary.

diarrhoea /daɪə'rɪə/ n. excessive evacuation of too fluid faeces.

diary /'daɪərɪ/ n. daily record of events etc.; book for keeping this or noting future engagements etc.

Diaspora /daɪ'æspərə/ n. dispersion of the Jews; Jews thus dispersed.

diastole /daɪ'æstəlɪ/ n. dilatation of heart alternating with systole in pulse.

diatomic /daɪə'tɒmɪk/ a. of two atoms.

diatonic /daɪə'tɒnɪk/ a. Mus. (of scale) involving only notes proper to key without chromatic alteration.

diatribe /'daɪətraɪb/ n. bitter criticism or denunciation.

dibble /'dɪbə(r)/ 1 n. (also **dibber**) garden tool for making holes to receive bulbs or plants. 2 v. plant (bulb etc.) thus.

dice 1 n. (pl. of **die²**, often used as sing.) small cube marked on each face with 1-6 spots etc., used in games of chance; game played with dice. 2 v. gamble with dice; take risks; cut into small cubes.

dicey /'daɪsɪ/ a. sl. risky, unreliable.

dichotomy /daɪ'kɒtəmɪ/ n. division into two.

dichromatic /daɪkrə'mætɪk/ a. of two colours.

dick n. US sl. detective.

dickens /'dɪkɪnz/ n. colloq. the Devil.

dicker /'dɪkə(r)/ v.i. haggle; hesitate.

dicky /'dɪkɪ/ 1 n. colloq. false shirt-front. 2 a. sl. shaky, unsound.

dicotyledon /daɪkɒtɪ'liːd(ə)n/ n. flowering plant with two cotyledons. **dicotyledonous** a.

Dictaphone /'dɪktəfəʊn/ n. (P) machine for recording and playing back dictated words.

dictate 1 /dɪk'teɪt/ v. say aloud (matter to be written down); lay down authoritatively; give peremptory order. 2 /'dɪkteɪt/ n. (usu. in pl.) authoritative instruction esp. *of* conscience or reason etc. **3 dictation** *n.*

dictator /dɪk'teɪtə(r)/ *n.* absolute ruler of State; person with absolute authority. **dictatorship** *n.*

dictatorial /dɪktə'tɔːrɪəl/ *a.* of a dictator; imperious, overbearing.

diction /'dɪkʃ(ə)n/ *n.* manner of enunciation; choice and use of words in speech or writing.

dictionary /'dɪkʃənərɪ/ *n.* book explaining, usu. in alphabetical order, words of a language, or giving their equivalents in another language; reference book of words and topics of subject arranged alphabetically.

dictum /'dɪktəm/ *n.* (*pl.* **-ta**) formal expression of opinion; maxim.

did *past* of **do**[1].

didactic /dɪ'dæktɪk/ *a.* meant to instruct; having manner of authoritarian teacher. **didacticism** *n.*

diddle /'dɪd(ə)l/ *v.t. sl.* cheat, swindle.

die[1] *v.i.* (*partic.* **dying**) cease to live; cease to exist; fade away; (of fire) go out. **be dying for, to**, have great desire; **die down** become less loud or strong; **die-hard** conservative or stubborn person; **die (of) laughing** laugh to exhaustion; **die out** become extinct, cease to exist.

die[2] *n.* see **dice**; engraved stamp for impressing design etc. on softer metal. **die-casting** process or product of making castings from metal moulds.

dielectric /daɪɪ'lektrɪk/ **1** *a. Electr.* that does not conduct electricity. **2** *n.* dielectric substance usable for insulating.

diesel /'diːz(ə)l/ *n.* internal-combustion engine in which fuel is ignited by heat of highly compressed air (in full **diesel engine**); fuel for or vehicle driven by diesel engine. **diesel-electric** driven by electric current from generator driven by diesel engine; **diesel oil** petroleum fraction used in diesel engines.

diet[1] /'daɪət/ **1** *n.* one's habitual food; prescribed course of food. **2** *v.* keep to special diet. **3 dietary** *a.*

diet[2] /'daɪət/ *n.* conference, congress.

dietetic /daɪə'tetɪk/ *a.* of diet and nutrition.

dietetics *n.pl.* scientific study of diet and nutrition.

dietitian /daɪə'tɪʃ(ə)n/ *n.* (also **-ician**) expert in dietetics.

differ /'dɪfə(r)/ *v.i.* be unlike; be distinguishable; diverge in opinion.

difference /'dɪfrəns/ *n.* being different or unlike; point in which things differ; degree or amount of unlikeness; remainder after subtraction; disagreement.

different /'dɪfrənt/ *a.* unlike, of other nature, form or quality; separate, unusual.

differential /dɪfə'renʃ(ə)l/ **1** *a.* varying with circumstances; constituting or relating to specific difference(s); *Math.* relating to infinitesimal differences. **2** *n.* differential gear; difference between rates of interest etc. or between wage-rates. **3 differential calculus** means of finding rates of change, maximum and minimum values, etc.; **differential gear** arrangement of gears enabling driving wheels to revolve at different speeds in rounding corners.

differentiate /dɪfə'renʃɪeɪt/ *v.* constitute difference between or of or in; discriminate; make or become different. **differentiation** *n.*

difficult /'dɪfɪk(ə)lt/ *a.* hard to do, deal with, or understand; troublesome.

difficulty /'dɪfɪkəltɪ/ *n.* being difficult; difficult point or situation; obstacle; in *pl.* trouble, esp. shortage of money.

diffident /'dɪfɪd(ə)nt/ *a.* lacking self-confidence. **diffidence** *n.*

diffract /dɪ'frækt/ *v.t.* break up (beam of light) into series of dark and light bands or coloured spectra. **diffraction** *n.*; **diffractive** *a.*

diffuse 1 /dɪ'fjuːz/ *v.* spread widely or thinly; (esp. of fluids) intermingle. **2** /dɪ'fjuːs/ *a.* spread out; not concentrated; verbose, not concise. **3 diffusible** *a.*; **diffusive** *a.*; **diffusion** *n.*

dig 1 *v.* (*past & p.p.* **dug**) turn up soil with spade etc. or with hands or claws etc.; excavate; thrust or plunge *in* or *into*; make search; prod, poke; *sl.* understand, admire. **2** *n.* piece of digging; archaeological excavation; thrust, poke; gibe; in *pl. colloq.* lodgings. **3 dig oneself in** prepare or occupy defensive position; **dig out, up**, get or find by digging.

digest 1 /dɪ'dʒest/ *v.t.* assimilate (food) in stomach and bowels; understand

and assimilate mentally; summarize. **2**
/'daɪdʒest/ *n.* compendium, esp. of
laws; periodical synopsis of current
news etc. **3 digestible** *a.*

digestion /dɪ'dʒestʃ(ə)n/ *n.* digesting;
power of digesting food.

digestive /dɪ'dʒestɪv/ *a.* of or promoting digestion. **digestive biscuit**
kind of wholemeal biscuit.

digger /'dɪɡə(r)/ *n.* person or thing that
digs; *colloq.* Australian, New
Zealander.

digit /'dɪdʒɪt/ *n.* any numeral from 0 to
9; finger or toe.

digital /'dɪdʒɪt(ə)l/ *a.* of digits. **digital
clock** etc. one showing time by displayed digits, not by hands; **digital
computer** one making calculations
with data represented by digits; **digital
recording** recording with sound-
information represented in digits.

digitalis /dɪdʒɪ'teɪlɪs/ *n.* heart stimulant drug made from foxglove.

dignified /'dɪɡnɪfaɪd/ *a.* having or
showing dignity.

dignify /'dɪɡnɪfaɪ/ *v.t.* give dignity to.

dignitary /'dɪɡnɪtərɪ/ *n.* holder of high
rank or office, esp. in Church.

dignity /'dɪɡnɪtɪ/ *n.* composed and serious manner or style; being worthy of
respect; high rank or position.

digraph /'daɪɡrɑːf/ *n.* group of two letters expressing single sound.

digress /daɪ'ɡres/ *v.i.* diverge temporarily from main track, esp. in
speech or writing. **digression** *n.*; **digressive** *a.*

dike **1** *n.* long ridge of earth, embankment; channel or ditch. **2** *v.t.* protect with dike(s).

dilapidated /dɪ'læpɪdeɪtɪd/ *a.* in disrepair or decay.

dilapidation /dɪlæpɪ'deɪʃ(ə)n/ *n.* state
of bad repair; falling into decay.

dilate /daɪ'leɪt/ *v.* widen or expand;
speak or write at length. **dilatation** *n.*;
dilation *n.*

dilatory /'dɪlətərɪ/ *a.* tending or designed to cause delay.

dilemma /dɪ'lemə/ *n.* position presenting choice between equally unwelcome possibilities.

dilettante /dɪlɪ'tæntɪ/ *n.* (*pl.* **-ti** /-tiː/
or **-tes**) person who dabbles in subject
without serious study. **dilettantism** *n.*

diligence /'dɪlɪdʒ(ə)ns/ *n.* persistent
effort or work. **diligent** *a.*

dill *n.* herb with scented leaves and
seeds. **dill pickle** pickled cucumber
etc. flavoured with dill.

dilly-dally /'dɪlɪdælɪ/ *v.i. colloq.* dawdle, vacillate.

dilute /daɪ'ljuːt/ **1** *v.t.* reduce in
strength by addition of water etc.; make
less forceful etc. **2** *a.* diluted. **3 dilution**
n.

diluvial /daɪ'luːvɪəl/ *a.* of flood, esp.
Flood in Genesis.

dim 1 *a.* deficient in brightness or clearness; obscure; indistinct; *colloq.* stupid.
2 *v.* make or become dim.

dime *n. US* 10-cent coin.

dimension /daɪ'menʃ(ə)n/ *n.* any of
the three linear measurements, length,
breadth, and depth; in *pl.* size or extent.
dimensional *a.*

diminish /dɪ'mɪnɪʃ/ *v.* make or become less; impair.

diminuendo /dɪmɪnjʊ'endəʊ/ **1** *adv.*
with decreasing volume of sound. **2** *n.*
(*pl.* **-dos**) passage to be played thus.

diminution /dɪmɪ'njuːʃ(ə)n/ *n.*
diminishing.

diminutive /dɪ'mɪnjʊtɪv/ **1** *a.* tiny,
undersized; (of word etc.) denoting or
implying smallness. **2** *n.* diminutive
word.

dimple /'dɪmp(ə)l/ **1** *n.* small hollow,
esp. in cheek or chin. **2** *v.* produce dimples in; show dimples.

din 1 *n.* continuous roar of confused
noise. **2** *v.* make din. **3 din into** teach
or weary by constant repetition.

dinar /'diːnɑː(r)/ *n.* currency unit in
Yugoslavia and several Middle Eastern
and N. African countries.

dine *v.* eat dinner; entertain to dinner.
dining-car railway coach where meals
are served; **dining-room** room in
which meals are eaten.

diner /'daɪnə(r)/ *n.* person who dines;
small dining-room; railway dining-car;
US restaurant.

ding-dong /'dɪŋdɒŋ/ **1** *n.* sound of
alternating strokes as of two bells. **2** *a.*
(of contest) in which each contestant
alternately has advantage. **3** *adv.* with
great energy.

dinghy /'dɪŋɡɪ/ *n.* small boat.

dingle /'dɪŋɡ(ə)l/ *n.* deep dell.

dingo /ˈdɪŋgəʊ/ n. (pl. -goes) Aus. wild dog.

dingy /ˈdɪndʒɪ/ a. dull-coloured; drab; dirty-looking. **dinginess** n.

dinkum /ˈdɪŋkəm/ a. Aus. sl. genuine, real.

dinky /ˈdɪŋkɪ/ a. colloq. pretty, small and neat.

dinner /ˈdɪnə(r)/ n. chief meal of day; formal evening meal in honour of person or event. **dinner-jacket** man's short usu. black coat for evening wear.

dinosaur /ˈdaɪnəsɔ:(r)/ n. extinct usu. large reptile.

dint 1 n. dent. 2 v.t. mark with dints. 3 **by dint of** by force or means of.

diocese /ˈdaɪəsɪs/ n. district under bishop's pastoral care. **diocesan** /daɪˈɒsɪs(ə)n/ a.

diode /ˈdaɪəʊd/ n. thermionic valve with two electrodes; semiconductor rectifier having two terminals.

dioxide /daɪˈɒksaɪd/ n. oxide with two atoms of oxygen to one of metal etc.

dip 1 v. put or let down into liquid, immerse; go under water and emerge quickly; go below any surface or level; lower for an instant and raise again; lower beam of (headlights); slope or extend downwards; put (hand etc.) into to take something out; look cursorily into book etc. 2 n. dipping; liquid into which thing is dipped; colloq. short bathe; downward slope; sauce etc. into which food is dipped before eating.

Dip. abbr. Diploma.

diphtheria /dɪfˈθɪərɪə/ n. infectious disease with inflammation of mucous membrane esp. of throat.

diphthong /ˈdɪfθɒŋ/ n. union of two vowels in one syllable. **diphthongal** a.

diploma /dɪˈpləʊmə/ n. certificate of educational qualification; document conferring honour, privilege, or licence.

diplomacy /dɪˈpləʊməsɪ/ n. management of international relations; tact.

diplomat /ˈdɪpləmæt/ n. person engaged in diplomacy; tactful person.

diplomatic /dɪpləˈmætɪk/ a. of or involved in diplomacy; tactful. **diplomatic bag** bag containing official mail from embassy etc.; **diplomatic immunity** exemption of diplomatic staff etc. abroad from arrest or taxation etc.

diplomatist /dɪˈpləʊmətɪst/ n. diplomat.

dipper /ˈdɪpə(r)/ n. thing that dips; kind of diving-bird.

dipsomania /dɪpsəˈmeɪnɪə/ n. abnormal craving for alcohol. **dipsomaniac** n. & a.

dipterous /ˈdɪptərəs/ a. two-winged.

diptych /ˈdɪptɪk/ n. pair of pictures or carvings on panels hinged together.

dire a. dreadful, ominous; urgent.

direct /dɪˈrekt/ 1 a. extending or moving in straight line or by shortest route, not crooked or oblique; straightforward, frank; without intermediaries. 2 adv. in a direct way or manner; by direct route. 3 v.t. control; guide; order; tell way to (place etc.); address (letter etc. to); send or point or utter etc. to or at or towards etc.; supervise acting etc. of (film, play, etc.). 4 **direct action** exertion of pressure on community by strikes etc. rather than by parliamentary means; **direct current** electric current flowing in one direction only; **direct debit** regular debiting of person's bank account at request of recipient; **direct grant** grant of money given to certain schools by Government not local authority; **direct object** primary object of verbal action; **direct speech** words as actually spoken, not as modified in reporting; **direct tax** tax levied on income.

direction /dɪˈrekʃ(ə)n/ n. directing; (usu. in pl.) orders or instructions; point to or from or along which person or thing looks or moves.

directional /dɪˈrekʃən(ə)l/ a. of or indicating direction; Radio sending or receiving signals in one direction only.

directive /dɪˈrektɪv/ 1 n. general instruction. 2 a. serving to direct.

directly /dɪˈrektlɪ/ 1 adv. in direct manner; at once, without delay. 2 conj. as soon as.

director /dɪˈrektə(r)/ n. person who directs, esp. member of board managing affairs of company etc.; person who directs film, play, etc. **directorial** a.; **directorship** n.

directorate /dɪˈrektərət/ n. office of director; board of directors.

directory /dɪˈrektərɪ/ n. book with list of telephone subscribers, inhabitants of town etc., members of profession, etc.

dirge *n.* song of mourning.

dirigible /'dɪrɪdʒɪb(ə)l/ **1** *a.* that can be steered. **2** *n.* dirigible balloon or airship.

dirk *n.* long dagger.

dirndl /'dɜːnd(ə)l/ *n.* full gathered skirt with tight waistband.

dirt *n.* unclean matter that soils; earth; foul or malicious talk; excrement. **dirt cheap** extremely cheap; **dirt road** *US* unmade road; **dirt-track** racing track with surface of earth or cinders etc.

dirty /'dɜːtɪ/ **1** *a.* soiled; unclean; sordid, obscene; mean, unfair; (of weather) rough; muddy-looking. **2** *v.* make or become dirty. **3 dirty look** *colloq.* look of disapproval or disgust. **4 dirtiness** *n.*

disability /dɪsə'bɪlɪtɪ/ *n.* thing or lack that prevents one doing something; physical incapacity.

disable /dɪ'seɪb(ə)l/ *v.t.* deprive of an ability; (esp. in *p.p.*) cripple, deprive of or reduce power of walking etc. **disablement** *n.*

disabuse /dɪsə'bjuːz/ *v.t.* free *of* false idea; disillusion.

disadvantage /dɪsəd'vɑːntɪdʒ/ *n.* unfavourable condition or circumstance. **disadvantageous** /dɪsədvɑːn'teɪdʒəs/ *a.*

disadvantaged *a.* in unfavourable conditions, esp. lacking normal social opportunities.

disaffected /dɪsə'fektɪd/ *a.* discontented; disloyal. **disaffection** *n.*

disagree /dɪsə'griː/ *v.i.* hold different opinion; fail to agree; quarrel. **disagree with** have bad effect on. **disagreement** *n.*

disagreeable /dɪsə'griːəb(ə)l/ *a.* unpleasant; bad-tempered.

disallow /dɪsə'laʊ/ *v.t.* reject; prohibit.

disappear /dɪsə'pɪə(r)/ *v.i.* pass from sight or existence; cease to be visible. **disappearance** *n.*

disappoint /dɪsə'pɔɪnt/ *v.t.* fail to fulfil desire or expectation of; frustrate. **disappointment** *n.*

disapprobation /dɪsæprə'beɪʃ(ə)n/ *n.* disapproval.

disapprove /dɪsə'pruːv/ *v.* have or express unfavourable opinion (*of*). **disapproval** *n.*

disarm /dɪs'ɑːm/ *v.* deprive of weapons; abandon or reduce military establishment; pacify hostility or suspicions of. **disarmament** *n.*

disarrange /dɪsə'reɪndʒ/ *v.t.* put into disorder; disorganize. **disarrangement** *n.*

disarray /dɪsə'reɪ/ *n.* disorder, confusion.

disaster /dɪ'zɑːstə(r)/ *n.* sudden or great misfortune; complete failure. **disastrous** *a.*

disavow /dɪsə'vaʊ/ *v.t.* say one does not know or have responsibility for or approve of. **disavowal** *n.*

disband /dɪs'bænd/ *v.* break up, disperse.

disbar /dɪs'bɑː(r)/ *v.t.* deprive of status of barrister. **disbarment** *n.*

disbelieve /dɪsbɪ'liːv/ *v.* refuse to believe; not believe (*in*). **disbelief** *n.*

disburden /dɪs'bɜːd(ə)n/ *v.t.* relieve of burden.

disburse /dɪs'bɜːs/ *v.* pay out (money). **disbursement** *n.*

disc *n.* round flat or apparently flat plate or surface or part; layer of cartilage between vertebrae; gramophone record; similar object used to store computer data etc. **disc brake** one using disc-shaped friction surfaces; **disc jockey** presenter of broadcast programme featuring records of popular music.

discard 1 /dɪs'kɑːd/ *v.t.* cast aside, give up; reject as unwanted. **2** /'dɪskɑːd/ *n.* discarded thing.

discern /dɪ'sɜːn/ *v.t.* perceive clearly with mind or senses; make out. **discernment** *n.*

discerning /dɪ'sɜːnɪŋ/ *a.* having good judgement or insight.

discharge /dɪs'tʃɑːdʒ/ **1** *v.* put forth, emit; send as missile; release, let go; dismiss; pay or perform (duty, debt); fire (gun etc.); relieve (bankrupt) of residual liability; relieve of cargo; unload. **2** *n.* (also /'dɪs-/) discharging or being discharged; matter or thing discharged.

disciple /dɪ'saɪp(ə)l/ *n.* person who takes another as his teacher or leader.

disciplinarian /dɪsɪplɪ'neərɪən/ *n.* maintainer of strict discipline.

disciplinary /dɪsɪ'plɪnərɪ/ *a.* of or enforcing discipline.

discipline /'dɪsɪplɪn/ **1** *n.* mental or moral training; orderly behaviour maintained (as) among persons under control or command; chastisement; branch of instruction. **2** *v.t.* train to obedience and order; punish.

disclaim /dɪs'kleɪm/ *v.t.* disown, deny.

disclaimer *n.* statement disclaiming something.

disclose /dɪs'kləʊz/ *v.t.* expose to view; make known, reveal. **disclosure** *n.*

disco /'dɪskəʊ/ *n.* (*pl.* **-cos**) *colloq.* discothèque.

discolour /dɪs'kʌlə(r)/ *v.* impair colour of; stain or become stained. **discoloration** *n.*

discomfit /dɪs'kʌmfɪt/ *v.t.* disconcert; baffle. **discomfiture** *n.*

discomfort /dɪs'kʌmfət/ *n.* uneasiness of body or mind.

discompose /dɪskəm'pəʊz/ *v.t.* disturb composure of. **discomposure** *n.*

disconcert /dɪskən'sɜːt/ *v.t.* disturb self-possession of; fluster.

disconnect /dɪskə'nekt/ *v.t.* break connection of or between; put (electrical apparatus) out of action by disconnecting parts. **disconnection** *n.*

disconnected *a.* incoherent, having abrupt transitions.

disconsolate /dɪs'kɒnsələt/ *a.* forlorn, unhappy; disappointed.

discontent /dɪskən'tent/ **1** *n.* dissatisfaction; lack of contentment. **2** *v.t.* make dissatisfied.

discontinue /dɪskən'tɪnjuː/ *v.t.* (cause to) cease; not go on with. **discontinuance** *n.*

discontinuous /dɪskən'tɪnjʊəs/ *a.* lacking continuity; intermittent. **discontinuity** /-'nju:-/ *n.*

discord /'dɪskɔːd/ *n.* disagreement, strife; harsh noise; lack of harmony. **discordance** *n.*; **discordant** *a.*

discothèque /'dɪskətek/ *n.* club etc. where records are played for dancing.

discount **1** /'dɪskaʊnt/ *n.* deduction from nominal value or price or amount. **2** *v.t.* /dɪs'kaʊnt/ disregard partly or wholly; deduct amount from (price etc.); give or get present value of (bill of exchange not yet due). **3 at a discount** below nominal or usual price, *fig.* depreciated.

discountenance /dɪs'kaʊntənəns/ *v.t.* refuse to approve of; disconcert.

discourage /dɪs'kʌrɪdʒ/ *v.t.* reduce confidence or spirits of; dissuade. **discouragement** *n.*

discourse 1 /'dɪskɔːs/ *n.* talk or conversation; lecture or sermon or other exposition. **2** /dɪs'kɔːs/ *v.i.* converse, speak or write at length.

discourteous /dɪs'kɜːtɪəs/ *a.* rude, uncivil. **discourtesy** *n.*

discover /dɪ'skʌvə(r)/ *v.t.* acquire knowledge or sight of by effort or chance; be first to do this in particular case.

discovery /dɪ'skʌvərɪ/ *n.* discovering, thing discovered.

discredit /dɪs'kredɪt/ **1** *v.t.* harm good reputation of; refuse to believe; cause to be disbelieved. **2** *n.* harm to reputation; cause of this; lack of credibility.

discreditable /dɪs'kredɪtəb(ə)l/ *a.* bringing discredit, shameful.

discreet /dɪ'skriːt/ *a.* prudent; cautious in speech or action; unobtrusive.

discrepancy /dɪ'skrepənsɪ/ *n.* difference; inconsistency. **discrepant** *a.*

discrete /dɪ'skriːt/ *a.* separate; distinct.

discretion /dɪ'skreʃ(ə)n/ *n.* prudence; judgement; liberty of deciding as one thinks fit.

discretionary /dɪ'skreʃənərɪ/ *a.* left to discretion.

discriminate /dɪ'skrɪmɪneɪt/ *v.* make or see a distinction (*between*), esp. as a basis for unfair treatment. **discrimination** *n.*; **discriminatory** *a.*

discursive /dɪs'kɜːsɪv/ *a.* rambling, not sticking to main subject.

discus /'dɪskəs/ *n.* heavy disc thrown in athletic exercises.

discuss /dɪs'kʌs/ *v.t.* examine by argument; debate; have argument about. **discussion** *n.*

disdain /dɪs'deɪn/ **1** *n.* scorn, contempt. **2** *v.t.* regard with disdain; think beneath oneself or one's notice. **3 disdainful** *a.*

disease /dɪ'ziːz/ *n.* unhealthy condition; (specific) disorder or illness.

diseased *a.* affected with disease; abnormal, disordered.

disembark /dɪsɪm'bɑːk/ *v.* put or go ashore. **disembarkation** *n.*

disembarrass /dɪsɪm'bærəs/ *v.t.* free from embarrassment; rid or relieve (*of*). **disembarrassment** *n.*

disembody /dɪsɪm'bɒdɪ/ v.t. separate (soul, voice, etc.) from body.

disembowel /dɪsɪm'baʊəl/ v.t. remove entrails of.

disenchant /dɪsɪn'tʃaːnt/ v.t. free from enchantment; disillusion. **disenchantment** n.

disencumber /dɪsɪn'kʌmbə(r)/ v.t. disburden; free from encumbrance.

disengage /dɪsɪn'geɪdʒ/ v. detach; loosen; release from engagement, become detached. **disengagement** n.

disengaged a. at leisure; not occupied.

disentangle /dɪsɪn'tæŋg(ə)l/ v.t. free or become free of tangles or complications. **disentanglement** n.

disestablish /dɪsɪ'stæblɪʃ/ v.t. deprive (Church) of State connection. **disestablishment** n.

disfavour /dɪs'feɪvə(r)/ n. dislike; disapproval.

disfigure /dɪs'fɪgə(r)/ v.t. spoil appearance of. **disfigurement** n.

disfranchise /dɪs'fræntʃaɪz/ v.t. deprive of franchise. **disfranchisement** n.

disgorge /dɪs'gɔːdʒ/ v.t. eject from throat; pour forth.

disgrace /dɪs'greɪs/ 1 n. loss of favour, downfall from position of honour; shame; cause of reproach. 2 v.t. bring shame or discredit on; dismiss from favour.

disgraceful /dɪs'greɪsfʊl/ a. causing disgrace; shameful.

disgruntled /dɪs'grʌnt(ə)ld/ a. discontented.

disguise /dɪs'gaɪz/ 1 v.t. conceal identity of, make unrecognizable; conceal, cover up. 2 n. (use of) changed dress or appearance for concealment or deception; disguised condition.

disgust /dɪs'gʌst/ 1 n. loathing, strong aversion; indignation. 2 v.t. cause disgust in.

disgusting a. distasteful; repellent.

dish 1 n. shallow flat-bottomed container for holding food; food served in dish or prepared for table; dish-shaped receptacle or object or cavity; colloq. attractive person. 2 v. make concave; colloq. defeat completely. 3 **dish out** sl. distribute; **dish up** (prepare to) serve meal; **dish-water** water in which dirty dishes etc. have been washed.

disharmony /dɪs'haːmənɪ/ n. lack of harmony, discord.

dishearten /dɪs'haːt(ə)n/ v.t. cause to lose courage or confidence. **disheartenment** n.

dishevelled /dɪ'ʃev(ə)ld/ a. ruffled, untidy.

dishonest /dɪs'ɒnɪst/ a. not honest; fraudulent; insincere. **dishonesty** n.

dishonour /dɪs'ɒnə(r)/ 1 v.t. bring dishonour upon; treat without honour or respect; refuse to pay (cheque etc.). 2 n. state of shame or disgrace; cause of this.

dishonourable /dɪ'sɒnərəb(ə)l/ a. causing disgrace; ignominious.

disillusion /dɪsɪ'luːʒ(ə)n/ 1 v.t. free from illusion or mistaken belief. 2 n. being disillusioned. 3 **disillusionment** n.

disincentive /dɪsɪn'sentɪv/ n. thing that tends to discourage.

disincline /dɪsɪn'klaɪn/ v.t. make unwilling. **disinclination** n.

disinfect /dɪsɪn'fekt/ v.t. cleanse of infection; remove bacteria from. **disinfection** n.

disinfectant /dɪsɪn'fekt(ə)nt/ 1 a. having disinfecting qualities. 2 n. disinfectant substance.

disinflation /dɪsɪn'fleɪʃ(ə)n/ n. reduction of inflation.

disingenuous /dɪsɪn'dʒenjʊəs/ a. insincere; not candid.

disinherit /dɪsɪn'herɪt/ v.t. deprive of right to inherit. **disinheritance** n.

disintegrate /dɪs'ɪntɪgreɪt/ v. separate into component parts; deprive of or lose cohesion. **disintegration** n.

disinter /dɪsɪn'tɜː(r)/ v.t. dig up (esp. corpse) from ground. **disinterment** n.

disinterested /dɪs'ɪntərestɪd/ a. not influenced by involvement or advantage. □ See page 666.

disjoin /dɪs'dʒɔɪn/ v.t. separate, disunite.

disjoint /dɪs'dʒɔɪnt/ v.t. separate at joints; dislocate.

disjointed a. disconnected, incoherent.

disjunction /dɪs'dʒʌŋkʃ(ə)n/ n. disjoining, separation.

disjunctive /dɪs'dʒʌŋktɪv/ a. involving separation or expressing alternative.

disk var. of **disc**.

dislike /dɪs'laɪk/ 1 n. feeling that thing etc. is unattractive, unpleasant, etc. 2 v.t. have dislike for.

dislocate /'dɪsləkeɪt/ v.t. disturb normal connection of; put out of order. **dislocation** n.

dislodge /dɪs'lɒdʒ/ v.t. move from established position. **dislodgement** n.

disloyal /dɪs'lɔɪəl/ a. unfaithful; lacking loyalty. **disloyalty** n.

dismal /'dɪzm(ə)l/ a. cheerless, dreary.

dismantle /dɪs'mænt(ə)l/ v.t. pull down, take to pieces; deprive of defences, equipment, etc.

dismay /dɪs'meɪ/ 1 n. feeling of intense disappointment and discouragement. 2 v.t. affect with dismay.

dismember /dɪs'membə(r)/ v.t. remove limbs from; partition (country etc.). **dismemberment** n.

dismiss /dɪs'mɪs/ v.t. send away, disband; allow to go; send away (esp. dishonourably); put out of one's thoughts; *Law* refuse further hearing to; *Crick.* put (batsman, side) out. **dismissal** n.; **dismissive** a.

dismount /dɪs'maʊnt/ v. (cause to) get off or down from cycle or horseback etc.; remove (thing) from mounting.

disobedience /dɪsə'biːdɪəns/ n. disobeying; rebelliousness. **disobedient** a.

disobey /dɪsə'beɪ/ v. fail or refuse to obey; disregard orders.

disoblige /dɪsə'blaɪdʒ/ v.t. refuse to consider convenience or wishes of. **disobliging** a.

disorder /dɪs'ɔːdə(r)/ 1 n. confusion; tumult, riot; bodily or mental ailment. 2 v.t. put into disorder, upset.

disorderly /dɪs'ɔːdəlɪ/ a. untidy; riotous.

disorganize /dɪs'ɔːgənaɪz/ v.t. upset order or system of; throw into confusion. **disorganization** n.

disorientate /dɪs'ɔːrɪənteɪt/ v.t. confuse (person) as to his bearings.

disown /dɪs'əʊn/ v.t. refuse to recognize or acknowledge; repudiate.

disparage /dɪs'pærɪdʒ/ v.t. speak slightingly of. **disparagement** n.

disparate /'dɪspərət/ a. essentially different, unrelated.

disparity /dɪs'pærɪtɪ/ n. inequality, difference.

dispassionate /dɪs'pæʃənət/ a. free from emotion; impartial.

dispatch /dɪs'pætʃ/ 1 v.t. send off; kill; get (business etc.) done promptly; eat quickly. 2 n. dispatching; rapidity; efficiency; official communication on State affairs. 3 **dispatch-box** case for dispatches and other papers; **dispatch-rider** motor-cyclist etc. carrying official messages.

dispel /dɪs'pel/ v.t. drive away; scatter.

dispensary /dɪs'pensərɪ/ n. place where medicines etc. are dispensed.

dispensation /dɪspen'seɪʃ(ə)n/ n. distributing, dealing out; ordering or management, esp. of world by Providence; exemption from penalty or obligation.

dispense /dɪs'pens/ v. distribute; administer; make up (medicine) from prescription or formula. **dispense with** do without.

dispenser n. person who dispenses something; device that dispenses selected quantity at a time.

disperse /dɪs'pɜːs/ v. (make) go various ways, scatter; put in circulation; separate (light) into coloured constituents. **dispersal** n.; **dispersion** n.

dispirit /dɪ'spɪrɪt/ v.t. make despondent.

displace /dɪs'pleɪs/ v.t. shift from proper position; oust, take the place of; remove from office. **displaced person** one who has had to leave his home country as result of war etc.

displacement n. displacing or being displaced; amount of fluid displaced by body floating or immersed in it.

display /dɪs'pleɪ/ 1 v.t. spread out to view; exhibit. 2 n. displaying; exhibition; ostentation.

displease /dɪs'pliːz/ v.t. offend; make angry; be unpleasing to.

displeasure /dɪs'pleʒə(r)/ n. disapproval, dissatisfaction, anger.

disport /dɪs'pɔːt/ v. *arch.* frolic, enjoy one*self*.

disposable /dɪs'pəʊzəb(ə)l/ a. that can be disposed of; designed to be thrown away after one use.

disposal /dɪs'pəʊz(ə)l/ n. disposing (*of*). **at one's disposal** available.

dispose /dɪs'pəʊz/ v. place suitably or in order; incline (*to*); bring into certain state; determine course of events. **dispose of** get rid of, deal with, finish.

disposition /dɪspə'zɪʃ(ə)n/ n. disposing or arrangement; temperament.

dispossess /dɪspə'zes/ v.t. oust or dislodge. **dispossession** n.

disproof /dɪs'pruːf/ n. disproving, refutation.

disproportion /dɪsprə'pɔːʃ(ə)n/ n. lack of proportion.

disproportionate /dɪsprə'pɔːʃənət/ a. relatively too large or too small.

disprove /dɪs'pruːv/ v.t. prove to be false.

disputable /dɪ'spjuːtəb(ə)l/ a. open to question.

disputant /dɪ'spjuːt(ə)nt/ n. person involved in dispute.

disputation /dɪspjuː'teɪʃ(ə)n/ n. argument, debate; formal discussion of question.

disputatious /dɪspjuː'teɪʃəs/ a. fond of argument.

dispute /dɪ'spjuːt/ □ See page 665. 1 v. hold debate; quarrel, controvert; contend; resist. 2 n. controversy, debate; quarrel; difference of opinion.

disqualify /dɪs'kwɒlɪfaɪ/ v.t. make or pronounce unfit or ineligible. **disqualification** n.

disquiet /dɪs'kwaɪət/ 1 n. uneasiness, anxiety. 2 v.t. cause disquiet to. 3 **disquietude** n.

disquisition /dɪskwɪ'zɪʃ(ə)n/ n. long or elaborate treatise or discourse.

disregard /dɪsrɪ'gɑːd/ 1 v.t. ignore, be uninfluenced by. 2 n. neglect.

disrepair /dɪsrɪ'peə(r)/ n. bad condition due to lack of repairs.

disreputable /dɪs'repjʊtəb(ə)l/ a. having a bad reputation; not respectable.

disrepute /dɪsrɪ'pjuːt/ n. lack of good repute; discredit.

disrespect /dɪsrɪ'spekt/ n. lack of respect. **disrespectful** a.

disrobe /dɪs'rəʊb/ v. undress.

disrupt /dɪs'rʌpt/ v.t. shatter; separate forcibly; cause disturbance in. **disruption** n.; **disruptive** a.

dissatisfaction /dɪsætɪs'fækʃ(ə)n/ n. discontent.

dissatisfy /dɪs'sætɪsfaɪ/ v.t. fail to satisfy; make discontented.

dissect /dɪ'sekt/ v.t. cut in pieces, esp. to examine parts or structure; criticize in detail. **dissection** n.; **dissector** n.

dissemble /dɪ'semb(ə)l/ v. conceal or disguise; be hypocritical.

disseminate /dɪ'semɪneɪt/ v.t. scatter about, spread. **dissemination** n.; **disseminator** n.

dissension /dɪ'senʃ(ə)n/ n. discord arising from difference in opinion.

dissent /dɪ'sent/ 1 v.i. disagree openly; think differently or express different opinion (from), esp. from established or orthodox church. 2 n. such difference of opinion; expression of this.

dissenter n. member of dissenting sect.

dissentient /dɪ'senʃɪənt/ 1 a. not agreeing, dissenting. 2 n. dissentient person.

dissertation /dɪsə'teɪʃ(ə)n/ n. detailed discourse, esp. as submitted for higher degree in university.

disservice /dɪs'sɜːvɪs/ n. harmful action.

dissident /'dɪsɪd(ə)nt/ 1 a. disagreeing, at variance. 2 n. person disagreeing or at variance, esp. with established government.

dissimilar /dɪ'sɪmɪlə(r)/ a. not similar. **dissimilarity** n.

dissimulate /dɪ'sɪmjʊleɪt/ v. dissemble. **dissimulation** n.; **dissimulator** n.

dissipate /'dɪsɪpeɪt/ v. dispel, disperse; squander or fritter away.

dissipated a. given to dissipation.

dissipation /dɪsɪ'peɪʃ(ə)n/ n. frivolous or dissolute way of life.

dissociate /dɪ'səʊsɪeɪt/ v. disconnect or separate in thought or fact. **dissociation** n.

dissolute /'dɪsəluːt/ a. lax in morals, licentious.

dissolution /dɪsə'luːʃ(ə)n/ n. dissolving or being dissolved; undoing or relaxing of bond or partnership etc.; dismissal or dispersal of assembly, esp. parliament.

dissolve /dɪ'zɒlv/ v. make or become liquid, esp. by immersion or dispersion in liquid; (cause to) vanish; dismiss or disperse (assembly); put an end to, annul.

dissonant /'dɪsənənt/ a. jarring, clashing, discordant. **dissonance** n.

dissuade /dɪ'sweɪd/ v.t. advise to refrain (from), persuade against. **dissuasion** n.; **dissuasive** a.

distaff /'dɪstɑːf/ n. cleft stick holding

wool etc. used in spinning. **distaff side** female branch of family.

distance /ˈdɪst(ə)ns/ 1 *n.* length from one point to another; being far off; remoteness; distant point. 2 *v.t.* place or cause to seem far off; leave behind in race etc.

distant /ˈdɪst(ə)nt/ *a.* at considerable or specified distance; reserved, cool.

distaste /dɪsˈteɪst/ *n.* dislike; aversion.

distasteful /dɪsˈteɪstfʊl/ *a.* causing distaste.

distemper¹ /dɪsˈtempə(r)/ *n.* catarrhal disease of dogs etc.

distemper² /dɪsˈtempə(r)/ 1 *n.* pigment used for painting on plaster etc. with powder colours mixed with size etc. 2 *v.t.* paint with distemper.

distend /dɪsˈtend/ *v.* swell out by pressure from within. **distensible** *a.*; **distension** *n.*

distich /ˈdɪstɪk/ *n.* verse couplet.

distil /dɪsˈtɪl/ *v.* subject to or undergo distillation; make or produce or extract or drive off etc. by distillation.

distillation /dɪstɪˈleɪʃ(ə)n/ *n.* vaporizing and subsequent condensation of substance to purify or decompose it; extracting of essence or making of whisky etc. thus.

distiller /dɪsˈtɪlə(r)/ *n.* person who distils, esp. maker of alcoholic liquor.

distillery /dɪsˈtɪlərɪ/ *n.* factory etc. for distilling liquor.

distinct /dɪsˈtɪŋkt/ *a.* separate, different in quality or kind; clearly perceptible, definite, positive.

distinction /dɪsˈtɪŋkʃ(ə)n/ *n.* seeing or making a difference; difference seen or made; thing that differentiates; excellence; individuality; mark of honour.

distinctive /dɪsˈtɪŋktɪv/ *a.* distinguishing, characteristic.

distingué /dɪsˈtæŋgeɪ/ *a.* having distinguished air, manners, etc. [F]

distinguish /dɪsˈtɪŋgwɪʃ/ *v.* observe or identify a difference in; draw distinctions between; characterize; make out by listening or looking etc.; make prominent or eminent.

distinguished *a.* eminent, having distinction.

distort /dɪsˈtɔːt/ *v.t.* pull or twist out of shape; misrepresent. **distortion** *n.*

distract /dɪsˈtrækt/ *v.t.* draw attention etc. away *from* or in different directions; bewilder.

distraction /dɪsˈtrækʃ(ə)n/ *n.* distracting or bring distracted; thing which distracts; interruption; amusement, relaxation; mental confusion.

distrain /dɪsˈtreɪn/ *v.* levy distraint (on).

distraint /dɪsˈtreɪnt/ *n.* seizure of goods as method of enforcing payment.

distrait /dɪsˈtreɪ/ *a.* not paying attention; distraught. [F]

distraught /dɪsˈtrɔːt/ *a.* much agitated in mind.

distress /dɪsˈtres/ 1 *n.* mental pain; exhaustion; lack of money or necessaries; *Law* distraint. 2 *v.t.* subject to distress; make unhappy.

distribute /dɪsˈtrɪbjuːt/ □ See page 665. *v.t.* divide and give share of to each of number; spread about; put at different points; arrange, classify. **distribution** *n.*

distributive /dɪsˈtrɪbjʊtɪv/ *a.* of or concerned with or effecting distribution; (of word etc.) referring to each individual of class, not collective.

distributor /dɪsˈtrɪbjʊtə(r)/ *n.* agent who markets goods; device in internal combustion engine for passing current to each sparking-plug in turn.

district *n.* /ˈdɪstrɪkt/ region; administrative division; province; territory. **district attorney** *US* public prosecutor of district; **district nurse** nurse visiting patients in their homes.

distrust /dɪsˈtrʌst/ 1 *n.* lack of trust; suspicion. 2 *v.t.* have no confidence in. 3 **distrustful** *a.*

disturb /dɪsˈtɜːb/ *v.t.* break rest or quiet of; worry; disorganize; in *p.p.* emotionally or mentally unstable or abnormal.

disturbance /dɪsˈtɜːbəns/ *n.* disturbing; disturbed state, tumult, disorder.

disunion /dɪsˈjuːnɪən/ *n.* separation; lack of union.

disunite /dɪsjuːˈnaɪt/ *v.* separate; divide. **disunity** *n.*

disuse 1 /dɪsˈjuːz/ *v.t.* cease to use. 2 /dɪsˈjuːs/ *n.* disused state.

disyllable /dɪsˈsɪləb(ə)l/ *n.* word or metrical foot of two syllables. **disyllabic** /-ˈlæb-/ *a.*

ditch 1 *n.* long narrow excavation esp.

to hold or conduct water or serve as boundary. 2 *v.* make or repair ditches; provide with ditches; drive (vehicle) into ditch; *sl.* make forced landing, land (aircraft) on sea; *sl.* abandon, discard, defeat.

dither /ˈdɪðə(r)/ 1 *v.i.* be nervously hesitant; tremble, quiver. 2 *n.* nervous excitement or apprehension.

dithyramb /ˈdɪθɪræm/ *n.* Greek choric hymn, wild in character; passionate or inflated speech or writing. **dithyrambic** /-ˈræmbɪk/ *a.*

ditto /ˈdɪtəʊ/ *n.* the aforesaid, the same or a similar thing.

ditty /ˈdɪtɪ/ *n.* short simple song.

diuretic /daɪjʊəˈretɪk/ 1 *a.* causing increased excretion of urine. 2 *n.* diuretic drug.

diurnal /daɪˈɜːn(ə)l/ *a.* in or of day; occupying one day.

diva /ˈdiːvə/ *n.* great woman singer.

divan /dɪˈvæn/ *n.* low couch or bed without back or ends.

dive 1 *v.i.* plunge, esp. head foremost, into water etc.; (of aircraft) descend steeply; (of submarine or diver) submerge; go down or out of sight suddenly; put one's hand *into.* 2 *n.* act of diving; *colloq.* disreputable place of resort. 3 **dive-bomb** drop bombs on from diving aircraft; **diving-board** sprung board for diving from.

diver /ˈdaɪvə(r)/ *n.* person who dives esp. person who works under water; diving bird.

diverge /daɪˈvɜːdʒ/ *v.i.* go in different directions from point or each other; go aside *from* track. **divergence** *n.*; **divergent** *a.*

divers /ˈdaɪvəz/ *a. arch.* various, several.

diverse /daɪˈvɜːs/ *a.* of differing kinds; varied.

diversify /daɪˈvɜːsɪfaɪ/ *v.t.* make diverse; vary; spread (investment) over several enterprises.

diversion /daɪˈvɜːʃ(ə)n/ *n.* diverting; recreation, pastime; alternative route for traffic.

diversity /daɪˈvɜːsɪtɪ/ *n.* being diverse.

divert /daɪˈvɜːt/ *v.t.* turn in another direction; ward off; draw off attention of; entertain, amuse.

divest /daɪˈvest/ *v.t.* unclothe, strip; deprive or rid *of.*

divide /dɪˈvaɪd/ 1 *v.* separate *into* parts; split or break up; separate (one thing) from another; become or be able to be divided; mark out into parts or groups; cause to disagree, set at variance; distribute; share *with* others; find how many times number contains another, be contained exact number of times; part (legislative assembly) into two sets for voting, be thus parted. 2 *n.* watershed; dividing-line.

dividend /ˈdɪvɪdend/ *n.* number to be divided by another; sum payable as interest or profit or share.

divider /dɪˈvaɪdə(r)/ *n.* screen etc. dividing room; in *pl.* measuring compasses.

divination /dɪvɪˈneɪʃ(ə)n/ *n.* divining the future; good guess.

divine /dɪˈvaɪn/ 1 *a.* of or from or like God or a god; sacred; *colloq.* excellent. 2 *n.* theologian. 3 *v.* discover by intuition or inspiration or guessing; foresee; conjecture; practise divination. 4 **divining-rod** dowser's forked twig.

diviner /dɪˈvaɪnə(r)/ *n.* expert in divination; dowser.

divinity /dɪˈvɪnɪtɪ/ *n.* being divine; god; theology.

divisible /dɪˈvɪzɪb(ə)l/ *a.* that can be divided. **divisibility** *n.*

division /dɪˈvɪʒ(ə)n/ *n.* dividing or being divided; one of parts into which thing is divided; administrative etc. district. **divisional** *a.*

divisor /dɪˈvaɪzə(r)/ *n.* number by which another is to be divided.

divorce /dɪˈvɔːs/ 1 *n.* legal dissolution of marriage; separation, severance. 2 *v.t.* legally dissolve marriage between; end marriage with by divorce; detach, separate.

divot /ˈdɪvət/ *n. Golf* piece of turf dislodged by club-head in making stroke.

divulge /daɪˈvʌldʒ/ *v.t.* disclose (secret); make public.

divvy /ˈdɪvɪ/ *colloq.* 1 *n.* dividend. 2 *v.* **divvy (up)** share out.

Dixie¹ /ˈdɪksɪ/ *n.* Southern States of US. **Dixieland** Dixie, kind of jazz.

dixie² /ˈdɪksɪ/ *n.* large iron pot for making stew etc.

DIY *abbr.* do-it-yourself.

dizzy /ˈdɪzɪ/ 1 *a.* giddy, dazed, unsteady; causing dizziness. 2 *v.t.* make dizzy.

DJ *abbr.* disc jockey; dinner jacket.

dl. *abbr.* decilitre.

D.Litt. *abbr.* Doctor of Letters.

dm. *abbr.* decimetre.

DNA *abbr.* deoxyribonucleic acid.

do /duː/ 1 *v.* (*past* **did**; *p.p.* **done** /dʌn/; 3 *sing. pres.* **does** /dʌz/) perform, carry out; produce, make; act or proceed; fare; operate on, deal with; bestow, impart; solve; be suitable, suffice; *colloq.* provide or cater for (*well* etc.); *sl.* swindle; exhaust. 2 *v. aux.* used esp. in questions and negative or emphatic statements and commands; also as *vbl. substitute* to avoid repetition of verb just used. 3 *n. colloq.* entertainment, elaborate operation etc.; swindle, hoax. 4 **do away with** abolish, kill; **do down** get the better of, swindle; **do for** be sufficient for, *colloq.* destroy or ruin or kill, *colloq.* do housework for; **do in** *sl.* kill, *colloq.* exhaust; **do-it-yourself** (to be) done or made by amateur handyman; **do up** fasten, wrap up, restore, repair; **do with** use, treat; **do without** forgo, complete one's task in the absence of.

do. *abbr.* ditto.

docile /ˈdəʊsaɪl/ *a.* submissive, easily managed. **docility** /-ˈsɪl-/ *n.*

dock[1] 1 *n.* artificial enclosed body of water for loading and repairing of ships; (usu. in *pl.*) range of docks with wharves, warehouses, etc. 2 *v.* bring or come into dock; join (spacecraft) together in space, be thus joined. 3 **dockyard** area with docks and shipbuilding and repairing equipment.

dock[2] *n.* enclosure in criminal court for accused.

dock[3] *n.* coarse weed with broad leaves.

dock[4] *v.t.* cut short (tail); reduce or deduct (money etc.).

docker /ˈdɒkə(r)/ *n.* labourer in docks.

docket /ˈdɒkɪt/ 1 *n.* document recording payment of customs, nature of goods delivered, jobs done, etc. 2 *v.t.* label with docket.

doctor /ˈdɒktə(r)/ 1 *n.* qualified medical practitioner; holder of doctorate. 2 *v.t.* treat medically; castrate, spay; tamper with.

doctoral /ˈdɒktər(ə)l/ *a.* of the degree of doctor.

doctorate /ˈdɒktərət/ *n.* higher university degree in any faculty.

doctrinaire /dɒktrɪˈneə(r)/ *a.* applying principles pedantically.

doctrine /ˈdɒktrɪn/ *n.* what is taught; principal of religious or political etc. belief. **doctrinal** /-ˈtraɪn(ə)l/ *a.*

document 1 /ˈdɒkjʊmənt/ *n.* something written or inscribed etc. that furnishes evidence or information on any subject. 2 /ˈdɒkjʊment/ *v.t.* prove by or provide with documents. 3 **documentation** *n.*

documentary /dɒkjʊˈmentərɪ/ 1 *a.* consisting of documents; factual, based on real events. 2 *n.* documentary film.

dodder /ˈdɒdə(r)/ *v.i.* shake, totter, be feeble. **doddery** *a.*

dodecagon /dəʊˈdekəgən/ *n.* plane figure with 12 sides and angles.

dodge 1 *v.* move quickly to one side; evade by cunning or trickery. 2 *n.* quick side-movement; trick, clever expedient.

dodgem /ˈdɒdʒəm/ *n.* small electrically-powered car at fun-fair, in which driver bumps into similar cars in enclosure.

dodo /ˈdəʊdəʊ/ *n.* (*pl.* **-dos**) large extinct flightless bird.

doe *n.* female of fallow deer or hare or rabbit. **doeskin** leather made from doe's skin.

DOE *abbr.* Department of the Environment.

does see **do**.

doff *v.t.* take off (hat etc.).

dog 1 *n.* 4-legged carnivorous animal of many breeds wild and domesticated; male of this or of fox or wolf; *colloq.* fellow; despicable person; mechanical device for gripping. 2 *v.t.* follow closely; pursue, track. 3 **dogcart** two-wheeled driving-cart with cross seats back to back; **dog-collar** *colloq.* clergyman's stiff collar that fastens at back; **dog days** hottest period of year; **dog-eared** (of corner of book-page etc.) turned down through use; **dog-end** *sl.* cigarette-end; **dogfight** fight (as) between dogs, *colloq.* fight between aircraft; **dogfish** small shark; **doghouse** *US* kennel (**in the doghouse** *sl.* in disgrace); **dogrose** wild hedge-rose; **dogsbody** *colloq.* drudge; **dog-star** Sirius; **dog-tired** tired out; **dog-watch** *Naut.* half-watch of 2 hrs.; **dogwood** shrub with whitish flowers and purple berries.

doge /dəʊdʒ/ n. hist. chief magistrate of Venice or Genoa.

dogged /ˈdɒgɪd/ a. tenacious.

doggerel /ˈdɒgərəl/ n. poor or trivial verse.

doggo /ˈdɒgəʊ/ adv. sl. **lie doggo** wait motionless or hidden.

doggy /ˈdɒgɪ/ a. of or like dogs; devoted to dogs.

dogma /ˈdɒgmə/ n. principle, tenet; doctrinal system.

dogmatic /dɒgˈmætɪk/ a. of dogma, doctrinal; authoritative, arrogant. **dogmatically** adv.; **dogmatism** n.

dogmatize /ˈdɒgmətaɪz/ v.i. make positive unsupported statements.

doh /dəʊ/ n. Mus. first note of scale in tonic sol-fa.

doily /ˈdɔɪlɪ/ n. small ornamental mat placed on plate for cakes etc.

doings /ˈduːɪŋz/ n.pl. activity, proceedings; sl. things needed.

Dolby /ˈdɒlbɪ/ n. (P) system used in tape-recording to reduce unwanted sounds at high frequency.

doldrums /ˈdɒldrəmz/ n.pl. low spirits; equatorial ocean region of calms.

dole 1 n. charitable (esp. niggardly) gift of food etc. or money; colloq. benefit claimable by the unemployed from the State. 2 v.t. deal out sparingly. 3 **on the dole** receiving State benefit for the unemployed.

doleful /ˈdəʊlfʊl/ a. dreary, dismal, melancholy.

doll 1 n. child's toy representing human figure; ventriloquist's dummy; sl. young woman. 2 v. dress up smartly.

dollar /ˈdɒlə(r)/ n. unit of currency in US and other countries.

dollop /ˈdɒləp/ n. colloq. clumsy or shapeless lump of food etc.

dolly /ˈdɒlɪ/ n. pet-name for doll; movable platform for cine-camera etc.

dolman sleeve /ˈdɒlmən/ loose sleeve cut in one piece with body of garment.

dolmen /ˈdɒlmən/ n. megalithic structure of large flat stone laid on upright ones.

dolomite /ˈdɒləmaɪt/ n. mineral or rock of calcium magnesium carbonate.

dolour /ˈdɒlə(r)/ n. sorrow, distress. **dolorous** a.

dolphin /ˈdɒlfɪn/ n. porpoise-like sea mammal.

dolt /dəʊlt/ n. stupid person. **doltish** a.

Dom n. title prefixed to names of some RC dignitaries and Carthusian and Benedictine monks.

domain /dəˈmeɪn/ n. lands held or ruled over; estate, realm; province, scope.

dome n. rounded vault as roof; domeshaped thing.

domed /dəʊmd/ a. having dome(s); shaped like dome; rounded.

domestic /dəˈmestɪk/ 1 a. of home, household, of family affairs; of one's own country; fond of home life; (of animal) kept by or living with man. 2 n. household servant.

domesticate /dəˈmestɪkeɪt/ v.t. tame, bring (animal) under human control; make fond of home life. **domestication** n.

domesticity /dɒmesˈtɪsɪtɪ/ n. being domestic; home life or privacy.

domicile /ˈdɒmɪsaɪl/ n. place of permanent residence.

domiciled a. having domicile at or in.

domiciliary /dɒmɪˈsɪlɪərɪ/ a. of a dwelling place; (of visit) to person's home.

dominant /ˈdɒmɪnənt/ 1 a. dominating, ruling, prevailing. 2 n. Mus. 5th note of scale. 3 **dominance** n.

dominate /ˈdɒmɪneɪt/ v. have commanding influence over; overlook, occupy commanding position in. **domination** n.

domineer /dɒmɪˈnɪə(r)/ v.i. behave overbearingly.

Dominican /dəˈmɪnɪkən/ n. friar or nun of order founded by St. Dominic.

dominion /dəˈmɪnɪən/ n. sovereignty or lordship; territory of sovereign or government; hist. title of self-governing territories of British Commonwealth.

domino /ˈdɒmɪnəʊ/ n. (pl. -noes) any of 28 oblong pieces marked with pips; in pl. game played with these; hooded cloak worn with half-mask to conceal identity.

don[1] n. head, fellow, or tutor of college esp. at Oxford or Cambridge; **Don** title of Spanish gentleman.

don[2] v.t. put on (garment).

donate /dəʊˈneɪt/ v.t. make donation of.

donation /dəʊˈneɪʃ(ə)n/ n. gift (esp. of money to fund or institution).

done 1 p.p. of **do**. 2 a. colloq. socially acceptable.

donkey /ˈdɒŋkɪ/ n. ass. **donkey jacket** thick weatherproof jacket; **donkey's years** a long time; **donkey-work** drudgery.

donna /ˈdɒnə/ n. title of Italian or Spanish or Portuguese lady.

donnish /ˈdɒnɪʃ/ a. like a college don; pedantic.

donor /ˈdəʊnə(r)/ n. giver of gift; person or animal providing blood for transfusion, organ for transplantation, etc.

don't /dəʊnt/ 1 v. do not. 2 n. prohibition.

doodle /ˈduːd(ə)l/ 1 v.i. scrawl or draw absentmindedly. 2 n. such scrawl.

doom /duːm/ 1 n. fate, destiny; ruin, death. 2 v.t. condemn to misfortune etc. 3 **doomsday** Last Judgement.

door /dɔː(r)/ n. hinged or sliding barrier of wood etc. closing entrance to building or room or cupboard etc.; doorway. **doormat** mat for wiping shoes on, fig. feebly subservient person; **doorstep** step or area immediately outside esp. outer door; **doorstop** device for keeping door open; **door-to-door** (of selling etc.) done at each house in turn; **doorway** opening flanked by door.

dope 1 n. thick liquid; varnish; sl. drug, esp. narcotic; sl. information; sl. stupid person. 2 v. drug; take drugs; apply dope to.

dopey /ˈdəʊpɪ/ a. slow-witted, stupid.

doppelgänger /ˈdɒpəlˈɡeŋə(r)/ n. wraith of living person. [G]

Doppler effect /ˈdɒplə(r)/ apparent change in pitch of sound or other waves when source or observer is moving.

dormant /ˈdɔːmənt/ a. lying inactive (as) in sleep; not acting or in use. **dormancy** n.

dormer n. /ˈdɔːmə(r)/ upright window set in sloping roof.

dormitory /ˈdɔːmɪtərɪ/ n. sleeping-room with several beds; (in full **dormitory town**) small town or suburb from which people travel to work in city.

dormouse /ˈdɔːmaʊs/ n. (pl. -mice) small hibernating rodent.

dormy /ˈdɔːmɪ/ a. Golf leading by as

many holes as there are holes left to play.

dorsal /ˈdɔːs(ə)l/ a. of or on back.

dory /ˈdɔːrɪ/ n. edible sea-fish.

dosage /ˈdəʊsɪdʒ/ n. giving of dose; size of dose.

dose /dəʊs/ 1 n. amount of medicine etc. to be taken at one time; amount of radiation received by person etc. exposed to it. 2 v. give medicine; treat with.

doss v.i. sl. sleep, esp. in doss-house. **doss down** sleep on makeshift bed; **doss-house** cheap lodging-house.

dossier /ˈdɒsɪə(r)/ n. set of documents relating to person or event.

dot n. 1 small spot, point; decimal point; shorter signal of two in Morse code. 2 v.t. mark or scatter with dot(s); scatter like dots; place dot over (letter i etc.), sl. hit. 3 **dotted line** line of dots for signature etc. on document; **on the dot** punctually.

dotage /ˈdəʊtɪdʒ/ n. feeble-minded senility.

dotard /ˈdəʊtəd/ n. person in his dotage.

dote v.i. be silly or infatuated. **dote on** be excessively fond of.

dotterel /ˈdɒtər(ə)l/ n. kind of plover.

dottle /ˈdɒt(ə)l/ n. tobacco left in pipe after smoking.

dotty /ˈdɒtɪ/ a. colloq. eccentric, silly.

double /ˈdʌb(ə)l/ 1 a. consisting of or combining two things; multiplied by two; twice as much or many or large etc.; of extra size or strength etc.; having some part double; (of flower) having more than one circle of petals; deceitful. 2 adv. twice the amount; two together. 3 n. double quantity or thing; double measure of spirits etc.; twice the amount or quantity; person or thing mistakable for another; in pl. game between two pairs of players; Racing cumulative bet on two horses. 4 v. make or become double; increase twofold; fold over upon itself; become folded; play two parts in same play etc.; turn sharply; Naut. get round (headland). 5 **at the double** running; **double agent** one who spies for two rival countries etc. **double-barrelled** (of gun) having two barrels, (of surname) hyphened; **double-bass** lowest-pitched instrument of violin kind; **dou-**

ble bed bed for two people; **double-breasted** (of garment) having fronts overlapping across body; **double chin** fold of flesh below chin; **double cream** thick cream with high fat content; **double-cross** deceive or betray; **double-dealing** duplicity; **double-decker** (bus etc.) with two decks, (sandwich) of several layers; **double Dutch** gibberish; **double eagle** figure of eagle with two heads; **double-edged** *fig.* damaging to user as well as opponent; **double figures** numbers from 10 to 99; **double glazing** two sheets of glass in window to reduce heat loss etc.; **double pneumonia** pneumonia of both lungs; **double standard** rule etc. applied more strictly to some persons than to others; **double-stopping** sounding of two notes at once on stringed instrument; **double take** delayed reaction to situation etc. immediately after first reaction; **double-talk** verbal expression that is (usu. deliberately) ambiguous.

double entendre /duːbl ɑːnˈtɑːndr/ phrase capable of two meanings, one usu. indecent. [F]

doublet /ˈdʌblɪt/ *n.* one of a pair of similar things; *hist.* man's close-fitting jacket.

doubloon /dʌˈbluːn/ *n. hist.* Spanish gold coin.

doubt /daʊt/ 1 *n.* feeling of uncertainty; inclination to disbelieve; uncertain state. 2 *v.* be in doubt or uncertainty; call in question, mistrust. 3 **no doubt** certainly, admittedly.

doubtful /ˈdaʊtful/ *a.* feeling or causing doubt; uncertain.

doubtless /ˈdaʊtlɪs/ *adv.* certainly, admittedly.

douche /duːʃ/ 1 *n.* jet of liquid applied to body externally or internally. 2 *v.* administer douche to; take douche.

dough /dəʊ/ *n.* kneaded moistened flour; bread-paste; *sl.* money. **doughnut** small spongy cake of dough fried in deep fat. **doughy** *a.*

doughty /ˈdaʊti/ *a. arch.* valiant.

dour /ˈdʊə(r)/ *a.* grim, stubborn.

douse /daʊs/ *v.t.* drench; extinguish (light).

dove /dʌv/ *n.* pigeon; person advocating negotiation rather than violence; gentle or innocent person.

dovecote pigeon-house; **dovetail** joint made with tenon shaped like dove's tail, (*v.*) fit together (as) with dovetails.

dowager /ˈdaʊdʒə(r)/ *n.* woman with title or property derived from her late husband.

dowdy /ˈdaʊdɪ/ *a.* lacking smartness, ill dressed.

dowel /ˈdaʊəl/ *n.* headless pin fastening together two pieces of wood etc.

dowelling *n.* round wooden rods for cutting into dowels.

dower /ˈdaʊə(r)/ 1 *n.* widow's share for life of husband's estate; *arch.* dowry. 2 *v.t. arch.* give dowry to; endow *with* talent etc.

down[1] /daʊn/ 1 *adv.* towards or in lower place or state or number; away from capital or university; to or in place in succession; from earlier to later time; on ground. 2 *prep.* downwards along or through or into; at lower part of. 3 *a.* directed downwards. 4 *v.t. colloq.* put or throw or knock or bring etc. down; swallow. 5 *n.* reverse of fortune. 6 **down and out** penniless, destitute; **downcast** dejected, (of eyes) looking down; **downfall** fall from prosperity or power, cause of this; **downgrade** lower in rank etc.; **down-hearted** despondent; **downhill** sloping down, declining, in descending direction, on a decline; **down in the mouth** down-hearted; **downpour** heavy fall of rain; **downright** plain, straightforward, blunt, thoroughly, quite; **downstairs** down the stairs; to or on or of lower floor of house etc.; **downstream** in direction of flow of stream etc., moving downstream; **down-to-earth** practical, realistic; **downtown** *US* central part of town or city; **downtrodden** oppressed; **down under** in Australia or NZ; **have a down on** *colloq.* dislike, be prejudiced against. 7 **downward** *a.* & *adv.*; **downwards** *adv.*

down[2] /daʊn/ *n.* fine soft short hair or feathers or fluff.

down[3] /daʊn/ *n.* open high land; esp. in *pl.* chalk uplands of S. England etc.

Down's syndrome congenital mental deficiency with mongoloid appearance.

downy /ˈdaʊnɪ/ *a.* of or like or covered with down; *sl.* knowing, sly.

dowry /'dauərɪ/ n. property brought by bride to her husband.

dowse /dauz/ v.i. search for hidden water or minerals with forked twig which dips suddenly when over right spot. **dowser** n.

doxology /dɒk'sɒlədʒɪ/ n. formula of praise to God.

doyen /'dɔɪən/ n. (fem. **doyenne** /dɔɪ'en/) senior member of a body of colleagues.

doz. abbr. dozen.

doze 1 v.i. sleep lightly, be half asleep. **2** n. short light sleep. **3 doze off** fall lightly asleep.

dozen /'dʌz(ə)n/ n. set of twelve.

D.Phil. abbr. Doctor of Philosophy.

Dr abbr. Doctor.

drab 1 a. dull, monotonous; of dull brownish colour. **2** n. drab colour.

drachm /dræm/ n. apothecaries' weight (60 grains).

drachma /'drækmə/ n. (pl. **-mas**) Greek currency unit.

Draconian /drə'kəʊnɪən/ adj. (of laws) rigorous, harsh.

draft /drɑːft/ **1** n. rough preliminary outline of scheme or speech or document etc.; order for drawing money; bill or cheque drawn; detachment of troops etc. from larger body; selection of this; US Mil. conscription. **2** v.t. prepare draft of; select as draft; US conscript.

draftsman /'drɑːftsmən/ n. (pl. **-men**) drafter of documents.

drag 1 v. draw along with effort or difficulty; (allow to) trail or go heavily; search (river-bed etc.) with grapnels and nets etc. **2** n. obstruction to progress, retarding force; colloq. boring or dreary task or person etc.; apparatus for dredging etc.; colloq. pull at cigarette; sl. women's clothes worn by men. **3 drag race** acceleration race between cars over short distance.

draggle /'dræg(ə)l/ v. make dirty and wet by trailing; hang trailing.

dragon /'drægən/ n. mythical monster like reptile, usu. with wings and claws and often breathing fire; fierce person.

dragonfly /'drægənflaɪ/ n. long-bodied gauzy-winged insect.

dragoon /drə'gu:n/ **1** n. cavalryman; hist. mounted infantryman; fierce fellow. **2** v.t. force into course of action.

drain 1 v. draw off liquid from; draw off (liquid); flow or trickle away; dry or become dry; exhaust; drink (liquid); empty (glass etc.). **2** n. channel or pipe carrying off water or sewage etc.; constant outlet or expenditure. **3 draining-board** sloping board on which washed dishes etc. are left to drain.

drainage /'dreɪnɪdʒ/ n. draining; system of drains; what is drained off.

drake n. male duck.

dram n. small drink of spirits etc.; drachm.

drama /'drɑːmə/ n. play for acting on stage or broadcasting; dramatic art; dramatic series of events.

dramatic /drə'mætɪk/ a. of drama; forcible, theatrical; striking.

dramatis personae /'dræmətɪs pɜː'səʊnaɪ/ characters in a play.

dramatist /'dræmətɪst/ n. writer of plays.

dramatize /'dræmətaɪz/ v. convert into play; make dramatic; behave dramatically. **dramatization** n.

drank past of drink.

drape 1 v. cover or hang or adorn with cloth etc.; arrange or hang in graceful folds. **2** n. US curtain.

draper /'dreɪpə(r)/ n. retailer of textile fabrics.

drapery /'dreɪpərɪ/ n. cloth or textile fabrics, draper's trade; clothing or hangings disposed in folds.

drastic /'dræstɪk/ a. acting strongly or severely; vigorous; violent.

drat v.t. curse, bother.

draught /drɑːft/ n. current of air; traction; depth of water needed to float ship; drawing of liquor from cask etc.; single act of drinking; amount so drunk; in pl. game played with 12 uniform pieces on each side, on **draught-board** like chess-board. **draught beer** beer drawn from cask, not bottled.

draughtsman /'drɑːftsmən/ n. (pl. **-men**) person who makes drawings; piece in game of draughts.

draughty /'drɑːftɪ/ a. liable to draughts of air.

draw /drɔ:/ **1** v. (past **drew**; p.p. **drawn**) pull, drag, haul; protract, stretch; attract; derive, deduce, infer; inhale; extract; entice; induce; elicit; take from or out; pull into or out of position; make (picture) by making lines; describe in words; write out (bill, cheque, etc.); bring (game etc.) to undecided conclusion; (of ship) require (stated depth of water); draw lots; obtain by lot; search (cover) for game etc.; (of chimney, pipe, etc.) promote or allow draught of air; make one's way, come, move. **2** *n.* act of drawing; thing that draws custom or attention; drawing of lots, lottery; drawn game. **3 draw back** withdraw; **drawback** thing that impairs satisfaction, disadvantage; **drawbridge** bridge hinged at one end for drawing up; **draw in** (of days etc.) become shorter; **draw out** prolong, induce to talk, (of days etc.) become longer; **draw-string** string that can be pulled to tighten mouth of bag or waist of garment etc.; **draw up** compose (document etc.), bring or come into regular order, come to a halt, make *oneself* stiffly erect.

drawer /'drɔːə(r)/ *n.* person who draws; (also /drɔː(r)/) receptacle sliding in and out of frame (**chest of drawers**) or of table etc.; in *pl.* undergarment worn next to body below waist.

drawing /'drɔːɪŋ/ *n.* art of representing by line with pencil etc.; picture etc. drawn thus. **drawing-board** board for stretching paper on while drawing is made; **drawing-pin** flat-headed pin for fastening paper to a surface.

drawing-room room for entertainment of company esp. in private house.

drawl 1 *v.* speak or utter with drawn-out vowel sounds. **2** *n.* drawling way of speaking.

dray *n.* low esp. brewer's cart for heavy loads.

dread /dred/ **1** *v.* be in great fear of; look forward to with terror. **2** *n.* great fear; awe. **3** *a.* dreaded, dreadful.

dreadful /'dredfʊl/ *a.* terrible; *colloq.* troublesome; very bad.

dream /driːm/ **1** *n.* series of pictures or events in mind of sleeping person; day-dream; ideal; aspiration or ambition. **2** *v.* (*past* & *p.p.* **dreamt** /dremt/ or **dreamed**) experience dream; imagine as in dream; (esp. with *neg.*) think of as a possibility; fall into reverie.

dreamy /'driːmɪ/ *a.* dreamlike; given to day-dreaming, impractical, vague.

dreary /'drɪərɪ/ *a.* dismal, gloomy, dull.

dredge¹ 1 *n.* apparatus for clearing out mud etc. or collecting oysters etc. from bottom of sea etc. **2** *v.* use dredge; clean or fetch *up* with dredge.

dredge² *v.t.* sprinkle with flour etc.

dredger¹ /'dredʒə(r)/ *n.* dredge; boat with dredge.

dredger² /'dredʒə(r)/ *n.* container with perforated lid for sprinkling flour etc.

dregs *n.pl.* sediment, grounds; worst part.

drench 1 *v.t.* wet thoroughly; force (animal) to take dose of medicine. **2** *n.* dose for animal; thorough wetting.

dress 1 *v.* clothe, clothe oneself; arrange or adorn; put dressing on (wound etc.); prepare (food); apply manure to. **2** *n.* clothing, esp. visible part of it; woman's or girl's one-piece garment of bodice and skirt. **3 dress-circle** first gallery in theatre; **dressmaker** person who makes esp. women's clothes; **dress rehearsal** (esp. final) one in costume; **dress up** put on special clothes, make more attractive.

dressage /'dresɑːʒ/ *n.* training of horse in obedience and deportment.

dresser¹ /'dresə(r)/ *n.* kitchen sideboard with shelves.

dresser² /'dresə(r)/ *n.* person who helps actor to dress for stage.

dressing /'dresɪŋ/ *n.* putting one's clothes on; sauce or seasoning etc. for food; ointment etc. applied to wound; manure. **dressing-down** scolding; **dressing-gown** loose robe worn while one is not fully dressed; **dressing-table** one with mirror etc. for use while dressing.

dressy /'dresɪ/ *a.* fond of smart dress.

drew *past* of **draw**.

drey *n.* squirrel's nest.

dribble /'drɪb(ə)l/ **1** *v.* allow saliva to flow from the mouth; (let) flow in drops; *Footb.* etc. move ball forward with repeated touches of feet etc. **2** *n.* act or process of dribbling; dribbling flow.

driblet /'drɪblɪt/ *n.* small quantity.

dried *past* & *p.p.* of **dry**.

drier /'draɪə(r)/ *n.* machine for drying hair or laundry etc.

drift 1 *n.* being driven by current; slow

movement or variation; snow etc. heaped by wind etc.; purpose, meaning, tenor; inaction; deviation due to current or wind etc. **2** *v.* be carried (as) by current; (of current) carry; heap or be heaped into drifts; move passively or casually or aimlessly. **3 drift-net** large net allowed to drift with tide, for catching herring etc.; **driftwood** wood washed ashore by sea.

drifter /'drɪftə(r)/ *n.* aimless person; boat with drift-net.

drill¹ 1 *n.* tool or machine for boring holes; exercising of soldiers etc.; routine; *colloq.* recognized procedure. **2** *v.* bore (hole etc.); subject to or undergo drill; impart (knowledge etc.) by strict method.

drill² 1 *n.* small furrow for sowing seed in; machine for furrowing, sowing, and covering seed. **2** *v.t.* sow or plant in drills.

drill³ *n.* coarse twilled fabric.

drill⁴ *n.* kind of baboon.

drink 1 *v.* (*past* **drank**; *p.p.* **drunk**) swallow liquid; take in with eager delight; take alcoholic liquor, esp. to excess; absorb moisture. **2** *n.* liquid for drinking; glass or portion of this, esp. alcoholic; intoxicating liquor. **3 the drink** *sl.* the sea; **drink to** toast, wish success to, by drinking.

drip 1 *v.* fall or let fall in drops; be so wet as to shed drops. **2** *n.* falling drop of liquid; liquid falling in drops; *colloq.* feeble person. **3 drip-dry** (of fabric etc.) that needs no ironing after hanging up to dry; **drip-feed** feeding (esp. intravenously) by liquid a drop at a time.

dripping /'drɪpɪŋ/ *n.* fat melted from roasting meat.

drive 1 *v.* (*past* **drove**; *p.p.* **driven** /'drɪv(ə)n/) urge onwards by force; throw or cause to go in some direction; operate and direct course of (vehicle etc.); convey or be conveyed in vehicle; *Golf* strike ball from tee; chase (game etc.) from large area into small; impel or carry along; force, constrain. **2** *n.* excursion in vehicle; driveway; forcible blow at cricket etc.; energy; energetic campaign; transmission of power to machinery or wheels of motor vehicle etc.; social gathering to play card-games etc. **3 drive at** seek, intend,

mean; **drive-in** (bank, restaurant, etc.) that may be used without getting out of one's car; **driveway** road for vehicles, esp. private one leading to house; **driving-licence** licence permitting one to drive motor vehicle; **driving-test** official test of competence to drive motor vehicle; **driving-wheel** wheel communicating motive power in machinery.

drivel /'drɪv(ə)l/ **1** *n.* silly nonsense. **2** *v.i.* talk silly nonsense; run at mouth or nose.

driver /'draɪvə(r)/ *n.* person who drives; golf-club for driving from tee.

drizzle /'drɪz(ə)l/ **1** *n.* fine dense rain. **2** *v.i.* fall in fine dense rain.

droll /drəʊl/ *a.* amusing, odd, queer.

drollery /'drəʊlərɪ/ *n.* quaint humour.

dromedary /'drɒmɪdərɪ/ *n.* swift usu. one-humped camel bred for riding.

drone 1 *n.* male or non-worker bee; idler; bass-pipe of bagpipes or its continuous note. **2** *v.* make deep humming sound; talk or utter monotonously.

drool *v.* dribble; show unrestrained admiration (*over*).

droop /druːp/ *v.* bend or hang down; languish, lose heart. **2** *n.* drooping attitude.

drop 1 *n.* small quantity of liquid such as falls or hangs or adheres to surface; thing in shape of drop, esp. sweet or pendant; in *pl.* liquid medicine to be measured in drops; minute quantity; act of dropping, fall, abrupt descent, distance dropped. **2** *v.* fall by force of gravity; allow to fall; leave hold of; fall or let fall or shed in drops; sink to ground; sink to lower level; lower (eyes etc.); allow oneself to fall *behind* etc.; break off acquaintance etc. with; cease, lapse; utter or be uttered casually; come or go casually *by* or *in* etc.; lose (money in transaction); omit; *Footb.* make (goal) by drop-kick. **3 drop-kick** kick at football made by dropping ball and kicking it as it touches ground; **drop off** fall asleep, decrease or depart gradually; **drop out** cease to appear or participate; **drop-out** person who drops out esp. of course of study or conventional society; **drop scone** one made by dropping spoonful of mixture on cooking surface; **drop-shot** *Tennis* shot dropping abruptly after clearing net.

droplet /ˈdrɒplɪt/ *n.* small drop of liquid.

dropper /ˈdrɒpə(r)/ *n.* device for releasing liquid in drops.

droppings /ˈdrɒpɪŋz/ *n.pl.* what falls or has fallen in drops; dung.

dropsy /ˈdrɒpsɪ/ *n.* disease with watery fluid collecting in body. **dropsical** *a.*

dross *n.* scum of molten metal; impurities; rubbish.

drought /draʊt/ *n.* abnormally prolonged spell of dry weather.

drove[1] *n.* moving herd or flock; crowd in motion.

drove[2] *past of* drive.

drover /ˈdrəʊvə(r)/ *n.* driver of or dealer in cattle.

drown /draʊn/ *v.* (cause to) suffocate by submersion; flood, drench; assuage (grief etc.) with drink; overpower (sound) by greater loudness.

drowse /draʊz/ *v.i.* be half asleep.

drowsy /ˈdraʊzɪ/ *a.* half asleep.

drub *v.t.* thrash, beat. **drubbing** *n.*

drudge 1 *n.* person who does dull, laborious, or menial work. 2 *v.i.* work hard or laboriously. 3 **drudgery** *n.*

drug 1 *n.* medicinal substance, esp. pain-killer, stimulant, narcotic, etc. (**dangerous drug** one causing addiction). 2 *v.* add drug to (drink, food, etc.); administer drugs to; indulge in narcotics etc. 3 **drug-store** *US* chemist's shop also selling miscellaneous articles, light refreshments, etc.

drugget /ˈdrʌgɪt/ *n.* coarse woven fabric for floor covering etc.

druggist /ˈdrʌgɪst/ *n.* pharmaceutical chemist.

Druid /ˈdruːɪd/ *n.* ancient Celtic priest; officer of a Gorsedd. **Druidical** *a.*; **Druidism** *n.*

drum 1 *n.* musical instrument sounded by striking skin stretched over frame; sound (as) of this; its player; cylindrical structure or object; cylinder used for storage etc.; tympanum of ear. 2 *v.* play drum; tap or thump repeatedly; drive facts etc. *into* person by persistence; (of bird etc.) make loud noise with wings. 3 **drum brake** kind in which shoes on vehicle press against drum on wheel; **drum major** leader of marching band; **drum majorette** female drum major;

drum out dismiss with ignominy; **drumstick** stick for beating drum, lower joint of cooked fowl's leg; **drum up** produce or obtain by vigorous effort.

drummer /ˈdrʌmə(r)/ *n.* player of drum.

drunk 1 *p.p.* of drink. 2 *a.* deprived of proper control of oneself by alcoholic liquor. 3 *n.* drunken person; *sl.* drinking-bout.

drunkard /ˈdrʌŋkəd/ *n.* person often drunk.

drunken /ˈdrʌŋkən/ *a.* drunk, often drunk; caused by or exhibiting drunkenness.

drupe *n.* stone-fruit.

dry 1 *a.* without or deficient in moisture; without rain; not yielding or using liquid; thirsty; teetotal, prohibiting sale of alcoholic liquor; solid, not liquid; without butter etc.; (of wine etc.) free from sweetness; stiff, cold, matter-of-fact; uninteresting. 2 *v.* make or become dry; preserve (food) by removal of moisture. 3 **dry-clean** clean (clothes etc.) with organic solvents, not using water; **dry-fly** (of fishing) using artificial fly floating on water; **dry ice** solid carbon dioxide; **dry out** become fully dry, (of alcoholic, drug addict, etc.) undergo treatment to cure addiction etc.; **dry rot** decay in wood not exposed to air, caused by fungus; **dry run** *colloq.* rehearsal; **dry-shod** without wetting one's shoes; **dry up** make or become completely dry, dry washed dishes.

dryad /ˈdraɪæd/ *n.* nymph inhabiting tree.

D.Sc. *abbr.* Doctor of Science.

DSC, DSM, DSO *abbrs.* Distinguished Service Cross, Medal, Order.

d.t.('s) *abbr.* delirium tremens.

dual /ˈdjuːəl/ 1 *a.* of two; twofold, double. 2 *n. Gram.* dual number or form. 3 **dual carriageway** road with dividing strip between traffic in opposite directions; **dual-control** (of vehicle etc.) that can be controlled by instructor as well as learner. 4 **duality** *n.*

dub[1] *v.t.* make (person) into knight; give title or nickname to.

dub[2] *v.t.* add sound effects etc. or new sound track, esp. in different language, to (film etc.).

dubbin /ˈdʌbɪn/ n. (also **dubbing**) grease for softening and waterproofing leather.

dubiety /djuːˈbaɪətɪ/ n. feeling of doubt.

dubious /ˈdjuːbɪəs/ a. doubtful; of questionable or suspected character.

ducal /ˈdjuːk(ə)l/ a. of or like duke.

ducat /ˈdʌkət/ n. gold coin formerly current in most European countries.

duchess /ˈdʌtʃɪs/ n. duke's wife or widow; woman with own rank of duke.

duchy /ˈdʌtʃɪ/ n. duke's territory.

duck[1] /dʌk/ n. kind of swimming-bird; female of this; its flesh as food; *Crick.* batsman's score of 0; darling. **2** v. bob down esp. to avoid blow etc.; dip head under water and emerge; plunge (person) in or *in* water. **3 duck-boards** narrow path of wooden slats over muddy ground; **duckweed** a plant that covers surface of still water.

duck[2] n. strong linen or cotton material; in *pl.* trousers of this.

duckling /ˈdʌklɪŋ/ n. young duck.

duct n. channel, tube; *Anat.* tube in body conveying secretions etc.

ductile /ˈdʌktaɪl/ a. capable of being drawn into wire; pliable; docile. **ductility** n.

ductless /ˈdʌktlɪs/ a. (of gland) secreting directly into bloodstream.

dud sl. **1** n. thing that fails to work, useless thing; in *pl.* clothes, rags. **2** a. defective, useless.

dude n. *US sl.* dandy; city man.

dudgeon /ˈdʌdʒ(ə)n/ n. resentment; state of wrath or indignation.

due 1 a. owing or payable as debt or obligation; merited, appropriate; to be ascribed or attributed *to* (cause etc.); under engagement *to* do something or arrive at certain time. **2** adv. exactly, directly. **3** n. what one owes; toll or fee legally demandable; what is owed to person.

duel 1 n. fight with weapons between two persons; contest. **2** v.i. fight duel(s). **3 duellist** n.

duenna /djuːˈenə/ n. older woman acting as chaperon to girls.

duet /djuːˈet/ n. musical composition for two performers.

duff 1 a. *sl.* useless, counterfeit. **2** n. boiled pudding.

duffer /ˈdʌfə(r)/ n. *colloq.* inefficient or stupid person.

duffle /ˈdʌf(ə)l/ n. (also **duffel**) coarse woollen cloth. **duffle bag** cylindrical canvas bag closed by draw-string; **duffle coat** short heavy overcoat with toggle fastenings.

dug[1] past & p.p. of **dig**.

dug[2] n. udder, teat.

dugong /ˈdjuːɡɒŋ/ n. Asian sea-mammal.

dug-out /ˈdʌɡaʊt/ n. hollowed tree as canoe; roofed shelter esp. for troops in trenches.

duke /djuːk/ n. British peer of highest hereditary rank; sovereign ruling duchy or small State. **dukedom** n.

dulcet /ˈdʌlsɪt/ a. sweet-sounding.

dulcimer /ˈdʌlsɪmə(r)/ n. musical instrument with metal strings struck by hammers held in hands.

dull 1 a. not bright; tedious; slow of understanding, stupid; listless, depressed. **2** v. make or become dull. **3 dully** /ˈdʌl·lɪ/ adv.

dullard /ˈdʌləd/ n. slow-witted person.

duly /ˈdjuːlɪ/ adv. in due time or manner; rightly, properly; sufficiently.

dumb /dʌm/ a. unable to speak; silent, taciturn; stupid, ignorant. **dumb-bell** short bar with weight at each end, used in pairs to exercise muscles; **dumb show** gestures instead of speech.

dumbfound /dʌmˈfaʊnd/ v.t. nonplus; make speechless with surprise.

dumdum bullet /ˈdʌmdʌm/ softnosed bullet that expands on impact.

dummy /ˈdʌmɪ/ **1** n. model of human form to hang clothes on or used by ventriloquist; imitation object, object serving to replace real or normal one; baby's rubber teat; stupid person; player or imaginary player in some card-games, whose cards are exposed and played by partner. **2** a. sham, imitation. **3** v.i. use feigned pass etc. in football. **4 dummy run** trial attempt.

dump 1 v.t. deposit as rubbish; put down firmly or clumsily; *colloq.* abandon; send (surplus goods) to foreign market at low price. **2** n. rubbish-heap; temporary depot of ammunition etc.; *colloq.* depressing place.

dumpling /ˈdʌmplɪŋ/ n. ball of dough boiled in stew or containing apple etc.

dumps n.pl. *colloq.* low spirits.

dumpy /'dʌmpɪ/ a. short and stout.

dun¹ 1 a. greyish-brown. 2 n. dun colour; dun horse.

dun² 1 v. ask persistently for payment of debt. 2 n. demand for payment.

dunce n. bad learner; dullard.

dunderhead /'dʌndəhed/ n. stupid person.

dune /dju:n/ n. mound of loose sand etc. formed by wind.

dung 1 n. excrement of animals; manure. 2 v.t. apply dung to (land). 3 **dunghill** heap of dung or refuse in farmyard.

dungaree /dʌŋgə'ri:/ n. strong coarse cotton cloth; in pl. overalls etc. of dungaree or similar material.

dungeon /'dʌndʒ(ə)n/ n. underground cell for prisoners.

dunk v. dip (bread etc.) into soup or beverage before eating it.

dunlin /'dʌnlɪn/ n. red-backed sandpiper.

dunnock /'dʌnək/ n. hedge-sparrow.

duo /'dju:əʊ/ n. (pl. **-os**) pair of performers; duet.

duodecimal /dju:əʊ'desɪm(ə)l/ a. of twelfths or 12; proceeding by twelves.

duodenum /dju:əʊ'di:nəm/ n. part of small intestine next to stomach. **duodenal** a.

duologue /'dju:əlɒg/ n. dialogue between two persons.

dupe /dju:p/ 1 n. victim of deception. 2 v.t. deceive and make use of.

duple /'dju:p(ə)l/ a. of two parts. **duple time** Mus. of two beats to bar.

duplex /'dju:pleks/ a. having two elements; twofold.

duplicate 1 /'dju:plɪkət/ a. exactly like thing already existing; doubled. 2 /'dju:plɪkət/ n. one of two things exactly alike. 3 /'dju:plɪkeɪt/ v.t. make exact copy of; repeat; double. 4 **duplication** n.

duplicator /'dju:plɪkeɪtə(r)/ n. machine for producing documents in multiple copies.

duplicity /dju:'plɪsɪtɪ/ n. deceitfulness.

durable /'djʊərəb(ə)l/ a. capable of lasting; resisting wear. **durability** n.

durance /'djʊərəns/ n. arch. imprisonment.

duration /djʊə'reɪʃ(ə)n/ n. time thing lasts.

duress /djʊə'res/ n. use of force or threats esp. illegally.

during /'djʊərɪŋ/ prep. throughout or at point in duration of.

dusk n. darker stage of twilight.

dusky /'dʌskɪ/ a. shadowy, dim; dark-coloured.

dust 1 n. light fine powder of earth or other matter; dead person's remains. 2 v. clear of dust; sprinkle with powder. 3 **dustbin** container for household refuse; **dust bowl** area denuded of vegetation and reduced to desert; **dust-cart** vehicle for collecting household refuse; **dust-cover, -jacket**, book's paper wrapper; **dustman** man employed to empty dustbins; **dustpan** pan into which dust is brushed from floor etc.; **dust-up** colloq. fight.

duster /'dʌstə(r)/ n. cloth for dusting.

dusty /'dʌstɪ/ a. covered with or full of or like dust.

Dutch 1 a. of the Netherlands. 2 n. Dutch language; the Dutch people. 3 **Dutch auction** sale in which price is reduced till purchaser is found; **Dutch barn** roof on poles over hay etc.; **Dutch courage** courage induced by drink; **Dutch treat** party or outing where each pays for his own share; **go Dutch** share expenses on outing. 4 **Dutchman** n.; **Dutchwoman** n.

duteous /'dju:tɪəs/ a. dutiful.

dutiable /'dju:tɪəb(ə)l/ a. liable to customs etc. duties.

dutiful /'dju:tɪfʊl/ a. doing or observant of one's duty.

duty /'dju:tɪ/ n. moral or legal obligation; office or function; tax levied on article or transaction. **on, off, duty** actually engaged, not engaged, in one's regular work or some obligation.

duvet /'du:veɪ/ n. thick soft quilt used as bedclothes.

dwarf /dwɔ:f/ 1 n. person or plant etc. much below ordinary size; small mythological being with magical powers. 2 a. of a kind very small in size. 3 v.t. stunt in growth; make look small by contrast.

dwell v.i. (past & p.p. **dwelt**) reside, live; keep attention fixed on; write or speak at length on.

dwelling /'dwelɪŋ/ n. house, residence.

dwindle /'dwɪnd(ə)l/ *v.i.* become gradually less or smaller; lose importance.

dye /daɪ/ **1** *n.* substance used to change colour of fabric or wood or hair etc.; colour produced by this. **2** *v.* (*partic.* **dyeing**) impregnate with dye; make (thing) specified colour; take dye.

dying *partic.* of **die**[1].

dyke var. of **dike**.

dynamic /daɪ'næmɪk/ *a.* of motive force; of force in operation; of dynamics; potent, forceful. **dynamically** *adv.*

dynamics *n.pl.* (usu. treated as *sing.*) branch of mechanics that treats of motion and of action of forces.

dynamism /'daɪnəmɪz(ə)m/ *n.* energizing or dynamic action or power.

dynamite /'daɪnəmaɪt/ **1** *n.* high explosive of nitroglycerine mixed with absorbent substance. **2** *v.t.* blow up with this.

dynamo /'daɪnəməʊ/ *n.* (*pl.* **-mos**) machine converting mechanical into electrical energy; energetic person.

dynast /'dɪnəst/ *n.* member of dynasty.

dynasty /'dɪnəstɪ/ *n.* line of hereditary rulers. **dynastic** /-'næs-/ *a.*

dyne *n.* *Phys.* unit of force.

dysentery /'dɪsəntərɪ/ *n.* inflammation of bowels.

dyslexia /dɪs'leksɪə/ *n.* abnormal difficulty in reading and spelling caused by a condition of the brain. **dyslexic** *a.*

dyspepsia /dɪs'pepsɪə/ *n.* indigestion. **dyspeptic** *a.*

dystrophy /'dɪstrəfɪ/ *n.* defective nutrition. **muscular dystrophy** hereditary progressive weakening of muscles.

E

E. *abbr.* east(ern).

each 1 *a.* every one of two or more taken separately. **2** *pron.* each person or thing. **3 each way** (of bet) backing horse etc. to win or to be placed.

eager /ˈiːgə(r)/ *a.* full of keen desire; enthusiastically impatient.

eagle /ˈiːg(ə)l/ *n.* large bird of prey; figure of eagle esp. as symbol of US; *Golf* score of 2 under par for hole. **eagle eye** keen sight or watchfulness.

ear¹ /ɪə(r)/ *n.* organ of hearing, esp. external part; sense of hearing; attention; faculty of discriminating sound; ear-shaped thing. **earache** pain in inner ear; **ear-drum** internal membrane of ear; **earmark** (*n.*) owner's mark on ear of sheep etc., (*v.t.*) mark (animal) thus, *fig.* assign (fund etc.) *for* some definite purpose; **earphone** device worn on ear to listen to radio or telephone communication; **ear-plug** device to protect ear from water, noise, etc., or to listen to radio etc. communication; **ear-ring** ornament worn on lobe of ear; **earshot** hearing-distance; **ear-trumpet** trumpet-shaped tube formerly used as hearing aid.

ear² /ɪə(r)/ *n.* seed-bearing head of cereal plant.

earl /ɜːl/ *n.* British nobleman ranking next below marquis. **Earl Marshal** officer of State with ceremonial duties. **earldom** *n.*

early /ˈɜːlɪ/ *a.* & *adv.* before due or usual or expected time, not far on in day or night etc. or in development etc.

earn /ɜːn/ *v.t.* obtain as reward of work or merit; bring as income or interest.

earnest¹ /ˈɜːnɪst/ *a.* serious; showing intense feeling. **in earnest** serious(ly).

earnest² /ˈɜːnɪst/ *n.* money paid as instalment to confirm contract; foretaste.

earnings /ˈɜːnɪŋz/ *n.pl.* money earned.

earth /ɜːθ/ **1** *n.* planet we live on; land and sea as opp. sky; dry land; ground; soil, mould; *Electr.* connection to earth as completion of circuit; hole of fox etc. **2** *v.t. Electr.* connect to earth; heap earth over (roots etc.). **3 earthwork** bank of earth in fortification; **earthworm** worm living in earth; **run to earth** find after long search.

earthen /ˈɜːθ(ə)n/ *a.* made of earth or of baked clay. **earthenware** baked clay, vessels made of this.

earthly /ˈɜːθlɪ/ *a.* of earth, terrestrial. **no earthly** *colloq.* absolutely no; **not an earthly** *sl.* no chance whatever.

earthquake /ˈɜːθkweɪk/ *n.* convulsion of earth's surface.

earthy /ˈɜːθɪ/ *a.* of or like earth or soil; grossly material.

earwig /ˈɪəwɪg/ *n.* insect with pincers at tail end.

ease /iːz/ **1** *n.* freedom from pain or trouble or constraint; facility. **2** *v.* relieve from pain etc.; relax, slacken; cause to move by gentle force. **3 ease (off)** become less burdensome or severe.

easel /ˈiːz(ə)l/ *n.* frame to support painting or blackboard etc.

easement /ˈiːzmənt/ *n. Law* right of way over another's property.

east 1 *n.* point of horizon where sun rises; eastern part of world or country or town etc. **2** *a.* towards or at or near or facing east; coming from east. **3** *adv.* towards or at or near east. **4 East End** eastern part of London. **5 eastward** *adv.*, *a.*, & *n.*; **eastwards** *adv.*

Easter /ˈiːstə(r)/ *n.* festival of Christ's resurrection. **Easter egg** artificial usu. chocolate egg as Easter gift.

easterly /ˈiːstəlɪ/ *a.* from or to east.

eastern /ˈiːst(ə)n/ *a.* of or in east. **Eastern Church** Orthodox Church.

easterner /ˈiːstənə(r)/ *n.* inhabitant of east.

easy /ˈiːzɪ/ **1** *a.* not difficult; free from bodily or mental pain or worry etc.; free from embarrassment or strictness etc.; compliant. **2** *adv.* in comfortable fashion; gently. **3 easy chair** large comfortable chair; **easygoing** not fussy, content with things as they are; **take it easy** proceed gently, relax.

eat *v.* (*past* **ate** /et/; *p.p.* **eaten**) chew and swallow (food); consume food, have meal; destroy, consume.

eatable /ˈiːtəb(ə)l/ **1** *a.* that may be eaten. **2** *n.* (usu. in *pl.*) food.

eau-de-Cologne /əʊdəkəˈləʊn/ *n.* perfume made orig. at Cologne.

eaves /iːvz/ *n.pl.* projecting lower edge of roof.

eavesdrop /ˈiːvzdrɒp/ v.i. listen secretly to private conversation.

ebb 1 n. outward movement of tide; decline, decay. 2 v.i. flow back; decline.

ebonite /ˈebənaɪt/ n. vulcanized rubber.

ebony /ˈebənɪ/ 1 n. hard heavy black wood. 2 a. made of or black as ebony.

ebullient /ɪˈbʌlɪənt/ a. exuberant; high-spirited. **ebullience** n.

ebullition /ebʊˈlɪʃ(ə)n/ n. boiling; outburst.

EC East Central.

eccentric /ɪkˈsentrɪk/ 1 a. odd or capricious in behaviour or appearance; not placed centrally, not having axis etc. placed centrally; not concentric; not circular. 2 n. eccentric person. 3 **eccentricity** /-ˈtrɪs-/ n.

ecclesiastic /ɪkliːzɪˈæstɪk/ n. clergyman.

ecclesiastical /ɪkliːzɪˈæstɪk(ə)l/ a. of the Church or clergy.

ECG abbr. electrocardiogram.

echelon /ˈeʃəlɒn/ n. formation of troops in parallel divisions, each with its end clear of those ahead or behind; any similar formation; level or rank in organization.

echidna /ɪˈkɪdnə/ n. Aus. egg-laying burrowing mammal.

echo /ˈekəʊ/ 1 n. (pl. -oes) repetition of sound by reflection of sound-waves; close imitation. 2 v. resound with echo; repeat, imitate; be repeated.

éclair /eɪˈkleə(r)/ n. finger-shaped cake filled with cream and iced.

éclat /eɪˈklɑː/ n. brilliant success; prestige.

eclectic /ɪˈklektɪk/ a. selecting ideas or beliefs from various sources. 2 n. eclectic person.

eclipse /ɪˈklɪps/ 1 n. interception of light of sun or moon etc. by another body; loss of brilliance or splendour. 2 v.t. intercept light of; fig. outshine, surpass.

ecliptic /ɪˈklɪptɪk/ n. sun's apparent path among stars during year.

eclogue /ˈeklɒg/ n. short pastoral poem.

ecology /ɪˈkɒlədʒɪ/ n. study of organisms in relation to one another and their surroundings. **ecological** a.; **ecologist** n.

economic /iːkəˈnɒmɪk/ a. of economics; maintained for profit; adequate to pay for expenses or costs; practical, utilitarian.

economical /iːkəˈnɒmɪk(ə)l/ a. thrifty; saving or avoiding waste (of).

economics /iːkəˈnɒmɪks/ n.pl. treated as sing. science of production and distribution of wealth; application of this to particular subject. **economist** n.

economize /ɪˈkɒnəmaɪz/ v. make economies; reduce expenditure.

economy /ɪˈkɒnəmɪ/ n. management of concerns and resources of State or business or household; frugality, instance of this.

ecru /ˈeɪkruː/ n. light fawn colour.

ecstasy /ˈekstəsɪ/ n. overwhelming feeling of joy; rapture. **ecstatic** /-ˈstæt-/ a.

ECT abbr. electroconvulsive therapy.

ectoplasm /ˈektəplæz(ə)m/ n. viscous substance supposed to emanate from body of spiritualistic medium during trance.

ecumenical /iːkjuːˈmenɪk(ə)l/ a. of or representing whole Christian world; seeking world-wide Christian unity; worldwide. **ecumenicalism** n. **ecumenism** n.

eczema /ˈeksɪmə/ n. kind of inflammation of skin.

ed. abbr. edited; edition; editor.

Edam /ˈiːdæm/ n. spherical Dutch cheese usu. with red rind.

eddy /ˈedɪ/ 1 n. small whirlpool; smoke etc. moving like this. 2 v. move in eddies.

edelweiss /ˈeɪdəlvaɪs/ n. white-flowered Alpine plant.

Eden /ˈiːd(ə)n/ n. (in full **Garden of Eden**) abode of Adam and Eve; delightful place or state.

edentate /ɪˈdenteɪt/ a. having few or no teeth.

edge 1 n. cutting side of blade; sharpness; effectiveness; crest of ridge, line where two surfaces meet abruptly; rim, narrow surface of thin or flat object; boundary, brink. 2 v. sharpen; give or form border to; advance esp. gradually and obliquely. 3 **edgeways**, **edgewise**, with edge foremost or uppermost; **have the edge on** have an advantage over; **on edge** excited or irritable.

edging /ˈedʒɪŋ/ n. border, fringe.

edgy /ˈedʒɪ/ a. irritable, on edge.

edible /'edɪb(ə)l/ **1** *a.* fit to be eaten. **2** *n.* edible thing. **3 edibility** *n.*

edict /'iːdɪkt/ *n.* order proclaimed by authority.

edifice /'edɪfɪs/ *n.* building, esp. large imposing one.

edify /'edɪfaɪ/ *v.t.* improve morally. **edification** *n.*

edit /'edɪt/ *v.t.* prepare for publication; act as editor of; cut and collate (films etc.) to make unified sequence; reword, modify.

edition /ɪ'dɪʃ(ə)n/ *n.* edited or published form of a book etc.; copies of book or newspaper etc. issued at one time.

editor /'edɪtə(r)/ *n.* person who edits; person who directs writing of newspaper or section of one; head of department of publishing house.

editorial /edɪ'tɔːrɪəl/ **1** *a.* of an editor. **2** *n.* newspaper article written or sanctioned by editor.

educate /'edjʊkeɪt/ *v.t.* train or instruct mentally and morally; provide schooling for. **educable** *a.*; **education** *n.*; **educator** *n.*; **educational** *a.*

educationist /edjʊ'keɪʃənɪst/ *n.* (also **educationalist**) expert in educational methods.

educe /ɪ'djuːs/ *v.t.* bring out, develop. **eduction** *n.*

Edwardian /ed'wɔːdɪən/ **1** *a.* of or characteristic of reign (1901–10) of Edward VII. **2** *n.* person of this period.

EEC *abbr.* European Economic Community.

EEG *abbr.* electroencephalogram.

eel *n.* snakelike fish.

eerie /'ɪərɪ/ *a.* strange; weird.

efface /ɪ'feɪs/ *v.t.* rub or wipe out; surpass, eclipse; make one*self* inconspicuous. **effacement** *n.*

effect /ɪ'fekt/ **1** *n.* result, consequence; efficacy; impression; in *pl.* property; in *pl.* sounds and visual features as accompaniment to play etc. **2** *v.t.* bring about; accomplish.

effective /ɪ'fektɪv/ *a.* having effect; impressive; actual; existing.

effectual /ɪ'fektjʊəl/ *a.* answering its purpose; valid.

effeminate /ɪ'femɪnət/ *a.* (of a man) unmanly, womanish. **effeminacy** *n.*

effervesce /efə'ves/ *v.i.* give off

bubbles of gas. **effervescent** *a.*; **effervescence** *n.*

effete /ɪ'fiːt/ *a.* worn out; feeble.

efficacious /efɪ'keɪʃəs/ *a.* producing desired effect. **efficacy** /'efɪkəsɪ/ *n.*

efficient /ɪ'fɪʃ(ə)nt/ *a.* productive with minimum waste of effort; competent, capable; producing desired result. **efficiency** *n.*

effigy /'efɪdʒɪ/ *n.* sculpture or model of person.

effloresce /eflə'res/ *v.i.* burst into flower. **efflorescence** *n.*; **efflorescent** *a.*

effluence /'efluəns/ *n.* flowing out (of liquid etc.); what flows out.

effluent /'efluənt/ **1** *a.* flowing out. **2** *n.* stream flowing from lake etc.; outflow from sewage tank or waste product of industrial process etc.

effluvium /ɪ'fluːvɪəm/ *n.* (*pl.* **-via**) outflow of substance, esp. unpleasant or harmful one.

effort /'efət/ *n.* exertion; vigorous attempt; force exerted; *colloq.* something accomplished.

effrontery /ɪ'frʌntərɪ/ *n.* impudence.

effulgent /ɪ'fʌldʒ(ə)nt/ *a.* bright, radiant. **effulgence** *n.*

effuse /ɪ'fjuːz/ *v.t.* pour forth.

effusion /ɪ'fjuːʒ(ə)n/ *n.* outpouring.

effusive /ɪ'fjuːsɪv/ *a.* demonstrative; gushing.

eft *n.* newt.

EFTA *abbr.* European Free Trade Association.

e.g. *abbr.* for example.

egalitarian /ɪgælɪ'teərɪən/ **1** *a.* of or advocating equal rights for all. **2** *n.* egalitarian person. **3 egalitarianism** *n.*

egg[1] *n.* oval body produced by female of birds etc., containing germ of new individual, esp. that of domestic fowl for eating; ovum. **egghead** *colloq.* intellectual; **egg-plant** aubergine; **egg-timer** device for timing boiling of egg.

egg[2] *v.t.* urge (person) *on*.

eglantine /'eglantaɪn/ *n.* sweet-brier.

ego /'iːgəʊ or 'e-/ *n.* the self; part of mind that has sense of individuality; self-esteem.

egocentric /egəʊ'sentrɪk/ *a.* self-centred.

egoism /'egəʊɪz(ə)m/ *n.* systematic

selfishness; egotism. **egoist** n.; **egoistic** a.

egotism /'egətɪz(ə)m/ n. practice of talking about oneself; self-conceit. **egotist** n.; **egotistic** a.

egregious /ɪ'griːdʒəs/ a. shocking; arch. remarkable.

egress /'iːgres/ n. going out; way out.

egret /'iːgret/ n. kind of white heron.

Egyptian /ɪ'dʒɪpʃ(ə)n/ 1 a. of Egypt. 2 n. native of Egypt; language of ancient Egyptians.

Egyptology /iːdʒɪp'tɒlədʒɪ/ n. study of Egyptian antiquities. **Egyptologist** n.

eh /eɪ/ int. expressing inquiry, surprise, etc.

eider /'aɪdə(r)/ n. northern species of duck. **eiderdown** quilt stuffed with down or other soft material.

eight /eɪt/ n. & a. one more than seven; 8-oared rowing-boat or its crew. **eightsome reel** lively Sc. dance for 8 persons. **eighth** /eɪtθ/ a. & n.

eighteen /eɪ'tiːn/ n. & a. one more than seventeen. **eighteenth** a. & n.

eighty /'eɪtɪ/ n. & a. eight times ten. **eightieth** /'eɪtɪɪθ/ a. & n.

eisteddfod /aɪ'steðvɒd/ n. Welsh congress of bards; national or local gathering for musical and literary competition.

either /'aɪðə(r) or 'iːðə(r)/ 1 pron. & a. one or other of two; each of two. 2 adv. introducing first alternative; (with neg. or interrog.) any more than the other.

ejaculate /ɪ'dʒækjʊleɪt/ v. utter suddenly, cry out; eject (fluid etc. esp. semen) from body. **ejaculation** n.; **ejaculatory** a.

eject /ɪ'dʒekt/ v.t. throw out, expel; emit. **ejection** n.

ejector seat device for ejection of pilot from aircraft etc. in emergency.

eke v.t. (with out) make (living) or support (existence) with difficulty; supply deficiencies of.

elaborate 1 /ɪ'læbərət/ a. minutely worked out; highly developed or complicated. 2 /ɪ'læbəreɪt/ v.t. work out or explain in detail. 3 **elaboration** n.; **elaborative** a.; **elaborator** n.

élan /eɪ'lɑ̃/ n. vivacity, dash. [F]

eland /'iːlənd/ n. large Afr. antelope.

elapse /ɪ'læps/ v.i. (of time) pass by.

elastic /ɪ'læstɪk/ 1 a. able to resume normal bulk or shape after dilation

etc.; buoyant; flexible; springy. 2 n. elastic cord or fabric usu. woven with strips of rubber. 3 **elasticity** n.

elasticated /ɪ'læstɪkeɪtɪd/ a. (of fabric) made elastic by weaving with rubber thread.

elate /ɪ'leɪt/ v.t. raise spirits of, excite. **elation** n.

elbow /'elbəʊ/ 1 n. joint between forearm and upper arm; part of sleeve of garment covering elbow; elbow-shaped thing. 2 v.t. thrust, jostle. 3 **elbowgrease** joc. vigorous polishing, hard work; **elbow-room** sufficient space to move or work in.

elder[1] /'eldə(r)/ 1 a. of greater age; senior. 2 n. person of greater age; official in early Christian and some modern Churches.

elder[2] /'eldə(r)/ n. white-flowered black-berried tree or shrub.

elderly /'eldəlɪ/ a. growing old.

eldest /'eldɪst/ a. first-born; oldest surviving.

eldorado /eldə'rɑːdəʊ/ n. (pl. -dos) fictitious region rich in gold.

eldritch /'eldrɪtʃ/ a. Sc. weird, hideous.

elect /ɪ'lekt/ 1 v.t. choose by voting; choose, decide. 2 a. chosen; (placed after n.) chosen but not yet in office.

election /ɪ'lekʃ(ə)n/ n. electing, being elected; process of electing esp. MPs.

electioneer /ɪlekʃə'nɪə(r)/ v.i. take part in election campaign.

elective /ɪ'lektɪv/ a. chosen or appointed by election; entitled to elect; optional.

elector /ɪ'lektə(r)/ n. person entitled to vote in election. **electoral** a.

electorate /ɪ'lektərət/ n. body of electors.

electric /ɪ'lektrɪk/ a. of or charged with or worked by electricity; startling. **electric blanket** one heated by internal wires; **electric chair** chair used for electrocution of criminals; **electric eel** eel-like fish able to give electric shock; **electric shock** effect of sudden discharge of electricity through body of person etc.

electrical /ɪ'lektrɪk(ə)l/ a. of or concerned with electricity; electric.

electrician /ɪlek'trɪʃ(ə)n/ n. person who installs and maintains electrical equipment professionally.

electricity /ɪlekˈtrɪsɪtɪ/ n. form of energy present in protons and electrons; supply of electricity; science of electricity.

electrify /ɪˈlektrɪfaɪ/ v.t. charge with electricity; convert to electric working; startle, excite. **electrification** n.

electro- /ɪˈlektrəʊ/ in comb. of or caused by electricity.

electrocardiogram /ɪlektrəʊˈkɑːdɪəgræm/ n. record of voltage generated by heartbeats.
electrocardiograph n. instrument for taking such records.

electroconvulsive /ɪlektrəʊkənˈvʌlsɪv/ a. (of therapy) making use of convulsive response to electric shocks.

electrocute /ɪˈlektrəkjuːt/ v.t. kill or execute by electric shock. **electrocution** n.

electrode /ɪˈlektrəʊd/ n. conductor through which electricity enters or leaves electrolyte or gas or vacuum etc.

electroencephalogram /ɪlektrəʊenˈsefələgræm/ n. record of electrical activity of brain; **electroencephalograph** n. instrument for taking such record.

electrolysis /ɪlekˈtrɒləsɪs/ n. chemical decomposition by action of electric current; breaking up of tumours or hairroots etc. thus.

electrolyte /ɪˈlektrəlaɪt/ n. solution able to conduct electric current; substance that can dissolve to produce this. **electrolytic** /-ˈlɪt-/ a.

electromagnet /ɪlektrəʊˈmægnɪt/ n. piece of material made into magnet by electric current through coil surrounding it.

electromagnetism /ɪlektrəʊˈmægnətɪz(ə)m/ n. magnetic forces produced by electricity; study of these.

electron /ɪˈlektrɒn/ n. stable elementary particle with indivisible charge of negative electricity, found in all atoms and acting as carrier of electricity in solids. **electron microscope** one with high magnification, using focused beam of electrons.

electronic /elɪkˈtrɒnɪk/ a. of electrons or electronics.

electronics n. pl. treated as sing. branch of physics and technology dealing with behaviour of electrons in vacuum or gas or semiconductor etc.

electroplate /ɪˈlektrəʊpleɪt/ 1 v.t. coat with chromium or silver etc. by electrolysis. 2 n. objects so produced.

elegant /ˈelɪgənt/ a. graceful, tasteful; of refined luxury. **elegance** n.

elegiac /elɪˈdʒaɪək/ a. suited to elegies, mournful.

elegy /ˈelədʒɪ/ n. song or poem of lamentation, esp. for dead.

element /ˈelɪmənt/ n. component part; *Chem.* any of substances which cannot be resolved by chemical means into simpler substances; *arch.* one of **the four elements** (earth, air, water, fire) formerly supposed to make up all matter; *Electr.* wire that gives out heat in electric heater or cooker etc.; in pl. rudiments, first principles; in pl. atmospheric agencies. **in one's element** in one's preferred surroundings.

elemental /elɪˈment(ə)l/ a. of or like the elements or the powers of nature; basic, essential.

elementary /elɪˈmentərɪ/ a. dealing with the simplest facts of subject, rudimentary, simple; that cannot be decomposed. **elementary particle** *Phys.* any of several subatomic particles not known to consist of simpler ones.

elephant /ˈelɪf(ə)nt/ n. largest living mammal, with trunk and ivory tusks.

elephantiasis /elɪfənˈtaɪəsɪs/ n. skin disease causing gross enlargement of limb etc.

elephantine /elɪˈfæntaɪn/ a. of elephants; huge, clumsy, unwieldy.

elevate /ˈelɪveɪt/ v.t. lift up, raise; in p.p. exalted.

elevation /elɪˈveɪʃ(ə)n/ n. elevating, being elevated; height above given level; angle above horizontal; drawing showing one side of building.

elevator /ˈelɪveɪtə(r)/ n. hoisting-machine; movable part of tailplane for changing aircraft's altitude; *US* lift.

eleven /ɪˈlev(ə)n/ n. & a. one more than ten; side of 11 persons at cricket etc. **eleventh** a. & n.

elevenses /ɪˈlevənzɪz/ n. light mid-morning refreshments.

elf n. (pl. **elves**) mythical dwarfish being; mischievous child. **elfish** a.

elfin /ˈelfɪn/ a. of elves, elflike.

elicit /ɪˈlɪsɪt/ v.t. (usu. *fig.*) draw out.

elide /ɪ'laɪd/ v.t. omit in pronunciation.

eligible /'elɪdʒɪb(ə)l/ a. fit or entitled to be chosen etc. (*for*); desirable or suitable esp. for marriage. **eligibility** n.

eliminate /ɪ'lɪmɪneɪt/ v.t. remove, get rid of; expel, exclude. **elimination** n.; **eliminator** n.

elision /ɪ'lɪʒ(ə)n/ n. omission of vowel or syllable in pronunciation.

élite /eɪ'liːt/ n. select group or class; *the* choice part (*of*).

élitism /eɪ'liːtɪz(ə)m/ n. advocacy of or reliance on dominance by a select group. **élitist** n.

elixir /ɪ'lɪksɪə(r)/ n. alchemist's preparation designed to change metal into gold or prolong life indefinitely.

Elizabethan /ɪlɪzə'biːθ(ə)n/ **1** a. of time of Elizabeth I or II. **2** n. person of this time.

elk n. large species of deer.

ell n. *hist.* measure of length (45 in.).

ellipse /ɪ'lɪps/ n. regular oval.

ellipsis /ɪ'lɪpsɪs/ n. (pl. **-ses** /-siːz/) omission of words needed to complete construction or sense.

elliptical /ɪ'lɪptɪk(ə)l/ a. of or like an ellipse or ellipsis.

elm n. tree with rough serrated leaves; its wood.

elocution /elə'kjuːʃ(ə)n/ n. style or art of expressive speaking. **elocutionary** a.; **elocutionist** n.

elongate /'iːlɒŋɡeɪt/ v.t. lengthen, extend, draw out. **elongation** n.

elope /ɪ'ləʊp/ v.i. run away to get secretly married. **elopement** n.

eloquence /'eləkwəns/ n. fluent and powerful use of language. **eloquent** a.

else /els/ adv. besides; instead; otherwise; if not. **elsewhere** in or to some other place.

elucidate /ɪ'luːsɪdeɪt/ v.t. throw light on, explain. **elucidation** n.; **elucidator** n.; **elucidatory** a.

elude /ɪljuː'd/ v.t. escape adroitly from; avoid; baffle.

elusive /ɪ'luːsɪv/ a. difficult to grasp or perceive or define.

elver /'elvə(r)/ n. young eel.

elves pl.of **elf**.

Elysium /ɪ'lɪzɪəm/ n. *Gk. myth.* abode of blessed after death; place of ideal happiness. **Elysian** a.

em n. *Print.* unit of measurement equal to space occupied by m.

emaciate /ɪ'meɪsɪeɪt/ v.t. make thin or feeble. **emaciation** n.

emanate /'eməneɪt/ v.i. (cause to) originate or proceed *from*. **emanation** n.

emancipate /ɪ'mænsɪpeɪt/ v.t. set free from legal or social or political or moral restraint. **emancipation** n.; **emancipator** n.

emasculate 1 /ɪ'mæskjʊleɪt/ v.t. castrate; enfeeble. **2** /ɪ'mæskjʊlət/ a. castrated; effeminate. **3 emasculation** n. **emasculatory** a.

embalm /ɪm'bɑːm/ v.t. preserve (corpse) from decay; preserve from oblivion; make fragrant. **embalmment** n.

embankment /ɪm'bæŋkmənt/ n. mound of earth, or stone structure etc., confining river, or carrying road or railway.

embargo /ɪm'bɑːɡəʊ/ n. (pl. **-goes**) order forbidding ships to enter or leave port; suspension of commerce; stoppage, prohibition.

embark /ɪm'bɑːk/ v. put or go on board ship; enter *on* (course etc.).

embarkation /embɑː'keɪʃ(ə)n/ n. embarking on ship.

embarrass /ɪm'bærəs/ v.t. make (person) awkward or ashamed; encumber. **embarrassment** n.

embassy /'embəsɪ/ n. ambassador's function or office or residence; deputation.

embattle /ɪm'bæt(ə)l/ v.t. set in battle array; furnish with battlements.

embed /ɪm'bed/ v.t. fix in surrounding mass.

embellish /ɪm'belɪʃ/ v.t. beautify, adorn; make fictitious additions to. **embellishment** n.

ember /'embə(r)/ n. (usu. in *pl.*) small piece of fuel in dying fire.

ember day /'embə(r)/ any of appointed days of fasting and prayer in each of four seasons.

embezzle /ɪm'bez(ə)l/ v.t. divert (money) fraudulently to one's own use. **embezzlement** n.

embitter /ɪm'bɪtə(r)/ v.t. arouse bitter feelings in, make bitter. **embitterment** n.

emblazon /ɪm'bleɪz(ə)n/ v.t. blazon.

emblem /'embləm/ n. symbol; distinctive badge. **emblematic** a.

embody /ɪm'bɒdɪ/ v.t. give concrete

form to; be an expression of; include, comprise. **embodiment** n.

embolden /ɪmˈbəʊld(ə)n/ v.t. encourage.

embolism /ˈembəlɪz(ə)m/ n. obstruction of artery etc. by blood-clot etc.

emboss /ɪmˈbɒs/ v.t. carve or decorate with design in relief. **embossment** n.

embrace /ɪmˈbreɪs/ 1 v.t. hold closely in arms, enclose; accept, adopt; include. 2 n. holding in arms, clasp.

embrasure /ɪmˈbreɪʒə(r)/ n. bevelling of wall at sides of window etc.; opening in parapet for gun.

embrocation /embrəˈkeɪʃ(ə)n/ n. liquid for rubbing on body to relieve muscular pain.

embroider /ɪmˈbrɔɪdə(r)/ v.t. ornament with needlework; embellish. **embroidery** n.

embroil /ɪmˈbrɔɪl/ v.t. bring into confusion; involve in hostility.

embryo /ˈembrɪəʊ/ n. (pl. -os) unborn or unhatched offspring; thing in rudimentary stage. **embryonic** /-ˈɒn-/ a.

emend /ɪˈmend/ v.t. correct, remove errors from (text of book etc.). **emendation** n.; **emendatory** a.

emerald /ˈemər(ə)ld/ n. bright-green precious stone; colour of emerald.

emerge /ɪˈmɜːdʒ/ v.i. come up or out into view or notice (from); come out.

emergency /ɪˈmɜːdʒənsɪ/ n. sudden state of danger or conflict etc., requiring immediate action.

emergent /ɪˈmɜːdʒ(ə)nt/ a. emerging; (of nation) newly independent. **emergence** n.

emeritus /ɪˈmerɪtəs/ a. retired and holding honorary title.

emery /ˈemərɪ/ n. coarse corundum for polishing metal etc.

emetic /ɪˈmetɪk/ 1 a. that causes vomiting. 2 n. emetic medicine.

emigrate /ˈemɪgreɪt/ v.i. go to settle in another country. **emigrant** a. & n.; **emigration** n.

émigré /ˈemɪgreɪ/ n. emigrant, esp. political exile. [F]

eminence /ˈemɪnəns/ n. recognized superiority; rising ground; **Eminence** cardinal's title of honour.

eminent /ˈemɪnənt/ a. distinguished, notable.

eminently adv. particularly; notably.

emir /eˈmɪə(r)/ n. title of various Muslim rulers.

emirate /ˈemɪərət/ n. position or reign or domain of emir.

emissary /ˈemɪsərɪ/ n. person sent on special diplomatic mission.

emission /ɪˈmɪʃ(ə)n/ n. emitting; what is emitted. **emissive** a.

emit /ɪˈmɪt/ v.t. give out, send forth.

emollient /ɪˈmɒlɪənt/ 1 a. softening; soothing. 2 n. emollient substance.

emolument /ɪˈmɒljʊmənt/ a. profit from employment; salary.

emotion /ɪˈməʊʃ(ə)n/ n. strong mental or instinctive feeling such as love or fear.

emotional /ɪˈməʊʃən(ə)l/ a. of or expressing emotion(s); liable to excessive emotion. **emotionalism** n.

emotive /ɪˈməʊtɪv/ a. of or tending to excite emotion.

empanel /ɪmˈpæn(ə)l/ v.t. enter (jury) on panel.

empathy /ˈempəθɪ/ n. power of identifying oneself mentally with person or object of contemplation. **empathize** v.

emperor /ˈempərə(r)/ n. ruler of empire.

emphasis /ˈemfəsɪs/ n. (pl. -ses /-siːz/) significant stress on word(s); importance; vigour of expression etc.

emphasize /ˈemfəsaɪz/ v.t. lay stress on.

emphatic /ɪmˈfætɪk/ a. forcible, strong; (of words) bearing emphasis.

emphysema /emfɪˈsiːmə/ n. swelling due to air in body tissues.

empire /ˈempaɪə(r)/ n. extensive group of States or countries under single supreme authority; supreme dominion; large commercial etc. organization owned or directed by one person.

empirical /ɪmˈpɪrɪk(ə)l/ a. based or acting on observation and experiment, not on theory. **empiricism** n; **empiricist** n.

emplacement /ɪmˈpleɪsmənt/ n. putting in position; platform for gun(s).

employ /ɪmˈplɔɪ/ 1 v.t. use services of esp. for wages; use (thing, time, energies, etc.); find occupation for. 2 n. **in the employ of** employed by.

employee /emplɔɪˈiː/ n. person employed for wages.

employer /ɪmˈplɔɪə(r)/ n. person who employs, esp. others for wages.

employment /ɪmˈplɔɪmənt/ a. employing or being employed; regular occupation or business. **employment exchange** State office concerned with finding employment for those needing it.

emporium /ɪmˈpɔːrɪəm/ n. centre of commerce; large shop, store.

empower /ɪmˈpaʊə(r)/ v.t. give power or authority to.

empress /ˈemprɪs/ n. wife or widow of emperor; woman emperor.

empty /ˈemptɪ/ **1** a. containing nothing; devoid (of); vacant; colloq. hungry; vacuous, foolish. **2** v. remove contents of; transfer (contents of); become empty; (of river) discharge itself. **3** n. emptied box or bottle etc.

emu /ˈiːmjuː/ n. large flightless Aus. bird.

emulate /ˈemjʊleɪt/ v.t. try to equal or excel; imitate. **emulation** n.; **emulative** a.; **emulator** n.

emulous /ˈemjʊləs/ a. zealously imitative (of); actuated by rivalry.

emulsify /ɪˈmʌlsɪfaɪ/ v.t. make emulsion of.

emulsion /ɪˈmʌlʃ(ə)n/ n. fine dispersion of one liquid in another, esp. as paint or medicine etc.

en n. Print. unit of measurement equal to space occupied by n.

enable /ɪˈneɪb(ə)l/ v.t. supply with means (to do); make possible.

enact /ɪˈnækt/ v.t. ordain; play (part); make into legislative act. **enactment** n.

enamel /ɪˈnæm(ə)l/ **1** n. glasslike coating on metal; any hard smooth coating; hard coating of teeth. **2** v.t. coat with enamel.

enamour /ɪˈnæmə(r)/ v.t. inspire with love; make fond of.

en bloc /ɑ̃ ˈblɒk/ in a block, all at the same time. [F]

encamp /ɪnˈkæmp/ v. settle in (esp. military) camp. **encampment** n.

encase /ɪnˈkeɪs/ v.t. confine (as) in a case.

encash /ɪnˈkæʃ/ v.t. convert into cash. **encashment** n.

encaustic /enˈkɔːstɪk/ **1** a. (of painting) with wax colours fixed by heat; (of tile etc.) inlaid with coloured clays burnt in. **2** n. art or product of this.

encephalitis /ensefəˈlaɪtɪs/ n. inflammation of brain.

enchain /ɪnˈtʃeɪn/ v.t. chain up; hold fast.

enchant /ɪnˈtʃɑːnt/ v.t. bewitch; delight. **enchantment** n.; **enchantress** n.

encircle /ɪnˈsɜːk(ə)l/ v.t. surround. **encirclement** n.

enclave /ˈenkleɪv/ n. territory of one State surrounded by that of another.

enclitic /ɪnˈklɪtɪk/ **1** a. (of word) so unemphatic as to be pronounced as if part of preceding word. **2** n. enclitic word.

enclose /ɪnˈkləʊz/ v.t. shut in on all sides; surround, fence in; shut up in receptacle (esp. in envelope besides letter); in p.p. (of religious community) secluded from outside world.

enclosure /ɪnˈkləʊʒə(r)/ n. enclosing; enclosed space or area; thing enclosed.

encode /ɪnˈkəʊd/ v.t. put into code.

encomium /ɪnˈkəʊmɪəm/ n. (pl. -iums or -ia) formal or high-flown praise.

encompass /ɪnˈkʌmpəs/ v.t. surround, contain.

encore /ˈɒŋkɔː(r)/ **1** n. call for further performance or repetition of item; such item. **2** v.t. call for repetition of or by. **3** int. again.

encounter /ɪnˈkaʊntə(r)/ **1** v.t. meet by chance; meet as adversary. **2** n. meeting by chance or in combat.

encourage /ɪnˈkʌrɪdʒ/ v.t. give courage to; urge; stimulate; promote. **encouragement** n.

encroach /ɪnˈkrəʊtʃ/ v.i. intrude on others' territory etc. **encroachment** n.

encrust v. /ɪnˈkrʌst/ cover with or form crust; overlay with crust of silver etc.

encumber /ɪnˈkʌmbə(r)/ v.t. be burden to; hamper, impede.

encumbrance /ɪnˈkʌmbrəns/ n. burden, impediment.

encyclical /enˈsɪklɪk(ə)l/ **1** a. for wide circulation. **2** n. papal encyclical letter.

encyclopaedia /ɪnˌsaɪkləˈpiːdɪə/ n. (also **encyclopedia**) book of information on many branches of knowledge or on many aspects of one subject. **encyclopaedic** a.

end 1 n. limit; farthest point; extreme point or part; remnant; conclusion, latter part; destruction; death; result; object. **2** v. bring or come to end. **3**

end-paper blank leaf of paper at beginning or end of book; **end-product** final product of process of manufacture etc.; **end up** reach certain state or action eventually. **4 endways, endwise**, advs.

endanger /ɪn'deɪndʒə(r)/ v.t. bring into danger.

endear /ɪn'dɪə(r)/ v.t. make dear (to).

endearment n. act or words expressing affection.

endeavour /ɪn'devə(r)/ **1** v.i. try, strive. **2** n. attempt, effort.

endemic /en'demɪk/ **1** a. regularly found among (specified) people or in (specified) area etc. **2** n. endemic disease or plant. **3 endemically** adv.

ending /'endɪŋ/ n. end of word or verse or story.

endive /'endɪv/ n. curly-leaved plant used as salad.

endless /'endlɪs/ a. infinite; continual; incessant.

endo- in comb. internal.

endocrine /'endəʊkraɪn/ a. (of gland) secreting directly into blood.

endogenous /en'dɒdʒɪnəs/ a. growing or originating from within.

endorse /ɪn'dɔːs/ v.t. confirm, approve; write on back of (document), esp. sign name on back of (cheque etc.); enter details of offence on (driving-licence etc.). **endorsement** n.

endow /ɪn'daʊ/ v.t. give permanent income to; (esp. in p.p.) provide with talent or ability. **endowment** n.

endue /ɪn'djuː/ v.t. provide (with quality etc.).

endurance /ɪn'djʊərəns/ n. habit or power of enduring.

endure /ɪn'djʊə(r)/ v. undergo; bear; last.

enema /'enɪmə/ n. injection of liquid etc. into rectum esp. to expel its contents; liquid or syringe used for this.

enemy /'enɪmɪ/ **1** n. person actively hostile to another; hostile army or nation; member of this; adversary, opponent. **2** a. of or belonging to enemy.

energetic /enə'dʒetɪk/ a. full of energy; powerfully active.

energize /'enədʒaɪz/ v.t. give energy to.

energy /'enədʒɪ/ n. force, vigour, activity; ability of matter or radiation to do work.

enervate /'enəveɪt/ v.t. deprive of vigour. **enervation** n.

enfant terrible /ɑ̃fɑ̃ te'riːbl/ person who causes embarrassment by indiscreet behaviour; unruly child. [F]

enfeeble /ɪn'fiːb(ə)l/ v.t. make feeble. **enfeeblement** n.

enfilade /enfɪ'leɪd/ **1** n. gunfire directed along line from end to end. **2** v.t. direct enfilade at.

enfold /ɪn'fəʊld/ v.t. wrap; embrace.

enforce /ɪn'fɔːs/ v.t. compel observance of; persist in; impose. **enforcement** n.

enfranchise /ɪn'fræntʃaɪz/ v.t. give (person) right to vote; free (slave etc.). **enfranchisement** /-tʃɪz-/ n.

engage /ɪn'geɪdʒ/ v. employ or hire; occupy; bind by contract or promise (esp. of marriage); cause parts of (gear) to interlock; fit, interlock (with); bring or come into conflict with enemy; take part in; pledge oneself. **engagement** n.

engender /ɪn'dʒendə(r)/ v.t. give rise to.

engine /'endʒɪn/ n. mechanical contrivance of parts working together esp. as a source of mechanical power; railway locomotive; means, instrument.

engineer /endʒɪ'nɪə(r)/ **1** n. person who works in a branch of engineering; person who makes or is in charge of engines etc.; person who designs and constructs military works. **2** v. construct or manage as engineer; colloq. contrive, bring about.

engineering /endʒɪ'nɪərɪŋ/ n. application of science for control and use of power in machines; road-building etc.

English /'ɪŋglɪʃ/ **1** a. of England. **2** n. language of England, now used in UK, US, and most Commonwealth countries; the people of England. **3 Englishman, Englishwoman**, native of England.

engraft /ɪn'grɑːft/ v.t. insert or incorporate into, (up)on.

engrave /ɪn'greɪv/ v.t. inscribe or cut (design) on hard surface; inscribe (surface) thus; impress deeply (on memory etc.).

engraving n. print made from engraved plate.

engross /ɪn'grəʊs/ v.t. fully occupy;

write in large letters or in legal form. **engrossment** *n*.

engulf /ɪnˈgʌlf/ *v.t.* flow over and swamp, overwhelm.

enhance /ɪnˈhɑːns/ *v.t.* heighten, intensify. **enhancement** *n*.

enigma /ɪˈnɪgmə/ *n*. puzzling person or thing; riddle. **enigmatic** *a*.

enjoin /ɪnˈdʒɔɪn/ *v.t.* command, order.

enjoy /ɪnˈdʒɔɪ/ *v.t.* find pleasure in; have use or benefit of; experience. **enjoy oneself** find pleasure, be happy. **enjoyable** *a*.; **enjoyment** *n*.

enkindle /ɪnˈkɪnd(ə)l/ *v.t.* cause to blaze up.

enlarge /ɪnˈlɑːdʒ/ *v*. expand; grow larger; describe in greater detail; reproduce on larger scale. **enlargement** *n*.

enlighten /ɪnˈlaɪt(ə)n/ *v.t.* instruct; inform; free from superstition. **enlightenment** *n*.

enlist /ɪnˈlɪst/ *v*. enrol for military service; get co-operation or support of. **enlistment** *n*.

enliven /ɪnˈlaɪv(ə)n/ *v.t.* make lively or cheerful; inspirit. **enlivenment** *n*.

en masse /ɑ̃ ˈmæs/ all together. [F]

enmesh /ɪnˈmeʃ/ *v.t.* entangle (as) in net.

enmity /ˈenmɪtɪ/ *n*. hatred, state of being an enemy.

ennoble /ɪˈnəʊb(ə)l/ *v.t.* make noble. **ennoblement** *n*.

ennui /ˈɒnwiː/ *n*. boredom.

enormity /ɪˈnɔːmɪtɪ/ *n*. great wickedness; crime, monstrous offence. □ See page 666.

enormous /ɪˈnɔːməs/ *a*. very large.

enough /ɪˈnʌf/ **1** *a*. as much or as many as required. **2** *n*. amount or quantity that is that is enough. **3** *adv*. to required degree; fairly; very, quite.

enquire, enquiry vars. of **inquire, inquiry**.

enrage /ɪnˈreɪdʒ/ *v.t.* make furious.

enrapture /ɪnˈræptʃə(r)/ *v.t.* delight intensely.

enrich /ɪnˈrɪtʃ/ *v.t.* make rich(er). **enrichment** *n*.

enrol /ɪnˈrəʊl/ *v.t.* insert name in list; enlist; incorporate as member; enrol oneself. **enrolment** *n*.

en route /ɑ̃ ruːt/ on the way. [F]

ensconce /ɪnˈskɒns/ *v.t.* establish in snug place.

ensemble /ɑ̃ˈsɑːb(ə)l/ *n*. thing viewed as whole; set of matching items of dress; group of musicians or dancers etc.; *Mus*. concerted passage for ensemble.

enshrine /ɪnˈʃraɪn/ *v.t.* enclose (as) in shrine; serve as shrine for.

enshroud /ɪnˈʃraʊd/ *v.t.* cover completely (as) with shroud.

ensign /ˈensaɪn/ *n*. banner, flag, esp. military or naval flag of nation; *hist*. lowest commissioned officer in infantry; *US* lowest commissioned officer in navy.

ensilage /ˈensɪlɪdʒ/ *n*. silage.

enslave /ɪnˈsleɪv/ *v.t.* make slave of. **enslavement** *n*.

ensnare /ɪnˈsneə(r)/ *v.t.* entrap.

ensue /ɪnˈsjuː/ *v*. happen later or as a result.

ensure /ɪnˈʃʊə(r)/ *v.t.* make safe or certain; secure.

ENT *abbr. Med*. ear, nose, and throat.

entail /ɪnˈteɪl/ **1** *v.t.* necessitate or involve unavoidably; settle (landed estate) on persons successively so that it cannot be bequeathed at pleasure. **2** *n*. entailing; entailed estate.

entangle /ɪnˈtæŋg(ə)l/ *v.t.* cause to get caught in snare etc.; involve in difficulties; complicate. **entanglement** *n*.

entente /ɒnˈtɒnt/ *n*. friendly understanding esp. between States.

enter /ˈentə(r)/ *v*. go or come in or into; come on stage; penetrate; put (name, fact, etc.) into list or record etc.; become member of; name, or name oneself, as competitor *for*; admit, obtain admission for. **enter into** engage in, sympathize with, form part of, bind oneself by; **enter (up)on** assume possession of, begin, begin to deal with.

enteric /enˈterɪk/ *a*. of intestines.

enteritis /entəˈraɪtɪs/ *n*. inflammation of intestines.

enterprise /ˈentəpraɪz/ *n*. bold undertaking; readiness to engage in enterprises.

enterprising *a*. showing courage or imaginativeness.

entertain /entəˈteɪn/ *v.t.* amuse; receive as guest; harbour; admit (idea) to consideration.

entertainment *n*. entertaining; thing that entertains, esp. before public audience.

enthral /ɪn'θrɔːl/ v.t. captivate; please greatly. **enthralment** n.

enthrone /ɪn'θrəʊn/ v.t. place on throne. **enthronement** n.

enthuse /ɪn'θjuːz/ v. colloq. show or fill with enthusiasm.

enthusiasm /ɪn'θjuːzɪæz(ə)m/ n. great eagerness, zeal. **enthusiast** n.; **enthusiastic** a.

entice /ɪn'taɪ/ v.t. persuade by offer of pleasure or reward. **enticement** n.

entire /ɪn'taɪə(r)/ a. complete; not broken; in one piece.

entirely adv. wholly.

entirety /ɪn'taɪərətɪ/ n. completeness; sum total.

entitle /ɪn'taɪt(ə)l/ v.t. give right or claim to; give title to. **entitlement** n.

entity /'entɪtɪ/ n. thing with real existence; thing's existence.

entomb /ɪn'tuːm/ v.t. place in tomb; serve as tomb for. **entombment** n.

entomology /entə'mɒlədʒɪ/ n. study of insects. **entomological** a.; **entomologist** n.

entourage /'ɒntʊəˈrɑːʒ/ n. people attending important person.

entr'acte /'ɒntrækt/ n. (performance in) interval in theatre etc.

entrails /'entreɪlz/ n.pl. inner parts; intestines.

entrance[1] /'entrəns/ n. coming or going in; right of admission; door or passage for entering.

entrance[2] /ɪn'trɑːns/ v.t. enchant, delight; put into trance.

entrant /'entrənt/ n. person who enters examination or profession etc.

entrap /ɪn'træp/ v.t. catch (as) in trap.

entreat /ɪn'triːt/ v.t. ask earnestly; beg.

entreaty /ɪn'triːtɪ/ n. earnest request.

entrecôte /'ɒntrəkəʊt/ n. boned steak cut off sirloin.

entrée /'ɒntreɪ/ n. right of admission; dish served between fish and meat courses; US main dish of meal.

entrench /ɪn'trentʃ/ v.t. establish firmly; surround or fortify with trench. **entrenchment** n.

entrepreneur /ɒntrəprə'nɜː(r)/ n. person who undertakes an enterprise, with chance of profit or loss; contractor. **entrepreneurial** a.

entropy /'entrəpɪ/ n. measure of the unavailability of a system's thermal energy for conversion into mechanical work; measure of the disorganization of the universe.

entrust /ɪn'trʌst/ v.t. charge with (duty, object of care); confide to.

entry /'entrɪ/ n. coming or going in; place of entrance; alley; entering; item entered.

entwine /ɪn'twaɪn/ v.t. twine round, interweave.

enumerate /ɪ'njuːməreɪt/ v.t. count; mention separately. **enumeration** n.; **enumerative** a.; **enumerator** n.

enunciate /ɪ'nʌnsɪeɪt/ v.t. pronounce (words); state definitely. **enunciation** n.; **enunciative** a.; **enunciator** n.

envelop /ɪn'veləp/ v.t. wrap up, cover; surround (enemy). **envelopment** n.

envelope /'envələʊp/ n. folded paper cover for letter etc.; wrapper, covering.

enviable /'envɪəb(ə)l/ a. such as to excite envy.

envious /'envɪəs/ a. feeling or showing envy.

environment /ɪn'vaɪərənmənt/ n. surroundings; surrounding objects or conditions etc. **environmental** a.

environmentalist /ɪnvaɪərən-'mentəlɪst/ n. person who is concerned with protection of natural environment.

environs /ɪn'vaɪərəns/ n.pl. district round town etc.

envisage /ɪn'vɪzɪdʒ/ v.t. visualize, imagine, contemplate.

envoy /'envɔɪ/ n. messenger; diplomatic minister ranking below ambassador.

envy /'envɪ/ **1** n. feeling of discontented longing aroused by another's better fortune etc.; object of this. **2** v.t. feel envy of.

enwrap /ɪn'ræp/ v.t. wrap, enfold.

enzyme /'enzaɪm/ n. Chem. substance produced by living cells catalysing reactions in organism.

EP abbr. extended-play (record).

epaulette /epə'let/ n. ornamental shoulder-piece worn on uniform.

ephedrine /'efədriːn/ n. alkaloid drug used to relieve asthma etc.

ephemera /ɪ'femərə/ n.pl. things of only short-lived use.

ephemeral /ɪ'femər(ə)l/ a. short-lived, transitory. **ephemerality** n.

epic /'epɪk/ **1** n. long poem narrating adventures of heroic figure etc.; book or film based on this. **2** *a.* like an epic, grand.

epicene /'episi:n/ *a.* having characteristics of both sexes.

epicentre /'episentə(r)/ *n.* point at which earthquake reaches earth's surface.

epicure /'epikjʊə(r)/ *n.* person with refined taste in food and drink. **epicurism** *n.*

epicurean /epikjʊə'riən/ **1** *a.* fond of pleasure and luxury. **2** *n.* person of epicurean tastes. **3 epicureanism** *n.*

epidemic /epi'demik/ **1** *a.* (of disease) prevalent among community at particular time. **2** *n.* epidemic disease.

epidemiology /epidi:mi'ɒlədʒi/ *n.* branch of medicine concerned with epidemics.

epidermis /epi'dɜ:mis/ *n.* outer layer of skin.

epidiascope /epi'daiəskəʊp/ *n.* optical projector giving images of both opaque and transparent objects.

epidural /epi'djʊər(ə)l/ **1** *a.* (of anaesthetic) injected into matter round spinal cord. **2** *n.* epidural injection.

epiglottis /epi'glɒtis/ *n.* cartilage at root of tongue, depressed in swallowing. **epiglottal** *a.*

epigram /'epigræm/ *n.* short poem with witty ending; pointed saying. **epigrammatic** *a.*; **epigrammatist** *n.*

epigraph /'epigrɑ:f/ *n.* inscription. **epigraphic** *a.*; **epigraphy** *n.*

epilepsy /'epilepsi/ *n.* nervous disorder with recurrent attacks of unconsciousness and convulsions etc. **epileptic** *a. & n.*

epilogue /'epilɒg/ *n.* concluding part of book etc.; short speech at end of play etc.

Epiphany /i'pifəni/ *n.* festival (6 Jan.) commemorating manifestation of Christ to Magi.

epiphyte /'epifait/ *n.* plant growing on another; vegetable parasite on animal.

episcopacy /i'piskəpəsi/ *n.* episcopal government; bishops collectively.

episcopal /i'piskəp(ə)l/ *a.* (of church) governed by bishops.

episcopalian /ipiskə'peiliən/ **1** *a.* of episcopacy. **2** *n.* adherent of episcopacy; member of Episcopal Church. **3 episcopalianism** *n.*

episcopate /i'piskəpət/ *n.* office or tenure of bishop; bishops collectively.

episode /'episəʊd/ *n.* incident in narrative; part of serial story; incidental narrative or digression. **episodic** /-'sɒd-/ *a.*

epistemology /episti'mɒlədʒi/ *n.* theory of method or grounds of knowledge. **epistemological** *a.*

epistle /i'pis(ə)l/ *n.* letter; poem etc. in form of letter.

epistolary /i'pistələri/ *a.* of or suitable for letters.

epitaph /'epitɑ:f/ *n.* words inscribed on or suitable for tomb.

epithelium /epi'θi:liəm/ *n. Biol.* tissue forming outer layer of body or lining open cavity. **epithelial** *a.*

epithet /'epiθet/ *n.* adjective expressing quality or attribute; descriptive word.

epitome /i'pitəmi/ *n.* person who embodies a quality etc. **epitomize** *v.t.*

EPNS *abbr.* electroplated nickel silver.

epoch /'i:pɒk/ *n.* period marked by special events; beginning of era. **epoch-making** notable, significant. **epochal** *a.*

eponym /'epənim/ *n.* person after whom place etc. is named. **eponymous** /i'pɒniməs/ *a.*

epoxy resin /i'pɒksi/ synthetic thermosetting resin.

Epsom salts /'epsəm/ magnesium sulphate used as purgative.

equable /'ekwəb(ə)l/ *a.* even; moderate; not easily disturbed. **equability** *n.*

equal /'i:kw(ə)l/ **1** *a.* same in number or size or merit etc.; evenly matched; having same rights or status. **2** *n.* person etc. equal to another. **3** *v.t.* be equal to; do something that is equal to.

equality /i'kwɒliti/ *n.* being equal.

equalize /'i:kwəlaiz/ *v.* make or become equal; (in games) equal opponent's score. **equalization** *n.*

equanimity /ekwə'nimiti/ *n.* composure, calm.

equate /i'kweit/ *v.t.* regard as equal or equivalent.

equation /i'kweiʒ(ə)n/ *n.* making equal, balancing; *Math.* statement of equality between two expressions; *Chem.* formula representing chemical reaction by means of symbols.

equator /ɪ'kweɪtə(r)/ *n.* imaginary line round the earth or other body, equidistant from poles.

equatorial /ekwə'tɔːrɪəl/ *a.* of or near the equator.

equerry /'ekwərɪ/ *n.* officer of British royal household, attending sovereign etc.

equestrian /ɪ'kwestrɪən/ **1** *a.* of horse-riding; on horseback. **2** *n.* rider or performer on horseback. **3 equestrianism** *n.*

equiangular /iːkwɪ'æŋɡʌʊlə(r)/ *a.* having equal angles.

equidistant /iːkwɪ'dɪst(ə)nt/ *a.* at equal distances.

equilateral /iːkɪ'lætər(ə)l/ *a.* having all sides equal.

equilibrium /iːkwɪ'lɪbrɪəm/ *n.* (*pl.* -ia or -iums) state of balance; composure.

equine /'ekwaɪn/ *a.* of or like horse.

equinoctial /iːkwɪ'nɒkʃ(ə)l/ **1** *a.* of or happening at or near equinox. **2** *n.* celestial equator.

equinox /'ekwɪnɒks/ *n.* time or date at which sun crosses equator and day and night are of equal length.

equip /ɪ'kwɪp/ *v.t.* supply with what is needed.

equipage /'ekwɪpɪdʒ/ *n.* requisites; outfit; carriage, horses, and attendants.

equipment /ɪ'kwɪpmənt/ *n.* equipping; necessary outfit, tools, apparatus, etc.

equipoise /'ekwɪpɔɪz/ *n.* equilibrium; counterbalancing thing.

equitable /'ekwɪtəb(ə)l/ *a.* fair, just; valid in equity.

equitation /ekwɪ'teɪʃ(ə)n/ *n.* riding on horse.

equity /'ekwɪtɪ/ *n.* fairness; principles of justice supplementing law; value of shares issued by company; in *pl.* stocks and shares not bearing fixed interest.

equivalent /ɪ'kwɪvələnt/ **1** *a.* equal in value or meaning etc.; corresponding. **2** *n.* equivalent amount etc. **3 equivalence** *n.*

equivocal /ɪ'kwɪvək(ə)l/ *a.* of double or doubtful meaning; dubious.

equivocate /ɪ'kwɪvəkeɪt/ *v.i.* use words ambiguously, esp. to conceal truth. **equivocation** *n.*

ER *abbr.* Queen Elizabeth (*Elizabeth Regina*); King Edward (*Edwardus Rex*).

era /'ɪərə/ *n.* system of chronology

starting from particular point; historical or other period.

eradicate /ɪ'rædɪkeɪt/ *v.t.* root out, get rid of. **eradication** *n.*

erase /ɪ'reɪz/ *v.t.* rub out, obliterate.

eraser *n.* piece of rubber etc. for rubbing out writing etc.

erasure /ɪ'reɪʒə(r)/ *n.* rubbing out; word etc. rubbed out.

ere /eə(r)/ *prep.* & *conj. arch.* before.

erect /ɪ'rekt/ **1** *a.* upright, vertical; (of part of body) enlarged and rigid esp. from sexual excitement. **2** *v.t.* raise, set upright; build. **3 erection** *n.*; **erector** *n.*

erectile /ɪ'rektaɪl/ *a.* that can become erect.

erg *n. Phys.* unit of work or energy.

ergo /'ɜːɡəʊ/ *adv.* therefore.

ergonomics /ɜːɡə'nɒmɪks/ *n.* study of efficiency of persons in their working environment. **ergonomist** *n.*

ergot /'ɜːɡət/ *n.* disease of rye etc. caused by fungus.

Erin /'erɪn/ *n. poet.* Ireland.

ermine /'ɜːmɪn/ *n.* animal of weasel kind; its white winter fur.

erne /ɜːn/ *n.* sea eagle.

Ernie /'ɜːnɪ/ *n.* device for drawing prize-winning numbers of Premium Bonds.

erode /ɪ'rəʊd/ *v.t.* eat away, wear out; destroy surface of.

erogenous /ɪ'rɒdʒɪnəs/ *a.* giving rise to sexual excitement.

erosion /ɪ'rəʊʒ(ə)n/ *n.* eroding or being eroded. **erosive** *a.*

erotic /ɪ'rɒtɪk/ *a.* of or arousing sexual desire or excitement. **eroticism** *n.*

erotica /ɪ'rɒtɪkə/ *n.pl.* erotic literature or art.

err /ɜː(r)/ *v.i.* make mistakes; be incorrect; sin.

errand /'erənd/ *n.* short journey on which person goes or is sent with message etc.; object of journey.

errant /'erənt/ *a.* erring; roaming in quest of adventure.

erratic /ɪ'rætɪk/ *a.* irregular or uncertain in movement or conduct etc.

erratum /ɪ'rɑːtəm/ *n.* (*pl.* -ta) error in printing etc.

erroneous /ɪ'rəʊnɪəs/ *a.* incorrect.

error /'erə(r)/ *n.* mistake; condition of being wrong in opinion or conduct;

wrong opinion; amount of inaccuracy in calculation or measurement.

ersatz /'3:zæts/ *a* & *n*. substitute; imitation.

erstwhile /'3:stwaɪl/ *adv*. & *a*. arch. former(ly).

eructation /erʌk'teɪʃ(ə)n/ *n*. belch.

erudite /'eru:daɪt/ *a*. learned. **erudition** /-dɪʃ-/ *n*.

erupt /ɪ'rʌpt/ *v.i.* break out or through; (of volcano) shoot out lava etc.; (of rash) appear on skin. **eruption** *n*.; **eruptive** *a*.

erysipelas /erɪ'sɪpələs/ *n*. acute inflammation of skin, with deep red coloration.

escalate /'eskəleɪt/ *v*. increase or develop by successive stages. **escalation** *n*.

escalator /'eskəleɪtə(r)/ *n*. moving staircase.

escalope /'eskəlɒp/ *n*. thin slice of meat, esp. veal.

escapade /'eskəpeɪd/ *n*. piece of irresponsible or unorthodox conduct.

escape /ɪs'keɪp/ **1** *v*. get free; find way out; leak; elude, avoid. **2** *n*. escaping; leakage; outlet; fire-escape. **3 escape clause** clause releasing contracting party from obligation in specified circumstances.

escapee /eskeɪ'pi:/ *n*. person who has escaped.

escapism /ɪ'skeɪpɪz(ə)m/ *n*. tendency to seek distraction or relief from reality. **escapist** *a*. & *n*.

escapology /eskə'pɒlədʒɪ/ *n*. methods and technique of escaping from confinement. **escapologist** *n*.

escarpment /ɪs'kɑ:pmənt/ *n*. long steep slope at edge of plateau etc.

eschatology /eskə'tɒlədʒɪ/ *n*. doctrine of death and afterlife. **eschatological** *a*.

escheat /ɪs'tʃi:t/ **1** *n*. lapse of property to Crown etc.; property so lapsing. **2** *v*. revert by escheat; confiscate.

eschew /ɪs'tʃu:/ *v.t.* abstain from.

escort 1 /'eskɔ:t/ *n*. body of armed men as guard; person(s) accompanying another for protection, or as courtesy, etc.; person accompanying another of opposite sex socially. **2** *v.t.* /ɪ'skɔ:t/ act as escort to.

escritoire /eskrɪ'twɑ:(r)/ *n*. writing-desk with drawers etc.

esculent /'eskjulənt/ **1** *a*. fit for food. **2** *n*. esculent substance.

escutcheon /ɪ'skʌtʃ(ə)n/ *n*. shield bearing coat of arms. **blot on one's escutcheon** stain on one's reputation.

Eskimo /'eskɪməʊ/ **1** *n*. (*pl*. **-mos**) member of people inhabiting Arctic coasts of N. Amer. etc.; their language. **2** *a*. of the Eskimos or their language.

ESN *abbr*. educationally sub-normal.

esoteric /i:səʊ'terɪk/ *a*. intelligible only to those with special knowledge.

ESP *abbr*. extra-sensory perception.

espadrille /espə'drɪl/ *n*. light canvas shoe with plaited fibre sole.

espalier /ɪ'spæliə(r)/ *n*. framework for training tree etc.; tree trained on espalier.

esparto /ɪ'spɑ:təʊ/ *n*. kind of grass used in paper-making.

especial /ɪ'speʃ(ə)l/ *a*. special, exceptional.

especially *adv*. particularly, more than in other cases.

Esperanto /espə'ræntəʊ/ *n*. artificial universal language.

espionage /'espɪənɑ:ʒ/ *n*. spying or using spies.

esplanade /'espləneɪd/ *n*. level space, esp. in front of fortress or used as public promenade.

espousal /ɪ'spaʊz(ə)l/ *n*. espousing; (usu. in *pl*.) marriage, betrothal.

espouse /ɪ'spaʊz/ *v.t.* support (cause); marry.

espresso /e'spresəʊ/ *n*. (*pl*. **-os**) coffee made under steam pressure; machine for making this.

esprit de corps /esprɪ də 'kɔ:(r)/ regard for honour and interests of body one belongs to. [F]

espy /ɪ'spaɪ/ *v.t.* catch sight of.

Esq. *abbr*. Esquire.

esquire /ɪ'skwaɪə(r)/ *n*. title of courtesy appended in writing to man's name; *arch*. squire.

essay 1 /'eseɪ/ *n*. short prose composition on a subject; attempt. **2** /e'seɪ/ *v.t.* attempt.

essayist /'eseɪɪst/ *n*. writer of essays.

essence /'es(ə)ns/ *n*. all that makes a thing what it is; indispensable quality or element; extract obtained by distillation etc.; perfume, scent.

essential /ɪ'senʃ(ə)l/ **1** *a*. necessary, indispensable; of or constituting a thing's essence. **2** n. indispensable element or thing. **3 essential oil** volatile oil with characteristic odour etc.

establish /ɪˈstæblɪʃ/ v.t. set up; settle; place beyond dispute. **Established Church** Church recognized by State.

establishment n. establishing or being established; public institution; house of business; staff, household, etc.; church system established by law. **the Establishment** social group exercising authority or influence and resisting change.

estate /ɪˈsteɪt/ n. landed property; residential or industrial district planned as a whole; person's collective assets and liabilities; order or class forming part of body politic. **estate agent** person whose business is sale and letting of houses and land; **estate car** saloon motor car with interior extended at rear for carrying passengers and goods; **estate duty** death duty.

esteem /ɪˈstiːm/ **1** v.t. think highly of; consider. **2** n. favourable opinion.

ester /estə(r)/ n. compound formed by interaction of an acid and an alcohol.

estimable /ˈestɪməb(ə)l/ a. worthy of esteem.

estimate 1 /ˈestɪmət/ n. approximate judgement of a number or value etc.; price quoted in advance for work. **2** /ˈestɪmeɪt/ v.t. form estimate of; fix by estimate *at*.

estimation /estɪˈmeɪʃ(ə)n/ n. judgement of worth.

estrange /ɪˈstreɪndʒ/ v.t. turn away feelings or affections of. **estrangement** n.

estuary /ˈestjʊərɪ/ n. tidal mouth of river.

etc. abbr. etcetera.

etcetera /et'setərə/ and the rest; and so on. **etceteras** n.pl. extras, sundries.

etch v. reproduce (picture etc.) by engraving metal plate with acid esp. in order to print copies; engrave (plate) thus; practise this craft; *fig.* impress deeply *on*.

etching /ˈetʃɪŋ/ n. print made from etched plate.

eternal /ɪˈtɜːn(ə)l/ a. existing always; without end or beginning; unchanging; constant, too frequent.

eternity /ɪˈtɜːnɪtɪ/ n. infinite time; endless life after death; being eternal.

ethane /ˈiːθeɪn/ n. hydrocarbon gas of paraffin series.

ether /ˈiːθə(r)/ n. volatile liquid used as anaesthetic and solvent; clear sky, upper air; medium formerly assumed to permeate space.

ethereal /ɪˈθɪərɪəl/ a. light, airy; delicate, esp. in appearance; heavenly. **ethereality** n.; **etherealize** v.t.

ethical /ˈeθɪk(ə)l/ a. relating to or treating of morals or ethics; moral, honourable; (of drug etc.) sold only on prescription.

ethics /ˈeθɪks/ n.pl. (also treated as *sing.*) science of morals, moral principles or code.

ethnic /ˈeθnɪk/ a. of group of mankind having common national or cultural tradition; (of clothes etc.) resembling those of an ethnic group.

ethnology /eθˈnɒlədʒɪ/ n. comparative study of peoples. **ethnological** a.

ethos /ˈiːθɒs/ n. characteristic spirit of community or people or system.

ethylene /ˈeθɪliːn/ n. a hydrocarbon of the olefin series.

etiolate /ˈiːtɪəleɪt/ v.t. make pale by excluding light; give sickly hue to. **etiolation** n.

etiquette /ˈetɪket/ n. conventional rules of social behaviour or professional conduct.

étude /eɪˈtjuːd/ n. short musical composition or exercise.

etymology /etɪˈmɒlədʒɪ/ n. word's origin and sense-development; account of this. **etymological** a.

eucalyptus /juːkəˈlɪptəs/ n. tall evergreen tree; oil obtained from it, used as antiseptic etc.

Eucharist /ˈjuːkərɪst/ n. Christian sacrament in which bread and wine are consecrated and consumed; consecrated elements, esp. bread. **Eucharistic** a.

euchre /ˈjuːkə(r)/ n. Amer. card-game.

eugenic /juːˈdʒenɪk/ a. of or concerning eugenics. **eugenically** adv.

eugenics n.pl. (usu. treated as *sing.*) science of improving the population by control of inherited qualities.

eulogize /ˈjuːlədʒaɪz/ v.t. extol; praise.

eulogy /ˈjuːlədʒɪ/ n. speech or writing in praise or commendation. **eulogistic** a.

eunuch /ˈjuːnək/ n. castrated man.

euphemism /'ju:fəmɪz(ə)m/ *n.* substitution of mild for blunt expression; such substitute. **euphemistic** *a.*

euphonium /ju:'fəʊnɪəm/ *n.* large brass wind instrument of tuba kind.

euphony /'ju:fənɪ/ *n.* pleasantness or smoothness of sounds, esp. in words. **euphonious** *a.*

euphoria /ju:'fɔːrɪə/ *n.* sense of well-being. **euphoric** *a.*

euphuism /'ju:fju:ɪz(ə)m/ *n.* affectedly high-flown style of writing. **euphuistic** *a.*

Eurasian /jʊə'reɪʒ(ə)n/ **1** *a.* of mixed European and Asian parentage; of Europe and Asia. **2** *n.* Eurasian person.

eureka /jʊə'ri:kə/ *int.* I have found it!

Eurocrat /'jʊərəʊkræt/ *n.* bureaucrat of EEC.

Eurodollar /'jʊərəʊdɒlə(r)/ *n.* dollar held in bank in Europe etc.

European /jʊərə'pɪən/ **1** *a.* of or in or extending over Europe. **2** *n.* native or inhabitant of Europe; descendant of such.

Eurovision /'jʊərəʊvɪʒ(ə)n/ *n.* television of European range.

Eustachian tube /ju:'steɪʃ(ə)n/ passage between middle ear and back of throat.

euthanasia /ju:θə'neɪzjə/ *n.* bringing about gentle and easy death, esp. in case of incurable and painful disease.

evacuate /ɪ'vækjʊeɪt/ *v.t.* send (people) away from place of danger; make empty, clear; withdraw from (place); empty (bowels). **evacuation** *n.*

evacuee /ɪvækjʊ'i:/ *n.* person sent away from place of danger.

evade /ɪ'veɪd/ *v.t.* escape from, avoid; avoid doing or answering directly.

evaluate /ɪ'væljʊeɪt/ *v.t.* find or state amount or value of; appraise, assess. **evaluation** *n.*

evanesce /evə'nes/ *v.i.* fade from sight; disappear. **evanescence** *n.*; **evanescent** *a.*

evangelical /i:væn'dʒelɪk(ə)l/ **1** *a.* of or according to gospel teaching; of Protestant school maintaining that doctrine of salvation by faith is essence of gospel. **2** *n.* member of evangelical school. **3 evangelicalism** *n.*

evangelist /ɪ'vændʒəlɪst/ *n.* writer of one of four Gospels; preacher of gospel. **evangelism** *n.*; **evangelistic** *a.*

evangelize /ɪ'vændʒəlaɪz/ *v.t.* preach gospel to. **evangelization** *n.*

evaporate /ɪ'væpəreɪt/ *v.* turn into vapour; (cause to) lose moisture as vapour; (cause to) be lost or disappear. **evaporation** *n.*

evasion /ɪ'veɪʒ(ə)n/ *n.* evading; evasive answer etc.

evasive /ɪ'veɪsɪv/ *a.* seeking to evade.

eve *n.* evening or day before festival etc.; time just before event; *arch.* evening.

even[1] /'i:v(ə)n/ **1** *a.* level, smooth; uniform; equal; equable, calm; divisible by two. **2** *v.t.* make even. **3** *adv.* inviting comparison with less strong assertion or negation etc. that might have been made.

even[2] /'i:v(ə)n/ *n.* evening. **evensong** evening service in Church of England; **eventide** *arch.* evening.

evening /'i:vnɪŋ/ *n.* end of day, esp. time from sunset to bedtime.

event /ɪ'vent/ *n.* thing that happens or takes place, esp. one of importance; fact of thing occurring; item in (esp. sports) programme. **in any event, at all events,** whatever happens.

eventful /ɪ'ventfʊl/ *a.* marked by noteworthy events.

eventual /ɪ'ventjʊəl/ *a.* finally resulting.

eventuality /ɪventjʊ'ælɪtɪ/ *n.* possible event.

eventuate /ɪ'ventjʊeɪt/ *v.i.* result, be the outcome.

ever /'evə(r)/ *adv.* at all times; always; at any time. **ever since** throughout period since (then); **ever so** *colloq.* very.

evergreen /'evəgri:n/ **1** *a.* retaining green leaves throughout year; always green or fresh. **2** *n.* evergreen tree or shrub.

everlasting /evə'lɑ:stɪŋ/ **1** *a.* lasting for ever or a long time; (of plant) retaining colour when dried. **2** *n.* eternity; everlasting flower.

evermore /evə'mɔ:(r)/ *adv.* for ever; always.

every /'evrɪ/ *a.* each; all taken separately. **everybody** every person; **everyday** occurring every day, ordinary; **Everyman** ordinary or typical human being; **everyone** everybody; **every other** each alternate; **every-**

thing all things, thing of first importance; **everywhere** in every place.

evict /ɪ'vɪkt/ v.t. expel (tenant) by legal process. **eviction** n.

evidence /'evɪd(ə)ns/ **1** n. indication, sign; information given to establish fact etc.; statement etc. admissible in court of law. **2** v.t. be evidence of, indicate.

evident /'evɪd(ə)nt/ a. obvious, manifest.

evidential /evɪ'denʃ(ə)l/ a. of or providing evidence.

evil /'iːvɪl/ **1** a. harmful; wicked. **2** n. evil thing; sin; harm. **3** **evildoer** sinner; **evil eye** supposed power of doing harm by look.

evince /ɪ'vɪns/ v.t. show, indicate.

eviscerate /ɪ'vɪsəreɪt/ v.t. disembowel. **evisceration** n.

evocative /ɪ'vɒkətɪv/ a. tending to evoke (feelings etc.).

evoke /ɪ'vəʊk/ v.t. call up (feeling etc.). **evocation** /evə'keɪʃ(ə)n/ n.

evolution /iːvə'luːʃ(ə)n/ n. evolving; origination of species by development from earlier forms; development; change of position of troops or ships. **evolutionary** a.

evolutionism /iːvə'luːʃənɪz(ə)m/ n. theory of evolution of species. **evolutionist** n.

evolve /ɪ'vɒlv/ v. develop gradually by natural process; work out or devise; unfold, open out; produce (heat etc.).

ewe /juː/ n. female sheep.

ewer /'juːə(r)/ n. pitcher; water-jug.

ex¹ prep. (of goods) sold from (warehouse etc.); outside. **ex-directory** not listed in telephone directory at subscriber's wish; **ex dividend** (of stocks and shares) not including next dividend.

ex² n. colloq. former husband or wife etc.

ex- in comb. formerly.

exacerbate /ek'sæsəbeɪt/ v.t. make worse; irritate. **exacerbation** n.

exact /ɪg'zækt/ **1** a. precise, accurate, strictly correct. **2** v.t. enforce payment of (fees etc.); demand, insist upon.

exaction /ɪg'zækʃ(ə)n/ n. exacting; illegal or exorbitant demand.

exactitude /ɪg'zæktɪtjuːd/ n. exactness.

exactly /ɪg'zæktlɪ/ adv. precisely; I agree.

exaggerate /ɪg'zædʒəreɪt/ v.t. make seem larger or greater than it really is; carry beyond truth; overstate. **exaggeration** n..

exalt /ɪg'zɔːlt/ v.t. raise in rank or power etc.; praise, extol; make lofty or noble. **exaltation** n.

exam /ɪg'zæm/ n. colloq. examination.

examination /ɪgzæmɪ'neɪʃ(ə)n/ n. examining or being examined; testing of knowledge or ability by questions; formal questioning of witness etc. in court.

examine /ɪg'zæmɪn/ v. investigate or inquire into; look closely at; test knowledge or proficiency of (pupils etc.) by questions; question formally. **examinee** n.; **examiner** n.

example /ɪg'zɑːmp(ə)l/ n. thing illustrating general rule; model, pattern; specimen; precedent; warning to others.

exasperate /ɪg'zɑːspəreɪt/ v.t. irritate (person). **exasperation** n.

ex cathedra /eks kə'θiːdrə/ with full authority, (esp. of papal pronouncement). [L]

excavate /'ekskəveɪt/ v.t. hollow out; make (hole etc.), reveal or extract by digging. **excavation** n.; **excavator** n.

exceed /ɪk'siːd/ v. be more or greater than; surpass; go beyond; be immoderate.

exceedingly /ɪk'siːdɪŋlɪ/ adv. very.

excel /ɪk'sel/ v. be superior to; be pre-eminent.

excellence /'eksələns/ n. great merit.

Excellency /'eksələnsɪ/ n. title of ambassador or governor etc.

excellent /'eksələns/ a. extremely good.

except /ɪk'sept/ **1** v. exclude from general statement etc. **2** prep. not including, with exception of. **3** **except for** if it were not for.

excepting /ɪk'septɪŋ/ prep. except.

exception /ɪk'sepʃ(ə)n/ n. excepting; thing or case excepted; objection.

exceptionable /ɪk'sepʃənəb(ə)l/ a. open to objection.

exceptional /ɪk'sepʃən(ə)l/ a. forming exception; unusual.

excerpt /'eksɜːpt/ **1** n. short extract

from book or film etc. **2** *v.t.* take excerpts from. **3 exception** *n.*

excess /ɪkˈses/ *n.* fact of exceeding; amount by which thing exceeds; intemperance in eating or drinking etc.; extreme degree. **2** /ˈekses/ *a.* that exceeds a limit or given amount.

excessive /ɪkˈsesɪv/ *a.* too much; too great.

exchange /ɪksˈtʃeɪndʒ/ **1** *n.* giving one thing and receiving another in its place; exchanging of money for equivalent in other currency; central office where telephone connections are made; building where merchants or stockbrokers etc. assemble to do business; employment exchange. **2** *v.* give or receive in exchange; interchange. **3 rate of exchange** price at which another country's money may be bought. **4 exchangeable** *a.*

exchequer /ɪksˈtʃekə(r)/ *n.* department charged with receipt and custody of public revenue; royal or national treasury; money of private person etc.

excise[1] /ˈeksaɪz/ *n.* duty or tax levied on goods produced or sold within the country, and on various licences etc.

excise[2] /ɪksˈaɪz/ *v.t.* cut out or away. **excision** /-ˈsɪʒ-/ *n.*

excitable /ɪkˈsaɪtəb(ə)l/ *a.* easily excited. **excitability** *n.*

excitation /eksɪˈteɪʃ(ə)n/ *n.* exciting, rousing; stimulation.

excite /ɪkˈsaɪt/ *v.t.* move to strong emotion; set in motion; stir up; stimulate to activity. **excitement** *n.*

exclaim /ɪksˈkleɪm/ *v.* cry out, esp. in anger or delight etc.; utter or say thus.

exclamation /ekskləˈmeɪʃ(ə)n/ *n.* exclaiming; word(s) etc. exclaimed. **exclamation mark** punctuation mark (!) denoting exclamation. **exclamatory** /-ˈklæm-/ *a.*

exclude /ɪksˈkluːd/ *v.t.* shut out (*from*), leave out; make impossible, preclude. **exclusion** *n.*

exclusive /ɪksˈkluːsɪv/ **1** *a.* excluding; not inclusive; (of society etc.) tending to exclude outsiders; not to be had or not published etc. elsewhere. **2** *n. colloq.* exclusive item of news or film etc. **3 exclusive of** not including, not counting.

excommunicate /ekskəˈmjuːnɪkeɪt/

v.t. deprive (person) of membership and sacraments of Church. **excommunication** *n.*; **excommunicator** *n.*

excoriate /eksˈkɔːrɪeɪt/ *v.t.* remove part of skin of by abrasion etc.; remove (skin); *fig.* censure severely. **excoriation** *n.*

excrement /ˈekskrɪmənt/ *n.* faeces. **excremental** *a.*

excrescence /ɪksˈkres(ə)ns/ *n.* abnormal or morbid outgrowth. **excrescent** *a.*

excreta /eksˈkriːtə/ *n.pl.* faeces and urine.

excrete /ɪksˈkriːt/ *v.t.* expel from the body as waste. **excretion** *n.*; **excretory** *a.*

excruciating /ɪksˈkruːʃɪeɪtɪŋ/ *a.* acutely painful; (of humour etc.) corny, very bad.

exculpate /ˈekskʌlpeɪt/ *v.t.* free from blame. **exculpation** *n.*; **exculpatory** *a.*

excursion /ɪksˈkɜːʃ(ə)n/ *n.* short journey or ramble; pleasure-trip, esp. one made by number of persons.

excursive /ɪksˈkɜːsɪv/ *a.* digressive.

excuse **1** /ɪksˈkjuːz/ *v.t.* try to lessen blame attaching to; forgive; grant exemption to; allow to leave. **2** /ɪksˈkjuːs/ *n.* reason put forward to mitigate or justify offence; apology. **3 excuse me** polite formula of apology for interrupting or disagreeing etc.

ex-directory, ex dividend see **ex**[1].

execrable /ˈeksɪkrəb(ə)l/ *a.* abominable.

execrate /ˈeksɪkreɪt/ *v.* express or feel abhorrence for; utter curses. **execration** *n.*

executant /ɪgˈzekjʊt(ə)nt/ *n.* performer, esp. of music.

execute /ˈeksɪkjuːt/ *v.t.* carry out, perform; put to death.

execution /eksɪˈkjuːʃ(ə)n/ *n.* carrying out, performance; capital punishment; skill in performing music.

executioner *n.* person carrying out sentence of death.

executive /ɪgˈzekjʊtɪv/ **1** *a.* concerned with execution of laws or policy etc. or with administration etc.; of an executive. **2** *n.* person or body having executive authority or in executive position in business etc.; executive branch of government etc.

executor /ɪgˈzekjʊtə(r)/ n. (fem. **executrix**) person appointed by testator to carry out terms of will. **executorial** a.

exegesis /eksɪˈdʒiːsɪs/ n. explanation, esp. of Scripture. **exegetic** a.

exemplar /ɪgˈzemplə(r)/ n. model; type.

exemplary /ɪgˈzemplərɪ/ a. fit to be imitated; serving as example.

exemplify /ɪgˈzemplɪfaɪ/ v.t. give or be example of. **exemplification** n.

exempt /ɪgˈzempt/ 1 a. free from obligation or liability imposed on others; not liable to. 2 v.t. make exempt (from). 3 **exemption** n.

exequies /ˈeksɪkwiːz/ n.pl. funeral rites.

exercise /ˈeksəsaɪz/ 1 n. use of muscles etc., esp. for health; task set for bodily or other training; employment (of faculties etc.); practice; (often in pl. military drill or manœuvres. 2 v. use; give exercise to; take exercise; perplex, worry.

exert /ɪgˈzɜːt/ v.t. use; bring to bear. **exert oneself** use efforts or endeavours. **exertion** n.

exfoliate /eksˈfəʊlɪeɪt/ v.i. come off in scales or layers. **exfoliation** n.

ex gratia /eks ˈɡreɪʃə/ done or given as concession and not under (esp. legal) compulsion. [L]

exhale /ɪksˈheɪl/ v. give off or be given off in vapour; breathe out. **exhalation** n.

exhaust /ɪgˈzɔːst/ 1 v.t. consume, use up; drain of energy or resources etc., tire out; empty of contents; draw off; deal with exhaustively. 2 n. expulsion or exit of steam or products of combustion etc. from engine etc.; such gases etc.; pipe or system through which they are expelled. 3 **exhaustible** a.; **exhaustion** n.

exhaustive /ɪgˈzɔːstɪv/ a. complete, comprehensive.

exhibit /ɪgˈzɪbɪt/ 1 v.t. display; manifest; show publicly. 2 n. thing exhibited. 3 **exhibitor** n.

exhibition /eksɪˈbɪʃ(ə)n/ n. display; public show; sum allowed to student from funds of college etc.

exhibitioner /eksɪˈbɪʃənə(r)/ n. student receiving exhibition.

exhibitionism /eksɪˈbɪʃənɪz(ə)m/ n. tendency towards display or extravagant behaviour; mental condition characterized by urge to expose genitals. **exhibitionist** n.

exhilarate /ɪgˈzɪləreɪt/ v.t. enliven, gladden. **exhilaration** n.

exhort /ɪgˈzɔːt/ v.t. admonish earnestly; urge (to). **exhortation** n.; **exhortative** a.; **exhortatory** a.

exhume /eksˈhjuːm/ v.t. dig out, unearth. **exhumation** n.

exigency /ˈeksɪdʒənsɪ/ n. (also **exigence**) urgent need; emergency. **exigent** a.

exiguous /eɡˈzɪɡjʊəs/ a. scanty, small. **exiguity** n.

exile /ˈeksaɪl/ 1 n. being expelled or long absence from one's country etc.; person in exile. 2 v.t. condemn to exile (from).

exist /ɪgˈzɪst/ v.i. be, have being; occur, be found; live, sustain life.

existence /ɪgˈzɪst(ə)ns/ n. fact or manner of existing or living; all that exists. **existent** a.

existential /egzɪˈstenʃ(ə)l/ a. of or relating to existence.

existentialism /egzɪˈstenʃəlɪz(ə)m/ n. philosophical theory emphasizing existence of individual as free and responsible agent determining his own development. **existentialist** a. & n.

exit /ˈeksɪt/ 1 n. going out; way out; departure. 2 v.i. make one's exit.

exodus /ˈeksədəs/ n. mass departure; **Exodus** that of Israelites from Egypt.

ex officio /eks əˈfɪʃɪəʊ/ by virtue of one's office.

exonerate /ɪgˈzɒnəreɪt/ v.t. free or declare free from blame. **exoneration** n.

exorbitant /ɪgˈzɔːbɪt(ə)nt/ a. grossly excessive. **exorbitance** n.

exorcize /ˈeksɔːsaɪz/ v.t. drive out (evil spirit) by invocation etc.; clear (person, place) thus. **exorcism** n.; **exorcist** n.

exordium /ɪgˈzɔːdɪəm/ n. (pl. **-diums** or **-dia**) introductory part of discourse or treatise. **exordial** a.

exotic /ɪgˈzɒtɪk/ 1 a. introduced from abroad; strange, bizarre. 2 n. exotic plant etc. 3 **exotically** adv.

expand /ɪkˈspænd/ v. increase in size

or bulk etc.; spread out; express at length; become genial.

expanse /ɪk'spæns/ *n*. wide area or extent of land or space etc.

expansion /ɪk'spænʃ(ə)n/ *n*. expanding or being expanded.

expansive /ɪk'spænsɪv/ *a*. able or tending to expand; extensive; genial.

expatiate /ɪk'speɪʃɪeɪt/ *v.i.* speak or write at length. **expatiation** *n*.

expatriate 1 /eks'pætrieɪt/ *v.t.* expel, remove *oneself* from one's native country. 2 /eks'pætriət/ *a*. expatriated. 3 /eks'pætriət/ *n*. expatriated person.

expect /ɪk'spekt/ *v.t.* regard as likely; assume as future event; look for as due; suppose.

expectant /ɪk'spekt(ə)nt/ *a*. expecting; expecting to become; pregnant. **expectancy** *n*.

expectation /ekspek'teɪʃ(ə)n/ *n*. looking forward; what one expects; probability; in *pl*. prospects of inheritance.

expectorant /ek'spektərənt/ 1 *a*. that causes one to expectorate. 2 *n*. expectorant medicine.

expectorate /ek'spektəreɪt/ *v*. cough or spit out from chest or lungs; spit. **expectoration** *n*.

expedient /ɪk'spiːdɪənt/ 1 *a*. suitable, advantageous; advisable on practical rather than moral grounds. 2 *n*. means of achieving one's end; resource. 3 **expedience** *n*.; **expediency** *n*.

expedite /'ekspədaɪt/ *v.t.* assist progress of; accomplish quickly.

expedition /ekspə'dɪʃ(ə)n/ *n*. journey or voyage for some definite purpose; people or ships etc. undertaking this; promptness, speed.

expeditionary /ekspə'dɪʃənərɪ/ *a*. of or used in an expedition.

expeditious /ekspə'dɪʃəs/ *a*. acting or done with speed and efficiency.

expel /ɪks'pel/ *v.t.* throw out; eject.

expend /ɪk'spend/ *v.t.* spend (money, time, care, etc.); use up, consume.

expendable /ɪk'spendəb(ə)l/ *a*. that can be spared; that may be sacrificed to gain one's ends.

expenditure /ek'spendɪtʃə(r)/ *n*. expending; amount expended.

expense /ɪk'spens/ *n*. cost, charge; in *pl*. costs incurred in doing job etc., reimbursement of this.

expensive /ɪk'spensɪv/ *a*. costing much; of high price.

experience /ɪk'spɪərɪəns/ 1 *n*. personal observation or contact; knowledge or skill based on this; event that affects one. 2 *v.t.* feel, undergo; have experience of.

experienced *a*. wise or skilful through experience.

experiment /ɪk'sperɪmənt/ 1 *n*. procedure adopted or operation carried out to test hypothesis or demonstrate known fact etc. 2 (also /-ment/) *v.i.* make experiment(s).

experimental /ɪksperɪ'ment(ə)l/ *a*. based on or done by way of experiment. **experimentalism** *n*.

expert /'eksp3ːt/ 1 *a*. trained by practice, well-informed, skilful. 2 *n*. person having special skill or knowledge.

expertise /eksp3ː'tiːz/ *n*. expert skill or knowledge.

expiate /'ekspieɪt/ *v.t.* make amends for (wrong); pay penalty of. **expiable** *a*.; **expiation** *n*.; **expiatory** *a*.

expire /ɪk'spaɪə(r)/ *v*. come to an end; become void; breathe out; die. **expiration** *n*.; **expiratory** *a*.

expiry /ɪk'spaɪərɪ/ *n*. ceasing; end of period of validity.

explain /ɪks'pleɪn/ *v.t.* make known; make intelligible; account for. **explanation** *n*.

explanatory /ɪk'splænətərɪ/ *a*. serving to explain.

expletive /ɪk'spliːtɪv/ 1 *n*. oath or exclamation; word used to fill out sentence. 2 *a*. serving as expletive.

explicable /'eksplɪkəb(ə)l/ *a*. explainable.

explicit /ɪk'splɪsɪt/ *a*. expressly stated or shown; definite; outspoken.

explode /ɪk'spləʊd/ *v*. expand violently with loud noise; cause (gas or bomb etc.) to do this; give vent suddenly to emotion or violence; (of population etc.) increase suddenly; discredit.

exploit 1 /'eksplɔɪt/ *n*. bold or daring feat. 2 /ɪk'splɔɪt/ *v.t.* use or develop for one's own ends; take advantage of. 3 **exploitation** *n*.

explore /ɪk'splɔː(r)/ *v.t.* examine (country etc.) by going through it; inquire into; examine by touch. **exploration** *n*.; **exploratory** *a*.

explosion /ɪkˈspləʊʒ(ə)n/ n. exploding; outbreak; sudden violent expansion.

explosive /ɪkˈspləʊsɪv/ 1 a. tending to explode; of or like explosion. 2 n. explosive substance. 3 **high explosive** one with violent local effect.

exponent /ɪkˈspəʊnənt/ n. person or thing that explains or interprets; type, representative; *Math.* symbol showing what power of a factor is to be taken.

exponential /ekspəˈnenʃ(ə)l/ a. (of increase) more and more rapid.

export /ˈekspɔːt/ 1 v.t. send (goods) for sale in another country. 2 n. exported article; (usu. in pl.) amount exported. 3 **exportation** n.

expose /ɪkˈspəʊz/ v.t. leave unprotected esp. from weather; disclose, reveal; subject (*to* risk etc.); *Photog.* subject (film, sensitized paper, etc.) to action of light.

exposé /ekˈspəʊzeɪ/ n. disclosure (of discreditable thing).

exposition /ekspəˈzɪʃ(ə)n/ n. expounding, explanation; exhibition.

ex post facto /eks pəʊst ˈfæktəʊ/ retrospective(ly). [L]

expostulate /ɪkˈspɒstjʊleɪt/ v.i. make protest, remonstrate. **expostulation** n.

exposure /ɪkˈspəʊʒə(r)/ n. exposing, being exposed; length of time photographic film etc. is exposed; unmasking or revealing of error or crime etc.

expound /ɪkˈspaʊnd/ v.t. set forth in detail; explain, interpret.

express /ɪkˈspres/ 1 v.t. represent by symbols etc. or in language; put into words; squeeze out (juice etc.); send by express service. 2 a. definitely stated, explicit; operating at high speed; delivered by special messenger or service; (of train etc.) with few intermediate stops. 3 n. express train or messenger etc. 4 adv. with speed; by express train etc. 5 **expressible** a.

expression /ɪkˈspreʃ(ə)n/ n. expressing; wording, word, phrase; expressive quality; aspect (of face), intonation (of voice); *Math.* symbols expressing quantity.

expressionism /ɪkˈspreʃənɪz(ə)m/ n. style of painting etc. in which artist seeks to express emotional experience

rather than depict external world. **expressionist** n. & a.

expressive /ɪkˈspresɪv/ a. serving to express; significant.

expressly /ɪkˈspreslɪ/ adv. explicitly; on purpose.

expropriate /eksˈprəʊprɪeɪt/ v.t. take away (property); dispossess. **expropriation** n.; **expropriator** n.

expulsion /ɪkˈspʌlʃ(ə)n/ n. expelling, being expelled. **expulsive** a.

expunge /ɪkˈspʌndʒ/ v.t. erase, strike out.

expurgate /ˈekspəgeɪt/ v.t. remove matter considered objectionable from (book etc.); cleanse (such matter). **expurgation** n.; **expurgator** n.

exquisite /ˈekskwɪzɪt/ 1 a. of extreme beauty or delicacy; acute, keen. 2 n. person of refined (esp. affected) tastes.

ex-serviceman /eksˈsɜːvɪsmən/ n. (pl. -men) former member of armed services.

extant /ekˈstænt/ a. still existing.

extempore /ekˈstempərɪ/ adv. & a. without preparation; off-hand. **extemporaneous** a.; **extemporary** a.

extemporize /ɪkˈstempəraɪz/ v. produce or speak extempore. **extemporization** n.

extend /ɪkˈstend/ v. lay out at full length; lengthen in space or time; reach or be continuous over certain area; have certain scope; offer or accord feeling or invitation etc.; tax powers of. **extendible** a.; **extensible** a.

extension /ɪkˈstenʃ(ə)n/ n. extending; enlargement, additional part; subsidiary telephone on same line as main one; its number; extramural instruction by university etc.

extensive /ɪkˈstensɪv/ a. large, far-reaching.

extent /ɪkˈstent/ n. space covered; width of application, scope.

extenuate /ɪkˈstenjʊeɪt/ v.t. lessen seeming seriousness of (guilt etc.) by partial excuse. **extenuation** n.

exterior /ɪkˈstɪərɪə(r)/ 1 a. outer, outward. 2 n. exterior aspect or part.

exterminate /ɪkˈstɜːmɪneɪt/ v.t. destroy utterly. **extermination** n.; **exterminator** n.

external /ɪkˈstɜːn(ə)l/ 1 a. outside; of or consisting in or belonging or referring to etc. outward world or what is outside; (of evidence) derived from source independent of thing discussed. **2** *n.* in *pl.* external features or circumstances. **3 externality** *n.*

externalize /ɪk'stɜːnəlaɪz/ *v.t.* give or attribute external existence to.

extinct /ɪk'stɪŋkt/ *a.* no longer existing, obsolete; no longer burning; (of volcano) that has ceased eruption.

extinction /ɪk'stɪŋkʃ(ə)n/ *n.* making or becoming extinct; dying out.

extinguish /ɪk'stɪŋgwɪʃ/ *v.t.* put out, quench; terminate, destroy; wipe out (debt).

extirpate /'ekstɜːpeɪt/ *v.t.* destroy; root out. **extirpation** *n.*

extol /ɪk'stəʊl/ *v.t.* praise enthusiastically.

extort /ɪk'stɔːt/ *v.t.* get by force or threats or intimidation etc.

extortion /ɪk'stɔːʃ(ə)n/ *n.* extorting, esp. of money; illegal exaction.

extortionate /ɪk'stɔːʃənət/ *a.* exorbitant.

extra /'ekstrə/ **1** *a.* additional; more than usual or necessary. **2** *adv.* more than usually; additionally. **3** *n.* extra thing; thing charged extra; person engaged to be one of crowd etc. in film etc.; special edition of newspaper; *Crick.* run not scored from hit with bat.

extra- /'ekstrə/ *in comb.* outside, not within scope of.

extract 1 /ɪk'strækt/ *v.t.* take out; draw forth; obtain (juices etc.) by pressure or distillation etc.; deduce, derive (from); copy out, quote; *Math.* find (root of number). **2** /'ekstrækt/ *n.* passage from book etc.; substance got by distillation etc.; concentrated preparation.

extraction /ɪk'strækʃ(ə)n/ *n.* extracting; lineage.

extractive /ɪk'stræktɪv/ *a.* (of industries) obtaining minerals etc. from the ground.

extractor fan /ɪk'stræktə(r)/ ventilating fan in window etc. to remove stale air.

extraditable /'ekstrədaɪtəb(ə)l/ *a.* liable to or (of crime) warranting extradition.

extradite /'ekstrədaɪt/ *v.t.* hand over (person accused of crime) to State where crime was committed. **extradition** *n.*

extramarital /ekstrə'mærɪt(ə)l/ *a.* (of sexual relationships) outside marriage.

extramural /ekstrə'mjʊər(ə)l/ *a.* additional to ordinary university teaching etc.

extraneous /ɪk'streɪnɪəs/ *a.* of external origin; not belonging.

extraordinary /ɪk'strɔːdɪnərɪ/ *a.* unusual or remarkable; out of the usual course; specially employed.

extrapolate /ɪk'stræpəleɪt/ *v.* estimate from known values or data etc. (others which lie outside the range of those known). **extrapolation** *n.*

extra-sensory /ekstrə'sensərɪ/ *a.* derived by means other than known senses.

extra-terrestrial /ekstrətə'restrɪəl/ *a.* outside the earth or its atmosphere.

extravagant /ɪk'strævəgənt/ *a.* spending (esp. money) excessively; costing much; wild, absurd. **extravagance** *n.*

extravaganza /ɪkstrævə'gænzə/ *n.* fantastic composition; spectacular theatrical procuction.

extreme /ɪk'striːm/ **1** *a.* reaching a high or the highest degree: going to great lengths, not moderate; outermost; utmost. **2** *n.* one or other of two things as remote or different as possible; thing at either end; extreme degree etc. **3 extreme unction** *RC Ch.* anointing by priest of dying person.

extremely *adv.* in extreme degree; very.

extremism /ɪk'striːmɪz(ə)m/ *n.* advocacy of extreme measures. **extremist** *a.* & *n.*

extremity /ɪk'stremɪtɪ/ *n.* extreme point, end; extreme adversity or danger etc.; in *pl.* hands and feet.

extricate /'ekstrɪkeɪt/ *v.t.* disentangle, release. **extrication** *n.*

extrinsic /ɪk'strɪnzɪk/ *a.* not inherent or intrinsic; extraneous. **extrinsically** *adv.*

extrovert /'ekstrəvɜːt/ **1** *a.* directing thoughts or interests to things outside oneself; sociable, unreserved. **2** *n.* extrovert person. **3 extroversion** *n.*

extrude /ɪk'struːd/ *v.t.* thrust or squeeze out; shape by forcing through mould. **extrusion** *n.*; **extrusive** *a.*

exuberant /ɪg'zuːbərənt/ *a.* lively,

effusive; high-spirited; luxuriant, prolific; copious, lavish. **exuberance** *n.*

exude /ɪgˈzjuːd/ *v.* ooze out; give off. **exudation** *n.*

exult /ɪgˈzʌlt/ *v.i.* rejoice, triumph (*at*, *in*, *over*). **exultant** *a.*; **exultation** *n.*

eye /aɪ/ **1** *n.* organ or faculty of sight; iris of eye; region round eye; gaze; perception; eyelike thing; leaf-bud of potato etc.; spot, hole, loop. **2** *v.t.*(*partic.* **eyeing**) observe, watch closely or suspiciously. **3 eyeball** ball of eye within lids and socket; **eyebath** vessel for applying lotion to eye; **eyebrow** hair growing on ridge over eye; **eyeglass** lens for defective eye, in *pl.* pair of these joined by bar over bridge of nose; **eyehole** hole to look through; **eyelash** any of hairs on edge of eyelid; **eyelid** movable fold of skin that can cover eye;

eye-liner cosmetic applied as line round eye; **eye-opener** surprising fact etc.; **eyepiece** lens(es) at eye-end of optical instrument; **eye-shade** device to protect eyes from strong light; **eye-shadow** cosmetic for eyelids; **eyesight** faculty or strength of sight; **eyesore** thing that offends sight; **eye-tooth** pointed tooth just under eye, canine; **eyewash** *sl.* nonsense; **eyewitness** one who can testify from his own observation.

eyeful /ˈaɪfʊl/ *n.* thing thrown or blown into eye; *colloq.* remarkable or attractive person.

eyelet /ˈaɪlɪt/ *n.* small hole for passing cord etc. through.

eyrie /ˈaɪərɪ/ *n.* nest of bird of prey or of bird that builds high up.

F

F *abbr.* Fahrenheit.

f *abbr.* forte[2].

FA *abbr.* Football Association.

fa var. of **fah**.

fable /ˈfeɪb(ə)l/ *n.* story not based on fact; short moral tale, esp. with animals for characters; myth, legend.

fabled *a.* celebrated in fable, legendary.

fabric /ˈfæbrɪk/ *n.* woven etc. material; walls, floor, and roof of building; structure; thing put together.

fabricate /ˈfæbrɪkeɪt/ *v.t.* construct, manufacture; invent (fact), forge (document). **fabrication** *n.*

fabulous /ˈfæbjʊləs/ *a.* celebrated in fable; incredible; *colloq.* marvellous.

façade /fəˈsɑːd/ *n.* face or front of building; outward (esp. deceptive) appearance.

face 1 *n.* front of head; expression, grimace; surface; front, right side; dial-plate of clock etc.; striking surface of bat or racket or golf-club etc.; effrontery; aspect. **2** *v.* look or front towards; be opposite to; meet firmly; supply (garment, wall, etc.) with facing. **3 face-lift** operation for removing wrinkles by tightening skin of face, *fig.* improvement in appearance; **face value** that stated on coin or note etc., apparent value; **lose face** be humiliated; **on the face of it** to judge by appearance; **save face** spare oneself humiliation.

faceless /ˈfeɪslɪs/ *a.* without identity, not identifiable.

facet /ˈfæsɪt/ *n.* particular aspect of thing; one side of many-sided body, esp. cut gem.

facetious /fəˈsiːʃəs/ *a.* intending or meant to be amusing, esp. inopportunely.

facia /ˈfeɪʃə/ *n.* instrument-panel of motor vehicle; plate over shop-front with name etc.

facial /ˈfeɪʃ(ə)l/ **1** *a.* of face. **2** *n.* beauty-treatment for face.

facile /ˈfæsaɪl/ *a.* easily achieved but of little value; easy; working easily; fluent.

facilitate /fəˈsɪlɪteɪt/ *v.t.* make easy, promote. **facilitation** *n.*

facility /fəˈsɪlɪtɪ/ *n.* absence of difficulty; dexterity; (usu. in *pl.*) opportunity or equipment for doing something.

facing /ˈfeɪsɪŋ/ *n.* material over part of garment etc. for contrast or strength; surface covering of different material.

facsimile /fækˈsɪmɪlɪ/ *n.* exact copy of writing or picture etc.

fact *n.* thing done; thing known to be true; what is true or existent, reality; **in fact** in reality, really, indeed.

faction /ˈfækʃ(ə)n/ *n.* small group with special aims within larger one, esp. political.

factious /ˈfækʃəs/ *a.* of a faction; characterized by factions.

factitious /fækˈtɪʃəs/ *a.* made for special purpose; artificial.

factor /ˈfæktə(r)/ *n.* thing contributing to result; any of numbers etc. whose product is given number etc.; business agent; *Sc.* land-steward.

factorial /fækˈtɔːrɪəl/ **1** *n.* the product of a number and all whole numbers below it. **2** *a.* of factor or factorial.

factorize /ˈfæktəraɪz/ *v.t.* resolve (number) into factors. **factorization** *n.*

factory /ˈfæktərɪ/ *n.* building(s) and equipment for manufacture of goods. **factory farm** one organized on industrial lines.

factotum /fækˈtəʊtəm/ *n.* employee doing all kinds of work.

factual /ˈfæktjʊəl/ *a.* based on or concerned with fact.

faculty /ˈfækəltɪ/ *n.* aptitude for particular action; physical or mental power; teaching staff of department of learning at university etc.; (esp. *Eccl.*) authorization.

fad *n.* craze, pet notion. **faddish** *a.*

faddy /ˈfædɪ/ *a.* having arbitrary likes and dislikes, esp. about food.

fade 1 *v.* (cause to) lose freshness or colour or strength; disappear gradually; bring sound or picture gradually *in* or *out* of perception. **2** *n.* action of fading.

faeces /ˈfiːsiːz/ *n.pl.* waste matter discharged from bowels. **faecal** /ˈfiːk(ə)l/ *a.*

fag[1] **1** *v.* toil, grow or make weary; (at schools) do service for seniors. **2** *n.* drudgery; *sl.* cigarette; schoolboy who fags. **3 fag-end** inferior remnant, cigarette-end.

fag² n. US sl. homosexual.

faggot /ˈfægət/ n. seasoned chopped liver etc. baked or fried as ball or roll; bundle of sticks for fuel; bundle of herbs or metal rods etc.; sl. unpleasant woman; US sl. homosexual.

fah n. Mus. fourth note of scale in tonic sol-fa.

Fahrenheit /ˈfærənhaɪt/ a. of scale of temperature on which water freezes at 32° and boils at 212°.

faience /faɪˈɑ̃s/ n. painted and glazed earthenware and porcelain.

fail 1 v. not succeed; be unsuccessful in (examination etc.); disappoint; neglect; not be able; be missing or deficient; break down; go bankrupt. **2** n. failure. **3 fail-safe** reverting to safe condition in event of breakdown etc.; **without fail** for certain, whatever happens.

failing /ˈfeɪlɪŋ/ **1** n. deficiency, fault; foible. **2** prep. in default of.

failure /ˈfeɪljʊə(r)/ n. failing; non-performance; cessation or impairment of vital function; unsuccessful person, thing, or attempt.

fain arch. **1** pred.a. willing; glad. **2** adv. gladly.

faint 1 a. dim, pale; weak from hunger etc.; timid; feeble. **2** v.i. lose consciousness; become faint. **3** n. act or state of fainting. **4 faint-hearted** cowardly.

fair¹ 1 a. just, equitable; blond, not dark; of moderate quality or amount; (of weather) favourable; beautiful. **2** adv. in fair manner. **3 fair and square** equitably, exactly; **fair copy** transcript free from corrections; **fair play** equitable conduct or conditions; **fair-weather friend** one not good in a crisis.

fair² n. periodical gathering for sale of goods, often with entertainments; funfair; trade exhibition.

Fair Isle /ˈfeər aɪl/ (of jersey etc.) knitted in characteristic coloured design.

fairly /ˈfeəlɪ/ adv. in a fair manner; moderately; to a noticeable degree.

fairway /ˈfeəweɪ/ n. navigable channel; mown grass between golf tee and green.

fairy /ˈfeərɪ/ n. small imaginary being with magical powers; sl. male homosexual. **fairy godmother** colloq. benefactress; **fairyland** home of fairies; **fairy lights** small coloured lights esp. for outdoor decorations; **fairy ring** ring of darker grass caused by fungi; **fairy story, -tale**, tale about fairies, incredible story, falsehood.

fait accompli /feɪt əˈkɒmplɪ/ thing done and past arguing about. [F]

faith n. trust; belief esp. in religious doctrine; religion; things believed; loyalty, trustworthiness. **faith-cure, -healing**, cure etc. depending on faith rather than treatment.

faithful /ˈfeɪθfʊl/ a. loyal, constant; true, accurate. **faithfully** adv. **yours faithfully** formula at end of business etc. letter.

faithless /ˈfeɪθlɪs/ a. disloyal, false.

fake 1 n. thing or person that is not genuine. **2** a. counterfeit, not genuine. **3** v.t. make (false thing) so that it appears genuine; feign.

fakir /ˈfeɪkɪə(r)/ n. Muslim or Hindu religious mendicant or ascetic.

falcon /ˈfɔːlkən/ n. small hawk trained to hunt game-birds for sport.

falconer /ˈfɔːlkənə(r)/ n. person who keeps or trains or hunts with hawks.

falconry /ˈfɔːlkənrɪ/ n. hunting with or breeding of hawks.

fall /fɔːl/ **1** v.i. (past **fell**; p.p. **fallen**) go or come down freely; cease to stand, lose balance; become detached and descend; slope or hang down; become lower, subside; lose high position; yield to temptation; occur; become. **2** n. falling; amount that falls; descent; drop; downfall, ruin; (often in pl.) waterfall; US autumn. **3 fall back on** have recourse to; **fall down (on)** colloq. fail (in); **fall for** be captivated or deceived by; **fall foul of** collide or quarrel with; **fall guy** sl. easy victim, scapegoat; **fall in** Mil. (cause to) take place in parade; **fall in with** meet (by chance), agree or coincide with; **fall off** decrease, deteriorate; **fall out** quarrel, result, occur, Mil. (cause to) leave place in parade; **fall-out** radioactive debris from nuclear explosion; **fall short of** fail to reach or amount to; **fall through** fail, come to nothing; **fall to** start working etc.

fallacy /ˈfæləsɪ/ n. mistaken belief;

faulty reasoning; misleading argument. **fallacious** /-'leɪʃ-/ a.

fallible /'fælɪb(ə)l/ a. capable of making mistakes. **fallibility** n.

Fallopian tube /fə'ləʊpɪən/ either of two tubes along which egg-cells travel from ovaries to womb.

fallow¹ /'fæləʊ/ 1 a. (of land) ploughed etc. but left unsown; uncultivated. 2 n. fallow land.

fallow² /'fæləʊ/ a. of pale brownish yellow. **fallow deer** kind smaller than red deer.

false /fɔːls/ a. wrong, incorrect; deceitful, treacherous; unfaithful to; deceptive; sham, artificial. **false alarm** alarm given without valid cause; **false pretences** misrepresentations meant to deceive. **falsity** n.

falsehood /'fɔːlshʊd/ n. untrue thing; lying, lie(s).

falsetto /fɔːl'setəʊ/ n. (pl. -os) high-pitched artificial voice esp. of male singer.

falsify /'fɔːlsɪfaɪ/ v.t. fraudulently alter; misrepresent. **falsification** n.

falter /'fɔːltə(r)/ v. go unsteadily; say or speak hesitatingly; waver.

fame n. renown, glory; arch. reputation.

famed /feɪmd/ a. famous, much spoken of.

familial /fə'mɪlɪəl/ a. of or relating to a family or its members.

familiar /fə'mɪlɪə(r)/ 1 a. well acquainted (with); well known; often encountered; (excessively) informal. 2 n. intimate friend; demon attending witch etc. 3 **familiarity** n.

familiarize /fə'mɪlɪəraɪz/ v.t. make (person etc.) familiar (with). **familiarization** n.

family /'fæmɪlɪ/ n. set of parents and children or of relatives; person's children; household; lineage; race; group of allied genera. **family allowance** allowance paid by State etc. to parent of family; **family man** man with family, domestic man; **family planning** birth-control; **family tree** genealogical chart.

famine /'fæmɪn/ n. extreme scarcity esp. of food.

famish /'fæmɪʃ/ v. reduce or be reduced to extreme hunger.

famous /'feɪməs/ a. well-known; celebrated; colloq. excellent.

fan¹ 1 n. rotating apparatus giving current of air; instrument, usu. folding and sector-shaped, for agitating air to cool face etc.; anything spreading out in fan shape. 2 v.t. move (air) with fan; drive air (as) with fan upon; increase (flames etc.) (as) by fanning; spread (out) in fan shape. 3 **fan-belt** belt transmitting torque from motor-vehicle engine to fan that cools radiator; **fan heater** heater in which fan drives air over electric heater into room etc.; **fanlight** window (orig. semi-circular) over door; **fantail** pigeon with fan-shaped tail.

fan² n. enthusiast, devotee. **fanmail** letters from fans.

fanatic /fə'nætɪk/ 1 n. person filled with excessive or mistaken enthusiasm, esp. in religion. 2 a. excessively enthusiastic. 3 **fanatical** a.; **fanaticism** n.

fancier /'fænsɪə(r)/ n. connoisseur.

fanciful /'fænsɪful/ a. imaginary; unreal; indulging in fancies.

fancy /'fænsɪ/ 1 n. faculty of imagination; supposition; caprice, whim; taste, liking. 2 a. ornamental, not plain; unusual. 3 v.t. imagine; colloq. feel inclination towards; colloq. find sexually attractive; colloq. have unduly high opinion of (oneself). 4 **fancy dress** fanciful costume, often historical or exotic; **fancy-free** not in love.

fandango /fæn'dæŋgəʊ/ n. (pl. -goes) lively Spanish dance.

fanfare /'fænfeə(r)/ n. short showy or ceremonious sounding of trumpets etc.

fang n. canine tooth esp. of dog etc.; serpent's venom-tooth; root of tooth or its prong.

fantasia /fæn'teɪzɪə/ n. musical etc. composition in which form is of minor importance.

fantasize /'fæntəsaɪz/ v. create fantasy (about).

fantastic /fæn'tæstɪk/ a. extravagantly fanciful; grotesque, quaint; colloq. excellent, extraordinary.

fantasy /'fæntəsɪ/ n. faculty of imagination; mental image, day-dream; fanciful invention or speculation etc.

far 1 adv. at or to great distance; by much. 2 a. distant, remote. 3 **far-away**

remote, as if from distance, dreamy; **Far East** countries of eastern Asia; **far-fetched** strained, unconvincing; **far-flung** widely extended; **far gone** very ill or drunk, much in debt, etc.; **far-off** remote; **far out** *colloq.* avant-garde, excellent; **far-reaching** of wide application or influence; **far-seeing** showing foresight, prudent; **far-sighted** far-seeing, seeing distant things best.

farad /ˈfærəd/ *n. Electr.* fundamental unit of capacitance.

farce *n.* comedy based on ludicrously improbable events; absurdly futile proceeding. **farcical** *a.*

fare /feə(r)/ 1 *n.* price charged to passenger on public transport; passenger; food. 2 *v.i.* progress; get on.

farewell /feəˈwel/ *int. & n.* goodbye.

farina /fəˈraɪnə/ *n.* flour or meal of corn or nuts or starchy roots. **farinaceous** /færɪˈneɪʃəs/ *a.*

farm 1 *n.* area of land and its buildings used for growing crops and raising animals etc.; place for breeding of animals; farmhouse. 2 *v.* use (land) for growing crops and raising animals etc.; breed (fish etc.) commercially; work as farmer; take proceeds of (tax) on payment of fixed sum. 3 **farmhouse** dwelling-place on farm; **farm out** delegate (work) to others; **farmstead** farm and its buildings; **farmyard** yard of farmhouse.

farmer /ˈfɑːmə(r)/ *n.* owner or manager of farm.

faro /ˈfeərəʊ/ *n.* gambling card-game.

farrago /fəˈrɑːɡəʊ/ *n.* (*pl.* **-gos**) medley, hotchpotch.

farrier /ˈfærɪə(r)/ *n.* smith who shoes horses. **farriery** *a.*

farrow /ˈfærəʊ/ 1 *v.i.* give birth to pigs. 2 *n.* farrowing; litter of pigs.

fart *vulg.* 1 *v.i.* emit wind from anus. 2 *n.* emission of wind from anus.

farther var. of **further**.

farthest var. of **furthest**.

farthing /ˈfɑːðɪŋ/ *n. hist.* quarter of old penny.

farthingale /ˈfɑːðɪŋɡeɪl/ *n. hist.* hooped petticoat.

fascia /ˈfeɪʃə/ *n.* long flat surface of wood or stone (*Archit.*); facia.

fascicle /ˈfæsɪk(ə)l/ *n.* instalment of book.

fascinate /ˈfæsɪneɪt/ *v.t.* capture interest of; charm irresistibly; paralyse (victim) with fear. **fascination** *n.*

Fascism /ˈfæʃɪz(ə)m/ *n.* extreme right-wing totalitarian political system or views, as orig. in Italy (1922–43). **Fascist** *n. & a.*

fashion /ˈfæʃ(ə)n/ 1 *n.* current popular custom or style, esp. in dress; manner of doing something. 2 *v.t.* form or make (*into*). 3 **in fashion** fashionable; **out of fashion** no longer fashionable.

fashionable /ˈfæʃənəb(ə)l/ *a.* of or conforming to (latest) fashion; characteristic of or patronized by those who are in fashion.

fast¹ /fɑːst/ 1 *a.* rapid; (of clock) showing later than correct time; firm, fixed; (of colour) not fading when washed etc.; (of person) dissipated. 2 *adv.* quickly; firmly, tightly. 3 **fast food** prepared food requiring minimum of further preparation before sale or serving etc.; **fast one** *sl.* unfair or deceitful action; **fast reactor** *Phys.* nuclear reactor using neutrons with high kinetic energy.

fast² /fɑːst/ 1 *v.i.* go without (some kinds of) food, esp. as religious observance. 2 *n.* fasting; going without food.

fasten /ˈfɑːs(ə)n/ *v.* attach, fix, secure; become tightly fixed.

fastener /ˈfɑːsənə(r)/ *n.* (also **fastening**) device that fastens something.

fastidious /fæˈstɪdɪəs/ *a.* easily disgusted, hard to please.

fastness /ˈfɑːstnɪs/ *n.* stronghold.

fat 1 *a.* well-fed, plump; oily; fertile, rich, rewarding. 2 *n.* oily substance esp. that found in animal bodies; fat part of thing. 3 **a fat lot** *colloq.* very little.

fatal /ˈfeɪt(ə)l/ *a.* causing or ending in death; destructive, ruinous.

fatalism /ˈfeɪtəlɪz(ə)m/ *n.* belief that all is predetermined and therefore inevitable. **fatalist** *n.*; **fatalistic** *a.*

fatality /fəˈtælɪtɪ/ *n.* death by accident, in war, etc.

fate 1 *n.* power predetermining events from eternity; what is destined; person's appointed lot; death, destruction. 2 *v.t.* in *p.p.* preordained.

fateful /ˈfeɪtfʊl/ *a.* controlled by fate; decisive; important.

father /ˈfɑːðə(r)/ *n.* male parent; forefather; originator; early leader; in *pl.* elders; priest; venerable person; oldest member. 2 *v.t.* beget; originate; fix paternity of, or responsibility for, *on*. 3 **father-in-law** wife's or husband's father; **fatherland** native country. 4 **fatherhood** *n.*

fatherly /ˈfɑːðəlɪ/ *a.* of or like a father.

fathom /ˈfæðəm/ 1 *n.* measure of 6ft., esp. in soundings. 2 *v.t.* comprehend; measure depth of (water).

fathomless /ˈfæðəmlɪs/ *a.* too deep to fathom.

fatigue /fəˈtiːɡ/ 1 *n.* weariness from exertion; weakness in metals etc. from variations of stress; soldier's non-combatant duty. 2 *v.t.* tire.

fatten /ˈfæt(ə)n/ *v.* make or become fat.

fatty /ˈfætɪ/ *a.* like or containing fat.

fatuous /ˈfætjʊəs/ *a.* vacantly silly; purposeless. **fatuity** *n.*

faucet /ˈfɔːsɪt/ *n.* tap for barrel etc.; *US* any tap.

fault /fɔːlt/ 1 *n.* defect, blemish; offence, misdeed; responsibility for something wrong; *Tennis* etc. incorrect serve; *Geol.* break in continuity of strata etc. 2 *v.* find fault with; cause fault in (strata etc.), show fault. 3 **find fault with** criticize unfavourably; **to a fault** excessively. 4 **faulty** *a.*

faun /fɔːn/ *n.* Latin rural deity with goat's horns, legs, and tail.

fauna /ˈfɔːnə/ *n.* (*pl.* **-nas**) the animals of a region or period.

faux pas /ˈfəʊ pɑː/ tactless mistake. [F]

favour /ˈfeɪvə(r)/ 1 *n.* liking, goodwill, approval; kind or helpful act; partiality; thing given or worn as mark of favour. 2 *v.t.* regard or treat with favour; support, facilitate; oblige; in *p.p.* having unusual advantages.

favourable /ˈfeɪvərəb(ə)l/ *a.* well disposed; approving; pleasing, satisfactory, helpful, suitable.

favourite /ˈfeɪvərɪt/ 1 *a.* preferred to all others. 2 *n.* favourite person or thing; person favoured by monarch or superior; competitor generally thought most likely to win.

favouritism /ˈfeɪvərɪtɪz(ə)m/ *n.* unfair favouring of one person or group.

fawn[1] 1 *n.* fallow deer in first year; light yellowish brown. 2 *a.* fawn-coloured. 3 *v.i.* give birth to fawn.

fawn[2] *v.i.* (of dog etc.) show affection

by frisking and grovelling etc.; lavish caresses *upon*; behave servilely.

fay *n. poet.* fairy.

FBI *abbr.* US Federal Bureau of Investigation.

FC *abbr.* Football Club.

fealty /ˈfiːəltɪ/ *n.* duty of feudal vassal to lord; faithful adherence.

fear /fɪə(r)/ 1 *n.* emotion caused by impending danger or pain etc.; alarm, dread. 2 *v.* be afraid (of); be anxious; hesitate; shrink from; revere (God).

fearful /ˈfɪəfʊl/ *a.* afraid; causing fear; *colloq.* annoying, extreme.

fearless /ˈfɪəlɪs/ *a.* feeling no fear; brave.

fearsome /ˈfɪəsəm/ *a.* formidable.

feasible /ˈfiːzɪb(ə)l/ *a.* practicable, possible; plausible. **feasibility** *n.*

feast 1 *n.* sumptuous meal; religious festival; something giving great pleasure. 2 *v.* partake of feast; eat and drink heartily (*on*); give feast to; regale.

feat *n.* remarkable act or achievement.

feather /ˈfeðə(r)/ 1 *n.* appendage of bird's skin with central shaft fringed with thin narrow barbs; piece of this as decoration etc.; piece(s) of feathers attached to end of arrow or dart; plumage; game-birds. 2 *v.* cover or line with feathers; turn (oar) so as to pass through air edgeways. 3 **feather bed** mattress stuffed with feathers; **feather-bed** make things easy for, pamper; **feather-brained, -headed,** silly; **featherweight** light person or thing, boxing-weight (up to 57 kg.). 4 **feathery** *a.*

feature /ˈfiːtʃə(r)/ *n.* part of face, esp. with regard to appearance; characteristic or prominent part; prominent article in newspaper etc.; feature film. 2 *v.* give prominence to; make or be special feature of; take part (*in*). 3 **feature film** main item in cinema programme.

featureless /ˈfiːtʃəlɪs/ *a.* lacking distinct features.

Feb. *abbr.* February.

febrile /ˈfiːbraɪl/ *a.* of fever.

February /ˈfebrʊərɪ/ *n.* second month of year.

feckless /ˈfeklɪs/ *a.* feeble, incompetent, helpless.

fecund /ˈfiːkənd/ *a.* fertile. **fecundity** *n.*

fecundate /'fiːkəndeɪt/ v.t. make fruitful; impregnate. **fecundation** n.

fed past & p.p. of **feed**. **fed up** sl. discontented or bored (with).

federal /'fedər(ə)l/ a. of system of government in which several states unite, but remain independent in internal affairs; of such States or their central government; US hist. of Northern States in Civil War. **federalism** n.; **federalist** n.; **federalize** v.

federate 1 /'fedəreɪt/ v. unite on federal basis or for common object. 2 /'fedərət/ a. so united.

federation /fedə'reɪʃ(ə)n/ n. act of federating; federal group. **federative** a.

fedora /fɪ'dɔːrə/ n. kind of soft felt hat.

fee n. sum payable to official or professional person etc. for services; charge esp. for instruction at school or entrance for examination etc.; money paid for transfer of footballer etc.; inherited estate.

feeble /'fiːb(ə)l/ a. weak; lacking energy or strength or effectiveness.

feed 1 v. (past & p.p. **fed**) supply with food; put food in mouth of; eat; graze; keep supplied or supply with; put material (*in*)*to*; comfort (*with*); nourish. 2 n. feeding; pasturage; fodder; meal (esp. for babies or *colloq.*). 3 **feedback** return to input of part of output of system or process, information about result of experiment, response; **feed on** consume, be nourished by.

feeder /'fiːdə(r)/ n. one that feeds in specified way; feeding apparatus in machine; child's bib; tributary; branch road or railway line.

feel 1 v. (past & p.p. **felt**) examine or perceive by touch; be conscious of, be consciously; experience; be affected by; have pity *for*; have vague or emotional impression; consider, think; seem. 2 n. sense of touch; sensation characterizing something. 3 **feel like** *colloq.* desire, be inclined towards doing.

feeler /'fiːlə(r)/ n. organ in certain animals for testing things by touch; tentative suggestion etc.

feeling /'fiːlɪŋ/ 1 n. sense of touch; physical sensation; emotion; in *pl.* susceptibilities; consideration for others; belief or opinion. 2 a. sensitive; sympathetic; heartfelt.

feet *pl.* of **foot**.

feign /feɪn/ v. pretend; simulate.

feint /feɪnt/ 1 n. sham attack or blow etc. to deceive opponent; pretence. 2 *v.i.* make feint. 3 a. (of paper etc.) having faintly ruled lines.

feldspar /'feldspɑː(r)/ n. common white or flesh-red mineral containing silicates.

felicitate /fɪ'lɪsɪteɪt/ v.t. congratulate. **felicitation** n.

felicitous /fɪ'lɪsɪtəs/ a. well-chosen, apt.

felicity /fɪ'lɪsɪtɪ/ n. great happiness; pleasing manner or style.

feline /'fiːlaɪn/ 1 a. of cats; catlike. 2 n. animal of cat family. 3 **felinity** /-'lɪn-/ n.

fell[1] v.t. cut down (tree); strike down; stitch down (seam).

fell[2] n. wild high stretch of country esp. in N. England.

fell[3] a. fierce; destructive.

fell[4] n. animal's hide or skin with hair.

fell[5] past of **fall**.

fellow /'feləʊ/ 1 n. comrade, associate; counterpart, equal; *colloq.* man or boy; incorporated senior member of college; member of learned society. 2 a. of same class; associated in joint action etc. 3 **fellow-feeling** sympathy; **fellow-traveller** sympathizer with but not member of political party.

fellowship /'feləʊʃɪp/ n. sharing; companionship; body of associates; position or income of college fellow.

felon /'felən/ n. person who has committed felony.

felony /'felənɪ/ n. crime regarded by law as grave. **felonious** a.

felspar var. of **feldspar**.

felt[1] 1 n. fabric of matted and pressed fibres of wool etc. 2 v. make into or form felt; cover with felt; become matted. 3 **felt pen** pen with felt point.

felt[2] past & p.p. of **feel**.

female /'fiːmeɪl/ 1 a. of offspring-bearing sex; (of plants) fruit-bearing; of women or female animals or plants; (of screw, socket, etc.) made hollow to receive corresponding inserted part. 2 n. female person or animal.

feminine /'femɪnɪn/ a. of women; womanly; *Gram.* of gender proper to women's names. **femininity** n.

feminism /'femɪnɪz(ə)m/ n. advocacy of women's rights. **feminist** n. & a.

femur /'fi:mə(r)/ n. (pl. **femurs** or **femora**) thigh-bone.

fen n. low marshy tract of land. **fenny** a.

fence 1 n. barrier or railing enclosing field or garden etc.; guard in machine; receiver of stolen goods. 2 v. surround (as) with fence; practise sword play; be evasive.

fencing /'fensɪŋ/ n. fences, material for fences; sword-fighting, esp. as sport.

fend v. ward or keep *off*; provide *for* (*oneself* etc.).

fender /'fendə(r)/ n. frame round hearth to keep in falling coals; thing used to keep something off; *US* bumper of motor vehicle.

fennel /'fen(ə)l/ n. fragrant herb with yellow flowers, used for flavouring.

fenugreek /'fenjʊgriːk/ n. leguminous plant with aromatic seeds.

feoff /fef/ n. fief.

feral /'fɪər(ə)l/ a. wild; in wild state after escape from captivity.

ferial /'fɪərɪəl/ a. (of day) not a festival or fast.

ferment 1 /'fɜːment/ n. fermenting agent; fermentation; excitement. 2 /fə'ment/ v. undergo or subject to fermentation; excite.

fermentation /fɜːmen'teɪʃ(ə)n/ n. chemical change involving effervescence and production of heat, induced by organic substance such as yeast; excitement.

fern n. kind of flowerless plant usu. with feathery fronds.

ferocious /fə'rəʊʃəs/ a. fierce, cruel. **ferocity** /-'rɒs-/ n.

ferret /'ferɪt/ 1 n. small animal like weasel, used in catching rabbits or rats etc. 2 v. hunt with ferrets; rummage or search *about* (*for*), search *out*. 3 **ferrety** a.

ferric, **ferrous**, /'ferɪk/ *adjs.* of or containing iron.

Ferris wheel /'ferɪs/ giant revolving vertical wheel with passenger cars, in amusement parks etc.

ferro- /'ferəʊ/ *in comb.* of or containing iron.

ferroconcrete /ferəʊ'kɒŋkriːt/ n. reinforced concrete.

ferrous: see **ferric**.

ferrule /'ferəl/ n. metal ring or cap at end of stick etc.

ferry /'ferɪ/ 1 v. take or go in boat, or work boat, over river or lake etc.; transport (persons or things) from place to place, esp. as regular service. 2 n. boat etc. for ferrying; ferrying place or service.

fertile /'fɜːtaɪl/ a. (of soil) producing abundant vegetation; fruitful; (of seed, egg, etc.) capable of becoming new individual; able to conceive young or produce fruit; inventive. **fertility** /-'tɪl-/ n.

fertilize /'fɜːtɪlaɪz/ v.t. make fertile; cause (egg etc. or female) to develop new individual. **fertilization** n.

fertilizer /'fɜːtɪlaɪzə(r)/ n. chemical plant food; manure.

fervent /'fɜːv(ə)nt/ a. ardent, impassioned. **fervency** n.

fervid /'fɜːvɪd/ a. fervent.

fervour /'fɜːvə(r)/ n. passion, zeal.

festal /'fest(ə)l/ a. of feast; bright, cheerful.

fester /'festə(r)/ v.i. make or become septic; cause continuing annoyance; rot; stagnate.

festival /'festɪv(ə)l/ n. day or time of celebration; series of musical etc. performances held regularly in town etc.

festive /'festɪv/ a. of feast; joyous.

festivity /fe'stɪvɪtɪ/ n. gaiety, festive celebration; in *pl.* festive proceedings.

festoon /fe'stuːn/ 1 n. chain of flowers or ribbons etc. hung in curve. 2 v.t. adorn with or form into festoons.

fetch v.t. go for and bring back; be sold for; draw forth; deal (blow).

fetching /'fetʃɪŋ/ a. attractive.

fête /feɪt/ 1 n. outdoor function to raise money for charity. 2 v.t. entertain; make much of (person).

fetid /'fetɪd/ a. stinking.

fetish /'fetɪʃ/ n. object worshipped by primitive peoples; anything irrationally reverenced; abnormal object of sexual desire. **fetishism** n.; **fetishist** n.

fetlock /'fetlɒk/ n. part of back of horse's leg where tuft of hair grows above hoof.

fetter /'fetə(r)/ 1 n. shackle for feet; in *pl.* captivity; restraint. 2 v.t. put into fetters, restrict.

fettle /'fet(ə)l/ n. condition, trim.

feud[1] /fjuːd/ 1 n. lasting mutual hostility esp. between two families or groups. 2 *v.i.* conduct feud.

feud² /fjuːd/ *n.* fief.

feudal /ˈfjuːd(ə)l/ *a.* of social system in medieval Europe whereby vassal held land from superior in exchange for allegiance and service. **feudalism** *n.*; **feudalistic** *a.*

fever /ˈfiːvə(r)/ 1 *n.* abnormally high body temperature; disease characterized by this; nervous agitation. 2 *v.t.* affect with fever or excitement.

feverfew /ˈfiːvəfjuː/ *n.* herb formerly used to reduce fever.

feverish /ˈfiːvərɪʃ/ *a.* having symptoms of fever; excited, restless.

few 1 *a.* not many. 2 *n.* a small number. 3 **a good few**, **quite a few**, *colloq.* a fair number. 4 **fewer** *a.* □ See page 667.

fey /feɪ/ *a.* strange, other-worldly; *Sc.* fated to die soon.

fez *n.* flat-topped conical red cap with tassel, worn by men in some Muslim countries.

ff. *abbr.* following pages etc.

ff *abbr.* fortissimo.

fiancé /fɪˈɒnseɪ/ *n.* (*fem.* **-cée** *pr.* same) person to whom a person is engaged to be married.

fiasco /fɪˈæskəʊ/ *n.* (*pl.* **-cos**) failure; ignominious result.

fiat /ˈfaɪæt/ *n.* authorization; decree.

fib 1 *n.* trivial lie. 2 *v.i.* tell fib.

fibre /ˈfaɪbə(r)/ *n.* one of the threadlike cells or filaments forming animal and vegetable tissue and textile substance; piece of glass in form of thread; roughage; substance formed of fibres; personal character. **fibre-board** board made of compressed wood etc. fibres; **fibreglass** glass in fibrous form woven as fabric or used as insulator etc.; **fibre optics** transmission of information by means of infra-red light signals along thin glass fibre.

fibril /ˈfaɪbrɪl/ *n.* small fibre.

fibroid /ˈfaɪbrɔɪd/ 1 *a.* like fibre or fibrous tissue. 2 *n.* fibroid tumour in uterus.

fibrositis /faɪbrəˈsaɪtɪs/ *n.* rheumatic inflammation of fibrous tissue.

fibrous /ˈfaɪbrəs/ *a.* of or like fibres.

fibula /ˈfɪbjʊlə/ *n.* (*pl.* **-lae** *or* **-las**) bone on outer side of lower leg.

fiche /fiːʃ/ *n.* (*pl.* same) microfiche.

fickle /ˈfɪk(ə)l/ *a.* inconstant, changeable.

fiction /ˈfɪkʃ(ə)n/ *n.* invention; invented statement or narrative; literature consisting of such narrative; conventionally accepted falsehood. **fictional** *a.*

fictitious /fɪkˈtɪʃəs/ *a.* imagined or made up, not real or genuine.

fiddle /ˈfɪd(ə)l/ 1 *n.* *colloq.* violin; *sl.* artful trick or piece of cheating. 2 *v.* fidget *with*; move aimlessly *about*; *sl.* falsify, swindle, get by cheating; play fiddle, play (tune) on fiddle. 3 **fiddlesticks** nonsense. 4 **fiddler** *n.*

fiddling /ˈfɪdlɪŋ/ *a.* *colloq.* petty, trivial.

fiddly /ˈfɪdlɪ/ *a.* awkward to do or use.

fidelity /fɪˈdelɪtɪ/ *n.* faithfulness, loyalty; accuracy, precision in sound reproduction.

fidget /ˈfɪdʒɪt/ 1 *v.* move restlessly; be or make uneasy, worry. 2 *n.* person who fidgets; restless state or mood. 3 **fidgety** *a.*

fiduciary /fɪˈdjuːʃərɪ/ 1 *a.* held or given in trust; (of currency) depending for its value on public confidence. 2 *n.* trustee.

fie /faɪ/ *int.* expressing disgust or shame.

fief /fiːf/ *n.* land held under feudal system; one's sphere of operation or control.

field /fiːld/ 1 *n.* area of open land, esp. for pasture or tillage or playing game; area rich in some natural product; all competitors or all except specified one(s); *Crick.* etc. fielding side; expanse of sea or snow etc.; scene of battle; area or sphere of action or influence etc.; *Computers* part of a record, representing a unit of information. 2 *v.* act as fieldsman, stop and return (ball); select (team or individual) to play in game. 3 **field-day** *Mil.* day of exercise in manoeuvres etc., review, day of brilliant or exciting events; **field-events** athletic events other than races; **field-glasses** binoculars for outdoor use; **field hospital** temporary hospital near battlefield; **Field Marshal** Army officer of highest rank; **fieldsman** *Crick.* player (other than bowler) opposed to batsman; **field sports** outdoor sports, esp. hunting, shooting, and fishing.

fielder /ˈfiːldə(r)/ n. Crick. etc. fieldsman.

fieldfare /ˈfiːldfeə(r)/ n. kind of thrush.

fiend /fiːnd/ n. devil; very wicked or cruel person; sl. addict, devotee. **fiendish** a.

fierce /fɪəs/ a. violent; ardent, eager; raging, vehemently aggressive; intense.

fiery /ˈfaɪərɪ/ a. consisting of fire, flaming; bright red; intensely hot; spirited, intense.

fiesta /fɪˈestə/ n. festival, holiday.

fife /faɪf/ n. small shrill flute.

fifteen /fɪfˈtiːn/ a. & n. one more than fourteen; Rugby Footb. side of fifteen players. **fifteenth** a. & n.

fifth /fɪfθ/ 1 a. next after fourth. 2 n. fifth person or thing; one of five equal parts of a thing. 3 **fifth column** group working for enemy within country at war etc.

fifty /ˈfɪftɪ/ a. & n. five times ten. **fifty-fifty** half-and-half, equally. **fiftieth** a. & n.

fig[1] n. soft pear-shaped fruit; tree bearing it; valueless thing. **fig-leaf** device for concealing something, esp. genitals.

fig[2] n. dress, equipment.

fig. abbr. figure.

fight /faɪt/ 1 v. (past & p.p. **fought** /fɔːt/) contend or struggle physically in battle or single combat; struggle (for); contend with; strive to overcome. 2 n. fighting; battle; power or inclination to fight; boxing-match. 3 **fight shy of** avoid.

fighter /ˈfaɪtə(r)/ n. person who fights; aircraft designed for attacking other aircraft.

fighting /ˈfaɪtɪŋ/ a. able and eager or bred or trained to fight; engaged in fighting. **fighting chance** chance of succeeding by great effort; **fighting fit** extremely fit.

figment /ˈfɪgmənt/ n. thing existing only in the imagination.

figurative /ˈfɪgərətɪv/ a. metaphorical; of pictorial or sculptural representation.

figure /ˈfɪgə(r)/ 1 n. external form, bodily shape; person as seen or viewed mentally; representation of human form; image; expression using words

differently from literal meaning; symbol of number, numeral, esp. 0–9; value, amount of money; in pl. arithmetical calculations; diagram, illustration; series of movements forming single unit in dancing or skating etc. 2 v. appear or be mentioned; represent in diagram or picture; imagine; embellish with pattern; calculate, estimate; US understand, consider; US colloq. be understandable. 3 **figure-head** carved image etc. over ship's prow, merely nominal leader etc.; **figure out** work out by arithmetic or logic.

figurine /fɪgəˈriːn/ n. statuette.

filament /ˈfɪləmənt/ n. threadlike strand or fibre; conducting wire or thread in electric bulb. **filamentary** a.

filbert /ˈfɪlbət/ n. nut of cultivated hazel; tree bearing it.

filch v.t. steal, pilfer.

file[1] 1 n. folder or box etc. for keeping papers for reference; papers so kept; collection of records for use by computer; row of persons or things one behind the other. 2 v.t. place in file or among records; submit (application for patent, petition for divorce, etc.); march in file.

file[2] 1 n. tool with rough surface for smoothing surfaces. 2 v.t. smooth or shape with file.

filial /ˈfɪlɪəl/ a. of or due from son or daughter.

filibuster /ˈfɪlɪbʌstə(r)/ 1 n. person who obstructs progress in legislative assembly; such obstruction. 2 v.i. act as filibuster.

filigree /ˈfɪlɪgriː/ n. fine ornamental tracery of gold or other wire; anything delicate and frail.

filings /ˈfaɪlɪŋz/ n.pl. particles rubbed off by file.

fill 1 v. make or become full; put filling into; spread over, pervade; block up (hole etc.); occupy. 2 n. as much as one wants; enough to fill thing. 3 **fill in** complete, fill completely, act as substitute, colloq. inform more fully; **fill out** enlarge, become enlarged, esp. to proper size; **fill up** fill completely, fill petrol tank of (motor vehicle).

filler /ˈfɪlə(r)/ n. person or thing that fills; material used to fill cavity or increase bulk.

fillet /ˈfɪlɪt/ 1 n. boneless piece of fish

or meat; band worn round head; hair ribbon; *Archit.* narrow flat band between mouldings. **2** *v.t.* remove bones from (fish etc.); divide (fish etc.) into fillets; bind or provide with fillet(s).

filling /ˈfɪlɪŋ/ *n.* material used to fill cavity in tooth; material between bread in sandwich. **filling-station** establishment selling petrol etc. to motorists.

fillip /ˈfɪlɪp/ **1** *n.* stimulus, incentive; flick with finger or thumb. **2** *v.* stimulate; flick.

filly /ˈfɪlɪ/ *n.* female foal; *sl.* young woman.

film 1 *n.* thin coating or layer; strip or sheet of plastic etc. coated with light-sensitive emulsion for exposure in camera; story etc. recorded on cinematographic film; slight veil of haze etc.; dimness over eyes. **2** *v.* make film or motion picture of; cover or become covered (as) with film. **3 film star** well-known actor or actress in films. **4 filmy** *a.*

filter /ˈfɪltə(r)/ **1** *n.* device for removing impurities from a liquid or gas; device for making coffee by letting hot water drip through ground beans; screen for absorbing or modifying light; electrical device for suppressing certain frequencies etc.; arrangement for filtering of traffic. **2** *v.* pass or flow through filter; make way (through, into, etc.), leak *out*; (of traffic) be allowed to pass in certain direction when other traffic is held up. **3 filter-tip** (cigarette with) filter for purifying smoke.

filth /fɪlθ/ *n.* loathsome dirt; garbage; obscenity. **filthy** *a.*

filtrate /ˈfɪltreɪt/ **1** *v.* filter. **2** *n.* filtered liquid. **3 filtration** *n.*

fin *n.* organ for propelling and steering, projecting from body of fish etc.; fin-like projection on aircraft or rocket etc.

finagle /fɪˈneɪɡ(ə)l/ *v. colloq.* act or obtain dishonestly or by trickery.

final /ˈfaɪn(ə)l/ **1** *a.* at the end, coming last; conclusive, decisive. **2** *n.* last or deciding heat or game or competition; last edition of day's newspaper; (usu. in *pl.*) final examination.

finale /fɪˈnɑːlɪ/ *n.* last movement or section of piece of music or drama etc.

finalist /ˈfaɪnəlɪst/ *n.* competitor in final.

finality /faɪˈnælɪtɪ/ *n.* quality or fact of being final.

finalize /ˈfaɪnəlaɪz/ *v.t.* put in final form; complete. **finalization** *n.*

finance /faɪˈnæns/ **1** *n.* management of money; money support for enterprise; in *pl.* money resources. **2** *v.t.* find capital for. **3 financial** *a.*

financier /faɪˈnænsɪə(r)/ *n.* person engaged in large-scale finance.

finch *n.* small passerine bird.

find /faɪnd/ **1** *v.t.* (*past & p.p.* **found** /faʊnd/) discover, or get possession of, by chance or search; become aware of, obtain; ascertain; supply; perceive, experience; *Law* judge and declare. **2** *n.* what is found; pleasing discovery. **3 find out** discover, detect.

finding /ˈfaɪndɪŋ/ *n.* conclusion reached by judicial inquiry.

fine¹ 1 *a.* of high quality; excellent; pure, refined; handsome, imposing; bright, free from rain; small or thin, in small particles; smart, showy; fastidious. **2** *adv.* finely. **3 fine arts** appealing to sense of beauty, esp. painting, sculpture, and architecture; **fine-spun** delicate, too subtle.

fine² 1 *n.* sum of money (to be) paid as penalty for offence. **2** *v.t.* punish by fine.

finery /ˈfaɪnərɪ/ *n.* showy dress or decoration.

finesse /fɪˈnes/ **1** *n.* subtle management; artfulness; *Cards* attempt to win trick by playing card that is not the highest held. **2** *v.* use finesse; manage by finesse; make finesse.

finger /ˈfɪŋɡə(r)/ **1** *n.* any of terminal members of hand (usu. excluding thumb); corresponding part of glove; finger-like object; breadth of finger, esp. that depth of liquor in glass. **2** *v.t.* touch or turn about with fingers; play (music or instrument) with fingers. **3 finger-bowl** bowl for rinsing fingers during meal; **fingerpost** signpost at road-junction; **fingerprint** impression made on surface by fingers, esp. used for identifying criminals, *fig.* distinctive characteristic; **fingerstall** cover to protect injured finger.

fingering¹ /ˈfɪŋɡərɪŋ/ *n.* proper use of fingers in playing music; indication of this in score.

fingering² /'fɪŋgərɪŋ/ *n.* fine wool for knitting.

finial /'fɪnɪəl/ *n.* ornamental top to gable or canopy etc.

finicky /'fɪnɪkɪ/ *a.* (also **finical, finicking**) excessively detailed; over-particular; fastidious.

finis /'fɪnɪs/ *n.* end, esp. of book.

finish /'fɪnɪʃ/ 1 *v.* bring or come to end, come to end of; put final touches to. 2 *n.* last stage, decisive result; completed state; mode of surface treatment.

finite /'faɪnaɪt/ *a.* limited, not infinite; *Gram.* (of verb) having specific number and person.

finnan /'fɪnən/ *n.* smoke-cured haddock.

fiord /fjɔːd/ *n.* narrow inlet of sea between cliffs.

fir *n.* kind of evergreen conifer with needles placed singly on shoots; its wood. **fir-cone** its fruit.

fire /faɪə(r)/ 1 *n.* state of combustion; flame, glow; destructive burning; burning fuel in grate etc.; electric or gas heater; firing of guns; fervour, spirit; burning heat. 2 *v.* shoot (gun etc. or missile from it); shoot gun or missile; detonate; dismiss (employee); set fire to; catch fire; supply with fuel; stimulate, fill with enthusiasm; bake or dry (pottery, bricks, etc.); become heated or excited. 3 **firearm** gun, pistol, etc.; **fire-ball** large meteor, ball of flame from nuclear explosion; **fire-bomb** incendiary bomb; **firebrand** piece of burning wood, trouble-maker; **fire-break** obstacle preventing spread of fire in forest etc.; **fire-brick** fire-proof brick used for grates etc.; **fire brigade** organized body of firemen; **fire-clay** clay used for fire-bricks etc.; **firedog** andiron; **fire-drill** rehearsal of procedure to be used if fire breaks out; **fire-engine** vehicle carrying equipment for extinguishing fires; **fire-escape** apparatus or emergency staircase for escape from building on fire; **firefly** insect emitting phosphorescent light; **fire-irons** tongs, poker, and shovel for tending domestic fire; **fireman** man employed to extinguish fires, man who tends furnace etc.; **fireplace** grate or hearth for domestic fire; **fire-power** destructive capacity of guns etc.; **fire-practice**

fire-drill; **fireside** area round fireplace, home, home-life; **fire-water** *colloq.* strong alcoholic liquor; **firework** device giving spectacular effect by use of combustible chemicals etc., *fig.* in *pl.* display of anger etc.; **under fire** being shot at, being criticized.

firing /'faɪərɪŋ/ *n.* discharge of guns; fuel. **firing-line** front line of battle; **firing-squad** group which fires salute at military funeral or shoots condemned person.

firkin /'fɜːkɪn/ *n.* small barrel.

firm¹ 1 *a.* of solid structure; fixed, steady; steadfast, resolute; (of offer etc.) not liable to cancellation after acceptance. 2 *v.* make or become firm or secure.

firm² 1 *n.* business concern or its members.

firmament /'fɜːməmənt/ *n.* sky regarded as vault.

first 1 *a.* foremost in time or order or importance. 2 *n.* first person or thing. 3 *adv.* before all or something else; for the first time. 4 **first aid** help given to injured until medical treatment is available; **first class** best category, best accommodation in train or ship etc., highest category of achievement in examination, class of mail most quickly delivered; **first-class** of or by first class; excellent; **first-foot** *Sc.* (be) first person to cross threshold in New Year; **firsthand** direct, original; **first night** first public performance of play etc.; **first-rate** excellent, very well. 5 **firstly** *adv.*

firth /fɜːθ/ *n.* inlet of sea, estuary.

fiscal /'fɪsk(ə)l/ 1 *a.* of public revenue. 2 *n.* *Sc.* procurator fiscal.

fish¹ 1 *n.* (*pl.* usu. same) vertebrate cold-blooded animal living in water; flesh of fish as food. 2 *v.* try to catch fish (in); search *for*; draw *out*; seek by indirect means *for*. 3 **fish-eye lens** wide-angled lens; **fish finger** small oblong piece of fish in breadcrumbs; **fishhook** barbed hook for catching fish; **fish-kettle** oval pan for boiling fish; **fishmeal** ground dried fish as fertilizer etc.; **fishmonger** dealer in fish; **fishslice** cook's flat implement for turning fish etc.; **fishwife** woman selling fish.

fish² *n.* piece of wood or iron for

strengthening mast etc.; **fish-plate** flat plate of iron etc. holding rails together.

fisherman /ˈfɪʃəmən/ n. (pl. **-men**) man who lives by fishing, angler.

fishery /ˈfɪʃərɪ/ n. place where fish are caught; business of fishing.

fishing /ˈfɪʃɪŋ/ n. sport of trying to catch fish.

fishy /ˈfɪʃɪ/ a. of or like fish; sl. dubious, open to suspicion.

fissile /ˈfɪsaɪl/ a. capable of undergoing nuclear fission; tending to split.

fission /ˈfɪʃ(ə)n/ 1 n. Biol. division of cell etc. as mode of reproduction; (in full **nuclear fission**) splitting of atomic nucleus. 2 v. (cause to) undergo fission.

fissure /ˈfɪʃə(r)/ 1 n. narrow opening; split; cleavage. 2 v. split.

fist n. clenched hand.

fistula /ˈfɪstjʊlə/ n. pipe-like ulcer; surgically made body-passage. **fistular** a.; **fistulous** a.

fit[1] 1 a. qualified, competent, worthy; in good health or condition; becoming, proper. 2 v. be in harmony (with); be or make of or adjust to right size and shape; join (on, together, up, etc.) parts that fit; adapt; make competent for or to; supply with. 3 n. way thing fits. **fit in** make room or time for, adapt oneself, conform, be adapted; **fit out**, **up**, equip.

fit[2] n. sudden seizure of epilepsy or hysteria or fainting etc.; attack of strong feeling; sudden transitory state; mood.

fitful /ˈfɪtfʊl/ a. active or occurring spasmodically or intermittently.

fitment /ˈfɪtmənt/ n. piece of fixed furniture.

fitter /ˈfɪtə(r)/ n. person who makes garments etc. fit; mechanic who fits together parts of engines etc..

fitting /ˈfɪtɪŋ/ 1 n. action of fitting on a garment; (usu. in pl.) fixture, fitment. 2 a. proper, befitting.

five a. & n. one more than four.

fiver /ˈfaɪvə(r)/ n. colloq. £5 note.

fives /faɪvz/ n. game in which ball is struck with hands or bat against walls of court.

fix 1 v. make firm or stable or permanent; fasten, secure; settle, specify; direct (eyes etc.) steadily on; attract and hold (attention etc.); identify, locate; mend, repair; arrange, make ready; sl. do for, get even with; colloq. tamper with or arrange result of etc., esp. by bribery; inject (oneself with narcotic); (of plant) assimilate (gas) by forming non-gaseous compound. 2 n. dilemma, difficult position; position determined by bearings etc.; sl. dose of narcotic drug.

fixate /fɪkˈseɪt/ v.t. Psych. cause to acquire abnormal attachment to person or things.

fixation /fɪkˈseɪʃ(ə)n/ n. act or process of being fixated; obsession; fixing, coagulation; process of combining gas to form solid.

fixative /ˈfɪksətɪv/ 1 a. tending to fix. 2 n. substance used to fix colours etc.

fixedly /ˈfɪksɪdlɪ/ adv. intently.

fixings /ˈfɪksɪŋz/ n. pl. US equipment; trimmings of dress or dish.

fixity /ˈfɪksɪtɪ/ n. fixed state; stability, permanence.

fixture /ˈfɪkstʃə(r)/ n. thing fixed in position; in pl. articles belonging to land or house; (date fixed for) sporting event.

fizz 1 v.i. effervesce; hiss or splutter. 2 n. fizzing sound; effervescence; colloq. effervescent drink. 3 **fizzy** a.

fizzle /ˈfɪz(ə)l/ 1 v.i. hiss or splutter feebly. 2 n. fizzling sound. 3 **fizzle out** fail feebly.

fjord var. of fiord.

fl. abbr. fluid.

flab n. colloq. fat, flabbiness.

flabbergast /ˈflæbəɡɑːst/ v.t. colloq. overwhelm with astonishment.

flabby /ˈflæbɪ/ a. limp, not firm; feeble.

flaccid /ˈflæksɪd/ a. flabby. **flaccidity** n.

flag[1] 1 n. piece of cloth or other material, attached by one edge to pole or rope etc. and used as standard or ensign or signal. 2 v.t. inform or signal to (as) with flag; mark with flag or tag. 3 **flag-day** day on which money is raised for cause by sale of small paper flags; **flag-officer** admiral or vice- or rear-admiral; **flag-pole** flagstaff; **flagship** ship with admiral on board; **flagstaff** pole on which flag is hung.

flag[2] v.i. become limp, feeble, or uninteresting.

flag[3] 1 n. flat slab of stone for paving; in pl. pavement of flags. 2 v.t. pave with flags. 3 **flagstone** flag.

flag⁴ *n.* plant with bladed leaf.

flagellant /ˈflædʒələnt/ **1** *n.* person who flagellates himself or others. **2** *a.* of flagellation.

flagellate /ˈflædʒəleɪt/ *v.t.* whip or flog, esp. as religious discipline or sexual stimulus. **flagellation** *n.*

flageolet /ˌflædʒəˈlet/ *n.* small wind-instrument like recorder.

flagon /ˈflægən/ *n.* rounded vessel to hold liquor.

flagrant /ˈfleɪɡrənt/ *a.* glaring, scandalous. **flagrancy** *n.*

flail 1 *n.* hand threshing-implement. **2** *v.* wave or swing wildly; beat (as) with flail.

flair *n.* selective instinct for what is good or useful etc.

flak *n.* anti-aircraft fire; *fig.* barrage of criticism.

flake 1 *n.* light fleecy piece esp. of snow; thin broad piece; layer. **2** *v.* take or come (*off* etc.) in flakes; fall in flakes, sprinkle with flakes. **3 flaky** *a.*

flambé /ˈflɑ̃beɪ/ *a.* (of food) covered with spirit and served alight. [F]

flamboyant /flæmˈbɔɪənt/ *a.* florid, showy. **flamboyance** *n.*

flame 1 *n.* (portion of) ignited gas; visible combustion; bright light; passion esp. of love; *colloq.* sweetheart. **2** *v.i.* emit flames; break *out*, blaze *up*, into anger; shine, gleam.

flamenco /fləˈmeŋkəʊ/ *n.* (*pl.* **-cos**) Spanish gipsy style of singing and dancing.

flaming /ˈfleɪmɪŋ/ *a.* burning with flames; very hot or bright; *colloq.* bloody, damned.

flamingo /fləˈmɪŋɡəʊ/ *n.* (*pl.* **-gos**) tall long-necked wading-bird with pink, scarlet, and black plumage.

flammable /ˈflæməb(ə)l/ *a.* inflammable.

flan *n.* pastry or sponge case filled or spread with jam or fruit or savoury mixture etc.

flange /flændʒ/ *n.* projecting flat rim or collar or rib.

flank 1 *n.* side of body between ribs and hip; side of mountain or body of troops etc. **2** *v.t.* be or be posted at or move along side(s) of.

flannel /ˈflæn(ə)l/ **1** *n.* woven woollen usu. napless cloth; in *pl.* flannel trousers; cloth used for washing oneself; *sl.*

nonsense, flattery. **2** *v.* wash with flannel; *sl.* flatter.

flannelette /ˌflænəˈlet/ *n.* napped cotton fabric resembling flannel.

flap 1 *v.* (cause to) swing or sway about or move up and down; drive (flies etc.) *away* with flat object; *colloq.* be agitated or panicky. **2** *n.* broad piece hinged or held by one side and usu. hanging down; action or sound of flapping; light blow usu. with something flat; *colloq.* state of agitation or fuss. **3 flapjack** sweet oatcake, small pancake.

flare /fleə(r)/ **1** *v.* blaze with bright unsteady flame; (cause to) widen or spread gradually. **2** *n.* unshaded flame in open air, esp. used as signal or guide; outburst of flame; bright unsteady light; flared shape. **3 flare path** line of lights to guide aircraft landing or taking off; **flare up** burst into flame or anger etc.

flash 1 *n.* sudden short blaze of flame or light; brief outburst or transient display; instant; brief news report; *Photog.* flashlight; *Mil.* cloth patch on uniform as emblem of unit etc. **2** *v.* produce a flash, gleam; *colloq.* show suddenly or ostentatiously; *sl.* briefly expose oneself indecently; send or reflect in flash(es); cause to shine briefly. **3** *a. colloq.* gaudy, showy. **4 flashback** return, esp. in a film, to past event; **flashbulb** bulb giving light for flashlight photograph; **flashlight** device producing brief bright light for indoor etc. photography, electric torch; **flashpoint** temperature at which vapour from oil etc. ignites.

flashing /ˈflæʃɪŋ/ *n.* strip of metal to prevent flooding or leakage at joint of roofing etc.

flashy /ˈflæʃɪ/ *a.* gaudy, showy.

flask /flɑːsk/ *n.* vacuum flask; narrow-necked bulbous bottle; pocket-bottle of metal or glass.

flat 1 *a.* horizontal, level; lying at full length; smooth, without bumps or indentation; absolute, downright; dull; dejected; without effervescence, insipid; (of battery) unable to generate electric current; (of tyre etc.) deflated or punctured; *Mus.* below correct or normal pitch. **2** *adv.* in a flat manner; *colloq.* downright, plainly; exactly. **3** *n.* group of rooms usu. on one floor, forming residence; flat surface or part; level ground; low-lying marshy land; *Mus.* note lowered by semitone, sign indicating this; section of stage scenery on frame; *colloq.* punctured tyre. **4 flat-fish** fish with flattened body, e.g. sole or plaice; **flat foot** foot with less than normal arch; **flat-footed** having flat feet, *colloq.* uninspired; **flat-iron** iron heated by external means, for smoothing linen; **flatlet** small flat; **flat out** at top speed, using all resources; **flat race** one over level ground without jumps; **flat rate** unvarying rate or charge; **flat spin** aircraft's nearly horizontal spin, *colloq.* panic, consternation.

flatten /ˈflæt(ə)n/ *v.* make or become flat; *colloq.* defeat decisively.

flatter /ˈflætə(r)/ *v.t.* fawn upon; overpraise; cause to feel honoured; (of portrait) exaggerate good looks of. **flattery** *n.*

flatulent /ˈflætjʊlənt/ *a.* causing, caused by, or troubled with, formation of gas in alimentary canal; inflated, pretentious. **flatulence** *n.*

flaunt /flɔːnt/ *v.* display proudly; show off, parade. □ See page 666.

flautist /ˈflɔːtɪst/ *n.* flute-player.

flavour /ˈfleɪvə(r)/ **1** *n.* mixed sensation of smell and taste; distinctive taste, characteristic quality. **2** *v.t.* give flavour to, season.

flavouring /ˈfleɪvərɪŋ/ *n.* thing used to flavour food or drink.

flaw 1 *n.* imperfection; blemish; crack, breach; defect in document etc. **2** *v.* make flaw in, spoil.

flax *n.* blue-flowered plant cultivated for its seeds and for textile fibre obtained from stem.

flaxen /ˈflæks(ə)n/ *a.* of flax; (of hair) pale yellow.

flay *v.t.* strip off skin or hide of; peel off; criticize severely.

flea *n.* small wingless jumping insect feeding on human or other blood. **flea market** *colloq.* street market selling second-hand goods etc.; **flea-pit** *sl.* dingy cinema.

fleck 1 *n.* spot of colour, freckle; small particle; speck. **2** *v.t.* mark with flecks.

fled *past* & *p.p.* of **flee**.

fledge *v.t.* provide with feathers or down; in *p.p.* able to fly, *fig.* mature.

fledgeling /ˈfledʒlɪŋ/ *n.* young bird; *fig.* inexperienced person.

flee *v.* (*past* & *p.p.* **fled**) run away (from); leave hurriedly.

fleece 1 *n.* woolly covering, esp. of sheep; wool shorn from sheep. **2** *v.t.* strip, plunder. **3 fleecy** *a.*

fleet 1 *n.* naval force, navy; ships sailing together; number of vehicles owned by one proprietor. **2** *a.* swift, nimble.

fleeting /ˈfliːtɪŋ/ *a.* brief, passing rapidly.

Flemish /ˈflemɪʃ/ **1** *a.* of Flanders. **2** *n.* language of Flanders.

flesh *n.* soft substance between skin and bones; meat; body as opp. to mind or soul; pulpy substance of fruit etc.; plumpness, fat. **flesh and blood** human body, human nature, mankind, one's (*own*) near relations; **flesh-colour** yellowish-pink; **flesh-pots** luxurious living; **flesh-wound** one not reaching bone or vital organ.

fleshly /ˈfleʃlɪ/ *a.* worldly; carnal.

fleshy /ˈfleʃɪ/ *a.* of or like flesh; plump.

fleur-de-lis /flɜːdəˈliː/ *n.* (*pl.* **fleurs-** pr. same) heraldic device of three petals; former royal arms of France.

flew *past* of **fly**[1].

flex[1] *n.* flexible insulated wire.

flex[2] *v.* bend (joint, limb); move (muscle) to bend joint.

flexible /ˈfleksɪb(ə)l/ *a.* easily bent; pliable; adaptable. **flexibility** *n.*

flexion /ˈflekʃ(ə)n/ *n.* bending, bent state or part.

flibbertigibbet /ˈflɪbətɪdʒɪbɪt/ *n.* gossiping or frivolous or restless person.

flick 1 *n.* sudden release of bent finger or thumb; quick light blow or stroke; jerk; in *pl. sl.* cinema. **2** *v.t.* strike or knock *away* or *off* with flick. **3 flick-knife** weapon with blade that springs out when button etc. is pressed; **flick through** look cursorily through (book etc.).

flicker /ˈflɪkə(r)/ *v.i.* shine or burn unsteadily; show fitful vibration. **2** *n.* flickering light or motion; brief feeling of hope etc.

flier var. of **flyer**.

flight[1] /flaɪt/ *n.* act or manner of flying; movement or path of thing through air; (regular) journey by airline; group of birds etc. flying together; volley (*of* arrows etc.); series (*of* stairs, hurdles etc. for racing, etc.); feather etc. on dart or arrow. **flight-deck** cockpit of large aircraft, deck of aircraft carrier; **flight lieutenant** RAF officer next below squadron leader; **flight-recorder** device in aircraft to record technical details for use in case of accident.

flight² /flaɪt/ *n.* running away; hasty retreat.

flighty /ˈflaɪtɪ/ *a.* frivolous; changeable.

flimsy /ˈflɪmzɪ/ *a.* easily damaged or knocked apart.

flinch *v.i.* draw back, shrink; wince.

fling 1 *v.* (*past & p.p.* **flung**) throw, hurl; rush, go violently. 2 *n.* throw, cast; vigorous dance; spell of self-indulgence.

flint *n.* hard stone found in pebbly lumps; piece of flint esp. as tool or weapon; piece of hard alloy used to produce spark. **flintlock** old type of gun discharged by spark from flint. **flinty** *a.*

flip¹ 1 *v.* turn over quickly, flick; toss (thing) so that it turns over. 2 *n.* action of flipping.

flip² *n.* drink of heated beer and spirit.

flip³ *a. colloq.* glib, flippant.

flippant /ˈflɪpənt/ *a.* treating serious things lightly; disrespectful. **flippancy** *n.*

flipper /ˈflɪpə(r)/ *n.* limb used by turtle or walrus etc. in swimming; rubber etc. attachment to foot for underwater swimming; *sl.* hand.

flirt 1 *v.* behave in amorous or enticing manner without serious intentions; superficially interest oneself *with*. 2 *n.* person who flirts. 3 **flirtation** *n.*; **flirtatious** *a.*

flit 1 *v.i.* pass lightly or rapidly (*about*); fly lightly and swiftly; abscond, disappear secretly, esp. to escape creditor. 2 *n.* act of flitting.

flitch *n.* side of bacon.

flitter /ˈflɪtə(r)/ *v.i.* flit about.

float 1 *v.* (cause to) rest or drift on surface of liquid; hover *before* eye or mind; (of currency) have fluctuating exchange rate; cause or allow to do this; launch (company, scheme). 2 *n.* thing that floats or rests on surface of liquid; raft; low-bodied cart etc. esp. used in procession; sum of money for minor expenditures or change-giving; tool for smoothing plaster etc.; in *sing.* or *pl.*

footlights. 3 **floating dock** floating structure usable as dry dock; **floating rib** rib not attached to breastbone in front; **floating voter** voter not committed to any political party.

floatation var. of **flotation**.

flocculent /ˈflɒkjʊlənt/ *a.* like tufts of wool.

flock¹ 1 *n.* number of animals esp. birds, sheep, or goats, regarded as a unit; large crowd of people; congregation in relation to its pastor. 2 *v.i.* move or assemble *together* in large numbers.

flock² *n.* lock or tuft of wool etc.; wool or cotton waste used as stuffing.

floe *n.* sheet of floating ice.

flog *v.t.* beat with whip or stick etc.; *sl.* sell.

flood /flʌd/ 1 *n.* (coming of) great quantity of water, esp. over land; outburst, outpouring; inflow of tide. 2 *v.* overflow; cover or be covered with flood; come in great quantities. 3 **the Flood** that described in Genesis; **floodgate** gate for admitting or excluding water; **floodlight** (illuminate with) copious artificial lighting directed on building etc.; **floodlit** lit thus.

floor /flɔː(r)/ *n.* lower surface of room; bottom of sea or cave etc.; rooms on one level in house; storey; part of legislative chamber where members sit and speak; right of speaking; level area. 2 *v.t.* provide with floor; knock down; baffle, nonplus; overcome. 3 **floor show** cabaret.

flop 1 *v.* move or fall or sit etc. *down* awkwardly or negligently or with soft thud; sway about heavily and loosely; *sl.* collapse, fail. 2 *n.* flopping motion or sound; *sl.* failure. 3 *adv.* with a flop. 4 **floppy** *a.*

flora /ˈflɔːrə/ *n.* (*pl.* **-ras**) the plants of a region or period.

floral /ˈflɔːr(ə)l/ *a.* of or decorated with flowers.

floret /ˈflɔːrɪt/ *n.* any of the small flowers of composite flower.

florid /ˈflɒrɪd/ *a.* ornate, showy; ruddy, high-coloured. **floridity** *n.*

florin /ˈflɒrɪn/ *n. hist.* gold or silver coin, esp. English two-shilling coin.

florist /ˈflɒrɪst/ *n.* person who deals in or grows flowers.

floruit /ˈflɒrʊɪt/ n. period at which person was alive or worked.

floss n. rough silk enveloping silkworm's cocoon; dental floss. **floss silk** rough silk used in cheap goods. **flossy** a.

flotation /fləˈteɪʃ(ə)n/ n. launching of a commercial enterprise etc.

flotilla /fləˈtɪlə/ n. small fleet, fleet of small ships.

flotsam /ˈflɒtsəm/ n. floating wreckage.

flounce¹ /flaʊns/ **1** v.i. go or move with agitated or violent motion. **2** n. flouncing movement.

flounce² /flaʊns/ **1** n. ornamental frill round woman's skirt etc. **2** v.t. trim with flounces.

flounder¹ /ˈflaʊndə(r)/ v.t. move or struggle clumsily; proceed in bungling or struggling fashion.

flounder² /ˈflaʊndə(r)/ n. small flat-fish.

flour /flaʊə(r)/ **1** n. powdery substance got by milling and usu. sifting cereals, esp. wheat. **2** v.t. sprinkle with flour. **3** **floury** a.

flourish /ˈflʌrɪʃ/ **1** v. grow vigorously; thrive, prosper; wave or throw about. **2** n. ornamental curve in writing; sweeping gesture with weapon or hand etc.; *Mus.* florid passage; fanfare.

flout /flaʊt/ v.t. express contempt for by word or act. □ See page 666.

flow /fləʊ/ v.i. glide along as stream; move like liquid; gush out; circulate; move easily; (of dress etc.) hang easily; be in flood; result (*from*). **2** n. flowing; copious supply; rise of tide. **3** **flow chart**, **diagram**, diagram of movement or actions etc. of things or persons in complex activity.

flower /flaʊə(r)/ **1** n. part of plant from which seed or fruit develops; flowering plant; state of blooming. **2** v. produce flowers; reach peak.

flowery /ˈflaʊərɪ/ a. abounding in flowers; full of fine words.

flown p.p. of fly¹.

flu n. colloq. influenza.

fluctuate /ˈflʌktjʊeɪt/ v.i. vary, rise and fall; be unstable. **fluctuation** n.

flue n. smoke-duct in chimney; channel for conveying heat.

fluent /ˈfluːənt/ a. expressing oneself

quickly and easily; copious and ready, flowing. **fluency** n.

fluff **1** n. light downy substance, e.g. that shed from fabric; *sl.* mistake made in speaking etc. **2** v. shake *up* or *out* into soft mass; *sl.* make mistake in speaking etc. **3** **fluffy** a.

fluid /ˈfluːɪd/ **1** n. substance capable of flowing freely, gas or liquid; liquid secretion. **2** a. able to flow freely, not solid or rigid or stable. **3** **fluid ounce** twentieth or (*US*) sixteenth of pint. **4** **fluidify** v.; **fluidity** n.

fluke¹ **1** n. lucky accidental stroke or success. **2** v. get or hit etc. by fluke. **3** **fluky** a.

fluke² n. flat-fish, flounder; parasitic flatworm in liver of sheep etc.

flummery /ˈflʌmərɪ/ n. sweet milk dish; empty talk; nonsense.

flummox /ˈflʌməks/ v.t. colloq. bewilder.

flung past & p.p. of fling.

flunk v. *US sl.* fail, esp. in examination.

flunkey /ˈflʌŋkɪ/ n. usu. derog. footman.

fluorescence /flʊəˈres(ə)ns/ n. light produced from some substances by action of radiation. **fluoresce** v.i.; **fluorescent** a.

fluoridate /ˈflʊərɪdeɪt/ v.t. add fluoride to (water supply). **fluoridation** n.

fluoride /ˈflʊəraɪd/ n. compound of fluorine with metal.

fluorine /ˈflʊəriːn/ n. pungent corrosive gaseous element.

fluorspar /ˈflʊəspɑː(r)/ n. calcium fluoride as mineral.

flurry /ˈflʌrɪ/ **1** n. gust, squall; nervous hurry, agitation. **2** v.t. agitate, confuse.

flush¹ **1** v. (cause to) glow or blush; cleanse (drain, lavatory, etc.) by flow of water; dispose of thus; spurt, rush out. **2** n. glow, blush; feeling of feverish heat; rush of emotion or elation; rush of water; cleansing by flushing; freshness, vigour. **3** a. level (*with*); colloq. having plenty of money etc.

flush² v. (cause to) fly up suddenly; reveal, drive *out*.

flush³ n. *Cards* hand of cards all of one suit.

fluster /ˈflʌstə(r)/ **1** v. confuse, agitate; bustle. **2** n. confused or agitated state.

flute **1** n. woodwind instrument, long pipe with holes stopped by keys and mouth-hole at side; vertical groove in pillar etc. **2** v. make grooves in; whistle or sing etc. in flute-like tones; play (on) flute.

fluting /ˈfluːtɪŋ/ n. series of ornamental grooves.

flutter /ˈflʌtə(r)/ **1** v. flap (wings) in flying or trying to fly; wave or flap quickly and irregularly; move restlessly; beat feebly and irregularly. **2** n. fluttering; tremulous excitement; rapid variation of pitch or loudness of sound; *colloq.* small bet or speculation.

fluty /ˈfluːtɪ/ a. soft and clear in tone.

fluvial /ˈfluːvɪəl/ a. of or found in rivers.

flux n. continuous succession of changes; flowing; inflow of tide; substance mixed with metal etc. to assist fusion.

fly¹ **1** v. (*past* **flew**; *p.p.* **flown** /fləʊn/) move through air with wings or in aircraft; control flight of (aircraft); flutter, wave, set or keep (flag, kite) flying; travel swiftly; hasten, rush; flee (from). **2** n. flying; flap on garment, esp. trousers, to contain or cover fastening; (*freq.* in pl.) this fastening; flap at entrance of tent; *Theatr.* in pl. space over proscenium; part of flag farthest from staff. **3 fly-half** *Rugby footb.* half-back who stands off from scrum-half; **flyleaf** blank leaf at beginning or end of book; **flyover** bridge carrying road etc. over another; **fly-past** ceremonial flight of aircraft past person or place; **fly-post** display (handbills etc.) in unauthorized places; **flywheel** heavy wheel regulating machinery or accumulating power.

fly² n. two-winged insect; disease of plants or animals caused by flies; natural or artificial fly used as bait. **fly-blown** tainted by flies' eggs; **flycatcher** bird that catches flies in air; **fly-spray** liquid sprayed from canister to kill flies; **flyweight** boxing-weight (up to 51 kg.).

fly³ a. sl. knowing, clever.

flyer /ˈflaɪə(r)/ n. airman; fast animal or vehicle.

flying /ˈflaɪɪŋ/ **1** n. flight. **2** a. that flies; hasty. **3 flying boat** seaplane with boatlike fuselage; **flying buttress** buttress slanting from column etc. to wall, usu. on arch; **flying fish** fish that can rise into air by winglike fins; **flying fox** fruit-eating bat; **flying officer** RAF officer next below flight-lieutenant; **flying saucer** unidentified saucer-shaped object reported as seen in sky; **flying squad** detachment of police organized for rapid movement; **flying start** start in which starting-point is passed at full speed, vigorous start, initial advantage.

FM *abbr.* Field Marshal; frequency modulation.

FO *abbr.* Flying Officer; *hist.* Foreign Office.

foal 1 n. young of horse or ass etc. **2** v.i. give birth to foal.

foam 1 n. froth formed in liquid; froth of saliva or perspiration; rubber or plastic in cellular mass. **2** v.i. emit foam; froth, gather foam. **3 foamy** a.

fob¹ n. ornamental attachment to watch-chain etc.; small pocket for watch etc. in waistband of trousers.

fob² v.t. (with *off*) deceive (person) into being satisfied (*with* inferior thing or excuse); palm or pass off (thing) *on* person.

focal /ˈfəʊk(ə)l/ a. of or at a focus. **focal length** distance between centre of lens etc. and its focus.

fo'c's'le var. of forecastle.

focus /ˈfəʊkəs/ **1** n. (*pl.* **-cuses** or **-ci** /-saɪ/) point at which rays etc. meet after reflection or refraction or from which rays etc. appear to proceed; point at which object must be situated to give clearly defined image; adjustment of eye or lens to produce clear image; state of clear definition; central or originating point. **2** v. bring into focus; adjust focus of (lens or eye); (cause to) converge to focus; concentrate or be concentrated *on*.

fodder /ˈfɒdə(r)/ **1** n. dried food, hay, etc. for cattle. **2** v.t. give fodder to.

foe n. enemy.

foetid var. of fetid.

foetus /ˈfiːtəs/ n. developed embryo in womb or egg. **foetal** a.

fog 1 n. vapour suspended at or near earth's surface; thick mist; cloudiness on photographic negative. **2** v.t. (*past* & *p.p.* **fogged**) envelop (as) in fog; perplex. **3 fog-horn** sounding instrument for warning ships in fog. **4 foggy** a.

fogy /ˈfəʊgɪ/ n. (also **fogey**) (**old**) **fogy** old-fashioned person.

foible /ˈfɔɪb(ə)l/ n. weak point, fault.

foil[1] v. baffle, frustrate, defeat.

foil[2] n. thin sheet or leaf of metal; thing that sets another off by contrast.

foil[3] n. blunt-edged fencing-sword.

foist v.t. fob (thing) (*off*) on person.

fold[1] /fəʊld/ 1 v. double (flexible thing) over upon itself; bend portion of; become or be able to be folded; clasp; envelop, wrap. 2 n. folding; hollow among hills; line made by folding. 3 **fold up** make more compact by folding, *colloq.* collapse, fail.

fold[2] /fəʊld/ 1 n. enclosure for sheep; body of believers. 2 v.t. enclose (sheep) in fold.

folder /ˈfəʊldə(r)/ n. folding cover or holder for loose papers etc.

foliaceous /fəʊlɪˈeɪʃəs/ a. of or like leaves; laminated.

foliage /ˈfəʊlɪɪdʒ/ n. leaves, leafage.

foliate 1 /ˈfəʊlɪət/ a. leaflike, having leaves. 2 /ˈfəʊlɪeɪt/ v. split into thin layers. 3 **foliation** n.

folio /ˈfəʊlɪəʊ/ 1 n. (pl. -os) leaf of paper etc. numbered only on front; sheet of paper folded once; volume made of such sheets. 2 a. (of book etc.) made of folios.

folk /fəʊk/ n. nation, race; in pl. people in general; people in general or of specified class; one's relatives; *attrib.* of popular origin. **folklore** traditional beliefs etc., study of these; **folk music** etc. music etc. traditional in a country, or in style of this; **folkweave** rough loosely-woven fabric.

folksy /ˈfəʊksɪ/ a. having characteristics of ordinary people; resembling folk art.

follicle /ˈfɒlɪk(ə)l/ n. small sac or vesicle; small gland or cavity containing hair-root. **follicular** a.

follow /ˈfɒləʊ/ v. go or come after; go along; come next in order or time; take as guide; understand meaning of; be aware of present state or progress of; provide *with* sequel or successor; result *from*; be necessary inference. **follow on** continue, *Crick.* bat again immediately after first innings; **follow suit** play card of same suit as was led, *fig.* conform to another's actions; **follow through** continue (action etc.) to conclusion; **follow up** pursue, develop, supplement.

follower /ˈfɒləʊə(r)/ n. supporter, devotee.

following /ˈfɒləʊɪŋ/ 1 n. body of supporters. 2 a. now to be mentioned.

folly /ˈfɒlɪ/ n. foolishness; foolish act or conduct or idea etc.; costly ornamental building.

foment /fəˈment/ v.t. instigate, stir up (trouble etc.). **fomentation** n.

fond a. tender, loving; doting; foolishly credulous or optimistic. **fond of** having liking for.

fondant /ˈfɒnd(ə)nt/ n. soft sweet of flavoured sugar.

fondle /ˈfɒnd(ə)l/ v. caress.

fondue /ˈfɒndjuː/ n. dish of flavoured melted cheese.

font n. receptacle for baptismal water.

food /fuːd/ n. substance taken into animal or plant to maintain life and growth; solid food. **food poisoning** illness due to bacteria etc. in food; **food processor** electric machine for chopping and mixing etc. food; **foodstuff** substance used as food.

fool[1] /fuːl/ 1 n. silly person, simpleton; unwise person; *hist.* jester, clown; dupe. 2 v. act in joking or teasing way; play or trifle; cheat, dupe. 3 **foolproof** so plain or simple as to be incapable of misuse or mistake; **fool's errand** fruitless one; **fool's paradise** illusory happiness; **make a fool of** make (person) look foolish; **play the fool** indulge in buffoonery.

fool[2] /fuːl/ n. dish of stewed crushed fruit mixed with cream, custard, etc.

foolery /ˈfuːlərɪ/ n. foolish acts or behaviour.

foolhardy /ˈfuːlhɑːdɪ/ a. foolishly bold; reckless.

foolish /ˈfuːlɪʃ/ a. lacking good sense; indiscreet; stupid.

foolscap /ˈfuːlskæp/ n. long folio writing or printing paper.

foot /fʊt/ 1 n. (pl. **feet**) end part of leg beyond ankle; lower part or end; linear measure of 12 in. (30.48 cm.); division of verse with one stressed syllable; step, pace, tread; *hist.* infantry. 2 v.t. pay (bill). 3 **foot-and-mouth (disease)** contagious virus disease of cattle etc.; **footfall** sound of footstep; **foothill** one lying at base of mountain or range;

foothold support for feet in climbing; **footlights** row of lights along front of stage; **footloose** free to act as one pleases; **footman** liveried servant; **footmark** footprint; **footnote** note at foot of page; **footpath** path for pedestrians only; **footplate** platform in locomotive for driver and fireman; **footprint** impression left by foot or shoe; **footsore** with sore feet, esp. from walking; **footstep** tread, footprint; **footstool** stool for resting feet on when sitting; **on foot** walking.

footage /ˈfʊtɪdʒ/ n. length in feet, esp. of cinema film.

football /ˈfʊtbɔːl/ n. large inflated usu. leather ball; game played with football. **football pool** form of gambling on results of football matches. **footballer** n.

footing /ˈfʊtɪŋ/ n. foothold; secure position; position or status of person etc. in relation to others.

footling /ˈfuːtlɪŋ/ a. trivial, silly.

fop n. dandy, vain man. **foppery** n.; **foppish** a.

for 1 prep. in defence or favour of; representing; at price of; with the object of; during; as regards; in direction of; because of, on account of; notwithstanding. 2 conj. seeing that, since.

forage /ˈfɒrɪdʒ/ 1 n. food for horses and cattle; foraging. 2 v. rummage, search (for); collect forage (from).

foray /ˈfɒreɪ/ 1 n. sudden attack, raid. 2 v.i. make foray.

forbad(e) past of **forbid**.

forbear[1] /fɔːˈbeə(r)/ v. (past **forbore**; p.p. **forborne**) abstain or refrain (from); be patient. **forbearance** n.; **forbearing** a.

forbear[2] var. of **forebear**.

forbid /fəˈbɪd/ v.t. (past **-bade** or **-bad** /-bæd/; p.p. **-bidden**) command not to do; not allow; prevent.

forbidding a. uninviting, repellent; stern.

force 1 n. strength, violence, intense effort; body of men; in pl. troops; body of police; compulsion; influence, effectiveness. 2 v.t. constrain, compel; strain, urge; break open by force; drive, propel; impose or press (up)on (person); cause or produce by effort; artificially hasten maturity of. 3 **forced landing** unavoidable landing of aircraft in emergency; **forced march**

lengthy and vigorous march, esp. of troops; **force-feed** feed (prisoner etc.) against his will; **force person's hand** compel him to act etc. prematurely or unwillingly.

forceful /ˈfɔːsfʊl/ a. powerful; impressive.

force majeure /fɔːs mæˈʒɜː(r)/ n. irresistible compulsion; circumstances beyond one's control. [F]

forcemeat /ˈfɔːsmiːt/ n. meat or other food chopped and seasoned for use as stuffing.

forceps /ˈfɔːseps/ n. (pl. same) surgical pincers.

forcible /ˈfɔːsɪb(ə)l/ a. done by or involving force; forceful.

ford 1 n. shallow place where river etc. may be crossed. 2 v.t. cross (water) at ford.

fore 1 a. situated in front. 2 n. front part; bow of ship. 3 int. Golf warning person in ball's line of flight. 4 **fore-and-aft** (of sails or rigging) set lengthwise, not on yards; **to the fore** conspicuous.

forearm[1] /ˈfɔːrɑːm/ n. arm from elbow to wrist or fingertips.

forearm[2] /fɔːˈrɑːm/ v.t. arm beforehand, prepare.

forebear /ˈfɔːbeə(r)/ n. ancestor.

forebode /fɔːˈbəʊd/ v.t. be advance sign of; portend.

foreboding n. expectation of trouble.

forecast /ˈfɔːkɑːst/ 1 v.t. (past & p.p. **-cast** or **-casted**) predict or estimate beforehand. 2 n. prediction or estimate, esp. of coming weather.

forecastle /ˈfəʊks(ə)l/ n. forward part of ship where formerly crew was accommodated.

foreclose /fɔːˈkləʊz/ v. gain possession of mortgaged property of (person) on non-payment of money due; stop (mortgage) from being redeemable; exclude, prevent. **foreclosure** n.

forecourt /ˈfɔːkɔːt/ n. enclosed space in front of building; part of filling station where petrol is supplied.

foredoom /fɔːˈduːm/ v.t. doom beforehand; predestine.

forefather /ˈfɔːfɑːðə(r)/ n. (usu. in pl.) ancestor, member of past generation etc.

forefinger /ˈfɔːfɪŋɡə(r)/ n. finger next to thumb.

forefoot /ˈfɔːfʊt/ n. (pl. **-feet**) front foot of animal.

forefront /ˈfɔːfrʌnt/ n. foremost part.

foregoing /fɔːˈɡəʊɪŋ/ a. previously mentioned.

foregone /ˈfɔːɡɒn/ a. previous, preceeding. **foregone conclusion** easily foreseeable result.

foreground /ˈfɔːɡraʊnd/ n. part of view nearest observer.

forehand /ˈfɔːhænd/ 1 n. Tennis etc. stroke made with palm turned forwards. 2 a. of or made with this stroke.

forehead /ˈfɒrɪd or ˈfɔːhed/ n. part of face above eyebrows.

foreign /ˈfɒrən/ a. of or in or with or characteristic of country or language other than one's own; of another district or society etc.; dissimilar or irrelevant to; introduced from outside.

foreigner /ˈfɒrənə(r)/ n. person born in or coming from another country.

foreknow /fɔːˈnəʊ/ v.t. (past **-knew**; p.p. **-known**) know beforehand. **foreknowledge** (/-ˈnɒlɪdʒ/) n.

foreland /ˈfɔːlənd/ n. promontory, cape.

foreleg /ˈfɔːleɡ/ n. animal's front leg.

forelock /ˈfɔːlɒk/ n. lock of hair just above forehead.

foreman /ˈfɔːmən/ n. (pl. **-men**) workman superintending others; principal juror.

foremast /ˈfɔːmɑːst/ n. mast nearest bow of ship.

foremost /ˈfɔːməʊst/ 1 a. first in place or order; chief, best. 2 adv. first.

forename /ˈfɔːneɪm/ n. first or Christian name.

forenoon /ˈfɔːnuːn/ n. arch. day till noon, morning.

forensic /fəˈrenzɪk/ a. of courts of law. **forensic medicine** application of medical knowledge to legal problems.

foreordain /fɔːrɔːˈdeɪn/ v.t. predestine.

foreplay /ˈfɔːpleɪ/ n. stimulation preceding sexual intercourse.

forerunner /ˈfɔːrʌnə(r)/ n. predecessor; advance messenger.

foresail /ˈfɔːseɪl/ n. principal sail on foremast.

foresee /fɔːˈsiː/ v.t. (past **-saw**; p.p. **-seen**) see or be aware of beforehand.

foreshadow /fɔːˈʃædəʊ/ v.t. be warning or indication of (future event).

foreshore /fɔːˈʃɔː(r)/ n. shore between high- and low-water marks.

foreshorten /fɔːˈʃɔːt(ə)n/ v.t. show or portray (object) with the apparent shortening due to visual perspective.

foresight /ˈfɔːsaɪt/ n. care for future; foreseeing.

foreskin /ˈfɔːskɪn/ n. loose skin covering end of penis.

forest /ˈfɒrɪst/ 1 n. large area of land covered chiefly with trees and undergrowth. 2 v.t. plant with trees; make into forest.

forestall /fɔːˈstɔːl/ v.t. act in advance of in order to prevent; deal with beforehand.

forester /ˈfɒrɪstə(r)/ n. officer in charge of forest; dweller in forest.

forestry /ˈfɒrɪstrɪ/ n. management of forests.

foretaste /ˈfɔːteɪst/ n. taste or experience of something in advance.

foretell /fɔːˈtel/ v.t. (past & p.p. **-told**) predict, prophesy; be precursor of.

forethought /ˈfɔːθɔːt/ n. care for the future; deliberate intention.

forever /fəˈrevə(r)/ adv. always, constantly.

forewarn /fɔːˈwɔːn/ v.t. warn beforehand.

forewoman /ˈfɔːwʊmən/ n. (pl. **-women** /-ˈwɪmɪn/) woman worker supervising others; woman foreman of jury.

foreword /ˈfɔːwɜːd/ n. preface.

forfeit /ˈfɔːfɪt/ 1 n. thing surrendered as a penalty. 2 v.t. lose or surrender as penalty. 3 a. lost or surrendered as a penalty. 4 **forfeiture** n.

forfend /fɔːˈfend/ v.t. arch. avert.

forgather /fɔːˈɡæðə(r)/ v.i. assemble; associate.

forgave past of **forgive**.

forge[1] 1 n. furnace etc. for melting or refining metal; workshop with this. 2 v. make or write in fraudulent imitation; shape by heating and hammering.

forge[2] v.i. advance gradually. **forge ahead** advance rapidly, take lead.

forgery /ˈfɔːdʒərɪ/ n. (making of) forged document.

forget /fəˈɡet/ v. (past **-got**; p.p. **-gotten**) lose remembrance of; neglect, overlook; cease to think of. **forget-**

me-not plant with small blue flowers; **forget oneself** act without due dignity, neglect one's interests.

forgetful /fə'getfʊl/ *a.* liable to forget.

forgive /fə'gɪv/ *v.t.* (*past* **-gave**; *p.p.* **-given** /-'gɪv(ə)n/) cease to resent; pardon; remit (debt). **forgiveness** *n.*

forgo /fɔː'gəʊ/ *v.t.* (*past* **-went**; *p.p.* **-gone** /-gɒn/) go without, relinquish.

fork 1 *n.* pronged instrument used in eating and cooking etc.; pronged implement for digging etc.; (place of) divergence into branches or limbs etc.; forked part, esp. of bicycle frame. 2 *v.* form fork; branch; take one road at fork; dig with fork. 3 **fork-lift (truck)** vehicle with pronged device for lifting and carrying loads; **fork out** *sl.* pay, usu. unwillingly.

forlorn /fə'lɔːn/ *a.* forsaken; in pitiful condition. **forlorn hope** the only faint hope that remains.

form 1 *n.* shape, arrangement of parts, visible aspect; mode in which thing exists or manifests itself; document with blanks to be filled up; class in school; behaviour according to rule or custom; set order of words; (of horse, athlete, etc.) condition of health and training; bench. 2 *v.* fashion, mould; take shape, become solid; make up, amount to; *Mil.* draw up in order, assume (formation).

formal /'fɔːm(ə)l/ *a.* according to recognized forms or rules; ceremonial, conventional; or of concerned with form; done as a matter of form, perfunctory; prim, stiff.

formaldehyde /fɔː'mældɪhaɪd/ *n.* colourless gas used in solution as preservative and disinfectant.

formalin /'fɔːməlɪn/ *n.* aqueous solution of formaldehyde.

formalism /'fɔːməlɪz(ə)m/ *n.* strict adherence to or concern with form. **formalist** *n.*

formality /fɔː'mælɪtɪ/ *n.* formal act or conduct; rigid observance of rules or convention.

formalize /'fɔːməlaɪz/ *v.t.* make formal; give definite (esp. legal) form to.

format /'fɔːmæt/ 1 *n.* shape and size (of book etc.); style or manner of arrangement etc. 2 *v.* (*past & p.p.* **formatted**) arrange in format.

formation /fɔː'meɪʃ(ə)n/ *n.* forming; thing formed; particular arrangement

(e.g. of troops); *Geol.* set of rocks or strata with common characteristic.

formative /'fɔːmətɪv/ *a.* serving to form; of formation.

former /'fɔːmə(r)/ 1 *a.* of the past, earlier. 2 *pron.* the first or first-named of two.

formerly *adv.* in former times.

formic acid /'fɔːmɪk/ colourless irritant volatile acid contained in fluid emitted by ants.

formidable /'fɔːmɪdəb(ə)l/ □ See page 665. *a.* inspiring fear or dread; difficult to overcome or resist etc.

formless /'fɔːmlɪs/ *a.* without definite or regular form.

formula /'fɔːmjʊlə/ *n.* (*pl.* **-las** or **-lae** /-liː/) set of chemical symbols showing constituents of substance; rule or fact expressed in figures; fixed form of words; list of ingredients; classification of racing car esp. by engine capacity. **formulaic** /-'leɪɪk/ *a.*

formulate /'fɔːmjʊleɪt/ *v.t.* express in a formula; express clearly and precisely. **formulation** *n.*

fornication /fɔːnɪ'keɪʃ(ə)n/ *n.* voluntary sexual intercourse between unmarried persons. **fornicate** *v.i.*; **fornicator** *n.*

forsake /fə'seɪk/ *v.t.* (*past* **forsook**; *p.p.* **forsaken**) give up, renounce; desert, abandon.

forsooth /fə'suːθ/ *adv.* arch. indeed.

forswear /fɔː'sweə(r)/ *v.t.* (*past* **-swore**; *p.p.* **-sworn**) abjure, renounce; perjure *oneself*; (in *p.p.*) perjured.

forsythia /fɔː'saɪθɪə/ *n.* ornamental shrub with bright yellow flowers.

fort *n.* fortified building or position. **hold the fort** act as temporary substitute.

forte[1] /'fɔːteɪ/ *n.* thing in which one excels.

forte[2] /'fɔːteɪ/ *Mus.* 1 *adv.* loudly. 2 *n.* passage to be performed thus.

forth /fɔːθ/ *adv.* forward; out of doors; onwards in time. **forthcoming** about to come forth, approaching, produced when wanted, informative or responsive; **forthright** straightforward, outspoken, decisive; **forthwith** immediately, without delay.

fortieth see **forty**.

fortification /fɔːtɪfɪ'keɪʃ(ə)n/ *n.* fortifying; (usu. in *pl.*) defensive work(s).

fortify /'fɔːtɪfaɪ/ v.t. strengthen; provide with defensive works; strengthen (wine etc.) with spirits; add extra nutrients to (food).

fortissimo /fɔː'tɪsɪməʊ/ Mus. **1** adv. very loudly. **2** n. (pl **-mos**) passage to be performed thus.

fortitude /'fɔːtɪtjuːd/ n. courage in pain or adversity.

fortnight /'fɔːtnaɪt/ n. two weeks.

fortnightly **1** a. done or produced or occurring once a fortnight. **2** adv. every fortnight. **3.** n. fortnightly magazine etc.

Fortran /'fɔːtræn/ n. computer language used esp. for scientific calculations.

fortress /'fɔːtrɪs/ n. fortified building or town.

fortuitous /fɔː'tjuːɪtəs/ a. happening by chance. **fortuity** n.

fortunate /'fɔːtjʊnət/ a. lucky, auspicious.

fortune /'fɔːtjuːn/ n. chance as power in human affairs; luck; person's destiny; prosperity, wealth; large sum of money. **fortune-teller** foreteller of future events etc.

forty /'fɔːtɪ/ a. & n. four times ten. **forty winks** short sleep. **fortieth** a. & n.

forum /'fɔːrəm/ n. place of public discussion; court, tribunal.

forward /'fɔːwəd/ **1** a. lying in one's line of motion, onward or towards front; relating to the future; precocious, presumptuous, pert; well-advanced. **2** n. attacking player in football etc. **3** adv. towards future; to front; progressively. **4** v.t. send (letter etc.) on; dispatch; help to advance, promote.

forwards adv. forward.

forwent past of forgo.

fosse /fɒs/ n. canal, ditch, trench.

fossil /fɒs(ə)l/ **1** n. remains or impression of (usu. prehistoric) plant or animal hardened in rock; antiquated or unchanging person or thing. **2** a. of or like fossil; dug from the ground.

fossilize /'fɒsəlaɪz/ v. (cause to) become fossil. **fossilization** n.

foster /'fɒstə(r)/ **1** v.t. promote growth of; nurse or bring up as foster-child; encourage or harbour (feeling). **2** a. having family connection by fostering and not birth. **3** **foster home** home in which foster-child is brought up.

fought past & p.p. of **fight**.

foul /faʊl/ **1** a. offensive, loathsome, stinking; dirty, soiled; obscene; (of weather) wet, rough; containing noxious matter; clogged, choked; unfair, against rules; in collision, entangled, etc. **2** n. foul blow or stroke etc.; collision, entanglement. **3** adv. unfairly. **4** v. make or become foul; commit foul on (player); entangle; become entangled; collide with. **5** **foul-mouthed** using obscene language; **foul play** unfair play, treacherous dealing, violence, murder; **foul up** block or jam (traffic etc.), make dirty or unpleasant. **6** **foully** /'faʊlɪ/ adv.

foulard /fuː'lɑːd/ n. thin soft smooth material of silk etc.

found[1] /faʊnd/ v.t. establish, originate; lay base of; base, build up.

found[2] /faʊnd/ v.t. melt and mould (metal), fuse (materials for glass); make thus.

found[3] past & p.p. of **find**.

foundation /faʊn'deɪʃ(ə)n/ n. (establishing of) endowed institution; solid ground or base; basis; underlying principle; base for application of cosmetics. **foundation garment** woman's supporting undergarment; **foundation-stone** one laid with ceremony to celebrate founding of building.

founder /'faʊndə(r)/ v.i. (of horse) collapse, fall lame; (of rider) fall to ground; (of plan) fail; (of ship) fill with water and sink.

foundling /'faʊndlɪŋ/ n. deserted infant of unknown parents.

foundry /'faʊndrɪ/ n. factory or workshop for founding metal or glass etc.

fount[1] /faʊnt/ n. set of printing type of same size and face.

fount[2] /faʊnt/ n. source, spring, fountain.

fountain /'faʊntɪn/ n. artificial jet(s) of water; spring; source. **fountain-head** source; **fountain-pen** pen with reservoir holding ink.

four /fɔː(r)/ a. & n. one more than three; 4-oared boat or its crew. **four-in-hand** vehicle with 4 horses driven by one person; **four-poster** bed with 4 posts supporting canopy; **foursome** party of 4, game between two pairs; **four-square** firmly placed, steady; **four-wheel** acting on all 4 wheels of vehicle. **fourfold** *a. & adv.*

fourteen /fɔːˈtiːn/ *a. & n.* one more than thirteen. **fourteenth** *a. & n.*

fourth /fɔːθ/ *a. & n.* next after third; one of four equal parts of thing.

fowl /faʊl/ **1** *n.* domestic cock or hen kept for eggs and flesh; bird. **2** *v.i.* hunt or shoot or snare wildfowl.

fox **1** *n.* wild four-legged animal with red fur and bushy tail; its fur; crafty person. **2** *v.t.* deceive; puzzle; discolour with brown spots. **3 foxglove** tall plant with purple or white flowers; **foxhole** *Mil.* hole in ground as shelter against missiles or as firing-point; **foxhound** hound bred to hunt foxes; **fox-terrier** small short-haired terrier; **foxtrot** ballroom dance with slow and quick steps.

foxy /ˈfɒksɪ/ *a.* foxlike; sly or cunning; reddish-brown.

foyer /ˈfɔɪeɪ/ *n.* entrance hall or open space of hotel or theatre etc.

Fr. *abbr.* Father; French.

fr. *abbr.* franc(s).

fracas /ˈfrækɑː/ *n.* (*pl.* same *pr.* /-kɑːz/) noisy quarrel.

fraction /ˈfrækʃ(ə)n/ *n.* numerical quantity that is not a whole number; small part or amount etc.; portion of mixture obtainable by distillation etc. **fractional** *a.*

fractious /ˈfrækʃəs/ *a.* unruly, peevish.

fracture /ˈfræktʃə(r)/ **1** *n.* breakage, esp. of bone. **2** *v.* cause fracture in, suffer fracture.

fragile /ˈfrædʒaɪl/ *a.* easily broken; of delicate constitution. **fragility** /-ˈdʒɪl-/ *n.*

fragment /ˈfrægmənt/ **1** *n.* part broken off; remains of otherwise lost whole. **2** *v.* (also /fræɡˈment/) break into fragments. **3 fragmentary** *a.*; **fragmentation** *n.*

fragrance /ˈfreɪɡrəns/ *n.* being fragrant; perfume.

fragrant /ˈfreɪɡrənt/ *a.* sweet-smelling.

frail *a.* fragile, delicate; morally weak.

frailty /ˈfreɪltɪ/ *n.* frail quality; weakness, foible.

frame **1** *v.t.* construct, put together or devise; adapt, fit; articulate (words); set in frame; serve as frame for; *sl.* concoct false accusation or contrive evidence against. **2** *n.* case or border enclosing picture etc.; construction, build, structure; framework; single picture on cinema film or transmitted by television; glazed structure to protect plants. **3 frame-up** *sl.* conspiracy, esp. to make innocent person appear guilty; **framework** essential supporting structure, basic system.

franc /fræŋk/ *n.* French or Belgian or Swiss etc. monetary unit.

franchise /ˈfræntʃaɪz/ *n.* right to vote; citizenship; authorization to sell company's goods etc. in particular area.

Franciscan /frænˈsɪskən/ **1** *a.* of order of St Francis. **2** *n.* Franciscan monk or nun.

frank **1** *a.* candid, open; outspoken; undisguised. **2** *v.t.* mark (letter etc.) to record payment of postage. **3** *n.* franking signature or mark.

frankfurter /ˈfræŋkfɜːtə(r)/ *n.* seasoned smoked sausage.

frankincense /ˈfræŋkɪnsens/ *n.* aromatic gum resin burnt as incense.

frantic /ˈfræntɪk/ *a.* wildly excited; characterized by great hurry or anxiety; desperate, violent.

fraternal /frəˈtɜːn(ə)l/ *a.* of brothers, brotherly.

fraternity /frəˈtɜːnɪtɪ/ *n.* religious body, guild, etc.; brotherliness; *US* male students' society in university etc.

fraternize /ˈfrætənaɪz/ *v.i.* associate, make friends. **fraternization** *n.*

fratricide /ˈfrætrɪsaɪd/ *n.* killing of one's brother or sister; person who does this.

fraud *n.* criminal deception; dishonest trick; impostor; disappointing person etc.

fraudulent /ˈfrɔːdjʊlənt/ *a.* of or involving or guilty of fraud. **fraudulence** *n.*

fraught /frɔːt/ *a.* filled or attended *with* (danger etc.); *colloq.* causing or suffering anxiety.

fray[1] *v.* rub; make or become ragged at edge.

fray[2] *n.* fight, conflict; brawl.

frazzle /ˈfræz(ə)l/ *n. colloq.* worn or exhausted state.

FRG *abbr.* Federal Republic of Germany (West Germany).

freak /friːk/ 1 *n.* capricious or unusual idea etc.; monstrosity; abnormal person or thing. 2 *v. sl.* (with *out*) (cause to) undergo drug etc. hallucinations or strong emotional experience; adopt unconventional life-style. 3 **freakish** *a.*

freckle /ˈfrek(ə)l/ 1 *n.* light brown spot on skin. 2 *v.* spot or be spotted with freckles.

free 1 *a.* (*compar.* **freer**; *superl.* **freest**) not a slave; at liberty; having personal rights and social and political liberty; unrestricted, unimpeded, not confined; spontaneous; not charged for; disengaged, available, permitted; lavish, unreserved; (of translation) not literal. 2 *adv.* freely; without cost or charge. 3 *v.t.* (*past & p.p.* **freed**) make free, set at liberty; disentangle. 4 **freeboard** part of ship's side between waterline and deck; **Free Church** a nonconformist Church; **free enterprise** freedom of private business from State control; **free fall** movement under force of gravity only; **free hand** liberty to act at one's own discretion; **free-hand** (of drawing) done without ruler or compasses etc.; **free house** public house not controlled by brewery; **free lance** person working for no fixed employer; **free-loader** *sl.* person who eats etc. at other's expense; **freeman** holder of freedom of city etc.; **free port** one open to all traders alike; **free-range** (of hens etc.) given freedom of movement in seeking food, (of eggs) from hens kept thus; **free-standing** not supported by another structure; **free-thinker** person who rejects authority in religious belief; **free trade** commerce left to its natural course without customs duties; **freeway** express highway; **free wheel** (in bicycle) driving-wheel able to revolve while pedals are at rest; **freewheel** ride bicycle with pedals stationary, drive car with clutch disengaged; **free will** power of directing one's actions voluntarily.

freebooter /ˈfriːbuːtə(r)/ *n.* pirate.

freedom /ˈfriːdəm/ *n.* being free; personal or civil liberty; liberty of action; undue familiarity; exemption (*from*); unrestricted use (*of*); membership or honorary citizenship (*of* company, city, etc.).

freehold /ˈfriːhəʊld/ *n.* land etc. held by owner in absolute possession; this tenure. **freeholder** *n.*

Freemason /ˈfriːmeɪs(ə)n/ *n.* member of society for mutual help etc. having elaborate secret rituals. **Freemasonry** *n.*

freesia /ˈfriːʒə/ *n.* fragrant flowering plant.

freeze 1 *v.* (*past* **froze**; *p.p.* **frozen**) turn into ice or other solid by cold; cover or be covered with ice; feel extreme cold; make or become cold and rigid, congeal or chill or be chilled by frost or cold or fear etc.; preserve (food) by refrigeration below freezing-point; fix at certain level; make (assets etc.) unrealizable, stabilize (prices etc.). 2 *n.* state of frost; coming or period of frost; fixing or stabilization of prices or wages etc. 3 **freeze-dry** freeze and dry by evaporation of ice in high vacuum; **freeze up** freeze completely, obstruct by formation of ice etc.; **freezing-point** temperature at which liquid freezes.

freezer *n.* refrigerated container or compartment in which food is preserved at very low temperature.

freight /freɪt/ 1 *n.* transport of goods by water or (*US*) land; goods transported, cargo; charge for transport of goods. 2 *v.t.* transport (goods) by freight; load (ship etc.).

freighter /ˈfreɪtə(r)/ *n.* ship or aircraft designed to carry freight.

French 1 *a.* of France. 2 *n.* French language; *the* French people. 3 **French bean** kind used as unripe pods or as ripe seeds; **French bread** bread in long crisp loaf; **French chalk** powdered talc used as marker or dry lubricant etc.; **French dressing** salad dressing of oil and vinegar; **French fried potatoes, French fries,** chips; **French horn** brass wind instrument with coiled tube; **French letter** *colloq.* condom; **Frenchman, Frenchwoman,** native of France; **French polish** shellac polish for wood; **French window** glazed door in outside wall.

frenetic /frəˈnetɪk/ *a.* frantic, frenzied. **frenetically** *adv.*

frenzy /ˈfrenzɪ/ 1 *n.* wild excitement;

delirious fury. **2** *v.t.* (usu. in *p.p.*) drive to frenzy.

frequency /ˈfriːkwənsɪ/ *n.* frequent occurrence; *Phys.* rate of recurrence (of vibration etc.); *Electr.* number of cycles of carrier wave per second.

frequent **1** /ˈfriːkwənt/ *a.* often occurring, common; habitual. **2** /frɪˈkwent/ *v.t.* go often or habitually to.

fresco /ˈfreskəʊ/ *n.* (*pl.* **-cos** *or* **-coes**) painting done in water-colour on fresh plaster.

fresh **1** *a.* newly made or obtained; not previously known or used; lately arrived *from*; not stale or faded; (of food) not preserved by tinning or freezing etc.; (of water) not salt; pure, untainted; refreshing; cheeky, amorously impudent; inexperienced. **2** *adv.* newly, recently.

freshen /ˈfreʃ(ə)n/ *v.* make or become fresh.

fresher /ˈfreʃə(r)/ *n.* freshman.

freshet /ˈfreʃɪt/ *n.* river flood.

freshman /ˈfreʃmən/ *n.* (*pl.* **-men**) university student in first year.

fret[1] **1** *v.* worry; annoy; distress oneself with regret or discontent; consume by gnawing or rubbing. **2** *n.* irritation, vexation.

fret[2] **1** *n.* ornamental pattern of continuous combinations of straight lines joined usu. at right angles. **2** *v.t.* adorn with fret etc. **3 fretsaw** narrow saw stretched on frame for cutting thin wood in patterns etc.; **fretwork** wood cut in patterns.

fret[3] *n.* bar or ridge on finger-board of guitar etc.

fretful /ˈfretfʊl/ *a.* querulous.

Freudian /ˈfrɔɪdɪən/ **1** *a.* of Freud's system of psychoanalysis. **2** *n.* adherent of Freud. **3 Freudian slip** unintentional error that seems to reveal subconscious feelings.

Fri. *abbr.* Friday.

friable /ˈfraɪəb(ə)l/ *a.* easily crumbled. **friability** *n.*

friar /ˈfraɪə(r)/ *n.* member of certain religious orders of men.

friary /ˈfraɪərɪ/ *n.* monastery of friars.

fricassee /ˈfrɪkəsiː/ **1** *n.* dish of fried or stewed pieces of meat with sauce. **2** *v.t.* make fricassee of.

fricative /ˈfrɪkətɪv/ **1** *a.* made by fric-

tion of breath in narrow opening. **2** *n.* fricative consonant.

friction /ˈfrɪkʃ(ə)n/ *n.* rubbing of one object against another; resistance object encounters in moving over another; *fig.* clash of wills or temperaments etc.

Friday /ˈfraɪdeɪ/ *n.* day of week following Thursday.

fridge *n. colloq.* refrigerator.

friend /frend/ *n.* person, usu. not relation or lover, who feels mutual affection and regard for another; sympathizer, helper; person who is not an enemy; **Friend** member of Society of Friends, Quaker.

friendly /ˈfrendlɪ/ *a.* acting or disposed to act as friend; on amicable terms. **Friendly Society** society for insurance against sickness etc. **friendliness** *n.*

friendship /ˈfrendʃɪp/ *n.* friendly relationship or feeling.

frieze /friːz/ *n.* part of entablature between architrave and cornice; band of decoration, esp. along wall near ceiling.

frigate /ˈfrɪɡət/ *n.* naval escort vessel like large corvette.

fright /fraɪt/ *n.* sudden or violent fear; grotesque-looking person.

frighten /ˈfraɪt(ə)n/ *v.t.* fill with fright; drive *away* or *into* etc. by fright.

frightful /ˈfraɪtfʊl/ *a.* dreadful, shocking; ugly; *colloq.* very great.

frigid /ˈfrɪdʒɪd/ *a.* lacking enthusiasm; dull; (of woman) sexually unresponsive; cold. **frigidity** *n.*

frill **1** *n.* ornamental strip of material or paper etc. gathered at one edge; in *pl.* unnecessary elaboration. **2** *v.t.* decorate with frill. **3 frilly** *a.*

fringe /frɪndʒ/ **1** *n.* bordering of loose threads or tassels or twists; front hair hanging over forehead; border, outskirts, margin; area or part of minor importance. **2** *v.t.* adorn with fringe; serve as fringe to. **3 fringe benefit** employee's benefit additional to wage or salary.

frippery /ˈfrɪpərɪ/ *n.* finery, needless or tawdry ornament; trifles.

frisk **1** *v.* leap or skip playfully; *sl.* search (person). **2** *n.* playful leap or skip.

frisky /ˈfrɪskɪ/ *a.* lively, playful.

fritter[1] /ˈfrɪtə(r)/ *v.t.* throw *away* in trifling and wasteful way.

fritter[2] /ˈfrɪtə(r)/ *n.* fried batter containing slice of fruit or meat etc.

frivolous /ˈfrɪvələs/ *a.* paltry, trifling; silly. **frivolity** /-ˈvɒl-/ *n.*

frizz 1 *v.* form (hair) into mass of small curls. 2 *n.* frizzed hair or state. 3 **frizzy** *a.*

frizzle[1] /ˈfrɪz(ə)l/ *v.* fry or toast or grill with sputtering noise; burn or shrivel *up*.

frizzle[2] /ˈfrɪz(ə)l/ 1 *v.* frizz (hair). 2 *n.* frizzed hair or state.

fro *adv.* **to and fro** backwards and forwards.

frock *n.* woman's or child's dress; monk's or priest's gown. **frock-coat** man's long-skirted coat not cut away in front.

frog[1] *n.* tailless amphibian with long web-footed hind legs. **frogman** underwater swimmer equipped with rubber suit and flippers; **frogmarch** hustle forward after seizing from behind and pinning arms.

frog[2] *n.* ornamental coat-fastening of spindle-shaped button and loop.

frolic /ˈfrɒlɪk/ 1 *v.i.* play about cheerfully. 2 *n.* prank, merry-making.

frolicsome /ˈfrɒlɪksəm/ *a.* playful.

from *prep.* expr. separation or origin.

frond *n.* leaf-like organ of ferns etc.

front /frʌnt/ 1 *n.* side or part normally nearer or towards spectator or direction of motion; scene of actual fighting; combination of forces etc. to achieve end; organized political group; appearance, demeanour; person etc. serving to cover subversive or illegal activities; part of seaside resort facing sea; *Meteor.* boundary between warm-air and cold-air masses; auditorium of theatre. 2 *a.* of or at front. 3 *v.* have front facing or directed (*on, to, towards,* etc.); *sl.* act as front *for*; furnish with front. 4 **front bench** seats for leading members of Government and Opposition in Parliament; **front line** foremost position of army in battle; **front runner** leading contestant.

frontage /ˈfrʌntɪdʒ/ *n.* land abutting on street or water; extent of front; front of building.

frontal /ˈfrʌnt(ə)l/ *a.* of or on front; of forehead.

frontier /ˈfrʌntɪə(r)/ *n.* boundary between States; border of settled or inhabited part; limits of attainment in science etc.

frontispiece /ˈfrʌntɪspiːs/ *n.* illustration facing title-page of book etc.

frost 1 *n.* freezing; frozen dew or vapour. 2 *v.t.* cover (as) with frost; injure (plant etc.) with frost; roughen surface of (glass etc.), make opaque. 3 **frost-bite** injury to body tissue due to freezing.

frosting /ˈfrɒstɪŋ/ *n.* icing for cakes.

frosty /ˈfrɒstɪ/ *a.* cold with frost; unfriendly.

froth /frɒθ/ 1 *n.* foam; idle talk. 2 *v.i.* emit or gather froth. 3 **frothy** *a.*

frown /fraʊn/ *v.* wrinkle brows; express displeasure or deep thought. 2 *n.* action of frowning, look of displeasure or deep thought.

frowsty /ˈfraʊstɪ/ *a.* stuffy, fusty.

frowzy /ˈfraʊzɪ/ *a.* fusty; slatternly, dingy.

froze, frozen *past* & *p.p.* of **freeze**.

FRS *abbr.* Fellow of the Royal Society.

fructify /ˈfrʌktɪfaɪ/ *v.* bear fruit; make fruitful. **fructification** *n.*

fructose /ˈfrʌktəʊz/ *n.* kind of sugar found in fruits and honey.

frugal /ˈfruːg(ə)l/ *a.* sparing, economical. **frugality** *n.*

fruit /fruːt/ 1 *n.* product of plant or tree that contains seed, this used as food; (usu. in *pl.*) vegetable products fit for food; product, result. 2 *v.i.* bear fruit. 3 **fruit-cake** cake containing dried fruit; **fruit machine** kind of slot-machine for gambling; **fruit sugar** fructose.

fruiterer /ˈfruːtərə(r)/ *n.* dealer in fruit.

fruitful /ˈfruːtfʊl/ *a.* fertile, prolific; productive.

fruition /fruːˈɪʃ(ə)n/ *n.* realization of aims or hopes etc.

fruitless /ˈfruːtlɪs/ *a.* not bearing fruit; useless, unsuccessful.

fruity /ˈfruːtɪ/ *a.* of or resembling fruit; of strong or rich quality. **fruitiness** *n.*

frump *n.* dowdy old-fashioned woman. **frumpish** *a.*; **frumpy** *a.*

frustrate /frʌsˈtreɪt/ *v.t.* prevent from achieving purpose; disappoint. **frustration** *n.*

fry[1] 1 *v.* cook in hot fat. 2 *n.* internal parts of animals, usu. eaten fried; fried food. **3 frying-pan** shallow long-handled pan for frying.

fry² /fraɪ/ *n.* young or freshly hatched fishes. **small fry** unimportant people, children.

ft. *abbr.* foot, feet.

fuchsia /'fjuːʃə/ *n.* ornamental shrub with drooping flowers.

fuddle /'fʌd(ə)l/ **1** *v.t.* intoxicate; confuse. **2** *n.* intoxication; confusion.

fuddy-duddy /'fʌdɪdʌdɪ/ **1** *a. sl.* fussy or old-fashioned. **2** *n.* such person.

fudge 1 *n.* soft toffee-like sweet; nonsense. **2** *v.t.* fit together or make up in makeshift or dishonest way; deal with incompetently.

fuel /'fjuːəl/ **1** *n.* material for burning as fire or as source of heat or power; thing that sustains or inflames passion etc. **2** *v.t.* supply with fuel.

fug *n. colloq.* stuffy atmosphere.

fugal /'fjuːg(ə)l/ *a.* of or resembling fugue.

fugitive /'fjuːdʒɪtɪv/ **1** *a.* fleeing; fleeting, transient. **2** *n.* one who flees (*from*).

fugue /fjuːg/ *n.* piece of music in which short melodic theme is introduced by one part and successively taken up by others.

fulcrum /'fʊlkrəm/ *n.* (*pl.* **-cra**) point against or on which lever is supported.

fulfil /fʊl'fɪl/ *v.t.* carry out; satisfy. **fulfilment** *n.*

full¹ /fʊl/ **1** *a.* holding all its limits will allow; replete; crowded; copious; abundant; complete, perfect; swelling. **2** *adv.* quite, exactly. **3 full back** football player behind half-backs; **full-blooded** vigorous, sensual, not hybrid; **full-bodied** rich in quality or tone etc.; **full brother, sister,** one having both parents the same; **full house** large or full attendance at theatre etc., *Poker* hand with three of a kind and a pair; **full-length** (of mirror, portrait, etc.) showing whole of human figure; **full moon** moon with whole disc illuminated; **full stop** punctuation mark (.) used at end of sentence, complete cessation.

full² /fʊl/ *v.t.* clean and thicken (cloth). **fuller** /'fʊlə(r)/ *n.* person who fulls cloth. **fuller's earth** clay used in fulling.

fully /'fʊlɪ/ *adv.* completely, quite.

fulmar /'fʊlmə(r)/ *n.* kind of petrel.

fulminant /'fʊlmɪnənt/ *a.* fulminating.

fulminate /'fʊlmɪneɪt/ *v.* express censure loudly and forcibly; explode, flash like lightning. **fulmination** *n.*

fulsome /'fʊlsəm/ *a.* cloying, disgustingly excessive. □ See page 666.

fumble /'fʌmb(ə)l/ **1** *v.* grope about; handle or deal with awkwardly. **2** *n.* act of fumbling.

fume 1 *n.* exuded smoke or vapour or gas etc. **2** *v.* emit fumes; be angry or irritated; subject to fumes; darken (oak etc.) thus.

fumigate /'fjuːmɪgeɪt/ *v.t.* subject to fumes, disinfect or purify thus. **fumigation** *n.*; **fumigator** *n.*

fun *n.* sport, amusement; source of this. **fun-fair** fair consisting of amusements and side-shows; **make fun of, poke fun at,** ridicule.

function /'fʌŋkʃ(ə)n/ **1** *n.* work thing is designed to do; official duty; public ceremony or occasion; *Math.* quantity whose value depends on varying values (*of* others). **2** *v.i.* fulfil function; operate.

functional /'fʌŋkʃən(ə)l/ *a.* of or serving a function; shaped, designed, etc. with regard mainly to function; utilitarian.

functionary /'fʌŋkʃənərɪ/ *n.* official.

fund 1 *n.* permanently available stock; stock of money, esp. one set apart for purpose; in *pl.* pecuniary resources. **2** *v.t.* provide with money; make (debt) permanent at fixed interest.

fundamental /fʌndə'ment(ə)l/ **1** *a.* of or serving as base or foundation; essential, primary. **2** *n.* fundamental rule etc.

fundamentalism /fʌndə'mentəlɪz(ə)m/ *n.* strict maintenance of traditional scriptural beliefs. **fundamentalist** *n.*

funeral /'fjuːnər(ə)l/ **1** *n.* burial or cremation of dead with ceremonies. **2** *a.* of or used at funeral.

funerary /'fjuːnərərɪ/ *a.* of funeral(s).

funereal /fjuː'nɪərɪəl/ *a.* of or appropriate to funeral; dismal, dark.

fungicide /'fʌndʒɪsaɪd/ *n.* substance that kills fungus.

fungus /'fʌŋgəs/ *n.* (*pl.* **-gi** /-gaɪ/) mushroom, toadstool, or allied plant;

spongy morbid growth. **fungoid** *a.*;
fungous *a.*

funicular /fjʊ'nɪkjʊlə(r)/ *n.* (in full **funicular railway**) cable railway with
ascending and descending cars
counterbalanced.

funk 1 *n. sl.* fear, panic; coward. 2 *v.* be
afraid of; evade, shirk.

funky /'fʌŋkɪ/ *a.* (of music etc.) un-
complicated, swinging, fashionable.

funnel /'fʌn(ə)l/ 1 *n.* narrowing tube
for guiding liquid etc. into small opening; chimney of steam-engine or ship. 2
v. (cause to) move (as) through funnel.

funny /'fʌnɪ/ *a.* comical, amusing;
strange. **funny-bone** part of elbow
over which ulnar nerve passes.

fur 1 *n.* short fine hair of some animals;
animal skin with fur on it; garment
made of or trimmed or lined with this;
collect. furred animals; crust or coating.
2 *v.* provide, clothe, coat, with fur; become coated with fur.

furbelow /'fɜːbɪləʊ/ *n.* flounce; pleated
border; in *pl.* showy ornaments.

furbish /'fɜːbɪʃ/ *v.t.* polish *up*;
renovate.

furcate /'fɜːkeɪt/ 1 *a.* forked, branched.
2 *v.* fork, divide. 3 **furcation** *n.*

furious /'fjʊərɪəs/ *a.* very angry, violent; raging, frantic.

furl *v.* roll up (sail, umbrella); become
furled.

furlong /'fɜːlɒŋ/ *n.* eighth of mile.

furlough /'fɜːləʊ/ *n.* leave of absence.

furnace /'fɜːnɪs/ *n.* apparatus with
chamber for applying intense heat;
closed fireplace for heating building;
very hot place.

furnish /'fɜːnɪʃ/ *v.t.* fit up with furniture; provide (*with*).

furniture /'fɜːnɪtʃə(r)/ *n.* movable contents of building or room; rigging and
stores etc. of ship; accessories, e.g.
handles and locks on doors.

furore /fjʊə'rɔːrɪ/ *n.* uproar; outburst
of popular enthusiasm.

furrier /'fʌrɪə(r)/ *n.* dealer in or
dresser of furs.

furrow /'fʌrəʊ/ 1 *n.* narrow trench
made by plough; rut; wrinkle. 2 *v.t.*
plough; make furrows in.

furry /'fɜːrɪ/ *a.* having or resembling
fur.

further /'fɜːðə(r)/ 1 *adv.* more far in
space or time; more, to greater extent;

in addition. 2 *a.* more distant or advanced; more, additional. 3 *v.t.*
promote, favour. 4 **further education**
education for persons above school
age; **furthermore** in addition, besides;
furthermost most distant.

furtherance /'fɜːðərəns/ *n.* furthering
(*of* plan etc.).

furthest /'fɜːðɪst/ 1 *a.* most distant. 2
adv. to or at the greatest distance.

furtive /'fɜːtɪv/ *a.* sly, stealthy.

fury /'fjʊərɪ/ *n.* fierce passion, wild
anger; violence; avenging spirit; angry
woman.

furze *n.* spiny yellow-flowered shrub,
gorse. **furzy** *a.*

fuse[1] /fjuːz/ 1 *v.* melt with intense heat;
blend (as) by melting; supply with
fuse(s); be put out of action by blowing
of fuse; cause fuse(s) of to blow. 2 *n.*
easily melted wire in circuit, designed
to melt when circuit is overloaded.

fuse[2] /fjuːz/ 1 *n.* cord etc. made so as to
burn in order to ignite explosive. 2 *v.t.*
fit fuse to.

fuselage /'fjuːzəlɑːʒ/ *n.* body of
aircraft.

fusible /'fjuːzɪb(ə)l/ *a.* that may be
melted. **fusibility** *n.*

fusilier /fjuːzɪ'lɪə(r)/ *n.* soldier of some
regiments formerly armed with light
muskets.

fusillade /fjuːzɪ'leɪd/ *n.* continuous
discharge of firearms; sustained outburst of criticism etc.

fusion /'fjuːʒ(ə)n/ *n.* fusing; blending,
coalition; (in full **nuclear fusion**)
union of atomic nuclei to form heavier
nuclei with release of energy.

fuss 1 *n.* bustle; excessive commotion;
excessive concern about trivial thing;
sustained protest. 2 *v.* make fuss; bustle; agitate, worry. 3 **fuss-pot** *colloq.*
person who is always making a fuss;
make a fuss complain vigorously;
make a fuss of treat with (excessive)
attention.

fussy /'fʌsɪ/ *a.* inclined to fuss; over-
elaborate; fastidious. **fussiness** *n.*

fustian /'fʌstɪən/ 1 *n.* thick twilled cotton cloth; bombast. 2 *a.* made of fustian;
bombastic, worthless.

fusty /'fʌstɪ/ *a.* musty, stuffy; stale-
smelling; antiquated. **fustiness** *n.*

futon /'fuːtɒn/ *n.* light orig. Japanese
kind of mattress.

futile /'fju:taɪl/ a. useless, frivolous, worthless. **futility** /-'tɪl-/ n.

future /'fju:tʃə(r)/ **1** a. about to happen or be or become; of time to come; *Gram.* (of tense) describing event yet to happen. **2** n. time to come; future condition or events etc.; prospect of success etc.

futurism /'fju:tʃərɪz(ə)m/ a. artistic and literary movement departing violently from tradition. **futurist** a. & n.

futuristic /fju:tʃə'rɪstɪk/ a. ultra-modern; pertaining to future; of futurism.

futurity /fju:'tjʊərɪtɪ/ n. future time, events, etc.

fuzz n. fluff; fluffy or frizzy hair; *sl.* police(man).

fuzzy /'fʌzɪ/ a. fluffy, frizzy; blurred, indistinct. **fuzziness** n.

G

g. *abbr.* gram(s).

gab *n. colloq.* talk, chatter.

gabardine /ˈgæbədiːn/ *n.* a strong twilled cloth.

gabble /ˈgæb(ə)l/ 1 *v.* talk or utter inarticulately or too fast. 2 *n.* rapid talk.

gabby /ˈgæbɪ/ *a. colloq.* talkative.

gaberdine var. of **gabardine**.

gable /ˈgeɪb(ə)l/ *n.* triangular part of wall at end of ridged roof.

gad *v.i.* go about idly or in search of pleasure. **gadabout** gadding person.

gadfly /ˈgædflaɪ/ *n.* cattle-biting fly.

gadget /ˈgædʒɪt/ *n.* small mechanical device or tool. **gadgetry** *n.*

Gaelic /ˈgeɪlɪk or ˈgælɪk/ *n.* Celtic language of Scots or Irish.

gaff 1 *n.* stick with hook for landing fish; barbed fishing-spear. 2 *v.t.* seize with gaff.

gaff *n. sl.* **blow the gaff** let out secret.

gaffe /gæf/ *n.* blunder, *faux pas.*

gaffer /ˈgæfə(r)/ *n. colloq.* old man; foreman, boss.

gag 1 *n.* thing thrust into mouth to prevent speech or hold it open etc.; joke, comic business, etc. 2 *v.* apply gag to, silence; make jokes; choke, retch.

gaga /ˈgɑːgɑː/ *a.* fatuous, senile.

gage¹ *n.* pledge, security; challenge.

gage² *n.* greengage.

gaggle /ˈgæg(ə)l/ *n.* flock (of geese); disorderly group.

gaiety /ˈgeɪətɪ/ *n.* being gay, mirth; amusement, merry-making.

gaily /ˈgeɪlɪ/ *adv.* in gay manner.

gain 1 *v.* obtain, secure; acquire, earn; improve or advance; (of clock etc.) become fast (by); win; reach; persuade. 2 *n.* increase of wealth, profit; money-making.

gainful /ˈgeɪnfʊl/ *a.* lucrative; paid.

gainsay /geɪnˈseɪ/ *v.t.* (*past & p.p.* **-said** /-ˈsed/) deny, contradict.

gait *n.* manner of or carriage in walking.

gaiter /ˈgeɪtə(r)/ *n.* covering of leather etc. for leg or ankle.

gal. *abbr.* gallon(s).

gala /ˈgɑːlə/ *n.* festive occasion; festive gathering for sports.

galactic /gəˈlæktɪk/ *a.* of galaxy.

galantine /ˈgæləntiːn/ *n.* cold dish of meat in jelly.

galaxy /ˈgæləksɪ/ *n.* independent system of stars etc. existing in space; brilliant company. **the Galaxy** Milky Way.

gale *n.* strong wind; outburst, esp. of laughter.

gall¹ /gɔːl/ *n.* bile; *colloq.* impudence; asperity, rancour. **gall-bladder** sac in body containing bile; **gallstone** small hard mass that forms in gall-bladder.

gall² /gɔːl/ 1 *n.* painful swelling, blister, etc.; sore. place rubbed bare. 2 *v.t.* rub sore; vex, humiliate.

gall³ /gɔːl/ *n.* growth produced on tree etc. by insect etc.

gallant /ˈgælənt/ 1 *a.* brave; fine, stately; (also /gəˈlænt/) attentive to women. 2 *n.* (also /gəˈlænt/) ladies' man.

gallantry /ˈgæləntrɪ/ *n.* bravery; polite act or speech.

galleon /ˈgælɪən/ *n. hist.* (usu. Spanish) ship of war.

gallery /ˈgælərɪ/ *n.* room for showing works of art; balcony over part of area of hall or church etc.; highest of such balconies in theatre; covered walk, colonnade; passage, corridor.

galley /ˈgælɪ/ *n. hist.* low flat one-decked vessel, usu. rowed by slaves or criminals; ship's or aircraft's kitchen; tray for set-up type; (in full **galley proof**) printer's proof in long narrow form.

Gallic /ˈgælɪk/ *a.* of Gaul or Gauls; French. **Gallicize** *v.*

Gallicism /ˈgælɪsɪz(ə)m/ *n.* French idiom.

gallinaceous /gælɪˈneɪʃəs/ *a.* of order of birds including domestic poultry.

gallivant /ˈgælɪvænt/ *v.i. colloq.* gad about.

gallon /ˈgælən/ *n.* measure of capacity (4546 cc).

gallop /ˈgæləp/ 1 *n.* horse's fastest pace; a ride at this pace. 2 *v.* go at gallop; make (horse) gallop; talk etc. very fast; progress rapidly.

gallows /ˈgæləʊz/ *n.pl.* (usu. treated as *sing.*) structure for hanging criminals.

Gallup poll /ˈgæləp/ assessment of public opinion by questioning representative sample.

galore /gəˈlɔː(r)/ *adv.* in plenty.

galosh /gə'lɒʃ/ *n.* waterproof overshoe.

galumph /gə'lʌmf/ *v.i. colloq.* go prancing exultantly; move noisily or clumsily.

galvanic /gæl'vænik/ *a.* producing an electric current by chemical action; (of electric current) produced thus; *fig.* stimulating, full of energy.

galvanize /'gælvənaiz/ *v.t.* stimulate (as) by electricity; *fig.* rouse by shock etc.; coat (iron) with zinc to protect from rust.

galvanometer /gælvə'nɒmitə(r)/ *n.* instrument for measuring electric currents.

gambit /'gæmbit/ *n. Chess* opening with sacrifice of pawn etc.; trick, device.

gamble /'gæmb(ə)l/ **1** *v.i.* play games of chance for money stakes; take risks (*with*). **2** *n.* risk, risky undertaking.

gambler /'gæmblə(r)/ *n.* person who gambles habitually.

gamboge /gæm'bu:dʒ/ *n.* gum-resin used as yellow pigment.

gambol /'gæmb(ə)l/ **1** *v.i.* jump about playfully. **2** *n.* caper.

game¹ 1 *n.* form of play or sport, esp. competitive one organized with rules etc.; portion of play forming scoring unit; winning score in game; in *pl.* athletic contests; scheme, undertaking; wild animals or birds etc. hunted for sport or food; their flesh as food. **2** *a.* spirited, ready. **3** *v.i.* gamble for money stakes. **4 game-cock** kind bred for cock-fighting; **gamekeeper** person employed to breed game and prevent poaching etc.; **gamesmanship** art of winning games by psychological means.

game² *a.* (of leg etc.) crippled.

gamete /'gæmi:t/ *n.* mature germ-cell uniting with another in sexual reproduction.

gamin /'gæmin/ *n.* street urchin, impudent child.

gamine /gə'mi:n/ *n.* girl with mischievous charm.

gamma /'gæmə/ *n.* third letter of Greek alphabet (*Γ, γ*). **gamma rays** very short X-rays emitted by radioactive substances.

gammon /'gæmən/ *n.* bottom piece of flitch of bacon with hind leg.

gammy /'gæmi/ *a. sl.* (of leg etc.) crippled.

gamut /'gæmət/ *n.* whole series of recognized notes in music; compass of voice; entire range or scope.

gamy /'geimi/ *a.* smelling or tasting like game kept until it is high.

gander /'gændə(r)/ *n.* male goose.

gang 1 *n.* set of associates, esp. for criminal purposes; set of workmen or slaves or prisoners. **2** *v.i. colloq.* join *up*; act in concert *with*.

ganger /'gæŋə(r)/ *n.* foreman of gang of workmen.

gangling /'gæŋgliŋ/ *a.* (of person) loosely built, lanky.

ganglion /'gæŋgliən/ *n.* (*pl.* **-glia**) knot on nerve forming centre for reception and transmission of impulses.

gangplank /'gæŋplæŋk/ *n.* plank for walking into or out of boat etc.

gangrene /'gæŋgri:n/ *n.* death of body tissue. **gangrenous** *a.*

gangster /'gæŋstə(r)/ *n.* member of gang of violent criminals.

gangue /gæŋ/ *n.* valueless earth in which ore is found.

gangway /'gæŋwei/ *n.* passage, esp. between rows of seats; opening in ship's bulwarks; bridge.

gannet /'gænit/ *n.* large sea-bird.

gantry /'gæntri/ *n.* structure supporting travelling crane or railway signals or equipment for rocket-launch etc.

gaol /dʒeil/ **1** *n.* prison. **2** *v.t.* put in prison. **3 gaolbird** habitual criminal.

gaoler /'dʒeilə(r)/ *n.* person in charge of gaol or prisoners in it.

gap *n.* breach in hedge or wall; interval; deficiency; wide divergence.

gape **1** *v.i.* open mouth wide; stare *at*; yawn. **2** *n.* yawn; stare.

garage /'gærɑ:dʒ/ **1** *n.* building for storing motor vehicle(s); establishment selling petrol etc. or repairing and selling motor vehicles. **2** *v.t.* put or keep in garage.

garb 1 *n.* clothing, esp. of distinctive kind. **2** *v.t.* dress.

garbage /'gɑ:bidʒ/ *n.* refuse; domestic waste; foul or rubbishy literature etc.

garble /'gɑ:b(ə)l/ *v.t.* distort or confuse (facts, statements, etc.).

garden /'gɑ:d(ə)n/ **1** *n.* piece of ground for growing flowers, fruit, and vegetables, esp. attached to a house; (esp. in *pl.*) pleasure-grounds. **2** *v.i.* cultivate or work in garden.

gardenia /gɑːˈdiːnɪə/ *n.* tree or shrub with fragrant white or yellow flower; this flower.

gargantuan /gɑːˈgæntjʊən/ *a.* gigantic.

gargle /ˈgɑːg(ə)l/ **1** *v.* rinse (throat) with liquid kept in motion by breath. **2** *n.* liquid so used.

gargoyle /ˈgɑːgɔɪl/ *n.* grotesque spout projecting from gutter of building.

garish /ˈgeərɪʃ/ *a.* obtrusively bright, gaudy.

garland /ˈgɑːlənd/ **1** *n.* wreath of flowers etc. as decoration. **2** *v.t.* crown or deck with garland.

garlic /ˈgɑːlɪk/ *n.* plant with pungent bulb; this bulb used in cookery.

garment /ˈgɑːmənt/ *n.* article of clothing.

garner /ˈgɑːnə(r)/ **1** *v.t.* store up, collect. **2** *n.* storehouse for corn etc.

garnet /ˈgɑːnɪt/ *n.* vitreous mineral, esp. red kind used as gem.

garnish /ˈgɑːnɪʃ/ **1** *v.t.* decorate, esp. dish of food. **2** *n.* decorative addition.

garret /ˈgærɪt/ *n.* room, esp. small and poor, on top floor.

garrison /ˈgærɪs(ə)n/ **1** *n.* troops stationed in town. **2** *v.t.* provide with or occupy as garrison.

garrotte /gəˈrɒt/ **1** *n.* Spanish capital punishment by strangulation; apparatus for this. **2** *v.t.* execute by garrotte.

garrulous /ˈgærələs/ *a.* talkative. **garrulity** *n.*

garter /ˈgɑːtə(r)/ *n.* band to keep sock or stocking up. **the Garter** (badge of) highest order of English knighthood; **garter stitch** pattern made by knitting all rows plain.

gas /gæs/ **1** *n.* (*pl.* **gases**) any airlike or completely elastic fluid, esp. one not liquid or solid at ordinary temperatures; such fluid, esp. coal gas or natural gas; gas used as anaesthetic; poisonous gas used in war; *US colloq.* petrol; *colloq.* empty talk, boasting. **2** *v.* expose to gas; *colloq.* talk emptily or boastfully. **3** **gasbag** *derog.* empty talker; **gas chamber** used to kill animals or prisoners by gas poisoning; **gasholder** gasometer; **gas mask** de-

vice worn over head for protection against harmful gases; **gas ring** ring pierced with small holes and fed with gas for cooking etc.; **gasworks** place where coal gas is manufactured.

gaseous /ˈgæsɪəs/ *a.* of or in form of gas.

gash 1 *n.* long deep cut or wound, cleft. **2** *v.t.* make gash in.

gasify /ˈgæsɪfaɪ/ *v.* convert into gas. **gasification** *n.*

gasket /ˈgæskɪt/ *n.* sheet or ring of rubber etc. to seal junction of metal surfaces; small cord securing furled sail to yard.

gasoline /ˈgæsəliːn/ *n. US* petrol.

gasometer /gæˈsɒmɪtə(r)/ *n.* large tank from which gas is distributed.

gasp /gɑːsp/ **1** *v.* catch breath with open mouth; utter with gasps. **2** *n.* convulsive catching of breath. **3** **at one's last gasp** at point of death, *fig.* exhausted.

gassy /ˈgæsɪ/ *a.* of or full of or like gas; verbose.

gastric /ˈgæstrɪk/ *a.* of stomach. **gastric flu** *colloq.* intestinal disorder of unknown cause; **gastric juice** digestive fluid secreted by stomach glands.

gastronome /ˈgæstrənəʊm/ *n.* connoisseur of cookery. **gastronomic** /-ˈnɒm-/ *a.*; **gastronomy** /-ˈstrɒn-/ *n.*

gastropod /ˈgæstrəpɒd/ *n.* mollusc that moves by means of ventral organ.

gate *n.* barrier, usu. hinged, used to close opening in wall or fence etc.; such opening; means of entrance or exit; numbered place of access to aircraft at airport; device regulating passage of water in lock etc.; number entering by payment at gates to see football match etc., money thus taken. **gatecrash** attend social gathering uninvited; **gatelegged** (of table) with legs in gateleg frame swinging back to allow top to fold down; **gateway** opening closed by gate.

gateau /ˈgætəʊ/ *n.* (*pl.* **-teaus**) large rich elaborate cake.

gather /ˈgæðə(r)/ **1** *v.* bring or come together, collect; infer, deduce; pluck (flowers etc.); increase (speed); draw together in folds or wrinkles; develop purulent swelling. **2** *n.* small fold or pleat.

gathering *n.* assembly; purulent swelling.

GATT *abbr.* General Agreement on Tariffs and Trade.

gauche /gəʊʃ/ *a.* tactless, socially awkward. **gaucherie** *n.*

gaucho /ˈgaʊtʃəʊ/ *n.* (*pl.* -os) mounted herdsman in S. Amer. pampas.

gaudy /ˈgɔːdɪ/ *a.* tastelessly showy.

gauge /geɪdʒ/ 1 *n.* standard measure; instrument for measuring or testing; capacity, extent; criterion, test. 2 *v.t.* measure exactly; measure contents of; estimate.

Gaul /gɔːl/ *n.* inhabitant of ancient Gaul. **Gaulish** *a.* & *n.*

gaunt /gɔːnt/ *a.* lean, haggard, grim.

gauntlet¹ /ˈgɔːntlɪt/ *n.* glove with long loose wrist, esp. for driving etc.; *hist.* armoured glove.

gauntlet² /ˈgɔːntlɪt/ *n.* **run the gauntlet** pass between two rows of men etc. armed with sticks etc., as punishment, *fig.* undergo criticism.

gauze /gɔːz/ *n.* thin transparent fabric or wire mesh etc. **gauzy** *a.*

gave *past of* **give**.

gavel /ˈgæv(ə)l/ *n.* auctioneer's or chairman's or judge's hammer.

gavotte /gəˈvɒt/ *n.* lively 18th-c. dance; music for this.

gawk /ˈgɔːk/ *v.i.* stare stupidly. 2 *n.* awkward or bashful person. 3 **gawky** *a.*

gawp /ˈgɔːp/ *v.i. colloq.* stare stupidly.

gay *a.* light-hearted, mirthful; *colloq.* homosexual; showy; dissolute.

gaze /geɪz/ 1 *v.i.* look fixedly. 2 *n.* intent look.

gazebo /gəˈziːbəʊ/ *n.* (*pl.* -bos) structure from which view may be had.

gazelle /gəˈzel/ *n.* small graceful antelope.

gazette /gəˈzet/ 1 *n.* newspaper, esp. official journal. 2 *v.t.* publish in official gazette.

gazetteer /gæzɪˈtɪə(r)/ *n.* geographical index.

gazump /gəˈzʌmp/ *v.t.* raise price after accepting offer from (buyer); swindle.

GB *abbr.* Great Britain.

GC *abbr.* George Cross.

GCE *abbr.* General Certificate of Education.

GCSE *abbr.* General Certificate of Secondary Education.

GDR *abbr.* German Democratic Republic (E. Germany).

gear /gɪə(r)/ 1 *n.* set of toothed wheels working together, esp. those connecting engine to road wheels; (often in *pl.*) particular setting of these; *colloq.* clothing, rigging. 2 *v.t.* put in gear; provide with gear; adapt or adapt *to*; harness (*up*). 3 **gearbox** case enclosing gears of machine or vehicle; **gearlever** lever moved to engage or change gear; **in gear** with gears engaged.

gecko /ˈgekəʊ/ *n.* (*pl.* -os) house lizard found in warm climates.

gee /dʒiː/ *int.* expr. surprise etc.

geese *pl. of* **goose**.

geezer /ˈgiːzə(r)/ *n. sl.* man, esp. old one.

Geiger counter /ˈgaɪgə(r)/ instrument for measuring radioactivity.

geisha /ˈgeɪʃə/ *n.* Japanese professional hostess and entertainer.

gel /dʒel/ *n.* semi-solid colloidal solution or jelly.

gelatine /ˈdʒelətiːn/ *n.* (also **gelatin** /-tɪn/) transparent tasteless substance used in cookery for making jelly etc. and in photography etc. **gelatinous** /-ˈlæt-/ *a.*

geld /geld/ *v.t.* castrate.

gelding /ˈgeldɪŋ/ *n.* castrated horse etc.

gelignite /ˈdʒelɪgnaɪt/ *n.* nitroglycerine explosive.

gem /dʒem/ 1 *n.* precious stone; thing of great beauty or worth. 2 *v.t.* adorn (as) with gems.

Gemini /ˈdʒemɪnaɪ/ *n.* third sign of zodiac.

gen /dʒen/ *colloq.* 1 *n.* information. 2 *v.* (with *up*) gain or give information.

Gen. *abbr.* General.

gendarme /ˈʒɒndɑːm/ *n.* soldier employed in police duties, esp. in France.

gender /ˈdʒendə(r)/ *n.* grammatical classification (or one of classes) roughly corresponding to two sexes and sexlessness.

gene /dʒiːn/ *n.* unit of heredity in chromosome, controlling particular inherited characteristic.

genealogy /dʒiːnɪˈælədʒɪ/ *n.* descent traced continuously from ancestor, pedigree; study of pedigrees. **genealogical** *a.*; **genealogist** *n.*

genera /ˈdʒenərə/ *pl. of* **genus**.

general /ˈdʒenər(ə)l/ 1 *a.* applicable to all, not partial or particular; prevalent, usual; vague, lacking detail; (in titles) chief, head. **2** *n.* Army officer next below Field Marshal; commander of army. **3 general anaesthetic** one affecting whole body; **general election** election of representatives to parliament etc. from whole country; **general knowledge** knowledge of miscellaneous facts; **general practitioner** doctor treating cases of all kinds; **in general** usually, for the most part.

generalissimo /dʒenərəˈlɪsɪməʊ/ *n.* (*pl.* **-mos**) commander of combined forces.

generality /dʒenəˈrælɪtɪ/ *n.* general statement; indefiniteness; majority *of.*

generalize /ˈdʒenərəlaɪz/ *v.* speak in general or indefinite terms, form general notion; reduce to general statement; infer (rule etc.) from particular cases; bring into general use. **generalization** *n.*

generally /ˈdʒenərəlɪ/ *adv.* in general sense; in most respects; usually.

generate /ˈdʒenəreɪt/ *v.t.* bring into existence, produce.

generation /dʒenəˈreɪʃ(ə)n/ *n.* procreation; production, esp. of electricity; step in pedigree; all persons born about same time; period of about 30 years.

generative /ˈdʒenərətɪv/ *a.* of procreation, productive.

generator /ˈdʒenəreɪtə(r)/ *n.* dynamo; apparatus for producing gas or steam etc.

generic /dʒɪˈnerɪk/ *a.* characteristic of or applied to genus or class; not specific or special.

generous /ˈdʒenərəs/ *a.* giving or given freely; magnanimous; abundant. **generosity** *n.*

genesis /ˈdʒenɪsɪs/ *n.* origin; mode of formation or generation.

genetic /dʒɪˈnetɪk/ *a.* of genetics; of or in origin.

genetics *n.pl.* treated as *sing.* study of heredity and variation in animals and plants.

genial /ˈdʒiːnɪəl/ *a.* kindly; sociable; mild, warm; cheering. **geniality** /-ˈæl-/ *n.*

genie /ˈdʒiːnɪ/ *n.* (*pl.* **genii** /ˈdʒiːnɪaɪ/) sprite or goblin of Arabian tales.

genital /ˈdʒenɪt(ə)l/ **1** *a.* of animal reproduction or reproductive organs. **2** *n.* in *pl.* external genital organs.

genitalia /dʒenɪˈteɪlɪə/ *n.pl.* genitals.

genitive /ˈdʒenɪtɪv/ *Gram.* **1** *a.* (of case) corresponding to *of* or *from* etc., with noun representing possessor or source etc. **2** *n.* genitive case.

genius /ˈdʒiːnɪəs/ *n.* (*pl.* **-iuses**) very high natural ability; person having this; tutelary spirit.

genocide /ˈdʒenəsaɪd/ *n.* deliberate extermination of a people or nation.

genre /ˈʒɑːnr/ *n.* kind or style etc. of art or literature; portrayal of scenes from ordinary life.

gent /dʒent/ *n. colloq.* gentleman.

genteel /dʒenˈtiːl/ *a.* affectedly polite or refined.

gentian /ˈdʒenʃ(ə)n/ *n.* mountain plant with usu. blue flowers. **gentian violet** dye used as antiseptic.

gentile /ˈdʒentaɪl/ **1** *a.* not Jewish; heathen. **2** *n.* gentile person.

gentility /dʒenˈtɪlɪtɪ/ *n.* social superiority; upper-class habits.

gentle /ˈdʒent(ə)l/ *a.* not rough or severe; kind, mild; well-born; quiet. **gently** *adv.*

gentlefolk /ˈdʒentəlfəʊk/ *n.* people of good family.

gentleman /ˈdʒentəlmən/ *n.* (*pl.* **-men**) man; chivalrous well-bred man; man of good social position.

gentlemanly *a.* behaving or looking like or befitting a gentleman.

gentlewoman /ˈdʒentəlwʊmən/ *n. arch.* (*pl.* **-women** /-wɪmɪn/) woman of good birth or breeding.

gentry /ˈdʒentrɪ/ *n.* people next below nobility; *derog.* people.

genuflect /ˈdʒenjuːflekt/ *v.i.* bend knee, esp. in worship. **genuflexion** *n.*

genuine /ˈdʒenjuːɪn/ *a.* really coming from its reputed source; not sham; properly so called.

genus /ˈdʒiːnəs/ *n.* (*pl.* **genera** /ˈdʒenərə/) group of animals, plants, etc., with common structural characteristics, usu. containing several species; kind, class.

geocentric /dʒiːəˈsentrɪk/ *a.* considered as viewed from earth's centre; having earth as centre.

geode /ˈdʒiːəʊd/ *n.* cavity lined with crystals; rock containing this.

geodesic /dʒiːəˈdiːsɪk/ *a.* (also **geodetic**) of geodesy. **geodesic line** shortest possible line on surface between two points.

geodesy /dʒiːˈɒdɪsɪ/ n. study of shape and area of the earth.

geography /dʒɪˈɒgrəfɪ/ n. science of earth's form and physical features etc.; features of place. **geographer** n.; **geographic(al)** a.

geology /dʒɪˈɒlədʒɪ/ n. science of earth's crust and strata. **geological** a.; **geologist** n.

geometry /dʒɪˈɒmɪtrɪ/ n. science of properties and relations of lines, surfaces, and solids. **geometric(al)** a.; **geometrician** n.

Geordie /ˈdʒɔːdɪ/ n. native of Tyneside.

georgette /dʒɔːˈdʒet/ n. thin crêpe of silk or other fabric.

Georgian /ˈdʒɔːdʒ(ə)n/ a. of time of Kings George I–IV or George V and VI.

geranium /dʒəˈreɪnɪəm/ n. herb or shrub with fruit shaped like crane's bill; cultivated pelargonium.

gerbil /ˈdʒɜːbɪl/ n. mouselike desert rodent with long hind legs.

geriatrics /dʒerɪˈætrɪks/ n.pl. treated as *sing*. branch of medical science dealing with old age and its diseases. **geriatric** a.; **geriatrician** n.

germ /dʒɜːm/ n. micro-organism or microbe; portion of organism capable of developing into new one; rudiment, elementary principle.

German[1] /ˈdʒɜːmən/ **1** a. of Germany. **2** n. native or language of Germany. **3 German measles** disease like mild measles; **German shepherd (dog)** dog of a wolfhound breed.

german[2] /ˈdʒɜːmən/ a. (placed after *brother* or *sister* etc.) having full relationship, not half-brother etc.

germander /dʒɜːˈmændə(r)/ n. plant of mint family, esp. speedwell.

germane /dʒɜːˈmeɪn/ a. relevant or pertinent (to).

Germanic /dʒɜːˈmænɪk/ a. having German characteristics.

germicide /ˈdʒɜːmɪsaɪd/ n. substance that destroys germs. **germicidal** a.

germinal /ˈdʒɜːmɪn(ə)l/ a. of germs; in earliest stage of development.

germinate /ˈdʒɜːmɪneɪt/ v. sprout, bud; cause to shoot, produce. **germination** n.

gerontology /dʒerɒnˈtɒlədʒɪ/ n. study of old age and ageing.

gerrymander /ˈdʒerɪˌmændə(r)/ v.t. manipulate boundaries of (constituency etc.) to gain unfair electoral advantage.

gerund /ˈdʒerənd/ n. verbal noun, in English ending in -*ing*.

Gestapo /geˈstɑːpəʊ/ n. Nazi secret police.

gestation /dʒeˈsteɪʃ(ə)n/ n. carrying in womb between conception and birth; period of this.

gesticulate /dʒeˈstɪkjʊleɪt/ v. use gestures with or instead of speech. **gesticulation** n.

gesture /ˈdʒestʃə(r)/ **1** n. significant movement of limb or body; action calculated to evoke response or convey intention. **2** v. gesticulate.

get /get/ v. (*past* **got**; *p.p.* **got** or *US* **gotten**) obtain, earn, gain, win, procure; fetch; go to reach or catch; prepare (meal); learn; experience or suffer; catch or contract, have inflicted; (cause to) reach some state or become; succeed in coming or going *to* or *away* etc., succeed in bringing or placing etc.; in *perf.* possess, have, be bound *to do* or *be*; induce; *colloq*. understand; *colloq*. annoy, attract, or obsess; beget. **get at** reach, get hold of, *colloq*. imply, *colloq*. tamper with; **get away** escape; **getaway** n.; **get by** *colloq*. be acceptable, cope; **get in** win election, obtain place at college etc.; **get on** advance, fare, live harmoniously *with*, become elderly; **get out of** avoid or escape; **get over** surmount, recover from; **gettogether** social assembly; **get up** rise esp. from bed, arrange appearance of; **get-up** style of equipment or costume etc.

geum /ˈdʒiːəm/ n. kind of rosaceous plant.

gewgaw /ˈgjuːgɔː/ n. gaudy plaything or ornament.

geyser /ˈgaɪzə(r)/ n. hot spring; /ˈgiːzə(r)/ apparatus for heating water.

ghastly /ˈgɑːstlɪ/ a. horrible, frightful; deathlike, pallid.

ghat /gɑːt/ n. (also **ghaut**) in India, steps leading to river; landing-place.

ghee /giː/ n. Indian clarified butter.

gherkin /ˈgɜːkɪn/ n. small cucumber for pickling.

ghetto /ˈgetəʊ/ n. (pl. -**os**) part of city occupied by minority group; Jews' quarter in city; segregated group or area.

ghost /gəʊst/ 1 *n.* apparition of dead person etc.; disembodied spirit; emaciated or pale person; semblance; secondary or duplicate image in defective telescope or television-picture. 2 *v.* act as ghost writer etc. 3 **ghost writer** writer doing work for which another takes credit. 4 **ghostly** *a.*

ghoul /guːl/ *n.* person morbidly interested in death etc.; spirit said to prey on corpses. **ghoulish** *a.*

GHQ *abbr.* General Headquarters.

ghyll var. of **gill³**.

GI /dʒiːˈaɪ/ 1 *n.* American private soldier. 2 *a.* of or for US armed forces.

giant /dʒaɪənt/ 1 *n.* mythical being of human form but superhuman size; very tall or large person or animal etc.; person of extraordinary ability. 2 *a.* gigantic. 3 **giant-killer** person who defeats more powerful opponent. 4 **giantess** *n.*

gibber /dʒɪbə(r)/ *v.i.* chatter inarticulately.

gibberish /dʒɪbərɪʃ/ *n.* unintelligible speech, meaningless sounds.

gibbet /dʒɪbɪt/ *n. hist.* gallows; post on which body of executed criminal was exposed.

gibbon /dʒɪbən/ *n.* long-armed ape.

gibbous /dʒɪbəs/ *a.* convex; (of moon etc.) with bright part greater than semicircle. **gibbosity** *n.*

gibe /dʒaɪb/ 1 *v.* jeer or mock (at). 2 *n.* jeering remark, taunt.

giblets /dʒɪblɪts/ *n.pl.* liver and gizzard etc. of bird removed before it is cooked.

giddy /gɪdɪ/ *a.* dizzy; tending to fall or stagger; making dizzy; excitable, flighty.

gift /gɪft/ 1 *n.* thing given, present; natural talent. 2 *v.t.* endow with gifts; present.

gig¹ /gɪg/ *n.* light two-wheeled one-horse carriage; light ship's-boat; rowing-boat esp. for race.

gig² /gɪg/ *n. colloq.* engagement to play jazz etc. esp. for one night.

gigantic /dʒaɪˈgæntɪk/ *a.* giant-like, huge.

giggle /gɪg(ə)l/ 1 *v.i.* give small bursts of half-suppressed laughter. 2 *n.* such laugh; *colloq.* amusing person or thing.

gigolo /dʒɪgələʊ/ *n.* (*pl.* **-los**) young man paid by older woman for his attentions.

gild¹ /gɪld/ *v.t.* (*p.p.* **gilded** or **gilt**) cover thinly with gold; tinge with golden colour.

gild² var. of **guild**.

gill¹ /gɪl/ *n.* usu. in *pl.* respiratory organ of fish etc.; vertical radial plate on under side of mushroom etc.; flesh below person's jaws and ears.

gill² /dʒɪl/ *n.* quarter-pint measure.

gill³ /gɪl/ *n.* deep wooded ravine; narrow mountain torrent.

gillie /gɪlɪ/ *n.* man or boy attending sportsman in Scotland.

gillyflower /dʒɪlɪflaʊə(r)/ *n.* clove-scented flower, e.g. wallflower.

gilt¹ /gɪlt/ 1 *a.* overlaid with gold. 2 *n.* gilding. 3 **gilt-edged** (of securities) having high degree of reliability.

gilt² /gɪlt/ *n.* young sow.

gimbals /dʒɪmb(ə)lz/ *n.pl.* contrivance of rings etc. for keeping things horizontal at sea.

gimcrack /dʒɪmkræk/ 1 *a.* flimsy, worthless. 2 *n.* showy ornament etc.

gimlet /gɪmlɪt/ *n.* small boring-tool.

gimmick /gɪmɪk/ *n. colloq.* tricky device or idea etc., esp. to attract attention. **gimmickry** *n.*; **gimmicky** *a.*

gimp /gɪmp/ *n.* twist of silk etc. with cord or wire running through.

gin¹ /dʒɪn/ *n.* spirit distilled from grain or malt and flavoured with juniper etc.

gin² /dʒɪn/ 1 *n.* snare, trap; machine separating cotton from seeds; kind of crane or windlass. 2 *v.t.* treat (cotton) in gin; trap.

ginger /dʒɪndʒə(r)/ 1 *n.* hot spicy root used in cooking and medicine; plant from which this comes; light reddish yellow; mettle, spirit. 2 *v.t.* flavour with ginger; liven *up.* 3 **ginger-ale, -beer,** ginger-flavoured aerated drinks; **gingerbread** ginger-flavoured treacle cake; **ginger group** one urging party or movement to more decided action; **ginger-nut, -snap,** kinds of ginger-flavoured biscuit. 4 **gingery** *a.*

gingerly /dʒɪndʒəlɪ/ 1 *a.* showing extreme care or caution. 2 *adv.* in gingerly manner.

gingham /gɪŋəm/ *n.* plain-woven cotton cloth, frequently striped or checked.

gingivitis /dʒɪndʒɪˈvaɪtɪs/ *n.* inflammation of the gums.

ginkgo /ˈɡɪŋkəʊ/ *n.* (*pl.* **-gos**) yellow-flowered Chinese and Japanese tree.

ginseng /ˈdʒɪnseŋ/ *n.* medicinal plant found in E. Asia and N. America; root of this.

gipsy var. of **gypsy**.

giraffe /dʒɪˈrɑːf/ *n.* large African four-legged animal with long neck.

gird /ɡɜːd/ (*past & p.p.* **girded** or **girt**) encircle or fasten (on) with waistbelt etc. **gird up one's loins** prepare for action.

girder /ˈɡɜːdə(r)/ *n.* iron or steel beam or compound structure forming span of bridge etc.; beam supporting joists.

girdle[1] /ˈɡɜːd(ə)l/ **1** *n.* cord or belt used to gird waist; thing that surrounds; corset; bony support for limbs. **2** *v.t.* surround with girdle.

girdle[2] /ˈɡɜːd(ə)l/ *n.* circular iron plate for baking scones etc. over heat.

girl /ɡɜːl/ *n.* female child; young woman; female servant; man's girlfriend. **girl guide** Guide. **girlhood** *n.*; **girlish** *a.*

giro /ˈdʒaɪrəʊ/ *n.* (*pl.* **-os**) system of credit transfer between banks or post offices etc.

girt *past & p.p.* of **gird**.

girth /ɡɜːθ/ *n.* distance round a thing; band round body of horse securing saddle.

gist /ˈdʒɪst/ *n.* substance or point or essence of a matter.

give /ɡɪv/ **1** *v.* (*past* **gave**; *p.p.* **given** /ˈɡɪv(ə)n/) transfer possession of gratuitously; grant, accord; deliver, administer; consign, put; pledge; devote; present, offer (one's hand, arm, etc.); exert; impart, be source of; assume, grant, specify; allow to have; collapse, yield, shrink. **2** *n.* elasticity; yielding to pressure. **3 give and take** exchange of talk or ideas, willingness to make concessions etc. **give away** transfer as gift, hand over (bride) to bridegroom, betray or expose; **give-away** *colloq.* unintentional disclosure; **give in** yield; **give off** emit; **give out** distribute, announce, emit, be exhausted, run short; **give over** devote *to*, hand over, *colloq.* desist; **give up** cease from effort or *doing*, part with, resign, surrender, re-

nounce hope (of); **give way** yield under pressure, give precedence.

given 1 *p.p.* of **give**. **2** *a.* disposed, prone (*to*); granted as basis of reasoning etc.; fixed, specified. **3 given name** forename.

gizzard /ˈɡɪzəd/ *n.* bird's second stomach, for grinding food.

glacé /ˈɡlæseɪ/ *a.* iced, sugared; (of cloth etc.) smooth, polished.

glacial /ˈɡleɪʃ(ə)l/ *a.* of ice, icy; *Geol.* characterized or produced by ice.

glaciated /ˈɡleɪsɪeɪtɪd/ *a.* covered with glaciers; affected by friction of moving ice. **glaciation** *n.*

glacier /ˈɡlæsɪə(r)/ *n.* slowly moving river or mass of ice.

glad *a.* pleased; joyful, cheerful. **glad rags** *colloq.* best clothes.

gladden /ˈɡlæd(ə)n/ *v.t.* make glad.

glade *n.* clear space in forest.

gladiator /ˈɡlædɪeɪtə(r)/ *n.* trained fighter in ancient Roman shows. **gladiatorial** *a.*

gladiolus /ɡlædɪˈəʊləs/ *n.* (*pl.* **-li** /-laɪ/) plant of iris kind with bright flower-spikes.

gladsome /ˈɡlædsəm/ *a. poet.* joyful, cheerful.

Gladstone bag /ˈɡlædst(ə)n/ kind of light portmanteau.

glair *n.* white of egg; similar viscous substance.

glamour /ˈɡlæmə(r)/ *n.* alluring or exciting beauty or charm. **glamorize** *v.t.*; **glamorous** *a.*

glance /ɡlɑːns/ **1** *v.i.* give brief or momentary look; glide *off.* **2** *n.* brief look; flash, gleam; swift oblique movement or impact. **3 glance at** make brief allusion to.

gland *n.* organ secreting substances required for particular function of body; similar organ in plant.

glanders /ˈɡlændəz/ *n.pl.* contagious horse-disease.

glandular /ˈɡlændjʊlə(r)/ *a.* of gland(s). **glandular fever** infectious disease with swelling of lymph-glands.

glare /ɡleə(r)/ **1** *v.i.* look fiercely; shine oppressively. **2** *n.* fierce look; oppressive light; tawdry brilliance.

glass /ɡlɑːs/ **1** *n.* substance, usu. transparent, lustrous, hard, and brittle, made by fusing sand with soda and potash etc.; glass objects collectively; glass drinking-vessel; looking-glass; lens; in *pl.* pair of spectacles or binoculars; barometer; microscope. **2** *v.t.* fit or cover with glass. **3 glass-cloth** cloth for drying glasses; **glass fibre** fabric made from or plastic reinforced by glass filaments; **glasshouse** greenhouse, *sl.* military prison; **glass-paper** paper covered with powdered glass, for smoothing etc.; **glass wool** fine glass fibres for packing and insulation.

glassy /ˈglɑːsɪ/ *a.* like glass; (of eye) dull, fixed.

glaucoma /glɔːˈkəʊmə/ *n.* eye-disease with pressure in eye-ball and gradual loss of sight.

glaze 1 *v.* fit with glass or windows; cover (pottery etc.) with vitreous substance or (surface) with smooth lustrous coating; (of eye) become glassy. **2** *n.* substance used for or surface produced by glazing.

glazier /ˈgleɪzɪə(r)/ *n.* person who glazes windows etc. professionally.

GLC *abbr.* Greater London Council.

gleam 1 *n.* subdued or transient light; faint or momentary show. **2** *v.i.* emit gleams.

glean *v.* pick up (facts etc.); gather (corn left by reapers). **gleanings** *n.pl.*

glebe *n.* piece of land yielding revenue to benefice.

glee *n.* mirth, lively delight; musical composition for several voices. **gleeful** *a.*

glen *n.* narrow valley.

glengarry /glenˈgærɪ/ *n.* kind of Highland cap.

glib *a.* speaking or spoken fluently but insincerely.

glide 1 *v.* pass or proceed by smooth continuous movement; (of aircraft) fly without engines; go stealthily. **2** *n.* gliding motion or flight.

glider /ˈglaɪdə(r)/ *n.* light aircraft without engine.

glimmer /ˈglɪmə(r)/ **1** *n.* faint light or gleam. **2** *v.i.* shine faintly or intermittently.

glimpse /glɪmps/ **1** *n.* brief view; faint transient appearance. **2** *v.t.* have brief view of.

glint *v.i.* & *n.* flash; glitter.

glissade /glɪˈsɑːd/ **1** *v.i.* make controlled slide down slope of ice etc. **2** *n.* glissading movement.

glisten /ˈglɪs(ə)n/ **1** *v.* shine like wet or polished surface; sparkle. **2** *n.* glistening.

glitter /ˈglɪtə(r)/ **1** *v.i.* shine with brilliant tremulous light. **2** *n.* glittering; material that glitters.

gloaming /ˈgləʊmɪŋ/ *n.* evening twilight.

gloat *v.i.* look or ponder with greedy or malicious pleasure (*over*).

global /ˈgləʊb(ə)l/ *a.* world-wide; all-embracing.

globe *n.* spherical object; *the* earth; spherical map of earth or constellations; thing shaped like this. **globe-trotting** travelling through many foreign countries.

globular /ˈglɒbjʊlə(r)/ *a.* globe-shaped; composed of globules. **globularity** *n.*

globule /ˈglɒbjuːl/ *n.* small globe or round particle, esp. of liquid.

glockenspiel /ˈglɒkənspiːl/ *n.* musical instrument of bells or tuned metal bars played with hammers.

gloom /gluːm/ **1** *n.* darkness; melancholy, depression. **2** *v.i.* look or be sullen or depressed; be dull.

gloomy /ˈgluːmɪ/ *a.* dark, depressed, depressing.

glorify /ˈglɔːrɪfaɪ/ *v.t.* make glorious; extol; make out to be more splendid than is the case; invest with radiance. **glorification** *n.*

glorious /ˈglɔːrɪəs/ *a.* possessing or conferring glory; splendid, excellent.

glory /ˈglɔːrɪ/ **1** *n.* renown, honourable fame; resplendent majesty or beauty etc.; halo of saint. **2** *v.i.* take pride (*in*).

gloss[1] **1** *n.* lustre of surface; deceptively attractive appearance. **2** *v.t.* make glossy. **3 gloss over** seek to conceal. **4 glossy** *a.*

gloss[2] **1** *n.* explanatory comment added to text; comment, interpretation. **2** *v.t.* insert glosses in, make or write gloss on; explain.

glossary /ˈglɒsərɪ/ *n.* dictionary of technical or special words.

glottal /ˈglɒt(ə)l/ *a.* of the glottis. **glottal stop** sound produced by sudden opening or shutting of glottis.

glottis /ˈglɒtɪs/ *n.* opening at upper end of windpipe and between vocal cords.

glove /glʌv/ **1** *n.* hand-covering, usu. with separated fingers, for warmth or protection etc.; boxing-glove. 2 *v.t.* cover or provide with gloves. 3 **glove compartment** recess for small articles in motor-car dashboard.

glow /glǝʊ/ 1 *v.* emit flameless light and heat; show warm colour; burn *with* bodily heat or emotion. 2 *n.* glowing state; ardour. 3 **glow-worm** beetle that emits green light from abdomen.

glower /'glaʊǝ(r)/ *v.i.* scowl (*at*).

glucose /'glu:kǝʊs/ *n.* kind of sugar found in fruits and blood etc.

glue 1 *n.* sticky substance used as adhesive. 2 *v.t.* attach (as) with glue; hold closely. **gluey** *a.*

glum *a.* dejected, sullen.

glut 1 *v.t.* feed or indulge to the full, satiate; overstock. 2 *n.* excessive supply; surfeit.

gluten /'glu:t(ǝ)n/ *n.* viscous part of flour.

glutinous /'glu:tɪnǝs/ *a.* sticky, gluelike, viscous.

glutton /'glʌt(ǝ)n/ *n.* excessive eater; person insatiably eager *for*; voracious animal of weasel kind. **gluttonous** *a.*; **gluttony** *n.*

glycerine /'glɪsǝri:n/ *n.* colourless sweet viscous liquid got from oils or fats.

gm. *abbr.* gram(s).

G-man /'dʒi:mæn/ *n.* US *sl.* Federal criminal-investigation officer.

GMT *abbr.* Greenwich Mean Time.

gnarled /nɑ:ld/ *a.* knobbly, rugged, twisted.

gnash /næʃ/ *v.* grind (one's teeth); (of teeth) strike together.

gnat /næt/ *n.* small biting fly.

gnaw /nɔ:/ *v.t.* bite persistently, wear *away* thus; corrode, torment.

gneiss /naɪs/ *n.* coarse-grained rock of quartz, feldspar, and mica.

gnome /nǝʊm/ *n.* goblin, dwarf; *colloq.* person with sinister influence, esp. in finance.

gnomic /'nǝʊmɪk/ *a.* of maxims, sententious.

gnomon /'nǝʊmɒn/ *n.* rod etc. showing time by its shadow on marked surface of sundial.

gnostic /'nɒstɪk/ 1 *a.* of knowledge; having special mystic knowledge. 2 *n.* **Gnostic**, early Christian heretic claiming mystical knowledge 3 **Gnosticism** *n.*

GNP *abbr.* gross national product.

gnu /nu:/ *n.* oxlike antelope.

go[1] 1 *v.i.* (*past* **went**; *p.p.* **gone** /gɒn/) walk, travel, proceed; depart; move, pass; become; (of money) be spent *in* or *on*; be functioning, moving, etc.; collapse, give way, fail; extend, reach; be successful or acceptable; be sold; give forth sound. 2 *n.* (*pl.* **goes**) animation, dash; *colloq.* state of affairs; success; turn, try (*at*). 3 **go-ahead** enterprising; **go by** be guided by, pass; **go-getter** enterprising pushful person; **go in for** compete or engage in; **go-kart** miniature racing-car with skeleton body; **go off** explode, deteriorate, (of event) succeed *well* etc., begin to dislike; **go out** leave room or house, be extinguished, cease to be fashionable, mix in society; **go round** pay informal visit, suffice for all; **go slow** work at deliberately slow pace as industrial protest; **go under** succumb, fail; **go without** not have, abstain from; **it's no go** *colloq.* nothing can be done; **on the go** *colloq.* in motion.

go[2] *n.* Japanese board-game.

goad 1 *n.* spiked stick for urging cattle; thing that incites or torments. 2 *v.t.* urge with goad; drive *by* annoyance.

goal *n.* structure into or through which ball is to be driven in certain games; point(s) so won; object of effort; destination; point where race ends. **goalkeeper** player protecting goal.

goalie /'gǝʊlɪ/ *n.* *colloq.* goalkeeper.

goat *n.* small horned ruminant; licentious man; fool. **get person's goat** *sl.* irritate him.

goatee /gǝʊ'ti:/ *n.* beard like goat's.

gob[1] *n.* *sl.* mouth. **gob-stopper** large hard sweet for sucking.

gob[2] *n.* *sl.* clot of slimy substance.

gobbet /'gɒbɪt/ *n.* extract from text set for translation or comment.

gobble[1] /'gɒb(ǝ)l/ *v.* eat hurriedly and noisily.

gobble[2] /'gɒb(ǝ)l/ *v.i.* (of turkey-cock) make gurgling sound in throat; speak thus.

gobbledegook /'gɒbǝldɪgu:k/ *n.* *colloq.* pompous official etc. jargon.

goblet /'gɒblɪt/ *n.* drinking-vessel with foot and stem.

goblin /'gɒblɪn/ *n.* mischievous demon.

goby /'gəʊbɪ/ n. small fish with ventral fins joined into disc or sucker.

god n. superhuman being worshipped as possessing divine power; (**God**) creator and ruler of universe; idol; adored person. **the gods** *Theatr.* (occupants of) gallery; **godchild** child in relation to godparent; **god-daughter** female godchild; **godfather** male godparent; **God-fearing** religious; **God-forsaken** dismal, forlorn; **godmother** female godparent; **godparent** sponsor at baptism; **godsend** unexpected welcome event or acquisition; **godson** male godchild.

goddess /'gɒdes/ n. female deity; adored woman.

godhead /'gɒdhed/ n. divine nature, deity.

godless /'gɒdlɪs/ a. not believing in God; impious, wicked.

godly /'gɒdlɪ/ a. pious, devout.

godwit /'gɒdwɪt/ n. marsh bird like curlew.

goer /'gəʊə(r)/ n. person or thing that goes; lively or vivacious person.

goggle /'gɒg(ə)l/ 1 v.i. look with wide-open eyes; (of eyes) be rolled, project; roll (eyes). 2 a. (of eyes) protuberant, rolling. 3 n.pl. spectacles for protecting eyes from glare or dust etc. 4 **goggle-box** sl. television set.

going /'gəʊɪŋ/ 1 n. condition of ground for riding etc.; progress. 2 a. in action; existing, available; currently valid. 3 **goings-on** strange conduct.

goitre /'gɔɪtə(r)/ n. abnormal enlargement of thyroid gland. **goitrous** a.

gold /gəʊld/ 1 n. precious yellow metal; coins or articles of this; wealth; colour of gold. 2 a. of or coloured like gold. 3 **gold-digger** sl. woman who wheedles money out of men; **goldfinch** bright-coloured song-bird; **goldfish** small golden-red Chinese carp; **gold-leaf** gold beaten into thin sheet; **gold medal** medal given usu. as first prize; **gold-rush** rush to newly-discovered goldfield; **goldsmith** worker in gold; **gold standard** financial system in which value of money is based on gold.

golden /'gəʊld(ə)n/ a. of gold; coloured or shining like gold; precious, excellent. **golden handshake** gratuity as compensation for dismissal or compulsory retirement; **golden mean** neither too much nor too little; **golden syrup** pale treacle; **golden wedding** 50th wedding anniversary.

golf 1 n. game in which small hard ball is struck with clubs over ground into series of small holes. 2 v.i. play golf. 3 **golf ball** ball used in golf, *colloq.* spherical unit carrying type in some electric typewriters; **golf-course** area of land on which golf is played.

golliwog /'gɒlɪwɒg/ n. black-faced soft doll with bright clothes and fuzzy hair.

golosh var. of **galosh**.

gonad /'gəʊnæd/ n. animal organ producing gametes, e.g. testis or ovary.

gondola /'gɒndələ/ n. light Venetian canal-boat; car suspended from airship.

gondolier /gɒndə'lɪə(r)/ n. rower of gondola.

gone *p.p.* of **go**[1].

goner /'gɒnə(r)/ n. *sl.* doomed or irrevocably lost person or thing.

gong n. metal disc giving resonant note when struck; saucer-shaped bell; *sl.* medal.

gonorrhoea /gɒnə'rɪə/ n. venereal disease with inflammatory discharge from urethra or vagina.

goo n. *colloq.* viscous or sticky substance. **gooey** a.

good /gʊd/ 1 a. (*compar.* **better**; *superl.* **best**) having right qualities, adequate; proper; virtuous, morally excellent; worthy; well-behaved; agreeable; suitable; considerable; valid. 2 n. good quality or circumstance; in *pl.* movable property, merchandise. 3 **good-for-nothing** worthless (person); **good humour** genial mood; **good-looking** handsome; **good-nature** kindly disposition; **goodwill** kindly feeling, heartiness, established custom or business etc.

goodbye /gʊd'baɪ/ 1 *int.* expressing good wishes at parting. 2 n. leave-taking, saying goodbye.

goodly /'gʊdlɪ/ a. handsome, of imposing size etc.

goodness /'gʊdnɪs/ n. virtue; excellence; kindness; nutriment.

goody /'gʊdɪ/ 1 n. something good or attractive esp. to eat; good person. 2 *int.* expr. childish delight.

goody-goody /'gʊdɪgʊdɪ/ **1** *a.* obtrusively virtuous. **2** *n.* such person.

goof /guːf/ *sl.* **1** *n.* foolish or stupid person or mistake. **2** *v.* blunder, bungle. **3 goofy** *a.*

googly /'guːglɪ/ *n. Crick.* ball bowled so as to bounce in unexpected direction.

goon /guːn/ *n. sl.* stupid person; hired ruffian.

goosander /guːˈsændə(r)/ *n.* kind of duck.

goose /guːs/ *n.* (*pl.* **geese** /'giːs/) large web-footed bird; female of this; simpleton; (*pl.* **gooses**) tailor's smoothing-iron. **goose-flesh** bristling state of skin due to cold or fright; **goose-step** parading-step of marching soldiers with knees kept stiff.

gooseberry /'gʊzbərɪ/ *n.* small green usu. sour berry; thorny shrub bearing it.

gopher /'gəʊfə(r)/ *n.* Amer. burrowing rodent.

gore[1] *n.* clotted blood.

gore[2] *v.t.* pierce with horn or tusk etc.

gore[3] **1** *n.* wedge-shaped piece in garment; triangular or tapering piece in umbrella or balloon etc. **2** *v.t.* shape with gore.

gorge **1** *n.* narrow opening between hills; surfeit; contents of stomach. **2** *v.* feed greedily; satiate.

gorgeous /'gɔːdʒəs/ *a.* richly coloured; splendid; *colloq.* very pleasant.

gorgon /'gɔːgən/ *n.* frightening or repulsive woman.

Gorgonzola /gɔːgənˈzəʊlə/ *n.* rich blue-veined Italian cheese.

gorilla /gəˈrɪlə/ *n.* large powerful anthropoid ape.

gormandize /'gɔːməndaɪz/ *v.i.* eat greedily.

gormless /'gɔːmlɪs/ *a. colloq.* foolish, lacking sense.

gorse /gɔːs/ *n.* prickly yellow-flowered shrub.

Gorsedd /'gɔːseð/ *n.* meeting of Welsh etc. bards and druids esp. at eisteddfod.

gory /'gɔːrɪ/ *a.* blood-stained; involving bloodshed.

gosh *int.* of surprise etc.

goshawk /'gɒshɔːk/ *n.* large short-winged hawk.

gosling /'gɒzlɪŋ/ *n.* young goose.

gospel /'gɒsp(ə)l/ *n.* teaching or revelation of Christ; **Gospel** each of four books of NT giving account of Christ's life; portion of this read at church service; thing regarded as absolutely true.

gossamer /'gɒsəmə(r)/ **1** *n.* filmy substance of small spiders' webs; delicate filmy material. **2** *a.* light and flimsy as gossamer.

gossip /'gɒsɪp/ **1** *n.* idle talk; informal talk or writing esp. about persons; person indulging in gossip. **2** *v.i.* talk or write gossip. **3 gossip column** regular newspaper column of gossip. **4 gossipy** *a.*

got *past & p.p.* of **get**.

Goth /gɒθ/ *n.* member of Germanic people who invaded Roman Empire in 3rd–5th c.

Gothic /'gɒθɪk/ *a.* of Goths; *Archit.* in the pointed-arch style prevalent in W. Europe in 12th–16th c.; (of novel etc.) in a horrific style popular in 18th–19th c.

gotten *US p.p.* of **get**.

gouache /guːˈɑːʃ/ *n.* painting with opaque water-colour; pigments used for this.

Gouda /'gaʊdə/ *n.* flat round usu. Dutch cheese.

gouge /gaʊdʒ/ **1** *n.* concave-bladed chisel. **2** *v.t.* cut or force (*out*) (as) with gouge.

goulash /'guːlæʃ/ *n.* stew of meat and vegetables seasoned with paprika.

gourd /gʊəd/ *n.* fleshy fruit of trailing or climbing plant; this plant; dried rind of this fruit used as bottle.

gourmand /'gʊəmænd/ *n.* glutton; gourmet.

gourmet /'gʊəmeɪ/ *n.* connoisseur of good food.

gout /gaʊt/ *n.* disease with painful inflammation of small joints; drop or splash, esp. of blood. **gouty** *a.*

govern /'gʌv(ə)n/ *v.* rule with authority; conduct policy and affairs of (State etc.); influence or determine; curb, control.

governance /'gʌvənəns/ *n.* act or manner or function of governing.

governess /'gʌvənɪs/ *n.* woman employed to teach children in private household.

government /'gʌvənmənt/ *n.* system of governing; persons governing State; particular ministry in office. **governmental** *a.*

governor /'gʌvənə(r)/ *n.* ruler; official

governing province or town etc.; executive head of State of US; one of governing body of institution; *sl.* one's employer or father; automatic regulator controlling speed of engine etc.

gown /gaʊn/ *n.* woman's, esp. formal or elegant, dress; robe of alderman or judge or clergyman or member of university etc.; surgeon's overall.

goy *n.* (*pl.* **goyim** or **goys**) Jewish name for non-Jew.

GP *abbr.* general practitioner.

GPO *abbr.* General Post Office.

gr. *abbr.* gram(s); gross.

grab 1 *v.* seize suddenly, snatch; take greedily; capture. 2 *n.* sudden clutch or attempt to seize; *Mech.* device for clutching or gripping.

grace 1 *n.* attractiveness, charm, esp. of elegant proportions or ease and refinement of movement or manner etc.; attractive feature, accomplishment; courteous good will; divine inspiring influence; delay granted; thanksgiving at meals. 2 *v.t.* add grace to; bestow honour on. 3 **grace-note** *Mus.* note embellishing melody; **His, Her, Your, Grace** titles used of or in addressing duke, duchess, or archbishop.

graceful /ˈɡreɪsfʊl/ *a.* full of grace or charm.

graceless /ˈɡreɪslɪs/ *a.* lacking grace or charm.

gracious /ˈɡreɪʃəs/ *a.* kindly, esp. to inferiors; merciful. **gracious living** elegant way of life.

gradate /ɡrəˈdeɪt/ *v.* (cause to) pass by gradations from one shade to another; arrange in gradations.

gradation /ɡrəˈdeɪʃ(ə)n/ *n.* stage of transition or advance; degree in rank or intensity etc.; arrangement in grades. **gradational** *a.*

grade 1 *n.* degree in rank or merit etc.; mark indicating quality of student's work; slope; *US* class or form in school. 2 *v.t.* arrange in grades; give grade to; reduce to easy gradients. 3 **make the grade** succeed.

gradient /ˈɡreɪdɪənt/ *n.* amount of slope in road etc.; sloping road etc.

gradual /ˈɡrædjʊəl/ *a.* happening by degrees; not steep or abrupt.

graduate 1 /ˈɡrædjʊət/ *n.* holder of academic degree. 2 /ˈɡrædjʊeɪt/ *v.* take academic degree; mark in degrees or

portions; arrange in gradations; apportion (tax) according to scale. 3 **graduation** *n.*

graffito /ɡrəˈfiːtəʊ/ *n.* (*pl.* **-ti** /-tiː/ □ See page 667.) drawing or writing on wall etc.

graft¹ /ɡrɑːft/ 1 *n.* shoot or scion planted in slit made in another stock; piece of transplanted living tissue; *sl.* hard work. 2 *v.* insert (graft) *in* or *on*; transplant (living tissue); fix or join (thing) permanently to another; *sl.* work hard.

graft² /ɡrɑːft/ 1 *n.* practices for securing illicit gains in politics or business; such gains. 2 *v.i.* seek or make graft.

Grail *n.* legendary cup or platter used by Christ at Last Supper.

grain 1 *n.* fruit or seed of cereal; *collect.* wheat or allied food-grass; corn; particle, least possible amount; unit of weight, 0.0648 gr.; texture in skin or wood or stone etc.; arrangement of lines of fibre in wood. 2 *v.* paint in imitation of grain of wood; form into grains.

grallatorial /ɡræləˈtɔːrɪəl/ *a.* of long-legged wading birds.

gram *n.* unit of weight in metric system.

graminaceous /ɡræmɪˈneɪʃəs/ *a.* of or like grass.

graminivorous /ɡræmɪˈnɪvərəs/ *a.* grass-eating.

grammar /ˈɡræmə(r)/ *n.* study or rules of a language's inflexions or other means of showing relation between words; book on grammar. **grammar school** secondary school with academic curriculum.

grammarian /ɡrəˈmeərɪən/ *n.* expert in grammar.

grammatical /ɡrəˈmætɪk(ə)l/ *a.* of or according to grammar.

gramme var. of **gram**.

gramophone /ˈɡræməfəʊn/ *n.* instrument reproducing recorded sound by stylus resting on rotating grooved disc. **gramophone record** such disc.

grampus /ˈɡræmpəs/ *n.* sea-animal resembling dolphin.

granary /ˈɡrænərɪ/ *n.* storehouse for grain; region producing much corn.

grand 1 *a.* splendid, imposing; chief, of chief importance; of highest rank;

colloq. excellent. **2** *n.* grand piano; *sl.* 1,000 pounds or dollars etc. **3 grand jury** jury to examine validity of accusation before trial; **grand piano** one with horizontal strings; **grand total** sum of other totals; **grand tour** *hist.* tour of Europe.

grandchild /'græntʃaɪld/ *n.* one's child's child.

granddaughter /'grændɔːtə(r)/ *n.* one's child's daughter.

grandee /græn'diː/ *n.* Spanish or Portuguese noble of highest rank; great personage.

grandeur /'grændjə(r)/ *n.* majesty, splendour, dignity; high rank, eminence.

grandfather /'grænfɑːðə(r)/ *n.* one's parent's father. **grandfather clock** clock in tall wooden case.

grandiloquent /græn'dɪləkwənt/ *a.* pompous or inflated in language. **grandiloquence** *n.*

grandiose /'grændɪəʊs/ *a.* imposing; planned on large scale. **grandiosity** *n.*

grandmother /'grænmʌðə(r)/ *n.* one's parent's mother.

grandparent /'grænpeərənt/ *n.* one's parent's parent.

Grand Prix /grɑ̃ priː/ international motor-racing championship.

grandson /'grænsʌn/ *n.* one's child's son.

grandstand /'grænstænd/ *n.* main stand for spectators at racecourse etc.

grange /greɪndʒ/ *n.* country-house with farm buildings.

granite /'grænɪt/ *n.* granular crystalline rock of quartz and mica etc.

granny /'grænɪ/ *n. colloq.* grandmother; (in full **granny knot**) reefknot crossed wrong way.

grant /grɑːnt/ **1** *v.t.* consent to fulfil; give formally, transfer legally; concede, admit. **2** *n.* thing, esp. money, granted; granting.

grantor /grɑːn'tɔː(r)/ *n.* person by whom property is legally transferred.

granular /'grænjʊlə(r)/ *a.* of or like grains or granules.

granulate /'grænjʊleɪt/ *v.* form into grains; roughen surface of. **granulation** *n.*

granule /'grænjuːl/ *n.* small grain.

grape *n.* green or purple berry growing in clusters on vine. **grape-shot** small

balls as scattering charge for cannon; **grapevine** vine, means of transmission of rumour.

grapefruit /'greɪpfruːt/ *n.* (*pl.* same) large round yellow citrus fruit.

graph /grɑːf/ *n.* symbolic diagram representing relation between two or more variables.

graphic /'græfɪk/ *a.* of writing or drawing or painting or etching etc.; vividly descriptive.

graphics *n.pl.* (usu. treated as *sing.*) production or use of diagrams etc. in calculation and design.

graphite /'græfaɪt/ *n.* crystalline form of carbon used in pencils or as lubricant etc.

graphology /grə'fɒlədʒɪ/ *n.* study of handwriting. **graphologist** *n.*

grapnel /'græpn(ə)l/ *n.* iron-clawed instrument for dragging or grasping; small many-fluked anchor.

grapple /'græp(ə)l/ **1** *v.* seize; grip with hands; come to close quarters with; contend in close fight *with.* **2** *n.* hold (as) of wrestler; close contest; clutching-instrument. **3 grappling-iron** grapnel.

grasp /grɑːsp/ **1** *v.* clutch, seize greedily; hold firmly; understand, realize. **2** *n.* firm hold, grip; mental hold, mastery.

grasping *a.* avaricious.

grass /grɑːs/ **1** *n.* herbage of which blade-like leaves are eaten by horses and cattle etc.; any species of this; pasture land; grass-covered ground; grazing; *sl.* marijuana; *sl.* informer. **2** *v.t.* cover with turf; *sl.* betray, inform police. **3 grass roots** fundamental level or source, esp. (*Polit.*) the voters; **grass snake** small non-poisonous snake; **grass widow** woman whose husband is temporarily absent. **4 grassy** *a.*

grasshopper /'grɑːshɒpə(r)/ *n.* jumping and chirping insect.

grate[1] *v.* rub to small particles on rough surface; grind, creak; have irritating effect.

grate[2] *n.* frame of metal bars holding fuel in fireplace etc.

grateful /'greɪtfʊl/ *a.* thankful; feeling or showing gratitude.

gratify /'grætɪfaɪ/ *v.t.* please, delight; indulge. **gratification** *n.*

grating /'greɪtɪŋ/ n. framework of parallel or crossed metal bars.

gratis /'greɪtɪs or 'grɑː-/ adv. & a. (given, done) for nothing, free.

gratitude /'grætɪtjuːd/ n. being thankful.

gratuitous /grə'tjuːɪtəs/ a. given or done gratis; uncalled for, motiveless.

gratuity /grə'tjuːɪtɪ/ n. money given in recognition of services.

gravamen /grə'veɪmen/ n. essence or worst part of accusation.

grave[1] n. hole dug for burial of corpse; mound or monument over it; being dead, death. **gravestone** inscribed stone over grave; **grave-yard** burial-ground.

grave[2] a. serious, weighty; dignified, solemn; low-pitched.

grave[3] v.t. (p.p. **graved** or **graven**) fix indelibly; arch. engrave, carve. **graven image** idol.

grave[4] /grɑːv/ n. accent (`) over vowel.

grave[5] v.t. clean (ship's bottom) by burning and tarring. **graving dock** dry dock.

gravel /'græv(ə)l/ 1 n. coarse sand and small stones; formation of crystals in bladder. 2 v.t. lay with gravel; puzzle, nonplus.

gravelly /'grævəlɪ/ a. of or like gravel; (of voice) deep and rough-sounding.

gravid /'grævɪd/ a. pregnant.

gravitate /'græviteɪt/ v.i. be attracted (towards); move or tend by force of gravity; sink (as) by gravity.

gravitation /grævɪ'teɪʃ(ə)n/ n. falling of bodies to earth; attraction of each particle of matter on every other; movement or tendency towards centre of this attraction. **gravitational** a.

gravity /'grævɪtɪ/ n. force that attracts body to centre of earth etc.; intensity of this; weight; importance, seriousness; solemnity.

gravy /'greɪvɪ/ n. (sauce made from) juices exuding from meat in and after cooking.

gray var. of **grey**.

grayling /'greɪlɪŋ/ n. silver-grey freshwater fish.

graze[1] 1 v. suffer slight abrasion of (part of body); touch lightly in passing, move (along, against, etc.) with such contact. 2 n. abrasion.

graze[2] v. feed on growing grass; pasture cattle.

grazier /'greɪzɪə(r)/ n. person who feeds cattle for market.

grazing /'greɪzɪŋ/ n. grassland suitable for pasturage.

grease /griːs/ 1 n. fatty or oily matter, esp. as lubricant; melted fat of dead animal. 2 v.t. lubricate or smear with grease. 3 **grease-paint** actor's make-up.

greasy /'griːsɪ/ a. of or like or smeared with or having too much grease; (of person, manner) too unctuous.

great /greɪt/ 1 a. large in bulk or number; considerable in extent or time; important, pre-eminent; of great ability; more than ordinary; colloq. very satisfactory. 2 n. great person or thing. 3 **greatcoat** large heavy overcoat.

great- /greɪt/ in comb. (of family relationships) one degree more remote (great-grandfather, great-niece, etc.).

greatly /'greɪtlɪ/ adv. much.

grebe n. a diving bird.

Grecian /'griːʃ(ə)n/ a. Greek.

greed n. excessive desire esp. for food or wealth.

greedy /'griːdɪ/ a. showing greed; gluttonous; eager to do thing.

Greek 1 a. of Greece. 2 n. native or language of Greece.

green 1 a. coloured like grass; unripe, young, inexperienced; not seasoned or dried or smoked etc. 2 n. green colour or paint or clothes etc.; piece of grassy public land; grass-plot for special purpose; in pl. green vegetables. 3 **green belt** area of open land for preservation round city; **green card** motorist's international insurance document; **greenfinch** bird with greenish plumage; **green fingers** colloq. skill in gardening; **greenfly** green aphid; **greengage** roundish green plum; **greenhorn** simpleton, novice; **greenhouse** structure with sides and roof mainly of glass, for rearing plants; **green pound** the agreed value of the pound for payments to agricultural producers in EEC; **green-room** room in theatre etc. for actors when off stage; **greenstone** kind of jade; **greenstuff** green vegetables; **greensward** grassy turf; **greenwood** woodlands in summer.

greenery /'gri:nəri/ n. green foliage.

greengrocer /'gri:ngrəʊsə(r)/ n. retailer of fruit and vegetables. **greengrocery** n.

greet v.t. address on meeting or arrival; salute, receive (with words etc.); meet (eye, ear, etc.).

greeting /'gri:tɪŋ/ n. act or words used to greet. **greetings card** decorative card for conveying goodwill message etc.

gregarious /grɪ'geərɪəs/ a. fond of company; living in flocks etc.

Gregorian /grɪ'gɔ:rɪən/ a. of plainsong. **Gregorian calendar** calendar introduced in 1582 by Pope Gregory XIII.

gremlin /'gremlɪn/ n. sl. mischievous sprite said to cause faults in machinery etc.

grenade /grɪ'neɪd/ n. small bomb thrown by hand or shot from rifle.

grenadier /grenə'dɪə(r)/ n. hist. soldier armed with grenades; **Grenadiers** first regiment of royal household infantry.

grew past of **grow**.

grey /greɪ/ 1 a. coloured like ashes or lead; clouded, dull; (of hair) turning white, (of person) with grey hair; anonymous, unidentifiable. 2 n. grey colour or paint or clothes etc.; grey horse. 3 v. make or become grey. 4 **Grey Friar** Franciscan monk; **grey matter** active part of brain.

greyhound /'greɪhaʊnd/ n. slender swift dog used in racing and coursing.

greylag /'greɪlæg/ n. European wild goose.

grid n. grating; system of numbered squares for map references; network of lines or electric-power connections etc.; gridiron.

griddle /'grɪd(ə)l/ n. = **girdle**².

gridiron /'grɪdaɪən/ n. barred metal frame for broiling or grilling.

grief /gri:f/ n. sorrow, deep trouble; **come to grief** meet with disaster.

grievance /'gri:v(ə)ns/ n. real or imagined cause for complaint.

grieve /gri:v/ v. (cause to) feel grief.

grievous /'gri:vəs/ a. severe; injurious, flagrant, heinous.

griffin /'grɪfɪn/ n. fabulous creature with eagle's head and wings and lion's body.

griffon /'grɪf(ə)n/ n. small coarse-haired terrier-like dog; large vulture; griffin.

grill 1 n. device on cooker for radiating heat downwards; gridiron; grilled food; grill room. 2 v. cook on gridiron or under grill; subject to severe questioning. 3 **grill room** small restaurant.

grille /grɪl/ n. grating, latticed screen; metal grid protecting motor-vehicle radiator.

grilse /grɪls/ n. young salmon that has been only once to the sea.

grim a. of harsh appearance; stern, merciless; ghastly, joyless; unpleasant.

grimace /'grɪməs/ 1 n. distortion of face expressing disgust etc. or to amuse. 2 v.i. make grimace.

grime 1 n. dirt deeply ingrained. 2 v.t. blacken, befoul. 3 **grimy** a.

grin 1 v.i. smile broadly, showing teeth. 2 n. act or action of grinning.

grind /graɪnd/ 1 v. (past **ground** /graʊnd/) crush to small particles; harass with exactions; sharpen; rub gratingly; study hard, toil. 2 n. grinding; hard dull work. 3 **grindstone** thick revolving abrasive disc for grinding and sharpening etc.

grip 1 v. grasp tightly; take firm hold; compel attention of. 2 n. firm hold, grasp; way of holding; mastery, intellectual hold; part of weapon etc. that is gripped; hair grip; US suitcase or travelling bag.

gripe 1 v. cause colic; affect with colic; sl. complain; clutch, grip. 2 n. in pl. colic pains; sl. complaint. 3 **gripewater** medicine to cure colic in babies.

grisly /'grɪzlɪ/ a. causing terror or horror.

grist n. corn for grinding.

gristle /'grɪs(ə)l/ n. tough flexible tissue; cartilage. **gristly** a.

grit 1 n. small particles of sand etc.; coarse sandstone; colloq. pluck, endurance. 2 v. spread grit on (icy roads etc.); grind or clench (teeth); make grating sound. 3 **gritty** a.

grits n.pl. oats husked but unground; coarse oatmeal.

grizzle /'grɪz(ə)l/ v.i. colloq. cry fretfully.

grizzled a. grey-haired.

grizzly /'grɪzlɪ/ 1 a. grey-haired. 2 n.

grizzly bear. **3 grizzly bear** large fierce
N. Amer. bear.

groan 1 v. make deep sound expressing
pain or grief or disapproval; be oppressed or loaded. **2** n. sound made in
groaning.

groat n. hist. silver fourpenny piece.

groats n.pl. hulled or crushed grain,
esp. oats.

grocer /ˈɡrəʊsə(r)/ n. dealer in food
and household provisions.

grocery /ˈɡrəʊsərɪ/ n. grocer's trade or
shop or (in pl.) goods.

grog n. drink of spirit (esp. rum) and
water.

groggy /ˈɡrɒɡɪ/ a. unsteady, tottering.

grogram /ˈɡrɒɡrəm/ n. coarse fabric
of silk and mohair etc.

groin 1 n. depression between belly
and thigh; edge formed by intersecting
vaults. **2** v.t. build with groins.

groom /ɡruːm/ **1** n. servant who tends
horses; bridegroom. **2** v.t. tend (horse);
give neat or attractive appearance to;
prepare (person) for office or occasion
etc.

groove 1 n. channel or hollow; spiral
cut in gramophone record for needle;
routine. **2** v.t. make groove(s) in.

groovy /ˈɡruːvɪ/ a. of or like a groove;
sl. excellent.

grope v.i. feel about as in dark; search
blindly. **grope one's way** move
cautiously.

grosgrain /ˈɡrəʊɡreɪn/ n. corded fabric of silk etc.

gross /ɡrəʊs/ **1** a. flagrant; total, not
net; coarse; indecent; overfed, bloated;
luxuriant, rank. **2** n. (pl. same) 12
dozen. **3** v.t. produce as gross profit.

grotesque /ɡrəʊˈtesk/ **1** a. comically
or repulsively distorted; incongruous,
absurd. **2** n. decoration interweaving
human and animal forms with foliage;
comically distorted figure or design.

grotto /ˈɡrɒtəʊ/ n. (pl. **-oes**) picturesque cave; structure imitating
cave.

grotty /ˈɡrɒtɪ/ a. sl. unpleasant, dirty,
ugly.

grouch /ɡraʊtʃ/ colloq. **1** v.i. grumble.
2 n. grumbler; complaint; sulky grumbling mood. **3 grouchy** a.

ground¹ /ɡraʊnd/ **1** n. surface of earth;
land; foundation, motive; area of special kind; surface worked upon in

painting; in pl. enclosed land attached
to house; in pl. dregs; bottom of sea or
water; floor or level. **2** v. run aground,
strand; prevent from taking off or
flying; instruct thoroughly; base upon
cause or principle; alight on ground; fix
or place on ground. **3 ground bass**
Mus. short bass phrase repeated with
varied upper parts; **ground floor**
storey on level of outside ground;
ground frost frost on surface of
ground; **ground-nut** peanut; **ground-
rent** rent for land leased for building;
groundsman person who maintains
sports-ground etc.; **ground speed** aircraft's speed relative to ground;
ground swell heavy sea due to distant
or past storm etc.; **groundwork** preliminary or basic work.

ground² past & p.p. of **grind**.

grounding /ˈɡraʊndɪŋ/ n. basic instruction in subject.

groundless /ˈɡraʊndlɪs/ a. without
motive or foundation.

groundsel /ˈɡraʊnds(ə)l/ n. yellow-
flowered weed.

group /ɡruːp/ **1** n. number of persons
or things near or belonging or classed
together; pop group; division of air
force. **2** v. form into group; place in
group(s). **3 group captain** RAF officer
next below air commodore; **group
practice**, medical practice in which
several doctors are associated.

grouse¹ /ɡraʊs/ n. game-bird with
feathered feet.

grouse² /ɡraʊs/ v.i. & n. sl. grumble.

grout /ɡraʊt/ **1** n. thin fluid mortar. **2**
v.t. apply grout to.

grove n. small wood; group of trees.

grovel /ˈɡrɒv(ə)l/ v.i. lie prone, humble
oneself.

grow /ɡrəʊ/ v. (past **grew**; p.p. **grown**)
increase in size or height or amount
etc.; develop or exist as living plant or
natural product; become by degrees;
produce by cultivation; let grow; in
pass. be covered with growth. **grown-
up** adult.

growl /ɡraʊl/ **1** n. guttural sound of
anger; rumble; murmur, complaint. **2**
v. make growl.

grown p.p. of **grow**.

growth /ɡrəʊθ/ n. increase; what has
grown or is growing; tumour. **growth**

industry one developing faster than others.

groyne /grɔɪn/ n. structure run out into sea etc. to stop shifting of beach.

grub 1 n. larva of insect; sl. food. 2 v. dig superficially; clear (ground) of roots etc.; dig up, out.

grubby /ˈgrʌbɪ/ a. dirty, grimy.

grudge 1 v.t. be unwilling to give or allow. 2 n. resentment, ill-will.

gruel /ˈgruːəl/ n. liquid food of oatmeal etc. boiled in milk or water.

gruelling /ˈgruːəlɪŋ/ a. exhausting, punishing.

gruesome /ˈgruːsəm/ a. grisly, disgusting.

gruff a. rough-voiced; surly.

grumble /ˈgrʌmb(ə)l/ 1 v. complain peevishly; be discontented; make rumbling sound. 2 n. act or sound of grumbling.

grummet /ˈgrʌmɪt/ n. insulating washer round electric conductor passing through hole in metal.

grumpy /ˈgrʌmpɪ/ a. ill-tempered.

grunt 1 n. low guttural sound characteristic of pig. 2 v. utter (with) grunt.

Gruyère /ˈgruːjeə(r)/ n. kind of orig. Swiss cheese with holes in.

gryphon var. of **griffin**.

G-string /ˈdʒiːstrɪŋ/ n. narrow strip of cloth etc. attached to string round waist, for covering genitals.

guano /ˈgwɑːnəʊ/ n. excrement of seafowl used as manure.

guarantee /gærənˈtiː/ 1 n. formal promise or assurance; giver of guaranty or security; thing serving as security. 2 v.t. give or serve as guarantee for; answer for; secure. 3 **guarantor** n.

guaranty /ˈgærəntɪ/ n. written or other undertaking to answer for performance of obligation; ground for security.

guard /gɑːd/ 1 n. vigilant state; watch; protector; sentry; official in charge of train; soldiers etc. protecting place or person; device to prevent injury or accident; defensive posture; in pl. household troops. 2 v. protect, defend; take precautions against; keep in check. 3 **guardhouse**, **guardroom**, room accommodating military guard or for keeping prisoners under guard; **guardsman** soldier of guards.

guardian /ˈgɑːdɪən/ n. keeper, protector; person having custody of person or property of minor etc. **guardianship** n.

guava /ˈgwɑːvə/ n. tropical Amer. tree; its edible orange acid fruit.

gubernatorial /guːbənəˈtɔːrɪəl/ a. US of governor.

gudgeon[1] /ˈgʌdʒ(ə)n/ n. small freshwater fish; credulous person.

gudgeon[2] /ˈgʌdʒ(ə)n/ n. kind of pivot or metal pin; socket for rudder.

guelder rose /ˈgeldə(r)/ shrub with round bunches of white flowers.

guernsey /ˈgɜːnzɪ/ n. thick knitted woollen jersey.

guerrilla /gəˈrɪlə/ n. person engaged in irregular fighting by small independently acting groups.

guess /ges/ 1 v. estimate without calculation or measurement; conjecture, think likely; conjecture rightly. 2 n. rough estimate, conjecture. 3 **guesswork** guessing.

guest /gest/ n. person invited to visit one's house or have meal etc. at one's expense, or lodging at hotel etc. **guesthouse** superior boarding-house.

guffaw /gʌˈfɔː/ 1 n. boisterous laugh. 2 v.i. utter guffaw.

guidance /ˈgaɪd(ə)ns/ n. guiding; advice.

guide /gaɪd/ 1 n. one who shows way; professional conductor of travellers or climber etc.; **Guide** member of girls' organization similar to Scouts; adviser; directing principle; guidebook. 2 v.t. act as guide to; lead, direct. 3 **guidebook** book of information about place etc.; **guided missile** one under remote control or directed by equipment within itself; **guide-dog** dog trained to lead blind person; **guided tour** tour accompanied by guide.

Guider /ˈgaɪdə(r)/ n. adult leader of Guides.

guild /gɪld/ n. society for mutual aid or with common object; medieval association of craftsmen. **guildhall** meeting-place of medieval guild, town hall.

guilder /ˈgɪldə(r)/ n. monetary unit of Netherlands.

guile /gaɪl/ n. treachery, deceit. **guileful** a.; **guileless** a.

guillemot /ˈgɪlɪmɒt/ n. kind of auk.

guillotine /ˈgɪlətiːn/ 1 n. beheading-machine; machine for cutting paper; *Parl.* method of shortening discussion of bill by fixing voting times. **2** *v.t.* use guillotine on.

guilt /gɪlt/ *n.* fact of having committed offence; (feeling of) culpability.

guiltless /ˈgɪltlɪs/ *a.* innocent; not having knowledge or possession *of*.

guilty /ˈgɪltɪ/ *a.* having or showing or due to guilt.

guinea /ˈgɪnɪ/ *n.* sum of £1.05. **guinea-fowl** domestic fowl with white-spotted grey plumage; **guinea-pig** small S. Amer. rodent common as pet, person used as subject of experiment etc.

guipure /ˈgiːpʊə(r)/ *n.* heavy lace of linen pieces joined by embroidery.

guise /gaɪz/ *n.* external, esp. assumed, appearance; pretence.

guitar /gɪˈtɑː(r)/ *n.* six-stringed musical instrument played with fingers or plectrum. **guitarist** *n.*

gulch *n. US* ravine, gully.

gulf *n.* large area of sea partly surrounded by land; deep hollow, chasm; wide difference of opinion etc. **Gulf Stream** warm current from Gulf of Mexico to Europe.

gull[1] *n.* long-winged web-footed sea-bird.

gull[2] *n. & v.t.* dupe, fool.

gullet /ˈgʌlɪt/ *n.* food-passage from mouth to stomach.

gullible /ˈgʌlɪb(ə)l/ *a.* easily persuaded or deceived. **gullibility** *n.*

gully /ˈgʌlɪ/ *n.* ravine cut by water; gutter, drain; *Crick.* fielding-position between point and slips.

gulp 1 *v.* swallow hastily or with effort; choke. **2** *n.* act of gulping; large mouthful.

gum[1] **1** *n.* sticky secretion of some trees and shrubs, used as glue etc.; chewing-gum; in *pl.* sweet made of gelatine etc. **2** *v.t.* apply gum to; fasten thus. **3 gum arabic** gum exuded from some kinds of acacia; **gumboot** rubber boot; **gum-tree** tree exuding gum, esp. eucalyptus; **gum up** *colloq.* interfere with, spoil.

gum[2] *n.* firm flesh around roots of teeth. **gumboil** small abscess on gum.

gummy[1] /ˈgʌmɪ/ *a.* sticky, exuding gum.

gummy[2] /ˈgʌmɪ/ *a.* toothless.

gumption /ˈgʌmpʃ(ə)n/ *n. colloq.* common sense; resourcefulness, enterprise.

gun *n.* metal tube for throwing missiles with explosive propellant; starting-pistol; device for discharging grease or electrons etc. in desired direction; member of shooting-party. **gunboat** small warship with heavy guns; **gun-carriage** wheeled support for gun; **gun-cotton** cotton steeped in acids, used for blasting; **gun dog** dog trained to assist at shoot; **gunfire** firing of guns; **gunman** armed lawbreaker; **gun-metal** bluish-grey alloy of copper and tin or zinc; **gunpowder** explosive of saltpetre, sulphur, and charcoal; **gunroom** room in warship, for junior officers; **gun-running** bringing guns into country illegally; **gunshot** shot from gun, the range of a gun.

gunner /ˈgʌnə(r)/ *n.* artillery soldier; *Naut.* warrant officer in charge of battery and magazine etc.; airman who operates gun.

gunnery /ˈgʌnərɪ/ *n.* construction and management of large guns.

gunny /ˈgʌnɪ/ *n.* coarse sacking usu. of jute fibre; sack made of this.

gunwale /ˈgʌn(ə)l/ *n.* upper edge of ship's or boat's side.

guppy /ˈgʌpɪ/ *n.* very small bright-coloured tropical fish.

gurgle /ˈgɜːg(ə)l/ **1** *n.* bubbling sound. **2** *v.* make gurgles; utter with gurgles.

gurnard /ˈgɜːnəd/ *n.* sea-fish with large spiny head.

guru /ˈguːruː/ *n.* Hindu spiritual teacher; influential or revered teacher.

gush 1 *n.* sudden or copious stream; effusiveness. **2** *v.* flow with gush; emit gush of; speak or behave effusively.

gusher /ˈgʌʃə(r)/ *n.* oil-well emitting unpumped oil.

gusset /ˈgʌsɪt/ *n.* piece let into garment etc. to strengthen or enlarge it.

gust 1 *n.* sudden violent rush of wind; burst of rain or smoke or anger etc. **2** *v.i.* blow in gusts. **3 gusty** *a.*

gustatory /ˈgʌstətərɪ/ *a.* connected with sense of taste.

gusto /ˈgʌstəʊ/ *n.* zest, enjoyment.

gut 1 *n.* intestine; in *pl.* bowels, entrails; in *pl. colloq.* force of character, staying power; material for violin etc. strings or surgical use or for fishing line. **2** *a.* instinctive, fundamental. **3** *v.t.* remove guts of; remove or destroy internal fittings of (building).

gutsy /'gʌtsɪ/ *a. colloq.* courageous; greedy.

gutta-percha /gʌtə'pɜːtʃə/ *n.* tough plastic substance from latex of various Malayan trees.

gutter /'gʌtə(r)/ **1** *n.* shallow trough below eaves, or channel at side of street, for carrying off rain-water; channel, groove. **2** *v.* (of candle) burn unsteadily and melt away.

guttering /'gʌtərɪŋ/ *n.* material for gutters.

guttersnipe /'gʌtəsnaɪp/ *n.* street urchin.

guttural /'gʌtər(ə)l/ **1** *a.* throaty; (of sound) produced in throat. **2** *n.* guttural consonant.

guy[1] /gaɪ/ **1** *n.* effigy of Guy Fawkes burnt on 5 Nov.; *sl.* man; grotesquely dressed person. **2** *v.t.* ridicule.

guy[2] /gaɪ/ **1** *n.* rope or chain etc. to steady crane-load etc. or secure tent. **2** *v.t.* secure with guy(s).

guzzle /'gʌz(ə)l/ *v.* drink or eat greedily.

gybe /dʒaɪb/ *v.* (of fore-and-aft sail or boom) swing to other side; (of boat etc.) change course thus.

gym /dʒɪm/ *n. colloq.* gymnasium, gymnastics. **gym-slip** sleeveless usu. belted garment worn by schoolgirls.

gymkhana /dʒɪm'kɑːnə/ *n.* meeting for competition between horse-riders etc.

gymnasium /dʒɪm'neɪzɪəm/ *n.* (*pl.* -siums) room etc. equipped for gymnastics.

gymnast /'dʒɪmnæst/ *n.* expert in gymnastics.

gymnastic /dʒɪm'næstɪk/ *a.* of gymnastics. **gymnastically** *adv.*

gymnastics *n.pl.* occas. treated as *sing.* exercises to develop muscles or demonstrate agility.

gynaecology /gaɪnə'kɒlədʒɪ/ *n.* science of physiological functions and diseases of women. **gynaecological** *a.*; **gynaecologist** *n.*

gypsum /'dʒɪpsəm/ *n.* mineral used to make plaster of Paris.

gypsy /'dʒɪpsɪ/ *n.* member of wandering dark-skinned people of Europe.

gyrate /dʒaɪ'reɪt/ *v.i.* move in circle or spiral. **gyration** *n.*; **gyratory** *a.*

gyro /'dʒaɪrəʊ/ *n.* (*pl.* -ros) *colloq.* gyroscope.

gyroscope /'dʒaɪrəskəʊp/ *n.* rotating wheel whose axis is free to turn but maintains fixed direction unless perturbed, esp. as used for stabilization. **gyroscopic** /-'skɒp-/ *a.*

H

H *abbr.* hard (pencil-lead).

h. *abbr.* hour(s); hot.

ha *int.* expr. surprise, triumph, etc.

ha. *abbr.* hectare(s).

habeas corpus /ˈheɪbɪəs ˈkɔːpəs/ writ requiring person to be brought before judge etc., esp. to investigate lawfulness of his imprisonment.

haberdasher /ˈhæbədæʃə(r)/ *n.* dealer in small articles of dress and sewing-goods. **haberdashery** *n.*

habiliments /həˈbɪlɪmənts/ *n.pl.* clothing.

habit /ˈhæbɪt/ **1** *n.* settled tendency or practice; practice that is hard to give up; constitution (of body or mind); clothes esp. of religious order. **2** *v.t.* clothe.

habitable /ˈhæbɪtəb(ə)l/ *a.* suitable for living in. **habitability** *n.*

habitat /ˈhæbɪtæt/ *n.* natural home of plant or animal.

habitation /hæbɪˈteɪʃ(ə)n/ *n.* house or home; inhabiting.

habitual /həˈbɪtjʊəl/ *a.* done as a habit; usual; given to a habit.

habituate /həˈbɪtjʊeɪt/ *v.t.* accustom (to). **habituation** *n.*

habitué /həˈbɪtjʊeɪ/ *n.* frequent visitor (*of*). [F]

hacienda /hæsɪˈendə/ *n.* plantation etc. with dwelling-house, in Spanish-speaking country.

hack[1] **1** *v.* cut or chop roughly; kick shin of; deal cutting blows (*at*). **2** *n.* kick with toe of boot, wound from this. **3** **hack-saw** saw for metal-cutting.

hack[2] **1** *n.* horse for ordinary riding; hired horse; person hired to do dull routine work, esp. as writer. **2** *v.i.* ride on horseback at ordinary pace. **3** *a.* used as hack; commonplace.

hacking *a.* (of cough) short, dry, and frequent.

hacker /ˈhækə(r)/ *n.* *colloq.* (excessively) enthusiastic computer user.

hackle /ˈhæk(ə)l/ *n.* long feathers on neck of domestic cock etc.; steel flax-comb. **with hackles up** angry, ready to fight.

hackney /ˈhæknɪ/ *v.t.* make common or trite by repetition. **hackney-cab, -carriage,** etc. taxi.

had *past* & *p.p.* of **have.**

haddock /ˈhædək/ *n.* common sea-fish used for food.

Hades /ˈheɪdiːz/ *n.* *Gk. myth.* abode of departed spirits; the underworld.

hadji /ˈhædʒɪ/ *n.* Muslim who has been to Mecca on pilgrimage.

haematite /ˈhiːmətaɪt/ *n.* red or brown iron ore.

haematology /hiːməˈtɒlədʒɪ/ *n.* study of physiology of the blood.

haemoglobin /hiːməˈɡləʊbɪn/ *n.* oxygen-carrying substance in red blood-cells.

haemophilia /hiːməˈfɪlɪə/ *n.* (hereditary) tendency to severe bleeding from even a slight injury through failure of blood to clot. **haemophiliac** *a.* & *n.*

haemorrhage /ˈhemərɪdʒ/ **1** *n.* escape of blood from blood-vessels, bleeding. **2** *v.i.* undergo haemorrhage.

haemorrhoid /ˈhemərɔɪd/ *n.* (usu. in *pl.*) swollen vein in tissue near anus.

haft /hɑːft/ *n.* handle (of knife etc.).

hag *n.* ugly old woman. **hagridden** afflicted by nightmares or fears.

haggard /ˈhæɡəd/ *a.* wild-looking (esp. from fatigue or worry etc.).

haggis /ˈhæɡɪs/ *n.* minced offal of sheep boiled in bag with oatmeal etc.

haggle /ˈhæɡ(ə)l/ *v.i.* & *n.* dispute, esp. *about* price or terms.

hagiography /hæɡɪˈɒɡrəfɪ/ *n.* writing of lives of saints.

ha ha *int.* representing laughter.

ha-ha *n.* fence placed along bottom of ditch, bounding park or garden.

haiku /ˈhaɪkuː/ *n.* Japanese 3-line poem of usu. 17 syllables.

hail[1] **1** *n.* pellets of frozen rain falling in shower (**hailstorm**); shower of questions etc. **2** *v.* pour down as or like hail. **3** **hailstone** pellet of hail.

hail[2] **1** *int.* of greeting. **2** *v.* salute; greet (*as*); call to; have come *from.* **3** *n.* hailing.

hair *n.* any or all of fine filaments growing from skin esp. of human head; hair-like thing. **haircloth** cloth made of hair; **haircut** (style of) cutting hair; **hair-do** *colloq.* style or process of woman's hairdressing; **hairdressing** cutting and styling of hair; **hair-grip** flat hairpin with ends close together; **hair-line** edge of person's hair on forehead, very narrow crack or line; **hair-piece** false hair augmenting person's natural hair; **hairpin** U-shaped pin for fastening the hair; **hairpin bend** very sharp doubling-back of road; **hair-raising** terrifying; **hair's breadth** minute distance; **hair shirt** ascetic's or penitent's shirt of haircloth; **hair-slide** clip for keeping hair in position; **hairspring** fine spring regulating balance-wheel of watch; **hair-style** particular way of arranging hair; **hair-trigger** trigger acting on very slight pressure. **hairy** *a.*

hajji var. of **hadji.**

hake *n.* codlike sea-fish.

halberd /'hælbəd/ *n. hist.* combined spear and battle-axe.

halcyon /'hælsɪən/ *a.* peaceful, quiet; (of period) happy, prosperous.

hale[1] *a.* strong and healthy.

hale[2] *v.t. arch.* drag forcibly.

half /hɑːf/ 1 *n.* (*pl.* **halves** /hɑːvz/) either of two (esp. equal) parts into which a thing is divided; half-price ticket; school term; *colloq.* half-back, half-pint, etc. 2 *a.* forming a half. 3 *adv.* in part; equally. 4 **half-and-half** being half one thing and half another; **half-back** player immediately behind forwards in football etc.; **half-baked** not thoroughly thought out; **half-breed** person of mixed race; **half-brother**, **-sister**, one having one parent in common; **half-caste** half-breed; **half-crown** former British coin worth 2s. 6d. (12½p); **half-hearted** lacking courage or zeal; **half-life** time after which radioactivity etc. is half its original value; **at half-mast** (of flag) lowered to half height of mast as symbol of mourning; **half moon** (shape of) moon with disc half illuminated; **half nelson** wrestling hold, with arm under opponent's arm and behind his head; **half-term** short holiday about halfway through school term; **half-timbered** having walls with spaces in timber frame filled with bricks or plaster; **half-time** time when half of game etc. is completed, interval occurring then; **half-tone** photograph representing tones by large or small dots; **half-truth** statement that conveys only part of truth; **half-volley** ball hit

or returned as soon as it touches ground; **half-wit** stupid or foolish person; **half-witted** *a.*

halfpenny /'heɪpnɪ/ *n.* (*pl.* **halfpence** /'heɪpəns/ or **halfpennies** /'heɪpnɪz/) former bronze coin worth half penny.

halibut /'hælɪbət/ *n.* large flat-fish.

halitosis /hælɪ'təʊsɪs/ *n.* unpleasant-smelling breath.

hall /hɔːl/ *n.* entrance room or passage of house; large room or building for meetings or meals or concerts etc.; large country house, esp. with landed estate; building for residence or instruction of students etc.; college dining-room; large public room; *US* corridor. **hallmark** mark used to show standard of gold, silver, and platinum, *fig.* token of excellence or quality.

hallelujah var. of **alleluia.**

halliard var. of **halyard.**

hallo /hə'ləʊ/ *int. & n.* calling attention or expr. surprise or greeting.

halloo /hə'luː/ 1 *int. & n.* cry inciting dogs to chase etc., or to attract attention. 2 *v.* cry halloo.

hallow /'hæləʊ/ *v.t.* make or honour as holy.

Hallowe'en /hæləʊ'iːn/ *n.* 31 Oct.

hallucinate /hə'luːsɪneɪt/ *v.i.* experience hallucination(s).

hallucination /həluːsɪ'neɪʃ(ə)n/ *n.* illusion of seeing objects or hearing sounds etc. not actually present. **hallucinatory** *a.*

hallucinogen /hə'luːsɪnədʒ(ə)n/ *n.* drug causing hallucinations. **hallucinogenic** /-'dʒen-/ *a.*

halo /'heɪləʊ/ 1 *n.* (*pl.* **-loes**) disc of light shown round head of saint etc. in paintings etc.; circle of light round sun or moon etc. 2 *v.t.* surround with halo.

halogen /'hæləʊdʒ(ə)n/ *n.* any of group of non-metallic elements (fluorine, chlorine, etc.) which form a salt by simple union with a metal.

halt[1] /hɔːlt or hɒlt/ 1 *n.* stoppage on march or journey; interruption of progress; railway stopping-place without regular station-buildings etc. 2 *v.* (cause to) make a halt.

halt[2] /hɔːlt or hɒlt/ 1 *v.i.* walk hesitatingly; limp. 2 *a.* lame.

halter /'hɔːltə(r)/ *n.* rope or strap with headstall for horses or cattle; woman's dress etc. with top held up by strap passing round back of neck.

halve /haːv/ v.t. divide into halves; reduce to half.

halyard /'hæljəd/ n. Naut. rope or tackle for raising and lowering sail etc.

ham 1 n. upper part of pig's leg salted and dried for food; back of thigh; thigh and buttock; inexpert but flamboyant performer or actor; operator of amateur radio station. **2** v. overact. **3 hamfisted** sl. heavy-handed, clumsy.

hamburger /'hæmbəːgə(r)/ n. fried cake of chopped beef, often eaten in a soft bread roll.

hamlet /'hæmlɪt/ n. small village, esp. without church.

hammer /'hæmə(r)/ **1** n. tool with heavy metal head at right angles to handle, used for breaking, driving nails, etc.; similar device, as for exploding charge in gun or striking strings of piano etc.; auctioneer's mallet; metal ball attached to a wire for throwing as athletic contest. **2** v. strike or drive (as) with hammer. **3 hammer and tongs** with great energy; **hammer-toe** toe bent permanently downwards.

hammock /'hæmək/ n. bed of canvas or netting suspended by cords at ends.

hamper[1] /'hæmpə(r)/ n. basketwork packing-case; food etc. packed up esp. as a present.

hamper[2] /'hæmpə(r)/ v.t. obstruct movement of; impede, hinder.

hamster /'hæmstə(r)/ n. small rodent often kept as pet.

hamstring /'hæmstrɪŋ/ **1** n. any of five tendons at back of human knee; (in quadruped) tendon at back of hock. **2** v.t. (past and p.p. **hamstrung**) cripple by cutting hamstring(s).

hand 1 n. end part beyond wrist of human arm; similar member of monkey; control, disposal; share (in doing); agency; handlike thing, esp. pointer of clock etc.; (right or left) side; pledge of marriage; skill or style esp. of writing; person who does or makes something; person etc. as source; manual worker in factory etc.; playing-cards dealt to player, round or game of cards; colloq. round of applause; forefoot of quadruped; measure of horse's height, = 4 in. **2** v.t. deliver or transfer (as) with

hand; serve (food round). **3 at hand** near by; **give, lend, a hand** help; **handbag** small bag esp. used by woman to hold purse etc.; **handbill** printed notice circulated by hand; **handbook** short manual or guidebook; **handcuff** secure (prisoner) with **handcuffs**, pair of lockable metal rings joined by short chain; **hand-out** food etc. given to needy person, information etc. distributed to press etc.; **hand over fist** with rapid progress; **handpicked** carefully chosen; **handrail** rail along edge of stairs etc.; **hands down** easily, without effort; **handwriting** (style of) writing by hand; **out of hand** without delay, out of control; **to hand** within reach.

h. & c. abbr. hot and cold (water).

handful /'hændfʊl/ n. enough to fill the hand; small number or quantity; colloq. troublesome person or task.

handicap /'hændɪkæp/ **1** n. disadvantage imposed on superior competitor to equalize chances; race etc. in which handicaps are imposed; disadvantage, disability. **2** v.t. impose handicap on; place at disadvantage; in p.p. suffering from physical or mental disability.

handicraft /'hændɪkrɑːft/ n. work that requires manual and artistic skill.

handiwork /'hændɪwɜːk/ n. thing done or made by hands or by particular person.

handkerchief /'hæŋkətʃɪf/ n. square of linen or cotton etc., used to wipe nose etc.

handle /'hænd(ə)l/ **1** n. part by which thing is held. **2** v.t. touch or feel with hands; manage; deal with; deal in (goods etc.). **3 handlebar** steering-bar of bicycle etc.

handler /'hændlə(r)/ n. person in charge of trained dog etc.

handmaid /'hændmeɪd/ n. arch. (also **-maiden**) female servant.

handsome /'hændsəm/ a. good-looking; generous; considerable.

handy /'hændɪ/ a. convenient to handle; ready to hand; clever with hands. **handyman** person able to do odd jobs.

hang 1 v. (past and p.p. **hung** exc. as below) (cause to) be supported from above; set up on hinges etc.; place (picture) on wall or in exhibition; attach (wallpaper); (*past* & *p.p.* **hanged**) suspend or be suspended by neck, esp. as capital punishment; let droop; remain or be hung. **2** *n.* way thing hangs. **3 get the hang of** get knack of, understand. **hang about, around** loiter, not move away; **hangdog** shamefaced; **hang fire** delay acting; **hang-glider** airborne frame controlled by movements of person standing or lying in it; **hangman** executioner by hanging; **hangnail** agnail; **hangover** after-effects of excess of alcohol; **hang up** hang from hook etc., end telephone conversation; **hang-up** *sl.* emotional inhibition.

hangar /ˈhæŋə(r)/ *n.* shed for housing aircraft etc.

hanger /ˈhæŋə(r)/ *n.* person or thing that hangs; shaped piece of wood etc. from which clothes may be hung. **hanger-on** follower, dependant.

hanging /ˈhæŋɪŋ/ *n.* usu. in *pl.* drapery for walls etc.

hank /hæŋk/ *n.* coil of yarn etc.

hanker /ˈhæŋkə(r)/ *v.i.* crave or long *after* or *for*.

hanky /ˈhæŋkɪ/ *n.* *colloq.* handkerchief.

hanky-panky /ˈhæŋkɪˈpæŋkɪ/ *n.* *sl.* trickery; misbehaviour.

hansom /ˈhænsəm/ *n.* (in full **hansom cab**) two-wheeled horse-drawn cab with driver seated behind.

haphazard /hæpˈhæzəd/ **1** *a.* casual, random. **2** *adv.* at random.

hapless /ˈhæplɪs/ *a.* unlucky.

happen /ˈhæpən/ *v.i.* occur; have the (good or bad) fortune (*to do* thing); be fate or experience of; come by chance *on*.

happy /ˈhæpɪ/ *a.* feeling or showing pleasure or contentment; fortunate, apt, pleasing. **happy-go-lucky** taking things cheerfully as they happen.

hara-kiri /ˈhærəˈkɪrɪ/ *n.* Japanese suicide by ritual disembowelling.

harangue /həˈræŋ/ **1** *n.* lengthy and earnest speech. **2** *v.* make harangue (to).

harass /ˈhærəs/ □ See page 665. *v.t.* worry, trouble; attack repeatedly. **harassment** *n.*

harbinger /ˈhɑːbɪndʒə(r)/ *n.* one who announces another's approach, forerunner.

harbour /ˈhɑːbə(r)/ **1** *n.* place of shel-

ter for ships; shelter. **2** *v.t.* give shelter to; entertain (thoughts etc.).

hard **1** *a.* firm, solid; unyielding; difficult to bear or do or understand; unfeeling, harsh, severe; (of drinks) strongly alcoholic; (of drug) potent and addictive; strenuous. **2** *adv.* strenuously, severely. **3 hard and fast** (of rule etc.) strict; **hardback** (book) bound in stiff covers; **hardbitten** tough; **hardboard** stiff board of compressed etc. wood-pulp; **hard-boiled** (of eggs) boiled until white and yolk are solid, *fig.* tough, shrewd; **hard cash** coins and banknotes, not cheques etc.; **hard copy** printed material produced by computer; **hard core** heavy material as road-foundation; **hard court** lawn-tennis court of asphalt etc.; **hard currency** currency not likely to fluctuate much in value; **hard-headed** practical, not sentimental; **hardhearted** unfeeling; **hard line** firm adherence to policy; **hard lines** worse fortune than one deserves; **hard of hearing** somewhat deaf; **hardpressed** closely pursued, burdened with urgent business; **hard sell** aggressive salesmanship; **hard shoulder** strip on side of motorway for use only in emergency; **hard up** short of money; **hardware** ironmongery, weapons, machinery, etc.; **hard water** water containing mineral salts that prevent soap from lathering easily; **hardwood** wood of deciduous tree.

harden /ˈhɑːd(ə)n/ *v.* make or become hard(er) or unyielding.

hardihood /ˈhɑːdɪhʊd/ *n.* boldness.

hardly /ˈhɑːdlɪ/ *adv.* with difficulty; scarcely; harshly, severely.

hardship /ˈhɑːdʃɪp/ *n.* severe suffering or privation.

hardy /ˈhɑːdɪ/ *a.* robust; capable of endurance; (of plant) able to grow in the open all year.

hare /heə(r)/ **1** *n.* mammal like large rabbit, with long ears, short tail, and divided upper lip. **2** *v.i.* run very fast. **3 hare-brained** rash, wild; **harelip** congenital fissure of upper lip.

harebell /ˈheəbel/ *n.* plant with pale-blue bell-shaped flowers.

harem /ˈhɑːriːm/ *n.* women of a Muslim household, living in separate part of house; their quarters.

haricot /ˈhærɪkəʊ/ n. (in full **haricot bean**) dried white seed of variety of bean.

hark v.i. listen. **hark back** revert (to subject).

harlequin /ˈhɑːlɪkwɪn/ 1 a. in various colours. 2 **Harlequin** n. pantomime character in mask and parti-coloured costume.

harlot /ˈhɑːlət/ n. arch. prostitute. **harlotry** n.

harm n. & v.t. damage, hurt.

harmful /ˈhɑːmfʊl/ a. that does harm.

harmless /ˈhɑːmlɪs/ a. that does no harm.

harmonic /hɑːˈmɒnɪk/ 1 a. of or relating to harmony; harmonious. 2 n. harmonic tone; component frequency of wave motion. 3 **harmonic tone** one produced by vibration of aliquot parts of strings etc.

harmonica /hɑːˈmɒnɪkə/ n. mouth-organ.

harmonious /hɑːˈməʊnɪəs/ a. sweet-sounding; forming a pleasant or consistent whole; free from dissent.

harmonium /hɑːˈməʊnɪəm/ n. keyboard musical instrument with bellows and metal reeds.

harmonize /ˈhɑːmənaɪz/ v. add notes to (melody) to form chords; bring into or be in harmony. **harmonization** n.

harmony /ˈhɑːmənɪ/ n. combination of notes to form chords; melodious sound; agreement, concord.

harness /ˈhɑːnɪs/ 1 n. gear of draught-horse etc.; arrangement of straps etc. for fastening thing to person etc. 2 v.t. put harness on; utilize (natural forces) for motive power.

harp 1 n. musical instrument with strings of graduated lengths played with fingers. 2 v.i. play harp; dwell tediously on. 3 **harpist** n.

harpoon /hɑːˈpuːn/ 1 n. spear-like missile for catching whales etc. 2 v.t. spear with harpoon.

harpsichord /ˈhɑːpsɪkɔːd/ n. keyboard musical instrument with strings plucked mechanically.

harpy /ˈhɑːpɪ/ n. Myth. monster with woman's face and bird's wings and claws; rapacious woman.

harridan /ˈhærɪd(ə)n/ n. ill-tempered old woman.

harrier /ˈhærɪə(r)/ n. hound used in hunting hares; in pl. cross-country runners; kind of falcon.

harrow /ˈhærəʊ/ 1 n. frame with metal teeth or discs for breaking clods of earth. 2 v.t. draw harrow over; distress greatly.

harry /ˈhærɪ/ v.t. ravage, spoil (land, people); harass.

harsh a. rough to hear or taste etc.; severe, unfeeling.

hart n. male of (esp. red) deer.

hartebeest /ˈhɑːtɪbiːst/ n. large Afr. antelope.

harum-scarum /heərəmˈskeərəm/ a. reckless, wild.

harvest /ˈhɑːvɪst/ 1 n. gathering in of crops etc.; season for this; season's yield; product of any action. 2 v.t. reap and gather in.

harvester n. reaper, reaping-machine.

has 3 pers. sing. pres. of **have**.

hash 1 n. dish of cooked meat cut into small pieces and recooked; mixture, jumble; re-used material. 2 v.t. make (meat) into hash. 3 **make a hash of** colloq. make a mess of, bungle; **settle person's hash** make end of or subdue him.

hashish /ˈhæʃiːʃ/ n. narcotic drug got from hemp.

hasp /hɑːsp/ n. hinged metal clasp passing over staple and secured by pin etc.

hassle /ˈhæs(ə)l/ 1 n. quarrel; struggle. 2 v. quarrel; harass.

hassock /ˈhæsək/ n. kneeling-cushion.

haste /heɪst/ 1 n. urgency of movement; hurry. 2 v.i. go in haste. 3 **make haste** be quick.

hasten /ˈheɪs(ə)n/ v. (cause to) proceed or go quickly.

hasty /ˈheɪstɪ/ a. hurried; acting or said or done too quickly.

hat n. head-covering esp. worn out of doors. **hat trick** Crick. taking 3 wickets with successive balls, Footb. etc. scoring of 3 goals by same player in same match.

hatch[1] n. opening in floor or wall etc.; opening or door in aircraft etc.; cover for hatchway. **hatchback** vehicle with rear door hinged at top; **hatchway** opening in ship's deck for lowering cargo.

hatch[2] 1 v. bring or come forth from

egg; incubate; devise (plot). **2** *n.* hatching; brood hatched.

hatch² *v.t.* mark with parallel lines.

hatchet /'hætʃɪt/ *n.* light short axe.

hate 1 *n.* hatred. **2** *v.t.* dislike strongly; bear malice to.

hateful /'heɪtfʊl/ *a.* arousing hatred.

hatred /'heɪtrɪd/ *a.* intense dislike; ill-will.

hatter /'hætə(r)/ *n.* maker or seller of hats.

haughty /'hɔːtɪ/ *a.* proud, arrogant.

haul /'hɔːl/ **1** *v.* pull or drag forcibly; transport by cart etc. **2** *n.* hauling; amount gained or acquired; distance to be traversed.

haulage /'hɔːlɪdʒ/ *n.* (charge for) conveyance of goods.

haulier /'hɔːlɪə(r)/ *n.* one who hauls, esp. firm or person engaged in road transport of goods.

haulm /hɔːm/ *n.* stalks of beans or peas or potatoes etc.

haunch *n.* fleshy part of buttock and thigh; leg and loin of deer etc. as food.

haunt 1 *v.t.* (of ghost etc.) visit frequently usu. with signs of its presence; be persistently in or with; obsess. **2** *n.* place frequented by person.

hautboy /'əʊbɔɪ/ *n.* old name for oboe.

haute couture /əʊt kuː'tjʊə(r)/ (world of) high fashion. [F]

hauteur /əʊ'tɜ:(r)/ *n.* haughtiness.

Havana /hə'vænə/ *n.* cigar of Cuban tobacco.

have /hæv/ **1** *v.* (**3** *sing. pres.* **has** /hæz/; *past & p.p.* **had**) hold in possession; possess, contain; enjoy, suffer; be burdened with; give birth to; engage in; permit (to); cause to be or do etc.; receive; *colloq.* deceive, get the better of. **2** *v. aux.* with *p.p.* of *vbs.* forming past tenses. **3** *n. sl.* one who has (esp. wealth etc.); **haves and have-nots** rich and poor); swindle. **4 have on** wear (clothes), have (engagement), *colloq.* play trick on; **have to** be obliged to, must.

haven /'heɪv(ə)n/ *n.* refuge; harbour.

haver /'heɪvə(r)/ *v.i.* hesitate; talk foolishly.

haversack /'hævəsæk/ *n.* canvas etc. bag carried on back or over shoulder.

havoc /'hævək/ *n.* devastation, confusion.

haw *n.* hawthorn berry.

hawk¹ 1 *n.* bird of prey with rounded wings; person who advocates aggressive policy. **2** *v.* hunt with hawk.

hawk² *v.* clear throat noisily; bring (phlegm etc.) *up* thus.

hawk³ *v.t.* carry about for sale.

hawker /'hɔːkə(r)/ *n.* person who hawks goods.

hawser /'hɔːzə(r)/ *n. Naut.* thick rope or cable for mooring ship.

hawthorn /'hɔːθɔːn/ *n.* thorny shrub or tree bearing red berries.

hay *n.* grass mown and dried for fodder. **hay fever** allergic irritation of nose and throat etc. caused esp. by pollen; **haymaking** mowing grass and spreading it to dry; **haystack** packed pile of hay; **haywire** tangled, in disorder, out of control.

hazard /'hæzəd/ **1** *n.* danger, risk; obstacle on golf-course. **2** *v.t.* risk; venture on (guess etc.).

hazardous /'hæzədəs/ *a.* risky.

haze *n.* slight mist; mental obscurity, confusion.

hazel /'heɪz(ə)l/ *n.* nut-bearing bush or small tree; light brown colour.

hazy /'heɪzɪ/ *a.* misty; vague.

HB *abbr.* hard black (pencil-lead).

H-bomb /'eɪtʃbɒm/ *n.* hydrogen bomb.

he 1 *pron.* (*obj.* **him**, *poss.* **his**) the male person or animal in question. **2** *n. & a.* male. **3 he-man** masterful or virile man.

HE *abbr.* high explosive; His or Her Excellency.

head /hed/ **1** *n.* uppermost part of human body; foremost part of body of animal; seat of intellect etc.; person, individual; top or front or upper end; thing like head in form or position; signal-converting device on tape-recorder etc.; foam on top of beer etc.; confined body of water or steam, pressure exerted by this; ruler, chief, leader, etc.; headmaster, headmistress; climax or crisis. **2** *v.* be or put oneself or be put or put thing at head of; form head of; *Footb.* strike (ball) with head; provide with head or heading. **3 headache** continuous pain in head, *colloq.* troublesome problem; **head-dress** (esp. ornamental) covering for head; **head-lamp, headlight**, lamp on front of car etc.; **headland** promontory; **headline** line at top of page or newspaper article etc. containing title etc., in *pl.* summary of broadcast news; **headlong** with head foremost, precipitately; **headmaster**, **headmistress**, principal master, mistress, of school; **head-on** (of collision etc.) head to head or front to front; **head-phone** pair of earphones held by band fitting over head; **headroom** overhead space; **headstall** part of bridle or halter fitting round horse's head; **head start** advantage granted or gained at beginning of race; **headstone** stone set up at head of grave; **headstrong** self-willed, obstinate; **headway** progress; **head wind** one blowing from directly in front; **off one's head** *colloq.* crazy.

header /'hedə(r)/ *n. Footb.* act of heading a ball; *colloq.* dive or plunge head first.

heading /'hedɪŋ/ *n.* title etc. at head of page etc.

headquarters /hed'kwɔːtəz/ *n.pl.* (occas. treated as *sing.*) centre of operations; chief place of business etc.

heady /'hedɪ/ *a.* (of liquor etc.) apt to intoxicate; impetuous.

heal *v.* restore to health; cure; become sound.

health /helθ/ *n.* state of being well in body or mind; condition of body; toast drunk in person's honour. **health food** food chosen for its unmodified natural qualities etc.; **health service** public medical service.

healthful /'helθfʊl/ *a.* health-giving.

healthy /'helθɪ/ *a.* having or conducive to good health.

heap 1 *n.* number of things lying one on another; in *sing.* or *pl. colloq.* large number or amount. 2 *v.t.* pile (*up*) in heap; load with large quantities.

hear *v.* (*past & p.p.* **heard** /hɜːd/) perceive with ear; listen to; listen judicially to; be informed; receive message etc. *from.* **hearsay** gossip.

hearing /'hɪərɪŋ/ *n.* faculty of perceiving sounds; range within which sounds may be heard; opportunity to be heard; giving of case in lawcourt. **hearing aid** small sound-amplifier worn by deaf person.

hearken /'hɑːkən/ *v.i. arch.* listen (*to*).

hearse /hɜːs/ *n.* vehicle for conveying coffin.

heart /hɑːt/ *n.* organ in body keeping up circulation of blood by expanding and contracting; seat of emotions or affections; soul, mind; courage; central or innermost part, essence; compact head of cabbage etc.; (conventionally) heart-shaped thing; playing-card of suit marked with red hearts. **at heart** in inmost feelings; **by heart** in or from memory; **have the heart** be hard-hearted enough (*to*); **heartache** mental anguish; **heart attack** sudden heart failure; **heart-breaking**, **heart-broken**, causing, crushed by, great distress; **heartburn** burning sensation in chest; **heartfelt** sincere; **heart-rending** distressing; **heartsick** despondent; **heart-strings** deepest affections or pity; **heart-throb** *sl.* object of romantic affections; **heart-to-heart** frank (talk); **heart-warming** emotionally moving and encouraging; **take to heart** be much affected by.

hearten /'hɑːt(ə)n/ *v.* encourage, cheer.

hearth /hɑːθ/ *n.* floor of fireplace; area in front of this.

heartless /'hɑːtlɪs/ *a.* unfeeling, pitiless.

hearty /'hɑːtɪ/ *a.* vigorous; genial; sincere; (of meal or appetite) copious.

heat 1 *n.* being hot, sensation of this; hot weather; warmth of feeling; anger; preliminary contest, winner(s) of which compete in final; receptive period of sexual cycle esp. in female mammals. 2 *v.* make or become hot; inflame. 3 **heat-stroke** illness caused by excessive heat; **heat wave** period of very hot weather.

heated /'hiːtɪd/ *a.* vehement, angry.

heath /hiːθ/ *n.* flat waste tract of land, esp. covered with low shrubs; undershrub of heather kind.

heathen /'hiːð(ə)n/ 1 *n.* person who is not a member of a widely-held religion. 2 *a.* of heathens, having no religion. 3 **heathenish** *a.*

heather /'heðə(r)/ *n.* purple-flowered plant of moors and heaths.

heave *v.* lift, raise; utter (sigh, groan) with effort; *colloq.* throw; *Naut.* (*past & p.p.* **hove**) haul; pull (at rope etc.); swell, rise; retch. 2 *n.* heaving. 3 **heave in sight** come into view; **heave to** bring vessel to standstill with head to wind.

heaven /'hev(ə)n/ n. place believed to be abode of God and of the righteous after death; place of bliss; sky.

heavenly a. of heaven, divine; of the sky; *colloq.* very pleasing.

heavy /'hevɪ/ 1 a. of great weight; of great density; laden; abundant; severe; extensive; striking or falling with force; hard to digest; (of ground) difficult to travel over; dull, tedious, oppressive, sad; *sl.* serious, important. 2 n. *Theatr.* villain. 3 **heavy-duty** designed to withstand hard use; **heavy-handed** clumsy, oppressive; **heavy hydrogen** deuterium; **heavy industry** that concerned with production of metal and machines etc.; **heavy water** oxide of deuterium; **heavyweight** boxing-weight with no upper limit.

Hebraic /hiː'breɪk/ a. of Hebrew or the Hebrews. **Hebraist** n.

Hebrew /'hiːbruː/ 1 n. member of a Semitic people in ancient Palestine; their language; modern form of this used esp. in Israel. 2 a. of or in Hebrew; of the Jews.

heckle /'hek(ə)l/ v.t. interrupt or harass (speaker).

hectare /'hektɛə(r)/ n. metric unit of square measure, about 2½ acres.

hectic /'hektɪk/ a. busy and confused; excited, feverish.

hectogram /'hektəgræm/ n. 100 grams.

hectolitre /'hektəliːtə(r)/ n. 100 litres.

hectometre /'hektəmiːtə(r)/ n. 100 metres.

hector /'hektə(r)/ v. bluster, bully.

hedge 1 n. fence of bushes or low trees; protection against loss. 2 v. surround with hedge; make or trim hedges; secure oneself against loss on (bet etc.); avoid committing oneself. 3 **hedge-hop** fly at low altitude; **hedgerow** row of bushes forming hedge; **hedgesparrow** common brown-backed bird.

hedgehog /'hedʒhɒg/ n. small spiny nocturnal insect-eating mammal.

hedonism /'hiːdənɪz(ə)m/ n. doctrine that pleasure is the only proper aim. **hedonist** n.; **hedonistic** a.

heed 1 v.t. attend to; take notice of. 2 n. care, attention.

heedless /'hiːdlɪs/ a. not giving care or attention.

hee-haw /'hiːhɔː/ n. & v.i. bray.

heel[1] 1 n. back part of human foot; corresponding part of quadruped's hind limb; part of sock etc. that covers heel; part of boot etc. that supports heel; heel-like thing; *US* contemptible person. 2 v. fit or renew heel on (shoe); *Rugby footb.* pass ball *out* at back of scrum with heel. 3 **heelball** shoemaker's polishing mixture of wax etc., esp. used in brass-rubbing.

heel[2] v. (of ship etc.) lean over; cause (ship) to do this. 2 n. heeling.

hefty /'heftɪ/ a. heavy; sturdy; stalwart.

hegemony /hɪ'gemənɪ/ n. leadership.

heifer /'hefə(r)/ n. young cow that has not had a calf.

heigh /heɪ/ int. expr. encouragement or inquiry. **heigh-ho** expr. boredom etc.

height /haɪt/ n. measure from base to top; elevation above ground or other level; high point; top; utmost degree.

heighten /'haɪt(ə)n/ v.t. raise higher; intensify; exaggerate.

heinous /'heɪnəs/ a. atrocious.

heir /eə(r)/ n. person entitled to property or rank as legal successor of former holder. **heir apparent** one whose claim cannot be superseded by birth of nearer heir; **heirloom** piece of property that has been in family for generations; **heir presumptive** one whose claim may be superseded by birth of nearer heir. **heiress** n.

held past & p.p. of **hold**[1].

helical /'helɪk(ə)l/ a. spiral.

helices pl. of **helix**.

helicopter /'helɪkɒptə(r)/ n. aircraft lifted and propelled by engine-driven blades revolving horizontally.

heliograph /'hiːlɪəgrɑːf/ 1 n. signalling apparatus reflecting flashes of sunlight. 2 v.t. send (message) thus.

heliotrope /'hiːlɪətrəʊp/ n. plant with small clustered purple flowers; light purple colour.

heliport /'helɪpɔːt/ n. place where helicopters take off and land.

helium /'hiːlɪəm/ n. light non-inflammable gaseous element.

helix /'hiːlɪks/ n. (pl. **helices** /'hiːlɪsiːz/) spiral.

hell n. abode of dead or damned; place or state of misery. **hellish** a.

hellebore /ˈhelɪbɔ:(r)/ *n.* plant of kind including Christmas rose.

Hellene /ˈheli:n/ *n.* Greek. **Hellenic** *a.*; **Hellenism** *n.*; **Hellenist** *n.*

hello var. of **hallo.**

helm *n.* tiller or wheel for managing rudder. **at the helm** in control; **helmsman** person who steers ship.

helmet /ˈhelmɪt/ *n.* protective headcover of soldier or fireman or motorcyclist etc.

helot /ˈhelət/ *n.* serf, esp. in ancient Sparta.

help 1 *v.t.* provide with means to what is needed or sought, be useful to; prevent, refrain from. **2** *n.* act of helping; person or thing that helps; domestic servant(s); employee(s); remedy etc. **3 help oneself (to)** take without seeking help or permission.

helpful /ˈhelpfʊl/ *a.* giving help, useful.

helping /ˈhelpɪŋ/ *n.* portion of food.

helpless /ˈhelplɪs/ *a.* unable to manage without help; without help or power.

helpmate /ˈhelpmeɪt/ *n.* helpful companion, esp. husband or wife.

helter-skelter /heltəˈskeltə(r)/ **1** *adv.* in disordered haste. **2** *n.* spiral slide at fun-fair.

helve *n.* handle of weapon or tool.

hem¹ 1 *n.* border of cloth where edge is turned under and sewn down. **2** *v.t.* sew edge thus. **3 hem in** enclose, confine; **hem-stitch** (make hem with) ornamental stitch.

hem² *int.* expr. hesitation or calling attention.

hemisphere /ˈhemɪsfɪə(r)/ *n.* half sphere; half earth, esp. as divided by equator or by line passing through poles; each half of brain. **hemispherical** /-ˈsfer-/ *a.*

hemlock /ˈhemlɒk/ *n.* poisonous plant with small white flowers; poison got from it.

hemp *n.* Asian herbaceous plant; its fibre used for rope etc.; any of several narcotic drugs got from it.

hempen /ˈhempən/ *a.* made of hemp.

hen *n.* female bird, esp. of domestic fowl; female crab or lobster or salmon. **hen-party** *colloq.* party of women only; **henpecked** (of husband) domineered over by his wife.

henbane /ˈhenbeɪn/ *n.* narcotic and poisonous plant.

hence *adv.* from now; for this reason. **henceforth, henceforward,** from this time forward.

henchman /ˈhentʃmən/ *n.* (*pl.*-men) trusty supporter.

henge *n.* monument of wood or stone as at *Stonehenge.*

henna /ˈhenə/ *n.* tropical shrub; reddish dye made from it and used esp. for hair.

hepatic /hɪˈpætɪk/ *a.* of the liver.

hepatitis /hepəˈtaɪtɪs/ *n.* inflammation of the liver.

hepta- /ˈheptə/ *in comb.* seven.

heptagon /ˈheptəgən/ *n.* plane figure with 7 sides and angles. **heptagonal** /-ˈtæg-/ *a.*

her *pron., obj.* and *poss.* case of **she,** with *abs.* form **hers.**

herald /ˈher(ə)ld/ **1** *n.* forerunner; messenger; *hist.* officer who made State proclamations etc. **2** *v.t.* proclaim approach of; usher in. **3 heraldic** /-ˈræld-/ *a.*

heraldry /ˈherəldrɪ/ *n.* knowledge or art of a herald; armorial bearings.

herb *n.* plant used for flavouring or medicine etc.; soft-stemmed plant dying down to ground after flowering. **herby** *a.*

herbaceous /hɜːˈbeɪʃəs/ *a.* of or like herbs. **herbaceous border** border in garden etc. containing esp. perennial flowering plants.

herbage /ˈhɜːbɪdʒ/ *n.* herbs; pasturage.

herbal /ˈhɜːb(ə)l/ **1** *a.* of herbs. **2** *n.* book about herbs.

herbalist /ˈhɜːbəlɪst/ *n.* dealer in medicinal herbs; writer on herbs.

herbarium /hɜːˈbeərɪəm/ *n.* collection of dried plants.

herbicide /ˈhɜːbɪsaɪd/ *n.* preparation used to destroy unwanted vegetation.

herbivorous /hɜːˈbɪvərəs/ *a.* feeding on plants. **herbivore** *n.*

herculean /hɜːkjʊˈlɪən/ *a.* extremely strong; (of task) of great difficulty.

herd 1 *n.* number of cattle etc. feeding or travelling together; large number of people. **2** *v.* collect or drive or go in herd; tend. **3 herdsman** keeper of herds.

here 1 *adv.* in or to this place; at this point. **2** *n.* this place or point. **3 hereabout(s)** somewhere near here; **hereafter** (in) future, (in) next world;

hereby by this means; **herein** in this place or book etc.; **hereinafter** below (in document); **hereof** of this; **hereto** to this; **heretofore** formerly; **hereupon** after or in consequence of this; **herewith** with this.

hereditable /hɪˈredɪtəb(ə)l/ *a.* that can be inherited. **hereditability** *n.*

hereditary /hɪˈredɪtərɪ/ *a.* descending by inheritance; transmitted from one generation to another; holding position by inheritance.

heredity /hɪˈredɪtɪ/ *n.* transmission of physical or mental characteristics from parents to children; these characteristics; genetic constitution.

heresy /ˈherəsɪ/ *n.* opinion contrary to orthodox (Christian) belief or to accepted doctrine.

heretic /ˈherətɪk/ *n.* believer in heresy. **heretical** *a.*

heritable /ˈherɪtəb(ə)l/ *a.* that can be inherited.

heritage /ˈherɪtɪdʒ/ *n.* what is or may be inherited; one's portion or lot; inherited cultural influence or tradition etc.

hermaphrodite /hɜːˈmæfrədaɪt/ 1 *n.* person or animal with characteristics or organs of both sexes. 2 *a.* having such characteristics. 3 **hermaphroditic** /-ˈdɪt-/ *a.*

hermetic /hɜːˈmetɪk/ *a.* with an airtight seal.

hermit /ˈhɜːmɪt/ *n.* person living in solitude.

hermitage /ˈhɜːmɪtɪdʒ/ *n.* place of hermit's retreat; secluded residence.

hernia /ˈhɜːnɪə/ *n. Med.* protrusion of internal part of organ through aperture in enclosing membrane etc.

hero /ˈhɪərəʊ/ *n.* (*pl.* **-roes**) man admired for great or noble deeds; chief male character in poem or story etc.

heroic /hɪˈrəʊɪk/ 1 *a.* having qualities of or suited to a hero; very brave. 2 *n.* in *pl.* over-dramatic talk or behaviour; heroic verse. 3 **heroic verse** form used in epic poetry.

heroin /ˈherəʊɪn/ *n.* sedative addictive drug prepared from morphine.

heroine /ˈherəʊɪn/ *n.* female hero.

heroism /ˈherəʊɪz(ə)m/ *n.* heroic conduct.

heron /ˈherən/ *n.* long-necked long-legged wading bird.

herpes /ˈhɜːpiːz/ *n.* virus disease of various kinds, causing blisters.

herring /ˈherɪŋ/ *n.* N. Atlantic edible fish. **herring-bone** stitch or weave suggesting bones of herring, zigzag pattern.

hers see **her.**

herself /hɜːˈself/ *pron., emphat. & refl.* form of **she.**

hertz *n.* (*pl.* same) unit of frequency, one cycle per second.

hesitant /ˈhezɪt(ə)nt/ *a.* hesitating. **hesitancy** *n.*

hesitate /ˈhezɪteɪt/ *v.i.* feel or show indecision; pause, be reluctant. **hesitation** *n.*

hessian /ˈhesɪən/ *n.* strong coarse cloth of mixed hemp and jute.

het *a.* **het up** *sl.* excited.

heterodox /ˈhetərədɒks/ *a.* not orthodox. **heterodoxy** *n.*

heterodyne /ˈhetərədaɪn/ *a. Radio* relating to production of lower (audible) frequency from combination of two high frequencies.

heterogeneous /hetərəˈdʒiːnɪəs/ *a.* diverse; composed of diverse elements. **heterogeneity** (/-ˈniːɪtɪ/) *n.*

heterosexual /hetərəˈseksjʊəl/ 1 *a.* characterized by being sexually attracted to opposite sex. 2 *n.* heterosexual person. 3 **heterosexuality** *n.*

heuristic /hjʊəˈrɪstɪk/ *a.* serving to discover; using trial and error.

hew *v.* (*p.p.* **hewed** or **hewn**) chop or cut with axe or sword etc.; cut into shape.

hexa- /heksə/ *in comb.* six.

hexagon /ˈheksəgən/ *n.* plane figure with 6 sides and angles. **hexagonal** *a.*

hexagram /ˈheksəgræm/ *n.* 6-pointed star formed by 2 intersecting equilateral triangles.

hexameter /hekˈsæmɪtə(r)/ *n.* line of 6 metrical feet.

hey /heɪ/ *int.* calling attention or expr. surprise or question. **hey presto!** conjuror's formula of command.

heyday /ˈheɪdeɪ/ *n.* time of greatest success, prime.

HF *abbr.* high frequency.

HGV *abbr.* heavy goods vehicle.

hi /haɪ/ *int.* calling attention or used as greeting.

hiatus /haɪˈeɪtəs/ *n.* gap in series etc.;

break between two vowels coming together but not in same syllable.

hibernate /'haɪbə(r)neɪt/ v.i. (of animal) spend winter in torpid state. **hibernation** n.

Hibernian /haɪ'bɜːnɪən/ 1 a. of Ireland. 2 n. native of Ireland.

hibiscus /hɪ'bɪskəs/ n. cultivated shrub with large bright-coloured flowers.

hiccup /'hɪkʌp/ (also **hiccough**) 1 n. involuntary audible spasm of respiratory organs. 2 v. make hiccup.

hick n. US yokel.

hickory /'hɪkərɪ/ n. N. Amer. tree related to walnut; its wood.

hid past of **hide**¹.

hidalgo /hɪ'dælgəʊ/ n. (pl. **-gos**) Spanish gentleman.

hidden p.p. of **hide**¹.

hide¹ 1 v. (past **hid**; p.p. **hidden**) put or keep out of sight; conceal (fact *from* person); conceal oneself. 2 n. place of concealment used in observing or hunting wild animals. 3 **hide-out** colloq. hiding-place.

hide² n. animal's skin, raw or dressed; joc. person's skin. **hidebound** rigidly conventional.

hideous /'hɪdɪəs/ a. repulsive, revolting.

hiding /'haɪdɪŋ/ n. thrashing.

hie v.i. & refl., poet. go quickly.

hierarchy /'haɪərɑːkɪ/ n. system in which grades of authority rank one above another. **hierarchical** a.

hieroglyph /'haɪərəglɪf/ n. picture or symbol representing word or syllable, esp. in ancient Egyptian writing. **hieroglyphic** a.; **hieroglyphics** n.pl.

hi-fi /'haɪfaɪ/ 1 a. colloq. high fidelity. 2 n. equipment for such sound-reproduction.

higgledy-piggledy /hɪgəldɪ'pɪgəldɪ/ adv. & a. in utter disorder.

high /haɪ/ 1 a. of great or specified upward extent; coming above normal level; of exalted rank or position, of superior quality; extreme, intense; (of opinion) favourable; (of sound) shrill; (of meat etc.) beginning to go bad; colloq. intoxicated by or *on* alcohol or drugs. 2 n. high or highest level or number; area of high barometric pressure; sl. euphoric state caused by drug etc. 3 adv. far up, aloft; in or to high degree;

at high price. 4 **highball** US drink of spirits and soda etc.; **highbrow** colloq. (person) of superior intellectual or cultural interests; **High Church** section of Church of England emphasizing ritual and priestly authority and sacraments; **High Commission** embassy from one Commonwealth country to another; **High Court** supreme court of justice for civil cases; **high explosive** explosive with violent local effect; **high fidelity** quality of sound-reproduction with little distortion; **high-flown** extravagant, bombastic; **high frequency** Radio 3–30 megahertz; **high-handed** overbearing; **high-level** conducted by persons of high rank; (of computer language) close to ordinary language; **highlight** moment or detail of vivid interest, bright part of picture, (v.t.) bring into prominence; **high-minded** of firm moral principles; **high priest** chief priest, head of cult; **high-rise** (of building) having many storeys; **high road** main road; **high school** school for secondary education; **high seas** seas outside territorial waters; **high-spirited** cheerful; **high tea** early evening meal of tea and cooked food; **high water** high tide; **high-water mark** recorded maximum in any fluctuation.

highland /'haɪlənd/ 1 n. (usu. in pl.) mountainous country, esp. (**Highlands**) of N. Scotland. 2 a. of highland or Sc. Highlands. 3 **highlander** n.

highly /'haɪlɪ/ adv. in high degree, favourably.

Highness /'haɪnɪs/ n. title of princes etc.

highway /'haɪweɪ/ n. public road, main route; conductor transmitting signals in computer. **Highway Code** official handbook for road-users; **highwayman** hist. (usu. mounted) robber of stage-coaches.

hijack /'haɪdʒæk/ 1 v.t. seize control of (lorry, aircraft in flight, etc.) illegally; steal (goods) in transit. 2 n. hijacking.

hike 1 n. long walk for pleasure or exercise. 2 v.i. go on hike.

hilarious /hɪ'leərɪəs/ a. cheerful, merry; extremely funny. **hilarity** n.

hill n. natural elevation of ground, small mountain; heap, mound. **hillbilly** US person from remote rural area. **hilly** a.

hillock /'hɪlək/ n. small hill, mound.

hilt n. handle of sword or knife etc.

him pron., obj. case of **he**.

himself /hɪm'self/ pron., emphat. & refl. form of **he**.

hind[1] /haɪnd/ a. situated at back. **hindquarters** rump and hind legs of quadruped; **hindsight** wisdom after event. **hindmost** a.

hind[2] /haɪnd/ n. female (esp. red) deer.

hinder[1] /'hɪndə(r)/ v.t. impede; prevent.

hinder[2] /'haɪndə(r)/ a. rear, hind.

Hindi /'hɪndɪ/ n. one of official languages of India; literary form of Hindustani; group of spoken languages in N. India.

hindrance /'hɪndrəns/ n. obstruction.

Hindu /hɪn'duː/ 1 n. adherent of Hinduism. 2 a. of Hindus or Hinduism.

Hinduism /'hɪnduːɪz(ə)m/ n. religious and social system esp. in India with worship of several gods etc.

Hindustani /hɪndu'staːnɪ/ n. language based on Hindi, used in N. India and Pakistan.

hinge 1 n. movable joint such as that by which door is hung on post; fig. principle on which all depends. 2 v. attach or be attached with hinge; depend (on).

hinny /'hɪnɪ/ n. offspring of she-ass by stallion.

hint 1 n. indirect suggestion; slight indication. 2 v. suggest indirectly. 3 **hint at** refer indirectly to.

hinterland /'hɪntəlænd/ n. district behind that lying along coast etc.

hip[1] n. projection of pelvis and upper part of thigh-bone at side of body.

hip[2] n. fruit of rose.

hip[3] int. used to introduce cheer.

hip[4] a. sl. stylish; well-informed.

hippie /'hɪpɪ/ n. sl. person (esp. in 1960s) rejecting materialism and formality in dress etc.

hippo /'hɪpəʊ/ n. (pl. **-os**) colloq. hippopotamus.

Hippocratic oath /hɪpə'krætɪk/ oath embodying code of medical ethics.

hippodrome /'hɪpədrəʊm/ n. name for theatre or cinema; course for chariot races etc.

hippopotamus /hɪpə'pɒtəməs/ n. (pl. **-muses**) large Afr. mammal with short legs and thick skin, inhabiting rivers etc.

hippy var. of **hippie**.

hipster /'hɪpstə(r)/ a. (of garment) hanging from hips rather than waist.

hire 1 v.t. obtain use of (thing) or services of (person) for payment; give use of thus. 2 n. hiring; payment for this. 3 **hire-purchase** system by which hired thing becomes hirer's property after number of payments.

hireling /'haɪəlɪŋ/ n. usu. derog. person who works for hire.

hirsute /'hɜːsuːt/ a. hairy.

his /hɪz/ pron., poss. case of **he**.

Hispanic /hɪ'spænɪk/ a. of Spain and other Spanish-speaking countries.

hiss /hɪs/ n. sharp sound of s. 2 v. make hiss; express disapproval of thus; utter with angry hiss.

histamine /'hɪstəmiːn/ n. substance occurring in animal tissues and causing some allergic reactions etc.

histology /hɪ'stɒlədʒɪ/ n. science of organic tissues.

historian /hɪ'stɔːrɪən/ n. writer of history books; person learned in history.

historic /hɪ'stɒrɪk/ a. famous in history or potentially so.

historical /hɪ'stɒrɪk(ə)l/ a. of history; belonging to or dealing with the past; not legendary; studying development over period of time.

historicity /hɪstə'rɪsɪtɪ/ n. historical truth or authenticity.

historiography /hɪstɔːrɪ'ɒgrəfɪ/ n. writing of history; study of this. **historiographer** n.

history /'hɪstərɪ/ n. continuous record of important or public events; past events, study of these; (eventful) career; story.

histrionic /hɪstrɪ'ɒnɪk/ 1 a. of acting; stagy. 2 n. in pl. theatricals; stagy behaviour (designed to impress others).

hit 1 v. (past & p.p. **hit**) strike with blow or missile; aim blow; have effect on, cause to suffer; propel (ball etc.) with bat etc.; colloq. encounter; light upon, find. 2 n. blow; stroke of satire etc.; successful attempt; success. 3 **hit it off** get on well (with); **hit-or-miss** colloq. casual, careless.

hitch 1 v. move (thing) with jerk; fasten with loop etc.; hitch-hike. 2 n. jerk; kind of noose or knot; temporary difficulty, snag. 3 **hitch-hike** travel by means of lifts in vehicles.

hither /ˈhɪðə(r)/ 1 *adv.* to this place. 2 *a.* situated on this side; the nearer. 3 **hitherto** *adv.* up to now.

hive 1 *n.* artificial home for bees; scene of busy activity. 2 *v.* place or live or store etc. (as) in hive. 3 **hive off** separate from larger group.

hives /haɪvz/ *n.pl.* skin eruption, esp. nettle-rash.

HM *abbr.* Her or His Majesty('s).

HMI *abbr.* Her or His Majesty's Inspector.

HMS *abbr.* Her or His Majesty's Ship.

HMSO *abbr.* Her or His Majesty's Stationery Office.

HNC, HND, *abbrs.* Higher National Certificate, Diploma.

ho *int.* expr. triumph or derision etc., or calling attention etc.

hoar /hɔː(r)/ *a.* grey with age; white. **hoar-frost** frozen water vapour on lawns etc.

hoard /hɔːd/ 1 *n.* store (esp. of money or treasure) laid by. 2 *v.* amass and put away, store *up*.

hoarding /ˈhɔːdɪŋ/ *n.* temporary board fence round building etc.; structure erected to carry advertisements.

hoarse /hɔːs/ *a.* (of voice) rough, husky; having hoarse voice.

hoary /ˈhɔːrɪ/ *a.* white or grey with age; aged; old and trite.

hoax 1 *v.t.* deceive esp. by way of joke. 2 *n.* such deception.

hob *n.* flat iron shelf at side of grate; array of hotplates etc. on top of cooker. **hob-nail** heavy-headed nail for boot-sole.

hobbit /ˈhɒbɪt/ *n.* one of an imaginary race of small people.

hobble /ˈhɒb(ə)l/ 1 *v.* walk lamely, limp; tie together legs of (horse etc.) to keep it from straying. 2 *n.* limping gait; rope etc. used to hobble horse.

hobby /ˈhɒbɪ/ *n.* favourite pursuit outside one's main work or business. **hobby-horse** stick with horse's head, used as toy, figure of horse used in morris-dancing, favourite theme, obsession.

hobgoblin /ˈhɒbgɒblɪn/ *n.* mischievous imp; bogy.

hob-nob *v.i.* associate or spend time (*with*).

hobo /ˈhəʊbəʊ/ *n.* (*pl.* **-bos**) *US* wandering workman or tramp.

hock[1] *n.* joint of quadruped's hind leg between knee and fetlock.

hock[2] *n.* German white wine.

hock[3] *US sl.* 1 *v.t.* pawn. 2 *n.* **in hock** in pawn, in prison, in debt.

hockey /ˈhɒkɪ/ *n.* team-game played with ball and curved sticks.

hocus-pocus /ˌhəʊkəsˈpəʊkəs/ *n.* trickery; conjuring formula.

hod *n.* trough on pole for carrying bricks etc.; container for shovelling and holding coal.

hodgepodge var. of **hotchpotch**

hoe 1 *n.* tool for scraping up weeds etc. 2 *v.* use hoe; weed (crops), loosen (soil) or dig *out* or *up* etc. with hoe.

hog 1 *n.* domesticated pig, esp. castrated male for slaughter; *colloq.* greedy person. 2 *v.* take greedily; hoard selfishly. 3 **go the whole hog** *sl.* do thing thoroughly; **hog's back** sharp hill-ridge; **hogwash** *fig.* worthless stuff.

hoggin /ˈhɒgɪn/ *n.* mixture of sand and gravel.

hogmanay /ˈhɒgməneɪ/ *n.* *Sc.* New Year's Eve.

hogshead /ˈhɒgzhed/ *n.* large cask; measure of beer (usu. about 50 gals.).

hoick *v.t.* *sl.* lift or jerk (*out* etc.).

hoi polloi /ˌhɔɪ pəˈlɔɪ/ ordinary people, the masses. [Gk]

hoist 1 *v.t.* raise or haul (*up*); raise with ropes and pulleys etc. 2 *n.* apparatus for hoisting things.

hoity-toity /ˌhɔɪtɪˈtɔɪtɪ/ *a.* *colloq.* haughty, petulant.

hokum /ˈhəʊkəm/ *n.* *sl.* false sentiment, sentimental or melodramatic nonsense.

hold[1] /həʊld/ 1 *v.* (*past* & *p.p.* **held**) keep thing in some position or condition; grasp; possess; have capacity for; conduct, celebrate; restrain; think; believe; not give way; keep going; be valid. 2 *n.* grasp; manner or means of holding; means of exerting influence *on* or *over*. 3 **holdall** large soft travelling bag; **hold down** repress, *colloq.* be competent enough to keep (job); **hold forth** speak at length or tediously; **hold on** maintain grasp, wait, not ring off; **hold out** offer (inducement etc.), maintain resistance, continue to make demand *for*; **hold over** postpone; **hold up** obstruct, sustain, rob by (threat of) violence; **hold-up** robbery of this kind, stoppage, delay; **hold water** (of reasoning) be sound; **hold with** *colloq.* approve of.

hold² /həʊld/ *n.* cavity below ship's deck for cargo.

holder /ˈhəʊldə(r)/ *n.* occupant of office etc.; device for holding something.

holding /ˈhəʊldɪŋ/ *n.* tenure of land; land or stocks held. **holding company** one formed to hold shares of other companies.

hole 1 *n.* cavity in solid body; opening through or sunken place on surface; burrow; *colloq.* small or gloomy place; *sl.* awkward situation; cavity into which ball must be got in some games, *Golf* section of course from tee to hole. 2 *v.* make hole(s) in; hit golf-ball into hole. 3 **hole-and-corner** underhand; **hole up** *sl.* hide oneself. 4 **holey** *a.*

holiday /ˈhɒlɪdeɪ/ *n.* break from work esp. for recreation; (freq. in *pl.*) period of this, esp. spent away from home.

holiness /ˈhəʊlɪnɪs/ *n.* being holy or sacred. **His Holiness** title of Pope.

holland /ˈhɒlənd/ *n.* linen fabric, freq. unbleached.

hollandaise /hɒlənˈdeɪz/ *n.* creamy sauce of butter and egg-yolks and vinegar etc.

holler /ˈhɒlə(r)/ *v. & n. US* shout.

hollow /ˈhɒləʊ/ 1 *a.* having hole or cavity or depression; not solid; empty; echoing, not full-toned; false, insincere. 2 *n.* hollow place; hole; valley. 3 *adv.* completely. 4 *v.t.* make hollow in.

holly /ˈhɒlɪ/ *n.* evergreen prickly-leaved shrub with red berries.

hollyhock /ˈhɒlɪhɒk/ *n.* tall plant with large showy flowers.

holm /həʊm/ *n.* (in full **holm-oak**) evergreen oak.

holocaust /ˈhɒləkɔːst/ *n.* wholesale destruction.

hologram /ˈhɒləɡræm/ *n.* photographic pattern that gives 3-dimensional image when specially illuminated.

holograph /ˈhɒləɡrɑːf/ 1 *a.* wholly in handwriting of person in whose name it appears. 3 *n.* such document.

holster /ˈhəʊlstə(r)/ *n.* leather case for carrying pistol or revolver on the person.

holy /ˈhəʊlɪ/ *a.* of high moral or spiritual excellence; belonging or devoted to God. **Holy Ghost** Holy Spirit; **holy orders** those of bishop, priest, and deacon; **Holy Spirit** Third Person of Trinity; **Holy Week** that preceding Easter Sunday; **Holy Writ** Bible.

homage /ˈhɒmɪdʒ/ *n.* tribute paid *to* person etc.; formal acknowledgement of allegiance.

Homburg /ˈhɒmbɜːɡ/ *n.* man's soft felt hat with narrow curled brim.

home 1 *n.* place where one lives; residence; native land; institution of refuge or rest; (in games) finishing line in race, home match or win etc. 2 *a.* of or connected with home; not foreign; played etc. on team's own ground; that affects one closely. 3 *adv.* to or at home; to point aimed at. 4 *v.i.* (of pigeon) make way home; (of missile etc.) be guided to destination. 5 **Home Counties** those lying round London; **home farm** one worked by owner of estate; **homeland** native land; **Home Office** British government department concerned with immigration and law and order etc.; **Home Rule** self-government; **Home Secretary** minister in charge of Home Office; **homesick** depressed by absence from home; **homespun** of yarn spun at home, plain and homely; **homestead** house with outbuildings, farm; **homework** lessons to be done by schoolchild at home. 6 **homeward** *a. & adv.*; *US* unattractive.

homely /ˈhəʊmlɪ/ *a.* plain; unpretentious; *US* unattractive.

homer /ˈhəʊmə(r)/ *n.* homing pigeon.

Homeric /həʊˈmerɪk/ *a.* of or in style of the ancient Gk poet Homer; of Bronze Age Greece.

homicide /ˈhɒmɪsaɪd/ *n.* killing of person by another; person who kills another. **homicidal** *a.*

homily /ˈhɒmɪlɪ/ *n.* sermon; moralizing lecture. **homiletic** *a.*

homing /ˈhəʊmɪŋ/ *a.* (of pigeon) trained to fly home from a distance; (of device) for guiding to target etc.

hominid /ˈhɒmɪnɪd/ 1 *a.* of the mammal family of existing and fossil man. 2 *n.* member of this.

hominoid /ˈhɒmɪnɔɪd/ 1 *a.* manlike. 2 *n.* animal resembling man.

homoeopathy /həʊmɪˈɒpəθɪ/ *n.* treatment of disease by drugs that in healthy person would produce similar symptoms. **homoeopath** *n.*; **homoeopathic** /-'pæθ-/ *a.*

homogeneous /hɒməʊ'dʒiːnɪəs/ *a.* of same kind or nature; uniform. **homogeneity** /-'niːɪtɪ/ *n.*

homogenize /hə'mɒdʒənaɪz/ *v.t.* treat (milk) so that cream does not separate.

homologous /hɒ'mɒləgəs/ *a.* having same relation or value; corresponding.

homology /hɒ'mɒlədʒɪ/ *n.* homologous relation, correspondence.

homonym /'hɒmənɪm/ *n.* word of same form as another but different meaning, **homonymous** *a.*

homophone /'hɒməfəʊn/ *n.* word having same sound as another, but different meaning.

homosexual /həʊməʊ'seksjʊəl/ **1** *a.* characterized by being sexually attracted to persons of same sex. **2** *n.* homosexual person. **3 homosexuality** *n.*

Hon. *abbr.* honorary; Honourable.

hone 1 *n.* whetstone, esp. for razors. **2** *v.t.* sharpen on hone.

honest /'ɒnɪst/ *a.* sincere; not lying or cheating or stealing; fairly earned.

honesty /'ɒnɪstɪ/ *n.* being honest, truthfulness; plant with purple flowers and flat round pods.

honey /'hʌnɪ/ *n.* sweet sticky yellow fluid made by bees from nectar collected from flowers; sweetness; darling.

honeycomb /'hʌnɪkəʊm/ **1** *n.* bees' wax structure of hexagonal cells for honey and eggs; pattern hexagonally arranged. **2** *v.t.* fill with cavities; mark with honeycomb pattern.

honeydew /'hʌnɪdjuː/ *n.* sweet substance excreted by aphids; sweet green-fleshed type of melon.

honeyed /'hʌnɪd/ *a.* sweet, sweet-sounding.

honeymoon /'hʌnɪmuːn/ **1** *n.* holiday of newly-married couple; *fig.* initial period of enthusiasm or goodwill. **2** *v.i.* spend honeymoon.

honeysuckle /'hʌnɪsʌk(ə)l/ *n.* climbing shrub with fragrant flowers.

honk 1 *n.* cry of wild goose or sound of motor horn. **2** *v.i.* make honk.

honorarium /ɒnə'reərɪəm/ *n.* (*pl.* -**riums**) voluntary payment for professional services.

honorary /'ɒnərərɪ/ *a.* conferred as honour; unpaid.

honorific /ɒnə'rɪfɪk/ *a.* implying respect.

honour /'ɒnə(r)/ **1** *n.* high respect, reputation; allegiance to what is right; thing conferred as distinction (esp. official award for bravery or achievement); privilege; person or thing that does credit to another; chastity, reputation for this; mark of respect; in *pl.* specialized degree-course or special distinction in examination; *Golf* right of driving off first; in *pl. Cards* 4 or 5 top cards in trump suit. **2** *v.t.* respect highly; confer honour on; accept or pay (bill, cheque) when due. **3 do the honours** perform duties of host etc.

honourable /'ɒnərəb(ə)l/ *a.* deserving or bringing honour; **Honourable** courtesy title of MPs and certain officials and children of certain ranks of the nobility.

hooch /huːtʃ/ *n. US sl.* alcoholic spirits, esp. inferior or illicit.

hood[1] /hʊd/ **1** *n.* covering for head and neck; garment worn as part of academic dress; thing like hood in shape or use, collapsible top or cover of motor vehicle etc.; *US* bonnet of car. **2** *v.t.* cover with hood.

hood[2] /hʊd/ *n. US* gangster, gunman.

hoodlum /'huːdləm/ *n.* hooligan; gangster.

hoodoo /'huːduː/ *US* **1** *n.* bad luck; thing that brings or causes this. **2** *v.t.* bring bad luck to.

hoodwink /'hʊdwɪŋk/ *v.t.* deceive, delude.

hooey /'huːɪ/ *n. sl.* nonsense.

hoof /huːf/ **1** *n.* (*pl.* **hoofs** or **hooves**) horny part of foot of horse etc. **2** *v.* **hoof it** *sl.* go on foot.

hook /hʊk/ **1** *n.* bent piece of wire etc. for catching hold or for hanging things on; curved cutting instrument; hooking stroke; short swinging blow in boxing. **2** *v.* grasp or secure or fasten or catch with hook; *Sport* send (ball) in curving or deviating path; *Rugby footb.* secure (ball) in scrum with foot. **3 hook and eye** small hook and loop as dress fastener; **hook-up** connection, esp. interconnection in broadcast transmission; **hookworm** kind of worm infesting intestines of humans and animals.

hookah /'hʊkə/ *n.* tobacco-pipe with long tube, drawing smoke through vase of water.

hooked /hʊkt/ *a.* bent like hook, hook-shaped. **hooked on** *colloq.* addicted to or captivated by.

hooker /'hʊkə(r)/ *n.* Rugby footb. player in front row of scrum who tries to hook ball; *US sl.* prostitute.

hooligan /'huːlɪgən/ *n.* young thug. **hooliganism** *n.*

hoop /huːp/ **1** *n.* circular band of metal or wood etc. esp. for binding cask etc.; wooden etc. circle trundled by child; iron arch through which balls are driven in croquet. **2** *v.t.* bind with hoops. **3 hoop-la** game in which rings are thrown to capture prizes.

hoopoe /'huːpuː/ *n.* bird with variegated plumage and fan-like crest.

hooray var. of **hurrah**.

hoot /huːt/ **1** *n.* owl's cry; sound of steam-whistle or car horn etc.; inarticulate shout of derision etc. **2** *v.* utter hoot(s); greet or drive away with hoots; sound (horn). **3 not care a hoot** or **two hoots** not care at all.

hooter /'huːtə(r)/ *n.* siren, steam whistle, esp. as signal for start or end of work; car horn; *sl.* nose.

Hoover /'huːvə(r)/ **1** (P) *n.* vacuum cleaner. **2 hoover** *v.t. colloq.* clean with vacuum cleaner.

hop¹ **1** *v.* spring on one foot; (of bird etc.) jump; hop over; move or go quickly or with leaping motion. **2** *n.* hopping; spring; *colloq.* dance; short flight in aircraft. **3 hop it** *sl.* go away; **hopscotch** child's game of hopping over lines marked on ground.

hop² **1** *n.* climbing plant with bitter cones used to flavour beer etc.; in *pl.* these cones. **2** *v.* flavour with hops. **3 hoppy** *a.*

hope **1** *n.* expectation and desire; trust; ground of hope; person or thing that encourages hope; what is hoped for. **2** *v.* feel hope; expect and desire.

hopeful /'həʊpfʊl/ *a.* feeling hope, promising.

hopefully *adv.* in a hopeful manner; *colloq.* (qualifying whole sentence) it is to be hoped that.

hopeless /'həʊplɪs/ *a.* feeling or admitting no hope; inadequate, incompetent.

hopper¹ /'hɒpə(r)/ *n.* one who hops, hopping insect etc.; funnel-like device for feeding grain into mill etc.

hopper² /'hɒpə(r)/ *n.* hop-picker.

horde /hɔːd/ *n.* large crowd or troop; troop of Tartar or other nomads.

horehound /'hɔːhaʊnd/ *n.* herb with aromatic bitter juice.

horizon /hə'raɪz(ə)n/ *n.* line at which earth and sky appear to meet; limit of mental perception or interest etc.

horizontal /hɒrɪ'zɒnt(ə)l/ **1** *a.* parallel to plane of horizon; level, flat. **2** *n.* horizontal line or bar etc.

hormone /'hɔːməʊn/ *n.* substance internally secreted that passes into the blood or sap and stimulates organs or growth etc.; similar synthetic substance. **hormonal** *a.*

horn /hɔːn/ *n.* hard outgrowth, often curved and pointed, on head of animal; horn-like projection; substance of horns, article made of this; brass wind instrument; instrument giving warning. **hornbeam** tough-wooded hedgerow tree; **hornbill** bird with hornlike excrescence on bill.

hornblende /'hɔːnblend/ *n.* dark-brown etc. mineral constituent of granite etc.

hornet /'hɔːnɪt/ *n.* large species of wasp.

hornpipe /'hɔːnpaɪp/ *n.* lively dance associated esp. with sailors; music for this.

horny /'hɔːnɪ/ *a.* of or like horn; hard; *sl.* lecherous.

horology /hə'rɒlədʒɪ/ *n.* clock-making. **horological** /-'lɒdʒ-/ *a.*

horoscope /'hɒrəskəʊp/ *n.* prediction of person's future based on relative position of stars at his birth.

horrible /'hɒrɪb(ə)l/ *a.* arousing horror; hideous, shocking; *colloq.* unpleasant.

horrid /'hɒrɪd/ *a.* horrible; *colloq.* disagreeable.

horrific /hə'rɪfɪk/ *a.* horrifying.

horrify /'hɒrɪfaɪ/ *v.t.* arouse horror in; shock.

horror /'hɒrə(r)/ *n.* intense dislike or fear; horrifying thing.

hors-d'œuvre /ɔː 'dɜːvr/ *n.* appetizer served at start of meal.

horse /hɔːs/ **1** *n.* solid-hoofed quadruped used as beast of burden and draught and for riding on; *collect.* cavalry; vaulting-block in gymnasium; frame for supporting things. **2** *v.u. colloq.* fool *around.* **3 horse-box** closed vehicle for transporting horse(s); **horse-chestnut** tree with conical clusters of white or pink flowers, its dark brown fruit; **Horse Guards** cavalry brigade of British household troops; **horsehair** hair from mane or tail of horse; **horse-laugh** loud coarse laugh; **horseman** (skilled) rider on horseback; **horsemanship** skill in riding; **horseplay** boisterous play; **horsepower** unit of rate of doing work; **horse-radish** plant with pungent root used to make sauce; **horse sense** *colloq.* plain common sense; **horseshoe** U-shaped iron shoe for horse, thing of this shape; **horsewhip** whip for horse, (*v.t.*) beat (person) with this; **horsewoman** (skilled) woman rider on horseback.

horsy /ˈhɔːsɪ/ *a.* of or like horse; concerned with horses.

hortative /ˈhɔːtətɪv/ *a.* (also **hortatory**) serving to exhort.

horticulture /ˈhɔːtɪkʌltʃə(r)/ *n.* art of gardening. **horticultural** *a.*; **horticulturist** *n.*

hosanna /həʊˈzænə/ *n.* cry of adoration.

hose /həʊz/ **1** *n.* flexible tube for conveying liquids; stockings; *hist.* breeches. **2** *v.* water or wash *down* (as) with a hose.

hosier /ˈhəʊzɪə(r)/ *n.* dealer in stockings and socks. **hosiery** *n.*

hospice /ˈhɒspɪs/ *n.* travellers' house of rest kept by religious order etc.; home for destitute or (esp. terminally) ill.

hospitable /ˈhɒspɪtəb(ə)l/ *a.* disposed to give hospitality.

hospital /ˈhɒspɪt(ə)l/ *n.* institution providing medical and surgical treatment for ill and injured persons; *hist.* charitable institution.

hospitality /hɒspɪˈtælɪtɪ/ *n.* friendly and generous reception of guests or strangers.

hospitalize /ˈhɒspɪtəlaɪz/ *v.t.* send to or treat in hospital. **hospitalization** *n.*

host¹ /həʊst/ *n.* large number; *arch.* army.

host² /həʊst/ *n.* person who entertains another as guest; landlord of inn; animal having parasite.

host³ /həʊst/ *n.* bread consecrated in celebration of Eucharist.

hostage /ˈhɒstɪdʒ/ *n.* person handed over or seized as pledge.

hostel /ˈhɒst(ə)l/ *n.* house of residence for students etc.

hostelry /ˈhɒstəlrɪ/ *n. arch.* inn.

hostess /ˈhəʊstɪs/ *n.* woman who entertains guests, or customers at night-club.

hostile /ˈhɒstaɪl/ *a.* of enemy; unfriendly.

hostility /hɒˈstɪlɪtɪ/ *n.* being hostile; enmity; warfare; in *pl.* acts of war.

hot 1 *a.* of or at high temperature, very warm; giving or feeling heat; pungent; ardent; excited; (of news) fresh; skilful, formidable; *sl.* (of goods) stolen. **2** *v.t. colloq.* heat *up.* **3 hot air** *sl.* excited or boastful talk; **hotbed** bed of earth heated by fermenting manure, *fig.* place that promotes growth; **hot dog** hot sausage sandwiched in bread roll; **hotfoot** in eager haste; **hothead** impetuous person; **hothouse** heated building with glass roof and sides, for growing plants; **hot line** direct communications link between distant places; **hotplate** heated metal plate for cooking food or keeping it hot; **hotpot** dish of stewed meat and vegetables; **hot seat** *sl.* awkward or responsible position, electric chair; **hot water** *colloq. fig.* disgrace, trouble; **hot-water bottle** container filled with hot water and used to warm bed etc.

hotchpotch /ˈhɒtʃpɒtʃ/ *n.* confused mixture, jumble, medley.

hotel /həʊˈtel/ *n.* place providing meals and accommodation for payment.

hotelier /həʊˈtelɪə(r)/ *n.* hotel-keeper.

hound /haʊnd/ **1** *n.* dog used in hunting; despicable man. **2** *v.t.* harass or pursue; urge *on.*

hour /aʊə(r)/ *n.* period of 60 minutes; period set aside for some purpose; in *pl.* fixed habitual time for work etc.; short time; time *for* action etc.; prayers said at any of 7 fixed times of day. **hourglass** reversible device with two glass bulbs containing sand that takes an hour to pass from upper to lower bulb.

houri /ˈhʊərɪ/ n. beautiful young woman (in Muslim paradise).

hourly /ˈaʊəlɪ/ 1 a. occurring etc. every hour. 2 adv. every hour.

house 1 /haʊs/ n. (pl. pr. /ˈhaʊzɪz/) building for habitation or specified purpose; building for keeping animals or goods; residential establishment, esp. of religious order; section of boarding-school etc.; family, dynasty; firm or institution; legislative etc. assembly, building where it meets; audience or performance in theatre etc. 2 /haʊz/ v.t. provide house for; receive or store (as) in house; fix in socket or mortise etc. 3 **house arrest** detention in one's own house; **houseboat** boat fitted up for living in; **house-bound** unable to leave one's house through illness etc.; **housebreaker** burglar; **housekeeper** woman managing affairs of house; **housemaid** female servant in house; **houseman** resident doctor of hospital or institution; **house-martin** bird which builds nests on house walls etc.; **housemaster** master in charge of school boarding-house; **house-plant** one grown indoors; **house-proud** preoccupied with care etc. of home; **house-trained** (of domestic animal) trained to be clean in house; **house-warming** party etc. celebrating move to new house; **housewife** mistress of house, domestic manager, /ˈhʌzɪf/ case for sewing requisites; **housewifely** a.; **housework** cleaning and cooking etc. in home.

household /ˈhaʊshəʊld/ n. occupants of house; domestic establishment. **household troops** those nominally employed to guard sovereign; **household word** familiar saying or name.

householder n. person who occupies house as his own dwelling; head of household.

housing /ˈhaʊzɪŋ/ n. (provision of) houses; protective casing. **housing estate** residential estate planned as a unit.

hove Naut. past & p.p. of **heave**.

hovel /ˈhɒv(ə)l/ n. small miserable dwelling.

hover /ˈhɒvə(r)/ v.i. (of bird etc.) remain in one place in air; loiter about.

hovercraft /ˈhɒvəkrɑːft/ n. (pl. same) vehicle moving on air-cushion over surface of sea or land.

how /haʊ/ 1 adv. in what way; by what means; in what condition; to what extent. 2 n. way thing is done. 3 **howbeit** /-ˈbiːt/ arch. nevertheless. **however** nevertheless, in or to whatever way or degree; **howsoever** /-səʊˈevə(r)/ in or to whatever manner or degree.

howdah /ˈhaʊdə/ n. seat, usu. with canopy, on elephant's back.

howitzer /ˈhaʊɪtsə(r)/ n. short gun firing shell at high elevation.

howl /haʊl/ 1 n. long doleful cry (as) of dog etc.; similar sound; loud cry of rage or derision or laughter etc. 2 v. make howl; utter with howl.

howler n. sl. glaring blunder.

hoy int. used to call attention.

hoyden /ˈhɔɪd(ə)n/ n. boisterous girl.

HP abbr. hire-purchase; horsepower.

HQ abbr. headquarters.

hr. abbr. hour.

HRH abbr. His or Her Royal Highness.

HT abbr. high tension.

hub n. central part of wheel, from which spokes radiate; centre of interest etc.

hubble-bubble /ˈhʌb(ə)lbʌb(ə)l/ n. form of hookah.

hubbub /ˈhʌbʌb/ n. din; tumult.

hubby /ˈhʌbɪ/ n. colloq. husband.

huckaback /ˈhʌkəbæk/ n. rough-surfaced linen or cotton fabric for towels etc.

huckleberry /ˈhʌkəlberɪ/ n. low shrub common in N. Amer.; its fruit.

huckster /ˈhʌkstə(r)/ 1 n. hawker; mercenary person. 2 v. haggle; be hawker.

huddle /ˈhʌd(ə)l/ 1 v. heap or crowd together; nestle closely. 2 n. confused heap etc.; sl. (secret) conference.

hue[1] n. colour, tint.

hue[2] n. hue and cry loud outcry.

huff 1 n. fit of petulance. 2 v. blow; Draughts remove (opponent's man) as forfeit. 3 **huffy** a.

hug 1 v.t. squeeze tightly in one's arms; keep close to (shore etc.); cling to. 2 n. close or rough clasp.

huge /hjuːdʒ/ a. very large or great.

hugely /ˈhjuːdʒlɪ/ adv. very much.

hugger-mugger /ˈhʌɡəmʌɡə(r)/ a. &

adv. secret(ly); confused(ly), in a muddle.

hula /'hu:lə/ *n.* women's dance of Hawaiian origin. **hula hoop** large hoop for spinning round the body.

hulk *n.* body of dismantled ship; large clumsy-looking person or thing.

hulking /'hʌlkɪŋ/ *a. colloq.* bulky, clumsy.

hull[1] *n.* body of ship etc.

hull[2] **1** *n.* pod of beans etc.; calyx of strawberry or raspberry etc. **2** *v.t.* remove hulls of.

hullabaloo /hʌləbə'lu:/ *n.* uproar.

hullo var. of **hallo**.

hum 1 *v.* make low continuous sound like bee; sing with closed lips; make slight inarticulate sound, esp. of hesitation. **2** *n.* humming sound; excl. of hesitation. **3 humming-bird** bird of kind whose wings hum.

human /'hju:mən/ **1** *a.* having or showing qualities distinctive of mankind; that is a person or consists of persons; not divine or animal or mechanical. **2** *n.* human being. **3 human interest** (newspaper etc. story) involving personal emotions; **human rights** those held to belong to all persons.

humane /hju:'meɪn/ *a.* benevolent, compassionate; (of studies) tending to civilize.

humanism /'hju:mənɪz(ə)m/ *n.* doctrine emphasizing human needs and seeking solely rational ways of solving human problems; system of thought etc. concerned with human rather than religious values; literary culture, esp. in Renaissance. **humanist** *n.*; **humanistic** *a.*

humanitarian /hju:mænɪ'teərɪən/ **1** *a.* concerned with promoting human welfare. **2** *n.* humanitarian person. **3 humanitarianism** *n.*

humanity /hju:'mænɪtɪ/ *n.* human nature; human race; humaneness; (usu. in *pl.*) learning or literature concerned with human culture.

humanize /'hju:mənaɪz/ *v.* make or become human or humane. **humanization** *n.*

humanly /'hju:mənlɪ/ *adv.* within human capabilities.

humble /'hʌmb(ə)l/ **1** *a.* having or showing low estimate of one's own importance; lowly, modest. **2** *v.t.* make

humble; lower rank of. **3 eat humble pie** submit to humiliation.

humbug /'hʌmbʌg/ **1** *n.* sham, deception; nonsense; impostor; kind of usu. peppermint-flavoured boiled sweet. **2** *v.t.* delude, cheat.

humdinger /'hʌmdɪŋə(r)/ *n. sl.* remarkable person or thing.

humdrum /'hʌmdrʌm/ *a.* dull, commonplace.

humerus /'hju:mərəs/ *n.* (*pl.* -**ri** /-raɪ/) bone of upper arm. **humeral** *a.*

humid /'hju:mɪd/ *a.* damp, moist.

humidity /hju:'mɪdɪtɪ/ *n.* humid state, degree of moisture esp. in atmosphere.

humiliate /hju:'mɪlɪeɪt/ *v.t.* harm dignity or self-respect of. **humiliation** *n.*

humility /hju:'mɪlɪtɪ/ *n.* humbleness; meekness.

hummock /'hʌmək/ *n.* low hill or hump.

hummus /'homəs/ *n.* paste of chickpeas and oil flavoured with lemon and garlic.

humorist /'hju:mərɪst/ *n.* humorous talker or writer etc.

humorous /'hju:mərəs/ *a.* full of humour, comic.

humour /'hju:mə(r)/ **1** *n.* quality of being amusing; ability to appreciate the comic; state of mind, mood; each of 4 fluids formerly held to determine physical and mental qualities. **2** *v.t.* keep (person) contented by indulging his wishes.

hump 1 *n.* protuberance esp. on back; rounded raised mass of earth etc.; *sl.* fit of depression. **2** *v.* make hump-shaped; *sl.* hoist or carry (pack etc.). **3 humpback** deformed back with hump, person having this; **humpback bridge** one with steep approach to top.

humph *int.* expr. dissatisfaction etc.

humus /'hju:məs/ *n.* organic constituent of soil formed by decomposition of plants etc.

hunch 1 *v.* bend or arch into a hump. **2** *n.* hump, hunk; intuitive feeling. **3 hunchback** humpback.

hundred /'hʌndrəd/ *n.* & *a.* ten times ten; *hist.* subdivision of county. **hundredweight** 112lb., *US* 100 lb. **hundredth** *a.* & *n.*

hundredfold *a.* & *adv.* a hundred times as much or many; consisting of a hundred parts.

hung *past* & *p.p.* of **hang**.

hunger /'hʌŋgə(r)/ 1 *n.* discomfort or painful sensation caused by lack of food; strong desire. 2 *v.i.* feel hunger; crave *for*. 3 **hunger-strike** refusal to take food.

hungry /'hʌŋgrɪ/ *a.* feeling or showing hunger; eager.

hunk *n.* large piece cut off.

hunt 1 *v.* pursue wild animals for food or sport; (of animal) pursue prey; search *for*; drive *out*. 2 *n.* hunting; hunting district or society. 3 **hunting-ground** place where one hunts (freq. *fig.*); **huntsman** hunter, person in charge of hounds.

hunter /'hʌntə(r)/ *n.* one who hunts; horse ridden for hunting; watch with cover protecting glass. **huntress** *n.*

hurdle /'hɜːd(ə)l/ 1 *n.* portable frame with bars etc. for temporary fence; frame to be jumped over in **hurdle-race**; in *pl.* hurdle-race; *fig.* obstacle. 2 *v.i.* run in hurdle-race.

hurdler /'hɜːdlə(r)/ *n.* hurdle-racer; hurdle-maker.

hurdy-gurdy /'hɜːdɪgɜːdɪ/ *n.* musical instrument with droning sound, played by turning handle; *colloq.* barrel-organ.

hurl 1 *v.t.* throw violently. 2 *n.* violent throw.

hurley /'hɜːlɪ/ *n.* Irish game resembling hockey.

hurly-burly /'hɜːlɪbɜːlɪ/ *n.* commotion, tumult.

hurrah /hə'rɑː/ *int.* & *n.* (also **hurray**) (shout) expr. joy or approval.

hurricane /'hʌrɪkən/ *n.* violent storm-wind, esp. W. Ind. cyclone. **hurricane lamp** one with flame protected from wind.

hurry /'hʌrɪ/ 1 *n.* great haste; eagerness; need for haste. 2 *v.* (cause to) move or act with haste; in *p.p.* hasty, done rapidly. 3 **hurry-scurry** (in) disorderly haste. 4 **hurriedly** *adv.*

hurt 1 *v.* (*past* & *p.p.* hurt) cause pain or injury or distress to; suffer pain. 2 *n.* injury; harm; offence. 3 **hurtful** *a.*

hurtle /'hɜːt(ə)l/ *v.i.* move swiftly esp. with clattering sound, come with crash.

husband /'hʌzbənd/ 1 *n.* married man in relation to his wife. 2 *v.t.* manage thriftily.

husbandry /'hʌzbəndrɪ/ *n.* farming; management of resources.

hush 1 *v.* silence; be silent. 2 *n.* silence. 3 **hush-hush** *colloq.* highly secret; **hush-money** sum paid to avoid exposure; **hush up** suppress (fact).

husk 1 *n.* dry outer covering of fruit or seed. 2 *v.t.* remove husk from.

husky[1] /'hʌskɪ/ *a.* full of or dry as husks; hoarse; *colloq.* big and strong.

husky[2] /'hʌskɪ/ *n.* Eskimo dog.

hussar /hə'zɑː(r)/ *n.* light-cavalry soldier.

hussy /'hʌsɪ/ *n.* pert girl; immoral woman.

hustings /'hʌstɪŋz/ *n.* (parliamentary) election proceedings.

hustle /'hʌs(ə)l/ 1 *v.* push roughly, jostle; hurry; push one's way, bustle. 2 *n.* hustling, bustle.

hut *n.* small simple or crude house or shelter; *Mil.* temporary housing for troops.

hutch *n.* boxlike pen for rabbits etc.

hyacinth /'haɪəsɪnθ/ *n.* bulbous plant with bell-shaped flowers.

hyaena /haɪ'iːnə/ var. of **hyena**.

hybrid /'haɪbrɪd/ 1 *n.* offspring of two animals or plants of different species etc.; thing of mixed origins. 2 *a.* bred as hybrid, cross-bred; heterogeneous. 3 **hybridism** *n.*; **hybridization** *n.*; **hybridize** *v.*

hydra /'haɪdrə/ *n.* thing hard to get rid of; water-snake; freshwater polyp.

hydrangea /haɪ'dreɪndʒə/ *n.* shrub with globular clusters of white or blue or pink flowers.

hydrant /'haɪdrənt/ *n.* water-pipe with nozzle for hose.

hydrate /haɪ'dreɪt/ 1 *n.* chemical compound of water with another compound etc. 2 *v.* (cause to) combine with water. 3 **hydration** *n.*

hydraulic /haɪ'drɔːlɪk/ *a.* of water etc. conveyed through pipes etc.; operated by movement of liquid.

hydraulics *n.pl.* usu. treated as *sing.* science of conveyance of liquids through pipes etc. esp. as motive power.

hydro /'haɪdrəʊ/ *n.* (pl. **-os**) *colloq.* hotel etc. providing hydropathic treatment; hydroelectric power plant.

hydro- /'haɪdrəʊ/ *in comb.* water; combined with hydrogen.

hydrocarbon /haɪdrəʊ'kɑːbən/ *n.* compound of hydrogen and carbon.

hydrocephalus /ˌhaɪdrəʊˈsefələs/ n. Med. condition, esp. in young children, with accumulation of fluid within cranium. **hydrocephalic** /-sɪˈfælɪk/ a.; **hydrocephalous** a.

hydrodynamics /ˌhaɪdrəʊdaɪˈnæmɪks/ n.pl. usu. treated as sing. science of forces exerted by liquids.

hydroelectric /ˌhaɪdrəʊɪˈlektrɪk/ a. producing electricity by water-power; (of electricity) produced by water-power.

hydrofoil /ˈhaɪdrəfɔɪl/ n. boat equipped with device for raising hull out of water at speed; this device.

hydrogen /ˈhaɪdrədʒ(ə)n/ n. light colourless odourless gas combining with oxygen to form water. **hydrogen bomb** immensely powerful bomb utilizing explosive fusion of hydrogen nuclei.

hydrogenate /haɪˈdrɒdʒəneɪt/ v.t. charge with or cause to combine with hydrogen. **hydrogenation** n.

hydrography /haɪˈdrɒɡrəfɪ/ n. study of seas, lakes, rivers, etc.

hydrolyse /ˈhaɪdrəlaɪz/ v.t. decompose by hydrolysis.

hydrolysis /haɪˈdrɒlɪsɪs/ n. decomposition by chemical reaction with water. **hydrolytic** /-lɪt-/ a.

hydrometer /haɪˈdrɒmɪtə(r)/ n. instrument for measuring density of liquids.

hydropathy /haɪˈdrɒpəθɪ/ n. medical treatment by external and internal application of water. **hydropathic** /-ˈpæθ-/ a.

hydrophobia /ˌhaɪdrəˈfəʊbɪə/ n. aversion to water, esp. as symptom of rabies in man; rabies. **hydrophobic** a.

hydroplane /ˈhaɪdrəpleɪn/ n. light fast motor boat; finlike device enabling submarine to rise or fall.

hydroponics /ˌhaɪdrəˈpɒnɪks/ n.pl. (usu. treated as sing.) art of growing plants without soil, in water etc. impregnated with chemicals.

hydrostatic /ˌhaɪdrəʊˈstætɪk/ a. of the equilibrium of liquids and the pressure exerted by liquids at rest.

hydrostatics n.pl. (usu. treated as sing.) study of properties of liquids.

hydrous /ˈhaɪdrəs/ a. containing water.

hyena /haɪˈiːnə/ n. carnivorous mammal allied to dog.

hygiene /ˈhaɪdʒiːn/ n. principles of maintaining health; sanitary science. **hygienic** a.; **hygienist** n.

hygrometer /haɪˈɡrɒmɪtə(r)/ n. instrument for measuring humidity of air etc.

hygroscopic /ˌhaɪɡrəˈskɒpɪk/ a. tending to absorb moisture from air.

hymen /ˈhaɪmən/ n. membrane partially closing external orifice of virgin's vagina.

hymenopterous /ˌhaɪməˈnɒptərəs/ a. of order of insects including wasp and ant etc., with 4 membranous wings.

hymn /hɪm/ 1 n. song of praise esp. to God. 2 v.t. praise or celebrate in hymns.

hymnal /ˈhɪmn(ə)l/ n. book of hymns.

hymnology /hɪmˈnɒlədʒɪ/ n. composition or study of hymns. **hymnologist** n.

hyoscine /ˈhaɪəsiːn/ n. alkaloid used as sedative etc.

hyper- /haɪpə(r)/ in comb. over-; excessive.

hyperbola /haɪˈpɜːbələ/ n. curve produced when cone is cut by plane making larger angle with base than side of cone makes. **hyperbolic** /-ˈbɒl-/ a.

hyperbole /haɪˈpɜːbəlɪ/ n. statement exaggerated for effect. **hyperbolical** /-ˈbɒl-/ a.

hypercritical /ˌhaɪpəˈkrɪtɪk(ə)l/ a. too critical.

hypermarket /ˈhaɪpəmɑːkɪt/ n. very large self-service store.

hypersensitive /ˌhaɪpəˈsensɪtɪv/ a. abnormally or excessively sensitive.

hypersonic /ˌhaɪpəˈsɒnɪk/ a. of speeds more than 5 times that of sound.

hypertension /ˌhaɪpəˈtenʃ(ə)n/ n. abnormally high blood-pressure; extreme tension.

hypertrophy /haɪˈpɜːtrəfɪ/ n. enlargement (of organ) due to excessive nutrition. **hypertrophic** /-ˈtrɒf-/ a.

hyphen /ˈhaɪf(ə)n/ 1 n. sign (-) used to join or divide words. 2 v.t. hyphenate.

hyphenate /ˈhaɪfəneɪt/ v.t. join or divide with hyphen.

hypnosis /hɪpˈnəʊsɪs/ n. (pl. **-noses** /-ˈnəʊsiːz/) state like sleep in which subject acts only on external suggestion; artificially induced sleep.

hypnotic /hɪp'nɒtɪk/ **1** *a*. of or causing hypnosis. **2** *n*. hypnotic drug or influence.

hypnotism /'hɪpnətɪz(ə)m/ *n*. production or process of hypnosis. **hypnotist** *n*.

hypnotize /'hɪpnətaɪz/ *v.t*. produce hypnosis in; fascinate.

hypo /'haɪpəʊ/ *n*. *Photog*. sodium thiosulphate, used in fixing.

hypocaust /'haɪpəkɔːst/ *n*. *Rom. ant*. hot-air channel under floor for heating house.

hypochondria /haɪpə'kɒndrɪə/ *n*. abnormal anxiety about one's health.

hypochondriac /haɪpə'kɒndrɪæk/ **1** *n*. person suffering from hypochondria. **2** *a*. of hypochondria.

hypocrisy /hɪ'pɒkrɪsɪ/ *n*. simulation of virtue; insincerity.

hypocrite /'hɪpəkrɪt/ *n*. person guilty of hypocrisy. **hypocritical** *a*.

hypodermic /haɪpə'dɜːmɪk/ **1** *a*. (of drug) introduced under the skin. **2** *n*. hypodermic injection or syringe. **3 hypodermic syringe** syringe with hollow needle for injecting under the skin.

hypostasis /haɪ'pɒstəsɪs/ *n*. (*pl*. **-ses** /-siːz/) *Metaphys*. underlying substance; *Theol*. any one of the three Persons of the Trinity. **hypostatic** *a*.

hypotenuse /haɪ'pɒtənjuːz/ *n*. side opposite right angle of right-angled triangle.

hypothermia /haɪpə'θɜːmɪə/ *n*. *Med*. condition of having abnormally low body temperature.

hypothesis /haɪ'pɒθɪsɪs/ *n*. (*pl*. **-ses** /-siːz/) supposition made as basis for reasoning etc.

hypothetical /haɪpə'θetɪk(ə)l/ *a*. of or resting on hypothesis.

hyssop /'hɪsəp/ *n*. small bushy aromatic herb.

hysterectomy /hɪstə'rektəmɪ/ *n*. surgical removal of womb. **hysterectomize** *v.t*.

hysteria /hɪ'stɪərɪə/ *n*. uncontrollable emotion or excitement; functional disturbance of nervous system.

hysteric /hɪ'sterɪk/ *n*. hysterical person. in *pl*. fit of hysteria.

hysterical /hɪ'sterɪk(ə)l/ *a*. of or caused by hysteria; suffering from hysteria; *colloq*. extremely funny.

Hz *abbr*. hertz.

I

I¹, i, Roman numeral 1.

I² /aɪ/ *pron.* (obj. **me**, poss. **my**) *pron.* of 1st person *sing*.

I. *abbr.* Island(s); Isle(s).

iambic /aɪˈæmbɪk/ **1** *a.* of or using iambuses. **2** *n.* (usu. in *pl.*) iambic verse.

iambus /aɪˈæmbəs/ *n.* metrical foot of one short and one long syllable.

IATA *abbr.* International Air Transport Association.

IBA *abbr.* Independent Broadcasting Authority.

ibex /ˈaɪbeks/ *n.* wild goat of Alps etc. with large backward-curving horns.

ibid. *abbr.* in same book or passage etc. (*ibidem*).

ibis /ˈaɪbɪs/ *n.* storklike bird with long curved bill.

ICBM *abbr.* intercontinental ballistic missile.

ice 1 *n.* frozen water; portion of ice-cream etc. **2** *v.t.* become covered (as) with ice; freeze; cool with ice; cover with icing. **3 ice age** glacial period; **ice-box** *US* refrigerator; **ice-breaker** boat with reinforced bow for breaking channel through ice; **ice-cap** mass of thick ice covering polar region etc.; **ice-cream** sweet creamy frozen food; **ice-field** extensive sheet of floating ice; **ice hockey** form of hockey played on ice with flat disc instead of ball; **ice lolly** kind of water-ice on stick.

iceberg /ˈaɪsbɜːg/ *n.* mass of floating ice at sea.

ichneumon /ɪkˈnjuːmən/ *n.* mongoose of N. Africa etc. **ichneumon-fly** kind of insect parasitic on other insects.

ichthyology /ɪkθɪˈɒlədʒɪ/ *n.* study of fishes. **ichthyological** *a.*; **ichthyologist** *n.*

icicle /ˈaɪsɪk(ə)l/ *n.* tapering hanging spike of ice.

icing /ˈaɪsɪŋ/ *n.* sugar etc. coating for cake etc.; formation of ice on aircraft. **icing sugar** finely powdered sugar.

icon /ˈaɪkɒn/ *n.* sacred painting or mosaic etc.

iconoclast /aɪˈkɒnəklɑːst/ *n.* person who assails cherished beliefs; breaker of images. **iconoclasm** *n.*; **iconoclastic** *a.*

iconography /aɪkəˈnɒgrəfɪ/ *n.* illustration of subject by drawings etc.; study of portraits esp. of one person.

ictus /ˈɪktəs/ *n.* rhythmical or metrical stress.

icy /ˈaɪsɪ/ *a.* very cold; covered with or abounding in ice; (of manner) unfriendly.

id *n. Psych.* part of mind comprising instinctive impulses of individual etc.

idea /aɪˈdɪə/ *n.* thing conceived by mind; vague belief, fancy; plan, intention, aim.

ideal /aɪˈdɪəl/ **1** *a.* perfect; existing only in idea; visionary. **2** *n.* perfect type; actual thing as standard for imitation.

idealism /aɪˈdɪəlɪz(ə)m/ *n.* forming or pursuing ideals; representation of things in ideal form; philosophy in which object of external perception is held to consist of ideas. **idealist** *n.*; **idealistic** *a.*

idealize /aɪˈdɪəlaɪz/ *v.t.* make or treat as ideal. **idealization** *n.*

identical /aɪˈdentɪk(ə)l/ *a.* same; agreeing in all details (with); (of twins) developed from single fertilized ovum and very similar in appearance.

identify /aɪˈdentɪfaɪ/ *v.* establish identity of; treat as identical; associate *with*; regard oneself as sharing characteristics *with*.

identity /aɪˈdentɪtɪ/ *n.* being specified person or thing; absolute sameness; individuality.

ideograph /ˈɪdɪəgrɑːf/ *n.* character in pictorial writing indicating idea, not name, of thing.

ideology /aɪdɪˈɒlədʒɪ/ *n.* scheme of ideas at basis of political etc. theory or system; characteristic way of thinking. **ideological** *a.*

idiocy /ˈɪdɪəsɪ/ *n.* mental condition of idiot; utter foolishness.

idiom /ˈɪdɪəm/ *n.* form of expression peculiar to language; language; characteristic mode of expression. **idiomatic** /-ˈmæt-/ *a.*

idiosyncrasy /ɪdɪəˈsɪŋkrəsɪ/ *n.* attitude or form of behaviour peculiar to person. **idiosyncratic** /-ˈkræt-/ *a.*

idiot /ˈɪdɪət/ *n.* person too deficient in mind to be capable of rational conduct; *colloq.* stupid person. **idiotic** /-ˈɒt-/*a.*

idle /ˈaɪd(ə)l/ **1** *a.* lazy, indolent; unoccupied; useless, purposeless. **2** v. be idle; pass (time) thus; (of engine) run slowly without doing any work. **3 idler** n.; **idly** adv.

idol /'aɪd(ə)l/ n. image as object of worship; object of devotion.

idolater /aɪ'dɒlətə(r)/ n. worshipper of idols; devout admirer. **idolatrous** a.; **idolatry** n.

idolize /'aɪdəlaɪz/ v.t. venerate or love to excess; treat as idol. **idolization** n.

idyll /'ɪdɪl/ n. account of picturesque scene or incident etc.; such scene etc. **idyllic** a.

i.e. abbr. that is to say (id est).

if conj. on condition or supposition that; whenever; whether.

igloo /'ɪgluː/ n. Eskimo dome-shaped snow house.

igneous /'ɪgnɪəs/ a. produced by volcanic action; of fire.

ignite /ɪg'naɪt/ v. set fire to; catch fire.

ignition /ɪg'nɪʃ(ə)n/ n. igniting; mechanism for starting combustion in cylinder of motor engine.

ignoble /ɪg'nəʊb(ə)l/ a. mean, base; of low birth or position.

ignominious /ɪgnə'mɪnɪəs/ a. humiliating.

ignominy /'ɪgnəmɪnɪ/ n. dishonour, infamy.

ignoramus /ɪgnə'reɪməs/ a. ignorant person.

ignorant /'ɪgnərənt/ a. lacking knowledge; uninformed (of). **ignorance** n.

ignore /ɪg'nɔː(r)/ v.t. refuse to take notice of.

iguana /ɪg'wɑːnə/ n. large S. Amer. tree lizard.

iguanodon /ɪg'wɑːnəd(ə)n/ n. large herbivorous dinosaur.

ikebana /ɪkɪ'bɑːnə/ n. Japanese art of flower-arrangement.

ikon var. of **icon**.

ilex /'aɪleks/ n. evergreen oak; Bot. plant of genus including holly.

iliac /'ɪlɪæk/ a. of flank or hip-bone.

ilk /ɪlk/ **1** a. Sc. same. **2** n. colloq. kind, sort. **3** of that ilk of ancestral estate of same name.

ill 1 a. in bad health, sick; harmful, unfavourable; faulty, deficient. **2** adv. badly, unfavourably; scarcely. **3** n. evil; harm; in pl. misfortunes. **4 ill-advised** unwise; **ill-bred** rude; **ill-favoured** unattractive; **ill-gotten** gained by evil

means; **ill-starred** unlucky; **ill-tempered** morose, irritable; **ill-timed** done or occurring at unsuitable time; **ill-treat, -use,** treat badly.

illegal /ɪ'liːg(ə)l/ a. contrary to law. **illegality** /-'gæl-/ n.

illegible /ɪ'ledʒɪb(ə)l/ a. not legible, unreadable. **illegibility** /-'bɪl-/ n.

illegitimate /ɪlɪ'dʒɪtɪmət/ a. (of child) born of parents not married to each other; not authorized by law; improper. **illegitimacy** n.

illiberal /ɪ'lɪbər(ə)l/ a. narrow-minded; sordid; stingy. **illiberality** n.

illicit /ɪ'lɪsɪt/ a. unlawful; forbidden.

illiterate /ɪ'lɪtərət/ **1** a. unable to read; uneducated. **2** n. illiterate person. **3 illiteracy** n.

illness /'ɪlnɪs/ n. ill health; disease.

illogical /ɪ'lɒdʒɪk(ə)l/ a. devoid of or contrary to logic. **illogicality** n.

illuminant /ɪ'luːmɪnənt/ **1** n. means of illumination. **2** a. serving to illuminate.

illuminate /ɪ'luːmɪneɪt/ v.t. light up; enlighten; help to explain; decorate with lights as sign of festivity; decorate (manuscript etc.) with gold etc. **illumination** n.; **illuminative** a.; **illuminator** n.

illumine /ɪ'luːmɪn/ v.t. light up; enlighten.

illusion /ɪ'luːʒ(ə)n/ n. false belief; deceptive appearance. **illusive** a.; **illusory** a.

illusionist /ɪ'luːʒənɪst/ n. producer of illusions, conjuror.

illustrate /'ɪləstreɪt/ v.t. provide with pictures; make clear, esp. by examples or drawings; serve as example of. **illustrator** n.

illustration /ɪlə'streɪʃ(ə)n/ n. illustrating; drawing etc. in book; explanatory example.

illustrative /'ɪləstrətɪv/ a. explanatory (of).

illustrious /ɪ'lʌstrɪəs/ a. distinguished, renowned.

image /'ɪmɪdʒ/ **1** n. imitation of object's external form, esp. figure of saint or divinity, idol; reputation, general impression of person or thing; simile, metaphor; mental representation; optical appearance produced by rays of light reflected from mirror or refracted through transparent medium; idea, conception. **2** *v.t.* make image of; mirror; picture.

imagery /'ɪmɪdʒərɪ/ *n.* figurative illustration; use of images in literature etc.; images, statuary.

imaginary /ɪ'mædʒɪnərɪ/ *a.* existing only in imagination.

imagination /ɪmædʒɪ'neɪʃ(ə)n/ *n.* mental faculty forming images of objects not present to senses; creative faculty of mind.

imaginative /ɪ'mædʒɪnətɪv/ *a.* having or showing high degree of imagination.

imagine /ɪ'mædʒɪn/ *v.t.* form mental image of, conceive; *colloq.* suppose, think.

imago /ɪ'meɪgəʊ/ *n.* (*pl.* **-gines** /-dʒɪniːz/) fully-developed stage of insect.

imam /ɪ'mɑːm/ *n.* prayer-leader of mosque; title of some Muslim leaders.

imbalance /ɪm'bæləns/ *n.* lack of balance; disproportion.

imbecile /'ɪmbɪsiːl/ **1** *n.* person of abnormally weak intellect; *colloq.* stupid person. **2** *a.* mentally weak; *colloq.* stupid. **3 imbecilic** *a.*; **imbecility** *n.*

imbed var. of **embed**.

imbibe /ɪm'baɪb/ *v.t.* drink in; drink; inhale; absorb.

imbroglio /ɪm'brəʊlɪəʊ/ *n.* (*pl.* **-os**) confused or complicated situation.

imbue /ɪm'bjuː/ *v.t.* inspire; saturate, dye.

imitable /'ɪmɪtəb(ə)l/ *a.* that can be imitated. **imitability** *n.*

imitate /'ɪmɪteɪt/ *v.t.* follow example of; mimic; be like. **imitative** *a.*; **imitator** *n.*

imitation /ɪmɪ'teɪʃ(ə)n/ *n.* imitating; copy; counterfeit.

immaculate /ɪ'mækjʊlət/ *a.* pure, spotless; faultless.

immanent /'ɪmənənt/ *a.* inherent; (of God) pervading universe. **immanence** *n.*

immaterial /ɪmə'tɪərɪəl/ *a.* not material; unimportant; irrelevant. **immateriality** *n.*

immature /ɪmə'tjʊə(r)/ *a.* not mature. **immaturity** *n.*

immeasurable /ɪ'meʒərəb(ə)l/ *a.* not measurable, immense.

immediate /ɪ'miːdɪət/ *a.* occurring at once; without intervening medium, direct; nearest. **immediacy** *n.*

immemorial /ɪmɪ'mɔːrɪəl/ *a.* ancient beyond memory.

immense /ɪ'mens/ *a.* vast, huge. **immensity** *n.*

immensely /ɪ'menslɪ/ *adv.* vastly, very much.

immerse /ɪ'mɜːs/ *v.t.* dip, plunge; put under water; involve deeply, embed. **immersible** *a.*

immersion /ɪ'mɜːʃ(ə)n/ *n.* immersing or being immersed. **immersion heater** electric heater designed to be immersed in liquid to be heated.

immigrant /'ɪmɪgrənt/ **1** *n.* person who immigrates. **2** *a.* immigrating; of immigrants.

immigrate /'ɪmɪgreɪt/ *v.t.* come as permanent resident (*into* country). **immigration** *n.*

imminent /'ɪmɪnənt/ *a.* soon to happen. **imminence** *n.*

immobile /ɪ'məʊbaɪl/ *a.* immovable; motionless. **immobility** *n.*

immobilize /ɪ'məʊbɪlaɪz/ *v.t.* prevent from being moved.

immoderate /ɪ'mɒdərət/ *a.* excessive.

immodest /ɪ'mɒdɪst/ *a.* indecent; impudent; conceited. **immodesty** *n.*

immolate /'ɪməleɪt/ *v.t.* kill as sacrifice. **immolation** *n.*

immoral /ɪ'mɒr(ə)l/ *a.* not conforming to, or opposed to, (esp. sexual) morality; dissolute, immorality. **immorality** *n.*

immortal /ɪ'mɔːt(ə)l/ **1** *a.* living for ever; famous for all time. **2** *n.* immortal being, esp. (in *pl.*) gods of antiquity. **3 immortality** *n.*; **immortalize** *v.t.*

immovable /ɪ'muːvəb(ə)l/ *a.* not movable; unyielding. **immovability** *n.*

immune /ɪ'mjuːn/ *a.* having immunity, exempt.

immunity /ɪ'mjuːnɪtɪ/ *n.* living organism's power of resisting and overcoming infection; freedom or exemption (*from*).

immunize /'ɪmjʊnaɪz/ *v.t.* make immune (*against*). **immunization** *n.*

immure /ɪ'mjʊə(r)/ *v.t.* imprison, shut in.

immutable /ɪ'mjuːtəb(ə)l/ *a.* unchangeable. **immutability** *n.*

imp *n.* little devil; mischievous child.

impact 1 /'ɪmpækt/ *n.* collision, striking; (immediate) effect or influence. **2** /ɪm'pækt/ *v.t.* drive or wedge together, in *p.p.* (of tooth) wedged between another tooth and jaw. **3 impaction** *n.*

impair /ɪmˈpeə(r)/ *v.t.* damage, weaken. **impairment** *n.*

impala /ɪmˈpɑːlə/ *n.* small S. Afr. antelope.

impale /ɪmˈpeɪl/ *v.t.* transfix on stake. **impalement** *n.*

impalpable /ɪmˈpælpəb(ə)l/ *a.* imperceptible to touch; not easily grasped.

impart /ɪmˈpɑːt/ *v.t.* give share of; communicate (to).

impartial /ɪmˈpɑːʃ(ə)l/ *a.* fair, not partial. **impartiality** /-ˈæl-/ *n.*

impassable /ɪˈpɑːsəb(ə)l/ *a.* that cannot be traversed. **impassability** *n.*

impasse /ˈæmpæs/ *n.* deadlock.

impassible /ɪmˈpæsɪb(ə)l/ *a.* not subject to suffering; impassive. **impassibility** *n.*

impassioned /ɪmˈpæʃ(ə)nd/ *a.* deeply moved; ardent.

impassive /ɪmˈpæsɪv/ *a.* not feeling or showing emotion. **impassivity** *n.*

impasto /ɪmˈpæstəʊ/ *n.* laying on of paint thickly.

impatient /ɪmˈpeɪʃ(ə)nt/ *a.* not patient; intolerant; eager. **impatience** *n.*

impeach /ɪmˈpiːtʃ/ *v.t.* accuse, esp. of treason etc.; call in question; disparage. **impeachment** *n.*

impeccable /ɪmˈpekəb(ə)l/ *a.* faultless; not liable to sin. **impeccability** *n.*

impecunious /ɪmprˈkjuːnɪəs/ *a.* having little or no money. **impecuniosity** *n.*

impedance /ɪmˈpiːd(ə)ns/ *n.* total effective resistance of electric circuit etc. to alternating current.

impede /ɪmˈpiːd/ *v.t.* retard; hinder.

impediment /ɪmˈpedɪmənt/ *n.* hindrance; defect in speech, esp. lisp or stammer.

impedimenta /ɪmpedɪˈmentə/ *n.pl.* baggage esp. of army.

impel /ɪmˈpel/ *v.t.* drive, force; propel.

impend /ɪmˈpend/ *v.i.* be imminent; hang (over).

impenetrable /ɪmˈpenɪtrəb(ə)l/ *a.* not penetrable; inscrutable; impervious. **impenetrability** *n.*

impenitent /ɪmˈpenɪt(ə)nt/ *a.* not penitent. **impenitence** *n.*

imperative /ɪmˈperətɪv/ **1** *a.* urgent, obligatory; *Gram.* of mood expressing command; peremptory. **2** *n.* imperative mood.

imperceptible /ɪmpəˈseptɪb(ə)l/ *a.* not perceptible; very slight or gradual.

imperfect /ɪmˈpɜːfɪkt/ **1** *a.* not perfect; incomplete; faulty; *Gram.* implying action going on but not completed. **2** *n.* imperfect tense.

imperfection /ɪmpəˈfekʃ(ə)n/ *n.* imperfectness; fault, blemish.

imperial /ɪmˈpɪərɪəl/ *a.* of empire or sovereign State ranking with this; of emperor; majestic; (of weights and measures) used by statute in UK.

imperialism /ɪmˈpɪərɪəlɪz(ə)m/ *n.* imperial system of government etc.; extension of country's power by acquisition of dependencies or (usu. *derog.*) through trade etc. **imperialist** *a.* & *n.*

imperil /ɪmˈperɪl/ *v.t.* endanger.

imperious /ɪmˈpɪərɪəs/ *a.* domineering; urgent.

imperishable /ɪmˈperɪʃəb(ə)l/ *a.* that cannot perish.

impermanent /ɪmˈpɜːmənənt/ *a.* not permanent. **impermanence** *n.*

impermeable /ɪmˈpɜːmɪəb(ə)l/ *a.* not permeable. **impermeability** *n.*

impersonal /ɪmˈpɜːsən(ə)l/ *a.* having no personality or personal feeling or reference; *Gram.* (of verb) used only in 3rd person *sing.* **impersonality** *n.*

impersonate /ɪmˈpɜːsəneɪt/ *v.* pretend to be, play part of. **impersonation** *n.*; **impersonator** *n.*

impertinent /ɪmˈpɜːtɪnənt/ *a.* insolent, saucy; irrelevant. **impertinence** *n.*

imperturbable /ɪmpəˈtɜːbəb(ə)l/ *a.* not excitable; calm. **imperturbability** *n.*

impervious /ɪmˈpɜːvɪəs/ *a.* impenetrable, inaccessible (to).

impetigo /ɪmpɪˈtaɪɡəʊ/ *n.* contagious skin disease.

impetuous /ɪmˈpetjʊəs/ *a.* acting rashly; moving violently or fast. **impetuosity** /-ˈɒs-/ *n.*

impetus /ˈɪmpɪtəs/ *n.* moving force; momentum; impulse.

impiety /ɪmˈpaɪətɪ/ *n.* lack of piety.

impinge /ɪmˈpɪndʒ/ *v.i.* make impact (*on*); encroach *upon.*

impious /ˈɪmpɪəs/ *a.* not pious; wicked.

impish /'ɪmpɪʃ/ a. of or like imp, mischievous.

implacable /ɪm'plækəb(ə)l/ a. not appeasable. **implacability** n.

implant 1 /ɪm'plɑːnt/ v.t. insert, fix; instil; plant. 2 /'ɪmplɑːnt/ n. thing implanted. 3 **implantation** n.

implement 1 /'ɪmplɪmənt/ n. tool, utensil. 2 /'ɪmplɪment/ v.t. carry into effect. 3 **implementation** n.

implicate /'ɪmplɪkeɪt/ v.t. include; involve; imply. **implication** n.

implicit /ɪm'plɪsɪt/ a. implied though not expressed; unquestioning.

implode /ɪm'pləʊd/ v. (cause to) burst inwards. **implosion** n.

implore /ɪm'plɔː(r)/ v.t. beg earnestly.

imply /ɪm'plaɪ/ v.t. mean; involve truth of; insinuate, hint. □ See page 666.

impolite /ɪmpə'laɪt/ a. uncivil, rude.

impolitic /ɪm'pɒlɪtɪk/ a. not politic, not advisable.

imponderable /ɪm'pɒndərəb(ə)l/ 1 a. that cannot be estimated; very light. 2 n. imponderable thing.

import 1 /ɪm'pɔːt/ v.t. bring in (esp. foreign goods) from abroad; imply, mean. 2 /'ɪmpɔːt/ n. article or (in pl.) amount imported; meaning, implication; importance. 3 **importation** n.

important /ɪm'pɔːt(ə)nt/ a. of great consequence, momentous; (of person) having position of authority or rank; pompous. **importance** n.

importunate /ɪm'pɔːtjʊnət/ a. making persistent or pressing requests. **importunity** /-'tjuːn-/ n.

importune /ɪm'pɔːtjuːn/ v.t. solicit pressingly; solicit for immoral purpose.

impose /ɪm'pəʊz/ v. lay (tax etc.) on; enforce compliance with; palm off (on). **impose (up)on** take advantage of, deceive, impress, overawe.

imposing /ɪm'pəʊzɪŋ/ a. impressive, esp. in appearance.

imposition /ɪmpə'zɪʃ(ə)n/ n. unfair demand or burden; tax, duty; work set as punishment at school; laying on (of hands in blessing etc.).

impossible /ɪm'pɒsɪb(ə)l/ a. not possible; not easy or convenient; colloq. outrageous, intolerable. **impossibility** n.

impost /'ɪmpəʊst/ n. tax, duty.

impostor /ɪm'pɒstə(r)/ n. person who assumes false character; swindler.

imposture /ɪm'pɒstʃə(r)/ n. fraudulent deception.

impotent /'ɪmpət(ə)nt/ a. powerless; decrepit; (of male) unable to achieve sexual intercourse. **impotence** n.

impound /ɪm'paʊnd/ v.t. confiscate; shut up in pound.

impoverish /ɪm'pɒvərɪʃ/ v.t. make poor. **impoverishment** n.

impracticable /ɪm'præktɪkəb(ə)l/ a. impossible in practice. **impracticability** n.

impractical /ɪm'præktɪk(ə)l/ a. not practical; not practicable. **impracticality** n.

imprecation /ɪmprɪ'keɪʃ(ə)n/ n. cursing; curse. **imprecatory** a.

impregnable /ɪm'pregnəb(ə)l/ a. safe against attack. **impregnability** n.

impregnate /ɪm'pregnet/ v.t. fill, saturate; make pregnant. **impregnation** n.

impresario /ɪmprɪ'sɑːrɪəʊ/ n. (pl. -os) organizer of public entertainments.

impress[1] /ɪm'pres/ v.t. affect or influence deeply; enforce, fix; imprint, stamp. 2 /'ɪmpres/ n. mark impressed; characteristic quality. 3 **impressible** a.

impress[2] /ɪm'pres/ v.t. hist. force to serve in army or navy. **impressment** n.

impression /ɪm'preʃ(ə)n/ n. effect produced on mind; belief; imitation of person or sound, done to entertain; impressing, mark impressed; unaltered reprint of book etc.; issue of book or newspaper etc.; print from type or engraving.

impressionable /ɪm'preʃənəb(ə)l/ a. easily influenced.

impressionism /ɪm'preʃənɪz(ə)m/ n. method of painting or writing so as to give general effect without detail. **impressionist** n.; **impressionistic** a.

impressive /ɪm'presɪv/ a. able to excite deep feeling esp. of approval or admiration.

imprimatur /ɪmprɪ'meɪtə(r)/ n. licence to print.

imprint 1 /ɪm'prɪnt/ v.t. impress mark on. 2 /'ɪmprɪnt/ n. impression; printer's or publisher's name in book etc.

imprison /ɪmˈprɪz(ə)n/ *v.t.* put into prison; confine. **imprisonment** *n.*

improbable /ɪmˈprɒbəb(ə)l/ *a.* not likely. **improbability** *n.*

improbity /ɪmˈprəʊbɪtɪ/ *n.* wickedness.

impromptu /ɪmˈprɒmptjuː/ **1** *adv.* & *a.* unrehearsed. **2** *n.* impromptu musical or other composition or performance.

improper /ɪmˈprɒpə(r)/ *a.* unseemly, indecent; inaccurate, wrong.

impropriety /ɪmprəˈpraɪətɪ/ *n.* incorrectness, unfitness; indecency.

improve /ɪmˈpruːv/ *v.* make or become better; make good use of (occasion, opportunity). **improvement** (*n.*)

improvident /ɪmˈprɒvɪd(ə)nt/ *a.* heedless, thriftless. **improvidence** *n.*

improvise /ˈɪmprəvaɪz/ *v.t.* compose extempore; use or construct from materials etc. not intended for the purpose. **improvisation** *n.*

imprudent /ɪmˈpruːd(ə)nt/ *a.* rash, indiscreet. **imprudence** *n.*

impudent /ˈɪmpjʊd(ə)nt/ *a.* impertinent; insolent. **impudence** *n.*

impugn /ɪmˈpjuːn/ *v.t.* challenge; call in question.

impulse /ˈɪmpʌls/ *n.* impelling; impetus; sudden tendency to act without reflection.

impulsive /ɪmˈpʌlsɪv/ *a.* apt to be moved or prompted by impulse.

impunity /ɪmˈpjuːnɪtɪ/ *n.* exemption from punishment or injurious consequences.

impure /ɪmˈpjʊə(r)/ *a.* adulterated, mixed; dirty; unchaste. **impurity** *n.*

impute /ɪmˈpjuːt/ *v.t.* ascribe (*to*); ascribe. **imputation** *n.*

in 1 *prep.* expr. inclusion or position within limits of space or time or circumstance etc. **2** *adv.* expr. position bounded by certain limits, or movement to point enclosed by them; into room etc.; at home etc.; in fashion or season or office; (of player etc.) having turn or right to play; (of fire etc.) burning. **3** *a.* internal, living etc. inside; fashionable. **4 inasmuch as** because; **ins and outs** details; **in so far as** to the extent that; **insomuch** to such an extent; **in-tray** tray for incoming documents etc.

in. *abbr.* inch(es).

inability /ɪnəˈbɪlɪtɪ/ *n.* being unable.

inaccessible /ɪnækˈsesɪb(ə)l/ *a.* not accessible; unapproachable. **inaccessibility** *n.*

inaccurate /ɪnˈækjʊrət/ *a.* not accurate. **inaccuracy** *n.*

inaction /ɪnˈækʃ(ə)n/ *n.* absence of action; sluggishness. **inactive** *a.*; **inactivity** *n.*

inadequate /ɪnˈædɪkwət/ *a.* insufficient; incompetent. **inadequacy** *n.*

inadmissible /ɪnədˈmɪsɪb(ə)l/ *a.* not allowable. **inadmissibility** *n.*

inadvertent /ɪnədˈvɜːt(ə)nt/ *a.* unintentional; inattentive. **inadvertence** *n.*; **inadvertency** *n.*

inalienable /ɪnˈeɪlɪənəb(ə)l/ *a.* not transferable to another owner.

inane /ɪˈneɪn/ *a.* silly, senseless; empty. **inanity** /-ˈnæn-/ *n.*

inanimate /ɪnˈænɪmət/ *a.* not endowed with life; spiritless, dull.

inanition /ɪnəˈnɪʃ(ə)n/ *n.* exhaustion from lack of nourishment.

inapplicable /ɪnˈæplɪkəb(ə)l/ *a.* irrelevant; unsuitable. **inapplicability** *n.*

inapposite /ɪnˈæpəzɪt/ *a.* not apposite.

inappropriate /ɪnəˈprəʊprɪət/ *a.* not appropriate.

inapt /ɪnˈæpt/ *a.* not suitable; unskilful. **inaptitude** *n.*

inarticulate /ɪnɑːˈtɪkjʊlət/ *a.* unable to express oneself clearly; not articulate, indistinct; dumb; not jointed.

inartistic /ɪnɑːˈtɪstɪk/ *a.* not following principles of or unskilled in art.

inattention /ɪnəˈtenʃ(ə)n/ *n.* lack of attention; negligence. **inattentive** *a.*

inaudible /ɪnˈɔːdɪb(ə)l/ *a.* that cannot be heard. **inaudibility** *n.*

inaugural /ɪnˈɔːgjʊr(ə)l/ **1** *a.* of inauguration. **2** *n.* inaugural speech or lecture.

inaugurate /ɪnˈɔːgjʊreɪt/ *v.t.* admit (person) to office; initiate or begin or introduce with ceremony. **inauguration** *n.*

inauspicious /ɪnɔːˈspɪʃəs/ *a.* not of good omen; unlucky.

inborn /ˈɪnbɔːn/ *a.* inherent by nature.

inbred /ɪnˈbred/ *a.* inborn; produced by inbreeding.

inbreeding /ɪnˈbriːdɪŋ/ *n.* breeding from closely related animals or persons.

Inc. *abbr.* Incorporated.

incalculable /ɪnˈkælkjʊləb(ə)l/ *a.* too great for calculation; uncertain. **incalculability** *n.*

incandesce /ɪnkænˈdes/ *v.* (cause to) glow with heat.

incandescent /ɪnkænˈdes(ə)nt/ *a.* glowing with heat, shining; (of artificial light) produced by glowing filament etc. **incandescence** *n.*

incantation /ɪnkænˈteɪʃ(ə)n/ *n.* spell, charm.

incapable /ɪnˈkeɪpəb(ə)l/ *a.* not capable; not capable of rational conduct. **incapability** *n.*

incapacitate /ɪnkəˈpæsɪteɪt/ *v.t.* make incapable or unfit.

incapacity /ɪnkəˈpæsɪtɪ/ *n.* inability; legal disqualification.

incarcerate /ɪnˈkɑːsəreɪt/ *v.t.* imprison. **incarceration** *n.*

incarnate 1 /ɪnˈkɑːnət/ *a.* embodied in flesh, esp. human form. **2** /ɪnˈkɑːneɪt/ *v.t.* embody in flesh; be living embodiment of (quality etc.).

incarnation /ɪnkɑːˈneɪʃ(ə)n/ *n.* embodiment in flesh. **the Incarnation** incarnation of God in Christ.

incautious /ɪnˈkɔːʃəs/ *a.* rash.

incendiary /ɪnˈsendɪərɪ/ **1** *a.* (of bomb) filled with material for causing fires; inflammatory; guilty of arson. **2** *n.* incendiary person or bomb.

incense¹ /ˈɪnsens/ *n.* gum or spice giving sweet smell when burned; smoke of this, esp. in religious ceremonial.

incense² /ɪnˈsens/ *v.t.* make angry.

incentive /ɪnˈsentɪv/ **1** *n.* thing inciting or encouraging to action; inducement, esp. to increase output etc. **2** *a.* inciting.

inception /ɪnˈsepʃ(ə)n/ *n.* beginning.

incertitude /ɪnˈsɜːtɪtjuːd/ *n.* uncertainty.

incessant /ɪnˈses(ə)nt/ *a.* continual; repeated.

incest /ˈɪnsest/ *n.* sexual intercourse of near relations. **incestuous** *a.*

inch 1 *n.* twelfth of (linear) foot, 2.54 cm.; used as unit of map scale (= 1 inch to one mile) or as unit of rainfall (= 1 inch depth of water). **2** *v.* move gradually.

inchoate /ˈɪnkəʊət/ *a.* undeveloped, just begun. **inchoation** *n.*

incidence /ˈɪnsɪd(ə)ns/ *n.* falling on or contact with thing; range, scope, extent; manner or range of occurrence.

incident /ˈɪnsɪd(ə)nt/ **1** *n.* event, occurrence; episode. **2** *a.* apt to occur, naturally attaching (*to*).

incidental /ɪnsɪˈdent(ə)l/ *a.* casual; not essential; (of music) played during or between scenes of play or film etc.

incidentally *adv.* by the way.

incinerate /ɪnˈsɪnəreɪt/ *v.t.* consume by fire. **incineration** *n.*

incinerator /ɪnˈsɪnəreɪtə(r)/ *n.* furnace or device for incineration.

incipient /ɪnˈsɪpɪənt/ *a.* beginning, in early stage.

incise /ɪnˈsaɪz/ *v.t.* make cut in; engrave. **incision** /-ˈsɪʒ(ə)n/ *n.*

incisive /ɪnˈsaɪsɪv/ *a.* sharp; clear and effective.

incisor /ɪnˈsaɪzə(r)/ *n.* any of front teeth between canines.

incite /ɪnˈsaɪt/ *v.t.* urge on, stir up. **incitement** *n.*

incivility /ɪnsɪˈvɪlɪtɪ/ *n.* rudeness.

inclement /ɪnˈklemənt/ *a.* (of weather) severe, cold or stormy. **inclemency** *n.*

inclination /ɪnklɪˈneɪʃ(ə)n/ *n.* propensity; liking, affection; slope, slant.

incline /ɪnˈklaɪn/ **1** *v.* (cause to) lean; bend forward or downward; dispose, be disposed; tend. **2** *n.* (also /ˈɪn-/) slope, inclined plane.

include /ɪnˈkluːd/ *v.t.* comprise, regard or treat as part of whole. **inclusion** *n.*

inclusive /ɪnˈkluːsɪv/ *a.* including; comprehensive; including all accessory payments.

incognito /ɪnkɒɡˈniːtəʊ/ **1** *adv.* under false name; with identity concealed. **2** *a.* acting incognito. **3** *n.* (*pl.* **-tos**) pretended identity; person who is incognito.

incoherent /ɪnkəʊˈhɪərənt/ *a.* not coherent. **incoherence** *n.*

incombustible /ɪnkəmˈbʌstɪb(ə)l/ *a.* that cannot be burnt up. **incombustibility** *n.*

income /ˈɪnkʌm/ *n.* money received, esp. periodically, from work or investments etc. **income tax** tax levied on income.

incoming /ˈɪnkʌmɪŋ/ *a.* coming in, succeeding.

incommensurable /ɪnkəˈmenʃərəb(ə)l/ *a.* not comparable in size or value etc.; having no common measure. **incommensurability** n.

incommensurate /mkə'menʃərət/ a. out of proportion; inadequate.

incommode /mkə'məʊd/ v.t. trouble, annoy; impede.

incommodious /mkə'məʊdɪəs/ a. not affording comfort, inconvenient.

incommunicable /mkə'mju:nɪkəb(ə)l/ a. that cannot be shared or told. **incommunicability** n.

incommunicado /mkəmju:nɪ'kɑːdəʊ/ a. without means of communication, in solitary confinement.

incomparable /m'kɒmpərəb(ə)l/ a. without an equal.

incompatible /mkəm'pætɪb(ə)l/ a. opposed; discordant; inconsistent. **incompatibility** n.

incompetent /m'kɒmpɪt(ə)nt/ a. not competent; not legally qualified. **incompetence** n.

incomplete /mkəm'pli:t/ a. not complete.

incomprehensible /mkɒmprɪ'hensɪb(ə)l/ a. that cannot be understood. **incomprehensibility** n.

inconceivable /mkən'si:vəb(ə)l/ a. that cannot be imagined. **inconceivability** n.

inconclusive /mkən'klu:sɪv/ a. (of argument etc.) not convincing or decisive.

incongruous /m'kɒŋgrʊəs/ a. out of keeping; absurd. **incongruity** n.

inconsequent /m'kɒnsɪkwənt/ a. irrelevant, disconnected; not following logically. **inconsequence** n.

inconsequential /mkɒnsɪ'kwenʃ(ə)l/ a. unimportant; inconsequent.

inconsiderable /mkən'sɪdərəb(ə)l/ a. not worth considering; of small size or value etc.

inconsiderate /mkən'sɪdərət/ a. not considerate of others; thoughtless.

inconsistent /mkən'sɪst(ə)nt/ a. not consistent; incompatible. **inconsistency** n.

inconsolable /mkən'səʊləb(ə)l/ a. that cannot be comforted.

inconspicuous /mkən'spɪkjʊəs/ a. not readily seen or noticed.

inconstant /m'kɒnst(ə)nt/ a. fickle; variable; irregular. **inconstancy** n.

incontestable /mkən'testəb(ə)l/ a. that cannot be disputed.

incontinent /m'kɒntɪnənt/ a. unable to control excretions voluntarily; lacking self-restraint. **incontinence** n.

incontrovertible /mkɒntrə'vɜːtɪb(ə)l/ a. indisputable.

inconvenience /mkən'vi:nɪəns/ 1 n. lack of ease or comfort; instance of this. 2 v.t. cause inconvenience to. 3 **inconvenient** a.

incorporate 1 /m'kɔːpəreɪt/ v.t. include as part or ingredient; constitute as legal corporation; combine into one substance or whole (with, in, into). 2 /m'kɔːpərət/ a. incorporated. 3 **incorporation** n.

incorporeal /mkɔː'pɔːrɪəl/ a. without substance or material existence.

incorrect /mkə'rekt/ a. untrue, inaccurate.

incorrigible /m'kɒrɪdʒɪb(ə)l/ a. incurably bad.

incorruptible /mkə'rʌptɪb(ə)l/ a. that cannot decay or be corrupted. **incorruptibility** n.

increase 1 /m'kri:s/ v. become or make greater or more numerous; intensify. 2 /'mkri:s/ n. growth, enlargement; increased amount. 3 **on the increase** increasing.

incredible /m'kredɪb(ə)l/ a. that cannot be believed; colloq. surprising. **incredibility** n.

incredulous /m'kredjʊləs/ a. unbelieving, showing disbelief. **incredulity** /-'dju:l-/ n.

increment /'mkrɪmənt/ n. amount of increase; added amount; profit.

incriminate /m'krɪmɪneɪt/ v.t. indicate as guilty; charge with crime. **incrimination** n.; **incriminatory** a.

incrustation /mkrʌs'teɪʃ(ə)n/ n. encrusting, being encrusted; crust, hard coating.

incubate /'mkjʊbeɪt/ v. hatch (eggs) by sitting on them or by artificial heat; sit on eggs; cause (bacteria etc.) to develop.

incubation /mkjʊ'beɪʃ(ə)n/ n. incubating or being incubated; development of disease germs before first symptoms appear.

incubator /'mkjʊbeɪtə(r)/ n. apparatus for hatching eggs or rearing babies born prematurely or for developing bacteria.

incubus /'mkjʊbəs/ n. oppressive person or thing; evil spirit believed to visit sleeper; nightmare.

inculcate /'mkʌlkeɪt/ v.t. urge, impress persistently (in etc.). **inculcation** n.

inculpate /'mkʌlpeɪt/ v.t. incriminate; accuse, blame. **inculpation** n.

incumbent /m'kʌmbənt/ 1 a. resting as duty (up)on. 2 n. holder of office, esp. benefice. 3 **incumbency** n.

incunabula /mkjʊ'næbjʊlə/ n.pl. early printed books, esp. from before 1501.

incur /m'kɜ:(r)/ v.t. bring on oneself.

incurable /m'kjʊərəb(ə)l/ 1 a. that cannot be cured. 2 n. incurable person. 3 **incurability** n.

incurious /m'kjʊərɪəs/ a. devoid of curiosity. **incuriosity** n.

incursion /m'kɜ:ʃ(ə)n/ n. invasion; sudden attack. **incursive** a.

indebted /m'detɪd/ a. owing money or gratitude (to).

indecent /m'di:s(ə)nt/ a. unbecoming; offending against decency; unsuitable. **indecent assault** sexual attack not involving rape. **indecency** n.

indecipherable /mdɪ'saɪfərəb(ə)l/ a. that cannot be deciphered.

indecision /mdɪ'sɪʒ(ə)n/ n. lack of decision, hesitation.

indecisive /mdɪ'saɪsɪv/ a. not decisive; irresolute.

indeclinable /mdɪ'klaɪnəb(ə)l/ a. Gram. (of word) having no inflexions.

indecorous /m'dekərəs/ a. improper, in bad taste.

indeed /m'di:d/ adv. in truth; really.

indefatigable /mdɪ'fætɪgəb(ə)l/ a. unwearying. **indefatigability** n.

indefeasible /mdɪ'fi:zɪb(ə)l/ a. that cannot be forfeited or annulled. **indefeasibility** n.

indefensible /mdɪ'fensɪb(ə)l/ a. that cannot be defended. **indefensibility** n.

indefinable /mdɪ'faɪnəb(ə)l/ a. that cannot be defined or exactly described.

indefinite /m'defɪnɪt/ a. vague, undefined.

indelible /m'delɪb(ə)l/ a. that cannot be blotted out; permanent. **indelibility** n.

indelicate /m'delɪkət/ a. immodest, tactless. **indelicacy** n.

indemnify /m'demnɪfaɪ/ v.t. secure against loss or legal responsibility;

compensate (for loss etc.). **indemnification** n.

indemnity /m'demnɪtɪ/ n. security against damage or loss; exemption from penalties etc.; compensation for damage.

indent 1 /m'dent/ v. make notches, dents, or recesses in; set back (beginning of line) inwards from margin; make requisition or written order for. 2 /'mdent/ n. official requisition, order; indentation; indenture. 3 **indentation** n.

indenture /m'dentʃə(r)/ 1 n. (usu. in pl.) sealed agreement, esp. binding apprentice to master. 2 v.t. bind by indentures.

independence /mdɪ'pend(ə)ns/ n. being independent. **Independence Day** US holiday (4 Jul.), anniversary of Declaration of Independence.

independent 1 a. not depending on authority (of); self-governing; not depending on something else for validity or efficiency etc. or on another person for one's livelihood or opinions; (of institution) not supported by public funds; (of income) making it unnecessary for one to earn one's livelihood; unwilling to be under obligation to others. 2 n. politician etc. independent of any political party.

indescribable /mdɪ'skraɪbəb(ə)l/ a. beyond description; vague. **indescribably** n.

indestructible /mdɪ'strʌktɪb(ə)l/ a. that cannot be destroyed. **indestructibility** n.

indeterminable /mdɪ'tɜ:mɪnəb(ə)l/ a. that cannot be ascertained or settled.

indeterminate /mdɪ'tɜ:mɪnət/ a. not fixed in extent or character etc.; vague.

index /'mdeks/ 1 n. (pl. **-dexes** or **-dices** /-dɪsi:z/) alphabetical list of subjects etc. with references, usu. at end of book; number expressing prices etc. in terms of a standard value; Math. exponent. 2 v.t. furnish (book) with index, enter in index. 3 **index finger** forefinger; **index-linked** related to value of price index.

India paper /'mdɪə/ very thin tough opaque printing-paper.

Indian /'mdɪən/ 1 a. of India; of the subcontinent comprising India and Pakistan and Bangladesh; of the original inhabitants of America and the W. Indies. **2** *n.* native of India; **Red Indian. 3 Indian club** bottle-shaped club for gymnastic exercises; **Indian corn** maize; **Indian file** single file; **Indian ink** black pigment; **Indian summer** period of calm dry warm weather in late autumn.

indiarubber /ɪndɪəˈrʌbə(r)/ *n.* rubber, esp. for rubbing out pencil marks etc.

indicate /ˈɪndɪkeɪt/ *v.t.* point out, make known, show; be sign of; require. **indication** *n.*

indicative /ɪnˈdɪkətɪv/ **1** *a.* suggestive, giving indications, *of*; *Gram.* of mood stating thing as fact, not conditional or subjunctive. **2** *n.* *Gram.* indicative mood.

indicator /ˈɪndɪkeɪtə(r)/ *n.* person or thing that indicates; recording instrument on machine etc.; board giving current information; device to show intended turn by vehicle.

indices *pl.* of **index**.

indict /ɪnˈdaɪt/ *v.t.* accuse, esp. by legal process. **indictment** *n.*

indictable /ɪnˈdaɪtəb(ə)l/ *a.* rendering person liable to be indicted; so liable.

indifference /ɪnˈdɪfərəns/ *n.* absence of interest or attention; unimportance.

indifferent *a.* showing indifference; neither good nor bad; rather bad.

indigenous /ɪnˈdɪdʒɪnəs/ *a.* native or belonging naturally (*to* soil etc.).

indigent /ˈɪndɪdʒ(ə)nt/ *a.* needy, poor. **indigence** *n.*

indigestible /ɪndɪˈdʒestɪb(ə)l/ *a.* difficult or impossible to digest.

indignant /ɪnˈdɪɡnənt/ *a.* moved by anger and scorn or sense of injury. **indignation** *n.*

indignity /ɪnˈdɪɡnɪtɪ/ *n.* humiliating treatment, insult, slight.

indigo /ˈɪndɪɡəʊ/ *n.* (*pl.* **-gos**) deep violet-blue; dye of this colour.

indirect /ɪndɪˈrekt/ *a.* not direct. **indirect object** *Gram.* person or thing affected by action of verb but not acted on; **indirect speech** reported speech; **indirect tax** tax paid as price increase for taxed goods.

indiscernible /ɪndɪˈsɜːnɪb(ə)l/ *a.* that cannot be discerned.

indiscipline /ɪnˈdɪsɪplɪn/ *n.* lack of discipline.

indiscreet /ɪndɪˈskriːt/ *a.* revealing secrets; injudicious, unwary.

indiscretion /ɪndɪˈskreʃ(ə)n/ *n.* indiscreet conduct or action.

indiscriminate /ɪndɪˈskrɪmɪnət/ *a.* confused; undiscriminating. **indiscrimination** *n.*

indispensable /ɪndɪˈspensəb(ə)l/ *a.* that cannot be dispensed with; necessary. **indispensability** *n.*

indispose /ɪndɪˈspəʊz/ *v.t.* make unfit or unable; make averse.

indisposed *a.* slightly unwell. **indisposition** *n.*

indisputable /ɪndɪˈspjuːtəb(ə)l/ *a.* beyond dispute.

indissoluble /ɪndɪˈsɒljʊb(ə)l/ *a.* cannnot be dissolved; lasting, stable.

indistinct /ɪndɪˈstɪŋkt/ *a.* not distinct; confused, obscure.

indistinguishable /ɪndɪˈstɪŋgwɪʃəb(ə)l/ *a.* not distinguishable.

indite /ɪnˈdaɪt/ *v.t.* put into words; *joc.* write (letter etc.).

individual /ɪndɪˈvɪdjʊəl/ **1** *a.* single; particular; characteristic of particular person etc.; of or for single person or thing. **2** *n.* single member of class or group etc.; single human being; *colloq.* person. **3 individuality** *n.*; **individualize** *v.t.*

individualism /ɪndɪˈvɪdjʊəlɪz(ə)m/ *n.* self-reliant action by individual; social theory favouring free action by individuals; egoism. **individualist** *n.*; **individualistic** *a.*

indivisible /ɪndɪˈvɪzɪb(ə)l/ *a.* not divisible.

indoctrinate /ɪnˈdɒktrɪneɪt/ *v.t.* imbue with doctrine etc.; teach. **indoctrination** *n.*

Indo-European /ɪndəʊjʊərəˈpɪən/ **1** *n.* family of languages spoken over most of Europe and in Asia as far as N. India. **2** *a.* of these languages.

indolent /ˈɪndələnt/ *a.* lazy, slothful. **indolence** *n.*

indomitable /ɪnˈdɒmɪtəb(ə)l/ *a.* unyielding.

indoor /ˈɪndɔː(r)/ *a.* done etc. in a building or under cover.

indoors /ɪnˈdɔːz/ *adv.* in(to) a building; under roof.

indorse var. of **endorse**.

indubitable /ɪnˈdjuːbɪtəb(ə)l/ *a.* beyond doubt.

induce /ɪnˈdjuːs/ v.t. prevail on, persuade; bring about; bring on (labour) artificially; produce by induction; infer. **inducible** a.

inducement n. thing that induces, attraction, motive.

induct /ɪnˈdʌkt/ v.t. install.

inductance /ɪnˈdʌkt(ə)ns/ n. Electr. amount of induction of current.

induction /ɪnˈdʌkʃ(ə)n/ n. inducting or inducing; Med. inducing (of labour); general inference from particular instances; Electr. production of electric or magnetic state by proximity of neighbouring circuit etc.

inductive /ɪnˈdʌktɪv/ a. based on or using induction.

indulge /ɪnˈdʌldʒ/ v. take one's pleasure freely in; yield freely to (desire etc.); gratify by compliance with wishes.

indulgence /ɪnˈdʌldʒ(ə)ns/ n. indulging; privilege granted; RC Ch. remission of punishment still due for sin after sacramental absolution.

indulgent a. willing to overlook faults; too lenient.

indurate /ˈɪndjʊəreɪt/ v. make or become hard. **induration** n.

industrial /ɪnˈdʌstrɪəl/ a. of industries; engaged in or connected with industry; having highly developed industries. **industrialize** v.t.

industrialism /ɪnˈdʌstrɪəlɪz(ə)m/ n. system involving prevalence of industries.

industrialist /ɪnˈdʌstrɪəlɪst/ n. person engaged in management of industry.

industrious /ɪnˈdʌstrɪəs/ a. hard-working.

industry /ˈɪndəstrɪ/ n. branch of trade or manufacture; trade or manufacture collectively; diligence.

inebriate 1 /ɪˈniːbrɪət/ a. drunken. **2** /ɪˈniːbrɪət/ n. drunkard. **3** /ɪˈniːbrɪeɪt/ v.t. make drunk. **4 inebriation** n.; **inebriety** /ɪnɪˈbraɪətɪ/ n.

inedible /ɪnˈedɪb(ə)l/ a. not edible.

ineducable /ɪnˈedjʊkəb(ə)l/ a. incapable of being educated.

ineffable /ɪnˈefəb(ə)l/ a. unutterable.

ineffective /ɪnɪˈfektɪv/ a. ineffectual.

ineffectual /ɪnɪˈfektjʊəl/ a. not producing desired effect; inefficient.

inefficient /ɪnɪˈfɪʃ(ə)nt/ a. not efficient or fully capable. **inefficiency** n.

inelastic /ɪnɪˈlæstɪk/ a. not elastic or adaptable; rigid. **inelasticity** n.

inelegant /ɪnˈelɪgənt/ a. ungraceful, unrefined; unpolished. **inelegance** n.

ineligible /ɪnˈelɪdʒɪb(ə)l/ a. not eligible, undesirable. **ineligibility** n.

ineluctable /ɪnɪˈlʌktəb(ə)l/ a. against which it is useless to struggle.

inept /ɪˈnept/ a. unskilful; absurd, silly; out of place. **ineptitude** n.

inequality /ɪnɪˈkwɒlɪtɪ/ n. lack of equality; variableness; unevenness.

inequitable /ɪnˈekwɪtəb(ə)l/ a. unfair, unjust.

ineradicable /ɪnɪˈrædɪkəb(ə)l/ a. that cannot be rooted out.

inert /ɪˈnɜːt/ a. without inherent power of action; chemically inactive; sluggish, slow.

inertia /ɪˈnɜːʃə/ n. inertness; property by which matter continues in existing state of rest or motion unless acted on by external force. **inertia reel** reel allowing automatic adjustment of safety-belt rolled round it; **inertia selling** sending of unordered goods in hope they will not be refused.

inescapable /ɪnɪˈskeɪpəb(ə)l/ a. that cannot be escaped or avoided.

inessential /ɪnɪˈsenʃ(ə)l/ a. & n. unnecessary (thing).

inestimable /ɪnˈestɪməb(ə)l/ a. too great etc. to be estimated.

inevitable /ɪnˈevɪtəb(ə)l/ a. unavoidable; bound to happen or appear. **inevitability** n.

inexact /ɪnɪgˈzækt/ a. not exact. **inexactitude** n.

inexcusable /ɪnɪksˈkjuːzəb(ə)l/ a. that cannot be justified.

inexhaustible /ɪnɪgˈzɔːstɪb(ə)l/ a. that cannot be exhausted.

inexorable /ɪnˈeksərəb(ə)l/ a. relentless. **inexorability** n.

inexpedient /ɪnɪkˈspiːdɪənt/ a. not expedient. **inexpediency** n.

inexpensive /ɪnɪkˈspensɪv/ a. cheap, offering good value.

inexperience /ɪnɪkˈspɪərɪəns/ n. lack of experience. **inexperienced** a.

inexpert /ɪnˈekspɜːt/ a. unskilful.

inexpiable /ɪnˈekspɪəb(ə)l/ a. that cannot be expiated.

inexplicable /ɪnˈeksp.lɪkəb(ə)l/ a. that cannot be explained. **inexplicability** n.

inexpressible /ɪnɪk'spresɪb(ə)l/ a. that cannot be expressed in words.

in extremis /ɪn ek'stri:mɪs/ at point of death; in great difficulties. [L]

inextricable /ɪ'nekstrɪkəb(ə)l/ a. that cannot be loosened or resolved or escaped from.

infallible /ɪn'fælɪb(ə)l/ a. incapable of erring; unfailing, sure. **infallibility** n.

infamous /'ɪnfəməs/ a. notoriously vile, evil; abominable.

infamy /'ɪnfəmɪ/ n. evil reputation; infamous conduct.

infant /'ɪnf(ə)nt/ n. child during earliest period of life; *Law* person under 18. **infancy** n.

infanta /ɪn'fæntə/ n. *hist.* daughter of Spanish or Portuguese king.

infanticide /ɪn'fæntɪsaɪd/ n. murder of infant soon after birth; person guilty of this.

infantile /'ɪnfəntaɪl/ a. of or like infants. **infantile paralysis** poliomyelitis.

infantry /'ɪnfəntrɪ/ n. foot-soldiers. **infantryman** soldier of infantry regiment.

infatuate /ɪn'fætjʊeɪt/ v.t. inspire with intense fondness. **infatuation** n.

infect /ɪn'fekt/ v.t. affect or contaminate with germ or virus or disease; imbue with opinion or feeling etc.

infection /ɪn'fekʃ(ə)n/ n. infecting or being infected; disease; communication of disease.

infectious /ɪn'fekʃəs/ a. transmissible by infection; apt to spread.

infelicitous /ɪnfɪ'lɪsɪtəs/ a. not felicitous.

infelicity /ɪnfɪ'lɪsɪtɪ/ n. unhappiness; infelicitous expression.

infer /ɪn'fɜ:(r)/ v.t. deduce, conclude. □ See page 666. **inference** /'ɪn-/ n.; **inferential** /-'ren-/ a.

inferior /ɪn'fɪərɪə(r)/ 1 a. lower in rank etc.; of poor quality; situated below. 2 n. inferior person.

inferiority /ɪnfɪərɪ'ɒrɪtɪ/ n. being inferior. **inferiority complex** unconscious feeling of inferiority to others, sometimes manifested in aggressive behaviour, *colloq.* sense of inferiority.

infernal /ɪn'fɜ:n(ə)l/ a. of hell; hellish.

inferno /ɪn'fɜ:nəʊ/ n. (pl. **-nos**) scene of horror or distress, esp. in fire; hell.

infertile /ɪn'fɜ:taɪl/ a. not fertile. **infertility** /-'tɪl-/ n.

infest /ɪn'fest/ v.t. overrun in large numbers. **infestation** n.

infidel /'ɪnfɪd(ə)l/ 1 n. disbeliever in (specified) religion. 2 a. unbelieving; of infidels.

infidelity /ɪnfɪ'delɪtɪ/ n. being unfaithful.

infighting /'ɪnfaɪtɪŋ/ n. hidden conflict in organization; boxing at closer quarters than arm's length.

infiltrate /'ɪnfɪltreɪt/ v. enter (territory, political party, etc.) gradually and imperceptibly; pass (fluid) by filtration (*into*); permeate by filtration. **infiltration** n.; **infiltrator** n.

infinite /'ɪnfɪnɪt/ a. boundless; endless; very great or many.

infinitesimal /ɪnfɪnɪ'tesɪm(ə)l/ a. infinitely or very small. **infinitesimal calculus** that dealing with such quantities.

infinitive /ɪn'fɪnɪtɪv/ a. & n. *Gram.* (verb-form) expressing verbal notion without particular subject or tense etc.

infinitude /ɪn'fɪnɪtju:d/ n. infinity; being infinite.

infinity /ɪn'fɪnɪtɪ/ n. infinite number or extent; immensity.

infirm /ɪn'fɜ:m/ a. weak; irresolute. **infirmity** n.

infirmary /ɪn'fɜ:mərɪ/ n. hospital; sick-quarters in school etc.

in flagrante delicto /ɪn flæ'græntɪ dɪ'lɪktəʊ/ in act of committing offence. [L]

inflame /ɪn'fleɪm/ v.t. provoke to strong feeling; cause inflammation in; (cause to) catch fire; make hot.

inflammable /ɪn'flæməb(ə)l/ a. easily set on fire or excited. **inflammability** n.

inflammation /ɪnflə'meɪʃ(ə)n/ n. condition of living tissue marked by heat and swelling and redness and usu. pain.

inflammatory /ɪn'flæmətərɪ/ a. tending to inflame; of inflammation.

inflate /ɪn'fleɪt/ v.t. distend with air or gas; puff up; raise (price) artificially; resort to inflation (of currency).

inflated /ɪn'fleɪtɪd/ a. (of language) bombastic.

inflation /ɪn'fleɪʃ(ə)n/ n. inflating or being inflated; general rise in prices, increase in supply of money regarded as cause of such rise. **inflationary** *a.*

inflect /ɪnˈflekt/ *v.t.* change or vary pitch of; modify (word) to express grammatical relation.

inflexible /ɪnˈfleksɪb(ə)l/ *a.* unbendable; unbending; unyielding. **inflexibility** *n.*

inflexion /ɪnˈflekʃ(ə)n/ *n.* modulation of voice etc.; inflected form; inflecting suffix etc.; inflecting. **inflexional** *a.*

inflict /ɪnˈflɪkt/ *v.t.* deal (blow etc.); impose (*up*)on. **infliction** *n.*

inflorescence /ɪnfləˈres(ə)ns/ *n.* arrangement of flowers or collective flower of plant; flowering.

inflow /ˈɪnfləʊ/ *n.* flowing in; that which flows in.

influence /ˈɪnflʊəns/ **1** *n.* action invisibly exercised; ascendancy; moral power; thing or person exercising this. **2** *v.t.* exert influence upon; affect.

influential /ɪnflʊˈenʃ(ə)l/ *a.* having great influence.

influenza /ɪnflʊˈenzə/ *n.* infectious virus disease with fever and severe aching and catarrh.

influx /ˈɪnflʌks/ *n.* flowing in.

inform /ɪnˈfɔːm/ *v.* give information to; bring charge (*against*); in *p.p.* knowing the facts.

informal /ɪnˈfɔːm(ə)l/ *a.* not formal; without formality. **informality** *n.*

informant /ɪnˈfɔːmənt/ *n.* giver of information.

information /ɪnfəˈmeɪʃ(ə)n/ *n.* what is told; knowledge; news; charge or accusation. **information science** study of processes for storing and retrieving information.

informative /ɪnˈfɔːmətɪv/ *a.* giving information, instructive.

infraction /ɪnˈfrækʃ(ə)n/ *n.* infringement.

infra dig. /ɪnfrə ˈdɪg/ beneath one's dignity.

infra-red /ɪnfrəˈred/ *a.* of or using invisible rays (just) beyond red end of spectrum.

infrastructure /ˈɪnfrəstrʌktʃə(r)/ *n.* subordinate parts of an undertaking, esp. permanent installations forming basis of defence.

infrequent /ɪnˈfriːkwənt/ *a.* not frequent. **infrequency** *n.*

infringe /ɪnˈfrɪndʒ/ *v.t.* transgress, act contrary to. **infringement** *n.*

infuriate /ɪnˈfjʊərɪeɪt/ *v.t.* enrage.

infuse /ɪnˈfjuːz/ *v.* cause to be saturated or filled *with* quality; instil; steep or be steeped in liquid to extract properties.

infusible /ɪnˈfjuːzɪb(ə)l/ *a.* that cannot be melted. **infusibility** *n.*

infusion /ɪnˈfjuːʒ(ə)n/ *n.* infusing; liquid extract so obtained; infused element.

ingenious /ɪnˈdʒiːnɪəs/ *a.* clever at contriving; cleverly contrived.

ingénue /ˈæʒeɪnjuː/ *n.* artless young woman, esp. as stage type. [F]

ingenuity /ɪndʒɪˈnjuːɪtɪ/ *n.* ingeniousness.

ingenuous /ɪnˈdʒenjʊəs/ *a.* artless; frank.

ingest /ɪnˈdʒest/ *v.t.* take in (food etc.). **ingestion** *n.*

ingle-nook /ˈɪŋgəlnʊk/ *n.* warm seat inside old-fashioned wide fireplace.

inglorious /ɪnˈglɔːrɪəs/ *a.* shameful; obscure.

ingoing /ˈɪŋgəʊɪŋ/ *a.* going in.

ingot /ˈɪŋgət/ *n.* mass of cast metal, esp. gold, silver, or steel.

ingrained /ɪnˈgreɪnd/ *a.* deeply embedded, inveterate.

ingratiate /ɪnˈgreɪʃɪeɪt/ *v.* bring oneself into favour *with*.

ingratitude /ɪnˈgrætɪtjuːd/ *n.* lack of gratitude.

ingredient /ɪnˈgriːdɪənt/ *n.* component part in mixture.

ingress /ˈɪngres/ *n.* going in; right to go in.

ingrowing /ˈɪngrəʊɪŋ/ *a.* (of nail) growing into the flesh.

inhabit /ɪnˈhæbɪt/ *v.t.* dwell in, occupy. **inhabitant** *n.*; **inhabitation** *n.*

inhalant /ɪnˈheɪlənt/ *n.* medicinal substance to be inhaled.

inhale /ɪnˈheɪl/ *v.* breathe in; take into lungs. **inhalation** *n.*

inhaler *n.* inhaling-apparatus.

inharmonious /ɪnhɑːˈməʊnɪəs/ *a.* not harmonious.

inhere /ɪnˈhɪə(r)/ *v.i.* be inherent.

inherent /ɪnˈhɪərənt/ *a.* existing or abiding in as essential quality.

inherit /ɪnˈherɪt/ *v.* receive as heir; derive from parents etc. **inheritor** *n.*

inheritance /ɪnˈherɪt(ə)ns/ *n.* what is inherited; inheriting.

inhibit /ɪnˈhɪbɪt/ *v.t.* hinder, restrain, or prevent; prohibit.

inhibition /ɪnhɪˈbɪʃ(ə)n/ *n.* inhibiting or being inhibited; restraint of direct expression of instinct; *colloq.* emotional resistance to thought or action.

inhospitable /ɪnˈhɒspɪtəb(ə)l/ *a.* not hospitable; affording no shelter.

inhuman /ɪnˈhjuːmən/ *a.* brutal, unfeeling, barbarous. **inhumanity** /-ˈmæn-/ *n.*

inimical /ɪˈnɪmɪk(ə)l/ *a.* hostile; harmful.

inimitable /ɪˈnɪmɪtəb(ə)l/ *a.* that cannot be imitated.

iniquity /ɪˈnɪkwɪtɪ/ *n.* wickedness; gross injustice. **iniquitous** *a.*

initial /ɪˈnɪʃ(ə)l/ **1** *a.* of or existing or occurring at beginning. **2** *n.* first letter of (esp. person's) name. **3** *v.t.* mark or sign with initials. **4 initially** *adv.*

initiate 1 /ɪˈnɪʃɪeɪt/ *v.t.* originate, set going; admit, introduce (*into*). **2** /ɪˈnɪʃɪət/ *n.* initiated person. **3 initiation** *n.*; **initiatory** *a.*

initiative /ɪˈnɪʃətɪv/ *n.* ability to initiate, enterprise; first step; lead.

inject /ɪnˈdʒekt/ *v.t.* force (fluid *into*) (as) by syringe; place (quality etc.) where needed in something. **injection** *n.*

injudicious /ɪndʒuːˈdɪʃəs/ *a.* unwise, ill-judged.

injunction /ɪnˈdʒʌŋkʃ(ə)n/ *n.* authoritative order; judicial process restraining from specified act or compelling restitution etc.

injure /ˈɪndʒə(r)/ *v.t.* hurt, harm, impair; do wrong to.

injurious /ɪnˈdʒʊərɪəs/ *a.* wrongful; harmful; defamatory.

injury /ˈɪndʒərɪ/ *n.* wrong; damage, harm. **injury time** extra time added to football match etc. because of that lost in dealing with injuries.

injustice /ɪnˈdʒʌstɪs/ *n.* unfairness; unjust act.

ink 1 *n.* coloured fluid for writing or printing; black liquid ejected by cuttlefish etc. **2** *v.t.* mark or cover or smear with ink. **3 inky** *a.*

inkling /ˈɪŋklɪŋ/ *n.* hint, slight knowledge or suspicion (*of*).

inland 1 /ˈɪnlænd/ *a.* in interior of country; remote from sea or border within a country. **2** /ɪnˈlænd/ *adv.* in or towards interior. **3** /ˈɪnlænd/ *n.* interior of country. **4 inland revenue** revenue from taxes and inland duties.

in-laws /ˈɪnlɔːz/ *n.pl. colloq.* relatives by marriage.

inlay 1 /ɪnˈleɪ/ *v.t.* (*past* & *p.p.* **-laid**) embed (thing in another); decorate (thing) thus. **2** /ˈɪnleɪ/ *n.* inlaid material or work.

inlet /ˈɪnlet/ *n.* small arm of sea etc.; way of admission.

inmate /ˈɪnmeɪt/ *n.* occupant (*of* house, hospital, prison, etc.).

in memoriam /ɪn məˈmɔːrɪæm/ in memory of. [L]

inmost /ˈɪnməʊst/ *a.* most inward.

inn *n.* house providing lodging etc. for payment, esp. for travellers; house providing alcoholic liquor. **innkeeper** keeper of inn; **Inns of Court** 4 legal societies admitting persons to practise at English bar.

innards /ˈɪnədz/ *n.pl. colloq.* entrails.

innate /ɪˈneɪt/ *a.* inborn.

inner /ˈɪnə(r)/ **1** *a.* interior, internal. **2** *n.* circle nearest bull's eye of target. **3 inner tube** separate inflatable tube in pneumatic tyre. **4 innermost** *a.*

innings /ˈɪnɪŋz/ *n.* (*pl.* same) *Crick.* etc. batsman's or side's turn at batting.

innocent /ˈɪnəs(ə)nt/ **1** *a.* not guilty; sinless; guileless; harmless. **2** *n.* innocent person, esp. young child. **3 innocence** *n.*

innocuous /ɪˈnɒkjʊəs/ *a.* harmless.

innovate /ˈɪnəveɪt/ *v.i.* bring in new ideas etc.; make changes. **innovation** *n.*; **innovative** *a.*; **innovator** *n.*

innuendo /ɪnjuːˈendəʊ/ *n.* (*pl.* **-oes**) allusive (usu. depreciatory) remark.

innumerable /ɪˈnjuːmərəb(ə)l/ *a.* countless.

innumerate /ɪˈnjuːmərət/ *a.* not knowing basic mathematics and science.

inoculate /ɪˈnɒkjʊleɪt/ *v.t.* treat with vaccine or serum, esp. as protective measure. **inoculation** *n.*

inoffensive /ɪnəˈfensɪv/ *a.* unoffending; not objectionable.

inoperable /ɪnˈɒpərəb(ə)l/ *a.* that cannot be cured by surgical operation.

inoperative /ɪnˈɒpərətɪv/ *a.* not working or taking effect.

inopportune /ɪˈnɒpətjuːn/ a. not appropriate, esp. as regards time.

inordinate /ɪˈnɔːdɪmət/ a. excessive.

inorganic /ɪnɔːˈgænɪk/ a. Chem. mineral not organic; without organized physical structure.

input /ˈɪnpʊt/ 1 n. what is put in; place of entry of energy or information etc. 2 v.t. (past & p.p. -put or -putted) put in; supply (data, programs, etc.) to computer.

inquest /ˈɪnkwest/ n. inquiry held by coroner into cause of death.

inquietude /ɪnˈkwaɪɪtjuːd/ n. uneasiness.

inquire /ɪnˈkwaɪə(r)/ v. ask question; seek information; make inqiry (into).

inquiry /ɪnˈkwaɪərɪ/ n. asking; question; investigation, esp. official.

inquisition /ɪnkwɪˈzɪʃ(ə)n/ n. investigation; official inquiry; **Inquisition** hist. RC Ch. ecclesiastical tribunal for suppression of heresy. **inquisitional** a.

inquisitive /ɪnˈkwɪzɪtɪv/ a. curious, prying.

inquisitor /ɪnˈkwɪzɪtə(r)/ n. investigator; officer of Inquisition.

inquisitorial /ɪnkwɪzɪˈtɔːrɪəl/ a. inquisitor-like; prying.

inroad /ˈɪnrəʊd/ n. hostile incursion; encroachment.

inrush /ˈɪnrʌʃ/ n. violent influx.

insalubrious /ɪnsəˈluːbrɪəs/ a. unhealthy.

insane /ɪnˈseɪn/ a. mad; extremely foolish.

insanitary /ɪnˈsænɪtərɪ/ a. not sanitary.

insanity /ɪnˈsænɪtɪ/ n. madness.

insatiable /ɪnˈseɪʃəb(ə)l/ a. that cannot be satisfied; greedy. **insatiability** n.

insatiate /ɪnˈseɪʃɪət/ a. never satisfied.

inscribe /ɪnˈskraɪb/ v.t. write (in, on); mark with characters; Geom. trace (figure) within another so that some points of their boundaries coincide; enter on list.

inscription /ɪnˈskrɪpʃ(ə)n/ n. words inscribed; inscribing.

inscrutable /ɪnˈskruːtəb(ə)l/ a. mysterious, impenetrable. **inscrutability** n.

insect /ˈɪnsekt/ n. small invertebrate animal with segmented body and 6 legs.

insecticide /ɪnˈsektɪsaɪd/ n. preparation used for killing insects.

insectivorous /ɪnsekˈtɪvərəs/ a. insect-eating. **insectivore** /-ˈsekt-/ n.

insecure /ɪnsɪˈkjʊə(r)/ a. not secure or safe; not feeling safe.

inseminate /ɪnˈsemɪneɪt/ v.t. introduce semen into; sow (seed etc.). **insemination** n.

insensate /ɪnˈsenseɪt/ a. without sensibility; stupid.

insensible /ɪnˈsensɪb(ə)l/ a. unconscious; unaware; callous; imperceptible. **insensibility** n.

insensitive /ɪnˈsensɪtɪv/ a. not sensitive.

insentient /ɪnˈsenʃ(ə)nt/ a. inanimate.

inseparable /ɪnˈsepərəb(ə)l/ a. that cannot be separated. **inseparability** n.

insert 1 /ɪnˈsɜːt/ v.t. place or put (thing into another). 2 /ˈɪnsɜːt/ n. thing inserted.

insertion /ɪnˈsɜːʃ(ə)n/ n. inserting, thing inserted.

inset 1 /ˈɪnset/ n. extra piece inserted in book or garment etc.; small map etc. within border of larger. 2 /ɪnˈset/ v.t. (past & p.p. -set) put in as inset.

inshore /ɪnˈʃɔː(r)/ adv. & a. close to shore.

inside /ɪnˈsaɪd/ 1 n. inner side or part; position on inner side; colloq. stomach and bowels. 2 a. (attrib. /ˈɪnsaɪd/) of or on or in the inside; nearer to centre of games field. 3 adv. on or in the inside; sl. in prison. 4 prep. within, on the inside of; in less than. 5 **inside information** information not accessible to outsiders; **inside job** colloq. burglary etc. by person living or working on premises; **inside out** turned so that inner becomes outer side; **know inside out** know thoroughly.

insidious /ɪnˈsɪdɪəs/ a. proceeding inconspicuously but harmfully.

insight /ˈɪnsaɪt/ n. mental penetration.

insignia /ɪnˈsɪgnɪə/ n.pl. badges or marks of office etc.

insignificant /ɪnsɪgˈnɪfɪkənt/ a. unimportant; trivial. **insignificance** n.

insincere /ɪnsɪnˈsɪə(r)/ a. not sincere or candid. **insincerity** /-ˈser-/ n.

insinuate /ɪnˈsɪnjʊeɪt/ v.t. hint obliquely; introduce gradually or subtly. **insinuation** n.

insipid /ɪn'sɪpɪd/ *a.* flavourless; dull, lifeless. **insipidity** *n.*

insist /ɪn'sɪst/ *v.* demand or maintain emphatically. **insistence** *n.*; **insistent** *a.*

in situ /ɪn 'sɪtjuː/ in its original place. [L]

insobriety /ɪnsə'braɪətɪ/ *n.* intemperance, esp. in drinking.

insole /'ɪnsəʊl/ *n.* removable inner sole for use in shoe.

insolent /'ɪnsələnt/ *a.* offensively contemptuous; insulting. **insolence** *n.*

insoluble /ɪn'sɒljʊb(ə)l/ *a.* that cannot be dissolved or solved. **insolubility** *n.*

insolvent /ɪn'sɒlv(ə)nt/ **1** *a.* unable to pay debts. **2** *n.* insolvent debtor. **3 insolvency** *n.*

insomnia /ɪn'sɒmnɪə/ *n.* sleeplessness.

insomniac /ɪn'sɒmnɪæk/ *n.* person suffering from insomnia.

insouciant /ɪn'suːsɪənt/ *a.* carefree, unconcerned. **insouciance** *n.*

inspect /ɪn'spekt/ *v.t.* look closely into; examine officially. **inspection** *n.*

inspector /ɪn'spektə(r)/ *n.* official employed to inspect or supervise; police officer next below superintendent.

inspectorate /ɪn'spektərət/ *n.* office of inspector; body of inspectors.

inspiration /ɪnspɪ'reɪʃ(ə)n/ *n.* inspiring; sudden brilliant idea; source of inspiring influence; divine influence in poetry and Scripture.

inspire /ɪn'spaɪə(r)/ *v.* stimulate (person) to creative activity; breathe in; animate; instil thought or feeling into.

inspirit /ɪn'spɪrɪt/ *v.t.* put life into, animate; encourage.

inst. *abbr.* instant, of current month.

instability /ɪnstə'bɪlɪtɪ/ *n.* lack of stability.

install /ɪn'stɔːl/ *v.t.* fix or establish (equipment, person, etc.); place *in* office with ceremony. **installation** *n.*

instalment *n.* any of successive parts of sum payable or of serial story etc.

instance /'ɪnst(ə)ns/ **1** *n.* example; particular case. **2** *v.t.* cite as instance.

instant /'ɪnst(ə)nt/ **1** *a.* immediate; (of food etc.) that can be prepared easily for immediate use; urgent, pressing; of current calendar month. **2** *n.* precise moment; short time, moment.

instantaneous /ɪnstən'teɪnɪəs/ *a.* occurring or done in an instant.

instantly /ɪn'stæntlɪ/ *adv.* immediately.

instead /ɪn'sted/ *adv.* as substitute or alternative; in place *of*.

instep /'ɪnstep/ *n.* top of foot between toes and ankle; part of shoe etc. fitting this.

instigate /'ɪnstɪgeɪt/ *v.t.* incite (*to*); bring about by persuasion. **instigation** *n.*; **instigator** *n.*

instil /ɪn'stɪl/ *v.t.* put (ideas etc. *into* mind etc.) gradually; put in by drops. **instillation** *n.*

instinct 1 /'ɪnstɪŋkt/ *n.* inborn pattern of behaviour; innate impulse; intuition. **2** /ɪn'stɪŋkt/ *a.* filled or charged (*with*). **3 instinctive** *a.*; **instinctual** *a.*

institute /'ɪnstɪtjuːt/ **1** *n.* organized body for promotion of scientific or other aim; its building. **2** *v.t.* establish; initiate.

institution /ɪnstɪ'tjuːʃ(ə)n/ *n.* instituting; (esp. charitable) institute; established law or custom; *colloq.* well-known person.

institutional /ɪnstɪ'tjuːʃən(ə)l/ *a.* of or like an institution; typical of charitable institutions. **institutionalize** *v.t.*

instruct /ɪn'strʌkt/ *v.t.* teach; inform; give information to; direct. **instructor** *n.*; **instructress** *n.*

instruction /ɪn'strʌkʃ(ə)n/ *n.* instructing; in *pl.* directions, orders. **instructional** *a.*

instructive /ɪn'strʌktɪv/ *a.* enlightening.

instrument /'ɪnstrʊmənt/ *n.* tool, implement; measuring-device, esp. in aircraft to find position in fog etc.; contrivance for producing musical sounds; formal (esp. legal) document.

instrumental /ɪnstrʊ'ment(ə)l/ *a.* serving as instrument or means (*to, in*); (of music) performed on instruments. **instrumentality** *n.*

instrumentalist /ɪnstrʊ'mentəlɪst/ *n.* performer on musical instrument.

instrumentation /ɪnstrʊmen'teɪʃ(ə)n/ *n.* arrangement of music for instruments.

insubordinate /ɪnsə'bɔːdɪnət/ *a.* disobedient; unruly. **insubordination** *n.*

insubstantial /ɪnsəb'stænʃ(ə)l/ *a.*

lacking solidity or substance; not real. **insubstantiality** n.

insufferable /ɪnˈsʌfərəb(ə)l/ a. unbearable.

insufficient /ɪnsəˈfɪʃ(ə)nt/ a. not enough, inadequate. **insufficiency** n.

insular /ˈɪnsjʊlə(r)/ a. narrow-minded; of or like islanders; of or forming an island. **insularity** n.

insulate /ˈɪnsjʊleɪt/ v.t. isolate, esp. by non-conductor of electricity or heat or sound etc. **insulation** n.; **insulator** n.

insulin /ˈɪnsjʊlɪn/ n. hormone produced in the pancreas, controlling sugar in body and used against diabetes.

insult 1 /ɪnˈsʌlt/ v.t. abuse scornfully; offend self-respect etc. of. 2 /ˈɪnsʌlt/ n. insulting remark or action.

insuperable /ɪnˈsuːpərəb(ə)l/ a. that cannot be got over. **insuperability** n.

insupportable /ɪnsəˈpɔːtəb(ə)l/ a. unbearable.

insurance /ɪnˈʃʊərəns/ n. procedure or contract securing compensation for loss or damage or injury on payment of premium; business of this; sum paid to effect insurance.

insure /ɪnˈʃʊə(r)/ v.t. effect insurance *against* or with respect to.

insurgent /ɪnˈsɜːdʒ(ə)nt/ 1 n. rebel. 2 a. in revolt; rebellious. 3 **insurgency** n.

insurmountable /ɪnsəˈmaʊntəb(ə)l/ a. insuperable.

insurrection /ɪnsəˈrekʃ(ə)n/ n. rising in resistance to authority; incipient rebellion. **insurrectionist** n.

insusceptible /ɪnsəˈseptɪb(ə)l/ a. not susceptible. **insusceptibility** n.

intact /ɪnˈtækt/ a. unimpaired; entire; untouched.

intaglio /ɪnˈtɑːlɪəʊ/ n. (pl. **-os**) engraved design; gem with incised design.

intake /ˈɪnteɪk/ n. action of taking in; place where water is taken into pipe, or fuel or air into engine; persons or things or quantity taken in.

intangible /ɪnˈtændʒɪb(ə)l/ a. that cannot be touched or mentally grasped. **intangibility** n.

integer /ˈɪntɪdʒə(r)/ n. whole number.

integral /ˈɪntɪgr(ə)l/ a. of or essential to a whole; complete; of or denoted by an integer.

integrate /ˈɪntɪgreɪt/ v. combine (parts) into whole; bring or come into equal membership of society; end racial etc. segregation. **integrated circuit** small piece of material replacing electrical circuit of many components. **integration** n.

integrity /ɪnˈtegrɪtɪ/ n. honesty; wholeness; soundness.

integument /ɪnˈtegjʊmənt/ n. skin, husk, or other (natural) covering.

intellect /ˈɪntəlekt/ n. faculty of knowing and reasoning; understanding.

intellectual /ɪntəˈlektjʊəl/ 1 a. of or requiring or using intellect; having highly-developed intellect. 2 n. intellectual person. 3 **intellectualism** n.; **intellectualize** v.t.

intelligence /ɪnˈtelɪdʒ(ə)ns/ n. intellect; quickness of understanding; news; (persons engaged in) obtaining of esp. secret information. **intelligence quotient** ratio of person's intelligence to the normal or average.

intelligent a. having or showing good intelligence, clever.

intelligentsia /ɪntelɪˈdʒentsɪə/ n. intellectuals as a class, esp. regarded as cultured and politically enterprising.

intelligible /ɪnˈtelɪdʒɪb(ə)l/ a. that can be understood. **intelligibility** n.

intemperate /ɪnˈtempərət/ a. immoderate; excessive in indulgence of appetite; addicted to drinking. **intemperance** n.

intend /ɪnˈtend/ v.t. have as one's purpose; design.

intended 1 a. done on purpose. 2 n. *colloq.* fiancé(e).

intense /ɪnˈtens/ a. existing in high degree; vehement; strenuous; feeling or apt to feel strong emotion. **intensity** n.

intensify /ɪnˈtensɪfaɪ/ v. make or become (more) intense. **intensification** n.

intensive /ɪnˈtensɪv/ a. thorough, vigorous; concentrated; increasing production of limited area etc.; emphasizing; of or in intensity. **intensive care** medical treatment with constant supervision of patient.

intent /ɪnˈtent/ 1 n. intention; purpose. 2 a. resolved, bent (*on*); attentively occupied; eager. 3 **to all intents (and purposes)** practically.

intention /ɪnˈtenʃ(ə)n/ n. intending; purpose, aim.

intentional /ɪnˈtenʃən(ə)l/ a. done on purpose.

inter /ɪnˈtɜː(r)/ v.t. place (corpse etc.) in earth or tomb; bury.

inter- /ɪntə(r)/ in comb. among, between; mutually, reciprocally.

interact /ɪntəˈrækt/ v.i. act on each other. **interaction** n.; **interactive** a.

interbreed /ɪntəˈbriːd/ v. (past & p.p. -bred) (cause to) produce hybrid individual.

intercalary /ɪntəˈkæləri/ a. inserted to harmonize calendar with solar year; having such additions; interpolated.

intercalate /ɪntəˈkəleɪt/ v.t. interpose; insert. **intercalation** n.

intercede /ɪntəˈsiːd/ v.i. mediate; plead (for another).

intercept /ɪntəˈsept/ v.t. seize or catch or stop etc. in transit; cut off. **interception** n.; **interceptor** n.

intercession /ɪntəˈseʃ(ə)n/ n. interceding. **intercessor** n.

interchange 1 /ɪntəˈtʃeɪndʒ/ v. put in each other's place; make exchange of; alternate. 2 /ˈɪntətʃeɪndʒ/ n. reciprocal exchange; alternation; road junction so arranged that paths of vehicles do not cross.

inter-city /ɪntəˈsɪti/ a. existing or travelling between cities.

intercom /ˈɪntəkɒm/ n. colloq. system of intercommunication operating like telephone.

intercommunicate /ɪntəkəˈmjuːnɪkeɪt/ v.i. have communication with each other. **intercommunication** n.

intercommunion /ɪntəkəˈmjuːnɪən/ n. mutual communion, esp. between religious bodies.

interconnect /ɪntəkəˈnekt/ v.i. connect with each other. **interconnection** n.

intercontinental /ɪntəkɒntɪˈnent(ə)l/ a. connecting or travelling between continents.

intercourse /ˈɪntəkɔːs/ n. social communication, dealings; sexual intercourse.

interdenominational /ɪntədɪnɒmɪˈneɪʃən(ə)l/ a. of or involving more than one Christian denomination.

interdependent /ɪntədɪˈpend(ə)nt/ a. mutually dependent. **interdependence** n.

interdict 1 /ɪntəˈdɪkt/ v.t. forbid; prohibit; restrain. 2 /ˈɪntədɪkt/ n. authoritative prohibition. 3 **interdiction** n.

interdisciplinary /ɪntədɪsɪˈplɪnəri/ a. of or involving different branches of learning.

interest /ˈɪntrest/ 1 n. concern or curiosity or attention; quality causing this; thing towards which one feels it; advantage; money paid for use of money borrowed etc.; legal concern or title or right. 2 v.t. arouse interest of; cause to take interest (in); in p.p. having private interest, not impartial.

interesting a. causing curiosity; holding the attention.

interface /ˈɪntəfeɪs/ n. surface forming common boundary of two regions; place where interaction occurs between two systems etc.

interfere /ɪntəˈfɪə(r)/ v.i. meddle, intervene; be an obstacle; clash (with).

interference /ɪntəˈfɪərəns/ n. interfering; fading of received radio signals.

interferon /ɪntəˈfɪərɒn/ n. protein inhibiting development of virus in cell.

interfuse /ɪntəˈfjuːz/ v.t. mix, blend. **interfusion** n.

interim /ˈɪntərɪm/ 1 n. intervening time. 2 a. provisional, temporary.

interior /ɪnˈtɪərɪə(r)/ 1 n. inner part; inland region; inside of room etc.; home affairs of country. 2 a. situated within; inland; internal, domestic.

interject /ɪntəˈdʒekt/ v.t. make (remark etc.) abruptly or parenthetically.

interjection /ɪntəˈdʒekʃ(ə)n/ n. exclamation.

interlace /ɪntəˈleɪs/ v. bind intricately together; interweave.

interlard /ɪntəˈlɑːd/ v.t. mix (speech etc.) with.

interleave /ɪntəˈliːv/ v.t. insert (usu. blank) leaves between leaves of (book).

interlink /ɪntəˈlɪŋk/ v. link together.

interlock /ɪntəˈlɒk/ 1 v. engage with each other by overlapping etc.; lock together. 2 a. (of fabric) knitted with closely interlocking stitches. 3 n. such fabric.

interlocutor /ɪntəˈlɒkjʊtə(r)/ n. person who takes part in conversation. **interlocutory** a.

interloper /ˈɪntələʊpə(r)/ n. intruder;

person who thrusts himself into others' affairs.

interlude /ˈɪntəluːd/ n. interval between parts of play etc., performance filling this; intervening time or event etc. of different kind.

intermarriage /ɪntəˈmærɪdʒ/ n. marriage between members of different families or races etc. **intermarry** v.i.

intermediary /ɪntəˈmiːdɪərɪ/ 1 n. mediator. 2 a. acting between parties; intermediate.

intermediate /ɪntəˈmiːdɪət/ 1 a. coming between in time or place or order. 2 n. intermediate thing.

interment /ɪnˈtɜːmənt/ n. burial.

intermezzo /ɪntəˈmetsəʊ/ n. (pl. -mezzi /-ˈmetsiː/) Mus. short connecting movement or composition.

interminable /ɪnˈtɜːmɪnəb(ə)l/ a. tediously long; endless.

intermingle /ɪntəˈmɪŋg(ə)l/ v. mix together, mingle.

intermission /ɪntəˈmɪʃ(ə)n/ n. pause, cessation; interval in cinema etc.

intermittent /ɪntəˈmɪt(ə)nt/ a. occurring at intervals, not continuous or steady.

intermix /ɪntəˈmɪks/ v. mix together.

intern 1 /ɪnˈtɜːn/ v.t. confine within prescribed limits. 2 /ˈɪntɜːn/ n. US recent graduate etc. living in hospital and acting as assistant physician or surgeon. 3 **internee** n.; **internment** n.

internal /ɪnˈtɜːn(ə)l/ a. of or in the inside of thing; relating to interior of the body; of domestic affairs of country; of students attending a university as well as taking its examinations; used or applying within an organization; intrinsic; of mind or soul. **internal-combustion engine** engine in which motive power comes from explosion of gas or vapour with air in cylinder.

international /ɪntəˈnæʃən(ə)l/ 1 a. existing or carried on between nations; agreed on by many nations. 2 n. contest (usu. in sports) between representatives of different nations; such representative; **International** one of four successive associations for socialist or communist action. 3 **internationality** n.

internationalism /ɪntəˈnæʃənəlɪz(ə)m/ n. advocacy of community of interests among nations; support of International. **internationalist** n.

internationalize /ɪntəˈnæʃənəlaɪz/ v.t. make international; bring under joint protection etc. of different nations.

internecine /ɪntəˈniːsaɪn/ a. mutually destructive.

interpenetrate /ɪntəˈpenɪtreɪt/ v. pervade; penetrate each other. **interpenetration** n.

interpersonal /ɪntəˈpɜːsən(ə)l/ a. between persons.

interplanetary /ɪntəˈplænɪtərɪ/ a. between planets.

interplay /ˈɪntəpleɪ/ n. reciprocal action.

Interpol /ˈɪntəpɒl/ n. International Criminal Police Commission.

interpolate /ɪnˈtɜːpəleɪt/ v.t. make (esp. misleading) insertions in; insert or introduce between other things. **interpolation** n.

interpose /ɪntəˈpəʊz/ v. insert (thing between others); introduce or use or say etc. as interruption or interference; intervene; interrupt. **interposition** n.

interpret /ɪnˈtɜːprɪt/ v. explain; render, represent; act as interpreter. **interpretation** n.

interpreter /ɪnˈtɜːprɪtə(r)/ n. person who translates orally.

interregnum /ɪntəˈregnəm/ n. (pl. -na or -nums) interval between successive reigns; interval, pause.

interrelated /ɪntərɪˈleɪtɪd/ a. related to each other. **interrelation(ship)** ns.

interrogate /ɪnˈterəgeɪt/ v.t. question closely or formally. **interrogation** n.; **interrogator** n.

interrogative /ɪntəˈrɒgətɪv/ 1 a. of or like or used in questions. 2 n. interrogative pronoun etc.

interrogatory /ɪntəˈrɒgətərɪ/ 1 a. questioning. 2 n. formal set of questions.

interrupt /ɪntəˈrʌpt/ v.t. break in upon; break continuity of; obstruct (view etc.). **interruption** n.

intersect /ɪntəˈsekt/ v. divide by passing or lying across; cross or cut each other.

intersection /ɪntəˈsekʃ(ə)n/ n. place where two roads intersect; point or line common to lines or planes that intersect.

intersperse /ɪntəˈspɜːs/ v.t. diversify

(*with* things scattered about); scatter, place here and there (*between*).

interstate /'ɪntəsteɪt/ *a.* existing etc. between states esp. of US.

interstellar /ɪntə'stelə(r)/ *a.* between stars.

interstice /ɪn'tɜːstɪs/ *n.* chink, crevice, gap.

interstitial /ɪntə'stɪʃ(ə)l/ *a.* of or in interstices.

intertwine /ɪntə'twaɪn/ *v.* twine closely together.

interval /'ɪntəv(ə)l/ *n.* intervening time or space; pause; break; *Mus.* difference of pitch between two sounds. **at intervals** here and there, now and then.

intervene /ɪntə'viːn/ *v.i.* occur in meantime; come between persons or things; interfere, mediate.

intervention /ɪntə'venʃ(ə)n/ *n.* intervening; interference; mediation.

interview /'ɪntəvjuː/ **1** *n.* meeting between reporter and person whose views he wishes to publish; oral examination of applicant; meeting of persons, esp. for discussion. **2** *v.t.* have interview with.

interweave /ɪntə'wiːv/ *v.t.* (*past* **-wove**; *p.p.* **-woven**) weave together; blend intimately.

intestate /ɪn'testeɪt/ **1** *a.* not having made a will before death. **2** *n.* intestate person. **3** *intestacy n.*

intestine /ɪn'testɪn/ *n.* lower part of alimentary canal. **intestinal** *a.*

intimate **1** /'ɪntɪmət/ *a.* closely acquainted; familiar; closely personal; close. **2** /'ɪntɪmət/ *n.* intimate friend. **3** /'ɪntɪmeɪt/ *v.t.* make known; state; imply. **4 intimacy** *n.*; **intimation** *n.*

intimidate /ɪn'tɪmɪdeɪt/ *v.t.* frighten, esp. in order to influence conduct.

into /ɪntuː/ *prep.* expr. motion or direction to point within, or change or condition or result; *colloq.* interested in.

intolerable /ɪn'tɒlərəb(ə)l/ *a.* that cannot be endured.

intolerant /ɪn'tɒlərənt/ *a.* not tolerant (*of*). **intolerance** *n.*

intonation /ɪntə'neɪʃ(ə)n/ *n.* intoning; modulation of voice, accent.

intone /ɪn'təʊn/ *v.t.* recite with prolonged sounds, esp. in monotone.

in toto /ɪn 'təʊtəʊ/ entirely. [L]

intoxicant /ɪn'tɒksɪkənt/ **1** *n.* intoxicating substance. **2** *a.* intoxicating.

intoxicate /ɪn'tɒksɪkeɪt/ *v.t.* make drunk; excite or elate beyond self-control. **intoxication** *n.*

intractable /ɪn'træktəb(ə)l/ *a.* not easily dealt with; stubborn. **intractability** *n.*

intramural /ɪntrə'mjʊər(ə)l/ *a.* situated or done within walls of city or house etc.

intransigent /ɪn'trænsɪdʒ(ə)nt/ **1** *a.* uncompromising. **2** *n.* such person. **3 intransigence** *n.*

intransitive /ɪn'trænsɪtɪv/ *a. Gram.* (of verb) not taking direct object.

intra-uterine /ɪntrə'juːtəraɪn/ *a.* within the womb.

intravenous /ɪntrə'viːnəs/ *a.* in(to) vein(s).

intrepid /ɪn'trepɪd/ *a.* fearless; brave. **intrepidity** *n.*

intricate /'ɪntrɪkət/ *a.* entangled; complicated. **intricacy** *n.*

intrigue /ɪn'triːg/ **1** *v.* carry on underhand plot; use secret influence; rouse interest or curiosity of. **2** *n.* (also /'ɪn-/) underhand plotting or plot; *arch.* secret love affair.

intrinsic /ɪn'trɪnzɪk/ *a.* inherent; essential.

introduce /ɪntrə'djuːs/ *v.t.* make (person) known to another; announce or present to audience; bring into use; bring before Parliament; draw attention to; insert; bring in; usher in, bring forward. **introducible** *a.*

introduction /ɪntrə'dʌkʃ(ə)n/ *n.* introducing; formal presentation; preliminary matter in book; introductory treatise. **introductory** *a.*

introspection /ɪntrə'spekʃ(ə)n/ *n.* examination of one's own thoughts. **introspective** *a.*

introvert /'ɪntrəvɜːt/ *n.* introverted person.

introverted *a.* principally interested in one's own thoughts; reserved, shy. **introversion** *n.*

intrude /ɪn'truːd/ *v.* thrust (*into*), force (*upon*); come uninvited, thrust oneself in. **intrusion** *n.*; **intrusive** *a.*

intuition /ɪntjʊ'ɪʃ(ə)n/ *n.* immediate apprehension by mind without reasoning; immediate insight. **intuitional** *a.*

intuitive /ɪnˈtjuːɪtɪv/ *a.* of or having or perceived by intuition.

inundate /ˈɪnʌndeɪt/ *v.t.* flood or overwhelm (*with*). **inundation** *n.*

inure /ɪˈnjʊə(r)/ *v.t.* habituate, accustom. **incurement** *n.*

invade /ɪnˈveɪd/ *v.t.* make hostile in-road into; encroach on.

invalid[1] /ˈɪnvəlɪd/ **1** *n.* (also -/liːd/) person enfeebled or disabled by illness or injury. **2** *a.* of or for invalids; being an invalid. **3** *v.t.* (also -/liːd/) remove from active service, send *home* etc. as invalid. **4** **invalidism** *n.*

invalid[2] /ɪnˈvælɪd/ *a.* not valid. **invalidity** *n.*

invalidate /ɪnˈvælɪdeɪt/ *v.t.* make invalid. **invalidation** *n.*

invaluable /ɪnˈvæljʊəb(ə)l/ *a.* beyond price, inestimable.

invariable /ɪnˈveərɪəb(ə)l/ *a.* always the same; *Math.* constant. **invariability** *n.*

invasion /ɪnˈveɪʒ(ə)n/ *n.* invading or being invaded. **invasive** *a.*

invective /ɪnˈvektɪv/ *n.* violent attack in words.

inveigh /ɪnˈveɪ/ *v.i.* speak or write violently *against.*

inveigle /ɪnˈveɪg(ə)l/ *v.t.* entice, tempt (*into*). **inveiglement** *n.*

invent /ɪnˈvent/ *v.t.* create by thought; originate; fabricate. **inventor** *n.*

invention /ɪnˈvenʃ(ə)n/ *n.* inventing; thing invented; inventiveness.

inventive /ɪnˈventɪv/ *a.* able to invent.

inventory /ˈɪnvəntərɪ/ **1** *n.* list of goods etc. **2** *v.t.* make inventory of; enter in inventory.

inverse /ɪnˈvɜːs/ **1** *a.* inverted in position or order or relation; (of ratio etc.) between two quantities one of which increases as other decreases. **2** *n.* inverted state; direct opposition.

inversion /ɪnˈvɜːʃ(ə)n/ *n.* inverting, esp. reversal of normal order of words.

invert /ɪnˈvɜːt/ **1** *v.t.* turn upside down; reverse position or order or relation etc. of. **2** /ˈɪnvɜːt/ *n.* homosexual. **3** **inverted commas** quotation-marks.

invertebrate /ɪnˈvɜːtɪbrət/ **1** *a.* without backbone or spinal column. **2** *n.* invertebrate animal.

invest /ɪnˈvest/ *v.t.* apply or use (money) for profit; endue (*with* qualities, insignia, etc.); clothe, dress; lay

siege to. **invest in** put money into (stocks etc.), *colloq.* buy. **investor** *n.*

investigable /ɪnˈvestɪgəb(ə)l/ *a.* that can be investigated.

investigate /ɪnˈvestɪgeɪt/ *v.t.* examine, inquire into. **investigation** *n.*; **investigator** *n.*

investiture /ɪnˈvestɪtʃ(r)/ *n.* formal investing of person with honours etc.

investment *n.* /ɪnˈvestmənt/ investing; money invested; property in which money is invested.

inveterate /ɪnˈvetərət/ *a.* deep-rooted, confirmed. **inveteracy** *n.*

invidious /ɪnˈvɪdɪəs/ *a.* likely to excite ill-will against performer or possessor etc.

invigilate /ɪnˈvɪdʒɪleɪt/ *v.i.* supervise examinees. **invigilation** *n.*; **invigilator** *n.*

invigorate /ɪnˈvɪgəreɪt/ *v.t.* give vigour to. **invigoration** *n.*; **invigorative** *a.*

invincible /ɪnˈvɪnsɪb(ə)l/ *a.* unconquerable. **invincibility** *n.*

inviolable /ɪnˈvaɪələb(ə)l/ *a.* not to be violated. **inviolability** *n.*

inviolate /ɪnˈvaɪələt/ *a.* not having been violated. **inviolacy** *n.*

invisible /ɪnˈvɪzɪb(ə)l/ *a.* that cannot be seen. **invisible exports, imports,** items for which payment is made by or to another country but which are not goods. **invisibility** *n.*

invite 1 /ɪnˈvaɪt/ *v.t.* request courteously to come or *to* do etc.; solicit courteously; attract. **2** /ˈɪnvaɪt/ *n. colloq.* invitation. **3** **invitation** /ɪnvɪˈteɪʃ(ə)n/ *n.*

inviting *a.* attractive.

invocation /ɪnvəˈkeɪʃ(ə)n/ *n.* invoking; calling upon in prayer. **invocatory** /-ˈvɒk-/ *a.*

invoice /ˈɪnvɔɪs/ **1** *n.* list of goods sent, with prices etc. **2** *v.t.* make invoice of; send invoice to.

invoke /ɪnˈvəʊk/ *v.t.* call on in prayer or as witness; appeal to; summon (spirit) by charms; ask earnestly for.

involuntary /ɪnˈvɒləntərɪ/ *a.* done etc. without exercise of will, not controlled by will.

involute /ˈɪnvəluːt/ *a.* intricate; curled spirally.

involution /ɪnvəˈluːʃ(ə)n/ *n.* involving, intricacy; curling inwards, part so curled.

involve /ɪn'vɒlv/ v.t. cause (person or thing) to share experience or effect; imply, make necessary; include or affect in its operation; in p.p. complicated. **involvement** n.

involved a. concerned (in); complicated.

invulnerable /ɪn'vʌlnərəb(ə)l/ a. that cannot be wounded. **invulnerability** n.

inward /'ɪnwəd/ 1 a. directed towards inside; situated within; mental, spiritual. 2 adv. inwards.

inwardly /'ɪnwədlɪ/ adv. on the inside; not aloud; in mind or spirit.

inwardness /'ɪnwədnɪs/ n. inner nature, spirituality.

inwards /'ɪnwədz/ adv. towards inside; within mind or soul.

inwrought /ɪn'rɔːt/ a. decorated (with); wrought (in, on).

iodine /'aɪədiːn/ n. black solid halogen element; solution of this used as antiseptic.

iodize /'aɪədaɪz/ v.t. impregnate with iodine.

IOM abbr. Isle of Man.

ion /'aɪən/ n. one of the electrically charged particles into which atoms and molecules of certain substances are dissociated by solution in water.

ionic /aɪ'ɒnɪk/ a. of or using ions.

ionize /'aɪənaɪz/ v.t. convert or be converted into ion(s). **ionization** n.

ionosphere /aɪ'ɒnəsfɪə(r)/ n. ionized region in upper atmosphere. **ionospheric** /-'sfer-/ a.

iota /aɪ'əʊtə/ n. ninth letter of Greek alphabet (I, ι); smallest amount.

IOU /aɪəʊ'juː/ n. signed document acknowledging debt.

IOW abbr. Isle of Wight.

IPA abbr. International Phonetic Alphabet.

ipecacuanha /ɪpɪkækjʊ'ɑːnə/ n. root of S. Amer. plant used as emetic etc.

ipso facto /ɪpsəʊ 'fæktəʊ/ by that very fact. [L]

IQ abbr. intelligence quotient.

IRA abbr. Irish Republican Army.

irascible /ɪ'ræsɪb(ə)l/ a. irritable; hot-tempered. **irascibility** n.

irate /aɪ'reɪt/ a. angry.

ire /aɪə(r)/ n. poet. anger. **ireful** a.

iridaceous /ɪrɪ'deɪʃəs/ a. Bot. of iris family.

iridescent /ɪrɪ'des(ə)nt/ a. showing rainbow-like colours. **iridescence** n.

iris /'aɪərɪs/ n. circular coloured membrane surrounding pupil of eye; bulbous or tuberous plant with sword-shaped leaves and showy flowers.

Irish /'aɪərɪʃ/ 1 a. of Ireland. 2 n. Celtic language of Ireland; the Irish people. 3 **Irish stew** dish of stewed mutton and onions and potatoes. 4 **Irishman** n.; **Irishwoman** n.

irk v.t. irritate or annoy.

irksome /'ɜːksəm/ a. tiresome.

iron /'aɪən/ 1 n. common strong grey metallic element; tool etc. of iron; implement heated to smooth clothes etc.; golf-club with iron or steel head; in pl. fetters, leg-supports to rectify malformations. 2 a. of iron; robust; unyielding. 3 v.t. smooth (clothes etc.) with heated iron. 4 **Iron Age** era characterized by use of iron weapons etc.; **Iron Curtain** fig. barrier to passage of persons and information at limit of Soviet sphere of influence; **ironing-board** narrow folding table etc. for ironing clothes on; **iron lung** rigid case over patient's body for prolonged artificial respiration; **ironmaster** manufacturer of iron; **ironmonger** dealer in tools and household implements etc.; **ironmongery** n.; **iron ration** (soldier's) small quantity of tinned etc. food for use in emergency; **ironstone** hard iron-ore, kind of hard white pottery.

ironic /aɪ'rɒnɪk/ a. (also **ironical**) using or displaying irony. **ironically** adv.

irony /'aɪərənɪ/ n. expression of meaning by use of words normally conveying opposite meaning; apparent perversity of fate or circumstances. **ironist** n.

irradiate /ɪ'reɪdɪeɪt/ v.t. subject to radiation; shine upon; throw light on; light up. **irradiation** n.

irrational /ɪ'ræʃən(ə)l/ a. unreasonable, illogical; not endowed with reason; Math. not commensurable with the natural numbers. **irrationality** n.

irreconcilable /ɪrekən'saɪləb(ə)l/

implacably hostile; incompatible. **irreconcilability** n.

irrecoverable /ırı'kʌvərəb(ə)l/ a. that cannot be recovered or remedied.

irredeemable /ırı'di:məb(ə)l/ a. that cannot be redeemed, hopeless.

irreducible /ırı'dju:sıb(ə)l/ a. not reducible.

irrefutable /ırı'fju:təb(ə)l/ a. that cannot be refuted. **irrefutability** n.

irregular /ı'regjolə(r)/ 1 a. uneven, varying; contrary to rule; (of troops) not in regular army. 2 n. member of irregular military force. 3 **irregularity** n.

irrelevant /ı'reləv(ə)nt/ a. not relevant. **irrelevance** n.

irreligion /ırı'lıdʒ(ə)n/ n. hostility or indifference to religion. **irreligious** a.

irremediable /ırı'mi:dıəb(ə)l/ a. that cannot be remedied.

irremovable /ırı'mu:vəb(ə)l/ a. not removable. **irremovability** n.

irreparable /ı'repərəb(ə)l/ a. that cannot be rectified or made good.

irreplaceable /ırı'pleısəb(ə)l/ a. that cannot be replaced.

irrepressible /ırı'presıb(ə)l/ a. that cannot be repressed.

irreproachable /ırı'prəʊtʃəb(ə)l/ a. faultless, blameless. **irreproachability** n.

irresistible /ırı'zıstıb(ə)l/ a. too strong or convincing or charming etc. to be resisted. **irresistibility** n.

irresolute /ı'rezəlu:t/ a. hesitating; lacking in resolution. **irresolution** n.

irrespective /ırı'spektıv/ a. **irrespective of** not taking into account, without reference to.

irresponsible /ırı'spɒnsıb(ə)l/ a. acting or done without due sense of responsibility; not responsible. **irresponsibility** n.

irretrievable /ırı'tri:vəb(ə)l/ a. not retrievable.

irreverent /ı'revərənt/ a. lacking in reverence. **irreverence** n.

irreversible /ırı'vɜ:sıb(ə)l/ a. that cannot be reversed. **irreversibility** n.

irrevocable /ı'revəkəb(ə)l/ □ See page 665. a. unalterable; gone beyond recall. **irrevocability** n.

irrigate /'ırıgeıt/ v.t. supply (land) with water; water (land) by system of artificial channels; *Med.* moisten (wound etc.) with constant flow of liquid. **irrigation** n.

irritable /'ırıtəb(ə)l/ a. easily annoyed; sensitive; inflamed, sore. **irritability** n.

irritant /'ırıt(ə)nt/ 1 a. causing irritation. 2 n. irritant substance or agent.

irritate /'ırıteıt/ v.t. excite to anger, annoy; inflame. **irritation** n.

irruption /ı'rʌpʃ(ə)n/ n. invasion; violent entry.

is /ız/ 3 pers. sing. pres. of **be**.

isinglass /'aızıŋglɑ:s/ n. kind of gelatin obtained from sturgeon etc.

Islam /'ızlɑ:m/ n. religion of Muslims, revealed through Prophet Muhammad; the Muslim world. **Islamic** /-'læm-/ a.

island /'aılənd/ n. piece of land surrounded by water; traffic island; detached or isolated thing.

islander /'aıləndə(r)/ n. inhabitant of island.

isle /aıl/ n. (usu. small) island.

islet /'aılıt/ n. small island.

isobar /'aısəbɑ:(r)/ n. line on map etc. connecting places with same atmospheric pressure. **isobaric** /-'bær-/ a.

isolate /'aısəleıt/ v.t. place apart or alone; separate (esp. infectious patient from others); insulate (electrical apparatus). **isolation** n.

isolationism /aısə'leıʃənız(ə)m/ n. policy of holding aloof from affairs of other countries or groups. **isolationist** n.

isomer /'aısəmɜ:(r)/ n. one of two or more substances whose molecules have same atoms in different arrangement. **isomeric** /-'mer-/ a.; **isomerism** /-'sɒm-/ n.

isosceles /aı'sɒsəli:z/ a. (of triangle) having two sides equal.

isotherm /'aısəθɜ:m/ n. line on map etc. connecting places with same temperature. **isothermal** a.

isotope /'aısətəʊp/ n. any of two or more forms of chemical element with different atomic weight and different nuclear but not chemical properties. **isotopic** /-'tɒp-/ a.

Israeli /ız'reılı/ 1 a. of modern State of Israel. 2 n. Israeli person.

issue /'ıʃu:/ 1 n. outgoing, outflow; giving out or circulation; copies of journal etc. issued at one time; one of regular series of magazine etc.; result, outcome; question, dispute; offspring. **2** *v.* go or come out; give or send out; publish, circulate; supply, supply *with* equipment etc.; emerge; be derived, result.

isthmus /'ɪsθməs/ *n.* neck of land; narrow connecting part.

it *pron.* (*poss.* **its**) thing named or in question; indefinite or undefined or impersonal action or condition or object etc.; *sl.* the very person or thing, perfection; *sl.* sexual intercourse, sex appeal.

Italian /ɪ'tælɪən/ *a.* of Italy. **2** *n.* native or language of Italy.

italic /ɪ'tælɪk/ **1** *a.* (of type etc.) of sloping kind; **Italic** of ancient Italy. **2** *n.* in *pl.* italic type.

italicize /ɪ'tælɪsaɪz/ *v.t.* print in italics.

itch 1 *n.* irritation in skin; disease with itch; restless desire. **2** *v.i.* feel itch.

item /'aɪtəm/ *n.* any one of enumerated things; detail of news etc.

itemize /'aɪtəmaɪz/ *v.t.* state by items. **itemization** *n.*

iterate /'ɪtəreɪt/ *v.t.* repeat; state repeatedly. **iteration** *n.*; **iterative** *a.*

itinerant /aɪ'tɪnərənt/ **1** *a.* travelling from place to place. **2** *n.* itinerant person.

itinerary /aɪ'tɪnərərɪ/ *n.* route; record of travel; guide-book.

its *pron., poss.* case of **it**.

itself /ɪt'self/ *pron., emphat. & refl.* form of **it**.

ITV *abbr.* independent television.

IUD *abbr.* intra-uterine (contraceptive) device.

ivory /'aɪvərɪ/ *n.* white substance of tusks of elephant etc.; colour of this; in *pl. sl.* dice, piano-keys, teeth, etc. **ivory tower** seclusion from harsh realities.

ivy /'aɪvɪ/ *n.* climbing evergreen with shining leaves.

J

jab 1 v.t. poke roughly; thrust abruptly. **2** n. abrupt blow with pointed thing or fist; *colloq.* hypodermic injection.

jabber /'dʒæbə(r)/ **1** v. chatter volubly; utter fast and indistinctly. **2** n. chatter, gabble.

jabot /'ʒæbəʊ/ n. frill at neck or down front opening of shirt or blouse etc.

jacaranda /dʒækə'rændə/ n. tropical Amer. tree with hard scented wood.

jacinth /'dʒæsɪnθ/ n. reddish-orange gem, kind of zircon.

jack 1 n. machine for lifting weights, esp. for lifting wheel of vehicle off ground; lowest-ranking court-card; ship's flag esp. one flown from bow and showing nationality; device using single plug to connect electrical circuit; device for turning spit; in *pl.* treated as *sing.* game played with jackstones; *Bowls* small white ball for players to aim at; (usu. young) pike. **2** v.t. hoist *up* (as) with jack. **3 jackboot** large boot with top reaching above knee, *fig.* oppressive behaviour; **jack in** *sl.* abandon; **jack-in-office** pompous official; **jack-in-the-box** toy figure that springs out when box is opened; **jack-knife** large clasp-knife, accidental folding of articulated vehicle (also v.); **jack of all trades** person who can do many kinds of work; **jackstone** small metal etc. object used with others in tossing-games.

jackal /'dʒæk(ə)l/ n. wild animal related to dog.

jackanapes /'dʒækəneɪps/ n. pert child or fellow.

jackass /'dʒækæs/ n. male ass; stupid person.

jackdaw /'dʒækdɔː/ n. bird of crow family.

jacket /'dʒækɪt/ n. sleeved short outer garment; outer covering round boiler etc. to prevent heat loss; outside wrapper of book; skin of potato.

jackpot /'dʒækpɒt/ n. accumulating prize in lottery etc.

Jacobean /dʒækə'bɪən/ a. of reign of James I of England.

Jacobite /'dʒækəbaɪt/ n. *hist.* supporter of exiled Stuarts.

Jacuzzi /dʒə'kuːzɪ/ n. (**P**) large bath with underwater jets of water.

jade¹ n. hard translucent green or blue or white stone; green colour of this.

jade² n. poor or worn-out horse; *joc.* hussy.

jaded /'dʒeɪdɪd/ a. tired out, sated.

jadeite /'dʒeɪdaɪt/ n. jadelike stone.

jag 1 n. sharp projection of rock etc. **2** v.t. cut or tear unevenly; make indentations in.

jagged /'dʒægɪd/ a. with unevenly cut or torn edge.

jaguar /'dʒægjʊə(r)/ n. large Amer. carnivorous spotted animal of cat family.

jail var. of **gaol**.

jalap /'dʒæləp/ n. purgative drug.

jalopy /dʒə'lɒpɪ/ n. *colloq.* dilapidated old motor vehicle.

jalousie /'ʒæluːzɪ/ n. blind or shutter with slats sloped upwards from outside.

jam¹ 1 v. squeeze; (cause to) become wedged; cause (machinery) to become wedged etc. so that it cannot work, become thus wedged; force or cram together; block by crowding; make (radio transmission) unintelligible by causing interference. **2** n. squeeze; stoppage; crowded mass esp. of traffic on road.

jam² n. conserve of fruit and sugar boiled until thick; *colloq.* something easy or pleasant to deal with. **jammy** a.

jamb /dʒæm/ n. side post or side of doorway or window etc.

jamboree /dʒæmbə'riː/ n. celebration, merry-making; large rally of Scouts.

Jan. *abbr.* January.

jangle /'dʒæŋg(ə)l/ **1** v. (cause to) make harsh metallic sound. **2** n. such sound.

janitor /'dʒænɪtə(r)/ n. doorkeeper; caretaker of building.

January /'dʒænjʊərɪ/ n. first month of the year.

japan /dʒə'pæn/ **1** n. hard usu. black varnish. **2** v.t. make black and glossy (as) with japan.

Japanese /dʒæpə'niːz/ **1** n. native or language of Japan. **2** a. of Japan.

jape n. practical joke.

japonica /dʒə'pɒnɪkə/ n. ornamental variety of quince with red flowers.

jar¹ 1 v. strike discordantly, grate; be at

variance (*with*). **2** *n.* jarring sound or shock or vibration.

jar² *n.* glass or pottery or plastic etc. vessel, usu. cylindrical.

jardinière /ʒɑːˈdɪˈnjeə(r)/ *n.* ornamental pot or stand for display of growing flowers.

jargon /ˈdʒɑːgən/ *n.* language peculiar to class or profession etc.; barbarous or debased language.

jasmine /ˈdʒæzmɪn/ *n.* shrub with white or yellow flowers.

jasper /ˈdʒæspə(r)/ *n.* red or yellow or brown opaque quartz.

jaundice /ˈdʒɔːndɪs/ **1** *n.* condition due to obstruction of bile and marked by yellowness of skin etc. **2** *v.t.* affect with jaundice; *fig.* affect (person etc.) with envy or resentment etc.

jaunt 1 *n.* pleasure excursion. **2** *v.i.* take a jaunt.

jaunty /ˈdʒɔːntɪ/ *a.* cheerful and self-confident; sprightly.

javelin /ˈdʒævəlɪn/ *n.* light spear thrown as weapon or in sports.

jaw 1 *n.* bone(s) containing teeth; in *pl.* mouth, gripping part of machine etc.; *colloq.* long or sermonizing talk. **2** *v.* *sl.* speak at length; admonish, lecture. **jaw-bone** lower jaw of mammals.

jay *n.* noisy European bird with vivid plumage. **jay-walker** pedestrian who walks in, or crosses, road carelessly.

jazz 1 *n.* music of US Negro origin usu. characterized by improvisation, syncopation, and marked rhythm. **2** *v.* brighten or liven *up*; play or dance to jazz.

jazzy /ˈdʒæzɪ/ *a.* of or like jazz; vivid.

jealous /ˈdʒeləs/ *a.* watchfully tenacious; suspicious or resentful of rivalry in love or affection; envious. **jealousy** *n.*

jean *n.* twilled cotton cloth; in *pl.* trousers of jean or denim.

Jeep *n.* (P) small sturdy motor vehicle with four-wheel drive.

jeer 1 *v.* scoff (*at*); deride. **2** *n.* gibe, taunt.

Jehovah /dʒɪˈhəʊvə/ *n.* OT name of God. **Jehovah's Witness** member of a fundamentalist Christian sect.

jejune /dʒɪˈdʒuːn/ *a.* meagre; poor, barren.

jell *v.i.* *colloq.* set as jelly; take definite form.

jellied /ˈdʒelɪd/ *a.* (of food etc.) set in jelly.

jelly /ˈdʒelɪ/ *n.* soft stiffish usu. semi-transparent food made of or with gelatin or of fruit-juice and sugar; substance of similar consistency; *sl.* gelignite. **jelly baby** gelatinous sweet in shape of baby; **jellyfish** marine animal with gelatinous body and stinging tentacles.

jemmy /ˈdʒemɪ/ *n.* burglar's crowbar.

jeopardize /ˈdʒepədaɪz/ *v.t.* endanger.

jeopardy /ˈdʒepədɪ/ *n.* danger esp. of severe harm.

jerboa /dʒɜːˈbəʊə/ *n.* small Afr. jumping rodent with long hind legs.

jeremiad /dʒerɪˈmaɪəd/ *n.* doleful complaint.

jerk¹ 1 *n.* sharp sudden pull or twist etc.; spasmodic twitch of muscle; *sl.* fool, stupid person. **2** *v.* move with a jerk; throw with suddenly arrested motion. **3** **jerky** *a.*

jerk² *v.t.* cure (esp. beef) by cutting in long slices and drying in the sun.

jerkin /ˈdʒɜːkɪn/ *n.* sleeveless jacket.

jeroboam /dʒerəˈbəʊəm/ *n.* wine-bottle of 6–12 times ordinary size.

jerrican var. of **jerrycan**.

jerry /ˈdʒerɪ/ *n.* *sl.* chamber-pot.

jerry-building building of unsubstantial houses with bad materials. **jerry-builder** *n.*; **jerry-built** *a.*

jerrycan /ˈdʒerɪkæn/ kind of petrol- or water-can.

jersey /ˈdʒɜːzɪ/ *n.* knitted usu. woollen pullover; knitted fabric.

Jerusalem artichoke /dʒəˈruːsələm/ kind of sunflower with edible tuber; this tuber.

jest 1 *n.* joke; fun; object of derision. **2** *v.* joke, make jests.

jester /ˈdʒestə(r)/ *n.* *hist.* professional joker at court etc.

Jesuit /ˈdʒezjʊɪt/ *n.* member of RC Society of Jesus. **Jesuitical** *a.*

jet¹ 1 *n.* stream of water or steam or flame etc. shot esp. from small opening; spout or nozzle for emitting water etc. thus; jet engine or plane. **2** *v.* spurt out in jet(s); *colloq.* travel or send by jet plane. **3 jet engine** one using jet propulsion for forward thrust esp. of aircraft; **jet lag** delayed bodily effects felt after long flight; **jet plane** one with jet engine; **jet-propelled** having jet propulsion, *fig.* very fast; **jet propulsion** propulsion by backward ejection of high-speed jet of gas etc.; **jet set** wealthy élite.

jet² *n.* hard black lignite taking brilliant polish. **jet-black** deep glossy black.

jetsam /'dʒetsəm/ *n.* goods thrown out of ship to lighten it and washed ashore.

jettison /'dʒetɪs(ə)n/ *v.t.* throw out (goods) from ship or aircraft esp. to lighten load; *fig.* abandon.

jetty /'dʒetɪ/ *n.* pier or breakwater constructed to defend harbour etc.; landing-pier.

Jew *n.* person of Hebrew descent or whose religion is Judaism. **Jewess** *n.*; **Jewish** *a.*

jewel /'dʒuːəl/ **1** *n.* precious stone; personal ornament containing jewel(s); precious thing etc. **2** *v.t.* adorn with jewels; fit (watch) with jewels for the pivot-holes.

jeweller /'dʒuːələ(r)/ *n.* dealer in jewels or jewellery.

jewellery /'dʒuːəlrɪ/ *n.* jewels or jewelled ornaments.

Jewry /'dʒuːrɪ/ *n.* Jews collectively.

Jezebel /'dʒezəbel/ *n.* shameless woman.

jib 1 *n.* triangular staysail from outer end of jib-boom to top of foremast or from bowsprit to mast-head. **2** *v.i.* (of horse or *fig.* of person) stop and refuse to go on. **3 jib at** object strongly to; **jib-boom** spar from end of bowsprit.

jibe¹ var. of **gibe**.

jibe² var. of **gybe**.

jiff *n.* *colloq.* (also **jiffy**) short time, moment.

jig 1 *n.* lively dance; music for this. **2** *v.* dance jig; move quickly up and down.

jigger¹ /'dʒɪgə(r)/ *n.* small glass or measure esp. for spirits.

jigger² /'dʒɪgə(r)/ var. of **chigoe**.

jiggery-pokery /dʒɪgərɪ'pəʊkərɪ/ *n.* *colloq.* deceitful or dishonest dealing; trickery.

jiggle /'dʒɪg(ə)l/ *v.t.* rock or jerk lightly.

jigsaw /'dʒɪgsɔː/ *n.* machine fretsaw; (in full **jigsaw puzzle**) picture pasted on board etc. and cut into irregular pieces to be reassembled as pastime.

jilt *v.t.* capriciously discard encouraged lover.

jingle /'dʒɪŋg(ə)l/ **1** *n.* mixed noise as of small bells or links of chain etc.;

repetition of same sounds in words; short verse of this kind used in advertising etc. **2** *v.* (cause to) make jingle.

jingo /'dʒɪŋgəʊ/ *n.* (*pl.* **-goes**) blustering patriot. **jingoism** *n.*; **jingoist** *n.*; **jingoistic** *a.*

jink 1 *v.* move elusively; elude by dodging. **2** *n.* act of jinking. **3 high jinks** boisterous fun.

jinnee /dʒɪ'niː/ *n.* (*pl.* **jinn**, also used as *sing.*) (in Muslim mythology) spirit of supernatural power.

jinx *n.* person or thing that brings bad luck.

jitter /'dʒɪtə(r)/ *colloq.* **1** *v.i.* be nervous, act nervously. **2** *n.* in *pl.* extreme nervousness. **3 jittery** *a.*

jive *sl.* **1** *n.* fast lively jazz music; dance done to this. **2** *v.i.* play or dance jive.

job 1 *n.* piece of work (to be) done; paid employment; *sl.* a crime, esp. a robbery; *colloq.* difficult task. **2** *v.* do jobs; hire, let out for time or job; buy and sell (stock etc.) as middleman; deal with corruptly. **3 jobcentre** government office displaying information about available jobs; **job lot** miscellaneous group of articles, esp. bought as speculation.

jobber /'dʒɒbə(r)/ *n.* stockjobber.

jobbery /'dʒɒbərɪ/ *n.* corrupt dealing.

jockey /'dʒɒkɪ/ **1** *n.* rider in horse-races. **2** *v.* cheat, trick; manoeuvre *for* advantageous position.

jock-strap /'dʒɒkstræp/ *n.* support or protection for male genitals worn esp. by sportsmen.

jocose /dʒə'kəʊs/ *a.* jocular. **jocosity** /-'kɒs-/ *n.*

jocular /'dʒɒkjʊlə(r)/ *a.* given to joking; humorous. **jocularity** *n.*

jocund /'dʒɒkənd/ *a.* merry, cheerful. **jocundity** *n.*

jodhpurs /'dʒɒdpəz/ *n.pl.* long riding-breeches, tight from knee to ankle.

jog 1 *v.* stimulate (memory); nudge, push, jerk; run slowly for exercise; walk or run or ride with jolting pace. **2** *n.* spell of jogging; slow walk or trot; push, jerk, nudge. **3 jog-trot** slow regular trot.

joggle /'dʒɒg(ə)l/ **1** *v.* move to and fro in jerks. **2** *n.* slight shake.

joie de vivre /ʒwɑː də 'viːvr/ feeling of exuberant enjoyment of life. [F]

join 1 *v.* put together, fasten, unite; connect (points) by line etc.; become member of; take one's place with or in; take part with others (*in*); unite or be united in marriage or alliance etc.; (of river or road) become continuous or connected with (another). **2** *n.* point or line or surface of junction.

joiner /ˈdʒɔɪnə(r)/ *n.* maker of furniture and light woodwork. **joinery** *n.*

joint 1 *n.* place at which or means by which two things join; structure by which two bones fit together; section of animal's carcase used for food; *sl.* place of meeting for drinking etc.; *sl.* marijuana cigarette. **2** *a.* held or done by, or belonging to, two or more persons etc. in common; sharing *with* others in possession etc. **3** *v.t.* connect by joint(s); divide (carcase) into joints or at a joint. **4 joint stock** capital held jointly.

jointure /ˈdʒɔɪntʃə(r)/ *n.* estate settled on wife for period during which she survives husband.

joist *n.* one of parallel timbers stretched from wall to wall to carry ceiling or floor boards.

jojoba /həʊˈhəʊbə/ *n.* desert shrub with bean yielding oil.

joke 1 *n.* thing said or done to excite laughter. **2** *v.i.* make jokes. **3 jokey** *a.*

joker /ˈdʒəʊkə(r)/ *n.* person who jokes; extra playing-card used in some games.

jollification /dʒɒlɪfɪˈkeɪʃ(ə)n/ *n.* merry-making.

jolly /ˈdʒɒlɪ/ **1** *a.* joyful; festive, jovial; *colloq.* pleasant, delightful. **2** *adv. colloq.* very. **3** *v.t. colloq.* coax or humour (person) *along*. **4 jollity** *n.*

jolt /dʒəʊlt/ **1** *v.* jerk from seat etc.; move along with jerks; give mental shock to. **2** *n.* such jerk or shock.

jonquil /ˈdʒɒŋkwɪl/ *n.* kind of narcissus with white or yellow fragrant flowers.

josh *US sl.* **1** *v.* make fun of, hoax. **2** *n.* good-natured joke.

joss *n.* Chinese idol. **joss-stick** stick of fragrant tinder and clay for incense.

jostle /ˈdʒɒs(ə)l/ **1** *v.* knock or shove (*against*); struggle. **2** *n.* jostling.

jot 1 *n.* small amount, whit. **2** *v.t.* write (*down*) briefly or hastily.

jotter /ˈdʒɒtə(r)/ *n.* small notebook etc.

joule /dʒuːl/ *n.* unit of work or energy.

jounce /dʒaʊns/ *v.* bump, bounce, jolt.

journal /ˈdʒɜːn(ə)l/ *n.* daily record of

events etc.; log-book; newspaper or other periodical; part of shaft or axle resting on bearings.

journalese /dʒɜːnəˈliːz/ *n.* hackneyed style of language characteristic of some newspaper writing.

journalism /ˈdʒɜːnəlɪz(ə)m/ *n.* work of journalist.

journalist /ˈdʒɜːnəlɪst/ *n.* person employed to write for journal or newspaper.

journey /ˈdʒɜːnɪ/ **1** *n.* act of going from one place to another; distance travelled. **2** *v.i.* make journey. **3 journeyman** qualified mechanic or artisan working for another.

joust /dʒaʊst/ *hist.* **1** *n.* combat with lances between two mounted knights. **2** *v.i.* engage in joust.

jovial /ˈdʒəʊvɪəl/ *a.* merry, convivial, hearty. **joviality** *n.*

jowl /dʒaʊl/ *n.* jaw, jawbone; cheek; loose skin on throat.

joy *n.* gladness, pleasure; cause of this. **joy-ride** *colloq.* (unauthorized) pleasure-ride in motor car etc.; **joystick** control lever of aircraft, *Computers* device for moving cursor on screen. **joyful** *a*; **joyous** *a.*

JP *abbr.* Justice of the Peace.

Jr. *abbr.* Junior.

jubilant /ˈdʒuːbɪlənt/ *a.* exultant.

jubilation /dʒuːbɪˈleɪʃ(ə)n/ *n.* exulting; rejoicing.

jubilee /ˈdʒuːbɪliː/ *n.* (esp. 50th) anniversary; time of rejoicing.

Judaic /dʒuːˈdeɪɪk/ *a.* Jewish.

Judaism /ˈdʒuːdeɪɪz(ə)m/ *n.* religion of the Jews.

Judas /ˈdʒuːdəs/ *n.* infamous traitor.

judder /ˈdʒʌdə(r)/ *v.i.* shake, shudder noisily. **2** *n.* instance of juddering.

judge 1 *n.* officer appointed to try causes in court of justice etc.; person appointed to decide dispute or contest; person fit to decide on merits of thing or question. **2** *v.* try (cause); pronounce sentence on (person); decide (contest, question); form opinion about, estimate; conclude, consider; act as judge.

judgement /ˈdʒʌdʒmənt/ *n.* critical faculty, discernment, good sense; opinion; decision of court of justice etc.; misfortune as sign of divine displeasure. **Last Judgement** judgement by God at end of world.

judicature /'dʒuːdɪkətʃə(r)/ *n.* administration of justice; body of judges.

judicial /dʒuː'dɪʃ(ə)l/ *a.* of or by court of law; of or proper to a judge; impartial.

judiciary /dʒuː'dɪʃərɪ/ *n.* judges collectively.

judicious /dʒuː'dɪʃəs/ *a.* sensible, prudent.

judo /'dʒuːdəʊ/ *n.* modern development of ju-jitsu.

jug 1 *n.* deep vessel for liquids, with handle and usu. spout; *sl.* prison. 2 *v.t.* stew (hare) in covered vessel.

juggernaut /'dʒʌgənɔːt/ *n.* large heavy motor vehicle; overpowering force or object.

juggins /'dʒʌgɪnz/ *n. sl.* simpleton.

juggle /'dʒʌg(ə)l/ *v.* perform feats of dexterity (*with* objects tossed up and caught); manipulate or arrange to suit purpose.

Jugoslav var. of **Yugoslav**.

jugular /'dʒʌgjʊlə(r)/ 1 *a.* of neck or throat. 2 *n.* jugular vein. 3 **jugular vein** either of veins of neck conveying blood from head.

juice /dʒuːs/ *n.* liquid content of vegetable or fruit or meat; bodily secretion; *sl.* petrol, electricity.

juicy /'dʒuːsɪ/ *a.* full of juice; *colloq.* interesting, (esp.) scandalous.

ju-jitsu /dʒuː'dʒɪtsuː/ *n.* Japanese system of wrestling.

ju-ju /'dʒuːdʒuː/ *n.* W.Afr. charm, fetish; magic attributed to this.

jujube /'dʒuːdʒuːb/ *n.* sweet fruit-flavoured lozenge of gelatin etc.

juke-box /'dʒuːkbɒks/ *n.* slot-machine that plays selected gramophone record.

Jul. *abbr.* July.

julep /'dʒuːlep/ *n.* drink of spirit and water iced and flavoured esp. with mint.

julienne /dʒuːlɪ'en/ 1 *n.* vegetables etc. cut into thin strips; clear soup to which such vegetables are added. 2 *a.* cut into thin strips.

Juliet cap /'dʒuːlɪet/ small or-namental cap worn by brides etc.

July /dʒuː'laɪ/ *n.* seventh month of the year.

jumble /'dʒʌmb(ə)l/ 1 *v.t.* mix (*up*) in confusion. 2 *n.* confused heap etc.;

muddle; articles for jumble sale. 3 **jumble sale** sale of miscellaneous usu. second-hand articles to raise funds for charity etc.

jumbo /'dʒʌmbəʊ/ 1 *n.* (*pl.* -bos) big animal (esp. elephant) or person or thing; jumbo jet. 2 *a.* very large of its kind. 3 **jumbo jet** large jet plane able to carry several hundred passengers.

jump 1 *v.* leap or spring from ground etc.; rise or move with sudden start; clear (obstacle) by jumping; come *to* or arrive *at* (conclusion etc.) hastily; (of train etc.) leave (rails); abscond from; pass over. 2 *n.* act of jumping; abrupt rise in price etc.; obstacle to be jumped, esp. by horse; sudden movement caused by shock etc. 3 **jump at** accept eagerly; **jumped-up** *a.* upstart; **jump the gun** make premature start; **jump-jet** jet plane that can take off and land vertically; **jump-lead** cable for conveying current from one battery to another; **jump-off** deciding round in show-jumping; **jump the queue** take unfair precedence; **jump suit** one-piece garment for whole body; **jump to it** act promptly and energetically.

jumper /'dʒʌmpə(r)/ *n.* knitted pullover; loose outer jacket worn by sailors; *US* pinafore dress.

jumpy /'dʒʌmpɪ/ *a.* nervous, easily startled.

Jun. *abbr.* June; Junior.

junction /'dʒʌŋkʃ(ə)n/ *n.* joining-point; place where railway lines or roads meet. **junction box** box containing junction of electric cables etc.

juncture /'dʒʌŋktʃə(r)/ *n.* state of affairs, crisis.

June *n.* sixth month of the year.

jungle /'dʒʌŋg(ə)l/ *n.* land overgrown with tangled vegetation esp. in tropics; tangled mass; place of bewildering complexity or ruthless struggle.

junior /'dʒuːnɪə(r)/ 1 *a.* the younger; inferior in age or standing or position. 2 *n.* junior person. 3 **junior school** one for younger pupils.

juniper /'dʒuːnɪpə(r)/ *n.* evergreen shrub, esp. with purple berry-like aromatic cones.

junk[1] *n.* discarded articles, rubbish; *sl.* narcotic drug, esp. heroin. **junk food** food which is not nutritious.

junk² *n.* flat-bottomed sailing vessel in China seas.

junket /'dʒʌŋkɪt/ **1** *n.* dish of milk curdled by rennet and sweetened and flavoured; feast; official's tour at public expense. **2** *v.i.* feast, picnic.

junkie /'dʒʌŋkɪ/ *n. sl.* drug-addict.

junta /'dʒʌntə/ *n.* political clique or faction holding power after revolution etc.

juridical /dʒʊə'rɪdɪk(ə)l/ *a.* of judicial proceedings, relating to the law.

jurisdiction /dʒʊərɪz'dɪkʃ(ə)n/ *n.* administration of justice; (extent or area of) authority.

jurisprudence /dʒʊərɪs'pruːd(ə)ns/ *n.* science or philosophy of law.

jurist /'dʒʊərɪst/ *n.* person versed in law. **juristic** *a.*

juror /'dʒʊərə(r)/ *n.* member of jury.

jury /'dʒʊərɪ/ *n.* body of persons sworn to render verdict in court of justice or coroner's court; judges of competition. **jury-box** enclosure in court for jury; **juryman, jurywoman,** juror.

just 1 *a.* upright, fair; deserved, due; well-grounded, right. **2** *adv.* exactly; barely; exactly or nearly at this or that moment; *colloq.* simply, merely, positively, quite; *sl.* really. **3 just now** at this moment, a little time ago.

justice /'dʒʌstɪs/ *n.* justness, fairness; judicial proceedings; judge, magistrate. **Justice of the Peace** lay magistrate.

justiciary /dʒʌs'tɪʃərɪ/ *n.* administrator of justice.

justify /'dʒʌstɪfaɪ/ *v.t.* show justice or truth of; be adequate ground for, warrant; *Print.* adjust (line of type) to fill space evenly. **justifiable** *a.*; **justification** *n.*; **justificatory** *a.*

jut 1 *v.i.* protrude. **2** *n.* projection.

jute *n.* fibre from bark of E. Ind. plants, used for sacking and mats etc.

juvenile /'dʒuːvənaɪl/ **1** *a.* youthful; of or for young persons. **2** *n.* young person; actor playing such part. **3 juvenile delinquency** offences committed by persons below age of legal responsibility; **juvenile delinquent** such offender. **4 juvenility** /-'nɪl-/ *n.*

juvenilia /dʒuːvə'nɪlɪə/ *n.pl.* works produced by author or artist in youth.

juxtapose /dʒuːkstə'pəʊz/ *v.t.* put side by side. **juxtaposition** *n.*

K

K. *abbr.* Köchel (list of Mozart's works).

k *abbr.* kilo-.

kaftan var. of **caftan**.

kaiser /'kaɪzə(r)/ *n. hist.* emperor esp. of Germany.

kale *n.* variety of cabbage, esp. **curly kale** with wrinkled leaves. **kaleyard** *Sc.* kitchen garden.

kaleidoscope /kə'laɪdəskəʊp/ *n.* tube containing angled mirrors and pieces of coloured glass, producing symmetrical patterns which can be altered by rotating the end of the tube; *fig.* constantly changing scene etc. **kaleidoscopic** /-'skɒp-/ *a.*

kamikaze /kæmɪ'kɑːzɪ/ *n. hist.* Japanese aircraft laden with explosives deliberately crashed by pilot on target.

kangaroo /kæŋgə'ruː/ *n.* Aus. marsupial with hind quarters strongly developed for jumping. **kangaroo court** illegal court held by strikers etc.

kaolin /'keɪəlɪn/ *n.* fine white clay used for porcelain.

kapok /'keɪpɒk/ *n.* fine cotton-like material from tropical tree used to stuff cushions etc.

kaput /kə'pʊt/ *a. sl.* done for, ruined, out of order.

karakul /'kærəkʊl/ *n.* Asian sheep whose lambs have dark curled fleece.

karate /kə'rɑːtɪ/ *n.* Japanese system of unarmed combat using hands and feet as weapons.

karma /'kɑːmə/ *n.* Buddhist's or Hindu's destiny as determined by his actions.

katydid /'keɪtɪdɪd/ *n.* large green grasshopper common in US.

kauri /'kaʊrɪ/ *n.* coniferous NZ timber-tree.

kayak /'kaɪæk/ *n.* Eskimo one-man canoe.

KBE *abbr.* Knight Commander of the Order of the British Empire.

KC *abbr.* King's Counsel.

kea /'keɪə/ *n.* green NZ parrot.

kebab /kɪ'bæb/ *n.* (usu. in *pl.*) small piece(s) of meat and vegetables etc. cooked on skewer.

kedge 1 *v.* move (ship) by hawser attached to small anchor. 2 *n.* small anchor for this purpose.

kedgeree /'kedʒərɪ/ *n.* dish of fish and rice and hard-boiled eggs etc.

keel 1 *n.* lengthwise timber on which ship's framework is built up. 2 *v.* turn (ship) keel upwards. 3 **keelhaul** haul (person) under keel as punishment. **keel over** capsize, (of person) fall over.

keen[1] *a.* eager, ardent; sharp; strong; acute, penetrating; competitive.

keen[2] 1 *n.* Irish funeral song accompanied with wailing. 2 *v.* utter the keen; utter in wailing tone.

keep 1 *v. (past & p.p.* **kept**) have charge of; retain possession of; maintain; provide for; maintain or remain in good or specified condition; restrain; pay due regard to, observe; protect; conduct or maintain, esp. for profit. 2 *n.* maintenance, food; *hist.* tower, stronghold. 3 **for keeps** *colloq.* permanently.

keeper /'kiːpə(r)/ *n.* person who keeps or looks after something; gamekeeper; custodian of museum etc. or forest; wicket-keeper.

keeping /'kiːpɪŋ/ *n.* custody, charge; agreement, harmony.

keepsake /'kiːpseɪk/ *n.* thing treasured for sake of giver.

keg *n.* small barrel. **keg beer** beer supplied from pressurized metal container.

kelp *n.* large seaweed; calcined ashes of this yielding iodine etc.

kelpie /'kelpɪ/ *n. Sc.* malevolent water-spirit.

Kelt var. of **Celt**.

ken 1 *v. Sc.* know. 2 *n.* range of knowledge or sight.

kendo /'kendəʊ/ *n.* Japanese sport of fencing with bamboo swords.

kennel /'ken(ə)l/ 1 *n.* small structure for shelter of house-dog or hounds; in *pl.* establishment where dogs are bred, or cared for during owners' absence. 2 *v.t.* put or keep in kennel.

kept *past & p.p.* of **keep**.

kerb *n.* stone edging to pavement etc.

kerchief /'kɜːtʃɪf/ *n.* cloth used to cover head.

kerfuffle /kə'fʌf(ə)l/ *n. colloq.* fuss, commotion.

kermes /'kɜːmɪz/ *n.* female of an insect that feeds on an evergreen oak; red dye made from these.

kernel /'kɜːn(ə)l/ n. part within hard shell of nut or stone fruit; seed within husk etc.; central or essential part.

kerosene /'kerəsiːn/ n. US fuel-oil distilled from petroleum or from coal or bituminous shale.

kestrel /'kestr(ə)l/ n. kind of small falcon.

ketch n. small two-masted coasting-vessel.

ketchup /'ketʃəp/ n. sauce made from tomatoes or mushrooms etc.

kettle /'ket(ə)l/ n. metal vessel with spout and handle, for boiling water. **kettledrum** tuned drum of hollow metal hemisphere with parchment etc. stretched across.

key /kiː/ 1 n. instrument for turning bolt of lock; instrument for winding clock etc. or for grasping screw or nut etc.; mechanical device for making or breaking electric circuit; one of set of levers pressed by finger on musical instrument or typewriter etc.; Mus. system of notes definitely related and based on particular note; solution; explanation, word or system for solving cipher or code; roughness of surface helping adhesion of plaster etc. 2 v. fasten with pin or wedge or bolt etc.; strike key(s) on keyboard of computer etc. 3 a. essential, of vital importance. 4 **keyboard** set of keys on piano or typewriter or computer etc.; **keyhole** hole by which key is put into lock; **keynote** Mus. note on which key is based, fig. dominant idea etc.; **key-pad** computer etc. keyboard, esp. small one held in hand; **key-ring** ring for keeping keys on; **keystone** central stone of arch, central principle; **key up** stimulate, increase nervous tension in.

KG abbr. Knight of the Order of the Garter.

kg. abbr. kilogram(s).

KGB n. secret police of USSR.

khaki /'kɑːkɪ/ 1 a. dull brownish yellow. 2 n. khaki colour or cloth or uniform.

khan /kɑːn/ n. title of rulers and officials in Central Asia. **khanate** n.

kHz abbr. kilohertz.

kibbutz /kɪ'buts/ n. (pl. **kibbutzim** /-tsiːm/) communal esp. farming settlement in Israel.

kibosh /'kaɪbɒʃ/ n. sl. **put the kibosh on** put an end to.

kick 1 v. strike out with foot; strike or move with foot; score (goal) by a kick; protest; sl. abandon (habit). 2 n. kicking action or blow; recoil of gun; colloq. temporary enthusiasm, sharp stimulant effect, thrill. 3 **kickback** recoil, payment esp. for illegal help; **kick off** Footb. begin game, colloq. start; **kick-off** n.; **kick out** colloq. expel forcibly, dismiss; **kick-start(er)** device to start engine of motor cycle etc. by downward thrust of pedal; **kick up a fuss** make vigorous protest etc.

kid 1 n. young goat; kid-skin leather; colloq. child. 2 v. give birth to kid; sl. hoax, deceive.

kidnap /'kɪdnæp/ v.t. carry off (person) illegally esp. to obtain ransom.

kidney /'kɪdnɪ/ n. either of pair of glandular organs serving to excrete urine; kidney of sheep or pig etc. as food; nature, kind. **kidney-bean** scarlet runner or dwarf French bean; **kidney machine** apparatus able to take over function of damaged kidney.

kill 1 v. deprive of life, put to death; put an end to; switch off; colloq. cause severe pain to; overwhelm (person) with amusement etc. 2 n. act of killing; animal(s) killed by sportsman. 3 **killjoy** depressing person.

killer /'kɪlə(r)/ n. person or thing that kills, esp. murderous person.

killing /'kɪlɪŋ/ 1 n. causing death; great financial success. 2 a. colloq. very attractive or amusing.

kiln n. furnace or oven for burning, baking, or drying.

kilo /'kiːləʊ/ n. (pl. **-os**) kilogram.

kilo- /'kɪləʊ/ in comb. 1,000.

kilocycle /'kɪləsaɪk(ə)l/ n. kilohertz.

kilogram /'kɪləgræm/ n. 1,000 grams.

kilohertz /'kɪləhɜːts/ n. unit of frequency, = 1,000 cycles per second.

kilolitre /'kɪləliːtə(r)/ n. 1,000 litres.

kilometre /'kɪləmiːtə(r)/ n. 1,000 metres, approx. 0.62 mile.

kiloton /'kɪlətʌn/ n. unit of explosive force equal to 1,000 tons of TNT.

kilotonne /'kɪlətʌn/ n. metric unit equivalent to kiloton.

kilowatt /'kɪləwɒt/ n. 1,000 watts. **kilowatt-hour** energy equal to 1 kilowatt working for 1 hour.

kilt 1 *n.* pleated skirt usu. of tartan, esp. worn by Highland man. **2** *v.t.* tuck up (skirts) round body; gather in vertical pleats.

kimono /kɪˈməʊnəʊ/ *n.* (*pl.* -os) long Japanese robe with wide sleeves; dressing-gown like this.

kin 1 *n.* one's relatives or family. **2** *pred. a.* related.

kind 1 *n.* class of similar or related things or animals etc.; natural way, fashion; character. **2** *a.* gentle, benevolent; friendly, considerate. **3 in kind** (of payment) in goods etc. instead of money, in same form.

kindergarten /ˈkɪndəgɑːt(ə)n/ *n.* school for young children.

kindle /ˈkɪnd(ə)l/ *v.* set on fire, light; *fig.* inspire; become kindled, glow.

kindling /ˈkɪndlɪŋ/ *n.* small pieces of wood etc. for lighting fires.

kindly /ˈkaɪndlɪ/ **1** *a.* kind, good-natured. **2** *adv.* in a kind manner; please.

kindred /ˈkɪndrɪd/ **1** *n.* blood relationship; one's relations. **2** *a.* related, allied, similar.

kine *n.pl. arch.* cows.

kinetic /kɪˈnetɪk/ *a.* of or due to motion. **kinetic energy** body's ability to do work by virtue of its motion.

king *n.* male sovereign ruler of independent state; man pre-eminent in specified field; largest kind of thing; chess piece to be protected from checkmate; crowned piece in draughts; court-card with picture of king. **King Charles spaniel** small black-and-tan kind; **kingcup** marsh marigold; **kingpin** main or large bolt, *fig.* essential person or thing; **king-size(d)** large. **kingly** *a.*

kingdom /ˈkɪŋdəm/ *n.* state or territory ruled by a king or queen; domain; division of nature. **kingdom-come** *sl.* the next world.

kingfisher /ˈkɪŋfɪʃə(r)/ *n.* small bird with brilliant blue plumage, which dives for fish.

kink 1 *n.* short backward twist in something straight or smooth; *fig.* mental twist. **2** *v.* (cause to) form kink.

kinky /ˈkɪŋkɪ/ *a.* having (many) kinks; bizarre; perverted.

kinsfolk /ˈkɪnzfəʊk/ *n.pl.* relations by blood. **kinsman** *n.*; **kinswoman** *n.*

kinship /ˈkɪnʃɪp/ *n.* blood relationship; similarity.

kiosk /ˈkiːɒsk/ *n.* light open structure for sale of newspapers or food etc.; structure in street etc. for public telephone.

kip 1 *sl. n.* sleep, bed. **2** *v.i.* sleep.

kipper /ˈkɪpə(r)/ **1** *n.* kippered fish, esp. herring. **2** *v.* cure (herring etc.) by splitting open, salting, drying, and smoking.

kirk *n. Sc.* church. **kirk-session** lowest court in Ch. of Scotland, composed of ministers and elders.

kirsch /kɪəʃ/ *n.* spirit distilled from wild cherries.

kismet /ˈkɪsmet/ *n.* destiny.

kiss 1 *n.* touch given with lips. **2** *v.t.* touch with lips, esp. as sign of love or affection or reverence etc.; touch gently. **3 kiss-curl** small curl of hair on forehead or nape of neck; **kiss hands** kiss those of sovereign on appointment to high office; **kissing-gate** one hung in U- or V-shaped enclosure.

kit 1 *n.* equipment or clothing etc. for particular activity; soldier's or traveller's pack or equipment; set of parts sold together from which whole thing can be made. **2** *v.t.* supply, fit *out* with kit. **3 kitbag** usu. cylindrical canvas etc. bag for carrying soldier's or traveller's kit.

kitchen /ˈkɪtʃɪn/ *n.* place where food is cooked. **kitchen garden** garden for growing fruit and vegetables.

kitchenette /kɪtʃɪˈnet/ *n.* small room or alcove fitted out as kitchen.

kite *n.* light framework covered with paper etc. and flown in wind at end of long string as toy; bird of prey of hawk family.

kith /kɪθ/ *n.* **kith and kin** friends and relations.

kitsch /kɪtʃ/ *n.* worthless pretentiousness in art; art of this type.

kitten /ˈkɪt(ə)n/ **1** *n.* young of cat. **2** *v.* give birth to (kittens).

kittiwake /ˈkɪtɪweɪk/ *n.* kind of small sea-gull.

kitty /ˈkɪtɪ/ *n.* joint fund; pool in some card games.

kiwi /ˈkiːwiː/ *n.* flightless NZ bird; **Kiwi** *colloq.* New Zealander.

kleptomania /kleptəˈmeɪnɪə/ *n.* irresistible tendency to steal. **klep-tomaniac** *a. & n.*

km. *abbr.* kilometre(s).

knack /næk/ *n.* acquired dexterity; trick, habit.

knacker /'nækə(r)/ **1** *n.* buyer of useless horses for slaughter. **2** *v.t. sl.* kill; exhaust, wear out.

knapsack /'næpsæk/ *n.* soldier's or traveller's bag strapped to back.

knapweed /'næpwi:d/ *n.* weed with purple flowers on globular head.

knave /neɪv/ *n.* unprincipled man, rogue; jack in cards. **knavery** *n.*; **knavish** *a.*

knead /ni:d/ *v.t.* work up into dough or paste; make (bread, pottery) thus; massage.

knee /ni:/ *n.* joint between thigh and lower leg; upper surface of thigh of sitting person; part of garment covering knee. **kneecap** convex bone in front of knee.

kneel /ni:l/ *v.i.* (*past & p.p.* **knelt**) rest or lower oneself on knees.

kneeler /'ni:lə(r)/ *n.* mat etc. for kneeling on.

knell /nel/ *n.* sound of bell esp. after death or at funeral; omen of death or extinction.

knelt *past & p.p.* of **kneel**.

knew *past* of **know**.

knickerbockers /'nɪkəbɒkəz/ *n.pl.* loose-fitting breeches gathered in at knee.

knickers /'nɪkəz/ *n.pl.* woman's or girl's undergarment covering body below waist and having separate legs or leg-holes.

knick-knack /'nɪknæk/ *n.* trinket or small ornament .

knife /naɪf/ **1** *n.* (*pl.* **knives**) blade with long sharpened edge fixed in handle and used as cutting instrument or weapon; cutting-blade in machine. **2** *v.t.* cut or stab with knife. **3 the knife** *colloq.* surgery; **knife-edge** edge of knife, *fig.* position of extreme uncertainty; **knife-pleat** one of series of overlapping narrow flat pleats.

knight /naɪt/ **1** *n.* man raised to rank below baronetcy as reward for personal merit or services; *hist.* man raised to honourable military rank by king etc.; chess piece usu. with shape of horse's head. **2** *v.t.* confer knight-hood on. **3 knight errant** medieval knight wandering in search of chivalrous adventures; **knight errantry** practice or conduct of knight errant. **4 knighthood** *n.*; **knightly** *a.*

knit /nɪt/ *v.* (*past & p.p.* **knitted** or **knit**) form (texture, garment) by interlocking loops of yarn or thread; treat (yarn etc.) thus; make (plain stitch) in knitting; wrinkle (brow); make or become close or compact; join, unite. **knitwear** knitted garments.

knitting /'nɪtɪŋ/ *n.* work being knitted. **knitting-needle** slender pointed rod used usu. in pairs in knitting.

knob /nɒb/ *n.* rounded protuberance e.g. handle of door or drawer etc., or for adjusting radio etc.; small lump (of butter, coal, etc.). **knobby** *a.*

knobbly /'nɒblɪ/ *a.* hard and lumpy.

knobkerrie /'nɒbkerɪ/ *n.* short stick with knobbed head as weapon of S. Afr. tribes.

knock /nɒk/ **1** *v.* strike with audible sharp blow; strike door or *at* door etc. for admittance; drive by striking; make by knocking; make knocking sound; *sl.* criticize. **2** *n.* sharp or audible blow; rap esp. at door. **3 knock about** treat roughly, wander about aimlessly; **knockabout** boisterous; **knock back** *sl.* eat or drink quickly; **knock down** strike to ground, demolish, dispose of *to* bidder at auction; **knock-down** (of price) very low, overwhelming; **knock knees** abnormal condition with legs curved inward at the knee; **knock-kneed** *a.*; **knock off** strike off with blow, leave off (work), *colloq.* do or make rapidly esp. without effort, *sl.* steal or kill; **knock-on effect** decision about one instance as affecting other instances; **knock out** render unconscious by blow to head, disable (boxer) so that he cannot recover in required time, defeat in knock-out competition; **knock-out** (blow) that knocks boxer out, (competition) in which loser of each match is eliminated, *sl.* outstanding person or thing; **knock together** construct hurriedly; **knock up** drive upwards with blow, make or arrange hastily, score (runs) at cricket, arouse (person) by knocking at door; **knock-up** practice game etc.

knocker /'nɒkə(r)/ *n.* hinged metal device on door for knocking to call attention.

knoll /nəʊl/ n. small hill, mound.

knop /nɒp/ n. ornamental knob; loop or tuft in yarn.

knot /nɒt/ 1 n. intertwining of parts of one or more ropes or strings etc., as fastening; tangled mass etc., cluster; hard mass formed in tree-trunk where branch grew out; round cross-grained piece in board caused by this; difficulty, problem; unit of ship's or aircraft's speed equal to one nautical mile per hour. 2 v. tie in knot; form knots; entangle. 3 **knot-grass** weed with intricate stems and pink flowers; **knot-hole** hole in wooden board, where knot has fallen out.

knotty /ˈnɒtɪ/ a. full of knots; puzzling.

know /nəʊ/ v. (past **knew**; p.p. **known**) be aware (of); have learnt; have understanding of; recognize, identify; be acquainted with. **in the know** knowing secret or inside information; **know-how** practical knowledge or skill.

knowing /ˈnəʊɪŋ/ a. cunning, shrewd.

knowingly adv. in a knowing manner; consciously, intentionally.

knowledge /ˈnɒlɪdʒ/ n. knowing; person's range of information; sum of what is known.

knowledgeable /ˈnɒlɪdʒəb(ə)l/ a. having much knowledge; well-informed.

known p.p. of **know**.

knuckle /ˈnʌk(ə)l/ 1 n. bone at finger-joint; projection of knee- or ankle-joint of quadruped; this as joint of meat. 2 v. strike or rub etc. with knuckles. 3 **knuckle down** apply oneself earnestly (to work etc.); **knuckle-duster** metal guard worn over knuckles in fist-fighting esp. to increase violence of blow; **knuckle under** give in, submit.

knurl /nɜːl/ n. small projecting ridge.

KO abbr. knock-out.

koala /kəʊˈɑːlə/ n. Aus. tailless arboreal marsupial with thick grey fur.

kohl /kəʊl/ n. powder used in eastern countries to darken eyelids etc.

kohlrabi /kəʊlˈrɑːbɪ/ n. cabbage with turnip-like edible stem.

kookaburra /ˈkʊkəbʌrə/ n. large Aus. kingfisher with loud discordant cry.

kooky /ˈkʊkɪ/ a. US sl. crazy or eccentric.

kopje /ˈkɒpɪ/ n. S.Afr. small hill.

Koran /kɔːˈrɑːn/ n. sacred book of Muslims.

kosher /ˈkəʊʃə(r)/ 1 a. (of food or food-shop) fulfilling requirements of Jewish law; colloq. correct, genuine. 2 n. kosher food or shop.

kowtow /kaʊˈtaʊ/ 1 v.i. act obsequiously; perform kowtow. 2 n. Chinese custom of touching ground with forehead as sign of worship or submission.

kraal /krɑːl/ n. S.Afr. village of huts enclosed by fence; enclosure for cattle.

kremlin /ˈkremlɪn/ n. citadel within Russian town, esp. that of Moscow. **the Kremlin** USSR government.

krill n. tiny plankton crustaceans eaten by whales etc.

kris /kriːs/ n. Malay dagger with wavy blade.

krugerrand /ˈkruːgərænd/ n. S. Afr. gold coin bearing portrait of President Kruger.

Kt. abbr. knight.

kudos /ˈkjuːdɒs/ n. colloq. glory, renown.

kukri /ˈkʊkrɪ/ n. heavy curved knife used by Gurkhas as weapon.

kümmel /ˈkʊm(ə)l/ n. liqueur flavoured with caraway seeds.

kumquat /ˈkʌmkwɒt/ n. tiny variety of orange.

kung fu /kʌŋ ˈfuː/ Chinese form of karate.

L

L, l, *n*. Roman numeral 50.

L *abbr.* learner(-driver).

L. *abbr.* Lake; Liberal.

l. *abbr.* left; line; litre(s).

la *var. of* **lah**.

lab *n. colloq.* laboratory.

Lab. *abbr.* Labour.

label /ˈleɪb(ə)l/ 1 *n*. slip attached to object to give some information about it; classifying phrase etc. 2 *v.t.* attach label to; assign to category.

labial /ˈleɪbɪəl/ 1 *a.* of lips; *Phonet.* pronounced with (closed) lips. 2 *n. Phonet.* labial sound.

laboratory /ləˈbɒrətərɪ/ *n.* place used for scientific experiments and research.

laborious /ləˈbɔːrɪəs/ *a.* needing much work; hard-working; showing signs of effort.

labour /ˈleɪbə(r)/ 1 *n.* bodily or mental work, exertion; task; the body of workers esp. as political force; **Labour** the Labour Party; process of giving birth, pains of this. 2 *v.* exert oneself, work hard; work as labourer; have difficulty; elaborate, work out in excessive detail. 3 **Labour Exchange** *colloq.* or *hist.* employment exchange; **labour force** body of workers employed; **Labour Party** *Polit.* party representing esp. workers' interests; **labour-saving** designed to reduce or eliminate work.

labourer /ˈleɪbərə(r)/ *n.* person who labours, esp. one employed to do unskilled manual work.

Labrador /ˈlæbrədɔː(r)/ *n.* (dog of) retriever breed with usu. black or golden coat.

laburnum /ləˈbɜːnəm/ *n.* poisonous tree with yellow hanging flowers.

labyrinth /ˈlæbərɪnθ/ *n.* network of passages, maze; tangled affairs. **labyrinthine** /-θaɪn/ *a.*

lace 1 *n.* cord etc. passed through eyelets or hooks for fastening or tightening shoes etc.; trimming-braid; fine open fabric of threads usu. with pattern. 2 *v.* fasten or tighten (*up*) with lace(s); trim with lace; add dash of spirits to.

lacerate /ˈlæsəreɪt/ *v.t.* tear roughly; wound (feelings etc.). **laceration** *n.*

lachrymal /ˈlækrɪm(ə)l/ *a.* of tears.

lachrymose /ˈlækrɪməʊz/ *a.* tearful, often weeping.

lack 1 *n.* deficiency or want *of.* 2 *v.* not have when needed, be without. 3 **lack-lustre** dull, lacking enthusiasm.

lackadaisical /lækəˈdeɪzɪk(ə)l/ *a.* languid; unenthusiastic.

lackey /ˈlækɪ/ *n.* footman; obsequious person.

lacking /ˈlækɪŋ/ *a.* undesirably absent; deficient (*in*).

laconic /ləˈkɒnɪk/ *a.* using or expressed in few words. **laconicism** *n.*

lacquer /ˈlækə(r)/ 1 *n.* hard shiny shellac or synthetic varnish; substance sprayed on hair to keep it in place. 2 *v.t.* coat with lacquer.

lacrosse /ləˈkrɒs/ *n.* team game played with ball carried in net at end of stick.

lactation /lækˈteɪʃ(ə)n/ *n.* suckling; secretion of milk.

lacteal /ˈlæktɪəl/ *a.* of milk; conveying chyle.

lactic /ˈlæktɪk/ *a.* of milk.

lactose /ˈlæktəʊs/ *n.* sugar present in milk.

lacuna /ləˈkjuːnə/ *n.* (*pl.* **-nas** or **-nae** /-niː/) gap, esp. in manuscript; missing part.

lacy /ˈleɪsɪ/ *a.* like lace fabric.

lad *n.* boy, young fellow.

ladder /ˈlædə(r)/ 1 *n.* pair of long pieces of wood or metal etc. joined at intervals by cross-pieces, used as means of ascent; vertical flaw in stocking etc.; *fig.* means of progress in career etc. 2 *v.* cause ladder in (stocking etc.); develop ladder.

lade *v.t.* (*p.p.* **laden**) load (ship); ship (goods); in *p.p.* loaded or burdened (*with*). **bill of lading** detailed list of ship's cargo.

la-di-da /lɑːdɪˈdɑː/ *a.* pretentious or affected, esp. in pronunciation.

ladle /ˈleɪd(ə)l/ 1 *n.* long-handled large bowled spoon for transferring liquids. 2 *v.t.* transfer with ladle.

lady /ˈleɪdɪ/ *n.* woman of good social standing; (polite or formal for) woman; **Lady** title used as prefix to name of peeress below duchess or to surname of knight's or baronet's wife or widow. **ladybird** small kind of beetle usu. reddish-brown with black spots; **Lady**

chapel chapel dedicated to Virgin Mary; **Lady Day** 25 Mar.; **ladylike** like or appropriate to a lady; **lady's maid** personal maidservant of lady.

ladyship /ˈleɪdɪʃɪp/ n. (with **her**, **your**, etc.) title used in addressing or referring to woman with rank of Lady.

lag[1] 1 v.i. go too slow; not keep pace; fall *behind*. 2 n. lagging, delay; *sl.* convict.

lag[2] v.t. enclose (boiler etc.) with insulating material.

lager /ˈlɑːɡə(r)/ n. kind of light beer.

laggard /ˈlæɡəd/ n. person lagging behind.

lagging /ˈlæɡɪŋ/ n. material used to lag boiler etc.

lagoon /ləˈɡuːn/ n. salt-water lake separated from sea by sandbank or enclosed by atoll.

lah n. *Mus.* sixth note of scale in tonic sol-fa.

laicize /ˈleɪɪsaɪz/ v.t. make secular.

laid past & p.p. of **lay**[1].

lain p.p. of **lie**[1].

lair n. place where animal habitually rests or eats; *fig.* hiding-place.

laird n. landed proprietor in Scotland.

laissez-faire /leɪseɪˈfeə(r)/ n. policy of non-interference. [F]

laity /ˈleɪtɪ/ n. laymen.

lake[1] n. large body of water surrounded by land.

lake[2] n. usu. reddish pigment made from dye and mordant.

lam v. *sl.* hit hard, thrash.

lama /ˈlɑːmə/ n. Tibetan or Mongolian Buddhist priest.

lamasery /ləˈmɑːsərɪ/ n. lama monastery.

lamb /læm/ 1 n. young sheep; its flesh as food; innocent or weak or dear person. 2 v.i. give birth to lamb.

lambaste /læmˈbeɪst/ v.t. *colloq.* thrash, beat.

lambent /ˈlæmbənt/ a. (of flame etc.) playing about a surface; gently brilliant. **lambency** n.

lame 1 a. disabled by injury or defect esp. in foot or leg; limping or unable to walk; (of excuse etc.) unsatisfactory; (of metre) halting. 2 v.t. make lame, disable. 3 **lame duck** person or firm unable to cope without help.

lamé /ˈlɑːmeɪ/ n. fabric with gold or silver thread woven in.

lament /ləˈment/ 1 n. passionate expression of grief, elegy. 2 v. express or feel grief for or about; utter lament; in *p.p.* mourned for.

lamentable /ˈlæmɪntəb(ə)l/ □ See page 665. a. deplorable, regrettable.

lamentation /læmɪnˈteɪʃ(ə)n/ n. lament, lamenting.

lamina /ˈlæmɪnə/ n. (*pl.* **-nae** /-niː/) thin plate or scale or flake or layer. **laminar** a.

laminate 1 /ˈlæmɪneɪt/ v.t. beat or roll into laminae, split into layers; overlay with plastic layer etc. 2 /ˈlæmɪnət/ n. laminated structure, esp. of layers fixed together. 3 **lamination** n.

lamp n. apparatus for giving light from electricity or gas or oil etc. **lampblack** pigment made from soot; **lamppost** post supporting street lamp; **lampshade** shade placed over lamp.

lampoon /læmˈpuːn/ 1 n. virulent or scurrilous satire. 2 v.t. write lampoon against.

lamprey /ˈlæmprɪ/ n. eel-like fish with sucker mouth.

Lancastrian /læŋˈkæstrɪən/ 1 a. of Lancaster or Lancashire; of House of Lancaster or its supporters in Wars of Roses. 2 n. Lancastrian person.

lance /lɑːns/ 1 n. long spear, esp. one used by horseman. 2 v.t. prick or open with lancet. 3 **lance-corporal** NCO below corporal.

lanceolate /ˈlɑːnsɪələt/ a. shaped like spearhead, tapering to each end.

lancer /ˈlɑːnsə(r)/ n. soldier of cavalry regiment orig. armed with lances; in *pl.* kind of square dance.

lancet /ˈlɑːnsɪt/ n. surgical instrument with point and two edges for small incisions; narrow pointed arch or window.

land 1 n. solid part of earth's surface; ground, soil, expanse of country; landed property; in *pl.* estates; country, State. 2 v. set or go ashore; bring (aircraft) down or come down to ground; bring to or reach certain place; deal (person blow etc.); bring (fish) to land; *fig.* win (prize, appointment, etc.). 3 **landfall** approach to land after sea or air journey; **landlady** woman keeping inn or lodgings, or having tenants; **land-locked** (almost) enclosed by land; **landlord** keeper of inn or lodgings, person who has tenants; **land-**

lubber person unfamiliar with sea and ships; **landmark** conspicuous object, notable event; **land mass** large area of land; **land-mine** explosive mine laid in or on ground; **landslide** landslip, *fig.* overwhelming majority for one side in election etc.; **landslip** sliding down of mass of land on cliff or mountain. 4 **landward** *a., adv.,* & *n.;* **landwards** *adv.*

landau /ˈlændɔː/ *n.* kind of 4-wheeled horse-drawn carriage.

landed /ˈlændɪd/ *a.* possessing or consisting of land.

landing /ˈlændɪŋ/ *n.* process of coming or bringing to land; place for disembarking; platform or passage at top of flight of stairs. **landing-craft** naval craft for putting ashore troops and equipment; **landing-gear** undercarriage of aircraft; **landing-stage** platform for disembarking passengers and goods.

landscape /ˈlændskeɪp/ 1 *n.* piece of inland scenery; picture of it. 2 *v.t.* improve by or engage in landscape gardening. 3 **landscape gardening** laying-out of grounds to imitate natural scenery.

lane *n.* narrow road or street; passage between rows of persons etc.; strip of road for one line of traffic; strip of track or water for competitor in race; regular course followed by ship or aircraft.

language /ˈlæŋgwɪdʒ/ *n.* words and their use; speech; form of this prevalent in one or more countries; method or style of expression; system of symbols and rules for computer programs.

languid /ˈlæŋgwɪd/ *a.* inert, lacking vigour etc.; apathetic; slow-moving.

languish /ˈlæŋgwɪʃ/ *v.i.* lose or lack vitality; live *under* depressing conditions; pine (*for*).

languor /ˈlæŋgə(r)/ *n.* languid state, soft or tender mood or effect. **languorous** *a.*

lank *a.* lean and tall; (of grass, hair, etc.) long and limp.

lanky /ˈlæŋkɪ/ *a.* ungracefully lean and tall or long.

lanolin /ˈlænəlɪn/ *n.* fat from sheep-wool used in ointments.

lantern /ˈlænt(ə)n/ *n.* transparent case protecting flame of candle etc.; light-chamber of lighthouse; erection on top

of dome or room, with glazed sides. **lantern jaws** long thin jaws.

lanyard /ˈlænjəd/ *n.* short cord for fastening or holding something.

lap¹ 1 *n.* front of sitting person's body from waist to knees; part of dress covering this; one circuit of race-track etc.; amount of overlap; single turn of thread etc. round reel etc. 2 *v.* lead (competitor in race) by one or more laps; fold or wrap (garment etc. *about, round*); enfold; (cause to) overlap. 3 **lap-dog** small pet dog.

lap² 1 *v.* drink by scooping with tongue; drink (*up*) greedily; make lapping sound. 2 *n.* act or sound of lapping.

lapel /ləˈpel/ *n.* part of coat-front folded back.

lapidary /ˈlæpɪdərɪ/ 1 *a.* concerned with stones; engraved on stone. 2 *n.* cutter or polisher or engraver of gems.

lapis lazuli /ˌlæpɪs ˈlæzjʊlɪ/ *n.* bright blue gem mineral, colour, and pigment.

lappet /ˈlæpɪt/ *n.* flap or fold of garment etc. or flesh.

lapse /læps/ 1 *n.* slight mistake; slip of memory etc.; passage *of* time. 2 *v.i.* fail to maintain position or state; fall *back* (*into*) former state); become void, elapse.

lapwing /ˈlæpwɪŋ/ *n.* peewit.

larboard /ˈlɑːbəd/ *n.* & *a. Naut.* = **port³.**

larceny /ˈlɑːsənɪ/ *n. Law* theft of personal property. **larcenous** *a.*

larch *n.* bright-foliaged deciduous coniferous tree; its wood.

lard 1 *n.* pig fat prepared for use in cooking etc. 2 *v.t.* insert strips of bacon in (meat etc.) before cooking; garnish (talk etc.) *with* strange terms etc.

larder /ˈlɑːdə(r)/ *n.* room or cupboard for storing provisions.

lardy-cake /ˈlɑːdɪkeɪk/ *n.* type of currant cake made with lard.

large *a.* of considerable or relatively great size or extent; of wide range, comprehensive. **at large** at liberty, as a body or whole, without specific aim.

largely /ˈlɑːdʒlɪ/ *adv.* to a great or preponderating extent.

largess /lɑːˈdʒes/ *n.* (also **largesse**) money or gifts freely given esp. on occasion of rejoicing.

largo /ˈlɑːgəʊ/ *Mus.* 1 *adv.* in slow time

with broad dignified treatment. **2** *n.* (*pl.* **-gos**) passage to be played thus.

lariat /ˈlærɪət/ *n.* tethering-rope; lasso.

lark[1] *n.* kind of small bird, esp. skylark.

lark[2] **1** *n.* frolic, spree; amusing incident; type of activity etc. **2** *v.i.* play *about*.

larkspur /ˈlɑːkspɜː(r)/ *n.* plant with spur-shaped calyx.

larrikin /ˈlærɪkɪn/ *n. Aus.* hooligan.

larva /ˈlɑːvə/ *n.* (*pl.* **-vae** /-viː/) insect in the stage between egg and pupa. **larval** *a.*

laryngeal /ləˈrɪndʒ(ə)l/ *a.* of the larynx.

laryngitis /lærɪnˈdʒaɪtɪs/ *n.* inflammation of larynx.

larynx /ˈlærɪŋks/ *n.* cavity in throat holding vocal cords.

Lascar /ˈlæskə(r)/ *n.* E. Indian seaman.

lascivious /ləˈsɪvɪəs/ *a.* lustful.

laser /ˈleɪzə(r)/ *n.* device giving strong beam of radiation in one direction.

lash 1 *v.* make sudden whiplike movement; pour, rush; hit or kick *out*; castigate in words; urge as with lash; fasten (*down, together*) with cord or twine. **2** *n.* stroke with whip etc.; flexible part of whip; eyelash.

lashings /ˈlæʃɪŋz/ *n.pl. sl.* plenty.

lass *n.* (also **lassie**) girl.

lassitude /ˈlæsɪtjuːd/ *n.* languor; disinclination to exert or interest oneself.

lasso /læˈsuː/ **1** *n.* (*pl.*-**os**) rope etc. with running noose used esp. for catching cattle. **2** *v.t.* catch with lasso.

last[1] /lɑːst/ **1** *a.* after all others; coming at end; most recent, utmost. **2** *adv.* after all others; on the last occasion before the present. **3** *n.* last-mentioned person or thing; end; last performance of certain acts. **4 at (long) last** in the end, after much delay.

last[2] /lɑːst/ *v.i.* remain unexhausted or adequate or alive for specified or long time.

last[3] /lɑːst/ *n.* shoemaker's model on which shoe etc. is shaped.

lasting /ˈlɑːstɪŋ/ *a.* permanent, durable.

lastly /ˈlɑːstlɪ/ *adv.* finally, in the last place.

lat. *abbr.* latitude.

latch 1 *n.* bar with catch as fastening of gate etc.; spring-lock as fastening of outer door. **2** *v.t.* fasten with latch. **3**

latchkey key of outer door; **latch on to** *colloq.* attach oneself to, understand.

late 1 *a.* (doing or done) after due or usual time; far on in day or night or period etc.; flowering or ripening etc. towards end of season; no longer alive or having specified status; of recent date. **2** *adv.* after due or usual time; far on in time; at or till late hour; formerly but not now. **3 of late** recently.

lateen sail /ləˈtiːn/ triangular sail on long yard at angle of 45° to mast.

lately /ˈleɪtlɪ/ *adv.* not long ago; in recent times.

latent /ˈleɪt(ə)nt/ *a.* concealed, dormant; existing but not developed or manifest. **latency** *n.*

lateral /ˈlætər(ə)l/ **1** *a.* of or at or towards or from side(s). **2** *n.* lateral shoot or branch. **3 lateral thinking** seeking to solve problems by indirect or illogical methods.

latex /ˈleɪteks/ *n.* milky fluid of (esp. rubber) plant; synthetic substance like this.

lath /lɑːθ/ *n.* thin narrow strip of wood.

lathe /leɪð/ *n.* machine for shaping wood or metal etc. by rotating article against cutting tools.

lather /ˈlɑːðə(r)/ **1** *n.* froth of soap etc. and water; frothy state of horse; state of agitation. **2** *v.* (of soap) form lather; cover with lather; thrash.

Latin /ˈlætɪn/ **1** *n.* language of ancient Rome; member of modern Latin people. **2** *a.* of or in Latin; (of peoples) speaking a language developed from Latin; of Roman Catholic Church. **3 Latin America** parts of Central and S. Amer. where Spanish or Portuguese is main language; **Latin Church** Western Church.

Latinate /ˈlætɪneɪt/ *a.* having character of Latin.

latitude /ˈlætɪtjuːd/ *n.* place's angular distance N. or S. of equator; (usu. in *pl.*) regions with reference to temperature; freedom from restriction in action or opinion.

latrine /ləˈtriːn/ *n.* communal lavatory, esp. in camp etc.

latter /ˈlætə(r)/ **1** *a.* mentioned later of two or last of three or more; recent; belonging to end of period etc. **2** *n. the* latter thing or person. **3 latter-day** modern, newfangled.

latterly *adv.* in later part of life or a period; of late.

lattice /'lætɪs/ *n.* structure of laths or bars crossing each other with spaces between; arrangement resembling this. **lattice window** one with small panes set in lead.

laud *v.t.* praise, extol.

laudable /'lɔːdəb(ə)l/ *a.* commendable. **laudability** *n.*

laudanum /'lɔːdənəm/ *n.* tincture of opium.

laudatory /'lɔːdətərɪ/ *a.* praising.

laugh /lɑːf/ 1 *v.* make sounds etc. usual in expressing amusement or exultation or scorn etc.; utter with laugh. 2 *n.* sound or act of laughing; *colloq.* comical person or thing. 3 **laugh at** ridicule.

laughable /'lɑːfəb(ə)l/ *a.* amusing; ridiculous.

laughing /'lɑːfɪŋ/ *n.* laughter. **laughing-gas** nitrous oxide as an anaesthetic; **laughing jackass** kookaburra; **laughing-stock** object of general derision.

laughter /'lɑːftə(r)/ *n.* act or sound of laughing.

launch[1] /lɔːntʃ/ 1 *v.* set (vessel) afloat; hurl, send forth; start or send off (*on* career etc.; *into* expense, abuse, etc.). 2 *n.* launching of ship.

launch[2] /lɔːntʃ/ *n.* large motor-boat; man-of-war's largest boat.

launcher *n.* structure to hold rocket during launching.

launder /'lɔːndə(r)/ *v.* wash and iron etc. (linen or other clothes).

launderette /lɔːndə'ret/ *n.* establishment with coin-operated automatic washing-machines for public use.

laundress /'lɔːndrɪs/ *n.* woman who launders.

laundry /'lɔːndrɪ/ *n.* place for laundering clothes etc.; batch of clothes to be laundered.

laureate /'lɒrɪət/ *a.* wreathed with laurel. **poet laureate** poet appointed to write poems for State occasions.

laurel /'lɒr(ə)l/ *n.* kind of shrub with dark green glossy leaves; in *sing.* or *pl.* wreath of bay-leaves as emblem of victory or poetic merit.

lava /'lɑːvə/ *n.* matter flowing from volcano and solidifying as it cools.

lavatory /'lævətərɪ/ *n.* receptacle for urine and faeces, usu. with means of disposal; room etc. containing this.

lave *v.t. literary* wash, bathe; wash against, flow along.

lavender /'lævɪndə(r)/ *n.* fragrant-flowered shrub; pale purplish colour of its flower. **lavender-water** a light perfume.

laver /'leɪvə(r)/ or /'lɑː-/ *n.* kind of edible seaweed.

lavish /'lævɪʃ/ 1 *v.t.* bestow or spend lavishly. 2 *a.* profuse, prodigal; (too) abundant.

law *n.* rule or body of rules established in a community and enjoining or prohibiting certain actions; such rules as social system or branch of study; *the* legal profession; *colloq. the* police; lawcourts, judicial remedy; statement of invariable sequence between specified conditions and phenomena. **law-abiding** obedient to the laws; **law-court** court of law; **Law Lord** member of House of Lords qualified to perform its legal work; **lawsuit** prosecution of claim in lawcourt.

lawful /'lɔːfʊl/ *a.* permitted or appointed or recognized by law; not illegal.

lawless /'lɔːlɪs/ *a.* having no laws; disobedient to laws; unbridled.

lawn[1] *n.* close-mown turf in gardens etc. **lawn-mower** machine for cutting grass of lawns; **lawn tennis** form of tennis played on outdoor grass or hard court.

lawn[2] *n.* kind of fine linen or cotton.

lawyer /'lɔːjə(r)/ *n.* person pursuing law as a profession, esp. solicitor; expert in law.

lax *a.* negligent, not strict, vague. **laxity** *n.*

laxative /'læksətɪv/ 1 *a.* tending to cause evacuation of bowels. 2 *n.* laxative medicine.

lay[1] 1 *v.t.* (*past* & *p.p.* **laid**) place on surface; put or bring into required position or state; make by laying; (of hen) produce (egg); cause to subside or lie flat; put down as wager; impose (*up*)*on*; make ready (trap, plan); prepare (table) for meal; put fuel ready to light (fire). 2 *n.* way or position or direction in which something lies. 3 **layabout** habitual loafer; **lay bare** expose, reveal; **lay-by** extra strip beside road for vehicles to park; **lay down** relinquish, pay or wager, formulate (rule), store (wine) in cellar, sacrifice (one's life); **lay in** provide oneself with stock of; **lay into** *sl.* punish or scold; **lay off** discharge temporarily owing to shortage of work, *colloq.* desist; **lay on** provide supply of; **lay out** spread, expose to view, prepare (body) for burial, expend (money), dispose (grounds etc.) according to a plan; **layout** disposing or arrangement of ground or printed matter etc.; **lay up** store, save (money), in *p.p.* confined to bed.

lay² *a.* not ordained into the clergy; not professionally qualified, esp. in law or medicine etc.; of or done by such persons. **layman** person not in holy orders or without professional or special knowledge; **lay reader** layman licensed to conduct some religious services.

lay³ *n.* minstrel's song, ballad.

lay⁴ *past* of **lie¹**.

layer /'leɪə(r)/ 1 *n.* thickness of matter, esp. one of several, spread over surface; shoot fastened down to take root. 2 *v.t.* arrange in layers; propagate by layers.

layette /leɪ'et/ *n.* clothes etc. prepared for new-born child.

lay figure artist's jointed wooden model of human figure; unreal character in novel etc.; person lacking individuality.

laze *colloq.* 1 *v.i.* indulge in laziness. 2 *n.* spell of lazing.

lazy /'leɪzɪ/ *a.* averse to work, doing little work; or of inducing idleness. **lazy-bones** lazy person.

lb. *abbr.* pound(s) weight.

l.b.w. *abbr.* leg before wicket.

l.c. *abbr.* lower case.

L/Cpl. *abbr.* lance-corporal.

lea *n.* piece of meadow or arable or pasture land.

LEA *abbr.* Local Education Authority.

leach *v.t.* make (liquid) percolate through some material; subject (material) to this; purge *away* or *out* thus.

lead¹ /li:d/ 1 *v.* (*past & p.p.* **led**) conduct or guide, esp. by going in front; direct movements or actions or opinions of; guide by persuasion (*to*); (of road etc.) go *to*; pass or spend (life); have first place in; go or be first; play (card) as first player in trick. 2 *n.* guidance, ex-

ample; leader's place; amount by which competitor is ahead of others; strap etc. for leading dog etc.; *Electr.* conductor conveying current to place of use; chief part in play etc.; player of this; *Cards* act or right of playing first. 3 **lead on** entice into going farther than was intended; **lead story** news item made most prominent; **lead to** have as result; **lead up to** form preparation for, serve to introduce, direct conversation towards.

lead² /led/ 1 *n.* heavy soft grey metal; graphite used in pencils; lump of lead used in sounding; in *pl.* strips of lead covering roof, piece of lead-covered roof; *Print.* metal strip to give space between lines. 2 *v.t.* cover or weight or frame or space with lead(s).

leaden /'led(ə)n/ *a.* of or like lead; heavy, inert, lead-coloured.

leader /'li:də(r)/ *n.* person or thing that leads; person followed by others; leading performer in orchestra or quartet etc.; leading article; shoot at apex of stem or main branch. **Leader of the House** member of Government with official initiative in business.

leading /'li:dɪŋ/ *a.* chief, most important. **leading aircraftman** one ranking just below NCO; **leading article** editorial expression of opinion in newspaper; **leading lady, man,** person taking chief part in play etc.; **leading light** prominent influential person; **leading note** seventh note of ascending scale; **leading question** one framed to prompt desired answer.

leaf 1 *n.* (*pl.* **leaves**) broad flat usu. green part of plant often on a stem; *collect.* leaves; single thickness of folded paper esp. in book; very thin sheet of metal etc.; hinged flap of table etc.; extra section that can be added to table. 2 *v.i.* **leaf through** turn over pages of (book etc.). 3 **leaf mould** soil composed chiefly of decaying leaves. 4 **leafy** *a.*

leafage /'li:fɪdʒ/ *n.* leaves of plant.

leaflet /'li:flɪt/ *n.* division of compound leaf; printed paper, single or folded, esp. for free distribution.

league¹ /li:g/ 1 *n.* agreement for mutual help, parties to it; group of sports clubs who contend for championship;

class of contestants. **2** v. join in league. **3 in league** allied.

league² /liːg/ n. arch. measure of travelling-distance, usu. about 3 miles.

leak 1 n. hole through which liquid etc. passes wrongly in or out; liquid etc. thus passing through; similar escape of electric charge; disclosure of secret information. **2** v. (let) pass out or in through leak; disclose (secret); **3 leak out** become known. **4 leaky** a.

leakage /ˈliːkɪdʒ/ n. action or result of leaking.

lean¹ 1 v. (past & p.p. **leaned** or **leant** /lent/) take or be in or put in sloping position; rest against for support; rely or depend on; be inclined or partial to. **2** n. inclination, slope. **3 lean-to** building with roof resting against larger building or wall.

lean² 1 a. having no superfluous fat; (of meat) consisting chiefly of muscular tissue, not fat; meagre. **2** n. lean part of meat. **3 lean years** time of scarcity.

leaning /ˈliːnɪŋ/ n. tendency or inclination.

leap v. (past & p.p. **leaped** or **leapt** /lept/) & n. jump. **leap-frog** game in which player vaults with parted legs over another bending down; **leap year** year with 29 Feb. as extra day.

learn /lɜːn/ v. (past **learned** or **learnt**) get knowledge of or skill in by study, experience, or being taught; commit to memory; find out.

learned /ˈlɜːnɪd/ a. deeply read, showing or requiring learning.

learner n. person learning, beginner; (in full **learner-driver**) person who is learning to drive motor vehicle but has not yet passed driving test.

learning n. knowledge got by study.

lease /liːs/ **1** n. contract by which owner of land or building allows another to use it for specified time usu. for rent. **2** v.t. grant or take on lease. **3 leasehold** tenure of or property held by lease; **leaseholder** n.; **a new lease of life** improved prospect of living or of use after repair.

leash 1 n. thong for holding dog(s). **2** v. put leash on, hold in leash.

least 1 a. smallest, slightest. **2** n. least amount. **3** adv. in the least degree.

leather /ˈleðə(r)/ **1** n. skin of animal prepared for use by tanning etc.; article

or piece of leather; polishing-cloth etc. **2** v.t. cover or polish with leather; beat, thrash. **3 leather-jacket** larva of crane-fly.

leatherette /leðəˈret/ n. imitation leather.

leathery /ˈleðərɪ/ a. like leather; tough.

leave¹ v. (past & p.p. **left**) go away (from); cause to or let remain; depart without taking; cease to reside at or belong to or work for etc.; abandon; bequeath; trust or commit to another; not consume or deal with.

leave² n. permission; permission to be absent from duty; period for which this lasts. **on leave** absent thus; **take one's leave of** bid farewell to.

leaven /ˈlev(ə)n/ **1** n. substance used to make dough ferment and rise; admixture of some quality. **2** v.t. ferment with leaven; permeate, transform; modify with tempering element.

leavings /ˈliːvɪŋz/ n.pl. what is left.

lecher /ˈletʃə(r)/ n. fornicator; debauchee.

lecherous /ˈletʃərəs/ a. lustful. **lechery** n.

lectern /ˈlektɜːn/ n. desk for holding bible etc. in church; similar desk for lecturer etc.

lecture /ˈlektʃə(r)/ **1** n. discourse delivered to class or other audience; admonition. **2** v. deliver lecture(s); admonish.

lecturer n. person who gives lectures, esp. in university.

lectureship /ˈlektʃəʃɪp/ n. university post as lecturer.

led past & p.p. of **lead¹**.

ledge n. narrow shelf or projection from vertical surface.

ledger /ˈledʒə(r)/ n. book in which a firm's accounts are kept.

lee n. shelter given by neighbouring object; side of thing away from the wind. **lee shore** shore to leeward of ship; **leeway** drift of ship to leeward, fig. allowable deviation.

leech n. blood-sucking worm formerly used medicinally for bleeding; fig. person who extorts profit from others.

leek n. vegetable of onion family with cylindrical white bulb.

leer n. & v.i. glance with lascivious or malign or sly expression.

leery /ˈlɪərɪ/ *a. sl.* knowing, sly; wary of.

lees /liːz/ *n.pl.* sediment of wine etc.; dregs.

leeward /ˈliːwəd or *Naut.* ˈluːəd/ 1 *a. & adv.* on or towards sheltered side. 2 *n.* this direction.

left¹ 1 *a.* on or towards side opposite **right**; of left in politics. 2 *adv.* on or to left side. 3 *n.* left part or region or direction; *Polit.* radicals collectively, more innovative etc. section of any group. 4 **left-handed** using left hand in preference to right, made by or for left hand, turning to left, awkward, clumsy, (of compliment etc.) ambiguous; **left-hander** left-handed person or blow; **left wing** group on left of army, football etc. team, or political party; **left-winger** member of this. 5 **leftward** *a. & adv.*; **leftwards** *adv.*

left² *past & p.p.* of **leave¹**.

leg 1 *n.* each of limbs on which person or animal walks and stands; leg of animal as food; artificial leg; part of garment covering leg; support of chair or other piece of furniture; *Crick.* part of field on side where batsman places his feet; each of progression of stages in journey or competition etc. 2 *v.t.* **leg it** walk or run hard. 3 **leg before wicket** (of batsman) out because of illegal obstruction of ball that would otherwise have hit his wicket; **pull person's leg** deceive him jokingly; **stretch one's legs** go for a walk.

legacy /ˈlegəsɪ/ *n.* gift left by will; anything handed down by predecessor.

legal /ˈliːg(ə)l/ *a.* of or based on or concerned with law; appointed or required or permitted by law.

legalism /ˈliːgəlɪz(ə)m/ *n.* unduly high regard for law or formula. **legalist** *n.*; **legalistic** *a.*

legality /lɪˈgælɪtɪ/ *n.* lawfulness.

legalize /ˈliːgəlaɪz/ *v.t.* make lawful; bring into harmony with law. **legalization** *n.*

legate /ˈlegət/ *n.* papal ambassador.

legatee /legəˈtiː/ *n.* recipient of legacy.

legation /lɪˈgeɪʃ(ə)n/ *n.* diplomatic minister and his suite; his residence.

legato /lɪˈgɑːtəʊ/ *Mus.* 1 *adv.* in smooth connected manner. 2 *n.* (*pl.* **-tos**) passage to be performed thus.

legend /ˈledʒ(ə)nd/ *n.* traditional story, myth; inscription on coin or medal etc.; caption; explanation on map of symbols used.

legendary /ˈledʒəndərɪ/ *a.* famous or existing only in legend.

legerdemain /ˌledʒədəˈmeɪn/ *n.* sleight of hand; trickery, sophistry.

leger line /ˈledʒə(r)/ short line added above or below staff for note(s) outside range of staff.

legging /ˈlegɪŋ/ *n.* (usu. in *pl.*) outer covering of leather etc. for leg from knee to ankle.

leggy /ˈlegɪ/ *a.* long-legged.

leghorn /ˈleghɔːn/ *n.* fine plaited straw; hat of this; **Leghorn** breed of domestic fowl.

legible /ˈledʒɪb(ə)l/ *a.* easily read. **legibility** *n.*

legion /ˈliːdʒ(ə)n/ *n.* division of 3,000-6,000 men in ancient Roman army; other large organized body.

legionary /ˈliːdʒənərɪ/ 1 *a.* of legions. 2 *n.* member of legion.

legionnaire /liːdʒəˈneə(r)/ *n.* member of legion. **legionnaire's disease** form of bacterial pneumonia.

legislate /ˈledʒɪsleɪt/ *v.i.* make laws. **legislator** *n.*

legislation /ledʒɪˈsleɪʃ(ə)n/ *n.* making laws; laws made.

legislative /ˈledʒɪslətɪv/ *a.* of or empowered to make legislation.

legislature /ˈledʒɪslətʃə(r)/ *n.* legislative body of a State.

legitimate /lɪˈdʒɪtɪmət/ *a.* (of child) born of parents married to one another; lawful, proper, regular; logically admissible. **legitimate theatre** plays of established merit or containing spoken lines only. **legitimacy** *n.*; **legitimation** *n.*

legitimatize /lɪˈdʒɪtəmətaɪz/ *v.t.* legitimize.

legitimize /lɪˈdʒɪtɪmaɪz/ *v.t.* make legitimate; serve as justification for. **legitimization** *n.*

legume /ˈlegjuːm/ *n.* leguminous plant; fruit or pod etc. of this.

leguminous /lɪˈgjuːmɪnəs/ *a.* of the family of plants with seeds in pods, e.g. peas and beans.

lei /ˈleɪ/ *n.* Polynesian garland of flowers.

leisure /ˈleʒə(r)/ *n.* free time, time at one's own disposal. **at leisure** not occupied, in unhurried manner; **at one's leisure** when one has time.

leisured *a.* having ample leisure.

leisurely 1 *a.* deliberate, unhurried. **2** *adv.* without hurry.

leitmotiv /ˈlaɪtməʊtiːf/ *n. Mus.* etc. theme associated throughout piece or work with some person or idea.

lemming /ˈlemɪŋ/ *n.* small arctic rodent reputed to rush in large numbers headlong into sea and drown, during migration.

lemon /ˈlemən/ *n.* yellow acid citrus fruit; its colour, tree bearing it. **lemon cheese, curd,** thick creamy lemon spread. **lemony** *a.*

lemon sole /ˈlemən/ kind of plaice.

lemonade /leməˈneɪd/ *n.* drink made from or flavoured like lemons, freq. aerated.

lemur /ˈliːmə(r)/ *n.* nocturnal mammal allied to monkeys.

lend *v.t.* (*past & p.p.* **lent**) grant temporary use of (thing); allow use of (money) at interest; bestow, contribute; accommodate *oneself to.*

length /leŋθ/ *n.* measurement from end to end; greatest of body's three dimensions; extent in or of or with regard to time; long stretch or extent; piece of certain length; full extent. **at length** in detail, at last, after a long time. **lengthways** *adv.*; **lengthwise** *adv. & a.*

lengthen /ˈleŋθ(ə)n/ *v.* make or become longer.

lengthy /ˈleŋθɪ/ *a.* of unusual length, prolix, tedious.

lenient /ˈliːnɪənt/ *a.* merciful, not severe, mild. **lenience** *n.*; **leniency** *n.*

lenity /ˈlenɪtɪ/ *n.* gentleness, mercifulness.

lens /lenz/ *n.* piece of transparent substance with one or both sides curved, used in spectacles and telescopes and cameras etc.; transparent substance behind iris of eye.

Lent[1] *n.* period of fasting and penitence from Ash Wednesday to Easter Eve. **Lenten** *a.*

lent[2] *past & p.p.* of **lend.**

lentil /ˈlentɪl/ *n.* edible seed of leguminous plant; this plant.

lento /ˈlentəʊ/ *a. & adv.* slow(ly).

Leo /ˈliːəʊ/ *n.* fifth sign of zodiac.

leonine /ˈliːənaɪn/ *a.* lionlike; of lions.

leopard /ˈlepəd/ *n.* large feline carnivore with dark-spotted fawn coat; panther.

leotard /ˈliːətɑːd/ *n.* close-fitting one-piece garment worn by dancers etc.

leper /ˈlepə(r)/ *n.* person with leprosy.

lepidopterous /lepɪˈdɒptərəs/ *a.* of the order of insects including moths and butterflies, with four scale-covered wings. **lepidopterist** *n.*

leprechaun /ˈleprɪkɔːn/ *n.* small mischievous sprite in Irish folklore.

leprosy /ˈleprəsɪ/ *n.* chronic infectious disease of skin and nerves, causing mutilations and deformities. **leprous** *a.*

lesbian /ˈlezbɪən/ **1** *n.* homosexual woman. **2** *a.* of homosexuality in women. **3 lesbianism** *n.*

lèse-majesté /liːzˈmædʒɪstɪ/ *n.* treason; affront to sovereign etc.; presumptuous conduct.

lesion /ˈliːʒ(ə)n/ *n.* damage, injury; *Path.* morbid change in action or texture of organ.

less 1 *a.* smaller; of smaller quantity; not so much. □ See page 667. **2** *adv.* to smaller extent, in lower degree. **3** *n.* smaller amount, quantity, or number. **4** *prep.* minus, deducting.

lessee /leˈsiː/ *n.* person holding property by lease.

lessen /ˈles(ə)n/ *v.* diminish.

lesser /ˈlesə(r)/ *a.* not so great as the other or the rest; minor.

lesson /ˈles(ə)n/ *n.* spell of teaching; thing learnt by pupil; experience that serves to warn or encourage; passage from Bible read aloud during church service.

lessor /ˈlesɔː(r)/ *n.* person who lets property by lease.

lest *conj.* in order that not, for fear that.

let[1] *v.* (*past & p.p.* **let**) allow or enable or cause to; grant use of (rooms, land) for rent or hire. **2** *n.* act of letting. **3 let alone** not interfere with, attend to, or do, not to mention; **let down** lower, fail to support at need, disappoint; **let fly** release, discharge; **let go** release, lose hold of, cease to restrain; **let in(to)** allow to enter, insert into surface of, make acquainted with (secret etc.); **let in for** involve in; **let loose** release; **let off** discharge, allow to go or escape, let (part of house etc.); **let on** *sl.* reveal secret; **let out** open door for exit of, allow to escape, slacken; **let-out** opportunity to escape; **let up** *colloq.* become less severe, diminish; **let-up** cessation, diminution.

let² 1 *n.* Tennis etc. obstruction of ball or player after which ball must be served again. 2 *v.t.* (*past* **letted** or **let**) *arch.* hinder, obstruct. 3 **without let or hindrance** unimpeded.

lethal /ˈliːθ(ə)l/ *a.* causing or sufficient to cause death.

lethargy /ˈleθədʒɪ/ *n.* torpid or apathetic state. **lethargic** /lɪˈθɑːdʒɪk/ *a.*

letter /ˈletə(r)/ 1 *n.* any of the symbols of which written words are composed; written or printed communication usu. sent by post or messenger; precise terms of statement; in *pl.* literature. 2 *v.t.* inscribe letters on; classify with letters. 3 **letter-bomb** terrorist explosive device sent by post; **letter-box** box for delivery or posting of letters, slit in door for delivery of letters; **letterhead** printed heading on stationery; **letterpress** printing from raised type.

lettuce /ˈletɪs/ *n.* garden plant with crisp leaves used as salad.

leucocyte /ˈljuːkəsaɪt/ *n.* white or colourless blood-corpuscle.

leukaemia /luːˈkiːmɪə/ *n.* progressive disease with abnormal accumulation of white corpuscles in tissues.

Levant /lɪˈvænt/ *n.* the East-Mediterranean region.

Levantine /lɪˈvæntaɪn/ 1 *a.* of or trading to the Levant. 2 *n.* inhabitant of the Levant.

levee¹ /ˈlevɪ/ *n.* assembly of visitors esp. at formal reception; *hist.* sovereign's assembly for men only.

levee² /ˈlevɪ/ *n.* US embankment against river floods.

level /ˈlev(ə)l/ 1 *n.* horizontal line or plane; social or moral or intellectual standard; plane of rank or authority; instrument for giving or testing a horizontal line or plane; height etc. reached; level surface, flat country. 2 *a.* horizontal; on a level or equality (*with*); even, uniform, well-balanced. 3 *v.* make or become level or even or uniform; place on same level; raze, abolish; take aim *at.* 4 **level-crossing** crossing of road and railway etc. at same level; **level-headed** mentally well-balanced, cool; **on the level** *colloq.* truthfully, honestly.

lever /ˈliːvə(r)/ 1 *n.* tool used in prizing; bar or other rigid structure used as lifting device; *fig.* means of moral pressure. 2 *v.* use lever; lift or move etc. (as) with lever.

leverage /ˈliːvərɪdʒ/ *n.* action or power of lever; *fig.* means of accomplishing a purpose.

leveret /ˈlevərɪt/ *n.* young hare.

leviathan /lɪˈvaɪəθ(ə)n/ *n. Bibl.* sea monster; anything very large of its kind.

levitate /ˈlevɪteɪt/ *v.* (cause to) rise and float in air. **levitation** *n.*

levity /ˈlevɪtɪ/ *n.* disposition to make light of weighty matters; frivolity.

levy /ˈlevɪ/ 1 *v.t.* impose or collect (payment etc.) compulsorily; enrol (troops etc.). 2 *n.* levying; payment etc. or (in *pl.*) troops levied.

lewd *a.* lascivious, indecent.

lexical /ˈleksɪk(ə)l/ *a.* of the words of a language; (as) of a lexicon.

lexicography /leksɪˈkɒɡrəfɪ/ *n.* making of dictionaries. **lexicographer** *n.*; **lexicographical** *a.*

lexicon /ˈleksɪkən/ *n.* dictionary.

ley /leɪ/ *n.* land temporarily under grass.

Leyden jar /ˈleɪd(ə)n/ kind of electrical condenser.

LF *abbr.* low frequency.

l.h. *abbr.* left hand.

liability /laɪəˈbɪlɪtɪ/ *n.* being liable; troublesome person or thing; in *pl.* debts for which one is liable.

liable /ˈlaɪəb(ə)l/ *pred.a.* legally bound; subject *to*; exposed or apt *to*; answerable *for.*

liaise /lɪˈeɪz/ *v.i. colloq.* establish cooperation or act as a link *with* or *between.*

liaison /lɪˈeɪzɒn/ *n.* comunication, co-operation; illicit sexual relationship.

liana /lɪˈɑːnə/ *n.* climbing and twining plant in tropical forests.

liar /ˈlaɪə(r)/ *n.* person who tells lies.

lias /ˈlaɪəs/ *n.* blue limestone rich in fossils.

Lib. *abbr.* Liberal; liberation.

libation /laɪˈbeɪʃ(ə)n/ *n.* drink-offering to god.

libel /ˈlaɪb(ə)l/ 1 *n.* false statement damaging to person's reputation; publishing of this; false defamatory statement. **2** *v.t.* (*past & p.p.* **libelled**) utter or publish libel against. **3 libellous** *a*.

liberal /'lɪbər(ə)l/ **1** *a*. given or giving freely; generous; abundant; unprejudiced; not rigorous; (of studies) directed to general broadening of mind; *Polit.* favouring moderate reforms. **2** *n*. person of liberal views, esp. **Liberal** member of Liberal Party. **3 liberalism** *n*.; **liberalize** *v.t.*; **liberalization** *n*.

liberality /lɪbə'rælɪtɪ/ *n*. generosity; breadth of mind.

liberate /'lɪbəreɪt/ *v.t.* set at liberty, release *from*; free from oppressive social conventions. **liberation** *n*.; **liberator** *n*.

libertarian /lɪbə'teərɪən/ **1** *a*. believing in free will; advocating liberty. **2** *n*. libertarian person.

libertine /'lɪbətiːn/ *n*. dissolute or licentious man.

liberty /'lɪbətɪ/ *n*. being free, freedom; right or power to do as one pleases; piece of presumption; in *pl*. privileges enjoyed by prescription or grant. **at liberty** free, disengaged, having right *to do*.

libidinous /lɪ'bɪdɪnəs/ *a*. lustful.

libido /lɪ'biːdəʊ/ *n*. (*pl.* **-dos**) psychic impulse or drive esp. that associated with sex instinct. **libidinal** *a*.

Libra /'liːbrə/ *n*. seventh sign of zodiac.

librarian /laɪ'breərɪən/ *n*. custodian or assistant in library.

library /'laɪbrərɪ/ *n*. a collection of books or of films or records etc.; room or building etc. where these are kept; series of books issued in similar bindings.

libretto /lɪ'bretəʊ/ *n*. (*pl.* **-ti** /-tɪ/ or **-tos**) text of opera etc. **librettist** *n*.

lice *pl.* of **louse**.

licence /'laɪs(ə)ns/ *n*. permit from government etc. to carry out some action etc. which without this would be illegal; permission, leave; excessive liberty of action, licentiousness.

license /'laɪs(ə)ns/ *v.t.* grant licence to; authorize use of (premises) for purpose esp. sale etc. of alcoholic liquor.

licensee /laɪsən'siː/ *n*. holder of licence esp. to sell alcoholic liquor.

licentiate /laɪ'senʃɪət/ *n*. holder of certificate of competence to practise certain profession.

licentious /laɪ'senʃəs/ *a*. immoral in sexual relations.

lichee var. of **litchi**.

lichen /'laɪkən/ *n*. plant organism composed of fungus and alga in association, growing on rocks and trees etc.

lich-gate /'lɪtʃgeɪt/ *n*. roofed gateway of churchyard.

licit /'lɪsɪt/ *a*. not forbidden.

lick **1** *v*. pass tongue over; take *off* or *up* by licking; play lightly over; *sl*. thrash, defeat. **2** *n*. act of licking with tongue; smart blow; *sl*. pace, speed.

lid *n*. hinged or removable cover esp. at top of container; eyelid.

lido /'liːdəʊ/ *n*. (*pl.* **-dos**) public open-air swimming-pool or bathing-beach.

lie[1] /laɪ/ **1** *v.i.* (*past* **lay**; *p.p.* **lain**; *partic.* **lying**) be in or assume horizontal position on supporting surface; be at rest on something; be situated or spread out to view etc.; remain, be; exist or be in certain position or manner; *Law* be admissible or sustainable. **2** *n*. way, position, or direction in which something lies. **3 lie in** *colloq.* remain in bed late in morning; **lie-in** *n*.; **lie low** keep quiet or unseen; **lie of the land** state of affairs.

lie[2] /laɪ/ **1** *n*. intentional false statement; imposture, false belief. **2** *v.i.* (*partic.* **lying**) tell lie(s); be deceptive.

lief /liːf/ *adv. arch.* willingly.

liege /liːdʒ/ *hist.* **1** *a*. entitled to receive or bound to give feudal service or allegiance. **2** *n*. liege lord; (usu. in *pl*) vassal, subject. **3 liege lord** feudal superior.

lien /'liːən/ *n*. right to hold another's property till debt on it is paid.

lieu /ljuː/ *n*. **in lieu** instead (*of*).

Lieut. *abbr.* Lieutenant.

lieutenant /lef'ten(ə)nt/ *n*. deputy or substitute who acts for a superior; army officer next below captain; naval officer next below lieutenant-commander. **lieutenant-colonel, -commander, -general**, officers ranking next below colonel etc. **lieutenancy** *n*.

life *n*. (*pl.* **lives**) capacity for growth and functional activity and continual change peculiar to animals and plants; state of existence as living individual; living things and their activity; period during which life lasts; period from birth to present time or from present time to death; manner of existence or particular aspect of this; energy, liveliness; business and pleasures of the world; written account of person's life; time for which manufactured or perishable product continues to function or be satisfactory etc.; sentence of imprisonment for life. **lifebelt** ring of buoyant material to support body in water; **life-blood** vitalizing influence; **lifeboat** boat for rescue in storms, ship's boat for emergency use; **life-buoy** lifebelt; **life cycle** *Biol.* cyclic series of changes undergone by an organism; **Life Guards** regiment of household cavalry; **life insurance** insurance for payment on death of insured person; **life jacket** upper garment of buoyant material to support body in water; **lifeline** rope used for life-saving, *fig.* sole means of communication; **life peer** peer whose title lapses at death; **life-size(d)** of same size as person or thing represented; **life-style** individual's way of life; **life-time** duration of person's life.

lifeless /ˈlaɪflɪs/ *a.* dead; lacking in animation.

lifelike /ˈlaɪflaɪk/ *a.* (of representation) realistic or vivid.

lifer /ˈlaɪfə(r)/ *n. sl.* person sentenced to imprisonment for life; such sentence.

lift 1 *v.* raise to higher level, take up, hoist; give upward direction to; elevate; (of cloud etc.) rise, disperse; go up, be raised; remove (restriction etc.); steal, plagiarize. 2 *n.* lifting; carrying of person without charge as passenger in vehicle; apparatus for raising and lowering persons or things from floor to floor in building, or for carrying persons up or down mountain etc.; supporting or elevating influence. 3 **lift-off** vertical take-off of spacecraft or rocket.

ligament /ˈlɪgəmənt/ *n.* band of tough fibrous tissue binding bones together.

ligature /ˈlɪgətʃə(r)/ 1 *n.* tie or bandage; *Mus.* slur, tie; *Print.* two or more letters joined (œ, fl, etc.). 2 *v.t.* bind or connect with ligature.

light¹ /laɪt/ 1 *n.* natural agent that makes things visible; medium or condition of space in which this is present; brightness of eyes or aspect; source of light; means of procuring fire; traffic light; aspect in which thing is viewed; mental illumination; in *pl.* one's mental powers; word to be deduced from cross-word clue. 2 *a.* well-provided with light, not dark; (of colours) pale. 3 *v.* (*past* lit; *p.p.* **lit** or **lighted**) set burning, begin to burn; give light to; show way etc. with light; (cause to) brighten (*up*) with animation. 4 **lighthouse** structure with beacon light to warn or guide ships at sea; **lightship** anchored ship with beacon light; **light-year** distance which light travels in one year.

light² /laɪt/ 1 *a.* of little weight, not heavy, easy to lift; relatively low in weight or amount or density or strength; deficient in weight; easy to digest; easily borne or done; intended only as entertainment, not profound; free from sorrow, cheerful; nimble; elegant. 2 *adv.* lightly; with light load. 3 *v.i.* (*past & p.p.* **lit** or **lighted**) come by chance (*upon*). 4 **light-fingered** apt to steal; **light-headed** giddy, delirious; **light-hearted** cheerful, untroubled; **light industry** that producing small or light articles; **lightweight** below average weight, of little ability or importance, (*n.*) lightweight person or thing, boxing weight (up to 60 kg.).

lighten¹ /ˈlaɪt(ə)n/ *v.* make or become less heavy; reduce weight or load of; bring relief to; mitigate.

lighten² /ˈlaɪt(ə)n/ *v.* shed light upon, make or become bright; emit lightning.

lighter¹ /ˈlaɪtə(r)/ *n.* device for lighting cigarettes etc.

lighter² /ˈlaɪtə(r)/ *n.* boat for transporting goods between ship and wharf etc.

lightning /ˈlaɪtnɪŋ/ *n.* visible electric discharge between clouds or cloud and ground. **lightning-conductor** metal rod or wire fixed to building etc. to divert lightning to earth.

lights /laɪts/ *n.pl.* lungs of sheep or pigs etc. as food, esp. for pets.

lightsome /ˈlaɪtsəm/ *a.* gracefully light; merry; agile.

ligneous /ˈlɪgnɪəs/ *a.* of the nature of wood.

lignite /ˈlɪgnaɪt/ *n.* brown coal of woody texture.

lignum vitae /ˈlɪgnəm ˈvaɪtiː/ a hard-wooded tree.

like¹ 1 *a.* similar, resembling; such as;

characteristic of; in suitable state or mood for. **2** *prep.* in the manner of, to the same degree as. **3** *conj. incorrect* as; □ See page 667 ; *US colloq.* as if. **4** *n.* counterpart, equal; like thing or person.

like² **1** *v.* find agreeable or satisfactory; feel attracted by, wish, prefer. **2** *n.* (usu. in *pl.*) thing one likes or prefers.

likeable /'laɪkəb(ə)l/ *a.* pleasant, easy to like.

likelihood /'laɪklɪhʊd/ *n.* probability.

likely /'laɪklɪ/ **1** *a.* probable; such as might well happen or be or prove true; to be expected *to*; promising, apparently suitable. **2** *adv.* probably.

liken /'laɪkən/ *v.t.* find or point out resemblance in (*to*).

likeness /'laɪknɪs/ *n.* resemblance; semblance; representation, portrait.

likewise /'laɪkwaɪz/ *adv.* also, moreover; similarly.

liking /'laɪkɪŋ/ *n.* one's taste; fondness or taste or fancy *for*.

lilac /'laɪlək/ **1** *n.* shrub with fragrant pale violet or white flowers; pale violet colour. **2** *a.* of lilac colour.

liliaceous /lɪlɪ'eɪʃəs/ *a.* of the lily family.

lilliputian /lɪlɪ'pjuːʃ(ə)n/ *a.* diminutive.

lilt **1** *n.* light pleasant rhythm; song or tune with this. **2** *v.* move or utter with lilt.

lily /'lɪlɪ/ *n.* bulbous plant with large showy flowers; its flower; heraldic fleur-de-lis. **lily of the valley** spring plant with fragrant white bell-shaped flowers.

limb¹ /lɪm/ *n.* leg, arm, or wing; large branch of tree; branch of cross. **out on a limb** *fig.* isolated, stranded.

limb² /lɪm/ *n. Astron.* specified edge of sun etc.

limber¹ /'lɪmbə(r)/ **1** *a.* flexible; lithe, agile. **2** *v.* make oneself limber in preparation for athletic etc. activity.

limber² /'lɪmbə(r)/ **1** *n.* detachable front of gun-carriage. **2** *v.t.* attach limber to (gun).

limbo¹ /'lɪmbəʊ/ *n.* (*pl.* **-bos**) supposed abode of pre-Christian righteous persons and of unbaptized infants; intermediate state or condition; condition of neglect or oblivion.

limbo² /'lɪmbəʊ/ *n.* (*pl.* **-bos**) W. Ind. dance in which dancer bends backwards to pass under horizontal bar.

lime¹ **1** *n.* white caustic substance got by heating limestone etc. **2** *v.t.* treat with lime. **3** **lime-kiln** kiln for heating limestone.

lime² *n.* round green acid fruit of lemon kind. **lime-green** yellowish-green colour.

lime³ *n.* ornamental tree with heart-shaped leaves.

limelight /'laɪmlaɪt/ *n.* intense white light used formerly in theatres; glare of publicity.

limerick /'lɪmərɪk/ *n.* humorous 5-line stanza.

limestone /'laɪmstəʊn/ *n.* rock composed mainly of calcium carbonate.

Limey /'laɪmɪ/ *n. US sl.* British person.

limit /'lɪmɪt/ **1** *n.* line etc. that may not or cannot be passed; greatest or smallest amount permitted. **2** *v.t.* set limits to, serve as limit to; restrict *to*.

limitation /lɪmɪ'teɪʃ(ə)n/ *n.* limiting or being limited; lack of ability; limiting rule or circumstance.

limn /lɪm/ *v.t. literary* paint (picture), portray.

limousine /lɪmʊ'ziːn/ *n.* motor car with closed body and partition behind driver.

limp¹ **1** *v.i.* walk lamely; proceed slowly or with difficulty; (of verse) be defective. **2** *n.* lame walk.

limp² *a.* easily bent and not springing back to shape; *fig.* without will or energy.

limpet /'lɪmpɪt/ *n.* mollusc with low conical shell adhering tightly to rocks.

limpid /'lɪmpɪd/ *a.* transparently clear. **limpidity** *n.*

linage /'laɪnɪdʒ/ *n.* number of lines in page etc.; payment by the line.

linchpin /'lɪntʃpɪn/ *n.* pin passed through axle-end to keep wheel on; *fig.* person or thing vital to organization etc.

linctus /'lɪŋktəs/ *n.* medicine, esp. soothing syrupy cough-mixture.

linden /'lɪnd(ə)n/ *n.* **lime³**.

line¹ **1** *n.* long narrow mark traced on surface; band of colour, furrow, wrinkle; extent of length without breadth; limit, boundary; row of persons or things; piece of cord or rope etc. serving usu. specified purpose; wire or cable for telephone or telegraph; connection by this; contour, outline, lineament; course of procedure or conduct; in *pl.* plan, draft, manner of procedure; row of printed or written words; a verse or in *pl.* a piece of poetry; in *pl.* words of actor's part; track or branch of railway; regular succession of ships or buses or aircraft etc. plying between certain places, company conducting this; lineage, stock; direction, track; department of activity, branch of business; class of commercial goods; *Mil.* connected series of field-works, arrangement of soldiers side by side; one of the very narrow horizontal sections forming television picture. **2** *v.* mark with lines; position or stand at intervals along. **3 line printer** machine that prints output from computer a line at a time; **linesman** umpire's or referee's assistant who decides whether ball falls within playing area or not; **line up** arrange or be arranged in lines; **line-up** *n.*

line² *v.t.* apply layer of usu. different material to inside of; serve as lining for; fill (purse etc.).

lineage /ˈlɪnɪɪdʒ/ *n.* lineal descent, ancestry.

lineal /ˈlɪnɪəl/ *a.* in the direct line of descent or ancestry.

lineament /ˈlɪnɪəmənt/ *n.* usu. in *pl.* distinctive feature or characteristic esp. of face.

linear /ˈlɪnɪə(r)/ *a.* of or in lines; long and narrow and of uniform breadth.

linen /ˈlɪnɪn/ **1** *n.* cloth woven from flax; articles made or orig. made of this, such as sheets, shirts, undergarments, etc. **2** *a.* made of linen.

liner¹ /ˈlaɪnə(r)/ *n.* ship or aircraft belonging to regular line and used for passenger transport.

liner² /ˈlaɪnə(r)/ *n.* removable lining.

ling¹ *n.* long slender sea-fish.

ling² *n.* kind of heather.

linger /ˈlɪŋɡə(r)/ *v.i.* be slow to depart; stay about, dally; be protracted.

lingerie /ˈlæʒərɪ/ *n.* women's underwear and night-clothes.

lingo /ˈlɪŋɡəʊ/ *n.* (*pl.* **-gos**) *derog.* foreign language.

lingual /ˈlɪŋɡw(ə)l/ *a.* of tongue; of speech or languages.

linguist /ˈlɪŋɡwɪst/ *n.* person skilled in languages or linguistics.

linguistic /lɪŋˈɡwɪstɪk/ *a.* of the study of languages; of language. **linguistically** *adv.*

linguistics *n.pl.* (usu. treated as *sing.*) study of languages.

liniment /ˈlɪnɪmənt/ *n.* embrocation, usu. made with oil.

lining /ˈlaɪnɪŋ/ *n.* layer of material used to line surface.

link **1** *n.* one loop or ring of chain etc.; thing or person that unites or provides continuity; member of series. **2** *v.* connect or join (*to, together, with*); clasp or intertwine.

linkage /ˈlɪŋkɪdʒ/ *n.* system of links; state of being linked.

links *n.pl.* (occas. treated as *sing.*) golf-course.

Linnaean /lɪˈniːən/ *a.* of Linnaeus or his classification of plants.

linnet /ˈlɪnɪt/ *n.* kind of song-bird.

lino /ˈlaɪnəʊ/ *n.* (*pl.* **-nos**) linoleum.

linocut design cut in relief on block of linoleum, print made from this.

linoleum /lɪˈnəʊlɪəm/ *n.* floor-covering of canvas thickly coated with a preparation of linseed oil etc.

Linotype /ˈlaɪnətaɪp/ *n.* **(P)** composing-machine producing lines of words as single slugs of metal.

linseed /ˈlɪnsiːd/ *n.* seed of flax.

linsey-woolsey /lɪnzɪ ˈwʊlzɪ/ *n.* fabric of coarse wool woven on cotton warp.

lint *n.* linen with one side made fluffy, used for dressing wounds; fluff.

lintel /ˈlɪnt(ə)l/ *n.* horizontal timber or stone over door or window.

lion /ˈlaɪən/ *n.* large powerful tawny carnivorous animal of cat family; celebrated person; brave person. **lioness** *n.*

lionize /ˈlaɪənaɪz/ *v.t.* treat as celebrity.

lip *n.* either edge of opening of mouth; edge of vessel or cavity etc.; *sl.* impudence. **lip-reading** method used esp. by deaf persons to understand speech from lip movements; **lip-read** *v.*; **lip-service** insincere expression of support; **lipstick** stick of cosmetic for colouring lips.

liquefy /ˈlɪkwɪfaɪ/ *v.* make or become liquid. **liquefaction** *n.*

liqueur /lɪˈkjʊə(r)/ *n.* drink made from a spirit sweetened and flavoured.

liquid /ˈlɪkwɪd/ 1 *a.* having consistency like that of water or oil; neither solid nor gaseous; having clearness of water; (of sounds) clear, pure; (of assets) easily convertible into cash. 2 *n.* liquid substance; sound of *l* or *r*. 3 **liquid crystal** liquid in state approaching that of crystalline solid.

liquidate /ˈlɪkwɪdeɪt/ *v.t.* wind up affairs of (company etc.); pay off (debt); put an end to, get rid of (often by violent means). **liquidator** *n.*

liquidation /lɪkwɪˈdeɪʃ(ə)n/ *n.* liquidating of company etc. **go into liquidation** be wound up and have assets apportioned.

liquidity /lɪˈkwɪdɪtɪ/ *n.* state of being liquid or having liquid assets.

liquidize /ˈlɪkwɪdaɪz/ *v.t.* reduce to liquid state.

liquidizer *n.* machine used for making purées etc.

liquor /ˈlɪkə(r)/ *n.* alcoholic (esp. distilled) drink; liquid used in or resulting from some process.

liquorice /ˈlɪkərɪs/ *n.* black substance used as sweet and in medicine; plant from whose root it is obtained.

lira /ˈlɪərə/ *n.* (*pl.* **lire** /ˈlɪəreɪ/ or **liras**) currency unit in Italy and Turkey.

lisle /laɪl/ *n.* fine smooth cotton thread used for stockings etc.

lisp 1 *v.* pronounce sibilants with sound like /θ/ or /ð/; say lispingly. 2 *n.* such pronunciation.

lissom /ˈlɪsəm/ *a.* lithe, agile.

list[1] 1 *n.* number of connected items or names etc. written or printed together; in *pl.* palisades enclosing tilting-ground. 2 *v.t.* arrange as or include in list. 3 **enter the lists** issue or accept challenge; **listed building** one of historical etc. importance having official protection from demolition etc.

list[2] 1 *v.i.* (of ship etc.) lean over to one side. 2 *n.* listing position, tilt.

listen /ˈlɪs(ə)n/ *v.i.* make effort to hear something, hear with attention; give attention with ear *to*; take notice. **listen in** tap communication made by telephone, listen to radio broadcast.

listless /ˈlɪstlɪs/ *a.* without energy or enthusiasm.

lit *past* & *p.p.* of **light**[1],[2].

litany /ˈlɪtənɪ/ *n.* series of supplications to God used in church services.

litchi /ˈliːtʃiː/ *n.* sweetish pulpy shelled fruit; tree bearing this.

literacy /ˈlɪtərəsɪ/ *n.* ability to read and write.

literal /ˈlɪtər(ə)l/ *a.* taking words in their usual sense without metaphor etc.; exactly corresponding to original. **literalism** *n.*

literary /ˈlɪtərərɪ/ *a.* of or concerned with or interested in literature.

literate /ˈlɪtərət/ 1 *a.* able to read and write. 2 *n.* literate person.

literati /lɪtəˈrɑːtɪ/ *n.pl.* literary or learned persons.

literature /ˈlɪtərətʃə(r)/ *n.* books and written works esp. of kind valued for form and style; the writings of a country or period etc.; *colloq.* printed matter.

lithe /laɪð/ *a.* flexible, supple.

litho /ˈlaɪθəʊ/ 1 *n.* (*pl.* -thos) lithographic process. 2 *a.* lithographic. 3 *v.t.* lithograph.

lithograph /ˈlɪθəgrɑːf/ 1 *n.* print produced by lithography. 2 *v.t.* produce such print of.

lithography /lɪˈθɒɡrəfɪ/ *n.* process of printing from stone or metal surface so treated that ink adheres only to the design to be printed. **lithographer** *n.*; **lithographic** *a.*

litigant /ˈlɪtɪɡənt/ 1 *n.* party to lawsuit. 2 *a.* engaged in lawsuit.

litigate /ˈlɪtɪɡeɪt/ *v.* go to law; contest (point) at law. **litigation** *n.*

litigious /lɪˈtɪdʒəs/ *a.* fond of litigation; contentious.

litmus /ˈlɪtməs/ *n.* blue colouring-matter turned red by acid and restored to blue by alkali.

litre /ˈliːtə(r)/ *n.* unit of capacity in metric system, about 1.75 pints.

litter /ˈlɪtə(r)/ 1 *n.* refuse, esp. paper, discarded on streets etc., odds and ends lying about; vehicle containing couch and carried on men's shoulders or by beasts of burden; kind of stretcher for sick and wounded; young animals brought forth at a birth; bedding for animals; material for filling receptacle for domestic cat etc. to urinate etc. in. 2 *v.t.* make (place) untidy; give birth to (young); provide (horse etc.) with bedding.

little /ˈlɪt(ə)l/ **1** *a.* small, not great or big; short in stature; of short distance or duration; working etc. on only small scale; trivial, mean; not much. **2** *n.* not much, only a small amount; *a* certain but no great amount; short time or distance. **3** *adv.* to a small extent only; not at all. **4 little by little** by degrees; **the little people** fairies.

littoral /ˈlɪtər(ə)l/ **1** *a.* of or on the shore. **2** *n.* region lying along the shore.

liturgy /ˈlɪtədʒɪ/ *n.* fixed form of public worship used in church. **liturgical** /-ˈtɜːdʒɪ-/ *a.*

live[1] /lɪv/ *v.* be alive, have life; continue alive; subsist or feed *on*; have one's home; conduct oneself; pass or spend; enjoy life to the full.

live[2] /laɪv/ *a.* that is alive, living; burning or glowing; capable of being exploded or kindled; charged with electricity; (of broadcast) heard or seen during occurrence of event, or undertaken with audience present; not obsolete or exhausted. **livestock** animals kept or dealt in for use or profit; **live wire** highly energetic forceful person.

liveable /ˈlɪvəb(ə)l/ *a.* worth living; fit to live in or *with*.

livelihood /ˈlaɪvlɪhʊd/ *n.* means of living; sustenance.

livelong /ˈlɪvlɒŋ/ *a.* in its entire length.

lively /ˈlaɪvlɪ/ *a.* full of life or energy or interest or vividness; cheerful, keen.

liven /ˈlaɪv(ə)n/ *v.* brighten or cheer (*up*).

liver[1] /ˈlɪvə(r)/ *n.* large glandular organ secreting bile; flesh of animal's liver as food; dark reddish-brown colour. **liver salts** salts for curing dyspepsia or biliousness.

liver[2] /ˈlɪvə(r)/ *n.* person who lives in specified way.

liverish /ˈlɪvərɪʃ/ *a.* suffering from disorder of liver; peevish.

liverwort /ˈlɪvəwɜːt/ *n.* lichen-like plant with lobed leaves.

livery /ˈlɪvərɪ/ *n.* distinctive clothes worn by male servant or member of City Company; distinctive guise or marking; allowance of provender for horses. **livery company** one of the London City Companies that formerly had distinctive costume; **livery stable** stable where horses are kept for owner or let out for hire.

livid /ˈlɪvɪd/ *a.* of bluish leaden colour; *colloq.* very angry.

living /ˈlɪvɪŋ/ **1** *n.* livelihood; position held by clergyman, providing income. **2** *a.* now alive; (of likeness) exact; (of language) still in vernacular use. **3 living-room** room for general day use; **living wage** wage on which one can live without privation; **withing living memory** that can still be remembered by living persons.

lizard /ˈlɪzəd/ *n.* reptile having usu. 4 legs and tail.

llama /ˈlɑːmə/ *n.* S. Amer. woolly-haired ruminant used as beast of burden.

Lloyd's /lɔɪdz/ *n.* incorporated society of underwriters in London. **Lloyd's Register** annual classified list of shipping.

lo *int. arch.* drawing attention.

loach *n.* small freshwater fish.

load 1 *n.* what is (to be) carried; amount usu. or actually carried; *fig.* weight of care or responsibility; *Electr.* amount of power supplied by generating station or carried by electric circuit; material object or force acting as a weight; in *pl. colloq.* plenty *of.* **2** *v.* put load on or aboard; place (load) aboard ship or on vehicle etc.; burden, strain; supply or assail overwhelmingly *with*; put ammunition in (firearm etc.); insert film in (camera); put (program, data, etc.) in computer memory. **3 load line** Plimsoll line.

loaded /ˈləʊdɪd/ *a.* (of question) carrying hidden implication; *sl.* rich, drunk, *US* drugged.

loadstone /ˈləʊdstəʊn/ *n.* magnetic oxide of iron; piece of it used as magnet; *fig.* thing that attracts.

loaf[1] *n.* (*pl.* **loaves**) quantity of bread baked alone or as part of batch; loaflike block of cooked minced meat etc.

loaf[2] *v.i.* spend time idly, hang about.

loam *n.* rich soil of clay and sand and decayed vegetable matter. **loamy** *a.*

loan 1 *n.* thing lent; sum to be returned with or without interest. **2** *v.t.* grant loan of. **3 loan-word** word adopted from one language from another.

loath /ləʊθ/ *pred.a.* disinclined, reluctant.

loathe /ləʊð/ *v.t.* regard with disgust. **loathing** *n.*

loathsome /ˈləʊðsəm/ a. repulsive, odious.

loaves pl. of **loaf**.

lob 1 v. send (ball) or send ball with slow or high-pitched motion. 2 n. such ball.

lobar /ˈləʊbə(r)/ a. of a lobe.

lobate /ˈləʊbeɪt/ a. having lobe(s).

lobby /ˈlɒbɪ/ 1 n. porch, entrance-hall; ante-room, corridor; (in House of Commons etc.) large hall open to public used esp. for interviews between MPs and others, one of two corridors to which members retire to vote; body of those who lobby. 2 v. seek to influence (MP etc.) by interviews etc. in lobby; solicit members' votes or influence of (person).

lobbyist /ˈlɒbɪɪst/ n. person who lobbies MP etc.

lobe /ləʊb/ n. lower soft pendulous part of outer ear; similar part of other organ.

lobelia /ləˈbiːlɪə/ n. herbaceous plant with brightly-coloured flowers.

lobotomy /ləˈbɒtəmɪ/ n. incision into frontal lobe of brain to relieve mental disorder.

lobster /ˈlɒbstə(r)/ n. large edible sea crustacean with heavy pincer-like claws; its flesh as food. **lobster-pot** basket in which lobsters are trapped.

lobworm /ˈlɒbwɜːm/ n. large earthworm used as fishing-bait.

local /ˈləʊk(ə)l/ 1 a. of place; belonging to or peculiar to certain place(s); of one's own neighbourhood; of or affecting a part and not the whole. 2 n. inhabitant of particular district; *colloq.* *the* local public house. 3 **local authority** body charged with administration of local government; **local colour** touches of detail in story etc. designed to provide convincing background; **local government** system of administration of county or district etc. by elected representatives of those who live there.

locale /ləˈkɑːl/ n. scene or locality of operations or events.

locality /ləʊˈkælɪtɪ/ n. thing's position; site or scene of something.

localize /ˈləʊkəlaɪz/ v.t. assign to particular place; invest with characteristics of place; decentralize. **localization** n.

locate /ləʊˈkeɪt/ v.t. discover exact place of; establish in a place; state locality of; in *pass.* be situated.

location /ləˈkeɪʃ(ə)n/ n. locating or being located; particular place; place other than studio where (part of) film is made.

loch /lɒx or lɒk/ n. Scottish lake or land-locked arm of the sea.

lock[1] n. mechanism for fastening door or lid etc.; section of canal or river confined within sluiced gates for shifting boats from one level to another; mechanism for exploding charge of gun; turning of front wheels of vehicle; interlocked or jammed state. 2 v. fasten with lock; shut *up* (house etc.); shut (person or thing) *up, in(to)*, or *out* by locking; be lockable; bring or come into rigidly fixed position; (cause to) jam or catch; store inaccessibly *up* or *away*. 3 **lockjaw** variety of tetanus in which jaws are rigidly closed; **lock-keeper** keeper of canal etc. lock; **lock-out** refusal by employer to allow employees access to place of work until they accept his conditions; **locksmith** maker and mender of locks; **lock-up** time or process of locking up, house or room for temporary detention of prisoners that is able to be locked.

lock[2] n. one of the portions into which the hair groups itself; in *pl.* the hair.

locker /ˈlɒkə(r)/ n. small lockable cupboard.

locket /ˈlɒkɪt/ n. small case containing portrait etc. usu. hung from neck.

locomotion /ləʊkəˈməʊʃ(ə)n/ n. (power of) motion from place to place, travel.

locomotive /ləʊkəˈməʊtɪv/ 1 n. locomotive engine. 2 a. of or effecting locomotion, not stationary. 3 **locomotive engine** engine for drawing trains.

locum /ˈləʊkəm/ n. deputy acting esp. for clergyman or doctor.

locus /ˈləʊkəs/ n. (*pl.* **loci** /ˈləʊsaɪ/) *Math.* curve etc. made by all points satisfying certain conditions or by defined motion of point or line or surface.

locust /ˈləʊkəst/ n. African or Asian grasshopper migrating in swarms and consuming all vegetation; any of various kinds of tree and their fruit.

locution /ləˈkjuːʃ(ə)n/ n. phrase or idiom; style of speech.

lode n. vein of metal ore. **lodestar** star used as guide in navigation, esp. polestar; **lodestone** var. of **loadstone**.

lodge 1 n. small house, esp. one at entrance to park or grounds of large house; porter's room etc.; members or meeting-place of branch of society such as Freemasons; beaver's or otter's lair. 2 v. provide with sleeping-quarters; reside as lodger; deposit for security or attention; fix in; settle, place.

lodger n. person paying for accommodation in another's house.

lodging n. accommodation in hired rooms, dwelling-place; in pl. room(s) rented for lodging in.

loft 1 n. attic; room over stable; gallery in church or hall; pigeon-house. 2 v.t. hit or throw or kick etc. (ball) high up.

lofty /ˈlɒftɪ/ a. of imposing height; haughty, keeping aloof; exalted, sublime.

log[1] 1 n. unhewn piece of felled tree; any large rough piece of wood; apparatus for ascertaining ship's speed; detailed record of ship's or aircraft's voyage or of progress or performance. 2 v.t. enter in ship's log-book; enter (data etc.) in regular record; cut into logs. 3 **log-book** log of ship etc., book showing registration details of motor vehicle; **log in, out**, begin, finish, operations at terminal of esp. multi-access computer.

log[2] n. logarithm.

loganberry /ˈləʊɡənbərɪ/ n. hybrid between raspberry and Amer. blackberry.

logan /ˈləʊɡən/ n. (in full **logan-stone**) poised heavy stone rocking at a touch.

logarithm /ˈlɒɡərɪð(ə)m/ n. one of a series of reckoning-numbers tabulated to simplify computation. **logarithmic** a.

loggerhead /ˈlɒɡəhed/ n. **at loggerheads** disagreeing or disputing (with).

loggia /ˈləʊdʒə/ n. open-sided gallery or arcade; open-sided extension to house.

logging /ˈlɒɡɪŋ/ n. felling, cutting, and transporting timber.

logic /ˈlɒdʒɪk/ n. science of reasoning; chain of reasoning, use of or ability in argument. **logician** n.

logical /ˈlɒdʒɪk(ə)l/ a. of logic; in conformity with laws of logic; rightly deducible; capable of correct reasoning. **logicality** n.

logistics /ləˈdʒɪstɪks/ n.pl. art of supplying and organizing (orig. military) services and equipment. **logistic** a.; **logistically** adv.

logo /ˈləʊɡəʊ/ n. (pl. **-gos**) logotype.

logotype /ˈlɒɡətaɪp/ n. non-heraldic device as badge of an organization; piece of type with this.

loin n. in pl. part of body on both sides of spine between ribs and hip-bones; in sing. joint of meat cut from loins. **loincloth** cloth worn round loins esp. as sole garment.

loiter /ˈlɔɪtə(r)/ v.i. linger on way; hang about.

loll v. recline or sit or stand in lazy attitude; (of tongue) hang out.

lollipop /ˈlɒlɪpɒp/ n. large boiled sweet on stick. **lollipop man** etc. colloq. official using circular sign on stick to stop traffic for children to cross road.

lollop /ˈlɒləp/ v.i. colloq. move or proceed in lounging or ungainly way; flop about.

lolly /ˈlɒlɪ/ n. colloq. lollipop; sl. money.

lone a. poet. solitary, uninhabited, lonely. **lone hand** hand played or player playing against the rest at cards, fig. person or action without allies; **lone wolf** loner.

lonely /ˈləʊnlɪ/ a. lacking friends or companions; sad because of this; solitary, isolated. **loneliness** n.

loner /ˈləʊnə(r)/ n. person or animal preferring not to associate with others.

lonesome /ˈləʊnsəm/ a. lonely; causing loneliness.

long[1] 1 a. measuring much from end to end in space or time; of specified length; seemingly more than stated amount; lasting or reaching far back or forward in time; of elongated shape; remarkable for or concerned with length or duration. 2 n. long interval or period; long vowel or syllable. 3 adv. for or by a long time; throughout specified time; in compar. after implied point of time. 4 **in the long run** ultimately; **longboat** sailing ship's largest boat; **longbow** one drawn by hand and shooting long arrow; **long-distance** travelling or operating between distant places; **long face** dismal expression; **longhand** ordinary handwriting; **long johns** *colloq.* underpants with full-length legs; **long jump** jump measured along ground; **long-life** (of milk etc.) treated to prolong shelf-life; **long odds** very uneven chances; **long-playing** (of gramophone record) playing about 15–30 minutes on each side; **long-range** having a long range, relating to long period of future time; **long-shore** found or employed on or frequenting the shore; **long shot** wild guess or venture; **long sight** ability to see clearly only what is comparatively distant; **long-sighted** having long sight or foresight; **long-suffering** bearing provocation patiently; **long-term** occurring in or relating to long period of time; **long-winded** inclined to talk or write at tedious length.

long² *v.i.* wish earnestly or vehemently (*for, to*).

long. *abbr.* longitude.

longevity /lɒnˈdʒevɪtɪ/ *n.* long life.

longitude /ˈlɒŋgɪtjuːd/ *n.* angular distance E. or W. of the meridian of Greenwich.

longitudinal /lɒŋgɪˈtjuːdɪn(ə)l/ *a.* of longitude; of or in length; lying longways.

longways /ˈlɒŋweɪz/ *adv.* (also **longwise**) in direction parallel with thing's length.

loo *n. colloq.* lavatory.

loofah /ˈluːfə/ *n.* dried pod of a kind of gourd used as rough sponge.

look /lʊk/ *v.* use or direct one's eyes; make search; have specified appearance, seem; contemplate, examine; face or be turned in specified direction; indicate by looks; expect *to do* thing. 2 *n.* act of looking; gaze or glance; expression of face; appearance; in *pl.* personal appearance. 3 **look after** attend to; **look down (up)on** consider oneself superior to; **look forward to** await eagerly or with specified feelings; **look in** make short visit; **looking-glass** glass mirror; **look into** investigate; **look on** be mere spectator; **look out** be vigilant or prepared (*for*); **look-out** watch, observation-post, person etc. stationed to look out, prospect of luck, person's own concern; **look up** search for in book of reference, improve; **look up to** respect.

loom¹ /luːm/ *n.* apparatus for weaving.

loom² /luːm/ *v.i.* appear dimly; be seen in vague and often magnified shape.

loon /luːn/ *n.* kind of diving bird; *sl.* crazy person.

loony /ˈluːnɪ/ *n. sl.* lunatic.

loop /luːp/ *n.* figure produced by curve or doubled string etc. crossing itself; similarly shaped attachment or ornament used as fastening etc.; endless strip of tape or film allowing continuous repetition. 2 *v.* form (string etc.) into loop; enclose (as) with loop; fasten with loops; form loop. 3 **loop-line** railway or telegraph line that diverges from main line and joins it again.

loophole /ˈluːphəʊl/ *n.* means of evading rule etc. without infringing letter of it; narrow vertical slit in wall.

loopy /ˈluːpɪ/ *a. sl.* crazy.

loose /luːs/ 1 *a.* released from bonds or restraint; detached or detachable from its place; not held together or fixed; slack; not compact or dense; inexact, vague; morally lax. 2 *v.* release, free, untie, undo; detach from moorings; relax. 3 **at a loose end** without definite occupation; **loose box** stall in which horse can move about; **loose change** money as coins in pocket etc.; **loose cover** removable cover for chair etc.; **loose-leaf** (of book) with each leaf separately removable; **loose-limbed** having supple limbs; **on the loose** having a spree.

loosen /ˈluːs(ə)n/ *v.* make or become less tight or compact or firm.

loot /luːt/ 1 *n.* booty, spoil; *sl.* money. 2 *v.* take loot (from); carry off (as) loot.

lop¹ *v.t.* cut away branches or twigs of; cut away.

lop² *v.i.* hang limply. **lop-eared** having drooping ears; **lop-sided** with one side lower, unevenly balanced.

lope /ləʊp/ 1 *v.i.* run with long bounding stride. 2 *n.* such stride.

loquacious /lɒˈkweɪʃəs/ *a.* talkative. **loquacity** *n.*

lord 1 *n.* master, ruler; *hist.* feudal superior; peer of realm; **Lord** prefixed as designation of certain ranks of peerage, or to Christian name of younger son of duke or marquis. **2** *int.* expr. surprise or consternation. **3** *v.* **lord it** domineer. **4 the Lord** God or Christ; **the Lords** the House of Lords; **Lord's day** Sunday; **Lord's Prayer** that beginning 'Our Father'; **Lord's Supper** Eucharist.

lordly /ˈlɔːdlɪ/ *a.* haughty, imperious; suitable for a lord.

lordship /ˈlɔːdʃɪp/ *n.* title used in addressing or referring to man with rank of Lord.

lore *n.* body of tradition and facts on a subject.

lorgnette /lɔːˈnjet/ *n.* pair of eyeglasses held to eyes by long handle.

lorn *a. arch.* desolate, forlorn.

lorry /ˈlɒrɪ/ *n.* motor truck for transporting goods etc.

lose /luːz/ *v.* (*past & p.p.* **lost**) be deprived of; cease to have; be unable to find; fail to keep in sight etc.; let pass from one's control; get rid of; be defeated in; forfeit; suffer loss or detriment; cause person the loss of; (of clock) become slow; in *pass.* disappear, perish.

loser /ˈluːzə(r)/ *n.* person who loses contest or game etc.; *colloq.* person who regularly fails.

loss *n.* losing; what is lost; detriment resulting from losing. **at a loss** *sold* etc. for less than was paid to buy it; **be at a loss** be puzzled or uncertain; **loss-leader** article sold at a loss to attract customers.

lost 1 *past & p.p.* of **lose**. **2** *a.* vanished; dead; deprived of help or salvation; astray.

lot *n. colloq.* considerable or (in *pl.*) great quantity or amount or number; each of set of objects used in securing chance selection; this method of deciding, share or office etc. given by it; destiny, fortune; piece or allotment of land; article or set of articles for sale at auction etc.; number or quantity of associated persons or things. **bad lot** disreputable etc. person; **the lot** total number or quantity.

loth var. of **loath.**

lotion /ˈləʊʃ(ə)n/ *n.* liquid preparation for skin as healing or cosmetic agent.

lottery /ˈlɒtərɪ/ *n.* arrangement for distributing prizes by chance among purchasers of numbered tickets, as a means of raising money.

lotto /ˈlɒtəʊ/ *n.* game of chance with numbers drawn at random.

lotus /ˈləʊtəs/ *n.* legendary plant inducing luxurious languor in the eater; kind of water-lily. **lotus position** cross-legged position of meditation

loud /laʊd/ **1** *a.* strongly audible; noisy; obtrusive. **2** *adv.* loudly. **3 loudspeaker** apparatus that converts electrical signals into sounds.

lough /lɒk or lɒx/ *n. Ir.* loch.

lounge /laʊndʒ/ **1** *v.i.* loll, recline; stand or move lazily, idle. **2** *n.* spell of or place for lounging; place in airport etc. with seats for waiting passengers; sitting-room in house. **3 lounge-suit** man's suit for ordinary day wear.

lour /ˈlaʊə(r)/ *v.i.* frown, look sullen; (of sky etc.) look dark and threatening.

louse /laʊs/ *n.* (*pl.* **lice**) kind of parasitic insect; *sl.* (*pl.* **louses**) contemptible person.

lousy /ˈlaʊzɪ/ *a.* infested with lice; *sl.* disgusting or bad; *sl.* abundantly supplied, swarming, *with.*

lout /laʊt/ *n.* hulking or rough-mannered fellow. **loutish** *a.*

louvre /ˈluːvə(r)/ *n.* one of set of overlapping boards etc. to admit air and exclude light or rain; domed erection on roof with side-openings for ventilation etc.

lovable /ˈlʌvəb(ə)l/ *a.* inspiring affection.

lovage /ˈlʌvɪdʒ/ *n.* herb used for flavouring etc.

love /lʌv/ **1** *n.* fondness, warm affection; sexual passion; sweetheart; beloved one; *colloq.* delightful person or thing; (in games) no score, nil. **2** *v.* be in love (with); feel affection for; delight in, admire; *colloq.* like, be delighted. **3 in love (with)** inspired with sexual love (for); **love-affair** relationship between two people in love; **love-bird** kind of parakeet; **love-in-a-mist** blue-flowered garden plant; **lovelorn** pining with unrequited love; **lovesick** languishing with love; **make love** pay amorous attentions *to*, have sexual intercourse.

loveless /ˈlʌvlɪs/ *a.* unloving, unloved.

lovely /ˈlʌvlɪ/ *a.* exquisitely beautiful; *colloq.* delightful. **loveliness** *n.*

lover /ˈlʌvə(r)/ n. person (esp. man) in love; admirer or devotee (of); in pl. pair in love.

loving /ˈlʌvɪŋ/ a. affectionate. **loving-cup** two-handled drinking-cup passed round at banquets.

low[1] /ləʊ/ 1 a. not high or tall or reaching far up; not elevated in position; of humble rank; of small or less than normal amount; lacking vigour, dejected; not shrill or loud; (of opinion) unfavourable; mean, vulgar. 2 n. low or lowest level or number; area of low barometric pressure. 3 adv. in or to low position; in low tone, at low pitch. 4 **keep a low profile** remain inconspicuous; **lowbrow** colloq. (person) not highly intellectual or cultured; **Low Church** section of Church of England giving low place to ritual and priestly authority and sacraments; **Low Countries** Netherlands, Belgium, and Luxembourg; **low-down** abject, dishonourable, (n.) sl. relevant information on; **Low Sunday** next Sunday after Easter; **low water** tide.

low[2] /ləʊ/ 1 n. sound made by cows. 2 v.i. make this sound.

lower[1] /ˈləʊə(r)/ v. let or haul down; make or become lower; diminish height or elevation of, degrade.

lower[2] var. of **lour**.

lowland /ˈləʊlənd/ 1 n. (usu. in pl.) low-lying country esp. (**Lowlands**) less mountainous part of Scotland. 2 a. of lowland or Sc. Lowlands. 3 **lowlander** n.

lowly /ˈləʊlɪ/ a. humble, unpretending. **lowliness** n.

loyal /ˈlɔɪəl/ a. faithful; true to allegiance; devoted to legitimate sovereign etc. **loyalty** n.

loyalist /ˈlɔɪəlɪst/ 1 a. remaining loyal to ruler or government etc. 2 n. loyalist person.

lozenge /ˈlɒzɪndʒ/ n. small sweet or medicinal etc. tablet to be dissolved in mouth; rhombus, diamond figure; lozenge-shaped thing.

LP abbr. long-playing (record).

L-plate /ˈelpleɪt/ n. sign bearing letter L, affixed to front and rear of motor vehicle to indicate that it is being driven by learner driver.

LSD abbr. lysergic acid diethylamide, a powerful hallucinogenic drug.

LT abbr. low tension.

Lt. abbr. Lieutenant.

Ltd. abbr. Limited.

lubber /ˈlʌbə(r)/ n. clumsy fellow, lout.

lubberly a. awkward, unskilful.

lubricant /ˈluːbrɪkənt/ n. substance used to reduce friction in machinery etc.

lubricate /ˈluːbrɪkeɪt/ v.t. apply lubricant to (machinery); make slippery. **lubrication** n.

lubricious /luːˈbrɪʃəs/ a. slippery; lewd. **lubricity** n.

lucerne /luːˈsɜːn/ n. alfalfa.

lucid /ˈluːsɪd/ a. expressing or expressed clearly. **lucidity** n.

luck n. good or ill fortune, chance; success due to chance.

luckless /ˈlʌklɪs/ a. invariably having ill luck; ending in failure.

lucky /ˈlʌkɪ/ a. having or resulting from good luck; bringing good luck. **lucky dip** tub containing articles from which one chooses at random.

lucrative /ˈluːkrətɪv/ a. yielding considerable profit.

lucre /ˈluːkə(r)/ n. pecuniary gain as motive; joc. money.

ludicrous /ˈluːdɪkrəs/ a. absurd, ridiculous, laughable.

ludo /ˈluːdəʊ/ n. board game played with dice and counters.

lug 1 v. drag with effort or violence; pull hard at. 2 n. hard or rough pull; projection on object by which it may be carried or fixed in place etc.; colloq. ear.

luggage /ˈlʌgɪdʒ/ n. bags etc. for containing traveller's belongings.

lugger /ˈlʌgə(r)/ n. small ship with 4-cornered sails (**lugsails**) set fore and aft.

lugubrious /luːˈguːbrɪəs/ a. doleful.

lukewarm /luːkˈwɔːm/ a. moderately warm, tepid; indifferent.

lull 1 v. send to sleep; soothe; quiet (suspicion) usu. by deception; (of storm or noise) lessen, fall quiet. 2 n. intermission in storm etc., interval of quiet.

lullaby /ˈlʌləbaɪ/ n. soothing song to send child to sleep.

lumbago /lʌmˈbeɪgəʊ/ n. rheumatic pain in muscles of loins.

lumbar /ˈlʌmbə(r)/ a. of loins.

lumber /'lʌmbə(r)/ **1** *n.* disused and cumbersome articles; useless stuff; partly prepared timber. **2** *v.* obstruct, encumber, *with*; move in blundering noisy way; cut and prepare forest timber. **3 lumberjack, lumberman**, feller or dresser or conveyor of lumber; **lumber-room** room where disused articles are kept.

luminary /'lu:mɪnərɪ/ *n.* natural light-giving body, esp. sun or moon; person noted for learning etc.

luminescent /lu:mɪ'nes(ə)nt/ *a.* emitting light without heat. **luminescence** *n.*

luminous /'lu:mɪnəs/ *a.* emitting light; phosphorescent and so visible in darkness. **luminosity** *n.*

lump¹ 1 *n.* compact shapeless mass; protuberance or swelling; heavy ungainly person etc. **2** *v.* class or mass *together*. **3 lump sugar** sugar in small lumps or cubes; **lump sum** sum including number of items or paid down all at once.

lump² *v.t. colloq.* (in contrast with *like*) put up with ungraciously.

lumpish /'lʌmpɪʃ/ *a.* heavy, clumsy, dull.

lumpy /'lʌmpɪ/ *a.* full of or covered with lumps.

lunacy /'lu:nəsɪ/ *n.* insanity; great folly.

lunar /'lu:nə(r)/ *a.* of or like or concerned with or determined by the moon. **lunar month** lunation, *pop.* period of four weeks.

lunate /'lu:neɪt/ *a.* crescent-shaped.

lunatic /'lu:nətɪk/ **1** *a.* insane; eccentric, outrageously foolish. **2** *n.* lunatic person.

lunation /lu:'neɪʃ(ə)n/ *n.* interval between new moons, about 29½ days.

lunch 1 *n.* midday meal; light refreshment at mid-morning. **2** *v.* take lunch; provide lunch for.

luncheon /'lʌntʃ(ə)n/ *n. formal* midday meal. **luncheon voucher** voucher given to employee as part of pay and exchangeable for food at restaurant etc.

lung *n.* either of pair of air-breathing organs in man and most vertebrates.

lunge 1 *n.* sudden throwing forward of body in thrusting or hitting; thrust. **2** *v.* deliver or make lunge; drive (weapon etc.) violently.

lupin /'lu:pɪn/ *n.* garden or fodder plant with long tapering spikes of flowers.

lupine /'lu:paɪn/ *a.* of or like wolves.

lupus /'lu:pəs/ *n.* ulcerous disease of skin.

lurch¹ 1 *n.* sudden shift of weight to one side. **2** *v.i.* make lurch, stagger.

lurch² *n.* **leave in the lurch** desert in difficulties.

lurcher /'lɜ:tʃə(r)/ *n.* cross-bred dog between collie and greyhound.

lure 1 *v.t.* entice; recall with lure. **2** *n.* thing used to entice, enticing quality; falconer's apparatus for recalling hawk.

lurid /'ljʊərɪd/ *a.* strong and glaring in colour etc.; sensational; horrifying; ghastly.

lurk *v.i.* keep out of sight, be hidden; be latent or elusive.

luscious /'lʌʃəs/ *a.* richly sweet in taste or smell; voluptuously attractive.

lush *a.* luxuriant and succulent.

lust 1 *n.* strong sexual desire; passionate desire *for* or enjoyment *of*; sensuous appetite. **2** *v.i.* have strong or excessive (esp. sexual) desire (*after*, *for*). **3** lustful *a.*

lustre /'lʌstə(r)/ *n.* gloss; shining surface; brilliance, splendour; (pottery or porcelain with) iridescent glaze. **lustrous** *a.*

lusty /'lʌstɪ/ *a.* healthy and strong; vigorous, lively.

lute¹ *n.* guitar-like musical instrument with pear-shaped body. **lutanist, lutenist, lutenist** *n.*

lute² *n.* composition for making joints airtight.

Lutheran /'lu:θərən/ **1** *a.* of Martin Luther or the Protestant doctrines associated with him. **2** *n.* follower of Luther; member of Lutheran Church. **3 Lutheranism** *n.*

luxuriant /lʌg'zjʊərɪənt/ *a.* growing profusely; exuberant, florid. **luxuriance** *n.*

luxuriate /lʌg'zjʊərɪeɪt/ *v.i.* revel or feel keen delight *in*.

luxurious /lʌg'zjʊərɪəs/ *a.* supplied with luxuries; very comfortable; fond of luxury.

luxury /'lʌkʃərɪ/ *n.* choice or costly

food, furniture, etc.; habitual use of these; thing desirable for comfort or enjoyment but not essential.

LV *abbr.* luncheon voucher.

lychgate var. of **lichgate**.

lye /laɪ/ *n.* water made alkaline with wood ashes etc.; other alkaline solution for washing.

lying *partic.* of **lie**¹,².

lymph /lɪmf/ *n.* colourless fluid from tissues or organs of body.

lymphatic /lɪm'fætɪk/ *a.* of or secreting or conveying lymph; (of person) flabby, pale.

lynch /lɪntʃ/ *v.t.* execute by mob action without legal trial.

lynx /lɪŋks/ *n.* animal of cat family with short tail, spotted fur, and proverbially keen sight.

lyre /laɪə(r)/ *n.* ancient U-shaped stringed instrument used esp. for accompanying song.

lyric /'lɪrɪk/ **1** *a.* (of poem) expressing writer's emotions; (of poet) writing lyric poetry; meant to be sung; of the nature of song. **2** *n.* lyric poem; (often in *pl.*) words of song. **3 lyricism** /-sɪz(ə)m/ *n.*

lyrical /'lɪrɪk(ə)l/ *a.* resembling or using language appropriate to lyric poetry; *colloq.* highly enthusiastic.

lyricist /'lɪrɪsɪst/ *n.* writer of lyrics.

M

M, m, *n*. Roman numeral 1,000.

M *abbr*. mega-; motorway.

M. *abbr*. Master; *Monsieur*.

m. *abbr*. metre(s); mile(s); million(s); milli-; minute(s); masculine; married; male.

ma /mɑː/ *n. colloq*. mother.

MA *abbr*. Master of Arts.

ma'am /mɑːm/ *n*. madam (esp. used in addressing royal lady or female officer etc.).

mac *n. colloq*. mackintosh.

macabre /məˈkɑːbr/ *a*. gruesome, grim.

macadam /məˈkædəm/ *n*. material for road-making with successive layers of broken stone compacted; tar macadam. **macadamize** *v.t.*

macaroni /mækəˈrəʊnɪ/ *n*. pasta formed into tubes.

macaroon /mækəˈruːn/ *n*. biscuit made of ground almonds etc.

macaw /məˈkɔː/ *n*. kind of parrot.

mace[1] *n*. staff of office, esp. symbol of Speaker's authority in House of Commons; *hist*. heavy usu. spiked club.

mace[2] *n*. dried outer covering of nutmeg used as spice.

macédoine /ˈmæsɪdwɑːn/ *n*. mixture of fruits or vegetables, esp. cut up small.

macerate /ˈmæsəreɪt/ *v*. make or become soft by soaking. **maceration** *n.*

machete /məˈtʃetɪ/ *n*. broad heavy knife used in Central America and W. Indies.

machiavellian /mækɪəˈvelɪən/ *a*. unscrupulous, cunning.

machination /mæʃɪˈneɪʃ(ə)n/ *n*. (usu. in pl.) intrigue, scheme, plot.

machine /məˈʃiːn/ 1 *n*. apparatus for applying mechanical power, having several parts each with definite function; bicycle; motor cycle, etc.; aircraft; computer; controlling system of an organization. 2 *v.t.* work or operate on with machine (esp. of sewing or printing). 3 **machine-gun** mounted automatic gun giving continuous fire; **machine readable** in form that computer can process; **machine tool** mechanically operated tool for working on metal, wood, or plastics.

machinery /məˈʃiːnərɪ/ *n*. machines;

mechanism; organized system, means arranged.

machinist /məˈʃiːnɪst/ *n*. person who works machine.

machismo /məˈtʃɪzməʊ/ *n*. virility, masculine pride.

Mach number /mɑːk/ ratio of speed of body to speed of sound in surrounding medium.

macho /ˈmætʃəʊ/ *a*. ostentatiously manly or virile.

mack var. of **mac**.

mackerel /ˈmækər(ə)l/ *n*. edible seafish. **mackerel sky** sky dappled with rows of small fleecy white clouds.

mackintosh /ˈmækɪntɒʃ/ *n*. waterproof coat or cloak; cloth waterproofed with rubber.

macramé /məˈkrɑːmɪ/ *n*. art of knotting cord or string in patterns; work so made.

macrobiotic /mækrəʊbaɪˈɒtɪk/ *a*. relating to or following diet intended to prolong life.

macrocosm /ˈmækrəʊkɒz(ə)m/ *n*. universe; any great whole.

mad *a*. with disordered mind, insane; frenzied; wildly foolish; infatuated; *colloq*. annoyed. **madcap** reckless person; **madhouse** *hist*. mental home or hospital, confused uproar; **madman**, **-woman**, mad person. **madness** *n.*

madam /ˈmædəm/ *n*. polite formal address to woman; woman brothelkeeper; *colloq*. conceited etc. young woman.

Madame /məˈdɑːm/ *n*. (*pl*. **Mesdames** /meɪˈdɑːm/) title uesd of or to Frenchspeaking woman.

madden /ˈmæd(ə)n/ *v.t.* make mad; irritate.

madder /ˈmædə(r)/ *n*. herbaceous climbing plant; red dye obtained from its root; synthetic substitute for this dye.

made *past* & *p.p.* of **make**.

Madeira /məˈdɪərə/ *n*. fortified wine from Madeira. **Madeira cake** kind of rich sweet sponge-cake.

Mademoiselle /mædəmwəˈzel/ *n*. (*pl*. **Mesdemoiselles** /meɪdmwəˈzel/) title used of or to unmarried Frenchspeaking woman. [F]

madonna /məˈdɒnə/ *n.* (*pl.* **-as**) (picture or statue of) Virgin Mary.

madras /məˈdrɑːs/ *n.* cotton fabric woven with coloured stripes etc.

madrigal /ˈmædrɪɡ(ə)l/ *n.* *Mus.* part-song for several voices, usu. unaccompanied.

maelstrom /ˈmeɪlstrəm/ *n.* great whirlpool.

maestro /ˈmaɪstrəʊ/ *n.* (*pl.* **-os**) eminent musical teacher or conductor.

Mafia /ˈmæfɪə/ *n.* organized international body of criminals.

Mafioso /mæfɪˈəʊsəʊ/ *n.* (*pl.* **-si** /-sɪ/) member of the Mafia.

magazine /mæɡəˈziːn/ *n.* periodical publication containing contributions by various writers; store for explosives, arms, or military provisions; chamber containing supply of cartridges fed automatically to breech of gun; similar device in camera, slide-projector, etc.

magenta /məˈdʒentə/ *n.* shade of crimson; aniline dye of this colour.

maggot /ˈmæɡət/ *n.* larva, esp. of blue-bottle. **maggoty** *a.*

Magi /ˈmeɪdʒaɪ/ *n. pl.* priests of ancient Persia; *the* 'wise men from the East' in the Gospel.

magic /ˈmædʒɪk/ **1** *n.* art of influencing events by occult control of nature or spirits; conjuring tricks; inexplicable or remarkable influence. **2** *a.* of or involving magic. **3 magic carpet** mythical carpet able to transport person on it to any place; **magic lantern** simple form of image-projector using slides.

magical /ˈmædʒɪk(ə)l/ *a.* of magic; resembling or involving or produced as if by magic.

magician /məˈdʒɪʃ(ə)n/ *n.* person skilled in magic; conjurer.

magisterial /mædʒɪˈstɪərɪəl/ *a.* authoritative; dictatorial; of a magistrate.

magistracy /ˈmædʒɪstrəsɪ/ *n.* magisterial office; magistrates.

magistrate /ˈmædʒɪstreɪt/ *n.* civil officer administering law, esp. one trying minor offences etc.

magnanimous /mæɡˈnænɪməs/ *a.* noble, generous, not petty, in feelings or conduct. **magnanimity** /-ˈnɪm-/ *n.*

magnate /ˈmæɡneɪt/ *n.* person of wealth, authority, etc.

magnesia /mæɡˈniːʃə/ *n.* magnesium oxide; hydrated magnesium carbonate used as antacid and laxative.

magnesium /mæɡˈniːzɪəm/ *n.* silver-white metallic element.

magnet /ˈmæɡnɪt/ *n.* piece of iron, steel, etc., having properties of attracting iron and of pointing approx. north when suspended; *fig.* person or thing that attracts.

magnetic /mæɡˈnetɪk/ *a.* having properties of magnet; produced or acting by magnetism; *fig.* very attractive. **magnetic field** area of influence of magnet; **magnetic north** point indicated by north end of compass-needle; **magnetic storm** disturbance of earth's magnetic field; **magnetic tape** impregnated or coated plastic strip for recording and reproduction of signals.

magnetism /ˈmæɡnɪtɪz(ə)m/ *n.* magnetic phenomena; science of these; *fig.* personal charm.

magnetize /ˈmæɡnɪtaɪz/ *v.t.* make into magnet; attract like magnet. **magnetization** *n.*

magneto /mæɡˈniːtəʊ/ *n.* (*pl.* **-tos**) electric generator using permanent magnets (esp. for ignition in internal combustion engine).

magnificent /mæɡˈnɪfɪs(ə)nt/ *a.* splendid; imposing; excellent. **magnificence** *n.*

magnify /ˈmæɡnɪfaɪ/ *v.t.* make (thing) appear larger than it is, as with lens (**magnifying glass**) etc.; exaggerate; *arch.* extol. **magnification** *n.*

magnitude /ˈmæɡnɪtjuːd/ *n.* largeness, size; importance.

magnolia /mæɡˈnəʊlɪə/ *n.* kind of flowering tree; very pale pinkish colour of its flowers.

magnum /ˈmæɡnəm/ *n.* two-quart bottle.

magpie /ˈmæɡpaɪ/ *n.* kind of crow with long tail and black-and-white plumage; random collector.

Magyar /ˈmæɡjɑː(r)/ **1** *n.* member of the people now predominant in Hungary; their language. **2** *a.* of this people.

maharaja /mɑːhəˈrɑːjə/ *n. hist.* (also **maharajah**) title of some Indian princes.

maharanee /mɑːhəˈrɑːnɪ/ *n. hist.* (also **maharani**) maharaja's wife or widow.

maharishi /mɑːhəˈrɪʃɪ/ *n*. great Hindu sage.

mahatma /məˈhætmə/ *n*. (in India etc.) person regarded with reverence.

mah-jong /mɑːˈdʒɒŋ/ *n*. (also **-jongg**) orig. Chinese game played with 136 or 144 pieces.

mahogany /məˈhɒgənɪ/ *n*. reddish-brown wood used for furniture etc.; colour of this.

mahout /məˈhaʊt/ *n*. elephant-driver.

maid *n*. female domestic servant; *arch*. girl, young woman. **maidservant** female domestic servant.

maiden /ˈmeɪd(ə)n/ 1 *n. arch*. girl, virgin, young unmarried woman; *Crick*. maiden over. 2 *a*. unmarried; (of voyage, speech by MP, etc.) first. 3 **maidenhair** delicate kind of fern; **maiden name** woman's surname before marriage; **maiden over** *Crick*. over in which no runs are scored. 4 **maidenly** *a*.

mail[1] 1 *n*. letters etc. conveyed by post; the post; vehicle carrying mail. 2 *v.t.* send by mail. 3 **mail order** purchase of goods by post.

mail[2] *n*. armour of metal rings or plates.

maim *v.t.* cripple, mutilate.

main 1 *a*. chief, principal, most important. 2 *n*. principal channel for water or gas etc. or (usu. in *pl*.) electricity; *arch*. high seas. 3 **in the main** for the most part; **mainland** continuous extent of land excluding neighbouring islands etc.; **mainmast** principal mast; **mainsail** lowest sail or sail set on after part of mainmast; **mainspring** principal spring of watch or clock, *fig*. chief motive power etc.; **mainstay** chief support; **mainstream** prevailing trend of opinion, fashion, etc.

mainly /ˈmeɪnlɪ/ *adv*. for the most part, chiefly.

maintain /meɪnˈteɪn/ *v.t.* keep up; keep going; keep in repair; support; assert as true.

maintenance /ˈmeɪntɪnəns/ *n*. maintaining or being maintained; (provision of) enough to support life; alimony.

maisonette /meɪzəˈnet/ *n*. part of house let or sold separately; small house.

maize /meɪz/ *n*. N: Amer. cereal plant; grain of this.

Maj. *abbr*. Major.

majestic /məˈdʒestɪk/ *a*. stately and dignified; imposing. **majestically** *adv*.

majesty /ˈmædʒɪstɪ/ *n*. stateliness of aspect, language, etc.; sovereign power; title used in speaking to or of sovereign or sovereign's wife or widow.

majolica /məˈjɒlɪkə/ *n*. kind of ornamented Italian earthenware.

major /ˈmeɪdʒə(r)/ 1 *a*. greater or relatively great in size etc.; of full legal age; unusually serious or significant; *Mus*. of or based on scale having semitone next above third and seventh notes. 2 *n*. army officer next below lieutenant-colonel; person of full legal age; *US* student's special subject or course. 3 *v.i. US* undertake major course, qualify *in* as a major. 4 **major-domo** (*pl*. **-mos**) house-steward; **major-general** army officer next below lieutenant-general.

majority /məˈdʒɒrɪtɪ/ *n*. greater number or part (*of*); number by which winning vote exceeds next; full legal age; rank of major.

make 1 *v*. (*past & p.p.* **made**) construct, frame, create, from parts or other substance; bring about, give rise to; prepare for consumption or use; write, compose; frame in the mind; establish, enact; gain, acquire, obtain as result; secure advancement or success of; cause to be or become; compel (to); execute, perform; represent as, consider (to be); constitute, amount to; accomplish; achieve place in. 2 *n*. way thing is made; origin of manufacture, brand. 3 **make believe** pretend; **make-believe** pretended, pretence; **make do** manage (*with* substitute etc.); **make for** be conducive to, proceed towards; **make good** compensate for, repair, fulfil (promise), succeed in an undertaking; **make off** depart hastily; **make out** draw up, write out, understand, distinguish by sight or hearing, pretend, make progress; **makeshift** (serving as) temporary substitute or device; **make up** serve or act to overcome (deficiency), complete, put together, prepare, invent (story), form or constitute, apply cosmetics (to); **make-up** disguise of actor, cosmetics etc., composition or constitution, person's temperament etc.; **make-weight** small quantity added to make full weight; **on the make** intent on gain.

maker /'meɪkə(r)/ *n.* one who makes, esp. (**Maker**) God.

making /'meɪkɪŋ/ *n.* in *pl.* essential qualities for becoming. **be the making of** ensure success etc. of; **in the making** in the course of being made.

malachite /'mæləkaɪt/ *n.* green mineral used for ornament.

maladjusted /mælə'dʒʌstɪd/ *a.* (of person) not satisfactorily adjusted to his environment etc. **maladjustment** *n.*

maladminister /mæləd'mɪnɪstə(r)/ *v.t.* manage badly or improperly. **maladministration** *n.*

maladroit /mælə'drɔɪt/ *a.* bungling, clumsy.

malady /'mælədɪ/ *n.* ailment, disease.

malaise /mə'leɪz/ *n.* feeling of illness or uneasiness.

malapropism /'mæləprɒpɪz(ə)m/ *n.* ludicrous confusion between words.

malaria /mə'leərɪə/ *n.* fever transmitted by mosquitoes. **malarial** *a.*

malcontent /'mælkəntent/ **1** *n.* discontented person. **2** *a.* discontented.

male 1 *a.* of sex that can beget offspring by performing fertilizing function; (of parts of machinery) designed to enter or fill corresponding female part. **2** *n.* male person or animal.

malediction /mælɪ'dɪkʃ(ə)n/ *n.* curse. **maledictory** *a.*

malefactor /'mælɪfæktə(r)/ *n.* criminal; evil-doer. **malefaction** *n.*

malevolent /mə'levələnt/ *a.* wishing ill to others. **malevolence** *n.*

malformation /mælfɔː'meɪʃ(ə)n/ *n.* faulty formation. **malformed** *a.*

malfunction /mæl'fʌŋkʃ(ə)n/ **1** *n.* failure to function in normal manner. **2** *v.i.* function faultily.

malice /'mælɪs/ *n.* ill-will; desire to do harm.

malicious /mə'lɪʃəs/ *a.* given to or arising from malice.

malign /mə'laɪn/ **1** *a.* malevolent, injurious. **2** *v.t.* speak ill of; slander. **3** **malignity** *n.*

malignant /mə'lɪgnənt/ *a.* (of tumour) cancerous; (of disease) very virulent;

feeling or showing intense ill-will. **malignancy** *n.*

malinger /mə'lɪŋgə(r)/ *v.i.* pretend illness to escape duty.

mallard /'mælɑːd/ *n.* kind of wild duck.

malleable /'mælɪəb(ə)l/ *a.* that can be shaped by hammering; pliable. **malleability** *n.*

mallet /'mælɪt/ *n.* hammer, usu. of wood; implement for striking croquet or polo ball.

mallow /'mæləʊ/ *n.* kind of flowering plant with hairy stems and leaves.

malmsey /'mɑːmzɪ/ *n.* strong sweet wine.

malnutrition /mælnjuː'trɪʃ(ə)n/ *n.* insufficient nutrition.

malodorous /mæl'əʊdərəs/ *a.* evil-smelling.

malpractice /mæl'præktɪs/ *n.* wrongdoing; illegal action for one's own benefit while in position of trust; physician's improper or negligent treatment of patient.

malt /mɔːlt/ **1** *n.* barley or other grain prepared for brewing etc.; malt whisky. **2** *v.t.* convert (grain) into malt. **3** **malted milk** drink made from dried milk and extract of malt; **malt whisky** whisky made from malted barley.

Maltese /mɔːl'tiːz/ **1** *a.* of Malta. **2** *n.* native or language of Malta. **3 Maltese cross** one with four equal limbs broadened at ends.

maltreat /mæl'triːt/ *v.t.* ill-treat. **maltreatment** *n.*

malversation /mælvə'seɪʃ(ə)n/ *n.* corrupt handling of public or trust money.

mamba /'mæmbə/ *n.* kind of venomous Afr. snake.

mamma /mə'mɑː/ *n. arch.* mother.

mammal /'mæm(ə)l/ *n.* animal of class characterized by secretion of milk to feed young. **mammalian** /-'meɪlɪən/ *a.*

mammary /'mæmərɪ/ *a.* of breasts.

Mammon /'mæmən/ *n.* wealth regarded as idol or evil influence.

mammoth /'mæməθ/ **1** *n.* large extinct species of elephant. **2** *a.* huge.

man 1 *n.* (*pl.* **men**) adult human male; human being; *collect.* the human race; person; husband; employee, workman; (usu. in *pl.*) soldiers, sailors, etc.; one of set of objects used in playing chess, draughts, etc. 2 *v.t.* furnish with man or men or person(s) for service or defence. 3 **manhole** opening giving person access to sewer, conduit, etc.; **man-hour** work done by one person in one hour; **man-of-war** armed ship of country's navy; **manpower** number of persons available for work or military service; **manservant** (*pl.* **menservants**) male domestic servant; **mantrap** trap set to catch esp. trespassers.

manacle /ˈmænək(ə)l/ 1 *n.* (usu. in *pl.*) fetter. 2 *v.t.* put manacles on.

manage /ˈmænɪdʒ/ *v.* organize or regulate; succeed in achieving, contrive; succeed with limited resources, cope; gain one's ends with; have effective control of. **manageable** *a.*

management /ˈmænɪdʒmənt/ *n.* managing or being managed; administration; persons managing a business.

manager /ˈmænɪdʒə(r)/ *n.* person conducting business etc.; person controlling activities of person or team etc.; person who manages money etc. in specified way. **manageress** *n.*; **managerial** /-ˈdʒɪərɪəl/ *a.*

mañana /mænˈjɑːnə/ *adv.* & *n.* tomorrow, indefinite future. [Sp.]

manatee /ˈmænətiː/ *n.* large tropical aquatic mammal feeding on plants.

Mancunian /mænˈkjuːnɪən/ 1 *n.* native of Manchester. 2 *a.* of Manchester.

mandarin /ˈmændərɪn/ *n.* influential person, esp. bureaucrat; *hist.* Chinese official; (**Mandarin**) former standard spoken language in China; small flat loose-skinned orange.

mandatary /ˈmændətərɪ/ *n.* receiver or holder of a mandate.

mandate /ˈmændeɪt/ 1 *n.* authoritative command; commission to act for another; political instructions from electorate. 2 *v.t.* give authority to (delegate); commit (territory) to mandatary.

mandatory /ˈmændətərɪ/ *a.* compulsory; of or conveying a command.

mandible /ˈmændɪb(ə)l/ *n.* jaw-bone, esp. lower one; either part of bird's beak; either half of crushing organ in mouth-parts of insect etc.

mandolin /ˈmændəlɪn/ *n.* musical instrument with paired metal strings, played with a plectrum.

mandrake /ˈmændreɪk/ *n.* narcotic plant with forked root.

mandrill /ˈmændrɪl/ *n.* kind of large baboon.

mane *n.* long hair on horse's or lion's neck; person's long hair.

manège /məˈneɪʒ/ *n.* training of horses; movements of trained horse.

manful /ˈmænfʊl/ *a.* brave, resolute.

manganese /ˈmæŋɡəniːz/ *n.* grey brittle metallic element; black oxide of this. etc.

mange /meɪndʒ/ *n.* skin disease of dogs etc.

mangel-wurzel /ˈmæŋɡ(ə)l ˌwɜːz(ə)l/ *n.* large kind of beet used as cattle-food.

manger /ˈmeɪndʒə(r)/ *n.* eating-trough in stable.

mangle[1] /ˈmæŋɡ(ə)l/ *v.t.* hack, cut about; mutilate, spoil.

mangle[2] /ˈmæŋɡ(ə)l/ 1 *n.* machine with rollers for pressing water out of washed clothes. 2 *v.t.* put through mangle.

mango /ˈmæŋɡəʊ/ *n.* (*pl.* **-goes**) tropical fruit with yellow flesh; tree bearing it.

mangrove /ˈmæŋɡrəʊv/ *n.* tropical sea-shore tree with interlacing roots above ground.

mangy /ˈmeɪndʒɪ/ *a.* having mange; squalid, shabby.

manhandle /ˈmænhænd(ə)l/ *v.t.* move by human effort alone, handle roughly.

manhood /ˈmænhʊd/ *n.* state of being a man; manliness; men of a country.

mania /ˈmeɪnɪə/ *n.* mental derangement marked by great excitement and (freq.) violence; craze, passion (*for*).

maniac /ˈmeɪnɪæk/ 1 *n.* person affected with mania. 2 *a.* of or affected with mania. 3 **maniacal** /məˈnaɪək(ə)l/ *a.*

manic /ˈmænɪk/ *a.* of or affected with mania. **manic-depressive** relating to mental disorder with alternating periods of elation and depression, person having such disorder.

manicure /ˈmænɪkjʊə(r)/ 1 *n.* cosmetic care and treatment of the hands. 2 *v.t.* apply manicure to. 3 **manicurist** *n.*

manifest /ˈmænɪfest/ 1 *a.* clear to sight

or mind; indubitable. **2** *v.t.* make manifest; reveal *itself*; appear. **3** *n.* cargo or passenger list. **4 manifestation** *n.*

manifesto /mænɪˈfestəʊ/ *n.* (*pl.* -**tos**) public declaration of policy or principles.

manifold /ˈmænɪfəʊld/ **1** *a.* many and various; having various forms or applications or component parts etc. **2** *n.* pipe etc. with several outlets.

manikin /ˈmænɪkɪn/ *n.* little man, dwarf.

manila /məˈnɪlə/ *n.* strong fibre of Philippine tree; brown wrapping-paper made of this.

manipulate /məˈnɪpjʊleɪt/ *v.t.* handle; deal skilfully with; manage craftily. **manipulation** *n.*; **manipulator** *n.*

mankind /mænˈkaɪnd/ *n.* human species.

manly /ˈmænlɪ/ *a.* having qualities associated with or befitting a man.

manna /ˈmænə/ *n.* food miraculously supplied to Israelites in wilderness.

mannequin /ˈmænɪkɪn/ *n.* person, usu. woman, employed to model clothes; dummy for display of clothes in shop.

manner /ˈmænə(r)/ *n.* way thing is done or happens; in *pl.* social behaviour; sort or kind; style.

mannered /ˈmænəd/ *a.* behaving in specified way; showing mannerism.

mannerism /ˈmænərɪz(ə)m/ *n.* distinctive gesture or feature of style; excessive use of these in art etc.

mannerly /ˈmænəlɪ/ *a.* well-behaved, polite.

mannish /ˈmænɪʃ/ *a.* characteristic of man as opp. to woman; (of woman, usu. *derog.*) like a man.

manœuvre /məˈnuːvə(r)/ **1** *n.* planned movement of vehicle or body of troops; in *pl.* large-scale exercise of troops etc.; deceptive or elusive movement; skilful plan. **2** *v.* perform or cause to perform manœuvres; force or drive or manipulate by scheming or adroitness; employ artifice. **3 manœuvrable** *a.*

manor /ˈmænə(r)/ *n.* large landed estate or its house; *hist.* territorial unit of feudal period. **manorial** *a.*

mansard roof /ˈmænsɑːd/ roof with each face having two slopes, the steeper below.

manse /mæns/ *n.* (esp. Sc. Presbyterian) minister's house.

mansion /ˈmænʃ(ə)n/ *n.* large grand house; in *pl.* block of flats.

manslaughter /ˈmænslɔːtə(r)/ *n.* criminal homicide without malice aforethought.

mantel /ˈmænt(ə)l/ *n.* structure above and around fireplace; mantelpiece. **mantelpiece** shelf above fireplace.

mantilla /mænˈtɪlə/ *n.* Spanish woman's lace scarf worn over head and shoulders.

mantis /ˈmæntɪs/ *n.* kind of predacious insect.

mantle /ˈmænt(ə)l/ **1** *n.* loose sleeveless cloak; covering; fragile hood round gas-jet to give incandescent light. **2** *v.t.* cover (as) with mantle; conceal, envelop.

manual /ˈmænjʊəl/ **1** *a.* of or done with hands. **2** *n.* book of instructions, reference book; organ keyboard played with hands not feet.

manufacture /mænjʊˈfæktʃə(r)/ **1** *v.t.* produce by labour, esp. on large scale; invent, fabricate. **2** *n.* manufacturing of articles; branch of such industry.

manure /məˈnjʊə(r)/ **1** *n.* fertilizer, esp. dung. **2** *v.t.* treat with manure.

manuscript /ˈmænjʊskrɪpt/ **1** *n.* book or document written by hand or typed, not printed. **2** *a.* written by hand.

Manx /mæŋks/ **1** *a.* of Isle of Man. **2** *n.* Celtic language of Isle of Man. **3 Manx cat** tailless variety.

many /ˈmenɪ/ **1** *a.* numerous, great in number. **2** *n.* many people or things; *the* multitude.

Maori /ˈmaʊrɪ/ **1** *n.* member of aboriginal NZ race; their language. **2** *a.* of this people.

map 1 *n.* flat representation of (part of) earth's surface, or of sky; diagram. **2** *v.t.* represent on map. **3 map out** arrange in detail.

maple /ˈmeɪp(ə)l/ *n.* kind of tree. **maple leaf** emblem of Canada; **maple sugar** sugar got by evaporating sap of some kinds of maple; **maple syrup** syrup got from maple sap or maple sugar.

maquette /məˈket/ *n.* preliminary model or sketch.

mar *v.t.* impair, spoil.

Mar. *abbr.* March.

marabou /'mærəbuː/ n. large W. Afr. stork; its down as trimming etc.

maraca /mə'rækə/ n. hand-held club-like gourd containing beans or beads etc., shaken as percussion instrument.

maraschino /mærə'skiːnəʊ/ n. liqueur made from cherries. **maraschino cherry** one preserved in this.

marathon /'mærəθ(ə)n/ n. long-distance foot-race; feat of endurance; undertaking of long duration.

maraud /mə'rɔːd/ v.i. make raid, pillage.

marble /'mɑːb(ə)l/ **1** n. kind of lime-stone used in sculpture and architecture; in pl. collection of sculpture; small ball of glass etc. as toy; in pl. game played with these. **2** v.t. give veined or mottled appearance to (esp. paper).

marcasite /'mɑːkəsaɪt/ n. crystalline iron sulphide; piece of this as ornament.

March[1] n. third month of year. **March hare** hare in breeding season.

march[2] **1** v. walk in military manner or with regular paces; proceed steadily; cause to march or walk. **2** n. marching of troops; procession as protest etc.; progress; piece of music suitable for marching to; distance covered in marching. **3** **march past** ceremonial march of troops past saluting-point.

march[3] hist. **1** n. boundary (often in pl.); tract of (often disputed) land between countries etc. **2** v.i. have common boundary (with).

marchioness /'mɑːʃənes/ n. fem. marquess's wife or widow; woman with own rank of marquess.

mare /meə(r)/ n. female of horse or other equine animal. **mare's nest** illusory discovery.

margarine /mɑːdʒə'riːn/ n. butter-substitute made from edible oils etc.

marge /mɑːdʒ/ n. colloq. margarine.

margin /'mɑːdʒɪn/ n. border, strip near edge of something; plain space round printed page etc.; extra amount over what is necessary. **margin of error** difference allowed for miscalculation or mischance.

marginal /'mɑːdʒɪn(ə)l/ a. written in margin; of or at edge; (of constituency) having elected MP with small majority;

close to limit esp. of profitability; barely adequate or provided for.

marguerite /mɑːgə'riːt/ n. ox-eye daisy or similar flower.

marigold /'mærɪgəʊld/ n. plant with golden or bright yellow flowers.

marijuana /mærɪ'hwɑːnə/ n. dried leaves etc. of common hemp smoked as intoxicant.

marimba /mə'rɪmbə/ n. Afr. and Central Amer. xylophone; orchestral instrument developed from this.

marina /mə'riːnə/ n. place with moorings for pleasure-boats.

marinade /'mærɪneɪd/ **1** n. mixture esp. of wine or vinegar with oil and herbs etc., for steeping fish or meat. **2** v. steep or be steeped in marinade.

marinate /'mærɪneɪt/ v. marinade.

marine /mə'riːn/ **1** a. of, found in, or produced by, the sea; for use at sea; of shipping. **2** n. member of corps trained to fight on land or sea; country's shipping fleet or navy.

mariner /'mærɪnə(r)/ n. sailor, seaman.

marionette /mærɪə'net/ n. puppet worked with strings.

marital /'mærɪt(ə)l/ a. of or between husband and wife; of marriage.

maritime /'mærɪtaɪm/ a. situated or living or found near the sea; connected with seafaring.

marjoram /'mɑːdʒərəm/ n. aromatic herb used in cookery.

mark[1] **1** n. visible sign left by person or thing; stain, scar etc.; written or printed symbol; this as assessment of conduct or proficiency; sign or indication (of); lasting effect or influence; unit of numerical award in examination; target, thing aimed at; line etc. serving to indicate position; (followed by numeral) particular design of piece of equipment. **2** v. make mark on; distinguish with mark; give distinctive character to, be a feature of; allot marks to (student's work etc.); in pass. have natural marks; see, notice, observe mentally; keep close to (opposing player) in games. **3** **mark down** reduce price of; **mark off** separate by boundary; **mark out** trace out boundary of, plan (course), destine; **mark time** lift feet as though marching while halted, fig. await opportunity to advance;

mark up increase price of; **mark-up** amount added by seller to cost-price of goods to cover profit margin etc.

mark² *n.* currency unit in Germany, Finland, etc.

marked /mɑːkt/ *a.* noticeable, conspicuous. **markedly** /-kɪdlɪ/ *adv.*

marker /'mɑːkə(r)/ *n.* thing that marks a position; scorer esp. at billiards.

market /'mɑːkɪt/ **1** *n.* gathering for sale of commodities or livestock etc.; space or building used for this; demand (*for* goods etc.); place where there is such demand; conditions as regards or opportunity for buying and selling. **2** *v.* sell, offer for sale; buy or sell goods in market. **3 market garden** place where vegetables are grown for market; **market-place** open space where market is held, *fig.* scene of actual dealings; **market research** study of possible buyers for one's goods; **market town** town where market is held; **market value** value as saleable thing; **on the market** offered for sale.

marking /'mɑːkɪŋ/ *n.* identification mark; colouring of feathers, skin, etc.

marksman /'mɑːksmən/ *n.* (*pl.* -**men**) skilled shot, esp. with rifle. **marksmanship** *n.*

marl *n.* soil composed of clay and lime, used as fertilizer.

marlinspike /'mɑːlɪnspaɪk/ *n.* pointed tool used to separate strands of rope or wire.

marmalade /'mɑːməleɪd/ *n.* conserve of oranges or other citrus fruit, made like jam.

marmoreal /mɑː'mɔːrɪəl/ *a.* of or like marble.

marmoset /'mɑːməzet/ *n.* small bushy-tailed monkey.

marmot /'mɑːmət/ *n.* burrowing rodent related to squirrel.

marocain /'mærəkeɪn/ *n.* thin fine dress-fabric of crêpe type.

maroon¹ /mə'ruːn/ *a.* & *n.* brownish-crimson.

maroon² /mə'ruːn/ *v.t.* put and leave ashore on desolate island or coast; leave stranded.

marquee /mɑː'kiː/ *n.* large tent.

marquess /'mɑːkwəs/ *n.* peer ranking between duke and earl.

marquetry /'mɑːkɪtrɪ/ *n.* inlaid work in wood etc.

marquis /'mɑːkwɪs/ *n.* rank in some European nobilities.

marquise /mɑː'kiːz/ *n.* marquis's wife or widow; woman with own rank of marquis.

marriage /'mærɪdʒ/ *n.* condition of man and woman legally united for the purpose of living together; act or ceremony etc. establishing this; particular matrimonial union. **marriage certificate**, **lines**, certificate stating that marriage has taken place.

marriageable /'mærɪdʒəb(ə)l/ *a.* old enough or fit for marriage.

marrow /'mærəʊ/ *n.* gourd with whitish flesh, cooked as vegetable; fatty substance in cavity of bones. **marrowbone** bone containing edible marrow; **marrowfat** kind of large pea.

marry /'mærɪ/ *v.* take or join or give in marriage; *fig.* unite intimately.

Marsala /mɑː'sɑːlə/ *n.* dark sweet fortified wine.

Marseillaise /mɑːseɪ'jeɪz/ *n.* national anthem of France.

marsh *n.* low-lying watery ground. **marsh gas** methane; **marsh mallow** shrubby herb, confection made from root of this; **marshmallow** soft sweet made from sugar and albumen and gelatine etc. **marshy** *a.*

marshal /'mɑːʃ(ə)l/ **1** *n.* high-ranking officer of state or in armed forces; officer arranging ceremonies, controlling procedure at races, etc. **2** *v.t.* arrange in due order; conduct (person) ceremoniously. **3 marshalling yard** railway yard in which goods trains etc. are assembled.

marsupial /mɑː'suːpɪəl/ **1** *n.* mammal of kind in which females usu. have pouch in which to carry their young. **2** *a.* of this class.

mart *n.* market.

Martello tower /mɑː'teləʊ/ small circular tower for coastal defence.

marten /'mɑːtɪn/ *n.* kind of weasel with valuable fur.

martial /'mɑːʃ(ə)l/ *a.* warlike; suited to or loving war. **martial arts** fighting sports such as judo or karate; **martial law** military government, by which ordinary law is suspended.

martin /'mɑːtɪn/ *n.* bird of swallow family.

martinet /mɑːtɪˈnet/ n. strict disciplinarian.

Martini /mɑːˈtiːniː/ n. (P) vermouth; cocktail of gin and vermouth.

martyr /ˈmɑːtə(r)/ 1 n. person who undergoes death or suffering for great cause, esp. adherence to Christian faith. 2 v.t. put to death as martyr; torment. 3 **martyr to** constant sufferer from.

martyrdom /ˈmɑːtədəm/ n. sufferings and death of martyr; torment.

marvel /ˈmɑːv(ə)l/ 1 n. wonderful thing; wonderful example of. 2 v.i. feel surprise or wonder.

marvellous /ˈmɑːvələs/ a. astonishing; excellent.

Marxism /ˈmɑːksɪz(ə)m/ n. doctrines of Marx, predicting abolition of private ownership of means of production. **Marxist** n. & a.

marzipan /ˈmɑːzɪpæn/ n. paste of ground almonds, sugar, etc.

mascara /mæsˈkɑːrə/ n. cosmetic for darkening eyelashes.

mascot /ˈmæskɒt/ n. person or animal or thing supposed to bring luck.

masculine /ˈmæskjʊlɪn/ a. of men, manly; mannish; Gram. of gender proper to men's names. **masculinity** /-ˈlɪn-/ n.

maser /ˈmeɪzə(r)/ n. device for amplifying microwaves.

mash 1 n. mashed potatoes (colloq.); mixture of boiled bran etc. given to horses. 2 v.t. reduce (potatoes etc.) to uniform mass by crushing; crush to pulp.

mask /mɑːsk/ 1 n. covering for all or part of face, worn as disguise or for protection, or by surgeon etc. to prevent infection of patient; respirator used to filter inhaled air or to supply gas for inhalation; likeness of person's face, esp. one made by taking mould from face; disguise. 2 v.t. cover or disguise with mask; conceal or protect.

masochism /ˈmæsəkɪz(ə)m/ n. pleasure in suffering physical or mental pain, e.g. as form of sexual perversion. **masochist** n.; **masochistic** a.

mason /ˈmeɪs(ə)n/ n. person who builds with stone; **Mason** Freemason. **Masonic** /məˈsɒnɪk/ a. of Freemasons. **masonry** /ˈmeɪsənrɪ/ n. mason's work; stonework; **Masonry** Freemasonry.

masque /mɑːsk/ n. amateur dramatic and musical entertainment, esp. in 16th–17th c.

masquerade /mɑːskəˈreɪd/ 1 n. false show, pretence; masked ball. 2 v.i. appear in disguise; assume false appearance.

mass[1] n. 1 n. coherent body of matter; dense aggregation, large number or amount (of); Phys. quantity of matter body contains; the majority or main part (of); in pl. the ordinary people. 2 v. gather into mass; assemble into one body. 3 a. of or relating to large numbers of people or things. 4 **mass media** means of communication to large numbers of people; **mass production** production of large quantities of standardized article by mechanical processes.

mass[2] n. celebration of Eucharist, esp. in RC Church; (musical setting of) liturgy used in this.

massacre /ˈmæsəkə/ 1 n. general slaughter. 2 v.t. make massacre of.

massage /ˈmæsɑːʒ/ 1 n. kneading and rubbing of muscles etc., usu. with hands. 2 v.t. treat thus.

masseur /mæˈsɜː(r)/ n. (fem. **masseuse** /mæˈsɜːz/) person who provides massage professionally.

massif /ˈmæsiːf/ n. mountain heights forming compact group.

massive /ˈmæsɪv/ a. large and heavy or solid; substantial; unusually large.

mast[1] /mɑːst/ n. upright to which ship's yards and sails are attached; post etc. to support radio or television aerial; flag-pole.

mast[2] /mɑːst/ n. fruit of beech or oak etc. esp. as food for pigs.

mastectomy /mæˈstektəmɪ/ n. surgical removal of a breast.

master /ˈmɑːstə(r)/ 1 n. person having control; male head of household; head of college etc.; owner of animal or slave; ship's captain; male teacher; skilled workman; holder of university degree above bachelor's; great artist; thing from which series of copies is made; **Master** title prefixed to name of boy. 2 a. commanding; main, principal; controlling others. 3 v.t. overcome, conquer; acquire complete knowledge of. 4 **master-key** one opening many different locks; **mastermind** (possessor of) outstanding intellect, plan and direct (enterprise); **Master of Ceremonies** person introducing speakers at banquet or entertainers at variety show; **masterpiece** outstanding piece of artistry, one's best work; **masterswitch** switch controlling electricity etc. supply to entire system.

masterful /ˈmɑːstəfʊl/ a. self-willed, imperious.

masterly /ˈmɑːstəlɪ/ a. worthy of a master; very skilful.

mastery /ˈmɑːstərɪ/ n. sway, dominion; masterly skill or knowledge.

mastic /ˈmæstɪk/ n. gum or resin exuded from certain trees; type of cement.

masticate /ˈmæstɪkeɪt/ v.t. chew. **mastication** n.

mastiff /ˈmæstɪf/ n. large strong kind of dog.

mastodon /ˈmæstədɒn/ n. extinct animal resembling elephant.

mastoid /ˈmæstɔɪd/ 1 a. shaped like woman's breast. 2 n. conical prominence on temporal bone; colloq. inflammation of mastoid.

masturbate /ˈmæstəbeɪt/ v. produce sexual arousal (of) by manual stimulation of genitals. **masturbation** n.; **masturbatory** a.

mat¹ 1 n. piece of coarse fabric as floor-covering or for wiping shoes on; small rug; piece of material laid on table etc. to protect surface. 2 v. bring or come into thickly tangled state. 3 **on the mat** colloq. being reprimanded.

mat² var. of **matt**.

matador /ˈmætədɔː(r)/ n. bullfighter whose task is to kill bull.

match¹ 1 n. contest, game; person or thing equal to or nearly resembling or corresponding to another; marriage; person in respect of eligibility for marriage. 2 v. be equal, correspond; find or be match for; place in competition with or contest against. 3 **matchboard** board fitting into others by tongue along one edge and groove along other; **matchmaker** person fond of scheming to bring about marriages; **match point** state of game when one side needs only one point to win match.

match² n. short thin piece of wood etc., tipped with composition that ignites when rubbed on rough or specially prepared surface. **matchbox** box for hold-

ing matches; **matchstick** stem of match; **matchwood** wood suitable for matches, minute splinters.

matchless /ˈmætʃlɪs/ a. incomparable.

mate¹ 1 n. companion, fellow worker; colloq. general form of address to equal; one of a pair esp. of birds; colloq. partner in marriage; subordinate officer on merchant ship; assistant to worker. 2 v. come or bring together for marriage or for breeding.

mate² n. & v.t. checkmate.

material /məˈtɪərɪəl/ 1 n. that from which thing is made; cloth, fabric; in pl. things needed for activity etc.; elements. 2 a. composed of or connected with matter; not spiritual; important, essential.

materialism /məˈtɪərɪəlɪz(ə)m/ n. belief that only matter is real or important; rejection of spiritual values etc. **materialist** n. & a.; **materialistic** a.

materialize /məˈtɪərɪəlaɪz/ v. become fact, happen; represent in or assume bodily form. **materialization** n.

maternal /məˈtɜːn(ə)l/ a. of or like a mother; motherly; related on mother's side.

maternity /məˈtɜːnɪtɪ/ n. motherhood; attrib. for women in pregnancy or childbirth.

matey /ˈmeɪtɪ/ a. familiar and friendly (with). **matily** adv.

mathematics /mæθəˈmætɪks/ n. pl. (also treated as sing.) science of space, number, and quantity. **mathematical** a.; **mathematician** /-məˈtɪʃ(ə)n/ n.

maths /mæθs/ n. colloq. mathematics.

matinée /ˈmætɪneɪ/ n. theatrical etc. performance in afternoon. **matinee coat** baby's short coat.

matins /ˈmætɪnz/ n. morning prayer.

matriarch /ˈmeɪtrɪɑːk/ n. woman who is head of family or tribe. **matriarchal** a.

matriarchy /ˈmeɪtrɪɑːkɪ/ n. social organization in which mother is head of family.

matricide /ˈmeɪtrɪsaɪd/ n. killing of one's mother; person who kills his mother. **matricidal** a.

matriculate /məˈtrɪkjʊleɪt/ v. admit (student) to university; be thus admitted. **matriculation** n.

matrimony /'mætrɪmənɪ/ n. marriage. **matrimonial** /-'məʊnɪəl/ a.

matrix /'meɪtrɪks/ n. (pl. -trices /-trɪsiːz/) mould in which thing is cast or shaped; mass of rock etc. enclosing gems etc.; Math. rectangular array of quantities treated as single quantity.

matron /'meɪtrən/ n. married woman; woman managing domestic arrangements of school etc.; woman in charge of nursing in hospital.

matronly /'meɪtrənlɪ/ a. of or like a matron, esp. stately or portly.

matt a. dull, without lustre.

matter /'mætə(r)/ 1 n. physical substance; thing(s), material; content as opp. form, substance; affair, concern; *the* thing that is amiss (*with*); purulent discharge. 2 v.i. be of importance; make difference (*to*). 3 **matter-of-fact** prosaic, unimaginative.

matting /'mætɪŋ/ n. fabric for mats.

mattock /'mætək/ n. tool like pickaxe with adze and chisel edge as ends of head.

mattress /'mætrɪs/ n. fabric case filled with soft or firm material or springs, used on or as bed.

mature /mətjʊə(r)/ 1 a. fully developed, ripe; adult; (of bill etc.) due for payment. 2 v. bring to or reach mature state. 3 **maturity** n.

matutinal /mætjuː'taɪn(ə)l/ a. of or in morning.

maty var. of **matey**.

maudlin /'mɔːdlɪn/ a. weakly sentimental.

maul /mɔːl/ 1 v.t. beat and bruise; injure by clawing etc.; handle roughly, damage. 2 n. heavy hammer, usu. of wood.

maulstick /'mɔːlstɪk/ n. stick used to support hand in painting.

maunder /'mɔːndə(r)/ v.i. talk ramblingly.

Maundy /'mɔːndɪ/ n. distribution of **Maundy money**, silver coins minted for English sovereign to give to the poor on **Maundy Thursday**, next before Easter.

mausoleum /mɔːsə'liːəm/ n. building erected as tomb and monument.

mauve /məʊv/ n. & a. pale purple.

maverick /'mævərɪk/ n. unorthodox or undisciplined person; *US* unbranded calf etc.

maw n. stomach of animal.

mawkish /'mɔːkɪʃ/ a. feebly sentimental.

maxillary /mæk'sɪlərɪ/ a. of the jaw.

maxim /'mæksɪm/ n. general truth or rule of conduct expressed in a sentence.

maximal /'mæksɪm(ə)l/ a. greatest possible in size, duration, etc.

maximum /'mæksɪməm/ 1 n. (pl. -ima) highest or greatest degree or magnitude or quantity. 2 a. greatest.

may[1] v. aux. (3 sing. **may**; *past* **might** /maɪt/) expr. possibility, permission, request, wish, etc.

May[2] fifth month of year; (**may**) hawthorn blossom. **May Day** 1 May, esp. as country festival and as international holiday in honour of workers; **mayfly** insect which lives briefly in spring; **maypole** flower-decked pole danced round on May Day; **may queen** girl chosen as queen of May Day festivities.

maybe /'meɪbɪ/ adv. perhaps.

mayday /'meɪdeɪ/ n. international radio distress-signal used by ships and aircraft.

mayhem /'meɪhem/ n. violent or damaging action; *hist.* crime of maiming.

mayonnaise /meɪə'neɪz/ n. creamy dressing of oil, egg-yolk, vinegar, etc.; dish dressed with this.

mayor /meə(r)/ n. head of municipal corporation of city or borough; head of district council with status of borough. **mayoral** a.

mayoralty /'meərəltɪ/ n. office of mayor; period of this.

mayoress /'meərɪs/ n. mayor's wife or woman fulfilling ceremonial duties of mayor's wife; woman mayor.

mazarine /mæzə'riːn/ n. & a. deep blue.

maze n. complex and baffling network of paths, lines, etc.; tangle, confusion.

mazurka /mə'zɜːkə/ n. lively Polish dance in triple time; music for this.

MB abbr. Bachelor of Medicine.

MBE abbr. Member of the Order of the British Empire.

MC abbr. Master of Ceremonies; Military Cross.

MCC abbr. Marylebone Cricket Club.

MD abbr. Doctor of Medicine; Managing Director.

me[1] /miː/ pron., obj. case of **I**.

me² /miː/ *n. Mus.* third note of scale in tonic sol-fa.

mead *n.* alcoholic drink of fermented honey and water.

meadow /ˈmedəʊ/ *n.* piece of grass-land, esp. used for hay; low-lying ground, esp. near river. **meadow-sweet** a fragrant flowering plant.

meagre /ˈmiːɡə(r)/ *a.* of poor quality and scanty in amount.

meal¹ *n.* occasion when food is eaten; food eaten on one occasion. **meal-ticket** source of income.

meal² *n.* grain or pulse ground to powder.

mealy /ˈmiːlɪ/ *a.* of, like, or containing meal; dry and powdery. **mealy-mouthed** afraid to speak plainly.

mean¹ *v.* (*past & p.p.* **meant** /ment/) have as one's purpose, design; be re-solved; intend to convey or indicate; in-volve, portend; be of (specified) significance *to* person.

mean² *a.* niggardly; not generous; ig-noble; of low degree or poor quality; *US* vicious, nastily behaved.

mean³ 1 *n.* condition or quality or course of action equally far from two extremes; quotient of the sum of sev-eral quantities and their number. 2 *a.* (of quantity) equally far from two ex-tremes. **3 in the mean time** meanwhile.

meander /mɪˈændə(r)/ 1 *v.i.* wind about; wander at random. 2 *n.* in *pl.* sinuous winding; winding path or course *etc.*

meaning /ˈmiːnɪŋ/ 1 *n.* what is meant; significance. 2 *a.* expressive; sig-nificant. **3 meaningful** *a.*; **mean-ingless** *a.*

means *n.pl.* (usu. treated as *sing.*) that by which result is brought about; money resources. **means test** official inquiry into financial resources of ap-plicant for assistance *etc.*

meantime, meanwhile, *advs.* in the intervening time; at the same time.

measles /ˈmiːz(ə)lz/ *n.* as *pl.* or *sing.* infectious virus disease with red rash.

measly /ˈmiːzlɪ/ *a.* of or affected with measles; *sl.* inferior or contemptible.

measure /ˈmeʒə(r)/ 1 *n.* size or quan-tity found by measuring; vessel, rod, tape, *etc.*, for measuring; degree, ex-tent; suitable action; legislative en-actment; that by which thing is measured; prescribed extent or am-ount; rhythm, metre, musical time. 2 *v.* find size, quantity, proportions, *etc.* of with measure; be of specified length *etc.*; deal *out*; bring into competition *with.* **3 measurement** *n.*

measureless /ˈmeʒəlɪs/ *a.* not measur-able; infinite.

meat *n.* animal flesh as food; chief part of.

meaty *a.* of or like meat; fleshy; full of meat or *fig.* substance.

mechanic /mɪˈkænɪk/ *n.* skilled worker, esp. one who makes or repairs or uses machinery.

mechanical /mɪˈkænɪk(ə)l/ *a.* of, working, or produced by, machines or mechanism; automatic; lacking orig-inality; of mechanics as a science.

mechanics /mɪˈkænɪks/ *n.pl.* (usu. treated as *sing.*) branch of applied mathematics dealing with motion; sci-ence of machinery; method of con-struction or operation.

mechanism /ˈmekənɪz(ə)m/ *n.* struc-ture or parts of machine; way machine works.

mechanize /ˈmekənaɪz/ *v.t.* introduce or use machines in; equip with ma-chines; give mechanical character to. **mechanization** *n.*

medal /ˈmed(ə)l/ *n.* piece of metal, usu. coin-shaped, commemorating event *etc.* or awarded as distinction.

medallion /mɪˈdælɪən/ *n.* large medal; thing so shaped, e.g. portrait.

medallist /ˈmedəlɪst/ *n.* winner of (specified) medal.

meddle *v.i.* busy oneself unduly (*with*); interfere (*in*).

meddlesome /ˈmed(ə)lsəm/ *a.* fond of meddling.

media *pl.* of **medium**. □ See page 667.

mediaeval var. of **medieval**.

medial /ˈmiːdɪəl/ *a.* situated in the middle.

median /ˈmiːdɪən/ 1 *a.* medial. 2 *n.* line from angle of triangle to middle of op-posite side.

mediate 1 /ˈmiːdɪeɪt/ *v.i.* act as go-between or peace-maker. 2 /ˈmiːdɪət/ *a.* connected through some other person or thing. **3 mediation** *n.*

medical /ˈmedɪk(ə)l/ 1 *a.* of medicine in general or as distinct from surgery.

2 *n. colloq.* medical examination. **3 medical certificate** certificate of fitness or unfitness to work etc.; **medical examination** examination to determine person's physical fitness.

medicament /mɪˈdɪkəmənt/ *n.* substance used in curative treatment.

medicate /ˈmedɪkeɪt/ *v.t.* treat medically; impregnate with medicinal substance. **medication** *n.*

medicinal /mɪˈdɪsɪn(ə)l/ *a.* of medicine; having healing properties.

medicine /ˈmedsɪn/ *n.* art of preserving and restoring health, esp. by other means than surgery; substance, esp. one taken internally, used in this. **medicine-man** witch-doctor.

medieval /medɪˈiːvl/ *a.* of or imitating Middle Ages.

mediocre /miːdɪˈəʊkə(r)/ *a.* of middling quality, second-rate.

mediocrity /miːdɪˈɒkrɪtɪ/ *n.* mediocre quality or person.

meditate /ˈmedɪteɪt/ *v.* exercise the mind in (esp. religious) contemplation; plan mentally. **meditation** *n.*; **meditative** /ˈmed-/ *a.*

Mediterranean /medɪtəˈreɪnɪən/ *a.* of or characteristic of the sea between Europe and N. Africa, or the countries bordering on it.

medium /ˈmiːdɪəm/ **1** *n.* (*pl.* **-dia** or **-diums**) middle quality or degree; environment; agency, means; in *pl. = mass media;* (*pl.* **-diums**) person claiming to communicate with spirits of the dead. **2** *a.* intermediate; average; moderate.

mediumistic /miːdɪəˈmɪstɪk/ *a.* of a spiritualist medium.

medlar /ˈmedlə(r)/ *n.* fruit like small apple, eaten when decayed; tree bearing it.

medley /ˈmedlɪ/ *n.* varied mixture.

medulla /mɪˈdʌlə/ *n.* bone or spinal marrow; hindmost segment of the brain. **medullary** *a.*

meek *a.* humbly submissive.

meerschaum /ˈmɪəʃəm/ *n.* creamy clay mineral used esp. for pipe-bowls; tobacco-pipe with meerschaum bowl.

meet[1] **1** *v.* (*past & p.p.* **met**) come into contact or company (*with*); make acquaintance of; be present at arrival of; assemble; confront; become per-

ceptible to; satisfy (need etc.); experience. **2** *n.* assembly for hunting etc.

meet[2] *a. arch.* fitting, proper.

meeting *n.* assembly of people for discussion or (Quaker) worship etc.

mega- *in comb.* great, large; one million.

megabyte /ˈmegəbaɪt/ *n.* one million bytes, esp. as unit of computer storage etc.

megalith /ˈmegəlɪθ/ *n.* large stone, esp. as monument. **megalithic** *a.*

megalomania /megələˈmeɪnɪə/ *n.* mental disorder involving exaggerated idea of one's own importance; passion for grandiose things. **megalomaniac** *a. & n.*

megaphone /ˈmegəfəʊn/ *n.* large funnel-shaped device for sending sound of voice to a distance.

megaton /ˈmegətʌn/ *n.* unit of explosive force equal to one million tons of TNT.

meiosis /maɪˈəʊsɪs/ *n.* (*pl.* **-ses** /-siːz/) ironical understatement.

melamine /ˈmeləmiːn/ *n.* resilient kind of plastic.

melancholia /melənˈkəʊlɪə/ *n.* mental illness marked by depression.

melancholic /melənˈkɒlɪk/ *a.* melancholy; liable to melancholy.

melancholy /ˈmelənkɒlɪ/ **1** *n.* pensive sadness; depression; tendency to this. **2** *a.* sad; depressing.

mêlée /ˈmeleɪ/ *n.* confused fight or struggle.

mellifluous /meˈlɪflʊəs/ *a.* sweet-sounding.

mellow /ˈmeləʊ/ **1** *a.* soft and rich in flavour, colour, or sound; softened by age etc.; genial. **2** *v.* make or become mellow.

melodic /mɪˈlɒdɪk/ *a.* of melody.

melodious /mɪˈləʊdɪəs/ *a.* of or producing melody, sweet-sounding.

melodrama /ˈmelədrɑːmə/ *n.* drama marked by crude appeals to emotion. **melodramatic** /-ˈmæt-/ *a.*

melody /ˈmelədɪ/ *n.* sweet music; arrangement of notes in musically expressive succession; principal part in harmonized music.

melon /ˈmelən/ *n.* sweet fruit of various gourds.

melt *v.* change from solid to liquid by heat; dissolve; soften, be softened; vanish (*away*). **melt down** reduce (metal) to molten state; **melting-point** temperature at which solid melts; **melting-pot** *fig.* place of reconstruction or vigorous mixing.

member *n.* person belonging to society, order, etc.; part of complex structure; limb or other bodily organ. **Member of Parliament** person elected to House of Commons.

membership *n.* being a member; number or body of members.

membrane /'membreɪn/ *n.* layer of connective tissue round organ, lining cavity, etc. in living organism. **membranous** *a.*

memento /mɪ'mentəʊ/ *n.* (*pl.* **-toes**) object serving as reminder or kept as memorial.

memo /'meməʊ/ *n.* (*pl.* **-mos**) *colloq.* memorandum.

memoir /'memwɑ:(r)/ *n.* record of events written from personal knowledge etc.; (esp. in *pl.*) (auto)biography.

memorable /'memərəb(ə)l/ *a.* likely or worthy to be remembered.

memorandum /memə'rændəm/ *n.* (*pl.* **-dums** *or* **-da**) *n.* note or record for future use; informal written message esp. in business etc.

memorial /mɪ'mɔːrɪəl/ **1** *n.* object or custom established in memory of person or event. **2** *a.* commemorative.

memorize /'meməraɪz/ *v.t.* learn by heart.

memory /'memərɪ/ *n.* faculty by which things are recalled to or kept in mind; what is remembered; posthumous repute; store for data etc. in computer

memsahib /'memsɑːɪb/ *n. Anglo-Ind.* European lady.

men *pl.* of **man**.

menace /'menɪs/ **1** *n.* threat; dangerous thing or person. **2** *v.t.* threaten.

ménage /meɪ'nɑːʒ/ *n.* domestic establishment.

menagerie /mɪ'nædʒərɪ/ *n.* collection of wild animals in captivity.

mend 1 *v.* restore to sound condition; repair; improve. **2** *n.* place where thing has been mended. **3 on the mend** improving.

mendacious /men'deɪʃəs/ *a.* lying, untruthful. **mendacity** /-'dæs-/ *n.*

mendicant /'mendɪkənt/ **1** *a.* begging. **2** *n.* beggar. **3 mendicancy** *n.*

menfolk /'menfəʊk/ *n.* men in general; men in family.

menhir /'menhɪə(r)/ *n.* prehistoric monumental monolith.

menial /'miːnɪəl/ **1** *a.* (of work) degrading, servile. **2** *n.* lowly domestic servant.

meningitis /menɪn'dʒaɪtɪs/ *n.* inflammation of membrane enclosing brain and spinal cord.

meniscus /mɪ'nɪskəs/ *n.* lens convex on one side and concave on the other.

menopause /'menəpɔːz/ *n.* period of life when menstruation ceases.

menses /'mensiːz/ *n.pl.* monthly flow of blood etc. from lining of womb.

menstrual /'menstrʊəl/ *a.* of menses.

menstruate /'menstrʊeɪt/ *v.i.* discharge menses. **menstruation** *n.*

mensurable /'mensjʊərəb(ə)l/ *a.* measurable.

mensuration /mensjʊə'reɪʃ(ə)n/ *n.* measuring; mathematical rules for computing length, area, etc.

mental /'ment(ə)l/ *a.* of or in mind; *sl.* affected with mental disorder. **mental age** stage of mental development reached by average child at specified age; **mental arithmetic** arithmetic performed without use of written figures; **mental hospital** establishment for care of mental patients; **mental patient** sufferer from mental illness.

mentality /men'tælɪtɪ/ *n.* mental character or outlook.

menthol /'menθɒl/ *n.* camphor-like substance got from oil of peppermint etc., used as flavouring or to relieve local pain etc.

mention /'menʃ(ə)n/ **1** *v.t.* speak of, refer to. **2** *n.* mentioning.

mentor /'mentɔ:(r)/ *n.* adviser, councillor.

menu /'menjuː/ *n.* list of dishes to be served or available in restaurant etc.; list of options displayed on computer screen.

MEP *abbr.* Member of European Parliament.

mercantile /'mɜːkəntaɪl/ *a.* of trade, commercial; trading. **mercantile marine** merchant navy.

mercenary /'mɜːsɪnərɪ/ **1** *a.* working

merely for money or reward; hired. **2** *n.* hired soldier in foreign service.

mercer /'mɜːsə(r)/ *n.* dealer in textile fabrics.

mercerized /'mɜːsəraɪzd/ *a.* (of cotton) having silky lustre given by treatment with caustic alkali.

merchandise /'mɜːtʃəndaɪz/ **1** *n.* commodities of commerce; goods for sale. **2** *v.* promote sales of; trade.

merchant /'mɜːtʃənt/ *n.* wholesale trader, esp. with foreign countries; *US* retail trader. **merchant bank** one dealing in commercial loans and financing; **merchant navy** shipping engaged in commerce; **merchantman**, **merchant ship**, ship carrying merchandise; **merchant prince** wealthy merchant.

merchantable /'mɜːtʃəntəb(ə)l/ *a.* saleable.

merciful /'mɜːsɪfʊl/ *a.* having or feeling or showing mercy.

merciless /'mɜːsɪlɪs/ *a.* cruel, pitiless.

mercurial /mɜːˈkjʊərɪəl/ *a.* of lively temperament; of or containing mercury.

mercury /'mɜːkjʊrɪ/ *n.* silver-white heavy normally liquid metal used in barometers, thermometers, etc. **mercuric** *a.*; **mercurous** *a.*

mercy /'mɜːsɪ/ *n.* refraining from infliction of suffering or punishment; disposition to forgive; act of mercy; thing to be thankful for. **at the mercy of** wholly in the power of or subject to; **mercy killing** killing out of pity for suffering person or animal.

mere[1] *a.* barely or only what it is said to be, nothing more than.

mere[2] *n. poet.* lake.

merely /'mɪəlɪ/ *adv.* just, only.

meretricious /merɪˈtrɪʃəs/ *a.* showily but falsely attractive.

merganser /mɜːˈgænsə(r)/ *n.* a diving duck.

merge *v.* join or blend gradually (*into*, *with*); lose or cause to lose character or identity in something else.

merger /'mɜːdʒə(r)/ *n.* combining of two commercial companies into one.

meridian /məˈrɪdɪən/ *n.* circle passing through given place and N. & S. poles; corresponding line on map etc.

meridional /məˈrɪdɪən(ə)l/ *a.* of the south, esp. of Europe, or its inhabitants.

meringue /məˈræŋ/ *n.* mixture of sugar and beaten egg-white baked crisp.

merino /məˈriːnəʊ/ *n.* (*pl.* **-nos**) kind of sheep; fine yarn or soft fabric of its wool; fine woollen yarn.

merit /'merɪt/ **1** *n.* quality of deserving well; excellence, worth; (usu. in *pl.*) thing that entitles to reward or gratitude. **2** *v.t.* deserve.

meritocracy /merɪˈtɒkrəsɪ/ *n.* government by persons selected for merit.

meritorious /merɪˈtɔːrɪəs/ *a.* praiseworthy.

merlin /'mɜːlɪn/ *n.* kind of falcon.

mermaid /'mɜːmeɪd/ *n.* legendary sea-creature with woman's head and trunk and fish's tail.

merriment /'merɪmənt/ *n.* hilarious enjoyment; mirth.

merry /'merɪ/ *a.* joyous, full of laughter or gaiety; *colloq.* slightly drunk. **merry-go-round** revoving machine carrying wooden horses, cars, etc., for riding on at fair etc.; **merry-making** festivity.

mesa /'meɪsə/ *n. US* high steep-sided tableland.

mésalliance /meɪzælɪɑ̃s/ *n.* marriage with social inferior. [F]

mescal /'meskæl/ *n.* peyote cactus. **mescal buttons** its disc-shaped dried tops.

mescaline /'meskəliːn/ *n.* hallucinogenic alkaloid present in mescal buttons.

Mesdames, Mesdemoiselles, *pl.* of **Madame, Mademoiselle**.

mesh **1** *n.* open space in net, sieve, etc.; network fabric; in *pl.* network. **2** *v.* (of toothed wheel etc.) engage, interlock; catch in net.

mesmerize /'mezməraɪz/ *v.t.* hypnotize; fascinate. **mesmerism** *n.*

meso- /mesəʊ/ *in comb.* middle.

mesolithic /mesəʊˈlɪθɪk/ *a.* of Stone Age between palaeolithic and neolithic.

meson /'miːzɒn/ *n. Phys.* elementary particle intermediate in mass between proton and electron.

Mesozoic /mesəʊˈzəʊɪk/ **1** *a.* of second geological era. **2** *n.* this era.

mess **1** *n.* dirty or untidy state; state of

confusion or trouble; spilt liquid etc.; domestic animal's excreta; disagreeable concoction; group of people who take meals together, esp. in armed services; room where such meals are taken; meal so taken; portion of liquid or pulpy food. **2** v. make dirty or untidy, muddle, bungle, (often with *up*); potter *about*; take meals *with*. **3 make a mess of** bungle.

message /'mesɪdʒ/ n. communication sent from one person to another; inspired communication of prophet, writer, etc.

messenger /'mesɪndʒə(r)/ n. person who carries message(s).

Messiah /mɪ'saɪə/ n. promised deliverer of Jews; Christ regarded as this. **Messianic** /mesɪ'ænɪk/ a.

Messieurs pl. of **Monsieur**.

Messrs /'mesəz/ abbr. pl. of **Mr**, as prefix to name of firm etc. or list of men's names.

messuage /'meswɪdʒ/ n. Law dwelling-house with outbuildings and land.

messy /'mesɪ/ a. untidy; causing or accompanied by a mess; difficult to deal with.

met past & p.p. of **meet**.

metabolism /mɪ'tæbəlɪz(ə)m/ n. process by which food is built up into living material or used to supply energy in living organism. **metabolic** /-'bɒl-/ a.

metacarpus /metə'kɑːpəs/ n. (pl. **-pi** /-paɪ/) part of hand between wrist and fingers. **metacarpal** a.

metal /'met(ə)l/ **1** n. any of class of elements such as gold, silver, iron, etc.; alloy of these; in pl. rails of railway; broken stone for roads. **2** a. made of metal. **3** v.t. furnish or supply with metal; make or mend (road) with metal.

metallic /mɪ'tælɪk/ a. (characteristic) of metal(s); sounding like struck metal.

metallurgy /mɪ'tælədʒɪ/ n. science of properties of metals; art of working metals, esp. of extracting them from ores. **metallurgical** a.; **metallurgist** n.

metamorphic /metə'mɔːfɪk/ a. Geol. (of rock) that has undergone transformation by natural agencies. **metamorphism** n.

metamorphose /metə'mɔːfəʊz/ v.

subject to or undergo metamorphosis or metamorphism.

metamorphosis /metə'mɔːfəsɪs/ n. (pl. **-ses** /-siːz/) change of form, esp. by magic or natural development; change of character or circumstances etc.

metaphor /'metəfə(r)/ n. application of name or descriptive term to object to which it is not literally applicable

metaphysics /metə'fɪzɪks/ n.pl. (often treated as sing.) theoretical philosophy of being, knowing, etc. **metaphysical** a.

metatarsus /metə'tɑːsəs/ n. (pl. **-si** /-saɪ/ part of foot betwwen ankle and toes. **metatarsal** n.

mete v.t. portion out.

meteor /'miːtɪə(r)/ n. small mass of matter from outer space made luminous by entering earth's atmosphere.

meteoric /miːtɪ'ɒrɪk/ a. of meteors; fig. dazzling, rapid.

meteorite /'miːtɪəraɪt/ n. fallen meteor; fragment of rock etc. reaching earth's surface from outer space.

meteorology /miːtɪə'rɒlədʒɪ/ n. study of atmospheric phenomena, esp. for weather forecasting. **meteorological** a.; **meteorologist** n.

meter /'miːtə(r)/ **1** n. instrument for recording quantity of substance supplied or time elapsed etc. **2** v.t. measure by meter.

methane /'miːθeɪn/ n. inflammable hydrocarbon gas of paraffin series.

methinks /mɪ'θɪŋks/ v.i. impers. (past **methought** /mɪ'θɔːt/) arch. it seems to me.

method /'meθəd/ n. way of doing something; orderliness.

methodical /mɪ'θɒdɪk(ə)l/ a. characterized by method or order.

Methodism /'meθədɪz(ə)m/ n. evangelistic religious movement founded in 18th. c. **Methodist** a. & n.

methought past of **methinks**.

meths /meθs/ n. colloq. methylated spirit.

methyl alcohol /'miːθaɪl/ a colourless volatile inflammable liquid.

methylate /'meθɪleɪt/ v.t. mix with methyl alcohol, esp. alcohol to make it unfit for drinking.

meticulous /mɪ'tɪkjʊləs/ a. (over-)

scrupulous about minute details; very careful or accurate.

métier /'metjeɪ/ *n.* one's trade or profession; one's forte. [F]

metonymy /mɪ'tɒnɪmɪ/ *n.* substitution of name of attribute for that of thing.

metre /'miːtə(r)/ *n.* metric unit of length (about 39.4 in.); any form of poetic rhythm.

metric /'metrɪk/ *a.* of or based on the metre. **metric system** decimal measuring system with metre, litre, and gram as units of length, capacity, and weight; **metric ton** 1,000 kg.

metrical /'metrɪk(ə)l/ *a.* of or in metre; involving measurement.

metronome /'metrənəum/ *n.* instrument marking musical time.

metropolis /mɪ'trɒpəlɪs/ *n.* chief city.

metropolitan /metrə'pɒlɪt(ə)n/ 1 *a.* of metropolis. 2 *n.* bishop with authority over bishops of province.

mettle /'met(ə)l/ *n.* quality of person's disposition or temperament; spirit, courage.

mettlesome /'metəlsəm/ *a.* spirited.

mew[1] 1 *n.* cat's cry. 2 *v.i.* utter mew.

mew[2] *n.* sea-gull.

mews *n.* series of private stables round open yard or lane, now often converted into dwellings.

mezzanine /'metsəniːn/ *n.* extra storey between two others, esp. ground and first floors.

mezzo /'metsəu/ *adv. Mus.* moderately, half. **mezzo forte**, **piano**, moderately loud, soft. [It.]

mezzo-soprano /metsəusə'prɑːnəu/ *n.* woman's singing voice between soprano and contralto in pitch; singer with mezzo-soprano voice; music for mezzo-soprano voice.

mezzotint /'metsəutɪnt/ *n.* kind of copper or steel engraving.

mf *abbr. mezzo-forte.*

mg *abbr.* milligram(s).

Mgr. *abbr. Monseigneur; Monsignor.*

mi *var. of* **me**[2].

MI *abbr.* Military Intelligence.

miaow /mɪ'au/ *n.* & *v.i.* = **mew**[1].

miasma /mɪ'æzmə/ *n.* infectious or noxious emanation. **miasmic** *a.*

mica /'maɪkə/ *n.* kind of mineral found as small glittering scales or crystals separable into thin plates.

mice *pl.* of **mouse.**

Michaelmas /'mɪkəlməs/ *n.* feast of St. Michael, 29 Sept. **Michaelmas daisy** aster flowering in autumn.

mickey /'mɪkɪ/ *n.* **take the mickey (out of)** tease or mock.

micro /'maɪkrəu/ *n. colloq.* microcomputer.

micro- *in comb.* small; one millionth of.

microbe /'maɪkrəub/ *n.* microorganism, esp. one causing disease or fermentation. **microbial** *a.*

microbiology /maɪkrəubaɪ'ɒlədʒɪ/ *n.* study of micro-organisms.

microchip /'maɪkrəutʃɪp/ *n.* tiny piece of semiconductor carrying many electrical circuits.

microcomputer /maɪkrəukəm-'pjuːtə(r)/ *n.* computer in which central processor is contained on microchip(s).

microcosm /'maɪkrəkɒz(ə)m/ *n.* complex thing regarded as epitome of greater system; miniature representation (*of*).

microdot /'maɪkrəudɒt/ *n.* photograph of document etc. reduced to very small size.

microfiche /'maɪkrəufiːʃ/ 1 *n.* (*pl.* same) piece of film bearing photograph of document etc. reduced to very small size.

microfilm /'maɪkrəufɪlm/ 1 *n.* length of film bearing series of document etc. reduced to very small size. 2 *v.t.* record on microfilm.

microlight /'maɪkrəulaɪt/ *n.* kind of motorized hang-glider.

micrometer /maɪ'krɒmɪtə(r)/ *n.* instrument for measuring small lengths or angles.

micron /'maɪkrɒn/ *n.* millionth of a metre.

micro-organism /'maɪkrəuːgænɪz(ə)m/ *n.* organism too small to be visible to the naked eye.

microphone /'maɪkrəfəun/ *n.* instrument for converting sound-waves into electrical energy.

microprocessor /'maɪkrəuprəusesə(r)/ *n.* data processor contained on microchip(s).

microscope /'maɪkrəskəup/ *n.* instrument for magnifying objects by means of lens(es) so as to reveal details invisible to naked eye.

microscopic /maɪkrə'skɒpɪk/ *a.* too

small to be visible (in detail) without microscope; of the microscope.

microscopy /maɪˈkrɒskəpɪ/ n. use of the microscope.

microsurgery /ˈmaɪkrəʊsɜːdʒərɪ/ n. surgery using microscope to see tissues and instruments.

microwave /ˈmaɪkrəʊweɪv/ n. electromagnetic wave of length between about 50 cm and 1 mm. **microwave oven** one using such waves to heat food quickly.

micturition /mɪktjʊˈrɪʃ(ə)n/ n. urination.

mid a. that is in the middle (of); intermediate. **midday** (time near) noon; **mid-off, -on,** Crick. fielder near bowler on off, on, side.

midden /ˈmɪd(ə)n/ n. dunghill; refuse-heap.

middle /ˈmɪd(ə)l/ 1 a. at equal distance from extremities; intermediate in rank, quality, etc.; average. 2 n. middle point or position; waist. **3 in the middle of** while or during; **middle age** middle part of normal lifetime; **Middle Ages** about 1000–1400; **middle class** social class including professional and business workers; **middleman** any of traders who handle commodity between its producer and its consumer; **middleweight** boxing-weight (up to 75 kg).

middling /ˈmɪdlɪŋ/ 1 a. moderately good; colloq. fairly well in health. 2 adv. fairly or moderately.

midge n. gnatlike insect.

midget /ˈmɪdʒɪt/ n. extremely small person or thing.

midland /ˈmɪdlənd/ a. of the middle part of country. **the Midlands** the inland counties of central England.

midnight /ˈmɪdnaɪt/ n. 12 o'clock at night; middle of night. **midnight sun** sun visible at midnight during summer in polar regions.

midriff /ˈmɪdrɪf/ n. region of front of body just above waist.

midshipman /ˈmɪdʃɪpmən/ n. (pl. -men) naval officer ranking next below sub-lieutenant.

midst n. middle.

midsummer /ˈmɪdsʌmə(r)/ n. period of or near summer solstice, about 21 June. **Midsummer's Day** 24 June.

midwife /ˈmɪdwaɪf/ n. (pl. -wives) person trained to assist at childbirth. **midwifery** /-ˈwɪfərɪ/ n.

mien /miːn/ n. person's bearing or look.

might[1] past of **may**[1].

might[2] /maɪt/ n. great power or strength or resources.

mighty /ˈmaɪtɪ/ a. 1 powerful, great. 2 adv. colloq. very.

mignonette /mɪnjəˈnet/ n. plant with fragrant grey-green flowers.

migraine /ˈmiːɡreɪn/ n. severe recurrent form of headache, often with disturbance of vision.

migrant /ˈmaɪɡrənt/ 1 a. that migrates. 2 n. migrant bird etc.

migrate /maɪˈɡreɪt/ v.i. move from one place, esp. one country, to another; (of bird etc.) come and go with seasons. **migration** n.; **migratory** a.

mikado /mɪˈkɑːdəʊ/ n. (pl. -dos) Emperor of Japan.

mike n. colloq. microphone.

milch /mɪltʃ/ a. (of domestic animal) giving or kept for milk.

mild /maɪld/ a. gentle; not severe or harsh or drastic; not strong or bitter. **mild steel** steel that is tough but not easily tempered.

mildew /ˈmɪldjuː/ 1 n. growth of minute fungi forming on surfaces exposed to damp. 2 v. taint or be tainted with mildew.

mile n. unit of linear measure (1760 yds.); race over one mile. **milestone** stone etc. set up on roadside to mark distance in miles, stage (in career etc.).

mileage /ˈmaɪlɪdʒ/ n. number of miles travelled; advantage to be gained from something.

miler /ˈmaɪlə(r)/ n. person or horse trained specially to run a mile.

milfoil /ˈmɪlfɔɪl/ n. common yarrow.

milieu /miːˈljɜː/ n. environment, social surroundings.

militant /ˈmɪlɪt(ə)nt/ 1 a. aggressively active; combative; engaged in warfare. 2 n. militant person. 3 **militancy** n.

militarism /ˈmɪlɪtərɪz(ə)m/ n. military spirit; reliance on military force and methods. **militarist** n.; **militaristic** a.

military /ˈmɪlɪtərɪ/ 1 a. of or for or done by soldiers or the armed forces. 2 n. the army. 3 **military band** combination of woodwind, brass, and percussion.

militate /ˈmɪlɪteɪt/ v.i. serve as argument or influence *against*. □ See page 666.

militia /mɪˈlɪʃə/ n. military force,esp. one raised from civilian population and supplementing regular army in emergency.

milk 1 n. opaque white fluid secreted by female mammals for feeding young; cow's milk as food; milk-like liquid. 2 v.t. draw milk from; get money out of, exploit. 3 **milk float** light vehicle used in delivering milk; **milkmaid** *arch.* woman who milks or works in dairy; **milkman** man who sells or delivers milk; **milk run** routine expedition or mission; **milk shake** drink of milk, flavouring, etc., mixed by shaking or whisking; **milksop** spiritless man or youth; **milk tooth** temporary tooth in young mammals.

milky /ˈmɪlkɪ/ a. of, like, or mixed with milk; (of) liquid) cloudy. **Milky Way** the Earth's galaxy.

mill 1 n. building fitted with mechanical apparatus for grinding corn; such apparatus; grinding-machine; building fitted with machinery for manufacturing process etc.; such machinery. 2 v. grind or treat in mill; produce grooves etc. in (metal, edge of coin, etc.); (of people or animals) move around in aimless manner. 3 **millpond** pond formed by damming stream to use water in mill; **mill-race** current of water driving mill-wheel; **millstone** circular stone for grinding corn, *fig.* heavy burden; **mill-wheel** wheel used to drive water-mill.

millennium /mɪˈlenɪəm/ n. thousand-year period; supposed coming time of happiness on earth. **millennial** a.

millepede /ˈmɪlɪpiːd/ n. small many-legged crawling animal.

miller /ˈmɪlə(r)/ n. person who works or owns a mill.

millesimal /mɪˈlesɪm(ə)l/ 1 a. thousandth; consisting of thousandths. 2 n. thousandth part.

millet /ˈmɪlɪt/ n. cereal plant with small nutritious seeds.

milli- *in comb.* one-thousandth.

milliard /ˈmɪljəd/ n. one thousand millions.

millibar /ˈmɪlɪbɑː(r)/ n. one-thousandth of a bar².

milligram /ˈmɪlɪgræm/ n. one-thousandth of a gram

millilitre /ˈmɪlɪliːtə(r)/ n. one-thousandth of a litre.

millimetre /ˈmɪlɪmiːtə(r)/ n. one-thousandth of a metre.

milliner /ˈmɪlɪnə(r)/ n. maker or seller of women's hats. **millinery** n.

million /ˈmɪljən/ n. one thousand thousand; million pounds, dollars, etc. **millionth** a. & n.

millionaire /mɪljəˈneə(r)/ n. person possessing a million pounds etc.; very rich person.

millipede var. of **millepede**.

milometer /maɪˈlɒmɪtə(r)/ n. instrument for recording number of miles travelled by vehicle.

milt n. roe of male fish.

mime 1 n. acting with gestures and usu. without words; performance involving this. 2 v. act or represent in mime.

mimeograph /ˈmɪmɪəgrɑːf/ 1 n. apparatus for making copies from stencils. 2 v.t. reproduce thus.

mimetic /mɪˈmetɪk/ a. of or given to imitation or mimicry.

mimic /ˈmɪmɪk/ 1 v.t. ridicule by imitating; imitate or resemble closely. 2 n. person who mimics. 3 **mimicry** n.

mimosa /mɪˈməʊzə/ n. kind of shrub esp. with small globular flower-heads.

min. *abbr.* minute(s); minimum.

Min. *abbr.* Minister; Ministry.

mina /ˈmaɪnə/ n. talking bird of starling family.

minaret /ˈmɪnəˈret/ n. tall slender tower of mosque.

minatory /ˈmɪnətərɪ/ a. threatening.

mince /mɪns/ 1 v. cut (meat etc.) very small, esp. in a machine; walk in affected way. 2 n. minced meat. 3 **mincemeat** mixture of currants, spices, suet, etc., chopped small; **mince pie** (usu. small round) pie of mincemeat.

mind /maɪnd/ 1 n. seat of consciousness, thought, volition, and feeling; intellectual powers; memory; opinion. 2 v. object to; take care or heed (of); have charge of; bear in mind.

minded /ˈmaɪndɪd/ a. disposed, inclined *to* do etc.

minder /'maɪndə(r)/ *n.* person whose business it is to look after person or thing.

mindful /'maɪndfʊl/ *a.* taking thought or care (*of*).

mindless /'maɪndlɪs/ *a.* stupidly ill-behaved; not involving mental effort.

mine¹ *pron.* & *a.* the one(s) belonging to me.

mine² 1 *n.* excavation for extracting metal or coal or salt etc.; *fig.* abundant source (*of*); receptacle filled with explosive placed in or on ground or in water. 2 *v.* obtain (minerals) from mine; dig in (earth etc.) for ore etc.; *Mil.* lay mines under or in. 3 **minefield** area where mines have been laid; **minesweeper** ship for clearing away explosive mines.

miner /'maɪnə(r)/ *n.* worker in mine.

mineral /'mɪnərəl/ 1 *n.* substance obtained by mining; natural inorganic substance in earth; artificial mineral water. 2 *a.* obtained by mining; not animal or vegetable. 3 **mineral water** water naturally or artificially impregnated with mineral substance, other non-alcoholic effervescent drink.

mineralogy /mɪnə'rælədʒɪ/ *n.* science of minerals. **mineralogical** *a.*; **mineralogist** *n.*

minestrone /mɪnɪ'strəʊnɪ/ *n.* soup containing vegetables and pasta or rice.

mingle /'mɪŋg(ə)l/ *v.* mix, blend.

mingy /'mɪndʒɪ/ *a. colloq.* stingy.

mini /'mɪnɪ/ *n. colloq.* miniskirt; (**Mini, P**) type of small car.

mini- /'mɪnɪ/ *in comb.* miniature, very small of its kind.

miniature /'mɪnɪtʃə(r)/ 1 *a.* much smaller than normal; represented on small scale. 2 *n.* small painted portrait etc.; miniature thing.

miniaturist /'mɪnɪtʃərɪst/ *n.* painter of miniatures.

miniaturize /'mɪnɪtʃəraɪŋ/ *v.t.* make miniature; produce in smaller version.

minibus /'mɪnɪbʌs/ *n.* small bus carrying about 12 passengers.

minicab /'mɪnɪkæb/ *n.* car like taxi but available only if ordered in advance.

minim /'mɪnɪm/ *n. Mus.* note half as long as semibreve.

minimal /'mɪnɪm(ə)l/ *a.* being or related to a minimum; very minute or slight.

minimize /'mɪnɪmaɪz/ *v.t.* reduce to or estimate at minimum; represent at less than true value etc.

minimum /'mɪnɪməm/ 1 *n.* (*pl.* -**ima**) least amount attainable, usual, etc. 2 *a.* that is a minimum.

minion /'mɪnjən/ *n. derog.* subordinate, assistant.

minister /'mɪnɪstə(r)/ 1 *n.* person at head of government department; clergyman, esp. in Presbyterian and Nonconformist Churches; diplomatic agent usu. ranking below ambassador; person employed in execution *of*. 2 *v.i.* render aid or service (*to*).

ministerial /mɪnɪ'stɪərɪəl/ *a.* of minister or his office; of government.

ministration /mɪnɪ'streɪʃ(ə)n/ *n.* (act of) ministering.

ministry /'mɪnɪstrɪ/ *n.* office or building or department of minister of State; ministers forming government; office as religious minister etc.

mink /mɪŋk/ *n.* small stoatlike animal; its fur.

minnow /'mɪnəʊ/ *n.* small freshwater fish.

Minoan /mɪ'nəʊən/ 1 *a.* of Cretan Bronze-Age civilization. 2 *n.* person of this civilization.

minor /'maɪnə(r)/ 1 *a.* lesser of two things, classes, etc.; under full legal age; comparatively unimportant; *Mus.* of or based on scale that has semitone next above second note. 2 *n.* person under full legal age; *US* student's subsidiary subject. 3 *v.i. US* (of student) undertake study in as minor.

minority /maɪ'nɒrɪtɪ/ *n.* smaller number or part, esp. in voting; group of persons differing from others in race, religion, language, etc.; state of being under full legal age, period of this.

minster /'mɪnstə(r)/ *n.* large church.

minstrel /'mɪnstr(ə)l/ *n.* medieval singer or musician; (usu. in *pl.*) one of band of entertainers with blackened faces etc.

minstrelsy /'mɪnstrəlsɪ/ *n.* minstrel's art or poetry.

mint¹ *n.* aromatic culinary herb; peppermint.

mint² 1 *n.* place where money is coined. 2 *v.t.* coin (money); invent.

minuet /mɪnjʊ'et/ *n.* slow stately

dance in triple time; music for this or in same style.

minus /'maɪnəs/ **1** *prep.* with subtraction of; *colloq.* deprived of. **2** *n.* minus sign (–); negative quantity.

minuscule /'mɪnəskjuːl/ **1** *a.* extremely small; lower-case. **2** *n.* lower-case letter.

minute[1] /'mɪnɪt/ **1** *n.* sixtieth part of hour or degree; short time; memorandum, summary; in *pl.* official record of proceedings. **2** *v.t.* record in minutes; send minute to.

minute[2] /maɪ'njuːt/ *a.* very small; precise, going into details.

minutiae /maɪ'njuːʃiː/ *n. pl.* trivial points, small details.

minx *n.* pert or sly girl.

miracle /'mɪrək(ə)l/ *n.* event due to supernatural agency; remarkable event or object. **miracle play** medieval dramatic representation based on Bible or lives of saints.

miraculous /mɪ'rækjʊləs/ *a.* supernatural; surprising.

mirage /mɪ'rɑːʒ/ *n.* optical illusion produced by atmospheric conditions; illusory thing.

mire /maɪə(r)/ **1** *n.* swampy ground, mud. **2** *v.* sink in or bespatter with mud.

mirror /'mɪrə(r)/ **1** *n.* smooth surface, esp. of amalgam-coated glass, reflecting image; *fig.* what gives faithful reflection. **2** *v.t.* reflect as in mirror. **3** **mirror image** reflection or copy in which left and right sides are reversed.

mirth /mɜːθ/ *n.* merriment, laughter. **mirthful** *a.*

miry /'maɪərɪ/ *a.* muddy.

misadventure /mɪsəd'ventʃə(r)/ *n.* piece of bad luck. **by misadventure** by accident.

misalliance /mɪsə'laɪəns/ *n.* unsuitable marriage.

misanthrope /'mɪsənθrəʊp/ *n.* hater of mankind. **misanthropic** /-'θrɒp-/ *a.*; **misanthropy** /-'sæn-/ *n.*

misapply /mɪsə'plaɪ/ *v.t.* apply or use wrongly. **misapplication** *n.*

misapprehend /mɪsæprɪ'hend/ *v.t.* misunderstand. **misapprehension** *n.*

misappropriate /mɪsə'prəʊprɪeɪt/ *v.t.* apply (another's money etc.) dishonestly to one's own use. **misappropriation** *n.*

misbegotten /mɪsbɪ'gɒt(ə)n/ *a.* contemptible; bastard.

misbehave /mɪsbɪ'heɪv/ *v.i.* behave improperly. **misbehaviour** *n.*

miscalculate /mɪs'kælkʊleɪt/ *v.* calculate wrongly. **miscalculation** *n.*

miscall /mɪs'kɔːl/ *v.t.* call by wrong name; call wrongly.

miscarriage /mɪs'kærɪdʒ/ *n.* spontaneous abortion; miscarrying of plan etc.

miscarry /mɪs'kærɪ/ *v.i.* be unsuccessful, go astray; have miscarriage.

miscast /mɪs'kɑːst/ *v.t.* (*past & p.p.* -**cast**) cast (actor) in unsuitable part.

miscegenation /mɪsɪdʒɪ'neɪʃ(ə)n/ *n.* interbreeding between races.

miscellaneous /mɪsə'leɪnɪəs/ *a.* of various kinds; of mixed composition or character.

miscellany /mɪ'selənɪ/ *n.* mixture, medley.

mischance /mɪs'tʃɑːns/ *n.* bad luck; misfortune.

mischief /'mɪstʃɪf/ *n.* troublesome but not malicious conduct, esp. of children; harm or injury caused esp. by person. **mischievous** /'mɪstʃɪvəs/ *a.*

misconceive /mɪskən'siːv/ *v.* have wrong idea of; misunderstand. **misconception** *n.*

misconduct /mɪs'kɒndʌkt/ *n.* improper conduct.

misconstrue /mɪskən'struː/ *v.t.* misinterpret. **misconstruction** *n.*

miscount /mɪs'kaʊnt/ **1** *v.* make wrong count, count (things) wrongly. **2** *n.* wrong count, esp. of votes.

miscreant /'mɪskrɪənt/ *n.* villain.

misdeal /mɪs'diːl/ **1** *v.* (*past & p.p.* -**dealt** /-'delt/) make mistake in dealing. **2** *n.* wrong deal.

misdeed /mɪs'diːd/ *n.* wrong action.

misdemeanour /mɪsdɪ'miːnə(r)/ *n.* misdeed; *Law* indictable offence.

misdirect /mɪsdaɪ'rekt/ *v.t.* direct wrongly. **misdirection** *n.*

mise en scène /miːz ɑ̃ 'sen/ scenery etc. of acted play; *fig.* surroundings of an event. [F]

miser /'maɪzə(r)/ *n.* person who hoards wealth and lives miserably. **miserly** *a.*

miserable /'mɪzərəb(ə)l/ *a.* wretchedly unhappy or uncomfortable; pitiable; mean.

misericord /mɪˈzerɪkɔːd/ n. projection under hinged seat in choir stall to support person standing.

misery /ˈmɪzərɪ/ n. wretched state of mind or outward circumstances; *colloq.* constantly grumbling person.

misfire /mɪsˈfaɪə(r)/ **1** v.i. fail to go off or start action or function regularly or have intended effect. **2** n. such failure.

misfit /ˈmɪsfɪt/ n. person ill-adapted to surroundings etc.; garment etc. that does not fit.

misfortune /mɪsˈfɔːtjuːn/ n. (instance of) bad luck.

misgive /mɪsˈgɪv/ v.t. (*past* **-gave**; *p.p.* **given**) (of person's mind etc.) fill him with suspicion or foreboding.

misgiving /mɪsˈgɪvɪŋ/ n. feeling of mistrust or apprehension.

misgovern /mɪsˈgʌv(ə)n/ v.t. govern badly. **misgovernment** n.

misguided /mɪsˈgaɪdɪd/ a. mistaken in thought or action.

mishandle /mɪsˈhænd(ə)l/ v.t. deal with ineffectually; handle roughly.

mishap /ˈmɪshæp/ n. unlucky accident.

mishear /mɪsˈhɪə(r)/ v. (*past* & *p.p.* **-heard** /-ˈhɜːd/) hear incorrectly or imperfectly.

misinform /mɪsɪnˈfɔːm/ v.t. give wrong information to. **misinformation** n.

misinterpret /mɪsɪnˈtɜːprɪt/ v.t. interpret wrongly. **misinterpretation** n.

misjudge /mɪsˈdʒʌdʒ/ v.t. judge wrongly. **misjudgement** n.

mislay /mɪsˈleɪ/ v.t. (*past* & *p.p.* **-laid**) put (thing) by accident where it cannot readily be found.

mislead /mɪsˈliːd/ v.t. (*past* & *p.p.* **-led**) lead astray; give wrong impression to.

mismanage /mɪsˈmænɪdʒ/ v.t. manage badly or wrongly. **mismanagement** n.

misnomer /mɪsˈnəʊmə(r)/ wrongly applied name.

misogynist /mɪˈsɒdʒɪnɪst/ n. person who hates all women. **misogyny** n.

misplace /mɪsˈpleɪs/ v.t. put in wrong place; bestow on ill-chosen object. **misplacement** n.

misprint **1** n. /ˈmɪsprɪnt/ error in printing. **2** v.t. /mɪsˈprɪnt/ print wrongly.

mispronounce /mɪsprəˈnaʊns/ v.t. pronounce wrongly. **mispronunciation** n.

misquote /mɪsˈkwəʊt/ v.t. quote wrongly. **misquotation** n.

misread /mɪsˈriːd/ v.t. (*past* & *p.p.* **-read** /-ˈred/) read or interpret wrongly.

misrepresent /mɪsreprɪˈzent/ v.t. give false account of; represent wrongly. **misrepresentation** n.

misrule /mɪsˈruːl/ **1** v.t. govern badly. **2** n. bad government.

miss[1] **1** v. fail to hit, reach, meet, find, catch, or perceive; pass over; regret absence of; fail. **2** n. failure. **3** *give thing a miss* avoid it, leave it alone; *miss out* omit.

Miss[2] n. title prefixed to name of or used to address unmarried woman or girl.

missal /ˈmɪs(ə)l/ n. RC mass-book.

missel-thrush /ˈmɪs(ə)l/ large kind of thrush.

misshapen /mɪsˈʃeɪpən/ a. deformed, distorted.

missile /ˈmɪsaɪl/ n. object or weapon capable of being thrown or projected; weapon directed by remote control or automatically.

missing /ˈmɪsɪŋ/ a. not present; not found; (of person) not traced but not known to be dead.

mission /ˈmɪʃ(ə)n/ n. persons sent out as envoys or evangelists; missionary post; task; operational sortie; vocation.

missionary /ˈmɪʃənərɪ/ **1** a. of religious etc. missions. **2** n. person doing missionary work.

missis /ˈmɪsɪz/ n. **the missis** *colloq.* my or your wife.

missive /ˈmɪsɪv/ n. letter.

misspell /mɪsˈspel/ v.t. (*past* & *p.p.* **-spelt** or **-spelled**) spell wrongly.

misspend /mɪsˈspend/ v.t. (*past* & *p.p.* **-spent**) spend wrongly or wastefully.

misstate /mɪsˈsteɪt/ v.t. state wrongly. **misstatement** n.

mist **1** n. water-vapour in drops smaller than rain; dimness, blurring, caused by tears etc. **2** v. cover or be covered (as) with mist.

mistake /mɪˈsteɪk/ **1** n. incorrect idea or opinion; thing incorrectly done or thought. **2** v. (*past* **-took**; *p.p.* **-taken**) come to wrong conclusion about, misinterpret; wrongly take (person or thing) *for* another; in *p.p.* due to error, misjudged.

mistime /mɪsˈtaɪm/ *v.t.* say or do at wrong time.

mistletoe /ˈmɪsəltəʊ/ *n.* parasitic white-berried plant.

mistral /ˈmɪstr(ə)l/ *n.* cold N. or NW wind in S. France.

mistress /ˈmɪstrɪs/ *n.* woman in authority or with power; female head of household; female teacher; woman having illicit sexual relationship with man.

mistrial /mɪsˈtraɪəl/ *n.* trial vitiated by error.

mistrust /mɪsˈtrʌst/ 1 *v.t.* feel no confidence in. 2 *n.* lack of confidence; suspicion. 3 **mistrustful** *a.*

misty /ˈmɪstɪ/ *a.* of, in, or like mist; of dim outline; obscure.

misunderstand /mɪsʌndəˈstænd/ *v.* (-stood) not understand rightly.

misuse 1 /mɪsˈjuːz/ *v.t.* use wrongly; ill-treat. 2 /mɪsˈjuːs/ *n.* wrong use.

mite *n.* small arachnid esp. of kind found in cheese etc.; modest contribution; small object or child.

mitigate /ˈmɪtɪɡeɪt/ *v.t.* make milder or less intense or severe. **mitigation** *n.* □ See page 666.

mitre /ˈmaɪtə(r)/ 1 *n.* bishop's tall pointed head-dress; joint of two pieces of wood such that line of junction bisects angle between them. 2 *v.t.* bestow mitre on; join with mitre.

mitt *n.* mitten; *sl.* hand.

mitten /ˈmɪt(ə)n/ *n.* glove with only one compartment for the 4 fingers; knitted etc. glove leaving fingertips and thumb-tip bare.

mix 1 *v.* put together, combine, (substances, groups, qualities, etc.) so that particles or members etc. of each are diffused among those of the other(s); prepare (compound, cocktail, etc.) by mixing ingredients; be sociable (*with*); join, be mixed; be compatible. 2 *n.* mixing, mixture; ingredients prepared commercially for making cake etc. or for process such as concrete-making.

mixed /mɪkst/ *a.* of diverse qualities or elements; of or for various classes, both sexes, etc. **mixed marriage** one between persons of different race or re-

ligion; **mixed-up** *colloq.* muddled, ill-adjusted.

mixer /ˈmɪksə(r)/ *n.* apparatus for mixing foods etc.; person who manages socially in specified way; non-alcoholic drink to be mixed with spirit etc.

mixture /ˈmɪkstʃə(r)/ *n.* mixing; what is mixed; combination of ingredients, qualities, etc.

mizen-mast /ˈmɪz(ə)n/ *Naut.* mast next aft of mainmast.

ml. *abbr.* mile(s); millilitre(s).

Mlle(s) *abbr.* *Mademoiselle, Mesdemoiselles.*

MM *abbr.* *Messieurs;* Military Medal.

mm. *abbr.* millimetre(s).

Mme(s) *abbr.* *Madame, Mesdames.*

mnemonic /nɪˈmɒnɪk/ 1 *a.* of or designed to aid memory. 2 *n.* mnemonic device; in *pl.* art of or system for improving memory.

mo *n.* (pl. **mos**) *sl.* moment.

MO *abbr.* Medical Officer; money order.

moan 1 *n.* low inarticulate sound expressing pain or grief; complaint. 2 *v.* utter moan; lament, complain.

moat *n.* defensive ditch round castle, town, etc., usu. filled with water.

mob 1 *n.* riotous crowd; rabble; *sl.* gang, associated group of persons. 2 *v.t.* attack in mob; crowd round and molest.

mob-cap *n.* *hist.* woman's indoor cap covering all the hair.

mobile /ˈməʊbaɪl/ 1 *a.* movable (readily or freely); (of face) of changing expression; (of shop etc.) accommodated in vehicle; (of person) able to change social status. 2 *n.* ornamental structure that may be hung so as to turn freely. 3 **mobility** /-ˈbɪl-/ *n.*

mobilize /ˈməʊbɪlaɪz/ *v.* call up, assemble, prepare, for warfare etc. **mobilization** *n.*

mobster /ˈmɒbstə(r)/ *n.* *sl.* gangster.

moccasin /ˈmɒkəsɪn/ *n.* soft heelless shoe as orig. worn by N. Amer. Indians.

mock 1 *v.* ridicule, scoff *at,* mimic; jeer, scoff. 2 *a.* sham; imitation. 3 **mock turtle soup** soup made from calf's head etc.; **mock-up** experimental model.

mockery /ˈmɒkərɪ/ *n.* derision, subject or occasion of this; travesty.

modal /ˈməʊd(ə)l/ *a.* of mode or form as opp. to substance; *Gram.* of or expressing mood or manner.

mode *n.* way in which thing is done; current fashion; *Mus.* scale system.

model /'mɒd(ə)l/ 1 *n.* representation in three dimensions of existing person or thing or of proposed structure, esp. on smaller scale; simplified description of system etc.; design or style of structure, esp. of motor vehicle; person or thing proposed for imitation; person employed to pose for artist, or to display clothes etc. by wearing them; (copy of) garment etc. by well-known designer. 2 *a.* exemplary, ideally perfect. 3 *v.* fashion or shape (figure) in clay, wax, etc.; form (thing) *after* or (*up*)*on* model; (of person acting as model) display (garment).

modem /'məʊdem/ *n.* device for sending and receiving computer data by means of telephone line.

moderate 1 /'mɒdərət/ *a.* avoiding extremes, temperate; not excessive; middling in quantity or quality. 2 /'mɒdərət/ *n.* person of moderate views. 3 /'mɒdəreɪt/ *v.t.* make or become less violent or excessive; act as moderator. 4 **moderation** *n.*

moderator /'mɒdəreɪtə(r)/ *n.* arbitrator, mediator; Presbyterian minister presiding over any ecclesiastical body.

modern /'mɒd(ə)n/ 1 *a.* of present and recent times; in current fashion, not antiquated. 2 *n.* person living in modern times. 3 **modernity** /-'dɜːn-/ *n.*

modernism /'mɒdənɪz(ə)m/ *n.* modern ideas or methods. **modernist** *a.* & *n.*

modernize /'mɒdənaɪz/ *v.* make modern; adapt to modern ideas, taste, etc. **modernization** *n.*

modest /'mɒdɪst/ *a.* having humble or moderate estimate of one's own merit; bashful; decorous; not excessive; unpretentious. **modesty** *n.*

modicum /'mɒdɪkəm/ *n.* small quantity.

modify /'mɒdɪfaɪ/ *v.t.* make less severe; tone down; make partial changes in. **modification** *n.*

modish /'məʊdɪʃ/ *a.* fashionable.

modular /'mɒdjʊlə(r)/ *a.* based on module(s).

modulate /'mɒdjʊleɪt/ *v.* regulate, adjust; adjust or vary tone or pitch of; alter amplitude or frequency of (wave)

by wave of lower frequency to convey signal; *Mus.* pass from one key to another. **modulation** *n.*

module /'mɒdjuːl/ *n.* standardized part or independent unit in construction esp. of furniture, building, spacecraft, or electronic system.

modus operandi /'məʊdəs ɒpə'rændɪ/ method of working. [L]

modus vivendi /'məʊdəs vɪ'vendɪ/ compromise pending settlement of dispute. [L]

mog *n. colloq.* (also **moggie**) cat.

mogul /'məʊg(ə)l/ *n.* great or important person.

mohair /'məʊheə(r)/ *n.* hair of Angora goat; yarn or fabric from this.

Mohammedan var. of **Muhammadan**.

moiety /'mɔɪətɪ/ *n.* half.

moil *v.i.* drudge.

moiré /'mwɑːreɪ/ *a.* (of silk) watered; like watered silk in appearance.

moist *a.* slightly wet, damp; rainy.

moisten /'mɔɪs(ə)n/ *v.* make or become moist.

moisture /'mɔɪstʃə(r)/ *n.* liquid diffused as vapour or condensed on surface.

moisturize /'mɔɪstʃəraɪz/ *v.t.* make less dry (esp. skin by use of cosmetic).

moke *n. sl.* donkey.

molar /'məʊlə(r)/ 1 *a.* serving to grind. 2 *n.* molar tooth.

molasses /mə'læsɪz/ *n.* syrup drained from raw sugar.

mole¹ *n.* small burrowing animal with short soft fur; *colloq.* spy established deep within organization. **molehill** mound thrown up by mole in burrowing.

mole² *n.* small permanent dark spot on human skin.

mole³ *n.* massive stone etc. structure as pier or breakwater.

molecule /'mɒlɪkjuːl/ *n.* smallest particle (usu. group of atoms) to which a substance can be reduced without losing its chemical identity. **molecular** /mə'lekjʊlə(r)/ *a.*

molest /mə'lest/ *v.t.* subject to intentional annoyance. **molestation** *n.*

moll *n. colloq.* prostitute; gangster's female companion.

mollify /'mɒlɪfaɪ/ *v.t.* soften, appease. **mollification** *n.*

mollusc /'mɒləsk/ *n.* one of a group of soft-bodied usu. hard-shelled animals including snails, oysters, etc.

mollycoddle /'mɒlɪkɒd(ə)l/ **1** *v.t.* coddle. **2** *n.* milksop.

molten /'məʊlt(ə)n/ *a.* liquefied by heat.

molto /'mɒltəʊ/ *adv. Mus.* very.

molybdenum /mə'lɪbdɪnəm/ *n.* silver-white metallic element used in steel for making high-speed tools etc.

moment /'məʊmənt/ *n.* point or brief space of time; importance, weight; *Phys.* product of force and distance of its line of action from centre of rotation.

momentary /'məʊməntərɪ/ *a.* lasting only a moment.

momentous /mə'mentəs/ *a.* having great importance.

momentum /mə'mentəm/ *n.* (*pl.* **-ta**) quantity of motion of moving body; impetus gained by movement.

Mon. *abbr.* Monday.

monarch /'mɒnək/ *n.* sovereign with title of king, queen, emperor, etc.; supreme ruler. **monarchic(al)** *a.*

monarchism /'mɒnəkɪz(ə)m/ *n.* advocacy or principals of monarchy. **monarchist** *n.*

monarchy /'mɒnəkɪ/ *n.* monarchical government; State with this.

monastery /'mɒnəstərɪ/ *n.* residence of community, usu. of monks.

monastic /mə'næstɪk/ *a.* of or like monks, nuns, etc.; of monasteries. **monasticism** /-'næs-/ *n.*

Monday /'mʌndeɪ/ *n.* day of week following Sunday.

monetarism /'mʌnɪtərɪz(ə)m/ *n.* control of money as chief method of stabilizing economy. **monetarist** *a. & n.*

monetary /'mʌnɪtərɪ/ *a.* of the currency in use, (consisting) of money.

money /'mʌnɪ/ *n.* current medium of exchange in form of coins and banknotes etc.; in *pl.* (**moneys** or **monies**) sums of money; wealth. **money-changer** person whose business it is to change money at stated rate; **money-lender** person lending money at interest; **money-market** sphere of operation of dealers in stocks and bills; **money order** post-office order for payment of specified sum; **money-**

spinner thing that brings in much profit, kind of small spider.

moneyed /'mʌnɪd/ *a.* rich.

Mongol /'mɒŋɡ(ə)l/ **1** *a.* of Asian people now inhabiting Mongolia; (**mongol**) having Down's syndrome. **2** *n.* Mongol person; (**mongol**) person with Down's syndrome.

Mongolian /mɒŋ'ɡəʊlɪən/ **1** *a.* of Mongolia; Mongol; Mongoloid. **2** *n.* native or language of Mongolia.

mongolism /'mɒŋɡəlɪz(ə)m/ *n.* Down's syndrome.

Mongoloid /'mɒŋɡəlɔɪd/ **1** *a.* resembling Mongolians in racial origin or in having broad flat (yellowish) face; mongol. **2** *n.* Mongoloid person.

mongoose /'mɒŋɡuːs/ *n.* small carnivorous tropical mammal.

mongrel /'mʌŋɡr(ə)l/ **1** *n.* dog of no definable breed or type; any animal or plant resulting from crossings of different breeds or types. **2** *a.* of mixed origin or character.

monitor /'mɒnɪtə(r)/ **1** *n.* pupil in school with disciplinary etc. duties; television receiver used in selecting or verifying the broadcast picture; person who listens to and reports on foreign broadcasts etc.; detector of radioactive contamination. **2** *v.* act as monitor (of); maintain regular surveillance (over).

monk /mʌŋk/ *n.* member of community of men living apart under religious vows. **monkish** *a.*

monkey /'mʌŋkɪ/ **1** *n.* mammal of a group closely allied to man; *sl.* £500. **2** *v.i.* play tricks (*with*). **3** **monkey-nut** peanut; **monkey-puzzle** kind of prickly tree; **monkey-wrench** wrench with adjustable jaw.

mono /'mɒnəʊ/ **1** *a.* monophonic. **2** *n.* such sound, reproduction, etc.

mono- *in comb.* one, alone, single.

monochromatic /mɒnəkrə'mætɪk/ *a.* (of light) containing only one colour or wavelength; executed in monochrome.

monochrome /'mɒnəkrəʊm/ *a.* having or using only one colour.

monocle /'mɒnək(ə)l/ *n.* single eye-glass.

monocular /mə'nɒkjʊlə(r)/ *a.* with or for one eye.

monody /'mɒnədɪ/ *n.* dirge or elegy.

monogamy /mə'nɒɡəmɪ/ *n.* state or

practice of being married to only one person at a time. **monogamous** *a.*

monogram /ˈmɒnəɡræm/ *n.* two or more letters, esp. initials, interwoven.

monograph /ˈmɒnəɡrɑːf/ *n.* treatise on single subject or aspect of it.

monolith /ˈmɒnəlɪθ/ *n.* single block of stone, esp. shaped into pillar etc.; person or thing like monolith in being massive, immovable, or solidly uniform. **monolithic** *a.*

monologue /ˈmɒnəlɒɡ/ *n.* scene in drama where person speaks alone; dramatic composition for one speaker; long speech by one person.

monomania /mɒnəˈmeɪnɪə/ *n.* obsession of mind by one idea or interest. **monomaniac** *n.*

monophonic /mɒnəˈfɒnɪk/ *a.* (of reproduction of sound) using only one channel of transmission.

monoplane /ˈmɒnəpleɪn/ *n.* aeroplane with one set of wings.

monopolist /məˈnɒpəlɪst/ *n.* holder or supporter of monopoly.

monopolize /məˈnɒpəlaɪz/ *v.t.* obtain exclusive possession or control of. **monopolization** *n.*

monopoly /məˈnɒpəlɪ/ *n.* exclusive trading privilege; sole possession or control.

monorail /ˈmɒnəʊreɪl/ *n.* railway in which track consists of single rail.

monosodium glutamate /mɒnəˈsəʊdɪəm ˈɡluːtəmeɪt/ substance added to food to enhance its flavour.

monosyllable /ˈmɒnəsɪləb(ə)l/ *n.* word of one syllable. **monosyllabic** *a.*

monotheism /ˈmɒnəθiːɪz(ə)m/ *n.* doctrine that there is only one God. **monotheist** *n;* **monotheistic** *a.*

monotone /ˈmɒnətəʊn/ *n.* sound continuing or repeated on one note or without change of pitch.

monotonous /məˈnɒtənəs/ *a.* lacking in variety, wearisome through sameness. **monotony** *n.*

monoxide /məˈnɒksaɪd/ *n.* oxide containing one oxygen atom.

Monseigneur /mɒ̃senˈjɜː(r)/ *n.* French title of princes, cardinals, etc. [F]

Monsieur /məˈsjɜː(r)/ *n.* (*pl. Messieurs* /mesˈjɜː/) title used of or to French-speaking man. [F]

Monsignor /mɒnsiːˈnjɔː(r)/ *n.* title of some RC prelates etc. [It.]

monsoon /mɒnˈsuːn/ *n.* seasonal wind prevailing in S. Asia; rainy season accompanying SW monsoon.

monster /ˈmɒnstə(r)/ **1** *n.* imaginary large and frightening creature; misshapen animal or plant; inhumanly cruel or wicked person; huge animal or thing. **2** *a.* huge.

monstrance /ˈmɒnstrəns/ *n. RC Ch.* vessel in which consecrated Host is exposed.

monstrosity /mɒnˈstrɒsɪtɪ/ *n.* misshapen or outrageous thing; monstrousness.

monstrous /ˈmɒnstrəs/ *a.* like a monster; huge; outrageous.

montage /ˈmɒntɑːʒ/ *n.* selection, cutting, and arrangement of shots in cinema film etc.; (picture etc. produced by) juxtaposition of (parts of) photographs etc.

month /mʌnθ/ *n.* any of 12 divisions of calendar year; any period between same dates in successive such portions; period of 28 days.

monthly /ˈmʌnθlɪ/ **1** *a.* produced or occurring once every month. **2** *adv.* every month. **3** *n.* monthly periodical.

monument /ˈmɒnjʊmənt/ *n.* anything designed or serving to commemorate someone or something.

monumental /mɒnjʊˈment(ə)l/ *a.* of or serving as monument; massive and permanent; great, stupendous.

moo 1 *n.* characteristic sound of cow. **2** *v.i.* make this sound.

mooch /muːtʃ/ *v.i. colloq.* loiter *about*; slouch *along*.

mood[1] /muːd/ *n.* state of mind or feeling.

mood[2] /muːd/ *n. Gram.* form(s) of verb serving to indicate whether it is to express fact or command or wish etc.; group of such forms.

moody /ˈmuːdɪ/ *a.* gloomy, sullen.

moon /muːn/ **1** *n.* natural satellite of the earth, revolving round it monthly, reflecting light from the sun; *poet.* month; natural satellite of any planet. **2** *v.i.* move or look listlessly. **3 moonbeam** ray of moonlight; **moonlight** light of moon, *colloq.* have other paid occupation besides official one; **moonlit** lighted by the moon; **moonshine**

visionary talk, illicit liquor; **moon-shot** launching of spacecraft to moon; **moonstone** feldspar with pearly appearance; **moonstruck** deranged in mind.

moony /'muːnɪ/ a. stupidly dreamy.

moor¹ /mʊə(r)/ n. tract of open waste land esp. if covered with heather. **moorhen** small water-hen; **moorland** country abounding in heather.

moor² /mʊə(r)/ v.t. attach (boat etc.) to fixed object.

Moor³ /mʊə(r)/ n. one of a Muslim people of NW Africa. **Moorish** a.

mooring /'mʊərɪŋ/ n. (usu.in pl.) permanent anchors and chains for ships to be moored to; place where vessel is moored.

moose /muːs/ n. (pl. same) N. Amer. elk.

moot /muːt/ 1 v.t. raise (question etc.) for discussion. 2 a. debatable. 3 n. hist. assembly.

mop 1 n. sponge or bundle of yarn etc. fixed to stick for use in cleaning; thick untidy head of hair. 2 v. clean or wipe (as) with mop; wipe up (as) with mop. 3 **mop up** sl. absorb, dispose of, Mil. complete occupation of (area etc.) by capturing or killing remaining enemy troops etc.

mope v.i. be dull, dejected, and spiritless.

moped /'məʊped/ n. motorized bicycle.

moquette /mə'ket/ n. fabric with pile, used for upholstery etc.

moraine /mɒ'reɪn/ n. pile of debris carried down and deposited by glacier.

moral /'mɒr(ə)l/ 1 a. concerned with character etc. or with right and wrong; good, virtuous. 2 n. moral lesson; in pl. moral habits. 3 **moral certainty** probability so great as to allow no reasonable doubt; **moral support** psychological rather than physical help.

morale /mɒ'rɑːl/ n. mental attitude or bearing of person or group.

moralist /'mɒrəlɪst/ n. person who teaches morality. **moralistic** a.

morality /mə'rælɪtɪ/ n. degree of conformity to moral principles; moral conduct; moralizing.

moralize /'mɒrəlaɪz/ v.i. indulge in moral reflection or talk. **moralization** n.

morass /mə'ræs/ n. marsh, bog; entanglement.

moratorium /mɒrə'tɔːrɪəm/ n. (pl. **-iums**) legal authorization to debtor to postpone payment; temporary prohibition or suspension.

morbid /'mɔːbɪd/ a. not natural and healthy; indicative etc. of disease. **morbidity** n.

mordant /'mɔːd(ə)nt/ 1 a. caustic, biting; (of acids etc.) corrosive. 2 n. mordant acid or substance.

more /mɔː/ 1 a. greater in quantity or degree. 2 n. greater quantity or number. 3 adv. to greater degree or extent or amount.

morello /mə'reləʊ/ n. (pl. **-os**) dark-coloured bitter cherry.

moreover /mɔː'rəʊvə(r)/ adv. besides, in addition.

mores /'mɔːriːz/ n.pl. social customs and moral principles etc. of class or group etc.

morganatic /mɔːgə'nætɪk/ a. (of marriage) between man of high rank and woman of lower rank who remains in her former station.

morgue /mɔːg/ n. mortuary; materials kept for reference by newspaper etc.

moribund /'mɒrɪbʌnd/ a. at point of death.

Mormon /'mɔːmən/ n. member of Church of Latter-day Saints. **Mormonism** n.

morn n. poet. morning.

morning /'mɔːnɪŋ/ n. early part of day till noon or midday meal. **morning coat** tail-coat with front sloped away; **morning dress** man's formal wear with morning coat; **morning glory** climbing plant with trumpet-shaped flowers; **morning star** Venus or other planet seen in east before sunrise.

morocco /mə'rɒkəʊ/ n. (pl. **-os**) fine flexible leather of goatskin tanned with sumac.

moron /'mɔːrɒn/ n. adult with mental development of child of about 8 or 12; colloq. stupid person. **moronic** /-'rɒn-/ a.

morose /mə'rəʊs/ a. sullen, gloomy, and unsocial.

morphia /'mɔːfɪə/ n. morphine.

morphine /'mɔːfiːn/ n. narcotic constituent of opium.

morphology /mɔː'fɒlədʒɪ/ n. study of

forms of animals and plants or of words and their structure. **morphological** *a.*

morris dance /ˈmɒrɪs/ traditional dance in fancy costume.

morrow /ˈmɒrəʊ/ *n.* following day.

Morse /mɔːs/ 1 *n.* the alphabet or code in which letters are represented by combinations of long and short signals. 2 *a.* of this alphabet or code.

morsel /ˈmɔːs(ə)l/ *n.* small quantity; mouthful.

mortal /ˈmɔːt(ə)l/ 1 *a.* subject to or causing death; (of enemy) implacable. 2 *n.* human being. 3 **mortal sin** one fatal to salvation.

mortality /mɔːˈtælɪtɪ/ *n.* being subject to death; loss of life on large scale; death-rate.

mortar /ˈmɔːtə(r)/ *n.* mixture of lime and sand and water, for joining stones or bricks; short gun for throwing shells etc. at high angles; vessel in which drugs, food, etc. are pounded with pestle. **mortar-board** board for holding mortar, stiff square-topped academic cap.

mortgage /ˈmɔːgɪdʒ/ 1 *n.* conveyance of property as security for debt until money is repaid; sum of money lent by this. 2 *v.t.* make over by mortgage; pledge in advance.

mortgagee /mɔːgəˈdʒiː/ *n.* creditor in mortgage.

mortgager /ˈmɔːgɪdʒə(r)/ *n.* (in *Law* **mortgagor**) debtor in mortgage.

mortician /mɔːˈtɪʃ(ə)n/ *n.* *US* undertaker.

mortify /ˈmɔːtɪfaɪ/ *v.* humiliate, wound; bring (body etc.) into subjection by self-denial etc.; be affected with gangrene. **mortification** *n.*

mortise /ˈmɔːtɪs/ 1 *n.* hole in framework to receive another part, esp. tenon. 2 *v.t.* join by mortise and tenon; cut mortise in. 3 **mortise lock** one recessed in frame of door etc.

mortuary /ˈmɔːtjʊərɪ/ 1 *n.* building in which dead bodies may be kept for a time. 2 *a.* of death or burial.

mosaic[1] /məˈzeɪɪk/ 1 *n.* picture or pattern made with small coloured pieces of stone, glass, etc. 2 *a.* of or like such work.

Mosaic[2] /məˈzeɪɪk/ of Moses.

moselle /məˈzel/ *n.* dry German white wine.

Moslem /ˈmɒzləm/ var. of **Muslim**.

mosque /mɒsk/ *n.* Muslim place of worship.

mosquito /mɒsˈkiːtəʊ/ *n.* (*pl.* **-toes**) gnat, esp. with long blood-sucking proboscis. **mosquito-net** net to keep off mosquitoes.

moss *n.* small flowerless plant growing on moist surfaces; swamp, peat-bog. **moss-rose** rose with mosslike growth on calyx and stalk. **mossy** *a.*

most /məʊst/ 1 *a.* greatest in quantity or degree; the majority of. 2 *n.* the greatest quantity or degree; the majority. 3 *adv.* in great or greatest degree.

mostly /ˈməʊstlɪ/ *adv.* for the most part.

mot /məʊ/ *n.* (*pl.* **mots** /məʊz/) witty saying. **mot juste** /ʒuːst/ exactly appropriate expression. [F]

MOT *abbr.* Ministry of Transport. **MOT test** *colloq.* compulsory annual test of motor vehicles over specified age.

mote *n.* particle of dust.

motel /məʊˈtel/ *n.* roadside hotel or group of cabins for motorists.

moth /mɒθ/ *n.* mainly nocturnal lepidopterous insect like butterfly; kind of moth breeding in cloth etc. on which its larvae feed. **mothball** piece of naphthalene etc. kept with clothes etc. to repel moths; **moth-eaten** damaged by moths, *fig.* antiquated.

mother /ˈmʌðə(r)/ 1 *n.* female parent; head of female religious community etc.; old woman. 2 *v.t.* act like mother to. 3 **mother country** country in relation to its colonies; **mother-in-law** wife's or husband's mother; **mother-of-pearl** iridescent lining of oyster and other shells; **mother tongue** native language. 4 **motherhood** *n.*; **motherly** *a.*

mothy /ˈmɒθɪ/ *a.* infested with moths.

motif /məʊˈtiːf/ *n.* distinctive feature or dominant idea of design, composition, etc.; ornament sewn or fastened on garment, vehicle, etc.

motion /ˈməʊʃ(ə)n/ 1 *n.* moving; gesture; formal proposal in deliberative assembly; application to judge or court for order etc.; evacuation of bowels. 2 *v.* make motion esp. to direct or guide person. 3 **motion picture** cinema film.

motionless *a.* not moving.

motivate /ˈməʊtɪveɪt/ v.t. supply motive or inducement to, be motive of; stimulate interest of. **motivation** n.

motive /ˈməʊtɪv/ **1** n. what induces person to act. **2** a. productive of motion or action.

motley /ˈmɒtlɪ/ **1** a. diversified in colour; of varied character. **2** n. hist. particoloured dress of jester.

motor /ˈməʊtə/ **1** n. motive agent or force; apparatus, esp. internal combustion engine, supplying motive power for vehicle or machinery; motor car. **2** a. giving, imparting, or producing motion; driven by motor; of or for motor vehicles. **3** v. go or convey by car. **4** **motor bike** colloq., **cycle**, 2-wheeled motor-driven road vehicle; **motor car** motor-driven car. 4-wheeled passenger road vehicle; **motorway** fast highway for motor vehicles.

motorcade /ˈməʊtəkeɪd/ n. procession or parade of motor cars.

motorist /ˈməʊtərɪst/ n. driver of motor car.

motorize /ˈməʊtəraɪz/ v.t. equip with motor transport; furnish with motor.

mottle /ˈmɒt(ə)l/ v.t. mark with spots or smears of colour.

motto /ˈmɒtəʊ/ n. (pl. **-oes**) maxim adopted as rule of conduct; inscription expressing appropriate sentiment or aspiration.

mould¹ /məʊld/ **1** n. hollow vessel in which fluid or plastic material is shaped or cast; pudding etc. shaped in mould; form or character. **2** v.t. shape (as) in mould; model.

mould² /məʊld/ n. furry growth of fungus on damp surface of organic material.

mould³ /məʊld/ n. loose earth; soil rich in organic matter.

moulder /ˈməʊldə(r)/ v.i. decay to dust; crumble away.

moulding /ˈməʊldɪŋ/ n. ornamental strip applied to building etc.; material, esp. of wood, for this.

mouldy /ˈməʊldɪ/ a. covered with mould; out-of-date; sl. dull or miserable.

moult /məʊlt/ **1** v. shed (feathers) or shed feathers in changing plumage; (of animal) shed (hair) or shed hair etc. **2** n. moulting.

mound /maʊnd/ **1** n. heap or bank esp. of earth. **2** v.t. heap up in mounds.

mount /maʊnt/ **1** v. climb on to; put upon or provide with animal for riding; ascend; provide with or fix on or in support(s) or setting; organize, arrange. **2** n. mountain, hill; horse for person to ride; margin round picture etc.; card etc. on which drawing etc. is mounted; setting for gem etc. **3** **mount guard** perform duty of guarding over thing etc.; **mount up** increase in amount.

mountain /ˈmaʊntɪn/ n. hill of impressive height; large heap or pile; large surplus stock. **mountain ash** scarlet-berried tree.

mountaineer /maʊntɪˈnɪə(r)/ **1** n. person skilled in mountain-climbing. **2** v.i. climb mountains as recreation.

mountainous /ˈmaʊntɪnəs/ a. having many mountains, huge.

mountebank /ˈmaʊntɪbæŋk/ n. swindler, charlatan.

Mountie /ˈmaʊntɪ/ n. colloq. member of Royal Canadian Mounted Police.

mourn /mɔːn/ v. feel sorrow or regret (for); grieve for loss of.

mourner n. person who mourns; person who attends funeral.

mournful /ˈmɔːnfʊl/ a. doleful, sad.

mourning /ˈmɔːnɪŋ/ n. (wearing of) black clothes as sign of sorrow.

mouse /maʊs/ **1** n. (pl. **mice**) small rodent; small vole or shrew; shy or timid person; Computers device for moving cursor on screen. **2** v.i. hunt mice. **3** **mousy** a.

mousse /muːs/ n. dish of cold flavoured whipped cream, eggs, etc.

moustache /məˈstɑːʃ/ n. hair on upper lip.

mouth /maʊθ/ **1** n. (pl. /maʊðz/) external opening in head, with cavity behind it containing organs for eating and speaking; opening of bag, cave, trumpet, volcano, etc.; place where river enters sea. **2** /maʊð/ v. utter or speak pompously; declaim; grimace; move lips silently. **3** **mouth-organ** thin rectangular musical instrument played by blowing and sucking air through it; **mouthpiece** part of pipe, musical instrument, telephone, etc., placed between or near lips; **mouthwash** liquid antiseptic etc. for use in mouth.

mouthful /ˈmaʊθfʊl/ n. quantity of

food or drink that fills the mouth; something difficult to say.

move /muːv/ 1 *v.* (cause to) change position, posture, place, or abode; move house; stir or rouse; affect with emotion; propose as resolution. 2 *n.* act or process of moving; change of residence, business premises, etc.; moving of piece at chess etc.; step or proceeding. 3 **move house** change one's place of residence; **move in** take possession of new residence etc., so **move out**. 4 **movable** *a.*

movement *n.* moving or being moved; moving part of mechanism; principal division of musical work; (group organized for) combined action or endeavour for particular end.

movie /ˈmuːvɪ/ *n. colloq.* cinema film.

mow /məʊ/ *v.* (*p.p.* **mowed** or **mown** /məʊn/) cut (grass etc.) with scythe or machine. **mower** *n.*

MP *abbr.* Member of Parliament.

mp *abbr. mezzo piano.*

m.p.g. *abbr.* miles per gallon.

m.p.h. *abbr.* miles per hour.

Mr /ˈmɪstə(r)/ *n.* title prefixed to name of man.

Mrs /ˈmɪsɪz/ *n.* title prefixed to name of married woman.

Ms /mɪz/ *n.* title prefixed to name of woman.

MS *abbr.* manuscript; multiple sclerosis.

M.Sc. *abbr.* Master of Science.

MSS /eˈmesɪz/ *abbr.* manuscripts.

Mt. *abbr.* Mount.

much /mʌtʃ/ 1 *a.* existing in great quantity. 2 *n.* great quantity; noteworthy thing. 3 *adv.* in great degree; often; by great deal. 4 **much of a muchness** very nearly the same.

mucilage /ˈmjuːsɪlɪdʒ/ *n.* viscous substance got from plants; adhesive gum.

muck 1 *n.* manure; dirt; filth; rubbish. 2 *v.* manure; make dirty; clean *out*; *sl.* fool or mess *about*. 3 **muck in** *sl.* share tasks etc. (*with*); **muck-raking** seeking out and publishing of scandals etc.; **muck up** *sl.* bungle, make mess of. 4 **mucky** *a.*

mucous /ˈmjuːkəs/ *a.* secreting or covered by mucus. **mucous membrane** skin lining nostrils and other cavities of body.

mucus /ˈmjuːkəs/ *n.* slimy substance secreted by mucous membrane.

mud *n.* wet soft earthy matter. **mud-guard** hood on wheel as protection against mud; **mud-slinging** abuse, slander.

muddle /ˈmʌd(ə)l/ 1 *v.* bewilder, confuse; bungle, mix *up*; act in confused ineffective manner. 2 *n.* muddled condition.

muddy /ˈmʌdɪ/ 1 *a.* like, covered in, or full of mud; confused; obscure. 2 *v.t.* make muddy.

muesli /ˈmuːzlɪ/ *n.* food of crushed cereals, dried fruit, nuts, etc.

muezzin /muːˈezɪn/ *n.* Muslim crier who proclaims hours of prayer from minaret.

muff[1] *n.* cover of fur etc. for hands.

muff[2] *v.t.* fail in, bungle; miss (catch etc.).

muffin /ˈmʌfɪn/ *n.* light flat yeast cake eaten toasted and buttered.

muffle /ˈmʌf(ə)l/ *v.t.* wrap *up* for warmth; wrap up to deaden sound.

muffler *n.* wrap or scarf worn for warmth.

mufti /ˈmʌftɪ/ *n.* plain clothes as opp. uniform.

mug[1] 1 *n.* drinking-vessel, usu. cylindrical and with handle; *sl.* mouth, face; *sl.* fool, gullible person. 2 *v.* rob with violence, esp. in public place; *sl.* make faces.

mug[2] *v. sl.* learn (subject) by hard study (with *up*).

muggins /ˈmʌgɪnz/ *n. colloq.* person who allows himself to be outwitted.

muggy /ˈmʌgɪ/ *a.* warm, damp, and oppressive.

Muhammadan /məˈhæməd(ə)n/ 1 *a.* of Muhammad; Muslim. 2 *n.* a Muslim.

mulatto /mjuːˈlætəʊ/ *n.* (*pl.* -**os**) person of mixed White and Black parentage.

mulberry /ˈmʌlbərɪ/ *n.* tree bearing purple or white edible berries; fruit of this.

mulch /mʌltʃ/ 1 *n.* wet straw, leaves, etc. put round plant's roots. 2 *v.t.* treat with mulch.

mulct /mʌlkt/ *v.t.* extract money from by fine or taxation or fraudulent means.

mule[1] /mjuːl/ *n.* offspring of mare and

he-ass; obstinate person; kind of spinning-machine.

mule² /mjuːl/ n. backless slipper or shoe.

muleteer /mjuːlɪˈtɪə(r)/ n. mule-driver.

mulish /ˈmjuːlɪʃ/ a. obstinate.

mull¹ v. ponder (over).

mull² v.t. heat and spice (wine, beer).

mullah /ˈmʌlə/ n. Muslim learned in Islamic law.

mullet /ˈmʌlɪt/ n. edible sea-fish.

mulligatawny /mʌlɪɡəˈtɔːnɪ/ n. highly seasoned soup orig. from India.

mullion /ˈmʌlɪən/ n. vertical bar dividing panes of window.

multi- /ˈmʌltɪ/ in comb. many.

multicoloured /-kʌləd/ a. of many colours.

multifarious /-ˈfeərɪəs/ a. having great variety.

multiform a. having many forms, of many kinds.

multilateral /-ˈlætər(ə)l/ a. (of treaty etc.) in which 3 or more parties participate; having many sides.

multilingual /-ˈlɪŋɡw(ə)l/ a. in or using many languages.

multinational /-ˈnæʃən(ə)l/ 1 a. (of manufacturing company etc.) operating in several countries. 2 n. such company.

multiple /ˈmʌltɪp(ə)l/ 1 a. having several or many parts, components, branches, kinds, etc. 2 n. Math. quantity exactly divisible by another. 3 **multiple sclerosis** kind spreading to all or many parts of body.

multiplicand /ˌmʌltɪplɪˈkænd/ n. quantity to be multiplied.

multiplication /ˌmʌltɪplɪˈkeɪʃ(ə)n/ n. multiplying.

multiplicity /ˌmʌltɪˈplɪsɪtɪ/ n. manifold variety, great number (of).

multiplier /ˈmʌltɪplaɪə(r)/ n. quantity by which multiplicand is multiplied.

multiply /ˈmʌltɪplaɪ/ v. find quantity produced by taking given quantity given number of times; make or become many.

multi-purpose a. serving more than one purpose.

multiracial /-ˈreɪʃ(ə)l/ a. composed of or concerning people of several races.

multitude /ˈmʌltɪtjuːd/ n. great num-

ber; throng; *the* common people. **multitudinous** a.

mum¹ a. silent. **mum's the word** say nothing.

mum² n. colloq. mother.

mumble /ˈmʌmb(ə)l/ 1 v. speak or utter indistinctly. 2 n. indistinct utterance.

mumbo-jumbo /mʌmbəʊˈdʒʌmbəʊ/ n. meaningless ritual; mystification, obscurity of language etc.

mummer /ˈmʌmə(r)/ n. actor in traditional mime.

mummery /ˈmʌmərɪ/ n. performance by mummers; ridiculous (esp. religious) ceremonial.

mummify /ˈmʌmɪfaɪ/ v. preserve (body) as mummy. **mummification** n.

mummy¹ /ˈmʌmɪ/ n. dead body preserved by embalming, esp. by ancient Egyptians.

mummy² /ˈmʌmɪ/ n. colloq. & childish mother.

mumps n.pl. infectious disease with swelling of neck and face.

munch /mʌntʃ/ v. chew steadily.

mundane /mʌnˈdeɪn/ a. dull, routine; of this world.

municipal /mjuːˈnɪsɪp(ə)l/ a. of municipality.

municipality /mjuːnɪsɪˈpælɪtɪ/ n. town or district with local self-government; its governing body.

munificent /mjuːˈnɪfɪs(ə)nt/ a. splendidly generous. **munificence** n.

muniment /ˈmjuːnɪmənt/ n. (usu. in pl.) document kept as evidence of rights or privileges.

munitions /mjuːˈnɪʃ(ə)nz/ n.pl. military weapons and ammunition and equipment and stores.

mural /ˈmjʊər(ə)l/ 1 a. of or in or on wall. 2 n. mural painting etc.

murder /ˈmɜːdə/ 1 n. unlawful and intentional killing of human being by another. 2 v.t. kill (human being) unlawfully; colloq. spoil by bad performance, mispronunciation, etc. 3 **murderer** n.; **murderess** n.; **murderous** a.

murky /ˈmɜːkɪ/ a. dark, gloomy.

murmur /ˈmɜːmə(r)/ 1 n. subdued continuous sound; hushed speech; subdued expression of discontent. 2 v. produce, say or speak in, murmur. 3 **murmurous** a.

murrain /'mʌrɪn/ n. infectious disease in cattle.

muscadine /'mʌskədi:n/ n. musk-flavoured kind of grape.

muscat /'mʌskət/ n. muscadine; wine made from this.

muscatel /mʌskə'tel/ n. muscadine; wine or raisin made from this.

muscle /'mʌs(ə)l/ 1 n. contractile fibrous band or bundle producing movement in animal body; lean flesh or meat; strength, power. 2 v.i. sl. force one's way in. 3 **muscle-bound** with muscles stiff through excessive exercise.

muscular /'mʌskjʊlə(r)/ a. of or affecting muscles; with well-developed muscles. **muscularity.** n.

muse¹ /mju:z/ v.i. ponder, meditate.

Muse² /mju:z/ n. Gk. myth. any of nine sister goddesses presiding over arts and sciences; **muse** poet's inspiration or genius.

museum /mju:'zi:əm/ n. place where objects illustrating antiquity, art, science, etc. are exhibited, studied, etc. **museum piece** object fit for museum, old-fashioned person etc.

mush /mʌʃ/ n. soft pulp; fig. feeble sentimentality; US maize porridge. **mushy** a.

mushroom /'mʌʃrʊm/ 1 n. edible fungus with stem and domed cap. 2 v.i. expand rapidly; take mushroom shape; gather mushrooms. 3 **mushroom cloud** characteristic cloud produced by nuclear explosion.

music /'mju:zɪk/ n. art of combining sounds for reproduction by voice or instrument(s) in rhythmic, melodic, and harmonic form; sounds so produced; record or score of these for reproduction; any pleasant sound. **music centre** item of equipment combining radio, record player, and tape recorder; **music-hall** variety theatre.

musical /'mju:zɪk(ə)l/ 1 a. of, fond of, skilled in, music; set to or accompanied by music; melodious. 2 n. play or film of which (esp. light) music is essential part.

musician /mju:'zɪʃ(ə)n/ n. person skilled in science or practice of music. **musicianship** n.

musicology /mju:zɪ'kɒlədʒɪ/ n. study

of history and forms of music. **musicological** a.; **musicologist** n.

musk n. substance secreted by male musk-deer used as basis of perfumes; plant with musky smell. **musk-deer** small hornless ruminant of Central Asia; **musk-melon** common melon; **musk-rat** (fur of) large N. Amer. aquatic rodent; **musk-rose** climbing rose with fragrant white flowers. **musky** a.

musket /'mʌskɪt/ n. hist. infantryman's (esp. smooth-bored) gun.

musketeer /mʌskɪ'tɪə(r)/ n. hist. soldier armed with musket.

musketry /'mʌskɪtrɪ/ n. muskets; art of using rifles or muskets.

Muslim /'mʊzlɪm/ 1 n. person believing in Allah as God according to revelations of Muhammad. 2 a. of Muslims or their religion.

muslin /'mʌzlɪn/ n. fine cotton fabric.

musquash /'mʌskwɒʃ/ n. musk-rat; its fur.

mussel /'mʌs(ə)l/ n. edible bivalve mollusc.

must¹ v.aux. (3 sing. **must**) be obliged to; be certain to. 2 n. colloq. something that cannot or should not be missed.

must² n. grape-juice before end of fermentation; new wine.

mustang /'mʌstæŋ/ n. wild horse of Mexico etc.

mustard /'mʌstəd/ n. plant with yellow flowers, seeds of which are ground and made into paste for use as condiment. **mustard gas** colourless oily liquid whose vapour is powerful irritant.

muster /'mʌstə(r)/ 1 v. bring or come together, collect; summon up (courage etc.). 2 n. assembling of persons for inspection etc. 3 **pass muster** be accepted as adequate.

musty /'mʌstɪ/ a. mouldy; antiquated, stale.

mutable /'mju:təb(ə)l/ a. liable to change; fickle. **mutability** n.

mutant /'mju:t(ə)nt/ 1 a. resulting from mutation. 2 n. mutant form.

mutation /mju:'teɪʃ(ə)n/ n. change; genetic change which when transmitted to offspring gives rise to heritable variation.

mute /mju:t/ 1 a. silent; refraining from speech; dumb; soundless. 2 n.

dumb person; device to deaden sound of musical instrument. **3** *v.t.* muffle or deaden sound of. **4 mute swan** common white swan.

mutilate /'mju:tɪleɪt/ *v.t.* injure, make imperfect, by depriving of part. **mutilation** *n.*

mutineer /mju:tɪ'nɪə(r)/ *n.* person who mutinies.

mutinous /'mju:tɪnəs/ *a.* rebellious.

mutiny /'mju:tɪnɪ/ **1** *n.* open revolt against authority, esp. by members of armed forces. **2** *v.i.* engage in mutiny.

mutt *n. sl.* stupid person.

mutter /'mʌtə/ **1** *v.* speak, utter, in low tone; grumble. **2** *n.* muttering.

mutton /'mʌt(ə)n/ *n.* flesh of sheep as food.

mutual /'mju:tʃʊəl/ *a.* felt or done by each to other; bearing same relation to each other; *colloq.* common to two or more. **mutuality** *n.*

muzzle /'mʌz(ə)l/ **1** *n.* projecting part of animal's head including nose and mouth; open end of gun-barrel; cage etc. put on animal's muzzle. **2** *v.t.* put muzzle on; silence.

muzzy /'mʌzɪ/ *a.* confused, dazed; indistinct.

MW *abbr.* megawatt(s).

my /maɪ/ *pron.*, *poss.* case of **I**, with *abs.* form **mine**.

mycology /maɪ'kɒlədʒɪ/ *n.* study of fungi.

myna(h) var. of **mina**.

myopia /maɪ'əʊpɪə/ *n.* shortsightedness. **myopic** /-'ɒp-/ *a.*

myriad /'mɪrɪəd/ **1** *n.* vast number. **2** *a.* innumerable.

myrmidon /'mɜ:mɪd(ə)n/ *n.* hired ruffian, menial servant.

myrrh /mɜ:/ *n.* gum resin used in perfumes and medicine and incense.

myrtle /'mɜ:t(ə)l/ *n.* evergreen shrub with fragrant white flowers.

myself /maɪ'self/ *pron. emphat.* and *refl.* form of **I**.

mysterious /mɪs'tɪərɪəs/ *a.* full of or wrapped in or enjoying mystery.

mystery /'mɪstərɪ/ *n.* inexplicable matter; secrecy, obscurity; fictional work dealing with puzzling crime; revealed religious truth, esp. one beyond human understanding; in *pl.* secret religious rites; miracle-play. **mystery tour** pleasure excursion to unspecified destination.

mystic /'mɪstɪk/ **1** *n.* person who seeks union with deity through contemplation etc. or believes in spiritual apprehension of truths beyond understanding. **2** *a.* spiritually mysterious; esoteric; enigmatic. **3 mystical** *a.*; **mysticism** *n.*

mystify /'mɪstɪfaɪ/ *v.t.* bewilder; confuse utterly. **mystification** *n.*

mystique /mɪs'ti:k/ *n.* atmosphere of mystery attending some activity or person.

myth /mɪθ/ *n.* traditional narrative usu. embodying esp. ancient popular belief or idea; fictitious person or thing; widely held but false idea. **mythical** *a.*

mythology /mɪ'θɒlədʒɪ/ *n.* body or study of myths. **mythological** *a.*; **mythologist** *n.*

myxomatosis /mɪksəmə'təʊsɪs/ *n.* virus disease in rabbits.

N

N. abbr. North(ern).

n n. Math. indefinite number.

n. abbr. name; neuter; note.

NAAFI /'næfɪ/ abbr. Navy, Army, and Air Force Institutes (canteen for servicemen).

nab v.t. sl. catch, arrest.

nacre /'neɪkə/ n. mother-of-pearl; shellfish yielding this. **nacreous** /'neɪkrɪəs/ a.

nadir /'neɪdɪə/ n. point of heavens opposite zenith; fig. lowest point.

nag¹ v. find fault (with) or scold persistently (at); (of pain etc.) be persistent.

nag² n. colloq. horse, esp. for riding.

naiad /'naɪæd/ n. water-nymph.

nail 1 n. horny covering of upper surface of tip of finger or toe; small usu. pointed and broad-headed metal spike. 2 v.t. fasten with nail(s); fix or hold tight; secure, catch.

nainsook /'neɪnsʊk/ n. fine cotton fabric.

naïve /nɑː'iːv/ a. artless, unaffected; amusingly simple. **naïvety** /nɑː'iːvətɪ/ n.

naked /'neɪkɪd/ a. unclothed, nude; without usual coverings or furnishings; unprotected; (of eye) unassisted.

namby-pamby /næmbɪ'pæmbɪ/ a. insipidly pretty; weakly sentimental.

name 1 n. word by which individual person, animal, place, or thing is spoken of or to; reputation, fame; family, clan. 2 v.t. give name to; speak of or to by name; nominate, appoint; identify; mention. 3 **name-day** day of saint after whom one is named; **namesake** person or thing of same name.

nameless /'neɪmlɪs/ a. obscure, left unnamed.

namely /'neɪmlɪ/ adv. that is to say, in other words.

nancy /'nænsɪ/ n. sl. effeminate or homosexual young man.

nankeen /næŋ'kiːn/ n. yellow cotton cloth.

nanny /'nænɪ/ n. child's nurse or minder. **nanny goat** female goat.

nano- /'nænəʊ/ in comb. one thousand millionth.

nap¹ 1 n. short sleep, esp. by day. 2 v.i. have nap.

nap² n. surface of cloth consisting of fibre-ends raised, cut even, and smoothed.

nap³ 1 n. card-game; racing tip claimed to be almost a certainty. 2 v.t. name (horse) as almost certain winner. 3 **go nap** risk everything one has.

napalm /'neɪpɑːm/ n. jellied petrol for use as incendiary.

nape n. back of neck.

naphtha /'næfθə/ n. inflammable oil distilled from coal etc.

naphthalene /'næfθəliːn/ n. white crystalline substance used in manufacture of dyes etc. and in moth-balls.

napkin /'næpkɪn/ n. piece of linen etc. for wiping lips etc. at table; nappy.

nappy /'næpɪ/ n. piece of absorbent material wrapped round waist and between legs of baby.

narcissism /'nɑːsɪsɪz(ə)m/ n. abnormal self-love or self-admiration. **narcissistic** a.

narcissus /nɑː'sɪsəs/ n. kind of flowering bulb including daffodil.

narcosis /nɑː'kəʊsɪs/ n. unconsciousness induced by narcotics.

narcotic /nɑː'kɒtɪk/ 1 a. inducing drowsiness, sleep, or insensibility. 2 n. narcotic drug or influence.

nark sl. 1 v.t. annoy, infuriate. 2 n. police spy, informer.

narrate /nə'reɪt/ v.t. recount, relate, give continuous account of. **narration** n.; **narrator** n.

narrative /'nærətɪv/ 1 n. spoken or written recital of connected events in order. 2 a. of or by narration.

narrow /'nærəʊ/ 1 a. of small width in proportion to length; restricted; with little margin; narrow-minded. 2 n. (usu. in pl.) narrow part of sound, strait, river, or pass. 3 v. make or become narrower; lessen, contract. 4 **narrow boat** canal boat; **narrow-minded** intolerant, restricted in one's views.

narwhal /'nɑːw(ə)l/ n. Arctic mammal of which male has long tusk.

nasal /'neɪz(ə)l/ 1 a. of nose; (of sounds) produced with nose passage open; (of voice etc.) having many nasal sounds. 2 n. nasal letter or sound.

nascent /'næs(ə)nt/ a. in process of birth; just beginning to be. **nascence** n.

nasturtium /nə'stɜːʃəm/ n. trailing garden plant with bright orange, red, or yellow flowers.

nasty /'nɑːstɪ/ a. unpleasant, disagreeable; ill-natured, spiteful.

Nat. abbr. National(ist).

natal /'neɪt(ə)l/ a. of or from birth.

nation /'neɪʃ(ə)n/ n. community of people having common descent, language, history, or political institutions.

national /'næʃən(ə)l/ 1 a. of nation; common to or characteristic of whole nation. 2 n. citizen of specified State. 3 **national grid** network of high-voltage electric power-lines between major power-stations; **National Insurance** system of compulsory contribution from employee and employer to provide State assistance in sickness, retirement, etc.; **national service** service by conscription in armed forces.

nationalism /'næʃənəlɪz(ə)m/ n. patriotic feeling or principles; policy of national independence. **nationalist** n.

nationality /næʃə'nælɪtɪ/ n. membership of nation; being national.

nationalize /'næʃənəlaɪz/ v.t. make national; convert (industry, etc.) into public ownership. **nationalization** n.

native /'neɪtɪv/ 1 a. inborn; by reason of (place of) one's birth; born in place, indigenous, of natives; occurring naturally. 2 n. person born in place; indigenous animal or plant.

nativity /nə'tɪvɪtɪ/ n. birth, esp. of Christ.

NATO /'neɪtəʊ/ abbr. (also **Nato**) North Atlantic Treaty Organization.

natter /'nætə/ colloq. 1 v.i. chatter idly, grumble. 2 n. aimless chatter.

natty /'nætɪ/ a. neat and trim.

natural /'nætʃər(ə)l/ 1 a. of or according to or provided by nature; physically existing; normal, not artificial; innate; to be expected; *Mus.* not flat or sharp. 2 n. person etc. naturally endowed, easy or obvious choice (for); *Mus.* natural note, sign indicating this. 3 **natural gas** fuel gas found in earth's crust; **natural history** study of animal and vegetable life; **natural selection**

process favouring survival of organisms best adapted to environment.

naturalism /'nætʃərəlɪz(ə)m/ n. adherence to nature in art and literature, realism; philosophy based on nature alone. **naturalistic** a.

naturalist /'nætʃərəlɪst/ n. student of animals and plants.

naturalize /'nætʃərəlaɪz/ v.t. admit (alien) to citizenship; adopt (foreign word etc.), introduce (plant etc.) into new environment. **naturalization** n.

naturally /'nætʃərəlɪ/ adv. in natural manner; as might be expected, of course.

nature /'neɪtʃə/ n. phenomena of material world, physical power causing these; thing's essential qualities; innate character; kind, sort, class.

naturist /'neɪtʃərɪst/ n. nudist. **naturism** n.

naught /nɔːt/ arch. 1 n. nothing. 2 pred.a. worthless.

naughty /'nɔːtɪ/ a. badly behaved; disobedient; wicked; indecent.

nausea /'nɔːzɪə/ n. feeling of sickness; loathing.

nauseate /'nɔːzɪeɪt/ v.t. affect with nausea.

nauseous /'nɔːzɪəs/ a. loathsome.

nautical /'nɔːtɪk(ə)l/ a. of sailors or navigation. **nautical mile** approx. 1.85 km.

nautilus /'nɔːtɪləs/ n. kind of mollusc with spiral shell.

naval /'neɪv(ə)l/ a. of navy; of ships.

nave[1] n. body of church not including chancel and aisles.

nave[2] n. hub of wheel.

navel /'neɪv(ə)l/ n. depression on belly left by detachment of umbilical cord; central point of anything. **navel orange** one with navel-like formation at top.

navigable /'nævɪgəb(ə)l/ a. affording passage for ships; that can be steered. **navigability** n.

navigate /'nævɪgeɪt/ v. voyage, sail ship; sail or steam on or through (sea, river, air); manage, direct course of; indicate correct route. **navigator** n.

navigation /nævɪ'geɪʃ(ə)n/ n. navigating; methods of determining ship's or aircraft's position and course.

navvy /'nævɪ/ n. labourer excavating for canals, roads, etc.

navy /'neɪvɪ/ n. State's warships with their crews and organization; officers and men of navy; fleet. **navy (blue)** very dark blue.

nay 1 adv. no; or rather, and even. 2 n. refusal.

Nazi /'nɑːtsɪ/ 1 n. member of German National Socialist party. 2 a. of this party.

NB abbr. note well (nota bene).

NCB abbr. National Coal Board.

NCO abbr. non-commissioned officer.

NE abbr. North-East(ern).

Neanderthal /nɪ'ændətɑːl/ a. of type of man found in palaeolithic Europe.

neap n. (in full **neap tide**) tide of minimum height.

Neapolitan /nɪə'pɒlɪt(ə)n/ 1 a. of Naples. 2 n. native of Naples.

near /nɪə(r)/ 1 adv. in or at a short distance in space or time; nearly; closely. 2 prep. near to in space, time, condition, or semblance. 3 a. close (to); closely related; (of way) direct, short; with little difference; left-hand; parsimonious. 4 v. draw near (to). 5 **near-sighted** short-sighted.

nearby /nɪə'baɪ/ a. close in position.

nearly /'nɪəlɪ/ adv. closely, almost. **not nearly** nothing like.

neat a. nicely made or proportioned; tidy, methodical; undiluted; cleverly done, phrased, etc.; deft, dextrous.

neaten /'niːt(ə)n/ v.t. make neat.

neath /niːθ/ prep. poet. beneath.

nebula /'nebjʊlə/ n. (pl. **-lae** /-liː/) luminous or dark patch in sky made by distant star-cluster or gas or dust. **nebular** a.

nebulous /'nebjʊləs/ a. cloudlike; hazy, vague. **nebulosity** n.

necessary /'nesəsərɪ/ 1 a. indispensable; that must be done; inevitable. 2 n. thing without which life cannot be maintained or is unduly harsh.

necessitate /nɪ'sesɪteɪt/ v.t. make necessary; involve as condition, result, etc.

necessitous /nɪ'sesɪtəs/ a. poor, needy.

necessity /nɪ'sesɪtɪ/ n. constraint or compulsion regarded as law governing all human action; imperative need; indispensable thing; in sing. or pl. pressing need.

neck 1 n. part of body connecting head with shoulders; narrow part of anything, esp. connecting wider parts; part of garment round neck. 2 v.i. sl. kiss and caress amorously. 3 **neckline** outline of garment-opening at neck; **neck-tie** band of material tied round shirt-collar.

necklace /'neklɪs/ n. ornament of jewels, beads, etc. round neck.

necklet /'neklɪt/ n. ornament or fur garment for neck.

necromancy /'nekrəmænsɪ/ n. dealings with dead as means of divination; magic. **necromancer** n.

necrophilia /nekrə'fɪlɪə/ n. abnormal attraction to corpses.

necropolis /ne'krɒpəlɪs/ n. cemetery.

necrosis /ne'krəʊsɪs/ n. (pl. **-ses** /-siːz/) death of piece of bone or tissue. **necrotic** /-'krɒt-/ a.

nectar /'nektə/ n. sweet fluid produced by plants and made into honey by bees; Myth. drink of gods.

nectarine /'nektərɪn/ n. downless kind of peach.

NEDC abbr. National Economic Development Council.

née /neɪ/ a. (before married woman's maiden name) born.

need 1 n. circumstances requiring some course of action; want, requirement; time of difficulty; destitution, poverty. 2 v. be in need of, require; be under necessity to do.

needful /'niːdfʊl/ a. requisite.

needle /'niːd(ə)l/ 1 n. pointed slender instrument pierced with eye for thread etc.; knitting-pin; instrument transmitting vibrations from revolving gramophone record; pointer of compass etc.; pointed instrument used in etching, surgery, etc.; pointed end of hypodermic syringe; leaf of fir or pine; sharp rock, peak; obelisk. 2 v.t. colloq. annoy, provoke. 3 **needlecord** finely ribbed fabric; **needle game**, **match**, etc., one closely contested or arousing exceptional personal feeling; **needlework** sewing or embroidery.

needless /'niːdlɪs/ a. unnecessary.

needy /'niːdɪ/ a. poor, destitute.

ne'er /neə/ adv. poet. never. **ne'er-do-well** good-for-nothing person.

nefarious /nɪ'feərɪəs/ a. wicked.

negate /nɪ'ɡeɪt/ *v.t.* nullify, deny existence of.

negation /nɪ'ɡeɪʃ(ə)n/ *n.* denying; negative statement etc.; negative or unreal thing.

negative /'neɡətɪv/ *a.* expressing or implying denial, prohibition, or refusal; lacking positive attributes; *Alg.* (of quantity) less than zero, to be subtracted; *Electr.* of, containing, producing, kind of charge carried by electrons, opposite to positive. **2** *n.* negative statement or word; *Photog.* developed film etc. bearing image having lights and shades of actual object reversed. **3** *v.t.* veto; serve to disprove; contradict; neutralize.

neglect /nɪ'ɡlekt/ **1** *v.t.* pay too little or no attention to; leave uncared for; leave undone. **2** *n.* neglecting or being neglected; negligence. **3** **neglectful** *a.*

négligé /'neɡlɪʒeɪ/ *n.* woman's light flimsy dressing-gown.

negligence /'neɡlɪdʒəns/ *n.* lack of proper care or attention; carelessness. **negligent** *a.*

negligible /'neɡlɪdʒɪb(ə)l/ *a.* that need not be considered.

negotiate /nɪ'ɡəʊʃɪeɪt/ *v.* confer with view to compromise or agreement; get or give money value for (bill, cheque); deal successfully with. **negotiable** *a.*; **negotiation** *n.*; **negotiator** *n.*

Negress /'niːɡres/ *n.* female Negro.

Negro /'niːɡrəʊ/ **1** *n.* (*pl.* -**groes**) member of black-skinned (orig.) African race. **2** *a.* of this race.

Negroid /'niːɡrɔɪd/ **1** *a.* of group having characteristics typical of Negroes. **2** *n.* Negroid person.

negus /'niːɡəs/ *n.* hot sweetened wine and water.

neigh /neɪ/ **1** *n.* cry of horse. **2** *v.i.* utter neigh.

neighbour /'neɪbə(r)/ *n.* person who lives next door or near by; fellow human being. **2** *v.* adjoin, border on or (*up*)*on*.

neighbourhood *n.* district; people of a district, vicinity.

neighbourly *a.* like good neighbour, friendly, helpful.

neither /'naɪðə(r) or 'niːðə(r)/ **1** *adv.* not either. **2** *a. & pron.* not the one or the other. **3** *conj. arch.* nor; nor yet.

nelson /'nels(ə)n/ *n.* wrestling hold in which arm is passed under opponent's arm from behind and hand applied to his neck.

nem. con. *abbr.* with no one dissenting (*nemine contradicente*).

nemesis /'neməsɪs/ *n.* justice bringing deserved punishment.

neo- *in comb.* new.

neolithic /niːə'lɪθɪk/ *a.* of later Stone Age.

neologism /niː'ɒlədʒɪz(ə)m/ *n.* new word; word-coining.

neon /'niːɒn/ *n.* inert gas giving orange-red glow when electricity is passed through it.

neophyte /'niːəfaɪt/ *n.* new convert; religious novice; beginner.

Neozoic /niːə'zəʊɪk/ *a.* of later period of geological history.

nephew /'nefjuː/ *n.* brother's or sister's son.

nephritic /ne'frɪtɪk/ *a.* of or in kidneys.

nephritis /ne'fraɪtɪs/ *n.* inflammation of kidneys.

nepotism /'nepətɪz(ə)m/ *n.* favouritism to relatives esp. in conferring offices etc.

nereid /'nɪərɪɪd/ *n. Gk myth.* sea-nymph; *Zool.* kind of marine worm.

nerve /nɜːv/ **1** *n.* fibrous connection conveying impulses of sensation or motion between brain and other parts; presence of mind; coolness in danger; *colloq.* impudent boldness; in *pl.* nervousness, condition of mental and physical stress; *Bot.* rib of leaf. **2** *v.t.* give strength, vigour, or courage to.

nerveless /'nɜːvlɪs/ *a.* lacking vigour or spirit.

nervous /'nɜːvəs/ *a.* having disordered or delicate nerves; highly strung; timid; of the nerves; full of nerves. **nervous breakdown** severe disorder of the nerves; **nervous system** nerves as a whole.

nervy /'nɜːvɪ/ *a.* nervous, tense.

ness *n.* headland.

nest **1** *n.* structure or place in which bird lays eggs and shelters young; breeding-place or lair; snug retreat, shelter; brood, swarm; cluster or accumulation of similar objects. **2** *v.i.* make or have nest; (of objects) fit one inside another. **3** **nest-egg** money saved up as reserve.

nestle /'nes(ə)l/ v. settle oneself or be settled comfortably; press close (to); lie half-hidden or sheltered.

nestling /'neslɪŋ/ n. bird too young to leave nest.

net[1] n. meshed fabric of cord, thread, hair, etc.; piece of this used for catching fish, keeping hair in place, enclosing area of ground e.g. in sport, etc. 2 v. cover, confine, catch, with net; send (ball) into net; make (cord etc.) into net. 3 **netball** game similar to basketball.

net[1] a. remaining after necessary deductions; (of price) off which discount is not allowed; (of weight) not including wrappings etc. 2 v.t. yield (sum) as net profit.

nether /'neðə/ a. lower. **nethermost** a.

nett var. of **net**[2].

netting /'netɪŋ/ n. netted fabric.

nettle /'net(ə)l/ 1 n. plant covered with stinging hairs; plant resembling this. 2 v.t. irritate, provoke. 3 **nettle-rash** skin eruption like nettle-stings.

network /'netwɜːk/ 1 n. arrangement of intersecting lines, complex system of; group of broadcasting stations connected for simultaneous broadcast of same programme. 2 v.t. broadcast thus.

neural /'njʊər(ə)l/ a. of nerves.

neuralgia /njʊə'rældʒə/ n. intermittent pain in nerves esp. of face and head. **neuralgic** a.

neurasthenia /ˌnjʊəræs'θiːnɪə/ n. debility of nerves causing fatigue etc. **neurasthenic** /-'θen-/ a.

neuritis /njʊə'raɪtɪs/ n. inflammation of nerve(s).

neurology /njʊə'rɒlədʒɪ/ n. scientific study of nerve systems. **neurological** a.; **neurologist** n.

neurone /'njʊərəʊn/ n. (also **neuron**) nerve-cell and its appendages.

neurosis /njʊə'rəʊsɪs/ n. (pl. -ses /-siːz/) disorder of nervous system producing depression or irrational behaviour.

neurotic /njʊə'rɒtɪk/ 1 a. caused by or suffering from neurosis; colloq. obsessively anxious. 2 n. neurotic person.

neuter /'njuːtə/ 1 a. Gram. neither masculine nor feminine. 2 n. neuter word etc.; neutered animal. 3 v.t. castrate.

neutral /'njuːtr(ə)l/ a. taking neither side; impartial; vague, indeterminate; (of colours) not strong or positive; Chem. neither acid nor alkaline; Electr. neither positive nor negative. 2 n. neutral State or person; position of gear mechanism in which engine is disconnected from driven parts. 3 **neutrality** n.

neutralize /'njuːtrəlaɪz/ v.t. make neutral; counterbalance; render ineffective. **neutralization** n.

neutrino /nuː'triːnəʊ/ n. Phys. (pl. -nos) elementary particle with zero electric charge and prob. zero mass.

neutron /'njuːtrɒn/ n. Phys. elementary particle of about same mass as proton but without electric charge.

never /'nevə/ adv. at no time, not ever; not at all; colloq. surely not. **never mind** it does not matter; the **never-never** colloq. hire-purchase.

nevermore /nevə'mɔː/ adv. at no future time.

nevertheless /nevəðə'les/ adv. for all that, notwithstanding.

new a. now first made, introduced, or discovered; fresh, additional; different, changed; recent; not worn. **newcomer** person recently arrived; **newfangled** different from what one is used to; **new moon** moon when first visible as crescent; **New Testament** part of Bible dealing with Christ and his followers; **New World** N. and S. America; **New Year's Day, Eve**, 1 Jan., 31 Dec.

newel /'njuːəl/ n. centre pillar of winding stair; top or bottom post of stair-rail.

newly /'njuːlɪ/ adv. recently, afresh.

news /njuːz/ n. new or interesting information; fresh events reported; broadcast report of news. **newsagent** dealer in newspapers etc.; **newsletter** printed informal bulletin of club etc.; **newspaper** /'njuːs-/ printed publication usu. daily or weekly with news etc.; **newsprint** paper for newspapers; **newsreader** radio or television broadcaster of news reports; **newsreel** cinema film of recent news; **newsroom** room where news is prepared for publication or broadcasting; **newsworthy** worth reporting as news. **newsy** a.

newt /njuːt/ n. small tailed amphibian.

next 1 a. nearest; immediately following or preceding. 2 adv. in next place or degree, on next occasion. **3** *n*. next person or thing. **4** *prep*. next to. **5 next of kin** nearest living relative.

nexus /ˈneksəs/ *n*. connected group or series.

NHS *abbr*. National Health Service.

NI *abbr*. National Insurance; Northern Ireland.

niacin /ˈnaɪəsɪn/ *n*. nicotinic acid.

nib *n*. pen-point; in *pl*. crushed coffee- or cocoa-beans.

nibble /ˈnɪb(ə)l/ **1** *v*. take small bites at; bite gently or cautiously. **2** *n*. act of nibbling, esp. at bait.

nice /naɪs/ *a*. agreeable; kind, friendly, considerate; subtle, fine; fastidious.

nicety /ˈnaɪsətɪ/ *n*. precision; subtle distinction or detail. **to a nicety** exactly.

niche /nɪtʃ, niːʃ/ *n*. shallow recess, esp. in wall; suitable place or position.

nick 1 *n*. small cut or notch; *sl*. prison, police station; *sl*. state, condition. **2** *v.t*. make nick(s) in; *sl*. catch, arrest, steal. **3 in the nick of time** only just in time.

nickel /ˈnɪk(ə)l/ *n*. silver-white met- allic element used esp. in alloys and as plating; *US* 5-cent coin.

nickname /ˈnɪkneɪm/ **1** *n*. name jok- ingly added to or substituted for reg- ular name. **2** *v.t*. give nickname to.

nicotine /ˈnɪkətiːn/ *n*. poisonous oily liquid got from tobacco.

nicotinic acid /nɪkəˈtɪnɪk/ vitamin of B group.

nictitate /ˈnɪktɪteɪt/ *v.i*. blink, wink. **nictitation** *n*.

niece /niːs/ *n*. brother's or sister's daughter.

nifty /ˈnɪftɪ/ *a*. *colloq*. neat, smart, clever.

niggard /ˈnɪgəd/ *n*. stingy person.

niggardly /ˈnɪgədlɪ/ *a*. stingy; given or giving grudgingly.

niggle /ˈnɪg(ə)l/ *v*. fuss over details, find fault in petty way; nag. **niggling** *a*.

nigh /naɪ/ *adv. & prep. arch*. near.

night /naɪt/ *n*. time from sunset to sun- rise; (period of) darkness; nightfall; evening. **nightcap** drink before going to bed; **night-club** club open late at night; **night-dress, gown**, woman's or girl's loose garment for sleeping in; **nightfall** end of daylight; **nightjar** nocturnal bird with harsh cry; **night-** life entertainment available at night; **nightmare** terrifying dream or *colloq*. experience; **night safe** safe with open- ing in outer wall of bank for deposit of money when bank is closed; **night- shade** any of various kinds of poison- ous plant; **nightshirt** long shirt for sleeping in.

nightingale /ˈnaɪtɪŋgeɪl/ *n*. small bird of thrush family, the male of which sings much at night.

nightly /ˈnaɪtlɪ/ **1** *a*. happening or done or existing in the night; recurring ev- ery night. **2** *adv*. every night.

nihilism /ˈnaɪɪlɪz(ə)m/ *n*. rejection of all religious and moral principles. **ni- hilist** *n.*; **nihilistic** *a*.

nil *n*. nothing.

nimble /ˈnɪmb(ə)l/ *a*. quick and light in movement; (of mind etc.) quick, clever.

nimbus /ˈnɪmbəs/ *n*. (*pl*. **-bi** /-baɪ/ or **-buses**) halo, aureole; *Meteor*. storm-cloud.

nincompoop /ˈnɪŋkəmpuːp/ *n*. foolish person.

nine *a. & n*. one more than eight. **nine- pins** kind of skittles. **ninefold** *a. & adv*. **ninth** *a. & n*.

nineteen /naɪnˈtiːn/ *a. & n*. one more than eighteen. **nineteenth** *a. & n*.

ninety /ˈnaɪntɪ/ *a. & n*. nine times ten. **ninetieth** *a. & n*.

ninny /ˈnɪnɪ/ *n*. foolish person.

nip[1] **1** *v*. pinch, squeeze sharply, bite; check growth of; *sl*. go nimbly. **2** *n*. pinch, sharp squeeze, bite; biting cold. **3 nip in the bud** *fig*. stop at very beginning.

nip[2] *n*. small quantity of spirits.

nipper /ˈnɪpə/ *n*. claw of crab etc.; in *pl*. implement with jaws for gripping or cutting; *sl*. young boy or girl.

nipple /ˈnɪp(ə)l/ *n*. point of mammal's breast; teat of baby's bottle; nipple-like protuberance.

nippy /ˈnɪpɪ/ *a*. *colloq*. cold; nimble.

nirvana /nɜːˈvɑːnə/ *n*. (in Buddhism and Hinduism) perfect bliss attained by extinction of individuality.

nit *n*. egg of louse or other parasite; *sl*. stupid person. **nit-picking** *colloq*. petty fault-finding.

nitrate /ˈnaɪtreɪt/ *n*. salt of nitric acid.

nitre /ˈnaɪtə/ *n*. saltpetre.

nitric acid /ˈnaɪtrɪk/ pungent cor- rosive caustic liquid.

nitrogen /ˈnaɪtrədʒ(ə)n/ *n.* gas forming four-fifths of atmosphere.

nitrogenous /naɪˈtrɒdʒɪnəs/ *a.* containing nitrogen.

nitro-glycerine /naɪtrəʊˈglɪsəriːn/ *n.* yellowish oily violently explosive liquid.

nitrous /ˈnaɪtrəs/ *a.* of, like, or impregnated with nitre.

nitty-gritty /nɪtɪˈgrɪtɪ/ *n. sl.* realities or basic facts of a matter.

nitwit /ˈnɪtwɪt/ *n. colloq.* stupid person.

nix *n. sl.* nothing.

NNE *abbr.* north north-east.

NNW *abbr.* north north-west.

no /nəʊ/ **1** particle used to express negative reply to question, request, etc. **2** *a.* not any, not one; not a. **3** *adv.* not; by no amount, not at all. **4** *n.* (*pl.* **noes**) word *no*, denial or refusal; in *pl.* voters against motion. **5** **no-ball** unlawfully delivered ball in cricket etc.; **no one** nobody; **no way** *colloq.* it is impossible.

No. *abbr.* number.

nob[1] *n. sl.* person of wealth or high social standing. **nobby** *a.*

nob[2] *n. sl.* head.

nobble /ˈnɒb(ə)l/ *v.t. sl.* tamper with (racehorse etc.); get hold of dishonestly; catch.

nobility /nəʊˈbɪlɪtɪ/ *n.* nobleness of character or rank; class of nobles.

noble /ˈnəʊb(ə)l/ **1** *a.* belonging to the aristocracy; of excellent character; magnanimous; of imposing appearance. **2** *n.* nobleman; noblewoman. **3** **nobleman, -woman,** peer(ess).

noblesse oblige /nəˈbles əˈbliːʒ/ privilege entails responsibility. [F]

nobody /ˈnəʊbədɪ/ **1** *pron.* no person. **2** *n.* person of no importance.

nock *n.* notch on bow or arrow for bowstring.

nocturnal /nɒkˈtɜːn(ə)l/ *a.* of or done or active in the night.

nocturne /ˈnɒktɜːn/ *n.* dreamy musical piece; picture of night scene.

nod /nɒd/ **1** *v.* incline head slightly and quickly; let head droop, be drowsy; bend and sway; make slip or mistake. **2** *n.* nodding of head esp. in assent.

noddle /ˈnɒd(ə)l/ *n. colloq.* head.

node *n.* knob on root or branch; point at which leaves spring; hard swelling; point or line of rest in vibrating body; point at which curve crosses itself;

intersecting-point esp. of planet's orbit and ecliptic. **nodal** *a.*

nodule /ˈnɒdjuːl/ *n.* small rounded lump of anything; small knotty tumour, ganglion. **nodular** *a.*

noggin /ˈnɒgɪn/ *n.* small mug; small measure of liquor.

Noh /nəʊ/ *n.* traditional Japanese drama.

noise /nɔɪz/ **1** *n.* sound, esp. loud or unpleasant one. **2** *v.t.* make public, spread *abroad*.

noisome /ˈnɔɪsəm/ *a.* noxious, disgusting.

noisy /ˈnɔɪzɪ/ *a.* loud; full of or making much noise; rowdy.

nomad /ˈnəʊmæd/ *n.* member of tribe roaming from place to place for pasture; wanderer. **nomadic** *a.*

nom de plume /nɒm də ˈpluːm/ *n.* writer's assumed name. [F]

nomenclature /nəˈmenklətʃə/ *n.* system of names or naming; terminology.

nominal /ˈnɒmɪn(ə)l/ *a.* of or like noun; in name or word only; not real or substantial.

nominate /ˈnɒmɪneɪt/ *v.t.* appoint to or propose for election to office. **nomination** *n.*; **nominator** *n.*

nominative /ˈnɒmɪnətɪv/ *Gram.* **1** *n.* case expressing subject of verb. **2** *a.* of or in nominative. **3** **nominatival** /-ˈtaɪv-/ *a.*

nominee /nɒmɪˈniː/ *n.* person who is nominated.

non- in *comb.* not. For the meanings of combinations not given below the main word should be consulted.

nonage /ˈnəʊnɪdʒ/ *n.* being under age.

nonagenarian /nəʊnədʒɪˈneərɪən/ *n.* person between 90 and 99 years old.

non-belligerent **1** *a.* taking no active or open part in war. **2** *n.* such State.

nonce /nɒns/ *n.* time being, present. **nonce-word** one coined for one occasion.

nonchalant /ˈnɒnʃəl(ə)nt/ *a.* unmoved, indifferent, cool. **nonchalance** *n.*

non-combatant **1** *a.* not fighting, esp. in war as being civilian, army chaplain, etc. **2** *n.* such person.

non-commissioned *a.* not holding commission (esp. of Army officers below second lieutenant).

non-committal *a.* not committing

oneself to definite view, course of action, etc.

non-conductor *n.* substance that does not conduct heat or electricity.

nonconformist *n.* person who does not conform, esp. **(Nonconformist)** member of Protestant sect dissenting from Anglican Church. **nonconformity** *n.*

non-contributory *a.* not involving contributions.

nondescript /'nɒndɪskrɪpt/ **1** *a.* hard to classify, indeterminate. **2** *n.* such person or thing.

none /nʌn/ **1** *pron.* not any ·*of*; no person(s). **2** *a.* no, not any. **3** *adv.* by no amount, not at all.

nonentity /nɒ'nentɪtɪ/ *n.* person of no importance; non-existence.

nonesuch var. of **nonsuch**.

non-event *n.* occurrence of no significance.

non-existent *a.* not existing. **non-existence** *n.*

non-fiction *n.* literary matter based on fact (opp. novels etc.).

non-interference *n.* policy of non-intervention.

non-intervention *n.* policy of not interfering in affairs of other State(s).

nonpareil /'nɒnpər(ə)l/ **1** *a.* unrivalled, unique. **2** *n.* such person or thing.

non-party *a.* independent of political parties.

nonplus /nɒn'plʌs/ *v.t.* **(nonplussed)** completely perplex.

nonsense /'nɒnsəns/ **1** *n.* absurd or meaningless words or ideas; foolish conduct. **2** *int.* you are talking nonsense. **3 nonsensical** /-'sen-/ *a.*

non sequitur /nɒn 'sekwɪtə/ conclusion that does not follow from the premises. [L]

non-skid *a.* that does not or is designed not to skid.

non-smoker *n.* person who does not smoke; compartment in train etc. where smoking is forbidden.

non-starter *n. fig.* idea, person, etc., not worth considering.

non-stick *a.* to which food will not adhere in cooking.

non-stop 1 *a.* (of train etc.) not stopping at intermediate stations; done

without stopping. **2** *adv.* without stopping.

nonsuch /'nʌnsʌtʃ/ *n.* unrivalled person or thing; paragon.

noodle¹ /'nu:d(ə)l/ *n.* strip of pasta used in soup etc.

noodle² /'nu:d(ə)l/ *n.* simpleton.

nook /nʊk/ *n.* secluded corner or recess.

noon /nu:n/ *n.* 12 o'clock in day, midday. **noonday** midday.

noose /nu:s/ **1** *n.* loop with running knot; snare. **2** *v.t.* catch with or enclose in noose.

nor *conj.* and not, neither, and no more.

Nordic /'nɔ:dɪk/ *a.* of tall blond Germanic people of N. Europe, esp. Scandinavia.

norm *n.* standard, type; standard amount; customary behaviour.

normal /'nɔ:m(ə)l/ **1** *a.* conforming to standard, usual, regular, typical. **2** *n.* usual state, level, etc. **3 normalcy** *n.*; **normality** *n.*; **normalize** *v.t.*

Norman /'nɔ:m(ə)n/ **1** *n.* native of Normandy. **2** *a.* of Normans or their style of medieval architecture; of Normandy.

Norse /nɔ:s/ **1** *n.* the Scandinavian language-group. **2** *a.* of ancient Scandinavia, esp. Norway.

north /nɔ:θ/ **1** *n.* point of horizon to left of person facing east; northern part of country etc. **2** *a.* situated etc. in or towards north; facing north; (of wind) blowing from north. **3** *adv.* towards or in north. **4 north-east, -west,** (compass-point) half-way between north and east; west; **North Star** polestar. **5 northward** *a.*, *adv.*, & *n.*; **northwards** *adv.*

northerly /'nɔ:ðəlɪ/ *a.* & *adv.* in northern position or direction; (of wind) blowing from north.

northern /'nɔ:ð(ə)n/ *a.* of or in the north. **northern lights** aurora borealis.

northerner /'nɔ:ðənə(r)/ *n.* native or inhabitant of the north.

Norwegian /nɔ:'wi:dʒən/ **1** *a.* of Norway. **2** *n.* native or language of Norway.

nose /nəʊz/ *n.* organ on face or head above mouth, used for smelling and breathing; sense of smell; odour or perfume; open end of nozzle of pipe etc.; projecting part, front end. **2** *v.* perceive smell of, discover by smell; smell *out*; thrust nose against or into; pry or search; make one's way cautiously forward. 3 **nosebag** fodder-bag hung on horse's head; **nosebleed** bleeding from nose; **nose-cone** cone-shaped nose of rocket, etc.; **nosedive** (make) steep downward plunge.

nosegay /'nəʊzgeɪ/ *n.* small bunch of flowers.

nosh *sl.* 1 *v.* eat or drink. 2 *n.* food or drink. 3 **nosh-up** large meal.

nostalgia /nɒs'tældʒə/ *n.* homesickness; sentimental yearning for the past. **nostalgic** *a.*

nostril /'nɒstrɪl/ *n.* either of two openings in nose.

nostrum /'nɒstrəm/ *n.* quack remedy, patent medicine; pet scheme.

nosy /'nəʊzɪ/ *a.* inquisitive, prying.

not *adv.* expressing negation, refusal, or denial. **not half** *sl.* very much, very.

notable /'nəʊtəb(ə)l/ 1 *a.* worthy of note, striking, eminent. 2 *n.* eminent person. 3 **notability** *n.*

notary /'nəʊtərɪ/ *n.* person with authority to draw up deeds and perform other legal formalities. **notarial** /-'teər-/ *a.*

notation /nəʊ'teɪʃ(ə)n/ *n.* representing of numbers, quantities, etc. by symbols; set of such symbols.

notch 1 *n.* V-shaped indentation on edge or surface. 2 *v.t.* make notches in; score (*up*) by notches.

note 1 *n.* brief record of facts etc.; short letter; annotation in book; banknote; formal diplomatic communication; notice, attention; eminence; written sign representing pitch and duration of musical sound; single tone of definite pitch made by instrument, voice, etc.; sign, characteristic. 2 *v.t.* observe, notice; set *down* as thing to be remembered; in *p.p.* celebrated, well known *for*. 3 **notebook** book for memoranda etc.; **notecase** wallet for banknotes; **notepaper** paper for private correspondence.

notelet /'nəʊtlɪt/ *n.* small folded card etc. for informal letter.

noteworthy /'nəʊtwɜːðɪ/ *a.* worthy of attention; remarkable.

nothing /'nʌθɪŋ/ 1 *n.* no thing, not anything, nought; thing of no importance; no amount. 2 *adv.* not at all; in no way.

nothingness *n.* non-existence; worthlessness.

notice /'nəʊtɪs/ 1 *n.* heed, attention; intimation, warning, announcement; formal declaration of intention to end agreement or employment; review or comment in newspaper etc. 2 *v.t.* perceive, take notice of; remark upon. 3 **noticeable** *a.*

notifiable /'nəʊtɪfaɪəb(ə)l/ *a.* (of disease etc.) that must be notified to the authorities.

notify /'nəʊtɪfaɪ/ *v.t.* report, give notice of; inform. **notification** *n.*

notion /'nəʊʃ(ə)n/ *n.* concept, idea; view, opinion; intention.

notional /'nəʊʃən(ə)l/ *a.* speculative, imaginary.

notorious /nəʊ'tɔːrɪəs/ *a.* well-known, esp. for unfavourable reason. **notoriety** /nəʊtə'raɪətɪ/ *n.*

notwithstanding /nɒtwɪð'stændɪŋ/ 1 *prep.* in spite of. 2 *adv.* nevertheless.

nougat /'nuːgɑː/ *n.* sweet made of sugar and honey and nuts etc.

nought /nɔːt/ *n.* figure 0; nothing.

noun /naʊn/ *n.* word used as name of person or thing etc.

nourish /'nʌrɪʃ/ *v.t.* sustain with food; foster, cherish, nurse.

nourishment *n.* sustenance, food.

nous /naʊs/ *n. colloq.* common sense.

Nov. *abbr.* November.

nova /'nəʊvə/ *n.* (*pl.* **-vae** /-viː/ *or* **-vas**) star showing sudden large increase of brightness and then subsiding.

novel /'nɒv(ə)l/ 1 *a.* of new kind, strange, hitherto unknown. 2 *n.* fictitious prose story published as complete book.

novelette /nɒvə'let/ *n.* short (esp. romantic) novel.

novelist /'nɒvəlɪst/ *n.* writer of novels.

novella /nə'velə/ *n.* short novel or narrative tale.

novelty /'nɒvəltɪ/ *n.* newness; new thing or occurrence; small toy etc.

November /nəʊ'vembə/ *n.* eleventh month of year.

novena /nə'viːnə/ *n. RC Ch.* special prayers or services on 9 successive days.

novice /'nɒvɪs/ *n.* probationary member of religious order; beginner.

noviciate /nə'vɪʃɪət/ *n.* (also **no-**

vitiate) period of being a novice; religious novice.

now /naʊ/ 1 *adv.* at present or mentioned time; in immediate past. 2 *conj.* (also with *that*) as, since. 3 *n.* this time; present. 4 **now and then** occasionally.

nowadays /'naʊədeɪz/ 1 *adv.* at the present day. 2 *n.* the present day.

nowhere /'naʊweə/ 1 *adv.* in or to no place. 2 *pron.* no place.

noxious /'nɒkʃəs/ *a.* harmful, unwholesome.

nozzle /'nɒz(ə)l/ *n.* spout of hose-pipe etc.

nr. *abbr.* near.

NSPCC *abbr.* National Society for Prevention of Cruelty to Children.

NSW *abbr.* New South Wales.

NT *abbr.* New Testament.

nuance /'njuːɑ̃s/ *n.* subtle difference in or shade of meaning, colour, etc.

nub *n.* point or gist (*of* matter etc.).

nubile /'njuːbaɪl/ *a. n.* (of woman) marriageable, sexually attractive. **nubility** /-'bɪl-/ *n.*

nuclear /'njuːklɪə/ *a.* of or relating to or constituting a nucleus; using nuclear energy. **nuclear energy** energy released or absorbed during reactions in atomic nuclei; **nuclear family** father, mother, and child(ren); **nuclear fuel** source of nuclear energy; **nuclear physics** physics dealing with atomic nuclei; **nuclear power** power derived from nuclear energy.

nucleic acid /njuː'klɪɪk/ either of two acids (DNA and RNA) present in all living cells.

nucleus /'njuːklɪəs/ *n.* (*pl.* **-clei** /-klɪaɪ/) central part or thing round which others collect; central part of atom, of seed, or of plant or animal cell; kernel.

nude /njuːd/ 1 *a.* naked, unclothed. 2 *n.* nude figure in painting etc.; nude person. 3 **the nude** unclothed state. 4 **nudity** *n.*

nudge /nʌdʒ/ 1 *v.t.* push with elbow to draw attention privately; push in gradual manner. 2 *n.* such push.

nudist /'njuːdɪst/ *n.* person who advocates or practises going unclothed. **nudism** *n.*

nugatory /'njuːɡətərɪ/ *a.* futile, trifling; inoperative, not valid.

nugget /'nʌɡɪt/ *n.* rough lump of gold etc.

nuisance /'njuːsəns/ *n.* source of annoyance; obnoxious act or circumstance or thing or person.

null *a.* void, not valid; expressionless. **nullity** *n.*

nullify /'nʌlɪfaɪ/ *v.t.* neutralize; make invalid. **nullification** *n.*

numb /nʌm/ 1 *a.* deprived of feeling or power of motion. 2 *v.t.* make numb.

number /'nʌmbə/ 1 *n.* aggregate of units, sum, company; word or symbol stating how many; numbered person or thing, esp. single issue of periodical etc.; item, song, etc., in programme. 2 *v.t.* count; mark or distinguish with number; include *in*, *with*, etc.; have or amount to specified number; in *p.p.* be restricted in number. 3 **number one** *colloq.* oneself; **number-plate** plate bearing number esp. of motor vehicle.

numberless /'nʌmbəlɪs/ *a.* innumerable.

numeral /'njuːmər(ə)l/ 1 *n.* word or symbol denoting a number. 2 *a.* of or denoting a number.

numerate /'njuːmərət/ *a.* familiar with basic elements of mathematics or science. **numeracy** *n.*

numeration /njuːmə'reɪʃ(ə)n/ *n.* numbering.

numerator /'njuːməreɪtə/ *n. Math.* number above line in vulgar fraction.

numerical /njuː'merɪk(ə)l/ *a.* of, in, denoting, etc. number(s).

numerology /njuːmə'rɒlədʒɪ/ *n.* study of occult significance of numbers.

numerous /'njuːmərəs/ *a.* many; consisting of many.

numinous /'njuːmɪnəs/ *a.* indicating presence or influence of a god.

numismatic /njuːmɪz'mætɪk/ *a.* of coins or medals.

numismatics *n.pl.* (usu. treated as *sing.*) study of coins and medals. **numismatist** /-'mɪz-/ *n.*

nun *n.* member of community of women living under religious vows.

nuncio /'nʌnʃɪəʊ/ *n.* (*pl.* **-cios**) Pope's diplomatic representative.

nunnery /'nʌnərɪ/ *n.* convent of nuns.

nuptial /'nʌpʃ(ə)l/ 1 *a.* of marriage or wedding. 2 *n.* in *pl.* wedding.

nurse /nɜːs/ 1 *n.* person trained for care of sick; woman employed to take charge of young children. **2** *v.* work as nurse; be nurse (of), tend; suckle; cherish; hold or treat carefully. **3 nursing home** private hospital.

nursemaid /'nɜːsmeɪd/ *n.* young woman in charge of child(ren).

nursery /'nɜːsərɪ/ *n.* room or place for children; place where plants are reared esp. for sale. **nurseryman** grower of plants etc. for sale; **nursery rhyme** traditional verse story for young children; **nursery school** school for young children under school age.

nurture /'nɜːtʃə(r)/ **1** *n.* bringing up, fostering, care; nourishment. **2.** *v.t.* bring up, rear.

nut *n.* fruit consisting of hard shell enclosing edible kernel; this kernel; small usu. hexagonal piece of metal with hole through it, screwed on end of bolt for securing it; *sl.* head; *sl.* crazy person; small lump of coal, butter, etc. **2** *v.* seek or gather nuts; *sl.* strike with the head. **3 nutcase** *sl.* crazy person; **nutcrackers** instrument for cracking nuts; **nuthatch** small climbing bird.

nutation /njuː'teɪʃ(ə)n/ *n.* nodding; oscillation of earth's axis.

nuthatch /'nʌthætʃ/ *n.* small climbing bird.

nutmeg /'nʌtmeg/ *n.* hard aromatic seed of E. Ind. tree used ground or grated as spice etc.

nutria /'njuːtrɪə/ *a.* fur of coypu.

nutrient /'njuːtrɪ(ə)nt/ **1** *a.* serving as or providing nourishment. **2** *n.* nutrient substance.

nutriment /'njuːtrɪm(ə)nt/ *n.* nourishing food.

nutrition /njuː'trɪʃ(ə)n/ *n.* food, nourishment. **nutritional** *a.*

nutritious /njuː'trɪʃəs/ *a.* efficient as food.

nutritive /'njuːtrɪtɪv/ *a.* of nutrition; nutritive.

nuts *pred.a. sl.* crazy.

nutshell /'nʌtʃel/ *n.* hard covering of nut. **in a nutshell** in a few words.

nutter /'nʌtə/ *n. sl.* crazy person.

nutty /'nʌtɪ/ *a.* full of nuts; tasting of nuts; *sl.* crazy.

nux vomica /nʌks 'vɒmɪkə/ seed of E. Indian tree, yielding strychnine.

nuzzle /'nʌz(ə)l/ *v.* prod or rub gently with nose; nestle, lie snug.

NW *abbr.* North-West(ern).

NY *abbr.* New York.

nylon /'naɪlɒn/ *n.* strong light synthetic polymer; fabric of this; in *pl.* stockings of nylon.

nymph /nɪmf/ *n.* mythological semidivine female spirit of sea or woods etc.; *Zool.* immature form of some insects.

nymphomania /nɪmfə'meɪnɪə/ *n.* excessive sexual desire in women. **nymphomaniac** *n.* & *a.*

NZ *abbr.* New Zealand.

O

O¹ /əʊ/ n. nought, zero.

O² /əʊ/ int. prefixed to name in vocative or expr. wish, entreaty, etc.

oaf n. awkward lout. **oafish** a.

oak n. forest tree with hard wood, acorns, and lobed leaves; its wood. **oak-apple, -gall**, kinds of excrescence produced on oak by gall-flies.

oakum /ˈəʊkəm/ n. loose fibre got by picking old rope to pieces.

OAP abbr. old-age pensioner.

oar /ɔː(r)/ n. pole with blade used to propel boat by leverage against water; rower.

oarsman /ˈɔːzmən/ n. (pl. **-men**) rower. **oarswoman** (pl. **-women**) n.

oasis /əʊˈeɪsɪs /n. (pl. **oases** /-siːz/) fertile spot in desert.

oast n. hop-drying kiln. **oast-house** building containing this.

oat n. in pl. cereal grown as food; grain of this; tall grass resembling oats. **oat-cake** thin unleavened cake of oatmeal; **oatmeal** meal ground from oats, greyish-fawn colour. **oaten** a.

oath /əʊθ/ n. (pl. /əʊðz/) solemn declaration or undertaking naming God etc. as witness; profanity, obscenity.

ob. abbr. died (obiit).

obbligato /ɒblɪˈɡɑːtəʊ/ n. (pl. **-tos**) Mus. part or accompaniment forming integral part of a composition.

obdurate /ˈɒbdjʊrət/ a. hardened; stubborn. **obduracy** n.

OBE abbr. Officer of the Order of the British Empire.

obedient /əʊˈbiːdɪənt/ a. obeying or ready to obey; submissive to another's will. **obedience** n.

obeisance /əʊˈbeɪs(ə)ns/ n. gesture expressing submission, respect, etc.; homage. **obeisant** a.

obelisk /ˈɒbəlɪsk/ n. tapering stone pillar of rectangular section; obelus.

obelus /ˈɒbələs/ n. (pl. **-li** /-laɪ/) dagger-shaped mark of reference (†).

obese /əʊˈbiːs/ a. very fat. **obesity** n.

obey /əʊˈbeɪ/ v. carry out command of; be obedient (to).

obfuscate /ˈɒbfəskeɪt/ v.t. darken; obscure, confuse; bewilder. **obfuscation** n.

obituary /əˈbɪtjʊərɪ/ 1 n. notice of death(s); brief biography of deceased person. 2 a. of or serving as obituary.

object 1 /ˈɒbdʒɪkt/ n. material thing; person or thing to which action or feeling is directed; thing sought or aimed at; Gram. word governed by transitive verb or preposition. 2 /əbˈdʒekt/ v. express opposition or feel dislike or reluctance (to); state as reason (against). 3 **no object** not an important factor; **object-glass** lens in telescope etc. nearest to object. 4 **objector** n.

objectify /ɒbˈdʒektɪfaɪ/ v.t. make objective, embody.

objection /əbˈdʒekʃ(ə)n/ n. expression of disapproval or dislike; objecting; adverse reason or statement.

objectionable a. open to objection; unpleasant, offensive.

objective /əbˈdʒektɪv/ 1 a. external to the mind; actually existing; dealing with outward things not thoughts or feelings; Gram. constructed as or appropriate to object. 2 n. object or purpose aimed at; Gram. objective case. 3 **objectivity** n.

objet d'art /ɒbʒeɪ ˈdɑː/ (pl. **-jets** pr. same) small decorative object.

objurgate /ˈɒbdʒəɡeɪt/ v.t. chide, scold.

oblate /ˈɒbleɪt/ a. (of spheroid) flattened at poles.

oblation /əˈbleɪʃ(ə)n/ n. thing offered to God; pious donation.

obligate /ˈɒblɪɡeɪt/ v.t. bind to do; oblige.

obligation /ɒbləˈɡeɪʃ(ə)n/ n. duty; binding agreement; indebtedness for service or benefit.

obligatory /əˈblɪɡətərɪ/ a. binding, compulsory.

oblige /əˈblaɪdʒ/ v. constrain, compel, require; be binding on; perform service (for); in pass. be bound (to) by gratitude.

obliging a. helpful, accommodating.

oblique /əˈbliːk/ 1 a. slanting; diverging from straight line or course; not going straight to the point, indirect; Gram. (of case) other than nominative or vocative. 2 n. oblique stroke. 3 **obliquity** n.

obliterate /əˈblɪtəreɪt/ v.t. blot out, leave no clear trace of. **obliteration** n.

oblivion /ə'blɪvɪən/ n. state of being forgotten or of being oblivious.

oblivious /ə'blɪvɪəs/ a. unaware or unconscious (with of or to).

oblong /'ɒblɒŋ/ 1 a. rectangular with adjacent sides unequal. 2 n. oblong figure or object.

obloquy /'ɒbləkwɪ/ n. abuse, being ill spoken of.

obnoxious /əb'nɒkʃəs/ a. offensive, objectionable; disliked.

oboe /'əʊbəʊ/ n. double-reeded woodwind musical instrument.

obscene /əb'siːn/ a. offensive, indecent; Law (of publication) tending to deprave or corrupt; colloq. highly offensive. **obscenity** /-'sen-/ n.

obscure /əb'skjʊə(r)/ 1 a. not clearly expressed or easily understood; dark, indistinct; hidden, undistinguished. 2 v.t. make obscure or invisible. 3 **obscurity** n.

obsequies /'ɒbsɪkwiːz/ n.pl. funeral.

obsequious /əb'siːkwɪəs/ a. fawning, servile.

observance /əb'zɜːv(ə)ns/ n. keeping or performance (of law, occasion, etc.); rite, ceremonial act.

observant a. good at observing.

observation /ɒbzə'veɪʃ(ə)n/ n. observing or being observed; comment, remark.

observatory /əb'zɜːvətərɪ/ n. building for astronomical or other observation.

observe /əb'zɜːv/ v. perceive, become aware of; watch; keep (rules etc.); celebrate (rite etc.); note and record; say esp. by way of comment.

obsess /əb'ses/ v.t. preoccupy, fill mind of. **obsession** n.; **obsessional** a. **obsessive** a.

obsidian /əb'sɪdɪən/ n. dark vitreous lava.

obsolescent /ɒbsə'les(ə)nt/ a. becoming obsolete. **obsolescence** n.

obsolete /'ɒbsəliːt/ a. no longer used, antiquated.

obstacle /'ɒbstək(ə)l/ n. thing obstructing progress.

obstetrics /əb'stetrɪks/ n.pl. usu. treated as sing. branch of medicine or surgery dealing with childbirth. **obstetrical** a.; **obstetrician** /-'trɪʃ-/ n.

obstinate /'ɒbstɪnət/ a. stubborn, intractable. **obstinacy** n.

obstreperous /əb'strepərəs/ a. noisy, unruly.

obstruct /əb'strʌkt/ v.t. block up; make hard or impossible to pass along or through; retard or prevent progress of.

obstruction /əb'strʌkʃ(ə)n/ n. obstructing, being obstructive; thing that obstructs; hindering. **obstructionist** n.

obstructive /əb'strʌktɪv/ a. causing or meant to cause obstruction.

obtain /əb'teɪn/ v. acquire; get; have granted; be prevalent or established.

obtrude /əb'truːd/ v.t. thrust importunately forward. **obtrusion** n.; **obtrusive** a.

obtuse /əb'tjuːs/ a. dull-witted, slow to understand; blunt, not sharp or pointed; (of angle) greater than one right angle and less than two.

obverse /'ɒbvɜːs/ n. side of coin or medal that bears head or principal design; front or top side; counterpart.

obviate /'ɒbvɪeɪt/ v.t. clear away, get rid of; get round.

obvious /'ɒbvɪəs/ a. easily seen or recognized or understood.

OC abbr. Officer Commanding.

ocarina /ɒkə'riːnə/ n. egg-shaped musical wind instrument.

occasion /ə'keɪʒ(ə)n/ 1 n. special event or happening; time marked by this; suitable juncture, opportunity; reason. 2 v.t. be occasion or cause of.

occasional /ə'keɪʒən(ə)l/ a. happening irregularly and infrequently; made or meant for, acting on, etc. special occasion(s). **occasional table** small table for use as required.

occasionally adv. sometimes; intermittently.

Occident /'ɒksɪd(ə)nt/ n. the West, esp. opp. Orient. **occidental** a.

occiput /'ɒksɪpʌt/ n. back of head. **occipital** /-'sɪp-/ a.

occlude /ə'kluːd/ v.t. stop up; obstruct; Chem. absorb (gases). **occlusion** n.

occult /ə'kʌlt/ a. involving the supernatural, mystical, magical; esoteric; recondite.

occupant /'ɒkjʊp(ə)nt/ n. person occupying a dwelling or office or position. **occupancy** n.

occupation /ɒkjʊ'peɪʃ(ə)n/ n. profession or employment; occupying or being occupied, esp. by armed forces of another country.

occupational *a.* pertaining to one's or an occupation. **occupational disease, hazard,** one to which a particular occupation renders one especially liable; **occupational therapy** mental or physical activity to assist recovery from disease or injury.

occupier /ˈɒkjʊpaɪə(r)/ *n.* person residing in house etc. as owner or tenant.

occupy /ˈɒkjʊpaɪ/ *v.t.* reside in; take up, fill, be in; take military possession of; place oneself in (building etc.) esp. as political demonstration; hold (office); keep busy or engaged.

occur /əˈkɜː(r)/ *v.i.* take place, happen; come into one's mind; be met with or found in some place or conditions.

occurrence /əˈkʌr(ə)ns/ *n.* happening, incident.

ocean /ˈəʊʃ(ə)n/ *n.* sea surrounding continents of the earth, esp. one of the five named divisions of this; *the* sea; immense expanse or quantity. **oceanic** /əʊʃɪˈænɪk/ *a.*

oceanography /əʊʃəˈnɒɡrəfɪ/ *n.* study of the oceans. **oceanographer** *n.*

ocelot /ˈɒsɪlɒt/ *n.* S. Amer. feline animal resembling leopard.

och /ɒx/ *int.* Sc. & Ir. oh, ah.

ochre /ˈəʊkə(r)/ *n.* earth used as pigment; pale brownish-yellow colour. **ochrous** *a.*

o'clock *adv.* of the clock, used to specify hour.

oct-, octa-, *in comb.* eight.

Oct. *abbr.* October.

octagon /ˈɒktəɡən/ *n.* plane figure with 8 sides and angles. **octagonal** /-ˈtæɡ-/ *a.*

octahedron /ɒktəˈhiːdrən/ *n.* solid figure contained by 8 plane faces (usu. triangles). **octahedral** *a.*

octane /ˈɒkteɪn/ *n.* hydrocarbon of paraffin series. **high-octane** (of fuel used in internal combustion engines) not detonating rapidly during power stroke.

octave /ˈɒktɪv/ *n. Mus.* note 7 diatonic degrees above or below another; interval between note and its octave; series of notes filling this.

octavo /ɒkˈteɪvəʊ/ *n.* (*pl.* **-vos**) size of book or page with sheets folded into 8 leaves.

octet /ɒkˈtet/ *n. Mus.* composition for group of 8 performers; the performers; group of 8.

octo- *in comb.* eight.

October /ɒkˈtəʊbə(r)/ *n.* tenth month of the year.

octogenarian /ɒktədʒɪˈneərɪən/ *n.* person between 80 and 89 years old.

octopus /ˈɒktəpʊs/ *n.* mollusc with 8 suckered tentacles.

ocular /ˈɒkjʊlə(r)/ *a.* of or connected with the eyes or sight; visual.

oculist /ˈɒkjʊlɪst/ *n.* specialist in treatment of eye disorders or defects.

odd *a.* extraordinary, strange; left over, detached from a set; casual; (of number) not even, not divisible by two. **odd-ball** eccentric person; **odd job** casual isolated piece of work.

oddity /ˈɒdɪtɪ/ *n.* strangeness; peculiar trait; strange person or thing.

oddment /ˈɒdm(ə)nt/ *n.* odd article; something left over.

odds *n.pl.* occas. treated as *sing.* ratio between amounts staked by parties to a bet; chances in favour of or against result; balance of advantage; advantageous difference. **at odds** in conflict (*with*); **odds and ends** remnants, stray articles; **odds-on** a state when success is more likely than failure; **over the odds** above general price etc.

ode *n.* lyric poem of exalted style and tone.

odious /ˈəʊdɪəs/ *a.* hateful, repulsive.

odium /ˈəʊdɪəm/ *n.* general dislike or disapproval.

odoriferous /əʊdəˈrɪfərəs/ *a.* diffusing (usu. pleasant) odours.

odour /ˈəʊdə(r)/ *n.* smell or fragrance; favour or repute. **odorous** *a.*

odyssey /ˈɒdɪsɪ/ *n.* long adventurous journey.

OED *abbr.* Oxford English Dictionary.

Oedipus complex /ˈiːdɪpəs/ attraction of child to parent of opposite sex (esp. son to mother). **Oedipal** *a.*

oesophagus /iːˈsɒfəɡəs/ *n.* canal from mouth to stomach, gullet.

of /ɒv/ *prep.* belonging to, from; concerning; out of; among; relating to.

off 1 *adv.* away, at or to distance; out of position; loose, separate, gone; discontinued, stopped. **2** *prep.* from; no longer upon. **3** *a.* further; far; right-hand; (of food) decaying; *Crick.*

towards or from or in side of field which batsman faces when playing. **4** *n.* off side. **5 off and on** occasionally, intermittently; **off-beat** unconventional, unusual; **off chance** remote possibility; **off colour** not in good health; **offhand** without preparation, casual, curt; **off-licence** shop selling alcoholic drink for consumption away from premises, licence for this; **off-peak** used or for use away from peak of electricity consumption, traffic, etc.; **off-print** reprint of part of publication; **off-putting** *colloq.* repellent, disconcerting; **offshoot** side-shoot or branch; **offside** (of player in field game) in position where he may not play the ball; **off white** white with grey or yellow tinge.

offal /'ɒf(ə)l/ *n.* edible organs of animal; refuse, waste stuff.

offence /ə'fens/ *n.* illegal act; transgression; wounding of person's feelings, wounded feelings; aggressive action.

offend /ə'fend/ *v.* cause offence to, upset; displease or anger; do wrong.

offensive /ə'fensɪv/ **1** *a.* causing offence; insulting; disgusting, nauseous; aggressive; intended for or used in attack. **2** *n.* aggressive attitude or action or campaign.

offer /'ɒfə(r)/ **1** *v.* present for acceptance or refusal; express readiness or show intention (*to* do); present by way of sacrifice. **2** *n.* expression of readiness to do or give or sell; proposal, esp. of marriage; bid.

offering *n.* thing offered.

offertory /'ɒfətərɪ/ *n.* collection of money at religious service.

office /'ɒfɪs/ *n.* room or building where administrative or clerical work is done; place for transacting business; department or local branch etc. for specified purpose; position with duties attached to it; tenure of official position; duty, task, function; authorized form of worship; in *pl.* parts of house devoted to household work etc.

officer /'ɒfɪsə(r)/ *n.* person holding position of authority or trust, esp. one with commission in armed forces; policeman; president; treasurer; etc. of society etc.

official /ə'fɪʃ(ə)l/ **1** *a.* of office or its ten-

ure; characteristic of persons in office; properly authorized. **2** *n.* person holding office or engaged in official duties. **3 officialdom** *n.*

officialese /əfɪʃə'liːz/ *n.* officials' jargon.

officiate /ə'fɪʃɪeɪt/ *v.i.* act in official capacity; perform divine service.

officious /ə'fɪʃəs/ *a.* aserting one's authority; intrusively kind.

offing *n.* **in the offing** *fig.* at hand, ready or likely to happen etc.

offset /'ɒfset/ **1** *n.* side-shoot of plant serving for propagation; compensation; sloping ledge; (in full **offset process**) method of printing by transferring ink from plate etc. to rubber roller and thence to paper. **2** *v.t.* (**-set**) counterbalance, compensate; print by offset process.

offspring /'ɒfsprɪŋ/ *n.* person's children or descendants; animal's young or descendants.

oft *adv. arch.* often.

often /'ɒf(ə)n/ *adv.* frequently; many times; at short intervals; in many instances.

ogee /'əʊdʒiː/ *n.* S-shaped curve; moulding with such section.

ogive /'əʊdʒaɪv/ *n.* diagonal rib of vault; pointed arch.

ogle /'əʊg(ə)l/ **1** *v.* look flirtatiously (at). **2** *n.* flirtatious glance.

ogre /'əʊgə(r)/ *n.* man-eating giant. **ogress** *n.*; **ogrish** *a.*

oh /əʊ/ *int.* expr. surprise, pain, etc.

ohm /əʊm/ *n.* unit of electrical resistance.

OHMS *abbr.* On Her (or His) Majesty's Service.

oho /əʊ'həʊ/ *int.* expressing surprise or exultation.

oil **1** *n.* viscous liquid with smooth and sticky feel; (often in *pl.*) oil-colour. **2** *v.t.* apply oil to, lubricate; treat with oil. **3 oilcake** compressed linseed etc. as cattle-food or manure; **oilcloth** fabric, esp. canvas, waterproofed with oil; **oil-colour** paint made by mixing powdered pigment in oil; **oilfield** district yielding mineral oil; **oil-painting** use of or picture in oil-colours; **oil rig** equipment for drilling an oil well; **oilskin** cloth waterproofed with oil, garment or (in *pl.*) suit of it; **oil-well** well from which mineral oil is drawn.

oily /'ɔɪlɪ/ *a.* of, like, covered or soaked with, oil; (of manner) fawning.

ointment /'ɔɪntm(ə)nt/ *n.* smooth greasy healing or beautifying preparation for skin.

OK /əʊ'keɪ/ *colloq.* 1 *a.* & *adv.* all right. 2 *n.* approval, sanction. 3 *v.t.* sanction.

okapi /əʊ'kɑːpɪ/ *n.* rare Afr. ruminant mammal.

okay var. of **OK**.

okra /'ɒkrə/ *n.* tall orig. Afr. plant with seed-pods used as food.

old /əʊld/ 1 *a.* advanced in age; not young or near its beginning; of specified age; dating from far back; long established; former. 2 *n.* old time. 3 **old age** later part of normal lifetime; **old-age pension** State retirement pension; **old-age pensioner** person receiving this; **old boy** former member of school, *colloq.* elderly man; **old-fashioned** in or according to fashion no longer current, antiquated; **old girl** former member of school, *colloq.* elderly woman; **Old Glory** *US* Stars and Stripes; **old guard** original or past or conservative members of group; **old hand** experienced or practised person; **old hat** *colloq.* thing tediously familiar; **old maid** elderly spinster; **old man** *colloq.* one's father or husband or employer etc.; **old master** great painter of former times, painting by such painter; **Old Testament** part of Bible dealing with pre-Christian times; **old-time** of former times, long-established; **old woman** *colloq.* one's wife or mother, *fig.* fussy or timid man.

olden /'əʊld(ə)n/ *a.* arch. of an earlier period.

oldie /'əʊldɪ/ *n.* colloq. old person or thing.

oleaginous /əʊlɪ'ædʒɪnəs/ *a.* having properties of or producing oil; oily.

oleander /əʊlɪ'ændə(r)/ *n.* evergreen flowering Mediterranean shrub.

oleaster /əʊlɪ'æstə(r)/ *n.* wild olive.

olefin /'əʊləfɪn/ *n.* hydrocarbon of type containing less than maximum amount of hydrogen.

O level ordinary level in GCE examination.

olfactory /ɒl'fæktərɪ/ *a.* concerned with smelling.

oligarch /'ɒlɪgɑːk/ *n.* member of oligarchy.

oligarchy /'ɒlɪgɑːkɪ/ *n.* government or State governed by small group of persons; members of such government. **oligarchic(al)** *a.*

olive /'ɒlɪv/ 1 *n.* oval hard-stoned fruit yielding oil; tree bearing it; colour of unripe olive, dull yellowish green. 2 *a.* coloured like unripe olive; (of complexion) yellowish-brown. 3 **olive-branch** *fig.* something done or offered for peace or reconciliation.

Olympiad /ə'lɪmpɪæd/ *n.* period of 4 years between Olympic games.

Olympian /ə'lɪmpɪən/ *a.* of Olympus; magnificent, condescending; aloof.

Olympic /ə'lɪmpɪk/ *a.* of the Olympic Games. 2 *n.* in *pl.* Olympic games. 3 **Olympic Games** ancient-Greek festival held every 4 years, or modern international revival of this.

OM *abbr.* (member of the) Order of Merit.

ombudsman /'ɒmbʊdzmən/ *n.* (*pl.* -men) official appointed to investigate individuals' complaints against public authorities.

omega /'əʊmɪgə/ *n.* last letter of Greek alphabet (Ω, ω); last of series.

omelette /'ɒmlɪt/ *n.* dish of beaten eggs cooked in a frying-pan.

omen /'əʊmən/ *n.* sign portending good or evil, prophetic significance.

ominous /'ɒmɪnəs/ *a.* of evil omen, inauspicious.

omit /ə'mɪt/ *v.t.* leave out, not include; leave undone, neglect. **omission** *n.*

omni- *in comb.* all.

omnibus /'ɒmnɪbəs/ 1 *n.* bus; volume containing several novels etc. previously published separately. 2 *a.* serving several objects at once; comprising several items.

omnipotent /ɒm'nɪpət(ə)nt/ *a.* all-powerful. **omnipotence** *n.*

omnipresent /ɒmnɪ'prez(ə)nt/ *a.* present everywhere. **omnipresence** *n.*

omniscient /ɒm'nɪsɪənt/ *a.* knowing everything. **omniscience** *n.*

omnivorous /ɒm'nɪvərəs/ *a.* feeding on many kinds of food; *joc.* reading everything that comes one's way.

on 1 *prep.* (so as to be) supported by or covering or attached to, etc.; (so as to be) close to, in direction of; at, near, concerning, about; added to. 2 *adv.* (so as to be) on something; in some direction, forward; in advance; in(to) movement or operation or activity; being shown or performed. **3** *a.* & *n.* Crick. (in, towards, from) side of field behind batsman as he plays. **4 on-line** directly controlled by or connected to computer; **on to** to a position on □ See page 666.

onager /'ɒnədʒə(r)/ *n.* wild ass.

onanism /'əʊnənɪz(ə)m/ *n.* masturbation.

ONC *abbr.* Ordinary National Certificate.

once /wʌns/ **1** *adv.* on one occasion only; at some time in past. **2** *conj.* as soon as. **3** *n.* one time, performance, etc. **4 at once** immediately, simultaneously; **once-over** *colloq.* rapid preliminary inspection.

oncoming /'ɒnkʌmɪŋ/ *a.* approaching from the front.

OND *abbr.* Ordinary National Diploma.

one /wʌn/ **1** *a.* single and integral in number; only, without others, identical, same. **2** *n.* lowest cardinal numeral; thing numbered with it; unit, unity; single thing, person, or example. **3** *pron.* any person; the speaker. **4 one-horse** *sl.* small, poorly equipped; **one-man** involving or operated by one person only; **one-off** *colloq.* made as the only one, not repeated; **one-sided** unfair, partial; **one-track mind** mind preoccupied with one subject; **one-way** allowing movement etc. in one direction only.

oneness /'wʌnnɪs/ *n.* singleness; uniqueness; agreement, sameness.

onerous /'əʊnərəs/ *a.* burdensome.

oneself /wʌn'self/ *pron.*, *emphat.* & *refl.* form of **one**.

ongoing /'ɒngəʊɪŋ/ *a.* continuing, in progress.

onion /'ʌnɪən/ *n.* vegetable with edible bulb of pungent smell and flavour.

onlooker /'ɒnlʊkə(r)/ *n.* spectator.

only /'əʊnlɪ/ **1** *a.* existing alone of its or their kind. **2** *adv.* solely, merely, exclusively. **3** *conj.* except that; but then. **4 if only** I wish that.

o.n.o. *abbr.* or near offer.

onomatopoeia /ɒnəmætə'pi:ə/ *n.* formation of word from sound associated with thing named. **onomatopoeic** *a.*

onset /'ɒnset/ *n.* attack, impetuous beginning.

onslaught /'ɒnslɔːt/ *n.* fierce attack.

onto *incorrect* □ See page 665 and **on**.

ontology /ɒn'tɒlədʒɪ/ *n.* department of metaphysics concerned with nature of being. **ontological** *a.*; **ontologist** *n.*

onus /'əʊnəs/ *n.* burden, duty, responsibility.

onward /'ɒnwəd/ **1** *adv.* onwards. **2** *a.* directed onwards.

onwards *adv.* further on; towards front; with advancing motion.

onyx /'ɒnɪks/ *n.* kind of chalcedony with coloured layers.

oodles /'uːd(ə)lz/ *n.pl. colloq.* very great amount.

ooh /uː/ *int.* expr. surprised pleasure, pain, excitement, etc.

oolite /'əʊəlaɪt/ *n.* granular limestone. **oolitic** /-'lɪt-/ *a.*

oomph /ʊmf/ *n. sl.* energy, enthusiasm.

ooze /uːz/ **1** *v.* pass slowly through pores etc.; exude; leak *out* or *away.* **2** *n.* wet mud; sluggish flow. **3 oozy** *a.*

op *n. colloq.* operation.

op. *abbr.* opus.

opacity /əʊ'pæsɪtɪ/ *n.* opaqueness.

opal /'əʊp(ə)l/ *n.* milk-white or bluish stone with iridescent reflections.

opalescent /əʊpə'les(ə)nt/ *a.* iridescent. **opalescence** *n.*

opaline /'əʊpəlaɪn/ *a.* opal-like; opalescent.

opaque /əʊ'peɪk/ *a.* not transmitting light, not transparent; obscure.

op. cit. *abbr.* in the work already quoted (*opere citato*).

OPEC /'əʊpek/ *abbr.* Organization of Petroleum Exporting Countries.

open /'əʊpən/ **1** *a.* not closed or locked or blocked up; not covered or confined; exposed; expanded, unfolded, spread out; manifest, public; accessible to visitors or customers; not restricted; communicative, frank. **2** *n. the* **open** air; open competition etc. **3** *v.* make or become open or more open; begin, make start; declare open. **4 open air** outdoors; **opencast** (of mining) on surface; **open-ended** with no limit or restriction; **open-handed** generous; **open-heart surgery** surgery with heart exposed and blood made to by-pass it; **open letter** one printed in newspaper etc. but addressed to person by name; **open mind** accessibility to new ideas, unprejudiced or undecided state; **open-plan** (of house, office, etc.) with few interior walls; **open prison** one with few physical restraints on prisoners; **open question** matter on which differences of opinion are legitimate; **open sandwich** one without bread on top.

opener *n.* device for opening tins or bottles etc.

opening 1 *n.* gap, aperture; beginning, initial part; opportunity. **2** *a.* initial, first.

openly *adv.* publicly, frankly.

opera[1] /'ɒpərə/ *n.* musical drama with sung or spoken dialogue. **operaglasses** small binoculars for use in theatres etc.; **opera-hat** man's collapsible top hat; **opera-house** theatre for operas.

opera[2] /'ɒpərə/ *pl.* of **opus**.

operable /'ɒpərəb(ə)l/ *a.* that can be operated; suitable for treatment by surgical operation.

operate /'ɒpəreɪt/ *v.* be in action, produce effect; perform or carry on operation(s); work (machine etc.); direct working of. **operating theatre** place in hospital where surgical operations are performed.

operatic /ɒpə'rætɪk/ *a.* of or like opera.

operation /ɒpə'reɪʃ(ə)n/ *n.* action, working; performance of surgery on a patient; military manœuvre; financial transaction. **operational** *a.*

operative /'ɒpərətɪv/ **1** *a.* in operation; practical; having principal relevance; of or by surgery. **2** *n.* worker, artisan.

operator /'ɒpəreɪtə(r)/ *n.* person who operates machine, esp. person making connections of lines in telephone exchange; person engaging in business.

operetta /ɒpə'retə/ *n.* light opera.

ophidian /ə'fɪdɪən/ **1** *n.* member of sub-order of reptiles including snakes. **2** *a.* of this order.

ophthalmia /ɒf'θælmɪə/ *n.* inflammation of eye.

ophthalmic /ɒf'θælmɪk/ *a.* of or for the eye; of or for or affected by ophthalmia. **ophthalmic optician** one qualified to prescribe as well as dispense spectacles.

ophthalmology /ɒfθæl'mɒlədʒɪ/ *n.* scientific study of the eye.

ophthalmoscope /ɒf'θælməskəʊp/ *n.* instrument for examining the eye.

opiate /'əʊpɪət/ **1** *a.* containing opium; soporific. **2** *n.* drug containing opium and easing pain or inducing sleep.

opine /əʊ'paɪn/ *v.t.* express or hold opinion (*that*).

opinion /ə'pɪnɪən/ *n.* belief based on grounds short of proof; view held as probable; professional advice; estimate.

opinionated /ə'pɪnjəneɪtɪd/ *a.* unduly confident in one's opinions.

opium /'əʊpɪəm/ *n.* drug made from juice of kind of poppy and used as narcotic or sedative.

opossum /ə'pɒsəm/ *n.* kind of small Amer. or Austral. marsupial.

opponent /ə'pəʊnənt/ *n.* person who opposes or belongs to opposing side.

opportune /'ɒpətjuːn/ *a.* (of time) suitable, favourable, well-selected; done etc. at opportune time.

opportunism /'ɒpətjuːnɪz(ə)m/ *n.* adaptation of policy to circumstances, esp. regardless of principle. **opportunist** *n.*

opportunity /ɒpə'tjuːnɪtɪ/ *n.* favourable occasion; good chance, opening.

oppose /ə'pəʊz/ *v.t.* place in opposition or contrast (to); set oneself against; resist; argue against. **as opposed to** in contrast with.

opposite /'ɒpəzɪt/ **1** *a.* having position on other side; facing; of contrary kind; diametrically different. **2** *n.* opposite thing or person or term. **3** *adv.* in opposite position. **4** *prep.* opposite to. **5** **opposite number** person in corresponding position in another set etc.

opposition /ɒpə'zɪʃ(ə)n/ *n.* antagonism, resistance; contrast; diametrically opposite position. **the Opposition** chief parliamentary party, or group of parties, opposed to that in office.

oppress /ə'pres/ *v.t.* govern tyrannically; treat with gross harshness or injustice; weigh down. **oppression** *n.*; **oppressor** *n.*

oppressive /ə'presɪv/ *a.* that oppresses; (of weather) sultry, close.

opprobrious /ə'prəʊbrɪəs/ *a.* severely scornful; abusive.

opprobrium /ə'prəʊbrɪəm/ *n.* disgrace, bad reputation; cause of this.

oppugn /əˈpjuːn/ v.t. controvert, call in question.

opt v.i. make choice; decide. **opt out (of)** choose not to take part etc. (in).

optic /ˈɒptɪk/ 1 a. of eye or sight. 2 n. (P) **Optic** device fastened to neck of bottle for measuring out spirits.

optical /ˈɒptɪk(ə)l/ a. visual; aiding sight; of or according to optics. **optical fibre** thin glass fibre used in fibre optics; **optical illusion** involuntary mental misinterpretation of thing seen, due to its deceptive appearance.

optician /ɒpˈtɪʃ(ə)n/ n. maker or prescriber of optical instruments, esp. spectacles.

optics /ˈɒptɪks/ n.pl. usu. treated as sing. science of light and vision.

optimal /ˈɒptɪm(ə)l/ a. best or most favourable.

optimism /ˈɒptɪmɪz(ə)m/ n. hopeful view or disposition; tendency or inclination to expect favourable outcome. **optimist** n.; **optimistic** a.

optimum /ˈɒptɪməm/ 1 n. (pl. -ma) most favourable conditions; best compromise. 2 a. optimal.

option /ˈɒpʃ(ə)n/ n. choice, choosing; right to choose; purchased right to buy, sell, etc., on specified conditions at specified time.

optional /ˈɒpʃən(ə)l/ a. not obligatory.

opulent /ˈɒpjʊl(ə)nt/ a. wealthy; abundant; luxurious. **opulence** n.

opus /ˈəʊpəs/ n. (pl. **opera**) musical composition numbered as one of composer's works.

or conj. introducing alternatives.

oracle /ˈɒrək(ə)l/ n. place at which ancient Greeks etc. consulted gods for advice or prophecy; response received there; person or thing regarded as source of wisdom etc. **oracular** /ɒˈrækjʊlə(r)/ a.

oral /ˈɔːr(ə)l/ 1 a. spoken, verbal; by word of mouth; done or taken by mouth. 2 n. colloq. spoken examination.

orange /ˈɒrɪndʒ/ 1 n. roundish reddish-yellow citrus fruit; its colour; tree bearing it. 2 a. orange-coloured.

orangeade /ɒrɪnˈdʒeɪd/ n. drink made from or flavoured like oranges, freq. aerated.

orang-utan /ɔːræŋuːˈtæn/ n. large anthropoid ape.

oration /əˈreɪʃ(ə)n/ n. formal or ceremonial speech.

orator /ˈɒrətə(r)/ n. maker of a speech; eloquent public speaker.

oratorio /ɒrəˈtɔːrɪəʊ/ n. (pl. -ios) semi-dramatic musical composition usu. on sacred theme.

oratory /ˈɒrətərɪ/ n. art of or skill in public speaking; small private chapel. **oratorical** /-ˈtɒr-/ a.

orb n. sphere, globe; globe surmounted by cross as part of regalia; poet. eye.

orbicular /ɔːˈbɪkjʊlə(r)/ a. spherical or circular.

orbit /ˈɔːbɪt/ 1 n. curved course of planet, comet, satellite, etc. round another body; range or sphere of action. 2 v. go round in orbit; put into orbit.

orbital /ˈɔːbɪt(ə)l/ a. of orbits; (of road) passing round outside of city.

Orcadian /ɔːˈkeɪdɪən/ 1 n. native or inhabitant of Orkney. 2 a. of Orkney.

orchard /ˈɔːtʃəd/ n. enclosed piece of land with fruit-trees.

orchestra /ˈɔːkɪstrə/ n. body of instrumental performers; area in theatre etc. assigned to them.

orchestral /ɔːˈkestr(ə)l/ a. of or for or performed by orchestra.

orchestrate /ˈɔːkɪstreɪt/ v.t. compose or arrange or score, for orchestral performance.

orchid /ˈɔːkɪd/ n. any of various plants, freq. with brilliantly coloured or grotesquely shaped flowers.

ordain /ɔːˈdeɪn/ v.t. confer holy orders on; destine; appoint, enact.

ordeal /ɔːˈdiːl/ n. severe or testing trial or experience.

order /ˈɔːdə(r)/ 1 n. state of regular arrangement and normal functioning; natural or moral system with definite tendencies; arrangement of things relative to each other, sequence; prevalence of obedience to law; system of rules or procedure; authoritative direction or instruction; direction to supply something, thing (to be) supplied; Banking etc. instruction to pay money or deliver property; social class or rank; kind or sort; religious fraternity; grade of Christian ministry; company of persons distinguished by particular honour or reward, insignia worn by its members; stated form of divine service; mode of treatment in architecture;

Biol. grouping of animals or plants below class and above family. **2** *v.t.* put in order; ordain; command, prescribe, direct; direct manufacturer, tradesman, etc., to supply or waiter to serve.

orderly /'ɔːdəlɪ/ **1** *a.* methodically arranged; tidy; not unruly. **2** *n.* soldier in attendance on officer; hospital attendant. **3 orderly room** room in barracks for company's business.

ordinal /'ɔːdɪn(ə)l/ **1** *a.* (of number) defining thing's position in a series. **2** *n.* ordinal number.

ordinance /'ɔːdɪnəns/ *n.* decree; religious rite.

ordinand /'ɔːdɪnænd/ *n.* candidate for ordination.

ordinary /'ɔːdɪnərɪ/ *a.* normal; not exceptional; commonplace. **ordinary level** lowest level in GCE examination; **ordinary seaman** one of lower rating than able seaman.

ordination /ɔːdɪ'neɪʃ(ə)n/ *n.* ordaining; conferring of holy orders.

ordnance /'ɔːdnəns/ *n.* artillery and military supplies; department for military stores etc. **Ordnance Survey** government survey of UK producing accurate maps.

ordure /'ɔːdjʊə(r)/ *n.* dung.

ore *n.* naturally-occurring mineral yielding metal.

oregano /ɒrɪ'gɑːnəʊ/ *n.* dried wild marjoram as seasoning.

organ /'ɔːgən/ *n.* musical instrument consisting of pipes that sound when air is forced through them, operated by keys and pedals; part of body serving some special function; medium of opinion, esp. newspaper. **organ-grinder** player of barrel-organ; **organ-stop** set of organ-pipes of similar tone-quality, handle bringing this into action.

organdie /'ɔːgəndɪ/ *n.* fine usu. stiffened muslin.

organic /ɔː'gænɪk/ *a.* of or affecting bodily organ(s); (of animals and plants) having organs or organized physical structure; (of food) produced without artificial fertilizers or pesticides; organized; inherent, structural; *Chem.* (of compound) containing carbon in its molecules. **organic chemistry** that of carbon compounds. **organically** *adv.*

organism /'ɔːgənɪz(ə)m/ *n.* individual animal or plant; organized body.

organist /'ɔːgənɪst/ *n.* player of organ.

organization /ɔːgənaɪ'zeɪʃ(ə)n/ *n.* organized body or system or society; organizing or being organized.

organize /'ɔːgənaɪz/ *v.* give orderly structure to; make arrangements for; make organic or into living tissue.

orgasm /'ɔːgæz(ə)m/ *n.* climax of sexual excitement. **orgasmic** /-'gæz-/ *a.*

orgy /'ɔːdʒɪ/ *n.* drunken or licentious party; excessive indulgence in an activity. **orgiastic** *a.*

oriel /'ɔːrɪəl/ *n.* window projecting from wall of house at upper level.

orient 1 /'ɔːrɪənt/ *n.* **Orient,** *the* East, the countries east of Mediterranean, esp. E. Asia. **2** /'ɔːrɪent/ *v.t.* establish *oneself* in relation to surroundings; place (building etc.) to face east; turn in specified direction; determine position of with regard to compass.

oriental /ɔːrɪ'ent(ə)l/ **1** *a.* of Eastern or Asian world or its civilization. **2** *n.* native of East. **3 orientalize** *v.*

orientate /'ɔːrɪənteɪt/ *v.t.* orient. **orientation** *n.*

orienteering /ɔːrɪən'tɪərɪŋ/ *n.* competitive sport of traversing rough country on foot with map and compass.

orifice /'ɒrɪfɪs/ *n.* aperture; mouth of cavity.

origami /ɒrɪ'gɑːmɪ/ *n.* Japanese art of folding paper into decorative shapes.

origanum /ɒrɪ'gɑːnəm/ *n.* wild marjoram.

origin /'ɒrɪdʒɪn/ *n.* source; starting-point; parentage.

original /ə'rɪdʒɪn(ə)l/ **1** *a.* existing from the first; primitive; earliest; not imitative or derived; creative. **2** *n.* pattern, archetype; thing from which another is copied or translated. **3 original sin** innate sinfulness held to be common to all human beings. **4 originality** *n.*

originate /ə'rɪdʒɪneɪt/ *v.* have origin; begin; initiate or give origin to, be origin of. **origination** *n.*; **originator** *n.*

oriole /'ɔːrɪəʊl/ *n.* kind of bird, esp. **golden oriole** with black and yellow plumage in male.

ormolu /'ɔːməluː/ *n.* gilded bronze; gold-coloured alloy; articles made of or decorated with these.

ornament 1 /'ɔːnəmənt/ *n.* thing used to adorn or decorate; decoration; quality or person bringing honour or distinction. **2** /'ɔːnəment/ *v.t.* adorn, beautify. **3 ornamental** *a.*; **ornamentation** *n.*

ornate /ɔː'neɪt/ *a.* elaborately adorned.

ornithology /ɔːnɪ'θɒlədʒɪ/ *n.* study of birds. **ornithological** *a.*; **ornithologist** *n.*

orotund /'ɒrətʌnd/ *a.* (of utterance) dignified, imposing, pompous.

orphan /'ɔːf(ə)n/ **1** *n.* child whose parents are dead. **2** *a.* being an orphan. **3** *v.t.* bereave of parent(s).

orphanage /'ɔːfənɪdʒ/ *n.* institution for orphans.

orrery /'ɒrərɪ/ *n.* clockwork model of planetary system.

orris-root /'ɒrɪs/ *n.* violet-scented iris root.

ortho- *in comb.* straight, correct.

orthodontics /ɔːθə'dɒntɪks/ *n.pl.* usu. treated as *sing.* correction of irregularities in teeth and jaws.

orthodox /'ɔːθədɒks/ *a.* holding usual or accepted views; not heretical; conventional. **Orthodox Church** Eastern or Greek branch of Christian Church and Russian etc. Churches in communion with it. **orthodoxy** *n.*

orthography /ɔː'θɒgrəfɪ/ *n.* spelling, esp. with reference to its correctness. **orthographic(al)** *a.*

orthopaedic /ɔːθə'piːdɪk/ *a.* curing or treating deformity in bone or muscle.

orthopaedics *n.pl.* usu. treated as *sing.* orthopaedic surgery.

OS *abbr.* Ordinary Seaman; Ordnance Survey; outsize.

Oscar /'ɒskə(r)/ *n.* statuette awarded annually for excellence in film acting, directing, etc.

oscillate /'ɒsɪleɪt/ *v.* (cause to) swing to and fro; vacillate; *Electr.* (of current) undergo high-frequency alternations. **oscillation** *n.*; **oscillator** *n.*

oscilloscope /ə'sɪləskəʊp/ *n.* device for recording oscillations esp. on screen of cathode ray tube.

osier /'əʊzɪə(r)/ *n.* willow used in basketwork; shoot of this.

osmosis /ɒz'məʊsɪs/ *n.* diffusion of fluid through semi-permeable partition into another fluid. **osmotic** /-'mɒt-/ *a.*

osprey /'ɒspreɪ/ *n.* large bird preying on inshore fish.

osseous /'ɒsɪəs/ *a.* bony; having bones.

ossify /'ɒsɪfaɪ/ *v.* turn into bone; harden; make or become rigid. **ossification** *n.*

ostensible /ɒs'tensɪb(ə)l/ *a.* professed; used to conceal real purpose or nature.

ostentation /ɒsten'teɪʃ(ə)n/ *n.* pretentious display; showing off. **ostentatious** *a.*

osteopath /'ɒstɪəpæθ/ *n.* person who treats disease by manipulation of bones. **osteopathy** /-'ɒp-/ *n.*

ostler /'ɒslə(r)/ *n.* stableman at inn.

ostracize /'ɒstrəsaɪz/ *v.t.* exclude from society, refuse to associate with. **ostracism** *n.*

ostrich /'ɒstrɪtʃ/ *n.* large flightless swift-running bird.

OT *abbr.* Old Testament.

other /'ʌðə(r)/ **1** *a.* not same; separate in identity; distinct in kind; alternative, further, or additional; *the* only remaining. **2** *n.* or *pron.* other person or thing. **3** *adv.* otherwise. **4 the other day, week,** etc., a few days etc. ago; **other world** life after death.

otherwise /'ʌðəwaɪz/ *adv.* in a different way; if circumstances are or were or had been different; in other respects; or else.

otiose /'əʊtɪəʊz/ *a.* not required, serving no practical purpose.

otter /'ɒtə(r)/ *n.* furred aquatic fish-eating mammal.

Ottoman /'ɒtəmən/ **1** *a. hist.* of Turkish Empire. **2** *n.* (*pl.* **-mans**) Turk of Ottoman period; **ottoman** cushioned seat without back or arms, storage-box with padded top.

OU *abbr.* Open University; Oxford University.

oubliette /uːblɪ'et/ *n.* secret dungeon with trapdoor entrance.

ouch /aʊtʃ/ *int.* expr. sharp or sudden pain.

ought /ɔːt/ *v.aux.* (3rd *sing.* **ought**) expr. duty, rightness, probability, etc.

Ouija /'wiːdʒə/ *n.* (**P**) (in full **Ouija-board**) board marked with alphabet used with movable pointer to obtain messages in spiritualist seances.

ounce /aʊns/ *n.* unit of weight, 1/16 lb. or 28 g.

our /aʊə(r)/ *pron.* & *a., poss.* case of **we**, with abs. form **ours**.

ourself /aʊə'self/ *pron.* corresponding to **myself** when used by sovereign, newspaper-writer, etc. who uses *we* instead of *I*.

ourselves /auə'selvz/ *pron.*, *emphat.* and *refl.* form of **we**.

ousel var. of **ouzel**.

oust /aust/ *v.t.* eject; drive out of office or power; seize place of.

out /aut/ **1** *adv.* away from or not in place, not in right or normal state; not at home; so as to be excluded; in(to) open, sight, notice, etc.; to or at an end; not in fashion, office, etc.; not burning. **2** *prep.* out of. **3 out of date** obsolete, antiquated; **out of doors** in(to) open air; **out of the way** unusual, remote, disposed of.

out- *in comb.* out of, external, to excess, so as to defeat or excel, etc.

outback /'autbæk/ *n. Austral.* remote inland districts.

outbid /aut'bɪd/ *v.t.* (*past* & *p.p.* **-bid**) bid higher than.

outboard /'autbɔːd/ *a.* towards outside of ship, aircraft, or vehicle, (of motor) attached externally to stern of boat; (of boat) using such motor.

outbreak /'autbreɪk/ *n.* breaking out of emotion, war, disease, fire, etc.

outbuilding /'autbɪldɪŋ/ *n.* outhouse.

outburst /'autbɜːst/ *n.* bursting out, esp. of emotion in vehement words.

outcast /'autkɑːst/ **1** *n.* person cast out from home and friends. **2** *a.* homeless, rejected.

outclass /aut'klɑːs/ *v.t.* surpass in quality.

outcome /'autkʌm/ *n.* result, issue.

outcrop /'autkrɒp/ *n.* rock etc. emerging at surface; *fig.* notable manifestation.

outcry /'autkraɪ/ *n.* loud protest; clamour.

outdated /aut'deɪtɪd/ *a.* out of date, obsolete.

outdistance /aut'dɪst(ə)ns/ *v.t.* get far ahead of.

outdo /aut'duː/ *v.t.* (*past* **-did**; *p.p.* **-done** /-'dʌn/) surpass, excel.

outdoor /'autdɔː(r)/ *a.* of or done for or use etc. out of doors.

outdoors 1 *n. the* open air. **2** *adv.* in(to) the open air.

outer /'autə(r)/ *a.* farther from centre or inside; on outside. **outer space** universe beyond earth's atmosphere. **outermost** *a.*

outface /aut'feɪs/ *v.t.* disconcert by staring or by confident manner.

outfall /'autfɔːl/ *n.* mouth of river, drain, etc.

outfield /'autfiːld/ *n.* outer part of cricket or baseball pitch.

outfit /'autfɪt/ *n.* set of equipment or clothes; *colloq.* (organized) group or company.

outfitter /'autfɪtə(r)/ *n.* supplier of equipment, esp. men's clothes.

outflank /aut'flæŋk/ *v.t.* get round the flank of; outmanoeuvre.

outflow /'autfləu/ *n.* outward flow; what flows out.

outgoing /'autgəuɪŋ/ **1** *a.* going out; retiring from office; friendly. **2** *n.* in *pl.* expenditure.

outgrow /aut'grəu/ *v.t.* (*past* **-grew**; *p.p.* **-grown** /-'grəun/) grow faster or get taller than; get too big for (clothes, etc.); leave behind as one develops.

outgrowth /'autgrəuθ/ *n.* offshoot.

outhouse /'authaus/ *n.* shed etc., esp. adjoining main house.

outing /'autɪŋ/ *n.* pleasure-trip.

outlandish /aut'lændɪʃ/ *a.* looking or sounding strange or foreign; bizarre.

outlast /aut'lɑːst/ *v.t.* last longer than.

outlaw /'autlɔː/ **1** *n.* person deprived of protection of law; lawless person. **2** *v.t.* declare outlaw; make illegal; proscribe. **outlawry** *n.*

outlay /'autleɪ/ *n.* expenditure.

outlet /'autlɪt/ *n.* means of exit; means of expressing feelings; market for goods.

outline /'autlaɪn/ **1** *n.* external boundary; line(s) enclosing visible object; contour; rough draft, summary; in *pl.* main features. **2** *v.t.* draw or describe in outline; mark outline of.

outlive /aut'lɪv/ *v.t.* live longer than or beyond or through.

outlook /'autluk/ *n.* view, prospect; what seems likely to happen; *fig.* mental attitude.

outlying /'autlaɪɪŋ/ *a.* far from centre; remote.

outmanoeuvre /autmə'nuːvə(r)/ *v.t.* outdo in manoeuvring.

outmatch /aut'mætʃ/ *v.t.* be more than a match for.

outmoded /aut'məudɪd/ *a.* out of fashion; obsolete.

outnumber /aʊt'nʌmbə(r)/ v.t. exceed in number.

outpace /aʊt'peɪs/ v.t. go faster than; outdo in contest.

out-patient /'aʊtpeɪʃ(ə)nt/ n. one not residing in hospital during treatment.

outpost /'aʊtpəʊst/ n. detachment on guard at some distance from army; outlying settlement etc.

output /'aʊtpʊt/ 1 n. amount produced; place where energy, information, etc., leaves a system; results etc. supplied by computer. 2 v.t. (past & p.p. -put or -putted) (of computer) supply (results etc.).

outrage /'aʊtreɪdʒ/ 1 n. forcible violation of others' rights, sentiments, etc.; gross offence or indignity; fierce resentment. 2 v.t. subject to outrage; insult; infringe violently; shock and anger.

outrageous /aʊt'reɪdʒəs/ a. immoderate, shocking; grossly cruel or offensive etc.

outrank /aʊt'ræŋk/ v.t. be superior in rank to.

outré /'uːtreɪ/ a. eccentric, violating decorum. [F]

outrider /'aʊtraɪdə(r)/ n. motor cyclist riding ahead of car(s) etc.

outrigger /'aʊtrɪgə(r)/ n. spar or framework projecting from or over ship's side; bracket bearing rowlocks outside boat; boat with these.

outright 1 /aʊt'raɪt/ adv. altogether, entirely; not gradually; without reservation. 2 /'aʊtraɪt/ a. complete; thorough.

outrun /aʊt'rʌn/ v.t. (past -ran; p.p. -run) run faster or farther than; escape; go beyond.

outsell /aʊt'sel/ v.t. (past & p.p. -sold /-'səʊld/) sell more than; be sold in greater quantities than.

outset /'aʊtset/ n. beginning.

outshine /aʊt'ʃaɪn/ v.t. (past & p.p. -shone /-'ʃɒn/) be more brilliant than.

outside /'aʊtsaɪd/ 1 n. external surface, outer part(s); external appearance; position on outer side; highest computation. 2 a. of, on, or nearer outside; not belonging to some circle or institution; greatest existent or possible. 3 /aʊt'saɪd/ adv. on or to outside; out of doors; not within. 4 /aʊt'saɪd/ prep. not in; to, or at the outside of; ex-

ternal to; beyond limits of. 5 **outside broadcast** one not made from a studio.

outsider /aʊt'saɪdə(r)/ n. non-member of circle, party, profession, etc.; competitor thought to have no chance.

outsize /'aʊtsaɪz/ 1 a. unusually large. 2 n. outsize garment etc.

outskirts /'aʊtskɜːts/ n.pl. outer area of town etc.

outsmart /aʊt'smɑːt/ v.t. colloq. outwit; be too clever for.

outspoken /aʊt'spəʊkən/a. frank, unreserved.

outspread /aʊt'spred/ a. spread out.

outstanding /aʊt'stændɪŋ/ a. conspicuous, esp. from excellence; still to be dealt with.

outstay /aʊt'steɪ/ v.t. stay longer than.

outstretched /aʊtstretʃt/ a. stretched out.

outstrip /aʊt'strɪp/ v.t. go faster than; surpass in progress, competition, etc.

outvote /aʊt'vəʊt/ v.t. defeat by majority of votes.

outward /'aʊtwəd/ 1 a. directed towards outside; going out; physical; external, superficial. 2 adv. outwards.

outwardly adv. in outward appearance; on the surface.

outwards adv. in outward direction; towards outside.

outweigh /aʊt'weɪ/ v.t. exceed in weight, value, influence, etc.

outwit /aʊt'wɪt/ v.t. be too clever for; overcome by greater ingenuity.

outwork /'aʊtwɜːk/ n. advanced or detached part of fortress etc.; work done outside shop, factory, etc.

outworn /aʊt'wɔːn/ a. worn out, obsolete.

ouzel /'uːz(ə)l/ n. small bird of thrush family.

ouzo /'uːzəʊ/ n. Greek drink of aniseed-flavoured spirits.

ova pl. of **ovum**.

oval /'əʊv(ə)l/ 1 a. shaped like egg, elliptical. 2 n. elliptical closed curve; thing with oval outline.

ovary /'əʊvərɪ/ n. ovum-producing organ in female animal; seed-vessel in plant. **ovarian** /-'veər-/ a.

ovation /əʊ'veɪʃ(ə)n/ n. enthusiastic applause or reception.

oven /'ʌv(ə)n/ n. enclosed chamber for baking or cooking in. **ovenware** dishes in which food can be cooked in oven.

over /'əʊvə(r)/ **1** *adv.* outward and downward from brink or from erect position; above in place or position; more than; covering whole surface; from one side, end, etc. to other; from beginning to end; at end; done with. **2** *n.* Crick. number of balls bowled from one end before change is made to other; play during this time. **3** *prep.* above; concerning; across; on or to other side, end, etc. of.

over- *in comb.* over; upper, outer; superior; excessive(ly).

overact /əʊvə'rækt/ *v.* act with exaggeration.

over-active /əʊvə'ræktɪv/ *a.* too active.

overall /'əʊvərɔːl/ **1** *a.* taking everything into account, inclusive, total. **2** *adv.* in all parts; taken as a whole. **3** *n.* protective outer garment; in *pl.* protective trousers or suit.

overarm /'əʊvərɑːm/ *a.* & *adv.* with arm raised above shoulder.

overawe /əʊvə'rɔː/ *v.t.* awe into submission.

overbalance /əʊvə'bæl(ə)ns/ *v.* (cause to) lose balance and fall.

overbear /əʊvə'beə(r)/ *v.t.* (*past* **-bore**; *p.p.* **-born**) bear down by weight or force; repress.

overbearing /əʊvə'beərɪŋ/ *a.* domineering, bullying.

overblown /əʊvə'bləʊn/ *a.* inflated or pretentious; past its prime.

overboard /'əʊvəbɔːd/ *adv.* from within ship into water. **go overboard** *colloq.* show extreme enthusiasm.

overbook /əʊvə'bʊk/ *v.* make too many bookings (for).

overcast /əʊvə'kɑːst/ *a.* (of sky) covered with cloud; (in sewing) edged with stitching.

overcharge /əʊvə'tʃɑːdʒ/ *v.* charge too high a price for or to; put too much (explosive, electric, etc.) charge into.

overcoat /'əʊvəkəʊt/ *n.* large coat worn over ordinary clothing.

overcome /əʊvə'kʌm/ *v.t.* (*past* **-came**; *p.p.* **-come**) prevail over, master; be victorious; in *p.p.* greatly affected or made helpless.

overcrowd /əʊvə'kraʊd/ *v.t.* cause too many people or things to be in (a place).

overdevelop /əʊvədɪ'veləp/ *v.* develop too much.

overdo /əʊvə'duː/ *v.t.* (*past* **-did**; *p.p.* **-done** /-dʌn/) carry to excess; cook too long; exhaust.

overdose /'əʊvədəʊs/ *n.* excessive dose esp. of drug etc.

overdraft /'əʊvədrɑːft/ *n.* overdrawing of bank account; amount by which account is overdrawn.

overdraw /əʊvə'drɔː/ *v.* (*past* **-drew**; *p.p.* **-drawn**) draw more from bank account) than amount in credit; in *p.p.* having overdrawn one's account.

overdress /əʊvə'dres/ *v.* dress ostentatiously or with too much formality.

overdrive /'əʊvədraɪv/ *n.* mechanism in vehicle providing gear ratio higher than that of ordinary top gear.

overdue /əʊvə'djuː/ *a.* past the time when due or ready; late, in arrears.

overestimate **1** /əʊvə'restɪmeɪt/ *v.t.* form too high an estimate of. **2** /əʊvə'restɪmət/ *n.* too high an estimate.

over-expose /əʊvərɪk'spəʊz/ *v.t.* expose too much or for too long.

overfish /əʊvə'fɪʃ/ *v.t.* fish (stream, sea, etc.) to depletion.

overflow **1** /əʊvə'fləʊ/ *v.* flow over, flood; extend beyond limits or capacity of; be so full that contents overflow; be very abundant. **2** /'əʊvəfləʊ/ *n.* what overflows or is superfluous; outlet for excess liquid.

overgrown /əʊvə'grəʊn/ *a.* covered with plants, weeds, etc.; grown too big.

overhang **1** /əʊvə'hæŋ/ *v.* (*past* & *p.p.* **-hung**) project or hang (over). **2** /'əʊvəhæŋ/ *n.* fact or amount of overhanging.

overhaul /əʊvə'hɔːl/ *v.t.* check over thoroughly and make necessary repairs to; overtake.

overhead **1** /əʊvə'hed/ *adv.* above one's head; in sky. **2** /'əʊvəhed/ *a.* placed overhead. **3** /'əʊvəhed/ *n.* in *pl.* routine administrative and maintenance expenses of a business.

overhear /əʊvə'hɪə(r)/ *v.t.* (*past* & *p.p.* **-heard** /-'hɜːd/) hear as unperceived or unintentional listener.

overjoyed /əʊvə'dʒɔɪd/ *a.* filled with extreme joy.

overkill /'əʊvəkɪl/ *n.* excess of capacity to kill or destroy.

overland **1** /əʊvə'lænd/ *adv.* by land

and not sea. **2** /ˈəʊvəlænd/ *a.* entirely or partly by land.

overlap **1** /əʊvəˈlæp/ *v.* partly cover; cover and extend beyond; partly coincide. **2** /ˈəʊvəlæp/ *n.* overlapping; overlapping part or amount.

overlay **1** /əʊvəˈleɪ/ *v.t.* (*past & p.p.* **-laid**) cover surface of *with* coating etc. **2** /ˈəʊvəleɪ/ *n.* thing laid over another.

overleaf /əʊvəˈliːf/ *adv.* on other side of leaf of book.

overlie /əʊvəˈlaɪ/ *v.t.* (*past* **-lay**; *p.p.* **-lain**) lie on top of.

overload **1** /əʊvəˈləʊd/ *v.t.* load too heavily. **2** /ˈəʊvələʊd/ *n.* amount by which thing is overloaded.

overlook /əʊvəˈlʊk/ *v.t.* fail to observe, take no notice of, condone; have view of from above.

overlord /ˈəʊvəlɔːd/ *n.* supreme lord.

overly /ˈəʊvəlɪ/ *adv.* excessively, too.

overman /əʊvəˈmæn/ *v.t.* provide with too many men as crew, staff, etc.

overmuch /əʊvəˈmʌtʃ/ *a.*, *n.*, & *adv.* too much.

overnight **1** /əʊvəˈnaɪt/ *adv.* during course of a night; on preceding evening; *colloq.* suddenly. **2** /ˈəʊvənaɪt/ *a.* done or for use etc. overnight.

overpass /ˈəʊvəpɑːs/ *n.* road that crosses another by a bridge.

overpower /əʊvəˈpaʊə(r)/ *v.t.* subdue, reduce to submission; be too intense or violent for.

over-produce /əʊvəprəˈdjuːs/ *v.t.* produce in excess of demand or of defined amount. **overproduction** *n.*

overrate /əʊvəˈreɪt/ *v.t.* have too high an opinion of.

overreach /əʊvəˈriːtʃ/ *v.* outwit, circumvent; **overreach oneself** defeat one's object by going too far.

over-react /əʊvərɪˈækt/ *v.i.* respond more violently etc. than is justified.

override /əʊvəˈraɪd/ *v.t.* (*past* **-rode**; *p.p.* **-ridden**) have precedence or superiority over, intervene and make ineffective.

overrider /əʊvəˈraɪdə(r)/ *n.* vertical attachment on motor vehicle bumper to prevent its becoming interlocked with another vehicle.

overrule /əʊvəˈruːl/ *v.t.* set aside by superior authority; annul decision of thus.

overrun /əʊvəˈrʌn/ *v.* (*past* **-ran**; *p.p.* **-run**) swarm or spread over; exceed time etc. allowed.

overseas /əʊvəˈsiːz/ *a.* & *adv.* across or beyond sea.

oversee /əʊvəˈsiː/ *v.t.* (*past* **-saw**; *p.p.* **-seen**) superintend. **overseer** *n.*

oversew /ˈəʊvəsəʊ/ *v.t.* (*p.p.* **-sewn**) sew (two edges) with stitches lying over them.

overshadow /əʊvəˈʃædəʊ/ *v.t.* appear much more prominent or important than; cast into shade.

overshoe /ˈəʊvəʃuː/ *n.* shoe worn over another for protection in wet weather etc.

overshoot /əʊvəˈʃuːt/ *v.* (*past & p.p.* **-shot**) pass or send beyond (target or limit).

oversight /ˈəʊvəsaɪt/ *n.* failure to notice; inadvertent omission or mistake; supervision.

oversimplify /əʊvəˈsɪmplɪfaɪ/ *v.t.* distort by putting in too simple terms.

oversleep /əʊvəˈsliːp/ *v.i.* (*past & p.p.* **-slept**) sleep beyond intended time of waking.

overspend /əʊvəˈspend/ *v.i.* (*past & p.p.* **-spent**) spend beyond one's means.

overspill /ˈəʊvəspɪl/ *n.* what is spilt over or overflows; *fig.* surplus population leaving one area for another.

overspread /əʊvəˈspred/ *v.t.* (*past & p.p.* **-spread**) cover surface of; in *pass.* be covered *with.*

overstate /əʊvəˈsteɪt/ *v.t.* state too strongly; exaggerate. **overstatement** *n.*

overstep /əʊvəˈstep/ *v.t.* pass beyond.

overstrain /əʊvəˈstreɪn/ *v.t.* damage by exertion; stretch too far.

overstrung /əʊvəˈstrʌŋ/ *a.* too highly strung or intensely strained.

oversubscribed /əʊvəsəbˈskraɪbd/ *a.* (of shares offered for sale) not enough to meet amount subscribed.

overt /əʊˈvɜːt/ *a.* openly done, unconcealed.

overtake /əʊvəˈteɪk/ *v.t.* (*past* **-took**; *p.p.* **-taken**) catch up and pass; come suddenly upon.

overtax /əʊvəˈtæks/ *v.t.* make excessive demands on; tax too highly.

overthrow **1** /əʊvəˈθrəʊ/ *v.t.* (*past* **-threw**; *p.p.* **-thrown**) remove forcibly from power; put an end to; conquer;

overtime /'əʊvətaɪm/ 1 *n*. time worked in addition to regular hours; payment for this. 2 *adv*. as or during overtime.

overtone /'əʊvətəʊn/ *n*. subtle extra quality or implication; *Mus*. any of tones above lowest in harmonic series.

overtop /əʊvə'tɒp/ *v.t*. be or become higher than, surpass.

overtrump /əʊvə'trʌmp/ *v*. play higher trump (than).

overture /'əʊvətjʊə(r)/ *n*. *Mus*. orchestral prelude; opening of negotiations; formal proposal or offer.

overturn /əʊvə'tɜːn/ *v*. (cause to) fall down or over; upset, overthrow.

overview /'əʊvəvjuː/ *n*. general survey.

overweening /əʊvə'wiːnɪŋ/ *a*. arrogant.

overweight 1 /əʊvə'weɪt/ *a*. beyond the weight allowed or desirable. 2 /'əʊvəweɪt/ *n*. excess weight.

overwhelm /əʊvə'welm/ *v.t*. overpower with emotion or *with* excess of business etc.; bury, submerge utterly.

overwhelming /əʊvə'welmɪŋ/ *a*. irresistible through force of numbers, influence, amount, etc.

overwork /əʊvə'wɜːk/ 1 *v*. (cause to) work too hard; weary or exhaust with work. 2 *n*. excessive work.

overwrought /əʊvə'rɔːt/ *a*. suffering reaction from excitement.

oviduct /'əʊvɪdʌkt/ *n*. tube through which ova pass from ovary.

oviform /'əʊvɪfɔːm/ *a*. egg-shaped.

ovine /'əʊvaɪn/ *a*. of or like sheep.

oviparous /əʊ'vɪpərəs/ *a*. egg-laying.

ovoid /'əʊvɔɪd/ *a*. (of solid) egg-shaped.

ovulate /'ɒvjʊleɪt/ *v.i*. discharge ovum or ova from ovary; produce ova. **ovulation** *n*.

ovule /'ɒvjuːl/ *n*. structure containing germ-cell in female plant.

ovum /'əʊvəm/ *n*. (*pl*. **ova**) female germ-cell in animals, from which by fertilization with male sperm the young is developed; egg.

ow /aʊ/ *int*. expr. sudden pain.

owe /əʊ/ *v*. be under obligation to (re)pay or render; be in debt (*for*); be indebted for (*to*).

owing /'əʊɪŋ/ *pred.a*. owed, yet to be paid. **owing to** caused by, because of.

owl /aʊl/ *n*. night bird of prey.

owlet /'aʊlɪt/ *n*. small or young owl.

owlish /'aʊlɪʃ/ *a*. like an owl; solemn and dull.

own /əʊn/ 1 *a*. (after possessive) not another's; (*absol*.) own property, kindred, etc. 2 *v*. have as property, possess; acknowledge authorship or paternity of; admit as valid, true, etc. 3 **hold one's own** maintain one's position, not be defeated; **of one's own** belonging to one; **on one's own** alone, independently, unaided; **own up** *colloq*. confess.

owner /'əʊnə(r)/ *n*. possessor. **owner-occupier** person who owns house he lives in. **ownership** *n*.

ox *n*. (*pl*. **oxen**) individual of kinds of large usu. horned ruminant; castrated male of domestic species of this. **ox-eye daisy** kind of plant with large white or yellow flowers.

oxalic acid /ɒk'sælɪk/ intensely sour poisonous acid found in wood sorrel and other plants.

Oxford shoe /'ɒksfəd/ low shoe laced over instep.

oxidation /ɒksɪ'deɪʃ(ə)n/ *n*. oxidization.

oxide /'ɒksaɪd/ *n*. compound of oxygen with another element or with radical.

oxidize /'ɒksɪdaɪz/ *v*. (cause to) combine with oxygen; rust; cover with coating of oxide. **oxidization** *n*.

oxy-acetylene /ɒksɪə'setɪliːn/ *a*. of or using mixture of oxygen and acetylene, esp. in cutting or welding metals.

oxygen /'ɒksɪdʒ(ə)n/ *n*. colourless odourless tasteless gas essential to life and to combustion. **oxygen tent** enclosure to allow patient to breathe air with increased oxygen content.

oxygenate /'ɒksɪdʒəneɪt/ *v.t*. supply or treat or mix with oxygen; oxidize.

oxymoron /ɒksɪ'mɔːrɒn/ *n*. figure of speech with pointed conjunction of apparent contradictions.

oyez /əʊ'jez/ *int*. uttered by public crier or court officer to call for attention.

oyster /'ɔɪstə(r)/ *n*. bivalve mollusc used as food; white colour with grey tinge.

oz. *abbr*. ounce(s).

ozone /'əʊzəʊn/ *n*. form of oxygen with pungent odour; *pop*. invigorating seaside air.

P

p *abbr.* penny, pence.

p. *abbr.* page.

p *abbr. Mus.* piano².

pa /pɑː/ *n. colloq.* father.

PA *abbr.* personal assistant; public address.

p.a. *abbr.* per annum.

pace¹ /peɪs/ **1** *n.* single step in walking or running; space traversed in this; speed, rate of progression; (of horse etc.) gait. **2** *v.* walk (over, about), esp. with slow or regular step; measure (distance) by pacing; set pace for. **3 pacemaker** person who sets pace; natural or electrical device for stimulating heart muscle.

pace² /ˈpeɪsɪ/ *prep.* with all due deference to.

pachyderm /ˈpækɪdɜːm/ *n.* large thick-skinned mammal, esp. elephant or rhinoceros. **pachydermatous** *a.*

pacific /pəˈsɪfɪk/ *a.* tending to peace, of peaceful disposition.

pacifist /ˈpæsɪfɪst/ *n.* person opposed to war. **pacifism** *n.*

pacify /ˈpæsɪfaɪ/ *v.t.* appease; bring to state of peace. **pacification** *n.*

pack¹ /pæk/ **1** *n.* collection of things wrapped or tied together for carrying; lot or set; set of playing-cards; group of wild animals or hounds; organized group of Cubs or Brownies; forwards of Rugby football team; medicinal or cosmetic substance applied to face; area of large crowded pieces of floating ice in sea; method of packing. **2** *v.* put (things) together into bundle, box, etc., fill (bag etc.) with clothes etc., for transport or storing; put closely together, cram, crowd together, form into pack; wrap tightly. **3 pack-drill** military punishment of walking up and down in full marching equipment; **pack-horse** horse for carrying packs; **pack up** *sl.* stop working, break down, retire from contest, activity, etc.; **packing-case** (usu. wooden) case for packing goods in; **send packing** *colloq.* dismiss summarily.

pack² *v.t.* select (jury etc.) so as to secure biased decision in one's favour.

package /ˈpækɪdʒ/ **1** *n.* parcel; box etc. in which goods are packed. **2** *v.t.* make up into or enclose in package. **3 package deal** *colloq.* transaction agreed to as a whole; **package holiday, tour**, etc., one with fixed inclusive price.

packet /ˈpækɪt/ *n.* small package; *colloq.* large sum of money; mail-boat.

pact *n.* agreement, treaty.

pad¹ **1** *n.* piece of soft stuff used to diminish jarring, raise surface, absorb fluid, etc.; number of sheets of blank paper fastened together at one edge; fleshy cushion forming sole of foot of some animals; leg-guard in games; flat surface for helicopter take-off; *sl.* lodging. **2** *v.t.* provide with pad, stuff; fill out or *out* with superfluous matter.

pad² *v.* walk softly; tramp (along) on foot; travel on foot.

padding /ˈpædɪŋ/ *n.* material used to pad.

paddle¹ /ˈpæd(ə)l/ **1** *n.* short oar with broad blade at one or each end; striking-board in paddle-wheel; fin or flipper; action or spell of paddling. **2** *v.* propel with paddle(s); row gently. **3 paddle-wheel** wheel for propelling ship, with boards round circumference so as to press backward against water.

paddle² /ˈpæd(ə)l/ **1** *v.i.* wade about in shallow water. **2** *n.* action or spell of paddling.

paddock /ˈpædək/ *n.* small field for keeping horses in; enclosure where horses or cars are assembled before race.

paddy¹ /ˈpædɪ/ *n.* field where rice is grown (in full **paddy-field**); rice before threshing or in the husk.

paddy² /ˈpædɪ/ *n. colloq.* rage, temper.

padlock /ˈpædlɒk/ **1** *n.* detachable lock hanging by hinged or pivoted hook. **2** *v.t.* secure with padlock.

padre /ˈpɑːdrɪ/ *n. colloq.* chaplain in army etc.

paean /ˈpiːən/ *n.* song of praise or triumph.

paederast var. of **pederast**.

paediatrics /piːdɪˈætrɪks/ *n.* branch of medicine dealing with children's diseases. **paediatric** *a.*; **paediatrician** /-ˈtrɪʃ-/ *n.*

paella /pɑːˈelə/ *n.* Spanish dish of rice, chicken, seafood, etc.

pagan /ˈpeɪgən/ *n. & a.* heathen. **paganism** *n.*

page[1] 1 n. leaf of book etc.; one side of this. 2 v.t. number pages of.

page[2] 1 n. boy employed as liveried servant or personal attendant. 2 v.t. call name of (person sought) in public rooms of hotel etc.

pageant /'pædʒ(ə)nt/ n. spectacular performance, usu. illustrative of historical events; any brilliant show.

pageantry /'pædʒəntrɪ/ n. spectacular show or display; what serves to make a pageant.

paginate /'pædʒɪneɪt/ v.t. number pages of (book etc.). **pagination** n.

pagoda /pə'gəʊdə/ n. temple or sacred tower in China etc.; ornamental imitation of this.

pah int. expr. disgust.

paid past & p.p. of **pay**. **put paid to** colloq. finish off.

pail n. bucket.

pain 1 n. bodily suffering caused by injury or disease; mental distress; in pl. trouble taken; in pl. throes of childbirth. 2 v.t. inflict pain on. 3 **painstaking** /'peɪnz-/ careful, industrious.

painful /'peɪnfʊl/ a. causing or suffering pain; causing trouble or difficulty.

painless /'peɪnlɪs/ a. not causing pain.

paint 1 n. colouring matter prepared for application to surface. 2 v. cover surface of with paint; portray or make pictures in colours; depict in words; apply liquid or cosmetic to. 3 **painted lady** butterfly with spotted orange-red wings.

painter[1] /'peɪntə(r)/ n. person who paints, esp. as artist or decorator.

painter[2] /'peɪntə(r)/ n. rope at bow of boat for tying it up.

painting /'peɪntɪŋ/ n. art of representing by colours on a surface; product of this.

pair /peə(r)/ 1 n. set of 2; thing with 2 corresponding parts not used separately; engaged or married or mated couple; (either of) 2 MPs etc. on opposite sides arranging both to be absent from division etc. 2 v. arrange or unite as pair or in pairs; mate. 3 **pair off** form into pairs.

Paisley /'peɪzlɪ/ a. having characteristic pattern of curved abstract figures.

pajamas var. of **pyjamas**.

Pakistani /pɑːkɪs'tɑːnɪ/ 1 n. native of Pakistan. 2 a. of Pakistan.

pal colloq. 1 n. friend. 2 v.i. (with up) make friends.

palace /'pælɪs/ n. official residence of sovereign, archbishop, or bishop; stately mansion or building.

paladin /'pælədɪn/ n. peer of Charlemagne's court; knight errant.

palaeo- /'pælɪəʊ/ in comb. ancient.

palaeography /pælɪ'ɒgrəfɪ/ n. study of ancient writing and inscriptions.

palaeolithic /pælɪəʊ'lɪθɪk/ a. of earlier Stone Age.

palaeontology /pælɪɒn'tɒlədʒɪ/ n. study of life in geological past.

Palaeozoic /pælɪəʊ'zəʊɪk/ 1 a. of geological era containing oldest forms of highly organized life. 2 n. this era.

palais /'pæleɪ/ n. dance hall.

palanquin /pælən'kiːn/ n. (also **palankeen**) Eastern covered litter.

palatable /'pælətəb(ə)l/ a. pleasant to taste; agreeable to the mind.

palatal /'pælət(ə)l/ 1 a. of the palate; (of sound) made with tongue against palate. 2 n. palatal sound.

palate /'pælət/ n. roof of mouth; sense of taste; liking.

palatial /pə'leɪʃ(ə)l/ a. like palace, splendid.

palaver /pə'lɑːvə(r)/ 1 n. fuss and bother; idle talk. 2 v. talk profusely; flatter, wheedle.

pale[1] 1 a. (of complexion etc.) whitish, not ruddy; faintly coloured; (of colour) faint, (of light) dim. 2 v. grow or make pale.

pale[2] n. stake etc. as part of fence; boundary. **beyond the pale** outside bounds of acceptable behaviour.

palette /'pælɪt/ n. artist's flat tablet for mixing colours on. **palette-knife** knife with long round-ended flexible blade.

palimpsest /'pælɪmpsest/ n. writing-material used for second time after original writing has been erased.

palindrome /'pælɪndrəʊm/ n. word or phrase etc. that reads same backwards as forwards. **palindromic** /-'drɒm-/ a.

paling /'peɪlɪŋ/ n. in sing. or pl. fence of pales; pale.

palisade /pælɪ'seɪd/ 1 n. fence of pointed stakes. 2 v.t. enclose with palisade.

pall[1] /pɔːl/ n. cloth spread over coffin etc.; ecclesiastical vestment; fig. dark covering. **pallbearer** person helping to carry coffin at funeral.

pall² /pɔːl/ v.i. become tiresome.

pallet¹ /'pælɪt/ n. straw bed, mattress.

pallet² /'pælɪt/ n. portable platform for transporting and storing loads.

palliasse /'pælɪæs/ n. straw mattress.

palliate /'pælɪeɪt/ v.t. alleviate without curing; excuse, extenuate. **palliation** n.; **palliative** a. & n.

pallid /'pælɪd/ a. pale, sickly-looking.

pallor /'pælə(r)/ n. paleness.

pally /'pælɪ/ a. colloq. friendly.

palm /pɑːm/ 1 n. inner surface of hand between wrist and fingers; kind of tree with unbranched stem and crown of large esp. fan-shaped leaves; leaf of this as symbol of victory; (prize for) supreme excellence. 2 v.t. conceal in hand. **3 palm off** impose or thrust fraudulently (on); **Palm Sunday** Sunday before Easter.

palmar /'pælmə(r)/ a. of or in palm of hand.

palmate /'pælmeɪt/ a. shaped like palm of hand.

palmetto /pæl'metəʊ/ n. (pl. **-os**) palm-tree, esp. of small size.

palmist /'pɑːmɪst/ n. teller of character or fortune from lines etc. in palm of hand. **palmistry** n.

palmy /'pɑːmɪ/ a. of or like or abounding in palms; flourishing.

palomino /pælə'miːnəʊ/ n. (pl. **-nos**) golden or cream-coloured horse with light-coloured mane and tail.

palpable /'pælpəb(ə)l/ a. that can be touched or felt; readily perceived. **palpability** n.

palpate /pæl'peɪt/ v.t. Med. examine by touch. **palpation** n.

palpitate /'pælpɪteɪt/ v.i. pulsate, throb; tremble. **palpitation** n.

palsy /'pɔːlzɪ/ 1 n. paralysis, esp. with involuntary tremors. 2 v.t. affect with palsy.

paltry /'pɔːltrɪ/ a. worthless; contemptible; trifling.

pampas /'pæmpəs/ n.pl. large treeless S. Amer. plains. **pampas-grass** large ornamental grass.

pamper /'pæmpə(r)/ v.t. over-indulge.

pamphlet /'pæmflɪt/ n. small unbound esp. controversial treatise.

pamphleteer /pæmflɪ'tɪə(r)/ n. writer of (esp. political) pamphlets.

pan¹ 1 n. flat-bottomed usu. metal vessel used in cooking etc.; shallow receptacle or tray; bowl of scales or of lavatory; hollow in ground. 2 v. colloq. criticize harshly. **3 pan out** (of gravel) yield gold, fig. succeed (well etc.).

pan² 1 v. cause film-camera to turn horizontally to follow movement etc.; (of camera) be moved thus. 2 n. panning movement.

pan- in comb. of or for all.

panacea /pænə'siːə/ n. universal remedy.

panache /pə'næʃ/ n. assertively confident style.

panama /pænəmɑː/ n. hat of straw-like material made from leaves of a pine-tree.

panatella /pænə'telə/ n. long thin cigar.

pancake /'pænkeɪk/ n. thin flat usu. fried batter-cake. **Pancake Day** Shrove Tuesday; **pancake landing** landing of aircraft descending vertically in level horizontal position.

panchromatic /pænkrə'mætɪk/ a. (of film etc.) sensitive to all visible colours of spectrum.

pancreas /'pænkrɪəs/ n. gland near stomach supplying digestive fluid and insulin. **pancreatic** /-'æt-/ a.

panda /'pændə/ n. large rare bear-like black-and-white animal of China (also **giant panda**); raccoon-like Himalayan animal. **panda car** police patrol car.

pandemic /pæn'demɪk/ a. (of disease) of world-wide distribution.

pandemonium /pændɪ'məʊnɪəm/ n. uproar; utter confusion; scene of this.

pander /'pændə(r)/ 1 v.i. (with to) indulge person or weakness. 2 n. go-between in illicit love affairs; procurer.

p. & p. abbr. postage and packing.

pane n. single sheet of glass in window or door.

panegyric /pænɪ'dʒɪrɪk/ n. laudatory discourse; eulogy. **panegyrist** n.; **panegyrize** v.t.

panel /'pæn(ə)l/ 1 n. distinct or separate part of surface, esp. of wall or door etc.; surface holding or displaying controls and switches and recording dials etc.; group of people assembled for discussion, consultation, etc.; list of jury. 2 v.t. fit with panels. **3 panel**

game quiz etc. played by panel of entertainers.

panellist /'pænəlist/ n. member of panel.

pang n. sudden sharp pain.

pangolin /pæŋ'gəʊlin/ n. scaly ant-eater.

panic /'pænik/ 1 n. sudden alarm; infectious fright. 2 a. of or connected with panic. 3 v. affect or be affected with panic. 4 **panic-stricken, -struck,** affected with panic. 5 **panicky** a.

panicle /'pænik(ə)l/ n. Bot. loose branching cluster of flowers.

panjandrum /pæn'dʒændrəm/ n. mock title of great personage.

pannier /'pæniə(r)/ n. one of pair of baskets or bags etc. carried by beast of burden or on bicycle or motor cycle etc.

panoply /'pænəpli/ n. full armour; fig. complete or splendid array.

panorama /pænə'rɑːmə/ n. picture or photograph containing wide view; continuous passing scene; unbroken view of surrounding region. **panoramic** /-'ræm-/ a.

pansy /'pænzi/ n. garden plant of violet family; colloq. effeminate man, male homosexual.

pant 1 v. gasp for breath; throb; yearn. 2 n. gasp; throb.

pantaloons /pæntə'luːnz/ n.pl. hist. trousers.

pantechnicon /pæn'teknikən/ n. furniture van.

pantheism /'pænθiɪz(ə)m/ n. doctrine that God is everything and everything God. **pantheist** n.; **pantheistic** a.

pantheon /'pænθiən/ n. temple of all gods; building with memorials of illustrious dead.

panther /'pænθə(r)/ n. leopard.

panties /'pæntiːz/ n.pl. colloq. short-legged or legless knickers.

pantile /'pæntaɪl/ n. curved roof-tile.

pantograph /'pæntəgrɑːf/ n. instrument for copying plan etc. on any scale.

pantomime /'pæntəmaɪm/ n. dramatic usu. Christmas entertainment based on fairy-tale; dumb show.

pantry /'pæntri/ n. room in which provisions, crockery, cutlery, etc. are kept.

pants n.pl. colloq. underpants; knickers; trousers.

pap[1] n. soft or semi-liquid food; mash, pulp.

pap[2] n. arch. nipple of breast.

papa /pə'pɑː/ n. arch. child's name for father.

papacy /'peɪpəsi/ n. Pope's office or tenure; papal system.

papal /'peɪp(ə)l/ a. of the Pope or his office.

papaw /pə'pɔː/ n. pulpy orange edible fruit; tropical Amer. tree bearing it.

paper /'peɪpə(r)/ 1 n. substance made in thin flexible sheets from pulp of wood or other fibrous material, used for writing, printing, wrapping, etc.; documents; newspaper; set of examination questions or answers; essay, memorandum. 2 a. made of paper; written on paper. 3 v.t. decorate (wall etc.) with paper. 4 **paper-boy, -girl,** one who delivers or sells newspapers; **paper-clip** clip of bent wire or plastic for holding sheets of paper together; **paper-hanger** person who decorates walls etc. with wallpaper; **paper-knife** blunt knife for opening envelopes etc.; **paper money** banknotes etc.; **paper-weight** small heavy object to hold papers down; **paperwork** office administration and record-keeping.

paperback /'peɪpəbæk/ 1 a. bound in stiff paper, not boards. 2 n. paperback book.

papier mâché /pæpɪeɪ 'mæʃeɪ/ moulded paper pulp used for making models etc.

papilla /pə'pɪlə/ n. (pl. **-lae** /-liː/) small nipple-like protuberance. **papillary** a.

papist /'peɪpɪst/ n. derog. Roman Catholic. **papistical** a.; **papistry** n.

papoose /pə'puːs/ n. young N. Amer. Indian child.

paprika /'pæprɪkə/ n. ripe red pepper; red condiment made from this.

papyrus /pə'paɪərəs/ n. (pl. **-ri** /-riː/) aquatic plant of sedge family; ancient writing-material made from stem of this; manuscript written on this.

par n. average or normal value or degree; equality, equal footing; Golf number of strokes needed by first-class player for hole or course; face value.

para- in comb. beside, beyond.

parable /'pærəb(ə)l/ n. narrative used to illustrate moral or spiritual truth.

parabola /pə'ræbələ/ n. plane curve

formed by intersection of cone with plane parallel to its side.

parabolic /pærə'bɒlɪk/ a. of or expressed in parable; of or like parabola. **parabolically** adv.

paracetamol /pærə'siːtəmɒl/ n. compound used to relieve pain and reduce fever; tablet of this.

parachute /'pærəʃuːt/ 1 n. umbrella-shaped apparatus allowing person or heavy object to descend safely from a height, esp. from aircraft. 2 v. convey or descend by parachute. 3 **parachutist** n.

parade /pə'reɪd/ 1 n. muster of troops etc. for inspection, public procession; display, ostentation; public square, parade-ground. 2 v. assemble for parade; march with display (through); display ostentatiously. 3 **parade-ground** place for muster of troops.

paradigm /'pærədaɪm/ n. example, pattern, esp. of inflexion of word.

paradise /'pærədaɪs/ n. heaven; region or state of supreme bliss; garden of Eden. **paradisiacal** /-dɪ'saɪək(ə)l/ a.

paradox /'pærədɒks/ n. seemingly absurd or self-contradictory though perhaps well-founded statement etc. **paradoxical** a.

paraffin /'pærəfɪn/ n. inflammable waxy or oily substance got by distillation from petroleum etc. **paraffin wax** solid paraffin.

paragon /'pærəgən/ n. model of excellence; excellent person or thing.

paragraph /'pærəgrɑːf/ n. distinct passage in book etc. usually marked by indentation of first line; mark of reference (¶); short separate item in newspaper etc.

parakeet /'pærəkiːt/ n. small long-tailed parrot.

parallax /'pærəlæks/ n. apparent difference in position or direction of object caused by change of observation point; angular amount of this. **parallactic** a.

parallel /'pærəlel/ 1 a. (of lines) continuously equidistant; precisely similar, analogous, or corresponding. 2 n. person or thing analogous to another; comparison; imaginary line on earth's surface or line on map marking degree of latitude. 3 v.t. be parallel or correspond to; represent as similar; compare. 4 **parallelism** n.

parallelepiped /pærəlelə'paɪped/ n. solid bounded by parallelograms.

parallelogram /pærə'leləgræm/ n. 4-sided rectilinear figure whose opposite sides are parallel.

paralyse /'pærəlaɪz/ v.t. affect with paralysis; render powerless, cripple.

paralysis /pə'rælɪsɪs/ n. (pl. **-ses** /-siːz/) incapacity to move or feel; powerless or immobile state.

paralytic /pærə'lɪtɪk/ 1 a. affected with paralysis; sl. very drunk. 2 n. person affected with paralysis.

paramedical /pærə'medɪk(ə)l/ a. supplementing and supporting medical work.

parameter /pə'ræmɪtə(r)/ n. Math. quantity constant in case considered, but varying in different cases; (esp. measurable or quantifiable) characteristic or feature. □ See page 666.

paramilitary /pærə'mɪlɪtərɪ/ a. ancillary to and similarly organized to military forces.

paramount /'pærəmaʊnt/ a. supreme. **paramountcy** n.

paramour /'pærəmʊə(r)/ n. arch. illicit lover.

paranoia /pærə'nɔɪə/ n. mental derangement with delusions of grandeur, persecution, etc.; abnormal tendency to suspect and mistrust others. **paranoiac** a. & n.; **paranoid** a. & n.

paranormal /pærə'nɔːm(ə)l/ a. lying outside the range of normal scientific investigations etc.

parapet /'pærəpɪt/ n. low wall at edge of roof, balcony, bridge, etc.; mound along front of trench.

paraphernalia /pærəfə'neɪlɪə/ n.pl. personal belongings, miscellaneous accessories, etc.

paraphrase /'pærəfreɪz/ 1 n. restatement of sense of passage etc. in other words. 2 v.t. express meaning of in other words.

paraplegia /pærə'pliːdʒə/ n. paralysis of lower part of body. **paraplegic** a. & n.

parapsychology /pærəsaɪ'kɒlədʒɪ/ n. study of mental phenomena outside sphere of ordinary psychology.

paraquat /'pærəkwɒt/ n. quick-acting

herbicide, becoming inactive on contact with soil.

parasite /'pærəsaɪt/ *n.* animal or plant living in or on another; self-seeking hanger-on. **parasitic** /-'sɪt-/ *a.*; **parasitism** *n.*

parasol /'pærəsɒl/ *n.* sunshade.

paratroops /'pærətruːps/ *n.pl.* airborne troops landing by parachute. **paratrooper** *n.*

paratyphoid /pærə'taɪfɔɪd/ *n.* fever resembling typhoid but caused by different bacterium.

parboil /'pɑːbɔɪl/ *v.t.* partly cook by boiling.

parcel /'pɑːs(ə)l/ 1 *n.* goods etc. packed up in single wrapping; piece of land. 2 *v.t.* wrap (*up*) into parcel; divide (*out*) into portions.

parch *v.* make or become hot and dry; slightly roast.

parchment /'pɑːtʃm(ə)nt/ *n.* skin, esp. of sheep or goat, prepared for writing etc.; manuscript written on this.

pardon /'pɑːd(ə)n/ 1 *n.* forgiveness; remission of punishment; courteous forbearance. 2 *v.t.* forgive; excuse.

pardonable /'pɑːdənəb(ə)l/ *a.* easily excused.

pare /peə(r)/ *v.t.* trim or reduce by cutting away edge or surface of; peel (fruit etc.); whittle away.

paregoric /pærɪ'ɡɒrɪk/ *n.* camphorated tincture of opium.

parent /'peər(ə)nt/ *n.* one who has begotten or borne offspring, father or mother; forefather; source, origin. **parentage** *n.*; **parental** /-'rent-/ *a.*

parenthesis /pə'renθəsɪs/ *n.* (*pl.* -ses /-siːz/) word or clause or sentence inserted as explanation etc. into passage independently of grammatical sequence; in *pl.* pair of round brackets used for this; *fig.* interlude. **parenthesize** *v.t.*; **parenthetic** /-'θet-/ *a.*

par excellence /pɑːr 'eksəlɑ̃s/ above all others that may be so called. [F]

parfait /'pɑːfeɪ/ *n.* rich iced pudding of whipped cream, eggs, etc.; layers of ice cream, fruit, etc., served in tall glass.

parget /'pɑːdʒɪt/ 1 *v.t.* plaster (wall etc.) with ornamental pattern; roughcast. 2 *n.* plaster, roughcast.

pariah /pə'raɪə/ *n.* member of low or no caste; social outcast.

parietal /pə'raɪət(ə)l/ *a.* of wall of body

or any of its cavities. **parietal bone** one of pair forming part of skull.

paring /'peərɪŋ/ *n.* strip pared off.

parish /'pærɪʃ/ *n.* division of diocese having its own church and clergyman; local-government district; inhabitants of parish.

parishioner /pə'rɪʃənə(r)/ *n.* inhabitant of parish.

parity /'pærɪtɪ/ *n.* equality; equal status etc.; equivalence; being at par.

park 1 *n.* large public garden in town; large enclosed piece of ground attached to country house or laid out or preserved for public use; place where vehicles may be parked. 2 *v.t.* place and leave (vehicle) temporarily. **parking-meter** mechanical device for collecting parking-fee esp. in street; **parking-ticket** notice of fine etc. imposed for parking vehicle illegally.

parka /'pɑːkə/ *n.* jacket with hood, as worn by Eskimos and mountaineers etc.

parky /'pɑːkɪ/ *a. sl.* chilly.

parkin /'pɑːkɪn/ *n.* oatmeal gingerbread.

parlance /'pɑːl(ə)ns/ *n.* way of speaking.

parley /'pɑːlɪ/ 1 *n.* meeting between representatives of opposed forces to discuss terms. 2 *v.i.* hold discussion on terms.

parliament /'pɑːləm(ə)nt/ *n.* legislative assembly; body consisting of House of Commons and House of Lords and forming (with Sovereign) legislature of UK.

parliamentarian /pɑːləmen'teərɪən/ *n.* skilled debater in parliament.

parliamentary /pɑːmə'mentərɪ/ *a.* of or in or concerned with or enacted by parliament.

parlour /'pɑːlə(r)/ *n.* sitting-room in private house; room in hotel or convent etc. for private conversation. **parlour game** indoor game, esp. word-game.

parlous /'pɑːləs/ *a. arch.* perilous; hard to deal with.

Parmesan /'pɑːmɪzæn/ *n.* hard cheese of kind made at Parma.

parochial /pə'rəʊkɪəl/ *a.* of a parish; of narrow range, merely local. **parochialism** *n.*

parody /'pærədɪ/ 1 *n.* humorous exaggerated imitation of author or style etc.;

travesty. **2** *v.t.* write or be parody of. **3 parodist** *n.*

parole /pə'rəʊl/ **1** *n.* release of prisoner for special purpose or before end of sentence, on promise of good behaviour; such promise; word of honour. **2** *v.t.* put (prisoner) on parole.

parotid /pə'rɒtɪd/ **1** *a.* situated near ear. **2** *n.* parotid gland. **3 parotid gland** salivary gland in front of ear.

paroxysm /'pærəksɪz(ə)m/ *n.* fit (*of* pain, rage, etc.).

parquet /'pɑːkeɪ/ **1** *n.* flooring of wooden blocks arranged in a pattern. **2** *v.t.* floor (room) thus.

parricide /'pærɪsaɪd/ *n.* person who kills his or her father; killing of one's father. **parricidal** *a.*

parrot /'pærət/ **1** *n.* kind of mainly tropical bird with short hooked bill, of which some species can be taught to repeat words; unintelligent imitator or chatterer. **2** *v.t.* (*past* & *p.p.* **parroted**) repeat mechanically.

parry /'pærɪ/ **1** *v.t.* ward off, avert. **2** *n.* act of parrying.

parse /pɑːz/ *v.t.* describe (word) or analyse (sentence) in terms of grammar.

parsec /'pɑːsek/ *n.* unit of stellar distance, about 3.25 light-years.

parsimony /'pɑːsɪmənɪ/ *n.* carefulness in use of money etc.; meanness. **parsimonious** /-'məʊn-/ *a.*

parsley /'pɑːslɪ/ *n.* herb used for seasoning and garnishing.

parsnip /'pɑːsnɪp/ *n.* plant with pale yellow tapering root used as vegetable; this root.

parson /'pɑːs(ə)n/ *n.* parish clergyman; *colloq.* any clergyman. **parson's nose** rump of cooked fowl. **parsonical** /-'sɒn-/ *a.*

parsonage /'pɑːsənɪdʒ/ *n.* parson's house.

part 1 *n.* some but not all; component, division, portion; share, allotted portion; assigned character or role; *Mus.* one of melodies making up harmony of concerted music; side in agreement or dispute; region, direction, way; in *pl.* abilities. **2** *v.* divide into parts; separate; make parting in (hair). **3** *adv.* partly, in part. **4 part and parcel** essential part *of*; **part exchange** transaction in which article is given as part of payment for more expensive one;

part-song song for 3 or more voice-parts; **part-time** employed for or taking up only part of working day etc.; **part-timer** part-time worker; **part with** give up, relinquish.

partake /pɑː'teɪk/ *v.i.* (*past* **-took**; *p.p.* **-taken**) take share (*in, of, with*); eat or drink some *of*; have some (*of* quality etc.).

parterre /pɑː'teə(r)/ *n.* level garden space filled with flower-beds etc.; pit of theatre.

partial /'pɑː∫(ə)l/ *a.* not total or complete; biased, unfair. **be partial to** like. **partiality** /-'æl-/ *n.*

participate /pɑː'tɪsɪpeɪt/ *v.i.* have share or take part (*in*). **participant** *n.* **participation** *n.*

participle /'pɑːtɪsɪp(ə)l/ *n.* adjective formed by inflexion from verb. **participial** /-'sɪp-/ *a.*

particle /'pɑːtɪk(ə)l/ *n.* minute portion of matter; smallest possible amount; minor esp. indeclinable part of speech; prefix or suffix with distinct meaning.

particoloured /'pɑːtɪkʌləd/ *a.* partly of one colour and partly of another.

particular /pə'tɪkjʊlə(r)/ **1** *a.* relating to one as distinguished from others; special; scrupulously exact; fastidious. **2** *n.* detail, item; in *pl.* detailed account. **3 particularity** /-'lær-/ *n.*

particularize /pə'tɪkjʊləraɪz/ *v.t.* name specially one by one; specify (items). **particularization** *n.*

particularly *adv.* very; to a special extent.

parting /'pɑːtɪŋ/ *n.* leave-taking; dividing line of combed hair.

partisan /pɑːtɪ'zæn/ *n.* adherent of party or side or cause; guerrilla. **partisanship** *n.*

partition /pɑː'tɪ∫(ə)n/ *n.* division into parts; such part; structure separating two such parts; thin wall. **2** *v.t.* divide into parts; divide *off* by partition.

partitive /'pɑːtɪtɪv/ *Gram.* **1** *a.* (*of* word) denoting part of collective whole. **2** *n.* partitive word.

partly /'pɑːtlɪ/ *adv.* with respect to a part; in some degree; not wholly.

partner /'pɑːtnə(r)/ *n.* sharer; person associated with others in business; either of pair in marriage etc. or dancing or game. **2** *v.t.* associate as partners; be partner of. **3 partnership** *n.*

partridge /'pɑːtrɪdʒ/ *n.* kind of game-bird.

parturition /pɑːtjʊəˈrɪʃ(ə)n/ *n.* act of bringing forth young; childbirth.

party /'pɑːtɪ/ *n.* social gathering; body of persons travelling or working together; body of persons united in cause or in opposition to another body; person consenting or contributing to affair; either side in lawsuit, contract, or other transaction. **party line** set policy of political party, shared telephone line; **party-wall** wall common to two adjoining rooms or buildings etc.

parvenu /'pɑːvənjuː/ *n.* (*fem.* -**nue**) person who has risen from obscurity; upstart.

Pascal /'pæskæl/ *n.* computer language designed for training.

paschal /'pæsk(ə)l/ *a.* of Passover; of Easter.

pasha /'pɑːʃə/ *n. hist.* Turkish officer of high rank.

pasque-flower /'pæskflaʊə(r)/ *n.* kind of anemone.

pass[1] /pɑːs/ 1 *v.* (*p.p.* **passed**, or as *adj.* **past**) move onward, proceed; go past; leave on one side or behind; surpass; (cause) to go; spend (time etc.); *Footb.* etc. kick, hand, or hit (ball etc.) to or to player of one's own side; discharge from body as or with excreta; be successful in (examination); (of candidate) satisfy examiner; change (*into*, *from*); die, come to an end; happen; be accepted as adequate; utter (judgement etc.); be sanctioned; allow (bill in Parliament, candidate for examination, etc.) to proceed after scrutiny; hand *round*. 2 *n.* passing, esp. of examination; status of degree without honours; written permission or ticket or order; *Footb.* etc. passing of ball; thrust in fencing; critical position. 3 **make a pass at** *colloq.* make advances to; **pass away** die; **passbook** book recording customer's transactions with bank etc.; **passer-by** person who goes past, esp. casually; **pass for** be accepted as; **passkey** master-key; **pass off** fade away, be carried through, misrepresent *as* something false, lightly dismiss; **pass out** become unconscious, complete military training; **pass over** omit, make no remark upon; **pass up** *colloq.* refuse or neglect (opportunity etc.); **password**

agreed secret word uttered to sentry etc. to allow one to proceed.

pass[2] /pɑːs/ *n.* narrow passage through mountains.

passable /'pɑːsəb(ə)l/ *a.* adequate, fairly good.

passage /'pæsɪdʒ/ *n.* passing, transit; passageway; right of conveyance as passenger by sea or air; journey by sea or air; transition from one state to another; short part of book or piece of music etc.; in *pl.* interchange of words.

passageway /'pæsɪdʒweɪ/ *n.* narrow way for passing along; corridor.

passé /'pæseɪ/ *a.* behind the times; past the prime. [F]

passenger /'pæsɪndʒə(r)/ *n.* traveller in public conveyance; traveller in car etc. who is not driving; ineffective member of team etc.

passerine /'pæsəraɪn/ 1 *a.* of sparrow kind. 2 *n.* passerine bird.

passim /'pæsɪm/ *adv.* throughout. [L]

passion /'pæʃ(ə)n/ *n.* strong emotion; anger; sexual love; strong enthusiasm; **Passion** *the* sufferings of Christ on cross, Gospel narrative of this or musical setting of it. **passion-flower** plant with flower supposed to suggest instruments of Crucifixion; **passion-fruit** edible fruit of some species of passion-flower.

passionate /'pæʃənət/ *a.* dominated by or easily moved to strong feeling; showing or caused by passion.

passive /'pæsɪv/ 1 *a.* acted upon, not acting; inert; submissive; *Gram.* of or in passive voice. 2 *n. Gram.* passive voice or form. 3 **passive voice** *Gram.* voice of verb indicating that subject undergoes action of the verb. 4 **passivity** /-'sɪv-/ *n.*

Passover /'pɑːsəʊvə(r)/ *n.* Jewish spring festival commemorating deliverance of Israelites from bondage in Egypt.

passport /'pɑːspɔːt/ *n.* official document showing identity and nationality etc. of traveller abroad.

past /pɑːst/ 1 *a.* (*p.p.* of **pass**[1]) gone by; just over. 2 *n.* past time; person's past life or career. 3 *prep.* beyond. 4 *adv.* by. 5 **past master** thorough master, expert.

pasta /'pæstə/ *n.* flour paste produced in various shapes; dish of this.

paste /peɪst/ 1 n. any moist fairly stiff mixture; dough of flour with fat and water etc.; flour and water or similar mixture as adhesive; easily spread preparation of pounded fish, meat, etc.; material used to make imitation gems. 2 v.t. fasten or coat with paste; sl. beat, thrash. 3 **pasteboard** stiff substance made by pasting together sheets of paper.

pastel /'pæst(ə)l/ n. crayon made of dry pigment-paste; drawing in pastel; light subdued colour.

pastern /'pæstɜːn/ n. part of horse's foot between fetlock and hoof.

pasteurize /'pæstʃəraɪz/ v.t. partially sterilize (milk etc.) by keeping for some time at high temperature. **pasteurization** n.

pastiche /pæs'tiːʃ/ n. musical or other medley made up from various sources; literary or other work imitating style of author or period etc.

pastille /'pæstɪl/ n. small sweet or lozenge.

pastime /'pɑːstaɪm/ n. recreation; sport or game.

pastor /'pɑːstə(r)/ n. minister of congregation; spiritual adviser.

pastoral /'pɑːstər(ə)l/ 1 a. of shepherds; of rural life; of pastor. 2 n. pastoral poem or picture; letter from bishop or other pastor to clergy or people.

pastrami /pæs'trɑːmɪ/ n. seasoned smoked beef.

pastry /'peɪstrɪ/ n. dough of flour, fat, and water; (item of) food made wholly or partly of this.

pasturage /'pɑːstʃərɪdʒ/ n. pasture land; pasturing.

pasture /'pɑːstʃə(r)/ 1 n. land covered with grass etc. for grazing animals; herbage for cattle. 2 v. put (cattle) to pasture; graze.

pasty[1] /'pæstɪ/ n. pie of meat etc. enclosed in pastry crust and baked without dish.

pasty[2] /'peɪstɪ/ a. of or like paste; pallid.

pat 1 v.t. strike gently with open hand or other flat surface. 2 n. patting touch or sound; small mass, esp. of butter, made (as) by patting. 3 a. apposite, opportune; ready for any occasion. 4 adv. in a pat manner.

patch 1 n. piece put on in mending; piece of plaster over wound; cover protecting injured eye; large or irregular spot on surface, distinct area or period; small plot of ground. 2 v.t. mend with patch(es); piece together; appear as patches on (surface). 3 **not a patch on** very much inferior to; **patch-pocket** pocket sewn on like patch; **patch up** repair, set to rights, esp. hastily; **patchwork** needlework using small pieces of different colours etc. sewn together.

patchy /'pætʃɪ/ a. uneven in quality; having patches.

pate n. colloq. head.

pâté /'pæteɪ/ n. smooth paste of meat etc. **pâté de foie gras** /də fwɑː grɑː/ pâté made from livers of fatted geese.

patella /pə'telə/ n. (pl. **-lae** /-liː/) kneecap.

paten /'pæt(ə)n/ n. plate for bread at Eucharist.

patent /'peɪt(ə)nt, 'pæt-/ 1 n. official document conferring right, title, etc., esp. sole right to make, use, or sell some invention; right granted by this; invention or process so protected. 2 a. conferred or protected by patent; (of food, medicine, etc.) proprietary; plain, obvious. 3 v.t. obtain patent for (invention). 4 **patent leather** leather with glossy varnished surface.

patentee /peɪtən'tiː/ n. holder of patent.

paternal /pə'tɜːn(ə)l/ a. of father, fatherly; related through father, on father's side.

paternalism /pə'tɜːnəlɪz(ə)m/ n. government etc. restricting freedom and responsibility by well-meant regulations. **paternalistic** a.

paternity /pə'tɜːnɪtɪ/ n. fatherhood; one's paternal origin.

paternoster /'pætənɒstə(r)/ n. Lord's Prayer, esp. in Latin.

path /pɑːθ/ n. footway; track; line along which person or thing moves.

pathetic /pə'θetɪk/ a. exciting pity or sadness or contempt.

pathogen /'pæθədʒ(ə)n/ n. agent causing disease. **pathogenic** /-'dʒen-/ a.

pathological /pæθə'lɒdʒɪk(ə)l/ a. of pathology; of or caused by mental or physical disorder.

pathology /pə'θɒlədʒɪ/ n. study of disease. **pathologist** n.

pathos /ˈpeɪθɒs/ n. quality that excites pity or sadness.

patience /ˈpeɪʃ(ə)ns/ n. endurance of hardship, provocation, pain, delay, etc.; perseverance; card-game, usu. for one person.

patient /ˈpeɪʃ(ə)nt/ 1 a. having or showing patience. 2 n. person under medical etc. treatment.

patina /ˈpætɪnə/ n. incrustation, usu. green, on surface of old bronze; gloss produced by age on woodwork etc.

patio /ˈpætɪəʊ/ n. (pl. -os) paved usu. roofless area adjoining house; roofless inner courtyard.

patois /ˈpætwɑː/ n. (pl. same /-wɑːz/) dialect of the common people of a district.

patriarch /ˈpeɪtrɪɑːk/ n. male head of family or tribe; bishop of certain sees in Orthodox and R.C. Churches; venerable old man. **patriarchal** a.

patriarchate /ˈpeɪtrɪɑːkət/ n. office or see or residence of patriarch.

patriarchy /ˈpeɪtrɪɑːkɪ/ n. patriarchal system of society etc.

patrician /pəˈtrɪʃ(ə)n/ 1 n. person of noble birth. 2 a. of nobility; aristocratic.

patricide /ˈpætrɪsaɪd/ n. parricide.

patrimony /ˈpætrɪmənɪ/ n. property inherited from father or ancestors.

patriot /ˈpætrɪət, ˈpeɪ-/ n. person devoted to and ready to defend his country. **patriotic** /-ˈɒt-/ a.; **patriotism** n.

patrol /pəˈtrəʊl/ 1 v. walk or travel round (area etc.) to supervise or supervise it; act as patrol. 2 n. patrolling; person(s) or vehicle(s) assigned or sent out to patrol; unit of usu. 6 in Scout troop or Guide company. 3 **patrol car** car used by police etc. for patrol; **patrolman** US police constable.

patron /ˈpeɪtrən/ n. person who gives financial or other support to; customer of shop etc. **patron saint** saint regarded as protecting person or place etc.

patronage /ˈpætrənɪdʒ/ n. patron's or customer's support; right of bestowing or recommending for appointments; patronizing airs.

patronize /ˈpætrənaɪz/ v.t. act as patron to; support, encourage; treat condescendingly.

patronymic /pætrəˈnɪmɪk/ n. name derived from that of father or ancestor.

patten /ˈpæt(ə)n/ n. wooden sole mounted on iron ring for raising wearer's shoe above mud etc.

patter[1] 1 v.i. (of rain etc.) make tapping sound; run with quick short steps. 2 n. sound of pattering.

patter[2] /ˈpætə(r)/ 1 n. language of profession or class; rapid often glib or deceptive talk. 2 v. say or talk with rapid utterance.

pattern /ˈpæt(ə)n/ 1 n. decorative design on surface; model or design or working instructions from which thing is to be made; excellent example; sample, esp. of cloth. 2 v.t. decorate with pattern.

patty /ˈpætɪ/ n. small pie or pasty.

paucity /ˈpɔːsɪtɪ/ n. smallness of number or quantity.

paunch /pɔːntʃ/ n. belly, stomach.

pauper /ˈpɔːpə(r)/ n. very poor person; hist. recipient of poor-law relief. **pauperism** n.; **pauperize** v.t.

pause /pɔːz/ 1 n. interval of inaction or silence; break made in speech or reading; Mus. mark denoting lengthening of note or rest. 2 v.i. make a pause; wait.

pavan /pəˈvæn/ n. (also **pavane**) stately dance in slow duple time; music for this.

pave v.t. cover with durable surface. **pave the way** make preparations for.

pavement /ˈpeɪvm(ə)nt/ n. paved footway at side of road.

pavilion /pəˈvɪljən/ n. light ornamental building; building on sports ground for spectators or players; large tent.

pavlova /pævˈləʊvə/ n. meringue cake with cream and fruit.

paw 1 n. foot of animal with claws; colloq. person's hand. 2 v. touch with paw; colloq. handle awkwardly, rudely, etc.; (of horse) strike (ground) with hoof.

pawky /ˈpɔːkɪ/ a. Sc. & dial. drily humorous; shrewd.

pawl n. lever with catch for teeth of wheel or bar; bar to prevent capstan etc. from recoiling.

pawn[1] n. chess-man of smallest size and value; fig. unimportant person subservient to others' plans.

pawn[2] 1 v.t. deposit (thing) as security for money borrowed; pledge. 2 n. state of being pawned. **3 pawnbroker** person who lends money at interest on security of personal property deposited with him; **pawnshop** his place of business.

pawpaw var. of **papaw**.

pay v. (past & p.p. **paid**) give as due; discharge debt to; bear cost; suffer penalty *for*; render, bestow (attention etc.); yield adequate return; let out (rope) by slackening it. **2** n. wages, salary. **3 in the pay of** employed by; **pay-as-you-earn** collection of income-tax by deduction at source from wages etc.; **pay-claim** demand for increase in pay; **payload** part of (esp. aircraft's) load from which revenue is derived; **paymaster** official who pays troops, workmen, etc.; **Paymaster General** head of Treasury department through which payments are made; **pay off** pay in full and discharge, *colloq.* yield good results; **pay-off** *sl.* climax, denouement; **payphone** coinbox telephone; **payroll** list of employees receiving regular pay.

payable /ˈpeɪəb(ə)l/ a. that must or may be paid.

PAYE abbr. pay-as-you-earn.

payee /peɪˈiː/ n. person to whom money is (to be) paid.

payment /ˈpeɪm(ə)nt/ n. paying, amount paid; recompense.

payola /peɪˈəʊlə/ n. bribe offered in return for illicit or unfair help in promoting commercial product.

PC abbr. Police Constable; Privy Councillor; personal computer.

p.c. abbr. per cent; postcard.

pd. abbr. paid.

PE abbr. physical education.

pea n. climbing plant bearing round seeds in pods and cultivated for food; one of the seeds; similar plant. **pea-souper** *colloq.* thick yellow fog.

peace /piːs/ n. quiet, calm; harmonious relations; freedom from or cessation of war; civil order. **peacemaker** person who brings about peace; **peacetime** time when country is not at war.

peaceable /ˈpiːsəb(ə)l/ a. disposed or tending to peace, peaceful.

peaceful /ˈpiːsfʊl/ a. characterized by or concerned with peace.

peach¹ /piːtʃ/ n. large roundish stone-fruit with downy delicately coloured skin; tree bearing it; *sl.* thing of superlative merit. **peach Melba** dish of ice cream and peaches. **peachy** a.

peach² v.i. *sl.* turn informer; inform.

peacock /ˈpiːkɒk/ n. male peafowl, bird with splendid plumage and fanlike tail. **peacock blue** bright lustrous blue of peacock's neck.

peafowl /ˈpiːfaʊl/ n. kind of pheasant, peacock or peahen.

peahen /ˈpiːhen/ n. female peafowl.

pea-jacket /ˈpiːdʒækɪt/ n. sailor's short thick double-breasted overcoat.

peak¹ 1 n. pointed top, esp. of mountain; projecting part of brim of cap; highest point of achievement, intensity, etc. **2** v.i. reach highest value, quality, etc.

peak² v.i. waste away; in p.p. pinched-looking.

peaky /ˈpiːkɪ/ a. sickly, puny.

peal 1 n. loud ringing of bell(s); set of bells; outburst of sound. **2** v. sound forth or ring (bells) in peal.

peanut /ˈpiːnʌt/ n. plant bearing underground pods containing seeds used as food and yielding oil; its seed; in pl. sl. trivial amount esp. of money. **peanut butter** paste of ground roasted peanuts.

pear /peə(r)/ n. fleshy fruit tapering towards stalk; tree bearing it.

pearl /pɜːl/ 1 n. lustrous usu. white concretion found in shell of certain oyster and prized as gem; imitation of this; precious thing, finest example. **2** v. fish for pearls; (of moisture) form drops, form drops on. **3 pearl barley** barley rubbed into small rounded grains; **pearl button** button of (real or imitation) mother-of-pearl; **pearl onion** very small onion used in pickles.

pearly /ˈpɜːlɪ/ 1 a. resembling a pearl; adorned with pearls. **2** n. in pl. costermongers' clothes decorated with pearl buttons. **3 Pearly Gates** gates of Heaven; **pearly king, queen**, wearers of pearlies.

peasant /ˈpez(ə)nt/ n. (in some countries) worker on land, farm labourer; small farmer.

peasantry /ˈpezəntrɪ/ n. peasants of a district etc.

pease pudding /piːz/ pudding of dried peas boiled in a cloth.

peat n. vegetable matter decomposed by water and partly carbonized; piece of this as fuel. **peat-bog** bog composed of peat. **peaty** a.

pebble /ˈpeb(ə)l/ n. small stone rounded by action of water. **pebble-dash** mortar with pebbles in it as wall-coating. **pebbly** a.

pecan /ˈpiːkən/ n. pinkish-brown smooth nut; kind of hickory producing it.

peccadillo /pekəˈdɪləʊ/ n. trivial offence.

peccary /ˈpekərɪ/ n. small wild pig of S. and Central Amer.

peck¹ 1 v. strike or pick up or pluck out or make (hole) with beak; eat fastidiously. 2 n. stroke with beak; hasty or perfunctory kiss.

peck² n. measure of capacity for dry goods, = 2 gallons.

pecker n. **keep your pecker up** sl. stay cheerful.

peckish /ˈpekɪʃ/ a. colloq. hungry.

pectin /ˈpektɪn/ n. gelatinous substance in ripe fruits, causing jam etc. to set.

pectoral /ˈpektər(ə)l/ 1 a. of or for breast or chest. 2 n. pectoral fin or muscle.

peculate /ˈpekjʊleɪt/ v. embezzle. **peculation** n.; **peculator** n.

peculiar /pɪˈkjuːlɪə(r)/ a. odd; exclusive to; belonging to the individual; particular; special.

peculiarity /pɪkjuːlɪˈærɪtɪ/ n. being peculiar; characteristic; oddity.

pecuniary /pɪˈkjuːnɪərɪ/ a. of or in money.

pedagogue /ˈpedəɡɒɡ/ n. schoolmaster; pedant.

pedagogy /ˈpedəɡɒdʒɪ/ n. science of teaching. **pedagogic(al)** a.

pedal /ˈped(ə)l/ 1 n. lever or key operated by foot, esp. in bicycle or motor vehicle or some musical instruments. 2 v. work pedals (of); ride bicycle. 3 a. of foot or feet.

pedant /ˈped(ə)nt/ n. person who overrates or parades learning or knowledge, or insists on strict adherence to formal rules. **pedantic** /-ˈdænt-/ a.; **pedantry** n.

peddle /ˈped(ə)l/ v. be pedlar; trade or deal in as pedlar.

pederast /ˈpedəræst/ n. man who commits pederasty.

pederasty /ˈpedəræstɪ/ n. sodomy with a boy.

pedestal /ˈpedɪst(ə)l/ n. base of column; block on which something stands.

pedestrian /pəˈdestrɪən/ 1 n. walker, traveller on foot. 2 a. prosaic, dull; going or performed on foot; of walking; for those on foot.

pedicure /ˈpedɪkjʊə(r)/ n. care or treatment of feet, esp. of toe-nails.

pedigree /ˈpedɪɡriː/ 1 n. genealogical table; ancestral line; ancient descent. 2 a. having known line of descent.

pediment /ˈpedɪm(ə)nt/ n. triangular part crowning front of building.

pedlar /ˈpedlə(r)/ n. travelling seller of small wares.

pedometer /pɪˈdɒmɪtə(r)/ n. instrument for estimating distance travelled on foot.

peduncle /pɪˈdʌŋk(ə)l/ n. Bot. stalk of flower or fruit or cluster, esp. main stalk bearing solitary flower.

pee colloq. 1 v.i. urinate. 2 n. urination; urine.

peek n. & v.i. peep, glance.

peel 1 n. rind or outer coating of fruit or potato etc. 2 v. strip peel or rind etc. from; take off (skin, peel, etc.); become bare of bark, skin, etc.; come off or like peel.

peeling /ˈpiːlɪŋ/ n. piece peeled off.

peep¹ 1 v.i. look furtively or through narrow aperture; come cautiously or partly into view; begin to appear. 2 n. furtive or peering glance; first light (of dawn, day). 3 **peep-hole** small hole to peep through; **Peeping Tom** furtive voyeur; **peep-show** exhibition of pictures etc. viewed through lens in peep-hole.

peep² n. & v.i. cheep, squeak.

peer¹ v.i. look searchingly; peep out.

peer² n. equal (esp. in civil standing or rank); duke, marquis, earl, viscount, or baron. **peer group** person's associates of same status.

peerage /ˈpɪərɪdʒ/ n. the peers; book listing these; rank of peer or peeress.

peeress /ˈpɪəres/ n. female holder of peerage; peer's wife.

peerless /ˈpɪəlɪs/ a. unequalled.

peeve /piːv/ sl. 1 v.t. irritate. 2 n. cause of annoyance.

peevish /ˈpiːvɪʃ/ a. querulous, irritable.

peewit /ˈpiːwɪt/ *n.* kind of plover named from its cry.

peg 1 *n.* wooden or metal etc. bolt or pin for holding things together or hanging things on, or as stopper or position indicator; forked wooden peg or similar device for hanging washing on line; drink, esp. of spirits. **2** *v.* fix or mark or hang out (as) with peg(s); keep (prices etc.) stable. **3 off the peg** (of clothes) ready-made; **peg away** work persistently (*at*); **peg-board** board with holes and pegs; **peg out** mark out boundaries of, *sl.* die.

pejorative /prɪˈdʒɒrətɪv/ **1** *a.* derogatory. **2** *n.* derogatory word.

peke *n. colloq.* Pekinese dog.

Pekinese /piːkɪˈniːz/ *n.* (also **Pekingese**) dog of small short-legged snub-nosed breed with long silky hair.

pelargonium /peləˈɡəʊnɪəm/ *n.* plant with showy flowers.

pelf *n.* money, wealth.

pelican /ˈpelɪkən/ *n.* large water-bird with pouch in bill for storing fish. **pelican crossing** road crossing-place with traffic lights operated by pedestrians.

pellagra /prɪˈlæɡrə/ *n.* deficiency disease with cracking of skin.

pellet /ˈpelɪt/ *n.* small ball of a substance; pill; small shot.

pellicle /ˈpelɪk(ə)l/ *n.* thin skin; membrane; film.

pell-mell /pelˈmel/ *adv.* in disorder; headlong.

pellucid /prɪˈljuːsɪd/ *a.* transparent, clear; free from obscurity.

pelmet /ˈpelmɪt/ *n.* pendent border concealing curtain-rods etc.

pelota /prɪˈləʊtə/ *n.* Basque game with ball and wicker racket in walled court.

pelt¹ **1** *v.* assail with missiles, abuse, etc.; (of rain) come down hard; run at full speed. **2** *n.* pelting.

pelt² *n.* skin of animal, esp. with hair or fur still on it.

pelvis /ˈpelvɪs/ *n.* lower abdominal cavity formed by haunch bones etc. **pelvic** *a.*

pen¹ **1** *n.* implement for writing with ink; writing or literary style. **2** *v.t.* compose and write (letter etc.). **3 penfriend** person with whom one corresponds without meeting; **penknife** small pocket-knife; **penmanship** skill in or style of handwriting; **pen-name** literary pseudonym.

pen² **1** *n.* small enclosure for cows, sheep, poultry, etc. **2** *v.t.* enclose; put or keep in confined space.

pen³ *n.* female swan.

penal /ˈpiːn(ə)l/ *a.* of or involving punishment; punishable.

penalize /ˈpiːnəlaɪz/ *v.t.* subject to penalty or comparative disadvantage; make punishable.

penalty /ˈpenltɪ/ *n.* fine or other punishment; disadvantage imposed by circumstances or for breaking rule or failing to fulfil condition etc.; (goal scored by) penalty kick. **penalty area** *Footb.* area in front of goal within which breach of rules involves penalty kick; **penalty kick** free kick at goal from close range.

penance /ˈpenəns/ *n.* act, esp. one imposed by priest, performed as expression of penitence.

pence *pl.* of **penny**.

penchant /ˈpãʃã/ *n.* inclination or liking (*for*). [F]

pencil /ˈpens(ə)l/ **1** *n.* instrument for drawing or writing, esp. of graphite enclosed in wooden cylinder or metal case with tapering end; something used or shaped like this. **2** *v.t.* draw or mark or write with pencil.

pendant /ˈpend(ə)nt/ *n.* ornament hung from necklace etc.

pendent /ˈpend(ə)nt/ *a.* hanging; overhanging; pending.

pending /ˈpendɪŋ/ **1** *a.* awaiting decision or settlement. **2** *prep.* until; during.

pendulous /ˈpendjʊləs/ *a.* hanging down; swinging.

pendulum /ˈpendjʊləm/ *n.* body suspended so as to be free to swing, esp. regulating movement of clock's works.

penetrate /ˈpenɪtreɪt/ *v.* make way into or through; pierce; permeate; see into or through; make a way. **penetrable** *a.*

penetrating *a.* having or showing insight; easily heard through or above other sounds.

penetration /penɪˈtreɪʃ(ə)n/ *n.* act or extent of penetrating; acute insight.

penguin /ˈpeŋgwɪn/ *n.* flightless seabird of southern hemisphere.

penicillin /penɪ'sɪlɪn/ *n.* antibiotic obtained from mould.

peninsula /pə'nɪnsjʊlə/ *n.* piece of land almost surrounded by water or projecting far into sea etc. **peninsular** *a.*

penis /'piːnɪs/ *n.* sexual and (in mammals) urinary organ of male animal.

penitent /'penɪt(ə)nt/ 1 *a.* repentant, contrite. 2 *n.* penitent person; person doing penance. **3 penitence** *n.*

penitential /penɪ'tenʃ(ə)l/ *a.* of penitence or penance.

penitentiary /penɪ'tenʃərɪ/ 1 *n. US* reformatory prison. 2 *a.* of penance or reformatory treatment.

pennant /'penənt/ *n.* tapering flag, esp. that at mast-head of ship in commission.

penniless /'penɪlɪs/ *a.* destitute.

pennon /'penən/ *n.* long narrow triangular or swallow-tailed flag; long pointed streamer of ship.

penny /'penɪ/ *n.* (*pl.* **pence** *or* **pennies**) British bronze coin worth 1/100 of pound, or formerly 1/12 of shilling. **penny farthing** early kind of bicycle with large front wheel and small rear one; **penny-pinching** niggardly; **a pretty penny** a large sum of money.

pennyroyal /penɪ'rɔɪəl/ *n.* kind of mint formerly used in medicine.

penology /piː'nɒlədʒɪ/ *n.* study of punishment and prison management. **penological** *a.*

pension /'penʃ(ə)n/ 1 *n.* periodic payment made to person above specified age or to retired or widowed or disabled etc. person. 2 *v.t.* grant pension to. 3 **pension off** dismiss with pension.

pensionable *a.* entitled or entitling person to pension.

pensionary /'penʃənərɪ/ 1 *a.* of pension. 2 *n.* recipient of pension.

pensioner /'penʃənə(r)/ *n.* recipient of (esp. retirement) pension.

pensive /'pensɪv/ *a.* deep in thought.

pent *a.* closely confined, shut *in* or *up*.

penta- *in comb.* five.

pentacle /'pentək(ə)l/ *n.* figure used as symbol, esp. in magic, e.g. pentagram.

pentagon /'pentəgən/ *n.* plane figure with 5 sides and angles. **the Pentagon** headquarters of leaders of US defence forces. **pentagonal** /-'tæg-/ *a.*

pentagram /'pentəgræm/ *n.* 5-pointed star.

pentameter /pen'tæmɪtə(r)/ *n.* line of 5 metrical feet.

Pentateuch /'pentətjuːk/ *n.* first 5 books of OT.

pentathlon /pen'tæθlən/ *n.* athletic contest comprising 5 different events for competitor.

Pentecost /'pentɪkɒst/ *n.* Jewish harvest festival 50 days after Passover; Whit Sunday. **pentecostal** *a.*

penthouse /'penthaʊs/ *n.* flat, house, etc. on roof of tall building; sloping roof supported against wall of building.

penultimate /pɪ'nʌltɪmət/ 1 *a.* & *n.* last but one.

penumbra /pɪ'nʌmbrə/ *n.* (*pl.* **-rae** /-riː/) partly shaded region round shadow of opaque body; partial shadow. **penumbral** *a.*

penurious /pɪ'njʊərɪəs/ *a.* poor; stingy.

penury /'penjʊərɪ/ *n.* destitution, poverty.

peon /pjuːn/ *n. Sp. Amer.* day-labourer.

peony /'piːənɪ/ *n.* garden plant with large globular flowers.

people /'piːp(ə)l/ 1 *n.* race or nation; persons in general; subjects; *the* body of enfranchised citizens; parents or other relatives. 2 *v.t.* fill with people; populate; inhabit.

pep 1 *n.* vigour, spirit. 2 *v.t.* fill *up*, inspire, with energy and vigour. 3 **pep pill** one containing stimulant drug; **pep talk** exhortation to greater effort or courage.

pepper /'pepə(r)/ 1 *n.* pungent aromatic condiment from dried berries of some plants; capsicum plant, its fruit. 2 *v.t.* sprinkle or flavour with pepper; pelt with missiles. 3 **pepper-and-salt** of closely mingled dark and light; **peppercorn** dried pepper berry, nominal rent; **pepper-mill** mill for grinding peppercorns.

peppermint /'pepəmɪnt/ *n.* species of mint grown for its strong fragrant oil; sweet flavoured with this oil; the oil.

peppery /'pepərɪ/ *a.* of or like or abounding in pepper; *fig.* hot-tempered.

pepsin /'pepsɪn/ *n.* enzyme contained in gastric juice.

peptic /'peptɪk/ a. digestive. **peptic ulcer** one in stomach or duodenum.

per prep. for each; by, by means or in-strumentality of.

peradventure /pərəd'ventʃə(r)/ adv. arch. perhaps, perchance; by chance.

perambulate /pə'ræmbjʊleɪt/ v. walk through or over or about. **per-ambulation** n.; **perambulatory** a.

perambulator /pə'ræmbjʊleɪtə(r)/ n. pram.

per annum /pɜːr 'ænəm/ for each year.

per capita /pɜː 'kæpɪtə/ for each person.

perceive /pə'siːv/ v.t. become aware of by one of senses; apprehend; understand.

per cent /pə 'sent/ in every hundred; percentage; one part in every hundred.

percentage /pə'sentɪdʒ/ n. rate or pro-portion per cent; proportion.

perceptible /pə'septɪb(ə)l/ a. that can be perceived. **perceptibility** n.

perception /pə'sepʃ(ə)n/ n. act or fac-ulty of perceiving.

perceptive /pə'septɪv/ a. of per-ception; quick to perceive or under-stand. **perceptivity** n.

perch[1] n. bird's resting place; fig. el-evated position; measure of length (5½ yds.). 2 v. rest or place on or as if on perch.

perch[2] n. kind of freshwater fish.

perchance /pə'tʃɑːns/ adv. arch. maybe.

percipient /pə'sɪpɪənt/ 1 a. per-ceiving; conscious.

percolate /'pɜːkəleɪt/ v. filter, esp. through pores or perforations. **per-colation** n.

percolator n. apparatus for making coffee by percolation.

percussion /pə'kʌʃ(ə)n/ n. forcible striking of body against another; Mus. instruments struck with stick or hand or struck together in pairs. **percussion cap** small metal or paper device con-taining explosive powder and exploded by fall of hammer. **percussive** a.

perdition /pə'dɪʃ(ə)n/ n. damnation.

peregrine /'perɪgrɪn/ n. kind of falcon.

peremptory /pə'remptərɪ/ a. im-perious; urgent.

perennial /pə'renɪəl/ 1 a. lasting through the year; lasting long or for

ever; (of plant) living several years. 2 n. perennial plant.

perfect /'pɜːfɪkt/ 1 a. complete, fault-less; not deficient; exact, precise; entire, unqualified; Gram. (of tense) ex-pressing completed action. 2 n. perfect tense. 3 v.t. (also /pə'fekt/) make per-fect. 4 **perfect pitch** Mus. ability to re-cognize pitch of note. 5 **perfectible** /-'fekt-/ a.; **perfectibility** n.

perfection /pə'fekʃ(ə)n/ n. being or making perfect; perfect state; perfect person, specimen, etc.

perfectionist /pə'fekʃənɪst/ n. person who aspires constantly to perfection.

perfectly adv. quite, completely.

perfidy /'pɜːfɪdɪ/ n. breach of faith, treachery. **perfidious** /-'fɪd-/ a.

perforate /'pɜːfəreɪt/ v. pierce, make hole(s); make row of small holes in (paper). **perforation** n.

perforce /pə'fɔːs/ adv. unavoidably, necessarily.

perform /pə'fɔːm/ v. carry into effect; accomplish; go through; execute; act, sing, etc. esp. in public; (of animals) do tricks etc.

performance /pə'fɔːməns/ n. carrying out, doing; execution; notable feat; per-forming of or in play etc.

perfume /'pɜːfjuːm/ 1 n. sweet smell; fragrant liquid, esp. for application to the body, scent. 2 v.t. impart perfume to.

perfumer /pə'fjuːmə(r)/ n. maker or seller of perfumes. **perfumery** n.

perfunctory /pə'fʌŋktərɪ/ a. done merely for sake of getting through a duty; superficial.

pergola /'pɜːgələ/ n. arbour or covered walk arched with climbing plants.

perhaps /pə'hæps/ adv. it may be, possibly.

perianth /'perɪænθ/ n. outer part of flower.

perigee /'perɪdʒiː/ n. point nearest to earth in orbit of moon etc.

perihelion /perɪ'hiːlɪən/ n. (pl. **-lia**) point nearest to sun in orbit of planet or comet etc. round it.

peril /'perɪl/ n. danger, risk. **perilous** a.

perimeter /pə'rɪmɪtə(r)/ n. cir-cumference or outline of closed figure; length of this; outer boundary.

period /'pɪərɪəd/ 1 n. amount of time

during which something runs its course; distinct portion of history, life, etc.; occurrence of menstruation, time of this; complete sentence; full stop. **2** a. of or characteristic of past period.

periodic /pɪərɪ'ɒdɪk/ a. appearing or recurring at regular intervals. **periodic table** arrangement of chemical elements by atomic number.

periodical /pɪərɪ'ɒdɪk(ə)l/ **1** a. periodic. **2** n. magazine etc. published at regular intervals.

periodicity /pɪərɪə'dɪsɪtɪ/ n. recurrence at intervals.

peripatetic /perɪpə'tetɪk/ a. going from place to place; itinerant.

peripheral /pə'rɪfər(ə)l/ **1** a. of periphery; of minor importance. **2** n. input or output device connected to computer.

periphery /pə'rɪfərɪ/ n. bounding line, esp. of round surface; outer or surrounding surface or area etc.

periphrasis /pə'rɪfrəsɪs/ n. (pl. -ses /-siːz/) roundabout speech or phrase, circumlocution. **periphrastic** /-'fræst-/ a.

periscope /'perɪskəʊp/ n. apparatus with tube and mirrors for viewing objects otherwise out of sight.

perish /'perɪʃ/ v. suffer destruction, lose life; come to untimely end; (cause to) lose natural qualities; (of cold etc.) reduce to distress.

perishable 1 a. subject to speedy decay. **2** n. in pl. perishable goods (esp. foods).

perisher n. sl. annoying person.

perishing a. colloq. intensely cold; confounded.

peritoneum /perɪtə'niːəm/ n. (pl. -neums) membrane lining abdominal cavity. **peritoneal** a.

peritonitis /perɪtə'naɪtɪs/ n. inflammation of peritoneum.

periwig /'perɪwɪg/ n. wig.

periwinkle[1] /'perɪwɪŋk(ə)l/ n. evergreen trailing plant with light-blue flower.

periwinkle[2] /'perɪwɪŋk(ə)l/ n. winkle.

perjure /'pɜːdʒə(r)/ v.refl. **perjure oneself** commit perjury; in p.p. guilty of perjury.

perjury /'pɜːdʒərɪ/ n. wilful utterance of false evidence while on oath.

perk[1] v. colloq. (cause to) recover cour-

age or confidence (usu. with up); raise (head etc.) briskly.

perk[2] n. sl. (usu. in pl.) perquisite.

perky /'pɜːkɪ/ a. lively and cheerful.

perm[1] **1** n. colloq. permanent wave. **2** v.t. give permanent wave to.

perm[2] **1** n. permutation. **2** v.t. make permutation of.

permafrost /'pɜːməfrɒst/ n. permanently frozen subsoil in polar regions.

permanence /'pɜːmənəns/ n. being permanent.

permanency /'pɜːmənənsɪ/ n. permanent thing or arrangement.

permanent /'pɜːmənənt/ a. lasting or intended to last indefinitely. **permanent wave** long-lasting artificial wave in hair; **permanent way** finished road-bed of railway.

permeable /'pɜːmɪəb(ə)l/ a. admitting passage of fluid etc. **permeability** n.

permeate /'pɜːmɪeɪt/ v. penetrate, saturate, pervade; be diffused. **permeation** n.

permissible /pə'mɪsɪb(ə)l/ a. allowable, that may be permitted. **permissibility** n.

permission /pə'mɪʃ(ə)n/ n. consent or liberty (to do).

permissive /pə'mɪsɪv/ a. tolerant, liberal; giving permission.

permit 1 /pə'mɪt/ v. give consent to or opportunity for; admit of. **2** /'pɜːmɪt/ n. written order giving permission.

permutation /pɜːmjʊ'teɪʃ(ə)n/ n. Math. variation of order of set of things; any one such arrangement; combination or selection of specified number of items from larger group.

pernicious /pə'nɪʃəs/ a. destructive, injurious.

pernickety /pə'nɪkɪtɪ/ a. colloq. fastidious, over-precise.

peroration /perə'reɪʃ(ə)n/ n. lengthy concluding part of speech.

peroxide /pə'rɒksaɪd/ **1** n. oxide containing maximum proportion of oxygen; (in full **hydrogen peroxide**) colourless liquid used in water solution, esp. to bleach hair. **2** v.t. bleach (hair) with hydrogen peroxide.

perpendicular /pɜːpən'dɪkjʊlə(r)/ **1** a. at right angles (to given line, plane, or surface); upright; very steep; **Perpendicular** of or in style of English

Gothic architecture of 15th-16th c. **2** *n.* perpendicular line etc. **3 perpendicularity** *n.*

perpetrate /'pɜːpɪtreɪt/ *v.t.* be guilty of; commit. **perpetration** *n.*; **perpetrator** *n.*

perpetual /pə'petjʊəl/ *a.* lasting for ever or indefinitely; continuous; *colloq.* frequent, repeated.

perpetuate /pə'petjʊeɪt/ *v.t.* make perpetual; cause to be always remembered. **perpetuation** *n.*

perpetuity /pɜːpɪ'tjuːɪtɪ/ *n.* perpetual continuance or possession. **in perpetuity** for ever.

perplex /pə'pleks/ *v.t.* bewilder, puzzle; complicate, tangle. **perplexity** *n.*

per pro. *abbr.* by proxy, through an agent (*per procurationem*).

perquisite /'pɜːkwɪzɪt/ *n.* extra profit additional to main income etc.; customary extra right or privilege.

perry /'perɪ/ *n.* drink made from fermented pear-juice.

per se /pɜː 'seɪ/ by or in itself, intrinsically. [L]

persecute /'pɜːsɪkjuːt/ *v.t.* subject to constant hostility and ill-treatment; harass, worry. **persecution** *n.*; **persecutor** *n.*

persevere /pɜːsɪ'vɪə(r)/ *v.i.* continue steadfastly, persist. **perseverance** *n.*

Persian /'pɜːʃ(ə)n/ **1** *n.* native or language of Persia (now Iran). **2** *a.* of Persia (Iran). **3 Persian cat** kind with long silky hair; **Persian lamb** silky curled fur of young karakul.

persiflage /'pɜːsɪflɑːʒ/ *n.* banter; light raillery.

persimmon /pɜː'sɪmən/ *n.* Amer. or E. Asian tree; its edible orange plumlike fruit.

persist /pə'sɪst/ *v.i.* continue to exist or do something in spite of obstacles. **persistence** *n.*; **persistent** *a.*

person /'pɜːs(ə)n/ *n.* individual human being; living body of human being; *Gram.* one of three classes of pronouns, verb-forms, etc., denoting respectively person etc. speaking, spoken to, or spoken of.

persona /pɜː'səʊnə/ *n.* (*pl.* **-nae** /-niː/) *Psychol.* aspect of personality as perceived by others. **persona grata** /-'ɡrɑːtə/ person, esp. diplomat, acceptable to certain others; **persona non grata** /-nɒn-/ person not acceptable.

personable /'pɜːsənəb(ə)l/ *a.* pleasing in appearance or demeanour.

personage /'pɜːsənɪdʒ/ *n.* person, esp important one.

personal /'pɜːsən(ə)l/ *a.* one's own; individual, private; done etc. in person; directed to or concerning individual; *Gram.* of or denoting one of the three persons. **personal column** part of newspaper devoted to short personal advertisements; **personal property** all property except land.

personality /pɜːsə'nælɪtɪ/ *n.* distinctive personal character; personal existence or identity; (esp. well-known) person; in *pl.* personal remarks.

personalize /'pɜːsənəlaɪz/ *v.t.* identify as belonging to particular person.

personally /'pɜːsənəlɪ/ *adv.* in person; for one's own part.

personate /'pɜːsəneɪt/ *v.t.* play part of; pretend to be. **personation** *n.*

personify /pɜː'sɒnɪfaɪ/ *v.t.* attribute personal nature to; symbolize by human figure; (esp. in *p.p.*) embody, exemplify typically. **personification** *n.*

personnel /pɜːsə'nel/ *n.* body of employees; persons engaged in particular service, profession, etc. **personnel department** department of firm etc. dealing with appointment and welfare of employees.

perspective /pə'spektɪv/ **1** *n.* art of drawing so as to give effect of solidity and relative position and size; relation or proportion between visible objects, parts of subject, etc.; view, prospect. **2** *a.* of or in perspective. **3 in perspective** according to rules of perspective, in proportion.

Perspex /'pɜːspeks/ *n.* (**P**) tough light transparent plastic.

perspicacious /pɜːspɪ'keɪʃəs/ *a.* having mental penetration or discernment. **perspicacity** /-'kæs-/ *n.*

perspicuous /pə'spɪkjʊəs/ *a.* expressed with clearness; lucid. **perspicuity** /-'kjuː-/ *n.*

perspire /pə'spaɪə(r)/ *v.* sweat. **perspiration** /pɜːspɪ'reɪʃ(ə)n/ *n.*

persuade /pə'sweɪd/ *v.t.* cause (person) by argument etc. to believe or do something; convince.

persuasion /pə'sweɪʒ(ə)n/ n. persuading; conviction; religious belief or sect.

persuasive /pə'sweɪsɪv/ a. able or tending to persuade.

pert a. forward, saucy.

pertain /pə'teɪn/ v.i. belong, relate.

pertinacious /pɜːtɪ'neɪʃəs/ a. persistent, obstinate. **pertinacity** /-'næs-/ n.

pertinent /'pɜːtɪn(ə)nt/ a. relevant; to the point. **pertinence** n.

perturb /pə'tɜːb/ v.t. throw into agitation; disquiet. **perturbation** n.

peruke /pə'ruːk/ n. wig.

peruse /pə'ruːz/ v.t. read; scan. **perusal** n.

pervade /pə'veɪd/ v.t. spread through, permeate, saturate. **pervasion** n.; **pervasive** a.

perverse /pə'vɜːs/ a. obstinately or wilfully in the wrong; wayward; peevish; wicked. **perversity** n.

perversion /pə'vɜːʃ(ə)n/ n. perverting or being perverted; preference for abnormal form of sexual activity.

pervert 1 /pə'vɜːt/ v.t. turn (thing) aside from proper or normal use; lead astray from right behaviour or belief etc.; in p.p. showing perversion. **2** /'pɜːvɜːt/ n. person who is perverted, esp. sexually.

pervious /'pɜːvɪəs/ a. permeable; allowing passage or access.

peseta /pə'seɪtə/ n. Spanish monetary unit.

peso /'peɪsəʊ/ n. (pl. **-sos**) monetary unit in several S. Amer. countries.

pessary /'pesərɪ/ n. instrument worn in vagina; vaginal suppository.

pessimism /'pesɪmɪz(ə)m/ n. tendency to take worst view or expect worst outcome. **pessimist** n.; **pessimistic** a.

pest n. troublesome or destructive person, animal, or thing.

pester /'pestə(r)/ v.t. trouble or annoy, esp. with persistent requests.

pesticide /'pestɪsaɪd/ n. substance for destroying harmful insects etc.

pestiferous /pes'tɪfərəs/ a. noxious; spreading infection; fig. pernicious.

pestilence /'pestɪl(ə)ns/ n. fatal epidemic disease, esp. bubonic plague.

pestilent /'pestɪlənt/ a. deadly or pestiferous; troublesome; obnoxious.

pestilential /pestɪ'lenʃ(ə)l/ a. of pestilence; pestilent.

pestle /'pes(ə)l/ n. instrument for pounding substances in a mortar.

pet[1] **1** n. domestic animal kept for pleasure or companionship; favourite. **2** a. of or for a pet; favourite; expressing fondness. **3** v.t. make pet of; fondle (esp. erotically).

pet[2] n. ill-humour, fit of peevishness.

petal /'pet(ə)l/ n. each division of flower corolla.

petard /pɪ'tɑːd/ n. hist. small bomb for breaking down door etc.

peter /'piːtə(r)/ v.i. peter out give out, come to an end.

petersham /'piːtəʃ(ə)m/ n. thick ribbed silk ribbon.

petiole /'petɪəʊl/ n. leaf-stalk.

petit /'petɪ/ a. **petit four** /fʊə(r)/ very small fancy cake etc.; **petit point** /pwæ̃/ embroidery on canvas using small stitches. [F]

petite /pə'tiːt/ a. (of woman) of small dainty build.

petition /pə'tɪʃ(ə)n/ **1** n. request, supplication; formal written request, esp. one signed by many people, to authorities etc. **2** v. make petition (to); ask humbly.

petrel /'petr(ə)l/ n. small sea-bird with black-and-white plumage.

petrify /'petrɪfaɪ/ v. paralyse with terror or astonishment etc.; turn or be turned into stone. **petrifaction** n.

petrochemical /petrəʊ'kemɪk(ə)l/ n. substance obtained from petroleum or natural gas.

petrodollar /'petrəʊdɒlə(r)/ n. dollar available in petroleum-exporting country.

petrol /'petr(ə)l/ n. refined petroleum used as fuel in motor vehicles, aircraft, etc. **petrol-pump** machine for transfering petrol esp. from underground reservoir to tank in motor vehicle; **petrol station** place where petrol can be bought.

petroleum /pɪ'trəʊlɪəm/ n. hydrocarbon oil found in upper strata of earth, refined for use as fuel etc. **petroleum jelly** translucent solid mixture of hydrocarbons got from petroleum and used as lubricant etc.

petticoat /'petɪkəʊt/ n. woman's or

child's undergarment hanging from waist or shoulders.

pettifogging /'petɪfɒgɪŋ/ a. quibbling; petty; dishonest.

pettish /'petɪʃ/ a. fretful, peevish.

petty /'petɪ/ a. unimportant, trivial; small-minded; minor, inferior. **petty cash** money kept for small items of expenditure; **petty officer** naval NCO.

petulant /'petjʊlənt/ a. peevishly impatient or irritable. **petulance** n.

petunia /pɪ'tju:nɪə/ n. plant with vivid funnel-shaped flowers.

pew n. (in church) enclosed compartment or fixed bench with back; colloq. seat.

pewit var. of **peewit**.

pewter /'pju:tə(r)/ n. grey alloy of tin and lead etc.; articles made of this.

peyote /peɪ'əʊtɪ/ n. a Mexican cactus; hallucinogenic drug prepared from it.

pfennig /'pfenɪg/ n. small German coin worth 1/100 of a mark.

phagocyte /'fægəsaɪt/ n. blood corpuscle etc. capable of absorbing foreign matter, esp. bacteria, in the body.

phalanx /'fælæŋks/ n. (pl. **-lanxes**) body of infantry in close formation; united or organized party or company.

phallus /'fæləs/ n. image of penis. **phallic** a.

phantasm /'fæntæz(ə)m/ n. illusion; phantom. **phantasmal** a.

phantasmagoria /fæntæzmə'gɔːrɪə/ n. shifting scene of real or imaginary figures. **phantasmagoric** a.

phantom /'fæntəm/ 1 n. spectre, apparition; mental illusion. 2 a. merely apparent, illusory.

Pharaoh /'feərəʊ/ n. title of ruler of ancient Egypt.

Pharisee /'færɪsiː/ n. member of ancient Jewish sect distinguished by strict observance of traditional and written law; self-righteous person; hypocrite. **Pharisaic** /-'seɪɪk/ a.

pharmaceutical /fɑːmə'sjuːtɪk(ə)l/ a. of pharmacy; of use or sale of medicinal drugs. **pharmaceutics** n.

pharmacist /'fɑːməsɪst/ n. person qualified to practise pharmacy.

pharmacology /fɑːmə'kɒlədʒɪ/ n. science of action of drugs on the body. **pharmacological** a.; **pharmacologist** n.

pharmacopoeia /fɑːməkə'piːə/ n. book with list of drugs and directions for use; stock of drugs.

pharmacy /'fɑːməsɪ/ n. preparation and dispensing of drugs; pharmacist's shop; dispensary.

pharynx /'færɪŋks/ n. cavity behind mouth and nose. **pharyngeal** /fæ'rɪndʒɪəl/ a.

phase /feɪz/ 1 n. stage of development or process or recurring sequence; aspect of moon or planet. 2 v.t. carry out by phases. 3 **phase in, out**, bring gradually into, out of, use.

Ph.D. abbr. Doctor of Philosophy.

pheasant /'fez(ə)nt/ n. long-tailed bright-plumaged game-bird.

phenomenal /fɪ'nɒmɪn(ə)l/ a. of or concerned with phenomena; extraordinary, remarkable.

phenomenon /fɪ'nɒmənən/ n. (pl. **-na**) observed or apparent object or fact or occurrence; remarkable person or thing.

phew /fjuː/ int. expr. disgust, relief, etc.

phial /'faɪəl/ n. small bottle.

philander /fɪ'lændə(r)/ v.i. (of man) flirt (with woman); flirt habitually.

philanthropy /fɪ'lænθrəpɪ/ n. love of all mankind; practical benevolence. **philanthropic** /-'θrɒp-/ a.; **philanthropist** n.

philately /fɪ'lætəlɪ/ n. stamp-collecting. **philatelic** /-'tel-/ a.; **philatelist** n.

philharmonic /fɪlhɑː'mɒnɪk/ a. devoted to music.

philippic /fɪ'lɪpɪk/ n. bitter invective.

philistine /'fɪlɪstaɪn/ 1 n. person who is hostile or indifferent to culture. 2 a. hostile or indifferent to culture. 3 **philistinism** n.

philology /fɪ'lɒlədʒɪ/ n. science of language. **philological** a.; **philologist** n.

philosopher /fɪ'lɒsəfə(r)/ n. person engaged in or learned in philosophy; person who acts philosophically.

philosophic(al) /fɪlə'sɒfɪk(ə)l/ a. of or according to philosophy; calm under adverse circumstances.

philosophize /fɪ'lɒsəfaɪz/ v.i. theorize; moralize.

philosophy /fɪ'lɒsəfɪ/ n. pursuit of wisdom or knowledge, esp. of ultimate reality or of general causes and principles; philosophical system; system for conduct of life; serenity, calmness.

philtre /'fɪlt(ə)r/ n. love-potion.

phlebitis /flɪ'baɪtɪs/ n. inflammation of walls of vein. **phlebitic** /-'bɪt-/ a.

phlegm /flem/ n. bronchial mucus ejected by coughing; calmness; sluggishness.

phlegmatic /fleg'mætɪk/ a. not easily agitated, sluggish.

phlox /flɒks/ n. plant with clusters of white or coloured flowers.

phobia /'fəʊbɪə/ n. abnormal fear or aversion. **phobic** a. & n.

phoenix /'fiːnɪks/ n. bird fabled to burn itself and rise from its ashes; unique person or thing.

phone /fəʊn/ n. & v. colloq. telephone.

phone-in broadcast programme in which listeners participate by telephone.

phonetic /fə'netɪk/ a. of or representing vocal sound; (of spelling) corresponding to pronunciation.

phonetics n.pl. usu. treated as sing. study or representation of vocal sounds. **phonetician** /fəʊ-/ n.

phoney /'fəʊnɪ/ sl. 1 a. false, sham, counterfeit. 2 n. phoney person or thing.

phonic /'fəʊnɪk/ a. of (vocal) sound.

phonograph /'fəʊnəgrɑːf/ n. early form of gramophone.

phonology /fə'nɒlədʒɪ/ n. study of sounds in a language. **phonological** a.

phosphate /'fɒsfeɪt/ n. salt of phosphoric acid, esp. used as fertilizer.

phosphoresce /fɒsfə'res/ v.i. show phosphorescence.

phosphorescence /fɒsfə'res(ə)ns/ n. emission of light without combustion or perceptible heat. **phosphorescent** a.

phosphoric, phosphorous, /fɒs-'fɒrɪk, 'fɒsfərəs/ adjs. of or containing phosphorus.

phosphorus /'fɒsfərəs/ n. non-metallic waxlike substance appearing luminous in dark.

photo /'fəʊtəʊ/ n. (pl. -tos) colloq. photograph. **photo finish** close finish of race in which winner is identified by photography.

photo- in comb. light; photography.

photocopier /'fəʊtəʊkɒpɪə(r)/ n. machine for photocopying documents.

photocopy /'fəʊtəʊkɒpɪ/ 1 n. photographic copy of document. 2 v.t. make photocopy of.

photoelectric /fəʊtəʊɪ'lektrɪk/ a. with or using emission of electrons from substances exposed to light. **photoelectric cell** device using this effect to generate current.

photogenic /fəʊtəʊ'dʒenɪk/ a. apt to be a good subject for photographs; producing light.

photograph /'fəʊtəgrɑːf/ 1 n. picture formed by chemical action of light on sensitive film. 2 v. take photograph (of). 3 **photographer** /-'tɒg-/ n.; **photographic** /-'græf-/ a.; **photography** /-'tɒg-/ n.

photogravure /fəʊtəʊgrə'vjʊə(r)/ n. picture produced from photographic negative transferred to metal plate and etched in.

photolithography /fəʊtəʊlɪ'θɒgrəfɪ/ n. lithographic process in which plates are made photographically.

photometer /fəʊ'tɒmɪtə(r)/ n. instrument for measuring light. **photometric** /-'met-/ a.; **photometry** n.

photon /'fəʊtɒn/ n. quantum of electromagnetic radiation energy.

Photostat /'fəʊtəʊstæt/ 1 (P) n. photocopy. 2 **photostat** v.t. make Photostat of.

photosynthesis /fəʊtəʊ'sɪnθəsɪs/ n. process in which energy of sunlight is used by green plants to form complex substances from carbon dioxide and water. **photosynthesize** v.

phrasal /'freɪz(ə)l/ a. consisting of a phrase.

phrase /freɪz/ 1 n. group of words forming conceptual unit but not sentence; short pithy expression; Mus. short sequence of notes. 2 v.t. express in words; group in phrases. 3 **phrase-book** book listing phrases and their foreign equivalents, for use by tourists etc.

phraseology /freɪzɪ'ɒlədʒɪ/ n. choice or arrangement of words. **phraseological** a.

phrenetic var. of frenetic.

phrenology /frɪ'nɒlədʒɪ/ n. study of external form of cranium as supposed indication of mental faculties etc. **phrenologist** n.

phthisis /'θaɪsɪs/ n. pulmonary tuberculosis. **phthisical** /'θɪzɪk(ə)l/ a.

phut *adv. colloq.* **go phut** collapse, *lit.* or *fig.*

phylactery /fɪˈlæktərɪ/ *n.* small box containing Hebrew texts, worn by Jews at prayer.

phylum /ˈfaɪləm/ *n.* (*pl.* **-la**) major division of plant or animal kingdom.

physic /ˈfɪzɪk/ *n.* medical art or profession; *arch.* medicine.

physical /ˈfɪzɪk(ə)l/ *a.* of matter; of the body; of nature or according to its laws; of physics.

physician /fɪˈzɪʃ(ə)n/ *n.* doctor, esp. specialist in medical diagnosis and treatment.

physics /ˈfɪzɪks/ *n.pl.* usu. treated as *sing.* science of properties and interaction of matter and energy. **physicist** *n.*

physiognomy /fɪzɪˈɒnəmɪ/ *n.* features or type of face; art of judging character from face and form; characteristic aspect. **physiognomist** *n.*

physiography /fɪzɪˈɒɡrəfɪ/ *n.* description of natural phenomena; physical geography. **physiographical** *a.*

physiology /fɪzɪˈɒlədʒɪ/ *n.* science of functioning of living organisms. **physiological** *a.*; **physiologist** *n.*

physiotherapy /fɪzɪəˈθerəpɪ/ *n.* treatment of injury or disease by exercise, heat, or other physical agencies. **physiotherapist** *n.*

physique /fɪˈziːk/ *n.* bodily structure and development.

pi /paɪ/ *n.* sixteenth letter of Greek alphabet (*Π, π*); *Math.* symbol of ratio of circumference of circle to diameter (approx. 3.14).

pia mater /pɪə ˈmeɪtə(r)/ inner membrane enveloping brain and spinal cord.

pianissimo /pɪəˈnɪsɪməʊ/ *Mus.* **1** *adv.* very softly. **2** *n.* (*pl.* **-os**) passage to be performed thus.

pianist /ˈpɪənɪst/ *n.* player of piano.

piano[1] /pɪˈænəʊ/ *n.* (*pl.* **-nos**) musical instrument played by keys which cause hammers to strike metal strings. **piano-accordion** accordion with melody played from small piano-like keyboard.

piano[2] /pɪˈɑːnəʊ/ *Mus.* **1** *adv.* softly. **2** *n.* (*pl.* **-nos**) passage to be performed thus.

pianoforte /pɪænəʊˈfɔːtɪ/ *n.* piano[1].

pibroch /ˈpiːbrɒk/ *n.* martial or funeral bagpipe music.

picador /ˈpɪkədɔː(r)/ *n.* mounted man with lance in bull-fight.

picaresque /pɪkəˈresk/ *a.* (of fiction) dealing with adventures of rogues.

piccalilli /pɪkəˈlɪlɪ/ *n.* pickle of chopped vegetables, mustard, and spices.

piccaninny /pɪkəˈnɪnɪ/ *n.* small Black or Aus. Aboriginal child.

piccolo /ˈpɪkələʊ/ *n.* (*pl.* **-los**) small high-pitched flute.

pick[1] *v.* select, esp. carefully; pluck, gather (flower, fruit, etc.); make hole in or break surface of with fingers or sharp instument; make (hole) thus; open (lock) with skeleton key etc.; probe with pointed instrument; clear (bone etc.) of adherent flesh. **2** *n.* picking, selection; *the* best part *of*; pickaxe; instrument for picking. **3 pick on** nag at, find fault with, select; **pickpocket** person who steals from pockets; **pick up** take hold of and lift, learn routinely, stop for and take with one, (of police) take into custody, acquire casually, make acquaintance of casually, detect, manage to receive (broadcast signal etc.), recover health, improve; **pick-up** picking up, person met casually, part of record-player carrying stylus, small open motor truck.

pick-a-back var. of *piggy-back*.

pickaxe /ˈpɪkæks/ *n.* tool with sharp-pointed iron cross-bar for breaking up ground etc.

picket /ˈpɪkɪt/ **1** *n.* one or more person(s) stationed to dissuade workers from working during strike etc.; small body of men on military police duty; pointed stake driven into ground. **2** *v.t.* place or act as picket outside; post as military picket; secure with stakes.

pickings /ˈpɪkɪŋz/ *n.pl.* perquisites, gleanings.

pickle /ˈpɪk(ə)l/ **1** *n.* vegetables etc. preserved in vinegar etc.; liquor used for preserving food etc.; *colloq.* plight. **2** *v.t.* preserve in or treat with pickle; in *p.p. sl.* drunk.

picnic /ˈpɪknɪk/ **1** *n.* pleasure party including outdoor meal. **2** *v.i.* (*past & p.p.* **picnicked**) take part in picnic.

picot /ˈpiːkəʊ/ *n.* one of series of small loops forming edging to lace etc.

pictograph /'pɪktəgrɑːf/ (also **pictogram**) *n.* pictorial symbol used as form of writing.

pictorial /pɪk'tɔːrɪəl/ *a.* of or expressed in a picture.

picture /'pɪktʃə(r)/ 1 *n.* likeness or representation of subject produced by painting or drawing or photography etc.; portrait; beautiful object; scene; mental image; photograph; image on television screen; cinema film; in *pl.* cinema (performance). 2 *v.t.* imagine; represent in picture; describe graphically. 3 **picture postcard** postcard with picture on one side; **picture window** large window facing attractive view.

picturesque /pɪktʃə'resk/ *a.* striking and pleasant to look at; (of language etc.) strikingly graphic.

piddle /'pɪd(ə)l/ *v.i.* work or act in trifling way; *colloq.* urinate.

pidgin /'pɪdʒɪn/ *n.* simplified language esp. used between persons of different nationality etc.; *colloq.* (a person's) business or particular concern.

pie[1] *n.* dish of meat or fruit etc., encased in or covered with pastry etc. and baked. **pie chart** diagram representing various quantities as sectors of circle.

pie[2] *n.* magpie.

piebald /'paɪbɔːld/ 1 *a.* having light and dark colour in irregular patches. 2 *n.* piebald animal.

piece /piːs/ 1 *n.* one of the distinct portions of which thing is composed or into which it is divided or broken; detached portion; example, specimen; item; picture, literary or musical composition; chess-man, man at draughts, etc. 2 *v.t.* form into a whole; join pieces of *together.* 3 **in pieces** broken; **of a piece** uniform or consistent (*with*); **piecegoods** textile fabrics woven in standard lengths; **piece-work**, work paid for according to amount done.

pièce de résistance /pɪes də reɪ'zɪstɑs/ most important or remarkable item. [F]

piecemeal /'piːsmiːl/ 1 *adv.* piece by piece, part at a time. 2 *a.* done etc. piecemeal.

pied /paɪd/ *a.* of black and white or of mixed colours.

pied-à-terre /pjeɪd ɑː 'teə(r)/ *n.* (*pl.*

pieds- pr. same) place kept available as temporary quarters when needed. [F]

pier /pɪə(r)/ *n.* structure running out into sea used as promenade and landing-stage or breakwater; support of spans of bridge; pillar; solid part of wall between windows etc. **pier-glass** large tall mirror.

pierce /pɪəs/ *v.* go through or into like spear or needle; make hole in.

pierrot /'pɪərəʊ/ *n.* French pantomime character; itinerant musical entertainer.

pietà /pjeɪ'tɑː/ *n.* picture or sculpture of Virgin Mary holding dead body of Christ. [It.]

pietism /'paɪətɪz(ə)m/ *n.* extreme or affected piety.

piety /'paɪətɪ/ *n.* piousness.

piffle /'pɪf(ə)l/ *sl.* 1 *n.* nonsense. 2 *v.i.* talk or act feebly.

pig 1 *n.* wild or domesticated animal with broad snout and stout bristly body; pork; *colloq.* greedy, dirty, obstinate, or annoying person; oblong mass of smelted iron or other metal. 2 *v.i.* live or behave like pig (esp. **pig it**). 3 **pigheaded** obstinate; **pig-iron** crude iron from smelting-furnace; **pigsty** sty for pigs; **pig-tail** plait of hair hanging from back of head.

pigeon /'pɪdʒɪn/ *n.* bird of dove family; person who is easily swindled. **pigeon-hole** one of set of compartments in cabinet etc. for papers etc., (*v.t.*) put in pigeon-hole, put aside for future consideration, classify mentally; **pigeon-toed** having toes turned inwards.

piggery /'pɪgərɪ/ *n.* place where pigs are bred; pigsty.

piggish /'pɪgɪʃ/ *a.* greedy, dirty.

piggy /'pɪgɪ/ *n.* little pig. **piggy-back** a ride on shoulders and back of another person; **piggy bank** pig-shaped hollow pot for saving money in.

piglet /'pɪglɪt/ *n.* young pig.

pigment /'pɪgmənt/ 1 *n.* colouring-matter. 2 *v.t.* colour (as) with natural pigment. 3 **pigmentation** *n.*

pigmy var. of **pygmy**.

pike *n.* large voracious freshwater fish; peaked top of hill; spear formerly used by infantry. **pikestaff** wooden shaft of pike (**plain as a pikestaff** quite obvious).

pilaff /ˈpɪlæf/ n. Oriental dish of rice with meat, spices, etc.

pilau /ˈpɪlaʊ/ n. pilaff.

pilaster /pɪˈlæstə(r)/ n. rectangular column, esp. one fastened into wall.

pilchard /ˈpɪltʃəd/ n. small sea-fish related to herring.

pile¹ 1 n. heap of things laid on one another; colloq. large amount esp. of money; building of imposing height; pyre; series of plates of dissimilar metals laid alternately for producing electric current; (in full **atomic pile**) nuclear reactor. 2 v. heap up or on; load; crowd in(to), on, out of, etc. 3 **pile up** accumulate, cause (vehicle or aircraft) to crash; **pile-up** collision of several motor vehicles.

pile² n. heavy beam driven vertically into ground as support for building etc.

pile³ n. nap of velvet or carpet etc.

pile⁴ n. (usu. in pl.) haemorrhoid.

pilfer /ˈpɪlfə(r)/ v. steal or thieve in petty way. **pilferage** n.

pilgrim /ˈpɪlɡrɪm/ n. person who journeys to sacred place; traveller. **Pilgrim Fathers** English Puritans who founded colony in Massachusetts 1620.

pilgrimage /ˈpɪlɡrɪmɪdʒ/ n. pilgrim's journey.

pill n. small ball or flat piece of medicinal substance to be swallowed whole. **the pill** colloq. contraceptive pill; **pillbox** small round shallow box for pills, hat shaped like this, Mil. small round concrete shelter, mainly underground.

pillage /ˈpɪlɪdʒ/ n. & v.t. plunder.

pillar /ˈpɪlə(r)/ n. slender upright structure used as support or ornament; column. **pillar-box** hollow pillar for posting letters in.

pillion /ˈpɪlɪən/ n. seat for passenger behind motor-cyclist etc.

pillory /ˈpɪlərɪ/ 1 n. hist. frame with holes for head and hands of offender exposed to popular ridicule. 2 v.t. set in pillory; fig. expose to ridicule.

pillow /ˈpɪləʊ/ 1 n. cushion as support for head, esp. in bed; pillow-shaped thing. 2 v.t. rest, prop up, (as) on pillow. 3 **pillowcase**, **-slip**, washable cover for pillow.

pilot /ˈpaɪlət/ 1 n. person operating flying controls of aircraft; person in charge of ships entering or leaving harbour etc.; guide. 2 v.t. act as pilot to; guide course of. 3 a. experimental, small-scale. 4 **pilot-light** small gas-burner kept alight to light another; **pilot officer** lowest commissioned rank in RAF, next below flying officer.

pimento /pɪˈmentəʊ/ n. (pl. **-tos**) allspice; sweet pepper.

pimp 1 n. person who solicits clients for prostitute or brothel. 2 v.i. act as pimp.

pimpernel /ˈpɪmpənel/ n. plant with small scarlet or blue flower.

pimple /ˈpɪmp(ə)l/ n. small hard inflamed spot on skin. **pimply** a.

pin 1 n. piece of thin stiff wire with point and head used as fastening; wooden or metal peg, rivet, etc.; skittle; in pl. sl. legs. 2 v.t. fasten with pin(s); fix responsibility for on; seize and hold fast; transfix with pin, lance, etc. 3 **pin-ball** game in which small metal balls are shot across sloping board and strike against obstacles; **pincushion** small pad for sticking pins in ready for use; **pin down** make (person) declare position or intentions; **pin-money** small sum of money, esp. earned by woman; **pinpoint** locate or define (target etc.) with minute precision; **pinprick** petty irritation; **pins and needles** tingling sensation in limb recovering from numbness; **pin-stripe** very narrow stripe in cloth; **pin-table** table used in pin-ball; **pintail** duck or grouse with pointed tail; **pin-tuck** narrow ornamental tuck; **pin-up** picture of attractive or famous person, pinned up on wall etc.; **pin-wheel** small Catherine wheel.

pinafore /ˈpɪnəfɔː(r)/ n. apron covering front of body above and below waist. **pinafore dress** dress without collar or sleeves, worn over blouse or jumper.

pince-nez /ˈpæsneɪ/ n. pair of eye-glasses with spring that clips on nose.

pincers /ˈpɪnsəz/ n.pl. gripping-tool forming pair of jaws; pincer-shaped claw in crustaceans etc. **pincer movement** Mil. converging movement against enemy position.

pinch 1 v. grip tightly between two surfaces, esp. tips of finger and thumb; affect painfully; (of cold etc.) nip, shrivel; stint, be niggardly; sl. steal, arrest. **2** *n.* pinching, squeezing; stress of poverty etc.; small amount. **3 at a pinch** in an emergency.

pinchbeck /ˈpɪntʃbek/ **1** *n.* goldlike copper and zinc alloy used in cheap jewellery etc. **2** *a.* spurious, sham.

pine¹ *n.* evergreen needle-leaved coniferous tree; its wood. **pine-cone** fruit of pine; **pine kernel** edible seed of some pine-trees.

pine² *v.i.* waste *away* with grief, disease, etc.; long (*for*).

pineal /ˈpɪnɪəl/ *a.* shaped like pine-cone. **pineal gland** conical gland in brain.

pineapple /ˈpaɪnæp(ə)l/ *n.* large juicy tropical fruit with yellow flesh and tough skin.

ping **1** *n.* abrupt single ringing sound. **2** *v.i.* emit ping.

ping-pong /ˈpɪŋpɒŋ/ *n.* table tennis.

pinion¹ /ˈpɪnɪən/ *n.* small cog-wheel engaging with larger.

pinion² /ˈpɪnɪən/ **1** *n.* outer joint of bird's wing; *poet.* wing; flight-feather. **2** *v.t.* cut off pinions to prevent flight; restrain by binding arms to sides.

pink¹ **1** *n.* pale-red colour; garden plant with clove-scented flowers; *the* point of perfection or excellence. **2** *a.* pink-coloured; *sl.* mildly socialist.

pink² *v.t.* pierce slightly; cut scalloped or zigzag edge in. **pinking shears** dressmaker's serrated shears for cutting zigzag edge.

pink³ *v.i.* (of vehicle engine) emit high-pitched explosive sounds when running faultily.

pinnace /ˈpɪnəs/ *n.* ship's small boat.

pinnacle /ˈpɪnək(ə)l/ *n.* small ornamental turret crowning buttress, roof, etc.; culmination or climax.

pinnate /ˈpɪnɪt/ *a. Bot.* (of compound leaf) with leaflets on each side of leaf-stalk.

pinny /ˈpɪnɪ/ *n. colloq.* pinafore.

pint /paɪnt/ *n.* measure of capacity, 0.56l.; *colloq.* pint of beer.

pinta /ˈpaɪntə/ *n. colloq.* pint of milk.

pintle /ˈpɪnt(ə)l/ *n.* bolt or pin, esp. one on which some other part turns.

pioneer /paɪəˈnɪə(r)/ **1** *n.* original explorer or settler etc.; beginner of enterprise etc. **2** *v.* act as pioneer (in).

pious /ˈpaɪəs/ *a.* devout, religious; dutiful. **pious fraud** deception meant to benefit victim.

pip¹ *n.* seed of apple, pear, orange, etc.

pip² *n.* each spot on dominoes, dice, or playing-cards; star on army officer's shoulder.

pip³ *v.t. colloq.* forestall; defeat.

pip⁴ *n.* short high-pitched sound.

pip⁵ *n.* disease of poultry etc. **the pip** *sl.* (fit of) depression or boredom or bad temper.

pipe **1** *n.* tube of earthenware, metal, etc., esp. for conveying gas, water, etc.; narrow tube with bowl at one end containing tobacco for smoking; quantity of tobacco held by this; musical wind-instrument; each tube by which sound is produced in organ; in *pl.* bagpipes; tubular organ etc. in body; boatswain's whistle; measure of capacity for wine (105 gals.). **2** *v.* convey (as) through pipes; transmit (recorded music etc.) by wire or cable; play on pipe; utter shrilly; summon or lead etc. by sound of pipe or whistle; trim with piping; furnish with pipe(s). **3 pipeclay** fine white clay for tobacco-pipes or for whitening leather etc.; **pipe-cleaner** piece of flexible tuft-covered wire to clean inside tobacco pipe; **pipe down** *colloq.* be quiet; **pipe-dream** extravagant fancy, impossible wish, etc.; **pipeline** pipe conveying oil etc. across country, *fig.* channel of supply or communication etc.; **pipe up** begin to play or speak etc.

piper /ˈpaɪpə(r)/ *n.* person who plays on pipe, esp. bagpipes.

pipette /pɪˈpet/ *n.* slender tube used for transferring or measuring small quantities of liquid.

piping /ˈpaɪpɪŋ/ **1** *n.* length or system of pipes; ornamentation of dress or upholstery etc. by means of cord enclosed in pipelike fold; ornamental cordlike lines of sugar on cake. **2** *a.* **piping hot** (of food or water) extremely hot.

pipit /ˈpɪpɪt/ *n.* small bird resembling lark.

pippin /ˈpɪpɪn/ *n.* apple grown from seed; dessert apple.

piquant /ˈpiːkənt/ *a.* agreeably pungent, sharp, appetizing, stimulating. **piquancy** *n.*

pique /piːk/ **1** *v.t.* wound pride or stir curiosity of. **2** *n.* enmity, resentment.

piquet /pɪˈket/ n. card-game for 2 players.

piracy /ˈpaɪrəsɪ/ n. activity of pirate.

piranha /pɪˈrɑːnə/ n. voracious S. Amer. freshwater fish.

pirate /ˈpaɪərət/ 1 n. sea-faring robber attacking other ships; ship used by pirate; person who infringes copyright or regulations or encroaches on rights of others etc. 2 v.t. reproduce (book etc.) without permission for one's own benefit. 3 piratical /-ˈræt/ a.

pirouette /pɪrʊˈet/ 1 n. ballet-dancer's spin on one foot or point of toe. 2 v.i. perform pirouette.

piscatorial /pɪskəˈtɔːrɪəl/ a. of fishing.

Pisces /ˈpaɪsiːz/ n. twelfth sign of zodiac.

pisciculture /ˈpɪsɪkʌltʃə(r)/ n. artificial rearing of fish.

piscina /pɪˈsiːnə/ n. (pl. **-nae** /-niː/ or **-nas**) stone basin in niche on south side of altar in church.

piss vulg. 1 v. urinate; discharge with urine; in p.p. sl. drunk. 2 n. urinating; urine. 3 **piss off** sl. go away, annoy, depress.

pistachio /pɪˈstæʃɪəʊ/ n. (pl. **-chios**) kind of nut with green kernel.

piste /piːst/ n. ski-track of compacted snow. [F]

pistil /ˈpɪstɪl/ n. female organ in flowers.

pistillate /ˈpɪstɪleɪt/ a. having pistils.

pistol /ˈpɪst(ə)l/ 1 n. small fire-arm. 2 v.t. shoot with pistol.

piston /ˈpɪst(ə)n/ n. sliding cylinder fitting closely in tube and moving up and down in it, used in steam or petrol engine to impart motion; sliding valve in trumpet etc. **piston-rod** rod connecting piston to other parts of machine.

pit 1 n. large hole in ground, esp. one made in digging for minerals etc.; coal-mine; covered hole as trap; depression in skin or any surface; floor of theatre auditorium, sunken area accommodating orchestra; sunken area in floor of workshop etc. for inspection or repair of underside of vehicle etc.; area to side of track where racing cars are refuelled etc. during race. 2 v.t. match against; make pit(s) in; store in pit. 3 **pitfall** unsuspected snare or danger, covered pit as trap; **pit-head** top of

shaft of coal-mine, area surrounding this; **pit of the stomach** hollow below bottom of breastbone.

pita /ˈpiːtə/ n. kind of flat bread orig. from Greece and Middle East.

pit-a-pat /ˈpɪtəpæt/ 1 n. sound as of light quick steps. 2 adv. with this sound.

pitch[1] 1 v. set up in chosen position; encamp; give chosen altitude or gradient or intensity or musical pitch or style or level etc. to; throw, fling, fall; (of ship etc.) plunge in longitudinal direction; sl. tell (yarn etc.). 2 n. act or process of pitching; area marked out for play in esp. outdoor game; Crick. part of ground between or near wickets; Mus. degree of highness or lowness of tone; place, esp. in street or market, where one is stationed; height, degree, intensity, gradient; distance between successive ridges of screw, teeth of cog-wheel, etc. 3 **pitched battle** one planned beforehand, not casual; **pitchfork** long-handled two-pronged fork for tossing hay etc., (v.t.) thrust forcibly or hastily into (office, position, etc.); **pitch in** colloq. set to work vigorously; **pitch into** colloq. attack vigorously.

pitch[2] 1 n. dark resinous tarry substance. 2 v.t. coat, smear, etc. with pitch. 3 **pitch black, dark**, etc., intensely dark; **pitch-pine** resinous kinds of pine.

pitchblende /ˈpɪtʃblend/ n. uranium oxide yielding radium.

pitcher[1] /ˈpɪtʃə(r)/ n. large jug, ewer. **pitcher-plant** plant with pitcher-shaped leaves.

pitcher[2] /ˈpɪtʃə(r)/ n. player who delivers ball in baseball.

pitchy /ˈpɪtʃɪ/ a. of, like, dark etc. as, pitch.

piteous /ˈpɪtɪəs/ a. deserving or arousing pity.

pith /pɪθ/ n. spongy tissue in stems of plants or lining rind of orange etc.; chief part; vigour, energy. **pith helmet** one made from dried pith of sola etc.

pithy /ˈpɪθɪ/ a. condensed and forcible, terse.

pitiable /ˈpɪtɪəb(ə)l/ a. deserving or arousing pity or contempt.

pitiful /ˈpɪtɪfʊl/ a. arousing pity; contemptible.

pitiless /ˈpɪtɪlɪs/ a. showing no pity.

piton /ˈpiːtɒn/ n. peg driven in to support climber or rope.

pittance /ˈpɪt(ə)ns/ n. scanty allowance, small amount.

pituitary /pɪˈtjuːɪtərɪ/ n. (in full **pituitary gland**) small ductless gland at base of brain.

pity /ˈpɪtɪ/ **1** n. sorrow for another's suffering; cause for regret. **2** v.t. feel pity for.

pivot /ˈpɪvət/ **1** n. shaft or pin on which something turns; cardinal or crucial person or point. **2** v. turn (as) on pivot; hinge (on); provide with pivot. **3** **pivotal** a.

pixie /ˈpɪksɪ/ (also **pixy**) n. supernatural being akin to fairy. **pixie hood** hood with pointed crown.

pizza /ˈpiːtsə/ n. flat piece of dough baked with savoury topping.

pizzicato /pɪtsɪˈkɑːtəʊ/ **1** adv. with the string of violin etc. plucked, not played with bow. **2** n. (pl. **-tos**) note or passage to be performed thus.

pl. abbr. place; plate; plural.

placable /ˈplækəb(ə)l/ a. easily appeased; mild-tempered. **placability** n.

placard /ˈplækɑːd/ **1** n. large notice for public display. **2** v.t. post placards on; advertise by placards.

placate /pləˈkeɪt/ v.t. conciliate, pacify. **placatory** /-ˈkeɪt-/ a.

place 1 n. particular part of space; space or room of or for person etc.; city, town, village, residence, building; building or spot devoted to specified purpose; office or employment; duties of this; rank, station, position. **2** v.t. put or dispose in place; assign rank or order or class to; give (order for goods etc.) to firm etc.; in pass. be among first 3 in race. **3 all over the place** in disorder; **in place** suitable, appropriate; **in place of** instead of; **out of place** unsuitable, inappropriate; **place-kick** Footb. kick made with ball placed on ground; **place-mat** small mat on table at person's place; **place-setting** set of dishes and implements for one person to eat with; **take place** happen; **take the place of** be substituted for. **4 placement** n.

placebo /pləˈsiːbəʊ/ n. (pl. **-bos**) medicine given to humour rather than cure patient; dummy pill etc.

placenta /pləˈsentə/ n. organ in uterus of pregnant mammal that nourishes foetus. **placental** a.

placer /ˈpleɪsə(r)/ n. deposit of gravel, sand, etc., on bed of stream containing minerals, esp. gold.

placid /ˈplæsɪd/ a. calm, unruffled; not easily disturbed. **placidity** /-ˈsɪd-/ n.

placket /ˈplækɪt/ n. opening or slit at top of skirt, for fastenings or access to pocket.

plagiarize /ˈpleɪdʒəraɪz/ v. take and use (another's writings etc.) as one's own. **plagiarism** n.; **plagiarist** n.

plague /pleɪg/ **1** n. deadly contagious disease; infestation of pest; great trouble or affliction. **2** v.t. afflict with plague; colloq. annoy, bother.

plaice /pleɪs/ n. kind of flat-fish.

plaid /plæd/ **1** n. long piece of woollen cloth as part of Highland costume; tartan cloth. **2** a. made of plaid, having plaidlike pattern.

plain /pleɪn/ **1** a. clear, evident; straightforward; ordinary, homely; not decorated or embellished or luxurious; not good-looking. **2** n. level tract of country; ordinary stitch in knitting. **3** adv. simply; clearly. **3 plain chocolate** chocolate made without milk; **plain clothes** civilian clothes as distinct from uniform; **plain sailing** simple situation or course of action; **plainsong** traditional church music sung in unison in medieval modes and free rhythm; **plain-spoken** frank.

plaint n. Law accusation, charge; poet. lamentation.

plaintiff /ˈpleɪntɪf/ n. party who brings suit into lawcourt.

plaintive /ˈpleɪntɪv/ a. mournful-sounding.

plait /plæt/ **1** n. interlacing of 3 or more strands of hair or ribbon etc.; material thus interlaced. **2** v.t. form into plait.

plan 1 n. method or procedure by which thing is to be done; drawing exhibiting relative position and size of parts of building etc., diagram, map. **2** v. arrange beforehand, scheme; make plan of; design.

planchette /plænˈʃet/ n. small board on castors, with pencil, said to trace letters etc. without conscious direction.

plane¹ 1 n. level surface; level of attainment etc.; aeroplane; main aerofoil. **2** a. level as or lying in a plane.

plane² 1 *n.* tool for smoothing surface of wood by paring shavings from it. 2 *v.t.* smooth, pare (*away* etc.), with plane.

plane³ *n.* tall spreading broad-leaved tree.

planet /ˈplænɪt/ *n.* any of heavenly bodies revolving round sun. **planetary** *a.*

planetarium /plænɪˈteərɪəm/ *n.* (*pl.* **-iums**) device for projecting image of night sky as seen at various times and places; building containing this.

plangent /ˈplændʒ(ə)nt/ *a.* loudly lamenting. **plangency** *n.*

plank 1 *n.* long flat piece of timber; item of political or other programme. 2 *v.t.* lay etc. with planks; *colloq.* put *down* (esp. money).

plankton /ˈplæŋkt(ə)n/ *n.* (chiefly microscopic) drifting or floating organisms found in sea or fresh water.

planner /ˈplænə(r)/ *n.* person who plans or makes plans, esp. with reference to controlled design of buildings and development of land. **planning** *n.*

plant /plɑːnt/ 1 *n.* organism capable of living wholly on inorganic substances and lacking power of locomotion; small plant (other than trees and shrubs); equipment for industrial process; *sl.* thing deliberately placed for discovery by others, hoax, trap. 2 *v.t.* place (seed etc.) in ground to grow; furnish (land etc.) with plants; fix firmly, establish; deliver (blow etc.); *sl.* conceal (stolen goods, evidence of complicity, etc.), esp. with view to misleading later discoverer.

plantain¹ /ˈplæntɪn/ *n.* herb yielding seed used as food for cage-birds.

plantain² /ˈplæntɪn/ *n.* tropical fruit like banana; treelike plant bearing it.

plantation /plɑːnˈteɪʃ(ə)n/ *n.* number of growing plants, esp. trees, planted together; estate for cultivation of cotton, tobacco, etc.; *hist.* colony.

planter /ˈplɑːntə(r)/ *n.* owner or manager of plantation; container for house plants.

plaque /plɑːk/ *n.* ornamental tablet of metal, porcelain, etc.; film on teeth, where bacteria proliferate.

plasma /ˈplæzmə/ *n.* colourless coagulable part of blood in which corpuscles etc. float; protoplasm; *Phys.*

gas of positive ions and free electrons in about equal numbers.

plaster /ˈplɑːstə(r)/ 1 *n.* mixture esp. of lime and sand and water spread on walls etc.; medicinal or protective substance etc. spread on fabric and applied to body; sticking-plaster; plaster of Paris. 2 *v.t.* cover with or like plaster; apply, stick, etc., like plaster to; coat, bedaub; *sl.* bomb heavily; in *p.p. sl.* drunk. 3 **plasterboard** board with core of plaster used for walls etc.; **plaster of Paris** fine white powder of gypsum used for making moulds or casts.

plastic /ˈplæstɪk/ 1 *n.* synthetic resinous etc. substance that can be moulded by heat or pressure. 2 *a.* made of plastic; capable of being moulded; giving form to clay, wax, etc. 3 **plastic arts** those concerned with modelling; **plastic surgery** repair or restoration of lost or damaged etc. tissue. 4 **plasticity** *n.*; **plasticize** *v.t.*

Plasticine /ˈplæstɪsiːn/ (**P**) *n.* plastic substance used for modelling.

plate 1 *n.* shallow usu. circular vessel from which food is eaten or served; table utensils of gold, silver, or other metal; engraved piece of metal; illustration printed from engraved plate etc.; thin sheet of metal, glass, etc. coated with sensitive film for photography; flat thin sheet of metal etc.; part of denture fitting to mouth and holding teeth. 2 *v.* cover (other metal) with thin coating of silver, gold, etc.; cover with plates of metal. 3 **plate glass** thick fine-quality glass for mirrors, windows, etc.; **platelayer** workman laying and repairing railway lines.

plateau /ˈplætəʊ/ *n.* (*pl.* **-teaux** /-təʊz/) area of level high ground; state of little variation following an increase.

platelet /ˈpleɪtlɪt/ *n.* small disc in blood, involved in clotting.

platen /ˈplæt(ə)n/ *n.* plate in printing-press by which paper is pressed against type; corresponding part in typewriter etc.

platform /ˈplætfɔːm/ *n.* raised level surface, esp. one from which speaker addresses audience, or one along side of line at railway station; thick sole of shoe; declared policy of political party.

platinum /ˈplætɪnəm/ *n.* white heavy

metallic element that does not tarnish. **platinum blonde** woman with silvery blonde hair, this colour.

platitude /'plætɪtjuːd/ n. commonplace remark. **platitudinous** a.

Platonic /plə'tɒnɪk/ a. of Plato or his philosophy; **platonic** confined to words or theory; (of love or friendship) purely spiritual, not sexual. **Platonism** n.; **Platonist** n.

platoon /plə'tuːn/ n. Mil. subdivision of infantry company.

platter /'plætə(r)/ n. flat plate or dish, esp. for food.

platypus /'plætɪpəs/ n. Aus. egg-laying mammal with ducklike beak.

plaudit /'plɔːdɪt/ n. (usu. in pl.) round of applause; commendation.

plausible /'plɔːzɪb(ə)l/ a. seeming reasonable or probable, (of person) persuasive but deceptive. **plausibility** n.

play 1 v. occupy or amuse oneself with some recreation or game or exercise etc.; do this with another; perform on (musical instrument), perform (piece of music etc.); perform (drama, role); act in drama etc., perform, execute; take part in (game); have as opponent in game; move piece in game, put card on table, strike ball, etc.; move about in lively or unrestrained manner; touch gently (on); allow (fish) to exhaust itself pulling against line. 2 n. recreation; amusement; playing of game, ball, etc.; dramatic piece; freedom of movement; fitful or light movement; gambling. 3 **play along** pretend to co-operate; **play back** make audible (what has been recorded); **play-back** n.; **playbill** poster announcing theatre programme; **play-boy** pleasure-seeking usu. wealthy man; **play down** minimize; **play-fellow** companion in childhood; **play-goer** person who goes often to the theatre; **playground** outdoor area for children to play on; **playgroup** group of pre-school children who play together under supervision; **playhouse** theatre; **playing-card** small oblong card used in games, one of set of usu. 52 divided into 4 suits; **playmate** play-fellow; **play-off** extra match played to decide draw or tie; **plaything** toy; **play up to** flatter to win favour etc.; **play-wright** dramatist.

PLC abbr. Public Limited Company.

plea n. appeal, entreaty; Law formal statement by or on behalf of defendant; excuse.

pleach v.t. entwine, interlace, (esp. branches to form a hedge).

plead v. address court as advocate or party; allege as plea; make appeal or entreaty. **plead guilty**, **not guilty**, admit, deny, liability or guilt; **plead with** make earnest appeal to.

pleading /'pliːdɪŋ/ n. (usu. in pl.) formal statement of cause of action or defence.

pleasant /'plez(ə)nt/ a. agreeable; giving pleasure.

pleasantry /'plezəntrɪ/ n. joking remark.

please /pliːz/ 1 v. be agreeable to; give joy or gratification to; choose, be willing, like. 2 int. or adv. as courteous qualification to request etc.

pleasurable /'pleʒərəb(ə)l/ a. causing pleasure.

pleasure /'pleʒə(r)/ n. satisfaction, delight; sensuous enjoyment; will, discretion, choice.

pleat 1 n. flattened fold in cloth etc. 2 v.t. make pleat(s) in.

pleb n. & a. colloq. plebeian.

plebeian /plə'biːən/ a. of common people. 2 n. plebeian person.

plebiscite /'plebɪsaɪt/ n. direct vote of all electors of State on important public question.

plectrum /'plektrəm/ n. small implement for plucking strings of musical instrument.

pledge 1 n. thing given to person as security for fulfilment of contract, payment of debt, etc.; thing put in pawn; token; solemn promise; drinking of health. 2 v.t. deposit as security, pawn; promise solemnly by pledge; bind by solemn promise; drink to the health of.

Pleiades /'plaɪədiːz/ n.pl. cluster of stars in constellation Taurus.

plenary /'pliːnərɪ/ a. not subject to limitation or exceptions; (of assembly) to be attended by all members.

plenipotentiary /plenɪpə'tenʃərɪ/ 1 n. person (esp. diplomat) having full power of independent action. 2 a. having such power.

plenitude /'plenɪtjuːd/ n. abundance; fullness; completeness.

plenteous /'plentɪəs/ a. plentiful.

plentiful /'plentɪfʊl/ a. existing in ample quantity.

plenty /'plentɪ/ 1 n. abundance; quite enough. 2 adv. colloq. fully.

pleonasm /'pliːənæz(ə)m/ n. use of more words than are needed to express meaning. **pleonastic** a.

plethora /'pleθərə/ n. over-supply, glut.

pleurisy /'plʊərɪsɪ/ n. inflammation of membrane enclosing lungs. **pleuritic** /-'rɪt-/ a.

plexus /'pleksəs/ n. Anat. network of nerves or vessels in animal body.

pliable /'paɪəb(ə)l/ a. easily bent or influenced; supple; accommodating. **pliability** n.

pliant /'plaɪənt/ a. pliable. **pliancy** n.

pliers /'plaɪəz/ n.pl. pincers with flat grip for bending wire etc.

plight[1] /plaɪt/ n. condition, state, esp. unfortunate one.

plight[2] /plaɪt/ v.t. arch. pledge; engage oneself.

plimsoll /'plɪmsəʊl/ n. rubber-soled canvas shoe. **Plimsoll line, mark**, marking on ship's side showing limit of legal submersion under various conditions.

plinth /plɪnθ/ n. base supporting vase or statue etc.

plod v.i. walk or work laboriously.

plonk n. sl. cheap or inferior wine.

plop 1 n. sound of smooth object dropping into water. 2 v. (cause to) fall with plop. 3 adv. with a plop.

plot 1 n. small piece of land; plan or essential facts of tale, play, etc.; secret plan, conspiracy. 2 v. make chart, diagram, graph, etc. of; hatch secret plans; devise secretly.

plough /plaʊ/ 1 n. implement for furrowing and turning up soil; similar instrument for clearing away snow etc. 2 v. turn up with plough; furrow, make (furrow); advance laboriously through; cut or force way; sl. fail in examination. 3 **plough back** plough (crop) into soil to enrich it, reinvest (profits etc.) in business etc.; **ploughman** guider of plough; **ploughman's lunch** meal of bread and cheese etc.; **ploughshare** blade of plough.

plover /'plʌvə(r)/ n. medium-sized wading bird.

ploy n. colloq. manœuvre to gain advantage.

pluck 1 v. pick or pull out or away; strip (bird) of feathers; pull at, twitch; tug or snatch at; plunder or swindle. 2 n. courage; animal's heart, liver, and lungs. 3 **pluck up courage** summon up one's courage.

plucky /'plʌkɪ/ a. brave, spirited.

plug 1 n. something fitting into and stopping or filling hole or cavity; device of metal pins etc. for making electrical connection; (piece of) tobacco pressed into cake or stick. 2 v. stop with plug; put plug into; sl. seek to make popular by frequent repetition, commendation, etc.; sl. shoot; colloq. work away at. 3 **plug in** connect electrically by inserting plug into socket.

plum n. roundish fleshy stone-fruit; tree bearing it; currant or raisin; good thing, best thing, prize. **plum pudding** Christmas pudding.

plumage /'pluːmɪdʒ/ n. bird's feathers.

plumb /plʌm/ 1 n. ball of lead attached to line for testing whether wall etc. is vertical; perpendicularity; sounding-lead. 2 a. vertical. 3 adv. exactly; vertically; US sl. quite, utterly. 4 v. sound (water); measure (depth); ascertain depth or get to bottom of; make vertical; work as plumber; fit as part of plumbing system. 5 **plumb-line** string with plumb attached.

plumber /'plʌmə(r)/ n. workman who fits and repairs water-pipes, cisterns, etc.

plumbing /'plʌmɪŋ/ n. system or apparatus of water-supply; plumber's work.

plume /pluːm/ 1 n. feather, esp. large and showy one; feathery ornament in hat, hair, etc.; feather-like formation, esp. of smoke. 2 v.t. furnish with plume; pride oneself (on); preen (feathers).

plummet /'plʌmɪt/ 1 n. plumb or plumb-line; sounding-lead. 2 v.i. fall rapidly.

plummy /'plʌmɪ/ a. colloq. good, desirable, (of voice) rich in tone.

plump 1 a. having full rounded fleshy shape. 2 v. make or become plump; vote for (candidate, or one of alternative choices). 3 adv. colloq. with sudden or heavy fall.

plunder /'plʌndə(r)/ v. rob forcibly,

esp. as in war; rob, steal, embezzle. **2** *n.* plundering; property plundered; *sl.* profit.

plunge **1** *v.* immerse completely; put suddenly, throw oneself, dive, (*into*); move with a rush; *sl.* run up gambling debts. **2** *n.* plunging; dive; *fig.* decisive step.

plunger /ˈplʌndʒə(r)/ *n.* part of mechanism that works with plunging or thrusting motion; rubber cup on handle for removing blockages by plunging action; *sl.* reckless gambler.

pluperfect /pluːˈpɜːfɪkt/ *Gram.* **1** *a.* expressing action completed prior to some past point of time. **2** *n.* pluperfect tense.

plural /ˈplʊər(ə)l/ **1** *a.* more than one in number. **2** *n.* plural number or form.

pluralism /ˈplʊərəlɪz(ə)m/ *n.* holding of more than one office at a time; form of society in which minority groups retain independent traditions. **pluralist** *n.*; **pluralistic** *a.*

plurality /plʊəˈrælɪtɪ/ *n.* state of being plural; majority (*of* votes etc.).

pluralize /ˈplʊərəlaɪz/ *v.t.* make plural; express as plural.

plus /plʌs/ **1** *prep.* with addition of; *colloq.* having gained. **2** *n.* symbol (+); additional or positive quantity; advantage. **3** *a.* additional, extra; (after number etc.) at least, rather better than; *Math.* positive.

plush /plʌʃ/ **1** *n.* cloth of silk, cotton, etc. with long soft pile. **2** *a.* made of plush, plushy.

plushy /ˈplʌʃɪ/ *a.* stylish, luxurious.

plutocracy /pluːˈtɒkrəsɪ/ *n.* State in which power belongs to rich; wealthy class. **plutocrat** *n.*; **plutocratic** *a.*

plutonium /pluːˈtəʊnɪəm/ *n.* radioactive metallic element.

pluvial /ˈpluːvɪəl/ *a.* of or caused by rain.

ply[1] /plaɪ/ *n.* fold, thickness, strand.

ply[2] /plaɪ/ *v.* wield vigorously; work *at*; supply continuously or assail vigorously (*with*); (of ship, vehicle, etc.) go to and fro (*between*).

plywood /ˈplaɪwʊd/ *n.* strong thin board made by gluing layers with the direction of the grain alternating.

PM *abbr.* Prime Minister.

p.m. *abbr.* after noon (*post meridiem*).

pneumatic /njuːˈmætɪk/ *a.* filled with wind or air; working by means of compressed air.

pneumonia /njuːˈməʊnɪə/ *n.* inflammation of lungs.

po *n.* (*pl.* **pos**) *colloq.* chamber-pot. **po-faced** solemn-faced, humourless.

PO *abbr.* Post Office; postal order; Petty Officer; Pilot Officer.

poach /pəʊtʃ/ *v.* cook (egg) without shell in boiling water; cook (fish etc.) by simmering in small amount of liquid; catch (game or fish) illicitly; encroach, trespass.

pock *n.* eruptive spot esp. in smallpox. **pock-marked** bearing marks like those left by smallpox.

pocket /ˈpɒkɪt/ **1** *n.* small bag inserted in or attached to garment for carrying small articles; pouchlike compartment in suitcase, car door, etc.; pecuniary resources; pouch at corner or on side of billiard-table into which balls are driven; cavity in earth, rock, etc., esp. filled with ore etc.; isolated area. **2** *a.* of suitable size for carrying in pocket; small, diminutive. **3** *v.t.* put into pocket; appropriate; submit to (affront etc.), conceal (feelings). **4** **in, out of, pocket** having gained, lost, in transaction; **pocket-book** notebook, small booklike case for papers, paper money, etc.; **pocket-knife** small folding knife; **pocket-money** money for occasional expenses, esp. allowance given to child.

pod **1** *n.* long seed-vessel esp. of pea or bean etc. **2** *v.* form pods; remove (peas etc.) from pods.

podgy /ˈpɒdʒɪ/ *a.* short and fat.

podium /ˈpəʊdɪəm/ *n.* (*pl.* **-dia**) continuous projecting base or pedestal round house etc.; conductor's or speaker's rostrum.

poem /ˈpəʊɪm/ *n.* metrical composition; elevated composition in prose or verse; something with poetic qualities.

poesy /ˈpəʊɪzɪ/ *n.* *arch.* poems or poetry.

poet /ˈpəʊɪt/ *n.* writer of poems. **poet Laureate** poet appointed to write poems for State occasions. **poetess** *n.*

poetaster /pəʊɪˈtæstə(r)/ *n.* inferior poet.

poetic /pəʊˈetɪk/ *a.* of or like poets or poetry. **poetic justice** well-deserved punishment or reward; **poetic licence** departure from truth etc. for effect.

poetical /pəʊˈetɪk(ə)l/ *a.* poetic; written in verse.

poetry /ˈpəʊɪtrɪ/ *n.* poet's art or work; poems; quality calling for poetical expression.

pogo /ˈpəʊɡəʊ/ *n.* (*pl.* **-gos**) stiltlike toy with spring, used to jump about on.

pogrom /ˈpɒɡrəm/ *n.* organized massacre (orig. of Jews in Russia).

poignant /ˈpɔɪnjənt/ *a.* painfully sharp, deeply moving; pleasantly piquant; arousing sympathy. **poignancy** *n.*

poinsettia /pɔɪnˈsetɪə/ *n.* plant with large scarlet bracts surrounding small yellowish flowers.

point 1 *n.* sharp end, tip, projection; very small mark on surface; particular place; stage or degree in progress or increase; precise moment; single item or particular; unit of scoring in games etc., or in evaluation etc.; significant thing, thing actually intended or under discussion; distinctive or salient feature; effectiveness, value; one of 32 directions marked on compass; (usu. in *pl.*) tapering movable rail to direct railway train from one line to another; power point; *Crick.* (position of) fielder near batsman on off side; promontory. **2** *v.* direct (finger, weapon, etc.) *at*; direct attention (as) by extending finger; aim or be directed; provide with point(s); give force to (words, action); fill joints of (brickwork etc.) with smoothed mortar or cement; (of dog) indicate presence of game by standing rigid looking towards it. **3 on the point of** on the verge of; **point-blank** with aim or weapon level, at close range, directly, flatly; **point-duty** (of policeman etc.) position at particular point to control traffic; **point of view** position from which thing is viewed, way of thinking about a matter; **point out** indicate, draw attention to; **point-to-point** horse-race over course defined only by landmarks; **point up** emphasize.

pointed /ˈpɔɪntɪd/ *a.* having point; (of remark etc.) cutting, emphasized.

pointer /ˈpɔɪntə(r)/ *n.* indicator on gauge etc.; rod used to point to words etc. on screen, blackboard, etc.; breed

of dog trained to point at game; *colloq.* hint.

pointless /ˈpɔɪntlɪs/ *a.* having no point; meaningless, purposeless.

poise /pɔɪz/ **1** *v.* balance or be balanced; hold suspended or supported. **2** *n.* equilibrium; composure; carriage (*of* head etc.).

poison /ˈpɔɪz(ə)n/ **1** *n.* substance that when absorbed by living organism kills or injures it; harmful influence. **2** *v.* administer poison to; kill or injure with poison; fill with prejudice; corrupt, pervert; spoil. **3 poison ivy** N. Amer. climbing plant secreting irritant oil from leaves; **poison pen** anonymous writer of scurrilous or libellous letters.

poke 1 *v.* push with (end of) finger, stick, etc.; stir (fire), make thrusts (*at* etc.) with stick etc.; thrust forward. **2** *n.* poking; thrust, nudge. **3 poke fun at** ridicule.

poker[1] /ˈpəʊkə(r)/ *n.* metal rod for poking fire.

poker[2] /ˈpəʊkə(r)/ *n.* card-game in which players bet on value of their hands. **poker-face** impassive countenance appropriate to poker-player, person with this.

poky /ˈpəʊkɪ/ *a.* (of room etc.) small and cramped.

polar /ˈpəʊlə(r)/ *a.* of or near either pole of earth; having electric or magnetic polarity; directly opposite in character. **polar bear** large white bear living in Arctic.

polarity /pəˈlærɪtɪ/ *n.* tendency of magnet etc. to point to earth's magnetic poles or of body to lie with axis in particular direction; possession of two poles having contrary qualities; electrical condition of body as positive or negative.

polarize /ˈpəʊləraɪz/ *v.* restrict vibrations of (light-waves etc.) so that they have different amplitudes in different planes; give polarity to; *fig.* divide into two opposing groups. **polarization** *n.*

pole[1] *n.* long slender rounded piece of wood or metal esp. as support for scaffolding, tent, etc.; measure of length (=**perch**[1]). **pole-jump, -vault,** vault over high bar with aid of pole held in hands.

pole[2] *n.* either end of earth's axis; either

of two points in celestial sphere about which stars appear to revolve; each of two opposite points on surface of magnet at which magnetic forces are concentrated; positive or negative terminal point of electric cell or battery etc.; each of two opposed principles etc. **pole-star** star near N. pole of heavens, thing serving as guide.

Pole³ *n.* native of Poland.

pole-axe 1 *n.* battle-axe; butcher's slaughtering axe. 2 *v.t.* kill or strike with pole-axe.

polecat /ˈpəʊlkæt/ *n.* small dark brown mammal of weasel family.

polemic /pəˈlemɪk/ 1 *n.* verbal attack; controversy. 2 *a.* controversial, involving dispute. 3 **polemical** *a.*

police /pəˈliːs/ 1 *n.* civil force responsible for maintaining public order; (as *pl.*) its members; similar force employed to enforce regulations etc. 2 *v.t.* control or provide with police; keep order in, control. 3 **police dog** dog trained and used by police to track criminals etc.; **policeman, police-officer, policewoman**, member of police force; **police state** totalitarian State regulated by esp. secret police; **police station** office of local police force.

policy¹ /ˈpɒlɪsɪ/ *n.* course of action adopted by government, party, etc.; prudent conduct.

policy² /ˈpɒlɪsɪ/ *n.* document containing contract of insurance.

polio /ˈpəʊlɪəʊ/ *n. colloq.* poliomyelitis.

poliomyelitis /ˌpəʊlɪəʊmaɪəˈlaɪtɪs/ *n.* infectious viral inflammation of nerve cells in spinal cord, with temporary or permanent paralysis.

polish¹ /ˈpɒlɪʃ/ 1 *v.* make or become smooth or glossy by rubbing; make elegant or cultured; smarten *up*; finish *off* quickly. 2 *n.* substance used to produce polished surface; smoothness, glossiness; refinement.

Polish² /ˈpəʊlɪʃ/ 1 *a.* of Poland. 2 *n.* language of Poland.

polite /pəˈlaɪt/ *a.* having refined manners, courteous; cultivated, cultured; refined, elegant.

politic /ˈpɒlɪtɪk/ *a.* judicious, expedient; sagacious, prudent.

political /pəˈlɪtɪk(ə)l/ *a.* of or taking part in politics; of State or its govern-

ment; of public affairs; relating to person's or organization's status etc. **political economy** study of economic problems of government; **political geography** that dealing with boundaries etc. of States; **political prisoner** person imprisoned for political offence.

politician /ˌpɒlɪˈtɪʃ(ə)n/ *n.* person engaged or interested in politics.

politicize /pəˈlɪtɪsaɪz/ *v.t.* give political character to.

politics /ˈpɒlɪtɪks/ *n.pl.* also treated as *sing.* science and art of government; political affairs or life or principles etc.

polity /ˈpɒlɪtɪ/ *n.* form of civil administration; organized society, State.

polka /ˈpɒlkə/ *n.* lively dance in duple time; music for this. **polka-dot** round dot as one of many forming regular pattern on textile fabric etc.

poll /pəʊl/ 1 *n.* voting; counting of voters; result of voting, number of votes recorded; questioning of sample of population to estimate trend of public opinion; head. 2 *v.* take votes of, vote, receive votes of; cut off top of (tree etc.) or horns of (cattle). 3 **polling-booth** place where vote is recorded at election; **poll-tax** tax levied on every person.

pollack /ˈpɒlək/ *n.* marine food-fish related to cod.

pollard /ˈpɒləd/ 1 *n.* tree polled to produce close head of young branches; hornless animal. 2 *v.t.* make pollard of (tree).

pollen /ˈpɒlən/ *n.* fertilizing powder discharged from flower's anther. **pollen count** index of amount of pollen in air.

pollinate /ˈpɒlɪneɪt/ *v.t.* sprinkle stigma of (flower) with pollen. **pollination** *n.*

pollock var. of **pollack**.

pollster /ˈpəʊlstə(r)/ *n.* person who organizes public opinion poll.

pollute /pəˈljuːt/ *v.t.* destroy purity of; contaminate or defile. **pollution** *n.*

polo /ˈpəʊləʊ/ *n.* game like hockey played on horseback. **polo-neck** high round turned-over collar.

polonaise /ˌpɒləˈneɪz/ *n.* slow processional dance; music for this.

polony /pəˈləʊnɪ/ *n.* kind of sausage.

poltergeist /ˈpɒltəgaɪst/ *n.* ghost

manifesting itself by noise, mischievous behaviour, etc.

poltroon /pɒlˈtruːn/ *n.* coward. **poltroonery** *n.*

poly- *in comb.* many.

polyandry /pɒlɪˈændrɪ/ *n.* polygamy in which one woman has more than one husband.

polyanthus /pɒlɪˈænθəs/ *n.* cultivated primula.

polychromatic /pɒlɪkrəʊˈmætɪk/ *a.* many-coloured.

polychrome /ˈpɒlɪkrəʊm/ **1** *a.* in many colours. **2** *n.* polychrome work of art.

polyester /pɒlɪˈestə(r)/ *n.* a synthetic resin or fibre.

polyethylene /pɒlɪˈeθɪliːn/ *n.* polythene.

polygamy /pəˈlɪgəmɪ/ *n.* practice of having more than one wife or husband at once. **polygamist** *n.*; **polygamous** *a.*

polyglot /ˈpɒlɪglɒt/ **1** *a.* knowing or using or written in several languages. **2** *n.* polyglot person.

polygon /ˈpɒlɪgən/ *n.* figure with many sides and angles. **polygonal** *a.*

polyhedron /pɒlɪˈhiːdrən/ *n.* (*pl.* **-dra**) solid figure with many faces. **polyhedral** *a.*

polymath /ˈpɒlɪmæθ/ *n.* person of varied learning, great scholar.

polymer /ˈpɒlɪmə(r)/ *n.* compound whose molecule is formed from many repeated units of one or more compounds. **polymeric** /-ˈmer-/ *a.*

polymerize /ˈpɒlɪməraɪz/ *v.* combine or be combined into polymer. **polymerization** *n.*

polyp /ˈpɒlɪp/ *n.* simple organism with tube-shaped body; small growth on mucous membrane.

polyphony /pəˈlɪfənɪ/ *n.* *Mus.* simultaneous combination of several individual melodies. **polyphonic** /-ˈfɒn-/ *a.*

polystyrene /pɒlɪˈstaɪriːn/ *n.* kind of hard plastic.

polysyllabic /pɒlɪsɪˈlæbɪk/ *a.* (of word) having many syllables; marked by polysyllables.

polysyllable /pɒlɪˈsɪləb(ə)l/ *n.* polysyllabic word.

polytechnic /pɒlɪˈteknɪk/ *n.* institution for higher education maintained by local authority and providing courses in esp. vocational subjects.

polytheism /ˈpɒlɪθiːɪz(ə)m/ *n.* belief in or worship of more than one god. **polytheist** *n.*; **polytheistic** *a.*

polythene /ˈpɒlɪθiːn/ *n.* a tough light plastic.

polyunsaturated /pɒlɪʌnˈsætʃəreɪtɪd/ *a.* of those kinds of fat or oil not associated with formation of cholesterol.

polyurethane /pɒlɪˈjʊərɪθeɪn/ *n.* a synthetic resin or plastic used esp. as foam.

polyvinyl chloride /pɒlɪˈvaɪnɪl/ *a* vinyl plastic used for insulation or as fabric.

pomade /pəˈmɑːd/ *n.* scented ointment for hair.

pomander /pəˈmændə(r)/ *n.* ball of mixed aromatic substances; container for this.

pomegranate /ˈpɒmɪgrænɪt/ *n.* large tough-rinded many-seeded fruit.

Pomeranian /pɒməˈreɪnɪən/ *n.* breed of small silky-haired dogs.

pommel /ˈpʌm(ə)l/ *n.* knob of sword-hilt; projecting front part of saddle.

pommy /ˈpɒmɪ/ *n.* *Aus.* & *NZ sl.* British person, esp. recent immigrant.

pomp *n.* splendour, splendid display; grandeur.

pom-pom[1] /ˈpɒmpɒm/ *n.* automatic quick-firing gun.

pom-pom[2] var. of **pompon**.

pompon /ˈpɒmpɒn/ *n.* decorative tuft or ball on hat or shoe etc.; small-flowered kind of chrysanthemum or dahlia.

pompous /ˈpɒmpəs/ *a.* showing self-importance; (of language) pretentious, unduly grand. **pomposity** /-ˈpɒs-/ *n.*

ponce 1 *n.* man who lives off prostitute's earnings; *sl.* effeminate man. **2** *v.i.* act as ponce; *sl.* move *about* effeminately.

poncho /ˈpɒntʃəʊ/ *n.* (*pl.* **-chos**) (orig. S. Amer.) cloak of rectangular piece of material with slit in middle for head.

pond *n.* small area of still water.

ponder /ˈpɒndə(r)/ *v.* think (*over*), muse.

ponderable /ˈpɒndərəb(ə)l/ *a.* having appreciable weight. **ponderability** *n.*

ponderous /ˈpɒndərəs/ *a.* heavy; unwieldy; dull, tedious. **ponderosity** *n.*

pong n. & v.i. colloq. stink.

poniard /'pɒnɪəd/ n. dagger.

pontiff /'pɒntɪf/ n. bishop; chief priest; Pope.

pontifical /pɒn'tɪfɪk(ə)l/ a. of or befitting pontiff; solemnly dogmatic.

pontificate 1 /pɒn'tɪfɪkeɪt/ v.i. speak or act pompously or dogmatically; officiate as bishop. 2 /pɒn'tɪfɪkət/ n. office of bishop or Pope; period of this.

pontoon¹ /pɒn'tuːn/ n. card-game in which players try to acquire cards with face-value totalling 21.

pontoon² /pɒn'tuːn/ n. flat-bottomed boat etc. as one of supports of temporary bridge.

pony /'pəʊnɪ/ n. horse of any small breed. **pony-tail** hair drawn back, tied, and hanging down behind head; **pony-trekking** travelling across country on ponies for pleasure.

poodle /'puːd(ə)l/ n. breed of dog with thick curling hair.

pooh /puː/ int. of contempt. **pooh-pooh** express contempt for, ridicule.

pool¹ /puːl/ n. small area of still water; puddle; deep place in river; swimming-pool.

pool² /puːl/ 1 n. common fund, e.g. of profits or of players' stakes in gambling; football pool; common supply of persons, vehicles, etc., for sharing by group; group of persons sharing duties etc.; arrangement between competing parties to fix prices and share business; game like billiards with usu. 16 balls. 2 v.t. put into common fund; share in common.

poop /puːp/ n. stern of ship; aftermost and highest deck.

poor /pʊə(r)/ a. having little money or means; deficient (in); inadequate; deserving pity; inferior; despicable; insignificant. **poor man's** inferior substitute for.

poorly /'pʊəlɪ/ 1 adv. in a poor manner; badly. 2 pred.a. unwell.

pop¹ 1 n. abrupt explosive sound; effervescing drink. 2 v. (cause to) make pop; go or come unexpectedly or suddenly; put quickly (in, down, etc.); sl. pawn. 3 adv. with sound of pop; suddenly. 4 **popcorn** maize which when heated bursts open to form fluffy balls; **pop-eyed** colloq. with eyes bulging or wide open; **popgun** toy gun shooting

pellet etc. by compressed air or spring.

popping-crease Crick. line in front of and parallel to wicket.

pop² 1 a. in popular modern style; performing or concerned with pop music. 2 n. pop music. 3 **pop music** music in popular modern style.

pop³ n. colloq. father.

pope n. bishop of Rome as head of RC Ch.

popery n. derog. papal system, RC religion.

popinjay /'pɒpɪndʒeɪ/ n. fop, conceited person.

popish /'pəʊpɪʃ/ a. derog. of popery.

poplar /'pɒplə(r)/ n. tree with straight trunk and often tremulous leaves.

poplin /'pɒplɪn/ n. closely-woven corded fabric.

poppadam /'pɒpədəm/ n. large thin crisp savoury Indian biscuit.

poppet /'pɒpɪt/ n. colloq. (esp. as term of endearment) small or dainty person.

poppy /'pɒpɪ/ n. plant with bright flowers and milky narcotic juice; artificial poppy worn on **Poppy Day** Remembrance Sunday.

poppycock /'pɒpɪkɒk/ n. sl. nonsense.

populace /'pɒpjʊləs/ n. the common people.

popular /'pɒpjʊlə(r)/ a. generally liked or admired; of or for the general public. **popularity** n.; **popularize** v.t.

populate /'pɒpjʊleɪt/ v.t. form population of; supply with inhabitants.

population /pɒpjʊ'leɪʃ(ə)n/ n. inhabitants of town, country, etc.; total number of these; degree to which place is populated.

populous /'pɒpjʊləs/ a. thickly inhabited.

porcelain /'pɔːsəlɪn/ n. fine earthenware, china; things made of this.

porch n. covered approach to entrance of building.

porcine /'pɔːsaɪn/ a. of or like pigs.

porcupine /'pɔːkjʊpaɪn/ n. rodent with body and tail covered with erectile spines.

pore¹ n. minute opening in surface through which fluids may pass.

pore² v.i. **pore over** be absorbed in studying (book etc.).

pork n. flesh of pig used as food.

porker /'pɔːkə(r)/ n. pig raised for pork.

pornography /pɔːˈnɒgrəfɪ/ n. explicit presentation of sexual activity in literature or films etc., to stimulate erotic rather than aesthetic feelings. **pornographer** n.; **pornographic** a.

porous /ˈpɔːrəs/ a. having pores; permeable. **porosity** n.

porphyry /ˈpɔːfɪrɪ/ n. hard rock with large crystals in fine-grained ground mass.

porpoise /ˈpɔːpəs/ n. sea mammal related to whale.

porridge /ˈpɒrɪdʒ/ n. oatmeal or other meal boiled in water or milk.

porringer /ˈpɒrɪndʒə(r)/ n. small soup-basin.

port¹ n. harbour; town or place possessing harbour.

port² n. strong sweet red fortified wine.

port³ 1 n. left-hand side of boat or aircraft etc. looking forward. 2 v. turn (helm) to port.

port⁴ n. opening in ship's side for entrance, loading, etc.; porthole. **porthole** (esp. glazed) aperture in ship's side to admit light and air.

port⁵ v.t. Mil. hold (rifle) diagonally in front of body.

portable /ˈpɔːtəb(ə)l/ a. that can be carried about, movable. **portability** n.

portage /ˈpɔːtɪdʒ/ n. carrying of boats or goods between two navigable waters.

portal /ˈpɔːt(ə)l/ n. gate; doorway.

portcullis /pɔːtˈkʌlɪs/ n. strong heavy grating raised and lowered in grooves as defence of gateway.

portend /pɔːˈtend/ v.t. foreshadow, as an omen; give warning of.

portent /ˈpɔːtent/ n. omen, significant sign; prodigy.

portentous /pɔːˈtentəs/ a. of or like portent; solemn; pompous.

porter¹ /ˈpɔːtə(r)/ n. person employed to carry luggage etc.; dark beer brewed from charred or browned malt. **porterhouse steak** a choice cut of beef.

porter² /ˈpɔːtə(r)/ n. gate-keeper or door-keeper, esp. of large building.

porterage /ˈpɔːtərɪdʒ/ n. hire of porters.

portfolio /pɔːtˈfəʊlɪəʊ/ n. (pl. -lios) case for loose drawings, sheets of paper, etc.; list of investments held by investor etc.; office of minister of State.

Minister without portfolio one not in charge of any department of State.

portico /ˈpɔːtɪkəʊ/ n. (pl. -coes) colonnade serving as porch to building.

portion /ˈpɔːʃ(ə)n/ 1 n. part allotted, share; helping; dowry; destiny or lot. 2 v.t. divide into portions, share out; give dowry to.

Portland n. **Portland cement** cement manufactured from chalk and clay; **Portland stone** valuable building limestone.

portly /ˈpɔːtlɪ/ a. corpulent and dignified.

portmanteau /pɔːtˈmæntəʊ/ n. (pl. -teaus) case for clothes etc. opening into two equal parts. **portmanteau word** invented word combining sounds and meanings of two others.

portrait /ˈpɔːtrɪt/ n. likeness of person or animal made by drawing or painting or photography; graphic description.

portraiture /ˈpɔːtrɪtʃə(r)/ n. portraying; portrait; graphic description.

portray /pɔːˈtreɪ/ v.t. make likeness of; describe. **portrayal** n.

Portuguese /pɔːtjʊˈgiːz/ 1 a. of Portugal. 2 n. native or language of Portugal.

pose /pəʊz/ 1 v. assume attitude, esp. for artistic purpose; set up, give oneself out, as; propound (question, problem); arrange in required attitude. 2 n. attitude of body or mind; affectation or pretence.

poser /ˈpəʊzə(r)/ n. puzzling question or problem.

poseur /pəʊˈzɜː(r)/ n. (fem. -seuse /-ˈzɜːz/) person who poses for effect.

posh a. colloq. smart, stylish; high-class.

posit /ˈpɒzɪt/ v.t. assume as fact, postulate.

position /pəˈzɪʃ(ə)n/ 1 n. place occupied by person or thing; proper place; way thing is placed; mental attitude; state of affairs; situation; rank or status; paid (official or domestic) employment; strategic point. 2 v.t. place in position. 3 **positional** a.

positive /ˈpɒzɪtɪv/ 1 a. formally or explicitly stated, definite, unquestionable; confident in opinion, cocksure; absolute, not relative; constructive; not negative; dealing only with matters of fact, practical; Alg. (of quantity) greater than zero; *Electr.* of, containing, producing, kind of charge produced by rubbing glass with silk; *Gram.* (of adj. etc.) expressing simple quality without comparison; *Photog.* showing lights and shades as seen in original image cast on film etc. **2** *n.* positive adjective, quantity, photograph, etc. **3 positive vetting** intensive enquiry into background etc. of candidate for senior post in civil service etc.

positivism /'pɒzɪtɪvɪz(ə)m/ *n.* philosophical system recognizing only positive facts and observable phenomena. **positivist** *n. & a.*; **positivistic** *a.*

positron /'pɒzɪtrɒn/ *n.* elementary particle with mass of electron and charge same as electron's but positive.

posse /'pɒsɪ/ *n.* body (*of* constables); strong force or company.

possess /pə'zes/ *v.t.* hold as property; own, have; (of demon etc.) occupy, dominate mind of. **possessor** *n.*

possession /pə'zeʃ(ə)n/ *n.* possessing or being possessed; thing possessed; occupancy; in *pl.* property.

possessive /pə'zesɪv/ **1** *a.* showing desire to possess or retain what one possesses; *Gram.* of or indicating possession. **2** *n. Gram.* possessive case or word.

possibility /pɒsɪ'bɪlɪtɪ/ *n.* state or fact of being possible; thing that may exist or happen.

possible /'pɒsɪb(ə)l/ **1** *a.* that can exist, be done, or happen; that may be or become. **2** *n.* possible candidate, member of team, etc.; highest possible score.

possibly /'pɒsɪblɪ/ *adv.* in accordance with possibility; perhaps, maybe.

possum /'pɒsəm/ *n. colloq.* opossum. **play possum** pretend to be unconscious.

post¹ /pəʊst/ **1** *n.* upright of timber or metal as support in building; stake or stout pole to mark boundary, carry notices, etc.; pole etc. marking start or finish in race. **2** *v.t.* (also with *up*) display (notice etc.) in prominent place; advertise by placard or in published list.

post² /pəʊst/ **1** *n.* official conveying of letters and parcels; single collection or delivery of these; place where letters etc. are dealt with. **2** *v.* put (letter etc.)

into post; supply with latest information; enter in ledger. **3 post-box** box for posting letters; **postcard** card conveying message by post without envelope; **postcode** group of letters and figures in postal address to assist sorting; **post-haste** with great speed; **postman** person who collects or delivers post; **postmark** official mark stamped on letters; **postmaster**, **postmistress**, official in charge of post office; **post office** room or building for postal business; **Post Office** public department or corporation providing postal etc. services.

post³ **1** *n.* situation of paid employment; appointed place of soldier etc. on duty; fort, trading-station. **2** *v.t.* place (soldier etc.) at his post, appoint to post or command.

post- *in comb.* after, behind.

postage /'pəʊstɪdʒ/ *n.* amount charged for sending letter etc. by post. **postage stamp** small adhesive label indicating amount of postage paid.

postal /'pəʊst(ə)l/ *a.* of or by post. **postal order** kind of money order issued by Post Office.

postdate /pəʊst'deɪt/ *v.t.* follow in time; give later than true date to.

poster /'pəʊstə(r)/ *n.* placard in public place; large printed picture.

poste restante /pəʊst re'stɑ̃t/ department in post office where letters are kept till called for.

posterior /pɒs'tɪərɪə(r)/ **1** *a.* hinder; later in time or order. **2** *n.* buttocks.

posterity /pɒs'terɪtɪ/ *n.* later generations; descendants.

postern /'pɒst(ə)n/ *n.* back or side entrance.

postgraduate /pəʊst'grædjʊət/ **1** *a.* (of course of study) carried on after taking first degree. **2** *n.* student taking such course.

posthumous /'pɒstjʊməs/ *a.* occurring after death; published after author's death; born after father's death.

postilion /pəs'tɪljən/ *n.* rider on near horse drawing coach etc. without coachman.

Post-Impressionism /pəʊst-/ *n.* artistic aims and methods directed to expressing individual artist's conception of objects represented. **Post-Impressionist** *n. & a.*

post-mortem /pəʊst'mɔːtəm/ 1 *n.* examination of body made after death; *colloq.* discussion after conclusion (of game etc.). 2 *a.* & *adv.* after death.

postnatal /pəʊst'neɪt(ə)l/ *a.* existing or occurring etc. after birth.

postpone /pəʊst'pəʊn/ *v.t.* cause to take place at later time. **postponement** *n.*

postscript /'pəʊstskrɪpt/ *n.* addition at end of letter etc. after signature.

postulant /'pɒstjʊlənt/ *n.* candidate esp. for admission to religious order.

postulate 1 /'pɒstjʊleɪt/ *v.t.* assume or require to be true; claim; take for granted. 2 /'pɒstjʊlət/ *n.* thing postulated.

posture /'pɒstʃə(r)/ 1 *n.* attitude of body or mind; relative position of parts esp. of body; condition or state (of affairs etc.). 2 *v.i.* assume posture esp. for effect.

post-war /pəʊst-/ *a.* occurring or existing after a war.

posy /'pəʊzɪ/ *n.* small bunch of flowers.

pot[1] 1 *n.* vessel of earthenware or metal or glass etc.; chamber-pot; teapot; contents of pot; *colloq.* large sum, cup, etc. won as prize; pot-belly. 2 *v.t.* plant in pot; pocket (ball) in billiards etc.; shoot; bag (game etc.); abridge, epitomize; preserve (food) in sealed pot. 3 **go to pot** *colloq.* be ruined; **pot-belly** protuberant belly; **pot-boiler** work of literature etc. done merely to earn money; **pot-herb** herb used in cooking; **pot-hole** deep cylindrical hole in rock, rough hole in road-surface; **pot luck** whatever is available; **pot-roast** braise, (*n.*) braised meat; **potsherd** piece of broken earthenware; **pot-shot** random shot.

pot[2] *n. sl.* marijuana.

potable /'pəʊtəb(ə)l/ *a.* drinkable.

potash /'pɒtæʃ/ *n.* potassium carbonate.

potassium /pə'tæsɪəm/ *n.* soft silver-white metallic element.

potation /pə'teɪʃ(ə)n/ *n.* drinking; a drink.

potato /pə'teɪtəʊ/ *n.* (*pl.* **-toes**) plant with tubers used as food; its tuber.

poteen /pɒ'tiːn/ *n. Ir.* whisky from illicit still.

potent /'pəʊt(ə)nt/ *a.* powerful; strong;

cogent; influential; (of a man) able to procreate. **potency** *n.*

potentate /'pəʊtənteɪt/ *n.* monarch, ruler.

potential /pə'tenʃ(ə)l/ 1 *a.* capable of coming into being. 2 *n.* capability for use or development; usable resources; quantity determining energy of mass in gravitational field or of charge in electric field etc. 3 **potentiality** *n.*

potheen var. of **poteen**.

pother /'pɒðə(r)/ *n.* fuss; din.

potion /'pəʊʃ(ə)n/ *n.* draught of medicine or poison.

pot-pourri /pəʊpʊ'riː/ *n.* scented mixture of dried petals and spices; musical or literary medley.

pottage /'pɒtɪdʒ/ *n. arch.* soup or stew.

potter[1] /'pɒtə(r)/ *v.i.* move (*about* etc.), work, etc. in aimless or desultory manner.

potter[2] /'pɒtə(r)/ *n.* maker of earthenware vessels.

pottery /'pɒtərɪ/ *n.* vessels etc. made of baked clay; potter's work or workshop.

potty[1] /'pɒtɪ/ *a. sl.* crazy; insignificant.

potty[2] /'pɒtɪ/ *n. colloq.* chamber-pot, esp. for child.

pouch /paʊtʃ/ 1 *n.* small bag; detachable pocket; baglike receptacle in which marsupials carry undeveloped young, other baglike natural receptacle. 2 *v.* put into pouch; take shape of or hang like pouch.

pouffe /puːf/ *n.* low stuffed seat or cushion.

poulterer /'pəʊltərə(r)/ *n.* dealer in poultry and usu. game.

poultice /'pəʊltɪs/ 1 *n.* soft usu. hot dressing applied to sore or inflamed part of body. 2 *v.t.* apply poultice to.

poultry /'pəʊltrɪ/ *n.* domestic fowls.

pounce /paʊns/ 1 *v.i.* make sudden attack (*up*)*on*; seize eagerly (*up*)*on*. 2 *n.* pouncing; sudden swoop.

pound[1] /paʊnd/ *n.* unit of weight equal to 16 oz. (454g.); monetary unit of UK (**pound sterling**) and some other countries.

pound[2] /paʊnd/ *v.* crush or beat with repeated strokes; thump, pummel; walk or run etc. heavily.

pound[3] /paʊnd/ *n.* enclosure where stray animals or officially removed vehicles etc. are kept until claimed.

poundage /'paʊndɪdʒ/ *n.* commission

or fee of so much per pound sterling or weight.

pounder /'paʊndə(r)/ n. thing that, or gun carrying shell that, weighs a pound or (-**pounder**) so many pounds (e.g. *six-pounder*).

pour /pɔː(r)/ v. (cause to) flow in stream or shower; rain heavily; discharge copiously.

pout /paʊt/ 1 v. protrude lips, (of lips etc.) protrude, esp. as sign of displeasure. 2 n. pouting expression.

pouter /'paʊtə(r)/ n. kind of pigeon with great power of inflating crop.

poverty /'pɒvətɪ/ n. being poor; want, scarcity or lack; inferiority, poorness. **poverty-stricken** poor; **poverty trap** situation in which increase of income incurs greater loss of State benefits.

POW abbr. prisoner of war.

powder /'paʊdə(r)/ 1 n. mass of fine dry particles; cosmetic or medicine in this form; gunpowder. 2 v. apply powder to; reduce to powder. 3 **powder blue** soft pale blue; **powder-puff** soft pad for applying cosmetic powder to skin; **powder-room** ladies' lavatory. 4 **powdery** a.

power /'paʊə(r)/ 1 n. ability to do or act; vigour, energy; control, influence, ascendancy; authority; influential person etc.; State with international influence; capacity for exerting mechanical force; electricity supply; *Math.* product obtained by multiplying a number by itself a specified number of times; magnifying capacity of lens. 2 v.t. supply with mechanical or electrical energy. 3 **power cut** temporary withdrawal or failure of electric power supply; **powerhouse** power-station, *fig.* source of drive or energy; **power-point** socket for connection of electrical appliance etc. to mains; **power-station** building etc. where electric power is generated for distribution.

powerful /'paʊəfʊl/ a. having great power or influence.

powerless /'paʊəlɪs/ a. without power; wholly unable (*to*).

pow-wow /'paʊwaʊ/ n. conference or meeting for discussion (orig. among N. Amer. Indians).

pox n. virus disease with pocks; *colloq.* syphilis.

pp. abbr. pages.

p.p. abbr. per pro.

pp abbr. pianissimo.

PPS abbr. Parliamentary Private Secretary; further postscript (*post postscriptum*).

PR proportional representation; public relations.

practicable /'præktɪkəb(ə)l/ a. that can be done or used etc. **practicability** n.

practical /'præktɪk(ə)l/ a. of or concerned with or shown in practice; inclined to action; able to do functional things well; that is such in effect though not in name, virtual. **practical joke** trick played on person. **practicality** n.

practically adv. virtually, almost; in a practical way.

practice /'præktɪs/ n. habitual action; established method; exercise to improve skill; action as opposed to theory; lawyer's or doctor's professional business. **in practice** in the realm of action, skilled by having recently had practice; **out of practice** no longer having former skill. □ See page 666.

practise /'præktɪs/ v. carry out in action; do repeatedly to improve skill; exercise oneself in or on; pursue profession; (in *p.p.*) expert. □ See page 666.

practitioner /præk'tɪʃənə(r)/ n. professional worker, esp. in medicine.

praetorian guard /prɪ'tɔːrɪən/ bodyguard of Roman emperor etc.

pragmatic /præg'mætɪk/ a. dealing with matters from a practical point of view; treating facts of history with reference to their practical lessons.

pragmatism /'prægmətɪz(ə)m/ n. matter-of-fact treatment of things; *Philos.* doctrine that evaluates assertions solely by practical consequences. **pragmatist** n.

prairie /'preərɪ/ n. large treeless tract of grassland esp. in N. Amer.

praise /preɪz/ 1 v.t. express warm approval of; commend; glorify. 2 n. praising; commendation. 3 **praiseworthy** worthy of praise.

praline /'prɑːliːn/ n. sweet made of almonds etc. browned in boiling sugar.

pram n. carriage for baby, pushed by person on foot.

prance /prɑːns/ 1 v.i. walk or move in

elated or arrogant manner; (of horse) spring from hind legs. **2** n. prancing; prancing movement.

prank n. practical joke.

prat n. sl. fool; buttocks.

prate v.i. chatter foolishly; talk too much.

prattle 1 v.i. talk in childish or artless way. **2** n. prattling talk.

prawn n. edible shellfish like large shrimp.

pray v. say prayers; make devout supplication (to); ask earnestly (for).

prayer /preə(r)/ n. solemn request or thanksgiving to God or object of worship; formula used in praying; entreaty. **prayer-book** book of forms of prayer, esp. liturgy of Church of England; **prayer-mat** small carpet used by Muslims when praying.

pre- pref. before (in time, place, order, or importance), freely used with Eng. words, only the more important of which are given below.

preach /priːtʃ/ v. deliver sermon; proclaim (the Gospel etc.); give obtrusive moral advice; advocate, inculcate.

preamble /priˈæmb(ə)l/ n. introductory part of statute, deed, etc.

pre-arrange /priəˈreɪndʒ/ v.t. arrange beforehand. **pre-arrangement** n.

prebend /ˈprebənd/ n. stipend of canon or member of chapter; portion of land etc. from which this is drawn. **prebendal** a.

prebendary /ˈprebəndərɪ/ n. holder of prebend; honorary canon.

precarious /prɪˈkeərɪəs/ a. uncertain; dependent on chance; perilous.

pre-cast /priːˈkɑːst/ a. (of concrete) cast in blocks before use.

precaution /prɪˈkɔːʃ(ə)n/ n. action taken beforehand to avoid risk or ensure good result. **precautionary** a.

precede /prɪˈsiːd/ v.t. come or go before in importance or place or time; cause to be preceded by.

precedence /ˈpresɪd(ə)ns/ n. priority; right of preceding others.

precedent /ˈpresɪd(ə)nt/ n. previous case taken as example or justification etc.

precentor /prɪˈsentə(r)/ n. member of cathedral clergy in general charge of music there.

precept /ˈpriːsept/ n. rule for action or conduct; writ, warrant.

preceptor /prɪˈseptə(r)/ n. teacher, instructor. **preceptorial** a.

precession /prɪˈseʃ(ə)n/ n. change by which equinoxes occur earlier in each successive sidereal year.

precinct /ˈpriːsɪŋkt/ n. space within boundaries of place or building; district in town where traffic is excluded; in pl. environs.

preciosity /preʃɪˈɒsɪtɪ/ n. overrefinement in art.

precious /ˈpreʃəs/ **1** a. of great price; valuable, highly valued; affectedly refined. **2** adv. colloq. extremely, very.

precipice /ˈpresɪpɪs/ n. vertical steep face of rock, cliff, mountain, etc.

precipitance /prɪˈsɪpɪt(ə)ns/ n. (also **precipitancy**) rash haste.

precipitate 1 /prɪˈsɪpɪteɪt/ v.t. hasten occurrence of; cause to go hurriedly or violently; throw down headlong; Chem. cause (substance) to be deposited in solid form from solution; Phys. condense (vapour) into drops. **2** /prɪˈsɪpɪtət/ a. headlong; rash; done too soon. **3** /prɪˈsɪpɪtət/ n. solid matter precipitated; moisture condensed from vapour.

precipitation /prɪsɪpɪˈteɪʃ(ə)n/ n. precipitating or being precipitated; rash haste; rain, snow, etc., falling to ground.

precipitous /prɪˈsɪpɪtəs/ a. of or like precipice; steep.

précis /ˈpreɪsiː/ **1** n. (pl. same) summary, abstract. **2** v.t. make précis of.

precise /prɪˈsaɪs/ a. accurately worded; definite, exact; punctilious.

precisely adv. in precise manner; in exact terms; quite so.

precision /prɪˈsɪʒ(ə)n/ n. accuracy; attrib. designed for exact work.

preclude /prɪˈkluːd/ v.t. prevent; make impossible.

precocious /prɪˈkəʊʃəs/ a. prematurely developed in some faculty or characteristic. **precocity** /-ˈkɒs-/ n.

precognition /priːkəgˈnɪʃ(ə)n/ n. (esp. supernatural) foreknowledge.

preconceive /priːkənˈsiːv/ v.t. form (opinion etc.) beforehand.

preconception /priːkənˈsepʃ(ə)n/ n. preconceiving; prejudice.

pre-condition /priːkənˈdɪʃ(ə)n/ n. condition that must be fulfilled beforehand.

precursor /priːˈkɜːsə(r)/ n. forerunner, harbinger; person who precedes in office etc.

predacious /prɪˈdeɪʃəs/ a. (of animal) predatory.

pre-date /priːˈdeɪt/ v.t. antedate.

predator /ˈpredətə(r)/ n. predatory animal.

predatory /ˈpredətərɪ/ a. (of animal) preying naturally on others; plundering or exploiting others.

predecease /priːdɪˈsiːs/ v.t. die before (another).

predecessor /ˈpriːdɪsesə(r)/ n. former holder of office or position; thing to which another has succeeded.

predestine /priːˈdestɪn/ v.t. determine or appoint beforehand; ordain by divine will or as if by fate. **predestination** n.

predetermine /priːdɪˈtɜːmɪn/ v.t. decree beforehand, predestine. **predetermination** n.

predicable /ˈpredɪkəb(ə)l/ a. that can be predicated or affirmed.

predicament /prɪˈdɪkəmənt/ n. difficult or unpleasant situation.

predicate 1 /ˈpredɪkeɪt/ v.t. assert, affirm, as true or existent. 2 /ˈpredɪkət/ n. what is predicated; *Gram.* what is said about subject of sentence. 3 **predication** n.

predicative /prɪˈdɪkətɪv/ a. *Gram.* (of adjective or noun) forming part or all of predicate.

predict /prɪˈdɪkt/ v.t. forecast; prophesy. **prediction** n.; **predictive** a.

predilection /priːdɪˈlekʃ(ə)n/ n. preference or special liking (*for*).

predispose /priːdɪsˈpəʊz/ v.t. render liable or inclined (*to*) beforehand. **predisposition** n.

predominate /prɪˈdɒmɪneɪt/ v.i. have chief power or influence; prevail; preponderate. **predominance** n.; **predominant** a.

pre-eminent /priːˈemɪnənt/ a. excelling others. **pre-eminence** n.

pre-empt /priːˈempt/ v.t. obtain by pre-emption; forestall.

pre-emption /priːˈempʃ(ə)n/ n. purchase of thing before it is offered to others; right to first refusal.

pre-emptive /priːˈemptɪv/ a. pre-empting; *Mil.* intended to prevent attack by disabling threatening enemy.

preen v.t. (of bird) trim (feathers) with beak; (of person) smarten (*oneself*). **preen oneself** show self-satisfaction.

pre-exist /priːɪgˈzɪst/ v.i. exist previously. **pre-existence** n.; **pre-existent** a.

prefab /ˈpriːfæb/ n. *colloq.* prefabricated building.

prefabricate /priːˈfæbrɪkeɪt/ v.t. manufacture sections of (building etc.) prior to assembly on a site. **prefabrication** n.

preface /ˈprefəs/ 1 n. introduction to book stating subject, scope, etc.; preliminary part of speech etc. 2 v.t. introduce or begin (as) with preface. 3 **prefatory** /ˈpref-/ a.

prefect /ˈpriːfekt/ n. chief administrative officer of certain departments in France etc.; senior pupil in school, authorized to maintain discipline. **prefectorial** a.

prefecture /ˈpriːfektjʊə(r)/ n. district under government of prefect; prefect's office or tenure.

prefer /prɪˈfɜː(r)/ v.t. choose rather, like better; submit (accusation etc. *against* offender); promote *to* office.

preferable /ˈprefərəb(ə)l/ □ See page 665. a. to be preferred, more desirable.

preference /ˈprefərəns/ n. preferring, thing preferred; favouring of one person etc. before others; prior right.

preferential /prefəˈrenʃ(ə)l/ a. of or giving or receiving preference.

preferment /prɪˈfɜːmənt/ n. promotion to office.

prefigure /priːˈfɪgə(r)/ v.t. represent or imagine beforehand.

prefix /ˈpriːfɪks/ 1 n. verbal element placed at beginning of word to qualify meaning; title placed before name. 2 v.t. add as introduction; join as prefix (*to* word).

pregnant /ˈpregnənt/ a. (of woman or female animal) having developing child or young in womb; significant, suggestive; plentifully furnished *with* (consequences etc.); fruitful in results. **pregnancy** n.

prehensile /prɪˈhensaɪl/ a. (of tail or limb etc.) capable of grasping.

prehistoric /priːhɪsˈtɒrɪk/ a. of period before written records. **prehistory** n.

prejudge /priːˈdʒʌdʒ/ v.t. pass judgement on before trial or proper inquiry. **prejudgement** n.

prejudice /ˈpredʒʊdɪs/ 1 n. preconceived opinion, bias; injury or detriment resulting from action or judgement. 2 v.t. impair validity of; cause (person) to have prejudice. 3 **prejudicial** /-ˈdɪʃ-/ a.

prelacy /ˈpreləsɪ/ n. church government by prelates; prelates collectively; office or rank of prelate.

prelate /ˈprelət/ n. high ecclesiastical dignitary, e.g. bishop.

preliminary /prɪˈlɪmɪnərɪ/ 1 a. preparatory, introductory. 2 n. (usu. in pl.) preliminary step or arrangement. 3 adv. preparatory.

prelude /ˈpreljuːd/ 1 n. action or event etc. serving as introduction (to); Mus. introductory movement or first piece of suite, short piece of music of similar type. 2 v.t. serve as prelude to, introduce (with prelude).

pre-marital /priːˈmærɪt(ə)l/ a. occurring etc. before marriage.

premature /ˈpremətjʊə(r)/ a. occurring or done before right or usual time; too hasty; (of baby) born 3-12 weeks before expected time. **prematurity** n.

premedication /priːmedɪˈkeɪʃ(ə)n/ n. medication in preparation for operation.

premeditate /priːˈmedɪteɪt/ v.t. (esp. in p.p.) think out or plan beforehand. **premeditation** n.

pre-menstrual /priːˈmenstrʊəl/ a. of the time immediately before menstruation.

premier /ˈpremɪə(r)/ 1 a. first in importance or order or time. 2 n. prime minister.

première /ˈpremɪeə(r)/ 1 n. first performance or showing of play, film, etc. 2 v.t. give premiere of.

premise /ˈpremɪs/ n. premiss; in pl. house or building with grounds etc.; in pl. Law the aforesaid houses, lands, or tenements. **on the premises** in the house etc. concerned.

premiss /ˈpremɪs/ n. previous statement from which another is inferred.

premium /ˈpriːmɪəm/ n. amount to be paid for contract of insurance; sum added to interest, wages, etc.; reward, prize. **at a premium** above nominal or usual price, fig. highly valued; **Premium (Savings) Bond** government security not bearing interest but with periodical chance of prize.

premonition /priːməˈnɪʃ(ə)n/ n. forewarning; presentiment. **premonitory** /-ˈmɒn-/ a.

pre-natal /priːˈneɪt(ə)l/ a. existing or occurring before birth.

preoccupation /priːɒkjʊˈpeɪʃ(ə)n/ n. state of being preoccupied; thing that engages one's mind.

preoccupy /priːˈɒkjʊpaɪ/ v.t. dominate or engross mind of.

pre-ordain /priːɔːˈdeɪn/ v.t. ordain or determine beforehand.

prep n. colloq. preparation of school work; time when this is done.

preparation /prepəˈreɪʃ(ə)n/ n. preparing or being prepared; substance specially prepared; work done by school pupils to prepare for lesson; (usu. in pl.) thing done to make ready.

preparatory /prɪˈpærətərɪ/ 1 a. serving to prepare; introductory. 2 adv. as a preparation (with to). 3 **preparatory school** where pupils are prepared for higher school or (US) for college.

prepare /prɪˈpeə(r)/ v. make or get ready; get oneself ready.

prepay /priːˈpeɪ/ v. (past & p.p. -paid) pay (charge) beforehand; pay postage on beforehand. **prepayment** n.

preponderate /prɪˈpɒndəreɪt/ v.i. be superior in influence, quantity, or number; be heavier. **preponderance** n.; **preponderant** a.

preposition /prepəˈzɪʃ(ə)n/ n. word governing (and normally preceding) noun or pronoun, expressing latter's relation to another word. **prepositional** a.

prepossess /priːpəˈzes/ v.t. take possession of; prejudice, usu. favourably. **prepossessing** a.; **prepossession** n.

preposterous /prɪˈpɒstərəs/ a. utterly absurd; perverse; contrary to reason.

prepuce /ˈpriːpjuːs/ n. foreskin.

Pre-Raphaelite /priːˈræfəlaɪt/ n. member of group of 19th-c. Eng. artists.

prerequisite /priːˈrekwɪzɪt/ 1 a. required as previous condition. 2 n. prerequisite thing.

prerogative /prɪˈrɒgətɪv/ n. right or privilege exclusive to individual or class.

Pres. abbr. President.

presage /ˈprɛsɪdʒ/ 1 n. omen; presentiment. 2 (also /prɪˈseɪdʒ/) v.t. portend; foretell, foresee.

presbyter /ˈprɛzbɪtə(r)/ n. priest of Episcopal Church; elder of Presbyterian Church.

Presbyterian /prɛzbɪˈtɪərɪən/ 1 a. (of church) governed by elders all of equal rank, esp. national Church of Scotland. 2 n. member of Presbyterian church. 3 **Presbyterianism** n.

presbytery /ˈprɛzbɪtərɪ/ n. body of presbyters, esp. court next above kirk-session; eastern part of chancel; RC priest's house.

prescient /ˈprɛsɪənt/ a. having fore-knowledge or foresight. **prescience** n.

prescribe /prɪˈskraɪb/ v.t. lay down authoritatively; advise use of (medicine etc.).

prescript /ˈpriːskrɪpt/ n. ordinance, command.

prescription /prɪˈskrɪpʃ(ə)n/ n. prescribing; physician's (usu. written) direction for composition and use of medicine, medicine thus prescribed.

prescriptive /prɪˈskrɪptɪv/ a. prescribing; laying down rules; based on prescription; preserved by custom.

presence /ˈprɛz(ə)ns/ n. being present; place where person is; personal appearance; person or thing that is present.

present[1] /ˈprɛz(ə)nt/ 1 a. being in place in question; now existing or occurring or being dealt with etc.; Gram. denoting present action etc. 2 n. the present time; present tense. 3 **at present** now; **for the present** for this time, just now.

present[2] /ˈprɛz(ə)nt/ n. gift.

present[3] /prɪˈzɛnt/ v.t. introduce; exhibit; hold out; offer, deliver, give. **present arms** hold rifle etc. in saluting position; **present person with** present to him, cause him to have.

presentable /prɪˈzɛntəb(ə)l/ a. of decent appearance; fit to be shown. **presentability** n.

presentation /prɛzənˈteɪʃ(ə)n/ n. presenting or being presented; thing presented.

presentiment /prɪˈzɛntɪmənt/ n. vague expectation, foreboding.

presently /ˈprɛz(ə)ntlɪ/ adv. before long; US & Sc. at present.

preservative /prɪˈzɜːvətɪv/ 1 n. substance for preserving food etc. 2 a. tending to preserve.

preserve /prɪˈzɜːv/ 1 v.t. keep safe; keep alive; maintain, retain; keep from decay; treat (food etc.) to prevent decomposition or fermentation; keep (game etc.) undisturbed for private use. 2 n. preserved fruit, jam; place where game etc. is preserved; fig. sphere regarded by person as being for him alone. 3 **preservation** /prɛzəˈveɪʃ(ə)n/ n.

pre-shrink /ˈpriːʃrɪŋk/ v.t. treat (fabric, garment) so as to shrink during manufacture, not after.

preside /prɪˈzaɪd/ v.i. be chairman or president; exercise control or authority.

presidency /ˈprɛzɪdənsɪ/ n. office of president; period of this.

president /ˈprɛzɪd(ə)nt/ n. elected head of republic; head of college or council or company etc.; person presiding over meetings and proceedings of society etc. **presidential** /-den-/ a.

presidium /prɪˈzɪdɪəm/ n. standing committee esp. in Communist organization.

press[1] 1 v. apply steady force to; squeeze; flatten, shape, take out (crease etc.), smooth (esp. clothes), etc. thus; exert pressure (on); be urgent, urge; crowd; hasten, urge one's way, on etc.; force (offer etc.) on. 2 n. pressing; device for compressing, flattening, extracting juice, etc.; machine for printing; the newspapers; printing-house; publishing company; crowding, crowd; pressure of affairs etc.; large usu. shelved cupboard for clothes, books, etc. 3 **press agent** person employed to attend to advertising and press publicity; **press conference** meeting with journalists; **press cutting** article, review, etc. cut from newspaper etc.; **press-gallery** gallery for reporters, esp. in legislative assembly; **press-stud** small device fastened by pressing to engage two parts; **press-up** (usu. in pl.) exercise in which prone body is raised by pressing down on hands to straighten arms.

press² *v.t. hist.* force to serve in army or navy; bring into use as makeshift. **press-gang** body of men employed to press men for navy; (*v.t.*) force into service.

pressing /'presɪŋ/ **1** *a.* urgent; insistent. **2** *n.* thing made by pressing, esp. gramophone record; series of records made at one time.

pressure /'preʃə(r)/ **1** *n.* exertion of continuous force, force so exerted, amount of this; urgency; constraining or compelling influence. **2** *v.t.* apply pressure to, coerce, persuade. **3** **pressure-cooker** apparatus for cooking under high pressure in short time; **pressure group** group seeking to influence policy by concerted action.

pressurize /'preʃəraɪz/ *v.t.* raise to high pressure; (esp. in *p.p.*) maintain normal atmospheric pressure in (aircraft cabin etc.) at high altitude.

prestidigitator /prestɪ'dɪdʒɪteɪtə(r)/ *n.* conjuror. **prestidigitation** *n.*

prestige /pres'tiːʒ/ **1** *n.* influence or reputation. **2** *a.* having or conferring prestige.

prestigious /pres'tɪdʒəs/ *a.* having or showing prestige.

presto /'prestəʊ/ *Mus.* **1** *adv.* in quick tempo. **2** *n.* (*pl.* **-tos**) movement etc. to be played thus.

pre-stressed /priː'strest/ *a.* (of concrete) strengthened by means of stretched wires etc. in it.

presumably /prɪ'zjuːməblɪ/ *adv.* it is or may reasonably be presumed.

presume /prɪ'zjuːm/ *v.* suppose to be true; take for granted; venture (*to*); be presumptuous. **presume upon** make unscrupulous use of.

presumption /prɪ'zʌmpʃ(ə)n/ *n.* arrogance, presumptuous behaviour; taking for granted; thing presumed to be true; ground for presuming.

presumptive /prɪ'zʌmptɪv/ *a.* giving ground for presumption.

presumptuous /prɪ'zʌmptjʊəs/ *a.* unduly confident, arrogant.

presuppose /priːsə'pəʊz/ *v.t.* assume beforehand; imply. **presupposition** /ˌzɪʃ-/ *n.*

pre-tax /priː'tæks/ *a.* (of income) before deduction of taxes.

pretence /prɪ'tens/ *n.* pretending, make-believe; pretext; claim; ostentation.

pretend /prɪ'tend/ *v.* claim or assert falsely; imagine in play; in *p.p.* falsely claimed to be. **pretend** to profess to have.

pretender *n.* person who claims throne or title etc.

pretension /prɪ'tenʃ(ə)n/ *n.* assertion of claim; pretentiousness.

pretentious /prɪ'tenʃəs/ *a.* making claim to great merit or importance, ostentatious.

preterite /'pretərɪt/ *Gram.* **1** *a.* expressing past action or state. **2** *n.* past tense.

preternatural /priːtə'nætʃər(ə)l/ *a.* outside ordinary course of nature, supernatural.

pretext /'priːtekst/ *n.* ostensible reason; excuse.

pretty /'prɪtɪ/ **1** *a.* attractive in delicate way; fine, good. **2** *adv.* fairly, moderately. **3** **pretty-pretty** too pretty; **sitting pretty** *colloq.* comfortably placed. **4** **prettiness** *n.*

pretzel /'prets(ə)l/ *n.* crisp knot-shaped salted biscuit.

prevail /prɪ'veɪl/ *v.i.* be victorious (*against* etc.); be the more usual or prominent; exist or occur in general use. **prevail (up)on** persuade.

prevalent /'prevələnt/ *a.* generally existing or occurring. **prevalence** *n.*

prevaricate /prɪ'værɪkeɪt/ *v.i.* make evasive or misleading statements. **prevarication** *n.*; **prevaricator** *n.*

prevent /prɪ'vent/ *v.t.* hinder, stop. **prevention** *n.*

preventative /prɪ'ventətɪv/ *a.* preventive.

preventive /prɪ'ventɪv/ **1** *a.* serving to prevent, esp. *Med.* to keep off disease. **2** *n.* preventive agent, measure, drug, etc.

preview /'priːvjuː/ **1** *n.* showing of film or play etc. before it is seen by general public. **2** *v.t.* view or show in advance of public presentation.

previous /'priːvɪəs/ *a.* coming before in time or order; prior *to*; done or acting hastily. **previous to** before.

pre-war /priː'wɔː(r)/ *a.* occurring or existing before a war.

prey /preɪ/ **1** *n.* animal hunted or killed

by other animal for food; victim. 2 *v.i.* **prey (up)on** seek or take as prey, exert harmful influence on.

price 1 *n.* money for which thing is bought or sold; what must be given, done, etc. to obtain thing; odds. 2 *v.t.* fix or find price of; estimate value of. 3 **at a price** at high cost.

priceless /'praɪslɪs/ *a.* invaluable; *sl.* very amusing or absurd.

pricey /'praɪsɪ/ *a. colloq.* expensive.

prick 1 *v.* pierce slightly, make small hole in; mark with pricks or dots; trouble mentally; feel pricking sensation. 2 *n.* pricking, mark of it; *vulg.* penis. 3 **prick out** plant (seedlings etc.) in small holes pricked in earth; **prick up one's ears** (of dog) erect the ears when on the alert, (of person) become suddenly attentive.

prickle /'prɪk(ə)l/ 1 *n.* small thorn; hard-pointed spine; prickling sensation. 2 *v.i.* feel sensation as of prick(s).

prickly /'prɪklɪ/ *a.* having prickles; irritable; tingling. **prickly heat** inflammation of skin near sweat glands with prickly sensation; **prickly pear** cactus with pear-shaped edible fruit, its fruit.

pride 1 *n.* feeling of elation and pleasure at one's achievements or possessions etc.; unduly high opinion of oneself; proper sense of one's own worth or position etc.; group (of lions etc.). 2 *v.refl.* **pride oneself (up)on** be proud of. 3 **take a pride in** be proud of.

prie-dieu /priː'djɜː/ *n.* kneeling-desk for prayer.

priest /priːst/ *n.* minister of religious worship; clergyman, esp. above deacon and below bishop.

priestess /'priːstes/ *n.* female priest of non-Christian religion.

priesthood /'priːsthʊd/ *n.* office or position of priest; *the* priests in general.

priestly /'priːstlɪ/ *a.* of or like or befitting priest.

prig *n.* self-righteously correct or moralistic person. **priggish** *a.*

prim *a.* consciously precise, formal; prudish.

prima /'priːmə/ *a.* **prima ballerina** chief female performer in ballet;

prima donna chief female singer in opera, temperamental person.

primacy /'praɪməsɪ/ *n.* pre-eminence; office of primate.

prima facie /praɪmə 'feɪʃɪ/ at first sight, (of evidence) based on first impression.

primal /'praɪm(ə)l/ *a.* primitive, primeval; fundamental.

primary /'praɪmərɪ/ 1 *a.* original; holding or sharing first place in time or importance or development. 2 *n.* thing that is primary; primary feather; *US* primary election. 3 **primary battery** one producing electricity by irreversible chemical action; **primary colour** one not obtained by mixing others; **primary education** first stage of education; **primary election** *US* election to select candidate(s) for principal election; **primary feather** large flight-feather of bird's wing; **primary school** school where primary education is given. 4 **primarily** □ See page 665. *adv.*

primate /'praɪmət/ *n.* archbishop; member of highest order of mammals including man and apes etc.

prime[1] 1 *a.* chief, most important; of highest quality; primary; fundamental. 2 *n.* state of highest perfection; best part; prime number. 3 **prime minister** chief minister of government; **prime number** number divisible only by itself and unity; **prime time** time at which television etc. audience is largest.

prime[2] *v.t.* prepare (explosive) for detonation; pour liquid into (pump) to start it working; cover (wood etc.) with first coat of paint or with oil etc. to prevent paint from being absorbed; equip (person *with* information).

primer[1] /'praɪmə(r)/ *n.* substance used to prime wood etc.

primer[2] /'praɪmə(r)/ *n.* elementary school-book; small introductory book.

primeval /praɪ'miːv(ə)l/ *a.* of first age of world; primitive, ancient.

primitive /'prɪmɪtɪv/ 1 *a.* ancient; at early stage of civilization; crude, simple. 2 *n.* untutored painter with naïve style; picture by such painter.

primogeniture /praɪməʊ'dʒenɪtʃə(r)/ *n.* principle by which property descends to eldest son.

primordial /praɪˈmɔːdɪəl/ a. existing at or from beginning, primeval.

primrose /ˈprɪmrəʊz/ n. plant bearing pale-yellow spring flower; this flower; pale yellow. **the primrose path** unjustified pursuit of pleasure.

primula /ˈprɪmjʊlə/ n. herbaceous perennial with flowers of various colours.

Primus /ˈpraɪməs/ n. (**P**) brand of portable stove burning vaporized oil.

prince /prɪns/ n. male member of royal family other than king; ruler esp. of small State; nobleman of some countries; fig. the greatest (of). **prince consort** husband of reigning queen who is himself a prince.

princely /ˈprɪnslɪ/ a. of or worthy of a prince, sumptuous, splendid.

princess /ˈprɪnses/ n. prince's wife; female member of royal family other than queen.

principal /ˈprɪnsɪp(ə)l/ **1** a. first in importance; chief, leading. **2** n. head of some institutions; principal actor or singer etc.; capital sum lent or invested; person for whom another acts as agent etc. **3 principal boy** actress playing leading male part in pantomime.

principality /prɪnsɪˈpælɪtɪ/ n. government of or State ruled by a prince. **the Principality** Wales.

principally /ˈprɪnsɪpəlɪ/ adv. for the most part, chiefly.

principle /ˈprɪnsɪp(ə)l/ n. fundamental truth or law as basis of reasoning or action; personal code of conduct; fundamental source or element. **in principle** as regards fundamentals but not necessarily in detail; **on principle** from settled moral motive.

principled a. based on or having (esp. praiseworthy) principles of behaviour.

prink v. smarten, dress up.

print 1 n. mark left on surface by pressure; impression left on paper by inked type or photography; reading-matter produced from type etc.; engraving, newspaper, photograph; printed fabric. **2** v.t. produce by means of printing-types etc.; express or publish in print; stamp or impress; write (letters etc.) without joining in imitation of printing; produce (photograph) from negative. **3 in print** in printed form, (of book etc.)

available from publisher; **out of print** (of book etc.) no longer available from publisher; **printed circuit** Electr. one with thin conducting strips printed on flat sheet; **printing-press** machine for printing from types etc.; **printout** computer output in printed form.

printer n. person who prints books; owner of printing-business; device that prints esp. computer output.

prior /ˈpraɪə(r)/ **1** a. earlier; coming before in time, order, or importance, (to). **2** n. superior of religious house; (in abbey) deputy of abbot. **3** adv. **prior to** before. **4 prioress** n.

priority /praɪˈɒrɪtɪ/ n. being earlier; precedence in rank etc.; interest having prior claim to attention.

priory /ˈpraɪərɪ/ n. religious house governed by prior or prioress.

prise /praɪz/ v.t. force open or out by leverage.

prism /ˈprɪz(ə)m/ n. solid figure whose two ends are equal parallel rectilineal figures, and whose sides are parallelograms; transparent body of this form with refracting surfaces.

prismatic /prɪzˈmætɪk/ a. of or like prism; (of colours) formed, distributed, etc. (as if) by transparent prism.

prison /ˈprɪz(ə)n/ n. place of captivity or confinement, esp. building to which persons are consigned while awaiting trial or for punishment.

prisoner /ˈprɪzənə(r)/ n. person kept in prison; fig. person or thing confined by illness, another's grasp, etc. **prisoner of war** one who has been captured in war.

prissy /ˈprɪsɪ/ a. prim, prudish.

pristine /ˈprɪstiːn/ a. in original condition; unspoilt. □ See page 666.

privacy /ˈprɪvəsɪ/ n. being private, freedom from publicity or observation.

private /ˈpraɪvət/ **1** a. belonging to an individual, personal, secret, confidential; not public or official; secluded; not provided or supported or managed by State. **2** n. private soldier. **3 in private** privately; **private detective** person who undertakes special enquiries for pay; **private enterprise** business(es) not under State control; **private eye** colloq. private detective; **private member** MP not holding Government appointment; **private**

parts genitals; **private soldier** ordinary soldier, not officer.

privateer /praɪvə'tɪə(r)/ n. privately owned and commissioned warship.

privation /praɪ'veɪʃ(ə)n/ n. lack of necessaries or comforts; hardship.

privatize /'praɪvətaɪz/ v.t. transfer from State to private ownership.

privet /'prɪvɪt/ n. bushy evergreen shrub used for hedges.

privilege /'prɪvɪlɪdʒ/ 1 n. right or advantage or immunity belonging to person or class or office; special advantage or benefit. 2 v.t. invest with privilege.

privy /'prɪvɪ/ 1 a. hidden, secluded, secret. 2 n. arch. lavatory. 3 **Privy Council** body of advisers chosen by sovereign; **Privy Counsellor** member of this; **privy purse** allowance from public revenue for monarch's private expenses; **privy seal** State seal formerly affixed to documents of minor importance (**Lord Privy Seal** senior cabinet minister without official duties); **privy to** in the secret of.

prize[1] 1 n. reward in lottery, competition, etc.; reward given as symbol of victory or superiority; thing (to be) striven for. 2 a. to which prize is awarded; excellent of its kind. 3 v.t. value highly. 4 **prize-fight** boxing-match for money.

prize[2] n. ship or property captured in naval warfare.

prize[3] var. of **prise**.

pro[1] n. (pl. **pros**) colloq. professional.

pro[2] 1 a. & prep. in favour (of). 2 n. reason in favour (esp. in **pros and cons**).

PRO abbr. public relations officer.

probability /prɒbə'bɪlɪtɪ/ n. being probable; likelihood; (most) probable event; extent to which thing is likely to occur, measured by ratio of favourable cases to all cases possible. **in all probability** most probably.

probable /'prɒbəb(ə)l/ 1 a. that may be expected to happen or prove true or correct; likely. 2 n. probable candidate or member of team etc.

probate /'prəʊbeɪt/ n. official proving of will.

probation /prə'beɪʃ(ə)n/ n. testing of person's conduct or character; system of suspending sentence on selected offenders subject to good behaviour under supervision of **probation officer. probationary** a.

probationer /prə'beɪʃənə(r)/ n. person on probation.

probe 1 n. blunt-ended surgical instrument for exploring wound etc.; unmanned exploratory spacecraft; probing, investigation. 2 v.t. explore with probe; fig. examine closely.

probity /'prəʊbɪtɪ/ n. uprightness, honesty.

problem /'prɒbləm/ n. doubtful or difficult question; thing hard to understand or deal with.

problematic /prɒblə'mætɪk/ a. (also **problematical**) attended by difficulty; doubtful, questionable.

proboscis /prə'bɒsɪs/ n. elephant's trunk; long flexible snout; elongated part of mouth of some insects.

procedure /prə'siːdjə(r)/ n. mode of conducting business; series of actions. **procedural** a.

proceed /prə'siːd/ v.i. go forward or on further; make one's way; continue or resume; adopt course of action; take legal proceedings; issue, originate.

proceeding /prə'siːdɪŋ/ n. action, piece of conduct; in pl. legal action, published report of discussions or conference.

proceeds /'prəʊsiːdz/ n.pl. money produced by sale or performance, etc.

process[1] /'prəʊses/ 1 n. course of action or proceeding, esp. series of stages in manufacture etc.; progress or course; natural or involuntary operation or series of changes; action at law; summons or writ; Biol. natural appendage or outgrowth of organism. 2. v.t. subject to manufacturing or legal process.

process[2] /prə'ses/ v.i. colloq. go in procession.

procession /prə'seʃ(ə)n/ n. array of persons etc. going along in orderly succession esp. as ceremony or on festive occasion.

processional /prə'seʃən(ə)l/ 1 a. of processions; used or carried or sung etc. in processions. 2 n. processional hymn.

processor /'prəʊsesə(r)/ n. machine that processes things; part of computer that controls activities of other units and performs actions specified in program.

proclaim /prə'kleɪm/ v.t. announce publicly and officially; declare to be. **proclamation** /prɒk-/ n.

proclivity /prə'klɪvɪtɪ/ n. natural tendency.

procrastinate /prə'kræstɪneɪt/ v.i. defer action, be dilatory. **procrastination** n.

procreate /'prəʊkrɪeɪt/ v. bring (offspring) into existence by natural process of reproduction; beget offspring. **procreation** n., **procreative** a.

proctor /'prɒktə(r)/ n. university official with disciplinary powers; **King's, Queen's, Proctor** official with power to intervene in cases of divorce etc. **proctorial** a.

procuration /prɒkjʊə'reɪʃ(ə)n/ n. procuring, action as another's agent.

procurator /'prɒkjʊəreɪtə(r)/ n. agent or proxy esp. with power of attorney. **procurator fiscal** coroner and public prosecutor of district in Scotland.

procure /prə'kjʊə(r)/ v. succeed in getting; bring about or cause by others' agency; act as procurer. **procurement** n.

procurer n. person who obtains women for prostitution. **procuress** n.

prod 1 v.t. poke with finger or end of stick etc.; stimulate to action. 2 n. poke, thrust; stimulus to action.

prodigal /'prɒdɪg(ə)l/ 1 a. wasteful; lavish (of). 2 n. spendthrift. 3 **prodigality** /-'gæl-/ n.

prodigious /prə'dɪdʒəs/ a. marvellous; enormous; abnormal.

prodigy /'prɒdɪdʒɪ/ n. person with exceptional qualities, esp. precocious child; marvellous thing.

produce 1 /prə'djuːs/ v.t. bring forward for inspection etc.; make or manufacture; bear or yield; bring into existence; cause or bring about; bring (play etc.) before public. 2 /'prɒdjuːs/ n. what is produced, esp. agricultural or natural products; amount produced.

producer n. person who produces articles or produce; person who directs performance of play or programme etc.; person in charge of financing and scheduling of film production.

product /'prɒdʌkt/ n. thing produced by natural process or manufacture;

Math. quantity obtained by multiplying.

production /prə'dʌkʃ(ə)n/ n. producing or being produced; thing(s) produced; literary or artistic work.

productive /prə'dʌktɪv/ a. producing esp. abundantly.

productivity /prɒdʌk'tɪvɪtɪ/ n. capacity to produce; effectiveness of productive effort esp. in industry.

proem /'prəʊɪm/ n. introductory discourse.

Prof. *abbr.* Professor.

profane /prə'feɪm/ 1 a. not sacred; irreverent, blasphemous. 2 v.t. treat with irreverence; pollute, violate. 3 **profanation** /prɒf-/ n.

profanity /prə'fænɪtɪ/ n. blasphemy.

profess /prə'fes/ v. claim openly to have; pretend; declare; affirm one's faith in or allegiance to.

professed a. self-acknowledged; alleged, ostensible. **professedly** /-'sɪdlɪ/ adv.

profession /prə'feʃ(ə)n/ n. occupation, esp. in branch of advanced learning or science; persons engaged in such branch; declaration, avowal.

professional /prə'feʃən(ə)l/ 1 a. of or belonging to or connected with or appropriate to a profession; engaged in specified activity as paid occupation. 2 n. professional person.

professionalism /prə'feʃənəlɪz(ə)m/ n. qualities or typical features of professionals.

professor /prə'fesə(r)/ n. holder of university chair, *US* university teacher; person who makes profession (of religion etc.). **professorial** /prɒfɪ'sɔːrɪəl/ a.; **professorship** n.

professoriate /prɒfɪ'sɔːrɪət/ n. the professors of a university etc.

proffer /'prɒfə(r)/ v.t. offer.

proficient /prə'fɪʃ(ə)nt/ a. expert, adept. **proficiency** n.

profile /'prəʊfaɪl/ n. side view or outline, esp. of human face; short biographical sketch.

profit /'prɒfɪt/ 1 n. advantage, benefit; pecuniary gain, excess of returns over outlay. 2 v. be of advantage (to); obtain advantage.

profitable /'prɒfɪtəb(ə)l/ a. beneficial; yielding profit, lucrative.

profiteer /prɒfɪ'tɪə(r)/ 1 v.i. make or

seek excessive profits out of others' needs esp. in times of scarcity. **2** *n.* person who profiteers.

profiterole /prə'fɪtərəʊl/ *n.* small hollow cake of choux pastry with filling.

profligate /'prɒflɪgət/ **1** *a.* licentious, dissolute; recklessly extravagant. **2** *n.* profligate person. **3 profligacy** *n.*

pro forma /prəʊ 'fɔːmə/ for form's sake; (in full **pro forma invoice**) invoice sent to purchaser in advance of goods for completion of business formalities.

profound /prə'faʊnd/ *a.* having or showing great knowledge or insight; requiring much study or thought; deep; intense. **profundity** *n.*

profuse /prə'fjuːs/ *a.* lavish, extravagant, copious, excessive. **profusion** *n.*

progenitor /prəʊ'dʒenɪtə(r)/ *n.* ancestor; predecessor, original.

progeny /'prɒdʒənɪ/ *n.* offspring; *fig.* issue, outcome.

progesterone /prəʊ'dʒestərəʊn/ *n.* a sex hormone that maintains pregnancy.

prognosis /prɒg'nəʊsɪs/ *n.* (*pl.* **-ses** /-siːz/) forecast of course of disease.

prognostic /prɒg'nɒstɪk/ **1** *n.* advance indication or omen; prediction. **2** *a.* foretelling, predictive (*of*).

prognosticate /prɒg'nɒstɪkeɪt/ *v.t.* foretell; betoken. **prognostication** *n.*

programme /'prəʊgræm/ (*US & Computers* **program**) **1** *n.* plan of intended proceedings; descriptive notice, list, of series of events etc.; such series of events; broadcast performance or entertainment; series of instructions to control operation of computer etc. **2** *v.t.* make programme of; express (problem) or instruct (computer) by means of program. **3 programmatic** *a.*

progress 1 /'prəʊgres/ *n.* forward movement; advance; development; *arch.* state journey, esp. by royal person. **2** /prə'gres/ *v.i.* move forward or onward; advance, develop. **3 in progress** in course of occurrence, going on.

progression /prə'greʃ(ə)n/ *n.* progressing; succession, series.

progressive /prə'gresɪv/ **1** *a.* moving forward; proceeding step by step; successive; favouring progress or reform; advanced in social conditions etc.; (of disease etc.) continuously increasing; (of taxation) at rates increasing with the sum taxed. **2** *n.* advocate of progressive policy.

prohibit /prə'hɪbɪt/ *v.t.* forbid, prevent.

prohibition /prəʊɪ'bɪʃ(ə)n/ *n.* forbidding or being forbidden; edict or order that forbids; forbidding by law of manufacture and sale of intoxicants.

prohibitive /prə'hɪbɪtɪv/ *a.* prohibiting; (of price) so high as to preclude purchase.

project 1 /'prɒdʒekt/ *n.* plan, scheme; planned undertaking, esp. piece of individual research by student(s). **2** /prə'dʒekt/ *v.* make plans for; cause (light, image) to fall on surface; send or throw outward or forward; protrude, jut out.

projectile /prə'dʒektaɪl/ **1** *n.* object to be hurled. **2** *a.* of or serving as a projectile.

projection /prə'dʒekʃ(ə)n/ *n.* projecting or being projected; part that protrudes; representation of earth etc. on plane surface; mental image viewed as objective reality.

projectionist /prə'dʒekʃənɪst/ *n.* person who operates projector.

projector /prə'dʒektə(r)/ *n.* apparatus for projecting image or film etc. on screen.

prolapse 1 /'prəʊlæps/ *n.* slipping downward or forward of part or organ, esp. of womb or rectum. **2** /prə'læps/ *v.i.* undergo prolapse.

prolate /'prəʊleɪt/ *a.* (of spheroid) lengthened along polar diameter.

prolegomena /prəʊlɪ'gɒmɪnə/ *n.pl.* preliminary matter prefixed to book etc.

proletarian /prəʊlɪ'teərɪən/ **1** *a.* of proletariat. **2** *n.* member of proletariat.

proletariat /prəʊlɪ'teərɪət/ *n.* class of industrial workers.

proliferate /prə'lɪfəreɪt/ *v.* reproduce itself or grow by multiplication of elementary parts; increase rapidly, multiply. **proliferation** *n.*

prolific /prə'lɪfɪk/ *a.* producing much offspring or output; abundantly productive.

prolix /'prəʊlɪks/ *a.* lengthy; long-winded; tedious. **prolixity** *n.*

prologue /ˈprəʊlɒg/ n. introduction to poem or play etc.; act or event serving as introduction (to).

prolong /prəˈlɒŋ/ v.t. make longer; cause to continue. **prolongation** /prəʊlɒŋˈgeɪʃ(ə)n/ n.

prom n. colloq. promenade; promenade concert.

promenade /prɒməˈnɑːd/ **1** n. place for walking, esp. paved area at seaside; leisure walk. **2** v. make promenade (on, through, etc.); lead about, esp. for display. **3 promenade concert** one at which (part of) audience is not provided with seats; **promenade deck** upper deck on liner.

prominent /ˈprɒmɪn(ə)nt/ a. jutting out, conspicuous; distinguished; well-known. **prominence** n.

promiscuous /prəˈmɪskjʊəs/ a. having casual sexual relations with many people; indiscriminate; of mixed and disorderly composition. **promiscuity** /prɒmɪsˈkjuːɪtɪ/ n.

promise /ˈprɒmɪs/ **1** n. explicit undertaking to do or not to do something; thing promised; favourable indications. **2** v. make promise (to) to give, do, etc.; seem likely (to), hold out good etc. prospect.

promising /ˈprɒmɪsɪŋ/ a. likely to turn out well; hopeful; full of promise.

promissory /ˈprɒmɪsərɪ/ a. conveying or implying promise. **promissory note** signed document containing promise to pay stated sum.

promontory /ˈprɒməntərɪ/ n. point of high land jutting out into sea etc.; headland.

promote /prəˈməʊt/ v.t. advance (person) to higher office or position; help forward or initiate process or formation of; publicize and sell. **promotion** n.; **promotional** a.

promoter n. person who promotes an enterprise financially, esp. formation of joint-stock company or holding of sporting event or theatrical production etc.

prompt **1** a. acting or done at once or without delay; punctual. **2** adv. punctually. **3** v.t. incite, move, inspire; help out (actor, speaker) by supplying words that come next. **4** n. thing said to help memory esp. of actor. **5 prompt side** side of stage to actor's left.

prompter /ˈprɒmptə(r)/ n. Theatr. person unseen by audience who prompts actors.

promptitude /ˈprɒmptɪtjuːd/ n. promptness.

promulgate /ˈprɒməlgeɪt/ v.t. make known to the public; proclaim. **promulgation** n.

prone a. lying face downwards; lying flat, prostrate; inclined, disposed (to).

prong n. spike of fork.

pronominal /prəˈnɒmɪn(ə)l/ a. of or of the nature of a pronoun.

pronoun /ˈprəʊnaʊn/ n. word serving as grammatical substitute for noun.

pronounce /prəˈnaʊns/ v. utter or speak, esp. with reference to correct manner; utter formally; give (as) one's opinion; pass judgement. **pronounceable** a.

pronounced a. strongly marked.

pronouncement n. formal statement, declaration.

pronto /ˈprɒntəʊ/ adv. sl. promptly, quickly.

pronunciation /prənʌnsɪˈeɪʃ(ə)n/ n. way in which word is pronounced; person's way of pronouncing words.

proof /pruːf/ **1** n. fact or evidence or reasoning that proves truth or existence of something; test or trial; trial impression of printed matter for correction; standard of strength of distilled alcoholic liquors. **2** a. impervious to penetration or damage or undesired action. **3** v.t. make proof, esp. against water or bullets. **4 proof-read** read and correct (printed proof); **proof-reader** person who does this; **proof spirit** mixture of alcohol and water used in computing alcoholic strength.

prop[1] **1** n. thing used to support something or keep it upright; supporter of cause etc. **2** v.t. support (as) by prop, hold up thus.

prop[2] n. colloq. aircraft propeller.

prop[3] n. Theatr. stage property.

propaganda /prɒpəˈgændə/ n. organized scheme for propagation of a doctrine etc.; ideas etc. so propagated; colloq. biased information.

propagate /ˈprɒpəgeɪt/ v. breed or reproduce from parent stock; (of plant etc.) reproduce (itself); disseminate. **propagation** n.

propane /'prəʊpeɪn/ n. a hydrocarbon of the paraffin series.

propel /prə'pel/ v.t. drive or push forward; give onward motion to.

propellant /prə'pelənt/ n. propelling agent.

propeller /prə'pelə(r)/ n. revolving device with blades for propelling ship or aircraft.

propensity /prə'pensɪtɪ/ n. inclination, tendency.

proper /'prɒpə(r)/ a. suitable, appropriate; accurate, correct; respectable, decent; strictly so called, genuine; belonging or relating exclusively or distinctively (to); colloq. thorough. **proper name** name of person or place etc.

property /'prɒpətɪ/ n. thing owned; landed estate; owning; being owned; attribute or quality; Theatr. movable article used on stage during performance of play.

prophecy /'prɒfəsɪ/ n. prophesying; prophetic utterance; prediction.

prophesy /'prɒfəsaɪ/ v. speak as prophet; predict.

prophet /'prɒfɪt/ n. inspired teacher; revealer or interpreter of divine will; person who predicts. **prophetess** n.

prophetic /prə'fetɪk/ a. of prophet; predicting or containing a prediction of.

prophylactic /prɒfɪ'læktɪk/ 1 a. tending to prevent disease or other misfortune. 2 n. prophylactic medicine or course of action.

prophylaxis /prɒfɪ'læksɪs/ n. (pl. -xes /-ksiːz/) preventive treatment against disease etc.

propinquity /prə'pɪŋkwɪtɪ/ n. nearness; close kinship.

propitiate /prə'pɪʃɪeɪt/ v.t. appease. **propitiation** n.; **propitiatory** a.

propitious /prə'pɪʃəs/ a. well-disposed, favourable (to); suitable for.

proponent /prə'pəʊnənt/ n. person who puts forward proposal.

proportion /prə'pɔːʃ(ə)n/ 1 n. comparative part; share; comparative relation, ratio; correct relation between things or parts of thing; in pl. dimensions. 2 v.t. make proportionate.

proportional /prə'pɔːʃən(ə)l/ a. in correct proportion; corresponding in degree or amount. **proportional representation** representation of parties

etc. in parliament in proportion to votes they receive.

proportionate /prə'pɔːʃənət/ a. in due proportion (to).

proposal /prə'pəʊz(ə)l/ n. proposing; scheme etc. proposed; offer of marriage.

propose /prə'pəʊz/ v. put forward for consideration; intend; set up as an aim; offer marriage (to); offer as subject for drinking of toast; nominate as member of society etc.

proposition /prɒpə'zɪʃ(ə)n/ 1 n. proposal; scheme proposed; statement, assertion; Math. formal statement of theorem or problem; colloq. task, problem, opponent. 2 v.t. colloq. put (esp. indecent) proposition to.

propound /prə'paʊnd/ v.t. offer for consideration or solution.

proprietary /prə'praɪətərɪ/ a. of proprietor; holding property; held in private ownership; manufactured and sold by one particular firm.

proprietor /prə'praɪətə(r)/ n. owner. **proprietorial** /-'tɔːr-/ a.; **proprietress** n.

propriety /prə'praɪətɪ/ n. fitness, rightness, correctness of behaviour or morals; in pl. the conventions of polite behaviour.

propulsion /prə'pʌlʃ(ə)n/ n. driving or pushing forward. **propulsive** a.

pro rata /prəʊ 'rɑːtə/ proportional; in proportion.

prorogue /prə'rəʊg/ v. discontinue meetings of (parliament) without dissolving it; be prorogued. **prorogation** n.

prosaic /prə'zeɪɪk/ a. like prose; unpoetic; commonplace. **prosaically** adv.

proscenium /prə'siːnɪəm/ n. (pl. -niums or -nia) part of theatre stage in front of curtain, esp. with enclosing arch.

proscribe /prə'skraɪb/ v.t. denounce or forbid; outlaw; banish, exile. **proscription** n.; **proscriptive** a.

prose /prəʊz/ 1 n. ordinary non-metrical form of language; plain speech. 2 v.i. talk tediously.

prosecute /'prɒsɪkjuːt/ v.t. institute legal proceedings against; pursue or carry on.

prosecution /prɒsɪˈkjuːʃ(ə)n/ n. prosecuting; prosecuting party.

prosecutor /ˈprɒsɪkjuːtə(r)/ n. person who prosecutes esp. in criminal court.

proselyte /ˈprɒsɪlaɪt/ n. Gentile convert to Jewish faith; any convert.

proselytism /ˈprɒsɪlɪtɪz(ə)m/ n. being a proselyte; practice of proselytizing.

proselytize /ˈprɒsɪlɪtaɪz/ v.t. seek to make proselyte of.

prosody /ˈprɒsədɪ/ n. science of versification. **prosodist** n.

prospect 1 /ˈprɒspekt/ n. what one is to expect; extensive view; mental scene; *colloq.* possible or likely customer etc. 2 /prəˈspekt/ v. explore (*for* gold etc.). 3 **prospector** n.

prospective /prəsˈpektɪv/ a. concerned with or applying to the future; expected, some day to be.

prospectus /prəsˈpektəs/ n. pamphlet etc. containing description of chief features of school or business etc.

prosper /ˈprɒspə(r)/ v.i. succeed, thrive.

prosperity /prɒˈsperɪtɪ/ n. state of prospering.

prosperous /ˈprɒspərəs/ a. successful, thriving; auspicious.

prostate gland /ˈprɒsteɪt/ large gland round neck of bladder, accessory to male genital organs. **prostatic** /-ˈtæt-/ a.

prostitute /ˈprɒstɪtjuːt/ 1 n. person who offers sexual intercourse for payment. 2 v.t. make prostitute of; sell or make use of unworthily. 3 **prostitution** n.

prostrate 1 /ˈprɒstreɪt/ a. lying with face to ground, esp. in submission or humility; lying horizontally; overthrown; exhausted. 2 /prɒsˈtreɪt/ v.t. throw or lay flat on ground; overcome; reduce to extreme physical weakness. 3 **prostration** n.

prosy /ˈprəʊzɪ/ a. tedious, commonplace, dull.

protagonist /prəˈtægənɪst/ n. chief person in drama or story etc. □ See page 666.

protean /ˈprəʊtɪən/ a. variable, versatile.

protect /prəˈtekt/ v.t. keep safe; shield; secure.

protection /prəˈtekʃ(ə)n/ n. protecting, defence; person or thing that pro-

tects; system or policy of protecting home industries by tariffs etc. **protectionism** n.; **protectionist** n. & a.

protective /prəˈtektɪv/ a. protecting; giving or intended for protection. **protective custody** detention of person for his own protection.

protector /prəˈtektə(r)/ n. person or thing that protects; regent in charge of kingdom during minority or absence of sovereign. **protectorship** n.; **protectress** n.

protectorate /prəˈtektərət/ n. office of protector of kingdom or State; period of this; protectorship of weak or underdeveloped State by stronger one; such territory.

protégé /ˈprɒteʒeɪ/ n. (*fem.* -**gée** *pr.* same) person under protection or patronage of another.

protein /ˈprəʊtiːn/ n. one of a class of nitrogenous compounds important in all living organisms.

pro tem /prəʊ ˈtem/ abbr. for the time being (*pro tempore*).

protest 1 /prəˈtest/ v. express disapproval or dissent; *US* object to; declare solemnly. 2 /ˈprəʊtest/ n. expression of dissent or disapproval; remonstrance. 3 **protestor** n.

Protestant /ˈprɒtɪst(ə)nt/ 1 n. member or adherent of any of the Christian bodies that separated from the Roman communion in the Reformation, or their offshoots. 2 a. of Protestants. 3 **Protestantism** n.

protestation /prɒtɪsˈteɪʃ(ə)n/ n. solemn affirmation.

protocol /ˈprəʊtəkɒl/ n. official formality and etiquette; observance of this; draft of diplomatic document, esp. of agreed terms of treaty.

proton /ˈprəʊtɒn/ n. *Phys.* elementary particle with unit positive electric charge, forming part or (in hydrogen) whole of atomic nucleus.

protoplasm /ˈprəʊtəʊplæz(ə)m/ n. viscous translucent substance forming main constituent of cells in organisms. **protoplasmic** a.

prototype /ˈprəʊtəʊtaɪp/ n. original thing or person in relation to a copy, improved form, etc.; trial model, esp. of aeroplane etc.

protozoon /prəʊtəˈzəʊən/ n. (*pl.* -**zoa**)

one-celled microscopic animal. **proto-zoan** a. & n.

protract /prəˈtrækt/ v.t. prolong, lengthen; make last long(er). **protraction** n.

protractor /prəˈtræktə(r)/ n. instrument for measuring angles, usu. in form of graduated semicircle.

protrude /prəˈtruːd/ v. stick out; thrust out. **protrusion** n.; **protrusive** a.

protuberant /prəˈtjuːbərənt/ a. bulging out; prominent. **protuberance** n.

proud /praʊd/ a. feeling or showing (proper) pride; haughty, arrogant; feeling greatly honoured; imposing, splendid; slightly projecting; (of flesh) overgrown round healing wound. **do proud** treat with great generosity or honour.

prove /pruːv/ v. (p.p. **proved** or esp. US, Sc., or literary **proven**) demonstrate to be true by evidence or argument; be found (to be); establish validity of (will); rise or cause (dough) to rise; arch. test.

provenance /ˈprɒvənəns/ n. origin; place of origin.

provender /ˈprɒvɪndə(r)/ n. fodder; joc. food for humans.

proverb /ˈprɒvɜːb/ n. short pithy saying in general use; person or thing that is widely known.

proverbial /prəˈvɜːbɪəl/ a. of or expressed in proverbs; notorious.

provide /prəˈvaɪd/ v. cause to have possession or use of; supply, make available; make due preparation; stipulate. **provide for** supply necessities of life for; **provided** (or **providing**) **(that)** on condition or understanding that.

providence /ˈprɒvɪd(ə)ns/ n. foresight, timely care; beneficent care of God or nature; **Providence** God.

provident /ˈprɒvɪd(ə)nt/ a. having or showing foresight, thrifty.

providential /prɒvɪˈdenʃ(ə)l/ a. of or by divine foresight or intervention; opportune, lucky.

province /ˈprɒvɪns/ n. principal administrative division of country; in pl. the whole of country outside capital; sphere of action; concern.

provincial /prəˈvɪnʃ(ə)l/ 1 a. of province(s); having restricted views or the interests or manners etc. attributed to inhabitants of the provinces. 2 n. inhabitant of province(s). 3 **provincialism** n.

provision /prəˈvɪʒ(ə)n/ n. providing; preparation for future contingency; provided amount of; in pl. supply of food and drink; formally stated condition.

provisional /prəˈvɪʒ(ə)n(ə)l/ a. providing for immediate needs only, temporary.

proviso /prəˈvaɪzəʊ/ n. (pl. -sos) stipulation; limiting clause. **provisory** a.

provocation /prɒvəˈkeɪʃ(ə)n/ n. incitement esp. to anger etc.; irritation; cause of annoyance.

provocative /prəˈvɒkətɪv/ a. tending or intended to cause provocation (of anger, lust, etc.)

provoke /prəˈvəʊk/ v.t. rouse, incite, (to); irritate; call forth, cause.

provost /ˈprɒvəst/ n. head of some colleges; Sc. head of municipal corporation or burgh; /prəˈvəʊ/ (in full **provost marshal**) head of military police in camp or on active service.

prow /praʊ/ n. part adjoining stem of boat or ship; pointed projecting front part.

prowess /ˈpraʊɪs/ n. skill, expertise; valour; gallantry.

prowl /praʊl/ 1 v. go about stealthily in search of prey or plunder; traverse (place) thus. 2 n. prowling.

prox. abbr. proximo.

proximate /ˈprɒksɪmət/ a. nearest, next before or after.

proximity /prɒkˈsɪmɪtɪ/ n. nearness; neighbourhood.

proximo /ˈprɒksɪməʊ/ a. of next month.

proxy /ˈprɒksɪ/ n. person authorized to act for another; agency of such a person; document authorizing person to vote on another's behalf; vote so given.

prude n. person of extreme propriety in conduct or speech, esp. as regards sexual matters. **prudery** n.; **prudish** a.

prudent /ˈpruːd(ə)nt/ a. showing care and foresight; discreet. **prudence** n.

prudential /pruːˈdenʃ(ə)l/ a. of or involving or marked by prudence.

prune[1] v.t. trim (tree etc.) by cutting away dead or overgrown parts; remove (superfluities); reduce (costs etc.); clear (*of* what is superfluous).

prune² *n*. dried plum.

prurient /'prʊərɪənt/ *a*. given to or arising from indulgence of lewd ideas. **prurience** *n*.

Prussian /'prʌʃ(ə)n/ **1** *a*. of Prussia. **2** *n*. native of Prussia. **3 Prussian blue** deep blue pigment.

prussic acid /'prʌsɪk/ a highly poisonous liquid.

pry /praɪ/ *v.i.* look or inquire etc. (*into*) inquisitively.

PS *abbr*. postscript.

psalm /sɑːm/ *n*. sacred song, hymn; **(Book of) Psalms** book of these in OT.

psalmist /'sɑːmɪst/ *n*. author of psalms.

psalmody /'sɑːmədɪ/ *n*. practice or art of singing psalms.

psalter /'sɔːltə(r)/ *n*. version or copy of Book of Psalms.

psaltery /'sɔːltərɪ/ *n*. ancient and medieval plucked stringed instrument.

psephology /se'fɒlədʒɪ/ *n*. study of trends in elections and voting. **psephologist** *n*.

pseudo- /'sjuːdəʊ/ *in comb*. false, apparent, supposed but not real.

pseudonym /'sjuːdənɪm/ *n*. fictitious name, esp. one assumed by author.

pseudonymous /sjuː'dɒnɪməs/ *a*. written under fictitious name.

psoriasis /sɔː'raɪəsɪs/ *n*. skin disease with red scaly patches.

PSV *abbr*. public service vehicle.

psyche /'saɪkɪ/ *n*. soul, spirit, mind.

psychedelic /saɪkə'delɪk/ *a*. hallucinatory, expanding the mind's awareness; having vivid colours or sounds etc.

psychiatry /saɪ'kaɪətrɪ/ *n*. study and treatment of mental disease. **psychiatric(al)** /saɪkɪ'ætrɪk(ə)l/ *a*.; **psychiatrist** *n*.

psychic /'saɪkɪk/ **1** *a*. psychical; able to exercise psychical or occult powers. **2** *n*. person susceptible to psychical influence, medium.

psychical /'saɪkɪk(ə)l/ *a*. of the soul or mind; of phenomena and conditions apparently outside domain of physical law.

psycho- /'saɪkəʊ/ *in comb*. mind, soul.

psycho-analysis /saɪkəʊə'nælɪsɪs/ *n*. therapeutic method for treating mental disorders by investigating interaction of conscious and unconscious elements in the mind. **psycho-analyse** *v.t.*; **psycho-analyst** *n.*; **psychoanalytical** /-'lɪt-/ *a*.

psychological /saɪkə'lɒdʒɪk(ə)l/ *a*. of the mind; of psychology. **psychological moment** the psychologically appropriate moment, *colloq*. the most appropriate time; **psychological warfare** achieving aims by acting on enemy's minds.

psychology /saɪ'kɒlədʒɪ/ *n*. science of human mind; treatise on or system of this; *colloq*. mental characteristics. **psychologist** *n*.

psychoneurosis /saɪkəʊnjʊə'rəʊsɪs/ *n*. (*pl*. -ses /-siːz/) neurosis esp. with indirect expression of emotional feelings. **psychoneurotic** /-'rɒt-/ *a*.

psychopath /'saɪkəpæθ/ *n*. person suffering chronic mental disorder esp. with abnormal social behaviour; mentally or emotionally unstable person. **psychopathic** *a*.

psychosis /saɪ'kəʊsɪs/ *n*. (*pl*. -ses /-siːz/) severe mental derangement involving whole personality.

psychosomatic /saɪkəʊsə'mætɪk/ *a*. of mind and body; (of disease) caused or aggravated by mental stress.

psychosurgery /saɪkəʊ'sɜːdʒərɪ/ *n*. brain surgery as means of treating mental disorder.

psychotherapy /saɪkəʊ'θerəpɪ/ *n*. treatment of mental disorder by psychological means. **psychotherapist** *n*.

psychotic /saɪ'kɒtɪk/ **1** *a*. of or suffering from psychosis. **2** *n*. psychotic person.

PT *abbr*. physical training.

pt. *abbr*. part; pint; point; port.

PTA *abbr*. parent-teacher association.

ptarmigan /'tɑːmɪgən/ *n*. bird of grouse family.

Pte. *abbr*. Private (soldier).

pterodactyl /terə'dæktɪl/ *n*. extinct winged reptile.

PTO *abbr*. please turn over.

ptomaine /'təʊmeɪn/ *n*. one of a group of compounds (some toxic) in putrefying animal and vegetable matter.

pub *n*. *colloq*. public house.

puberty /'pjuːbətɪ/ *n*. stage at which

person becomes capable of procreating.

pubes /ˈpjuːbiːz/ *n.* lower part of abdomen.

pubescence /pjuːˈbes(ə)ns/ *n.* arrival at puberty; soft down on plant or animal. **pubescent** *a.*

pubic /ˈpjuːbɪk/ *a.* of pubes or pubis.

pubis /ˈpjuːbɪs/ *n.* (*pl.* **-bes** /-biːz/) bone forming front of each half of pelvis.

public /ˈpʌblɪk/ 1 *a.* of or concerning community as a whole; open to or shared by people in general; open to general observation, done etc. in public. 2 *n.* (members of) community as a whole; section of community. 3 **in public** publicly, openly; **public-address system** equipment of loudspeakers etc.; **public house** place licensed for and chiefly concerned with selling of alcoholic drink; **public lending right** right of authors to payment when their books are lent by public libraries; **public relations** relations between organization and the public; **public school** endowed independent fee-paying school, *Sc.* & *US* etc. school managed by public authorities; **public-spirited** ready to do things for the benefit of people in general; **public transport** buses, trains, etc., available to public and having fixed routes; **public utility** organization supplying water or gas or electricity etc. 4 **publicly** *adv.*

publican /ˈpʌblɪkən/ *n.* keeper of public house.

publication /pʌblɪˈkeɪʃ(ə)n/ *n.* publishing; published book, periodical, etc.

publicist /ˈpʌblɪsɪst/ *n.* publicity agent; writer on public concerns.

publicity /pʌbˈlɪsɪtɪ/ *n.* public attention or the means of attracting it; business of advertising; being open to general observation.

publicize /ˈpʌblɪsaɪz/ *v.t.* bring to public notice, esp. by advertisement etc.

publish /ˈpʌblɪʃ/ *v.t.* prepare and issue copies of (book, magazine, etc.) for sale to public; make generally known; formally announce.

publisher *n.* person or firm that issues copies of book, magazine, etc.

puce /pjuːs/ *a.* & *n.* brownish-purple.

puck[1] *n.* rubber disc used in ice-hockey.

puck[2] *n.* mischievous sprite. **puckish** *a.*

pucker /ˈpʌkə(r)/ 1 *v.* contract or gather (*up*) into wrinkles or folds or bulges. 2 *n.* such bulge etc.

pudding /ˈpʊdɪŋ/ *n.* sweet food eaten as course of meal; food containing or enclosed in mixture of flour etc. and cooked by baking or boiling; kind of sausage.

puddle /ˈpʌd(ə)l/ *n.* small dirty pool; clay made into watertight coating.

pudenda /pjuːˈdendə/ *n.pl.* genitals, esp. of woman.

puerile /ˈpjʊəraɪl/ *a.* childish; trivial. **puerility** /-ˈrɪl-/ *n.*

puerperal /pjuːˈɜːpər(ə)l/ *a.* of or due to childbirth.

puff 1 *n.* short quick blast of breath or wind; sound (as) of this; smoke or vapour sent out by it; pad for applying powder to skin; (piece of) light pastry; unduly laudatory review or advertisement etc. 2 *v.* emit puff or puffs; smoke in puffs; pant; blow *out* or *up*, inflate; advertise in exaggerated terms. 3 **puff-adder** large venomous Afr. viper; **puff-ball** ball-shaped fungus; **puff pastry** light flaky pastry; **puff sleeve** short full sleeve gathered into band.

puffin /ˈpʌfɪn/ *n.* N. Atlantic auk with short striped bill.

puffy /ˈpʌfɪ/ *a.* puffed out, swollen; short-winded.

pug *n.* small snub-nosed breed of dog. **pug-nosed** having short snub or flat nose.

pugilist /ˈpjuːdʒɪlɪst/ *n.* boxer. **pugilism** *n.* **pugilistic** *a.*

pugnacious /pʌɡˈneɪʃəs/ *a.* disposed to fight. **pugnacity** /-ˈnæs-/ *n.*

puisne /ˈpjuːnɪ/ *n.* judge of superior court who is inferior in rank to chief justice.

puissant /ˈpwiːs(ə)nt/ *a. literary* wielding great power; mighty. **puissance** *n.*

puke /pjuːk/ *v.* & *n.* vomit.

pukka /ˈpʌkə/ *a. colloq.* real, genuine.

pulchritude /ˈpʌlkrɪtjuːd/ *n.* beauty. **pulchritudinous** *a.*

pull /pʊl/ 1 *v.* exert force on (thing etc.) to move it to oneself; cause to move towards oneself or in direction so regarded; exert pulling force; damage (muscle etc.) by abnormal strain; proceed with effort; attract; make (grimace) by distorting muscles. **2** *n.* act of pulling; force thus exerted; means of exerting influence; advantage; deep draught of liquor; handle etc. for applying pull; printer's rough proof. **3 pull back** retreat; **pull down** demolish, lower in health etc.; **pull in** move towards near side, into parking-place, etc., **pull-in** place for doing this; **pull off** win, manage successfully; **pull oneself together** recover control of oneself; **pull out** move away, move towards off side; **pull one's punches** fail to give full force in boxing or argument etc.; **pull round, through**, recover from (illness); **pull strings** exert (esp. clandestine) influence; **pull up** (cause) to stop moving, check oneself, pull out of ground; **pull one's weight** do fair share of work.

pullet /'pʊlɪt/ *n.* young domestic fowl before first moult.

pulley /'pʊlɪ/ *n.* grooved wheel for cord etc. to run over, mounted in block and used to lift weight etc.; wheel or drum mounted on shaft and turned by belt, used to increase speed or power.

Pullman /'pʊlmən/ *n.* railway carriage or motor coach with specially comfortable seats etc.; sleeping-car.

pullover /'pʊləʊvə(r)/ *n.* knitted garment put on over the head.

pullulate /'pʌljʊleɪt/ *v.* grow or develop; abound *with*. **pullulation** *n.*

pulmonary /'pʊlmənərɪ/ *a.* of or in or connected with lungs; affected with or subject to lung-disease.

pulp 1 *n.* fleshy part of fruit, animal body, etc.; soft shapeless mass, esp. of materials for paper-making. **2** *v.* reduce to pulp; become pulp. **3 pulpy** *a.*

pulpit /'pʊlpɪt/ *n.* raised enclosed platform for preaching from; *the* profession of preaching.

pulsar /'pʌlsɑː(r)/ *n.* cosmic source of regularly and rapidly pulsating radio signals.

pulsate /pʌl'seɪt/ *v.i.* expand and contract rhythmically; throb, vibrate, quiver. **pulsation** *n.*

pulse¹ /pʌls/ **1** *n.* rhythmical throbbing of arteries; point where this can be felt externally; single vibration of sound or light or electric signal etc.; throb, thrill, of life or emotion. **2** *v.i.* pulsate.

pulse² /pʌls/ *n.* as *sing.* or *pl.* edible seeds of peas, beans, lentils, etc.

pulverize /'pʌlvəraɪz/ *v.* reduce or crumble to powder or dust; demolish, crush, smash. **pulverization** *n.*

puma /'pjuːmə/ *n.* large tawny Amer. feline.

pumice /'pʌmɪs/ *n.* (also **pumicestone**) light porous lava used as abrasive; piece of this.

pummel /'pʌm(ə)l/ *v.t.* strike repeatedly, esp. with fists.

pump¹ 1 *n.* machine or device of various kinds for raising or moving liquids or gases. **2** *v.* work pump; remove or raise or compress or inflate etc. (as) by pumping; elicit information from (person) by persistent or artful questions. **3 pump-room** room at spa where medicinal water is dispensed; **pump up** inflate (pneumatic tyre etc.)

pump² *n.* plimsoll; light shoe for dancing etc.

pumpernickel /'pʌmpənɪkəl/ *n.* wholemeal rye bread.

pumpkin /'pʌmpkɪn/ *n.* large orange-coloured fruit used as vegetable; plant bearing it.

pun 1 *n.* humorous use of word to suggest different meanings, or of different words of same sound, etc. **2** *v.i.* make pun(s).

punch¹ 1 *v.* strike with fist; make hole in (as) with punch; pierce (hole) thus. **2** *n.* blow with fist; *sl.* vigour, effective force; instrument or machine for cutting holes or impressing design in leather or metal or paper etc. **3 punchball** inflated or stuffed ball used for practice in punching; **punch-drunk** stupefied with repeated punches; **punch-line** words giving point of joke etc.; **punch-up** *sl.* fight with fists, brawl.

punch² *n.* mixture of spirit or wine with (hot) water and spices etc. **punch-bowl** bowl in which punch is mixed; round deep hollow in hill(s).

punch³ *n.* short-legged thickset draught horse.

Punch⁴ *n.* grotesque humpbacked figure in puppet-show called *Punch and Judy.*

punchy /'pʌntʃɪ/ *a.* having vigour, forceful.

punctilio /pʌŋk'tɪlɪəʊ/ *n.* (*pl.* **-lios**) delicate point of ceremony or honour; petty formality.

punctilious /pʌŋk'tɪliəs/ a. attentive to formality or etiquette; precise in behaviour.

punctual /'pʌŋktjʊəl/ a. observant of appointed time; not late. **punctuality** n.

punctuate /'pʌŋktjʊeɪt/ v.t. insert punctuation marks in; interrupt at intervals.

punctuation /pʌŋktjʊ'eɪʃ(ə)n/ n. punctuating. **punctuation mark** any of the marks used in writing to separate sentences and phrases etc.

puncture /'pʌŋktʃə(r)/ 1 n. prick or pricking; hole made by it. 2 v. make puncture in; suffer puncture.

pundit /'pʌndɪt/ n. learned Hindu; learned person, expert.

pungent /'pʌndʒ(ə)nt/ a. having strong sharp taste or smell; stinging, caustic, biting. **pungency** n.

punish /'pʌnɪʃ/ v.t. cause (offender) to suffer for offence; inflict penalty for (offence); tax severely the powers of; subject to severe treatment. **punishment** n.

punitive /'pju:nɪtɪv/ a. inflicting or intended to inflict punishment.

punk n. colloq. worthless person or thing; colloq. punk rock, fan of this. **punk rock** type of pop music using aggressive and outrageous effects.

punkah /'pʌŋkə/ n. large swinging fan on frame worked by cord or electrically.

punnet /'pʌnɪt/ n. small basket for fruit etc.

punster /'pʌnstə(r)/ n. maker of puns.

punt¹ 1 n. flat-bottomed boat propelled by long pole thrust against bottom of river etc. 2 v. propel with or use punt-pole; travel or convey in punt.

punt² 1 v. kick (football) dropped from hands before it reaches ground. 2 n. such kick.

punt³ v.i. (in some card games) lay stake against bank; colloq. bet, speculate in shares, etc.

puny /'pju:nɪ/ a. undersized, feeble.

pup 1 n. puppy; young wolf, rat, seal, etc. 2 v.i. (of bitch) give birth to pups.

pupa /'pju:pə/ n. (pl. -pae /-pi:/) insect in passive development between larva and imago.

pupil /'pju:pɪl/ n. person being taught; opening in centre of iris of eye.

puppet /'pʌpɪt/ n. kind of doll representing human being etc. and moved by various means as entertainment; person whose acts are controlled by another. **puppet state** country apparently independent but actually under control of some greater power. **puppetry** n.

puppy /'pʌpɪ/ n. young dog; conceited young man. **puppy-fat** temporary fatness of child or adolescent.

purblind /'pɜ:blaɪnd/ a. partly blind, dim-sighted; obtuse, dull.

purchase /'pɜ:tʃɪs/ 1 v.t. buy. 2 n. buying; thing bought; firm hold on thing, leverage.

purdah /'pɜ:də/ n. system of screening Muslim or Hindu women from strangers, by means of curtain.

pure /pjʊə(r)/ a. unmixed, unadulterated; morally or sexually undefiled; guiltless; mere, simple; not discordant; (of science) dealing with abstract concepts and not practical applications.

purée /'pjʊəreɪ/ 1 n. pulp of vegetables or fruit etc. reduced to uniform mass. 2 v.t. (past & p.p. puréed) make purée of.

purely /'pjʊəlɪ/ adv. merely; exclusively; solely; entirely.

purgative /'pɜ:gətɪv/ 1 a. serving to purify; strongly laxative. 2 n. purgative thing.

purgatory /'pɜ:gətərɪ/ n. condition or place of spiritual cleansing; place of temporary suffering or expiation. **purgatorial** a.

purge /pɜ:dʒ/ 1 v.t. make physically or spiritually clean; remove by cleansing process; rid of persons regarded as undesirable; clear (bowels) by evacuation; Law atone for or wipe out (offence etc.). 2 n. purging; purgative. 3 **purgation** n.

purification /pjʊərɪfɪ'keɪʃ(ə)n/ n. purifying; ritual cleansing.

purify /'pjʊərɪfaɪ/ v.t. make pure, cleanse; clear of extraneous elements.

purist /'pjʊərɪst/ n. stickler for correctness esp. in language. **purism** n.

Puritan /'pjʊərɪt(ə)n/ 1 n. hist. member of English Protestant party regarding Reformation as incomplete; **puritan** person of extreme strictness in religion or morals. **2** *a.* **puritan** of Puritans; scrupulous in religion or morals. **3 puritanical** *a.*; **puritanism** *n.*

purity /ˈpjʊərɪtɪ/ *n.* freedom from physical or moral pollution.

purl [1] *n.* stitch in knitting with needle moved in opposite to normal direction; chain of minute loops. **2** *v.t.* make (stitch) purl.

purl [2] *v.i.* flow with babbling sound.

purler /ˈpɜːlə(r)/ *n. colloq.* heavy fall.

purlieu /ˈpɜːljuː/ *n.* (usu. in *pl.*) outskirts, outlying region.

purlin /ˈpɜːlɪn/ *n.* horizontal beam running along length of roof.

purloin /pɜːˈlɔɪn/ *v.t.* steal, pilfer.

purple /ˈpɜːp(ə)l/ **1** *n.* colour between red and blue; purple robe, esp. as dress of emperor etc.; cardinal's scarlet official dress. **2** *a.* of purple. **3** *v.* make or become purple.

purport 1 /ˈpɜːpət/ *n.* ostensible meaning; tenor of document or speech. **2** /pəˈpɔːt/ *v.t.* profess, be intended to seem (*to* do); have as its meaning.

purpose /ˈpɜːpəs/ **1** *n.* thing to be attained, thing intended; intention to act; resolution, determination. **2** *v.t.* have as one's purpose, intend. **3 on purpose** intentionally; **to good, little, no,** etc. **purpose** with good, little, etc. effect or result; **to the purpose** relevant.

purposeful /ˈpɜːpəsfʊl/ *a.* having or indicating purpose; intentional.

purposely /ˈpɜːpəslɪ/ *adv.* on purpose.

purposive /ˈpɜːpəsɪv/ *a.* having or serving or done with a purpose; purposeful.

purr /pɜː(r)/ **1** *v.* make low vibratory sound of cat expressing pleasure; (of machinery etc.) make similar sound. **2** *n.* such sound.

purse /pɜːs/ **1** *n.* small pouch for carrying money in; funds; sum given as present or prize. **2** *v.* contract (esp. lips) in wrinkles; become wrinkled. **3 hold the purse strings** have control of expenditure.

purser /ˈpɜːsə(r)/ *n.* ship's officer who keeps accounts, esp. head steward in passenger vessel.

pursuance /pəˈsjuːəns/ *n.* carrying out or observance (*of* plan, rules, etc.).

pursuant /pəˈsjuːənt/ *adv.* conformably *to*.

pursue /pəˈsjuː/ *v.* follow with intent to overtake or capture or do harm to; seek after; persistently assail; proceed along; continue; continue to investigate etc.; follow (profession etc.).

pursuit /pəˈsjuːt/ *n.* pursuing; occupation or activity pursued.

purulent /ˈpjʊərʊlənt/ *a.* of or containing or discharging pus. **purulence** *n.*

purvey /pəˈveɪ/ *v.* provide or supply (provisions) as one's business. **purveyor** *n.*

purview /ˈpɜːvjuː/ *n.* range of physical or mental vision.

pus /pʌs/ *n.* yellowish viscous matter produced from inflamed or infected tissue.

push /pʊʃ/ **1** *v.* exert force on (thing etc.) to move it away from oneself; cause to move thus; exert such force; thrust forward or upward or *out* or *forth*; make one's way forcibly or persistently; make persistent demands *for*; urge, impel; sell (drug) illegally; tax abilities or tolerance of. **2** *n.* act of pushing; force thus exerted; vigorous effort; determination; use of influence to advance person. **3 the push** *sl.* dismissal; **push-bike** *colloq.* pedal cycle; **push-chair** child's folding chair on wheels; **push off** *sl.* go away; **push-over** opponent or difficulty easily overcome.

pusher *n.* illegal seller of drugs.

pushing *a. colloq.* pushy; having nearly reached (specified age).

pushy *a. colloq.* self-assertive; showing determination to get on.

pusillanimous /pjuːsɪˈlænɪməs/ *a.* lacking courage, timid. **pusillanimity** /-ˈnɪm-/ *n.*

puss /pʊs/ *n.* cat; playful or coquettish girl.

pussy /ˈpʊsɪ/ *n. colloq.* cat. **pussyfoot** tread softly or lightly, move or act warily; **pussy-willow** kind of willow with silky catkins.

pustulate /ˈpʌstjʊleɪt/ *v.* form into pustules.

pustule /ˈpʌstjuːl/ *n.* pimple. **pustular** *a.*

put /pʊt/ **1** *v.* (*past* & *p.p.* **put**) move to or cause to be in specified place or position or state; impose; substitute (thing *for* another); express in words; hurl (*the shot*) from hand as athletic exercise. **2** *n.* throw of shot. **3 put about** spread (rumour); **put across** make acceptable or effective or understood; **put away** *colloq.* imprison, *colloq.* consume (food or drink); **put down** suppress, snub, record in writing, consider *as*, attribute *to*, kill (old etc. animal); **put in** install, formally present, perform (spell of work), *colloq.* spend (time); **put off** postpone, evade (person *with* excuse), dissuade, repel, disconcert; **put on** clothe (oneself) with, cause (electric light, apparatus) to operate, feign, develop additional (weight of body); **put out** disconcert, annoy, extinguish, dislocate; **put over** = *put across*; **put through** connect by telephone, cause to undergo or experience, complete; **put together** make from parts, combine (parts) into whole; **put up** build, raise, lodge and entertain, propose, offer for sale etc., pack for sale etc.; **put-up** fraudulently concocted; **put upon** *colloq.* unfairly burdened or deceived; **put up to** inform of, instigate in; **put up with** submit to, tolerate.

putative /ˈpjuːtətɪv/ *a.* reputed, supposed.

putrefy /ˈpjuːtrɪfaɪ/ *v.* become putrid, go bad, rot; fester. **putrefaction** *n.*; **putrefactive** *a.*

putrescent /pjuːˈtresənt/ *a.* of or in process of rotting. **putrescence** *n.*

putrid /ˈpjuːtrɪd/ *a.* decomposed, rotten; stinking. **putridity** *n.*

putsch /pʊtʃ/ *n.* attempt at revolution.

putt /pʌt/ **1** *v.* strike (golf-ball) gently to roll it into hole. **2** *n.* putting stroke. **3 putting-green** smooth turf round hole.

puttee /ˈpʌti/ *n.* long strip of cloth wound spirally round leg for protection and support.

putter /ˈpʌtə(r)/ *n.* golf-club used in putting.

putty /ˈpʌti/ **1** *n.* paste of chalk and linseed oil etc. for fixing panes of glass etc. **2** *v.t.* fix or fill with putty.

puzzle /ˈpʌz(ə)l/ **1** *n.* difficult or confusing problem; problem or toy designed to test ingenuity etc. **2** *v.* perplex, be perplexed; puzzle *out* by exercising ingenuity etc. **3 puzzlement** *n.*

PVC *abbr.* polyvinyl chloride.

pyaemia /paɪˈiːmɪə/ *n.* severe bacterial infection of blood.

pygmy /ˈpɪgmɪ/ **1** *n.* one of group of very short people in equatorial Africa; very small person or thing. **2** *a.* of pygmies; dwarf.

pyjamas /pəˈdʒɑːməz/ *n.pl.* suit of trousers and top for sleeping in etc.

pylon /ˈpaɪlɒn/ *n.* tall structure erected as support, esp. for overhead electric cables.

pyorrhoea /paɪəˈriːə/ *n.* discharge of pus, esp. in disease of tooth-sockets.

pyramid /ˈpɪrəmɪd/ *n.* monumental (esp. ancient Egyptian) stone structure with square base and sloping sides meeting at apex; solid of this shape with base of three or more sides; pyramid-shaped thing. **pyramidal** /-ˈræm-/ *a.*

pyre /paɪə(r)/ *n.* pile of combustible material esp. for burning corpse.

pyrethrum /paɪˈriːθrəm/ *n.* chrysanthemum with finely divided leaves; insecticide made from its dried flowers.

Pyrex /ˈpaɪreks/ *n.* (**P**) a hard heat-resistant glass.

pyrites /paɪˈraɪtiːz/ *n.* native sulphide of iron or copper and iron.

pyromania /paɪrəʊˈmeɪnɪə/ *n.* uncontrollable impulse to start fires. **pyromaniac** *n.* & *a.*

pyrotechnics /paɪrəʊˈtekniks/ *n.pl.* art of making fireworks; display of fireworks. **pyrotechnic** *a.*

pyrrhic /ˈpɪrɪk/ *a.* (of victory) achieved at too great cost.

python /ˈpaɪθ(ə)n/ *n.* large snake that crushes its prey.

pyx /pɪks/ *n.* vessel in which concrated bread for Eucharist is kept.

Q

Q *abbr.* Queen.

QC *abbr.* Queen's Counsel.

QED *abbr.* which was to be proved (*quod erat demonstrandum*).

QM *abbr.* Quartermaster.

qr. *abbr.* quarter(s).

qt. *abbr.* quart(s).

qua /kwɑː/ *conj.* in the capacity of.

quack¹ **1** *n.* harsh cry of ducks. **2** *v.i.* utter quack; talk loudly and foolishly.

quack² *n.* pretender to skill esp. in medicine etc.; charlatan. **quackery** *n.*

quad /kwɒd/ *colloq.* **1** *n.* quadrangle; quadruplet; quadraphony. **2** *a.* quadraphonic.

quadrangle /ˈkwɒdræŋg(ə)l/ *n.* 4-sided figure, esp. square or rectangle; 4-sided court esp. in college etc. **quadrangular** *a.*

quadrant /ˈkwɒdrənt/ *n.* quarter of circle or sphere; instrument for taking angular measurements etc.

quadraphonic /kwɒdrəˈfɒnɪk/ *a.* (of sound-reproduction) using 4 transmission channels. **quadraphony** *n.*

quadratic /kwɒdˈrætɪk/ **1** *a.* involving the square and no higher power of unknown quantity or variable. **2** *n.* quadratic equation.

quadrennial /kwɒdˈrenɪəl/ *a.* lasting 4 years; recurring every 4 years.

quadrilateral /kwɒdrɪˈlætər(ə)l/ **1** *a.* 4-sided. **2** *n.* quadrilateral figure.

quadrille /kwəˈdrɪl/ *n.* square dance; music for it.

quadroon /kwɒˈdruːn/ *n.* person of quarter-Negro blood.

quadruped /ˈkwɒdrʊped/ *n.* 4-footed animal.

quadruple /ˈkwɒdrʊp(ə)l/ **1** *a.* fourfold; of 4 parts or parties; being 4 times as many or much as. **2** *n.* quadruple number or amount. **3** *v.* multiply by 4.

quadruplet /ˈkwɒdrʊplet/ *n.* one of 4 children born at one birth.

quadruplicate 1 /kwɒˈdruːplɪkət/ *a.* fourfold; of which 4 copies are made. **2** /kwɒˈdruːplɪkeɪt/ *v.t.* multiply by 4; make 4 copies of.

quaff /kwɒf/ *v.* drink in copious draughts.

quagmire /ˈkwæɡmaɪə(r)/ *n.* quaking bog, marsh, slough.

quail¹ *n.* bird related to partridge.

quail² *v.i.* flinch, show fear.

quaint *a.* unfamiliar or old-fashioned; daintily odd.

quake 1 *v.i.* tremble; rock to and fro. **2** *n. colloq.* earthquake.

Quaker /ˈkweɪkə(r)/ *n.* member of Society of Friends. **Quakerism** *n.*

qualification /kwɒlɪfɪˈkeɪʃ(ə)n/ *n.* qualifying; accomplishment; thing that modifies or limits. **qualificatory** *a.*

qualify /ˈkwɒlɪfaɪ/ *v.* make or become competent or fit or entitled or eligible etc. (*for, to*); modify, limit; moderate, mitigate; attribute quality to, describe as.

qualitative /ˈkwɒlɪtətɪv/ *a.* concerned with or depending on quality.

quality /ˈkwɒlɪtɪ/ *n.* degree of excellence, attribute; relative nature or kind or character; timbre.

qualm /kwɑːm/ *n.* misgiving; scruple of conscience; momentary faint or sick feeling.

quandary /ˈkwɒndərɪ/ *n.* perplexed state; dilemma.

quango /ˈkwæŋɡəʊ/ *n.* semi-public administrative body appointed by government.

quanta *pl.* of **quantum**.

quantify /ˈkwɒntɪfaɪ/ *v.t.* express as quantity.

quantitative /ˈkwɒntɪtətɪv/ *a.* of or measured or measurable by quantity.

quantity /ˈkwɒntɪtɪ/ *n.* size or extent or weight or amount or number; in *pl.* large amounts or numbers; length or shortness of sound or syllable; thing having quantity. **quantity surveyor** person who measures and prices the work of builders.

quantum /ˈkwɒntəm/ *n.* (*pl.* **-ta**) unit quantity of energy proportional to frequency of radiation; required or desired or allowed amount.

quarantine /ˈkwɒrəntiːn/ **1** *n.* isolation imposed on ship or person or animal etc. to prevent infection or contagion; period of this. **2** *v.t.* put in quarantine.

quark /kwɑːk/ *n. Phys.* component of elementary particles.

quarrel /ˈkwɒr(ə)l/ **1** *n.* severe or angry dispute; break in friendly relations; cause of complaint. **2** *v.i.* have quarrel, dispute fiercely; find fault *with*. **3 quarrelsome** *a*.

quarry[1] /'kwɒrɪ/ **1** *n*. place from which stone is extracted for building etc. **2** *v*. extract from quarry. **3 quarry tile** unglazed floor-tile.

quarry[2] /'kwɒrɪ/ *n*. intended prey; object of pursuit.

quart /kwɔːt/ *n*. liquid measure equal to a quarter of gallon.

quarter /'kwɔːtə(r)/ **1** *n*. one of 4 equal parts; period of 3 months, esp. ending on quarter-day; point of time 15 minutes before or after any hour o'clock; 25 US or Canadian cents, coin worth this; division of town; point of compass, region at this; direction, district; source of supply; in *pl*. lodgings, abode, station of troops; mercy towards enemy etc. on condition of surrender; grain-measure of 8 bushels, weight of 28 or *US* 25 lb. **2** *v.t.* divide into quarters; put (troops, etc.) into quarters; provide with lodgings. **3 quarter-day** day on which quarterly payments are due; **quarterdeck** part of upper deck between stern and after-mast; **quarter-final** match or round preceding semifinal; **quarter-finalist** *n*.; **quarter-light** side-window other than main door-window in car etc.; **quartermaster** *Mil.* regimental officer in charge of quartering, rations, etc., *Naut.* officer in charge of steering, hold-stowing, etc.

quartering *n*. division into quarters; in *pl. Her.* coats of arms arranged on one shield to denote alliances of families.

quarterly /'kwɔːtəlɪ/ **1** *adv*. once in every quarter of year. **2** *a*. done or published or due quarterly. **3** *n*. quarterly magazine.

quartet /kwɔː'tet/ *n. Mus.* composition for group of 4 performers; the performers; group of 4.

quarto /'kwɔːtəʊ/ *n*. (*pl.* **-os**) size of book or page given by folding sheet of standard size to form 4 leaves; book or page of this size.

quartz /kwɔːts/ *n*. silica in various mineral forms. **quartz clock** one operated by electric vibrations of quartz crystal.

quasar /'kweɪzɑː(r)/ *n*. starlike object with large red-shift.

quash /kwɒʃ/ *v.t.* annul; reject as not valid; suppress, crush.

quasi- /'kweɪzaɪ/ *in comb.* seeming(ly), not real(ly), almost.

quassia /'kwɒʃə/ *n*. S. Amer. tree; its wood or bark or root; bitter tonic made from this.

quaternary /kwə'tɜːnərɪ/ *a*. having 4 parts.

quatrain /'kwɒtreɪn/ *n*. 4-line stanza.

quatrefoil /'kætrəfɔɪl/ *n*. 4-cusped figure; 4-lobed leaf or flower.

quaver /'kweɪvə(r)/ **1** *v*. (of voice or sound) vibrate, shake, tremble; say in trembling tones. **2** *n*. tremulousness in speech; trill; *Mus.* note equal to half crotchet. **3 quavery** *a*.

quay /kiː/ *n*. artificial landing-place for loading or unloading ships.

queasy /'kwiːzɪ/ *a*. inclined to sickness or nausea; liable to qualms or scruples.

queen 1 *n*. female sovereign of kingdom; king's wife; woman or country etc. pre-eminent in specified field; perfect fertile female of bee or ant etc.; most powerful piece in chess; court-card bearing representation of queen; *sl.* male homosexual. **2** *v*. convert (pawn in chess) to queen when it reaches opponent's end of board; (of pawn) be thus converted. **3 queen it** act like queen; **queen mother** king's widow who is mother of sovereign; **Queen's** or **King's Bench** division of High Court of Justice; **Queen's** or **King's Counsel** counsel to the Crown, taking precedence over other barristers. **4 queenly** *a*.

queer /kwɪə(r)/ **1** *a*. strange, odd, eccentric; of questionable character; out of sorts; *sl.* (esp. of man) homosexual. **2** *n. sl.* (esp. male) homosexual. **3** *v.t. sl.* spoil, put out of order.

quell *v.t.* suppress, crush.

quench *v.t.* satisfy (thirst); extinguish (fire); cool; stifle or suppress.

quern *n*. hand-mill for grinding corn etc.

querulous /'kweruːləs/ *a*. complaining; peevish.

query /'kwɪərɪ/ **1** *n*. question, question mark, esp. indicating doubt of correctness of statement etc. **2** *v.t.* call in question, question accuracy of.

quest 1 *n*. search, seeking; thing sought; inquiry. **2** *v.i.* search *about*.

question /'kwestʃ(ə)n/ **1** *n.* sentence phrased, punctuated, or spoken so as to elicit information; doubt or dispute; subject of discussion; problem for solution; matter depending on conditions *of.* **2** *v.t.* ask questions of; subject to examination; throw doubt on. **3 in question** being mentioned or discussed; **out of the question** too impracticable to be worth discussing; **question mark** punctuation mark (?) indicating question; **question-master** chairman of broadcast quiz etc.; **question time** period in parliament when MPs may question ministers.

questionable /'kwestʃənəb(ə)l/ *a.* of doubtful truth or honesty or wisdom.

questionnaire /kwestʃə'neə(r)/ *n.* series of questions for obtaining information on special points.

queue /kju:/ **1** *n.* line of persons or vehicles etc. awaiting their turn; pigtail. **2** *v.i.* (often with *up*) stand in or join queue.

quibble /'kwɪb(ə)l/ **1** *n.* petty objection; merely verbal or trivial point of criticism; play on words; equivocation, evasion. **2** *v.i.* use quibbles.

quiche /ki:ʃ/ *n.* open pie with usu. savoury filling.

quick 1 *a.* taking only a short time (to do thing or things); arriving after only a short time, prompt; lively, alert, intelligent. **2** *adv.* quickly. **3** *n.* sensitive flesh below nails or skin; seat of feeling or emotion. **4 quicklime** unslaked lime; **quicksand** loose wet sand readily swallowing up heavy objects; **quickset** (of hedge) formed of living plants set to grow in ground; **quicksilver** mercury; **quickstep** fast foxtrot.

quicken *v.* make or become quicker; accelerate; give life to; (of foetus) make perceptible movements.

quid¹ *n. sl.* (*pl.* same) one pound sterling.

quid² *n.* lump of tobacco for chewing.

quiddity /'kwɪdɪtɪ/ *n.* essence, real nature.

quid pro quo /kwɪd prəʊ 'kwəʊ/ thing given as compensation.

quiescent /kwɪ'es(ə)nt/ *a.* inert, dormant. **quiescence** *n.*

quiet /'kwaɪət/ **1** *a.* with little or no sound or motion; of gentle disposition; unobtrusive; tranquil. **2** *n.* undisturbed state; tranquillity, repose; calm, silence. **3** *v.* quieten.

quieten /'kwaɪətən/ *v.* make or become quiet, calm.

quietism /'kwaɪətɪz(ə)m/ *n.* passive attitude towards life, esp. as form of religious mysticism. **quietist** *n. & a.*

quietude /'kwaɪətju:d/ *n.* quietness.

quietus /kwaɪ'i:təs/ *n.* death; finishing stroke.

quiff *n.* lock of hair brushed upwards in front.

quill *n.* large feather of wing or tail; hollow stem of this; pen etc. made of quill; (usu. in *pl.*) porcupine's spine(s).

quilt 1 *n.* bed-cover, esp. of quilted material. **2** *v.t.* make from padding kept in place between two layers of material by lines of stitching.

quin *n. colloq.* quintuplet.

quince *n.* (tree bearing) hard pear-shaped fruit used in jams etc.

quincentenary /kwɪnsen'ti:nərɪ/ **1** *n.* 500th anniversary; celebration of this. **2** *a.* of a quincentenary.

quinine /'kwɪni:n/ *n.* bitter drug used in treatment of malaria and as tonic.

Quinquagesima /kwɪŋkwə'dʒesɪmə/ *n.* Sunday before Lent.

quinquennial /kwɪŋ'kwenɪəl/ *a.* lasting 5 years; recurring every 5 years.

quinsy /'kwɪnzɪ/ *n.* abscess that forms around tonsils.

quintessence /kwɪn'tes(ə)ns/ *n.* purest form or manifestation *of* some quality etc.; highly refined extract. **quintessential** /-'sen-/ *a.*

quintet /kwɪn'tet/ *n. Mus.* composition for group of 5 performers; the performers; group of 5.

quintuple /'kwɪntʊp(ə)l/ **1** *a.* fivefold; having 5 parts; being 5 times as many or much as. **2** *n.* quintuple number or amount. **3** *v.* multiply by 5.

quintuplet /'kwɪntjʊplɪt/ *n.* one of 5 children born at one birth.

quip 1 *n.* clever saying, epigram. **2** *v.i.* make quips.

quire /kwaɪə(r)/ *n.* 25 sheets of writing-paper; one of the folded sheets that are sewn together in book-binding.

quirk *n.* trick of action or behaviour. **quirky** *a.*

quisling /'kwɪzlɪŋ/ *n.* collaborator with invading enemy.

quit 1 *v.* give up, abandon; leave; stop. **2** *pred.a.* rid *of*.

quitch *n.* couch-grass.

quite *adv.* completely, altogether, absolutely; rather, to some extent.

quits *pred.a.* on even terms by retaliation or repayment.

quittance /'kwɪt(ə)ns/ *n.* release *from* obligation; acknowledgement of payment.

quiver¹ /'kwɪvə(r)/ **1** *v.i.* tremble or vibrate with slight rapid motion. **2** *n.* quivering motion or sound.

quiver² /'kwɪvə(r)/ *n.* case for arrows.

qui vive /ki: 'vi:v/ **on the *qui vive*** on the alert. [F]

quixotic /kwɪk'sɒtɪk/ *a.* extravagantly and romantically chivalrous. **quixotically** *adv.*

quiz 1 *n.* questioning or series of questions, esp. as entertainment or competition. **2** *v.t.* examine by questioning.

quizzical /'kwɪzɪk(ə)l/ *a.* mocking, gently amused.

quod *n. sl.* prison.

quoin /kɔɪn/ *n.* external angle of building, corner-stone; wedge used in printing or gunnery.

quoit /kɔɪt/ *n.* rubber ring thrown at mark or to encircle peg etc.; in *pl.* game played with quoits.

quondam /'kwɒndæm/ *a.* that was; former.

quorate /'kwɔ:reɪt/ *a.* (of meeting etc.) having quorum present.

quorum /'kwɔ:rəm/ *n.* number that must be present to constitute valid meeting.

quota /'kwəʊtə/ *n.* share to be contributed to or received from total by one of parties concerned; total number or amount required or permitted.

quotable /'kwəʊtəb(ə)l/ *a.* worth quoting. **quotability** *n.*

quotation /kwəʊ'teɪʃ(ə)n/ *n.* quoting; passage or price quoted. **quotation-marks** punctuation marks (' ' or " ") used at beginning and end of quoted words.

quote 1 *v.* cite as example, authority, etc.; repeat or copy out passage from; make quotations (*from*); state price (of). **2** *n. colloq.* passage or price quoted; (usu. in *pl.*) quotation-mark.

quoth /kwəʊθ/ *v.t. arch.* (only with *I* or *he* or *she* placed after) said.

quotidian /kwɒ'tɪdɪən/ *a.* daily, of every day; commonplace.

quotient /'kwəʊʃ(ə)nt/ *n.* result given by dividing one quantity by another.

q.v. *abbr.* which see (*quod vide*).

qy. *abbr.* query.

R

R *abbr.* registered as trademark.

R. *abbr. Regina; Rex;* River.

r. *abbr.* right.

RA *abbr.* Royal Academician; Royal Academy; Royal Artillery.

rabbet /'ræbɪt/ **1** *n.* step-shaped channel cut along edge or face of wood etc. to receive edge or tongue of another piece. **2** *v.t.* join with rabbet; cut rabbet in.

rabbi /'ræbaɪ/ *n.* Jewish religious leader; Jewish scholar or teacher esp. of the law. **rabbinical** /-'bɪn-/ *a.*

rabbit /'ræbɪt/ **1** *n.* gregarious burrowing mammal of hare family; *colloq.* poor performer at game. **2** *v.i.* hunt rabbits; *sl.* talk at length. **3 rabbit punch** punch on back of neck. **4 rabbity** *a.*

rabble /'ræb(ə)l/ *n.* disorderly crowd, mob; contemptible or inferior set of people; *the* lowest classes. **rabble-rouser** person who stirs up rabble for social or political change.

Rabelaisian /ræbə'leɪzɪən/ *a.* exuberantly and coarsely humorous.

rabid /'ræbɪd/ *a.* furious, unreasoning; affected with rabies, mad. **rabidity** *n.*

rabies /'reɪbiːz/ *n.* contagious virus disease of dogs etc., hydrophobia.

RAC *abbr.* Royal Automobile Club.

raccoon var. of **racoon**.

race[1] **1** *n.* contest of speed; in *pl.* series of these for horses etc.; onward movement; strong current in sea or river; channel. **2** *v.* compete in speed (with); cause to race; go at full speed; attend races. **3 racecourse** ground for horseracing; **racehorse** one bred or kept for racing; **race-meeting** horse-racing fixture; **race-track** course for racing horses or vehicles etc.

race[2] *n.* each of the major divisions of mankind; group of persons or animals etc. (regarded as) of common stock; posterity *of.*

raceme /rə'siːm/ *n.* flower-cluster with flowers attached by short stalks along central stem.

racial /'reɪʃ(ə)l/ *a.* of or characteristic of race[2]; concerning or caused by race[2].

racialism /'reɪʃəlɪz(ə)m/ *n.* belief in superiority of particular race; antagonism between races. **racialist** *n.* & *a.*

racism /'reɪsɪz(ə)m/ *n.* racialism; theory that human abilities etc. are determined by race. **racist** *n.* & *a.*

rack[1] **1** *n.* framework, usu. with rails or bars etc. for holding things; cogged or indented rail or bar gearing with wheel, pinion, etc.; *hist.* instrument of torture for stretching victim's joints. **2** *v.t.* torture on rack; inflict suffering on. **3 rack one's brains** make great mental effort; **rack-rent** extortionate rent.

rack[2] *n.* destruction (usu. **rack and ruin**).

racket[1] *n.* network of cord, catgut, etc. stretched across round or oval frame with handle, used as bat in tennis etc.; in *pl.* ball-game with rackets in court of 4 plain walls.

racket[2] **1** *n.* uproar, din; way of making money etc. by dubious or illegal means; *sl.* game, line of business. **2** *v.i.* move *about* noisily.

racketeer /rækɪ'tɪə(r)/ *n.* person who operates dishonest scheme. **racketeering** *n.*

rackety /'rækɪtɪ/ *a.* noisy, rowdy.

raconteur /rækɒn'tɜː(r)/ *n.* teller of anecdotes.

racoon /rə'kuːn/ *n.* bushy-tailed N. Amer. nocturnal mammal.

racy /'reɪsɪ/ *a.* lively, spirited; of distinctive quality or vigour.

RADA *abbr.* Royal Academy of Dramatic Art.

radar /'reɪdɑː(r)/ *n.* system for determination of direction and range of objects by radio devices; apparatus used for this. **radar trap** arrangement using radar to detect vehicles travelling faster than speed limit.

raddle /'ræd(ə)l/ **1** *n.* red ochre. **2** *v.t.* colour with raddle, or with much rouge crudely used.

radial /'reɪdɪəl/ **1** *a.* of or arranged like rays or radii; having spokes or lines radiating from a centre; acting or moving along such lines; (of tyre) having fabric layers parallel and tread strengthened. **2** *n.* radial-ply tyre. **3 radial-ply** (of tyre) radial.

radian /'reɪdɪən/ *a.* angle at centre of circle formed by radii of arc with length equal to radius.

radiant /'reɪdɪənt/ *a.* emitting rays;

beaming with joy etc.; bright or dazzling; issuing in rays. **2** *n.* point or object from which heat or light radiates. **3 radiance** *n.*; **radiancy** *n.*

radiate /ˈreɪdɪeɪt/ *v.* diverge or emit from centre; emit rays of light, heat, etc.; be arranged like spokes; disseminate; show clearly.

radiation /reɪdɪˈeɪʃ(ə)n/ *n.* radiating; emission of energy as electromagnetic waves; energy thus transmitted, esp. invisibly. **radiation sickness** that caused by exposure to excessive radiation.

radiator /ˈreɪdɪeɪtə(r)/ *n.* apparatus for heating room etc. by radiation of heat; engine-cooling apparatus in motor vehicle or aeroplane.

radical /ˈrædɪk(ə)l/ **1** *a.* fundamental, far-reaching, thorough; advocating fundamental reforms; forming the basis, primary; of the root of a number. **2** *n.* person holding radical political opinions; atom or group of atoms forming base of compound and remaining unchanged during reactions; quantity forming or expressed as root of another. **radicalism** *n.*

radicle /ˈrædɪk(ə)l/ *n.* part of seed that develops into root.

radio /ˈreɪdɪəʊ/ **1** *n.* (*pl.* **-os**) transmission and reception of messages etc. by electromagnetic waves without connecting wires; apparatus for receiving signals by radio; broadcasting station; sound broadcasting. **2** *a.* of or relating to or sent by or used in or using radio. **3** *v.* send (message), send message to (person), by radio; communicate or broadcast by radio. **4 radio car** etc. vehicle equipped with radio for communication.

radio- *in comb.* connected with rays, radiation, radioactivity, or radio.

radioactive /reɪdɪəʊˈæktɪv/ *a.* of or exhibiting radioactivity.

radioactivity /reɪdɪəʊækˈtɪvɪtɪ/ *n.* property of spontaneous disintegration of atomic nuclei usu. with emission of penetrating radiation or particles.

radio-carbon /reɪdɪəʊˈkɑːbən/ *n.* radioactive isotope of carbon used in dating ancient organic materials.

radiogram /ˈreɪdɪəʊgræm/ *n.* combined radio and gramophone; telegram sent by raio; picture obtained by X-rays etc.

radiograph /ˈreɪdɪəʊgrɑːf/ **1** *n.* picture obtained by X-rays etc. **2** *v.t.* obtain such picture of. **3 radiographer** /-ˈɒg-/ *n.*; **radiography** /-ˈɒg-/*n.*

radiology /reɪdɪˈɒlədʒɪ/ *n.* scientific study of X-rays and other high-energy radiation. **radiologist** *n.*

radioscopy /reɪdɪˈɒskəpɪ/ *n.* examination by X-rays etc. of objects opaque to light. **radioscopic** /-ˈskɒp-/ *a.*

radio-telegraphy /reɪdɪəʊteˈlegrəfɪ/ *n.* telegraphy using radio.

radio-telephony /reɪdɪəʊteˈlefənɪ/ *n.* telephony using radio.

radio-therapy /reɪdɪəʊˈθerəpɪ/ *n.* treatment of disease by X-rays or other forms of radiation.

radish /ˈrædɪʃ/ *n.* plant with crisp pungent root eaten raw; this root.

radium /ˈreɪdɪəm/ *n.* radioactive metallic element.

radius /ˈreɪdɪəs/ *n.* (*pl.* **-dii** /-dɪaɪ/) straight line from centre to circumference of circle or sphere; any of set of lines diverging from point like radii of circle; bone of forearm on same side as thumb.

radix /ˈreɪdɪks/ *n.* (*pl.* **-dices** /-dɪsiːz/) number or symbol used as basis of numeration scale.

RAF *abbr.* Royal Air Force.

raffia /ˈræfɪə/ *n.* soft fibre from leaves of kind of palm.

raffish /ˈræfɪʃ/ *a.* of dissipated appearance; disreputable.

raffle /ˈræf(ə)l/ **1** *n.* sale of articles by lottery. **2** *v.t.* sell by raffle.

raft /rɑːft/ *n.* flat floating structure of wood or fastened logs etc., used in water for transport or as emergency boat.

rafter /ˈrɑːftə(r)/ *n.* any of sloping beams forming framework of roof.

rag[1] *n.* torn or frayed piece of woven material; remnant; in *pl.* tattered clothes; *derog.* newspaper. **rag doll** stuffed cloth doll; **ragtime** form of jazz with much syncopation; **rag trade** *colloq.* the clothing business; **ragwort** yellow-flowered wild plant.

rag[2] **1** *n.* annual programme of stunts etc. staged by students esp. to collect money for charity; *colloq.* prank; disorderly scene, rowdy celebration. **2** *v.*

sl. tease; play rough jokes on; engage in rag.

ragamuffin /'rægəmʌfɪn/ *n.* person in ragged dirty clothes.

rage 1 *n.* violent anger; fit of this; object of widespread temporary popularity. **2** *v.i.* rave, storm; be violent, be at the height; be full of anger.

ragged /'rægɪd/ *a.* torn, frayed; in ragged clothes; having broken jagged outline or surface; lacking finish or smoothness or uniformity.

raglan /'ræglən/ *n.* garment in which top of sleeve is carried up to neck. **raglan sleeve** one of this kind.

ragout /'rægu:/ *n.* stew of meat with vegetables.

raid 1 *n.* rapid surprise attack, in warfare or to steal or do harm; surprise visit by police etc. to arrest suspected persons or seize illicit goods. **2** *v.* make raid (on).

rail¹ 1 *n.* level or sloping bar or series of bars used to hang things on or as protection against falling etc. or as part of fence etc.; steel bar making part of track of railway; railway. **2** *v.t.* provide or enclose with rail(s). **3 railhead** farthest point reached by railway, point where rail transport ends; **railroad** *US* railway.

rail² *v.i.* complain fiercely or abusively.

rail³ *n.* small wading bird.

railing *n.* fence or barrier with rails.

raillery /'reɪlərɪ/ *n.* good-humoured ridicule.

railway /'reɪlweɪ/ *n.* track or set of tracks for passage of trains; tracks of this kind worked by single company; organization and persons required for their working. **railwayman** railway employee.

raiment /'reɪmənt/ *n. arch.* clothing.

rain 1 *n.* condensed moisture of atmosphere falling in drops; fall of these; in *pl.* season of these; falling liquid or particles or objects etc., rainlike descent of these. **2** *v.* fall or send down like rain; send down rain. **3 it rains** rain falls; **raincoat** waterproof coat; **rainfall** total amount of rain falling within given area in given time; **rain forest** tropical forest with heavy rainfall.

rainbow /'reɪnbəʊ/ **1** *n.* arch showing sequence of colours formed in sky by

refraction and dispersion of sun's rays in falling raindrops etc. **2** *a.* many-coloured. **3 rainbow trout** large trout orig. of N. Amer.

rainy /'reɪnɪ/ *a.* (of weather, day, region, etc.) in or on which rain is falling or much rain usually falls. **rainy day** *fig.* time of need.

raise /reɪz/ **1** *v.t.* put or take into higher position, cause to stand up or *up*, bring to vertical position; rouse; build up or *up*; levy, collect; cause to be heard or considered; educate; breed; increase amount of; remove (barrier). **2** *n.* increase in amount; *US* rise in salary. **3 raise Cain, hell,** etc. *colloq.* raise a disturbance; **raise a laugh** cause others to laugh; **raise one's eyebrows** look supercilious or shocked; **raising agent** substance causing bread and cakes etc. to rise.

raisin /'reɪz(ə)n/ *n.* dried grape.

raison d'être /reɪzɔ̃ 'detr/ purpose that accounts for or justifies or originally caused thing's existence. [F]

raj /rɑ:dʒ/ *n.* British rule in India.

raja /'rɑ:dʒə/ (also **rajah**) *n. hist.* Indian king or prince.

rake¹ 1 *n.* implement of pole with comb-like crossbar for drawing hay etc. together, smoothing loose soil, etc.; implement resembling rake used for other purposes. **2** *v.* collect, draw *together,* (as) with rake; use rake; ransack, search (*through* etc.); sweep with eyes, shot, etc. **3 rake-off** *colloq.* (share of) profit, commission.

rake² *n.* dissipated or immoral man of fashion.

rake³ *v.* set or be set at sloping angle; (of mast, funnel, etc.) incline towards stern or rear. **2** *n.* raking position or build; amount by which thing rakes.

rakish /'reɪkɪʃ/ *a.* like a rake²; dashing, jaunty.

rallentando /rælən'tændəʊ/ *Mus.* **1** *adv.* with gradual decrease of speed. **2** *n.* (*pl.* **-dos**) passage to be played thus.

rally¹ /'rælɪ/ **1** *v.* bring or come together for united effort; revive by effort of will; throw off illness; (of prices etc.) increase after fall. **2** *n.* act of rallying; recovery of energy or spirit; mass meeting; competition for motor vehicles over public roads; *Tennis* etc.

series of strokes before point is decided.

rally² /'rælɪ/ v.t. subject to good-humoured ridicule.

ram 1 n. uncastrated male sheep; battering-ram; pile-driving or hydraulic or pumping-machine or parts of them. 2 v.t. beat firm; force home; pack closely; collide violently with, charge or crash into; impress by repetition.

RAM abbr. Royal Academy of Music; random-access memory.

Ramadan /'ræmədɑːn/ n. ninth month of Muslim year, with strict fast during daylight hours.

ramble /'ræmb(ə)l/ 1 v.i. walk for pleasure; talk in desultory or irrelevant way. 2 n. walk taken for pleasure.

rambler /'ræmblə(r)/ n. person who rambles; straggling or climbing rose.

rambling /'ræmblɪŋ/ a. irregularly arranged; (of plant) straggling, climbing.

RAMC abbr. Royal Army Medical Corps.

ramekin /'ræmɪkɪn/ n. small dish for baking and serving individual portion of food; food served in this.

ramify /'ræmɪfaɪ/ v. form branches or sub-divisions; develop into complicated system. **ramification** n.

ramp¹ 1 n. slope joining two levels of ground or floor etc.; stairs for entering or leaving aircraft. 2 v. furnish or construct with ramp; take threatening posture.

ramp² n. sl. swindle; charging of extortionate prices.

rampage 1 /ræm'peɪdʒ/ v.i. rush about; rage, storm. 2 /'ræmpeɪdʒ/ n. violent behaviour. **3 on the rampage** rampaging. **4 rampageous** a.

rampant /'ræmpənt/ a. Her. (esp. of lion etc.) standing on one hind leg with forefeet in air; extravagant, unrestrained, rank, luxuriant. **rampancy** n.

rampart /'ræmpɑːt/ n. defensive broad-topped wall; defence, protection.

ramrod /'ræmrɒd/ n. hist. rod for ramming home charge of muzzle-loading firearm; fig. thing that is very straight or rigid.

ramshackle /'ræmʃæk(ə)l/ a. rickety, tumbledown.

ran past of **run**.

ranch /rɑːntʃ/ 1 n. cattle-breeding establishment esp. in US & Canada; farm where other animals are bred. 2 v.i. conduct ranch.

rancid /'rænsɪd/ a. smelling or tasting like rank stale fat. **rancidity** n.

rancour /'ræŋkə(r)/ n. malignant hate; bitterness. **rancorous** a.

rand n. monetary unit of S. Afr. countries.

R & D abbr. research and development.

random /'rændəm/ a. made or done etc. without method or conscious choice. **at random** without aim or purpose or principle; **random-access** (of computer memory) having all parts directly accessible.

randy /'rændɪ/ a. colloq. lustful.

ranee /'rɑːnɪ/ n. raja's wife or widow.

rang past of **ring**².

range /reɪndʒ/ 1 n. area over which thing is found or has effect or relevance; scope; region between limits of variables, such limits; distance attainable or to be covered by gun or projectile; distance that can be covered by vehicle etc. without refuelling; row or series, esp. of mountains; open or enclosed area with targets for shooting; cooking fireplace; stretch of grazing or hunting ground. 2 v. place in row(s) or in specified arrangement; rove, wander; extend, reach; vary between limits; go all about. **3 range-finder** instrument for estimating distance of object for shooting or photography.

ranger /'reɪndʒə(r)/ n. keeper of royal park or forest; **Ranger** senior Guide.

rangy /'reɪndʒɪ/ a. tall and slim.

rani var. of **ranee**.

rank¹ 1 n. position in hierarchy; grade of advancement; distinct social class, grade of dignity, high social position; place in scale; row, queue; soldiers in single line abreast; place where taxis await customers. 2 v. have rank or place; assign rank to; arrange in rank. **3 rank and file** ordinary undistinguished people; **the ranks** common soldiers.

rank² a. too luxuriant; coarse; offensive, loathsome; flagrant; gross.

rankle /'ræŋk(ə)l/ v.i. cause persistent annoyance or pain or resentment.

ransack /'rænsæk/ v.t. pillage, plunder; thoroughly search.

ransom /'rænsəm/ 1 *n*. sum of money or value paid for release of prisoner; liberation of prisoner in return for this. 2 *v.t.* buy freedom or restoration of; hold to ransom; release for a ransom. 3 **hold to ransom** keep prisoner and demand ransom.

rant 1 *v.* use bombastic language; preach noisily. 2 *n.* piece of ranting.

ranunculus /rə'nʌŋkjuləs/ *n.* (*pl.* -**luses**) plant of genus including buttercup.

rap[1] 1 *n.* smart slight blow; sound (as) of this; *sl.* blame, punishment. 2 *v.* strike smartly; make sound of rap; criticize adversely. 3 **rap out** utter abruptly.

rap[2] *n.* the least bit.

rapacious /rə'peɪʃəs/ *a.* grasping, extortionate, predatory. **rapacity** /-'pæs-/.

rape[1] 1 *n.* forcible or fraudulent sexual intercourse esp. imposed on woman; violent assault or interference. 2 *v.t.* commit rape on.

rape[2] *n.* plant grown as fodder and for its oil-yielding seed.

rapid /'ræpɪd/ 1 *a.* speedy, swift. 2 *n.* (usu. in *pl.*) steep descent in river-bed with swift current. 3 **rapidity** /-'pɪd-/ *n.*

rapier /'reɪpɪə(r)/ *n.* light slender sword used for thrusting.

rapine /'ræpaɪn/ *n.* plundering.

rapist /'reɪpɪst/ *n.* man who commits rape.

rapport /ræ'pɔː(r)/ *n.* communication, sympathetic relationship.

rapprochement /ræ'prɒʃmã/ *n.* restoration of harmonious relations esp. between States. [F]

rapscallion /ræp'skælɪən/ *n.* arch. rascal.

rapt *a.* absorbed; intent; carried away in spirit.

raptorial /ræp'tɔːrɪəl/ 1 *a.* predatory. 2 *n.* predatory animal or bird.

rapture /'ræptʃə(r)/ *n.* ecstatic delight; in *pl.* great enthusiasm or expression of it. **rapturous** *a.*

rare[1] *a.* seldom done or found or occurring; uncommon; exceptionally good; of less than usual density.

rare[2] *a.* (of meat) underdone.

rarebit: see **Welsh rabbit**.

rarefy /'reərɪfaɪ/ *v.* lessen density or solidity of; refine, become less dense. **rarefaction** *n.*

rarely /'reəlɪ/ *adv.* seldom, not often.

raring /'reərɪŋ/ *a.* colloq. eager (*to go* etc.).

rarity /'reərɪtɪ/ *n.* rareness; rare thing.

rascal /'rɑːsk(ə)l/ *n.* dishonest or mischievous person. **rascally** *a.*

rase var. of **raze**.

rash[1] *a.* hasty, impetuous; reckless.

rash[2] *n.* skin eruption in spots or patches; *fig.* sudden widespread onset of.

rasher /'ræʃə(r)/ *n.* thin slice of bacon or ham.

rasp /rɑːsp/ 1 *n.* coarse file; grating sound or effect. 2 *v.* scrape with rasp; scrape roughly; grate upon; make grating sound.

raspberry /'rɑːzbərɪ/ *n.* small usu. red fruit like blackberry; bramble bearing this; *sl.* sound expressing derision or dislike.

Rastafarian /ræstə'feərɪən/ 1 *n.* member of orig. Jamaican sect. 2 *a.* of this sect.

rat 1 *n.* rodent like large mouse; *sl.* unpleasant or treacherous person. 2 *v.i.* hunt or kill rats; act as informer. 3 **rat on** desert or betray (person); **rat race** fiercely competitive struggle; **smell a rat** begin to suspect treachery etc.

ratafia /rætə'fiːə/ *n.* liqueur flavoured with almonds or fruit-kernels; biscuit similarly flavoured.

ratchet /'rætʃɪt/ *n.* set of teeth on edge of bar or wheel with catch allowing motion in one direction only; ratchet-wheel. **ratchet-wheel** wheel with rim so toothed.

rate[1] 1 *n.* stated numerical proportion between two sets of things; standard or way of reckoning; value or cost, measure of this; (relative) speed; assessment on buildings and land owned, levied by local authorities; in *pl.* amount thus paid by householder. 2 *v.* estimate worth or value of; consider, regard as; rank or be rated *as*; subject to payment of local rate. 3 **ratepayer** person liable to pay rates.

rate[2] *v.t.* scold angrily.

rateable /'reɪtəb(ə)l/ *a.* liable to local rates. **rateable value** value at which house etc. is assessed for rates.

rather /'rɑːðə(r)/ *adv.* by preference;

more truly; to a greater extent; somewhat; *colloq.* most emphatically, assuredly.

ratify /'rætɪfaɪ/ *v.t.* confirm or accept by signature or other formality. **ratification** *n.*

rating /'reɪtɪŋ/ *n.* placing in rank or class; non-commissioned sailor; estimated standing of person as regards credit etc.; estimated size of audience to show popularity of a broadcast.

ratio /'reɪʃɪəʊ/ *n.* (*pl.* **-ios**) quantitative relation between similar magnitudes; proportion.

ratiocinate /rætɪ'ɒsɪneɪt/ *v.i.* reason, esp. formally. **ratiocination** *n.*

ration /'ræʃ(ə)n/ *n.* 1 *n.* fixed allowance or individual share of provisions, fuel, clothing, etc. 2 *v.t.* limit (food etc.) to fixed ration; share (*out*) in fixed quantities.

rational /'ræʃən(ə)l/ *a.* able to reason; sensible; moderate; of or based on reasoning; *Math.* expressible as ratio of integers. **rationality** *n.*

rationale /ræʃə'nɑːl/ *n.* fundamental reason or logical basis.

rationalism /'ræʃənəlɪz(ə)m/ *n.* practice of treating reason as basis of belief and knowledge. **rationalist** *n.* & *a.*; **rationalistic** *a.*

rationalize /'ræʃənəlaɪz/ *v.* offer rational but specious explanation of (behaviour or attitude); make logical and consistent; make (an industry etc.) more efficient by reducing waste. **rationalization** *n.*

ratline /'rætlɪn/ (also **ratlin**) *n.* any of the small lines fastened across ship's shrouds like ladder-rungs.

rattan /rə'tæn/ *n.* palm with long thin many-jointed stems; cane of this.

rattle /'ræt(ə)l/ 1 *v.* give out rapid succession of short sharp sounds; cause such sounds by shaking something; move or travel with rattling noise; say or recite rapidly; *sl.* disconcert, alarm. 2 *n.* rattling sound; instrument or plaything made to rattle. 3 **rattlesnake** venomous Amer. snake making rattling noise with tail; **rattletrap** rickety vehicle etc.

rattling 1 *a.* brisk, vigorous. 2 *adv.* remarkably (*good* etc.).

raucous /'rɔːkəs/ *a.* harsh-sounding; hoarse.

ravage /'rævɪdʒ/ 1 *v.* lay waste, plunder; make havoc. 2 *n.* (esp. in *pl.*) destructive effects *of.*

rave 1 *v.* talk wildly or deliriously; speak with rapturous admiration (*about*, *over*). 2 *n. colloq.* highly enthusiastic review. 3 **rave-up** *sl.* lively party.

ravel /'ræv(ə)l/ *v.* entangle, become entangled; confuse, complicate; fray out.

raven[1] /'reɪv(ə)n/ 1 *n.* large black hoarse-voiced crow. 2 *a.* of glossy black.

raven[2] /'ræv(ə)n/ *v.* seek *after* prey or plunder; devour voraciously.

ravenous /'rævənəs/ *a.* very hungry; voracious; rapacious.

ravine /rə'viːn/ *n.* deep narrow gorge.

ravioli /rævɪ'əʊlɪ/ *n.* small pasta cases containing meat etc.

ravish /'rævɪʃ/ *v.t.* enrapture, fill with delight; commit rape on.

raw *a.* uncooked; in natural state, not processed or manufactured; inexperienced, unskilled; stripped of skin; sore, sensitive to touch; (of weather) damp and chilly; crude. **in the raw** in its natural state, naked; **raw-boned** gaunt; **raw deal** unfair treatment; **rawhide** untanned leather; **raw material** that from which process of manufacture makes articles.

Rawlplug *n.* (**P**) thin cylindrical plug for holding screw in masonry.

ray[1] *n.* single line or narrow beam of light or other radiant energy; remnant or beginning of enlightening influence; any of set of radiating lines, parts, or things; marginal part of daisy etc.

ray[2] *n.* large marine food-fish related to skate.

ray[3] *n. Mus.* second note of scale in tonic sol-fa.

rayon /'reɪɒn/ *n.* textile fibre or fabric made from cellulose.

raze *v.t.* completely destroy, tear down.

razor /'reɪzə(r)/ *n.* instrument for shaving. **razor-bill** auk with sharp-edged bill; **razor-blade** flat piece of metal with usu. two sharp edges, used in safety razor; **razor-edge** keen edge, sharp mountain ridge, critical situation, sharp line of division.

razzle /'ræz(ə)l/ *n. sl.* spree.

razzle-dazzle *n.* excitement, bustle.

RC *abbr.* Roman Catholic.

RCA *abbr.* Royal College of Art.

RCM *abbr.* Royal College of Music.

RCS *abbr.* Royal College of Science; Royal College of Surgeons; Royal Corps of Signals.

Rd. *abbr.* Road.

re[1] /ri:/ *prep.* in the matter of; *colloq.* about, concerning.

re[2] var. of **ray**[3].

re- *pref.* attachable to almost any verb or verbal derivative, denoting once more, again, anew, afresh, repeated, back. For words with this prefix, if not found below, the root-words should be consulted.

RE *abbr.* Royal Engineers.

reach /ri:tʃ/ 1 *v.* stretch *out*, extend; stretch out hand etc.; get as far as, attain to, arrive at; amount to; pass or take with outstretched hand etc.; *Naut.* sail with wind abeam. 2 *n.* act of reaching; range of hand etc.; scope; continuous extent, tack. 3 **reach-me-down** *colloq.* ready-made.

react /rɪˈækt/ *v.i.* respond *to* stimulus; undergo change or show behaviour under some influence; be activated by repulsion *against*; tend in reverse or backward direction.

reaction /rɪˈækʃ(ə)n/ *n.* reacting; responsive feeling; occurrence of condition after its opposite; *Polit.* tendency to oppose change or to return to former system.

reactionary /rɪˈækʃənərɪ/ 1 *a. Polit.* showing reaction. 2 *n.* reactionary person.

reactivate /rɪˈæktɪveɪt/ *v.t.* restore to state of activity.

reactive /rɪˈæktɪv/ *a.* showing reaction.

reactor /rɪˈæktə(r)/ *n.* (in full **nuclear reactor**) assembly of materials in which controlled nuclear chain reaction takes place.

read /ri:d/ *v.* (*past* & *p.p.* **read** /red/) reproduce mentally or vocally (written or printed words etc.) while following their symbols with the eyes; (be able to) convert into intended words or meaning (written or printed words, figures, markings, etc.); interpret in certain sense; find written or printed; show, convey when read, record, indicate; study by reading; (of computer) copy or transfer (data).

readable /ˈri:dəb(ə)l/ *a.* able to be read esp. with interest. **readability** *n.*

reader /ˈri:də(r)/ *n.* person who reads, esp. aloud; book containing passages for instruction or exercise etc.; device to produce image that can be read from microfilm etc.; senior university lecturer; publisher's employee who reports on submitted MSS; printer's proof-corrector.

readership /ˈri:dəʃɪp/ *n.* readers of a newspaper etc.

readily /ˈredɪlɪ/ *adv.* without reluctance; willingly; easily.

readiness /ˈredmɪs/ *n.* prepared state; willingness, facility; quickness in argument or action.

reading /ˈri:dɪŋ/ *n.* entertainment at which something is read; literary knowledge; figure etc. shown by instrument or dial etc.; interpretation or view taken, rendering; word(s) read or given by editor as text; presentation of bill to legislative assembly. **reading-lamp** lamp giving light for reading.

ready /ˈredɪ/ 1 *a.* with preparations complete; in fit state; willing; within reach; fit for immediate use or action; prompt, enthusiastic. 2 *adv.* beforehand; in readiness. 3 *n. sl.* ready money. 4 *v.t.* prepare. 5 **at the ready** ready for action; **ready-made** (esp. of clothes) made in standard shapes and sizes, not to measure; **ready money** cash, actual coin; **ready reckoner** book or table of results of arithmetical calculations.

reagent /ri:ˈeɪdʒ(ə)nt/ *n.* substance used to produce chemical reaction.

real 1 *a.* actually existing or occurring; objective; genuine; consisting of immovable property; appraised by purchasing power. 2 *adv. Sc.* & *US colloq.* really, very. 3 **real tennis** original form of tennis played on indoor court.

realism /ˈri:əlɪz(ə)m/ *n.* practice of regarding things in their true nature and dealing with them as they are; fidelity to nature in representation. **realist** *n.*

realistic /rɪəˈlɪstɪk/ *a.* regarding things as they are; based on facts rather than ideals.

reality /rɪˈælɪtɪ/ *n.* what is real or existent or underlies appearances; real existence; being real; likeness to original. **in reality** in fact.

realize /'riːəlaɪz/ *v.t.* be fully aware of; present or conceive as real; understand clearly; convert into fact; convert into money; be sold for. **realization** *n.*

really /'riːəlɪ/ *adv.* in fact; I assure you; as expression of mild protest or surprise.

realm /relm/ *n.* kingdom; sphere, domain.

realty /'riːəltɪ/ *n.* real estate.

ream *n.* twenty quires of paper; (usu. in *pl.*) large quantity of writing.

reap *v.* cut (grain etc.) with sickle or machine; harvest; *fig.* receive as consequences of actions.

rear[1] *n.* back part of anything; space or position at back. **2** *a.* at the back. **3 bring up the rear** come last; **rear-admiral** flag officer below vice-admiral; **rearguard** troops etc. detached to protect rear, esp. in retreat; **rearguard action** engagement between rearguard and enemy. **4 rear-most** *a.*

rear[2] *v.* bring up, foster, educate; cultivate; (of horse etc.) rise on hind feet; raise, build.

rearm /riːˈɑːm/ *v.* arm again, esp. with improved weapons. **rearmament** *n.*

rearward /'rɪəwəd/ **1** *n.* rear. **2** *a.* at the rear. **3** *adv.* rearwards.

rearwards *adv.* towards the rear.

reason /'riːz(ə)n/ **1** *n.* motive or cause or justification; fact adduced or serving as this; intellectual faculty by which conclusions are drawn from premisses; sense, sanity; sensible conduct; moderation. **2** *v.* form or try to reach conclusions by connected thought; think *out*; use argument *with* by way of persuasion.

reasonable /'riːzənəb(ə)l/ *a.* having sound judgement; sensible, moderate; inexpensive, not extortionate; tolerable.

reassure /riːəˈʃʊə(r)/ *v.t.* restore confidence to; confirm again in opinion etc.

rebarbative /rɪˈbɑːbətɪv/ *a.* forbidding, repellent.

rebate[1] /'riːbeɪt/ *n.* deduction from sum to be paid, discount.

rebate[2] /'ræbɪt, rɪˈbeɪt/ var. of **rabbet**.

rebel 1 /'reb(ə)l/ *n.* person who fights against or resists or refuses allegiance to established government; person who resists authority or control. **2** /rɪˈbel/ *v.i.* act as rebel (*against*); feel or show opposition, repugnance, etc. (*against*).

rebellion /rɪˈbeljən/ *n.* open resistance to any authority, esp. organized armed resistance to established government.

rebellious /rɪˈbeljəs/ *a.* in rebellion; disposed to rebel; unmanageable, refractory.

rebound 1 /rɪˈbaʊnd/ *v.i.* spring back after impact; recoil. **2** /'riːbaʊnd/ *n.* rebounding, recoil; reaction after emotion.

rebuff /rɪˈbʌf/ **1** *n.* rejection of person who makes advances or offers help etc.; repulse. **2** *v.t.* give rebuff to.

rebuke /rɪˈbjuːk/ **1** *v.t.* express condemnation of or censure authoritatively. **2** *n.* rebuking or being rebuked.

rebus /'riːbəs/ *n.* riddling representation of name or word etc. by pictures etc. suggesting its parts.

rebut /rɪˈbʌt/ *v.t.* refute, disprove; force back. **rebuttal** *n.*

recalcitrant /rɪˈkælsɪtrənt/ *a.* obstinately disobedient or refractory. **recalcitrance** *n.*

recall /rɪˈkɔːl/ **1** *v.t.* summon back; bring back *to* memory; (cause to) remember; revive, resuscitate; revoke, annul. **2** *n.* recalling or being recalled.

recant /rɪˈkænt/ *v.* withdraw and renounce as erroneous or heretical; disavow former opinion etc. **recantation** *n.*

recap /'riːkæp/ **1** *v. colloq.* recapitulate. **2** *n.* recapitulation.

recapitulate /riːkəˈpɪtjʊleɪt/ *v.* summarize, restate briefly. **recapitulation** *n.*

recast /riːˈkɑːst/ *v.t.* (*past* & *p.p.* **-cast**) put into new form; improve arrangement of.

recce /'rekɪ/ *sl.* **1** *n.* reconnaissance. **2** *v.* reconnoitre.

recede /rɪˈsiːd/ *v.i.* go or shrink back; be left at an increasing distance; slope backwards; decline in force or value etc.

receipt /rɪˈsiːt/ **1** *n.* receiving or being received; written acknowledgement of receipt of payment etc.; (usu. in *pl.*) amount of money received. **2** *v.t.* write or give receipt on or for.

receive /rɪˈsiːv/ *v.* take into one's hands or possession, have sent to one;

acquire, get; have conferred etc. on one; stand force or weight of; consent to hear or consider; admit, submit to; convert (broadcast signals) into sound or picture; entertain as guest, greet, welcome; (esp. in *p.p.*) accept as authoritative or true.

receiver /rɪˈsiːvə(r)/ *n.* person appointed to administer property of bankrupt etc. or property under litigation; person who receives stolen goods; apparatus for receiving transmitted signals.

recent /ˈriːs(ə)nt/ *a.* not long past, that happened or existed lately; not long established, modern.

receptacle /rɪˈseptək(ə)l/ *n.* vessel, space, or place for receiving or holding.

reception /rɪˈsepʃ(ə)n/ *n.* receiving or being received; way in which person or thing is received; social occasion for receiving guests, esp. after wedding; place where visitors register on arriving at hotel, business premises, etc.; receiving of broadcast signals; quality of this. **reception room** one available or suitable for receiving guests.

receptionist /rɪˈsepʃənɪst/ *n.* person employed to receive guests, patients, clients, etc.

receptive /rɪˈseptɪv/ *a.* able or quick to receive ideas etc. **receptivity** /-ˈtɪv-/ *n.*

recess /rɪˈses/ 1 *n.* space set back from line of wall etc.; remote or secret place; temporary cessation from work etc., esp. of Parliament. 2 *v.* set back; provide with recess(es); *US* take recess.

recession /rɪˈseʃ(ə)n/ *n.* temporary decline in activity or prosperity; receding, withdrawal.

recessive /rɪˈsesɪv/ *a.* tending to recede; (of inherited characteristic) remaining latent when dominant contrary characteristic is present.

recherché /rəˈʃeəʃeɪ/ *a.* (excessively) far-fetched or carefully thought out.

recidivism /rɪˈsɪdɪvɪz(ə)m/ *n.* habitual relapse into crime. **recidivist** *n.*

recipe /ˈresɪpɪ/ *n.* statement of ingredients and procedure for preparing dish etc.

recipient /rɪˈsɪpɪənt/ *n.* person who receives thing.

reciprocal /rɪˈsɪprək(ə)l/ 1 *a.* in return; mutual; *Gram.* expressing mutual relation. 2 *n. Math.* function or

expression so related to another that their product is unity.

reciprocate /rɪˈsɪprəkeɪt/ *v.* interchange; requite, make return (*with*); go with alternate backward and forward motion. **reciprocation** *n.*

reciprocity /resɪˈprɒsɪtɪ/ *n.* reciprocal condition, mutual action; give-and-take.

recital /rɪˈsaɪt(ə)l/ *n.* act of reciting; detailed account or narration of facts etc.; programme of music performed by one musician with or without accompanist, or by small group of musicians.

recitation /resɪˈteɪʃ(ə)n/ *n.* reciting esp. as entertainment; piece recited.

recitative /resɪtəˈtiːv/ *n.* musical declamation of kind usual in narrative and dialogue parts of opera and oratorio.

recite /rɪˈsaɪt/ *v.* repeat aloud or declaim from memory; mention in order, enumerate.

reckless /ˈreklɪs/ *a.* regardless of consequences or danger etc.

reckon /ˈrekən/ *v.* ascertain number or amount (of) by counting or calculation; count; settle accounts *with*; rely or base plans (*up*)on; *colloq.* conclude, suppose.

reckoning *n.* calculating; opinion; settlement of account. **day of reckoning** time when something must be atoned for or avenged.

reclaim /rɪˈkleɪm/ *v.t.* ask for return of (one's property); bring (land) under cultivation from sea or from waste state; win back from vice or error. **reclamation** /rek-/ *n.*

recline /rɪˈklaɪn/ *v.* (cause to) assume or be in horizontal or leaning position.

recluse /rɪˈkluːs/ *n.* person living in retirement or isolation.

recognition /rekəgˈnɪʃ(ə)n/ *n.* recognizing or being recognized.

recognizable /ˈrekəgnaɪzəb(ə)l/ *a.* that can be recognized, identified, or detected. **recognizability** *n.*

recognizance /rɪˈkɒgnɪzəns/ *n.* bond by which person engages before court or magistrate to observe some condition; sum pledged as surety for such observance.

recognize /ˈrekəgnaɪz/ *v.t.* know again, identify as known before; accord notice or consideration to; acknowledge or realize validity or quality or character or claims etc. of.

recoil /rɪˈkɔɪl/ 1 *v.i.* start back, shrink, in horror or disgust or fear; rebound; (of gun) be driven backwards by discharge. 2 (also /ˈriːkɔɪl/) *n.* act or fact or sensation of recoiling.

recollect /rekəˈlekt/ *v.t.* succeed in remembering, call to mind.

recollection /rekəˈlekʃ(ə)n/ *n.* act or power of recollecting; thing recollected; person's memory, time over which it extends.

recommend /rekəˈmend/ *v.t.* suggest as fit for favour or trial; advise (course of action etc., person *to* do etc.); make acceptable or desirable; commit *to* care of. **recommendation** *n.*

recompense /ˈrekəmpens/ 1 *v.t.* make amends for; requite; compensate. 2 *n.* reward; requital; compensation.

reconcile /ˈrekənsaɪl/ *v.t.* make friendly after estrangement; make resigned; harmonize; make compatible; show compatibility of. **reconciliation** *n.*

recondite /ˈrekəndaɪt/ *a.* abstruse; obscure.

recondition /riːkənˈdɪʃ(ə)n/ *v.t.* overhaul, renovate, make usable again.

reconnaissance /rɪˈkɒnɪs(ə)ns/ *n.* military etc. examination of region to locate enemy or ascertain strategic features; preliminary survey.

reconnoitre /rekəˈnɔɪtə(r)/ *v.* make reconnaissance (of).

reconsider /riːkənˈsɪdə(r)/ *v.t.* consider again, esp. for possible change of decision.

reconstitute /riːˈkɒnstɪtjuːt/ *v.t.* reconstruct or reorganize; restore previous constitution of. **reconstitution** *n.*

reconstruct /riːkənˈstrʌkt/ *v.t.* build again; restore mentally; reorganize. **reconstruction** *n.*

record 1 /rɪˈkɔːd/ *v.* put in writing or other permanent form; set down for remembrance or reference; put into permanent form for later reproduction. 2 /ˈrekɔːd/ *n.* being recorded, recorded state; recorded evidence or information etc.; document or monument preserving it; facts known about person's past; disc from which recorded sound can be reproduced; best performance or most remarkable event of its kind. 3 **have a record** have been

convicted on previous occasion; **off the record** unofficially, confidentially; **on record** legally or otherwise recorded; **recorded delivery** Post Office service whereby safe delivery is recorded; **record-player** gramophone.

recorder /rɪˈkɔːdə(r)/ *n.* judge in certain courts; recording apparatus; woodwind musical instrument.

recording /rɪˈkɔːdɪŋ/ *n.* process of recording sound etc. for later reproduction; sound etc. thus recorded; television programme recorded on film.

recount /rɪˈkaʊnt/ *v.t.* narrate; tell in detail.

re-count 1 /riːˈkaʊnt/ *v.t.* count again. 2 /ˈriːkaʊnt/ *n.* re-counting, esp. of votes.

recoup /rɪˈkuːp/ *v.t.* recover or regain (loss); compensate or reimburse for loss. **recoup oneself** recover loss. **recoupment** *n.*

recourse /rɪˈkɔːs/ *n.* resorting to possible source of help; person or thing resorted to.

recover /rɪˈkʌvə(r)/ *v.* regain possession or use or control of; come back to life or health or normal state or position; secure by legal process; make up for; retrieve. **recovery** *n.*

recreant /ˈrekrɪənt/ 1 *a.* craven, cowardly. 2 *n.* coward.

re-create /riːkrɪˈeɪt/ *v.t.* create anew.

recreation /rekrɪˈeɪʃ(ə)n/ *n.* (means of) entertaining oneself; pleasurable exercise or employment.

recriminate /rɪˈkrɪmɪneɪt/ *v.i.* make mutual or counter accusations. **recrimination** *n.*; **recriminatory** *a.*

recrudesce /riːkruːˈdes/ *v.i.* (of disease or sore etc.) break out again. **recrudescence** *n.*; **recrudescent** *a.*

recruit /rɪˈkruːt/ 1 *n.* newly enlisted soldier; person who joins society etc. 2 *v.* enlist recruits (for), enlist (person); replenish, reinvigorate. 3 **recruitment** *n.*

rectal /ˈrekt(ə)l/ *a.* of or by means of rectum.

rectangle /ˈrektæŋg(ə)l/ *n.* 4-sided plane rectilinear figure with 4 right angles. **rectangular** /-ˈtæŋ-/ *a.*

rectify /ˈrektɪfaɪ/ *v.t.* adjust or make right; *Chem.* purify, esp. by redistilling;

change (electric current) from alternating to direct. **rectification** n.

rectilinear /rektɪ'lɪnɪə(r)/ a. bounded or characterized by straight lines; in or forming straight line.

rectitude /'rektɪtjuːd/ n. moral uprightness.

recto /'rektəʊ/ n. (pl. **-tos**) right-hand page of open book; front of leaf.

rector /'rektə(r)/ n. incumbent of parish where all tithes formerly passed to incumbent; head priest of church etc.; head of university or college or religious institution. **rectorship** n.

rectory /'rektərɪ/ n. rector's house.

rectum /'rektəm/ n. (pl. **-tums**) final section of large intestine.

recumbent /rɪ'kʌmbənt/ a. lying down, reclining.

recuperate /rɪ'kuːpəreɪt/ v. recover from exhaustion or illness or loss etc.; regain (health or losses etc.). **recuperation** n.; **recuperative** a.

recur /rɪ'kɜː(r)/ v.i. occur again; go back in thought or speech; Math. (of decimal figure etc.) be repeated indefinitely.

recurrent /rɪ'kʌrənt/ a. recurring. **recurrence** n.

recusant /'rekjʊz(ə)nt/ n. person refusing submission or compliance; hist. person who refused to attend Anglican services. **recusancy** n.

recycle /riː'saɪk(ə)l/ v.t. return (material) to previous stage of cyclic process, esp. convert (waste) to reusable material.

red 1 a. of colour from crimson to orange; (of hair) reddish-brown; having to do with bloodshed, burning, violence, or revolution; communist. **2** n. red colour, paint, clothes, etc.; debit side of account; socialist or communist. **3 in the red** in debt; **red-blooded** virile, vigorous; **redbreast** robin; **redbrick** (of university) founded relatively recently; **redcap** military policeman; **redcoat** hist. British soldier; **Red Cross** international relief organization; **red flag** symbol of revolution, danger signal; **red-handed** in act of crime; **redhead** person with red hair; **red herring** irrelevant diversion; **red-hot** heated to redness, furious, excited; **Red Indian** N. Amer. Indian; **red lead** red oxide of lead as

pigment etc.; **red-letter day** joyfully memorable day; **red light** stop signal, warning; **red pepper** cayenne pepper, red capsicum; **red rag** thing that excites rage; **redshank** kind of sandpiper; **red-shift** Astron. movement of spectrum to longer wavelengths in light from distant galaxies; **redskin** Red Indian; **redstart** red-tailed songbird; **red tape** excessive bureaucracy or formalities esp. in public business; **redwing** kind of thrush; **redwood** tree yielding red wood. **4 reddish** a.

redcurrant /'redkʌrənt/ n. small round red berry; shrub bearing it.

redden /'red(ə)n/ v. make or become red.

redeem /rɪ'diːm/ v.t. recover by expenditure of effort; make single payment to cancel (regular charge etc.); convert (tokens or bonds) into goods or cash; deliver from sin and damnation; make amends or compensate for; save, rescue, reclaim; fulfil (promise).

redeemer n. one who redeems, esp. Christ.

redemption /rɪ'dempʃ(ə)n/ n. redeeming or being redeemed. **redemptive** a.

redeploy /riːdɪ'plɔɪ/ v.t. send (troops, workers) to new place or task. **redeployment** n.

rediffusion /riːdɪ'fjuːʒ(ə)n/ n. relaying of broadcast programmes esp. by wire from central receiver.

redolent /'redələnt/ a. strongly smelling or suggestive of. **redolence** n.

redouble /riː'dʌb(ə)l/ v. make or grow greater or more intense or numerous; double again.

redoubt /rɪ'daʊt/ n. detached outwork without flanking defences.

redoubtable /rɪ'daʊtəb(ə)l/ a. formidable.

redound /rɪ'daʊnd/ v.i. make great contribution to one's advantage etc.; recoil on or upon.

redress /rɪ'dres/ **1** v.t. remedy, make up for; put right again. **2** n. compensation, reparation; redressing.

reduce /rɪ'djuːs/ v. make or become smaller or less; bring by force or necessity to some state or action; convert to or to other (esp. simpler) form; subdue; bring lower; lessen one's weight or size; weaken; impoverish. **reducible** *a.*

reduction /rɪˈdʌkʃ(ə)n/ *n.* reducing or being reduced; amount by which prices etc. are reduced; reduced copy of picture etc.

redundant /rɪˈdʌnd(ə)nt/ *a.* superfluous; that can be omitted without loss of significance; (of worker) no longer needed for any available job and therefore liable to dismissal. **redundancy** *n.*

reduplicate /rɪˈdjuːplɪkeɪt/ *v.t.* make double; repeat. **reduplication** *n.*

re-echo /riːˈekəʊ/ *v.* echo repeatedly; resound.

reed *n.* firm-stemmed water or marsh plant; tall straight stalk of this; vibrating part of some musical wind instruments; in *pl.* such instruments. **reed-mace** tall waterside plant with brown flower-spikes.

reedy /ˈriːdɪ/ *a.* full of reeds; like reed; like reed instrument in tone.

reef¹ *n.* ridge of rock or sand etc. at or near surface of water; lode of ore, bedrock surrounding this.

reef² 1 *n.* one of several strips along top or bottom of sail that can be taken in and rolled up. 2 *v.t.* take in reef(s) of (sail). 3 **reef-knot** symmetrical double knot.

reefer /ˈriːfə(r)/ *n.* marijuana cigarette.

reek 1 *v.i.* smell unpleasantly (*of*); have suspicious associations. 2 *n.* foul or stale smell; smoke, vapour, exhalation.

reel 1 *n.* cylindrical device on which thread, paper, film, wire, etc., are wound; device for winding and unwinding line as required esp. in fishing; lively Sc. dance, music for this. 2 *v.* wind on reel; draw *in* or *up* by means of reel; rattle *off* without pause or apparent effort; stand or walk unsteadily; be shaken physically or mentally; dance reel.

re-entrant /riːˈentrənt/ *a.* (of angle) pointing inwards.

re-entry /riːˈentrɪ/ *n.* act of entering again, esp. (of spacecraft etc.) of re-entering earth's atmosphere.

reeve¹ *n. hist.* chief magistrate of town or district.

reeve² *v.t.* (*past* **rove**) *Naut.* thread (rope, rod, etc.) *through* ring etc.; fasten (rope, block) thus.

ref *n. colloq.* referee.

refectory /rɪˈfektərɪ/ *n.* room for meals in monastery, college, etc. **refectory table** long narrow table.

refer /rɪˈfɜː(r)/ *v.* (*past & p.p.* **referred**) trace or ascribe *to*; assign *to*; send on or direct *to* some authority or source of information; make allusion or have relation *to*. **referable** *a.*

referee /refəˈriː/ 1 *n.* arbitrator, person chosen to decide between opposing parties; umpire, esp. in football or boxing; person willing to testify to character of applicant for employment etc. 2 *v.* act as referee (for).

reference *n.* referring to some authority; scope given to such authority; relation or respect or allusion etc. *to*; direction *to* page, book, etc. where information may be found; written testimonial, person giving it. **reference book** book for occasional consultation at particular points for information; **reference library** library of books that may be consulted but not taken away. **referential** *a.*

referendum /refəˈrendəm/ *n.* (*pl.* **-dums** □ See page 667) referring of question to electorate for direct decision.

referral /rɪˈfɜːr(ə)l/ *n.* referring esp. of person to medical specialist etc.

refill 1 /riːˈfɪl/ *v.t.* fill again. 2 /ˈriːfɪl/ *n.* what serves to refill anything.

refine /rɪˈfaɪn/ *v.* free from impurities or defects; make or become more elegant or cultured.

refinement *n.* refining or being refined; fineness of feeling or taste; elegance; instance of added development; piece of subtle reasoning, fine distinction.

refinery /rɪˈfaɪnərɪ/ *n.* place where oil etc. is refined.

refit 1 /riːˈfɪt/ *v.* make or become fit again (esp. of ship undergoing repairs etc.). 2 /ˈriːfɪt/ *n.* refitting. 3 **refitment** *n.*

reflate /riːˈfleɪt/ *v.t.* cause reflation of (currency, economy, etc.).

reflation /riːˈfleɪʃ(ə)n/ *n.* inflation of financial system to restore previous condition after deflation.

reflect /rɪˈflekt/ *v.* throw back (light, heat, sound); (of mirror etc.) show image of, reproduce to eye or mind; bring credit, discredit, etc., on; meditate, consider.

reflection /rɪˈflekʃ(ə)n/ n. reflecting or being reflected; reflected light or heat or colour or image; thing bringing discredit; reconsideration; comment.

reflective /rɪˈflektɪv/ a. (of surface) giving back reflection or image; concerned in reflection or thought; thoughtful, given to meditation.

reflector /rɪˈflektə(r)/ n. piece of glass or metal for reflecting light etc. in required direction; telescope etc. using mirror to produce images.

reflex /ˈriːfleks/ 1 a. (of angle) larger than 180°; (of action) independent of the will. 2 n. reflex action; reflected light or image. 3 **reflex camera** camera in which image is reflected by mirror to allow focusing up to moment of exposure.

reflexion var. of **reflection**.

reflexive /rɪˈfleksɪv/ 1 a. Gram. (of word or form) implying subject's action on himself or itself. 2 n. reflexive word or form.

reform /rɪˈfɔːm/ 1 v. make or become better; abolish or cure (abuse etc.). 2 n. removal of abuses esp. in politics; improvement. 3 **reformative** a.

reformation /refəˈmeɪʃ(ə)n/ n. reforming or being reformed, esp. radical change for the better in political or religious or social affairs; **the Reformation** 16th-c. movement for reform of abuses in Roman Church ending in establishment of Reformed or Protestant Churches.

reformatory /rɪˈfɔːmətərɪ/ 1 a. tending or intended to produce reform. 2 n. US institution to which young offenders are sent to be reformed.

reformer /rɪˈfɔːmə(r)/ n. advocate of reform; leader in Reformation.

refract /rɪˈfrækt/ v.t. deflect (light) at certain angle when it enters obliquely a medium of different density. **refraction** n.; **refractive** a.

refractor /rɪˈfræktə(r)/ n. refracting medium or lens; telescope using lens to produce image.

refractory /rɪˈfræktərɪ/ a. stubborn, unmanageable; rebellious; resistant to heat, treatment, etc.

refrain¹ /rɪˈfreɪn/ v. hold back, keep oneself (from thing or action).

refrain² /rɪˈfreɪn/ n. recurring phrase or lines esp. at end of stanzas.

refresh /rɪˈfreʃ/ v.t. give fresh spirit or vigour to; freshen up (memory).

refresher n. extra fee to counsel in prolonged lawsuit.

refreshment n. refreshing or being refreshed in mind or body; thing esp. (usu. in pl.) food or drink that refreshes.

refrigerant /rɪˈfrɪdʒərənt/ 1 n. substance used for refrigeration. 2 a. refrigerating.

refrigerate /rɪˈfrɪdʒəreɪt/ v. make or become cool or cold; subject (food etc.) to low temperature, esp. to preserve it. **refrigeration** n.

refrigerator /rɪˈfrɪdʒəreɪtə(r)/ n. cabinet or room in which food etc. is refrigerated.

reft pred.a. taken or torn (away, from).

refuge /ˈrefjuːdʒ/ n. shelter from pursuit or danger or trouble; person or place offering this.

refugee /refjuˈdʒiː/ n. person taking refuge, esp. in foreign country from war or persecution or natural disaster.

refulgent /rɪˈfʌldʒ(ə)nt/ a. shining, gloriously bright. **refulgence** n.

refund 1 /rɪˈfʌnd/ v. pay back; reimburse. 2 /ˈriːfʌnd/ n. repayment, money etc. repaid.

refurbish /riːˈfɜːbɪʃ/ v.t. brighten up, redecorate.

refusal /rɪˈfjuːz(ə)l/ n. refusing or being refused; chance of taking thing before it is offered to others.

refuse¹ /rɪˈfjuːz/ v. withhold acceptance of or consent to; indicate unwillingness; not grant request made by (person); (of horse) be unwilling to jump (fence etc.).

refuse² /ˈrefjuːs/ n. what is rejected as worthless; waste.

refute /rɪˈfjuːt/ v.t. prove falsity or error of; rebut by argument. □ See page 666. **refutation** /refjuːˈteɪʃ(ə)n/ n.

regain /riːˈgeɪn/ v.t. gain back possession of; reach (place) again.

regal /ˈriːg(ə)l/ a. of or by king(s); magnificent. **regality** n.

regale /rɪˈgeɪl/ v.t. entertain lavishly (with); give delight to.

regalia /rɪˈgeɪlɪə/ n.pl. insignia of royalty used at coronation etc.; insignia of an order or of civic dignity.

regard /rɪˈgɑːd/ 1 *v.* gaze upon; give heed to, take into account; look upon or contemplate mentally in specified way. 2 *n.* look; attention, heed, care, concern; esteem; in *pl.* expression of friendly feelings. 3 **as regards** about, in respect of; **with regard to** in respect of.

regardful /rɪˈgɑːdfʊl/ *a.* not neglectful *of.*

regarding /rɪˈgɑːdɪŋ/ *prep.* concerning, related to.

regardless /rɪˈgɑːdlɪs/ 1 *a.* without regard or consideration (*of*); without paying attention.

regatta /rɪˈgætə/ *n.* meeting for boat or yacht races.

regency /ˈriːdʒənsɪ/ 1 *n.* office of regent; commission acting as regent; regent's or regency commission's period of office. **the Regency** 1810–20. 2 *a.* of or in style of Regency.

regenerate 1 /riːˈdʒenəreɪt/ *v.* generate again, bring or come into renewed existence; improve moral condition; breathe more vigorous life into; invest with new and higher spiritual nature. 2 /riːˈdʒenərət/ *a.* spiritually born again; reformed. 3 **regeneration** *n.*; **regenerative** *a.*

regent /ˈriːdʒ(ə)nt/ 1 *n.* person appointed to administer kingdom during minority, absence, or incapacity of monarch. 2 *a.* (placed after *n.*) acting as regent.

reggae /ˈregeɪ/ *n.* W. Ind. style of music with strongly accented subsidiary beat.

regicide /ˈredʒɪsaɪd/ *n.* person who kills or takes part in killing a king; killing of a king. **regicidal** *a.*

regime /reɪˈʒiːm/ *n.* method of government; prevailing system of things.

regimen /ˈredʒɪmen/ *n.* prescribed course of treatment, way of life, or esp. diet.

regiment /ˈredʒɪmənt/ 1 *n.* permanent unit of army consisting of several battalions or troops or companies; large array or number. 2 *v.t.* organize in groups or according to system; form into regiment(s). 3 **regimentation** *n.*

regimental /redʒɪˈment(ə)l/ 1 *a.* of a regiment. 2 *n.* in *pl.* military uniform, esp. of particular regiment.

region /ˈriːdʒ(ə)n/ *n.* area of land or division of the earth's surface, having

definable characteristics; administrative district, esp. in Scotland; part of body; sphere or realm *of.* **regional** *a.*

register /ˈredʒɪstə(r)/ 1 *n.* official list; book in which items are recorded for reference; device recording speed etc.; adjustable plate for regulating draught etc.; compass of voice or instrument. 2 *v.* record in writing; enter or cause to be entered in register; send (letter) by registered post; enter one's name in register; record automatically, indicate; make mental note of; show (emotion etc.) in face etc.; make impression. 3 **registered post** postal procedure with special precautions and compensation in case of loss; **register office** place where civil marriages are conducted.

registrar /ˈredʒɪstrɑː(r)/ *n.* person charged with keeping register; doctor undergoing hospital training as specialist.

registration /redʒɪsˈtreɪʃ(ə)n/ *n.* registering or being registered. **registration mark, number,** combination of letters and numbers identifying motor vehicle.

registry /ˈredʒɪstrɪ/ *n.* place where registers or records are kept. **registry office** register office.

Regius professor /ˈriːdʒəs/ holder of university chair founded by sovereign or filled by Crown appointment.

regress 1 /rɪˈgres/ *v.i.* move backwards. 2 /ˈriːgres/ *n.* going back; backward tendency.

regression /rɪˈgreʃ(ə)n/ *n.* backward movement; relapse; return to earlier stage of development. **regressive** *a.*

regret /rɪˈgret/ 1 *v.t.* feel or express sorrow or repentance or distress over (action or loss); say with sorrow or remorse. 2 *n.* sorrow or repentance etc. over action or loss etc. 3 **regretful** *a.*

regrettable *a.* undesirable, unwelcome; deserving censure.

regular /ˈregjʊlə(r)/ 1 *a.* conforming to a rule or principle; consistent; systematic; habitual; (of soldier) being member of regular army; not capricious or casual; acting or done uniformly in time or manner; correct; *Eccl.* bound by religious rule, belonging to monastic order. 2 *n.* regular soldier;

regular customer or visitor etc.; one of regular clergy. **3 regular army** army of professional soldiers. **4 regularity** *n.*; **regularize** *v.t.*; **regularization** *n.*

regulate /'regjʊleɪt/ *v.t.* control by rule, subject to restrictions; adapt to requirements; adjust (clock, watch, etc.) to work accurately. **regulator** *n.*

regulation /regjʊ'leɪʃ(ə)n/ **1** *n.* regulating or being regulated; prescribed rule. **2** *a.* in accordance with regulations, of correct pattern etc.

regurgitate /ri:'gɜːdʒɪteɪt/ *v.t.* bring (swallowed food) up again to mouth; pour or cast out again. **regurgitation** *n.*

rehabilitate /ri:hə'bɪlɪteɪt/ *v.t.* restore to rights or reputation etc. or to previous condition or normal health or capacity, etc. **rehabilitation** *n.*

rehash 1 /ri:'hæʃ/ *v.t.* put into new form, without significant change or improvement. **2** /'ri:hæʃ/ *n.* rehashing, material rehashed.

rehearsal /rɪ'hɜːs(ə)l/ *n.* rehearsing, trial performance or practice.

rehearse /rɪ'hɜːs/ *v.* practise before performing in public; recite or say over; give list of, enumerate.

Reich /raɪx/ *n.* the former German State, esp. **(Third Reich)** Nazi regime.

reign /reɪn/ **1** *n.* sovereignty, rule; sovereign's period of rule. **2** *v.i.* be king or queen; prevail.

reimburse /ri:ɪm'bɜːs/ *v.t.* repay (person); refund. **reimbursement** *n.*

rein /reɪn/ **1** *n.* long narrow strap used to guide horse; *fig.* means of control. **2** *v.t.* check, pull *back* or *up* or hold *in* with reins; *fig.* govern, control.

reincarnation /ri:ɪnkɑː'neɪʃ(ə)n/ *n.* rebirth of soul in new body. **reincarnate** /-'kɑːnət/ *a.*

reindeer /'reɪndɪə(r)/ *n.* subarctic deer with large antlers.

reinforce /ri:ɪn'fɔːs/ *v.t.* support or strengthen by additional men or material. **reinforced concrete** concrete with metal bars etc. embedded in it.

reinforcement *n.* reinforcing or being reinforced; in *pl.* additional men, ships, aircraft, etc., for military or naval force.

reinstate /ri:ɪn'steɪt/ *v.t.* re-establish in or restore to lost position or privileges etc. **reinstatement** *n.*

reinsure /ri:ɪn'ʃʊə(r)/ *v.* insure again (esp. of insurer securing himself by transferring risk to another insurer). **reinsurance** *n.*

reiterate /ri:'ɪtəreɪt/ *v.t.* repeat over again or several times. **reiteration** *n.*; **reiterative** *a.*

reject 1 /rɪ'dʒekt/ *v.* refuse to accept or believe in; put aside or send back as not to be used or done or complied with. **2** /'ri:dʒekt/ *n.* rejected thing or person. **3 rejection** *n.*

rejoice /rɪ'dʒɔɪs/ *v.* feel joy, be glad; take delight *in* or *at*; cause joy to.

rejoin[1] /ri:'dʒɔɪn/ *v.* join again; reunite.

rejoin[2] /rɪ'dʒɔɪn/ *v.* say in answer; retort.

rejoinder /rɪ'dʒɔɪndə(r)/ *n.* what is rejoined or said in reply.

rejuvenate /rɪ'dʒuːvəneɪt/ *v.t.* make young again. **rejuvenation** *n.*; **rejuvenator** *n.*

relapse /rɪ'læps/ **1** *v.i.* fall back *into* worse state after improvement. **2** *n.* relapsing, esp. deterioration in patient's condition after partial recovery.

relate /rɪ'leɪt/ *v.* narrate, recount; bring into relation; have reference *to*; bring oneself into relation *to*; in *p.p.* connected, akin by blood or marriage.

relation /rɪ'leɪʃ(ə)n/ *n.* connection between persons or things; kinsman, kinswoman, relative; narration, narrative. **relational** *a.*

relationship /rɪ'leɪʃənʃɪp/ *n.* state of being related; condition or character due to being related; connection between persons or things; kinship.

relative /'relətɪv/ **1** *a.* in relation or proportion to something else; implying comparison or relation; having application or reference *to*; *Gram.* (of word, clause, etc.) referring to expressed or implied antecedent, attached to antecedent by such word. **2** *n.* person connected by blood or marriage; species related to another by common origin; relative word, esp. pronoun.

relativity /relə'tɪvɪtɪ/ *n.* relativeness; theory based on principle that all motion is relative and that light has constant velocity in a vacuum.

relax /rɪ'læks/ *v.* make or become less stiff or rigid or tense or formal or strict; reduce or abate.

relaxation /ri:læk'seɪʃ(ə)n/ n. relaxing; recreation, amusements.

relay /'ri:leɪ/ 1 n. fresh set of people or horses to replace tired ones; gang of men, supply of materials, etc. similarly used; relay race; *Electr.* device activating a circuit. 2 (also /rɪ'leɪ/) v.t. receive (esp. broadcast message) and transmit to others. 3 **relay race** one between teams of which each member in turn covers part of total distance.

release /rɪ'li:s/ 1 v.t. set free, liberate, unfasten; allow to move from fixed position; make (information) public; exhibit etc. (film etc.) generally or for first time. 2 n. liberation from confinement or fixed position or trouble etc.; handle or catch etc. that releases part of machine etc.; document etc. made available for publication; film or record etc. that is released; releasing of document or film etc.

relegate /'relɪgeɪt/ v.t. consign or dismiss to inferior position; transfer (team) to lower division of league. **relegation** n.

relent /rɪ'lent/ v.i. relax severity; yield to compassion.

relentless /rɪ'lentlɪs/ a. unrelenting.

relevant /'relɪv(ə)nt/ a. bearing upon or pertinent *to* matter in hand. **relevance** n.

reliable /rɪ'laɪəb(ə)l/ a. that may be relied upon. **reliability** n.

reliance /rɪ'laɪəns/ n. trust, confidence. **reliant** a.

relic /'relɪk/ n. part of holy person's body or belongings kept as object of reverence; in *pl.* dead body, remains, of person, what has survived destruction or wasting; surviving trace or memorial *of*.

relict /'relɪkt/ n. object which has survived in primitive form.

relief /rɪ'li:f/ n. alleviation of or deliverance from pain or distress etc.; feature etc. that diversifies monotony or relaxes tension; assistance given to persons in special danger or need; replacing of person(s) on duty by another or others; persons thus bringing relief; thing supplementing another in some service; method of carving, moulding, etc., in which design projects from surface; piece of sculpture etc. in relief; effect of being done in relief given by

colour or shading etc.; delivery of place from siege. **relief map** one showing hills and valleys by shading or colouring etc.

relieve /rɪ'li:v/ v.t. bring or give or be relief to; release (person) from duty by taking his place or providing a substitute. **relieve oneself** urinate or defecate.

religion /rɪ'lɪdʒ(ə)n/ n. belief in superhuman controlling power, esp. in a personal God or gods entitled to obedience; system of faith and worship; life under monastic conditions.

religious /rɪ'lɪdʒəs/ 1 a. imbued with religion, devout; of or concerned with religion. 2 n. (pl. same) person bound by monastic vows.

relinquish /rɪ'lɪŋkwɪʃ/ v.t. give up, let go, resign, surrender. **relinquishment** n.

reliquary /'relɪkwərɪ/ n. receptacle for relics.

relish /'relɪʃ/ 1 n. liking or enjoyment *for*; appetizing flavour, attractive quality; thing eaten with plainer food to add flavour; distinctive flavour or taste *of*. 2 v. get pleasure out of, enjoy greatly.

relocate /ri:ləʊ'keɪt/ v. locate in or move to new place. **relocation** n.

reluctant /rɪ'lʌkt(ə)nt/ a. unwilling, disinclined. **reluctance** n.

rely /rɪ'laɪ/ v.i. depend with confidence (*up*)*on* (person or thing).

remain /rɪ'meɪn/ v.i. be left over; stay in same place or condition; be left behind; continue to be.

remainder /rɪ'meɪndə(r)/ 1 n. residue; remaining persons or things; *Arith.* number left after subtraction or division; copies of book left unsold. 2 v.t. dispose of remaining stocks of (book) at reduced price.

remains /rɪ'meɪnz/ n.pl. what remains over; surviving parts or amount; relics of antiquity etc.; dead body.

remand /rɪ'mɑ:nd/ 1 v.t. send back (prisoner) into custody to allow of further inquiry. 2 n. recommittal to custody. 3 **remand centre, home,** place of detention for juvenile offenders.

remark /rɪ'mɑ:k/ v. say by way of comment; make comment (*up*)*on*; take notice of. 2 n. comment; noticing; thing said.

remarkable /rɪˈmɑːkəb(ə)l/ a. worth notice; exceptional, striking.

REME abbr. Royal Electrical and Mechanical Engineers.

remedial /rɪˈmiːdɪəl/ a. affording or intended as a remedy; (of teaching) for slow or backward children.

remedy /ˈremədɪ/ 1 n. healing medicine or treatment; means of removing anything undesirable; redress. 2 v.t. rectify, make good. 3 **remediable** /-ˈmiːd-/ a.

remember /rɪˈmembə(r)/ v.t. retain in or recall to memory; not forget; convey greetings from; make present to, tip.

remembrance /rɪˈmembrəns/ n. remembering or being remembered; keepsake, souvenir; in pl. greetings conveyed through third person.

remind /rɪˈmaɪnd/ v.t. cause (person) to remember or think of.

reminder /rɪˈmaɪndə(r)/ n. thing that reminds or is memento (of).

reminisce /remɪˈnɪs/ v.i. indulge in reminiscence(s).

reminiscence /remɪˈnɪs(ə)ns/ n. remembering of things past; in pl. account of things remembered, esp. in literary form.

reminiscent /remɪˈnɪs(ə)nt/ a. reminding or suggestive of; concerned with reminiscence.

remiss /rɪˈmɪs/ a. careless of duty; negligent.

remission /rɪˈmɪʃ(ə)n/ n. shortening of prison sentence on account of good behaviour; remittance of debt etc.; diminution of force etc.; forgiveness of sins etc.

remit 1 /rɪˈmɪt/ v. (past & p.p. **remitted**) refrain from exacting or inflicting (debt, punishment, etc.); abate, slacken; send (esp. money); refer to some authority, send back to lower court; postpone, defer; pardon (sins, etc.). 2 /ˈriːmɪt/ n. terms of reference of committee etc.

remittance /rɪˈmɪt(ə)ns/ n. money sent to person; sending of money.

remittent /rɪˈmɪt(ə)nt/ a. that abates at intervals.

remnant /ˈremn(ə)nt/ n. small remaining quantity; piece of cloth etc. left when greater part has been used or sold.

remonstrate /ˈremənstreɪt/ v. make protest with (person). **remonstrance** /-ˈmɒn-/ n.; **remonstration** n.

remorse /rɪˈmɔːs/ n. bitter repentance; compunction. **remorseful** a.

remorseless /rɪˈmɔːslɪs/ a. without compassion.

remote /rɪˈməʊt/ a. far apart or away in place or time; out-of-the-way, secluded; not closely related; aloof, not friendly. **remote control** control of apparatus etc. from a distance.

remould 1 /riːˈməʊld/ v.t. mould again, refashion; reconstruct tread of (tyre). 2 /ˈriːməʊld/ n. remoulded tyre.

removal /rɪˈmuːv(ə)l/ n. removing or being removed; transfer of furniture etc. to different house.

remove /rɪˈmuːv/ 1 v. take off or away from place occupied; convey to another place; dismiss; change one's residence, go away from; in p.p. distant or remote from. 2 n. distance, degree of remoteness; stage in gradation; form or division in some schools.

removed /rɪˈmuːvd/ a. (of cousins) **once**, **twice**, etc. **removed** with difference of one, two, etc., generations.

remunerate /rɪˈmjuːnəreɪt/ v.t. pay for service rendered.

remuneration /rɪmjuːnəˈreɪʃ(ə)n/ n. remunerating or being remunerated; what is received as pay.

remunerative /rɪˈmjuːnərətɪv/ a. profitable.

Renaissance /rɪˈneɪs(ə)ns/ n. revival of arts and literature in 14th-16th cc.; style of art and architecture developed by it; **renaissance** any similar revival.

renal /ˈriːn(ə)l/ a. of kidneys.

renascent /rɪˈnæs(ə)nt/ a. springing up anew; being reborn. **renascence** n.

rend v. (past & p.p. **rent**) arch. tear or wrench; split or divide.

render /ˈrendə(r)/ v.t. cause to be or become; give in return; pay as due; present, submit; reproduce, portray; perform, translate; melt (fat) down; give (first) coat of plaster etc. to.

rendezvous /ˈrɒndeɪvuː/ 1 n. (pl. same /-vuːz/) agreed or regular meeting-place; meeting by appointment. 2 v.i. (3 sing. -**vouses** /-vuːz/; past & p.p. -**voused** /-vuːd/; partic. -**vousing** /-vuːɪŋ/) meet at rendezvous.

rendition /renˈdɪʃ(ə)n/ n. rendering, performance, interpretation.

renegade /ˈrenɪgeɪd/ n. deserter of party or principles.

renege /rɪˈniːg/ v.i. go back on promise; back out.

renew /rɪˈnjuː/ v. make new again; restore to original state; replace; repeat; continue or resume; grant or be granted continuation of (licence etc.). **renewal** n.

rennet /ˈrenɪt/ n. curdled milk from calf's stomach, or artificial preparation, used in curdling milk for cheese or junket etc.

renounce /rɪˈnaʊns/ v.t. consent formally to abandon; repudiate; decline further association with.

renovate /ˈrenəveɪt/ v.t. restore to good condition; repair. **renovation** n.

renown /rɪˈnaʊn/ n. fame, high distinction.

renowned /rɪˈnaʊnd/ a. famous; celebrated.

rent[1] 1 n. periodical payment for use of land or premises; payment for hire of machinery etc. 2 v. take or occupy or use for rent; let or hire for rent; be let (at).

rent[2] n. tear in garment etc.; gap, cleft, fissure.

rent[3] past & p.p. of **rend**.

rental /ˈrent(ə)l/ n. amount paid or received as rent; act of renting; income from rents.

rentier /ˈrɑ̃tieɪ/ n. person living on income from property or investments. [F]

renunciation /rɪnʌnsɪˈeɪʃ(ə)n/ n. renouncing, self-denial, giving up of things.

rep[1] n. corded upholstery fabric.

rep[2] n. colloq. representative, esp. commercial traveller.

rep[3] n. colloq. repertory theatre or company.

repair[1] 1 v.t. restore to good condition after damage or wear; set right or make amends for. 2 n. restoring to sound condition; good or relative condition for working or using.

repair[2] v.i. resort; go (to).

reparable /ˈrepərəb(ə)l/ a. that can be repaired or made good.

reparation /repəˈreɪʃ(ə)n/ n. making of amends; compensation.

repartee /repɑːˈtiː/ n. witty retort; making of witty retorts.

repast /rɪˈpɑːst/ n. meal.

repatriate 1 /riːˈpætrɪeɪt/ v.t. return to native land. 2 /riːˈpætrɪət/ n. repatriated person. 3 **repatriation** n.

repay /riːˈpeɪ/ v. (past & p.p. -paid) pay back; return, retaliate; requite, recompense. **repayment** n.

repeal /rɪˈpiːl/ 1 v.t. annul, revoke. 2 n. repealing.

repeat /rɪˈpiːt/ 1 v. say or do over again; recite, report; reproduce; recur. 2 n. repeating; repeated broadcast programme; Mus. passage intended to be repeated.

repeatedly /rɪˈpiːtɪdlɪ/ adv. several times.

repeater /rɪˈpiːtə(r)/ n. person or thing that repeats; firearm that fires several shots without reloading; watch that strikes last quarter etc. again when required.

repel /rɪˈpel/ v.t. (past & p.p. **repelled**) drive back; ward off; be repulsive or distasteful to.

repellent /rɪˈpelənt/ 1 a. that repels. 2 n. substance that repels, esp. insects etc.

repent /rɪˈpent/ v. feel sorrow or regret for what one has done or left undone; think with regret or contrition of. **repentance** n.; **repentant** a.

repercussion /riːpəˈkʌʃ(ə)n/ n. indirect effect or reaction (of); recoil after impact.

repertoire /ˈrepətwɑː(r)/ n. stock of pieces etc. that performer or company knows or is prepared to perform.

repertory /ˈrepətərɪ/ n. repertoire; theatrical performance of various plays for short periods by one company.

repetition /repɪˈtɪʃ(ə)n/ n. repeating or being repeated; thing repeated, copy. **repetitious** a.; **repetitive** /-ˈpet-/ a.

repine /rɪˈpaɪn/ v.i. fret, be discontented.

replace /rɪˈpleɪs/ v.t. put back in place; take or fill up place of, be or provide substitute for; in pass. be succeeded or superseded (by).

replacement n. replacing or being replaced; person or thing that takes the place of another.

replay 1 /riːˈpleɪ/ v.t. play (match, recording, etc.) again. 2 /ˈriːpleɪ/ n. replaying (of match, recording of incident in game, etc.).

replenish /rɪˈplenɪʃ/ v.t. fill up again (with). **replenishment** n.

replete /rɪˈpliːt/ a. filled or well supplied with; sated. **repletion** n.

replica /ˈreplɪkə/ n. exact copy, model; duplicate made by original artist.

replicate /ˈreplɪkeɪt/ v.t. make replica of. **replication** n.

reply /rɪˈplaɪ/ 1 v. make an answer, respond. 2 n. replying; what is replied.

report /rɪˈpɔːt/ 1 v. bring back or give account of; tell as news; make official or formal statement; inform against; take down, write description of, etc., for publication; present oneself to (person); be responsible to. 2 n. account given or opinion formally expressed after investigation; description, reproduction, or epitome of speech, law case, scene, etc., esp. for newspaper publication; common talk, rumour; repute; account by teacher of pupil's conduct and progress; sound of explosion.

reporter n. person employed to report news etc. for newspaper or broadcast.

repose¹ /rɪˈpəʊz/ 1 n. rest; sleep; peaceful state, tranquillity; restful effect. 2 v. rest, lay to rest, give rest to; be lying; be supported or based on. 3 **reposeful** a.

repose² /rɪˈpəʊz/ v.t. place (trust etc.) in.

repository /rɪˈpɒzɪtərɪ/ n. place where things are stored or may be found; receptacle; recipient of secrets etc.

repp var. of **rep¹**.

reprehend /reprɪˈhend/ v.t. rebuke, blame.

reprehensible /reprɪˈhensɪb(ə)l/ a. blameworthy.

represent /reprɪˈzent/ v.t. stand for, correspond to; symbolize; present likeness of to mind or senses; describe or depict as; declare to be; allege that; show or play part of in action or show; be substitute or deputy for, esp. be accredited deputy for in legislative assembly etc. **representation** n.

representational /reprɪzenˈteɪʃən(ə)l/ a. (of art) seeking to portray objects etc. realistically.

representative /reprɪˈzentətɪv/ 1 a. typical of class; containing typical specimens of all or many classes; of or

based on representation of body of persons, esp. whole people, in government or legislation. 2 n. sample, specimen; typical embodiment of; agent; person representing another or a section of community etc.

repress /rɪˈpres/ v.t. keep under; put down; suppress. **repression** n.; **repressive** a.

reprieve /rɪˈpriːv/ 1 v.t. postpone or remit execution of. 2 n. remission or commutation of capital sentence; respite.

reprimand /ˈreprɪmɑːnd/ 1 n. official rebuke. 2 v.t. rebuke officially.

reprint 1 /riːˈprɪnt/ v.t. print again. 2 /ˈriːprɪnt/ n. new printing of book etc., esp. without alterations; book etc. reprinted.

reprisal /rɪˈpraɪz(ə)l/ n. act of retaliation.

reprise /rɪˈpriːz/ n. Mus. repeated passage or song etc.

reproach /rɪˈprəʊtʃ/ 1 v.t. express disapproval to (person) for fault etc.; rebuke. 2 n. rebuke, censure; thing that brings discredit.

reproachful /rɪˈprəʊtʃfʊl/ a. inclined to or expressing reproach.

reprobate /ˈreprəbeɪt/ n. unprincipled or immoral person.

reprobation /reprəˈbeɪʃ(ə)n/ n. strong condemnation.

reproduce /riːprəˈdjuːs/ v. produce copy or representation of; produce further members of same species by natural means; produce offspring of (oneself, itself). **reproducible** a.

reproduction /riːprəˈdʌkʃ(ə)n/ n. reproducing; copy of painting etc.; attrib. (of furniture etc.) made in imitation of earlier style. **reproductive** a.

reproof /rɪˈpruːf/ n. blame; words expressing blame.

reprove /rɪˈpruːv/ v.t. rebuke, scold.

reptile /ˈreptaɪl/ n. member of class of cold-blooded vertebrates including snakes; mean grovelling person. **reptilian** /-ˈtɪl-/ a.

republic /rɪˈpʌblɪk/ n. State in which supreme power is held by the people or its elected representatives.

republican /rɪˈpʌblɪkən/ 1 a. of or characterizing etc. republic(s); advocating or supporting republican government. 2 n. supporter or advocate of republican government; **Re-**

publican *US* member of Republican party. **3 republicanism** *n*.

repudiate /rɪˈpjuːdɪeɪt/ *v*. disown, disavow, deny; refuse to recognize or obey (authority) or discharge (obligation or debt). **repudiation** *n*.

repugnance /rɪˈpʌɡn(ə)ns/ *n*. aversion, antipathy; inconsistency or incompatibility of ideas, tempers, etc.

repugnant /rɪˈpʌɡn(ə)nt/ *a*. distasteful, contradictory, (*to*).

repulse /rɪˈpʌls/ 1 *v.t*. drive back; rebuff, reject. 2 *n*. defeat, rebuff.

repulsion /rɪˈpʌlʃ(ə)n/ *n*. aversion, disgust; *Phys*. tendency of bodies to repel each other.

repulsive /rɪˈpʌlsɪv/ *a*. causing aversion or loathing.

reputable /ˈrepjʊtəb(ə)l/ □ See page 665 *a*. of good repute, respectable.

reputation /repjʊˈteɪʃ(ə)n/ *n*. what is generally said or believed about character of person or thing; credit, respectability; credit or discredit.

repute /rɪˈpjuːt/ 1 *n*. reputation. 2 *v.t*. in *pass*. be generally considered.

request /rɪˈkwest/ 1 *n*. asking for something, thing asked for; being sought after, demand. 2 *v.t*. make request for or of; seek permission *to do*.

requiem /ˈrekwɪəm/ *n*. Mass for the dead; musical setting for this.

require /rɪˈkwaɪə(r)/ *v.t*. need; depend on for success etc.; lay down as imperative; demand or insist on.

requirement *n*. thing required; need.

requisite /ˈrekwɪzɪt/ 1 *a*. required, necessary. 2 *n*. thing needed (*for* some purpose).

requisition /rekwɪˈzɪʃ(ə)n/ 1 *n*. official order laying claim to use of property or materials; formal demand, usu. in writing. 2 *v.t*. demand use or supply of.

requite /rɪˈkwaɪt/ *v.t*. make return for; reward or avenge; give in return. **requital** *n*.

reredos /ˈrɪədɒs/ *n*. ornamental screen covering wall above back of altar.

resale /riːˈseɪl/ *n*. sale of thing bought.

rescind /rɪˈsɪnd/ *v.t*. abrogate, revoke, cancel. **rescission** /-ˈsɪʒ(ə)n/ *n*.

rescript /ˈriːskrɪpt/ *n*. edict or official pronouncement.

rescue /ˈreskjuː/ 1 *v.t*. save or set free from danger or harm. 2 *n*. rescuing or being rescued.

research /rɪˈsɜːtʃ/ 1 *n*. careful search or inquiry into subject to discover facts by study or investigation. 2 *v*. make researches (into or for).

resemble /rɪˈzemb(ə)l/ *v.t*. be like; have similarity to. **resemblance** *n*.

resent /rɪˈzent/ *v.t*. show or feel indignation at; feel injured or insulted by. **resentment** *n*.

resentful /rɪˈzentfʊl/ *a*. feeling resentment.

reservation /rezəˈveɪʃ(ə)n/ *n*. reserving or being reserved; thing reserved (e.g. room in hotel); express or tacit limitation or exception; strip of land between carriageways of road; tract of land reserved esp. for exclusive occupation of group, tribe, etc.

reserve /rɪˈzɜːv/ 1 *v.t*. put aside or keep back for later occasion or special use; order to be retained or allocated for person at particular time; retain or secure; in *p.p.* reticent, uncommunicative. 2 *n*. thing reserved for future use; limitation or exception attached to something; self-restraint, coolness of manner; company's profit added to capital; in *sing*. or *pl*. assets kept readily available; troops withheld from action to reinforce or protect others; forces outside regular ones but available in emergency; extra player chosen as possible substitute in team; tract of land reserved for special use, esp. for occupation by animals.

reservist /rɪˈzɜːvɪst/ *n*. member of reserve forces.

reservoir /ˈrezəvwɑː(r)/ *n*. large natural or artificial lake as source of area's water supply; receptacle for fluid; supply *of* facts etc.

reshuffle /riːˈʃʌf(ə)l/ 1 *v.t*. shuffle again; interchange posts of (Government ministers etc.). 2 *n*. reshuffling.

reside /rɪˈzaɪd/ *v.i*. have one's home; (of right etc.) be vested *in*; (of quality) be present *in*.

residence /ˈrezɪd(ə)ns/ *n*. residing; place where one resides; abode. **in residence** dwelling at specified place.

resident /ˈrezɪd(ə)nt/ 1 *n*. permanent inhabitant; guest staying at hotel. 2 *a*. having quarters on the spot; located *in*; residing; in residence.

residential /rezɪˈdenʃ(ə)l/ *a*. suitable

for or occupied by private houses; used as residence; connected with residence.

residual /rɪ'zɪdjʊəl/ *a.* left as residue or residuum.

residuary /rɪ'zɪdjʊərɪ/ *a.* of the residue of an estate; residual.

residue /'rezɪdju:/ *n.* remainder, what is left over; what remains of estate when liabilities have been discharged.

residuum /rɪ'zɪdjʊəm/ *n.* (*pl.* **-dua**) what remains esp. after combustion or evaporation.

resign /rɪ'zaɪn/ *v.* give up office; relinquish, surrender; reconcile *oneself to*.

resignation /rezɪg'neɪʃ(ə)n/ *n.* resigning esp. of an office; uncomplaining endurance.

resigned /rɪ'zaɪnd/ *a.* having resigned oneself; content to endure; full or indicative of resignation.

resilient /rɪ'zɪlɪənt/ *n.* resuming original form after compression etc.; (of person) readily recovering from depression etc. **resilience** *n.*

resin /'rezɪn/ **1** *n.* sticky secretion of trees and plants; similar synthetic substance, esp. organic compound made by polymerization etc. and used in plastics. **2** *v.t.* rub or treat with resin. **3** **resinous** *a.*

resist /rɪ'zɪst/ *v.* withstand action or effect of; abstain from (pleasure etc.); strive against, oppose; offer resistance. **resistible** *a.*

resistance /rɪ'zɪst(ə)ns/ *n.* act of resisting; power to resist; impeding effect exerted by material thing on another; *Phys.* property of resisting passage of electric current or heat etc.; *Electr.* resistor; secret organization resisting authority, esp. in conquered country. **resistant** *a.*

resistor /rɪ'zɪstə(r)/ *n.* *Electr.* device having resistance to passage of current.

resoluble /rɪ'zɒljʊb(ə)l/ *a.* resolvable, analysable *into*.

resolute /'rezəlju:t/ *a.* determined; bold; not vacillating or shrinking.

resolution /rezə'lju:ʃ(ə)n/ *n.* resolute temper or character or conduct; thing resolved on; formal expression of opinion of meeting; solving *of* question etc.; resolving or being resolved.

resolve /rɪ'zɒlv/ **1** *v.* make up one's mind; cause to do this; pass resolution

by vote; (cause to) separate into constituent parts, analyse; solve; settle; *Mus.* convert (discord), or be converted, into concord. **2** *n.* mental decision; determination.

resonant /'rezən(ə)nt/ *a.* echoing, resounding; continuing to sound; causing reinforcement or prolongation of sound, esp. by vibration. **resonance** *n.*

resonate /'rezəneɪt/ *v.i.* produce or show resonance. **resonator** *n.*

resort /rɪ'zɔːt/ **1** *n.* place frequented esp. for holidays etc.; thing to which recourse is had, recourse; frequenting or being frequented. **2** *v.i.* turn for aid etc. *to*; go often or in numbers *to*. **3 in the last resort** when all else has failed.

resound /rɪ'zaʊnd/ *v.i.* ring or echo; produce echoes, go on sounding, fill place with sound; be much mentioned or repeated.

resounding *a.* unmistakable, emphatic.

resource /rɪ'sɔːs/ *n.* expedient, device; in *pl.* means of supplying what is needed; stock that can be drawn on; skill in devising expedients.

resourceful /rɪ'sɔːsfʊl/ *a.* good at devising expedients.

respect /rɪ'spekt/ **1** *n.* deferential esteem; heed or regard *of*; detail, aspect; reference or relation (*to*); in *pl.* polite greetings. **2** *v.* treat or regard with deference or esteem; treat with consideration, spare.

respectable /rɪ'spektəb(ə)l/ *a.* deserving respect; of fair social standing, honest and decent; of acceptably great amount or size or merit; befitting respectable persons. **respectability** *n.*

respectful /rɪ'spektfʊl/ *a.* showing deference.

respecting *prep.* with regard to.

respective /rɪ'spektɪv/ *a.* concerning or appropriate to each of several individually; comparative.

respectively *adv.* for each separately or in turn, and in the order mentioned.

respiration /respɪ'reɪʃ(ə)n/ *n.* breathing; plant's absorption of oxygen and emission of carbon dioxide; single inspiration and expiration. **respiratory** /-'spɪr-/ *a.*

respirator /'respɪreɪtə(r)/ *n.* apparatus worn over mouth and nose to filter etc. inhaled air; apparatus for maintaining artificial respiration.

respire /rɪ'spaɪə(r)/ v. breathe; take breath; (of plant) carry out respiration.

respite /'respaɪt/ **1** n. interval of rest or relief; delay permitted in discharge of obligation or suffering of penalty. **2** v.t. grant or bring respite to.

resplendent /rɪ'splend(ə)nt/ a. brilliant, glittering. **resplendence** n.

respond /rɪ'spɒnd/ v.i. make answer; act etc. in response (to).

respondent /rɪ'spɒnd(ə)nt/ **1** n. defendant in appeal or divorce case. **2** a. in position of defendant.

response /rɪ'spɒns/ n. answer; action, feeling, etc. caused by stimulus etc.; part of liturgy said or sung in answer to priest.

responsibility /rɪspɒnsɪ'bɪlɪtɪ/ n. being responsible; charge, trust.

responsible /rɪ'spɒnsɪb(ə)l/ a. liable to be called to account; morally accountable for actions; of good credit and repute; trustworthy; involving responsibility.

responsive /rɪ'spɒnsɪv/ a. responding readily to some influence; sympathetic; answering; by way of answer.

respray 1 /riː'spreɪ/ v.t. spray again (esp. to change colour of paint on vehicle). **2** /'riːspreɪ/ n. respraying.

rest¹ 1 v. cease from exertion or action; be still; lie in sleep or death; give relief or repose to; place or lie or lean or rely or base or depend etc. (upon). **2** n. repose or sleep; resting; prop or support for steadying something; Mus. interval of silence, sign denoting this. **3 at rest** not moving, not agitated or troubled; **lay to rest** bury; **set at rest** settle, reassure.

rest² 1 n. the remainder or remaining parts or individuals (of). **2** v.i. remain in specified state. **3 for the rest** as regards anything else; **rest with** be in hands or charge or choice of.

restaurant /'restərɒnt/ n. public premises where meals may be had.

restaurateur /restərə'tɜː(r)/ n. restaurant-keeper.

restful /'restfʊl/ a. quiet, soothing.

restitution /restɪ'tjuːʃ(ə)n/ n. restoring of property etc. to its owner; reparation.

restive /'restɪv/ a. fidgety; intractable, resisting control.

restless /'restlɪs/ a. finding or affording no rest; uneasy, agitated, fidgeting.

restoration /restə'reɪʃ(ə)n/ n. restoring or being restored; model or drawing representing supposed original form of extinct animal, ruined building, etc. **the Restoration** return of Charles II to throne of England in 1660.

restorative /rɪ'stɒrətɪv/ **1** a. tending to restore health or strength. **2** n. restorative food or medicine etc.

restore /rɪ'stɔː(r)/ v.t. bring back to original state by rebuilding, repairing, etc.; give back; reinstate; bring back to former place or condition or use; make restoration of (extinct animal, ruined building, etc.).

restrain /rɪ'streɪn/ v.t. check or hold in (from); keep under control; repress; confine.

restraint /rɪ'streɪnt/ n. restraining or being restrained; agency or influence that restrains; self-control; avoidance of exaggeration; reserve.

restrict /rɪ'strɪkt/ v.t. confine, limit. **restriction** n.

restrictive /rɪ'strɪktɪv/ a. restricting. **restrictive practice** agreement or practice that limits efficiency or output in industry etc.

result /rɪ'zʌlt/ **1** n. consequence; issue; answer etc. got by calculation; (often in pl.) announcement of score or winner etc. in sporting event or examination. **2** v.i. arise as consequence, effect, or conclusion (from); end in.

resultant /rɪ'zʌlt(ə)nt/ **1** a. resulting. **2** n. force etc. equivalent to two or more forces acting in different directions at same point.

resume /rɪ'zjuːm/ v. begin again; recommence; take again or back. **resumption** n.; **resumptive** a.

résumé /'rezjuːmeɪ/ n. summary.

resurface /riː'sɜːfɪs/ v. put new surface on; return to surface.

resurgent /rɪ'sɜːdʒ(ə)nt/ a. rising or arising again. **resurgence** n.

resurrect /rezə'rekt/ v.t. revive practice or memory of; take from grave.

resurrection /rezə'rekʃ(ə)n/ n. rising from the dead; revival from disuse or decay etc.

resuscitate /rɪ'sʌsɪteɪt/ v. revive from unconsciousness or apparent death; revive (old custom etc.). **resuscitation** n.

retail /'riːteɪl/ 1 n. sale of goods to the public in small quantities. 2 a. of retail. 3 adv. by retail. 4 v. sell by retail; be retailed; (also /rɪ'teɪl/) recount.

retain /rɪ'teɪn/ v.t. keep possession of, continue to have or use or recognize etc.; keep in mind; keep in place, hold fixed; secure services of (esp. barrister) by preliminary fee.

retainer /rɪ'teɪnə(r)/ n. person or thing that retains; fee for retaining barrister etc.; hist. dependant or follower of person of rank.

retaliate /rɪ'tælɪeɪt/ v. repay in kind; attack in return. **retaliation** n.; **retaliatory** a.

retard /rɪ'tɑːd/ v.t. make slow or late; delay progress or accomplishment of; in p.p. backward in mental or physical development. **retardation** n.

retch v.i. make motion of vomiting.

retention /rɪ'tenʃ(ə)n/ n. retaining or being retained.

retentive /rɪ'tentɪv/ a. tending to retain; (of memory) not forgetful.

rethink 1 /riː'θɪŋk/ v.t. (past & p.p. -thought /-'θɔːt/) consider afresh, esp. with view to making changes. 2 /'riːθɪŋk/ n. rethinking.

reticence /'retɪs(ə)ns/ n. avoidance of expressing all one knows or feels; uncommunicativeness. **reticent** a.

reticulate 1 /rɪ'tɪkjʊleɪt/ v. divide or be divided in fact or appearance into network. 2 /rɪ'tɪkjʊlət/ a. reticulated. 3 **reticulation** n.

reticule /'retɪkjuːl/ n. arch. woman's handbag.

retina /'retɪnə/ n. (pl. -nas) layer at back of eyeball sensitive to light. **retinal** a.

retinue /'retɪnjuː/ n. suite or train of persons attending important person.

retire /rɪ'taɪə(r)/ v. leave office or employment, esp. because of age; cause (employee) to retire; withdraw, retreat, seek seclusion or shelter; go to bed.

retired a. who has retired; withdrawn from society, secluded.

retirement n. condition of having retired; seclusion, secluded place. **retirement pension** pension paid by State to retired people above certain age.

retiring /rɪ'taɪərɪŋ/ a. shy, fond of seclusion.

retort¹ /rɪ'tɔːt/ 1 n. incisive or witty or angry reply. 2 v. say by way of retort; repay in kind.

retort² /rɪ'tɔːt/ n. vessel with long downward-bent neck for distilling liquids; vessel for heating coal to generate gas.

retouch /riː'tʌtʃ/ v.i. amend or improve (esp. photograph) by new touches.

retrace /riː'treɪs/ v.t. go back over; trace back to source or beginning.

retract /rɪ'trækt/ v. draw or be drawn back or in; withdraw (statement or opinion). **retraction** n.

retractile /rɪ'træktaɪl/ a. retractable. **retractility** n.

retread 1 /riː'tred/ v.t. put new tread on (tyre). 2 /'riːtred/ n. retreaded tyre.

retreat /rɪ'triːt/ 1 v.i. go back, retire; recede. 2 n. act of retreating; withdrawing into seclusion; place of seclusion or shelter; temporary retirement for religious exercises; military signal for retreating.

retrench /rɪ'trentʃ/ v. reduce amount of, cut down; economize. **retrenchment** n.

retrial /riː'traɪəl/ n. retrying of case.

retribution /retrɪ'bjuːʃ(ə)n/ n. recompense, usu. for evil, vengeance. **retributive** /-'trɪb-/ a.

retrieve /rɪ'triːv/ v. regain possession of; find again; (of dog) find and bring in game; rescue from bad state etc., restore to good state; repair. **retrieval** n.

retriever /rɪ'triːvə(r)/ n. dog of breed used for retrieving game.

retro- /retrəʊ/ in comb. backwards, back.

retroactive /retrəʊ'æktɪv/ a. having retrospective effect.

retrograde /'retrəʊgreɪd/ 1 a. directed backwards; reverting, esp. to inferior state. 2 v.i. move backwards; decline, revert.

retrogress /retrəʊ'gres/ v.i. move backwards; deteriorate. **retrogression** n.; **retrogressive** a.

retro-rocket /'retrəʊrɒkɪt/ n. auxiliary rocket for slowing down spacecraft etc.

retrospect /'retrəspekt/ *n.* survey of or reference to past time or events. **in retrospect** when looked back on.

retrospection /retrə'spekʃ(ə)n/ *n.* action of looking back, esp. into the past.

retrospective /retrə'spektɪv/ *a.* looking back on or dealing with the past; (of statute etc.) applying to the past as well as to the future.

retroussé /rə'tru:seɪ/ *a.* (of nose) turned up at tip. [F]

retry /ri:'traɪ/ *v.t.* (*past & p.p.* **-tried**) try (defendant, law case) again.

return /rɪ'tɜ:n/ 1 *v.* come or go back; bring or put or send back; give in response; say in reply; send (ball) back in tennis etc.; state in answer to formal demand; elect as MP. 2 *n.* returning or being returned; coming round again; return ticket; what is returned; proceeds or profit; coming in of these; formal report. 3 **returning officer** official conducting election in constituency etc. and announcing result; **return match** second match between same opponents; **return ticket** ticket for journey to place and back again.

reunion /ri:'ju:nɪən/ *n.* reuniting or being reunited; social gathering.

reunite /ri:ju:'naɪt/ *v.* bring or come together again; join again.

rev *colloq.* 1 *n.* revolution (of engine). 2 *v.* (*past & p.p.* **revved**) (of engine) revolve; rev up. 3 **rev up** cause (engine) to run quickly.

Rev. *abbr.* Reverend.

revamp /ri:'væmp/ *v.t.* renovate, revise; patch up.

Revd *abbr.* Reverend.

reveal /rɪ'vi:l/ *v.t.* display, show, allow to appear; disclose, divulge.

reveille /rɪ'vælɪ/ *n.* military waking-signal.

revel /'rev(ə)l/ 1 *v.i.* (*past & p.p.* **revelled**) make merry, be riotously festive; take keen delight *in.* 2 *n.* revelling; in *sing.* or *pl.* merry-making.

revelation /revə'leɪʃ(ə)n/ *n.* revealing; knowledge disclosed by divine or supernatural agency; striking disclosure; (**the**) **Revelation** last book of NT.

revelry /'revəlrɪ/ *n.* revelling.

revenge /rɪ'vendʒ/ 1 *n.* (act of) retaliation; desire for this. 2 *v.t.* inflict

punishment or exact retribution for; avenge.

revengeful /rɪ'vendʒfʊl/ *a.* eager for revenge.

revenue /'revənju:/ *n.* annual income, esp. of State; department collecting State revenue.

reverberate /rɪ'vɜ:bəreɪt/ *v.* (of sound, light, heat) be returned or reflected; return (sound etc.) thus. **reverberant** *a.*; **reverberation** *n.*; **reverberative** *a.*

revere /rɪ'vɪə(r)/ *v.t.* regard with deep and affectionate or religious respect.

reverence /'revərəns/ 1 *n.* revering or being revered; deep respect. 2 *v.t.* revere.

reverend /'revərənd/ *a.* deserving reverence; **Reverend** title of clergyman.

reverent /'revərənt/ *a.* feeling or showing reverence.

reverential /revə'renʃ(ə)l/ *a.* of the nature of or due to or characterized by reverence.

reverie /'revərɪ/ *n.* fit of musing; day-dream.

revers /rə'vɪə(r)/ *n.* turned-back front edge of garment.

reversal /rɪ'vɜ:s(ə)l/ *n.* reversing or being reversed.

reverse /rɪ'vɜ:s/ 1 *v.* turn the other way round or up or inside out; convert to opposite character or effect; make (vehicle) travel backwards; (of vehicle) travel backwards; make work in contrary direction; revoke, annul. 2 *a.* opposite or contrary (*to*); inverted, back(ward); upside down. 3 *n. the* contrary (*of*); piece of misfortune, disaster; reverse gear or motion; reverse side; side of coin etc. bearing secondary design; verso of leaf. 4 **reverse the charges** make recipient of telephone call responsible for payment; **reverse gear** gear used to make vehicle etc. travel backwards; **reversing light** light at rear of vehicle operated when vehicle is in reverse gear. 5 **reversible** *a.*

reversion /rɪ'vɜ:ʃ(ə)n/ *n.* legal right (esp. of original owner) to possess or succeed to property on death of present possessor; return to previous state or earlier type.

revert /rɪ'vɜ:t/ *v.i.* return *to* former condition or practice etc.; recur *to* in thought or talk; return by reversion. **revertible** *a.*

review /rɪ'vju:/ **1** *n*. general survey, inspection; retrospect; revision, reconsideration; published account or criticism of book etc.; periodical in which events, books, etc. are reviewed. **2** *v*. survey, look back on; hold review of (troops, etc.); write review of (book etc.).

revile /rɪ'vaɪl/ *v.t.* criticize abusively.

revise /rɪ'vaɪz/ **1** *v.t.* examine and improve or amend; read again. **2** *n*. proof-sheet embodying corrections made in earlier proof.

revision /rɪ'vɪʒ(ə)n/ *n*. revising; revised edition or form.

revisionism /rɪ'vɪʒənɪz(ə)m/ *n*. policy of revision or modification, esp. of Marxist-Leninist doctrine.

revisory /rɪ'vaɪzərɪ/ *a*. of revision.

revival /rɪ'vaɪv(ə)l/ *n*. reviving or being revived; new production of old play; reawakening of religious fervour; campaign to promote this.

revivalism /rɪ'vaɪvəlɪz(ə)m/ *n*. organization of religious revival. **revivalist** *n*.

revive /rɪ'vaɪv/ *v*. come or bring back to consciousness, life, vigour, use, or notice.

revivify /ri:'vɪvɪfaɪ/ *v.t.* restore to life or strength or activity. **revivification** *n*.

revocable /'revəkəb(ə)l/ *a*. that can be revoked.

revoke /rɪ'vəʊk/ **1** *v*. rescind, withdraw, cancel; *Cards* fail to follow suit though able to. **2** *n*. revoking at cards. **3 revocation** *n*.

revolt /rɪ'vəʊlt/ **1** *v*. rise in rebellion against authority; affect with disgust; feel revulsion. **2** *n*. insurrection; sense of loathing, rebellious mood.

revolting *a*. disgusting, horrible.

revolution /revə'lu:ʃ(ə)n/ *n*. forcible substitution of new government or ruler for old; fundamental change; revolving; single completion of orbit or rotation.

revolutionary /revə'lu:ʃənərɪ/ **1** *a*. involving great change; of political revolution. **2** *n*. instigator or supporter of political revolution.

revolutionize /revə'lu:ʃənaɪz/ *v.t.* completely change or reconstruct.

revolve /rɪ'vɒlv/ *v*. turn round; rotate; move in orbit; ponder in the mind.

revolver *n*. pistol with revolving chambers enabling user to fire several shots without reloading.

revue /rɪ'vju:/ *n*. theatrical entertainment consisting of a series of items.

revulsion /rɪ'vʌlʃ(ə)n/ *n*. abhorrence; sudden violent change of feeling.

reward /rɪ'wɔ:d/ **1** *n*. return or recompense for service or merit; requital for good or evil; sum offered for detection of criminal or recovery of lost property etc. **2** *v.t.* give or serve as reward to.

rewind /ri:'waɪnd/ *v.t.* (*past & p.p.* **-wound** /-'waʊnd/) wind (film, tape, etc.) back towards beginning.

rewire /ri:'waɪə(r)/ *v.t.* renew electrical wiring of (building).

RHA *abbr*. Regional Health Authority.

rhapsodize /'ræpsədaɪz/ *v.i.* utter or write rhapsodies. **rhapsodist** *n*.

rhapsody /'ræpsədɪ/ *n*. enthusiastic high-flown utterance or composition. **rhapsodical** *a*.

rhesus /'ri:səs/ *n*. small Indian monkey. **Rhesus factor** antigen occurring in red blood cells of most persons and some animals. **Rhesus-positive** (or **-negative**) having (or not having) Rhesus factor.

rhetoric /'retərɪk/ *n*. art of persuasive speaking or writing; inflated or exaggerated language. **rhetorician** /-'rɪʃ-/ *n*.

rhetorical /rɪ'tɒrɪk(ə)l/ *a*. expressed with a view to persuasive or impressive effect; of the nature of rhetoric. **rhetorical question** question asked not for information but to produce effect.

rheumatic /ru:'mætɪk/ **1** *a*. of or caused by or suffering from rheumatism. **2** *n. in pl. colloq.* rheumatism. **3 rheumatic fever** fever with pain in the joints. **4 rheumatically** *a*.

rheumatism /'ru:mətɪz(ə)m/ *n*. disease marked by inflammation and pain in the joints etc.

rheumatoid /'ru:mətɔɪd/ *a*. having the character of rheumatism. **rheumatoid arthritis** chronic progressive disease causing inflammation and stiffening of joints.

rhinestone /'raɪnstəʊn/ *n*. imitation diamond.

rhino /'raɪnəʊ/ n. (pl. **-nos**) colloq. rhinoceros.

rhinoceros /raɪ'nɒsərəs/ n. large thick-skinned animal with horn or two horns on nose.

rhizome /'raɪzəʊm/ n. rootlike stem growing along or under ground and producing both roots and shoots.

rhododendron /rəʊdə'dendrən/ n. evergreen shrub with large flowers.

rhomboid /'rɒmbɔɪd/ 1 a. like a rhombus. 2 n. quadrilateral of which only opposite sides and angles are equal. 3 **rhomboidal** a.

rhombus /'rɒmbəs/ n. (pl. **-buses**) oblique equilateral parallelogram, e.g. diamond on playing-card.

rhubarb /'ruːbɑːb/ n. plant with fleshy leaf-stalks cooked and eaten as fruit; these stalks.

rhyme /raɪm/ 1 n. identity of sound at ends of words or verse-lines; rhymed verse; word providing rhyme; poem, poetry. 2 v. (of words or lines) end in rhymes; be or use as rhyme (to, with); versify, write rhymes.

rhythm /'rɪð(ə)m/ n. measured flow of words in verse or prose; Mus. periodical accent and duration of notes; movement or pattern with regulated succession of strong and weak elements; regularly occurring sequence of events. **rhythm method** contraception by avoiding sexual intercourse near times of ovulation. **rhythmic(al)** a.

rib 1 n. each of the curved bones protecting thoracic cavity and its organs; ridge or long raised piece often of stronger or thicker material across surface or through structure, serving to support or strengthen; combination of plain and purl stitches producing ribbed somewhat elastic fabric. 2 v.t. provide or mark (as) with ribs; colloq. tease.

ribald /'rɪbəld/ a. irreverent, coarsely humorous. **ribaldry** n.

riband /'rɪbənd/ n. ribbon.

ribbing a. ribs or riblike structure.

ribbon /'rɪbən/ n. narrow strip or band of fabric; material in this form; ribbon of special colour worn to indicate some honour or membership of sports team etc.; long narrow strip; in pl. ragged strips. **ribbon development** building

of houses along main road outwards from town.

ribonucleic acid /raɪbəʊnjuː'kliːk/ substance controlling protein synthesis in cells.

rice n. grain from a kind of grass grown esp. in Asia; this grass. **rice-paper** edible paper made from pith of an oriental tree and used for painting and in cookery.

rich /rɪtʃ/ a. having much wealth; splendid, costly; abundant, ample; abounding in; fertile; (of food) containing much fat or spice etc.; mellow, strong and full; highly amusing.

riches /'rɪtʃɪz/ n.pl. abundant means; valuable possessions.

richly /'rɪtʃlɪ/ adv. fully, thoroughly.

rick¹ n. stack of hay etc.

rick² 1 v.t. slightly strain or sprain. 2 n. slight strain or sprain.

rickets /'rɪkɪts/ n. as sing. or pl. children's deficiency disease with softening of the bones.

rickety /'rɪkɪtɪ/ a. shaky, insecure; suffering from rickets.

rickshaw /'rɪkʃɔː/ n. light two-wheeled hooded vehicle drawn by one or more persons.

ricochet /'rɪkəʃeɪ/ 1 n. rebounding of projectile etc. from object it strikes; hit made after this. 2 v.i. skip or rebound once or more on surface.

rid v.t. (past & p.p. **rid**) make (person, place) free of.

riddance /'rɪd(ə)ns/ n. **good riddance** welcome freedom from unwanted thing or person.

ridden p.p. of **ride**.

riddle¹ /'rɪd(ə)l/ 1 n. question designed to test ingenuity in divining answer or meaning; puzzling fact or thing or person. 2 v.i. speak in or propound riddles.

riddle² /'rɪd(ə)l/ 1 v.t. sift; make many holes in esp. with gunshot; in p.p. filled with (faults etc.). 2 n. coarse sieve.

ride 1 v. (past **rode**; p.p. **ridden**) sit on and be carried by horse etc.; go on horseback or bicycle or in train or other conveyance; manage horse; lie at anchor; float buoyantly; in p.p. dominated or infested (with). 2 n. journey in vehicle; spell of riding; path (esp. through woods) for riding on. 3 **ride up** (of garment) work upwards when worn; **take for a ride** sl. make fool of.

rider /ˈraɪdə(r)/ n. person riding; additional clause amending or supplementing document; corollary; recommendation added to verdict.

ridge n. line of junction in which two sloping surfaces meet; long narrow hill-top; mountain range; any narrow elevation along surface. **ridge-pole** horizontal pole of long tent; **ridgeway** road along ridge.

ridicule /ˈrɪdɪkjuːl/ **1** n. derision, mockery. **2** v.t. make fun of; subject to ridicule; laugh at.

ridiculous /rɪˈdɪkjʊləs/ a. deserving to be laughed at; unreasonable.

riding /ˈraɪdɪŋ/ n. former division of Yorkshire.

rife pred. a. of common occurrence; prevailing, current, numerous.

riff n. short repeated phrase in jazz and similar music.

riff-raff /ˈrɪfræf/ n. the rabble, disreputable people.

rifle /ˈraɪf(ə)l/ **1** n. gun with rifled barrel; in pl. troops armed with these. **2** v.t. search and rob; make spiral grooves in (gun, etc.) to make bullets spin.

rift n. crack, split; cleft; disagreement, dispute. **rift valley** one formed by subsidence of section of earth's crust.

rig¹ 1 v.t. provide (ship) with spars and ropes etc.; fit (out, up) with clothes or equipment; set up hastily or as makeshift. **2** n. arrangement of ship's masts and sails etc.; equipment for special purpose; oil-rig. **3 rig-out** colloq. outfit, costume.

rig² v.t. manage or conduct fraudulently.

rigging /ˈrɪgɪŋ/ n. ropes etc. used to support masts and work or set sails etc.

right /raɪt/ **1** a. morally good, just; correct, true; in good or normal condition; not mistaken; on or towards side of human body which in majority of persons has the more-used hand, or on or towards that part of an object which is analogous to person's right side. **2** n. what is just; fair treatment; fair claim; being entitled to privilege or immunity, thing one is entitled to; in pl. right condition, true state; right part, region, or direction; *Polit.* conservatives collectively. **3** v.t. restore to proper or straight or vertical position; make reparation for, avenge; vindicate, re-

habilitate; correct, set in order. **4** adv. straight; all the way (*round, to*, etc.); completely; quite, very; justly, properly, correctly, truly; on or to right side. **5 by rights** if right were done; **in the right** having justice or truth on one's side; **right angle** angle of 90° (**at right angles** placed with right angle); **right-hand** placed on right side; **right-handed** using right hand in preference to left, made by or for right hand, turning to right; **right-hander** right-handed person or blow; **right-hand man** indispensable or chief assistant; **right-minded** having sound views and principles; **right of way** right to pass over another's ground, path subject to such right, precedence in passing granted to one vehicle over another; **right side** side of fabric etc. meant to show; **right wing** group on right of army or football etc. team or political party; **right-winger** member of this; **set to rights** arrange properly. **6 rightward** a. & adv.; **rightwards** adv.

righteous /ˈraɪtʃəs/ a. virtuous, upright, just, honest.

rightful /ˈraɪtfʊl/ a. legitimately entitled to position etc.; that one is entitled to.

rightly /ˈraɪtlɪ/ adv. justly, correctly, properly, justifiably.

rigid /ˈrɪdʒɪd/ a. not flexible; that cannot be bent; inflexible, harsh. **rigidity** n.

rigmarole /ˈrɪgmərəʊl/ n. rambling or meaningless talk.

rigor mortis /ˌrɪgə ˈmɔːtɪs/ stiffening of body after death.

rigour /ˈrɪgə(r)/ n. severity, strictness, harshness; strict application or observance etc. (*of*). **rigorous** a.

rile v.t. colloq. anger, irritate.

rill n. tiny stream.

rim n. raised edge or border; outer ring of wheel on which tyre is fitted.

rime¹ 1 n. hoar-frost. **2** v.t. cover with rime.

rime² var. of **rhyme**.

rimmed /rɪmd/ a. edged, bordered.

rind /raɪnd/ n. tough outer layer or covering of fruit and vegetables or cheese or bacon etc.

ring¹ 1 n. circlet usu. of precious metal and often set with gem(s) worn esp. on finger; circular band of any material; line or band round cylindrical or circular object; mark or part etc. having form of circular band; enclosure for circus, boxing, betting at races, etc.; persons or things arranged in circle, such arrangement; combination of traders, politicians, spies, etc., acting together for control of operations. **2** *v.t.* encompass; encircle; put ring on (bird etc.). **3 ring-dove** large species of pigeon; **ring-finger** third finger esp. of left hand; **ringleader** instigator in crime or mischief etc.; **ring main** electrical supply through cable in continuous ring; **ringmaster** director of circus performance; **ring road** bypass encircling town; **ringworm** skin-disease forming circular patches.

ring² *v.* (*past* **rang**; *p.p.* **rung**) give clear resonant sound; make (bell) ring; make telephone call (to); (of place) resound, re-echo; (of ears) be filled with sensation of ringing; ring bell; announce or signal or summon by sound of bell. **2** *n.* ringing sound or tone; act of ringing bell, sound caused by this; *colloq.* telephone call; set of (church) bells. **3 ring off** end telephone call; **ring up** make telephone call (to), record (amount) on cash register.

ringlet /ˈrɪŋlɪt/ *n.* curly lock of hair.

rink *n.* stretch or sheet of ice (used for skating or game of curling); floor for roller-skating; strip of bowling-green used for match.

rinse /rɪns/ **1** *v.t.* pour water into and out of to remove dirt etc.; wash lightly, pour liquid over; put through clean water to remove soap; remove by rinsing. **2** *n.* rinsing; solution for temporary tinting of hair.

riot /ˈraɪət/ **1** *n.* tumult, disorder; disturbance of peace by crowd; loud revelry; lavish display *of*; very amusing thing or person. **2** *v.i.* make or engage in riot. **3 run riot** throw off all restraint. **4 riotous** *a.*

rip¹ **1** *v.* cut or tear quickly or forcibly away or apart; make (hole etc.) thus; make long cut or tear in; come violently apart, split. **2** *n.* long tear or cut; act of ripping. **3 let rip** not check speed of or interfere; **rip-cord** cord for releasing parachute from its pack; **rip off** *sl.* defraud, steal; **rip-off** *n.*

rip² *n.* dissolute person, rake.

RIP *abbr.* may he or she or they rest in peace.

riparian /raɪˈpeərɪən/ *a.* of or on river-bank.

ripe *a.* ready to be reaped or picked or eaten; mature, in fit state *for.*

ripen /ˈraɪpən/ *v.* make or become ripe.

riposte /rɪˈpɒst/ **1** *n.* retort; quick return thrust in fencing. **2** *v.i.* deliver riposte.

ripple /ˈrɪp(ə)l/ **1** *n.* ruffling of water's surface; small wave(s); gentle lively sound that rises and falls. **2** *v.* form or flow in ripples; sound like ripples; make ripples.

rise /raɪz/ **1** *v.i.* (*past* **rose** /rəʊz/; *p.p.* **risen** /ˈrɪz(ə)n/) come or go up; project or swell upwards; come to surface; get up from lying or sitting or kneeling; get out of bed; cease to sit for business; make revolt; ascend, soar; have origin, begin to flow. **2** *n.* rising; upward slope; social advancement; increase in rank or price or amount or wages etc.; origin. **3 give rise to** cause, induce; **take a rise out of** cause to display temper etc.

riser /ˈraɪzə(r)/ *n.* vertical piece between treads of staircase.

risible /ˈrɪzɪb(ə)l/ *a.* laughable; inclined to laugh. **risibility** *n.*

rising /ˈraɪzɪŋ/ *n.* insurrection.

risk 1 *n.* chance of injury or loss or bad consequence; person or thing causing risk. **2** *v.t.* expose to risk; venture on, take chances of.

risky /ˈrɪskɪ/ *a.* full of risk; *risqué.*

risotto /rɪˈzɒtəʊ/ *n.* (*pl.* **-tos**) Italian dish of rice with stock, meat, onions, etc.

risqué /ˈrɪskeɪ/ *a.* (of story etc.) slightly indecent. [F]

rissole /ˈrɪsəʊl/ *n.* fried ball or cake of minced meat with breadcrumbs etc.

rite *n.* religious or solemn ceremony or observance.

ritual /ˈrɪtjʊəl/ **1** *n.* prescribed order for performing religious service; performance of actions in rite; procedure regularly followed. **2** *a.* of or done with rites.

ritualism /ˈrɪtjʊəlɪz(ə)m/ *n.* regular or excessive practice of ritual. **ritualist** *n.*; **ritualistic** *a.*

rival /ˈraɪv(ə)l/ **1** *n.* person or thing

that competes with another. **2** *v.t.* be rival of or comparable to.

rivalry /ˈraɪvəlrɪ/ *n.* being rivals; emulation.

riven /ˈrɪv(ə)n/ *a.* split, torn violently.

river /ˈrɪvə(r)/ *n.* large natural stream of water flowing in channel; copious flow *of*.

rivet /ˈrɪvɪt/ **1** *n.* nail or bolt for holding together metal plates etc. **2** *v.t.* (*past &* *p.p.* **riveted**) join or fasten with rivets; concentrate, direct intently (*upon*); engross attention of.

rivulet /ˈrɪvjʊlɪt/ *n.* small stream.

RM *abbr.* Royal Marines.

RN *abbr.* Royal Navy.

RNA *abbr.* ribonucleic acid.

roach /rəʊtʃ/ *n.* small freshwater fish.

road *n.* way, esp. with prepared surface, for pedestrians, riders, and vehicles; way of getting *to*; route; (usu. in *pl.*) piece of water near shore in which ships can ride at anchor. **on the road** travelling; **road-block** obstruction on road to detain traffic; **road fund licence** *colloq.* vehicle excise tax certificate; **road-hog** reckless or inconsiderate motorist etc.; **roadhouse** inn or restaurant on main road in country district; **roadstead** sea road for ships; **road test** test of vehicle by use on road; **roadway** part of road, bridge, etc. used by vehicles; **roadworks** construction or repair of roads; **roadworthy** (of vehicle) fit to be used on road.

roadie /ˈrəʊdɪ/ *n.* *colloq.* assistant of touring pop group etc., responsible for equipment.

roadster /ˈrəʊdstə(r)/ *n.* open car without rear seats; horse or bicycle for use on roads.

roam *v.* ramble, wander or travel unsystematically (about).

roan **1** *a.* (of animal) with coat of which prevailing colour is thickly interspersed with another. **2** *n.* roan horse or cow.

roar /rɔː(r)/ **1** *n.* loud deep hoarse sound as of lion. **2** *v.* utter roar; say or shout in roar; travel in vehicle at high speed.

roaring /ˈrɔːrɪŋ/ *a.* riotous, noisy, brisk.

roast **1** *v.* cook or heat by exposure to an open fire or in oven; undergo roast-

ing. **2** *attrib.a.* roasted. **3** *n.* dish of roast meat; meat for roasting.

rob *v.* take unlawfully from or deprive *of* esp. by violence; deprive (*of*); commit robbery. **robbery** *n.*

robe **1** *n.* long loose garment, esp. as indication of rank, office, etc.; dressing-gown. **2** *v.* dress; put on robes; clothe in robe.

robin /ˈrɒbɪn/ *n.* small brown red-breasted bird.

robot /ˈrəʊbɒt/ *n.* automaton with human appearance; automatic mechanical device; machine-like person. **robotic** /-ˈbɒt-/ *a.*

robust /rəʊˈbʌst/ *a.* of strong health and physique; not slender or weakly; vigorous.

roc *n.* gigantic bird of Eastern legend.

rock[1] *n.* solid part of earth's crust; material or mass of this; large detached stone or boulder; hard sweet usu. in form of stick and flavoured with peppermint. **on the rocks** *colloq.* short of money, having broken down, (of drink) served with ice cubes; **rock-bottom** *colloq.* very lowest; **rock-cake** bun with rugged surface; **rock crystal** crystallized quartz; **rock-garden** rockery; **rock-plant** plant that grows on or among rocks; **rock salmon** dogfish as sold for food; **rock-salt** common salt as solid mineral.

rock[2] **1** *v.* move gently to and fro; set or keep or be in such motion; sway from side to side; oscillate; shake, reel. **2** *n.* rocking motion; popular modern music with strong beat. **3 rock and roll** popular music with heavy beat and simple melody; **rock group** group playing rock music; **rocking-chair** chair mounted on rockers; **rocking-horse** wooden horse on rockers for child.

rocker *n.* each of the curved bars on which cradle etc. rocks; rocking-chair.

rockery /ˈrɒkərɪ/ *n.* pile of rough stones with soil between them for growing rock-plants on.

rocket /ˈrɒkɪt/ **1** *n.* firework or signal in form of cylindrical case that can be projected to distance or height by ignition of contents; shell or bomb or spacecraft projected by rocket propulsion. **2** *v.t.* (*past & p.p.* **rocketed**) move rapidly upwards or away; bombard with rockets. **3 rocket pro-**

pulsion propulsion by reaction of jet of gases released in combustion of propellant.

rocketry /'rɒkɪtrɪ/ n. science or practice of rocket propulsion.

rocky[1] /'rɒkɪ/ a. of or like rock; full of rocks.

rocky[2] /'rɒkɪ/ a. colloq. unsteady, tottering.

rococo /rə'kəʊkəʊ/ 1 a. of ornate style of art, music, and literature in 18th-c. Europe. 2 n. this style.

rod n. slender straight round stick or metal bar; cane or birch for flogging; fishing-rod; measure of length (=**perch**[1]).

rode past of **ride**.

rodent /'rəʊd(ə)nt/ n. animal with strong incisors and no canine teeth (e.g. rat, squirrel, beaver).

rodeo /'rəʊdeɪəʊ/ n. (pl. -**deos**) exhibition of cowboys' skills; round-up of cattle for branding etc.

roe[1] n. **hard roe** mass of eggs in female fish; **soft roe** male fish's milt.

roe[2] n. small kind of deer. **roebuck** male roe.

roentgen /'rʌntjən/ n. unit of ionizing radiation.

rogation /rə'geɪʃ(ə)n/ n. (usu. in pl.) litany of the saints chanted on the 3 days (**Rogation days**) before Ascension Day.

roger /'rɒdʒə(r)/ int. used to indicate that message has been received and understood; sl. I agree.

rogue /rəʊg/ n. dishonest or unprincipled person; mischievous person; wild animal driven or living apart from herd and of savage temper; inferior or defective specimen among many acceptable ones. **roguery** n.; **roguish** a.

roister /'rɔɪstə(r)/ v.i. revel noisily, be uproarious.

role n. actor's part; person's or thing's function.

roll /rəʊl/ 1 n. cylinder formed by turning paper, cloth, etc. over and over on itself without folding; thing of similar form; small loaf of bread for one person; official list or register; rolling motion or gait; continuous sound of thunder or drum or shouting. 2 v. move or send or go in some direction by turning over and over on axis; make into or form roll; make by rolling; flatten with roller; walk with swaying gait; sway or rock; undulate, show undulating motion or surface; sound with vibration. 3 **roll-call** calling of list of names to establish presence; **rolled gold** thin coating of gold applied by roller to base metal; **rolling-mill** machine or factory for rolling metal into shape; **rolling-pin** roller for pastry; **rolling-stock** company's railway or (US) road vehicles; **rollmop** rolled pickled herring fillet; **roll-top desk** desk with flexible cover sliding in curved grooves; **roll-up** hand-rolled cigarette; **strike off the rolls** debar from practising as solicitor.

roller /'rəʊlə(r)/ n. hard cylinder used for smoothing or flattening or crushing or spreading ink or paint etc.; small cylinder on which hair is rolled for setting; long swelling wave. **roller-coaster** switchback at fair etc.; **roller-skate** skate mounted on set of small rollers; **roller-towel** towel with ends joined, hung on roller.

rollicking /'rɒlɪkɪŋ/ a. jovial and boisterous.

roly-poly /'rəʊlɪ'pəʊlɪ/ 1 n. pudding of suet pastry covered with jam and rolled up and boiled. 2 a. podgy, plump.

Roman /'rəʊmən/ 1 a. of ancient Rome or its territory or people; of medieval or modern Rome; Roman Catholic. 2 n. inhabitant of Rome, member of ancient-Roman State; Roman Catholic; **roman** roman type. 3 **Roman alphabet** letters A-Z as in W. Eur. languages; **Roman candle** tubular firework discharging coloured sparks; **Roman Catholic** of part of Christian Church acknowledging Pope as its head, member of this; **Roman nose** one with high bridge; **Roman numerals** numbers expressed in letters of Roman alphabet; **roman type** plain upright type used in ordinary print.

romance /rə'mæns/ 1 n. episode or story centred on imaginative scenes of love or heroism etc.; romantic character or quality; love affair; medieval tale of chivalry; exaggeration, picturesque falsehood. 2 a. **Romance** of any of the languages developed from Latin. 3 v.i. exaggerate, invent or tell fantastic stories.

Romanesque /rəʊməˈnɛsk/ *n.* style in architecture etc. prevalent between classical and Gothic periods.

romanize /ˈrəʊmənaɪz/ *v.t.* make Roman or Roman Catholic in character; put into Roman alphabet or roman type. **romanization** *n.*

romantic /rəˈmæntɪk/ **1** *a.* marked by or suggestive of or given to romance; imaginative, visionary; (of literature or music etc.) concerned more with emotion than with form. **2** *n.* romantic person, esp. writer, painter, or musician.

romanticism /rəˈmæntɪsɪz(ə)m/ *n.* adherence to romantic style in literature or art etc. **romanticist** *n.*

romanticize /rəˈmæntɪsaɪz/ *v.* make romantic; indulge in romance.

Romany /ˈrɒmənɪ/ *n.* gypsy; language of gypsies.

romp **1** *v.i.* play in lively and boisterous manner; *colloq.* succeed easily. **2** *n.* spell of romping.

rompers *n.pl.* young child's play-garment.

rondeau /ˈrɒndəʊ/ *n.* short poem with two rhymes only, and opening words used as refrains.

rondel /ˈrɒnd(ə)l/ *n.* rondeau.

rondo /ˈrɒndəʊ/ *n.* (*pl.* **-os**) *Mus.* movement or composition in which principal theme recurs several times.

Röntgen rays /ˈrʌntjən/ X-rays.

rood /ruːd/ *n.* crucifix, esp. on roodscreen; quarter-acre. **rood-screen** carved screen separating nave and chancel.

roof /ruːf/ **1** *n.* upper covering of building; top of covered vehicle etc. **2** *v.t.* cover with roof; be roof of. **3 roof of the mouth** palate; **roof-rack** framework to carry luggage etc. on motor-car roof.

rook[1] /rʊk/ **1** *n.* black bird of crow kind that nests in colonies. **2** *v.t.* swindle or cheat, esp. at cards etc.; charge extortionately.

rook[2] /rʊk/ *n.* chess piece with battlement-shaped top.

rookery /ˈrʊkərɪ/ *n.* colony of rooks or penguins or seals.

rookie /ˈrʊkɪ/ *n. sl.* recruit.

room /ruːm/ **1** *n.* space that is or might be occupied by something; part of house etc. enclosed by walls or partitions; in *pl.* apartments or lodgings;

opportunity, scope. **2** *v.i. US* have room(s), lodge.

roomy /ˈruːmɪ/ *a.* having much room, spacious.

roost /ruːst/ **1** *n.* bird's resting-place. **2** *v.i. n.* (of bird) settle for sleep; be perched or lodged for the night.

rooster /ˈruːstə(r)/ *n. US* domestic cock.

root[1] /ruːt/ **1** *n.* part of plant that fixes it to earth etc. and conveys nourishment from soil; in *pl.* fibres or branches of this; plant with edible root, such root; embedded part of hair or tooth etc.; in *pl.* emotional attachment to a place; source, means of growth, basis; *Math.* number which multiplied by itself a given number of times yields a given number, esp. *square root*; ultimate element of language. **2** *v.* (cause to) take root; fix or establish firmly; pull up by root. **3 root out** find and get rid of; **root-stock** rhizome, source from which offshoots have arisen; **take root** begin to draw nourishment from the soil, become established.

root[2] /ruːt/ *v.* turn up ground, turn *up* (ground etc.) in search of food; search *out*, hunt *up.* **root for** *US sl.* encourage by applause or support.

rope **1** *n.* stout cord made by twisting together strands of hemp or wire etc.; string *of* pearls; in *pl. the* ropes enclosing boxing-ring etc. **2** *v.t.* fasten or secure or connect with rope, put rope on; enclose or mark *off* with rope. **3 know the ropes** be familiar with conditions in some sphere of action; **rope in** persuade to take part.

ropy /ˈrəʊpɪ/ *a. colloq.* poor in quality.

Roquefort /ˈrɒkfɔː(r)/ *n.* (**P**) blue cheese orig. made from ewe's milk.

rorqual /ˈrɔːkw(ə)l/ *n.* kind of whale with dorsal fin.

rosaceous /rəʊˈzeɪʃəs/ *a.* of the family of plants including the rose.

rosary /ˈrəʊzərɪ/ *n. RC Ch.* form of devotion made up of repeated prayers; string of beads for keeping count in this.

rose[1] /rəʊz/ **1** *n.* prickly shrub bearing fragrant flower usu. of red, yellow, or white colour; similar flowering plant; light crimson colour, pink; representation of the flower; rose-shaped design or object; nozzle of watering-can etc. **2** *a.* coloured like pale red rose, of warm pink. **3 rosebud** bud of rose, pretty girl; **rose-coloured** rosy, *fig.* sanguine, cheerful, optimistic; **rose-water** fragrant liquid distilled from roses; **rose-window** circular window, usu. with roselike tracery; **rosewood** close-grained fragrant kind used in making furniture.

rose² *past of* **rise**.

rosé /ˈrəʊzeɪ/ *n.* light pink wine. [F]

roseate /ˈrəʊzɪət/ *a.* rose-coloured.

rosemary /ˈrəʊzmərɪ/ *n.* evergreen fragrant shrub used as culinary herb.

rosette /rəʊˈzet/ *n.* rose-shaped ornament made of ribbons etc. or carved in stone etc.

rosin /ˈrɒzɪn/ **1** *n.* resin, esp. in solid form. **2** *v.t.* rub with rosin.

RoSPA /ˈrɒspə/ *abbr.* Royal Society for the Prevention of Accidents.

roster /ˈrɒstə(r)/ *n.* list or plan showing turns of duty etc.

rostrum /ˈrɒstrəm/ *n.* (*pl.* **-tra**) platform for public speaking etc.

rosy /ˈrəʊzɪ/ *a.* coloured like pink or red rose; cheerful, hopeful.

rot 1 *v.* undergo decay by putrefaction or from lack of use; cause to rot, make rotten. **2** *n.* decay, rottenness; *sl.* nonsense; *sl.* series of failures. **3 rot-gut** inferior or harmful liquor.

rota /ˈrəʊtə/ *n.* list of persons acting, or duties to be done, in rotation.

rotary /ˈrəʊtərɪ/ *a.* rotating, acting by rotation.

rotate /rəʊˈteɪt/ *v.* move round axis or centre, revolve; arrange or take in rotation. **rotatory** *a.*

rotation /rəʊˈteɪʃ(ə)n/ *n.* rotating or being rotated; recurrent series or period; regular succession of members of a group. **rotational** *a.*

rote *n.* mechanical process of memory.

rotisserie /rəˈtɪsərɪ/ *n.* cooking-device for roasting food on revolving spit.

rotor /ˈrəʊtə(r)/ *n.* rotary part of machine; rotating system of helicopter.

rotten /ˈrɒt(ə)n/ *a.* perishing from decay; morally or politically corrupt; worthless; *sl.* disagreeable, ill-advised.

rotter /ˈrɒtə(r)/ *n.* *sl.* objectionable person.

rotund /rəʊˈtʌnd/ *a.* rounded, plump; sonorous, grandiloquent. **rotundity** *n.*

rotunda /rəʊˈtʌndə/ *n.* circular building, esp. one with dome.

rouble /ˈruːb(ə)l/ *n.* monetary unit of USSR.

roué /ˈruːeɪ/ *n.* debauchee, rake.

rouge /ruːʒ/ **1** *n.* red cosmetic used to colour cheeks and lips. **2** *v.* colour with rouge; adorn oneself thus.

rough /rʌf/ **1** *a.* having uneven surface, not smooth or level; not mild or quiet or gentle; violent, harsh, unfeeling, unpleasant; deficient in finish etc.; approximate, preliminary. **2** *adv.* in rough manner. **3** *n.* hardship; hooligan; rough ground; *the* unfinished or natural state. **4** *v.t.* make rough; sketch *in* or plan *out* roughly. **5 rough-and-ready** rough or crude but effective, not elaborate or over-particular; **rough-and-tumble** irregular, disorderly, (*n.*) haphazard fight; **roughcast** plaster of lime and gravel, (*v.t.*) coat with this; **rough house** disturbance, rough fight; **rough it** do without ordinary comforts; **rough justice** treatment that is approximately fair; **roughneck** *colloq.* driller on oil rig, *US sl.* rough person; **roughshod** (of horse) having shoes with nail-heads projecting (**ride roughshod over** treat inconsiderately or arrogantly).

roughage /ˈrʌfɪdʒ/ *n.* indigestible material in food that stimulates intestinal action.

roughen /ˈrʌf(ə)n/ *v.* make or become rough.

roulette /ruːˈlet/ *n.* gambling game played on table with revolving compartmented wheel in which ball rolls randomly.

round /raʊnd/ **1** *a.* shaped like circle or sphere or cylinder; done with circular motion; (of number etc.) without odd units; entire, continuous, complete, candid. **2** *n.* round object; revolving motion, circular or recurring course, series; route on which goods are regularly delivered; single provision (*of* drinks etc.); one spell of play etc., one stage in competition; playing of all holes in golf-course once; ammunition to fire one shot; slice of bread, sandwich made from whole slices of bread; rung of ladder; circumference, extent, *of*; *Mus.* canon for voices at same pitch or in octaves. **3** *adv.* with circular motion, with return to starting-point or change to opposite position; to or at or affecting all or many points of circumference or area or members of company etc.; in every direction from a centre; measuring (specified distance) in girth. 4 *prep.* so as to encircle or enclose; at or to points on circumference of; in various directions from; so as to pass in curved course, having thus passed. 5 *v.* give or take round shape; make (number etc.) round by omitting units etc.; pass round (corner etc.). 6 **in the round** with all features shown or considered, with audience all round theatre stage; **Roundhead** member of Parliamentary party in English Civil War; **round off** bring to complete or symmetrical state; **round on** attack unexpectedly; **round robin** petition with signatures in circle to conceal order of writing; **roundsman** tradesman's employee who delivers goods; **round-table conference** one with discussion by members round table; **round trip** circular tour, outward and return journey; **round up** gather or bring together; **round-up** rounding up, summary.

roundabout /ˈraʊndəbaʊt/ 1 *n.* road junction with traffic passing in one direction round central island; merry-go-round. 2 *a.* circuitous.

roundel /ˈraʊnd(ə)l/ *n.* small disc; rondeau.

roundelay /ˈraʊndəleɪ/ *n.* short simple song with refrain.

rounders /ˈraʊndəz/ *n.* team-game with bat and ball where players run round a series of bases.

roundly /ˈraʊndlɪ/ *adv.* bluntly, severely.

rouse /raʊz/ *v.* stir up from sleep or quiescence; cease to sleep; become active.

rout¹ /raʊt/ 1 *n.* disorderly retreat of defeated troops. 2 *v.t.* defeat utterly.

rout² var. of **root**².

route /ruːt/ *n.* way taken in getting from starting-point to destination. 2 *v.t.* (*partic.* **routeing**) send etc. along particular route. 3 **route march** training-march of soldiers etc.

routine /ruːˈtiːn/ 1 *n.* regular course of procedure, unvarying performance of certain acts; set sequence in per-

formance, esp. dance; sequence of instructions to computer. 2 *a.* performed as routine.

rove¹ *v.* wander without settled destination; (of eyes) look in changing directions.

rove² var. of **reeve**².

rover¹ /ˈrəʊvə(r)/ *n.* wanderer.

rover² /ˈrəʊvə(r)/ *n.* pirate.

row¹ /rəʊ/ *n.* line of persons or things; line of seats in theatre etc. **in a row** *colloq.* in succession.

row² /rəʊ/ 1 *v.* propel boat with oars; convey in boat. 2 *n.* spell of rowing. 3 **rowing-boat** boat propelled with oars.

row³ /raʊ/ *colloq.* 1 *n.* disturbance, noise, dispute; being reprimanded. 2 *v.t.* make or engage in a row; reprimand.

rowan /ˈraʊən, ˈrəʊən/ *n.* mountain ash; its scarlet berry.

rowdy /ˈraʊdɪ/ 1 *a.* noisy and disorderly. 2 *n.* rowdy person. 3 **rowdyism** *n.*

rowel /ˈraʊəl/ *n.* spiked revolving disc at end of spur.

rowlock /ˈrɒlək/ *n.* appliance serving as point of support for oar.

royal /ˈrɔɪəl/ 1 *a.* of or suited to or worthy of king or queen; in service or under patronage of king or queen; belonging to or of family of king or queen; splendid, on great scale. 2 *n. colloq.* member of royal family. 3 **royal blue** deep vivid blue; **royal warrant** warrant authorizing tradesman to supply goods to royal person.

royalist /ˈrɔɪəlɪst/ *n.* supporter of monarchy or of the royal side in civil war etc.

royalty /ˈrɔɪəltɪ/ *n.* being royal; royal persons; member of royal family; sum paid to patentee for use of patent or to author etc. for each copy of his book etc. sold or for each public performance of his work; royal right (now esp. over minerals) granted by sovereign to individual or corporation.

r.p.m. *abbr.* revolutions per minute.

RSM *abbr.* Regimental Sergeant-Major.

RSPCA *abbr.* Royal Society for the Prevention of Cruelty to Animals.

RSVP *abbr.* please answer (*répondez s'il vous plaît*).

Rt. Hon. *abbr.* Right Honourable.

Rt. Revd. *abbr.* Right Reverend.

rub 1 v. slide hand or object along or over surface of; polish or clean or abrade or chafe or make dry or sore by rubbing; take (stain etc.) *out*; freshen or brush *up*; come into or be in sliding contact, exercise friction *against* etc.; get frayed or worn by friction; get *along* etc. with more or less restraint or difficulty. **2** n. action or spell of rubbing; impediment or difficulty. **3 rub off** be transferred by contact; **rub (up) the wrong way** irritate.

rubato /ruː'bɑːtəʊ/ n. *Mus.* (pl. -tos) temporary disregarding of strict tempo.

rubber[1] /'rʌbə(r)/ n. elastic substance made from latex of tropical plants or synthetically; piece of this or other substance for erasing pencil-marks; *US* in pl. galoshes. **rubber band** loop of rubber to hold papers etc.; **rubber-neck** *US* (be) gaping sightseer; **rubber plant** plant yielding rubber, esp. kind grown as house plant; **rubber stamp** device for inking and imprinting on surface; **rubber-stamp** approve automatically without proper consideration. **rubbery** a.

rubber[2] /'rʌbə(r)/ n. three successive games between same sides or persons at bridge etc. or cricket.

rubbish /'rʌbɪʃ/ n. waste or worthless matter; litter; trash, nonsense. **rubbishy** a.

rubble /'rʌb(ə)l/ n. waste fragments of stone, brick, etc.

rubella /ruː'belə/ n. German measles.

rubicund /'ruːbɪkʌnd/ a. ruddy, red-faced.

rubric /'ruːbrɪk/ n. direction for conduct of divine service inserted in liturgical book; explanatory words; general instruction; heading or passage in red or special lettering.

ruby /'ruːbɪ/ **1** n. crimson or rose-coloured precious stone; glowing red colour. **2** a. ruby-coloured.

ruche /ruːʃ/ **1** n. frill or gathering of lace etc. **2** v.t. gather into or trim with ruche(s).

ruck[1] n. main body of competitors not likely to overtake leaders; undistinguished crowd of persons or things.

ruck[2] v. crease, wrinkle.

rucksack /'rʌksæk/ n. bag slung by straps from both shoulders and resting on back.

ruction /'rʌkʃ(ə)n/ n. *colloq.* dispute, row.

rudder /'rʌdə(r)/ n. flat piece hinged to vessel's stern or rear of aeroplane for steering with.

ruddy /'rʌdɪ/ a. freshly or healthily red; reddish; *sl.* bloody, damnable.

rude a. impolite, offensive; roughly made; primitive; uneducated; abrupt, sudden; vigorous, hearty.

rudiment /'ruːdɪmənt/ n. in pl. elements or first principles (*of*), imperfect beginning of something undeveloped; in *sing.* part or organ imperfectly developed as having no function.

rudimentary /ruːdɪ'mentərɪ/ a. not advanced or developed; of the nature of a rudiment.

rue[1] v.t. (*partic.* **ruing**) repent of; wish undone or non-existent.

rue[2] n. evergreen shrub with bitter strong-scented leaves.

rueful /'ruːfʊl/ a. expressing (mock) sorrow.

ruff[1] n. projecting starched frill worn round neck; projecting or conspicuous band of feathers or hair round bird's or animal's neck; kind of pigeon.

ruff[2] **1** v. trump at cards. **2** n. trumping.

ruffian /'rʌfɪən/ n. violent lawless person. **ruffianly** a.

ruffle /'rʌf(ə)l/ **1** v.t. disturb smoothness or tranquillity of. **2** n. frill of lace etc.; ripple.

rufous /'ruːfəs/ a. reddish-brown.

rug n. floor-mat; thick woollen wrap or coverlet.

Rugby /'rʌgbɪ/ n. (in full **Rugby football**) game played with oval ball that may be kicked or carried.

rugged /'rʌgɪd/ a. of rough uneven surface; harsh; austere.

rugger /'rʌgə(r)/ n. *colloq.* Rugby football.

ruin /'ruːɪn/ **1** n. fallen or wrecked state; downfall; loss of property or position; (often in pl.) remains of building etc. that has suffered ruin; cause of ruin. **2** v.t. reduce to ruins; bring to ruin; damage irrecoverably, destroy, bankrupt. **3 ruination** n.

ruinous /'ruːɪnəs/ a. bringing ruin; disastrous; in ruins.

rule /ruːl/ 1 *n.* principle to which action conforms or should conform; prevailing custom, standard, normal state of things; government, dominion; graduated straight measure; *Print.* thin line or dash; code of discipline of religious order. 2 *v.* exercise sway or decisive influence over; keep under control; have sovereign control of or *over*; pronounce authoritatively (*that*); make parallel lines across (paper), make (straight line) with ruler etc. 3 **as a rule** usually; **rule of thumb** method or procedure based on experience or practice, not theory; **rule out** exclude.

ruler /ˈruːlə(r)/ *n.* person exercising government or dominion; straight strip of wood etc. used for drawing or measuring lines.

ruling /ˈruːlɪŋ/ *n.* authoritative pronouncement.

rum¹ *n.* spirit distilled from sugar-cane or molasses.

rum² *a. colloq.* queer, strange.

rumba /ˈrʌmbə/ *n.* ballroom dance of Cuban origin; music for this.

rumble¹ /ˈrʌmb(ə)l/ 1 *v.* make continuous deep sound as of thunder; (of person or vehicle) go *along* making such sound. 2 *n.* rumbling sound.

rumble² /ˈrʌmb(ə)l/ *v.t. sl.* see through, detect.

rumbustious /rʌmˈbʌstʃəs/ *a. colloq.* boisterous, uproarious.

ruminant /ˈruːmɪn(ə)nt/ 1 *n.* animal that chews the cud. 2 *a.* of ruminants; ruminating.

ruminate /ˈruːmɪneɪt/ *v.i.* chew the cud; meditate, ponder. **rumination** *n.*; **ruminative** *a.*

rummage /ˈrʌmɪdʒ/ 1 *v.* search thoroughly or untidily (in); find among other things. 2 *n.* search. 3 **rummage sale** jumble sale.

rummy /ˈrʌmɪ/ *n.* card-game played usu. with two packs.

rumour /ˈruːmə(r)/ 1 *n.* general talk or report or hearsay, of doubtful accuracy. 2 *v.t.* report by way of rumour.

rump *n.* tail-end or buttocks of animal or bird or person. **rump steak** cut of beef from rump.

rumple /ˈrʌmp(ə)l/ *v.t.* crease, crumple.

rumpus /ˈrʌmpəs/ *n. colloq.* row, uproar.

run 1 *v.* (*past* **ran**; *p.p.* **run**) go at pace faster than walk; flee; go or travel hurriedly or briefly etc.; advance (as) by rolling or on wheels or smoothly; be in action or operation; be current or operative or valid; (of bus or train etc.) travel or be travelling on its route; extend; compete in race etc.; enter for race or contest; seek election; flow or emit contents; spread rapidly; set or keep going, control operations of; own and use (vehicle); smuggle. 2 *n.* act or spell of running; short excursion; distance travelled; general tendency; regular route; continuous stretch or spell or course; high general demand; general or average type or class; point scored in cricket or baseball; permission for free use *of*; animal's regular track; enclosure for fowls etc.; range of pasture; ladder in stocking. 3 **on the run** fleeing; **run across** happen to meet; **run after** pursue; **run away** leave quickly or secretly; **runaway** fugitive; **run down** knock down or collide with, reduce numbers of (staff), (of clockwork) stop for lack of winding, (of person or health etc.) become enfeebled, discover after search, disparage; **run-down** reduction in numbers, detailed analysis, (*a.*) decayed from prosperity; **run dry** cease to flow; **run in** bring (new engine etc.) into good working order, *colloq.* arrest; **run into** incur (debt), collide with, happen to meet, reach as many as; **run low** become depleted, have few left; **run off** flee, produce (copies) on machine, decide (race) after tie or heats, write or recite fluently; **run-of-the-mill** ordinary, not special; **run out** come to an end, exhaust one's stock *of*, put down wicket of (running batsman); **run out on** desert; **run over** overflow, (of vehicle) pass over (animal, prostrate person, etc.), review; **run short** = *run low*; **run through** examine or rehearse briefly, deal successively with; **run to** have money or ability for, reach (amount etc.), show tendency to; **run up** accumulate quickly, build or make hurriedly, raise (flag); **run up against** meet with (difficulty etc.); **runway** specially prepared airfield surface for taking off and landing.

rune *n.* letter of earliest Germanic alphabet; similar character of mysterious or magic significance. **runic** *a.*

rung[1] *n.* short stick fixed as crossbar, esp. in ladder.

rung[2] *p.p.* of **ring**[2].

runnel /ˈrʌn(ə)l/ *n.* brook; gutter.

runner /ˈrʌnə(r)/ *n.* racer; messenger; creeping plant-stem that can take root; groove or rod for thing to slide along; sliding ring on rod etc.; long narrow ornamental cloth or rug. **runner bean** kind of climbing bean; **runner-up** competitor taking second place.

running 1 *n.* act or manner of running; management. 2 *a.* continuous; consecutive. 3 **in the running** with chance of winning or success; **make the running** set the pace; **running commentary** oral description of events in progress; **running jump** one in which jumper runs to take-off; **running knot** one that slips along rope etc. and changes size of loop; **running repairs** minor repairs and replacements; **running water** water available from stream or taps.

runny /ˈrʌnɪ/ *a.* tending to run or flow; excessively fluid.

runt *n.* undersized person or animal; smallest of litter.

rupee /ruːˈpiː/ *n.* monetary unit of India, Pakistan, etc.

rupture /ˈrʌptʃə(r)/ 1 *n.* breaking, breach; breach of harmonious relations; abdominal hernia. 2 *v.* burst (cell, membrane, etc.); sever (connection); affect with or suffer hernia.

rural /ˈrʊər(ə)l/ *a.* in or of or suggesting country. **rurality** /-ˈræl-/ *n.*; **ruralize** *v.t.*

ruse /ruːz/ *n.* stratagem.

rush[1] 1 *v.* go or move or pass precipitately or with great speed; impel or carry along rapidly; force (person) to act hastily; attack or capture by sudden assault. 2 *n.* act of rushing; violent advance or attack; period of great activity; sudden migration of large numbers; strong run *on* or *for* a commodity; in *pl. Cinema* preliminary showings of film before cutting. 3 **rush-hour** time each day when traffic

etc. is heaviest.

rush[2] *n.* marsh plant with slender pith-filled stem; its stem; rushes as material. **rushlight** candle made by dipping pith of rush in tallow.

rusk *n.* slice of bread rebaked as kind of light biscuit esp. for infants.

russet /ˈrʌsɪt/ 1 *a.* reddish-brown. 2 *n.* russet colour; rough-skinned russet apple.

Russian /ˈrʌʃ(ə)n/ 1 *a.* of Russia. 2 *n.* native or language of Russia. 3 **Russian roulette** firing of revolver held to one's head after spinning cylinder with one chamber loaded; **Russian salad** mixed diced cooked vegetables with mayonnaise.

rust 1 *n.* reddish- or yellowish-brown corrosive coating formed on iron by oxidation; plant-disease with rust-coloured spots. 2 *v.* become rusty; affect with rust; lose quality or efficiency by disuse or inactivity.

rustic /ˈrʌstɪk/ 1 *a.* of or like country people or peasants; uncouth; of simple workmanship; made of untrimmed branches or rough timber, with rough surface. 2 *n.* countryman. 3 **rusticity** *n.*

rusticate /ˈrʌstɪkeɪt/ *v.* expel temporarily from university as punishment; retire to or live in the country. **rustication** *n.*

rustle /ˈrʌs(ə)l/ 1 *v.* (cause to) make sound as of dry leaves blown in breeze; go with rustle; steal (cattle or horses). 2 *n.* rustling sound. 3 **rustle up** *colloq.* produce when needed.

rusty /ˈrʌstɪ/ *a.* rusted, affected with rust; impaired by age or disuse; discoloured by age.

rut[1] *n.* track sunk by passage of wheels; fixed pattern of behaviour difficult to change.

rut[2] 1 *n.* periodic sexual excitement of male deer etc. 2 *v.i.* be affected with rut. 3 **ruttish** *a.*

ruthless /ˈruːθlɪs/ *a.* having no pity or compassion.

RV *abbr.* Revised Version (of Bible).

rye /raɪ/ *n.* cereal plant used for bread and as fodder etc.; grain of this; (in full **rye whisky**) whisky distilled from rye.

S

S. *abbr.* south; southern.

s. *abbr.* second(s); shilling(s); singular; son.

SA *abbr.* Salvation Army; sex appeal; South Africa; South Australia.

sabbatarian /sæbə'teərɪən/ *n.* person observing sabbath strictly. **sabbatarianism** *n.*

sabbath /'sæbəθ/ *n.* religious rest-day appointed for Jews on last, and for Christians on first, day of the week.

sabbatical /sə'bætɪk(ə)l/ **1** *a.* of sabbath; (of leave) granted at intervals to university teacher etc. for study or travel. **2** *n.* period of sabbatical leave.

sable /'seɪb(ə)l/ **1** *n.* small dark-furred arctic mammal; its skin or fur; the colour black. **2** *a.* black, gloomy.

sabot /'sæbəʊ/ *n.* wooden or wooden-soled shoe.

sabotage /'sæbətɑːʒ/ **1** *n.* deliberate destruction or damage, esp. for industrial or political purpose. **2** *v.t.* commit sabotage on; damage or destroy.

saboteur /sæbə'tɜː(r)/ *n.* person who commits sabotage.

sabre /'seɪbə(r)/ *n.* cavalry sword with curved blade; light fencing-sword. **sabre-rattling** display or threats of military force.

sac *n.* membranous bag in animal or vegetable organism.

saccharin /'sækərɪn/ *n.* very sweet substance used as substitute for sugar.

saccharine /'sækəriːn/ *a.* intensely sweet, cloying.

sacerdotal /sækə'dəʊt(ə)l/ *a.* of priests or priestly office.

sachet /'sæʃeɪ/ *n.* small bag or packet esp. of perfumed substance or shampoo etc.

sack[1] **1** *n.* large bag made of coarse flax or hemp etc.; amount held by sack. **2** *v.t.* put in sack(s); *colloq.* dismiss from employment. **3 the sack** *colloq.* dismissal; **sackcloth** coarse fabric of flax or hemp etc.

sack[2] *v.t.* plunder and destroy. **2** *n.* sacking of town etc.

sack[3] *n. hist.* white wine from Spain etc.

sackbut /'sækbʌt/ *n.* early form of trombone.

sacking /'sækɪŋ/ *n.* sackcloth.

sacral /'seɪkr(ə)l/ *a.* of sacrum.

sacrament /'sækrəmənt/ *n.* symbolic religious ceremony, esp. Eucharist; sacred thing, influence, etc. **sacramental** *a.*

sacred /'seɪkrɪd/ *a.* connected with religion; dedicated or appropriated to a god or *to* some person or purpose; safeguarded or required by religion or tradition etc.; inviolable. **sacred cow** idea or institution unreasonably held to be above criticism.

sacrifice /'sækrɪfaɪs/ **1** *n.* giving up something for sake of something else, thing given up thus; loss entailed; slaughter of animal or person or surrender of a possession as offering to a deity; what is thus slaughtered or surrendered. **2** *v.* give up, devote *to*; offer or kill (as) sacrifice. **3 sacrificial** /-'fɪʃ-/ *a.*

sacrilege /'sækrɪlɪdʒ/ *n.* violation of what is sacred. **sacrilegious** *a.*

sacristan /'sækrɪst(ə)n/ *n.* person in charge of sacristy and church contents.

sacristy /'sækrɪstɪ/ *n.* repository for church's vestments and vessels etc.

sacrosanct /'sækrəsæŋkt/ *a.* most sacred; inviolable. **sacrosanctity** *n.*

sacrum /'seɪkrəm/ *n.* composite bone forming back of pelvis.

sad *a.* sorrowful; showing or causing sorrow; incorrigible; deplorably bad.

sadden /'sæd(ə)n/ *v.* make or become sad.

saddle /'sæd(ə)l/ **1** *n.* seat of leather etc. fastened on horse etc.; seat for rider of bicycle etc.; joint of meat consisting of the two loins; ridge rising to a summit at each end. **2** *v.t.* put saddle on (horse etc.); burden *with* task etc. **3 saddle-bag** one of pair of bags laid across back of horse etc.; bag attached behind saddle of bicycle etc.

saddler /'sædlə(r)/ *n.* maker of or dealer in saddles and harness. **saddlery** *n.*

sadism /'seɪdɪz(ə)m/ *n.* enjoyment of cruelty to others; sexual perversion characterized by this. **sadist** *n.*; **sadistic** /-'dɪs-/ *a.*

s.a.e. *abbr.* stamped addressed envelope.

safari /sə'fɑːrɪ/ *n.* hunting or scientific expedition esp. in Africa. **safari park**

area where wild animals are kept in open for viewing.

safe 1 *a.* free of danger or injury; affording security or not involving danger; reliable; sure; prevented from escaping or doing harm; cautious. **2** *n.* strong lockable cupboard for valuables; ventilated cupboard for provisions. **3 safe conduct** immunity from arrest or harm; **safe deposit** building containing safes or strong-rooms let separately.

safeguard /'seɪfgɑːd/ 1 *n.* proviso or circumstance etc. that tends to prevent something undesirable. **2** *v.t.* guard or protect (rights etc.).

safety /'seɪftɪ/ *n.* being safe; freedom from danger. **safety belt** strap securing person safely, esp. seat-belt; **safety-catch** contrivance for locking gun-trigger or preventing accidental operation of machinery; **safety curtain** fireproof curtain in theatre to divide auditorium from stage in case of fire etc.; **safety match** match that ignites only on specially prepared surface; **safety net** net placed to catch acrobat etc. in case he falls; **safety-pin** pin with point that is bent back to head and held in guard when closed; **safety razor** razor with guard protecting skin from cuts; **safety-valve** valve relieving excessive pressure of steam, *fig.* means of harmlessly releasing excitement or anger etc.

saffron /'sæfrən/ 1 *n.* orange-coloured stigmas of crocus used for colouring and flavouring; colour of this. **2** *a.* saffron-coloured.

sag 1 *v.i.* sink or subside; have downward bulge or curve in middle. **2** *n.* state or amount of sagging.

saga /'sɑːgə/ *n.* medieval Icelandic or Norwegian prose tale; story of heroic achievement or adventure; long family chronicle.

sagacious /sə'geɪʃəs/ *a.* having or showing insight or good judgement. **sagacity** /-'gæs-/ *n.*

sage[1] *n.* aromatic herb with dull greyish-green leaves.

sage[2] 1 *a.* wise, judicious, experienced. **2** *n.* person credited with profound wisdom.

Sagittarius /sædʒɪ'teərɪəs/ *n.* ninth sign of zodiac.

sago /'seɪgəʊ/ *n.* starch prepared from palm-pith and used for puddings etc.

sahib /sɑːɪb/ *n.* former title of address to European men in India.

said *past & p.p.* of **say**.

sail 1 *n.* piece of canvas etc. extended on rigging to catch wind and propel vessel; *collect.* ship's sails; voyage or excursion in sailing-vessel; wind-catching apparatus attached to arm of windmill. **2** *v.* travel on water by use of sails or engine-power; traverse sea; navigate ship; start on voyage; glide or move smoothly or easily. **3 sailcloth** canvas for sails, kind of coarse linen; **sailing-boat, -ship** etc. one moved by sails; **sailplane** kind of glider.

sailor /'seɪlə(r)/ *n.* seaman or mariner, esp. below officer's rank. **bad, good, sailor** person very liable, not liable, to seasickness.

sainfoin /'sænfɔɪn/ *n.* pink-flowered fodder-plant.

saint 1 *n.* holy or canonized person, regarded as having place in heaven; very virtuous person. **2** *attrib.* as prefix to name. **3** *v.t.* canonize; in *p.p.* sacred, worthy of sainthood. **4 sainthood** *n.*; **saintly** *a.*

sake[1] /seɪk/ *n.* **for the sake of, for my** etc. **sake** out of consideration for, in the interest of, in order to please or get etc.

sake[2] /'sɑːkɪ/ *n.* Japanese fermented liquor made from rice.

salaam /sə'lɑːm/ 1 *n.* oriental salutation; low bow. **2** *v.i.* make salaam.

salacious /sə'leɪʃəs/ *a.* erotic; lecherous. **salacity** /-'læs-/ *n.*

salad /'sæləd/ *n.* mixture of raw or cold vegetables etc. often eaten with or including cold meat or cheese etc.; vegetable or herb suitable for eating raw. **salad days** one's period of youthful inexperience; **salad-dressing** mixture of oil and vinegar etc., used with salad.

salamander /'sæləmændə(r)/ *n.* lizard-like animal formerly supposed to live in fire; kind of tailed amphibian.

salami /sə'lɑːmɪ/ *n.* highly-seasoned sausage, orig. Italian.

sal ammoniac /sæl ə'məʊnɪæk/ ammonium chloride.

salary /'sælərɪ/ 1 *n.* fixed regular payment made by employer to employee. **2** *v.t.* (esp. in *p.p.*) pay salary to.

sale *n.* exchange of commodity for money etc.; act or instance of selling; amount sold; occasion when goods are sold; offering of goods at reduced prices for a period. **for, on, sale** offered for purchase; **sale-room** room where auctions are held; **salesman, salesperson, saleswoman,** person employed to sell goods etc.

saleable /'seɪləb(ə)l/ *a.* fit to be sold; finding purchasers. **saleability** *n.*

salesmanship /'seɪlzmənʃɪp/ *n.* skill in selling.

salient /'seɪlɪənt/ 1 *a.* prominent, conspicuous; standing or pointing outwards. 2 *n.* salient angle; *Mil.* bulge in line of attack or defence.

saline /'seɪlaɪn/ 1 *a.* of salt(s); containing or tasting of salt(s). 2 *n.* saline substance; salt lake or spring etc. **salinity** /-'lɪn-/ *n.*

saliva /sə'laɪvə/ *n.* colourless liquid produced by glands in mouth. **salivary** *a.*

salivate /'sælɪveɪt/ *v.i.* secrete or discharge saliva esp. in excess.

sallow[1] /'sæləʊ/ *a.* (of complexion) of sickly yellow or yellowish brown.

sallow[2] /'sæləʊ/ *n.* low-growing willow; shoot or wood of this.

sally /'sælɪ/ 1 *n.* rush from besieged place upon enemy; witticism, piece of banter. 2 *v.i.* make sally; go *forth* or *out* for walk etc.

salmon /'sæmən/ 1 *n.* large silver-scaled fish with orange-pink flesh. 2 *a.* orange-pink. 3 **salmon-trout** sea trout.

salmonella /sælmə'nelə/ *n.* kind of bacterium causing food poisoning.

salon /'sælɒn/ *n.* reception-room of large house; meeting here of eminent people; room or establishment where hairdresser or couturier etc. receives clients.

saloon /sə'luːn/ *n.* large room or hall for assemblies etc. or for specified purpose; public room on ship; *US* drinking-bar; saloon car. **saloon bar** first-class bar in public house; **saloon car** motor car with closed body and no partition behind driver.

salsify /'sælsɪfɪ/ *n.* plant with long fleshy root cooked as vegetable.

salt /sɔːlt/ 1 *n.* substance that gives sea-water its characteristic taste, got by mining or by evaporation of sea-water etc., and used esp. for seasoning or preserving food; *Chem.* substance formed when part of the hydrogen in an acid is replaced by a metal or metal-like radical; (often in *pl.*) substance resembling salt in taste or form etc.; in *pl.* such substance used as laxative; piquancy, pungency, wit. 2 *a.* containing or tasting of or treated with salt. 3 *v.t.* preserve or season or treat with salt; *sl.* make fraudulent entries in (accounts etc.). 4 **salt away, down,** *colloq.* save or put away for the future; **salt-cellar** vessel holding salt for table use; **salt-marsh** marsh overflowed by sea; **salt-mine** mine yielding rock-salt, *fig.* place of unremitting toil; **salt of the earth** finest people, those who keep society wholesome; **saltpan** hollow near sea where salt is got by evaporation; **take with a grain** or **pinch of salt** be sceptical about; **worth one's salt** having merit.

SALT *abbr.* Strategic Arms Limitation Talks.

salting /'sɔːltɪŋ/ *n.* salt marsh.

saltire /'sɔːltaɪə(r)/ *n.* X-shaped cross.

saltpetre /sɔːltpiːtə(r)/ *n.* white crystalline salty substance used in gunpowder, in preserving meat, and medicinally.

salty /'sɔːltɪ/ *a.* containing or tasting of salt; pungent, witty.

salubrious /sə'luːbrɪəs/ *a.* health-giving. **salubrity** *n.*

saluki /sə'luːkɪ/ *n.* large slender silky-coated dog.

salutary /'sæljʊtərɪ/ *a.* producing good effects.

salutation /sælju'teɪʃ(ə)n/ *n.* sign or expression of greeting or respect; use of these.

salute /sə'luːt/ 1 *n.* gesture expressing respect or courteous recognition etc.; *Mil.* etc. prescribed movement or use of flags or discharge of gun(s) in sign of respect. 2 *v.* make salute to; greet with polite gesture; express respect for.

salvage /'sælvɪdʒ/ 1 *n.* rescue of property from loss at sea or by fire, payment made or due for this; saving and utilization of waste material; property or materials salvaged. 2 *v.t.* save from wreck or fire etc.; make salvage of.

salvation /sæl'veɪʃ(ə)n/ *n.* act of sav-

ing or being saved, esp. from sin and
its consequences; person or thing that
preserves from loss or calamity etc.
Salvation Army religious missionary
body organized on quasi-military lines.
Salvationist /sæl'veɪʃənɪst/ n. member of Salvation Army. **Salvationism**
n.

salve[1] /sælv/ 1 n. healing ointment;
something that soothes. 2 v.t. soothe.

salve[2] /sælv/ v.t. save from wreck or
fire etc.

salver /'sælvə(r)/ n. tray for handing
refreshments or letters etc.

salvo /'sælvəʊ/ n. (pl. **-voes**) simultaneous firing of artillery or other
guns; round of applause.

sal volatile /sæl və'lætɪlɪ/ solution of
ammonium carbonate, used as restorative in faintness etc.

Samaritan /sə'mærɪt(ə)n/ n. charitable or helpful person (also **good Samaritan**); member of organization
helping people in mental distress.

samba /'sæmbə/ 1 n. ballroom dance
of Brazilian origin; music for this. 2 v.i.
dance samba.

same 1 a. identical; unchanged; unvarying; previously referred to. 2 pron.
the same the same thing. 3 adv. **the
same** in the same manner. 4 **just the
same** nevertheless.

samovar /'sæməvɑː(r)/ n. Russian urn
for making tea.

Samoyed /'sæməjed/ n. white Arctic
breed of dog.

sampan /'sæmpæn/ n. small boat used
in Far East.

samphire /'sæmfaɪə(r)/ n. cliff plant
used in pickles.

sample /'sɑːmp(ə)l/ 1 n. small part
taken from quantity to show what
whole is like; specimen; typical example. 2 v.t. take samples of, try qualities
of; get representative experience of.

sampler /'sɑːmplə(r)/ n. piece of embroidery worked to show proficiency.

samurai /'sæmʊraɪ/ n. (pl. same) Japanese army officer; hist. member of
military caste in Japan.

sanatorium /sænə'tɔːrɪəm/ n. (pl.
-iums) establishment for treatment of
invalids, esp. convalescents and the
chronically sick; accommodation for
sick persons in school etc.

sanctify /'sæŋktɪfaɪ/ v.t. consecrate,

make or observe as holy; purify from
sin. **sanctification** n.

sanctimonious /sæŋktɪ'məʊnɪəs/ a.
making a show of being holy.

sanction /'sæŋkʃ(ə)n/ 1 n. approval
given to action etc. by custom or tradition; express permission; penalty or
reward attached to law; consideration
causing any rule to be obeyed; in pl.
economic or military action to coerce a
State to conform to agreement etc. 2 v.t.
authorize, countenance, permit.

sanctity /'sæŋktɪtɪ/ n. sacredness,
holiness.

sanctuary /'sæŋktjʊərɪ/ n. holy place;
place where wild animals and birds etc.
are protected; esp. hist. place of refuge.

sanctum /'sæŋktəm/ n. holy place;
person's private room.

sand 1 n. substance resulting from
wearing down of esp. siliceous rocks;
in pl. grains of sand, expanse of sand,
sandbank. 2 v.t. smooth or polish with
sandpaper; sprinkle or treat with sand.
3 **sandbag** bag filled with sand esp. for
making temporary defences, (v.t.) defend or hit with sandbag(s); **sandbank**
deposit of sand forming shallow place
in sea or river; **sand-blast** jet of sand
driven by compressed air or steam,
(v.t.) clean or treat with this; **sandcastle** structure of sand made esp. by
child on beach; **sand-hill** dune; **sandmartin** bird nesting in sandy banks;
sandpaper paper with abrasive coating for smoothing or polishing, (v.t.)
treat with this; **sandpiper** bird inhabiting wet sandy places; **sandstone**
sedimentary rock of compressed sand;
sandstorm storm with clouds of sand
raised by wind.

sandal /'sænd(ə)l/ n. shoe with openwork upper or no upper, fastened with
straps.

sandalwood /'sændəlwʊd/ n. kind of
scented wood; tree with this.

sandwich /'sænwɪdʒ/ 1 n. two or more
slices of bread or toast etc. with filling
between; cake of two or more layers
with jam or cream etc. between. 2 v.t.
put (thing, statement, etc.) between two
others of different kind. 3 **sandwich-
board** board carried by sandwich-
man; **sandwich course** course of
study in which periods of theoretical
and practical work alternate;

sandwich-man man walking in street with advertisement boards hanging in front and behind.

sandy /'sændɪ/ a. covered with sand; sand-coloured, (of hair) yellowish-red.

sane a. of sound mind, not mad; (of opinion etc.) sensible, rational.

sang past of **sing**.

sang-froid /sã'frwɑː/ n. calmness in danger or difficulty.

sanguinary /'sæŋgwɪnərɪ/ a. accompanied by or delighting in bloodshed; bloodthirsty; bloody.

sanguine /'sæŋgwɪn/ a. optimistic; (of complexion) bright and florid.

Sanhedrin /'sænɪdrɪn/ n. court of justice and supreme council in ancient Jerusalem.

sanitarium /sænə'teərɪəm/ n. US sanatorium.

sanitary /'sænɪtərɪ/ a. of or aimed at or assisting the protection of health; hygienic. **sanitary towel** absorbent pad used during menstruation.

sanitation /sænɪ'teɪʃ(ə)n/ n. sanitary conditions, maintenance or improvement of these; disposal of sewage and refuse etc.

sanitize /'sænɪtaɪz/ v.t. make sanitary.

sanity /'sænɪtɪ/ n. being sane.

sank past of **sink**.

Sanskrit /'sænskrɪt/ **1** n. ancient and sacred language of Hindus in India. **2** a. of or in Sanskrit. **3 Sanskritic** a.

Santa Claus /'sæntə klɔːz/ person said to fill children's stockings with presents at Christmas.

sap[1] **1** n. vital juice of plants; vitality; sl. foolish person. **2** v.t. drain of sap; exhaust vigour of. **3 sappy** a.

sap[2] **1** n. tunnel or trench to conceal assailants' approach to fortified place. **2** v. make saps; undermine (wall etc.); destroy insidiously, weaken.

sapid /'sæpɪd/ a. savoury; not tasteless; not insipid. **sapidity** n.

sapient /'seɪpɪənt/ a. wise; pretending to be wise. **sapience** n.

sapling /'sæplɪŋ/ n. young tree.

sapper /'sæpə(r)/ n. private of Royal Engineers.

sapphire /'sæfaɪə(r)/ **1** n. transparent blue precious stone; its colour. **2** a. of sapphire blue.

saprophyte /'sæprəfaɪt/ n. vegetable organism living on dead organic matter.

saraband /'særəbænd/ n. slow Spanish dance; music for this.

Saracen /'særəs(ə)n/ n. Arab or Muslim of time of crusades. **Saracenic** a.

sarcasm /'sɑːkæz(ə)m/ n. bitter or wounding remark(s), esp. ironically worded. **sarcastic** a.

sarcophagus /sɑː'kɒfəgəs/ n. (pl. -gi /-gaɪ/) stone coffin.

sardine /sɑː'diːn/ n. small fish related to herring, often tinned tightly packed in oil.

sardonic /sɑː'dɒnɪk/ a. grimly jocular; full of bitter mockery; cynical.

sardonyx /sɑː'dɒnɪks/ n. onyx in which white layers alternate with yellow or orange ones.

sargasso /sɑː'gæsəʊ/ n. (pl. -os) seaweed with berry-like air-vessels.

sarge /sɑːdʒ/ n. sl. sergeant.

sari /'sɑːrɪ/ n. length of material wrapped round body, worn as main garment by Hindu women.

sarong /sə'rɒŋ/ n. garment of long strip of cloth tucked round waist or under armpits.

sarsaparilla /sɑːsəpə'rɪlə/ n. tropical Amer. smilax; its dried roots; tonic made from these.

sarsen /'sɑːs(ə)n/ n. sandstone etc. boulder, relict carried by ice in glacial period.

sarsenet /'sɑːsnɪt/ n. soft silk fabric used for linings etc.

sartorial /sɑː'tɔːrɪəl/ a. of clothes or tailoring.

sash[1] n. long strip or loop of cloth worn over one shoulder or round waist esp. as part of uniform or insignia.

sash[2] n. frame holding window-glass, usu. made to slide up and down in grooves.

sassafras /'sæsəfræs/ n. a medicinal bark; N. Amer. tree with this.

Sassenach /'sæsənæx/ n. Sc. & Ir. usu. derog. English person.

sat past & p.p. of **sit**.

Sat. abbr. Saturday.

Satan /'seɪt(ə)n/ n. the Devil.

satanic /sə'tænɪk/ a. of or like Satan; devilish, evil.

satchel /'sætʃ(ə)l/ n. small bag, esp. for carrying school-books.

sate v.t. satiate.

sateen /sæˈtiːn/ n. glossy cotton fabric woven like satin.

satellite /ˈsætəlaɪt/ n. heavenly or artificial body revolving round earth or other planet; hanger-on, follower; country etc. controlled by or dependent on another.

satiate /ˈseɪʃɪeɪt/ v.t. gratify fully, surfeit. **satiation** n.

satiety /səˈtaɪətɪ/ n. state of being glutted; feeling of having had too much.

satin /ˈsætɪn/ n. silk etc. fabric with glossy surface on one side. **satinwood** kind of choice glossy timber. **satiny** a.

satire /ˈsætaɪə(r)/ n. use of ridicule or irony etc. to expose folly or vice etc.; work or composition using satire. **satirical** /-ˈtɪr-/ a.

satirist /ˈsætɪrɪst/ n. writer or performer of satires.

satirize /ˈsætɪraɪz/ v.t. attack with satire; describe satirically.

satisfaction /sætɪsˈfækʃ(ə)n/ n. satisfying or being satisfied; thing that satisfies desire or gratifies feeling; payment of debt; atonement; amends for injury.

satisfactory /sætɪsˈfæktərɪ/ a. causing satisfaction; adequate.

satisfy /ˈsætɪsfaɪ/ v.t. meet expectations or wishes of; be accepted by (person etc.) as adequate; please; pay, fulfil, comply with; put an end to (an appetite or want), rid (person) of an appetite or want; convince.

satsuma /sætˈsuːmə/ n. kind of mandarin orange.

saturate /ˈsætʃəreɪt/ v.t. fill with moisture, soak; imbue *with* or steep *in*; cause (substance) to absorb, hold, or combine with greatest possible amount of another substance.

saturation /sætʃəˈreɪʃ(ə)n/ n. act or result of being saturated. **saturation point** stage beyond which no more can be absorbed or accepted.

Saturday /ˈsætədeɪ/ n. day of week following Friday.

Saturnalia /sætəˈneɪlɪə/ n. ancient-Roman festival of Saturn; **saturnalia** scene or time of wild revelry.

saturnine /ˈsætənaɪn/ a. of gloomy temperament or appearance.

satyr /ˈsætə(r)/ n. *Gk. & Rom. myth.* half-human half-animal woodland deity; lustful or sensual man.

sauce /sɔːs/ 1 n. liquid or soft prep-

aration used as relish with food; something that adds piquancy; *colloq.* sauciness. 2 v.t. *colloq.* be impudent to. 3 **sauce-boat** shallow jug in which sauce is served; **saucepan** metal cooking-vessel with long handle, for use on top of stove.

saucer /ˈsɔːsə(r)/ n. small shallow dish, esp. for standing cup on.

saucy /ˈsɔːsɪ/ a. impudent, cheeky; *colloq.* smart-looking.

sauerkraut /ˈsaʊəkraʊt/ n. German dish of pickled cabbage.

sauna /ˈsɔːnə/ n. Finnish-style steam-bath.

saunter /ˈsɔːntə(r)/ 1 v.i. walk in leisurely way. 2 n. leisurely ramble or gait.

saurian /ˈsɔːrɪən/ 1 n. animal of lizard family. 2 a. of or like a lizard.

sausage /ˈsɒsɪdʒ/ n. minced meat seasoned and stuffed into cylindrical case of thin membrane; sausage-shaped object. **sausage-dog** *colloq.* dachshund; **sausage roll** sausage-meat baked in cylindrical pastry-case.

sauté /ˈsəʊteɪ/ 1 a. quickly and lightly fried in a little fat. 2 n. food cooked thus. 3 v.t. (*past & p.p.* **sautéd**) cook thus.

savage /ˈsævɪdʒ/ 1 a. uncivilized, in primitive state; fierce, cruel; *colloq.* angry. 2 n. member of savage tribe; brutal or barbarous person. 3 v.t. attack and bite or trample; attack fiercely.

savagery /ˈsævɪdʒərɪ/ n. savage behaviour or state.

savannah /səˈvænə/ n. grassy plain in tropical or subtropical region.

savant /ˈsæv(ə)nt/ n. learned person.

save 1 v. rescue or preserve *from* danger or harm; keep for future use (also with *up*); obviate need for, avoid wasting; relieve from need or obligation or experience; prevent loss of; effect spiritual salvation of; *Footb.* etc. prevent opponent from scoring. 2 n. act of saving in football etc. 3 *prep.* except, but.

saveloy /ˈsævəlɔɪ/ n. highly seasoned sausage.

saving /ˈseɪvɪŋ/ 1 n. act of rescuing or preserving; in *pl.* amount of money saved. 2 a. redeeming; that makes economical use of; making reservation or exception. **3** *prep*. except. **4 savings-bank** bank receiving small deposits at interest.

saviour /ˈseɪvɪə(r)/ *n*. deliverer, redeemer; person who saves others from harm or danger.

savoir-faire /sævwɑːˈfeə(r)/ *n*. quickness to see and do right thing; tact.

savory /ˈseɪvərɪ/ *n*. aromatic herb used in cookery.

savour /ˈseɪvə(r)/ **1** *n*. characteristic taste or flavour; tinge or hint *of*. **2** *v*. appreciate flavour of, enjoy; suggest presence *of*.

savoury /ˈseɪvərɪ/ **1** *a*. with appetizing taste or smell; of stimulating or piquant flavour, not sweet. **2** *n*. savoury dish, esp. at end of meal or as appetizer.

savoy /səˈvɔɪ/ *n*. rough-leaved winter cabbage.

savvy /ˈsævɪ/ *sl*. **1** *v*. know. **2** *n*. knowingness, understanding.

saw[1] **1** *n*. implement with toothed blade for cutting wood etc. **2** *v*. (*p.p*. **sawn** or **sawed**) cut or make with saw; make to-and-fro motion as of saw or sawing. **3** *sawdust* fine wood-fragments produced in sawing; *sawfish* large sea-fish with toothed end of snout; *sawmill* mill for mechanical sawing of wood into planks etc.; **saw-toothed** serrated.

saw[2] *n*. old saying, maxim.

saw[3] *past of* **see**[1].

sawyer /ˈsɔːjə(r)/ *n*. workman who saws timber.

sax *n. colloq*. saxophone.

saxe /sæks/ *n*. (also **saxe blue**) light blue with greyish tinge.

saxifrage /ˈsæksɪfrɪdʒ/ *n*. kind of rock plant.

Saxon /ˈsæks(ə)n/ **1** *a*. of Germanic people by whom parts of England were occupied in 5th–6th cc.; Anglo-Saxon. **2** *n*. member or language of the Saxon people.

saxophone /ˈsæksəfəʊn/ *n*. keyed brass reed instrument with gradually widening tube. **saxophonist** /sækˈsɒf-/ *n*.

say **1** *v*. (3rd. *sing. pres*. **says** /sez/; *past* & *p.p*. **said** /sed/) utter; state; speak words of; express; convey information, indicate; adduce or plead; decide. **2** *n*. what one wishes to say, opportunity of saying this; share in decision. **3 say-so** power of decision, mere assertion.

saying /ˈseɪɪŋ/ *n*. common remark, maxim.

sc. *abbr*. scilicet.

scab *n*. crust formed over sore in healing; kind of skin-disease or plant-disease; blackleg in strike. **scabby** *a*.

scabbard /ˈskæbəd/ *n*. sheath of sword etc.

scabies /ˈskeɪbiːz/ *n*. contagious skin-disease causing itching.

scabious /ˈskeɪbɪəs/ *n*. a wild or garden flower.

scabrous /ˈskeɪbrəs/ *a*. rough-surfaced; indecent.

scaffold /ˈskæf(ə)ld/ *n*. platform on which criminal is executed; scaffolding.

scaffolding *n*. temporary structure of poles and planks providing builders etc. with platform(s); materials for this.

scald /skɔːld/ **1** *v.t*. burn with hot liquid or vapour; heat (liquid, esp. milk) to near boiling-point; cleanse with boiling water. **2** *n*. injury to skin by scalding.

scale[1] **1** *n*. set of marks at measured distances on line for use in measuring; basis of numerical notation; relative dimensions, ratio of reduction or enlargement in map or picture etc.; series of degrees; ladder-like arrangement, graded system; *Mus*. set of sounds belonging to a key, arranged in order of pitch. **2** *v.t*. climb up with ladder or by clambering; represent in dimensions different from but proportional to actual ones. **3 scale down** or **up** make smaller or larger in proportion, reduce or increase in size; **to scale** with uniform reduction or enlargement.

scale[2] **1** *n*. one of thin horny overlapping plates protecting skin of many fishes and reptiles; thin plate or flake resembling this; incrustation inside boiler etc.; tartar on teeth. **2** *v*. remove scale(s) from; form or come off in scales. **3 scaly** *a*.

scale[3] **1** *n*. pan of weighing-balance; in *pl*. weighing-instrument. **2** *v.t*. be found to weigh (specified amount).

scalene /ˈskeɪliːn/ *a*. (of triangle) having unequal sides.

scallion /ˈskælɪən/ *n*. spring onion.

scallop /ˈskɒləp/ **1** *n*. bivalve shellfish with fan-shaped ridged shells; one shell of this esp. used for cooking or serving food on; in *pl*. ornamental edging in fabric etc. **2** *v.t.* cook in scallop; ornament with scallops.

scallywag /'skælɪwæg/ *n. sl.* scamp, rascal.

scalp **1** *n.* skin and hair of top of head; this cut off as trophy by Amer. Indian. **2** *v.t.* take scalp of.

scalpel /'skælp(ə)l/ *n.* small surgical knife.

scamp **1** *n.* rascal, rogue. **2** *v.t.* do (work etc.) perfunctorily or inadequately.

scamper /'skæmpə(r)/ **1** *v.i.* move or run hastily or impulsively. **2** *n.* act of scampering.

scampi /'skæmpɪ/ *n.pl.* large prawns.

scan **1** *v.* look at all parts of successively; look over quickly; traverse systematically with radar beam etc.; resolve (picture) into elements of light and shade for television transmission; analyse metre of (line etc.) by examining feet and syllables; be metrically correct. **2** *n.* act or process of scanning.

scandal /'skænd(ə)l/ *n.* general feeling of outrage or indignation, thing causing this; malicious gossip. **scandalmonger** /-mʌŋgə(r)/ person who spreads scandal.

scandalize /'skændəlaɪz/ *v.t.* offend moral feelings or sense of propriety of.

scandalous /'skændələs/ *a.* containing or arousing scandal; outrageous, shocking.

Scandinavian /skændɪ'neɪvɪən/ **1** *a.* of Scandinavia. **2** *n.* native or inhabitant, or family of languages, of Scandinavia.

scansion /'skænʃ(ə)n/ *n.* metrical scanning.

scant *a.* barely sufficient; deficient.

scanty /'skæntɪ/ *a.* of small amount or extent; barely sufficient.

scapegoat /'skeɪpgəʊt/ *n.* person blamed or punished for faults of others.

scapula /'skæpjʊlə/ *n.* (*pl.* **-lae** /-liː/) shoulder-blade.

scapular /'skæpjʊlə(r)/ **1** *a.* of scapula. **2** *n.* monastic short cloak.

scar[1] **1** *n.* mark left on skin etc. by wound etc. **2** *v.* mark with or form scar(s).

scar[2] *n.* precipitous craggy part of mountain-side.

scarab /'skærəb/ *n.* gem cut in form of beetle.

scarce /skeəs/ **1** *a.* not plentiful; insufficient, rare. **2** *adv. arch.* scarcely. **3** **make oneself scarce** go away, keep out of the way.

scarcely /'skeəslɪ/ *adv.* hardly, only just; surely not.

scarcity /'skeəsɪtɪ/ *n.* being scarce; insufficiency.

scare /skeə(r)/ **1** *v.t.* strike with sudden terror, frighten (*away, off,* etc.); in *p.p.* frightened (*of, to* do). **2** *n.* sudden fright or alarm, esp. general alarm caused by baseless or exaggerated rumours. **3** **scarecrow** device for frightening birds away from crops, badly dressed or grotesque person; **scaremonger** /-mʌŋgə(r)/ person who starts or spreads scare(s).

scarf[1] *n.* (*pl.* **scarves**) long strip of material worn round neck for ornament or warmth; square piece of material worn round neck or over woman's hair.

scarf[2] **1** *n.* joint made by thinning ends of two pieces of timber etc. so that they overlap without increase of thickness. **2** *v.t.* join with scarf.

scarify /'skeərɪfaɪ/ *v.t.* loosen surface of (soil etc.); *Surg.* make slight incisions in; scratch; criticize etc. mercilessly. **scarification** *n.*

scarlatina /skɑːlə'tiːnə/ *n.* scarlet fever.

scarlet /'skɑːlɪt/ **1** *a.* of brilliant red colour inclining to orange. **2** *n.* scarlet colour or pigment or clothes etc. **3 scarlet fever** infectious fever with scarlet rash; **scarlet runner** scarlet-flowered climbing bean.

scarp **1** *n.* steep slope, esp. inner side of ditch in fortification. **2** *v.t.* make steep or perpendicular.

scarper /'skɑːpə(r)/ *v.i. sl.* escape, run away.

scat *n.* wordless jazz song using voice as instrument.

scathing /'skeɪðɪŋ/ *a.* (of criticism etc.) harsh, severe.

scatology /skæ'tɒlədʒɪ/ *n.* preoccupation with the obscene or with excrement. **scatological** *a.*

scatter /'skætə(r)/ **1** *v.* throw or send or go in many different directions; cover by scattering; rout or be routed; dissipate; *Phys.* deflect or diffuse (light, particles, etc.); in *p.p.* not situated together, wide apart. **2** *n.* act of scattering; small amount scattered; extent of distribution. **3 scatter-brain** thoughtless or flighty person; **scatter cushions** ones to be placed here and there in a room.

scatty /'skætɪ/ a. sl. lacking concentration, disorganized.

scavenge /'skævɪndʒ/ v. be or act as scavenger; remove dirt or waste etc. from.

scavenger /'skævɪndʒə(r)/ n. person who searches among or collects things unwanted by others; animal or bird that feeds on carrion.

scenario /sɪ'nɑːrɪəʊ/ n. (pl. **-rios**) script or synopsis of film or play etc.; imagined sequence of future events.

scene /siːn/ n. place of actual or fictitious occurrence; piece of continuous action that forms part of play; action, episode, situation; stormy action or encounter or outburst, esp. with display of temper; landscape or view; painted canvas and properties etc. representing scene of action, stage set with these; sl. area or subject of activity or interest. **behind the scenes** out of view of audience, out of sight or hearing or knowledge of general public; **scene-shifter** person who changes scenes in theatre.

scenery /'siːnərɪ/ n. furnishings used in theatre to represent scene; features (esp. picturesque) of landscape.

scenic /'siːnɪk/ a. picturesque; of or on stage; of scenery.

scent /sent/ 1 n. characteristic odour of something; fragrance; liquid perfume; smell or trail left by animal; line of investigation etc.; power of scenting. 2 v.t. discern by smell; begin to suspect presence or existence of; make fragrant, perfume.

sceptic /'skeptɪk/ n. person who questions truth of (esp. religious) doctrine or theory etc.; sceptical person. **scepticism** n.

sceptical /'skeptɪk(ə)l/ a. of scepticism; critical, doubtful, incredulous, hard to convince.

sceptre /'septə(r)/ n. staff borne as symbol of sovereignty.

schedule /'ʃedjuːl/ 1 n. timetable or programme of planned events; table of details etc., esp. as appendix to document. 2 v.t. make schedule of, include in schedule; appoint time for; include (building etc.) in list of those to be preserved. **3 on schedule** at time appointed; **scheduled flight** one operated on regular timetable.

schematic /skɪ'mætɪk/ a. of or like scheme or diagram; systematic, formalized.

schematize /'skiːmətaɪz/ v.t. put in schematic form.

scheme /skiːm/ 1 n. systematic arrangement; outline, syllabus; plan of action; artful or underhand design. 2 v.i. make plans, plan esp. in secret or underhand way.

scherzo /'skeətsəʊ/ n. (pl. **-zos**) Mus. vigorous and lively movement or composition.

schism /'sɪz(ə)m/ n. separation or division in religious group. **schismatic** a.

schist /ʃɪst/ n. fine-grained rock with components arranged in layers.

schizo /'skɪtsəʊ/ n. (pl. **-zos**) colloq. schizophrenic.

schizoid /'skɪtsɔɪd/ 1 a. of or resembling schizophrenia or a schizophrenic. 2 n. schizoid person.

schizophrenia /skɪtsə'friːnɪə/ n. mental disorder marked by disconnection between thought, feelings, etc., and actions. **schizophrenic** /-'fren-/ a. & n.

schmaltz /ʃmɔːlts/ n. sickly sentimentality.

schnapps /ʃnæps/ n. strong kind of gin.

schnitzel /'ʃnɪts(ə)l/ n. veal cutlet.

schnorkel var. of **snorkel**.

scholar /'skɒlə(r)/ n. learned person; person who learns; holder of scholarship. **scholarly** a.

scholarship /'skɒləʃɪp/ n. award of money towards education; learning, erudition.

scholastic /skə'læstɪk/ a. of schools or education; academic.

school¹ /skuːl/ 1 n. institution for educating children or giving instruction; its buildings; its pupils; time given to teaching; being educated in school; circumstances etc. serving to discipline or instruct; branch of study at university; group of artists or disciples etc. following or holding similar principles or opinions etc. 2 v.t. send to school; discipline, bring under control, train or accustom *to*. **3 schoolboy**, **schoolchild**, **schoolgirl**, one who attends school; **school-leaver** person who has just left school; **schoolmaster**, **schoolmistress**, **schoolteacher**, teacher in school; **schoolroom** room used for lessons, esp. in private house.

school² /skuːl/ *n.* shoal of fish or whales etc.

schooner /ˈskuːnə(r)/ *n.* two-masted fore-and-aft rigged ship; large glass of sherry.

schottische /ʃɒˈtiːʃ/ *n.* kind of slow polka.

sciatic /saɪˈætɪk/ *a.* of hip or sciatic nerve; of or having sciatica. **sciatic nerve** large nerve from pelvis to thigh.

sciatica /saɪˈætɪkə/ *n.* neuralgia of hip and thigh.

science /ˈsaɪəns/ *n.* branch of knowledge, esp. one dealing with material phenomena and based on observation, experiment, and induction; systematic and formulated knowledge; pursuit of this; skilful technique. **science fiction** imaginative fiction based on postulated scientific discoveries etc.

scientific /saɪənˈtɪfɪk/ *a.* of or concerned with science; according to principles of science; having or requiring trained skill.

scientist /ˈsaɪəntɪst/ *n.* student or expert in science.

scilicet /ˈsaɪlɪset/ *adv.* that is to say, namely.

scimitar /ˈsɪmɪtə(r)/ *n.* curved oriental sword.

scintillate /ˈsɪntɪleɪt/ *v.i.* sparkle, twinkle; talk or act cleverly or wittily. **scintillation** *n.*

scion /ˈsaɪən/ *n.* shoot cut for grafting; young member *of* family.

scissors /ˈsɪzəz/ *n.pl.* (also **pair of scissors**) cutting-instrument of pair of blades pivoted together.

sclerosis /sklɪəˈrəʊsɪs/ *n.* abnormal hardening of tissue. **sclerotic** /-ˈrɒt-/ *a.*

scoff¹ **1** *v.i.* speak derisively; mock or jeer *at*. **2** *n.* mocking words; taunt.

scoff² *v.t. sl.* eat greedily.

scold /skəʊld/ **1** *v.* rebuke severely or noisily; find fault noisily. **2** *n.* nagging or complaining woman.

sconce /skɒns/ *n.* wall-bracket holding candlestick or light-fitting.

scone /skɒn or skəʊn/ *n.* soft flat cake of flour etc. baked quickly.

scoop /skuːp/ **1** *n.* short-handled deep shovel; long-handled ladle; excavating part of digging-machine etc.; device for serving portions of ice cream etc.; act or motion of scooping; large profit made quickly; exclusive item in newspaper etc. **2** *v.* lift (*up*) or hollow (*out*) (as) with scoop; secure by sudden action or stroke of luck; forestall (rival newspaper etc.) with news scoop.

scoot /skuːt/ *v.i. colloq.* dart, shoot along; make off.

scooter /ˈskuːtə(r)/ *n.* child's toy of narrow foot-board on wheels propelled by pushes of one foot on ground; low-powered kind of motor cycle.

scope *n.* reach or sphere of observation or action, range; opportunity.

scorch /skɔːtʃ/ **1** *v.* burn or discolour surface of with dry heat; become so discoloured etc.; *sl.* go at very high speed. **2** *n.* mark of scorching. **3 scorched earth policy** policy of destroying everything that might be of use to invading enemy.

scorcher *n. colloq.* extremely hot day.

score *n.* number of points or goals etc. made by player or side in game etc.; detailed table of these; (set of) 20; *Mus.* copy of composition with parts on series of staves; point or reason; *colloq.* remark or act by which person scores off another; scratch or notch or line made on surface; record of money owing. **2** *v.* make (points etc.) in game; win or gain; record or keep score; enter in score, record, esp. mentally (often with *up*); secure an advantage, have good luck; mark with incisions or lines; make (line etc.) with something that marks; *Mus.* orchestrate or arrange (*for* instruments). **3 score off** *colloq.* defeat in argument etc., humiliate.

scoria /ˈskɔːrɪə/ *n.* (*pl.* **-riae** /rɪiː/) slag; clinker-like mass of lava.

scorn 1 *n.* disdain, contempt, derision; object of contempt. **2** *v.t.* hold in contempt; abstain from or refuse *to* do as unworthy.

scornful /ˈskɔːnfʊl/ *a.* contemptuous (*of*).

Scorpio /ˈskɔːpɪəʊ/ *n.* eighth sign of zodiac.

scorpion /'skɔ:pɪən/ n. lobster-like arachnid with jointed stinging tail.

Scot n. native of Scotland.

Scotch[1] 1 a. Scots, Scottish. 2 n. Scotch whisky. 3 **Scotch broth** soup made from beef or mutton with pearl barley and vegetables; **Scotch egg** hard-boiled egg enclosed in sausage-meat; **Scotch fir** common N. Eur. pine; **Scotch mist** thick mist and drizzle; **Scotch terrier** small rough-coated short-legged terrier; **Scotch whisky** whisky distilled in Scotland.

scotch[2] v.t. decisively put an end to; arch. wound without killing.

scot-free a. unharmed, unpunished.

Scots 1 a. of Scotland. 2 n. form of English spoken in (esp. Lowlands of) Scotland. 3 **Scotsman**, **Scotswoman**, native of Scotland; **Scots pine** = Scotch fir.

Scottish /'skɒtɪʃ/ a. of Scotland or its inhabitants.

scoundrel /'skaʊndr(ə)l/ n. unscrupulous person; villain. **scoundrelly** a.

scour[1] /skaʊə(r)/ 1 v.t. rub bright or clean; clean out; clear off, out, etc. 2 n. act or process of scouring.

scour[2] /skaʊə(r)/ v. search rapidly or thoroughly; hasten esp. in search or pursuit.

scourer /'skaʊərə(r)/ n. abrasive pad or powder for scouring.

scourge /skɜ:dʒ/ n. person or thing regarded as instrument of divine or other vengeance etc.; whip. 2 v.t. chastise; afflict; whip.

scouse /skaʊs/ sl. 1 a. of Liverpool. 2 n. native of Liverpool; Liverpool dialect.

scout[1] /skaʊt/ 1 n. person sent out to get information or reconnoitre; **Scout** member of boys' organization intended to develop character. 2 v.i. act as scout. 3 **scout about, around**, search (for).

scout[2] /skaʊt/ v.t. reject with scorn or ridicule.

Scouter /'skaʊtə(r)/ n. adult leader in Scout Association.

scowl /skaʊl/ 1 n. sullen or bad-tempered look. 2 v.i. wear scowl.

scrabble /'skræb(ə)l/ 1 v.i. scratch or grope busily (about). 2 n. **Scrabble** (P) game in which players build up words from letter-blocks on board.

scrag 1 n. inferior end of neck of mutton (also **scrag end**); skinny person or animal. 2 v.t. strangle, hang; seize roughly by the neck; beat up.

scraggy /'skrægɪ/ a. thin and bony.

scram v.i. sl. go away.

scramble /'skræmb(ə)l/ 1 v. make way by clambering etc.; struggle with competitors (for thing or share of it); cook (eggs) by stirring in heated pan with butter etc.; alter frequency of sound etc. in telephoning etc. so as to make message unintelligible without special receiver; go rapidly or hastily. 2 n. climb or rough walk; motor-cycle race over rough ground; eager struggle or competition (for).

scrap[1] 1 n. small detached piece; shred or fragment; waste material, discarded metal for reprocessing; in pl. odds and ends, bits of uneaten food. 2 v.t. discard as useless. 3 **scrap-book** book in which cuttings etc. are kept; **scrap-heap** collection of waste material; **scrap yard** place where scrap is collected.

scrap[2] colloq. 1 n. fight or rough quarrel. 2 v.i. have scrap.

scrape 1 v. clean or abrade etc. by causing hard edge to move across surface; take away or off or out etc. by scraping; draw or move with sound (as) of scraping; produce such sound (from); move while (almost) touching; get along or by or through etc. with difficulty; gain with effort or by parsimony; be economical; make clumsy bow. 2 n. act or sound of scraping; awkward predicament esp. resulting from escapade.

scraper /'skreɪpə(r)/ n. device used for scraping.

scrappy /'skræpɪ/ a. consisting of scraps, incomplete.

scratch 1 v. score or wound superficially with sharp or pointed thing; rub with the nails to relieve itching; make hole or strike out or mark through etc. by scratching; erase name of or withdraw from list of competitors etc. 2 n. wound or mark or sound made by scratching; act of scratching oneself; colloq. trifling wound; starting-line for race etc.; position of those receiving no handicap. 3 a. collected by chance, collected or made from whatever is available; with no handicap given. 4 **from scratch** from the beginning without any help or advantage; **up to scratch** up to required standard.

scratchy /'skrætʃɪ/ a. tending to make scratches or scratching noise; tending to cause itchiness; done in scratches or carelessly.

scrawl 1 v. write in hurried untidy way. **2** n. hurried writing; scrawled note.

scrawny /'skrɔːnɪ/ a. lean, scraggy.

scream 1 v. utter piercing cry (as) of terror or pain; utter in or with scream; laugh uncontrollably. **2** n. screaming cry or sound; *colloq.* irresistibly funny occurrence or person etc.

scree n. in *sing.* or *pl.* small loose stones; mountain slope covered with these.

screech /skriːtʃ/ **1** n. loud shrill harsh cry or sound. **2** v. make or utter with screech. **3 screech-owl** barn-owl.

screed n. long and tiresome letter or harangue.

screen 1 n. fixed or movable upright partition designed to shelter from observation or draughts or excess of heat etc.; thing used as shelter, esp. from observation; measure adopted for concealment; windscreen; blank surface on which images are projected; *the* cinema industry; large sieve; system for showing presence or absence of disease or quality etc. **2** v.t. shelter, hide partly or completely; protect from detection or censure etc.; show (film etc.) on screen; prevent from causing electrical interference; sieve; test (person) for presence or absence of disease or quality etc., esp. for reliability or loyalty. **3 screen off** shut off or hide with screen; **screenplay** script of film; **screen-printing** process like stencilling with ink forced through prepared sheet of fine material.

screw 1 n. cylinder or cone with spiral ridge running round it outside (**male screw**) or inside (**female screw**); metal male screw with slotted head for holding pieces of wood etc. together; wooden or other screw used to exert pressure; revolving shaft with spiral blades for propelling ship or aircraft etc.; one turn of screw; small twisted-up paper (*of*); oblique curling motion; *sl.* prison warder; *sl.* salary. **2** v. fasten or tighten (as) with screw; press hard

on, oppress; extort *out of*; contort, distort. **3 screwball** *US sl.* crazy or eccentric person; **screwdriver** tool for turning screws by slot; **screw up** contract or contort, summon up (courage etc.), *sl.* bungle or mismanage.

screwy /'skruːɪ/ a. *sl.* mad, eccentric, absurd.

scribble /'skrɪb(ə)l/ **1** v. write hurriedly or carelessly; be author or writer. **2** n. scrawl; hasty note etc.

scribe n. ancient or medieval copyist of manuscripts. **scribal** a.

scrim n. open-weave fabric for lining or upholstery etc.

scrimmage /'skrɪmɪdʒ/ **1** n. tussle, confused struggle, brawl. **2** v.i. engage in scrimmage.

scrimp v. skimp.

scrip n. provisional certificate of money subscribed to company etc.; *collect.* such certificates.

script 1 n. handwriting; type-face imitating handwriting; alphabet or system of writing; text of play or film or broadcast etc.; examinee's written answer. **2** v.t. write script for (film etc.).

scripture /'skrɪptʃə(r)/ n. sacred book; the Bible. **scriptural** a.

scrivener /'skrɪvənə(r)/ n. *hist.* drafter of documents; notary.

scrofula /'skrɒfjʊlə/ n. disease with glandular swellings. **scrofulous** a.

scroll /skrəʊl/ **1** n. roll of parchment or paper; book of ancient roll form; ornamental design imitating roll of parchment. **2** v.t. move (display on VDU screen) up or down etc. as new material appears.

scrotum /'skrəʊtəm/ n. (pl. **-ta**) pouch of skin enclosing testicles. **scrotal** a.

scrounge /skraʊndʒ/ v. *colloq.* obtain (things) illicitly or by cadging.

scrub[1] **1** v. rub hard so as to clean, esp. with hard brush; pass (gas etc.) through scrubber; *sl.* cancel (plan, order, etc.). **2** n. scrubbing or being scrubbed.

scrub[2] n. brushwood or stunted trees etc.; land covered with this; stunted or insignificant person etc. **scrubby** a.

scrubber /'skrʌbə(r)/ n. scrubbing-brush; apparatus for removing impurities from gases.

scruff n. back of neck.

scruffy /'skrʌfɪ/ a. shabby, slovenly, untidy.

scrum *n.* scrummage. **scrum-half** half-back who puts ball into scrum.

scrummage /ˈskrʌmɪdʒ/ *n. Rugby footb.* grouping of all forwards on each side to push against those of the other and seek possession of ball thrown on ground between them.

scrumptious /ˈskrʌmpʃəs/ *a. colloq.* delicious.

scrunch *n. & v.* crunch.

scruple /ˈskruːp(ə)l/ **1** *n.* doubt or hesitation in regard to morality or propriety of an action; unit of apothecaries' weight (20 grains). **2** *v.t.* hesitate owing to scruples *to* do.

scrupulous /ˈskruːpjʊləs/ *a.* careful to avoid doing wrong; conscientious even in small matters; (over-)attentive to details. **scrupulosity** *n.*

scrutineer /skruːtɪˈnɪə(r)/ *n.* person who scrutinizes ballot-papers.

scrutinize /ˈskruːtɪnaɪz/ *v.t.* subject to scrutiny.

scrutiny /ˈskruːtɪnɪ/ *n.* critical gaze; close or detailed examination; official examination of ballot-papers to check their validity or accuracy of their counting.

scuba /ˈskuːbə/ *n.* self-contained underwater breathing apparatus.

scud *v.i.* run or fly straight and fast; skim along; *Naut.* run before wind.

scuff 1 *v.* walk with dragging feet; graze or brush against; mark or wear out (shoes etc.) thus. **2** *n.* mark of scuffing.

scuffle /ˈskʌf(ə)l/ **1** *n.* confused struggle or disorderly fight. **2** *v.i.* engage in scuffle.

scull 1 *n.* each of pair of small oars; oar used to propel boat from stern. **2** *v.* row or propel boat with scull(s).

scullery /ˈskʌlərɪ/ *n.* back kitchen where dishes are washed etc.

sculpt *v. colloq.* sculpture.

sculptor /ˈskʌlptə(r)/ *n.* person who does sculpture. **sculptress** *n.*

sculpture /ˈskʌlptʃə(r)/ **1** *n.* art of forming representations by chiselling, carving, casting, or modelling; a work of sculpture. **2** *v.* represent in or adorn with sculpture; practise sculpture. **3** **sculptural** *a.*

scum 1 *n.* impurities that rise to surface of liquid; *the* worst part, refuse (*of*). **2** *v.* remove scum from; form scum (on). **3** **scummy** *a.*

scupper /ˈskʌpə(r)/ **1** *n.* hole in ship's side draining water from deck. **2** *v.t. sl.* sink (ship, crew); defeat or ruin (plan etc.).

scurf *n.* flakes of dead skin, esp. in hair. **scurfy** *a.*

scurrilous /ˈskʌrɪləs/ *a.* grossly or obscenely abusive. **scurrility** /-ˈrɪl-/ *n.*

scurry /ˈskʌrɪ/ **1** *v.i.* run hurriedly, scamper. **2** *n.* scurrying, bustle, rush; flurry (*of* snow etc.).

scurvy /ˈskɜːvɪ/ **1** *n.* deficiency disease resulting from lack of vitamin C. **2** *a. arch.* paltry, contemptible.

scut *n.* short tail, esp. of rabbit, hare, or deer.

scutter /ˈskʌtə(r)/ *v.i. colloq.* scurry.

scuttle[1] /ˈskʌt(ə)l/ *n.* receptacle for carrying and holding small supply of coal; part of motor-car body between windscreen and bonnet.

scuttle[2] /ˈskʌt(ə)l/ **1** *n.* hole with lid in ship's deck or side. **2** *v.t.* let water in (ship) esp. to sink it.

scuttle[3] /ˈskʌt(ə)l/ **1** *v.i.* scurry; make off, retreat in undignified way. **2** *n.* hurried gait; precipitate flight or departure.

scythe /saɪð/ **1** *n.* mowing and reaping implement with long thin slightly curved blade. **2** *v.t.* cut with scythe.

SE *abbr.* South-East(ern).

sea *n.* expanse of salt water; ocean; swell of sea, large wave; vast quantity or expanse *of*. **at sea** in ship on the sea, confused; **sea anchor** bag to retard drifting of ship; **seaboard** coastal region; **sea-dog** old sailor; **seafaring** travelling by sea, esp. regularly; **seafood** edible marine fish or shellfish; **sea front** part of seaside town facing sea; **seagoing** designed for open sea; **sea-gull** = **gull**[1]; **sea-horse** small fish with head suggestive of horse's head; **sea-kale** herb with young shoots used as vegetable; **sea-legs** ability to walk on deck of rolling ship; **sea-level** mean level of sea's surface, used in reckoning heights of hills etc. and as barometric standard; **sea-lion** large kind of seal; **seaman** sailor, navigator, sailor below rank of officer; **seaplane** aircraft designed to take off from and land on water; **seaport** town with harbour; **sea-salt** salt got by evaporating sea-water; **seascape** picture or view of the sea; **sea shell** shell of salt-water mollusc; **seasick** suffering sickness caused by motion of ship etc.; **seaside** sea coast, esp. as holiday resort; **sea trout** trout resembling salmon; **sea-urchin** marine animal covered with spines; **seaweed** plant growing in sea; **seaworthy** fit to put to sea.

seal[1] 1 *n.* piece of wax etc. impressed with design and attached to document as evidence of authenticity etc., or to envelope or receptacle or door to prevent its being opened without owner's knowledge; metal stamp etc. used in making seal; act or thing etc. regarded as confirmation or guarantee; decorative adhesive stamp. 2 *v.t.* stamp or fasten or certify as correct with seal; fix seal to; close securely or hermetically; settle or decide. 3 **sealing-wax** mixture of shellac and rosin softened by heating and used for seals; **seal off** prevent entry to and exit from (area).

seal[2] 1 *n.* kind of amphibious marine animal with flippers. 2 *v.i.* hunt seals.

sealer /'siːlə(r)/ *n.* ship or man engaged in seal-hunting.

Sealyham /'siːləm/ *n.* wiry-haired short-legged terrier.

seam 1 *n.* line of junction between two edges, esp. those of two pieces of cloth etc. sewn together; fissure between parallel edges; wrinkle; stratum of coal etc. 2 *v.t.* join with seam; (esp. in *p.p.*) mark or score with seam or fissure or scar.

seamstress /'semstrɪs/ *n.* woman who sews, esp. professionally.

seamy /'siːmɪ/ *a.* showing seams. **seamy side** disreputable or unattractive side.

seance /'seɪɑ̃s/ *n.* meeting for exhibition or investigation of spiritualistic phenomena.

sear /sɪə(r)/ *v.t.* scorch, cauterize; make callous.

search /sɜːtʃ/ 1 *v.* examine thoroughly, esp. to find something; make search or investigation. 2 *n.* act of searching, investigation. 3 **searchlight** lamp designed to throw strong beam of light in any desired direction, light or beam from this; **search-party** group of persons going out to look for lost person or thing; **search-warrant** official authority to enter and search building.

season /'siːz(ə)n/ 1 *n.* each of four divisions of year; proper or suitable time, time when something is plentiful or active or in vogue etc.; indefinite period; season-ticket. 2 *v.* flavour or make palatable with condiments etc.; temper, moderate; make or become suitable or in desired condition, esp. by exposure to air or weather. 3 **in season** (of food) available plentifully, (of animal) on heat; **season-ticket** one entitling holder to any number of journeys or admittances etc. in a given period.

seasonable /'siːznəb(ə)l/ *a.* suitable to season; opportune. □ See page 666.

seasonal /'siːzən(ə)l/ *a.* of or depending on or varying with seasons. □ See page 666.

seasoning /'siːzənɪŋ/ *n.* flavouring for food.

seat 1 *n.* thing made or used for sitting on; buttocks, part of garment covering them; part of chair etc. on which sitter's weight directly rests; place for one person in theatre etc.; occupation of seat or right to occupy it, esp. as member of House of Commons; site, location; country-house. 2 *v.t.* cause to sit; provide sitting accommodation for; place (*oneself*) in sitting posture; establish in position. 3 **seat-belt** safety-belt for seated person in vehicle or aircraft.

seating /'siːtɪŋ/ *n.* seats collectively; sitting accommodation.

sebaceous /sɪ'beɪʃəs/ *a.* fatty; secreting or conveying oily matter.

sec *a.* (of wine) dry. [F]

Sec. *abbr.* Secretary.

sec. *abbr.* second(s).

secateurs /'sekətɜːz/ *n.pl.* pruning-clippers.

secede /sɪ'siːd/ *v.i.* withdraw formally from political or religious body.

secession /sɪ'seʃ(ə)n/ *n.* seceding. **secessionist** *n.*

seclude /sɪ'kluːd/ *v.t.* keep retired or away from company, screen from view.

seclusion /sɪ'kluːʒ(ə)n/ *n.* secluded state or place.

second[1] /'sekənd/ 1 *a.* next after first; other, another, additional; of subordinate importance or value; inferior. 2 *n.* second person or class etc.; supporter or helper esp. of boxer or duellist; in *pl.* goods of second quality, second helping of food. 3 *v.t.* back up, give one's support to; /sɪ'kɒnd/ transfer (person) temporarily to another department etc. **4 second-best** next after the best; **second class** second-best group or category or accommodation; **second cousin** child of parent's first cousin; **second fiddle** subordinate position; **second-hand** (of goods) bought after use etc. by previous owner, (of information etc.) obtained from others and not by original observation etc.; **second nature** acquired tendency that has become instinctive; **second-rate** inferior; **second sight** supposed power of perceiving future events; **second string** person or thing kept in reserve; **second thoughts** new opinion reached after consideration; **second wind** renewed capacity for effort after tiredness.

second² /'sekənd/ *n.* sixtieth part of minute of time or angle.

secondary /'sekəndərɪ/ *a.* coming after or next below what is primary; derived from or depending on or supplementing what is primary. **secondary colour** one made by mixing two primary colours; **secondary education** education for those who have had primary education; **secondary school** school where secondary education is given.

secondly /'sekəndlɪ/ *adv.* in the second place, furthermore.

secrecy /'si:krəsɪ/ *n.* keeping of secrets; being secret.

secret /'si:krɪt/ **1** *a.* kept from general knowledge or view; not (to be) made known; working etc. in secret. **2** *n.* thing (to be) kept secret; thing for which explanation is unknown or not widely known. **3 in secret** secretly; **secret agent** spy; **secret police** police operating in secret for political ends; **secret service** government department concerned with espionage.

secretariat /sekrɪ'teərɪət/ *n.* administrative office or department; its members or premises.

secretary /'sekrətərɪ/ *n.* person employed to deal with correspondence and keep records and make appointments etc.; principal assistant of minister or ambassador etc. **secretary-bird** long-legged crested Afr. bird; **Secretary-General** principal administrative officer of or-

ganization etc.; **Secretary of State** head of major government department, *US* Foreign Secretary. **secretarial** *a.*

secrete /sɪ'kri:t/ *v.t.* conceal; *Physiol.* separate (substance) in gland etc. from blood or sap for function in the organism or for excretion.

secretion /sɪ'kri:ʃ(ə)n/ *n.* act of secreting; secreted substance.

secretive /'si:krətɪv/ *a.* inclined to make or keep secrets, uncommunicative.

secretory /sɪ'kri:tərɪ/ *a.* of physiological secretion.

sect *n.* body of persons sharing (usu. unorthodox) religious doctrines; religious denomination.

sectarian /sek'teərɪən/ **1** *a.* of or concerning sect(s); bigoted in following one's sect. **2** *n.* member of a sect. **sectarianism** *n.*

section /'sekʃ(ə)n/ **1** *n.* part cut off; one of parts into which something is divided; subdivision of book or statute or group of people etc.; *US* area of land, district of town; subdivision of platoon; separation by cutting; cutting of solid by plane, resulting figure or area of this; thin slice cut off for microscopic examination. **2** *v.t.* arrange in or divide into sections. **3 section mark** sign (§) used to indicate start of section of book etc.

sectional /'sekʃən(ə)l/ *a.* of a section; made up of sections; local rather than general.

sector /'sektə(r)/ *n.* branch of an activity; *Geom.* plane figure enclosed between two radii of circle etc.; *Mil.* portion of battle area.

secular /'sekjʊlə(r)/ *a.* concerned with the affairs of this world; not sacred; not monastic or ecclesiastical; occurring once in an age or century. **secularity** *n.*; **secularize** *v.t.*

secularism /'sekjʊlərɪz(ə)m/ *n.* doctrine that morality or education should not be based on religion. **secularist** *n.*

secure /sɪ'kjʊə(r)/ **1** *a.* untroubled by danger or fear; impregnable; safe, reliable, firmly fixed or fastened or established etc. **2** *v.t.* make secure or safe; fasten or close securely; obtain.

security /sɪ'kjʊərɪtɪ/ *n.* secure condition or feeling; thing that guards or guarantees; safety of State or company etc. against espionage or theft etc.; organization for ensuring this; thing deposited or pledged as guarantee of fulfilment of undertaking or repayment of loan; document as evidence of loan, certificate of stock or bond etc. **security risk** person of doubtful loyalty.

sedan /sɪ'dæn/ n. sedan-chair; *US* saloon car. **sedan-chair** *hist.* vehicle for one person, usu. carried on poles by two men.

sedate /sɪ'deɪt/ **1** a. tranquil, equable, serious. **2** v.t. put under sedation.

sedation /sɪ'deɪʃ(ə)n/ n. treatment by sedatives.

sedative /'sedətɪv/ **1** a. tending to calm or soothe. **2** n. sedative medicine etc.

sedentary /'sedəntərɪ/ a. sitting; (of work etc.) characterized by much sitting and little physical exercise; (of person) having or inclined to work etc. of this kind.

sedge n. grasslike plant growing in marshes or by water. **sedgy** a.

sediment /'sedɪmənt/ n. matter that settles to bottom of liquid, dregs; *Geol.* material carried by water or wind which settles and consolidates to make rock. **sedimentary** /-'men-/ a.; **sedimentation** n.

sedition /sɪ'dɪʃ(ə)n/ n. conduct or language inciting to rebellion. **seditious** a.

seduce /sɪ'djuːs/ v.t. tempt or entice into sexual activity or into wrongdoing; coax or lead astray.

seduction /sɪ'dʌkʃ(ə)n/ n. seducing or being seduced; tempting or attractive thing or quality.

seductive /sɪ'dʌktɪv/ a. tending to seduce; alluring, enticing.

sedulous /'sedjʊləs/ a. persevering, diligent, painstaking. **sedulity** n.

see[1] v. (*past* **saw**; *p.p.* **seen**) have or use power of perceiving with eye; discern mentally; understand; consider, foresee; watch, look at; meet, grant interview to; take view of; visit to consult; imagine; escort or conduct. **see about** attend to; **see off** accompany to place of departure; **see over** tour and examine; **see red** become enraged; **see through** not be deceived by, support (person) during difficult time, not abandon project) before its completion; **see-**

through transparent; **see to** attend to, repair.

see[2] n. office or position or jurisdiction of bishop.

seed 1 n. flowering plant's unit of reproduction capable of developing into another such plant; *collect.* seeds in any quantity esp. as collected for sowing; semen; prime cause, beginning; offspring; seeded player. **2** v. place seed(s) in; sow seeds; sprinkle (as) with seed; produce or drop seed; remove seeds from (fruit etc.); place crystal etc. in (cloud) to produce rain; *Tennis* etc. designate (competitor in knock-out tournament) so that strong competitors do not meet each other until later rounds. **3 go, run, to seed** cease flowering as seed develops, *fig.* become degenerate or unkempt etc.; **seed-bed** bed of fine soil in which to sow seeds; **seed pearl** very small pearl; **seed-potato** one kept for planting; **seedsman** dealer in seeds.

seedling /'siːdlɪŋ/ n. young plant raised from seed.

seedy /'siːdɪ/ a. full of seed; shabby; unwell.

seeing /'siːɪŋ/ **1** n. use of eyes. **2** *conj.* (also **seeing that**) considering that; since, because.

seek v. (*past & p.p.* **sought** /sɔːt/) go in search of, look *for*; make a search; try to obtain or bring about, try to do; ask for, request.

seem v.i. have air or appearance of; appear to be or exist or be true etc. or *to* be or do.

seeming /'siːmɪŋ/ a. apparent but not real.

seemly /'siːmlɪ/ a. decorous, becoming.

seen *p.p.* of **see**[1].

seep v.i. ooze, percolate.

seepage /'siːpɪdʒ/ n. act of seeping; quantity that seeps.

seer /sɪə(r)/ n. person who sees; person who sees visions; prophet.

seersucker /'sɪəsʌkə(r)/ n. thin cotton etc. fabric with puckered surface.

see-saw /'siːsɔː/ **1** a. & *adv.* with backward-and-forward or up-and-down motion. **2** n. long board supported in middle so that ends on which children etc. sit move alternately up and down; game played on this. **3** v.i.

seethe

self-

play at or move up and down as on see-saw; vacillate.

seethe /siːð/ v. boil, bubble; be agitated.

segment /'segmənt/ n. part cut off or separable from other parts; *Geom.* part of circle or sphere cut off by line or plane intersecting it. 2 v. divide into segments. 3 **segmental** a.; **segmentation** n.

segregate /'segrɪgeɪt/ v. put or come apart, isolate; separate (esp. racial group) from the rest of the community. **segregation** n.

seigneur /sem'jɜː(r)/ n. feudal lord. **seigneurial** a.

seine /seɪn/ n. large vertical fishing-net with ends drawn together to enclose fish.

seismic /'saɪzmɪk/ a. (also **seismical**) of earthquake(s).

seismograph /'saɪzməɡrɑːf/ n. instrument for recording earthquake tremors.

seismography /saɪz'mɒɡrəfɪ/ n. study or recording of seismic phenomena. **seismographer** n.

seismology /saɪz'mɒlədʒɪ/ n. seismography. **seismologist** n.

seize /siːz/ v. take or hold possession of esp. forcibly or suddenly or by legal power; comprehend quickly or clearly; *Law* put in possession *of*. **seize up** (of mechanism) become stuck or jammed from undue heat or friction etc.

seizure /'siːʒə(r)/ n. seizing or being seized; sudden attack of apoplexy etc., stroke.

seldom /'seldəm/ adv. rarely; not often.

select /sɪ'lekt/ 1 v.t. choose, esp. as best or most suitable. 2 a. chosen for excellence; picked, choice; exclusive. 3 **selector** n.

selection /sɪ'lekʃ(ə)n/ n. selecting; what is selected; things from which choice may be made; *Biol.* process by which some animals or plants thrive more than others, as factor in evolution.

selective /sɪ'lektɪv/ a. using or characterized by selection; able to select. **selectivity** n.

selenium /sɪ'liːnɪəm/ n. non-metallic element of sulphur group.

self 1 n. (pl. **selves**) person's or thing's

own individuality or essence; person or thing as object of reflexive action; one's own interests or pleasure, concentration on these; *Commerc.* or *colloq.* myself, yourself, himself, etc. 2 a. of same colour throughout.

self- in comb. expr. reflexive action, automatic or independent action, or sameness. **self-abuse** masturbation; **self-addressed** addressed to oneself; **self-assertive** determined to assert oneself or one's claims etc.; **self-assertion** n.; **self-assurance** self-confidence; **self-catering** providing one's own meals; **self-centred** preoccupied with oneself or one's own affairs; **self-confident** having confidence in one's own abilities etc.; **self-confidence** n.; **self-conscious** embarrassed or ill at ease from awareness of oneself; **self-contained** complete in itself, uncommunicative; **self-control** control of oneself or one's behaviour etc.; **self-defence** defence of oneself or one's reputation etc.; **self-denial** going without things one would like; **self-determination** free will, choice of form of government or allegiance exercised by nation; **self-employed** working as owner of business etc.; **self-esteem** good opinion of oneself; **self-evident** needing no demonstration; **self-governing** governing itself or oneself; **self-government** n.; **self-help** use of one's own abilities etc. to achieve success; **self-important** having exaggerated idea of one's own importance; **self-importance** n.; **self-indulgent** indulging one's own desires for ease or pleasure etc.; **self-indulgence** n.; **self-interest** one's personal interests or advantage; **self-interested** activated by self-interest; **self-made** having risen from obscurity or poverty by one's own efforts; **self-opinionated** obstinate in one's own opinion; **self-pity** pity for oneself; **self-portrait** artist's portrait of himself; **self-possessed** unperturbed, cool; **self-possession** n.; **self-preservation** keeping oneself from death and harm, instinct for this; **self-raising** (of flour) containing its own raising agent; **self-reliant** relying on one's own abilities; **self-reliance** n.; **self-respect** proper regard for one's dignity or standard of conduct etc.; **self-righteous** convinced of one's own righteousness; **self-sacrifice** sacrifice of one's interests and desires to those of others; **self-same** the very same; **self-satisfied** conceited; **self-satisfaction** n.; **self-seeking** seeking one's own welfare before that of others; **self-service** in or at which customers help themselves and pay cashier afterwards; **self-starter** electric device for starting internal-combustion engine; **self-styled** having taken name or description without justification; **self-sufficient** capable of supplying one's own needs; **self-sufficiency** n.; **self-willed** determined to follow one's own wishes or intentions etc.

selfish /'selfɪʃ/ a. deficient in consideration for others; actuated by or appealing to self-interest.

selfless /'selflɪs/ a. disregarding oneself, unselfish.

sell 1 v. (past & p.p. **sold** /səʊld/) make over or dispose of in exchange for money; deal in, keep stock of for sale; betray for money or other reward; promote sales (of); advertise or publish merits of; persuade or convince of value or importance of something; cause to be sold. 2 n. colloq. manner of selling; deception, disappointment. 3 **seller's market** situation when goods are scarce and expensive; **sell off** sell remainder of at reduced prices; **sell out** sell (all) one's stock or shares etc., betray, be treacherous; **sell-out** selling of all tickets for show etc., commercial success, betrayal; **sell short** disparage, underestimate; **sell up** sell one's business or house etc.

Sellotape /'seləteɪp/ n. (P) adhesive usu. transparent cellulose tape.

selvage /'selvɪdʒ/ n. edge of cloth so woven that it cannot unravel.

semantic /sɪ'mæntɪk/ a. of meaning in language.

semantics n.pl. (usu. treated as sing.) branch of linguistics concerned with meanings.

semaphore /'seməfɔː(r)/ 1 n. signalling by person holding flag in each hand. 2 v. signal or send by semaphore.

semblance /'sembləns/ n. outward or superficial appearance of something.

semen /'siːmən/ n. reproductive fluid of males, containing spermatozoa.

semester /sɪ'mestə(r)/ n. half-year term in (esp. German and US) universities.

semi /'semɪ/ n. colloq. semi-detached house.

semi- in comb. half-, partly, occurring etc. twice in specified period.

semibreve /'semɪbriːv/ n. Mus. longest note in common use.

semicircle /'semɪsɜːk(ə)l/ n. half of circle or its circumference. **semicircular** a.

semicolon /semɪ'kəʊlən/ n. punctuation mark (;) of intermediate value between comma and full stop.

semiconductor /semɪkən'dʌktə(r)/ n. substance that in certain conditions has electrical conductivity intermediate between insulators and metals.

semi-detached /semɪdɪ'tætʃt/ a. (of house) joined to another on one side only.

semifinal /semɪ'faɪn(ə)l/ n. match or round preceding final. **semifinalist** n.

seminal /'semɪn(ə)l/ a. of seed or semen; germinal, reproductive; (of idea etc.) providing basis for future development.

seminar /'semɪnɑː(r)/ n. small class for discussion etc.; short intensive course of study.

seminarist /'semɪnərɪst/ n. student in seminary.

seminary /'semɪnərɪ/ n. training-college for priests etc.

semi-permeable /semɪ'pɜːmɪəb(ə)l/ a. (of membrane etc.) allowing small molecules to pass through but not large ones.

semiprecious /semɪ'preʃəs/ a. (of gem) of less value than a precious stone.

semiquaver /'semɪkweɪvə(r)/ n. Mus. note equal to half a quaver.

Semite /'siːmaɪt/ n. member of any of races supposedly descended from Shem, including Jews and Arabs.

Semitic /sɪ'mɪtɪk/ a. of languages of family including Hebrew and Arabic; of Semites, esp. of Jews.

semitone /'semɪtəʊn/ n. half a tone in musical scale.

semi-trailer /semɪ'treɪlə(r)/ n. trailer

having wheels at back and supported at front by towing vehicle.

semivowel /ˈsemivauəl/ n. sound intermediate between vowel and consonant; letter representing this.

semolina /seməˈliːnə/ n. hard round grains of wheat used for puddings etc.

sempstress var. of **seamstress**.

Sen. abbr. Senator; Senior.

senate /ˈsenɪt/ n. upper house of legislature in some countries; governing body of some universities; Rom. hist. State council.

senator /ˈsenətə(r)/ n. member of senate. **senatorial** a.

send v. (past & p.p. **sent**) order or cause to go or be conveyed (to); send message or letter; grant, bestow, inflict, cause to be. **send down** rusticate or expel from university; **send for** summon, order by post; **send off** get despatched, send away (for), attend departure of; **send-off** demonstration of goodwill etc. at departure of person; **send on** transmit to further destination; **send up** colloq. satirize; **send-up** n.

senescent /sɪˈnes(ə)nt/ a. growing old. **senescence** n.

seneschal /ˈsenɪʃ(ə)l/ n. steward of medieval great house.

senile /ˈsiːnaɪl/ a. of or characteristic of old age; having symptoms and weakness of old age. **senility** /-ˈnɪl-/ n.

senior /ˈsiːnɪə(r)/ 1 a. older in age or standing; of higher degree. 2 n. person of advanced age or long service; one's elder or superior. 3 **senior citizen** old person, esp. old-age pensioner. 4 **seniority** /-ˈɒr-/ n.

senna /ˈsenə/ n. cassia; laxative prepared from this.

señor /senˈjɔː(r)/ n. (pl. **señores** /senˈjɔːrez/) title used of or to Spanish-speaking man. [Sp.]

señora /senˈjɔːrə/ n. title used of or to Spanish-speaking married woman. [Sp.]

señorita /senjəˈriːtə/ n. title used of or to Spanish-speaking unmarried woman. [Sp.]

sensation /senˈseɪʃ(ə)n/ n. consciousness of perceiving or seeming to perceive some condition of body or senses or mind etc.; excited or violent feeling esp. in community; cause or manifestation of this.

sensational /senˈseɪʃən(ə)l/ a. causing or intended to cause a sensation. **sensationalism** n.; **sensationalist** a. & n.

sense /sens/ 1 n. any of special bodily faculties through which sensation is caused; ability to perceive; consciousness of; appreciation or instinct; practical wisdom; conformity to this; meaning of word etc.; intelligibility or coherence; prevailing opinion; in pl. person's sanity or normal state of mind. 2 v.t. perceive by sense(s); be vaguely aware of; (of machine) detect.

senseless /ˈsenslɪs/ a. unconscious; wildly foolish; meaningless, purposeless.

sensibility /sensɪˈbɪlɪtɪ/ n. capacity to feel; sensitiveness or susceptibility; in pl. tendency to feel offended etc.

sensible /ˈsensɪb(ə)l/ a. having or showing good sense; judicious; perceptible by senses; aware of.

sensitive /ˈsensɪtɪv/ a. acutely affected by external impressions; having sensibility to; touchy or quick to take offence; responsive to or recording slight changes of condition, readily affected by or susceptible to (light, agency, etc.); (of topic) subject to restriction of discussion to prevent embarrassment etc. **sensitive plant** kind of mimosa that droops or closes when touched. **sensitivity** n.

sensitize /ˈsensɪtaɪz/ v.t. make sensitive. **sensitization** n.

sensor /ˈsensə(r)/ n. device to detect or record or measure a physical property.

sensory /ˈsensərɪ/ a. of sensation or senses.

sensual /ˈsensjuəl/ a. of or connected with the body and the senses; self-indulgent, esp. sexually. **sensualism** n.; **sensuality** /-ˈæl-/ n.

sensuous /ˈsensjuəs/ a. of or derived from or affecting senses, esp. aesthetically.

sent past & p.p. of **send**.

sentence /ˈsent(ə)ns/ 1 n. series of words grammatically complete in itself; punishment allotted to person convicted in criminal trial; declaration of this. 2 v.t. declare sentence of, condemn to.

sententious /senˈtenʃəs/ a. affectedly

or pompously moralizing; aphoristic, moralistic.

sentient /'senʃ(ə)nt/ a. that feels or is capable of feeling. **sentience** n.

sentiment /'sentɪmənt/ n. mental feeling, view; emotional thought expressed in words etc.; tendency to be swayed by feeling; mawkish tenderness.

sentimental /sentɪ'ment(ə)l/ a. of or characterized by sentiment; showing or affected by emotion rather than reason. **sentimentalism** n.; **sentimentalist** n.; **sentimentality** n.; **sentimentalize** v.

sentinel /'sentɪn(ə)l/ n. sentry.

sentry /'sentrɪ/ n. soldier etc. stationed to keep guard. **sentry-box** wooden cabin large enough to shelter standing sentry; **sentry-go** duty of pacing up and down as sentry.

sepal /'sep(ə)l/ n. leaf or division of calyx.

separable /'sepərəb(ə)l/ a. that can be separated. **separability** n.

separate 1 /'sepərət/ a. divided or withdrawn from others; independent, distinct, individual, of individuals. 2 /'sepərət/ n. in pl. separate articles of dress suitable for wearing together in various combinations. 3 /'sepəreɪt/ v. make separate, sever; prevent union or contact of; cease to live together as married couple; go different ways; secede *from*; divide or sort into parts or sizes. 4 **separator** n.

separation /sepə'reɪʃ(ə)n/ n. separating or being separated; separation of husband and wife without dissolution of marriage.

separatist /'sepərətɪst/ n. person who favours separation, esp. for political or ecclesiastical independence. **separatism** n.

sepia /'si:pɪə/ n. dark reddish-brown colour or paint.

sepoy /'si:pɔɪ/ n. *hist.* Indian soldier under European, esp. British, discipline.

sepsis /'sepsɪs/ n. (pl. -ses /-si:z/) septic condition.

sept n. clan, esp. in Ireland.

Sept. *abbr.* September.

September /sep'tembə(r)/ n. ninth month of year.

septet /sep'tet/ n. musical composition

for 7 performers; the performers; group of 7.

septic /'septɪk/ a. putrefying; contaminated by bacteria. **septic tank** tank in which sewage is disintegrated through bacterial activity.

septicaemia /septɪ'si:mɪə/ n. blood-poisoning.

septuagenarian /septjʊədʒɪ'neərɪən/ n. person between 70 and 79 years old.

Septuagesima /septjʊə'dʒesɪmə/ n. third Sunday before Lent.

Septuagint /'septjʊəgɪnt/ n. ancient Greek version of OT.

septum /'septəm/ n. (pl. **-ta**) partition such as that between nostrils.

sepulchral /sɪ'pʌlkr(ə)l/ a. of tomb or burial; gloomy, dismal.

sepulchre /'sepəlkə(r)/ 1 n. tomb, burial vault or cave. 2 v.t. lay in sepulchre.

sequel /'si:kw(ə)l/ n. what follows after; novel or film etc. that continues story of earlier one.

sequence /'si:kwəns/ n. succession; order of succession; set of things belonging next to one another; unbroken series; episode or incident in film etc.

sequential /sɪ'kwenʃ(ə)l/ a. forming sequence or consequence.

sequester /sɪ'kwestə(r)/ v.t. seclude, isolate; sequestrate.

sequestrate /sɪ'kwestreɪt/ v.t. *Law* confiscate, take temporary possession of (debtor's estate etc.). **sequestration** /si:kwe'streɪʃ(ə)n/ n.

sequin /'si:kwɪn/ n. circular spangle on dress etc.

sequoia /sɪ'kwɔɪə/ n. Californian coniferous tree of immense height.

sera pl. of **serum**.

seraglio /sə'rɑ:lɪəʊ/ n. (pl. **-ios**) harem; *hist.* Turkish palace.

seraph /'serəf/ n. (pl. **-phim** or **-phs**) member of highest of 9 orders of angels. **seraphic** /-'ræf-/ a.

serenade /serə'neɪd/ 1 n. piece of music (suitable to be) sung or played at night, esp. by lover under lady's window; orchestral suite for small ensemble. 2 v.t. sing or play serenade to.

serendipity /serən'dɪpɪtɪ/ n. faculty of making happy discoveries by accident. **serendipitous** a.

serene /sə'ri:n/ a. clear and calm; placid, unperturbed. **serenity** /-'ren-/ n.

serf *n. hist.* labourer not allowed to leave the land on which he worked; oppressed person, drudge. **serfdom** *n.*

serge *n.* durable twilled worsted or fabric.

sergeant /'sɑːdʒ(ə)nt/ *n.* non-commissioned army or RAF officer next below warrant officer; police officer next below inspector. **sergeant-major** warrant officer assisting adjutant of regiment or battalion.

serial /'sɪərɪəl/ **1** *n.* story published or broadcast etc. in instalments. **2** *a.* of in or forming series; (of story etc.) in form of serial.

serialize /'sɪərɪəlaɪz/ *v.t.* publish or produce in instalments. **serialization** *n.*

series /'sɪəriːz/ *n.* (*pl.* same) number of things or events etc. of which each is similar to or connected with the preceding one; number of radio or television programmes or films etc. with same actors and theme etc. but each complete in itself. **in series** (of set of electrical circuits) arranged so that same current passes through each circuit.

serif /'serɪf/ *n.* fine cross-line finishing off stroke of letter.

serious /'sɪərɪəs/ *a.* thoughtful, earnest; important; requiring thought; not slight or negligible; sincere, in earnest.

serjeant /'sɑːdʒ(ə)nt/ *n. hist.* barrister of highest rank. **serjeant-at-arms** official of court or city or parliament with ceremonial duties.

sermon /'sɜːmən/ *n.* discourse on religious or moral subject, esp. delivered from pulpit; admonition, reproof.

sermonize /'sɜːmənaɪz/ *v.* deliver moral lecture (to).

serous /'sɪərəs/ *a.* of or like serum, watery.

serpent /'sɜːpənt/ *n.* snake, esp. of large kind; treacherous or cunning person.

serpentine /'sɜːpəntaɪn/ **1** *a.* of or like serpent; writhing, coiling, sinuous. **2** *n.* soft usu. dark green rock, sometimes mottled.

serrated /sə'reɪtɪd/ *a.* with toothed edge like a saw. **serration** *n.*

serried /'serɪd/ *a.* (of ranks esp. of soldiers) close together.

serum /'sɪərəm/ *n.* (*pl.* **-ra** or **-rums**) liquid separating from clot when blood coagulates, esp. used for inoculation; watery fluid in animal bodies.

servant /'sɜːv(ə)nt/ *n.* person who carries out orders of employer, esp. one engaged in household work; person willing to serve another.

serve **1** *v.* be servant to; do service for; carry out duty; be employed (*in* organization, esp. armed forces); meet needs (of), perform function, be suitable, suffice; go through due period of (office or apprenticeship or prison sentence etc.); set (food) on table, distribute, dish *out* or *up*; act as waiter; act towards or treat in specified way; make legal delivery of (writ etc.); set (ball) in play at tennis etc.; (of male animal) copulate with (female). **2** *n. Tennis* etc. act or manner of serving ball; person's turn to serve. **3 serve person right** be his deserved misfortune.

server /'sɜːvə(r)/ *n.* person who serves, esp. *Eccl.* celebrant's lay assistant.

service /'sɜːvɪs/ **1** *n.* work done or doing of work for employer or for community etc.; assistance or benefit given to someone; provision of some public need, e.g. transport or (in *pl.*) water, gas, etc.; being servant; employment or position as servant; department of royal or public employ, persons or employment in it; in *pl. the* armed forces; meeting of congregation for worship; liturgical form for use on some occasion; maintenance and repair work, esp. by vendor or manufacturer after sale; serving of food etc.; set of dishes etc. for serving meal; serve in tennis etc., game in which one serves. **2** *v.t.* provide service for, do routine maintenance work on. **3 at person's service** ready to serve him; **of service** useful; **service area** area near road for supply of petrol and refreshments etc.; **service charge** additional charge for service rendered; **service flat** one in which domestic service etc. is provided by the management; **service industry** one providing services not goods; **serviceman, servicewoman,** person in armed services; **service road** one giving access to houses lying back from main road; **service station** place beside road selling petrol etc. to motorists.

serviceable /'sɜːvɪsəb(ə)l/ *a.* useful or usable; durable, hard-wearing.

serviette /sɜːvɪ'et/ *n.* table-napkin.

servile /'sɜːvaɪl/ *a.* of or like slave(s); slavish, fawning, completely dependent. **servility** /-'vɪl-/ *n.*

servitor /'sɜːvɪtə(r)/ *n. arch.* attendant, servant.

servitude /'sɜːvɪtjuːd/ *n.* slavery, subjection.

servo- *in comb.* power-assisted.

sesame /'sesəmɪ/ *n.* E. Ind. herbaceous plant with oil-yielding seeds; its seeds.

sesqui- *in comb.* one and a half.

sessile /'sesaɪl/ *a. Biol.* attached directly by base without stalk or peduncle etc.

session *n.* assembly for deliberative or judicial business; single meeting for such purpose; period during which such meetings are regularly held; academic year; period devoted to an activity. **in session** assembled for business, not on vacation. **sessional** *a.*

set¹ 1 *v.* (*past & p.p.* **set**) put or lay or stand in certain position; fix or place ready; dispose suitably for use or action or display; (of sun, moon, etc.) move towards or below earth's horizon; adjust hands or mechanism of (clock, trap, etc.); lay (table) for meal; solidify or harden; fix (hair) while damp so that it dries in desired style; (of face) assume hard expression; insert (jewel) in ring or framework etc.; ornament or provide (surface) *with*; bring into specified state, cause to be; present or impose as work to be done or material to be dealt with or problem to be solved etc.; initiate (fashion etc.); es'ablish (a record etc.); determine, decide; join, attach, fasten; appoint, establish; (of tide, current, etc.) have certain motion or direction; put parts of (broken or dislocated bone, limb, etc.) into correct position for healing; provide (song, words) with music; arrange (type) or type for (book etc.); (of blossom) form into fruit; (of hunting dog) take rigid attitude indicating presence of game. 2 *n.* direction or position in which something sets or is set; setting or stage furniture etc. for play or film etc.; setting of sun or star etc.; (also **sett**) badger's

burrow, paving-block, young plant or bulb ready to be planted. 3 *a.* prescribed or determined in advance; unchanging, fixed; prepared for action. 4 **set about** begin, take steps towards, attack; **set back** impede or reverse progress of, *sl.* cost (person) specified amount; **set-back** reversal or arrest of progress; **set down** record in writing; **set eyes on** catch sight of; **set forth** begin journey or expedition; **set in** begin, become established, insert; **set off** begin journey, initiate, stimulate, cause (person) to start laughing etc., serve as adornment or foil to, use as compensating item *against*; **set on** set upon, instigate, (*a.*) determined to get or achieve etc.; **set out** begin journey, exhibit, arrange; **set piece** formal or elaborate arrangement esp. in art or literature, fireworks arranged on scaffolding etc.; **set square** right-angled triangular plate for drawing lines at certain angles; **set to** begin doing something vigorously; **set-to** fight or argument; **set up** place in position or view, start or establish, prepare, equip; **set-up** arrangement or organization, manner or structure of this; **set upon** attack, cause or urge to attack.

set² *n.* number of things or persons that belong or are usually found together; collection, group; section of society having similar interests etc.; collection of implements or vessels etc. needed for specified purpose; radio or television receiver; *Tennis* etc. group of games counting as unit towards match for player or side that wins greater number of games; *Math.* collection of things sharing a property.

sett *n.* see **set¹**.

settee /se'tiː/ *n.* long seat with back and usu. arms, for more than one person.

setter /'setə(r)/ *n.* kind of sporting dog trained to stand rigid on scenting game.

setting /'setɪŋ/ *n.* position or manner in which thing is set; surroundings, environment, scene; scenery etc. of play or film etc.; frame in which jewel etc. is set; music to which words are set; cutlery for one person at table.

settle¹ /'set(ə)l/ *v.* establish or become established in abode or place or way of life; (cause to) sit or come down to stay;

cease from wandering or change or disturbance etc.; determine, agree upon, decide, appoint; deal effectually with; get rid of; pay (bill); subside, sink; become colonists or dwellers in. **settle down** begin to live routine life; **settle on** give (property etc.) to (person) esp. for rest of his life; **settle up** pay money owed etc.

settle² /'set(ə)l/ n. bench with high back and arms.

settlement /'setəlmənt/ n. settling or being settled; place occupied by settlers; arrangement ending dispute; terms on which property is given to person; deed stating these.

settler /'setlə(r)/ n. person who settles in newly developed (tract of) country.

seven /'sev(ə)n/ a. & n. one more than six. **seventh** a. & n.

seventeen /sevən'ti:n/ a. & n. one more than sixteen. **seventeenth** a. & n.

seventy /'sevəntɪ/ a. & n. seven times ten. **seventieth** a. & n.

sever /'sevə(r)/ v. divide, break, make separate, esp. by cutting; end employment contract of (person).

several /'sevər(ə)l/ a. & pron. a few, more than two; separate or respective.

severally adv. separately, respectively.

severance /'sevərəns/ n. severing; severed state. **severance pay** amount paid to employee on termination of contract.

severe /sɪ'vɪə(r)/ a. harsh and rigorous; serious; extreme or forceful; arduous, exacting; unadorned. **severity** /-'ver-/ n.

sew /səʊ/ v. (p.p. **sewn** or **sewed**) fasten or join or make etc. by passing thread again and again through material by means of a needle; use needle and thread or sewing-machine. **sewing-machine** machine for sewing or stitching.

sewage /'su:ɪdʒ/ n. waste matter conveyed in sewers. **sewage farm**, **works**, place where sewage is treated.

sewer /'su:ə(r)/ n. (usu. underground) pipe or conduit for carrying off drainage water and waste matter.

sewerage /'su:ərɪdʒ/ n. system of or drainage by sewers.

sewn p.p. of **sew**.

sex 1 n. being male or female; males or females collectively; sexual instincts or desire or activity etc.; sexual intercourse. **2** v.t. determine sex of; in p.p. having specified sexual appetite. **3 sex appeal** sexual attractiveness; **sex change** apparent change of sex by surgical means.

sexagenarian /seksədʒə'neərɪən/ n. person between 60 and 69 years old.

Sexagesima /seksə'dʒesɪmə/ n. second Sunday before Lent.

sexism /'seksɪz(ə)m/ n. prejudice or discrimination against people (esp. women) because of their sex. **sexist** a. & n.

sexless /'sekslɪs/ a. neither male nor female; lacking sexual desire or attractiveness.

sextant /'sekst(ə)nt/ n. instrument with graduated arc of 60° used in navigation and surveying for measuring angular distance of objects by means of mirrors.

sextet /seks'tet/ n. musical composition for 6 performers; the performers; group of 6.

sexton /'sekst(ə)n/ n. person who looks after church and churchyard, often acting as bell-ringer and grave-digger.

sextuple /'sekstjʊp(ə)l/ a. sixfold.

sextuplet /'sekstjʊplɪt/ n. each of 6 children born at one birth.

sexual /'seksjʊəl/ a. of or connected with sex or sexes. **sexual intercourse** insertion of man's penis into woman's vagina.

sexuality /seksjʊ'ælɪtɪ/ n. sexual characteristics or activity.

sexy /'seksɪ/ a. colloq. sexually attractive or provocative.

SF abbr. science fiction.

Sgt. abbr. Sergeant.

sh int. hush.

shabby /'ʃæbɪ/ a. dingy and faded from wear or exposure; worn, dilapidated; poorly dressed; contemptible, dishonourable.

shack 1 n. roughly built hut or cabin. **2** v.i. sl. **shack up** cohabit with or together.

shackle /'ʃæk(ə)l/ **1** n. metal loop or link closed by bolt, coupling link; fetter, fig. restraint. **2** v.t. fetter, impede.

shad n. large edible fish.

shade 1 *n.* comparative darkness caused by shelter from direct light and heat; place or area sheltered from the sun; darker part of picture etc.; a colour, esp. with regard to its depth or as distinguished from one nearly like it; slight amount or difference; translucent cover for lamp etc.; screen excluding or moderating light; ghost. 2 *v.* screen from light; darken, esp. with parallel pencil lines to represent shadow etc.; change or pass by degrees. 3 **in the shade** in comparative obscurity.

shadow /ˈʃædəʊ/ 1 *n.* shade; patch of shade; dark figure projected by body intercepting rays of light; person's inseparable attendant or companion; person secretly following another; insubstantial remnant; shaded part of picture; gloom or sadness. 2 *v.t.* cast shadow over; follow closely, persistently, and usu. secretly. 3 **shadow-boxing** boxing against imaginary opponent; **Shadow Cabinet** members of opposition party serving as spokesmen for affairs for which Cabinet ministers have responsibility. 4 **shadowy** *a.*

shady /ˈʃeɪdɪ/ *a.* giving or situated in shade; of doubtful honesty, disreputable.

shaft /ʃɑːft/ *n.* arrow or spear; its long slender stem; *fig.* remark aimed to hurt or stimulate; ray (*of* light); stroke (*of* lightning); handle of tool etc.; long narrow space, usu. vertical, for access to a mine or for a lift in a building or for ventilation etc.; long and narrow part supporting or connecting or driving part(s) of greater thickness etc.; part of column between base and capital; one of pair of poles between which horse of vehicle is harnessed.

shag *n.* rough mass of hair; coarse tobacco; (crested) cormorant.

shaggy /ˈʃægɪ/ *a.* hairy, rough-haired; tangled. **shaggy-dog story** long inconsequential narrative or joke.

shagreen /ʃæˈɡriːn/ *n.* kind of untanned leather with granulated surface; shark-skin.

shah /ʃɑː/ *n.* former ruler of Iran.

shake 1 *v.* (*past* **shook** /ʃʊk/; *p.p.* **shaken** /ˈʃeɪkən/) move violently or quickly up and down or to and fro;

(cause to) tremble or rock or vibrate; agitate, shock, disturb; weaken or impair. 2 *n.* shaking or being shaken; jerk, shock; *colloq.* moment. 3 **shake down** settle or cause to fall by shaking, become comfortably settled or established; **shake-down** makeshift bed esp. on floor; **shake hands** clasp hands (*with* person), esp. at meeting or parting or as sign of bargain; **shake off** get rid of, evade; **shake up** mix (ingredients) by shaking, disturb or make uncomfortable, rouse from lethargy etc.; **shake-up** upheaval, reorganization.

shaker *n.* container for shaking together ingredients of cocktails etc.

Shakespearian /ʃeɪkˈspɪərɪən/ *a.* of Shakespeare.

shako /ˈʃækəʊ/ *n.* (*pl.* **-kos**) military cap with peak and upright plume or tuft.

shaky /ˈʃeɪkɪ/ *a.* unsteady, trembling, infirm, tottering, wavering.

shale /ʃeɪl/ *n.* soft rock that splits easily, resembling slate. **shaly** *a.*

shall *v. aux.* (*pres.* **shall**, *past* **should** /ʃʊd/) expr. future event or situation etc. or (strong) intention or condition or command or duty or obligation or likelihood or tentative suggestion. ▫ See page 667.

shallot /ʃəˈlɒt/ *n.* onion-like plant with cluster of small bulbs.

shallow /ˈʃæləʊ/ 1 *a.* of little depth; superficial, trivial. 2 *n.* shallow place. 3 *v.* make or become shallow(er).

sham 1 *n.* imposture, pretence; person or thing pretending or pretended to be what he or it is not. 2 *a.* pretended, counterfeit. 3 *v.* feign; pretend (to be).

shamble /ˈʃæmb(ə)l/ 1 *v.i.* walk or run in shuffling or ungainly way. 2 *n.* shambling gait.

shambles *n.pl.* (usu. treated as *sing.*) *colloq.* mess, muddle; butchers' slaughter-house; scene of carnage.

shambolic /ʃæmˈbɒlɪk/ *a. colloq.* disorganized, chaotic.

shame 1 *n.* feeling of humiliation excited by consciousness of guilt or folly; capacity for experiencing this; state of disgrace or ignominy or discredit; person or thing that brings disgrace; *colloq.* regrettable or unlucky thing. 2 *v.t.* make ashamed, bring disgrace on;

force by shame *into* or *out of* etc. 3
shamefaced bashful, ashamed,
abashed.
shameful /'ʃeɪmfʊl/ *a.* disgraceful,
scandalous.
shameless /'ʃeɪmlɪs/ *a.* having or
showing no shame; impudent.
shammy /'ʃæmɪ/ *n.* chamois-leather.
shampoo /ʃæm'puː/ 1 *n.* liquid or
cream used to wash hair; similar substance for washing carpet or car etc. 2
v.t. wash with shampoo.
shamrock /'ʃæmrɒk/ *n.* kind of
trefoil, used as national emblem of
Ireland.
shandy /'ʃændɪ/ *n.* mixture of beer
with ginger-beer or lemonade.
shanghai /ʃæŋ'haɪ/ *v.t.* force (person)
to be sailor on ship, usu. by trickery.
shank *n.* leg, lower part of leg; stem or
shaft of nail or key or anchor etc.
shan't /ʃɑːnt/ *colloq.* = shall not.
shantung /ʃæn'tʌŋ/ *n.* soft undressed
Chinese silk, usu. undyed.
shanty[1] /'ʃæntɪ/ *n.* hut, cabin. **shanty
town** suburb etc. of shanties.
shanty[2] /'ʃæntɪ/ *n.* song sung by
sailors while hauling ropes etc.
shape 1 *n.* configuration, form; external appearance, guise; orderly arrangement, proper condition; pattern
or mould. 2 *v.* fashion into desired or
definite shape; form, devise, plan; direct (one's course etc.); develop (*into*).
shapeless /'ʃeɪplɪs/ *a.* lacking proper
shape or shapeliness.
shapely /'ʃeɪplɪ/ *a.* well-formed; of
pleasing shape.
shard /ʃɑːd/ *n.* broken piece of pottery
or glass etc.
share /ʃeə(r)/ 1 *n.* portion that person
gives to or receives from common
amount or commitment; each of equal
parts into which company's capital is
divided entitling owner to proportion
of profits. 2 *v.* get or give or have share
(of); participate in; divide and distribute (often with *out*); give away part
of. 3 **shareholder** owner of shares in
a company; **share index** number indicating how prices of shares have fluc-
tuated; **share-out** division and
distribution.
shark *n.* large voracious sea-fish; extortioner, swindler. **shark-skin** skin

of shark, smooth fabric with dull
surface.
sharp 1 *a.* having edge or point able to
cut or pierce; tapering to a point or
edge; abrupt or angular or steep; severe; intense; shrill, piercing; harsh;
acute, sensitive; clever; unscrupulous;
acid, pungent; vigorous or brisk; *Mus.*
above true pitch, a semitone higher
than note named. 2 *n. Mus.* sharp note;
sign indicating this; *colloq.* swindler,
cheat. 3 *adv.* punctually, suddenly; at a
sharp angle; *Mus.* above true pitch. 4
sharp practice barely honest dealings; **sharp-shooter** skilled
marksman.
sharpen /'ʃɑːpən/ *v.* make or become
sharp.
sharper /'ʃɑːpə(r)/ *n.* swindler esp. at
cards.
shatter /'ʃætə(r)/ *v.* break suddenly in
pieces; wreck, utterly destroy; *fig.*
severely discompose.
shave 1 *v.* (*p.p.* **shaved** or esp. as *a.*
shaven) cut (growing hair) from face
etc. with razor; remove hair from face
etc. (of); cut thin slices from surface of
(wood etc.) to shape it; pass close to
without touching, miss narrowly. 2 *n.*
shaving or being shaved; narrow miss
or escape; tool for shaving wood etc.
3 **shaving-brush** brush for lathering
chin etc. before shaving; **shaving-
cream, -soap**, etc., substance applied
to chin etc. to assist shaving.
shaver /'ʃeɪvə(r)/ *n.* electrical appliance for shaving face etc.; *colloq.*
youngster.
Shavian /'ʃeɪvɪən/ *a.* of the writer G.
B. Shaw.
shaving /'ʃeɪvɪŋ/ *n.* (esp. in *pl.*) thin
paring of wood.
shawl *n.* rectangular piece of fabric
freq. folded into triangle, worn over
shoulders etc. or wrapped round baby.
she 1 *pron.* (*obj.* **her**, *poss.* **her**) the female person or animal in question. 2 *n.*
& *a.* female.
sheaf 1 *n.* (*pl.* **sheaves**) group of things
laid lengthwise together and usu. tied,
esp. bundle of corn-stalks tied after
reaping. 2 *v.t.* make into sheaves.
shear 1 *v.* (*p.p.* **shorn** or **sheared**) cut
(off) with scissors or shears etc.; clip
wool off (sheep etc.); *fig.* strip bare *of*,
deprive *of*; distort or be distorted or

break *off*. **2** *n.* strain produced by pressure in structure of substance; in *pl.* (also **pair of shears**) clipping or cutting instrument shaped like scissors.

sheath /ʃiːθ/ *n.* close-fitting cover, esp. for blade or tool; condom. **sheath-knife** dagger-like knife carried in sheath.

sheathe /ʃiːð/ *v.t.* put into sheath; encase or protect with sheath.

shebeen /ʃɪˈbiːn/ *n. Ir.* unlicensed house selling alcoholic liquor.

shed[1] *n.* one-storeyed building for storage or shelter or as workshop etc.

shed[2] *v.t.* (*past & p.p.* shed) let fall off, lose; cause to fall or flow; disperse, diffuse, radiate.

sheen *n.* brightness, lustre. **sheeny** *a.*

sheep *n.* (*pl.* same) animal with thick woolly coat, esp. kept in flocks for its wool or meat; bashful or timid or silly person; (usu. in *pl.*) member of minister's congregation. **sheep-dip** preparation for cleansing sheep of vermin etc., place where sheep are dipped in this; **sheep-dog** dog trained to guard and herd sheep, type of dog suitable for this; **sheep-fold** enclosure for sheep; **sheepshank** knot used to shorten rope temporarily; **sheepskin** garment or rug of sheep's skin with wool on.

sheepish /ʃiːpɪʃ/ *a.* bashful or embarrassed in manner.

sheer[1] *a.* mere, unqualified, absolute; (of cliff, ascent, etc.) perpendicular; (of textile) thin, diaphanous. **2** *adv.* perpendicularly; directly.

sheer[2] *v.i.* swerve or change course. **sheer off** go away, esp. from person that one dislikes or fears.

sheet[1] *n.* rectangular piece of cotton or linen etc. as part of bedclothes; broad thin flat piece of glass or paper etc.; wide expanse *of* water or flame etc. **2** *v.* cover with sheet; form into sheets. **3** **sheet metal** metal formed into thin sheets by rolling or hammering etc.; **sheet music** music published in separate sheets.

sheet[2] *n.* rope or chain at lower corner of sail to extend it or alter its direction. **sheet-anchor** large anchor used only in emergencies, thing depended on as one's last hope.

sheikh /ʃeɪk/ *n.* chief or head of Arab tribe or family etc.; Muslim leader.

sheila /ʃiːlə/ *n. Aus. & NZ sl.* young woman, girl.

shekel /ʃek(ə)l/ *n.* currency unit of Israel; ancient Jewish etc. weight and coin; in *pl. colloq.* money.

sheldrake /ʃeldreɪk/ *n.* (*fem. & pl.* **shelduck**) bright-plumaged wild duck.

shelf *n.* (*pl.* **shelves**) horizontal slab or board projecting from wall or forming one tier of bookcase or cupboard; ledge on cliff-face etc.; reef or sandbank. **on the shelf** put aside, (past of unmarried woman) considered past marriageable age; **shelf-life** time for which stored thing remains usable; **shelf-mark** mark on book to show its place in library.

shell **1** *n.* hard outer case enclosing nut-kernel or egg or seed or fruit or animal or part of it; framework or case for something; walls of unfinished or gutted building or ship etc.; explosive artillery projectile; light rowing-boat for racing; outward show, mere semblance. **2** *v.t.* take out of shell, remove shell or pod from; fire shells at. **3 come out of one's shell** become communicative; **shellfish** water animal with shell (mollusc or crustacean); **shell out** *sl.* pay (money); **shell-shock** nervous breakdown resulting from prolonged exposure to battle conditions.

shellac /ʃəˈlæk/ **1** *n.* resinous substance used for making varnish etc. **2** *v.t.* (*past & p.p.* **shellacked**) varnish with shellac.

shelter /ʃeltə(r)/ **1** *n.* protection from danger or the elements etc.; place providing this. **2** *v.* act or serve as shelter to; shield; take shelter.

shelve *v.* put on shelf; defer consideration of; remove from active work etc.; provide with shelves; (of ground) slope gently.

shelving /ʃelvɪŋ/ *n.* shelves; material for shelves.

shepherd /ʃepəd/ **1** *n.* man who tends sheep; *fig.* pastor. **2** *v.t.* tend or drive sheep; marshal or guide like sheep. **3** **shepherd's pie** minced meat baked with covering of (esp. mashed) potato. **4 shepherdess** *n.*

sherbet /ʃɜːbət/ *n.* fizzy flavoured drink; the powder for making this.

sherd *n.* potsherd.

sheriff /'ʃerɪf/ n. chief executive officer of Crown in county, with legal and ceremonial duties; Sc. chief judge of county or district; US chief law-enforcing officer of county.

sherry /'ʃerɪ/ n. white usu. fortified wine orig. from Spain, drunk esp. as aperitif.

Shetland /'ʃetlənd/ a. **Shetland pony** pony of small hardy breed; **Shetland wool** fine wool from Shetland sheep.

shew /ʃəʊ/ arch. var. of **show**.

shibboleth /'ʃɪbəleθ/ n. old-fashioned doctrine or formula of party etc., catchword; word or custom etc. regarded as revealing person's orthodoxy.

shield /ʃiːld/ 1 n. piece of defensive armour carried in hand or on arm to protect the body when fighting; person or thing serving as protection or defence; representation of shield for displaying person's coat of arms; shield-shaped thing, esp. sports trophy; protective plate etc. in machinery etc. 2 v.t. protect or defend.

shift 1 v. change or move from one position to another; change form or character; use expedients; manage, get along; sl. move quickly. 2 n. change of place or character etc.; group of workers working at same time; period for which they work; expedient, device, trick; woman's loose straight dress; change of position of typewriter type-bars to type capitals etc.; displacement of lines of spectrum; US gear-change in motor vehicle.

shiftless /'ʃɪftlɪs/ a. lazy, inefficient; lacking in resource.

shifty /'ʃɪftɪ/ a. not straightforward, evasive, deceitful.

Shiite /'ʃiːaɪt/ 1 n. member of esp. Iranian Muslim sect opposed to Sunnites. 2 a. of this sect.

shillelagh /ʃɪ'leɪlɪ/ n. Irish cudgel.

shilling /'ʃɪlɪŋ/ n. former British monetary unit and coin, worth 1/20 of pound; monetary unit in some other countries.

shilly-shally /'ʃɪlɪʃælɪ/ v.i. vacillate, hesitate or be undecided.

shimmer /'ʃɪmə(r)/ 1 n. tremulous or faint diffused light. 2 v.i. shine with shimmer. 3 **shimmery** a.

shin 1 n. front of leg below knee. 2 v.i. climb (up) by using arms and legs. 3

shin-bone inner and usu. larger of two bones from knee to ankle.

shindig /'ʃɪndɪg/ (also **shindy**) n. colloq. festive gathering, esp. boisterous one; brawl, disturbance.

shine 1 v. (past & p.p. **shone** /ʃɒn/) emit or reflect light, be bright, glow; be brilliant, excel; cause to shine; colloq. (past and p.p. **shined**) polish (boots etc.). 2 n. light, brightness, sunshine; lustre, sheen; polishing. 3 **take a shine to** colloq. take a liking to.

shiner /'ʃaɪnə(r)/ n.sl. black eye.

shingle¹ /'ʃɪŋg(ə)l/ n. small rounded pebbles on sea-shore. **shingly** a.

shingle² /'ʃɪŋg(ə)l/ 1 n. rectangular piece of wood used as roof-tile etc.; shingled hair. 2 v.t. roof with shingles; cut (woman's hair) short and tapering from back of head to nape of neck.

shingles /'ʃɪŋg(ə)lz/ n.pl. painful virus infection of nerves with outbreaks of small blisters, esp. round waist.

shinty /'ʃɪntɪ/ n. game resembling hockey.

shiny /'ʃaɪnɪ/ a. shining, polished, rubbed bright.

ship 1 n. large seagoing vessel; colloq. spacecraft, US aircraft. 2 v. send or take or put in ship; deliver (goods) to agent for forwarding; fix (mast, rudder) in its place on ship; embark; (of sailor) engage for service on ship; take (oars) from rowlocks and lay them inside boat. 3 **ship-canal** canal allowing ships to go inland; **shipmate** person sailing on same ship as another; **shipshape** in good order, neat and tidy; **shipwreck** destruction of ship by storm or collision etc., ruin of one's hopes etc., (v.) suffer this, cause to suffer this; **shipwright** shipbuilder, ship's carpenter; **shipyard** place where ships are built.

shipment /'ʃɪpmənt/ n. putting of goods etc. on board; goods shipped.

shipper /'ʃɪpə(r)/ n. importer or exporter.

shipping /'ʃɪpɪŋ/ n. ships collectively.

shire /ʃaɪə(r)/ n. county. **shire-horse** heavy powerful draught-horse.

shirk v.t. avoid or get out of (duty, work, etc.) from laziness or cowardice.

shirr v.t. gather with several parallel threads. **shirring** n.

shirt n. loose sleeved garment of cotton

etc. for upper part of body; **in shirtsleeves** not wearing jacket; **shirt dress** dress with bodice like shirt; **shirtwaister** shirt dress.

shirting /ˈʃɜːtɪŋ/ n. material for shirts.

shirty /ˈʃɜːtɪ/ a. sl. annoyed.

shiver¹ /ˈʃɪvə(r)/ 1 v.i. tremble esp. with cold or fear. 2 n. momentary shivering movement. 3 **shivery** a.

shiver² /ˈʃɪvə(r)/ 1 n. small fragment, splinter. 2 v. break into shivers.

shoal¹ 1 n. crowd, great number, esp. of fish swimming together. 2 v.i. form shoal(s).

shoal² 1 n. shallow place in sea; submerged sandbank. 2 v.i. become shallow.

shock¹ 1 n. violent concussion or impact; sudden and disturbing physical or mental impression; acute state of prostration following sudden violent emotion or severe injury etc.; electric shock; violent shake or tremor of earth's surface in earthquake; great disturbance of or injury to organization, stability, etc. 2 v.t. affect with electrical or mental shock; appear scandalous or outrageous to. 3 **shock absorber** device on vehicle etc. for absorbing vibration and shock; **shock therapy** electroconvulsive therapy.

shocker /ˈʃɒkə(r)/ n. person or thing that shocks; very bad specimen of anything; sensational novel or film etc.

shocking /ˈʃɒkɪŋ/ a. scandalous; improper; colloq. very bad.

shod past & p.p. of **shoe**.

shoddy /ˈʃɒdɪ/ a. of poor quality, counterfeit, shabby.

shoe /ʃuː/ 1 n. outer covering of leather etc. for foot, esp. one not reaching above ankle; thing like shoe in shape or use; metal rim nailed to underside of horse's hoof. 2 v. (past & p.p. **shod**; partic. **shoeing**) fit with shoe(s); (in p.p.) having shoes of specified kind. 3 **shoehorn** curved piece of metal etc. for easing heel into back of shoe; **shoelace** cord for lacing shoe; **shoe-string** shoe-lace, colloq. small or inadequate amount of money; **shoe-tree** shaped block for keeping shoe in shape.

shone past & p.p. of **shine**.

shoo 1 int. used to frighten birds etc. away. 2 v. utter such sound; drive away thus.

shook past of **shake**.

shoot /ʃuːt/ 1 v. (past & p.p. **shot**) cause (weapon) to discharge missile; kill or wound (person, animal) with missile from weapon; send out or discharge rapidly; hunt game etc. with gun; come or go swiftly or suddenly; Footb. etc. take shot at goal; take film or photograph of; (of plant) put forth buds, (of bud) appear. 2 n. young branch or sucker; expedition or party for shooting game; land on which game is shot. 3 **shooting-brake** estate-car; **shooting-gallery** place for shooting at targets with rifles etc.; **shooting star** small meteor appearing like star, moving quickly and disappearing; **shooting-stick** spiked walking-stick with handle that can be used as seat.

shop 1 n. place for retail sale of goods or services etc.; workshop or place of manufacture; one's work or profession as subject of conversation. 2 v. go to shops to make purchases; sl. inform against. 3 **shop around** look for best bargain; **shop-assistant** employee in retail shop; **shop-floor** production area in factory etc., workers as distinct from management; **shopkeeper** owner or manager of shop; **shoplifting** stealing of goods from display in shop; **shop-soiled** soiled or faded by being shown in shop; **shop-steward** person elected by fellow workmen as their spokesman; **shopwalker** supervisor in large shop.

shopping /ˈʃɒpɪŋ/ n. going to shops; goods bought in shop(s). **shopping centre** area containing many shops.

shore¹ n. land that adjoins sea or large body of water; **on shore** ashore.

shore² 1 n. prop, beam set obliquely against wall etc. as support. 2 v.t. support or prop up with shore(s).

shorn p.p. of **shear**.

short 1 a. measuring little from end to end in space or time, or from head to foot; concise, brief; curt, uncivil; deficient, inadequate in quantity, scarce; (of pastry) easily crumbled; (of vowel or syllable) having the less of two recognized durations. 2 adv. abruptly, suddenly; before the natural or expected time or place; in short manner. 3 n. short thing, esp. short syllable or vowel or film; colloq. short circuit, short drink; in *pl.* trousers reaching only to or above knees, *US* underpants. **4** *v.* short-circuit. **5 shortbread, shortcake**, rich crumbly cake made of flour and butter and sugar; **short-change** rob or cheat esp. by giving insufficient change; **short circuit** electric circuit through small resistance, esp. instead of through normal circuit; **short-circuit** cause short circuit in, have short circuit, *fig.* shorten or avoid by taking short cut; **shortcoming** failure to reach required standard, deficiency; **short cut** path or course shorter than usual or normal; **short drink** small drink of spirits etc.; **shortfall** deficit; **shorthand** method of rapid writing for keeping pace with speaker, *fig.* abbreviated or symbolic means of expression; **short-handed** undermanned, understaffed; **shorthorn** breed of cattle; **short list** list of candidates from whom final selection will be made; **short-list** put on short list; **short-lived** having short life, ephemeral; **short of** not having enough of, less than, without reaching; **short-range** having short range, relating to short period of future time; **short shrift** curt attention or treatment; **short sight** ability to see clearly only what is comparatively near; **short-sighted** having short sight, *fig.* lacking imagination or foresight; **short-tempered** easily angered; **short-term** occurring in or relating to a short period of time; **short-winded** easily becoming breathless.

shortage /ˈʃɔːtɪdʒ/ *n.* deficiency; amount of this.

shorten /ˈʃɔːt(ə)n/ *v.* become or make short(er).

shortening /ˈʃɔːtənɪŋ/ *n.* fat used for making esp. short pastry.

shortly /ˈʃɔːtlɪ/ *adv.* soon, in a short time; in a short manner.

shot¹ *n.* discharge of gun etc.; sound of this; attempt to hit something by shooting or throwing etc.; stroke or kick in ball-game; attempt to do something; person of specified skill in shooting; single missile for gun or cannon etc.; small lead pellet of which several are used for single charge; (as *pl.*) these collectively; heavy metal ball thrown in shot-put; scene etc. photographed,

photograph, photographing; injection of drug etc.; *colloq.* dram of spirits. **shotgun** gun for firing small shot at short range; **shotgun wedding** wedding enforced esp. because of bride's pregnancy; **shot-put** athletic contest of throwing heavy metal ball.

shot² **1** *past* & *p.p.* of **shoot**. **2** *a.* woven or dyed so as to show different colours at different angles.

should *v.aux.* expr. duty or obligation, possible or expected future event, or conditional or indefinite mood. □ See also **shall** and page 667.

shoulder /ˈʃəʊldə(r)/ **1** *n.* part of body to which arm or foreleg or wing is attached; part of garment covering shoulder; animal's upper foreleg as joint of meat; in *pl.* upper part of back; part or projection resembling human shoulder; strip of land adjoining metalled road-surface. **2** *v.* push with shoulder, jostle; take (burden) on one's shoulder, assume (responsibility etc.). **3 shoulder-blade** either flat bone of upper back; **shoulder-strap** strap passing over shoulder to support something, strap from shoulder to collar of garment, esp. with indication of military rank.

shout /ʃaʊt/ **1** *n.* loud cry calling attention or expr. joy or defiance or approval etc. **2** *v.* utter shout; speak or say loudly, call out. **3 shout down** reduce to silence by shouting.

shove /ʃʌv/ **1** *n.* (strong) push. **2** *v.* push, esp. vigorously or roughly; *colloq.* put. **3 shove-halfpenny** game in which coins etc. are driven along polished board by blow with hand; **shove off** *colloq.* depart.

shovel /ˈʃʌv(ə)l/ **1** *n.* spadelike scoop used to shift earth or coal etc. **2** *v.t.* move (as) with shovel or spade. **shovelboard** game played on ship's deck by pushing discs over marked surface.

shoveller /ˈʃʌvələ(r)/ *n.* duck with shovel-like beak.

show /ʃəʊ/ **1** *v.* (*p.p.* **shown** or **showed**) allow or cause to be seen; disclose, manifest; offer for inspection; exhibit; demonstrate, make understand; be or become visible or noticeable. **2** *n.* showing; spectacle, exhibition, display;

public entertainment or performance; *sl.* concern, undertaking, business; outward appearance, impression produced; ostentation, mere display. **3 show business** the entertainment profession; **show-case** glazed case for displaying goods or exhibits; **show-down** final test or battle etc., disclosure of achievements or possibilities; **show-jumping** competitive jumping on horseback; **showman** proprietor or organizer of public entertainment, person skilled in showmanship; **showmanship** capacity for exhibiting one's wares or capabilities to best advantage; **show off** display to advantage, try to impress people by displaying one's skill or wealth etc.; **show-piece** excellent specimen suitable for display; **show-place** place that tourists etc. go to see; **showroom** room where goods are exhibited or kept for inspection; **show round** take (person) to all points of interest; **show trial** judicial trial regarded as intended to impress public opinion; **show up** make or be visible or conspicuous, expose, humiliate, *colloq.* appear or arrive.

shower /ˈʃaʊə(r)/ 1 *n.* brief fall of rain or hail or sleet; great number of missiles or gifts or questions or kisses etc.; shower-bath. **2** *v.* descend or send or give in shower; bestow lavishly *upon*; take shower-bath. **3 shower-bath** bath in which water is sprayed from above.

showery /ˈʃaʊərɪ/ *a.* of or characterized by rain-showers.

showing /ˈʃəʊɪŋ/ *n.* quality or appearance of performance or achievement etc.; evidence, putting of case etc.

shown *p.p.* of **show**.

showy /ˈʃəʊɪ/ *a.* striking, making good display; gaudy.

shrank *past* of **shrink**.

shrapnel /ˈʃræpn(ə)l/ *n.* fragments of metal scattered from exploding projectile.

shred 1 *n.* small torn or broken or cut piece; scrap, fragment; least amount. **2** *v.* tear or cut etc. to shreds.

shrew *n.* small long-snouted mouselike animal; scolding woman.

shrewd *a.* showing astute powers of judgement; clever.

shrewish /ˈʃruːɪʃ/ *a.* ill-tempered and scolding.

shriek /ʃriːk/ 1 *n.* loud shrill piercing cry or sound. **2** *v.* make a shriek; say in shrill tones.

shrike *n.* bird with strong hooked beak.

shrill 1 *a.* piercing and high-pitched. **2** *v.* sound or utter shrilly.

shrimp *n.* small edible crustacean; *derog.* very small person.

shrine *n.* casket or tomb holding relics; sacred or revered place.

shrink *v.* (*past* **shrank**; *p.p.* **shrunk** or as *a.* **shrunken**) become or make smaller, esp. by action from moisture or heat or cold; recoil or flinch (*from*). **shrink-wrap** enclose (article) in material that shrinks tightly round it.

shrinkage /ˈʃrɪŋkɪdʒ/ *n.* process or degree of shrinking; allowance for loss by theft or wastage.

shrivel /ˈʃrɪv(ə)l/ *v.* contract into wrinkled or curled-up state.

shroud /ʃraʊd/ 1 *n.* wrapping for a corpse; something which conceals; in *pl.* ropes supporting ship's mast. **2** *v.t.* clothe (corpse) for burial; cover or disguise.

Shrove Tuesday day before Ash Wednesday.

shrub *n.* woody plant smaller than tree and usu. branching from near ground. **shrubby** *a.*

shrubbery /ˈʃrʌbərɪ/ *n.* area planted with shrubs.

shrug 1 *v.* draw up shoulders momentarily as gesture of indifference etc. **2** *n.* shrugging movement.

shrunk(en) *p.p.* of **shrink**.

shudder /ˈʃʌdə(r)/ 1 *n.* sudden or convulsive shivering due to horror or cold etc. **2** *v.i.* experience shudder; have vibrating movement.

shuffle /ˈʃʌf(ə)l/ 1 *v.* move with dragging or sliding or difficult motion; intermingle or rearrange (esp. cards); keep shifting one's position; prevaricate, be evasive. **2** *n.* shuffling action or movement; general change of relative positions; shuffling dance. **3 shuffle off** remove or get rid of.

shun *v.t.* avoid, keep clear of.

shunt 1 *v.* move (train etc.) to another track; (of train) be shunted; redirect. **2** *n.* shunting or being shunted; *Electr.* conductor joining two points in electric circuit for diversion of current; *sl.* collision.

shush /ʃʊʃ/ v. & int. colloq. hush.

shut v. (past & p.p. **shut**) move (door, window, lid, etc.) into position to block opening; become or admit of being shut; shut door etc. of; bring (book, hand, telescope) into folded or contracted state; bar access to (place). **shut down** close, cease working; **shut-eye** sl. sleep; **shut off** stop flow of (water, gas, etc.), separate, cut off; **shut out** exclude, prevent; **shut up** close securely or decisively or permanently, imprison, put away in box etc., colloq. stop talking.

shutter /ˈʃʌtə(r)/ 1 n. movable hinged cover for window; device for opening and closing aperture of camera. 2 v.t. provide or close with shutter(s). 3 **put up the shutters** close business for the day or permanently.

shuttle /ˈʃʌt(ə)l/ 1 n. weaving-implement by which weft-thread is carried between threads of warp; thread-carrier for lower thread in sewing-machine; train or bus or aircraft etc. used in shuttle service; space shuttle. 2 v. (cause to) move to and fro like shuttle. 3 **shuttlecock** object struck to and fro in badminton, consisting of rounded piece of cork with feathers in or of imitation of this; **shuttle service** transport system operating to and fro over relatively short distance.

shy[1] 1 a. self-conscious or uneasy in company, bashful; easily startled, wary; (as suffix) showing fear or distaste for. 2 v.i. (esp. of horse) start aside in alarm (at). 3 n. shying.

shy[2] v. & n. colloq. throw, fling.

shyster /ˈʃaɪstə(r)/ n. colloq. person, esp. lawyer, who acts unscrupulously or unprofessionally.

si /siː/ n. Mus. te.

SI abbr. international system of units of measurement (Système International).

Siamese /saɪəˈmiːz/ 1 a. of Siam (now Thailand). 2 n. native or language of Siam. 3 **Siamese cat** cream-coloured brown-faced short-haired breed of cat; **Siamese twins** twins joined together at birth.

sibilant /ˈsɪbɪlənt/ 1 a. hissing, sounding like hiss. 2 n. sibilant speech sound. 3 **sibilance** n.

sibling /ˈsɪblɪŋ/ n. one of two or more children having one or both parents in common.

sibyl /ˈsɪbɪl/ n. pagan prophetess.

sibylline /ˈsɪbɪlaɪn/ a. uttered by or characteristic of a sibyl, mysteriously prophetic.

sic adv. thus used or spelt etc. (confirming form of quoted words). [L]

sick 1 a. ill, unwell; vomiting or disposed to vomit; of or for those who are sick; surfeited and tired of; (of humour) making fun of misfortune or macabre things. 2 v.t. colloq. vomit (esp. with up). 3 n. vomit. 4 **sick-bay** place for sick persons.

sicken /ˈsɪkən/ v. make or become sick or disgusted etc. **sicken for** be in first stages of (illness).

sickle /ˈsɪk(ə)l/ n. short-handled implement with semicircular blade for reaping or lopping etc.

sickly /ˈsɪklɪ/ a. liable to be ill, of weak health; causing or suggesting sickness; faint, pale; mawkish, weakly sentimental.

sickness /ˈsɪknɪs/ n. being ill; disease; vomiting, nausea.

side 1 n. one of inner or outer surfaces of object, esp. as distinct from top and bottom or front and back or ends; one of lines bounding triangle or rectangle etc.; either surface of thing regarded as having only two; right or left part of person's or animal's body; part of object or place etc. that faces specified direction or that is in observer's right or left; region nearer or farther than, or to right or left of, a real or imaginary dividing line; marginal part of area or thing; each of sets of opponents in war or game etc.; cause represented by this; team; line of descent through father or mother; spinning motion given to ball by striking it on side; sl. swagger, assumption of superiority. 2 a. of or on or from or to side; oblique, indirect; subordinate, subsidiary, not main. 2 v.i. take part or be on same side with. 3 **side-bet** one additional to ordinary stakes; **sideboard** table or flat-topped chest with drawers and cupboards for crockery etc.; **sideburns** short side-whiskers; **side by side** standing close together esp. for mutual encouragement; **side-car** passenger car attachable to side of motor cycle; **side-drum** small double-headed drum; **sidekick** *colloq.* close associate; **sidelight** light from side, small light at front of vehicle etc., piece of incidental information etc.; **sideline** work etc. carried on in addition to one's main activity, in *pl.* lines bounding sides of football-pitch or tennis-court etc., space just outside these, place for spectators as opp. participants; **side-saddle** saddle *esp.* for woman made so that rider may have both feet on same side of horse, (*adv.*) sitting thus on horse; **side-show** minor show attached to principal one (freq. *fig.*); **sideslip** skid, movement sideways, (*v.i.*) move sideways (esp. of aircraft); **sidesman** assistant churchwarden; **side-step** step taken sideways, (*v.t.*) avoid, evade; **side-track** divert from course or purpose etc.; **sidewalk** US pavement at side of road; **side-whiskers** hair left unshaven on cheeks.

sidelong /ˈsaɪdlɒŋ/ 1 *a.* directed to the side. 2 *adv.* to the side.

sidereal /saɪˈdɪərɪəl/ *a.* of or measured or determined by stars.

sideways /ˈsaɪdweɪz/ *a.* & *adv.* with side foremost; to or from a side.

siding /ˈsaɪdɪŋ/ *n.* short track by side of railway line for shunting line.

sidle /ˈsaɪd(ə)l/ *v.i.* walk obliquely, esp. in furtive or unobtrusive manner.

siege /siːdʒ/ 1 *n.* surrounding and blockading of fortified place. **lay siege to** conduct siege of; **raise siege** end it.

sienna /sɪˈenə/ *n.* kind of clay used as pigment; its colour of reddish- or yellowish-brown.

sierra /sɪˈerə/ *n.* long jagged mountain-chain in Spain or Spanish America.

siesta /sɪˈestə/ *n.* afternoon nap or rest in hot countries.

sieve /sɪv/ 1 *n.* utensil with network or perforated bottom through which liquids or fine particles can pass. 2 *v.t.* sift.

sift *v.* separate with or cause to pass through sieve; sprinkle; closely examine details of, analyse; fall (as) from or through sieve.

sigh /saɪ/ 1 *n.* long deep audible breath expressing dejection or weariness or longing or relief etc. 2 *v.* give sigh or

sound resembling it; express with sighs; yearn *for*.

sight /saɪt/ 1 *n.* faculty of seeing; seeing or being seen; range of or region open to vision; thing seen or visible or worth seeing; *colloq.* person or thing of ridiculous or repulsive appearance; in *pl.* noteworthy or attractive features of a place; precise aim with gun or observation with optical instrument; device for assisting this; *colloq. a* great quantity. 2 *v.t.* get sight of; observe presence of; aim (gun etc.) with sights. 3 **at first sight** on first glimpse or impression; **on sight** as soon as person or thing is seen; **out of sight** not visible; **sight-read** play (music) at sight; **sight-screen** *Crick.* large white screen placed near boundary in line with wicket to help batsman see ball; **sight-seer** person visiting sights of place; **sight-seeing** *n.*

sightless /ˈsaɪtlɪs/ *a.* blind.

sightly /ˈsaɪtlɪ/ *a.* attractive to sight.

sign /saɪn/ 1 *n.* indication or suggestion or symptom *of* or *that*; symbol or word etc. representing phrase or idea or instruction etc.; mark traced on surface etc.; motion or gesture used instead of words to convey information or demand etc.; one of the 12 divisions of the zodiac; signboard. 2 *v.* write one's name on (document etc.) to show that one is the author etc. or that one accepts or agrees with contents; write (one's name) thus; communicate by gesture. 3 **signboard** board bearing name or symbol etc. displayed outside shop or inn etc.; **sign-language** series of signs used esp. by deaf or dumb people for communication; **sign off** end contract or work etc.; **sign on** register to obtain unemployment benefit; **signpost** post etc. showing directions of roads, (*v.t.*) provide with signpost(s).

signal /ˈsɪgn(ə)l/ 1 *n.* sign, esp. prearranged one, conveying information or direction esp. to person(s) at a distance; message made up of such signs; device on railway giving instructions or warnings to train-drivers etc.; event which causes immediate activity; *Electr.* transmitted impulses or radio waves; sequence of these. 2 *v.* make signal(s) (to); transmit or announce or direct (*to* do) by signal(s). 3 *a.*

remarkably good or bad, noteworthy. **4**
signal-box building from which railway signals are controlled; **signalman** person responsible for displaying or operating signals.

signalize /ˈsɪgnəlaɪz/ v.t. make conspicuous or remarkable.

signatory /ˈsɪgnətərɪ/ **1** a. that has signed an agreement, esp. a treaty. **2** n. signatory party.

signature /ˈsɪgnətʃ(ə)r/ n. person's name or initials used in signing; act of signing; *Mus.* indication of key or tempo following clef; section of book made from one sheet folded and cut; letter or figure indicating sequence of these. **signature tune** tune used esp. in broadcasting to announce a particular programme or performer etc.

signet /ˈsɪgnɪt/ n. small seal, esp. one set in finger-ring (**signet ring**).

significance /sɪgˈnɪfɪkəns/ n. being significant; meaning, import; importance.

significant /sɪgˈnɪfɪkənt/ a. having or conveying meaning; highly expressive; important. **significant figure** *Math.* digit conveying information about a number containing it, not a zero filling vacant place at beginning or end.

signification /sɪgnɪfɪˈkeɪʃ(ə)n/ n. exact meaning or sense.

signify /ˈsɪgnɪfaɪ/ v. be sign or symbol of; represent, mean, denote; make known, be of importance, matter.

signor /ˈsiːnjɔː(r)/ n. (pl. **-ri** /-riː/) title used of or to Italian man. [It.]

signora /siːˈnjɔːrə/ n. title used of or to Italian married woman. [It.]

signorina /siːnjəˈriːnə/ n. title used of or to Italian unmarried woman. [It.]

silage /ˈsaɪlɪdʒ/ n. storage in silo; green fodder so stored.

silence /ˈsaɪləns/ **1** n. absence of sound; abstinence from speech or noise; reticence; neglect or omission to mention or write etc. **2** v.t. make silent, reduce to silence; put down, repress.

silencer /ˈsaɪlənsə(r)/ n. device for reducing noise made by gun or vehicle's exhaust etc.

silent /ˈsaɪlənt/ a. making or accompanied by little or no sound or speech.

silhouette /sɪluˈet/ **1** n. dark outline or shadow in profile against lighter back-

ground; contour, outline, profile; portrait in profile cut from paper or done in solid black on white. **2** v.t. represent or show in silhouette.

silica /ˈsɪlɪkə/ n. hard mineral occurring as quartz and as main constituent of sand etc. **siliceous** /sɪˈlɪʃəs/ a.

silicate /ˈsɪlɪkət/ n. compound of metal(s), silicon, and oxygen.

silicon /ˈsɪlɪkən/ n. non-metallic element occurring in silica and silicates. **silicon chip** tiny piece of silicon containing integrated circuit.

silicone /ˈsɪlɪkəʊn/ n. any of group of silicon compounds, used in polishes and paints and lubricants etc.

silicosis /sɪlɪˈkəʊsɪs/ n. lung disease caused by inhaling dust containing silica.

silk n. fine strong soft lustrous fibre produced by silkworms; thread or cloth made from this; in *pl.* kinds or garments of silk; *colloq.* KC or QC; *attrib.* made of silk. **silk hat** tall cylindrical hat covered with silk plush; **silk-screen printing** = *screen-printing*; **silkworm** caterpillar which spins cocoon of silk; **take silk** become KC or QC.

silken /ˈsɪlkən/ a. of or resembling silk; soft or smooth or lustrous.

silky /ˈsɪlkɪ/ a. like silk in smoothness or softness etc.; suave.

sill n. shelf or slab of wood or stone etc. at base of window or doorway.

sillabub var. of **syllabub**.

silly 1 a. foolish, imprudent, thoughtless; weak-minded; *Crick.* (of fielder or his position) very close to batsman. **2** n. *colloq.* silly person.

silo /ˈsaɪləʊ/ n. (pl. **-los**) pit or airtight structure in which green crops are stored for fodder; tower or pit for storage of grain or cement etc.; underground place where guided missile is kept ready for firing.

silt 1 n. sediment deposited by water in channel or harbour etc. **2** v. block or be blocked (*up*) with silt.

silvan /ˈsɪlv(ə)n/ a. of the woods; wooded; rural.

silver /ˈsɪlvə(r)/ **1** n. white lustrous precious metal; coins or articles made of or looking like this; colour of silver. **2** a. of or coloured like silver. **3** v. coat or plate with silver; give silvery appearance to; provide (mirror-glass) with backing of tin amalgam etc.; (of hair) turn grey or white. **4 silver birch** common birch with silver-coloured bark; **silver-fish** silver-coloured fish, silvery wingless insect; **silver jubilee** 25th anniversary; **silver medal** medal awarded as second prize; **silver paper** tin foil; **silver plate** articles plated with silver; **silver-plated** plated with silver; **silver sand** fine pure kind used in gardening; **silverside** upper side of round of beef; **silversmith** worker in silver; **silver wedding** 25th anniversary of wedding.

silvery /ˈsɪlvərɪ/ *a.* like silver in colour or appearance; having clear soft ringing sound.

simian /ˈsɪmɪən/ **1** *a.* resembling ape or monkey. **2** *n.* ape or monkey.

similar /ˈsɪmɪlə(r)/ *a.* like, alike, having resemblance (*to*), of same kind or nature or shape or amount. **similarity** /-ˈlær-/ *n.*

simile /ˈsɪmɪlɪ/ *n.* comparison of two things for purpose of illustration or ornament.

similitude /sɪˈmɪlɪtjuːd/ *n.* guise or outward appearance; simile.

simmer /ˈsɪmə(r)/ **1** *v.* be or keep just below boiling-point; be in state of suppressed anger or laughter. **2** *n.* simmering state. **3 simmer down** become less agitated.

simnel /ˈsɪmn(ə)l/ *n.* rich decorated fruit-cake, usu. with almond paste.

simony /ˈsaɪmənɪ/ *n.* buying or selling of ecclesiastical offices.

simoom /sɪˈmuːm/ *n.* hot dry dust-laden desert wind.

simper /ˈsɪmpə(r)/ **1** *v.* smile in silly affected way; utter with simper. **2** *n.* such smile.

simple /ˈsɪmp(ə)l/ *a.* easily understood or done, presenting no difficulty; not complicated or elaborate; unsophisticated, natural; consisting of or involving only one element or operation etc.; foolish, feeble-minded. **simple-minded** unsophisticated, ingenuous, feeble-minded.

simpleton /ˈsɪmpəlt(ə)n/ *n.* stupid or gullible person.

simplicity /sɪmˈplɪsɪtɪ/ *n.* quality of being simple.

simplify /ˈsɪmplɪfaɪ/ *v.t.* make simple, make easy to do or understand. **simplification** *n.*

simplistic /sɪmˈplɪstɪk/ *a.* excessively simple or simplified. **simplistically** *adv.*

simply /ˈsɪmplɪ/ *adv.* in simple manner; absolutely; merely.

simulate /ˈsɪmjʊleɪt/ *v.t.* pretend to be or have or feel; counterfeit; imitate conditions of (situation etc.) e.g. for training. **simulation** *n.*; **simulator** *n.*

simultaneous /sɪməlˈteɪnɪəs/ *a.* occurring or operating at same time (*with*). **simultaneity** *n.*

sin 1 *n.* transgression against divine law or principles of morality; offence against good taste etc. **2** *v.i.* commit sin; offend *against*.

since 1 *prep.* from (specified time) till now, within period between (specified past time) and now. **2** *conj.* from time that; seeing that, because. **3** *adv.* since that time or event.

sincere /sɪnˈsɪə(r)/ *a.* free from pretence or deceit, genuine, frank, not assumed or put on. **sincerity** /-ˈser-/ *n.*

sincerely *adv.* in sincere manner; **yours sincerely** formula for closing letter.

sine *n. Math.* ratio of side opposite angle (in right-angled triangle) to hypotenuse.

sinecure /ˈsɪnɪkjʊə(r)/ *n.* position that requires little or no work but usu. yields profit or honour.

sine die /ˈsaɪnɪ ˈdaɪiː/ adjourned indefinitely with no appointed date. [L]

sine qua non /ˈsɪneɪ kwɑː ˈnəʊn/ indispensable condition or qualification. [L]

sinew /ˈsɪnjuː/ *n.* tough fibrous tissue joining muscle to bone; piece of this; in *pl.* muscles, strength; *fig.* that which strengthens or sustains. **sinewy** *a.*

sinful /ˈsɪnfʊl/ *a.* committing or involving sin; wicked.

sing *v.* (*past* **sang**; *p.p.* **sung**) utter words or sounds in tuneful succession, esp. in set tune; produce vocal melody, utter (song, tune); make melodious humming or whistling etc. sounds; celebrate in verse. **sing out** *colloq.* call out loudly; **singsong** uttered with monotonous rhythm or cadence, singsong manner, session of informal singing.

singe /sɪndʒ/ 1 v. (*partic.* **singeing**) burn superficially or slightly, burn ends or edges (of); suffer singeing. 2 n. superficial burn; singeing.

Singhalese var. of **Sinhalese**.

single /'sɪŋg(ə)l/ 1 a. one only, not double or multiple; individual; of or for one person or thing; solitary, unaided; unmarried; taken separately; (of ticket) valid for one journey only, not return. 2 n. single ticket; pop record with one piece of music on each side; hit for one run in cricket; (usu. in *pl.*) game with one player on each side. 3 v.t. choose *out* for special attention. 4 **single-breasted** (of coat etc.) with only one set of buttons, not overlapping; **single file** line of persons etc. going one behind another; **single-handed** without assistance from others; **single-minded** keeping one purpose in view.

singlet /'sɪŋglɪt/ n. sleeveless vest; athlete's garment like vest.

singleton /'sɪŋgəlt(ə)n/ n. player's only card of suit.

singular /'sɪŋgjʊlə(r)/ 1 a. extraordinary, uncommon, surprising; strange, peculiar; *Gram.* denoting one person or thing. 2 n. *Gram.* singular word or form. 3 **singularity** /-'lær-/ n.

Sinhalese /sɪnhə'liːz/ 1 a. of a people from N. India now forming majority of population of Sri Lanka. 2 n. member or language of this people.

sinister /'sɪnɪstə(r)/ a. suggestive of evil; harmful; wicked, corrupt, evil; villainous; *Her.* on left side of shield etc.

sink 1 v. (*past* **sank**; *p.p.* **sunk** or as a. **sunken**) fall or come slowly downwards, decline, disappear below horizon or surface of liquid; get to bottom of sea etc.; settle down, droop, gradually expire or perish or cease; cause or allow to sink; dig (well), bore (shaft), invest (money) so that it is not readily realizable or is lost; cause (ball) to enter pocket at billiards or hole at golf etc.; cause failure of; penetrate or make way *in* or *into*; be absorbed *in* or *into* mind etc. 2 n. fixed basin with water supply and outflow pipe; place where foul liquid collects, *fig.* place of rampant vice etc. 3 **sinking-fund** money set aside for gradual repayment of debt.

sinker /'sɪŋkə(r)/ n. weight used to sink fishing- or sounding-line.

Sino- /'saɪnəʊ/ *in comb.* Chinese.

sinology /saɪ'nɒlədʒɪ/ n. study of China and its language and history etc. **sinologist** n.; **sinologue** /'sɪnəlɒg/ n.

sinter /'sɪntə(r)/ 1 n. solid coalesced by heating. 2 v. form into sinter.

sinuous /'sɪnjʊəs/ a. with many curves, undulating. **sinuosity** n.

sinus /'saɪnəs/ n. cavity, esp. either of cavities in skull communicating with nostrils.

sinusitis /saɪnə'saɪtɪs/ n. inflammation of sinus.

sip 1 v. drink in repeated small mouthfuls or spoonfuls. 2 n. small mouthful of liquid; action of taking this.

siphon /'saɪf(ə)n/ 1 n. pipe or tube bent so that one leg is longer than other, used for drawing off liquids by atmospheric pressure; bottle from which aerated water is forced out by pressure of gas. 2 v. conduct or flow (as) through siphon.

sir /sɜː(r)/ n. polite or respectful form of address or reference to a man; **Sir** title of honour placed before Christian name of knight or baronet.

sire /saɪə(r)/ 1 n. male parent of animal, esp. stallion kept for breeding; *arch.* as form of address to king; *arch.* father or other male ancestor. 2 v.t. beget.

siren /'saɪərən/ n. device for making loud prolonged signal or warning sound; *Gk. Myth.* any of several women or winged creatures whose singing lured unwary sailors on to rocks; dangerously fascinating woman.

sirloin /'sɜːlɔɪn/ n. best part of loin of beef.

sirocco /sɪ'rɒkəʊ/ n. (*pl.* **-os**) hot moist wind in S. Europe.

sisal /'saɪz(ə)l/ n. fibre from leaves of agave.

siskin /'sɪskɪn/ n. small song-bird.

sissy /'sɪsɪ/ 1 n. effeminate or cowardly man. 2 a. characteristic of sissy.

sister /'sɪstə(r)/ n. daughter of same parents; female fellow-member of class or sect or human race; member of religious sisterhood; head nurse of ward in hospital etc. **sister-in-law** husband's or wife's sister, brother's wife. **sisterly** a.

sisterhood /ˈsɪstəhʊd/ n. relationship (as) of sisters; society of women bound by monastic vows or devoting themselves to religious or charitable work.

sit v. (past & p.p. **sat**) take or be in position in which body is supported more or less upright by buttocks; cause to sit, place in sitting position; (of bird) perch; (of animal) rest with hind legs bent and body close to ground; pose for portrait; be MP for constituency; (of bird) remain on nest to hatch eggs; be candidate for examination; undergo (examination etc.); (of parliament, court, etc.) be in session; keep or have one's seat on (horse etc.). **sit back** relax one's efforts; **sit down** sit after standing, cause to sit, suffer tamely (under humiliation etc.); **sit in** occupy place as protest; **sit-in** n.; **sit in on** be present as guest etc. at (meeting); **sit on** be member of (committee etc.), colloq. delay action about, sl. repress or snub; **sit out** take no part in, stay till end of, sit outdoors; **sit tight** colloq. remain firmly in one's place, not yield; **sit up** rise from lying to sitting position, sit erect without lolling, not go to bed.

sitar /sɪˈtɑː(r)/ n. long-necked Indian guitar-like instrument.

sitcom /ˈsɪtkɒm/ n. colloq. situation comedy.

site 1 n. ground on which town or building etc. stands or stood or is to stand; ground set apart for some purpose. 2 v.t. locate, place.

sitter /ˈsɪtə(r)/ n. person who sits for portrait etc.; baby-sitter; sl. easy catch or shot.

sitting /ˈsɪtɪŋ/ 1 n. time during which person or assembly etc. sits. 2 a. having sat down; (of animal or bird) not running or flying. 1 **sitting-room** room containing easy chairs.

situate /ˈsɪtjʊeɪt/ v.t. place or put in position or situation etc. 2 /ˈsɪtjʊət/ a. arch. situated.

situation /sɪtjʊˈeɪʃ(ə)n/ n. place and its surroundings; set of circumstances, position of affairs, condition; employee's position or job. **situation comedy** broadcast comedy involving same characters in series of episodes. **situational** a.

six a. & n. one more than five. **hit, knock, for six**, colloq. utterly surprise or defeat; **six-gun**, **-shooter**, 6-chambered revolver.

sixpence /ˈsɪkspəns/ n. sum of 6p.; formerly sum of 6d, silver coin worth this. **sixpenny** a.

sixteen /sɪksˈtiːn/ a. & n. one more than fifteen. **sixteenth** a. & n.

sixth 1 a. next after fifth. 2 n. one of 6 equal parts. 3 **sixth form** in secondary school for pupils of 16–18 years old; **sixth form college** college with special courses for such pupils; **sixth sense** supposed faculty giving intuitive or extra-sensory knowledge.

sixty /ˈsɪkstɪ/ a. & n. six times ten. **sixtieth** a. & n.

size¹ 1 n. relative bigness or extent of a thing; dimensions, magnitude; each of classes into which things are divided by size. 2 v.t. sort in sizes or by size. 3 **size up** estimate size of, colloq. form judgement of.

size² 1 n. gelatinous solution used for glazing paper and stiffening textiles etc. 2 v.t. treat with size.

sizeable /ˈsaɪzəb(ə)l/ a. fairly large.

sizzle /ˈsɪz(ə)l/ 1 v.i. make sputtering or hissing noise, as of frying. 2 n. sizzling sound.

SJ abbr. Society of Jesus.

skate¹ 1 n. each of pair of steel blades (or boots with blades attached) for gliding over ice; roller-skate. 2 v. move or glide or perform (as) on skates; pass lightly over. 3 **skateboard** short narrow board on roller-skate wheels for riding on standing up; **skating-rink** place with specially-prepared surface for skating.

skedaddle /skɪˈdæd(ə)l/ v.i. colloq. run away, retreat hastily.

skein /skeɪn/ n. quantity of yarn etc. coiled and usu. loosely twisted; flock of wild geese etc. in flight.

skeleton /ˈskelɪt(ə)n/ n. hard framework of bones or shell or woody fibre etc. supporting or containing animal or vegetable body; dried bones of body fastened together in same relative position as in life; very thin person or animal; remaining part of something after usefulness etc. has gone; outline sketch; attrib. having only the essential or minimum number of persons or parts etc. **skeleton key** key fitting many locks. **skeletal** /ˈskelɪt(ə)l/ a.

skep *n*. wooden or wicker basket or hamper; straw or wicker beehive.

skerry /'skerɪ/ *n*. rocky reef or islet.

sketch 1 *n*. rough or unfinished drawing or painting; rough draft, general outline; short usu. humorous play. 2 *v*. make or give sketch of; make sketches.

sketchy /'sketʃɪ/ *a*. insubstantial or imperfect, esp. through haste.

skew 1 *a*. oblique, slanting, not symmetrical. 2 *n*. slant. 3 *v*. make skew; move obliquely.

skewbald /'skju:bɔ:ld/ 1 *a*. (of animal) with irregular patches of white and another colour. 2 *n*. skewbald animal, esp. horse.

skewer /'skju:ə(r)/ 1 *n*. wooden or metal pin for holding meat compactly together while cooking. 2 *v.t*. fasten together or pierce (as) with skewer.

ski /ski:/ 1 *n*. each of pair of long narrow pieces of wood etc. fastened under feet for travelling over snow; similar device under vehicle. 2 *v.i*. (*past & p.p.* **ski'd** or **skied** /ski:d/; *partic*. **skiing**) travel on skis. 3 **skier** *n*.

skid 1 *v*. (of vehicle etc.) slide esp. sideways or obliquely on slippery road etc.; cause (vehicle) to skid. 2 *n*. act of skidding; braking device, esp. wooden or metal shoe, on wheel of vehicle; runner used as part of landing-gear of aircraft. 3 **skid-pan** slippery surface prepared for vehicle-drivers to practise control of skidding; **skid row** *US sl*. district frequented by vagrants.

skied[1] *past & p.p.* of **ski**.

skied[2] *past & p.p.* of **sky**.

skiff *n*. small light boat, esp. for rowing or sculling.

skilful /'skɪlfʊl/ *a*. having or showing skill.

skill *n*. practised ability, expertness, facility; craft or art etc. requiring skill.

skilled /skɪld/ *a*. skilful; properly trained or experienced; requiring skill and experience.

skillet /'skɪlɪt/ *n*. metal cooking utensil, usu. with feet and long handle; *US* frying-pan.

skim *v*. take scum or cream etc. from surface of (liquid); pass over surface or along etc. rapidly and lightly with close approach or very slight contact; read superficially. **skim milk** milk with cream removed.

skimp *v*. supply meagrely, use too little of; be parsimonious.

skimpy /'skɪmpɪ/ *a*. meagre, insufficient.

skin 1 *n*. flexible continuous covering of human or animal body; skin removed from animal, material made from this; complexion; outer layer or covering; container for liquid, made of animal's skin; ship's planking or plating. 2 *v*. strip skin from; cover or become covered (as) with skin; *sl*. swindle, fleece. 3 **skin-deep** merely superficial; **skin-diver** person who swims under water without diving-suit; **skin-diving** *n*.; **skinflint** miserly person; **skin-graft** surgical transplanting of skin, skin thus transferred; **skin-tight** very close-fitting.

skinful /'skɪnfʊl/ *n*. *colloq*. enough alcoholic liquor to make one drunk.

skinny /'skɪnɪ/ *a*. thin, emaciated.

skint *a*. *sl*. having no money.

skip[1] 1 *v*. move along lightly, esp. by taking two steps with each foot in turn; jump lightly from ground; spring or leap over rope revolved over head and under feet; shift quickly from one subject etc. to another; omit or make omissions in reading; *colloq*. not participate in; *colloq*. leave hurriedly. 2 *n*. skipping movement or action.

skip[2] *n*. large container for refuse etc.; cage or bucket etc. in which men or materials are lowered or raised in mines or quarries.

skipper /'skɪpə(r)/ 1 *n*. captain of ship or aircraft or team etc. 2 *v.t*. act as captain of.

skirl 1 *n*. shrill sound of bagpipes. 2 *v.i*. make skirl.

skirmish /'skɜ:mɪʃ/ 1 *n*. minor fight esp. between detached or outlying bodies of troops etc.; short argument. 2 *v.i*. engage in skirmish.

skirt 1 *n*. woman's outer garment hanging from waist, or this part of complete dress; part of coat etc. that hangs below waist; hanging part round base of hovercraft; border or outlying part; flank of beef etc. 2 *v*. go or be along or round edge or border of. 3 **skirting-board** narrow board round bottom of room-wall.

skit *n*. light piece of satire, burlesque.

skittish /ˈskɪtɪʃ/ a. lively; playful, (of horse etc.) nervous, inclined to shy.

skittle /ˈskɪt(ə)l/ n. pin used in game of **skittles**, in which number of wooden pins are set up to be bowled or knocked down.

skive v. sl. evade (a duty). **skive off** depart evasively.

skivvy /ˈskɪvɪ/ n. colloq. derog. female domestic servant.

skua /ˈskjuːə/ n. large predatory sea-bird.

skulduggery /skʌlˈdʌɡərɪ/ n. trickery, unscrupulous behaviour.

skulk v.i. lurk or conceal oneself or move stealthily, esp. in cowardly or sinister way, or to shirk duty.

skull n. bony case of brain; bony framework of head; representation of this; head as site of intelligence. **skull-cap** close-fitting brimless cap.

skunk n. black white-striped bushy-tailed Amer. animal, emitting powerful stench when attacked; sl. contemptible person.

sky /skaɪ/ 1 n. region of the atmosphere and outer space seen from the earth. 2 v.t. (past & p.p. **skied** /skaɪd/) hit (cricket-ball etc.) high into air. 3 **sky-blue** bright clear blue; **sky-diving** parachuting in which parachute is opened only at last safe moment; **skyjack** sl. hijack (aircraft); **skylark** lark that soars while singing, (v.i.) play tricks and practical jokes; **skylight** window in roof; **skyline** outline of hills or buildings etc. defined against sky; **sky-rocket** rocket exploding high in air, (v.i.) rise steeply; **skyscraper** very tall building.

Skye /skaɪ/ n. short-legged long-haired Scotch terrier.

slab n. flat broad thickish piece of solid material.

slack¹ 1 a. lacking firmness or tautness; lacking energy or activity; sluggish; negligent; (of tide etc.) neither ebbing nor flowing. 2 n. slack period; slack part of rope etc.; colloq. spell of inactivity; in pl. trousers for casual wear. 3 v. slacken; colloq. take a rest, be lazy. 4 **slack off** loosen, (cause to) lose vigour; **slack up** reduce speed.

slack² n. coal-dust.

slacken /ˈslækən/ v. make or become slack, slack off.

slacker /ˈslækə(r)/ n. shirker; idler.

slag n. refuse left after ore has been smelted etc. **slag-heap** hill of refuse from mine etc.

slain p.p. of **slay**.

slake v.t. assuage or satisfy (thirst etc.); cause (lime) to heat and crumble by action of water.

slalom /ˈslɑːləm/ n. downhill ski-race on zigzag course between artificial obstacles.

slam¹ 1 v. shut or throw or put down violently, with bang; sl. criticize severely. 2 n. sound or action of slamming.

slam² n. winning of all tricks at cards. **grand slam** winning of all 13 tricks in bridge, winning of all of group of championships in a sport.

slander /ˈslɑːndə(r)/ 1 n. false report maliciously uttered to person's injury. 2 v.t. utter slander about. 3 **slanderous** a.

slang 1 n. language in common informal use but not regarded as standard in a language; words or uses of them peculiar to profession or class etc. 2 v. use abusive language (to). 3 **slanging-match** prolonged exchange of abuse. 4 **slangy** /ˈslæŋɪ/ a.

slant 1 v. slope; be or put in oblique position; present (news etc.) in biased or unfair way. 2 n. slope, oblique position; point of view, esp. biased one. 3 a. sloping, oblique.

slantwise /ˈslɑːntwaɪz/ adv. aslant.

slap 1 v. strike (as) with palm of hand; lay forcibly; put hastily or carelessly. 2 n. slapping stroke or sound. 3 **slap-dash** hasty, careless; **slap-happy** colloq. cheerfully casual; **slapstick** boisterous knockabout comedy; **slap-up** sl. done regardless of expense.

slash 1 v. cut (at) with sweep of sharp weapon or implement; make gashes in, slit; lash with whip; reduce (prices etc.) drastically; criticize harshly. 2 n. slashing cut.

slat n. long narrow strip of wood or plastic etc., used in sets in Venetian blind or fence or bedstead etc.

slate 1 n. fine-grained grey rock easily split into thin smooth plates; trimmed plate of this used esp. in roofing or for writing on. 2 v.t. cover with slates; colloq. criticize severely; US make arrangements for (event etc.), nominate for office. **3 slaty** a.

slattern /'slætɜːn/ n. slovenly woman. **slatternly** a.

slaughter /'slɔːtə(r)/ **1** n. killing of animals for food; killing of many persons or animals at once. **2** v.t. kill thus. **3 slaughterhouse** place for slaughter of animals for food.

Slav /slɑːv/ **1** n. member of group of peoples of East & Central Europe speaking Slavonic languages.

slave 1 n. person who is owned by another and has to work for him; drudge, person working very hard; helpless victim *of* or *to* some dominating influence. **2** v.i. work very hard. **3 slave-driver** overseer of slaves at work, hard taskmaster; **slave-trade** procuring, transporting, and selling slaves, esp. African Blacks.

slaver[1] /'sleɪvə(r)/ n. ship or person engaged in slave-trade.

slaver[2] /'slævə(r)/ **1** n. saliva running from mouth. **2** v. let saliva run from mouth; drool.

slavery /'sleɪvərɪ/ n. condition or work of slave; drudgery; custom of having slaves.

slavish /'sleɪvɪʃ/ a. of or like slaves; without originality.

Slavonic /slə'vɒnɪk/ **1** a. of group of languages including Russian and Polish etc. **2** n. Slavonic group of languages.

slay v.t. (past **slew**; p.p. **slain**) kill.

sleazy /'sliːzɪ/ a. squalid; tawdry; slatternly.

sled n. & v.t. US sledge.

sledge 1 n. vehicle on runners instead of wheels for conveying loads or passengers esp. over snow. **2** v. travel or convey in sledge.

sledge-hammer n. large heavy hammer.

sleek 1 a. (of hair, skin, etc.) smooth and glossy; of well-fed comfortable appearance. **2** v.t. make sleek.

sleep 1 n. condition in which eyes are closed, muscles and nerves relaxed, and consciousness suspended; spell of this; inert condition of some hibernating animals. **2** v. (past & p.p. **slept**) be or fall asleep; spend the night *at* or *in*; provide sleeping accommodation for; have sexual intercourse *with* or *to-*

gether; be inactive or dead. **3 sleeping-bag** lined or padded bag to sleep in esp. when camping etc.; **sleeping-car**, **-carriage**, railway coach with beds or berths; **sleeping partner** partner not sharing in actual work of a firm; **sleeping-pill** pill to induce sleep; **sleep-walker** person who walks during sleep; **sleep-walking** n.

sleeper /'sliːpə(r)/ n. sleeping person; one of beams on which rails of railway etc. rest; sleeping car; ring worn in pierced ear to keep hole from closing.

sleepy /'sliːpɪ/ a. feeling need of sleep; lacking activity or bustle.

sleet 1 n. snow and rain together; snow or hail falling in half-melted state. **2** v.i. fall as sleet. **3 it sleets** sleet falls. **4 sleety** a.

sleeve n. part of garment covering arm; cover for gramophone record; tube enclosing another tube etc. **up one's sleeve** concealed but ready for use.

sleigh /sleɪ/ **1** n. sledge, esp. as passenger-vehicle drawn by horses. **2** v.i. travel in sleigh.

sleight /slaɪt/ n. **sleight-of-hand** conjuring, dexterity.

slender /'slendə(r)/ a. of small girth or breadth; slim; scanty, slight, meagre.

slept past & p.p. of **sleep**.

sleuth /sluːθ/ n. detective. **sleuth-hound** bloodhound.

slew[1] v. turn or swing *round* to new position. **2** n. such turn.

slew[2] past of **slay**.

slice 1 n. thin broad piece or wedge cut from something; cooking- or serving-implement with thin broad blade; *Golf* slicing stroke. **2** v. cut into slices, cut *off*; cut cleanly or easily; strike ball so that it deviates away from one.

slick 1 a. colloq. skilful or efficient; shrewd, wily; sleek, smooth. **2** n. patch or film of oil on water. **3** v.t. colloq. make smooth or sleek.

slide 1 v. (past & p.p. **slid**) (cause to) move along smooth surface touching it always with same part; move or go smoothly or quietly; pass gradually (*into* state or condition); glide over ice on foot without skates. **2** n. act of sliding; smooth slope down which persons or things can slide; track for sliding esp. on ice; part of machine or instrument that slides; mounted transparency viewed by means of projector etc.; piece of glass holding object for microscope. **3 let things slide** be negligent, allow deterioration; **slide-rule** ruler with sliding central piece, graduated logarithmically to allow ease in calculations; **sliding scale** scale of fees or taxes or wages etc. that varies as a whole according to changes in some standard.

slight /slaɪt/ 1 *a.* small, inconsiderable; not serious or important; inadequate; slender, slim. **2** *v.t.* treat with indifference or disrespect, disdain, ignore. **3** *n.* instance of slighting or being slighted.

slim 1 *a.* slender; not fat or overweight; clever, artful. **2** *v.* make or become slim, esp. by dieting etc.

slime *n.* oozy or sticky substance.

slimy /slaɪmɪ/ *a.* of or like or covered or smeared with slime; disgustingly obsequious.

sling[1] 1 *n.* strap etc. used to support or raise thing; bandage supporting injured arm; strap or string used to throw small missile. **2** *v.t.* (*past & p.p.* **slung**) hurl, throw; suspend with sling; arrange so as to be held or moved from above. **3 sling-back** shoe held in place by strap round back of heel; **sling one's hook** *sl.* make off.

sling[2] *n.* sweetened drink of spirit, esp. gin, with water.

slink *v.i.* (*past & p.p.* **slunk**) go in stealthy, guilty, or sneaking manner.

slinky /slɪŋkɪ/ *a.* slinking; (of garment) close-fitting and sinuous.

slip[1] 1 *v.* slide momentarily by accident; lose footing or balance thus; go with sliding motion; get away by being hard to grasp; make one's way quietly or unobserved; make casual mistake; fall below normal standard; place stealthily or casually; release from restraint or connection; put *on*, *off*, get *into*, etc. easily or casually. **2** *n.* act of slipping; accidental or slight error; loose covering or garment, petticoat; slope on which boats are landed or ships are built or repaired etc.; *Crick.* fielder behind wicket on off side, in *pl.* this part of field; finely ground clay mixed with water for coating or decorating earthenware. **3 give person the slip**

evade or escape from him; **slip-knot** knot that can be undone by pull, knot of running noose; **slip-on** (of shoes or clothes) that can be easily slipped on or off; **slip-over** (esp. sleeveless) pullover; **slipped disc** displaced vertebra; **slip-road** road for entering or leaving motorway etc.; **slip-stream** current of air or water driven backwards by propeller; **slipway** shipbuilding or landing slip.

slip[2] *n.* small piece of paper for making notes etc.; cutting from plant for grafting or planting.

slipper /slɪpə(r)/ *n.* light loose indoor shoe.

slippery /slɪpərɪ/ *a.* with smooth or polished or oily etc. surface making foothold etc. insecure or object etc. difficult to grasp or hold; elusive, unreliable, shifty.

slippy /slɪpɪ/ *a. colloq.* slippery.

slipshod /slɪpʃɒd/ *a.* slovenly, careless; having shoes down at heel.

slit 1 *n.* long narrow incision or opening. **2** *v.* (*past & p.p.* **slit**) make slit in; cut in strips.

slither /slɪðə(r)/ 1 *v.i.* slide or slip unsteadily. **2** *n.* act of slithering. **3 slithery** *a.*

sliver /slɪvə(r)/ 1 *n.* splinter; small narrow slice or piece. **2** *v.* cut or split into slivers.

slob *n. colloq.* large and coarse or stupid person.

slobber /slɒbə(r)/ 1 *v.* slaver, show excessive sentiment (*over*). **2** *n.* slaver. **3 slobbery** *a.*

sloe *n.* blackthorn; its small bluish-black fruit.

slog 1 *v.* hit hard and usu. unskilfully; work or walk doggedly. **2** *n.* heavy random hit; hard steady work; spell of this.

slogan /sləʊgən/ *n.* short catchy phrase used in advertising etc.; party cry, watchword.

sloop /sluːp/ *n.* small one-masted fore-and-aft rigged vessel.

slop 1 *v.* spill or flow over edge of vessel; allow to do this; spill or splash liquid on. **2** *n.* liquid spilled or splashed; in *pl.* dirty water or liquid, waste contents of kitchen vessels or chamber-pot etc.; in *sing.* or *pl.* unappetizing liquid food. **3 slop-basin** basin for receiving dregs of tea-cups.

slope 1 *n.* inclined position or direction or state; piece of rising or falling ground; difference in level between two ends or sides of a thing; place for skiing. **2** *v.* have or show slope; slant; cause to slope. **3 slope off** *sl.* go away, esp. to evade work etc.

sloppy /ˈslɒpɪ/ *a.* wet, watery, too liquid; unsystematic, careless; untidy, ill-fitting; weakly emotional.

slosh 1 *v.* splash or flounder (*about* etc.); *sl.* hit heavily; *colloq.* pour (liquid) clumsily; in *p.p. colloq.* drunk. **2** *n.* slush; sound or act of splashing; *sl.* heavy blow.

slot 1 *n.* slit or other aperture in machine etc. for something (esp. coin) to be inserted; allotted place in arrangement. **2** *v.t.* put or be placed (as if) into slot; provide with slot(s). **3 slot-machine** machine worked by insertion of coin, esp. delivering small purchased articles or providing amusement.

sloth /sləʊθ/ *n.* laziness, indolence; slow-moving arboreal mammal of tropical America.

slothful /ˈsləʊθfʊl/ *a.* indolent, lazy.

slouch /slaʊtʃ/ **1** *v.* stand or move or sit etc. in drooping or ungainly fashion. **2** *n.* slouching posture or movement; downward droop of hat-brim; *sl.* incompetent or slovenly worker. **3 slouch hat** soft hat with wide flexible brim.

slough¹ /slaʊ/ *n.* swamp, miry place. **Slough of Despond** state of hopeless depression.

slough² /slʌf/ **1** *n.* dead skin or other part of animal (esp. snake) cast off. **2** *v.* cast or drop off or *off* as slough.

sloven /ˈslʌv(ə)n/ *n.* person of careless or untidy or dirty habits.

slovenly /ˈslʌvənlɪ/ *a.* careless and untidy; unmethodical.

slow /sləʊ/ **1** *a.* taking relatively long time to do thing(s); acting or moving or done without speed; (of clock etc.) showing earlier than correct time; dull-witted, stupid; tedious; (of fire, oven, etc.) not very hot; reluctant *to do*. **2** *adv.* slowly. **3** *v.* (with *down, up*) (cause to) move or act or work less quickly or energetically. **4 slowcoach** slow or indolent person; **slow motion** speed of film in which actions appear

much slower than usual, simulation of this in real action.

slow-worm /ˈsləʊwɜːm/ *n.* small Eur. legless lizard.

sludge *n.* thick greasy mud; sewage; muddy or slushy sediment or deposit. **sludgy** *a.*

slue var. of **slew¹**.

slug¹ *n.* slimy shell-less gastropod; irregularly shaped bullet etc.; missile for airgun; line of type in Linotype printing; *US* tot of liquor.

slug² *US* hit hard.

sluggard /ˈslʌgəd/ *n.* lazy person.

sluggish /ˈslʌgɪʃ/ *a.* inert, slow-moving.

sluice /sluːs/ **1** *n.* (also **sluice-gate**) sliding gate or other contrivance for regulating flow or level of water; water regulated by this; (also **sluice-way**) artificial water-channel; place for rinsing. **2** *v.* provide or wash with sluice(s); rinse; pour water freely upon.

slum 1 *n.* dirty squalid overcrowded street or district etc. **2** *v.i.* live in slum-like conditions; visit slums esp. in search of amusement. **3 slummy** *a.*

slumber /ˈslʌmbə(r)/ *n.* & *v.i.* sleep. **slumb(e)rous** *a.*

slump 1 *n.* sudden severe or continued fall in prices and demand etc. **2** *v.i.* undergo slump; sit or fall down limply.

slung *past* & *p.p.* of **sling**.

slunk *past* & *p.p.* of **slink**.

slur 1 *v.* sound or write (words, musical notes, etc.) so that they run into one another; put slur upon (person, character); pass lightly or deceptively *over*. **2** *n.* imputation of wrongdoing, reproach; action of slurring; *Mus.* curved line over or under notes to be slurred.

slurp *colloq.* **1** *v.t.* eat or drink noisily. **2** *n.* sound of slurping.

slurry /ˈslʌrɪ/ *n.* thin sloppy cement or mud etc.

slush *n.* thawing snow; watery mud; silly sentiment. **slush fund** fund for illegal purposes, esp. bribery. **slushy** *a.*

slut *n.* slovenly woman, hussy. **sluttish** *a.*

sly *a.* crafty, wily; secretive; underhand; knowing, mischievous. **on the sly** secretly.

smack¹ *n.* sharp slap or blow; hard hit; sharp sound as of surface struck with palm of hand; loud kiss. **2** *v.* slap; move with smack. **3** *adv. colloq.* with a smack, suddenly, violently.

smack² 1 *v.i.* taste *of*, suggest presence *of*. **2** *n.* flavour or suggestion *of*.

smack³ *n.* single-masted sailing-boat.

smacker /'smækə(r)/ *n. sl.* loud kiss; *sl.* £1, *US* $1.

small /smɔːl/ **1** *a.* not large or big; comparatively little in size or importance or number etc.; doing thing on small scale; petty, mean, paltry. **2** *n. the* slenderest part (esp. *of* back); in *pl. colloq.* small articles of laundry, esp. underwear. **3** *adv.* into small pieces, on small scale, etc. **4 small arms** portable firearms; **small change** coins as opp. notes; **smallholding** piece of agricultural land smaller than farm; **small hours** night-time after midnight; **smallpox** acute contagious disease with fever and pustules usu. leaving permanent marks; **small print** matter printed small, esp. limitations in contract; **small talk** trivial social conversation; **small-time** unimportant, petty.

smarmy /'smɑːmɪ/ *a. colloq.* ingratiating.

smart 1 *a.* clever, ingenious, quick-witted; bright and fresh in appearance, neat; fashionable; stylish; conspicuous in society; quick, brisk; painfully severe, sharp, vigorous. **2** *v.i.* feel or give acute pain or distress; rankle. **3** *n.* bodily or mental sharp pain, stinging sensation.

smarten /'smɑːt(ə)n/ *v.* make or become smart (usu. with *up*).

smash 1 *v.* break to pieces; bring or come to disaster; utterly defeat; bring or drive violently *down, into,* etc.; *Tennis* hit (ball) hard downwards over net. **2** *n.* act or sound of smashing; very successful play or song etc. **3** *adv.* with smash. **4 smash-and-grab** *colloq.* (of robbery) with goods snatched from broken shop-window etc.

smashing /'smæʃɪŋ/ *a. sl.* very fine, wonderful.

smattering /'smætərɪŋ/ *n.* slight knowledge (*of*).

smear /smɪə(r)/ **1** *v.* daub with greasy or sticky substance; smudge; (seek to) discredit or defame. **2** *n.* action or result of smearing; material smeared on microscope slide etc. for examination;

specimen of this; discrediting or defaming; attempt at this. **3** *smeary a.*

smell 1 *n.* sense by which odours are perceived, property perceived by this; unpleasant odour; act of inhaling to ascertain smell. **2** *v.* (past & p.p. **smelt** or **smelled**) perceive or detect by smell; emit smell; be redolent *of;* stink; have or use sense of smell. **3 smelling-salts** sharp-smelling substances to be sniffed to relieve faintness.

smelly /'smelɪ/ *a.* evil-smelling, stinking.

smelt¹ *v.t.* fuse or melt (ore) to extract metal; obtain (metal) thus.

smelt² *n.* small edible fish with tender oily flesh.

smelt³ *past & p.p.* of **smell**.

smilax /'smaɪlæks/ *n.* a climbing plant.

smile 1 *v.* make or have facial expression of amusement or pleasure, usu. with parting of lips and upward turning of their ends; express by smiling; give (smile); be propitious. **2** *n.* act of smiling; smiling expression or aspect.

smirch /smɜːtʃ/ *v.t. & n.* stain, smear.

smirk 1 *n.* silly or conceited smile. **2** *v.i.* give smirk.

smite *v.* (past **smote;** p.p. **smitten**) *arch.* strike, hit, chastise; defeat; seize *with* disease or emotion etc.

smith /smɪθ/ *n.* worker in metal; blacksmith; *fig.* person who creates specified thing.

smithereens /smɪðə'riːnz/ *n.pl. colloq.* small fragments.

smithy /'smɪðɪ/ *n.* blacksmith's workshop, forge.

smitten *p.p.* of **smite**.

smock 1 *n.* loose-fitting short shirtlike outer garment, freq. with gathers or smocking at yoke. **2** *v.t.* adorn with smocking.

smocking /'smɒkɪŋ/ *n.* ornamentation on cloth made by gathering it tightly with stitches.

smog *n.* dense smoky fog. **smoggy** *a.*

smoke 1 *n.* visible vapour from burning substance; *colloq.* spell of smoking tobacco etc.; *sl.* cigar, cigarette. **2** *v.* emit smoke or visible vapour; inhale and exhale smoke of (tobacco etc.); do this habitually; darken or preserve by action of smoke. **3 smoke-bomb** bomb emitting dense smoke on bursting; **smoke out** drive out by means of smoke, drive out of hiding etc.; **smoke-screen** cloud of smoke to conceal military or naval operations etc., device for disguising activities; **smoke-stack** funnel of locomotive or steamship.

smoker /ˈsməʊkə(r)/ n. person who smokes tobacco habitually; part of railway coach where smoking is permitted.

smoky /ˈsməʊkɪ/ a. producing or emitting much smoke; covered or filled with smoke; obscured (as) with smoke; suggestive of or having the colour of smoke.

smooth /smuːð/ 1 a. having even surface; free from projections and roughness; (of progress, passage, etc.) not interrupted or disturbed by obstacles or storms etc.; conciliatory or plausible or flattering. 2 v. make or become smooth; get rid of impediments etc. from. 3 n. smoothing touch or stroke. 4 **smooth-tongued** insincerely flattering.

smorgasbord /ˈsmɔːgəsbɔːd/ n. Swedish hors-d'œuvres; buffet meal with variety of dishes.

smote past of **smite**.

smother /ˈsmʌðə(r)/ 1 v.t. suffocate, stifle; overwhelm with kisses or gifts etc.; cover entirely with or with; extinguish (fire) by heaping with ashes etc.; have difficulty in breathing; suppress or conceal. 2 n. cloud of smoke or dust etc.; obscurity caused by this.

smoulder /ˈsməʊldə(r)/ 1 v.i. burn and smoke without flame (freq. fig.). 2 n. such burning.

smudge 1 n. dirty mark or blur or smear. 2 v. make smudge on or with; become blurred or smeared. 3 **smudgy** a.

smug a. complacent, self-satisfied; consciously respectable.

smuggle /ˈsmʌg(ə)l/ v. import or export (goods) illegally, esp. without paying customs duties; convey secretly in or out etc.

smut 1 n. small piece of soot; spot or smudge made by this; obscene talk or pictures or stories; cereal-disease turning parts of plant to black powder. 2 v. mark or infect with smut(s); contract smut disease. 3 **smutty** a.

snack n. slight or casual or hasty meal.

snack-bar place where snacks are sold.

snaffle /ˈsnæf(ə)l/ n. simple bridle-bit without curb. 2 v.t. put snaffle on; sl. take, steal.

snag 1 n. hidden or unexpected obstacle or drawback; jagged projecting stump or point; tear in material caused by snag. 2 v.t. catch or tear on snag.

snail n. slow-moving mollusc with spiral shell.

snake 1 n. long limbless reptile; treacherous or ungrateful person. 2 v. move or twist etc. like a snake. 3 **snake in the grass** secret enemy; **snakes and ladders** game with counters moved along board, with sudden advances and reverses.

snaky /ˈsneɪkɪ/ a. of or like a snake; sinuous; treacherous.

snap 1 v. break sharply; (cause to) emit sudden sharp sound; open or close with snapping sound; speak with sudden irritation; make sudden audible bite; move quickly; take snapshot of. 2 n. act or sound of snapping; catch that fastens with a snap; small crisp biscuit; snapshot; sudden brief spell of cold weather; card-game in which players call 'snap' when two cards of equal rank are exposed. 3 adv. with snapping sound. 4 a. taken or made suddenly or without notice or warning or preparation etc. 5 **snapdragon** plant with flowers that can be made to gape; **snap fastener** press-stud; **snap one's fingers at** defy; **snap out of** sl. get out of (mood) by sudden effort; **snapshot** photograph taken informally or casually; **snap up** buy hastily or eagerly.

snapper /ˈsnæpə(r)/ n. kind of food-fish.

snappish /ˈsnæpɪʃ/ a. peevish, irritable, petulant.

snappy /ˈsnæpɪ/ a. colloq. brisk; full of zest; neat and elegant.

snare /sneə(r)/ 1 n. trap, esp. with noose, for catching birds or animals; thing that tempts one to risk capture or defeat etc.; arrangement of twisted gut or wire etc. stretched across lower head of side-drum to produce buzzing sound. 2 v.t. catch in snare, ensnare. 3 **snare-drum** side-drum with snare.

snarl¹ 1 v. make angry growl with

bared teeth; speak irritably or cynically. **2** *n.* act or sound of snarling.

snarl² **1** *v.* (often with *up*) tangle, confuse and hamper movement of (traffic etc.). **2** *n.* tangle.

snatch **1** *v.* seize quickly or eagerly or unexpectedly; take suddenly *away*, *from*, etc. **2** *n.* act of snatching; fragment of song or talk etc.; short spell of activity etc.

snazzy /'snæzɪ/ *a. sl.* smart, attractive, excellent.

sneak **1** *v.* go or take furtively; *sl.* carry off unobserved; *sl.* tell tales. **2** *n.* mean-spirited or underhand person; tell-tale. **3** *a.* acting or done without warning, secret. **4 sneak-thief** person who steals what is in reach without breaking into buildings, petty thief.

sneakers /'sni:kəz/ *n.pl. sl.* soft-soled shoes.

sneaking /'sni:kɪŋ/ *a.* (of feeling, suspicion, etc.) unavowed, persistent and puzzling.

sneer **1** *n.* derisive smile or remark. **2** *v.* make sneer (*at*); utter sneeringly.

sneeze **1** *n.* sudden involuntary explosive expulsion of air from irritated nostrils. **2** *v.i.* make sneeze. **3 not to be sneezed at** not contemptible, worth having.

snick **1** *v.t.* make slight notch or cut in; *Crick.* deflect (ball) slightly with bat. **2** *n.* such notch or deflection.

snicker *v.i. & n.* snigger.

snide *a. colloq.* sneering, slyly derogatory; counterfeit.

sniff **1** *v.* draw up air audibly through nose; smell scent of, draw (*up*), take (*in*), etc., by sniffing. **2** *n.* act or sound of sniffing. **3 sniff at** show contempt for or disapproval of.

sniffle /'snɪf(ə)l/ **1** *v.i.* sniff repeatedly or slightly. **2** *n.* act of sniffling; in *pl.* cold in the head causing sniffling.

snifter /'snɪftə(r)/ *n. sl.* small drink of alcoholic liquor.

snigger /'snɪgə(r)/ **1** *n.* half-suppressed laugh. **2** *v.i.* utter snigger.

snip **1** *v.* cut with scissors etc., esp. in small quick strokes. **2** *n.* act of snipping; piece snipped off; *sl.* something cheaply acquired or easily done.

snipe **1** *n.* wading bird with long straight bill. **2** *v.* fire shots from hiding usu. at long range; *fig.* make sly critical attack *at*.

snippet /'snɪpɪt/ *n.* small piece cut off; (usu. in *pl.*) scrap or fragment of information or knowledge etc.

snitch *v. sl.* steal.

snivel /'snɪv(ə)l/ *v.i.* (*past* & *p.p.* **snivelled**) sniffle; be tearful; show maudlin emotion. **2** *n.* act of snivelling.

snob *n.* person with exaggerated respect for social position or wealth or who despises people with inferior rank or tastes etc. **snobbery** *n.*; **snobbish** *a.*

snood /snu:d/ *n.* loose net worn by woman to keep hair in place.

snook /snu:k/ *n. colloq.* contemptuous gesture with thumb to nose and fingers spread. **cock a snook at** make this gesture, show contempt for.

snooker /'snu:kə(r)/ **1** *n.* game played with 15 red and 6 other coloured balls on billiard-table; position in this game where direct shot would lose points. **2** *v.t.* subject (player) to snooker; *sl.* (esp. in *p.p.*) thwart, defeat.

snoop /snu:p/ *colloq.* **1** *v.i.* pry into another's private affairs; sneak *about* or *around* looking for infringements of rules etc. **2** *n.* act of snooping.

snooty /'snu:tɪ/ *a. sl.* supercilious, snobbish.

snooze /snu:z/ **1** *n.* short sleep, esp. in daytime. **2** *v.i.* take snooze.

snore **1** *n.* snorting or grunting sound in breathing during sleep. **2** *v.i.* make such sounds.

snorkel /'snɔ:k(ə)l/ **1** *n.* device for supplying air to underwater swimmer or submerged submarine. **2** *v.i.* (*past* & *p.p.* **snorkelled**) swim with snorkel.

snort **1** *n.* loud or harsh sound made by driving breath violently through nose, usu. expr. indignation or incredulity etc.; noise resembling this; *colloq.* small drink of liquor. **2** *v.* make snorting sound; express or utter with snorts.

snorter /'snɔ:tə(r)/ *n. sl.* something notably vigorous or difficult etc.

snot *n. vulg.* nasal mucus.

snotty /'snɒtɪ/ *a. sl.* running or foul with nasal mucus; *colloq.* contemptible, bad-tempered; supercilious.

snout /snaʊt/ *n.* projecting nose (and mouth) of animal; *derog.* person's nose; pointed front of thing.

snow /snəʊ/ **1** *n.* frozen vapour falling

to earth in light white flakes; fall of this, layer of it on ground; anything resembling snow in whiteness or texture etc.; *sl.* cocaine. **2** *v.i.* fall as or like snow; come in large numbers or quantities. **3 it snows** snow falls; **snowball** snow pressed or rolled into ball, esp. for use as missile, (*v.*) pelt with or throw snowballs, increase rapidly; **snow-blind** temporarily blinded by glare of sun on snow; **snow-bound** prevented by snow from going out; **snowdrift** bank of snow piled up by wind; **snowdrop** spring-flowering plant with white drooping flowers; **snowed in** snow-bound; **snowed under** covered with snow, overwhelmed with numbers etc.; **snowed up** snow-bound; **snowflake** each of the small collections of crystals in which snow falls; **snow goose** arctic white goose; **snow-line** level above which snow never melts entirely; **snowman** figure made of snow; **snow-plough** device for clearing road or railway of snow; **snow-shoe** one of pair of light racket-shaped strung frames enabling wearer to walk on surface of snow; **snow-storm** heavy fall of snow esp. with wind; **snow-white** pure white. **4 snowy** *a.*

SNP *abbr.* Scottish National Party.

Snr. *abbr.* Senior.

snub 1 *v.t.* rebuff, humiliate, in sharp or cutting manner. **2** *n.* snubbing, rebuff. **3** *a.* (of nose) short and turned up.

snuff¹ **1** *v.* remove snuff from (candle). **2** *n.* charred part of candle-wick. **3 snuff it** *sl.* die; **snuff out** extinguish (candle) by covering or pinching flame, kill or put an end to (hopes etc.), *sl.* die.

snuff² **1** *n.* powdered tobacco or medicine taken by sniffing it up nostrils. **2** *v.* take snuff; sniff.

snuffle /ˈsnʌf(ə)l/ *v.* sniff, esp. audibly or noisily; speak like person with a cold. **2** *n.* snuffling sound or speech.

snug 1 *a.* sheltered, well enclosed; closely fitting; comfortable; (of income etc.) sufficing for comfort. **2** *n.* bar-parlour of inn.

snuggle /ˈsnʌg(ə)l/ *v.* move or lie close *up to* for warmth etc.

so¹ /səʊ/ *adv.* & *conj.* in this or that way, in the manner or position or state de-scribed or implied, to that extent; to a great or notable degree; consequently, therefore; indeed, in actual fact; also. **so-and-so** particular person or thing not needing to be specified, *colloq.* unpleasant or contemptible person; **so-called** called or named thus (but perhaps wrongly or inaccurately); **so long** *colloq.* goodbye; **so long as** provided that; **so-so** *colloq.* only moderately well or good.

so² var. of **soh**.

soak 1 *v.* make or become thoroughly wet through saturation with or in liquid; (of rain etc.) drench; take (liquid) *in* or *up*; drink heavily; *sl.* extort money from. **2** *n.* soaking, *colloq.* hard drinker. **3 soak-away** arrangement for disposal of waste water by percolation through soil.

soap 1 *n.* cleansing substance yielding lather when rubbed in water. **2** *v.t.* apply soap to; rub with soap. **3 soap-box** makeshift stand for street orator; **soap opera** sentimental domestic broadcast serial; **soap powder** preparation of soap usu. with additives, for washing clothes etc.; **soapstone** steatite; **soap-suds** froth of soapy water in water.

soapy /ˈsəʊpɪ/ *a.* of or like soap; containing or smeared with soap; unctuous, flattering.

soar /sɔ:(r)/ *v.i.* fly or rise high; reach high level or standard; fly without flapping of wings or use of motor power.

sob 1 *v.* draw breath in convulsive gasps usu. with weeping; utter with sobs. **2** *n.* act or sound of sobbing. **3 sob-story** *colloq.* narrative meant to evoke sympathy; **sob-stuff** *colloq.* pathos, sentimental writing or behaviour.

sober /ˈsəʊbə(r)/ **1** *a.* not drunk; not given to drink; moderate, sane, tranquil; (of colour) quiet. **2** *v.* (often with *down* or *up*) make or become sober.

sobriety /səˈbraɪətɪ/ *n.* soberness.

sobriquet /ˈsəʊbrɪkeɪ/ *n.* nickname.

Soc. *abbr.* Socialist; Society.

soccer /ˈsɒkə(r)/ *n. colloq.* Association football.

sociable /ˈsəʊʃəb(ə)l/ *a.* fitted for or liking society of other people; friendly. **sociability** *n.*

social /ˈsəʊʃ(ə)l/ **1** *a.* of society or its organization; concerned with mutual relations of (classes of) human beings; living in communities; gregarious; unfitted for solitary life. **2** *n.* social gathering. **3 social science** scientific study of human society and social relationships; **social security** State assistance to those lacking adequate money or welfare; **social services** welfare services such as education, health, housing, pensions, etc., provided by the State; **social worker** person working, esp. for local authority, to alleviate social problems.

socialism /'səʊʃəlɪz(ə)m/ *n.* political and economic principle that community as whole should have ownership and control of all means of production and distribution; policy or practice based on this theory. **socialist** *n.*; **socialistic** *a.*

socialite /'səʊʃəlaɪt/ *n.* person prominent in fashionable society.

socialize /'səʊʃəlaɪz/ *v.* behave sociably; make social; organize in socialistic manner.

society /sə'saɪətɪ/ *n.* organized and interdependent community, the system and organization of living in this; distinguished or fashionable members of a community, the upper classes; mixing with other people, companionship, company; association of persons sharing common aim or interest etc.

sociology /səʊsɪ'ɒlədʒɪ/ *n.* study of society and social problems. **sociological** *a.*; **sociologist** *n.*

sock[1] *n.* short stocking usu. not reaching knee; insole.

sock[2] *sl.* **1** *v.t.* hit hard. **2** *n.* hard blow. **3 sock it to** attack or address vigorously.

socket /'sɒkɪt/ *n.* natural or artificial hollow for thing to fit into etc.; hollow or cavity holding eye or tooth etc.; device receiving electrical plug or lightbulb etc., to make connection.

Socratic /sə'krætɪk/ *a.* of the ancient-Gk philosopher Socrates or his philosophy.

sod[1] *n.* turf, piece of turf; surface of ground.

sod[2] *vulg.* **1** *n.* unpleasant or despised person. **2** *v.* damn.

soda /'səʊdə/ *n.* compound of sodium in common use; soda-water. **soda-fountain** device supplying soda-water, shop serving ice-cream and soft drinks

etc.; **soda-water** water made effervescent with carbon dioxide and used as drink alone or with spirits etc.

sodden /'sɒd(ə)n/ *a.* saturated with liquid; soaked through; rendered stupid or dull etc. with drunkenness.

sodium /'səʊdɪəm/ *n.* soft silver-white metallic element. **sodium lamp** lamp giving yellow light from electrical discharge in sodium vapour.

sodomite /'sɒdəmaɪt/ *n.* person practising sodomy.

sodomy /'sɒdəmɪ/ *n.* unnatural sexual act, esp. between males.

sofa /'səʊfə/ *n.* long seat with raised ends and back.

soffit /'sɒfɪt/ *n.* under-surface of arch or lintel etc.

soft **1** *a.* not hard; yielding to pressure; malleable, plastic, easily cut; smooth or fine textured; mild; (of water) not containing mineral salts which prevent lathering; not loud or strident; not sharply defined; gentle, conciliatory; compassionate, sympathetic; feeble, effeminate; silly; *sl.* easy; (of drug) not likely to cause addiction. **2** *adv.* softly. **3 soft drink** non-alcoholic drink; **soft fruit** highly perishable fruit, esp. small berries etc.; **soft furnishings** curtains and rugs etc.; **soft-hearted** easily affected by others' pain or grief etc.; **soft option** easier alternative; **soft palate** back part of palate; **soft pedal** pedal on piano making tone softer; **soft-pedal** refrain from emphasizing; **soft sell** restrained salesmanship; **soft soap** liquid soap, *fig.* flattery; **soft spot** sentimental affection *for*; **soft touch** *sl.* person readily parting with money; **software** programs etc. for computer; **softwood** wood of coniferous tree.

soften /'sɒf(ə)n/ *v.* make or become soft(er). **soften up** reduce strength or resistance etc. of.

softie /'sɒftɪ/ *n. colloq.* weak or silly person.

soggy /'sɒgɪ/ *a.* sodden, waterlogged.

soh *n. Mus.* fifth note of scale in tonic sol-fa.

soil[1] *n.* upper layer of earth, in which plants grow; the ground.

soil[2] **1** *v.* smear or stain with dirt etc.; defile; bring discredit to. **2** *n.* dirty mark; filth, refuse matter. **3 soil-pipe** discharge-pipe of water-closet.

soirée /'swɑːreɪ/ n. evening party.

sojourn /'sɒdʒɜːn/ 1 n. temporary stay. 2 v.i. make sojourn.

sola n. pithy-stemmed E. Ind. swamp plant. **sola topi** sun-helmet made from pith of this.

solace /'sɒlɪs/ 1 n. comfort in distress or disappointment. 2 v.t. give solace to.

solan /'səʊlən/ n. large gooselike gannet.

solar /'səʊlə(r)/ a. of or reckoned by sun. **solar battery, cell,** device converting solar radiation into electricity; **solar plexus** complex of radiating nerves at pit of stomach; **solar system** sun and the heavenly bodies whose motion is governed by it.

solarium /sə'leərɪəm/ n. (pl. -ria) place for enjoyment or medical use of sunshine.

sold past & p.p. of **sell**.

solder /'səʊldə(r)/ 1 n. fusible alloy used for joining less fusible metals or wires etc. 2 v.t. join with solder. 3 **soldering-iron** tool for melting and applying solder.

soldier /'səʊldʒə(r)/ 1 n. member of army, esp. private or NCO; man of military skill and experience. 2 v.i. serve as soldier. 3 **soldier on** colloq. persevere doggedly. 4 **soldierly** a.

soldiery /'səʊldʒərɪ/ n. soldiers collectively.

sole¹ 1 n. under-surface of foot; part of shoe or stocking below foot, esp. part other than heel; lower surface or base of plough or golf-club head etc. 2 v.t. provide with sole.

sole² n. flat-fish used as food.

sole³ a. one and only; single; exclusive.

solecism /'sɒlɪsɪz(ə)m/ n. offence against grammar or idiom or etiquette etc.

solemn /'sɒləm/ a. serious and dignified; formal; accompanied by ceremony; impressive; pompous. **solemnity** /-'lem-/ n.

solemnize /'sɒləmnaɪz/ v.t. duly perform (esp. marriage ceremony); make solemn. **solemnization** n.

solenoid /'səʊlɪnɔɪd/ n. Electr. cylindrical coil of wire acting as magnet when carrying electric current.

sol-fa /'sɒl'fɑː/ n. Mus. system of syllables representing musical notes.

solicit /sə'lɪsɪt/ v.t. ask repeatedly or earnestly for or seek or invite; (of prostitute) accost (man) for immoral purpose. **solicitation** n.

solicitor /sə'lɪsɪtə(r)/ n. member of legal profession qualified to advise clients and instruct barristers.

solicitous /sə'lɪsɪtəs/ a. troubled, concerned; anxious, eager (to do).

solicitude /sə'lɪsɪtjuːd/ n. being solicitous, anxiety, concern.

solid /'sɒlɪd/ 1 a. of stable shape, not liquid or fluid; of solid substance throughout, not hollow etc.; alike all through; rigid, hard and compact; of three dimensions; concerned with solids; sound and reliable; unanimous. 2 n. solid substance or body; in pl. solid food. 3 **solid-state** using electronic properties of solids to replace those of valves. 4 **solidity** n.

solidarity /sɒlɪ'dærɪtɪ/ n. unity, agreement of feelings and action, community of interests, mutual dependence.

solidify /sə'lɪdɪfaɪ/ v. make or become solid.

soliloquy /sə'lɪləkwɪ/ n. talking to oneself or without addressing any person; period of this. **soliloquize** v.i.

solipsism /'sɒlɪpsɪz(ə)m/ n. view that self is all that exists or can be known.

solitaire /'sɒlɪteə(r)/ n. jewel set by itself; game played on special board by one person who removes objects one at a time by jumping others over them; card-game for one person.

solitary /'sɒlɪtərɪ/ a. alone, living alone; without companions; single; secluded, lonely. 2 n. recluse; sl. solitary confinement. 3 **solitary confinement** isolation of prisoner in separate cell.

solitude /'sɒlɪtjuːd/ n. being solitary, solitary place.

solo /'səʊləʊ/ 1 n. (pl. -los) piece of music performed by one person with or without subordinate accompaniment; performance by one person; flight by unaccompanied pilot in aircraft; solo whist. 2 a. & adv. performed as solo, unaccompanied, alone. 3 **solo whist** card-game like whist in which one player may oppose the others.

soloist /'səʊləʊɪst/ n. performer of solo.

solstice /'sɒlstɪs/ n. either of two times (**summer, winter, solstice**) when sun is farthest from equator.

soluble /'sɒljʊb(ə)l/ a. that can be dissolved or solved. **solubility** n.

solution /sə'lu:ʃ(ə)n/ n. solving or means of solving a problem or difficulty; conversion of solid or gas into liquid form by mixture with liquid; state or substance resulting from this; dissolving or being dissolved.

solve v.t. explain, resolve; find answer to.

solvency /'sɒlvənsı/ n. being financially solvent.

solvent /'sɒlv(ə)nt/ 1 a. that dissolves or can dissolve; able to pay all debts or liabilities. 2 n. liquid capable of or used for dissolving something.

somatic /sə'mætık/ a. of the body, not of the mind.

sombre /'sɒmbə(r)/ a. dark, gloomy, dismal.

sombrero /sɒm'breərəʊ/ n. (-ros) broad-brimmed hat worn esp. in Latin American countries.

some /sʌm/ 1 a. an unspecified amount or number of; an unknown or unnamed; approximately so many or so much of; a considerable amount or number of; at least a small amount of; such to a certain extent; sl. notably such; 2 pron. some people or things; some number or amount. 3 adv. colloq. to some extent. 4 **somebody** some person, important person; **somehow** in some indefinite or unspecified way, by some means or other; **someone** somebody; **something** some thing esp. unspecified or unknown or unimportant or forgotten, a quantity or quality expressed or understood, important or notable person or thing; **sometime** former(ly); **sometimes** at some times; **somewhat** to some extent; **somewhere** in or to some place.

somersault /'sʌməsɔːlt/ 1 n. leap or roll in which one turns head over heels. 2 v.i. perform somersault.

somnambulism /sɒm'næmbjʊlɪz(ə)m/ n. sleep-walking. **somnambulant** a.; **somnambulist** n.

somnolent /'sɒmnələnt/ a. sleepy, drowsy; inducing drowsiness. **somnolence** n.

son /sʌn/ n. male child in relation to his parents; male descendant; male member of family etc.; product, native,

follower. **son-in-law** daughter's husband.

sonar /'səʊnɑː(r)/ n. system of detecting objects under water by reflection of sonic and ultrasonic waves; apparatus for this.

sonata /sə'nɑːtə/ n. musical composition for one or two instruments in several related movements.

song n. singing, vocal music; piece of music or set of words for singing; poem. **for a song** very cheaply; **songbird** bird with musical song; **song thrush** common thrush.

songster /'sɒŋstə(r)/ n. singer; songbird. **songstress** n.

sonic /'sɒnık/ a. of or involving sound or sound-waves. **sonic bang, boom**, noise made when aircraft passes speed of sound.

sonnet /'sɒnıt/ n. poem of 14 lines arranged in one of certain definite rhyme-schemes.

sonny /'sʌnı/ n. familiar form of address to young boy.

sonorous /'sɒnərəs/ a. having a loud or full or deep sound; (of speech etc.) imposing. **sonority** /-'nɒr-/ n.

soon /su:n/ adv. not long after present or time in question; early; readily, willingly. **sooner or later** at some future time.

soot /sʊt/ 1 n. black powdery substance rising in smoke and deposited by it on surfaces. 2 v.t. cover with soot.

soothe /su:ð/ v.t. calm, tranquillize; reduce force or intensity of.

soothsayer /'su:θseıə(r)/ n. person who foretells future events.

sooty /'sʊtı/ a. of or like or as black as or black with soot.

sop 1 n. piece of bread etc. dipped in liquid before eating or cooking; something given to pacify or bribe. 2 v. soak (up).

sophism /'sɒfız(ə)m/ n. false argument, esp. one meant to deceive.

sophist /'sɒfıst/ n. captious or fallacious reasoner. **sophistic(al)** a.

sophisticate 1 /sə'fıstıkeıt/ v.t. (esp. in p.p.) make (person etc.) worldly-wise or cultured or refined; make (equipment, technique) highly developed or complex. 2 /sə'fıstıkət/ n. sophisticated person. 3 **sophistication** n.

sophistry /ˈsɒfɪstrɪ/ n. use of soph-isms; a sophism.

sophomore /ˈsɒfəmɔː(r)/ n. US second-year university or high-school student.

soporific /sɒpəˈrɪfɪk/ 1 a. tending to produce sleep. 2 n. soporific drug or in-fluence. 3 **soporifically** adv.

sopping /ˈsɒpɪŋ/ a. drenched.

soppy /ˈsɒpɪ/ a. soaked, wet; colloq. mawkish, foolishly sentimental.

soprano /səˈprɑːnəʊ/ n. (pl. **-nos**) high-est singing voice of women or boys; singer with soprano voice; music for so-prano voice.

sorbet /ˈsɔːbeɪ/ n. water-ice; sherbet.

sorcerer /ˈsɔːsərə(r)/ n. magician, wiz-ard. **sorceress** n.; **sorcery** n.

sordid /ˈsɔːdɪd/ a. dirty, squalid; ignoble, mercenary.

sore 1 a. painful from injury or disease; suffering pain, aggrieved, vexed (at); arousing painful feelings, irritating. 2 n. sore place or subject etc. 3 adv. arch. grievously, severely.

sorely /ˈsɔːlɪ/ adv. very much, severely.

sorghum /ˈsɔːgəm/ n. tropical cereal grass.

sorority /səˈrɒrɪtɪ/ n. devotional sis-terhood; US women's college or uni-versity society.

sorrel¹ /ˈsɒr(ə)l/ n. sour-leaved herb.

sorrel² /ˈsɒr(ə)l/ 1 a. of light reddish-brown colour. 2 n. this colour; sorrel animal, esp. horse.

sorrow /ˈsɒrəʊ/ 1 n. mental distress caused by loss or disappointment etc.; thing causing sorrow. 2 v.i. feel sorrow; mourn. 3 **sorrowful** a.

sorry /ˈsɒrɪ/ a. pained at or regretful over something; feeling pity (for); wret-ched, paltry, of poor quality.

sort 1 n. kind, variety; colloq. person of specified sort. 2 v.t. arrange according to sort. 3 **of sorts** colloq. of not very satisfactory kind; **out of sorts** slightly unwell, in low spirits; **sort out** sepa-rate into sorts, select from mis-cellaneous group, disentangle, put into order, solve, sl. deal with or punish.

sortie /ˈsɔːtiː/ n. sally, esp. from be-sieged garrison; operational flight by military aircraft.

SOS n. international code-signal of ex-treme distress; colloq. urgent appeal for help.

sot n. habitual drunkard. **sottish** a.

sotto voce /ˈsɒtəʊ ˈvəʊtʃeɪ/ in an undertone. [It.]

sou /suː/ n. former French coin of low value; colloq. very small amount of money.

soubrette /suːˈbret/ n. pert maid-servant etc. in comedy; actress taking such part.

soubriquet var. of **sobriquet**.

soufflé /ˈsuːfleɪ/ n. light spongy dish made with stiffly-beaten egg-white.

sough /saf or saʊ/ 1 n. moaning or whispering sound, as of wind in trees. 2 v.i. make this sound.

sought /sɔːt/ past & p.p. of **seek**. **sought-after** much in demand.

souk /suːk/ n. market-place in Muslim countries.

soul /səʊl/ n. spiritual or immaterial part of man; moral or emotional or in-tellectual nature of person or animal; personification or pattern of; an in-dividual; animating or essential part; emotional or intellectual energy or in-tensity; Black American culture or mu-sic etc. **soul-destroying** deadeningly monotonous etc.; **soul mate** person ideally suited to another; **soul-searching** examining one's conscience.

soulful /ˈsəʊlfʊl/ a. having or ex-pressing or evoking deep feeling.

soulless /ˈsəʊllɪs/ a. lacking sensitivity or noble qualities; undistinguished, uninteresting.

sound¹ /saʊnd/ 1 n. sensation pro-duced in organs of hearing when sur-rounding air etc. vibrates; vibrations causing this; what is or may be heard. 2 v. (cause to) emit sound; utter, pro-nounce; convey specified impression; give audible signal for; test condition of by noting sound produced. 3 **sound-barrier** high resistance of air to ob-jects moving at speeds near that of sound; **sound-effect** sound other than speech or music produced artificially for film or broadcast etc.; **sounding-board** canopy projecting sound towards audience; **sound off** colloq. talk loudly, express one's opinions forcefully; **soundproof** impervious to sound, (v.t.) make soundproof; **sound-**

track strip on side of cinema film or videotape for recording sound, the sound itself; **sound wave** wave of condensation and rarefaction by which sound is transmitted in air etc.

sound² /saʊnd/ a. healthy, free from disease or defects or corruption; correct, orthodox, valid; financially secure; (of sleep) unbroken; thorough. **2** adv. soundly, fast asleep.

sound³ /saʊnd/ v.t. test depth or quality of bottom of water, esp. with line and lead etc.; (also with out) inquire into views etc. of (person) esp. in cautious or indirect manner.

sound⁴ /saʊnd/ n. strait (of water).

sounding n. measurement of depth of water; in pl. region near enough to shore to allow sounding.

soup /suːp/ **1** n. liquid food made by stewing bones and vegetables etc. **2** v.t. (usu. with up) colloq. increase power of (engine, car, etc.). **3 in the soup** sl. in difficulties, in trouble; **soup-kitchen** establishment supplying free soup etc. to the poor in times of distress. **4 soupy** a.

soupçon /ˈsuːpsɔ̃/ n. dash or trace (of).

sour /saʊə(r)/ **1** a. having acid taste or smell (as) from unripeness or fermentation; peevish, morose; (of soil) cold and wet. **2** v. make or become sour. **3 sour grapes** said when person disparages what he desires but cannot attain; **sourpuss** sl. bad-tempered person.

source /sɔːs/ n. place from which thing comes or is got; person or book etc. providing information; place from which river or stream issues. **at source** at point of origin or issue.

souse /saʊs/ **1** v. immerse in pickle or other liquid; soak (thing in liquid); in p.p. sl. drunk. **2** n. pickle made with salt; US food in pickle.

soutane /suːˈtɑːn/ n. cassock of RC priest.

south /saʊθ/ **1** n. point of horizon opposite north; southern part of country etc. **2** a. situated etc. in or towards south; facing south; (of wind) coming from south. **3** adv. towards or in south. **4 south-east, south-west,** (compass-point) half-way between south and east, west; **southpaw** colloq. left-handed person esp. boxer. **5 southward** a., adv., & n.; **southwards** adv.

southerly /ˈsʌðəlɪ/ a. & adv. in southern position or direction; (of wind) blowing from south.

southern /ˈsʌð(ə)n/ a. of or in the south. **Southern Cross** constellation with stars forming cross; **southern lights** aurora australis.

southerner /ˈsʌðənə(r)/ n. native or inhabitant of south.

souvenir /suːvəˈnɪə(r)/ n. thing kept as reminder of person or place or event etc.

sou'wester /saʊˈwestə(r)/ n. waterproof hat with broad flap at back; wind from SW.

sovereign /ˈsɒvrɪn/ **1** n. supreme ruler, esp. monarch; hist. British gold coin worth nominally £1. **2** a. supreme; independent; (of remedy etc.) very good. **3 sovereignty** n.

soviet /ˈsəʊvɪət/ **1** n. council elected in district of USSR. **2** a. **Soviet** of the Soviet Union. **3 Soviet Union** USSR.

sow¹ /səʊ/ v.t. (p.p. **sowed** or **sown**) scatter (seed) on or in earth, plant with seed; initiate, arouse.

sow² /saʊ/ n. adult female pig.

soy n. sauce made from pickled soya beans.

soya /ˈsɔɪə/ n. leguminous plant yielding edible oil and flour. **soya bean** seed of this plant.

sozzled /ˈsɒz(ə)ld/ a. sl. very drunk.

spa /spɑː/ n. curative mineral spring; place with this.

space 1 n. continuous expanse in which things exist and move; amount of this taken by particular thing or available for purpose; interval between points or objects; interval of time; expanse of paper used in writing or printing etc.; universe beyond earth's atmosphere; Print. piece of metal separating words etc. **2** attrib.a. of or used for travelling outside earth's atmosphere. **3** v. set or arrange at intervals, put spaces between; spread out. **4 space age** era of space travel; **space-bar** bar on typewriter for making spaces between words etc.; **spacecraft** craft for travelling in outer space; **space-heater** self-contained device for heating room; **spaceman** traveller in outer space; **spaceship** spacecraft; **space shuttle**

spacecraft for repeated use; **space station** artificial satellite as base for operations in outer space; **spacesuit** garment allowing wearer to survive in outer space; **space-time** fusion of concepts of space and time as 4-dimensional continuum.

spacious /'speɪʃəs/ a. having ample space, roomy.

spade¹ n. tool for digging etc., usu. with flattish rectangular blade on long handle; anything resembling this in form or use. **spadework** hard preparatory work.

spade² n. playing card of suit marked with black figures resembling inverted heart with short stem.

spaghetti /spə'getɪ/ n. pasta in long thin strings.

span 1 n. full extent from end to end; maximum lateral extent of aeroplane or its wing; each part of bridge between supports; maximum distance between tips of thumb and little finger, esp. as measure, = 9 in. 2 v.t. extend from side to side or end to end of; bridge (river etc.).

spandrel /'spændr(ə)l/ n. space between curve of arch and surrounding rectangular framework, or between curves of adjoining arches and moulding above.

spangle /'spæŋg(ə)l/ 1 n. small piece of glittering material esp. one of many as ornament of dress etc. 2 v.t. cover (as) with spangles.

Spaniard /'spænɪəd/ n. native of Spain.

spaniel /'spænɪəl/ n. dog with long silky coat and drooping ears.

Spanish /'spænɪʃ/ 1 a. of Spain. 2 n. language of Spain.

spank 1 v.t. slap on buttocks. 2 n. slap given in spanking.

spanker /'spæŋkə(r)/ n. Naut. fore-and-aft sail on mizen-mast.

spanking /'spæŋkɪŋ/ colloq. 1 a. striking, excellent; brisk. 2 adv. strikingly; excellently.

spanner /'spænə(r)/ n. tool for turning nut on bolt etc. **spanner in the works** upsetting element or influence.

spar¹ n. stout pole esp. of kind used for ship's mast etc.

spar² 1 v.i. use fists (as) in boxing, make motions of boxing, dispute, engage in argument. 2 n. sparring; boxing-match. 3 **sparring-partner** boxer employed to practise with another in training for a fight, person with whom one enjoys arguing.

spar³ n. easily split crystalline mineral.

spare /speə(r)/ 1 v. refrain from hurting or destroying or using or bringing into operation; dispense with; afford to give; let (person) have (thing etc. esp. that one does not need); be parsimonious or grudging (with). 2 a. superfluous, not required for ordinary or present use; reserved for emergency or occasional use; (of person) lean, thin, frugal. 3 n. spare part. 4 **go spare** sl. become very angry; **spare part** duplicate to replace lost or damaged part; **spare-rib** closely trimmed rib of meat, esp. pork; **spare time** leisure; **spare tyre** colloq. circle of fatness round or above waist.

sparing /'speərɪŋ/ a. economical, frugal, grudging.

spark 1 n. fiery particle of burning substance; flash of light accompanying electrical discharge; electric spark for firing explosive mixture in internal-combustion engine; flash of wit etc.; minute amount of a quality etc.; lively person. 2 v. emit spark(s); (also with off) stir into activity, initiate. 3 **spark-plug, sparking-plug**, device for making spark in internal-combustion engine.

sparkle /'spɑːk(ə)l/ v.i. emit or seem to emit sparks; glitter, flash, scintillate; (of wine etc.) effervesce. 2 n. sparkling; glitter.

sparkler /'spɑːklə(r)/ n. sparkling firework; sl. diamond.

sparrow /'spærəʊ/ n. small brownish-grey bird. **sparrow-hawk** a small hawk.

sparse /spɑːs/ a. thinly scattered. **sparsity** n.

Spartan /'spɑːt(ə)n/ 1 a. of ancient Sparta; **spartan** austere, hardy, rigorous. 3 n. native of Sparta; **spartan** person of courage and endurance.

spasm /spæz(ə)m/ n. sudden involuntary muscular contraction; sudden convulsive movement or emotion etc.

spasmodic /spæz'mɒdɪk/ a. of or occurring in spasms; intermittent.

spastic /'spæstɪk/ **1** *a.* suffering from cerebral palsy with spasm of muscles. **2** *n.* spastic person.

spat¹ *n.* (usu. in *pl.*) short gaiter covering instep and ankle.

spat² *past* & *p.p.* of **spit¹**.

spate *n.* river-flood; large or excessive amount.

spathe /speɪð/ *n. Bot.* large bract(s) enveloping flower-cluster.

spatial /'speɪʃ(ə)l/ *a.* of space.

spatter /'spætə(r)/ **1** *v.* splash or scatter in drips. **2** *n.* spattering; pattering.

spatula /'spætjʊlə/ *n.* broad-bladed implement used esp. by artists and in cookery.

spawn 1 *v.* (of fish or frog etc.) produce (eggs), be produced as eggs or young; *fig.* produce or generate in large numbers. **2** *n.* eggs of fish or frogs etc.; *derog.* human or other offspring; white fibrous matter from which fungi grow.

spay *v.t.* sterilize (female animal) by removing ovaries.

speak *v.* (*past* **spoke**; *p.p.* **spoken**) utter words in ordinary way; say something; hold conversation; deliver speech; utter or pronounce; use (specified language) in speaking; reveal, indicate. **speak for** express views or sentiments of; **speaking clock** telephone service giving correct time in words; **speak out, up**, speak freely, speak loud(er).

speaker /'spiːkə(r)/ *n.* person who speaks esp. in public; person of specified skill in speech-making; person who speaks specified language; loudspeaker; **Speaker** presiding officer of legislative assembly.

spear 1 *n.* thrusting or hurling weapon with long shaft and sharp-pointed head. **2** *v.t.* pierce or strike (as) with spear. **3 spearhead** *fig.* person(s) leading an attack or challenge, (*v.t.*) act as spearhead of (attack); **spearmint** common garden mint.

spec *n. colloq.* speculation; specification. **on spec** experimentally, as a gamble.

special /'speʃ(ə)l/ **1** *a.* of particular or peculiar kind; not general; for particular purpose; exceptional. **2** *n.* special constable or edition of newspaper or dish on menu etc. **3 Special Branch** police department dealing with pol-

itical security; **special constable** person assisting police in routine duties or in emergencies; **special licence** licence allowing marriage to take place without publication of banns; **special pleading** biased reasoning.

specialist /'speʃəlɪst/ *n.* person who specializes in particular branch of profession etc., esp. medicine.

speciality /speʃɪ'ælɪtɪ/ *n.* special feature; special thing or activity; special product; thing in which a person or place specializes.

specialize /'speʃəlaɪz/ *v.* devote oneself to particular branch of profession etc. (with *in*); become or make special. **specialization** *n.*

specialty /'speʃəltɪ/ *n.* speciality.

specie /'spiːʃiː/ *n.* coin as opp. to paper money.

species /'spiːʃiːz/ *n.* (*pl.* same) class of things having common characteristics; group of animals or plants within genus; kind, sort.

specific /spə'sɪfɪk/ **1** *a.* particular or clearly defined; exact, giving full details; particular, relating to particular thing; (of medicine etc.) for particular disease or condition etc. **2** *n.* specific medicine or aspect. **3 specific gravity** ratio between weight of substance and that of same volume of water or air. **4 specifically** *adv.*; **specificity** /-'fɪs-/ *n.*

specification /spesɪfɪ'keɪʃ(ə)n/ *n.* (usu. in *pl.*) detailed description of work (to be) undertaken or invention or patent etc.

specify /'spesɪfaɪ/ *v.* name expressly, mention definitely; include in specifications.

specimen /'spesɪmən/ *n.* individual or part taken as example of class or whole, esp. serving for investigation etc.; *colloq.* person etc. of specified sort.

specious /'spiːʃəs/ *a.* seeming good or correct but not being really so; plausible.

speck 1 *n.* small spot or stain; particle. **2** *v.t.* (esp. in *p.p.*) mark with specks.

speckle /'spek(ə)l/ **1** *n.* speck, esp. one of many markings on skin etc. **2** *v.t.* (esp. in *p.p.*) mark with speckles.

specs *n.pl. colloq.* (pair of) spectacles.

spectacle /'spektək(ə)l/ *n.* object of sight, esp. of public attention; impressive or ridiculous sight; public show; in *pl.* pair of lenses set in frame supported on nose, to correct or assist defective eyesight or to protect eyes.

spectacled *a.* wearing spectacles.

spectacular /spek'tækjʊlə(r)/ **1** *a.* of or like a public show; striking, lavish. **2** *n.* spectacular performance.

spectator /spek'teɪtə(r)/ *n.* person who watches a show or game or incident etc. **spectator sport** sport which attracts many spectators.

spectra *pl.* of **spectrum**.

spectral /'spektr(ə)l/ *a.* of spectres or spectra; ghostly.

spectre /'spektə(r)/ *n.* ghost; haunting presentiment.

spectroscope /'spektrəskəʊp/ *n.* instrument for producing and examining spectra. **spectroscopic** /-'skɒp-/ *a.*; **spectroscopy** /-'trɒs-/ *n.*

spectrum /'spektrəm/ *n.* (*pl.* **-tra**) band of colours as seen in rainbow etc.; entire or wide range of anything arranged by degree or quality etc.

speculate /'spekjʊleɪt/ *v.i.* engage in conjectural thought or writing; buy or sell commodities etc. in expectation of rise or fall in market value; engage in risky financial transactions. **speculation** *n.*; **speculative** /'spek-/ *a.*; **speculator** *n.*

sped *past* & *p.p.* of **speed**.

speech *n.* act or faculty or manner of speaking; thing said; public address; language, dialect. **freedom of speech** right to express one's views freely; **speech-day** annual prize-giving day in school; **speech therapy** remedial treatment of defective speech.

speechify /'spiːtʃɪfaɪ/ *v.i. colloq.* make speeches.

speechless /'spiːtʃlɪs/ *a.* temporarily deprived of speech by emotion etc.

speed 1 *n.* rapidity, quickness; rate of progress or motion etc.; gear on bicycle; relative sensitivity of photographic film to light. **2** *v.* (*past* & *p.p.* **sped**) go or send quickly; travel at excessive or illegal speed; *arch.* be or make prosperous or successful. **3 speedboat** fast motor boat; **speed limit** maximum permitted speed of vehicle on road etc.; **speedway** motorcycle racing, arena for this, *US* road intended for fast motor vehicles.

speedometer /spiː'dɒmɪtə(r)/ *n.* device indicating speed of vehicle.

speedwell /'spiːdwel/ *n.* small blue-flowered herbaceous plant.

speedy /'spiːdɪ/ *a.* rapid, swift; prompt.

speleology /spelɪ'ɒlədʒɪ/ *n.* scientific study of caves etc. **speleologist** *n.*

spell[1] *n.* words used as charm; fascination, attraction. **spellbound** held as if by spell, fascinated.

spell[2] *v.* (*past* & *p.p.* **spelt** *or* **spelled**) name or write correctly the letters of (word); form (word); imply, involve, mean. **spell out** make out laboriously, spell aloud, explain in detail.

spell[3] **1** *n.* period of time or work; period of some activity. **2** *v.t.* relieve or take turns with (person etc.).

spelt[1] *n.* kind of wheat giving very fine flour.

spelt[2] *past* & *p.p.* of **spell**[2].

spend *v.* (*past* & *p.p.* **spent**) pay out (money); use up, consume; pass or occupy (time); in *p.p.* having lost force or strength. **spendthrift** extravagant person.

sperm *n.* semen; spermatozoon. **sperm-whale** large whale yielding spermaceti.

spermaceti /spɜːmə'setɪ/ *n.* white waxy substance used for ointments etc.

spermatozoon /spɜːmətə'zəʊən/ *n.* (*pl.* **-zoa**) fertilizing cell of male organism.

spermicide /'spɜːmɪsaɪd/ *n.* substance that kills spermatozoa. **spermicidal** *a.*

spew *v.* vomit.

sphagnum /'sfægnəm/ *n.* moss growing in swampy places, used as packing etc.

sphere /sfɪə(r)/ *n.* figure or body having all points of its surface equidistant from point within it; ball, globe; field of action or influence etc.; place in society; each of several hollow globes in which heavenly bodies were formerly thought to be set.

spherical /'sferɪk(ə)l/ *a.* shaped like sphere; of spheres.

spheroid /'sfɪərɔɪd/ *n.* spherelike but not perfectly spherical body. **spheroidal** *a.*

sphincter /'sfɪŋktə(r)/ *n.* ring of muscle closing and opening orifice.

sphinx /sfɪŋks/ *n.* (in Egyptian antiquity) figure of recumbent lion with head of man or animal; *Gk myth* winged monster with woman's head and lion's body; enigmatic or mysterious person.

spice 1 *n.* aromatic or pungent vegetable substance used as flavouring; spices collectively; *fig.* thing that adds zest or excitement etc. 2 *v.t.* flavour with spice; enhance.

spick and span smart, trim, new-looking.

spicy /ˈspaɪsɪ/ *a.* of or flavoured with spice; piquant; improper.

spider /ˈspaɪdə(r)/ *n.* eight-legged arthropod, many species of which spin webs esp. to capture insects as food; thing resembling spider.

spidery /ˈspaɪdərɪ/ *a.* of or like spider; very thin or long.

spiel /spiːl/ *sl.* 1 *n.* speech or story, esp. glib or persuasive one. 2 *v.i.* talk lengthily or glibly.

spigot /ˈspɪɡət/ *n.* small peg or plug; device for controlling flow of liquor from cask etc.

spike[1] 1 *n.* sharp point; pointed piece of metal, e.g. one of set forming top of iron fence or worn on bottom of running-shoe to prevent slipping; in *pl.* running-shoes fitted with spikes; large nail. 2 *v.t.* put spikes on or into; fix on spike; *colloq.* add alcohol to (drink). 3 **spike person's guns** defeat his plans.

spike[2] *n.* long cluster of flowers on short stalks on central stem.

spikenard /ˈspaɪknɑːd/ *n.* tall sweet-smelling plant; aromatic ointment formerly made from this.

spiky /ˈspaɪkɪ/ *a.* like a spike; having spikes; *colloq.* dogmatic, bad-tempered.

spill[1] 1 *v.* (*past & p.p.* **spilt** or **spilled**) allow (liquid etc.) to fall or run out from vessel, esp. accidentally or wastefully; (of liquid etc.) run out thus; shed (others' blood); cause to fall from horse or vehicle. 2 *n.* spilling or being spilt; throw or fall, esp. from horse or vehicle; tumble. 3 **spill the beans** *sl.* divulge secret etc.

spill[2] *n.* strip of wood or paper etc. for lighting candle etc.

spillikin /ˈspɪlɪkɪn/ *n.* small thin rod of wood etc.; in *pl.* game in which heap of these is removed by taking one at a time without disturbing others.

spilt *past & p.p.* of **spill**[1].

spin 1 *v.* (*past & p.p.* **spun**) turn rapidly on its own axis, cause to do this; make (yarn) by drawing out and twisting together fibres of wool etc.; make (web etc.) by extrusion of fine viscous thread; (of person's head) be in a whirl; toss (coin); tell or compose (story etc.). 2 *n.* revolving motion, whirl; secondary revolving or twisting motion e.g. of cricket or tennis ball; short or brisk excursion, esp. in motor vehicle. 3 **spin bowler** *Crick.* one who imparts spin to ball; **spin-drier** machine for drying clothes etc. by spinning them in rotating drum; **spin-dry** *v.*; **spinning-wheel** household implement for spinning yarn, with spindle driven by wheel with crank or treadle; **spin-off** incidental result, esp. as benefit from industrial or technological development; **spin out** prolong (discussion etc.).

spina bifida /ˌspaɪnə ˈbɪfɪdə/ congenital defect of spine, with protruding membranes.

spinach /ˈspɪnɪdʒ/ *n.* plant with succulent leaves used as vegetable. **spinach beet** kind of beet with leaves used like spinach.

spinal *a.* of spine. **spinal column** spine; **spinal cord** cylindrical nervous structure within spine.

spindle /ˈspɪnd(ə)l/ *n.* slender rod used to twist or wind thread in spinning; pin or axis on which something revolves.

spindly /ˈspɪndlɪ/ *a.* long or tall and thin.

spindrift /ˈspɪndrɪft/ *n.* spray blown along surface of sea.

spine *n.* articulated series of vertebrae extending from skull, backbone; sharp needle-like outgrowth of animal or plant; part of book visible when it is one of row on shelf; ridge, sharp projection. **spine-chilling** causing thrill of terror.

spineless /ˈspaɪnlɪs/ *a.* lacking backbone or resoluteness, timid, weak.

spinet /sprˈnet/ *n. hist.* small keyboard instrument of harpsichord kind.

spinnaker /ˈspɪnəkə(r)/ *n.* large three-cornered extra sail of racing-yacht.

spinner /ˈspɪnə(r)/ *n.* person or thing that spins; manufacturer engaged in spinning; spin bowler; revolving bait for fishing.

spinneret /ˈspɪnərɛt/ n. spinning-organ in spider or silkworm etc.

spinney /ˈspɪnɪ/ n. small wood, thicket.

spinster /ˈspɪnstə(r)/ n. unmarried woman.

spiny /ˈspaɪnɪ/ a. having (many) spines.

spiraea /spaɪəˈrɪə/ n. garden plant related to meadowsweet.

spiral /ˈspaɪər(ə)l/ 1 a. coiled in a plane or as round a cylinder or cone; having this shape. 2 n. spiral curve; progressive rise or fall. 3 v.i. move in spiral course. 4 **spiral staircase** staircase rising round central axis.

spirant /ˈspaɪərənt/ 1 a. uttered with continuous expulsion of breath. 2 n. spirant consonant.

spire /spaɪə(r)/ n. tapering structure in form of tall cone or pyramid rising above tower.

spirit /ˈspɪrɪt/ 1 n. animating or vital principle; person's soul; person from intellectual or moral view; disembodied person or incorporeal being; mental or moral nature or qualities; attitude, mood; vigour, courage, vivacity; general meaning or feeling (of); distilled essence, alcoholic solution of; (usu. in pl.) distilled alcoholic liquor. 2 v.t. convey mysteriously away etc. 3 **in high, low, spirits** cheerful, depressed; **spirit gum** quick-drying gum for attaching false hair; **spirit-lamp** lamp burning methylated or other volatile spirit; **spirit-level** device used to test levelness.

spirited a. full of spirit, lively; courageous; having specified spirit(s).

spiritual /ˈspɪrɪtjʊəl/ 1 a. of or concerned with spirit; religious, divine, inspired. 2 n. religious song, esp. of Amer. Blacks. 3 **spirituality** n.

spiritualism /ˈspɪrɪtjʊəlɪz(ə)m/ n. belief that spirits of dead can communicate with living, esp. through mediums. **spiritualist** a. & n.; **spiritualistic** a.

spirituous /ˈspɪrɪtjʊəs/ a. alcoholic; distilled as well as fermented.

spit[1] v. 1 v. (past & p.p. **spat**) eject from mouth; eject saliva from mouth; do this as gesture of contempt; utter vehemently; make spitting sound as sign of anger or hostility; (of rain etc.) fall lightly. 2 n. spittle; spitting. 3 **the**

(very) **spit** spitting image of; **spitfire** fiery-tempered person; **spitting image** exact counterpart or likeness (of).

spit[2] 1 n. rod on which meat is fixed for roasting over fire etc.; small point of land projecting into sea; spade-depth of earth. 2 v.t. pierce (as) with spit.

spite 1 n. ill will, malice. 2 v.t. thwart, annoy. 3 **in spite of** notwithstanding, regardless of.

spiteful /ˈspaɪtfʊl/ a. full of spite, malicious.

spittle /ˈspɪt(ə)l/ n. saliva, esp. as ejected from mouth.

spittoon /spɪˈtuːn/ n. vessel to spit into.

spiv n. sl. man, esp. flashily-dressed one, living from shady dealings rather than regular work.

splash 1 v. agitate (liquid) so that drops of it fly about; wet or stain by splashing; (of liquid) fly about in drops; step or fall etc. into etc. with splashing; mark or mottle with irregular patches of colour etc.; colloq. display conspicuously esp. in print; spend (money) recklessly or ostentatiously. 2 n. splashing, sound or mark made by it; quantity splashed; large irregular patch of colour etc.; striking or ostentatious display or effect; colloq. small quantity of soda-water etc. (in drink). 3 **splashback** panel behind sink etc. to protect wall from splashes; **splash-down** alighting of spacecraft on sea; **splash out** spend money freely.

splatter /ˈsplætə(r)/ v. & n. splash, esp. with continuous or noisy action, spatter.

splay 1 v. spread apart; (of opening) have sides diverging; make (opening) have divergent sides. 2 n. surface at oblique angle to another. 3 a. splayed.

spleen n. abdominal organ maintaining proper condition of blood; moroseness, irritability, spite.

splendid /ˈsplendɪd/ a. magnificent, admirable, glorious, excellent.

splendiferous /splenˈdɪfərəs/ a. colloq. splendid.

splendour /ˈsplendə(r)/ n. great brightness; magnificence.

splenetic /splɪˈnetɪk/ a. bad-tempered; peevish.

splenic /ˈspliːnɪk/ a. of or in spleen.

splice 1 v.t. join pieces of (rope) by interweaving strands; join (pieces of wood or tape etc.) in overlapping position; *colloq.* join in marriage. **2** *n.* junction made by splicing.

splint 1 *n.* strip of more or less rigid material holding broken bone in right position while it heals. **2** *v.t.* secure with splint.

splinter /'splɪntə(r)/ **1** *n.* rough or sharp-edged or thin fragment broken or split off from some hard material. **2** *v.* split into splinters; come off as or like splinter. **3 splinter group** small esp. political group that has split off from larger one. **4 splintery** *a.*

split 1 *v.* (*past & p.p.* **split**) break, esp. lengthwise or with grain or plane of cleavage; break forcibly; divide into parts or thicknesses; divide into disagreeing or hostile parties; cause fission of (atom); *sl.* reveal secret, inform *on.* **2** *n.* splitting; fissure; disagreement, schism; something formed by splitting; in *pl.* feat of sitting down or leaping with legs widely spread out at right angles to body. **3 split hairs** make over-subtle distinctions; **split infinitive** one with adverb etc. inserted between *to* and verb; **split-level** built or having components at more than one level; **split personality** change of personality as in schizophrenia; **split pin** pin or bolt etc. held in place by splaying of its split end; **split ring** metal ring, with usu. two spiral turns, for holding keys etc.; **split second** very short period of time; **split up** separate, esp. (of married couple etc.) cease living together.

splotch 1 *n.* large irregular spot or patch of colour etc., blotch. **2** *v.t.* mark with splotches. **3 splotchy** *a.*

splurge 1 *n.* noisy or ostentatious display or effort. **2** *v.i.* make splurge.

splutter /'splʌtə(r)/ **1** *v.* speak or emit with spitting sound; emit spitting sounds; speak rapidly or incoherently. **2** *n.* spluttering speech or sound.

spoil 1 *v.* (*past & p.p.* **spoilt** or **spoiled**) make or become useless or unsatisfactory; ruin character of by indulgence; decay, go bad. **2** *n.* in *sing.* or *pl.* plunder, stolen goods; *fig.* profits, advantages accruing from success or public office etc. **3 spoil-sport** person who spoils others' enjoyment.

spoiler /'spɔɪlə(r)/ *n.* device on aircraft to retard it by interrupting air flow; device on vehicle to increase contact with ground at speed.

spoke¹ *n.* any of bars running from hub to rim of wheel; rung of ladder. **put a spoke in person's wheel** hinder or thwart his purpose.

spoke² *past* of **speak**.

spoken *p.p.* of **speak**.

spokesman /'spəʊksmən/ *n.* (*pl.* -men) person who speaks for others, representative. **spokeswoman** *n.*

spoliation /spəʊlɪ'eɪʃ(ə)n/ *n.* plundering, pillage.

sponge /spʌndʒ/ **1** *n.* sea animal with porous body-wall and tough elastic skeleton; this skeleton or piece of porous rubber etc. used as absorbent in bathing or cleansing surfaces etc.; thing of spongelike absorbency or consistency; sponge-cake; act of sponging. **2** *v.* wipe or cleanse with sponge; wipe *out* or efface (as) with sponge; take *up* (water etc.) (as) with sponge; live parasitically off others. **3 sponge-bag** waterproof bag for holding toilet articles; **sponge-cake, pudding,** one of light spongelike consistency; **sponge rubber** rubber made porous like sponge.

sponger /'spʌndʒə(r)/ *n.* person who habitually sponges on others.

spongy /'spʌndʒɪ/ *a.* like a sponge; porous, elastic, absorbent.

sponsor /'spɒnsə(r)/ **1** *n.* person who makes himself responsible for another or presents candidate for baptism or introduces legislation or contributes to charity in return for specified activity by another; advertiser who pays for broadcast or sporting event etc., to advertise his wares. **2** *v.t.* be sponsor for. **3 sponsorship** *n.*

spontaneous /spɒn'teɪnɪəs/ *a.* acting or done or occurring without external cause; automatic; instinctive, natural, unconstrained. **spontaneity** /-'niːɪtɪ/ *n.*

spoof /spuːf/ *n. & v.t. colloq.* parody; hoax, swindle.

spook /spuːk/ *n. colloq.* ghost. **spooky** *a.*

spool /spuːl/ **1** *n.* reel on which something is wound; revolving cylinder of angler's reel. **2** *v.t.* wind on spool.

spoon /spuːn/ **1** *n.* utensil with oval or round bowl and handle for conveying food to mouth or stirring etc.; spoon-shaped thing; spoon-bait. **2** *v.* take liquid (*up, out*) with spoon; hit (ball) feebly upwards; *colloq.* behave in amorous way, esp. foolishly. **3 spoon-bait** revolving spoon-shaped metal fish-lure; **spoonbill** wading-bird with broad flat tip of bill; **spoon-feed** feed (baby etc.) with spoon, give help etc. to (person) without demanding any effort from recipient. **4 spoonful** *n.*

spoonerism /ˈspuːnərɪz(ə)m/ *n.* transposition, usu. accidental, of initial sounds of two or more words.

spoor /spʊə(r)/ *n.* animal's track or scent.

sporadic /spəˈrædɪk/ *a.* occurring in isolated instances or very small numbers; scattered, occasional.

spore /spɔː(r)/ *n.* minute reproductive cell of ferns, fungi, protozoa, etc.

sporran /ˈspɒrən/ *n.* pouch worn in front of kilt.

sport 1 *n.* game or competitive activity usu. involving physical exertion; these collectively; in *pl.* meeting for competition in athletics; amusement, fun; *colloq.* sportsman, good fellow; animal or plant that deviates from type. **2** *v.* engage in sport; wear or exhibit esp. ostentatiously. **3 sports car** low-built fast car; **sports coat** men's jacket for informal wear; **sportsman**, **sportswoman**, person fond of sport, person who behaves fairly and generously; **sportsmanlike** *a.*

sporting /ˈspɔːtɪŋ/ *a.* interested in sport; sportsmanlike. **sporting chance** some possibility of success.

sportive /ˈspɔːtɪv/ *a.* playful.

sporty /ˈspɔːtɪ/ *a. colloq.* fond of sport; *colloq.* rakish, showy.

spot 1 *n.* small mark differing in colour etc. from surface it is on; blemish, pimple; particular place, definite locality; particular part of one's body or character; *colloq.* one's (regular) position in organization or programme etc.; *colloq.* small quantity of something; spotlight. **2** *v.* mark or become marked with spot(s); make spots, rain slightly; *colloq.* pick out, recognize, catch sight of; watch for and take note of (trains, talent, etc.). **3 in a spot** *colloq.* in difficulties; **on the spot** at scene of action or event, in position such that response or action is required; **spot cash** money paid immediately after sale; **spot check** sudden or random check; **spotlight** beam of light directed on small area, full attention or publicity, (*v.t.*) illuminate with spotlight; **spot-on** *colloq.* precise(ly).

spotless /ˈspɒtlɪs/ *a.* absolutely clean, unblemished.

spotted *a.* marked with spots. **spotted dick** *sl.* suet pudding containing currants.

spotty /ˈspɒtɪ/ *a.* marked with spots, patchy, irregular.

spouse /spaʊs/ *n.* husband or wife.

spout /spaʊt/ **1** *n.* projecting tube or lip through which liquid is poured or issues from teapot or jug or roof-gutter or fountain etc.; jet of liquid. **2** *v.* discharge or issue forcibly in jet; utter in declamatory manner. **3 up the spout** *sl.* in a bad way or hopeless position, in pawn.

sprain 1 *v.t.* wrench (ankle, wrist, etc.) so as to cause pain and swelling. **2** *n.* such injury.

sprang *past of* **spring**.

sprat *n.* small sea-fish.

sprawl 1 *v.* fall or lie etc. with limbs spread out in careless or ungainly way; straggle, spread untidily. **2** *n.* sprawling movement or attitude; straggling group or mass.

spray¹ 1 *n.* water or other liquid flying in small drops; preparation intended for spraying; instrument or apparatus for spraying. **2** *v.* scatter or diffuse as spray; sprinkle (as) with spray. **3 spray-gun** apparatus for spraying paint etc.

spray² *n.* slender shoot or twig, graceful branch with flowers etc.; jewel or other ornament in form of spray.

spread /spred/ **1** *v.* (*past & p.p.* **spread**) extend surface of or cause to cover larger surface; have wide or specified or increasing extent; (cause to) become widely known; cover surface of. **2** *n.* action or capability or extent of spreading; breadth, diffusion; range; elaborate meal; paste for spreading on bread etc.; printed matter spread across more than one column. **3 spread eagle** figure of eagle with legs and wings extended as emblem; **spread-eagle** place (person) in position with arms and legs spread out, defeat utterly.

spree *n.* lively outing, bout of drinking etc. **shopping, spending,** etc. **spree** occasion of lavish spending.

sprig *n.* small branch, twig, spray; ornament resembling this, esp. on fabric.

sprigged /ˈsprɪgd/ *a.* ornamented with sprigs.

sprightly /ˈspraɪtlɪ/ *a.* vivacious, lively.

spring 1 *v.* (*past* **sprang**; *p.p.* **sprung**) rise rapidly or suddenly, leap; move rapidly (as) by action of a spring, originate or arise (*from*); (cause to) act or appear unexpectedly; contrive escape of (person *from* prison etc.); develop (leak); (usu. in *p.p.*) provide with springs. **2** *n.* jump, leap; recoil, elasticity; elastic device usu. of bent or coiled metal used esp. to drive clockwork or for cushioning furniture or in vehicles; season of year between winter and summer; early stage *of* life etc.; place where water or oil etc. wells up from earth; basin or flow so formed; motive for or origin of action or custom etc. **3 spring balance** device measuring weight by tension of spring; **springboard** springy board giving impetus in leaping or diving etc., *fig.* source of impetus; **spring-clean** thorough cleaning of house or room esp. in spring, (*v.t.*) clean thus; **spring onion** young onion eaten raw; **spring tide** tide of maximum height; **springtime** season of spring.

springbok /ˈsprɪŋbɒk/ *n.* S. Afr. gazelle.

springer /ˈsprɪŋə(r)/ *n.* small spaniel.

springy /ˈsprɪŋɪ/ *a.* elastic.

sprinkle /ˈsprɪŋk(ə)l/ **1** *v.* scatter in small drops or particles; subject (ground, object) to sprinkling (*with*); (of liquid etc.) fall thus on. **2** *n.* light shower (*of* rain etc.).

sprinkler /ˈsprɪŋklə(r)/ *n.* contrivance for sprinkling water on lawn or to extinguish fires.

sprinkling /ˈsprɪŋklɪŋ/ *n.* a few or a little here and there.

sprint 1 *v.i.* run etc. at top speed, esp. for short distance. **2** *n.* such run; similar short effort in cycling or swimming etc.

sprit *n.* small diagonal spar reaching from mast to upper outer corner of sail. **spritsail** sail extended by sprit.

sprite *n.* elf or fairy.

sprocket /ˈsprɒkɪt/ *n.* projection on rim of wheel engaging with links of chain etc.

sprout /spraʊt/ **1** *v.* put forth (shoots), begin to grow. **2** *n.* shoot, new growth; in *pl. colloq.* Brussels sprouts.

spruce[1] **1** *a.* of trim smart appearance. **2** *v.* smarten (*up*), make spruce.

spruce[2] *n.* conifer with dense conical foliage; its wood.

sprung *p.p.* of **spring**.

spry /spraɪ/ *a.* active, nimble, lively.

spud 1 *n.* small narrow spade for digging up weeds etc.; *sl.* potato. **2** *v.t.* dig (*out, up*) with spud.

spume /spjuːm/ *n.* & *v.i.* froth, foam. **spumy** *a.*

spun *past* & *p.p.* of **spin**. **spun silk** cheap material of short-fibred and waste silk, often mixed with cotton.

spunk *n.* *colloq.* mettle, spirit; *sl.* semen. **spunky** *a.*

spur 1 *n.* device with small spike or spiked wheel, attached to rider's heel for urging horse forward; stimulus, incentive; spur-shaped thing, esp. hard projection on cock's leg; projection from mountain (range); branch road or railway. **2** *v.* prick (horse) with spur; incite, stimulate; ride hard; (esp. in *p.p.*) provide with spurs. **3 on the spur of the moment** on a momentary impulse.

spurge *n.* plant with acrid milky juice.

spurious /ˈspjʊərɪəs/ *a.* not genuine or authentic; not what it purports to be.

spurn *v.t.* reject with contempt or disdain; repel with foot.

spurt 1 *v.* (cause to) gush out in jet or stream; make spurt. **2** *n.* sudden gushing out, jet; short sudden effort or burst of speed esp. in racing.

sputnik /ˈspʊtnɪk/ *n.* Russian artificial earth satellite.

sputter /ˈspʌtə(r)/ *v.* & *n.* splutter.

sputum /ˈspjuːtəm/ *n.* (*pl.* **-ta**) saliva; expectorated matter esp. used to diagnose disease.

spy 1 *n.* person secretly collecting and reporting information esp. relating to another country or rival firm etc.; person keeping secret watch on others. **2** *v.* discern, make out; act as spy (*on*). **3** **spyglass** small telescope; **spyhole** peep-hole; **spy out** explore or discover, esp. secretly.

sq. *abbr.* square.

Sqn. Ldr. *abbr.* Squadron Leader.

squab /skwɒb/ *n.* young esp. unfledged pigeon; thickly stuffed loose cushion, esp. as part of seat in motor car; sofa.

squabble /'skwɒb(ə)l/ **1** *n.* petty or noisy quarrel. **2** *v.i.* engage in squabble.

squad /skwɒd/ *n.* small group of people sharing task etc., esp. small number of soldiers. **squad car** *US* police car having radio link with headquarters.

squaddie /'skwɒdɪ/ *n. sl.* private soldier.

squadron /'skwɒdrən/ *n.* organized body of persons etc., esp. cavalry division of 2 troops; detachment of warships employed on particular service; unit of RAF with 10 to 18 aircraft. **squadron leader** RAF officer commanding squadron, next below wing commander.

squalid /'skwɒlɪd/ *a.* dirty, filthy, mean in appearance; wretched, sordid.

squall /skwɔːl/ **1** *n.* sudden violent gust or storm; discordant cry; scream. **2** *v.* scream loudly or discordantly. **3** **squally** *a.*

squalor /'skwɒlə(r)/ *n.* filthy or squalid state.

squander /'skwɒndə(r)/ *v.t.* spend wastefully.

square /skweə(r)/ **1** *n.* rectangle with 4 equal sides; object or area of (roughly) this shape; open space, esp. enclosed by houses etc., buildings surrounding this; product of number multiplied by itself; L- or T-shaped instrument for measuring or testing right angles. **2** *a.* having shape of square; having or in form of a right angle; designating unit of measure equal in area to square whose side is one of the unit specified; level or parallel; balanced, equal; solid, sturdy; fair, honest; *sl.* conventional, old-fashioned. **3** *adv.* squarely. **4** *v.* make square; multiply (number) by itself; make or be consistent (*with*), reconcile; mark out in squares; settle (*up*) account etc.; place (shoulders etc.) squarely facing forwards; pay or bribe;

make scores etc. equal or level. **5** **square dance** one in which 4 couples face inwards from 4 sides; **square deal** fair bargain or treatment; **square leg** *Crick.* position of fielder on batsman's leg-side nearly in line with stumps; **square meal** substantial one; **square-rigged** having principal sails at right angles to length of ship; **square root** number that when multiplied by itself gives specified number.

squash¹ /skwɒʃ/ **1** *v.* crush or be squeezed flat or into pulp; force *into* small space; crowd; snub, suppress. **2** *n.* crowded state; crowd; drink made of crushed fruit; (in full **squash rackets**) game played with rackets and fairly soft ball in closed court. **3** **squashy** *a.*

squash² /skwɒʃ/ *n.* trailing annual plant; gourd of this.

squat /skwɒt/ **1** *v.* sit on one's heels, or on ground with knees drawn up, or in hunched posture; put into squatting position; *colloq.* sit down; act as squatter. **2** *a.* squatting; short and thick, dumpy. **3** *n.* squatting posture; place occupied by squatter(s); being squatter.

squatter /'skwɒtə(r)/ *n.* person who takes unauthorized possession of unoccupied premises etc.; *Aus.* sheep-farmer.

squaw *n.* N. Amer. Indian woman or wife.

squawk **1** *n.* harsh cry; complaint. **2** *v.i.* make squawk.

squeak **1** *n.* short high-pitched cry or sound; (also **narrow squeak**) narrow escape. **2** *v.* emit squeak, utter in squeaking voice; *sl.* turn informer. **3** **squeaky** *a.*

squeal **1** *n.* prolonged shrill sound or cry. **2** *v.* make a squeal; utter (words) with squeal; *sl.* turn informer; protest vociferously.

squeamish /'skwiːmɪʃ/ *a.* easily nauseated; fastidious, over-scrupulous.

squeegee /'skwiːdʒiː/ **1** *n.* implement with rubber blade or roller used to remove liquid from surfaces. **2** *v.t.* clean etc. with squeegee.

squeeze **1** *v.* exert pressure on from opposite or all sides, esp. to extract moisture; reduce size of or alter shape of by squeezing; force or make one's way into or through small or narrow space; harass; bring pressure to bear on; get by entreaty or extortion. **2** *n.* action or result of squeezing; crowd, crowded state; small quantity produced by squeezing; restriction on borrowing and investment.

squelch /skweltʃ/ **1** *v.* tread or walk heavily in water or wet ground, make sound (as) of this; disconcert, silence. **2** *n.* act or sound of squelching.

squib *n.* small hissing firework thrown by hand; short satirical composition.

squid *n.* 10-armed marine cephalopod.

squiffy /'skwɪfɪ/ *a. sl.* slightly drunk.

squiggle /'skwɪg(ə)l/ *n.* short curling line, esp. in handwriting. **squiggly** *a.*

squint 1 *v.i.* have eyes turned in different directions; look sidelong. **2** *n.* squinting condition of eyes; *colloq.* look, glance; oblique opening through wall of church etc.

squire /skwaɪə(r)/ **1** *n.* country gentleman, esp. chief landed proprietor in district; man escorting or attending on woman; *hist.* attendant on knight. **2** *v.t.* (of man) escort (woman).

squirearchy /'skwaɪərɑːkɪ/ *n.* landowners collectively.

squirm 1 *v.i.* writhe, wriggle; *fig.* show or feel embarrassment. **2** *n.* squirming movement.

squirrel /'skwɪr(ə)l/ **1** *n.* bushy-tailed usu. arboreal rodent. **2** *v.t.* hoard (*away*).

squirt 1 *v.* eject (liquid etc.) in a jet; be ejected thus. **2** *n.* jet of water etc.; device for ejecting this; *colloq.* insignificant person.

squish 1 *n.* slight squelching sound. **2** *v.i.* move with squish. **3 squishy** *a.*

Sr. *abbr.* Senior.

SRN *abbr.* State Registered Nurse.

SS *abbr.* Saints; steamship; *hist.* Nazi special police force.

SSE *abbr.* south-south-east.

SSW *abbr.* south-south-west.

St. *abbr.* Saint; Street.

st. *abbr.* stone.

stab 1 *v.* pierce or wound with pointed tool or weapon; aim blow with such weapon (*at*); cause sharp pain to. **2** *n.* act or result of stabbing; *colloq.* attempt. **3 stab in the back** treacherous attack.

stability /stə'bɪlɪtɪ/ *n.* being stable.

stabilize /'steɪbɪlaɪz/ *v.t.* make or become stable. **stabilization** *n.*

stabilizer /'steɪbɪlaɪzə(r)/ *n.* device to keep aircraft or child's bicycle steady.

stable /'steɪb(ə)l/ **1** *a.* firmly fixed or established, not fluctuating or changing, not easily shaken or decomposed or destroyed etc. **2** *n.* building in which horses are kept; establishment for training racehorses; racehorses of particular stable; persons or products etc. having common origin or affiliation; such origin or affiliation. **3** *v.t.* put or keep (horse) in stable.

stabling /'steɪblɪŋ/ *n.* accommodation for horses etc.

staccato /stə'kɑːtəʊ/ *a.* & *adv.* esp. *Mus.* with each sound or spoken phrase sharply distinct from the others.

stack 1 *n.* pile or heap, esp. in orderly arrangement; *colloq.* large quantity; number of chimneys standing together; smoke-stack; tall factory chimney; part of library where books are compactly stored. **2** *v.t.* pile in stack(s); arrange (cards, or *fig.* circumstances etc.) secretly for cheating; cause (aircraft) to fly round at different levels while waiting to land.

stadium /'steɪdɪəm/ *n.* (*pl.* **-diums**) athletic or sports ground with tiers of seats for spectators.

staff /stɑːf/ **1** *n.* stick or pole as weapon or support or as symbol of office; group of persons carrying on work under manager etc.; those in authority in a school etc.; body of officers in army etc. assisting officer in high command; *Mus.* (*pl.* **staves**) set of usu. 5 parallel lines to indicate pitch of notes by position. **2** *v.t.* provide (institution etc.) with staff. **3 staff nurse** one ranking just below a sister; **staff officer** *Mil.* officer serving on staff.

stag *n.* male deer; *St. Exch.* person who seeks to buy new shares and sell at once for profit. **stag-beetle** large beetle with antler-like mandibles; **stag-party** party for men only.

stage 1 *n.* point or period of development or progress; platform, esp. raised one on which plays etc. are performed; *the* theatre or acting profession; scene of action; regular stopping-place on route; interval between stopping-places; section of space-rocket with separate means of propulsion. **2** *v.* put (play etc.) on stage, organize and carry out. **3 stage-coach** *hist.* coach running regularly between two places; **stage direction** instruction in text of play about actor's movement or sounds heard etc.; **stage door** entrance from street to backstage part of theatre; **stage fright** nervousness at appearing before audience; **stage-manage** arrange or control etc. as or like stage-manager; **stage-manager** person responsible for lighting and mechanical arrangements etc. of play; **stage-struck** strongly wishing to be actor or actress; **stage whisper** loud whisper meant to be heard by others than person addressed.

stager *n.* **old stager** experienced person.

stagger /'stægə(r)/ **1** *v.* walk or move unsteadily; cause shock or confusion to; arrange (events, hours of work, etc.), so that they do not coincide; arrange (objects) so that they are not in line. **2** *n.* staggering movement; in *pl.* disease, esp. of horses and cattle, causing staggering.

staggering /'stægərɪŋ/ *a.* bewildering, astonishing.

staging /'steɪdʒɪŋ/ *n.* presentation of play etc.; (temporary) platform; shelving, esp. for plants in greenhouse etc. **staging post** regular stopping-place, esp. on air route.

stagnant /'stægnənt/ *a.* not flowing or running, without motion or current; inert, sluggish, without activity. **stagnancy** *n.*

stagnate /stæg'neɪt/ *v.i.* be or become stagnant. **stagnation** *n.*

stagy /'steɪdʒɪ/ *a.* theatrical, artificial, or exaggerated.

staid *a.* sober, steady, sedate.

stain 1 *v.* discolour or be discoloured by action of liquid sinking in; spoil or damage; colour (wood or glass) with substance that penetrates the material; treat with colouring agent. **2** *n.* discoloration or mark, esp. one not easily removable; dye etc. for staining; blot, blemish.

stainless /'steɪnlɪs/ *a.* without stains; not liable to stain. **stainless steel** chrome steel that resists rust and corrosion.

stair *n.* each of a set of fixed indoor steps; in *pl.* set or flight of these. **below**

stairs in or to basement, esp. as servants' part of house; **staircase** flight or series of flights of stairs, part of building containing staircase; **stair-rod** rod for securing carpet in angle between 2 steps; **stairway** staircase.

stake 1 *n.* stick or post pointed for driving into ground; *hist.* post to which person was tied for burning alive; money etc. wagered on event; interest or concern, esp. financial; in *pl.* money offered as prize in horse-race; such race. **2** *v.t.* secure or support with stake(s); mark (area) *off* or *out* with stakes; wager (money etc. *on* event); *US colloq.* give financial or other support to. **3 at stake** wagered, risked, to be won or lost; **stake out** place under surveillance; **stake-out** *n.*

stalactite /'stæləktaɪt/ *n.* deposit of calcium carbonate hanging like icicle from roof of cave etc.

stalagmite /'stæləgmaɪt/ *n.* deposit of calcium carbonate rising like spike from floor of cave etc.

stale *a.* not fresh; the worse for age or use; lacking novelty, trite; (of athlete, musician, etc.) having ability impaired by excessive exertion or practice etc. **2** *v.* become or make stale.

stalemate /'steɪlmeɪt/ **1** *n.* state of chess-game in which one player cannot move without going into check; deadlock in proceedings. **2** *v.t.* bring (player) to stalemate; bring to standstill.

stalk¹ /stɔːk/ **1** *n.* stem, esp. main stem of herbaceous plant; attachment or support of leaf or flower or animal organ etc.

stalk² /stɔːk/ **1** *v.* pursue or approach (wild animal, enemy) stealthily; stride, walk in stately or haughty manner. **2** *n.* stalking of game; imposing gait. **3 stalking-horse** screen etc. behind which hunter hides, pretext concealing one's real intentions or actions.

stall¹ /stɔːl/ *n.* stable or cowhouse; compartment for one animal in this; trader's booth in market etc.; fixed seat in choir or chancel, (partly) enclosed at back and sides; any of seats on ground floor of theatre; stalling of engine or aircraft. **2** *v.* (of motor vehicle or its engine) stop because of inadequate fuel-supply or overloading of engine etc.; (of aircraft) get out of control because speed is insufficient; cause (engine) to stall; put or keep in stalls.

stall² /stɔːl/ v. play for time when being questioned etc.; delay or obstruct (person etc.).

stallion /ˈstæliən/ n. uncastrated male horse.

stalwart /ˈstɔːlwət/ 1 a. sturdy, strong; courageous, resolute. 2 n. stalwart person, esp. loyal uncompromising partisan.

stamen /ˈsteimən/ n. male fertilizing organ of flowering plant.

stamina /ˈstæminə/ n. ability to endure prolonged physical or mental strain.

stammer /ˈstæmə(r)/ 1 v. speak with halting articulation, esp. with pauses or rapid repetitions of same syllable; (often with *out*) utter (words) thus. 2 n. act or habit of stammering.

stamp 1 v. bring down (one's foot) heavily on ground etc., crush or flatten thus; impress (pattern or mark) on; impress with pattern or mark etc.; affix postage or other stamp to; *fig.* assign specific character to, mark out. 2 n. instrument for stamping; mark or design made by this; postage stamp; mark impressed on or label etc. fixed to commodity as evidence of quality etc.; act or sound of stamping of foot; characteristic mark of quality. 3 **stamp-duty** duty imposed on certain kinds of legal document; **stamping-ground** favourite place of resort or action; **stamp out** produce by cutting out with die etc., put an end to.

stampede /stæmˈpiːd/ 1 n. sudden rush of (usu. frightened) cattle or people etc.; uncontrolled or unreasoning action by large number of people. 2 v. (cause to) take part in stampede.

stance /stɑːns/ n. player's position for making stroke; pose, attitude, standpoint.

stanch /stɑːntʃ/ v.t. stop flow of (esp. blood); stop flow from (esp. wound).

stanchion /ˈstænʃ(ə)n/ n. upright post or support; device for confining cattle in stall etc.

stand 1 v. (past & p.p. **stood** /stʊd/) have or take or maintain stationary upright position; be situated; be of specified height; be in specified condition;

set upright or in specified position; move to and remain in specified condition; remain valid; *Naut.* hold specified course; endure, tolerate; provide at one's expense; offer oneself for election etc. 2 n. act or condition of standing; resistance to attack or compulsion; position adopted; rack or pedestal etc. on or in which things may be placed; stall in market etc.; standing-place for vehicles; raised structure with seats at sports ground etc.; *US* witness-box; halt made by touring-company etc. to give performance(s); group of growing trees etc. 3 **stand by** stand ready for action, look on without interfering, uphold or support (person), adhere to (terms, beliefs, etc.); **stand-by** thing or person ready if needed in emergency; **stand down** withdraw from position or candidacy; **stand for** represent, signify, imply, be candidate for (esp. public office), *colloq.* endure, tolerate; **stand in** deputize *for*; **stand-in** deputy, substitute, esp. for actor or actress; **stand off** move or keep away, temporarily dispense with services of (employee); **stand-off half** *Rugby footb.* half-back who forms link between scrum-half and three-quarters; **stand-offish** cold or distant in manner; **stand on** insist on, observe scrupulously; **stand out** be prominent or conspicuous, persist in resistance *against* or support *for*; **standpipe** vertical pipe, esp. with spout or nozzle, for attachment to water-main; **standpoint** point of view; **standstill** stoppage, inability to proceed; **stand to** abide by, be likely or certain to; **stand to reason** be obvious or logical; **stand up** get on one's feet, maintain upright position, be valid, *colloq.* fail to keep appointment with; **stand-up** (of meal) eaten standing, (of fight) violent, thorough, (of collar) upright; **stand up for** support, side with; **stand up to** face courageously, be resistant to.

standard /ˈstændəd/ 1 n. object or quality or measure to which others (should) conform or against which others are judged; required degree of excellence etc.; ordinary procedure etc.; distinctive flag; upright support or pipe; treelike shrub with or grafted on upright stem. 2 a. serving or used as standard; of normal or prescribed quality or size etc. 3 **standard-bearer** person who carries distinctive flag, prominent leader in cause; **standard lamp** lamp set on tall holder standing on floor etc.; **standard of living** degree of material comfort enjoyed by person or group; **standard time** time established legally or by custom in region etc.

standardize /ˈstændədaɪz/ v.t. (cause to) conform to standard. **standardization** n.

standing /ˈstændɪŋ/ 1 n. established repute or position; duration. 2 a. of permanent kind; constantly ready for use; (of jump) made without run. 3 **standing order** instruction to banker to make regular payments; **standing orders** rules governing procedure in Parliament or council etc.; **standing room** space to stand in.

stank past of **stink**.

stanza /ˈstænzə/ n. group of lines forming division of song or poem.

staphylococcus /ˌstæfɪləˈkɒkəs/ n. (pl. -ci /-kaɪ/) form of pus-producing bacterium. **staphylococcal** a.

staple[1] /ˈsteɪp(ə)l/ 1 n. piece of wire or metal bent into U-shape for driving into wood etc.; various similar contrivances, esp. bent wire for fastening sheets of paper together. 2 v.t. furnish or fasten with staple(s).

staple[2] /ˈsteɪp(ə)l/ 1 a. principal; important as product or export. 2 n. important or principal product or article of commerce; chief element or material; textile fibre with respect to its quality or length.

star 1 n. celestial body appearing as point of light; celestial body considered as influencing human affairs or person's fate; rayed figure or object representing star as ornament etc.; asterisk; brilliant or prominent person, esp. chief actor or actress. 2 v. mark or adorn (as) with star(s); present or perform as star actor etc. 3 **starfish** star-shaped sea creature; **star-gazer** colloq. astronomer or astrologer; **starlight** light of stars; **Stars and Stripes** US national flag; **star turn** principal item or attraction.

starboard /ˈstɑːbəd/ 1 n. right-hand side of ship or aircraft etc. looking forward. 2 v.t. turn (helm) to starboard.

starch 1 n. white carbohydrate forming important constituent of human food; preparation of this for stiffening linen etc.; fig. stiffness of manner or conduct. 2 v.t. stiffen with starch. 3 **starchy** a.

stardom /ˈstɑːdəm/ n. being star, status of star.

stare /steə(r)/ 1 v. look fixedly with eyes wide open, esp. with curiosity or surprise or horror. 2 n. staring gaze. 3 **stare person in the face** be clearly evident or imminent.

stark 1 a. desolate, bare; sharply evident; downright, sheer; completely naked; arch. stiff, rigid. 2 adv. completely, wholly.

starlet /ˈstɑːlɪt/ n. young film actress likely to become star.

starling /ˈstɑːlɪŋ/ n. small gregarious chattering lustrous-plumaged bird.

starry /ˈstɑːrɪ/ a. set with stars; bright as star; starlike. **starry-eyed** colloq. romantic but unpractical.

start 1 v. set in motion or action; cause beginning of; set oneself in motion or action; begin journey; cause (machine etc.) to begin operating; (of engine) begin running; found or establish; give signal to (persons) to start in race; make sudden movement from surprise or pain etc.; rouse (game) from lair. 2 n. beginning; starting-place of race; advantage granted in beginning a race; advantageous initial position in life or business etc.; sudden movement of surprise or pain etc. 3 **starting-block** shaped block against which runner braces feet at start of race; **starting-gate** mechanically operated barrier used to start horse-races; **starting-price** final odds before start of horse-race etc.

starter /ˈstɑːtə(r)/ n. apparatus for starting engine of motor vehicle etc.; person giving signal to start race; competitor starting in race; first course of meal.

startle /ˈstɑːt(ə)l/ v.t. give shock or surprise to.

starve v. (cause to) die or suffer acutely from lack of food etc.; colloq. feel hungry; (cause to) be deprived of; force into or out etc. by starvation. **starvation** n.

starveling /'staːvlɪŋ/ n. starving person or animal.

stash sl. 1 v.t. conceal, put away in safe place. 2 n. hiding-place.

state 1 n. existing position or condition; colloq. excited or agitated condition of mind or feeling; (often **State**), organized political community under one government; civil government; pomp. 2 a. of or concerned with the State or its ceremonial occasions. 3 v.t. express, esp. fully or clearly, in speech or writing; specify; put into form of statement. 4 **lie in state** be laid in public place of honour before burial; **State Department** US Department of Foreign Affairs; **state of affairs** existing conditions. **stateroom** state apartment, private compartment in passenger ship; **the States** USA.

stately /'steɪtlɪ/ a. dignified, imposing. **stately home** large magnificent house, esp. one open to visits by the public.

statement /'steɪtmənt/ n. stating or being stated; thing stated; formal account of facts, esp. of transactions in bank account or of amount due to tradesman etc.

statesman /'steɪtsmən/ n. (pl. -men) person skilled in affairs of State; sagacious far-sighted politician. **statesmanlike** a.; **statesmanship** n.

static /'stætɪk/ 1 a. stationary, not active or changing; concerned with forces in equilibrium or bodies at rest. 2 n. static electricity; atmospherics. 3 **static electricity** electricity produced by friction, not flowing as current.

statics n.pl. (usu. treated as sing.) science of static bodies or forces; atmospherics.

station /'steɪʃ(ə)n/ 1 n. place or building etc. where person or thing stands or is placed or where particular activity, esp. public service, is based or organized; regular stopping-place on railway line, buildings of this; establishment engaged in broadcasting; military or naval base; position in life, rank, status; Aus. sheep- or other farm. 2 v.t. assign station to; put in position. **station-master** official in charge of railway-station; **Stations of the Cross** series of scenes from the Passion successively venerated in

some churches; **station-wagon** estate car.

stationary /'steɪʃənərɪ/ a. not moving or movable; not changing in amount or quantity.

stationer /'steɪʃənə(r)/ n. dealer in stationery.

stationery /'steɪʃənərɪ/ n. writing materials, office supplies, etc.

statistic /stə'tɪstɪk/ n. statistical fact or item.

statistics n.pl. numerical facts systematically collected; (usu. treated as sing.) science of collecting or using statistics. **statistician** /stætɪs'tɪʃ(ə)n/ a.

statistical /stə'tɪstɪk(ə)l/ a. of or concerned with statistics.

statuary /'stætjʊərɪ/ 1 a. of or for statues. 2 n. sculpture, statues.

statue /'stætjuː/ n. sculptured or cast or moulded figure of person or animal etc., usu. of or above life size.

statuesque /stætjʊ'esk/ a. like statue, esp. in beauty or dignity.

statuette /stætjʊ'et/ n. small statue.

stature /'stætjʊə(r)/ n. bodily height; eminence, mental or moral quality.

status /'steɪtəs/ n. social or legal position or condition; rank, prestige; superior social etc. position. **status quo** /kwəʊ/ existing or unchanged position; **status symbol** possession considered to show person's high social status.

statute /'stætjuːt/ n. law passed by legislative body; permanent rule of corporation etc.

statutory /'stætjʊtərɪ/ a. enacted or required by statute.

staunch /stɔːntʃ/ a. trustworthy, loyal.

stave 1 n. each of narrow shaped vertical strips forming sides of cask; stanza of song etc.; Mus. staff. 2 v.t. (past & p.p. **stove** or **staved**) break hole in, knock out of shape. 3 **stave in** crush by forcing inwards; **stave off** avert or defer (danger, misfortune, etc.).

staves see **staff**.

stay[1] 1 v. continue to be in same place or condition, not depart or change; dwell temporarily; (cause to) stop or pause; postpone (judgement etc.); assuage (hunger etc.) esp. for short time; show endurance. 2 n. action or period of staying; suspension or postponement of execution of sentence etc.

3 **stay-at-home** person remaining habitually at home; **staying-power** endurance; **stay put** *colloq.* remain where it is put or where one is.

stay² *n.* prop, support; rope etc. supporting mast or flagstaff etc.; tie-piece in aircraft; in *pl.* corset, esp. stiffened with whalebone etc. **staysail** sail extended on stay.

stayer /'steɪə(r)/ *n.* person or animal etc. of great endurance.

STD *abbr.* subscriber trunk dialling.

stead /sted/ *n.* **in person's** or **thing's stead** as substitute for him or it; **stand in good stead** be of advantage or service to (person).

steadfast /'stedfɑːst/ *a.* constant, firm, unwavering.

steady /'stedɪ/ *a.* firm, stable, not faltering or shaking or rocking or wavering etc.; settled; regular, maintained at even rate of action or change etc.; serious and dependable. 2 *v.* make or become steady. 3 *adv.* steadily. 4 *n. colloq.* regular boy-friend or girl-friend. 5 **steady state** unvarying condition, esp. in physical process.

steak /steɪk/ *n.* thick slice of meat (esp. beef) or fish, usu. grilled or fried. **steak-house** restaurant specializing in beef steaks.

steal /stiːl/ *v.* (*past* **stole**; *p.p.* **stolen**) take dishonestly and esp. secretly what is another's; obtain surreptitiously or by surprise, etc.; move secretly or silently. 2 *n. colloq.* stealing, theft; bargain, easy task. 3 **steal a march on** gain advantage over by acting surreptitiously; **steal the show** outshine other performers.

stealth /stelθ/ *n.* secret or surreptitious behaviour.

stealthy /'stelθɪ/ *a.* practising or done by stealth.

steam 1 *n.* gas into which water is changed by boiling; condensed vapour formed from this; power obtained from steam; *colloq.* power, energy. 2 *v.* give out steam; cook or soften etc. with steam; move by power of steam. 3 **let off steam** *fig.* relieve pent-up energy or feelings; **steamboat** one propelled by steam; **steam-engine** one worked or propelled by steam; **steam iron** electric iron emitting steam from its flat surface; **steamroller** heavy slow-moving locomotive with roller used in road-making, *fig.* a crushing power or force, (*v.t.*) crush or move along (as) with steam-roller; **steamship** one propelled by steam; **steam train** train pulled by steam-engine; **steam up** cover or become covered with condensed steam, *sl.* (esp. in *p.p.*) make (person) excited or angry; **under one's own steam** *fig.* without help from others. 4 **steamy** *a.*

steamer /'stiːmə(r)/ *n.* steamboat; utensil for steaming food etc.

steatite /'stiːətaɪt/ *n.* kind of usu. grey talc with greasy feel.

steed *n. poet.* horse.

steel 1 *n.* malleable alloy of iron and carbon, used for tools and weapons and machines etc.; steel rod for sharpening knives. 2 *v.t.* harden, make resolute. 3 **steel band** musical band of orig. W. Ind. kind, with instruments made from oil-drums; **steel wool** fine steel shavings used as abrasive; **steelyard** weighing-apparatus with graduated arm along which weight slides.

steely /'stiːlɪ/ *a.* of or like steel; inflexible, obdurate.

steep¹ 1 *a.* sloping sharply; (of rise or fall) rapid; *colloq.* (of price etc.) exorbitant; incredible. 2 *n.* steep hill, precipice.

steep² 1 *v.* soak or be soaked in liquid. 2 *n.* action of or liquid for steeping. 3 **steep in** *fig.* pervade or imbue with, make deeply acquainted with (subject etc.).

steepen /'stiːpən/ *v.* make or become steep(er).

steeple /'stiːp(ə)l/ *n.* tall tower, esp. with spire, above roof of church. **steeplechase** horse-race with obstacles such as fences to jump, cross-country foot-race; **steeplejack** man who repairs steeples and tall chimneys etc.

steer¹ *v.* guide (vehicle or ship etc.) by wheel or rudder etc.; direct or guide in specified direction. **steer clear of** take care to avoid; **steering column** column on which steering-wheel is mounted; **steering committee** one deciding order of business or general course of operations etc.; **steering-wheel** wheel by which vehicle or vessel etc. is steered; **steersman** person who steers ship.

steer² *n.* young male ox, esp. bullock.

steerage /'stɪərɪdʒ/ *n.* steering; part of ship allotted to passengers travelling at cheapest rate.

stein /staɪn/ *n.* large earthenware mug for beer etc.

stela /'stiːlə/ *n.* (*pl.* **-lae** /-liː/) (also **stele** /'stiːlɪ/) *Archaeol.* upright slab or pillar, usu. inscribed and sculptured, esp. as gravestone.

stellar /'stelə(r)/ *a.* of stars; star-shaped.

stem¹ 1 *n.* main body or stalk of plant; stalk supporting fruit or flower or leaf; stem-shaped part, e.g. slender part of wineglass between body and foot; *Gram.* root or main part of noun or verb etc. to which case-endings etc. are added; main upright timber at bow of ship. 2 *v.i.* spring or originate *from*.

stem² *v.* check, stop, make headway against, (stream etc.).

Sten *n.* (in full **Sten gun**) lightweight machine-gun.

stench *n.* foul or offensive smell.

stencil /'stens(ə)l/ 1 *n.* thin sheet in which pattern is cut, used to produce corresponding pattern on surface beneath it by applying ink or paint etc.; pattern so produced. 2 *v.t.* produce (pattern) with stencil; mark (surface) thus.

stenography /ste'nɒgrəfɪ/ *n.* shorthand. **stenographer** *n.*

stentorian /sten'tɔːrɪən/ *a.* (of voice) extremely loud.

step 1 *n.* complete action of moving and placing one leg in walking or running; distance covered by this; measure or (in *pl.*) course of action taken; flat-topped structure, esp. one of series, to facilitate movement from one level to another, stair, tread; in *pl.* step-ladder; short distance; mark or sound made by setting foot down; degree in scale, advance from one degree to another. 2 *v.* lift and set down foot or alternate feet in walking etc.; go or come in specified direction by stepping; make progress; measure (distance) by stepping; perform (dance). 3 **in step** stepping in time *with* other person(s) or music, moving or acting etc. in conformity or harmony or agreement (*with*); **mind**, **watch**,

one's step take care; **out of step** not in step; **step down** resign; **step in** enter, intervene; **step-ladder** short self-supporting ladder with flat steps; **step on it** *colloq.* hurry; **step out** take long steps, *colloq.* go out for entertainment etc.; **stepping-stone**, raised stone, usu. as one of set in stream etc. to help in crossing, *fig.* means of progress; **step up** come up or forward, increase rate or volume etc. of.

step- *in comb.* related by remarriage of parent. **stepchild**, **stepdaughter**, **stepson**, spouse's child by previous marriage; **stepfather**, **stepmother**, **step-parent**, mother's or father's later spouse; **stepbrother**, **stepsister**, child of previous marriage of one's step-parent.

stephanotis /stefə'nəʊtɪs/ *n.* fragrant tropical climbing plant.

steppe /step/ *n.* level treeless plain.

stereo /'steriəʊ/ 1 *n.* (*pl.* **-os**) stereophonic record-player etc.; stereophony; stereoscope; stereotype. 2 *a.* stereophonic; stereoscopic.

stereo- *in comb.* solid; three-dimensional.

stereophonic /steriəʊ'fɒnɪk/ *a.* using two or more transmission channels to give effect of naturally-distributed sound. **stereophony** /steri'ɒf-/ *n.*

stereoscope /'steriəskəʊp/ *n.* instrument for combining two pictures of object etc. from slightly different points of view, to give effect of three dimensions. **stereoscopic** /-'skɒp-/ *a.*

stereotype /'steriətaɪp/ 1 *n.* unduly fixed mental impression; conventional idea; printing-plate cast from mould of composed type. 2 *v.t.* formalize, make typical or conventional (usu. in *p.p.*); print from stereotype; make stereotype of.

sterile /'steraɪl/ *a.* not able to produce seed or offspring, barren; free from living germs; lacking originality or emotive power etc. **sterility** /-'rɪl-/ *n.*

sterilize /'sterɪlaɪz/ *v.t.* make sterile; deprive of power of reproduction. **sterilization** *n.*

sterling /'stɜːlɪŋ/ 1 *a.* of or in British money; genuine, of standard value or purity; of solid worth, reliable. 2 *n.* British money. 3 **sterling silver** silver of 92½% purity.

stern¹ *a.* severe, strict; enforcing discipline or submission.

stern² *n.* rear part of ship or aircraft etc.; any rear part. **stern-post** central upright timber etc. of stern, usu. bearing rudder.

sternum /'stɜːnəm/ *n.* (*pl.* **-nums** or **-na**) breastbone. **sternal** *a.*

steroid /'stɪərɔɪd/ *n.* any of various organic compounds incl. some hormones and vitamins.

sterol /'stɪərɒl/ *n.* one of class of complex solid alcohols.

stertorous /'stɜːtərəs/ *a.* (of breathing etc.) producing snoring or rasping sound.

stet *v.* (usu. as instruction written on proof-sheet etc.) ignore or cancel correction or alteration, let original form stand.

stethoscope /'steθəskəʊp/ *n.* instrument used for listening to heart and lungs etc. **stethoscopic** /-'skɒp-/ *a.*

stetson /'stets(ə)n/ *n.* slouch hat with wide brim and high crown.

stevedore /'stiːvədɔː(r)/ *n.* man employed in loading and unloading ships.

stew 1 *v.* cook by long simmering in closed vessel with liquid; make (tea) bitter or strong with too long standing; *colloq.* swelter. 2 *n.* dish of stewed meat etc.; *colloq.* state of great alarm or excitement.

steward /'stjuːəd/ 1 *n.* person employed to manage another's property or to arrange supplies of food for college or club or ship etc.; passengers' attendant on ship or aircraft or train; official managing race-meeting or show etc. **stewardship** *n.*

stewardess /'stjuːədes/ *n.* female steward, esp. in ship or aircraft.

stick¹ *n.* thin branch or piece of wood, esp. trimmed for use as support or as weapon; thin rod of wood etc. for particular purpose; more or less cylindrical piece of something; punishment, criticism; *colloq.* person, esp. one who is dull or unsociable. **stick-insect** insect with twiglike body.

stick² *v.* (*past & p.p.* **stuck**) thrust (point or pointed thing) *in(to)* or *through*; stab; fix or be fixed (as) by point *in(to)* or *on*; fix or become or remain fixed by adhesive etc.; lose or deprive of power of motion or action

through friction or jamming etc.; *colloq.* put or remain in specified place; *sl.* endure, tolerate. **stick around** *sl.* remain in same place; **stick at** *colloq.* work persistently at; **sticking-plaster** adhesive plaster for wounds etc.; **stick-in-the-mud** unprogressive or old-fashioned person; **stick out** (cause to) protrude, hold out persistently *for*; **stick up** (cause to) protrude, be or make erect, *sl.* rob or threaten (person etc.) with gun; **stick up for** support or defend.

sticker /'stɪkə(r)/ *n.* adhesive label.

stickleback /'stɪk(ə)lbæk/ *n.* small spiny-finned fish.

stickler /'stɪklə(r)/ *n.* person who insists on something.

sticky /'stɪkɪ/ *a.* tending or intended to stick or adhere, glutinous, viscous; (of weather) humid; *colloq.* making or likely to make objections; *sl.* very unpleasant or painful. **sticky wicket** difficult situation.

stiff 1 *a.* rigid, not flexible; not working freely, sticking, not supple; aching from exertion; thick and viscous, not fluid; hard to cope with, trying; unbending, unyielding; severe or strong; formal, constrained, haughty; (of alcoholic drink) strong. 2 *n. sl.* corpse. 3 **stiff-necked** obstinate or haughty; **stiff upper lip** firmness, fortitude.

stiffen /'stɪf(ə)n/ *v.* make or become stiff.

stifle /'staɪf(ə)l/ *v.* smother; cause or experience constraint of breathing or suppression of utterance etc.

stigma /'stɪgmə/ *n.* mark or sign of disgrace or discredit; *Bot.* part of pistil which receives pollen in pollination; (usu. in *pl.*, **stigmata**) marks corresponding to those left on Christ's body by the Crucifixion.

stigmatize /'stɪgmətaɪz/ *v.t.* characterize; describe opprobriously.

stile *n.* set of steps etc. to enable people to pass over fence or wall etc.

stiletto /stɪ'letəʊ/ *n.* (*pl.* **-tos**) short dagger; small pointed implement for making eyelet-holes etc. **stiletto heel** high narrow heel on shoe.

still¹ 1 *a.* without motion or sound, silent, quiet, calm; (of wine etc.) not effervescent. 2 *n.* silence; ordinary photograph, esp. illustration from cinema film. **3** *adv.* without motion or change; now, then, as before; even then, even now; nevertheless; even, yet; always. **4** *v.* make or become still, quieten. **5 still birth** birth of dead child; **stillborn** born dead, *fig.* abortive; **still life**, painting of inanimate objects.

still² *n.* apparatus for distilling. **still-room** housekeeper's store-room in large house.

stilt *n.* each of pair of poles with supports for feet enabling user to walk at a distance above the ground; each of set of piles or posts supporting building etc.

stilted /'stɪltɪd/ *a.* highflown; stiff and unnatural.

Stilton /'stɪlt(ə)n/ *n.* rich blue-veined cheese.

stimulant /'stɪmjʊlənt/ **1** *a.* that stimulates, esp. that increases bodily or mental activity. **2** *n.* stimulant substance or influence.

stimulate /'stɪmjʊleɪt/ *v.t.* animate, excite, rouse. **stimulation** *n.*; **stimulative** *a.*; **stimulator** *n.*

stimulus /'stɪmjʊləs/ *n.* (*pl.* -**li** /-laɪ/) stimulating thing or effect.

sting 1 *n.* sharp wounding organ of insect or snake or nettle etc.; inflicting of wound with this, the wound or the pain caused by it; wounding or painful quality or effect; keenness, vigour. **2** *v.* (*past & p.p.* **stung**) wound with sting; be able to do this; feel or cause tingling physical pain or sharp mental pain; incite by such mental effect; *sl.* charge heavily, swindle. **3 stinging-nettle** nettle that stings; **sting-ray** broad flat-fish with stinging tail.

stingy /'stɪndʒɪ/ *a.* niggardly, mean.

stink 1 *v.* (*past* **stank** or **stunk**; *p.p.* **stunk**) have strong offensive smell; *colloq.* be or seem very unpleasant. **2** *n.* strong offensive smell; *colloq.* loud complaint or fuss. **3 stink-bomb** device emitting stink when exploded; **stink out** drive out by stink, fill (place) with stink.

stinker /'stɪŋkə(r)/ *n. sl.* particularly annoying or unpleasant person; very difficult problem etc.; letter etc. conveying strong disapproval.

stinking /'stɪŋkɪŋ/ **1** *a.* that stinks; *sl.*

obnoxious, objectionable. **2** *adv. sl.* extremely and usu. objectionably.

stint 1 *v.t.* supply or give in niggardly or grudging way; keep on short allowance. **2** *n.* limitation of supply or effort; fixed or allotted amount of work etc.

stipend /'staɪpend/ *n.* salary, esp. of clergyman.

stipendiary /staɪ'pendɪərɪ/ **1** *a.* receiving stipend. **2** *n.* person receiving stipend. **3 stipendiary magistrate** paid magistrate.

stipple /'stɪp(ə)l/ **1** *v.* draw or paint with dots instead of lines; roughen surface of (paint or cement etc.). **2** *n.* stippling, effect of stippling.

stipulate /'stɪpjʊleɪt/ *v.* demand or specify as part or bargain or agreement. **stipulation** *n.*

stir 1 *v.* move spoon etc. round and round in (liquid etc.) to mix ingredients; move esp. slightly; be or begin to be in motion; arouse, inspire, excite. **2** *n.* act of stirring; commotion, excitement, sensation. **3 stir up** mix thoroughly by stirring, stimulate, incite.

stirrup /'stɪrəp/ *n.* support for rider's foot, suspended by strap from saddle. **stirrup-cup** drink offered to person about to depart, orig. on horseback; **stirrup-pump** small portable water-pump with stirrup-shaped foot-rest.

stitch 1 *n.* single pass of needle, or result of this, in sewing or knitting or crochet etc.; thread between two needle-holes; particular method of sewing or knitting etc.; least bit of clothing; acute pain in side induced by running etc. **2** *v.* sew, make stitches (in). **3 in stitches** *colloq.* laughing uncontrollably.

stoat *n.* ermine, esp. in its brown summer coat.

stock 1 *n.* store of goods etc. ready for sale or distribution; supply of things for use; equipment or raw material for trade; farm animals or implements; capital of business company; shares in this; money lent to government at fixed interest; one's reputation or popularity; line of ancestry; liquid made by stewing bones and vegetables etc., as basis for soup etc.; base or support or handle for implement or machine;

plant into which graft is inserted; fragrant garden plant; in *pl.* timbers on which ship rests while building; in *pl. hist.* wooden framework with holes for feet, where offenders were confined as public punishment; wide band of material worn round neck. **2** *a.* kept regularly in stock for sale or use; commonly used, constantly recurring. **3** *v.t.* keep (goods) in stock; equip with goods or requisites etc. **4 stockbroker** person who buys and sells stocks on commission; **stock-car** car used in racing where deliberate bumping is allowed; **stock exchange** place where stocks and shares are publicly bought and sold, dealers working there; **stock-in-trade** all requisites for particular trade or occupation etc.; **stockjobber** member of stock exchange dealing in stocks on his own account; **stock-market** stock exchange, transactions on this; **stockpile** reserve supply of raw materials or commodities etc., (*v.*) accumulate stockpile (of); **stock-pot** cooking-pot in which stock is made and kept; **stock-still** motionless; **stock-taking** making inventory of goods in shop etc.; **stock up** provide with or get stocks or supplies; **stock up with** gather stock of (food, fuel, etc.); **stock-yard** enclosure for sorting or temporary keeping of cattle etc.; **take stock** make inventory of merchandise etc. in hand, make review or estimate (*of*).

stockade /stɒˈkeɪd/ **1** *n.* line of upright stakes as a defence etc. **2** *v.t.* fortify with stockade.

stockinet /stɒkɪˈnet/ (also **-nette**) *n.* elastic knitted material.

stocking /ˈstɒkɪŋ/ *n.* covering for foot and all or part of leg, usu. knitted of nylon or silk or wool etc. **stocking mask** nylon stocking worn over head as criminal's disguise; **stocking-stitch** knitting-stitch of alternate rows of plain and purl.

stockist /ˈstɒkɪst/ *n.* person who stocks specified goods for sale.

stocky /ˈstɒkɪ/ *a.* short and strongly built.

stodge *n.* food esp. of thick heavy kind; unimaginative person or work.

stodgy /ˈstɒdʒɪ/ *a.* (of food) heavy, filling; dull, heavy, uninteresting.

stoic /ˈstəʊɪk/ *n.* person having great self-control in adversity. **stoical** *a.*; **stoicism** *n.*

stoke *v.* (often with *up*) feed and tend (furnace, fire, etc.); *colloq.* consume food esp. steadily and in large quantities. **stokehold** place where steamer's fires are tended; **stokehole** space for stokers in front of furnace.

stoker /ˈstəʊkə(r)/ *n.* person who stokes furnace esp. of ship or locomotive.

stole[1] *n.* woman's long garment like scarf worn over shoulders; strip of silk etc. worn as vestment by priest.

stole[2] *past* of **steal**.

stolen *p.p.* of **steal**.

stolid /ˈstɒlɪd/ *a.* slow to feel or show feeling; not easily excited or moved. **stolidity** *n.*

stomach /ˈstʌmək/ **1** *n.* internal organ in which food is digested; lower front of body; appetite or inclination etc. *for.* **2** *v.t.* endure, tolerate. **3 stomach-pump** syringe for emptying stomach or forcing liquid into it.

stomp *n.* lively jazz dance usu. with heavy stamping. **2** *v.* tread heavily (on); dance stomp.

stone **1** *n.* solid non-metallic mineral matter of which rock is made; small piece of this; piece of stone of definite shape or purpose; hard morbid concretion in kidney etc.; hard case of kernel in some fruits; precious stone; (*pl.* same) unit of weight (14 lb.). **2** *a.* made of stone. **3** *v.t.* pelt with stones; rid (fruit) of stone(s). **4 Stone Age** stage of civilization marked by use of stone implements and weapons; **stone-cold** completely cold; **stonecrop** creeping plant; **stone-dead** completely dead; **stone-deaf** completely deaf; **stone-fruit** fruit with flesh or pulp enclosing stone; **stone's throw** short distance; **stonewall** obstruct by evasive answers, *Crick.* bat with excessive caution; **stoneware** hard dense pottery of flinty clay; **stonework** masonry.

stony /ˈstəʊnɪ/ *a.* full of stones; hard or unfeeling; unresponsive. **stony-broke** *sl.* entirely without money.

stood *past* & *p.p.* of **stand**.

stooge /stuːdʒ/ **1** *n.* person acting as foil for comedian etc.; subordinate, puppet. **2** *v.i.* move *about* or *around* esp. in aimless way; act as stooge.

stool /stuːl/ *n.* seat without arms or back; footstool; faeces; root or stump of felled tree. **stool-pigeon** decoy, police informer.

stoop[1] /stuːp/ **1** *v.* bend down; carry head and shoulders bowed forward; deign or condescend (*to*). **2** *n.* stooping posture.

stoop[2] /stuːp/ *n.* US porch or small veranda or steps in front of house.

stop 1 *v.* put an end to progress or motion or operation etc. (of); effectively hinder or prevent; discontinue; come to an end; (cause to) cease action; defeat; *colloq.* remain or stay for short time; block or close up (hole, leak, etc., often with *up*); not permit or supply as usual; put filling in (tooth); *Mus.* obtain desired pitch from (string of violin etc.) by pressing at appropriate point with finger. **2** *n.* stopping or being stopped; place where bus or train etc., regularly stops; sign to show pause in written matter; device for stopping motion at particular point; *Mus.* change of pitch effected by stopping string; (in organ) set of pipes of one character, knob etc. operating these; *Photog.* etc. diaphragm, effective diameter of lens, device reducing this; plosive sound. **3 pull out all the stops** make extreme effort; **stopcock** externally operated valve to regulate flow in pipe etc.; **stop dead** stop abruptly; **stopgap** temporary substitute; **stop off**, **over**, break one's journey; **stop-press** late news inserted in newspaper after printing has begun; **stop short** stop abruptly; **stop-watch** watch with mechanism for instantly starting and stopping it, used in timing of races etc.

stoppage /ˈstɒpɪdʒ/ *n.* condition of being blocked or stopped.

stopper /ˈstɒpə(r)/ *n.* plug for closing bottle etc.

stopping /ˈstɒpɪŋ/ *n.* filling for tooth.

storage /ˈstɔːrɪdʒ/ *n.* storing of goods or data etc.; method of or space for or cost of storing. **storage battery** accumulator; **storage heater** electric heater accumulating heat outside peak hours for later release.

store 1 *n.* quantity of something ready to be drawn on; in *pl.* articles of particular kind or for special purpose; in *pl.* supply of things needed, stocks, reserves; storehouse; large shop selling goods of many different kinds; *US* shop; device in computer for storing retrievable data etc. **2** *v.t.* put in store; lay up for future use; stock or provide with something useful. **3 in store** in reserve, to come, waiting, *for*; **storehouse** place where things are stored; **storekeeper** person in charge of stores; *US* shopkeeper; **store-room** place where household or other supplies are kept.

storey /ˈstɔːrɪ/ *n.* each stage or portion into which building is divided horizontally.

stork *n.* large long-legged wading bird.

storm 1 *n.* violent disturbance of atmosphere, with high winds and freq. rain and thunder etc.; violent disturbance or tumult in human affairs; heavy discharge or shower (*of* blows, abuse, etc.); assault on (and capture of) fortified place. **2** *v.* rage, be violent; bluster; rush violently; take by storm. **3 storm-centre** comparatively calm central area of cyclonic storm, centre round which storm of controversy etc. rages; **storm-cloud** heavy rain-cloud; **storm troops** shock troops, Nazi political militia; **take by storm** take by assault, quickly captivate.

stormy /ˈstɔːmɪ/ *a.* of or affected by storm(s); violent, full of feeling or outbursts.

story /ˈstɔːrɪ/ *n.* account of real or fictitious events; narrative, tale, anecdote; course of life of person or institution etc.; plot of novel or play etc.; article in newspaper, material for this; *colloq.* lie. **story-teller** person who tells or writes stories, *colloq.* liar.

stoup /stuːp/ *n.* holy-water basin; *arch.* flagon, beaker.

stout /staʊt/ **1** *a.* rather fat, corpulent; of considerable thickness or strength; undaunted, resolute. **2** *n.* strong dark type of beer.

stove[1] *n.* enclosed apparatus to contain burning fuel or consume electricity etc. for heating or cooking etc. **stove-enamel** heat-proof enamel; **stove-pipe** pipe carrying off smoke etc. from stove.

stove[2] *past* & *p.p.* of **stave**.

stow /stəʊ/ v.t. pack (away) esp. closely or compactly; sl. desist from. **stow away** conceal oneself on ship etc., esp. to avoid paying fare; **stowaway** person who stows away.

stowage /'stəʊɪdʒ/ n. stowing; place for this.

straddle /'stræd(ə)l/ 1 v. stand or sit across with legs wide apart; spread legs wide apart; drop shots or bombs short of and beyond (target). 2 n. act of straddling.

strafe /strɑːf/ 1 v.t. bombard; harass with gunfire. 2 n. act of strafing.

straggle /'stræg(ə)l/ 1 v.i. lack or lose compactness or tidiness; stray from main body, be dispersed or scattered. 2 n. straggling group. 3 **straggly** a.

straight /streɪt/ 1 a. without curve or bend or flare, not crooked or curly; direct, successive; level, tidy, in proper order or place or condition; honest, candid; unmodified; undiluted; sl. conventional, respectable, heterosexual. 2 n. straight part of something, esp. concluding stretch of racecourse; straight condition; sl. straight person. 3 adv. in a straight line, direct; in right direction, correctly. 4 **go straight** live honestly after being criminal; **straight away** immediately; **straight face** serious expression, esp. avoiding smile though amused; **straight fight** contest between two candidates only; **straightforward** honest, open, presenting no complications; **straight man** performer who says things for comedian to make jokes about; **straight off** colloq. immediately, without hesitation etc.; **straight out** frankly, outspokenly.

straighten /'streɪt(ə)n/ v. make or become straight. **straighten up** stand erect after bending.

strain¹ 1 v. stretch tightly; make or become taut or tense (oneself, senses, powers, etc.) intensely or excessively; press to extremes, make intense effort; distort from true intention or meaning; overtask or injure by over-use or excessive demands; clear (liquid) of solid matter by passing it through sieve etc.; in p.p. constrained, artificial. 2 n. act of straining; force exerted in straining; injury caused by straining muscle etc.; severe demand on resources, exertion needed to meet

this; snatch or spell of music or poetry; tone or tendency in speech or writing.

strain² n. breed or stock of animals or plants etc.; moral tendency as part of character.

strainer /'streɪnə(r)/ n. utensil for straining liquids.

strait 1 n. narrow water-passage connecting two large bodies of water; in pl. difficult position, need. 2 a. arch. narrow, strict. 3 **strait-jacket** strong garment put on violent person to confine arms, fig. restrictive measures; **strait-laced** severely virtuous, puritanical.

straiten /'streɪt(ə)n/ v.t. restrict; in p.p. of or marked by poverty.

strand¹ 1 v. run aground; (in p.p.) in difficulties, without money or means of transport. 2 n. margin of sea or river etc., esp. foreshore.

strand² n. any of strings or wires twisted together to form rope etc.; constituent filament of necklace or hair etc.; fig. element in character, theme in story, etc.

strange /streɪndʒ/ a. unusual, peculiar, surprising, eccentric; unfamiliar, alien, foreign; unaccustomed to, not at ease.

stranger /'streɪndʒə(r)/ n. person in place or company etc. that he does not know or belong to; person one does not know.

strangle /'stræŋg(ə)l/ v.t. kill by external compression of throat; hinder growth of by overcrowding; suppress. **stranglehold** deadly grip (usu. fig.).

strangulate /'stræŋgjʊleɪt/ v.t. constrict so as to prevent circulation or passage of fluid.

strangulation /stræŋgjʊ'leɪʃ(ə)n/ n. strangling; strangulating.

strap 1 n. flat strip of leather etc., esp. with buckle etc., for holding things together; loop for grasping to steady oneself in moving vehicle. 2 v.t. secure or bind (up) with strap; thrash with strap.

strapping /'stræpɪŋ/ 1 a. stalwart; tall and strong. 2 n. strip(s) of adhesive plaster.

strata pl. of **stratum**. □ See page 667.

stratagem /'strætədʒəm/ n. cunning plan or scheme; trick.

strategic /strə'tiːdʒɪk/ a. of or serving the ends of strategy; (of materials) essential in war; (of bombing) designed to disorganize or demoralize the enemy; (of nuclear weapons etc.) able to reach the enemy's home territory rather than for use at close quarters.

strategy /'strætɪdʒɪ/ n. art of war; art of planning and directing larger movements and operations of campaign or war; plan of action or policy in business or politics etc. **strategist** n.

strathspey /stræθ'speɪ/ n. slow Sc. country dance; music for this.

stratify /'strætɪfaɪ/ v. arrange in strata or layers etc. **stratification** n.

stratosphere /'stætəsfɪə(r)/ n. region of atmosphere above troposphere.

stratum /'strɑːtəm/ n. (pl. **-ta**) layer of rock; layer of deposits in excavation etc.; social grade or class etc.

straw n. dry cut stalks of various cereals; single stalk or piece of straw; hollow tube for sucking drink through; insignificant thing; pale yellow colour. **straw vote** unofficial ballot as test of opinion.

strawberry /'strɔːbərɪ/ n. pulpy red fruit having surface studded with yellow seeds; plant bearing this. **strawberry-mark** reddish birthmark.

stray 1 v.i. wander from the right place, become separated from one's companions etc.; go astray; deviate. **2** n. strayed domestic animal; homeless friendless person. **3** a. strayed; isolated, occasional.

streak 1 n. thin irregular line or band of different colour or substance from surface etc. in which it appears; flash of lightning; strain, element, trait. **2** v. mark with streaks; go at full speed; colloq. run naked through public place.

streaky /'striːkɪ/ a. marked with streaks; (of bacon) with fat and lean in layers or streaks.

stream 1 n. body of running water, esp. small river; current or flow; group of schoolchildren selected as being of similar ability. **2** v. flow or move as or in stream; run with liquid; emit stream of; float or wave in wind; arrange (schoolchildren) in streams. **3 on stream** in active operation or production.

streamer /'striːmə(r)/ n. long narrow flag; long narrow ribbon of paper.

streamline /'striːmlaɪn/ v.t. give form which presents least resistance to motion; make simple or more efficient or better organized.

street n. road in town or village with houses on each side. **man in the street** ordinary person; **on the streets** living as prostitute; **streetcar** US tram; **street-walker** prostitute seeking customers in street.

strength n. quality or extent or manner of being strong; what makes one strong; number of persons present or available. **on the strength of** relying on, arguing from.

strengthen /'streŋθ(ə)n/ v. make or become stronger.

strenuous /'strenjʊəs/ a. making or requiring great exertions, energetic.

streptococcus /streptə'kɒkəs/ n. (pl. **-cocci** /-'kɒkaɪ/) bacterium causing serious infections. **streptococcal** a.

streptomycin /streptə'maɪsɪn/ n. an antibiotic drug.

stress 1 n. pressure, tension; quantity measuring this; demand on physical or mental energy; emphasis. **2** v.t. lay stress on, accent, emphasize; subject to stress.

stressful /'stresfʊl/ a. causing stress.

stretch 1 v. draw or be drawn or admit of being drawn out into greater length or size; make or become taut; place or lie at full length or spread out; extend limbs to tighten muscles; have specified length or extension; extend; strain or exert to utmost or beyond legitimate extent; exaggerate. **2** n. stretching or being stretched; continuous expanse or tract or period; sl. term of imprisonment. **3 at a stretch** without intermission, continuously; **stretch one's legs** exercise oneself by walking; **stretch out** extend (hand, foot, etc.), prolong, last for longer period; **stretch a point** agree to something not normally allowed.

stretcher /'stretʃə(r)/ n. oblong frame with handles at each end for carrying sick or injured etc. person; any of various devices for stretching; brick etc. laid with length in direction of wall.

stretchy /'stretʃɪ/ a. colloq. able or tending to stretch.

strew v.t. (p.p. **strewn** or **strewed**)

scatter over surface; cover (surface etc.) *with* small objects scattered.

striated /straɪ'eɪtɪd/ *a.* marked with slight ridges or furrows etc. **striation** *n.*

stricken 1 *arch. p.p.* of **strike**. **2** *a.* afflicted with disease or grief etc.

strict *a.* precisely limited or defined; without exception or deviation; requiring complete obedience or exact performance.

stricture /'strɪktʃə(r)/ *n.* (usu. in *pl.*) adverse criticism, critical remark.

stride 1 *v.* (*past* **strode**; *p.p.* **stridden**) walk with long steps; pass over with one step; bestride. **2** *n.* single walking or running step; distance covered by long step; (usu. in *pl.*) progress. **3 take in one's stride** manage without difficulty.

strident /'straɪd(ə)nt/ *a.* loud and harsh. **stridency** *n.*

strife *n.* conflict, struggle, dispute.

strike 1 *v.* (*past* **struck**; *p.p.* **struck** or *arch. exc. in comb.* **stricken**) subject to impact, deliver (blow) or inflict blow on; come or bring sharply into contact with, propel or divert with blow; (cause to) penetrate; ignite (match) or produce (sparks) by rubbing; make (coin) by stamping; produce (musical note) by striking; (of clock) indicate (time) by sounding of bell etc.; (of time) be indicated thus; afflict; cause to become suddenly; reach or achieve; agree on (bargain); put oneself theatrically into (attitude); discover or come across; find (oil) by drilling; come to attention of or appear to; (of employees) engage in strike, cease work as protest; lower or take down (flag, tent, etc.); take specified direction. **2** *n.* act of striking; employees' concerted refusal to work until some grievance is remedied; similar refusal to participate in other expected activity; sudden find or success; attack, esp. from the air. **3 on strike** taking part in industrial strike; **strikebreaker** person working or engaged in place of striker; **strike home** deal effective blow; **strike off** remove with stroke, delete; **strike out** hit out, act vigorously, delete; **strike pay** allowance paid to strikers by trade union; **strike up** start (acquaintance, con-versation) casually, begin playing (tune etc.).

striker /'straɪkə(r)/ *n.* person or thing that strikes; employee on strike; *Footb.* etc. player whose main function is to try to score goals.

striking /'straɪkɪŋ/ *a.* noticeable, impressive.

string 1 *n.* twine or fine cord; length of this or some other material serving to tie or attach or lace or activate puppet etc.; piece of catgut or wire etc. on musical instrument, producing note by vibration; in *pl.* stringed instruments in orchestra etc.; in *pl.* awkward condition attached to offer etc.; set of things strung together; group of racehorses trained at particular stable; tough fibre etc. **2** *v.* (*past & p.p.* **strung**) supply with string(s); thread on string; connect or put together or arrange in series or row(s) etc.; remove strings from (bean-pod etc.). **3 string along** *colloq.* deceive; **string-course** raised horizontal band of bricks etc. on building; **string up** hang up on strings, kill by hanging.

stringed /strɪŋd/ *a.* (of musical instrument) having strings.

stringent /'strɪndʒ(ə)nt/ *a.* strict, binding, requiring exact performance. **stringency** *n.*

stringer /'strɪŋə(r)/ *n.* longitudinal structural member in framework esp. of ship or aircraft; newspaper correspondent not on regular staff.

stringy /'strɪŋɪ/ *a.* fibrous; like string.

strip¹ 1 *v.* remove clothes or covering from, undress; deprive (person) of property or titles; leave bare of accessories etc.; remove old paint etc. from; damage thread of (screw). **2** *n.* act of stripping, esp. of undressing in strip-tease; *colloq.* clothes worn by member of sports team etc. **3 strip club** club where strip-tease is performed; **strip-tease** entertainment in which performer gradually undresses before audience.

strip² *n.* long narrow piece. **strip cartoon** comic strip; **strip light** tubular fluorescent light; **tear person off a strip** *sl.* rebuke him.

stripe *n.* long narrow band differing in colour or texture from surface on either side; *Mil.* chevron etc. indicating rank; *arch.* (usu. in *pl.*) blow with scourge or lash. **stripy** *a.*

striped /straɪpt/ *a.* having stripes.

stripling /ˈstrɪplɪŋ/ *n.* youth not fully grown.

stripper /ˈstrɪpə(r)/ *n.* device or solvent for removing paint etc.; performer of strip-tease.

strive *v.i.* (*past* **strove**; *p.p.* **striven** /ˈstrɪv(ə)n/) try hard; struggle or contend *against.*

strobe *n. colloq.* stroboscope.

stroboscope /ˈstrəʊbəskəʊp/ *n.* lamp producing regular intermittent flashes. **stroboscopic** /-ˈskɒp-/ *a.*

strode *past* of **stride.**

stroke 1 *n.* act of striking; sudden disabling attack esp. of apoplexy; action or movement esp. as one of series or in game etc.; slightest such action; effort or action of specified kind; sound made by striking clock etc.; movement in one direction of pen or paintbrush etc.; detail contributing to general effect; mode or action of moving oar; mode of moving limbs in swimming; oarsman nearest stern, who sets time of stroke; act or spell of stroking. 2 *v.t.* pass hand gently along surface of; act as stroke of (boat, crew).

stroll /strəʊl/ 1 *v.i.* walk in leisurely fashion. 2 *n.* leisurely walk. 3 **strolling players** actors etc. going from place to place performing.

strong 1 *a.* physically or morally or mentally powerful or vigorous or robust; powerful in numbers or equipment etc.; performed with muscular strength; difficult to capture or break into or escape from etc.; energetic, effective, decided; powerfully affecting senses or mind etc.; (of drink) with large proportion of alcohol or flavouring ingredient etc.; (of verb) forming inflexions by vowel change in root syllable. 2 *adv.* strongly, vigorously. 3 **going strong** thriving; **strong-arm** use of force; **strong-box** strongly made box for valuables; **stronghold** fortress, citadel, centre of support for a cause etc.; **strong language** swearing; **strong-minded** with vigorous or determined mind; **strong point** fortified position, *fig.* thing at which one excels; **strong-room** strongly-built room for valuables;

strong suit suit at cards in which one can take tricks, *fig.* thing in which one excels.

strontium /ˈstrɒntɪəm/ *n.* soft silver-white metallic element. **strontium 90** radioactive isotope of this.

strop 1 *n.* device, esp. strip of leather, for sharpening razors. 2 *v.t.* sharpen on or with strop.

stroppy /ˈstrɒpɪ/ *a. sl.* bad-tempered, awkward to deal with.

strove *past* of **strive.**

struck *past* & *p.p.* of **strike.**

structuralism /ˈstrʌktʃərəlɪz(ə)m/ *n.* doctrine that structure rather than function is important. **structuralist** *a.* & *n.*

structure /ˈstrʌktʃə(r)/ 1 *n.* way in which thing is constructed; supporting framework or essential parts; thing constructed; complex whole. 2 *v.t.* give structure to, organize. 3 **structural** *a.*

strudel /ˈstruːd(ə)l/ *n.* confection of thin pastry filled esp. with apple.

struggle /ˈstrʌg(ə)l/ 1 *v.i.* throw one's limbs or body about in violent effort to get free; make great efforts under difficulties; contend *with* or *against* etc.; make one's way with difficulty. 2 *n.* act or period of struggling; hard or confused contest.

strum 1 *v.* play on (stringed or keyboard instrument) esp. carelessly or unskilfully. 2 *n.* strumming sound.

strumpet /ˈstrʌmpɪt/ *n. arch.* prostitute.

strung *past* & *p.p.* of **string.**

strut 1 *n.* bar inserted in framework to resist pressure; strutting gait. 2 *v.* walk in stiff pompous way; brace with strut(s).

'struth /struːθ/ *int. colloq.* exclamation of surprise.

strychnine /ˈstrɪkniːn/ *n.* highly poisonous vegetable alkaloid.

stub 1 *n.* remnant of pencil or cigarette etc., after use; counterfoil of cheque or receipt etc.; stump, stunted tail, etc. 2 *v.t.* strike (one's toe) against something; (usu. with *out*) extinguish (cigarette etc.) by pressing lighted end against something.

stubble /ˈstʌb(ə)l/ *n.* cut stalks of cereals left sticking up after harvest; short stubble-like growth of hair, esp. on unshaven face. **stubbly** *a.*

stubborn /'stʌbən/ a. obstinate, inflexible; intractable.

stubby /'stʌbɪ/ a. short and thick.

stucco /'stʌkəʊ/ 1 n. (pl. **-oes**) plaster or cement for coating walls or moulding into architectural decorations. 2 v.t. coat with stucco.

stuck past & p.p. of **stick**. **get stuck into** sl. start in earnest; **stuck for** at a loss for, needing; **stuck-up** colloq. conceited, snobbish; **stuck with** colloq. unable to get rid of.

stud[1] 1 n. projecting nail-head or similar knob on surface; device for fixing separate collar to shirt. 2 v.t. set with studs; in p.p. thickly set or strewn with (jewels, stars, etc.).

stud[2] n. number of horses kept for breeding etc.; place where these are kept; stallion; stud poker. **stud-book** book giving pedigrees of thoroughbred horses; **stud-farm** place where horses are bred; **stud poker** poker with betting after dealing of successive cards face up.

student /'stju:d(ə)nt/ n. person who is studying, esp. at university or other place of higher education; attrib. studying in order to become (nurse, teacher, etc.).

studied /'stʌdɪd/ a. deliberate, intentional, artificial.

studio /'stju:dɪəʊ/ n. (pl. **-dios**) workroom of sculptor or painter or photographer etc.; room or premises used for transmission of broadcasts etc. or making films or recordings etc. **studio couch** couch that can be converted into a bed.

studious /'stju:dɪəs/ a. assiduous in study or reading; painstaking, deliberate.

study /'stʌdɪ/ 1 n. giving one's attention to acquiring information esp. from books; in pl. pursuit of knowledge; piece of work, esp. in painting, done as exercise or preliminary experiment; careful examination or observation of; Mus. composition designed to develop player's skill; room used for reading or writing etc.; thing that is or deserves to be investigated. 2 v. make object of study; apply oneself to study; scrutinize; devote time and thought to understanding subject etc. or assuring desired result.

stuff 1 n. material that thing is made of; substance or things of uncertain kind or quality or not needing to be specified; particular knowledge or activity; woollen fabric; trash, nonsense. 2 v. pack, cram; fill out skin to restore original shape of (bird, animal, etc.); fill (receptacle, cushion-cover, etc.) with; fill (inside of bird, piece of meat, etc.) with minced seasoning etc. before cooking; eat greedily, overeat oneself; push, esp. hastily or clumsily; block up.

stuffing /'stʌfɪŋ/ n. padding used for stuffing cushions; savoury mixture used to stuff fowls etc.

stuffy /'stʌfɪ/ a. lacking ventilation; close, oppressive; old-fashioned or narrow-minded.

stultify /'stʌltɪfaɪ/ v.t. make ineffective or useless; reduce to foolishness or absurdity. **stultification** n.

stumble /'stʌmb(ə)l/ 1 v.i. lurch forward or have partial fall from catching or striking foot etc.; make blunder(s) in speaking etc.; come accidentally across or (up)on. 2 n. act of stumbling. 3 **stumbling-block** obstacle, circumstance causing difficulty or hesitation.

stump 1 n. projecting remnant of felled or fallen tree; part remaining of broken branch or tooth or amputated limb etc.; stub; Crick. each of 3 uprights of wicket. 2 v. be too difficult for, cause to be at a loss; Crick. put batsman out by touching stumps with ball while he is out of his crease; walk stiffly or clumsily and noisily; traverse (district) making political speeches. 3 **stump up** sl. produce or pay over money required.

stumpy /'stʌmpɪ/ a. stocky, short and thick.

stun v.t. knock senseless; stupefy, bewilder, shock.

stung past & p.p. of **sting**.

stunk past & p.p. of **stink**.

stunner /'stʌnə(r)/ n. colloq. stunning person or thing.

stunning /'stʌnɪŋ/ a. colloq. extremely good or attractive.

stunt[1] v.t. retard growth or development of, dwarf, cramp.

stunt[2] colloq. 1 n. something unusual done to attract attention; trick or daring manoeuvre. 2 v.i. perform stunts. 3 **stunt man** man employed to take actor's place in performing dangerous stunts.

stupefy /'stju:pɪfaɪ/ v.t. make stupid or insensible; astonish. **stupefaction** n.

stupendous /stju:'pendəs/ a. amazing; of vast size or importance.

stupid /'stju:pɪd/ a. unintelligent; slow-witted; uninteresting; in state of stupor. **stupidity** n.

stupor /'stju:pə(r)/ n. dazed or torpid state; utter amazement.

sturdy /'stɜ:dɪ/ a. robust, hardy, strongly built.

sturgeon /'stɜ:dʒ(ə)n/ n. large edible fish yielding caviare.

stutter /'stʌtə(r)/ v. & n. stammer.

sty[1] /staɪ/ n. enclosure for pigs; filthy room or dwelling.

sty[2] /staɪ/ n. inflamed swelling on edge of eyelid.

Stygian /'stɪdʒɪən/ a. of or like Styx or Hades; murky, gloomy.

style /staɪl/ 1 n. kind, sort; manner of writing or speaking or doing; distinctive manner of person or school or period; correct way of designating person or thing; superior quality or manner; fashion in dress etc.; implement for scratching or engraving; Bot. narrow extension of ovary supporting stigma. 2 v.t. design or make etc. in particular style; designate in specified way.

stylish /'staɪlɪʃ/ a. fashionable, elegant.

stylist /'staɪlɪst/ n. person having or aiming at good style in writing etc.; person who styles hair.

stylistic /staɪ'lɪstɪk/ a. of literary or artistic style.

stylize /'staɪlaɪz/ v.t. (usu. in p.p.) make conform to rules of conventional style, conventionalize. **stylization** n.

stylus /'staɪləs/ n. (pl. **-li** /laɪ/) needle-like point for producing or following groove in gramophone record; ancient pointed writing-implement.

stymie /'staɪmɪ/ v.t. obstruct, thwart.

styptic /'stɪptɪk/ 1 a. serving to check bleeding. 2 n. styptic substance.

suave /swɑ:v/ a. urbane, gracious, refined. **suavity** n.

sub colloq. 1 n. submarine; subscription; substitute; sub-editor. 2 v. act as substitute; sub-edit.

sub- in comb. under, below; more or less, roughly, not quite, on the borders of; subordinate(ly), secondary, further.

subaltern /'sʌbəlt(ə)n/ n. Mil. officer of rank next below captain.

subaqua /sʌ'bækwə/ a. (of sport etc.) taking place under water.

subatomic /sʌbə'tɒmɪk/ a. occurring in or smaller than an atom.

subcommittee /'sʌbkəmɪtɪ/ n. committee formed from main committee for special purpose.

subconscious /sʌb'kɒnʃəs/ 1 n. part of mind that is not fully conscious but is able to influence actions etc. 2 a. of the subconscious.

subcontinent /sʌb'kɒntɪnənt/ n. land-mass of great extent not classed as continent.

subcontract 1 /sʌbkɒn'trækt/ n. arrangement by which person who has contracted to do work arranges for it to be done by others. 2 /sʌbkən'trækt/ v. make subcontract (for). 3 **subcontractor** n.

subculture /'sʌbkʌltʃə(r)/ n. social group or its culture within a larger culture.

subcutaneous /sʌbkju:'teɪnɪəs/ a. under the skin.

subdivide /sʌbdɪ'vaɪd/ v. divide again after first division.

subdivision /sʌbdɪ'vɪʒ(ə)n/ n. subdividing; subordinate division.

subdue /səb'dju:/ v.t. conquer, suppress; tame; soften, tone down.

sub-edit /sʌb'edɪt/ v.t. act as sub-editor of.

sub-editor /sʌb'edɪtə(r)/ n. assistant editor; person who prepares material for printing in newspaper or book etc. **sub-editorial** a.

sub-heading /sʌb'hedɪŋ/ n. subordinate division of subject etc.; subordinate heading or title.

subhuman /sʌb'hju:mən/ a. less than human; not fully human.

subject 1 /'sʌbdʒɪkt/ n. theme of discussion or description or representation or music, matter (to be) studied or thought about; person under political rule; member of State or of subject State; circumstance or person or thing that gives occasion for specified feeling or action; branch of study; Gram. etc. thing about which something is predicated; thinking or feeling entity, conscious self; person with specified usu. undesirable bodily or mental tendency. **2** /ˈsʌbdʒɪkt/ *a.* under government; (with *to*) conditional upon; owing obedience *to*; liable exposed or prone *to*. **3** /ˈsʌbdʒɪkt/ *adv.* (with *to*) conditionally upon, on the assumption of. **4** /səbˈdʒekt/ *v.t.* expose or make liable *to*; subdue (nation etc.). **5 subject-matter** matter dealt with in book or lawsuit etc. **6 subjection** *n.*

subjective /səbˈdʒektɪv/ *a.* of or due to the consciousness or thinking or percipient subject as opp. real or external things, not objective, imaginary; *Gram.* of the subject. **subjectivity** *n.*

subjoin /səbˈdʒɔɪn/ *v.t.* add at the end.

sub judice /sʌb ˈdʒuːdɪsɪ/ under judicial consideration, not yet decided. [L]

subjugate /ˈsʌbdʒʊgeɪt/ *v.t.* conquer, bring into subjection. **subjugation** *n.*

subjunctive /səbˈdʒʌŋktɪv/ *Gram.* **1** *a.* (of mood) expressing wish or supposition or possibility. **2** *n.* subjunctive mood or form.

sublease **1** /ˈsʌbliːs/ *n.* lease granted to subtenant. **2** /sʌbˈliːs/ *v.t.* lease by sublease.

sublet /sʌbˈlet/ *v.t.* (*past & p.p.* **-let**) lease to subtenant.

sublimate **1** /ˈsʌblɪmeɪt/ *v.t.* divert energy of (primitive impulse etc.) into culturally higher activity; sublime (substance); refine, purify. **2** /ˈsʌblɪmət/ *n.* sublimated substance. **3 sublimation** *n.*

sublime /səˈblaɪm/ **1** *a.* of most exalted kind; inspiring awe. **2** *v.t.* convert (substance) from solid into vapour by heat (and usu. allow to solidify again); (of substance) undergo this process; make sublime. **3 sublimity** /-ˈlɪm-/ *n.*

subliminal /səbˈlɪmɪn(ə)l/ *a. Psych.* below threshold of consciousness; too faint or rapid to be consciously perceived.

sub-machine-gun /sʌbməˈʃiːngʌn/ *n.* lightweight machine-gun held by hand.

submarine /sʌbməˈriːn/ **1** *a.* existing or occurring or done below surface of sea. **2** *n.* vessel which can be submerged and navigated under water.

submerge /səbˈmɜːdʒ/ *v.* place or go

beneath water. **submergence** *n.*; **submersion** *n.*

submersible /səbˈmɜːsɪb(ə)l/ **1** *a.* capable of submerging. **2** *n.* submersible vehicle.

submicroscopic /sʌbmaɪkrəˈskɒpɪk/ *a.* too small to be seen by microscope.

submission /sʌbˈmɪʃ(ə)n/ *n.* submitting or being submitted; thing submitted; submissive attitude etc.

submissive /səbˈmɪsɪv/ *a.* willing to submit; unresisting, meek.

submit /səbˈmɪt/ *v.* surrender (*oneself*) to the control or authority of another, cease to resist or oppose; present for consideration or decision; subject *to* a process or treatment.

subnormal /sʌbˈnɔːm(ə)l/ *a.* less than normal; below normal.

subordinate **1** /səˈbɔːdɪnət/ *a.* of inferior importance or rank, secondary, subservient. **2** /səˈbɔːdɪnət/ *n.* subordinate person. **3** /səˈbɔːdɪneɪt/ *v.t.* make subordinate; treat or regard as of minor importance. **4 subordinate clause** clause serving as noun or adjective or adverb within sentence. **5 subordination** *n.*

suborn /səˈbɔːn/ *v.t.* induce esp. by bribery to commit perjury or other crime.

subpoena /səbˈpiːnə/ **1** *n.* writ commanding person's attendance in lawcourt. **2** *v.t.* (*past & p.p.* **-poenaed** /-ˈpiːnəd/) serve subpoena on.

sub rosa /sʌb ˈrəʊzə/ (done) in confidence or in secret. [L]

subscribe /səbˈskraɪb/ *v.* pay (specified sum) esp. regularly for membership of an organization or receipt of a publication etc.; agree to pay (such sum); contribute *to* a fund or *for* a purpose; write (esp. one's name) at foot of document etc., sign (document) thus. **subscribe to** arrange to receive (periodical etc.) regularly, agree with (opinion or resolution).

subscriber /səbˈskraɪbə(r)/ *n.* person who subscribes, esp. person paying regular sum for hire of telephone. **subscriber trunk dialling** making of trunk-calls by subscriber without assistance of operator.

subscript /ˈsʌbskrɪpt/ **1** *a.* written or printed below. **2** *n.* subscript number or symbol.

subscription /səb'skrɪpʃ(ə)n/ *n.* amount subscribed, act of subscribing.

subsequent /'sʌbsɪkwənt/ *a.* following a specified or implied event. **subsequent to** later than, after.

subservient /sʌb'sɜːvɪənt/ *a.* subordinate *to*; obsequious; of use in minor role. **subservience** *n.*

subside /səb'saɪd/ *v.i.* sink or settle to lower level; cave in, sink; become less active or intense or prominent; (of person) sink into a chair etc. **subsidence** *n.*

subsidiary /səb'sɪdɪərɪ/ **1** *a.* serving to help or supplement, subordinate, secondary; (of company) controlled by another. **2** *n.* subsidiary company or person or thing.

subsidize /'sʌbsɪdaɪz/ *v.t.* pay subsidy to; support by subsidies.

subsidy /'sʌbsɪdɪ/ *n.* money contributed by State or public body etc., to keep prices at desired level or to assist in meeting expenses etc.

subsist /səb'sɪst/ *v.i.* exist, continue to exist; maintain or support oneself.

subsistence *n.* subsisting; means of supporting life. **subsistence farming** farming in which almost all crops are consumed by farmer's household; **subsistence level, wage,** merely enough to provide bare necessities of life.

subsoil /'sʌbsɔɪl/ *n.* soil just below surface soil.

subsonic /sʌb'sɒnɪk/ *a.* relating to speeds less than that of sound.

subspecies /'sʌbspiːʃiːz/ *n. Biol.* grouping within a species.

substance /'sʌbst(ə)ns/ *n.* particular kind of material; essence of what is spoken or written; reality, solidity; wealth and possessions.

substandard /sʌb'stændəd/ *a.* inferior; of lower than desired standard.

substantial /səb'stænʃ(ə)l/ *a.* of real importance or value, of considerable amount; of solid structure; having substance, not illusory; well-to-do; in essentials, virtual. **substantiality** *n.*

substantiate /səb'stænʃɪeɪt/ *v.t.* support or prove truth of. **substantiation** *n.*

substantive /'sʌbstəntɪv/ **1** *a.* having separate existence; not subordinate; actual, real, permanent. **2** *n.* noun. **3 substantival** *a.*

substitute /'sʌbstɪtjuːt/ **1** *n.* person or thing acting or serving in place of another. **2** *v.* put in place of another; act as substitute (*for*). **3** *a.* acting as substitute. **4 substitution** *n.*

substratum /'sʌbstrɑːtəm/ *n.* (*pl.* **-ta**) underlying layer; basis.

subsume /səb'sjuːm/ *v.t.* include under particular rule or class etc.

subtenant /'sʌbtenənt/ *n.* person renting room or house etc. from one who is a tenant. **subtenancy** *n.*

subtend /sʌb'tend/ *v.t.* (of line) be opposite (angle, arc).

subterfuge /'sʌbtəfjuːdʒ/ *n.* evasion, esp. in argument or excuse.

subterranean /sʌbtə'reɪnɪən/ *a.* underground.

subtitle /'sʌbtaɪt(ə)l/ **1** *n.* subordinate or additional title of book etc.; caption of cinema film, esp. translating dialogue in foreign film. **2** *v.t.* provide with subtitle(s).

subtle /'sʌt(ə)l/ *a.* hard to detect or describe, fine, delicate; ingenious, clever. **subtlety** *n.*

subtract /səb'trækt/ *v.t.* deduct (number etc. *from* greater number). **subtraction** *n.*

subtropical /sʌb'trɒpɪk(ə)l/ *a.* bordering on the tropics; characteristic of such regions.

suburb /'sʌbɜːb/ *n.* outlying district of city.

suburban /sə'bɜːbən/ *a.* of or characteristic of suburbs; *derog.* provincial in outlook. **suburbanite** *n.*

Suburbia /sə'bɜːbɪə/ *n.* usu. *derog.* suburbs and their inhabitants etc.

subvention /səb'venʃ(ə)n/ *n.* subsidy.

subversion /səb'vɜːʃ(ə)n/ *n.* weakening or overthrow, esp. of government; attempt at this.

subversive /səb'vɜːsɪv/ **1** *a.* attempting subversion. **2** *n.* subversive person.

subvert /səb'vɜːt/ *v.t.* effect or attempt subversion of.

subway /'sʌbweɪ/ *n.* underground passage, esp. for pedestrians; *US* underground railway.

succeed /sək'siːd/ *v.* have success (*in*); prosper; follow in order, be subsequent (to or *to*); come by inheritance or in due order (*to* title, office, etc.).

success /sək'ses/ *n.* favourable outcome; attainment of object or wealth or fame etc.; person or thing that succeeds or is successful.

successful /sək'sesful/ a. having success, prosperous.

succession /sək'seʃ(ə)n/ n. following in order; series of things in succession; succeeding to inheritance or office or esp. throne, right of this; set of persons with such right. **in succession** one after another.

successive /sək'sesɪv/ a. following in succession, consecutive.

successor /sək'sesə(r)/ n. person or thing that succeeds (*to*) another.

succinct /sək'sɪŋkt/ a. brief, concise.

succour /'sʌkə(r)/ 1 n. aid given in time of need. 2 v.t. come to assistance of.

succulent /'sʌkjʊlənt/ 1 a. juicy; (of plant) thick and fleshy. 2 n. succulent plant. 3 **succulence** n.

succumb /sə'kʌm/ v.i. give way *to*; be overcome; die.

such /sʌtʃ/ 1 a. of kind or degree or extent indicated or suggested; of the same kind; so great or extreme. 2 pron. such person(s) or thing(s). 3 **as such** as being what has been specified; **such-and-such** particular but unspecified; **suchlike** colloq. of such a kind.

suck 1 v. draw (liquid) into mouth using lip-muscles etc.; draw liquid or sustenance or advantage from; *fig.* imbibe or gain (knowledge, advantage, etc.); roll tongue round and squeeze (sweet etc.) in mouth; use sucking action or make sucking sound. 2 n. act or period of sucking. 3 **suck up** absorb; **suck up to** sl. seek favour of, flatter.

sucker /'sʌkə(r)/ n. shoot springing from plant's root beside stem; organ in animal, or part of apparatus, adapted for adhering by suction to surfaces; sl. gullible person, simpleton.

sucking /'sʌkɪŋ/ a. not yet weaned.

suckle /'sʌk(ə)l/ v. feed (young) at breast or udder.

suckling /'sʌklɪŋ/ n. unweaned child or animal.

sucrose /'suːkrəʊz/ n. kind of sugar obtained from cane or beet etc.

suction /'sʌkʃ(ə)n/ n. sucking; production of partial vacuum so that external atmospheric pressure forces

fluid into vacant space or causes adhesion of surfaces.

sudden /'sʌd(ə)n/ a. coming or happening or performed etc. unexpectedly or without warning, abrupt. **all of a sudden** suddenly.

sudorific /suːdə'rɪfɪk/ 1 a. causing sweating. 2 n. sudorific drug.

suds n.pl. froth of soap and water. **sudsy** a.

sue v. begin lawsuit against (person); plead, appeal (*for*).

suede /sweɪd/ n. leather with flesh side rubbed into nap.

suet /'suːɪt/ n. hard fat surrounding kidneys of cattle and sheep, used in cooking etc. **suety** a.

suffer /'sʌfə(r)/ v. undergo pain or grief etc.; undergo or be subjected to (pain, loss, punishment, grief, etc.); tolerate; arch. permit.

sufferance /'sʌfərəns/ n. tacit permission or toleration. **on sufferance** tolerated but not supported.

suffering /'sʌfərɪŋ/ n. pain etc. suffered.

suffice /sə'faɪs/ v. be enough; meet needs of.

sufficiency /sə'fɪʃənsɪ/ n. a sufficient amount.

sufficient /sə'fɪʃ(ə)nt/ a. sufficing; adequate.

suffix /'sʌfɪks/ 1 n. verbal element attached to end of word in inflexion or word-formation etc. 2 v.t. add as suffix.

suffocate /'sʌfəkeɪt/ v. kill or stifle or choke by stopping respiration; be or feel suffocated. **suffocation** n.

suffragan /'sʌfrəgən/ n. bishop assisting diocesan bishop in particular part of diocese.

suffrage /'sʌfrɪdʒ/ n. right of voting in political elections.

suffragette /sʌfrə'dʒet/ n. hist. woman who agitated for women's suffrage.

suffuse /sə'fjuːz/ v.t. (of colour or moisture etc.) spread throughout or over. **suffusion** n.

sugar /'ʃʊgə(r)/ n. sweet crystalline substance obtained from juices esp. of sugar-cane and sugar-beet and used in cookery and confectionery etc.; *Chem.* any of a group of soluble sweet carbohydrates; *fig.* flattery etc. 2 v.t. sweeten or coat with sugar; make sweet or agreeable. 3 **sugar-beet** kind of white beet from which sugar is manufactured; **sugar-cane** tall stout perennial tropical grass cultivated as source of sugar; **sugar-daddy** *sl.* elderly man who lavishes gifts on young woman; **sugar-loaf** conical moulded mass of hard refined sugar.

sugary /'ʃʊgərɪ/ *a.* containing or resembling sugar; cloying, sentimental.

suggest /sə'dʒest/ *v.t.* propose for consideration or as a possibility; cause (idea) to present itself, bring (idea) into the mind.

suggestible /sə'dʒestɪb(ə)l/ *a.* capable of being influenced by suggestion. **suggestibility** *n.*

suggestion /sə'dʒestʃ(ə)n/ *n.* suggesting; thing suggested; insinuation of belief or impulse into the mind; hint or slight trace *of*.

suggestive /sə'dʒestɪv/ *a.* conveying a suggestion (*of*); suggesting something indecent.

suicidal /suːɪ'saɪd(ə)l/ *a.* of or tending to suicide; (of person) liable to commit suicide; destructive to one's own interests.

suicide /'suːɪsaɪd/ *n.* intentional self-killing; person who intentionally kills himself; action destructive to one's own interests etc.

sui generis /suːiː 'dʒenərɪs/ of its own kind, unique. [L]

suit /suːt/ **1** *n.* set of clothes for wearing together, esp. of same cloth and consisting usu. of jacket and trousers or skirt; clothing for particular purpose; set *of* pyjamas or armour etc.; any of the 4 sets into which pack of cards is divided; lawsuit; *arch.* suing, seeking of woman's hand in marriage. **2** *v.* meet requirements of; agree with; be in harmony with; adapt or make appropriate *to*; be agreeable or convenient; in *p.p.* well adapted or fitted etc. to. **3 suitcase** flat case for carrying clothes, usu. with hinged lid.

suitable /'suːtəb(ə)l/ *a.* suited *to* or *for*; well fitted for purpose; appropriate to occasion. **suitability** *n.*

suite /swiːt/ *n.* set of rooms or furniture etc.; group of attendants; *Mus.* set of instrumental pieces.

suitor /'suːtə(r)/ *n.* man who woos woman; plaintiff or petitioner in lawsuit.

sulk 1 *v.i.* be sulky. **2** *n.* (usu. in *pl.*) sulky fit.

sulky /'sʌlkɪ/ *a.* sullen and unsociable from resentment or ill temper.

sullen /'sʌlən/ *a.* ill-humoured, moody, morose, gloomy.

sully /'sʌlɪ/ *v.t.* spoil purity or splendour of (reputation etc.).

sulphate /'sʌlfeɪt/ *n.* salt of sulphuric acid.

sulphide /'sʌlfaɪd/ *n.* compound of sulphur with element or radical.

sulphite /'sʌlfaɪt/ *n.* salt of sulphurous acid.

sulphonamide /sʌl'fɒnəmaɪd/ *n.* kind of antibiotic drug.

sulphur /'sʌlfə(r)/ *n.* pale-yellow non-metallic element burning with blue flame and stifling smell; yellow butterfly.

sulphureous /sʌl'fjʊərɪəs/ *a.* of or like sulphur.

sulphuric /sʌl'fjʊərɪk/ *a.* of or containing sulphur in a higher valency. **sulphuric acid** dense highly corrosive oily acid.

sulphurous /'sʌlfərəs/ *a.* of or like sulphur; (also /sʌl'fjʊərəs/) containing sulphur in a lower valency. **sulphurous acid** unstable weak acid used e.g. as bleaching agent.

sultan /'sʌlt(ə)n/ *n.* Muslim sovereign.

sultana /sʌl'tɑːnə/ *n.* kind of seedless raisin; sultan's wife or mother or concubine or daughter.

sultanate /'sʌltənət/ *n.* position of or territory ruled by sultan.

sultry /'sʌltrɪ/ *a.* (of weather) oppressively hot; (of person) passionate, sensual.

sum 1 *n.* number resulting from addition of items; amount of money; arithmetical problem; working out of this; sum total; summary. **2** *v.* find sum of. **3 in sum** briefly, to sum up; **sum total** total resulting from addition of items, summary; **sum up** find or give total of, express briefly or summarize, form or express judgement or opinion of, (esp. of judge) recapitulate evidence or argument.

sumac /'suːmæk/ *n.* shrub yielding leaves which are dried and ground for use in tanning and dyeing; these leaves.

summarize /'sʌməraɪz/ *v.t.* make or be summary of.

summary /'sʌmərɪ/ 1 *n.* brief account giving chief points. 2 *a.* brief, without details or formalities.

summation /sʌ'meɪʃ(ə)n/ *n.* finding of total or sum; summarizing.

summer /'sʌmə(r)/ *n.* warmest season of year; year of life or age. **summer-house** light building in garden etc. for use in summer; **summer school** course of lectures etc. held during summer vacation; **summer time** time shown by clocks advanced in summer for daylight saving; **summer-time** season or weather of summer. **summery** *a.*

summit /'sʌmɪt/ *n.* highest point, top; highest level of achievement or status; (in full **summit conference, meeting**) discussion between heads of governments.

summon /'sʌmən/ *v.t.* require presence or attendance of; call together; call upon (*to* do, appear, etc.); muster *up* (courage etc.).

summons /'sʌmənz/ 1 *n.* authoritative call to attend or do something, esp. to appear in court. 2 *v.t.* serve with summons.

sump *n.* casing holding oil in internal-combustion engine; pit or well for collecting water etc.

sumptuary /'sʌmptjʊərɪ/ *a.* regulating (esp. private) expenditure.

sumptuous /'sʌmptjʊəs/ *a.* costly, splendid, magnificent.

sun 1 *n.* the star round which the earth travels and from which it receives light and warmth; this light or warmth; any fixed star. 2 *v.* expose (oneself) to the sun. 3 **sunbathe** expose one's body to the sun; **sun-beam** ray of sun; **sunburn** inflammation of skin from exposure to sun; **sunburnt** affected by sunburn; **sundial** instrument showing time by shadow of pointer in sunlight; **sundown** sunset; **sunflower** tall garden-plant with large golden-rayed flowers; **sun-glasses** tinted spectacles to protect eyes from glare; **sun-lamp** lamp giving ultra-violet rays for therapy or artificial sun-tan; **sun lounge** room designed to receive much sunlight; **sunrise** (time of) sun's rising; **sunset** (time of) sun's setting; **sun-shade** light umbrella used to give shade from sun; **sunshine** sunlight,

area illuminated by it, cheerfulness or bright influence; **sunspot** dark patch on sun's surface; **sunstroke** acute prostration from excessive heat of sun; **sun-tan** tanning of skin by exposure to sun; **sun-trap** sunny place, esp. sheltered from wind.

Sun. *abbr.* Sunday.

sundae /'sʌndeɪ/ *n.* confection of ice cream with fruit, nuts, syrup, etc.

Sunday /'sʌndeɪ/ *n.* day of week following Saturday; newspaper published on Sundays. **month of Sundays** very long period; **Sunday school** school held on Sundays for religious instruction of children.

sunder /'sʌndə(r)/ *v.t.* literary sever, keep apart.

sundry /'sʌndrɪ/ 1 *a.* various, several. 2 *n.* in *pl.* oddments, accessories; items not needing to be specified. 3 **all and sundry** everyone.

sung *p.p.* of **sing**.

sunk *p.p.* of **sink**.

sunken /'sʌŋkən/ *a.* that has sunk; lying below general surface; (of eyes, cheeks, etc.) shrunken, hollow.

Sunni /'sʌnɪ/ *n.* member of Muslim sect opposed to Shi'ites.

sunny /'sʌnɪ/ *a.* bright with or as sunlight; exposed to or warm with sun; cheerful.

sup 1 *v.* drink by sips or spoonfuls; take supper. 2 *n.* sip or spoonful of liquid.

super /'suːpə(r)/ 1 *a. sl.* excellent, unusually good. 2 *n. colloq.* supernumerary; superintendent.

super- *in comb.* on top, over, beyond, besides, exceeding, transcending, of higher kind, more than usually.

superannuate /suːpər'ænjʊeɪt/ *v.t.* dismiss or discard as too old; discharge with pension; in *p.p.* too old for work.

superannuation /suːpərænjʊ-'eɪʃ(ə)n/ *n.* pension; payment made to obtain pension.

superb /suː'pɜːb/ *a.* magnificent, splendid; *colloq.* excellent.

supercargo /'suːpəkɑːgəʊ/ *n.* (*pl.* -**goes**) person in merchant ship managing sales etc. of cargo.

supercharge /'suːpətʃɑːdʒ/ *v.t.* charge to extreme or excess; use supercharger on.

supercharger /'suːpətʃɑːdʒə(r)/ *n.* device forcing extra air or fuel into internal-combustion engine.

supercilious /suːpəˈsɪlɪəs/ a. haughtily contemptuous.

supererogation /suːpərerəˈgeɪʃ(ə)n/ n. doing of more than duty requires.

superficial /suːpəˈfɪʃ(ə)l/ a. of or on the surface; without depth of knowledge or feeling etc.; (of measure) square. **superficiality** /-ˈæl-/ n.

superfluity /suːpəˈfluːɪtɪ/ n. superfluous amount or thing; being superfluous.

superfluous /suːˈpɜːfluəs/ a. more than is needed or wanted, useless.

supergrass /ˈsuːpəgrɑːs/ n. sl. large-scale police informer.

superhuman /suːpəˈhjuːmən/ a. exceeding (normal) human capacity or power.

superimpose /suːpərɪmˈpəʊz/ v.t. place (thing) on or (up)on or above something else. **superimposition** n.

superintend /suːpərɪnˈtend/ v. manage, watch over (work etc.). **superintendence** n.

superintendent /suːpərɪnˈtend(ə)nt/ n. person who superintends; director of institution etc.; police officer above rank of inspector.

superior /suːˈpɪərɪə(r)/ 1 a. higher in rank or quality etc., (to); better or greater in some respect; high-quality; priggish; unlikely to yield or not resorting to; situated above; written or printed above the line. 2 n. person superior to another esp. in rank; head of monastery. 3 **superiority** /-ˈɒr-/ n.

superlative /suːˈpɜːlətɪv/ 1 a. of highest degree; excellent; Gram. (of degree, inflexional form, adjective or adverb) expressing highest or very high degree of quality etc. denoted by simple word. 2 n. superlative degree or (form of) word.

superman /ˈsuːpəmæn/ n. (pl. -men) man of superhuman powers or achievement.

supermarket /ˈsuːpəmɑːkɪt/ n. large self-service store usu. selling food and some household goods.

supernatural /suːpəˈnætʃər(ə)l/ a. of or manifesting phenomena not explicable by natural or physical laws.

supernova /suːpəˈnəʊvə/ n. (pl. -vae /-viː-/ or vas) Astron. star that suddenly increases very greatly in brightness.

supernumerary /suːpəˈnjuːmərərɪ/ 1 a. in excess of normal number; engaged for extra work; (of actor) with non-speaking part. 2 n. supernumerary person or thing.

superphosphate /suːpəˈfɒsfeɪt/ n. fertilizer made from phosphate rock.

superpower /ˈsuːpəpaʊə(r)/ n. extremely powerful nation.

superscribe /ˈsuːpəskraɪb/ v.t. write (inscription) at top of or outside document etc.

superscript /ˈsuːpəskrɪpt/ 1 a. written above. 2 n. superscript number or symbol.

superscription /suːpəˈskrɪpʃ(ə)n/ n. superscribed words.

supersede /suːpəˈsiːd/ v.t. take place of; put or use another in place of. **supersession** n.

supersonic /suːpəˈsɒnɪk/ a. of or having speed greater than that of sound.

superstition /suːpəˈstɪʃ(ə)n/ n. belief in the existence or power of the supernatural; irrational fear of unknown or mysterious; a religion or practice or opinion based on such tendencies; widely held but wrong idea. **superstitious** a.

superstructure /ˈsuːpəstrʌktʃə(r)/ n. structure built on top of something else; upper part of building or ship etc.

supertanker /ˈsuːpətæŋkə(r)/ n. very large tanker.

supertax /ˈsuːpətæks/ n. & v.t. surtax.

supervene /suːpəˈviːn/ v.i. occur as interruption in or change from some state. **supervention** n.

supervise /ˈsuːpəvaɪz/ v.t. oversee, superintend. **supervision** n.; **supervisor** n.; **supervisory** a.

supine /ˈsuːpaɪn/ 1 a. lying face upwards; inactive, indolent. 2 n. type of Latin verbal noun.

supper /ˈsʌpə(r)/ n. meal taken late in day, esp. evening meal less formal and substantial than dinner.

supplant /səˈplɑːnt/ v.t. take the place of, esp. by underhand means.

supple /ˈsʌp(ə)l/ a. easily bent, pliant, flexible.

supplement 1 /ˈsʌplɪmənt/ n. thing or part added to remedy deficiencies or amplify information; separate addition to newspaper etc. **2** /ˈsʌplɪmənt/ *v.t.* make supplement to. **3 supplemental** *a.*; **supplementation** *n.*

supplementary /ˌsʌplɪˈmentərɪ/ *a.* supplemental. **supplementary benefit** payment made by State in cases of hardship.

suppliant /ˈsʌplɪənt/ **1** *n.* humble petitioner. **2** *a.* supplicating; expressing supplication.

supplicate /ˈsʌplɪkeɪt/ *v.* make humble petition to or for. **supplication** *n.*; **supplicatory** *a.*

supply /səˈplaɪ/ **1** *v.t.* furnish or provide (with) thing needed; make up for (deficiency etc.). **2** *n.* provision of what is needed; stock, store; in *pl.* necessaries for army or expedition etc.; person, esp. teacher or minister, supplying vacancy or acting as substitute. **3 supply and demand** quantities available and required, as factors regulating price of commodities.

support /səˈpɔːt/ **1** *v.t.* carry all or part of weight of; keep from falling or sinking or failing; provide for; strengthen, encourage, give help or corroboration to; speak in favour of; take secondary part to (actor etc.); endure, tolerate. **2** *n.* supporting or being supported; person or thing that supports. **3 supportive** *a.*

supporter /səˈpɔːtə(r)/ *n.* person or thing that supports; person who is interested in a particular team or sport.

suppose /səˈpəʊz/ *v.t.* assume, be inclined to think; take as possibility or hypothesis; require as condition; in *p.p.* generally accepted as being so. **be supposed to** be expected or required to, (with *neg.*, *colloq.*) not be allowed to.

supposedly /səˈpəʊzɪdlɪ/ *adv.* as is generally supposed.

supposition /ˌsʌpəˈzɪʃ(ə)n/ *n.* what is supposed or assumed.

supposititious /ˌsʌpəˈzɪʃəs/ *a.* hypothetical.

suppositious /səˈpɒzɪˈtɪʃəs/ *a.* spurious.

suppository /səˈpɒzɪtərɪ/ *n.* medical preparation inserted into rectum or vagina to melt.

suppress /səˈpres/ *v.t.* put an end to existence or activity of; withhold or withdraw from publication; keep secret or unexpressed; *Electr.* partially or

wholly eliminate (interference etc.), equip (device) to reduce interference due to it. **suppression** *n.*; **suppressor** *n.*

suppurate /ˈsʌpjʊreɪt/ *v.i.* form or secrete pus; fester. **suppuration** *n.*

supra- *in comb.* above.

supranational /ˌsuːprəˈnæʃən(ə)l/ *a.* transcending national limits.

supremacy /suːˈpreməsɪ/ *n.* being supreme, supreme authority.

supreme /suːˈpriːm/ *a.* highest in authority or rank; greatest; of highest quality or degree or amount.

supremo /suːˈpriːməʊ/ *n.* (*pl.* **-mos**) supreme leader.

surcease /sɜːˈsiːs/ *arch.* **1** *n.* cessation. **2** *v.i.* cease.

surcharge /ˈsɜːtʃɑːdʒ/ **1** *n.* additional charge or payment; excessive or additional load. **2** *v.t.* exact surcharge from; exact (sum) as surcharge; overload.

surd 1 *a.* (of number) irrational; (of sound) uttered with breath and not voice. **2** *n.* surd number or sound.

sure /ʃʊə(r)/ **1** *a.* having or seeming to have adequate reason for belief, convinced (*of, that*); having certain prospect or confident anticipation or satisfactory knowledge *of*; reliable or unfailing; certain (*to* do); undoubtedly true or truthful. **2** *adv. colloq.* certainly. **3 make sure** make or become certain, ensure; **sure-fire** *colloq.* certain (to succeed); **sure-footed** never stumbling; **to be sure** it is undeniable or admitted.

surely /ˈʃʊəlɪ/ *adv.* with certainty or safety; as appeal to likelihood or reason.

surety /ˈʃʊərətɪ/ *n.* person undertaking to be liable for another's default or non-appearance etc.

surf 1 *n.* swell and white foamy water of sea breaking on rock or (esp. shallow) shore. **2** *v.i.* engage in surf-riding. **3 surf-board** long narrow board for riding over heavy surf to shore; **surf-riding** sport of riding on surf-board.

surface /ˈsɜːfɪs/ **1** *n.* the outside of a thing; any of the limits terminating a solid; the top of a liquid or of soil etc.; outward aspect, what is apprehended of something on casual view or consideration; *Geom.* that which has length or breadth but no thickness. **2** *attrib.a.* of the surface (only), superficial. **3** *v.* give (special) surface to; come to the surface; become visible or known or *colloq.* conscious; bring (submarine) to the surface. **4 surface mail** mail not carried by air; **surface tension** tension of surface of liquid, tending to minimize its surface area.

surfeit /'sɜːfɪt/ **1** *n.* excess, esp. in eating or drinking; satiety. **2** *v.t.* overfeed; satiate *with*, cloy.

surge 1 *v.i.* move to and fro (as) in waves; move suddenly and powerfully. **2** *n.* wave(s), surging motion; impetuous onset.

surgeon /'sɜːdʒ(ə)n/ *n.* person skilled in surgery; medical practitioner qualified to practise surgery.

surgery /'sɜːdʒərɪ/ *n.* manual or instrumental treatment of injuries or disorders of body; place where or time when doctor or dentist etc. gives advice and treatment, or *colloq.* MP or lawyer etc. is available for consultation.

surgical /'sɜːdʒɪk(ə)l/ *a.* of or by surgery or surgeons; (of appliance) used for surgery or in conditions suitable for surgery. **surgical spirit** methylated spirits used for cleansing etc.

surly /'sɜːlɪ/ *a.* bad-tempered, unfriendly.

surmise /sə'maɪz/ **1** *n.* conjecture. **2** *v.* infer doubtfully or conjecturally; guess.

surmount /sə'maʊnt/ *v.t.* overcome, prevail over, get over; in *p.p.* capped or crowned (*by, with*).

surname /'sɜːneɪm/ **1** *n.* name common to all members of family. **2** *v.t.* give surname to.

surpass /sə'pɑːs/ *v.t.* outdo, be better than.

surpassing /sə'pɑːsɪŋ/ *a.* greatly exceeding or excelling others.

surplice /'sɜːplɪs/ *n.* loose full-sleeved white vestment worn by clergy etc.

surplus /'sɜːpləs/ **1** *n.* amount left over when requirements have been met. **2** *a.* in excess of what is needed or used.

surprise /sə'praɪz/ **1** *n.* unexpected or astonishing thing; catching of person(s) unprepared; emotion excited by the unexpected. **2** *v.t.* affect with surprise; shock, scandalize; capture by surprise;

attack or come upon unawares; lead unawares or betray *into doing* etc.

surrealism /sə'rɪəlɪz(ə)m/ *n.* 20th-c. movement in art and literature aiming to express subconscious mind. **surrealist** *a.* & *n.*; **surrealistic** *a.*

surrender /sə'rendə(r)/ **1** *v.* hand over, relinquish possession of; accept enemy's demand for submission; submit (*to*); give *oneself* over *to* habit or emotion etc.; give up rights under (insurance policy) in return for smaller sum received immediately. **2** *n.* surrendering.

surreptitious /sʌrəp'tɪʃəs/ *a.* done by stealth; underhand.

surrogate /'sʌrəgət/ *n.* deputy esp. of bishop; substitute. **surrogate mother** woman who conceives and gives birth to child on behalf of woman unable to do so.

surround /sə'raʊnd/ **1** *v.t.* come or be all round. **2** *n.* border or edging esp. area between walls and carpet.

surroundings /sə'raʊndɪŋz/ *n.pl.* things in neighbourhood of, or conditions affecting, a person or thing.

surtax /'sɜːtæks/ **1** *n.* additional tax, esp. on incomes above a certain amount. **2** *v.t.* impose surtax on.

surveillance /sə'veɪləns/ *n.* supervision; close watch esp. on suspected person.

survey 1 /sə'veɪ/ *v.t.* take or present general view of; examine condition of (building etc.); determine boundaries and extent and ownership etc. of (district etc.). **2** /'sɜːveɪ/ *n.* act or result of surveying; inspection or investigation; map or plan made by surveying.

surveyor /sə'veɪə(r)/ *n.* person who surveys land and buildings, esp. professionally.

survival /sə'vaɪv(ə)l/ *n.* surviving; relic of earlier time.

survive /sə'vaɪv/ *v.* continue to live or exist; live or exist longer than; come alive through or continue to exist in spite of (danger, accident, etc.). **survivor** *n.*

sus /sʌs/ *sl.* **1** *n.* suspicion, suspect. **2** *v.t.* (*past* & *p.p.* **sussed**) investigate, inspect, understand (often *with out*).

susceptible /sə'septɪb(ə)l/ *a.* impressionable, sensitive; readily touched with emotion; accessible or sensitive *to*; admitting *of*. **susceptibility** *n*.

suspect 1 /səs'pekt/ *v.t.* have an impression of the existence or presence of; half believe *to be*; be inclined to think (*that*); mentally accuse *of*; doubt the innocence or genuineness or truth of. 2 /'sʌspekt/ *n.* suspected person. 3 /'sʌspekt/ *a.* subject to suspicion or distrust.

suspend /səs'pend/ *v.t.* hang up; keep inoperative or undecided for a time; debar temporarily from function or office etc.; in *p.p.* (of solid in fluid) sustained or floating between top and bottom. **suspended sentence** judicial sentence remaining unenforced on condition of good behaviour.

suspender *n.* attachment to hold up stocking or sock by its top; in *pl.* US pair of braces. **suspender belt** woman's undergarment with suspenders.

suspense /səs'pens/ *n.* state of anxious uncertainty or expectation.

suspension /səs'penʃ(ə)n/ *n.* suspending or being suspended; means by which vehicle is supported on its axles; substance consisting of particles suspended in fluid. **suspension bridge** bridge with roadway suspended from cables supported by towers.

suspicion /səs'pɪʃ(ə)n/ *n.* feeling or state of mind of one who suspects; suspecting or being suspected; slight trace (*of*).

suspicious /səs'pɪʃəs/ *a.* prone to or feeling suspicion; indicating or justifying suspicion.

sustain /səs'teɪn/ *v.t.* bear weight of or support, esp. for long period; endure, stand; undergo or suffer (defeat, injury, loss, etc.); (of court etc.) decide in favour of, uphold; substantiate or corroborate; keep up (effort etc.).

sustenance /'sʌstɪn(ə)ns/ *n.* nourishment, food, means of support.

suture /'suːtʃə(r)/ 1 *n. Surg.* joining of edges of wound by stitching; stitch or thread etc. used for this. 2 *v.t.* stitch (wound).

suzerain /'suːzəreɪn/ *n.* feudal overlord; sovereign or State having some control over another State that is internally autonomous. **suzerainty** *n.*

svelte /svelt/ *a.* slim, slender, graceful.

SW *abbr.* South-West(ern).

swab /swɒb/ 1 *n.* mop or absorbent pad or cloth for cleansing or mopping up etc.; absorbent pad used in surgery; specimen of secretion etc. taken for examination. 2 *v.t.* clean or wipe (as) with swab.

swaddle /'swɒd(ə)l/ *v.t.* swathe in bandages or wrappings etc. **swaddling-clothes** narrow bandages wrapped round new-born child to restrain its movements.

swag *n.* ornamental festoon of flowers etc.; representation of this; *sl.* thief's booty; *Aus.* traveller's bundle.

swagger /'swægə(r)/ 1 *v.i.* walk or behave arrogantly or self-importantly; talk boastfully. 2 *n.* swaggering gait or manner.

swain *n. arch.* a country youth; *poet.* young lover or suitor.

swallow[1] /'swɒləʊ/ 1 *v.* make or let pass down one's throat; perform muscular action (as) of swallowing something; accept meekly or credulously; repress (emotion); engulf. 2 *n.* act of swallowing; amount swallowed.

swallow[2] /'swɒləʊ/ *n.* migratory insect-eating bird with forked tail. **swallow-dive** dive with arms spread sideways; **swallow-tail** deeply forked tail, butterfly etc. with this.

swam *past of* **swim**.

swamp /swɒmp/ 1 *n.* piece of wet spongy ground. 2 *v.t.* submerge, inundate; cause to fill with water and sink; overwhelm with numbers or quantity. 3 **swampy** *a.*

swan /swɒn/ *n.* large web-footed usu. white water-bird with long flexible neck. **swansdown** down of swan used in trimmings etc., thick cotton cloth with soft nap on one side; **swan-song** person's final composition or performance etc.; **swan-upping** annual taking up and marking of Thames swans.

swank 1 *colloq. n.* ostentation, swagger. 2 *v.i.* behave with swank. 3 **swanky** *a.*

swannery /'swɒnərɪ/ *n.* place where swans are kept.

swap /swɒp/ *colloq.* 1 *v.* exchange by barter. 2 *n.* act of swapping; thing suitable for swapping.

sward /swɔːd/ *n. literary* expanse of short grass.

swarm /swɔːm/ **1** *n.* large or dense body or multitude of persons or insects etc., esp. moving about; cluster of bees leaving hive etc. with queen bee to establish new hive. **2** *v.i.* move in or form swarm; be overrun or crowded *with*.

swarm² /swɔːm/ *v.* climb (*up*) clasping or clinging with arms and legs.

swarthy /ˈswɔːðɪ/ *a.* dark-complexioned, dark in colour.

swashbuckler /ˈswɒʃbʌklə(r)/ *n.* swaggering bully or ruffian. **swashbuckling** *a.* & *n.*

swastika /ˈswɒstɪkə/ *n.* cross with equal arms, each arm with limb of same length at right angles to its end.

swat /swɒt/ **1** *v.t.* hit hard, crush (fly etc.) with blow. **2** *n.* act of swatting.

swatch /swɒtʃ/ *n.* sample, esp. of cloth; collection of samples.

swath /swɔːθ/ *n.* (*pl.* /swɔːθs, swɔːðz/) row or line of grass or corn etc. as it falls when cut; space covered or width of grass etc. cut by sweep of scythe.

swathe¹ /sweɪð/ *v.t.* bind or enclose in bandages or garments etc.

swathe² var. of **swath**.

sway **1** *v.* (cause to) move in different directions alternately; oscillate irregularly; waver; have influence over; rule over. **2** *n.* swaying motion; rule, government.

swear /sweə(r)/ *v.* (*past* **swore**; *p.p.* **sworn**) take oath; state or promise on oath; cause to take oath; use profane oaths. **swear by** appeal to as witness or guarantee of oath, *colloq.* have great confidence in; **swear in** admit to office etc. by administering oath; **swear off** renounce; **swear to** *colloq.* say that one is certain of; **swear-word** profane or obscene word.

sweat /swet/ **1** *n.* moisture exuded from skin esp. when one is hot or nervous; state or period of sweating; *colloq.* state of anxiety; *colloq.* drudgery, effort, laborious task or undertaking; condensed moisture on a surface. **2** *v.* exude sweat; *fig.* be terrified, suffer, etc.; emit like sweat; make (horse, athlete, etc.) sweat by exercise; (cause to) toil or drudge. **3** **sweat-band** band of absorbent material inside hat or round wrist etc. to soak up sweat; **sweated labour** workers employed for long hours at low wages; **sweat-shirt** sleeved cotton sweater; **sweat-shop** workshop where sweated labour is employed. **4 sweaty** *a.*

sweater /ˈswetə(r)/ *n.* woollen etc. pullover.

Swede *n.* native of Sweden; **swede** large yellow variety of turnip.

Swedish /ˈswiːdɪʃ/ **1** *a.* of Sweden. **2** *n.* language of Sweden.

sweep **1** *v.* (*past & p.p.* **swept**) clean or clear with or as with a broom; clean room etc. thus; collect or remove (dirt etc.) by sweeping; clear *off* or *away* etc. forcefully; traverse swiftly or lightly; impart sweeping motion to; glide swiftly; go majestically; have continuous extent. **2** *n.* act or motion of sweeping; moving in continuous curve; curve in road etc.; range or scope; chimney-sweep; sortie by aircraft; *colloq.* sweepstake; long oar. **3 sweep the board** win all the money in gambling-game, win all possible prizes etc.; **sweepstake** form of gambling on horse-races etc., in which money staked is divided among those who have drawn numbered tickets for winners.

sweeping *a.* of wide range, regardless of limitations or exceptions.

sweet **1** *a.* tasting like sugar or honey etc.; pleasing to sense of smell, fragrant; melodious; fresh; not sour or bitter; gratifying; dear, beloved; amiable, gentle; *colloq.* pretty. **2** *n.* small shaped piece of sugar or chocolate confectionery; sweet dish forming course of meal; in *pl.* delights, gratifications; darling. **3 sweetbread** pancreas or thymus gland of animal, as food; **sweet-brier** kind of single-flowered fragrant-leaved rose; **sweet chestnut** edible chestnut; **sweet corn** sweet-flavoured maize; **sweetheart** either of pair of lovers; **sweetmeat** a sweet; **sweet pea** climbing garden annual with showy scented flowers; **sweet pepper** mild-flavoured kind of capsicum; **sweet potato** tropical plant with tuberous roots used for food; **sweet tooth** liking for sweet-tasting things; **sweet-william** garden plant with close clusters of sweet-smelling flowers.

sweeten /'swiːt(ə)n/ *v.* make or become sweet(er).

sweetener /'swiːtənə(r)/ *n.* thing that sweetens; *colloq.* bribe.

sweetie /'swiːtɪ/ *n. colloq.* a sweet; sweetheart.

swell 1 *v.* (*p.p.* **swollen** /'swəʊlən/ or **swelled**) (cause to) grow bigger or louder or more intense; rise or raise up; bulge *out.* **2** *n.* act or state of swelling; heaving of sea etc. with long rolling waves that do not break; *Mus.* crescendo; mechanism in organ etc. for gradually varying volume; *colloq.* fashionable or stylish person, person of distinction or ability. **3** *a. colloq.* smart, finely dressed, distinguished, first-rate.

swelling /'swelɪŋ/ *n.* abnormally swollen place esp. on body.

swelter /'sweltə(r)/ **1** *v.i.* be uncomfortably hot. **2** *n.* sweltering condition.

swept *past* & *p.p.* of **sweep. swept-wing** (of aircraft) having wings placed at acute angle to axis.

swerve 1 *v.* (cause to) change direction, esp. suddenly. **2** *n.* swerving motion.

swift 1 *a.* rapid, speedy, quick, prompt. **2** *n.* swift-flying long-winged insectivorous bird.

swig *colloq.* **1** *v.* drink in large draughts. **2** *n.* swallow of liquid, esp. of large amount.

swill 1 *v.* rinse (*out*), pour water over or through; drink greedily. **2** *n.* swilling; mainly liquid refuse as pig-food; inferior liquor.

swim 1 *v.* (*past* **swam**; *p.p.* **swum**) progress in water by working limbs or body; float on or at surface of liquid; appear to undulate or reel or whirl, have dizzy effect or sensation; be flooded *with* moisture. **2** *n.* spell or act of swimming; main current of affairs. **3** **swimming-bath, -pool,** pool constructed for swimming; **swimming-costume, swim-suit,** bathing-suit.

swimmingly /'swɪmɪŋlɪ/ *adv.* with easy unobstructed progress.

swindle /'swɪnd(ə)l/ **1** *v.* cheat; defraud. **2** *n.* act of swindling; person or thing represented as what it is not.

swine *n.* (*pl.* same) pig; *colloq.* disgusting or unpleasant person or thing.

swing 1 *v.* (*past* & *p.p.* **swung**) (cause to) move with to-and-fro or curving motion; sway or hang like pendulum or door etc.; oscillate; move by gripping something and leaping etc.; go with swinging gait; attempt to hit or punch (*at* person etc.); play (music) with swing rhythm; *sl.* be lively or up-to-date etc.; have decisive influence on (voting etc.). **2** *n.* act or motion or extent of swinging; swinging or smooth gait or rhythm or action; seat slung by ropes or chains etc. for swinging on or in, spell of swinging thus; smooth rhythmic jazz or jazzy dance music; amount by which votes etc. change from one side to another. **3** **swing-boat** boat-shaped swing at fairs etc.; **swing bridge** bridge that can be swung aside to let ships etc. pass; **swing-door** door that swings in either direction and closes by itself when released; **swing-wing** (of aircraft) having wings that can be moved backwards and forwards.

swingeing /'swɪndʒɪŋ/ *a.* forcible; daunting, huge.

swinish /'swaɪnɪʃ/ *a.* bestial, filthy.

swipe 1 *v. colloq.* hit hard and recklessly; *sl.* steal. **2** *n. colloq.* reckless hard hit or attempt to hit.

swirl 1 *v.* move or flow or carry along with whirling motion. **2** *n.* swirling motion; twist, curl.

swish 1 *v.* swing (cane, scythe, etc.) audibly through air or grass etc.; cut (flower etc.) *off* thus; move with or make swishing sound. **2** *n.* swishing action or sound. **3** *a. colloq.* smart, fashionable.

Swiss 1 *a.* of Switzerland. **2** *n.* (*pl.* same) native of Switzerland. **3** **Swiss roll** thin flat sponge-cake spread with jam etc. and rolled up.

switch 1 *n.* device for making and breaking connection in electric circuit; transfer, change-over, deviation; flexible shoot cut from tree, light tapering rod; railway points. **2** *v.t.* turn *on* or *off* etc. with switch; change or transfer (position or subject etc.); reverse positions of; swing or snatch (thing) suddenly; whip or flick with switch. **3** **switchback** railway at fair etc. in which train's ascents are achieved by momentum of previous descents, railway or road with alternate sharp ascents and descents; **switchboard** apparatus for varying connections between electric circuits, esp. in telephony.

swivel /'swɪv(ə)l/ **1** *n*. coupling between two parts etc. so that one can turn freely without the other. **2** *v*. turn (as) on swivel, swing round. **3 swivel chair** chair with seat turning horizontally on pivot.

swizz *n*. *sl*. swindle, disappointment.

swizzle /'swɪz(ə)l/ *n*. *colloq*. compounded intoxicating drink esp. of rum or gin and bitters made frothy; *sl*. swizz. **swizzle-stick** stick used for frothing or flattening drinks.

swollen *p.p*. of **swell**.

swoon /swuːn/ *v.i*. & *n*. *literary* faint.

swoop /swuːp/ **1** *v.i*. come down with rush like bird of prey; make sudden attack (*on*). **2** *n*. act of swooping, sudden pounce. **3 at one fell swoop** at a single blow or stroke.

swop var. of **swap**.

sword /sɔːd/ *n*. weapon with long blade for cutting or thrusting. **cross swords** have fight or dispute (*with*); **put to the sword** kill; **sword-dance** dance in which performer brandishes swords or steps about swords laid on ground; **swordfish** large sea-fish with sword-like upper jaw; **sword-play** fencing, repartee or lively arguing; **swordsman** person of (usu. specified) skill with sword; **sword-stick** hollow walking-stick containing sword-blade.

swore *past* of **swear**.

sworn 1 *p.p*. of **swear**. **2** *a*. bound (as) by oath.

swot *sl*. **1** *v*. work hard, esp. at books. **2** *n*. person who works hard, esp. at learning; hard work or study. **3 swot up** study hurriedly or for particular occasion.

swum *p.p*. of **swim**.

swung *past* & *p.p*. of **swing**.

sybarite /'sɪbəraɪt/ *n*. self-indulgent or luxury-loving person. **sybaritic** /-'rɪt/ *a*.

sycamore /'sɪkəmɔː(r)/ *n*. large species of maple.

sycophant /'sɪkəfænt/ *n*. flatterer, toady. **sycophancy** *n*.; **sycophantic** /-'fæn-/ *a*.

syllabary /'sɪləbərɪ/ *n*. set of written characters representing syllables.

syllabic /sɪ'læbɪk/ *a*. of or in syllables.

syllable /'sɪləb(ə)l/ *n*. unit of pronunciation forming whole or part of word and usu. having one vowel-sound often with consonant(s) before or after; character(s) representing syllable; least amount of speech or writing.

syllabub /'sɪləbʌb/ *n*. dish of cream or milk curdled or whipped with wine etc.

syllabus /'sɪləbəs/ *n*. (*pl*. **-buses**) programme or conspectus of a course of study or teaching etc.

syllogism /'sɪlədʒɪz(ə)m/ *n*. form of reasoning in which from two propositions a third is deduced. **syllogistic** *a*.

sylph /sɪlf/ *n*. elemental spirit of air; slender graceful woman.

sylvan var. of **silvan**.

symbiosis /sɪmbaɪ'əʊsɪs/ *n*. (*pl*. **-oses** /-'əʊsiːz/) (usu. mutually advantageous) association of two different organisms living attached to one another etc. **symbiotic** /-'ɒt/ *a*.

symbol /'sɪmb(ə)l/ *n*. thing generally regarded as typifying or representing or recalling something; mark or character taken as conventional sign of some object or idea or process etc. **symbolic** *a*.; **symbolically** *adv*.

symbolism /'sɪmbəlɪz(ə)m/ *n*. symbols; use of symbols; artistic movement or style using symbols to express ideas or emotions etc. **symbolist** *n*.

symbolize /'sɪmbəlaɪz/ *v.t*. be symbol of; represent by symbol.

symmetry /'sɪmɪtrɪ/ *n*. correct proportion; beauty resulting from this; structure that allows an object to be divided into parts of equal shape and size; possession of such structure; repetition of exactly similar parts facing each other or a centre. **symmetric(al)** *a*.

sympathetic /sɪmpə'θetɪk/ *a*. of or showing or expressing or due to sympathy; likeable, not antagonistic. **sympathetic magic** magic seeking to affect person through associated object. **sympathetically** *adv*.

sympathize /'sɪmpəθaɪz/ *v.i*. feel or express sympathy (*with*).

sympathy /'sɪmpəθɪ/ *n*. state of sharing or tendency to share emotion or sensation or condition etc. of another person or thing; mental participation in another's trouble, compassion; disposition to agree (with) or approve, favourable attitude of mind. **in sympathy** having or showing or resulting from sympathy (*with* another).

symphony /'sɪmfənɪ/ *n.* musical composition in several movements for full orchestra. **symphony orchestra** large orchestra playing symphonies etc. **symphonic** /-'fɒn-/ *a.*

symposium /sɪm'pəʊzɪəm/ *n.* (*pl.* **-sia**) meeting or conference for discussion of subject; collection of opinions delivered or articles contributed by number of persons on special topic.

symptom /'sɪmptəm/ *n.* aspect of physical or mental condition as sign of disease or injury; sign of the existence of something. **symptomatic** /-'mæt-/ *a.*

synagogue /'sɪnəɡɒɡ/ *n.* (building for) regular assembly of Jews for religious instruction and worship.

sync /sɪŋk/ *colloq.* (also **synch**) **1** *n.* synchronization. **2** *v.t.* synchronize.

synchromesh /'sɪŋkrəmeʃ/ **1** *n.* system of gear-changing, esp. in motor vehicles, in which gear-wheels revolve at same speed during engagement. **2** *a.* of this system.

synchronize /'sɪŋkrənaɪz/ *v.* make or be synchronous with. **synchronization** *n.*

synchronous /'sɪŋkrənəs/ *a.* existing or occurring at same time (*with*); operating at same rate and simultaneously.

syncopate /'sɪŋkəpeɪt/ *v.* displace beats or accents in (music); shorten (word) by omitting syllable or letter(s) in middle. **syncopation** *n.*

syncope /'sɪŋkəpɪ/ *n.* syncopation; *Med.* unconsciousness through fall of blood-pressure.

syncretic /sɪŋ'kriːtɪk/ *a.* attempting, esp. inconsistently, to unify or reconcile differing schools of thought. **syncretism** *n.*; **syncretize** *v.*

syndicalism /'sɪndɪkəlɪz(ə)m/ *n.* movement for transfer of control and ownership of means of production and distribution to workers' unions. **syndicalist** *n.*

syndicate 1 /'sɪndɪkət/ *n.* combination of persons or commercial firms etc. to promote some common interest; as-

sociation supplying material simultaneously to a number of periodicals. **2** *v.* /'sɪndɪkeɪt/ form into syndicate; publish (material) through a syndicate. **3 syndication** *n.*

syndrome /'sɪndrəʊm/ *n.* group of concurrent symptoms of disease; characteristic combination of opinions or emotions etc.

synecdoche /sɪ'nekdəkɪ/ *n.* figure of speech in which part or individual is put for whole or class.

synod /'sɪnəd/ *n.* church council of senior clergy and officials.

synonym /'sɪnənɪm/ *n.* word or phrase that means exactly or nearly the same as another in same language. **synonymous** /-'nɒn-/ *a.*

synopsis /sɪ'nɒpsɪs/ *n.* (*pl.* **-ses** /-siːz/) summary; outline.

synoptic /sɪ'nɒptɪk/ *a.* of or giving synopsis. **Synoptic Gospels** those of Matthew, Mark, and Luke.

syntax /'sɪntæks/ *n.* grammatical arrangement of words; rules or analysis of this. **syntactic** *a.*

synthesis /'sɪnθəsɪs/ *n.* (*pl.* **-ses** /-siːz/) putting together of parts or elements to make up complex whole; artificial production of (esp. organic) substances from simpler ones.

synthesize /'sɪnθəsaɪz/ *v.t.* make synthesis of.

synthesizer /'sɪnθəsaɪzə(r)/ *n.* electronic musical instrument producing a great variety of sounds.

synthetic /sɪn'θetɪk/ **1** *a.* produced by synthesis; artificial. **2** *n.* synthetic substance.

syphilis /'sɪfɪlɪs/ *n.* a contagious venereal disease. **syphilitic** *a. & n.*

syringa /sɪ'rɪŋɡə/ *n.* shrub with white scented flowers.

syringe /'sɪrɪndʒ/ **1** *n.* device for drawing in quantity of liquid and ejecting it in fine stream. **2** *v.t.* sluice or spray with syringe.

syrup /'sɪrəp/ *n.* water (nearly) saturated with sugar, often flavoured or medicated; condensed sugar-cane juice, molasses, treacle; excessive sweetness of manner. **syrupy** *a.*

system /'sɪstəm/ *n.* complex whole; set of connected things or parts; organized body of things; the animal body as organized whole; method, considered principles of procedure or classification; orderliness; major group of geological strata. **systems analysis** analysis of an operation to decide how a computer may best be used to perform it.

systematic /sɪstə'mætɪk/ *a.* methodical; according to system; deliberate.

systematize /'sɪstəmətaɪz/ *v.t.* make systematic. **systematization** *n.*

systemic /sɪs'temɪk/ *a.* of the bodily system as a whole; (of insecticide etc.) entering plant tissues via roots and shoots. **systemically** *adv.*

systole /'sɪstəlɪ/ *n.* contraction of heart rhythmically alternating with diastole.

T

T, t, *n.* **cross the t's** be minutely accurate; **to a T** exactly, to a nicety; **T-junction** junction, esp. of two roads, in shape of T; **T-shirt** usu. buttonless casual shirt of knitted cotton etc.; **T-square** T-shaped instrument for measuring or obtaining right angles.

t. *abbr.* ton(s); tonne(s).

ta /tɑː/ *int. colloq.* thank you.

TA *abbr.* Territorial Army.

tab *n.* short broad strap or flat loop or tag etc., by which things can be taken hold of or fastened or identified etc.; *colloq.* account. **keep tabs on** have under observation or in check.

tabard /'tæbɑːd/ *n.* herald's short official coat emblazoned with arms of sovereign; woman's or child's garment of similar shape; *hist.* knight's short emblazoned garment worn over armour.

tabby /'tæbɪ/ *n.* grey or brownish cat with dark stripes.

tabernacle /'tæbənæk(ə)l/ *n. Jewish hist.* tent used as sanctuary by Israelites in the wilderness; canopied niche or receptacle; Nonconformist meeting-house.

tabla /'tæblə/ *n.* pair of small Indian drums played with hands.

table /'teɪb(ə)l/ **1** *n.* piece of furniture with flat top on which things may be placed for use or display; food provided at table; set of facts or figures systematically arranged esp. in columns; flat surface; slab of wood or stone etc., matter inscribed on it. **2** *v.t.* bring forward for discussion or consideration. **3 at table** while taking meal; **tableland** plateau of land; **tablespoon** large spoon for serving etc. and used as measure; **table tennis** indoor game based on lawn tennis, played with small bats and celluloid ball bouncing on table divided by net; **turn the tables** cause complete reversal of state of affairs.

tableau /'tæbləʊ/ *n.* (*pl.* **-leaux** /-ləʊz/) picturesque presentation, esp. of group of persons etc.; dramatic or effective situation suddenly brought about.

table d'hôte /tɑːbl 'dəʊt/ meal in restaurant etc. served at fixed price and at stated hour(s).

tablet /'tæblɪt/ *n.* fixed amount of drug compressed into small convenient shape; small flat piece of prepared substance, e.g. soap; small slab esp. for display of inscription.

tabloid /'tæblɔɪd/ *n.* newspaper, usu. popular in style, printed on sheets of half size of usual newspaper.

taboo /tə'buː/ **1** *n.* act or system of setting apart person or thing as sacred or accursed; ban, prohibition. **2** *a.* avoided or prohibited, esp. by social custom. **3** *v.t.* put under taboo; exclude or prohibit by authority or social influence.

tabor /'teɪbə(r)/ *n.* small drum.

tabu var. of **taboo**.

tabular /'tæbjʊlə(r)/ *a.* of or arranged in tables.

tabulate /'tæbjʊleɪt/ *v.t.* arrange (figures, facts) in tabular form. **tabulation** *n.*

tabulator /'tæbjʊleɪtə(r)/ *n.* attachment to typewriter for advancing to sequence of set positions in tabular work.

tachograph /'tækəgrɑːf/ *n.* device in motor vehicle to record speed and travel-time.

tacit /'tæsɪt/ *a.* implied or understood without being stated.

taciturn /'tæsɪtɜːn/ *a.* saying little, uncommunicative. **taciturnity** *n.*

tack[1] **1** *n.* small sharp usu. broad-headed nail; long stitch used in fastening materials lightly or temporarily together; direction in which vessel moves as determined by position of sails, one of consecutive series of changes of direction; course of action or policy. **2** *v.* fasten (*down* etc.) with tacks; stitch lightly together; annex, append; change ship's course by turning head to wind, make series of such tacks; change one's conduct or policy etc.

tack[2] *n.* riding-harness and saddles etc.

tackle /'tæk(ə)l/ **1** *n.* gear or appliances esp. for fishing or other sport; rope(s) and pulley(s) etc. used in working sails or hoisting weights etc.; *Footb.* etc. tackling. **2** *v.t.* grapple with; grasp with endeavour to hold or manage or overcome etc.; enter into discussion with; *Footb.* etc. intercept or stop (opponent in possession of ball etc.).

tacky /'tækɪ/ a. (of glue, varnish, etc.) in the sticky stage before complete dryness.

tact n. adroitness in dealing with persons or circumstances; intuitive perception of right thing to do or say. **tactful** a.

tactic /'tæktɪk/ n. piece of tactics.

tactical /'tæktɪk(ə)l/ a. of tactics; (of bombing etc.) done in immediate support of military or naval operation; adroitly planning or planned.

tactics /'tæktɪks/ n.pl. also treated as *sing.* art of disposing armed forces esp. in contact with enemy; procedure calculated to gain some end, skilful device(s). **tactician** n.

tactile /'tæktaɪl/ a. of or connected with sense of touch; perceived by touch. **tactility** /-'tɪl-/ n.

tadpole /'tædpəʊl/ n. larva of frog or toad etc. at stage of living in water and having gills and tail.

taffeta /'tæfɪtə/ n. fine plain-woven lustrous silk or silklike fabric.

taffrail /'tæfreɪl/ n. rail round ship's stern.

tag 1 n. metal point of shoelace etc.; loop or flap or label for handling or hanging or marking thing; loose or ragged end; trite quotation, stock phrase. 2 v. furnish with tag(s); tack or fasten *on* etc.; *colloq.* follow, trail behind; go along (*with*).

tail¹ 1 n. hindmost part of animal esp. when prolonged beyond body; thing like tail in form or position, esp. part of shirt below waist, hanging part of back of coat, end of procession etc.; inferior or weaker part of anything; in *pl. colloq.* tailcoat, evening dress with this; (usu. in *pl.*) reverse of coin turning up in toss. 2 v. remove stalks of (fruit etc.); follow (inconspicuously) and keep watch on. 3 **tail away**, **off**, fall away in straggling line, diminish and cease; **tail-back** long queue of traffic extending back from an obstruction; **tail-board** hinged or removable back of lorry etc.; **tailcoat** man's coat divided at back into tails and cut away in front; **tail-gate** tail-board, hinged rear door of estate car; **tail-light** light carried at back of train or car etc.; **tail-piece** final part of thing, decoration at end of chapter or book etc.; **tailplane**

horizontal stabilizing surface of tail of aircraft; **tail-spin** aircraft's spinning dive, *fig.* state of panic; **tail wind** one blowing in direction of one's travel.

tail² *Law* 1 n. limitation of ownership, esp. of estate limited to person and his heirs. 2 a. so limited.

tailor /'teɪlə(r)/ 1 n. maker of (esp. men's) outer garments, esp. to order. 2 v. be or work as tailor; make by tailor's methods; (esp. in *p.p.*) furnish with clothes; adapt or fit *to* requirements etc. 3 **tailor-made** made by tailor, *fig.* entirely appropriate to purpose.

taint 1 n. spot or trace of decay or corruption or disease; corrupt condition, infection. 2 v. introduce corruption or disease into; infect, be infected.

take 1 v. (*past* **took** /tʊk/, *p.p.* **taken**) lay hold of, grasp, seize; capture; obtain, get possession of, acquire, use; be successful or effective; consume, use up; have as necessary accompaniment or requirement or part; cause to come or go with one; remove, dispossess person of; catch, be infected with; ascertain and record; grasp mentally, understand; accept, submit to; deal with; teach, be taught or examined in; make (photograph). 2 n. amount taken or caught; *Cinemat.* scene or sequence photographed at one time without stopping camera. 3 **take after** resemble (parent etc.); **take against** begin to dislike; **take away** remove or carry elsewhere, subtract; **take-away** (cooked meal) bought at restaurant for eating elsewhere, restaurant selling this; **take back** retract, convey to original position; **take care** be careful; **take care of** look after, deal with; **take down** write down (spoken words), dismantle (structure); **take-home** (of pay etc.) given to employee after deduction of tax etc.; **take in** include, make (garment etc.) smaller, understand, cheat; **take in hand** start doing or dealing with, undertake control or reform of; **take it out of** exhaust strength of; **take it out on** relieve frustration by attacking; **take off** remove (clothing) from body, deduct, mimic, jump from ground, become airborne; **take-off** act of mimicking or becoming airborne, place from which one jumps; **take on** undertake, acquire, engage, agree to oppose at game, *colloq.* show violent emotion; **take out** remove, escort on outing, procure (patent, summons, etc.); **take over** succeed to management or ownership of, assume control; **take-over** *n.*; **take place** happen; **take to** begin, have recourse to, form liking for; **take up** begin, consume, adopt as protégé or pursuit, begin to consort *with*, interrupt or correct (speaker).

taker /'teɪkə(r)/ *n.* person who takes esp. a bet etc.

taking /'teɪkɪŋ/ 1 *a.* attractive, captivating. 2 *n.* in *pl.* money taken in business.

talc *n.* translucent mineral often found in thin glasslike plates; talcum powder.

talcum /'tælkəm/ *n.* talc. **talcum powder** (usu. perfumed) powdered talc, for toilet use.

tale *n.* narrative or story, esp. fictitious; idle or mischievous gossip, malicious report.

talent /'tælənt/ *n.* special aptitude or gift (*for*); high mental or artistic ability; *colloq.* persons of talent; ancient weight and money unit. **talent scout** person engaged in searching for talented people, esp. theatrical etc. **talented** /'tæləntɪd/ *a.* having high ability.

talisman /'tælɪsmən/ *n.* thing believed to bring good luck or protect from harm. **talismanic** /-'mæn-/ *a.*

talk /tɔːk/ 1 *v.* convey or exchange ideas or information etc. by speech, have or exercise faculty of speech, utter words; express or utter or discuss in words; gossip; use (language). 2 *n.* conversation; mode of speech; short address or lecture; rumour or gossip, its theme; discussion. 3 **talk down** silence by louder or more effective talking, speak patronizingly *to*, bring (aircraft) in to land by verbal instruction to pilot from ground; **talk into** persuade by talking; **talk over** discuss; **talk round** persuade to change opinion etc.; **talk to** speak to, *colloq.* reprove.

talkative /'tɔːkətɪv/ *a.* fond of talking.

tall /tɔːl/ *a.* of more than average height, or of specified height; higher than surroundings; *sl.* extravagant, excessive. **tallboy** tall chest of drawers;

tall order exorbitant or unreasonable demand.

tallow /'tæləʊ/ *n.* harder kinds of (esp. animal) fat melted down for use in making candles or soap etc. **tallowy** *a.*

tally 1 *v.i.* agree or correspond (*with*). 2 *n.* reckoning of debt or score; mark registering fixed number of objects delivered or received; *hist.* piece of wood scored with notches for items of account; distinguishing mark or ticket or label; counterpart, duplicate.

tally-ho /tælɪ'həʊ/ *int.* huntsman's cry as signal on seeing fox.

Talmud /'tælmʊd/ *n.* body of Jewish civil and ceremonial law. **Talmudic** *a.*

talon /'tælən/ *n.* claw esp. of bird of prey.

tamarind /'tæmərɪnd/ *n.* tropical tree with fruit whose acid pulp is used for medicinal or cooling drinks; this fruit.

tamarisk /'tæmərɪsk/ *n.* feathery-leaved evergreen shrub growing in sandy places.

tambour /'tæmbʊə(r)/ *n.* drum; circular frame for stretching embroidery-work on.

tambourine /tæmbə'riːn/ *n.* musical instrument of hoop with parchment stretched over one side and pairs of loose jingling discs in slots round circumference.

tame 1 *a.* (of animal) domesticated, not wild or shy; lacking spirit; uninteresting, insipid. 2 *v.t.* make tame, domesticate; break in; humble, subdue.

Tamil /'tæmɪl/ 1 *n.* member of a people inhabiting S. India and Sri Lanka; their language. 2 *a.* of this people or their language.

tam-o'-shanter /tæmə'ʃæntə/ *n.* round woollen Scottish etc. cap.

tamp *v.t.* pack or ram down tightly.

tamper /'tæmpə(r)/ *v.t.* meddle or interfere *with*.

tampon /'tæmpɒn/ 1 *n.* plug of cotton-wool etc. used to absorb secretions or stop haemorrhage. 2 *v.t.* plug with tampon.

tan 1 *n.* bronzed colour of skin exposed to sun etc. or weather; yellowish-brown colour; crushed or bruised bark of oak etc. used for tanning. 2 *a.* yellowish-brown. 3 *v.* make or become brown by exposure to sun or weather; convert (hide) into leather by steeping in liquid containing tannic acid or by use of mineral salts etc.; *sl.* thrash.

tandem 1 *n.* bicycle etc. with 2 or more seats behind each other; vehicle driven tandem. 2 *adv.* with two or more horses etc. harnessed one behind another. 3 **in tandem** one behind the other.

tandoor /'tænduə(r)/ *n.* Indian etc. clay oven.

tandoori /tæn'duəri/ *n.* food cooked in a tandoor.

tang *n.* strong or penetrating taste or smell; characteristic property; part of tool by which blade is held firm in handle.

tangent /'tændʒ(ə)nt/ *n.* straight line touching but not intersecting curve; *Math.* ratio of sides opposite and adjacent to angle in right-angled triangle **at a tangent** diverging from previous course of action or thought etc. **tangential** /-'dʒen-/ *a.*

tangerine /tændʒə'riːn/ *n.* kind of small flat sweet-scented orange.

tangible /'tændʒɪb(ə)l/ *a.* perceptible by touch; definite, clearly intelligible, not elusive or visionary. **tangibility** *n.*

tangle 1 *v.* intertwine or become twisted or involved in confused mass; entangle; complicate. 2 *n.* tangled condition or mass. 3 **tangly** *a.*

tango /'tæŋgəʊ/ 1 *n.* (*pl.* **-gos**) S. Amer. slow ballroom dance; music for this. 2 *v.i.* dance tango.

tank *n.* large receptacle for liquid or gas etc.; receptacle for fuel in motor vehicle; *Mil.* armoured motor vehicle carrying guns and mounted on Caterpillar tracks.

tankard /'tæŋkəd/ *n.* tall mug of pewter etc. for beer.

tanker /'tæŋkə(r)/ *n.* ship or aircraft or road vehicle for carrying liquids (esp. mineral oils) in bulk.

tannery /'tænəri/ *n.* place where hides are tanned.

tannic /'tænɪk/ *a.* of tan. **tannic acid** tannin.

tannin /'tænɪn/ *n.* any of several substances extracted from tree-barks etc. and used in tanning etc.

Tannoy /'tænɔɪ/ *n.* (**P**) type of public-address system.

tansy /'tænzɪ/ *n.* aromatic herb with yellow flowers.

tantalize /'tæntəlaɪz/ *v.t.* torment with disappointment, raise and then dash the hopes of. **tantalization** *n.*

tantalus /'tæntələs/ *n.* stand in which spirit-decanters are locked up but visible.

tantamount /'tæntəmaʊnt/ *pred.a.* equivalent *to.*

tantra /'tæntrə/ *n.* any of a class of Hindu or Buddhist mystical or magical writings.

tantrum /'tæntrəm/ *n.* outburst of bad temper or petulance.

tap[1] 1 *n.* device by which flow of liquid or gas from pipe or vessel can be controlled; act of tapping telephone. 2 *v.t.* provide (cask) with tap, let out (liquid) thus; draw sap from (tree) by cutting into it; draw supplies or information from; divert part of current from (telegraph or telephone wires etc.) to detect message; make screw-thread in. 3 **on tap** ready to be drawn off, ready for immediate use; **taproom** room where liquor on tap is sold and drunk; **taproot** tapering root growing vertically downwards.

tap[2] 1 *v.* strike (with) light or gentle blow; knock gently; cause to strike lightly *against* etc. 2 *n.* light blow or sound. 3 **tap-dancing** stage dancing with rhythmical tapping of feet.

tape 1 *n.* narrow woven strip of cotton etc. used as string; piece of tape stretched across race-course at winning-post; strip of paper or transparent film etc. coated with adhesive for fastening packages etc.; magnetic tape; tape-recording; continuous strip of paper on which messages are printed; tape-measure. 2 *v.t.* tie up or join with tape; record on magnetic tape; measure with tape. 3 **have person, thing, taped** *sl.* have summed him up, fully understand it; **tape-machine** device for receiving and recording telegraph messages; **tape-measure** strip of tape or thin flexible metal marked for measuring length; **tape-recorder** apparatus for recording sounds etc. on magnetic tape and afterwards reproducing them; **tape-recording** *n.*; **tapeworm** tapelike worm parasitic in alimentary canal.

taper 1 *n.* wick coated with wax etc. for conveying flame. 2 *v.* diminish in width or thickness towards one end; cause to do this. **3 taper off** make or become gradually less.

tapestry /'tæpɪstrɪ/ *n.* thick textile fabric in which coloured weft threads are woven (orig. by hand) to form pictures or designs; embroidery usu. in wools on canvas imitating this; piece of such embroidery.

tapioca /tæpɪˈəʊkə/ *n.* starchy granular foodstuff prepared from cassava.

tapir /'teɪpə(r)/ *n.* small piglike mammal with short flexible snout.

tappet /'tæpɪt/ *n.* arm or cam etc. used in machinery to impart intermittent motion.

tar¹ 1 *n.* dark thick inflammable liquid distilled from wood or coal etc.; similar substance formed in combustion of tobacco. 2 *v.t.* cover with tar. **3 tar macadam** road-making material of crushed stone etc. bound with tar.

tar² *colloq.* sailor.

taradiddle /'tærədɪd(ə)l/ *n. colloq.* fib; nonsense.

tarantella /tærənˈtelə/ *n.* rapid whirling S. Italian dance; music for this.

tarantula /təˈræntjʊlə/ *n.* large black spider of S. Europe; large hairy tropical spider.

tarboosh /tɑːˈbuːʃ/ *n.* cap like fez.

tardy /'tɑːdɪ/ *a.* slow to act or come or happen; behind time.

tare¹ /teə(r)/ *n.* vetch, esp. as corn-weed or fodder; in *pl.* injurious corn-weed.

tare² /teə(r)/ *n.* allowance made for weight of box etc. in which goods are packed; weight of motor vehicle without fuel or load.

target /'tɑːgɪt/ *n.* mark for shooting at, esp. with concentric circles round central ring or spot; anything aimed at.

tariff /'tærɪf/ *n.* table of fixed charges; duty on particular class of goods; list of duties or customs to be paid.

tarlatan /'tɑːlət(ə)n/ *n.* thin stiff muslin.

Tarmac /'tɑːmæk/ 1 *n.* **(P)** tar macadam; area surfaced with Tarmac. 2 *v.t.* **tarmac** (*past* & *p.p.* **tarmacked**) apply Tarmac to.

tarn *n.* small mountain lake.

tarnish /'tɑːnɪʃ/ 1 *v.* lessen or destroy lustre of; impair (reputation etc.); lose lustre. 2 *n.* tarnished state; stain, blemish.

taro /'tɑːrəʊ/ *n.* (*pl.* **-ros**) tropical plant of arum family with tuberous root used as food.

tarot /'tærəʊ/ *n.* pack of 78 playing-cards used in fortune-telling.

tarpaulin /tɑːˈpɔːlɪn/ *n.* waterproof cloth esp. of tarred canvas; sheet or covering of this.

tarragon /'tærəgən/ *n.* aromatic herb.

tarry¹ /'tɑːrɪ/ *a.* of or smeared with tar.

tarry² /'tærɪ/ *v.i.* delay, be late; linger.

tarsus /'tɑːsəs/ *n.* (*pl.* **-si** /-saɪ/) collection of small bones forming ankle. **tarsal** *a.*

tart¹ *n.* pastry case containing fruit or jam etc.

tart² 1 *n. sl.* prostitute, immoral woman. 2 *v. colloq.* dress *up* gaudily, smarten *up*.

tart³ *a.* sharp-tasting, acid; cutting, biting.

tartan /'tɑːt(ə)n/ *n.* pattern of coloured stripes crossing at right angles, worn orig. by Scottish Highlanders in distinctive patterns denoting their clans; cloth woven in such pattern.

tartar¹ /'tɑːtə(r)/ *n.* hard deposit that forms on teeth; substance deposited in cask by fermentation of wine. **cream of tartar** preparation of tartaric acid used in cookery.

Tartar² /'tɑːtə(r)/ *n.* native of Tartary; intractable or violent-tempered person. **tartar sauce** mayonnaise with chopped gherkins etc.

tartaric /tɑːˈtærɪk/ *a.* of tartar. **tartaric acid** organic acid present in many plants.

tartlet /'tɑːtlɪt/ *n.* small tart.

task /tɑːsk/ 1 *n.* piece of work to be done. 2 *v.t.* make great demands on. 3 **take to task** accuse of fault, rebuke; **task force** specially organized unit for task; **taskmaster** person who imposes task or burden.

tassel /'tæs(ə)l/ *n.* tuft of hanging threads etc. as ornament; tassel-like catkin.

taste /teɪst/ 1 *n.* sensation caused in tongue etc. by contact with some substances, flavour; sense by which this is perceived; small portion of food etc. taken as sample; liking, predilection, (*for*); aesthetic discernment in art or literature or conduct, conformity to its dictates. **2** *v.* perceive or learn flavour of; have specified flavour; eat small portion of, sample; have experience of. **3 taste-bud** organ of taste in mouth, esp. on tongue.

tasteful /'teɪstfʊl/ *a.* done in or having good taste.

tasteless /'teɪstlɪs/ *a.* flavourless; having or done in bad taste.

taster /'teɪstə(r)/ *n.* person employed to judge teas or wines etc. by taste; *colloq.* small sample of food etc.

tasty /'teɪstɪ/ *a. colloq.* of pleasing flavour, appetizing.

tat[1] *n. colloq.* tatty thing(s) or person; tattiness.

tat[2] *v.* do or make by tatting.

tatter /'tætə(r)/ *n.* (usu. in *pl.*) rag, irregularly torn piece, esp. hanging loose; *fig.* useless remains.

tattered /'tætəd/ *a.* in tatters.

tatting /'tætɪŋ/ *n.* kind of knotted lace made by hand with small shuttle.

tattle /'tæt(ə)l/ **1** *v.i.* gossip idly; repeat or discuss scandal. **2** *n.* gossip, idle talk.

tattoo[1] /tə'tuː/ *n.* evening signal recalling soldiers to quarters; elaboration of this with music and marching etc. as entertainment; drumming, rapping; drumbeat.

tattoo[2] /tə'tuː/ **1** *v.t.* mark (skin) by puncturing and inserting pigment; make (design) thus. **2** *n.* such design.

tatty /'tætɪ/ *a. colloq.* tattered; shabby, inferior, tawdry.

taught *past* & *p.p.* of **teach**.

taunt 1 *n.* insulting or provoking gibe. **2** *v.t.* reproach or mock at insultingly or contemptuously.

Taurus /'tɔːrəs/ *n.* second sign of zodiac.

taut *a.* drawn tight; stiff, tense; (of ship etc.) in good condition.

tauten /'tɔːt(ə)n/ *v.* make or become taut.

tautology /tɔː'tɒlədʒɪ/ *n.* saying of same thing twice over in different words. **tautological** *a.*; **tautologous** *a.*

tavern /'tæv(ə)n/ *n.* inn, public-house.

tawdry /'tɔːdrɪ/ *a.* showy or gaudy without real value.

tawny /'tɔːnɪ/ *a.* of orange-brown colour.

tax 1 *n.* contribution to State revenue

legally levied on person or property or business etc.; strain or heavy demand (*up*)*on*. **2** *v.t.* impose tax on; pay tax on; make demands on; charge (*with*), call to account. **3 tax-deductible** (of expenses) that may be paid out of income before deduction of income tax; **tax return** declaration of income etc. for taxation purposes.

taxation /tæk'seɪʃ(ə)n/ *n.* imposition or payment of tax(es).

taxi /'tæksɪ/ **1** *n.* (in full **taxi-cab**) motor car plying for hire and usu. fitted with taximeter. **2** *v.* (of aircraft) go along ground or surface of water under machine's own power before or after flying; go or convey in taxi.

taxidermy /'tæksɪdɜːmɪ/ *a.* art of preparing, stuffing, and mounting skins of animals with lifelike effect. **taxidermist** *n.*

taximeter /'tæksɪmiːtə(r)/ *n.* automatic device indicating fare due fitted to taxi.

taxonomy /tæk'sɒnəmɪ/ *n.* classification, esp. in biology; principles of this. **taxonomical** *a.*; **taxonomist** *n.*

TB *abbr.* tubercle bacillus; *colloq.* tuberculosis.

te /tiː/ *n. Mus.* seventh note of scale in tonic sol-fa.

tea *n.* evergreen shrub or small tree grown in China and India etc.; its dried leaves; infusion of these leaves as drink; infusion made from leaves etc. of other plants or beef extract etc.; meal at which tea is served, esp. light meal in afternoon or evening. **tea-bag** small permeable bag holding tea-leaves for infusion; **tea-break** interruption of work allowed for drinking tea; **teacake** light flat usu. sweet bun; **tea-chest** light metal-lined wooden box in which tea is exported; **tea-cloth** cloth for teatable, tea-towel; **tea-leaf** leaf of tea, esp. in *pl.* after infusion; **teapot** vessel with handle and spout, in which tea is made; **tea-rose** rose with scent like tea; **teaspoon** small spoon for stirring tea etc. or used as measure; **tea-towel** cloth for drying washed crockery etc.

teach *v.* (*past* & *p.p.* **taught** /tɔːt/) give systematic information to (person) or about (subject or skill); enable (person) to do something by instruction; advocate as moral etc. principle. **teach-in**

series of lectures and discussions on subject of public interest.

teachable /'ti:tʃəb(ə)l/ *a.* apt at learning; that can be taught.

teacher /'ti:tʃə(r)/ *n.* person who teaches esp. in school.

teaching /'ti:tʃɪŋ/ *n.* what is taught; doctrine; teachers' profession. **teaching hospital** one where medical students are taught.

teak *n.* heavy durable timber; Asian tree yielding this.

teal *n.* (*pl.* same) small freshwater duck.

team 1 *n.* set of players etc. in game or sport; set of persons working together; set of draught animals. 2 *v.* join (*up*) as team or in common action (*with*). 3 **team-work** combined effort, co-operation.

teamster /'ti:mstə(r)/ *n.* driver of team; *US* lorry-driver.

tear[1] /teə(r)/ 1 *v.* (*past* **tore**; *p.p.* **torn**) pull (apart) with some force; make (hole, rent) thus; move violently or impetuously; undergo tearing. 2 *n.* hole made or damage caused by tearing; torn part of cloth etc. 3 **tearaway** hooligan, ruffian.

tear[2] /tɪə(r)/ *n.* drop of clear salty liquid appearing in or flowing from eye as result of emotion, esp. grief, or physical irritation etc. **in tears** weeping; **tear-gas** gas that disables by causing severe irritation to the eyes.

tearful /'tɪəfʊl/ *a.* in or given to or accompanied with tears.

tearing /'teərɪŋ/ *a.* extreme, overwhelming.

tease /ti:z/ 1 *v.* irritate playfully or maliciously with jests or petty annoyances etc.; pick (wool etc.) into separate fibres; dress (cloth) with teasels etc. 2 *n. colloq.* person fond of teasing others.

teasel /'ti:z(ə)l/ *n.* plant with prickly flower-heads; such head dried and used for raising nap on cloth.

teaser /'ti:zə(r)/ *n. colloq.* difficult question or problem.

teat *n.* mammary nipple esp. of animal; device of rubber etc. for sucking milk from bottle.

tec *n. sl.* detective.

Tech /tek/ *n. colloq.* Technical college or school.

technical /'teknɪk(ə)l/ *a.* of or in-

volving the mechanical arts and applied sciences; of or relating to a particular subject or craft etc.; requiring special knowledge to be understood; in strict legal sense.

technicality /teknɪ'kælɪtɪ/ *n.* being technical; technical expression; technical point or detail.

technician /tek'nɪʃ(ə)n/ *n.* expert in practical application of science; person skilled in technique of art or subject.

technique /tek'ni:k/ *n.* mechanical skill in art or craft etc.; method of achieving purpose; manner of execution or performance in music or painting etc.

technocracy /tek'nɒkrəsɪ/ *n.* government or control by technical experts.

technocrat 'teknəkræt/ *n.* advocate of technocracy.

technology /tek'nɒlədʒɪ/ *n.* study or use of the mechanical arts and applied sciences; these subjects collectively. **technological** *a.*; **technologist** *n.*

teddy bear /'tedɪ/ child's toy bear.

tedious/'ti:dɪəs/ *a.* tiresomely long, wearisome.

tedium /'ti:dɪəm/ *n.* tediousness.

tee[1] *n.* letter T.

tee[2] *Golf* 1 *n.* cleared space from which ball is struck at beginning of play for each hole, small pile of sand or small appliance of wood or rubber etc., on which ball is placed before being thus struck. 2 *v.* place (ball) on tee. 3 **tee off** make first stroke in golf, start, begin.

teem[1] *v.i.* swarm *with*; be abundant.

teem[2] *v.i.* pour (esp. of rain).

teenage /'ti:neɪdʒ/ *a.* of or characteristic of teenagers.

teenager /'ti:neɪdʒə(r)/ *n.* person in teens.

teens *n.pl.* years of one's age from 13 to 19.

teeny /'ti:nɪ/ *a. colloq.* tiny.

teeter /'ti:tə(r)/ *v.* totter, stand or move unsteadily.

teeth *pl.* of **tooth**.

teethe /ti:ð/ *v.i.* grow or cut teeth, esp. milk-teeth. **teething troubles** initial troubles in an enterprise etc.

teetotal /ti:'təʊt(ə)l/ *a.* advocating or practising total abstinence from intoxicants. **teetotalism** *n.*; **teetotaller** *n.*

tele- /telɪ/ *in comb.* far; at a distance; television.

telecommunication /telɪkəmjuːnɪˈkeɪʃ(ə)n/ *n.* communication over long distances by cable or telegraph or telephone or radio; in *pl.* this branch of technology.

telegram /ˈtelɪɡræm/ *n.* message sent by telegraph.

telegraph /ˈtelɪɡrɑːf/ 1 *n.* transmission of messages to a distance by making and breaking electrical connection; apparatus for this. 2 *v.* send message by telegraph; send (message) thus.

telegraphist /tɪˈleɡrəfɪst/ *n.* person skilled or employed in telegraphy.

telegraphic /telɪˈɡræfɪk/ *a.* of telegraphs or telegrams; (of style) economically worded. **telegraphically** *adv.*

telegraphy /tɪˈleɡrəfɪ/ *n.* use or construction of telegraph.

telemeter /ˈtelɪmiːtə(r)/ *n.* apparatus for recording readings of instrument at distance, usu. by radio. **telemetry** /tɪˈlemɪtrɪ/ *n.*

teleology /telɪˈɒlədʒɪ/ *n.* view that events etc. are due to purpose or design that is served by them; study of final causes. **teleological** *a.*

telepathy /tɪˈlepəθɪ/ *n.* communication between minds other than by known senses. **telepathic** /-ˈpæθ-/ *a.*

telephone /ˈtelɪfəʊn/ 1 *n.* apparatus for transmitting speech and other signals to a distance; transmitting and receiving instrument used in this; system of communication by network of telephones. 2 *v.* send message or speak to by telephone; make telephone call. 3 **telephone book, directory,** book listing names and numbers of telephone subscribers; **telephone booth, box, kiosk,** structure containing telephone for public use; **telephone number** number assigned to particular subscriber and used in making connections to his telephone. 4 **telephonic** /-ˈfɒn-/ *a.*; **telephonically** *adv.*

telephonist /tɪˈlefənɪst/ *n.* operator in telephone exchange or a switchboard.

telephony /tɪˈlefənɪ/ *n.* use or system of telephones.

telephotography /telɪfəˈtɒɡrəfɪ/ *n.* photographing distant object with combined lenses giving large image. **telephoto** *a.*; **telephotographic** *a.*

teleprinter /ˈtelɪprɪntə(r)/ *n.* telegraph instrument for sending messages by typing.

telescope /ˈtelɪskəʊp/ 1 *n.* optical instrument using lenses or mirrors to make distant objects appear nearer and larger; (in full **radio telescope**) apparatus for collecting radio waves from celestial objects. 2 *v.* press or drive (sections of tube etc.) one into another like sections of telescope; close or be driven or be capable of closing thus; compress.

telescopic /telɪˈskɒpɪk/ *a.* of or made with telescope; consisting of sections that telescope. **telescopic sight** small telescope used as sight for firearm etc.

televise /ˈtelɪvaɪz/ *v.t.* transmit by television.

television /ˈtelɪvɪʒ(ə)n/ *n.* system for reproducing on a screen visual images transmitted (with sound) by radio signals; (in full **television set**) apparatus for displaying pictures transmitted by television.

televisual /telɪˈvɪzjʊəl/ *a.* of television.

telex /ˈteleks/ 1 *n.* system of telegraphy using teleprinters and public telecommunication network. 2 *v.t.* send or communicate with by telex.

tell *v.* (*past & p.p.* **told** /təʊld/) relate or narrate; utter or express in words; inform or give information *of* etc.; divulge, reveal; betray secret; ascertain, decide about, distinguish; instruct or order (*to* do etc.); be of account or weight, produce marked effect (*on*). **tell off** *colloq.* scold, reprimand; **tell-tale** person who tells tales, automatic registering device, *attrib.* serving to reveal or betray something; **tell tales** report discreditable fact about another.

teller /ˈtelə(r)/ *n.* person employed to receive and pay out money in bank etc.; person appointed to count votes.

telling /ˈtelɪŋ/ *a.* having marked effect, striking.

telly /ˈtelɪ/ *n. colloq.* television.

temerity /tɪˈmerɪtɪ/ *n.* rashness, audacity.

temp *n. colloq.* temporary employee, esp. secretary.

temper /ˈtempə(r)/ 1 *n.* habitual or temporary disposition of mind esp. as regards composure; irritation, anger; condition of metal as regards hardness and elasticity. **2** *v.t.* bring (clay, metal) to proper consistency or hardness; moderate or mitigate by blending *with* another quality. **3 lose one's temper** become angry.

tempera /'tempərə/ *n.* method of painting using emulsion e.g. of pigment with egg.

temperament /'tempərəmənt/ *n.* person's distinct nature and character, which permanently affects behaviour.

temperamental /tempərə'ment(ə)l/ *a.* liable to erratic or peculiar moods.

temperance /'tempərəns/ *n.* moderation or self-restraint, esp. in eating and drinking; total or partial abstinence from alcoholic drink.

temperate /'tempərət/ *a.* avoiding excess, moderate; (of climate) not exhibiting extremes of heat or cold.

temperature /'tempərətʃ(ə)r/ *n.* degree or intensity of heat of body or at mosphere, esp. as shown by thermometer; *colloq.* body temperature above normal.

tempest /'tempist/ *n.* violent storm.

tempestuous /tem'pestjʊəs/ *a.* stormy, turbulent.

template /'templeit/ *n.* thin board or plate used as guide in cutting or drilling.

temple[1] /'temp(ə)l/ *n.* building treated as the dwelling-place, or devoted to worship, of god(s). **Inner, Middle, Temple** two Inns of Court in London.

temple[2] /'temp(ə)l/ *n.* flat part of side of head between forehead and ear.

tempo /'tempəʊ/ *n.* (*pl.* **-pos** or **-pi** /-piː/) speed at which music is (to be) played; rate of motion or activity.

temporal /'tempər(ə)l/ *a.* of worldly as opposed to spiritual affairs, secular; of or denoting time; of the temples of the head.

temporary /'tempərəri/ **1** *a.* lasting or meant to last only for a time. **2** *n.* person employed temporarily. **3 temporarily** *n.* □ See page 665.

temporize /'tempəraiz/ *v.i.* avoid committing oneself, act so as to gain time; comply temporarily with requirements of occasion. **temporization** *n.*

tempt *v.t.* entice, incite; allure, attract; risk provoking.

temptation /temp'teiʃ(ə)n/ *n.* tempting or being tempted; incitement esp. to sin; attractive thing or course of action.

ten *a.* & *n.* one more than nine. **tenfold** *a.* & *adv.*; **tenth** *a.* & *n.*

tenable /'tenəb(ə)l/ *a.* that can be maintained against attack or objection; that can be held *for* period or *by* person etc.

tenacious /ti'neiʃəs/ *a.* keeping firm hold (*of*); retentive; holding tightly, not easily separable, tough. **tenacity** /-næs-/ *n.*

tenancy /'tenənsi/ *n.* tenant's position.

tenant /'ten(ə)nt/ *n.* person who rents land or (part of) house from landlord; occupant of place.

tenantry /'tenəntri/ *n.* tenants.

tench *n.* (*pl.* same) freshwater fish of carp family.

tend[1] *v.i.* be apt or inclined, conduce (*to*); be moving or directed in certain direction.

tend[2] *v.t.* take care of, look after.

tendency /'tendənsi/ *n.* tending, leaning, inclination.

tendentious /ten'denʃəs/ *a. derog.* designed to advance a cause.

tender[1] /'tendə(r)/ *a.* not tough or hard; easily touched or wounded; delicate, fragile; loving, affectionate. **tenderfoot** novice, newcomer; **tenderloin** middle part of loin of pork.

tender[2] /'tendə(r)/ **1** *v.* offer, hand in, present; offer as payment; make tender (*for*). **2** *n.* offer, esp. to execute work or supply goods at fixed price. **3 legal tender** currency that cannot legally be refused in payment of debt.

tender[3] /'tendə(r)/ *n.* vessel attending larger one to supply stores etc.; truck attached to steam locomotive and carrying fuel etc.

tenderize /'tendəraiz/ *v.t.* render (meat) tender by beating etc.

tendon /'tend(ə)n/ *n.* tough fibrous tissue connecting muscle to bone etc.

tendril /'tendril/ *n.* one of the slender leafless shoots by which some climbing plants cling.

tenement /'tenəmənt/ *n.* dwelling-house; portion of house occupied separately; house divided into and let in tenements.

tenet /'tenit/ *n.* doctrine held by group or person etc.

tenner /'tenə(r)/ *n. colloq.* £10 note.

tennis /'tenɪs/ n. (in full **lawn tennis**) ball game played with rackets on court divided by net.

tenon /'ten(ə)n/ n. projection shaped to fit into mortise.

tenor /'tenə(r)/ n. adult male voice between male alto and baritone; singer with tenor voice; music for tenor voice; general purport; prevailing course of one's life or habits.

tense[1] 1 a. stretched tight; strained or highly strung. 2 v. make or become tense.

tense[2] n. form taken by verb to indicate time of action etc.; set of such forms for various persons and numbers.

tensile /'tensaɪl/ a. of tension; capable of being stretched. **tensility** /-'sɪl-/ n.

tension /'tenʃ(ə)n/ n. stretching or being stretched; mental strain or excitement; strained state; effect produced by forces pulling against each other; electromotive force.

tent n. portable shelter or dwelling of canvas etc.

tentacle /'tentək(ə)l/ n. slender flexible appendage of animal, used for feeling, grasping, or moving.

tentative /'tentətɪv/ a. done by way of trial, experimental; hesitant, not definite.

tenterhooks /'tentəhʊks/ n.pl. **on tenterhooks** in suspense, distracted by uncertainty.

tenuous /'tenjʊəs/ a. slight, of little substance; subtle; thin, slender. **tenuity** n.

tenure /'tenjʊə(r)/ n. holding of property or office; conditions or period of this.

tepee /'tiːpiː/ n. N. Amer. Indian's conical tent.

tepid /'tepɪd/ a. slightly warm, lukewarm. **tepidity** n.

tequila /te'kiːlə/ n. Mexican liquor made from agave.

tercentenary /tɜːsen'tiːnərɪ/ n. 300th anniversary; celebration of this.

terebinth /'terɪbɪnθ/ n. S. Eur. tree yielding turpentine.

tergiversation /tɜːdʒɪvə'seɪʃ(ə)n/ n. desertion of party or principles; making of conflicting statements.

term 1 n. word used to express definite concept esp. in branch of study etc.; in pl. language used, mode of expression; in pl. relation, footing; in pl. conditions, stipulations, charge, price; limited period; period of action or of contemplated results; period during which instruction is given in school or university or during which lawcourt holds sessions; Math. each quantity in ratio or series, item of compound algebraic expression. 2 v.t. denominate, call. 3 **come to terms with** reconcile oneself to; **terms of reference** points referred to an individual or body of persons for decision or report, scope of inquiry etc., definition of this.

termagant /'tɜːməgənt/ n. overbearing woman, virago.

terminable /'tɜːmɪnəb(ə)l/ a. that may be terminated.

terminal /'tɜːmɪn(ə)l/ 1 a. of or forming the last part or terminus; Med. forming or undergoing last stage of fatal disease; of or done etc. each term. 2 n. terminating thing, extremity; terminus; point of connection for closing electric circuit; air terminal; apparatus for transmission of messages to and from computer or communications system etc.

terminate /'tɜːmɪneɪt/ v. bring or come to an end; end in etc.

termination /tɜːmɪ'neɪʃ(ə)n/ n. ending, way something ends; word's final syllable or letter(s).

terminology /tɜːmɪ'nɒlədʒɪ/ n. system of terms used in particular subject. **terminological** a.

terminus /'tɜːmɪnəs/ n. (pl. **-nuses** or **-ni** /-naɪ/) point at end of railway or bus route or pipeline etc.

termite /'tɜːmaɪt/ n. antlike insect destructive to timber.

tern n. sea-bird with long pointed wings and forked tail.

ternary /'tɜːnərɪ/ a. composed of 3 parts.

terrace /'terɪs/ n. raised level space, natural or artificial, esp. for walking or standing; row of houses built in one block of uniform style; (usu. in pl.) flight of wide shallow steps as for spectators at sports ground.

terracotta /terə'kɒtə/ n. unglazed usu. brownish-red fine pottery; its colour.

terra firma /terə 'fɜːmə/ dry land, firm ground.

terrain /təˈreɪn/ n. tract of country as regards its natural features.

terrapin /ˈterəpɪn/ n. N. Amer. edible freshwater tortoise.

terrarium /teˈreərɪəm/ n. (pl. -riums) place for keeping small land animals; ornamental transparent structure containing growing plants.

terrestrial /teˈrestrɪəl/ a. of or on the earth; of or on dry land.

terrible /ˈterɪb(ə)l/ a. causing or fit to cause terror; dreadful; colloq. very great or bad, incompetent.

terribly /ˈterɪblɪ/ adv. in a terrible manner; colloq. very, extremely.

terrier /ˈterɪə(r)/ n. small active hardy dog.

terrific /təˈrɪfɪk/ a. causing terror; colloq. of great size or intensity; colloq. excellent.

terrify /ˈterɪfaɪ/ v.t. fill with terror, frighten.

terrine /təˈriːn/ n. pâté or similar food; earthenware vessel for holding this.

territorial /terɪˈtɔːrɪəl/ 1 a. of territory or districts. 2 n. **Territorial** member of Territorial Army. 3 **Territorial Army** volunteer reserve force organized by localities; **territorial waters** waters under State's jurisdiction, esp. part of sea within stated distance of shore.

territory /ˈterɪtərɪ/ n. extent of land under jurisdiction of sovereign or State etc.; **Territory**, organized division of a country esp. if not yet admitted to full rights of a State; sphere of action or thought, province; area over which commercial traveller etc. operates; area defended by animal against others of same species or by team etc. in game.

terror /ˈterə(r)/ n. extreme fear; terrifying person or thing; colloq. troublesome or tiresome person, esp. child.

terrorism /ˈterərɪz(ə)m/ n. practice of using violent and intimidating methods, esp. to secure political ends. **terrorist** n.

terrorize /ˈterəraɪz/ v. fill with terror; coerce by terrorism. **terrorization** n.

terry /ˈterɪ/ n. pile fabric with loops left uncut.

terse /tɜːs/ a. concise, brief and forcible in style; curt.

tertiary /ˈtɜːʃərɪ/ a. of third order or rank etc.

Terylene /ˈterɪliːn/ n. (P) synthetic polyester used as textile fabric.

tessellated /ˈtesəleɪtɪd/ a. of or resembling mosaic; having finely chequered surface. **tessellation** n.

test 1 n. critical examination or trial of qualities or nature of person or thing; means or standard or circumstances suitable for or serving such examination; colloq. test match. 2 v.t. subject to test, make trial of; try severely, tax. 3 **test bed** equipment for testing aircraft engines etc. before general use; **test case** Law case whose decision is taken as settling other similar cases; **test match** one of series of (esp. cricket) matches between different countries; **test-tube** thin glass tube closed at one end used to hold substance undergoing chemical test etc.; **test-tube baby** colloq. baby conceived by artificial insemination or developed elsewhere than in a mother's body.

testaceous /tesˈteɪʃəs/ a. having hard continuous shell.

testacy /ˈtestəsɪ/ n. being testate.

testament /ˈtestəmənt/ n. a will; colloq. written statement of one's beliefs etc. **Old, New, Testament** main divisions of Bible.

testamentary /testəˈmentərɪ/ a. of or by or in a will.

testate /ˈtesteɪt/ 1 a. having left valid will at death. 2 n. testate person.

testator /tesˈteɪtə(r)/ n. person who has made a will, esp. one who dies testate.

testatrix /tesˈteɪtrɪks/ n. female testator.

testes pl. of testis.

testicle /ˈtestɪk(ə)l/ n. male organ that secretes spermatozoa, esp. one of pair in scrotum behind penis of man and most male mammals.

testify /ˈtestɪfaɪ/ v. bear witness; give evidence; affirm, declare, be evidence of.

testimonial /testɪˈməʊnɪəl/ n. certificate of character or conduct or qualifications; gift presented as mark of esteem.

testimony /ˈtestɪmənɪ/ n. Law oral or written statement made under oath or affirmation; evidence.

testis /ˈtestɪs/ n. (pl. -tes /-tiːz/) testicle.

testosterone /tes'tɒstərəʊn/ *n.* male sex hormone.

testy /'testɪ/ *a.* irascible, short-tempered.

tetanus /'tetənəs/ *n.* bacterial disease with continuous painful contraction of voluntary muscles.

tetchy /'tetʃɪ/ *a.* peevish, irritable.

tête-à-tête /teɪtɑː'teɪt/ 1 *n.* private conversation or interview between two persons. 2 *adv.* together in private.

tether /'teðə(r)/ 1 *n.* rope etc. by which grazing animal is confined. 2 *v.t.* fasten with tether. 3 **end of one's tether** extreme limit of one's strength or patience etc.

tetra- *in comb.* four.

tetrad /'tetræd/ *n.* group of 4.

tetragon /'tetrəgən/ *n.* plane figure with 4 sides and angles. **tetragonal** /-'træg-/ *a.*

tetrahedron /tetrə'hiːdrən/ *n.* (*pl.* **-drons**) 4-sided triangular pyramid. **tetrahedral** *a.*

tetralogy /te'trælədʒɪ/ *n.* group of 4 related literary or dramatic works.

Teutonic /tjuː'tɒnɪk/ *a.* of Germanic peoples or languages.

text *n.* main body of book; wording of anything written or printed, esp. opp. to translation or commentary etc.; passage of Scripture quoted or chosen as subject of sermon etc.; subject, theme; in *pl.* books prescribed for study. **textbook** manual of instruction, standard book in any branch of study.

textile /'tekstaɪl/ 1 *n.* woven material. 2 *a.* of weaving; woven.

textual /'tekstjʊəl/ *a.* of or in or concerning a text.

texture /'tekstʃə(r)/ 1 *n.* quality of a surface or substance when felt or looked at; arrangement of threads in textile fabric. 2 *v.t.* give particular esp. rough texture to. 3 **textural** *a.*

thalidomide /θə'lɪdəmaɪd/ *n.* sedative drug found in 1961 to cause malformation of limbs of embryo when taken by mother early in pregnancy.

than /ðæn/ *conj.* introducing second element in comparison or statement of difference.

thane /θeɪn/ *n. hist.* holder of land from Engl. king by military service, or from Sc. king and ranking below earl; clan-chief.

thank /θæŋk/ 1 *v.t.* express gratitude to. 2 *n.* in *pl.* gratitude, expression of gratitude. 3 **thank-offering** gift made in gratitude; **thanksgiving** expression of gratitude esp. to God; **Thanksgiving (Day)** US annual holiday on fourth Thurs. in Nov.; **thanks to** as good or bad result of; **thank you** polite formula acknowledging gift or service or accepted offer, etc.; **no thank you** polite refusal of offer.

thankful /'θæŋkfʊl/ *a.* grateful, pleased, expressive of thanks.

thankless /'θæŋklɪs/ *a.* not feeling or expressing gratitude; (of task etc.) unprofitable.

that /ðæt/ 1 *pron.* (*pl.* **those** /ðəʊz/) the person or thing indicated or named or understood; coupled or contrasted with **this**; the one, the person, etc.; used to introduce defining clause. 2 *a.* (*pl.* **those**) designating the person or thing indicated etc. 3 *adv.* to such a degree, so. 4 *conj.* introducing subordinate clause indicating esp. statement or hypothesis or purpose or result. 5 **at that** too, besides; **that is** in other words, more correctly or intelligibly.

thatch /θætʃ/ 1 *n.* roofing of straw or reeds etc. 2 *v.t.* roof with thatch.

thaw /θɔː/ 1 *v.* release or escape from frozen state; warm into liquid state or into life or animation or cordiality. 2 *n.* thawing; warmth of weather that thaws.

the (before vowel /ðɪ/, before consonant /ðə/, *emphat.* /ðiː/) 1 *a.* serving to particularize as needing no further identification, or to describe as unique or assist in defining or distinguish as best-known, or to confer generic or representative or distributive value on. 2 *adv.* (preceding comparatives in expressions of proportional variation) in or by that degree, on that account.

theatre /'θɪətə(r)/ *n.* building or outdoor area for dramatic performances; plays and acting; room or hall for lectures etc. with seats in tiers; scene or field of operation; operating theatre.

theatrical /θɪ'ætrɪk(ə)l/ 1 *a.* of or for theatre or acting; calculated for effect, showy. 2 *n.* in *pl.* dramatic performances. 3 **theatricality** *n.*

thee /ðiː/ *pron. obj.* case of **thou**.

theft /θeft/ *n.* stealing.

their /ðeər/ *pron.*, *poss.* case of **they** with *absol.* form **theirs**.

theism /ˈθiːɪz(ə)m/ *n.* belief in divine creation and conduct of the universe. **theist** *n.*; **theistic** *a.*

them /ðem/ *pron. obj.* case of **they**.

theme /θiːm/ *n.* subject or topic (*of* talk etc.); *US* school exercise on given subject; *Mus.* leading melody in a composition. **theme song, tune**, signature tune. **thematic** /-ˈmæt-/ *a.*

themselves /ðəmˈselvz/ *pron.*, *emphat.* and *refl.* form of **they**.

then /ðen/ 1 *adv.* at that time; after that, next; in that case, accordingly. **2** *a.* existing etc. at that time. **3** *n.* that time. **4 then and there** immediately and on the spot.

thence /ðens/ *adv.* from that place, for that reason. **thenceforth, thenceforward**, from that time on.

theo- /θɪəʊ/ *in comb.* God or god.

theocracy /θɪˈɒkrəsɪ/ *n.* form of government by God or god directly or through a priestly order etc. **theocratic** *a.*; **theocratically** *adv.*

theodolite /θɪˈɒdəlaɪt/ *n.* surveying-instrument for measuring angles.

theology /θɪˈɒlədʒɪ/ *n.* study or system of (esp. Christian) religion. **theologian** /-ˈləʊdʒ-/ *n.*; **theological** *a.*

theorem /ˈθɪərəm/ *n.* general proposition not self-evident but demonstrable by argument.

theoretical /θɪəˈretɪk(ə)l/ *a.* concerned with knowledge but not with its practical application; based on theory rather than experience.

theoretician /θɪərəˈtɪʃ(ə)n/ *n.* person concerned with theoretical part of a subject.

theorist /ˈθɪərɪst/ *n.* holder or inventor of a theory.

theorize /ˈθɪəraɪz/ *v.i.* evolve or indulge in theories.

theory /ˈθɪərɪ/ *n.* supposition or system of ideas explaining something, esp. one based on general principles; speculative view; sphere of abstract knowledge or speculative thought; exposition of principles of a science etc.; *Math.* collection of propositions to illustrate principles of a subject.

theosophy /θɪˈɒsəfɪ/ *n.* philosophy professing to achieve knowledge of God by direct intuition or spiritual ecstasy etc. **theosophical** *a.*

therapeutic /θerəˈpjuːtɪk/ *a.* of or for or tending to the cure of diseases.

therapeutics *n.pl.* (usu. treated as *sing.*) branch of medicine concerned with remedial treatment of ill health.

therapy /ˈθerəpɪ/ *n.* curative medical etc. treatment. **therapist** *n.*

there /ðeə(r)/ 1 *adv.* in or at that place; to that place or point; at that point; in that respect. **2** *n.* that place or point. **3** *int.* drawing attention to anything. **4 thereabout(s)** near that place or amount or time; **thereafter** *formal* after that; **thereby** by that means or agency; **therefore** for that reason, accordingly, consequently; **therein** in that place or respect; **thereof** *formal* of that, of it; **thereto** to that or it, in addition; **thereupon** in consequence of that, directly after that.

therm /θɜːm/ *n.* unit of heat, esp. statutory unit of calorific value in gas-supply (100,000 British thermal units).

thermal /ˈθɜːm(ə)l/ 1 *a.* of or for or producing heat. **2** *n.* rising current of heated air. **3 British thermal unit** amount of heat required to raise 1 lb. of water 1° F.

thermionic valve /θɜːmɪˈɒnɪk/ device giving flow of electrons in one direction from heated substance, used esp. in rectification of current and in radio reception.

thermo- *in comb.* heat.

thermodynamics /θɜːməʊdaɪˈnæmɪks/ *n.pl.* usu. treated as *sing.* science of relationship between heat and other forms of energy.

thermometer /θəˈmɒmɪtə(r)/ *n.* instrument for measuring temperature, esp. graduated glass tube containing mercury or alcohol. **thermometric** /-ˈmet-/ *a.*; **thermometry** *n.*

thermonuclear /θɜːməʊˈnjuːklɪə(r)/ *a.* relating to nuclear reactions that occur only at very high temperatures; (of bomb etc.) using such reactions.

thermoplastic /θɜːməʊˈplæstɪk/ 1 *a.* becoming soft and plastic on heating and hardening on cooling. **2** *n.* thermoplastic substance.

Thermos /ˈθɜːmɒs/ *n.* (P) vacuum flask.

thermosetting /ˈθɜːməʊˈsetɪŋ/ a. (of plastics) setting permanently when heated.

thermostat /ˈθɜːməstæt/ n. device for automatic regulation of temperature. **thermostatic** a.

thesaurus /θɪˈsɔːrəs/ n. (pl. -ri /-raɪ/) dictionary of synonyms etc.

these pl. of **this**.

thesis /ˈθiːsɪs/ n. (pl. -ses /-siːz/) proposition to be maintained or proved; dissertation esp. by candidate for university degree.

Thespian /ˈθespɪən/ 1 a. of tragedy or dramatic art. 2 n. actor or actress.

thews /θjuːz/ n.pl. literary person's muscular strength.

they /ðeɪ/ pron. (obj. **them** poss. **their** /ðeɪ(r)/) pl. of **he**, **she**, and **it**.

thick /θɪk/ 1 a. of great or specified depth between opposite surfaces; (of line etc.) broad, not fine; closely set; numerous; crowded; abounding or packed with; firm in consistency; made of thick material; muddy, not clear; colloq. dull, stupid; (of voice) indistinct; colloq. intimate. 2 n. thick part of anything. 3 adv. thickly. 4 **a bit thick** sl. unreasonable, too much to tolerate; **in the thick of it** in the busiest part of an activity etc.; **thick-headed** stupid; **thickset** set or growing close together, heavily or solidly built; **thick-skinned** not sensitive to criticism or rebuff; **through thick and thin** under all conditions, in spite of all difficulties.

thicken /ˈθɪkən/ v. make or become thick(er).

thicket /ˈθɪkɪt/ n. dense growth of small trees or shrubs etc.

thief /θiːf/ n. (pl. **thieves**) one who steals, esp. secretly and without violence.

thieve /θiːv/ v. be a thief; steal. **thievery** n.

thievish /ˈθiːvɪʃ/ a. given to stealing.

thigh /θaɪ/ n. part of leg between hip and knee.

thimble /ˈθɪmb(ə)l/ n. metal or plastic cap worn to protect finger and push needle in sewing.

thimbleful n. small quantity esp. of liquid to drink.

thin /θɪn/ 1 a. having opposite surfaces close together, of small thickness or diameter; (of line etc.) narrow, fine; made of thin material; lean, not plump; not dense or copious; of slight consistency; weak, lacking an important ingredient; (of excuse etc.) transparent, flimsy; sl. wretched and uncomfortable. 2 v. make or become thin(ner). 3 adv. thinly. 4 **thin out** reduce number of; **thin-skinned** sensitive to criticism.

thine /ðaɪn/ poss. a. belonging to thee; what is thine.

thing /θɪŋ/ n. any possible object of thought including persons, material objects, events, qualities, ideas, utterances, and acts; colloq. one's special interest or concern; in pl. personal belongings or (esp. outer) clothing or equipment; in pl. the world in general. **the thing** what is conventionally proper or fashionable, what is needed or required or most important; **have a thing about** be obsessed or prejudiced about.

thingummy /ˈθɪŋəmɪ/ n. colloq. (also **thingamajig** etc.) person or thing whose name one forgets or does not know.

think /θɪŋk/ 1 v. (past & p.p. thought /θɔːt/) be of opinion; consider; exercise mind; form connected ideas; conceive notion of doing; form conception of; contemplate. 2 n. colloq. act of thinking. **think about** consider; **think of** consider, imagine, intend, contemplate, entertain ideas of, hit upon; **think out** consider carefully, devise; **think over** reflect upon; **think-tank** body of experts providing advice and ideas on national and commercial problems; **think twice** avoid hasty action etc.; **think up** colloq. devise, produce by thought.

thinker /ˈθɪŋkə(r)/ n. person who thinks in specified way; person with skilled or powerful mind.

thinking /ˈθɪŋkɪŋ/ 1 a. thoughtful; intellectual. 2 n. opinion, judgement.

third /θɜːd/ 1 a. next after second. 2 n. third person or class etc.; one of 3 equal divisions of whole. 3 **third class** class next after second in accommodation or examination-list etc.; **third degree** severe and protracted interrogation by police etc.; **third man** Crick. fieldsman near boundary behind slips; **third party** another party besides the two principals, bystander etc.; **third-party**

insurance insurance against damage or injury suffered by person other than the insured; **third-rate** inferior, very poor; **Third World** developing countries of Africa, Asia, and Latin America.

thirst /θɜːst/ 1 *n.* desire for a drink; suffering caused by lack of drink; ardent desire, craving. 2 *v.i.* feel thirst.

thirsty /ˈθɜːstɪ/ *a.* feeling thirst; (of country or season) dry, parched; *fig.* eager (*for*, *after*); *colloq.* causing thirst.

thirteen /θɜːˈtiːn/ *a. & n.* one more than twelve. **thirteenth** *a. & n.*

thirty /ˈθɜːtɪ/ *a. & n.* three times ten. **thirtieth** *a. & n.*

this /ðɪs/ 1 *pron.* (*pl.* **these** /ðiːz/) the person or thing near or present or just mentioned or understood; contrasted with **that**. 2 *a.* (*pl.* **these**) designating the person or thing close at hand etc.; the present or current. 3 *adv.* to this degree or extent.

thistle /ˈθɪs(ə)l/ *n.* prickly herbaceous plant usu. with globular heads of purple flowers; this as Scottish national emblem. **thistledown** down containing thistle-seeds. **thistly** *a.*

thither /ˈðɪðə(r)/ *adv. arch.* to that place.

thole /θəʊl/ *n.* pin in gunwale of boat as fulcrum for oar; each of two such pins between which oar works.

thong /θɒŋ/ *n.* narrow strip of hide or leather.

thorax /ˈθɔːræks/ *n.* (*pl.* **-races** /-rəsiːz/) part of the body between neck and abdomen. **thoracic** /-ˈræs-/ *a.*

thorn /θɔːn/ *n.* stiff sharp-pointed projection on plant; thorn-bearing shrub or tree.

thorny /ˈθɔːnɪ/ *a.* having many thorns; *fig.* (of subject) hard to handle without offence.

thorough /ˈθʌrə/ *a.* complete, unqualified, not superficial; acting or done with great care etc. **thoroughbred** of pure breed, high-spirited, (*n.*) such animal, esp. horse; **thoroughfare** public way open at both ends, esp. main road; **thoroughgoing** uncompromising, extreme.

those *pl.* of **that**.

thou /ðaʊ/ *pron.* (*obj.* **thee** *poss.* **thine** and **thy**) of 2nd pers. *sing.*, now *arch.* or *poet.*

though /ðəʊ/ 1 *conj.* in spite of the fact that; even if, granting that; as though, as if. 2 *adv. colloq.* however, all the same.

thought[1] /θɔːt/ *n.* process or power or faculty etc. of thinking; sober reflection, consideration; idea, notion; way of thinking; intention, purpose; (usu. in *pl.*) one's opinion. **thought-reader** person able to perceive another's thoughts.

thoughtful /ˈθɔːtfʊl/ *a.* engaged in or given to meditation; considerate.

thoughtless /ˈθɔːtlɪs/ *a.* careless of consequences or of others' feelings; caused by lack of thought.

thousand /ˈθaʊz(ə)nd/ *a. & n.* ten hundred. **thousandth** *a. & n.*

thrall /θrɔːl/ *n.* slave; slavery. **thraldom** *n.*

thrash /θræʃ/ *v.t.* beat, esp. with stick or whip; conquer, surpass; thresh; move violently *about* etc. **thrash out** discuss to conclusion.

thread /θred/ 1 *n.* spun-out cotton or silk or glass etc.; length of this; thin cord of twisted yarns used esp. in sewing and weaving; anything regarded as threadlike with ref. to its continuity or connectedness; spiral ridge of screw. 2 *v.t.* pass thread through (needle's eye, beads); arrange (material in strip form, e.g. film) in proper position on equipment; pick one's way through (maze, crowded place, etc.). 3 **threadbare** (of cloth) so worn that nap is lost and threads showing, (of person) shabby, (of idea etc.) commonplace, hackneyed.

threat /θret/ *n.* declaration of intention to punish or hurt; indication of proximity of something undesirable; person or thing regarded as dangerous.

threaten /ˈθret(ə)n/ *v.t.* use threats towards; be sign or indication of (something undesirable); announce one's intention (*to* do); give warning of infliction of (harm etc.).

three /θriː/ *a. & n.* one more than two. **three-cornered** triangular, (of contest etc.) between 3 persons; **three-decker** ship with 3 decks, sandwich with 3 slices of bread, 3-volume novel; **three-dimensional** having or appearing to have length, breadth, and depth; **three-legged race** race between pairs with right leg of one tied to other's left leg; **threepence** /'θrepəns/ sum of 3 pence; **threepenny** /'θrepənɪ/ costing or worth 3 pence; **three-ply** (wool etc.) having 3 strands, (plywood) having 3 layers; **three-point turn** method of turning vehicle round in narrow space; **three-quarter** *Rugby footb.* any of 3 or 4 players just behind half-backs; **three-score** *arch.* 60. **threefold** *a.*

threesome /'θriːsəm/ *n.* group of 3 persons.

threnody /'θrenədɪ/ *n.* song of lamentation.

thresh *v.* beat out or separate grain from husks of corn etc.

threshold /'θreʃhəʊld/ *n.* plank or stone forming bottom of doorway; point of entry; limit below which stimulus causes no reaction.

threw *past* of **throw**.

thrice *adv.* three times.

thrift *n.* frugality, economical management. **thrifty** *a.*

thrill 1 *n.* wave or nervous tremor of emotion or sensation; throb, pulsation. 2 *v.* (cause to) experience thrill; quiver or throb (as) with emotion.

thriller /'θrɪlə(r)/ *n.* sensational or exciting play or story etc.

thrive *v.i.* (*past* **throve** or **thrived**; *p.p.* **thriven** /'θrɪv(ə)n/ or **thrived**) prosper; grow vigorously.

throat *n.* gullet or windpipe; front of neck; narrow passage or entrance.

throaty /'θrəʊtɪ/ *a.* (of voice) deficient in clarity, hoarsely resonant.

throb 1 *v.i.* palpitate, pulsate; (of heart etc.) beat strongly; quiver, vibrate. 2 *n.* throbbing, violent beat or pulsation.

throe *n.* (usu. in *pl.*) violent pang. **in the throes of** *colloq.* struggling with the task of.

thrombosis /θrɒm'bəʊsɪs/ *n.* (*pl.* **-ses** /-siːz/) coagulation of blood in blood-vessel or organ during life.

throne 1 *n.* chair of state for sovereign or bishop etc.; sovereign power. 2 *v.t.* enthrone.

throng 1 *n.* crowd, multitude, esp. in small space. 2 *v.* come or go or press in multitudes; fill (as) with crowd.

throstle /'θrɒs(ə)l/ *n.* song thrush.

throttle /'θrɒt(ə)l/ 1 *n.* valve controlling flow of steam or fuel in engine; throat. 2 *v.* choke, strangle; control (engine etc.) with throttle. 3 **throttle**

back, down, reduce speed of (engine etc.) by throttling.

through /θruː/ 1 *prep.* from end to end or side to side of; between or among; from beginning to end of; by agency or means or fault of; by reason of; *US* up to and including. 2 *adv.* through something; from end to end; to the end. 3 *a.* (concerned with) going through; going all the way without change of line or vehicle etc.; (of traffic) going through a place to its destination. 4 **be through** have finished (*with*), cease to have dealings (*with*); **through and through** thoroughly, completely; **throughput** amount of material put through a manufacturing etc. process or a computer.

throughout /θruː'aʊt/ 1 *prep.* from end to end of; in every part of. 2 *adv.* in every part or respect.

throve *past* of **thrive**.

throw /θrəʊ/ 1 *v.* (*past* **threw**; *p.p.* **thrown**) release (thing) after imparting motion, propel through space, send forth or dismiss esp. with some violence; compel to be in specified condition; project (rays, light, etc.); cast (shadow); bring to the ground; *colloq.* disconcert; put (clothes etc.) carelessly or hastily *on* or *off* etc.; cause (dice) to fall on table etc., obtain (specified number) thus; cause to pass or extend suddenly to another state or position; move (switch or lever) to on position; shape (pottery) on wheel; have (fit, tantrum, etc.); *colloq.* give (a party). 2 *n.* act of throwing; distance a missile is or may be thrown; being thrown in wrestling. 3 **throw away** part with as unwanted, lose by neglect, waste, fail to make use of; **throw-away** (thing) to be thrown away after (one) use, deliberately under-emphasized; **throw back** (usu. in *pass.*) compel to rely *on*; **throwback** reversion to ancestral character, instance of this; **throw in** add as makeweight, interpose (word, remark), throw (football) from edge of pitch where it has gone out of play; **throw off** discard, contrive to get rid of, write or utter in offhand manner; **throw out** put out forcibly or suddenly, reject, confuse or distract; **throw over** desert, abandon; **throw up** abandon, resign from, vomit, erect, bring to notice.

thrum 1 v. play monotonously or unskilfully on or *on*; drum or tap idly on or *on*. 2 n. such playing; resultant sound.

thrush[1] n. kind of small bird.

thrush[2] n. fungoid infection of throat esp. in children, or of vagina.

thrust 1 v. (*past* & *p.p.* **thrust**) push with sudden impulse or with force; impose (thing) forcibly *on*; make lunge or stab *with* weapon; force oneself *through* or *past* etc. 2 n. sudden or forcible push or lunge; forward force exerted by propeller or jet etc.; strong attempt to penetrate enemy's line or territory; remark aimed at person; stress between parts of arch etc. 3 **thrust oneself in** obtrude, interfere.

thud /θʌd/ 1 n. low dull sound as of blow on non-resonant thing. 2 v.i. make thud; fall with thud.

thug /θʌg/ n. vicious or brutal ruffian. **thuggery** n.

thumb /θʌm/ 1 n. short thick digit, set apart from the fingers on hand; part of glove for thumb. 2 v.t. soil or wear with thumb; turn over pages (as) with thumb; make request for (lift) by sticking out thumb. 3 **thumb-index** set of lettered grooves cut in fore-edge of dictionary etc. to assist use; **thumb-nail sketch** brief verbal description; **thumb-screw** instrument of torture for squeezing thumbs; **under person's thumb** dominated by him.

thump /θʌmp/ 1 n. heavy blow, sound of this. 2 v. beat heavily, esp. with fist; deliver heavy blows.

thumping /'θʌmpɪŋ/ a. colloq. big.

thunder /'θʌndə(r)/ 1 n. loud noise accompanying lightning; any loud deep rumbling or resounding noise; authoritative censure or threats. 2 v. sound with or like thunder; utter or emit in loud or impressive manner; move with loud noise; make violent threats. 3 **thunderbolt** flash of lightning with crash of thunder, imaginary bolt or shaft as destructive agent; **thunderclap** crash of thunder; **thunderstorm** storm with thunder and lightning; **thunderstruck** amazed. 4 **thundery** a.

thundering /'θʌndərɪŋ/ a. colloq. very big or great.

thunderous /'θʌndərəs/ a. as loud as thunder.

thurible /'θjʊərɪb(ə)l/ n. censer.

Thurs. abbr. Thursday.

Thursday /'θɜːzdɪ/ n. fifth day of week.

thus /ðʌs/ adv. in this way, like this; accordingly, and so; to this extent, number, or degree.

thwack n. & v.t. hit esp. with stick.

thwart /θwɔːt/ 1 v.t. frustrate, foil. 2 n. seat across boat for rower etc.

thy /ðaɪ/ pron. poss. case of **thou**.

thyme /taɪm/ n. shrubby herb with fragrant aromatic leaves.

thymol /'θaɪmɒl/ n. antiseptic made from oil of thyme.

thymus /'θaɪməs/ n. ductless gland near base of neck.

thyroid /'θaɪərɔɪd/ n. thyroid gland. **thyroid cartilage** large cartilage of larynx, projection of which in man forms Adam's apple; **thyroid gland** large ductless gland near larynx secreting a hormone which regulates growth and development, extract of this.

thyself /ðaɪ'self/ pron. emphat. and refl. form of **thou**.

ti var. of **te**.

tiara /tɪ'ɑːrə/ n. jewelled ornamental band worn on front of woman's hair; Pope's 3-crowned diadem.

tibia /'tɪbɪə/ n. (pl. **-biae** /-bɪiː/) shin-bone.

tic n. habitual spasmodic contraction of muscles, esp. of face.

tick[1] 1 n. slight recurring click, esp. that of watch or clock; colloq. moment, instant; small mark set against items in list etc. in checking. 2 v. make sound of tick; mark (*off*) with tick. 3 **tick off** sl. reprimand; **tick over** (of engine or fig.) idle; **tick-tack** kind of manual semaphore signalling by racecourse bookmakers.

tick[2] n. parasitic arachnid or insect on animals.

tick[3] n. colloq. credit.

tick[4] n. case of mattress or bolster; ticking.

ticker /'tɪkə(r)/ n. colloq. heart; watch, tape-machine. **ticker-tape** US paper strip from tape-machine, esp. as thrown from windows to greet a celebrity.

ticket /'tɪkɪt/ 1 n. piece of paper or card

entitling holder to enter place or participate in event or travel by public transport etc.; certificate of discharge from army or of qualification as ship's master or pilot etc.; label attached to thing and giving price etc.; notification of traffic offence etc.; list of candidates put forward by group, esp. political party, principles of party. **2** *v.t.* attach ticket to. **3 the ticket** *sl.* the correct or desirable thing.

ticking /'tɪkɪŋ/ *n.* strong usu. striped linen or cotton material to cover mattress etc.

tickle /'tɪk(ə)l/ **1** *v.* touch or stroke lightly so as to excite nerves and usu. produce laughter; feel this sensation; excite agreeably, amuse. **2** *n.* act or sensation of tickling.

ticklish /'tɪklɪʃ/ *a.* sensitive to tickling; difficult, requiring careful handling.

tidal /'taɪd(ə)l/ *a.* of or due to or affected by or resembling tides. **tidal wave** exceptionally large ocean wave (e.g. one attributed to earthquake etc.), widespread manifestation of feeling etc.

tiddler /'tɪdlə(r)/ *n. colloq.* small fish, esp. stickleback or minnow; unusually small thing.

tiddly /'tɪdlɪ/ *a. sl.* slightly drunk.

tiddly-winks /'tɪdlɪwɪŋks/ *n.* game of flipping small counters into receptacle.

tide 1 *n.* regular rise and fall of sea due to attraction of moon and sun; water as moved by this; trend of opinion or fortune or events; *arch.* time, season. **2** *v.* be carried by the tide. **3 tide-mark** mark made by tide at high water, *colloq.* line of dirt round bath, or on body of person showing extent of washing; **tide person over** help him through temporary need; **tideway** tidal part of river.

tidings /'taɪdɪŋz/ *n. as sing.* or *pl.* news.

tidy /'taɪdɪ/ **1** *a.* neat, orderly; neatly arranged; *colloq.* considerable. **2** *n.* receptacle for odds and ends. **3** *v.t.* make tidy; put in order.

tie 1 *v.* (*partic.* **tying**) attach or fasten with cord etc.; form into knot or bow; tie strings etc. of; restrict, bind; make same score as another competitor; bind (rafters etc.) by crosspiece etc.; *Mus.* unite notes by tie; in *p.p.* (of dwelling-house) occupied subject to tenant's working for house's owner, (of public house etc.) bound to supply only particular brewer's liquor. **2** *n.* cord or chain etc. used for fastening; necktie; thing that unites or restricts persons; equality of score or draw or dead heat among competitors; match between any pair of players or teams; rod or beam holding parts of structure together; *Mus.* curved line above or below two notes of same pitch that are to be joined as one. **3 tie-break** means of deciding winner when competitors have tied; **tie-clip, -pin,** ornamental clip, pin, to hold necktie in place; **tie up** fasten with cord etc., invest (money etc.) so that it is not immediately available for use, obstruct.

tier /tɪə(r)/ **1** *n.* row or rank or unit of structure, as one of several placed one above another. **2** *v.t.* arrange in tiers.

tiff *n.* slight or petty quarrel.

tiffin /'tɪfɪn/ *n. Anglo-Ind.* lunch.

tiger /'taɪgə(r)/ *n.* (*fem.* **tigress**) large Asian animal of cat family, with yellowish and black stripes; fierce or energetic person; *colloq.* formidable opponent in game. **tiger-cat** any moderate-sized feline resembling tiger; **tiger-lily** tall garden lily with dark-spotted orange flowers.

tight /taɪt/ **1** *a.* closely held or drawn or fastened or fitting or constructed; impermeable, impervious; tense, stretched; *colloq.* drunk; (of money or materials) not easily obtainable; produced by or requiring great exertion or pressure; stringent, demanding; *colloq.* presenting difficulties; *colloq.* tight-fisted. **2** *adv.* tightly. **3** *n.* in *pl.* thin close-fitting elastic garment covering legs and lower half of body. **4 tight-fisted** stingy; **tight-lipped** restraining emotion; **tightrope** tightly stretched rope or wire on which acrobats etc. perform.

tighten /'taɪt(ə)n/ *v.* make or become tight(er).

'til *incorrect* □ See page 665 and **till**[1].

tilde /'tɪldə/ *n.* mark (˜) placed over letter, e.g. Spanish *n* in *señor*.

tile 1 *n.* thin slab of baked clay or other material for covering roof or floor etc. **2** *v.t.* cover with tiles.

till[1] **1** *prep.* up to, as late as. **2** *conj.* up to time when; to degree that.

till² *n.* money-drawer in counter of bank or shop etc., esp. with device recording amount of each purchase.

till³ *v.t.* cultivate (land).

tillage /'tɪlɪdʒ/ *n.* preparation of land for crop-bearing; tilled land.

tiller /'tɪlə(r)/ *n.* bar by which rudder is turned.

tilt 1 *v.* (cause to) assume sloping position or heel over; thrust or run *at* with lance etc.; engage in contest *with*. **2** *n.* tilting; sloping position; (of medieval knights etc.) charging with lance against opponent or mark. **3 at full tilt** at full speed, with full force.

tilth /tɪlθ/ *n.* tillage, cultivation; cultivated soil.

timber /'tɪmbə(r)/ *n.* wood for building or carpentry etc.; piece of wood, beam, esp. as rib of vessel; large standing trees.

timbered /'tɪmbəd/ *a.* made (partly) of timber; wooded.

timbre /'tæbr/ *n.* distinctive character of musical sound or voice apart from its pitch and intensity.

timbrel /'tɪmbr(ə)l/ *n.* *arch.* tambourine.

time 1 *n.* indefinite continuous duration regarded as dimension; finite duration as distinct from eternity; more or less definite portion of this, historical or other period; allotted or available portion of time; definite or fixed point or portion of time; season; occasion; in *pl.* (preceded by numeral etc.) expressing multiplication; lifetime; in *pl.* prevailing circumstances of period; prison sentence; apprenticeship; measured amount of time worked; rhythm or measure of musical composition. **2** *v.t.* choose time for, do at chosen or appropriate time; ascertain time taken by. **3 at the same time** simultaneously, nevertheless; **at times** now and then; **behind the times** old-fashioned; **from time to time** occasionally; **in no time** rapidly, in a moment; **in time** not late, early enough, sooner or later, following time of music etc.; **on time** punctually; **time-and-motion** concerned with measuring efficiency of industrial etc. operations; **time bomb** one designed to explode at pre-set time; **time-honoured** respected on account of antiquity, traditional; **timekeeper** person who takes or records time, watch or clock esp. in respect of accuracy; **time-lag** interval between cause etc. and effect; **time off, out,** time used for rest or different activity; **timepiece** clock or watch; **time-server** person who adapts himself to opinions of the times or of persons in power; **time-sharing** use of computer by several persons for different operations at the same time, use of holiday home by several joint owners at different times of year; **time-signal** audible indication of exact time of day; **time-signature** *Mus.* indication of tempo; **time-switch** one operating automatically at set time; **timetable** table showing times of public transport services, scheme of school work etc.; **time zone** range of longitudes where a common standard time is used.

timeless /'taɪmlɪs/ *a.* not affected by passage of time.

timely /'taɪmlɪ/ *a.* opportune, coming at right time.

timer /'taɪmə(r)/ *n.* person or device that measures time taken.

timid /'tɪmɪd/ *a.* easily alarmed; shy. **timidity** *n.*

timing /'taɪmɪŋ/ *n.* way thing is timed.

timorous /'tɪmərəs/ *a.* timid, frightened.

timpani /'tɪmpənɪ/ *n.pl.* kettledrums. **timpanist** *n.*

tin 1 *n.* white metal used esp. in alloys and in making tin plate; vessel of tin or tin plate esp. for preserving food; tin plate. **2** *v.t.* pack (food) in tin for preservation; cover or coat with tin. **3 tin foil** thin sheet of tin or aluminium or tin alloy, used to wrap food for cooking or keeping fresh etc.; **tin hat** *sl.* modern soldier's steel helmet; **tin-pan alley** world of composers and publishers of popular music; **tin plate** sheet iron or steel coated with tin; **tinpot** cheap, inferior; **tin-tack** tinned iron tack.

tincture /'tɪŋktʃə(r)/ *n.* **1** slight flavour or tinge (*of*); medicinal solution *of* drug in alcohol. **2** *v.t.* colour slightly, tinge, flavour; affect slightly (*with* quality).

tinder /'tɪndə(r)/ *n.* dry substance readily taking fire from spark. **tindery** *a.*

tine *n.* prong or tooth or point of fork or comb or antler etc.

tinge /tɪndʒ/ **1** *v.t.* colour slightly (*with*). **2** *n.* tendency to or trace of some colour; slight admixture of a feeling or quality.

tingle /'tɪŋg(ə)l/ **1** *v.i.* feel or cause slight pricking or stinging sensation. **2** *n.* tingling sensation.

tinker /'tɪŋkə(r)/ **1** *n.* itinerant mender of kettles and pans etc.; *Sc. & Ir.* gipsy; *colloq.* mischievous person or animal. **2** *v.i.* work in amateurish or clumsy fashion *at* or *with* (thing) by way of repair or alteration; work as tinker.

tinkle /'tɪŋk(ə)l/ **1** *n.* sound (as) of small bell. **2** *v.* (cause to) make tinkle.

tinny *a.* like tin; flimsy; sounding like struck tin.

tinsel /'tɪns(ə)l/ *n.* glittering decorative metallic strips or threads etc.; superficial brilliance or splendour.

tint **1** *n.* a variety of a colour; tendency towards or admixture of a different colour; faint colour spread over surface. **2** *v.t.* apply tint to, colour.

tintinnabulation /tɪntɪmæbjʊ'leɪʃ(ə)n/ *n.* ringing of bells.

tiny /'taɪnɪ/ *a.* very small.

tip¹ **1** *n.* extremity, esp. of small or tapering thing; small piece or part attached to tip, esp. mouthpiece of cigarette. **2** *v.t.* provide with tip. **3 tiptop** first-rate, of highest excellence.

tip² **1** *v.* (cause to) lean or slant; overturn, cause to overbalance; discharge contents of (jug, wagon, etc.) thus; give usu. small present of money to, esp. for service; name as likely winner of race or contest; strike or touch lightly. **2** *n.* small present of money given esp. for service; piece of useful private or special information, or prediction, given by expert; piece of advice; slight push or tilt; place where refuse etc. is tipped; light touch or blow. **3 tip-off** a hint; **tip person off** give him warning or hint or inside information; **tip-up** able to be tipped, e.g. of seat as used in theatre to allow passage past.

tippet /'tɪpɪt/ *n.* small cape or collar of fur etc.

tipple /'tɪp(ə)l/ **1** *v.* drink intoxicating liquor habitually or repeatedly in small quantities. **2** *n. colloq.* alcoholic drink.

tipster /'tɪpstə(r)/ *n.* person who gives tips about horse-racing etc.

tipsy /'tɪpsɪ/ *a.* slightly intoxicated; caused by or showing intoxication.

tiptoe /'tɪptəʊ/ **1** *n.* the tips of the toes. **2** *v.i.* walk on tiptoe or stealthily. **3** *adv.* on tiptoe, with heels off the ground.

TIR *abbr.* International Road Transport (*Transport International Routier*).

tirade /taɪə'reɪd/ *n.* long vehement denunciation or declamation.

tire¹ /taɪə(r)/ *v.* make or grow weary; exhaust patience or interest of; in *p.p.* having had enough *of*.

tire² *US* var. of **tyre**.

tireless /'taɪəlɪs/ *a.* of inexhaustible energy.

tiresome /'taɪəsəm/ *a.* tedious; *colloq.* annoying.

tiro /'taɪərəʊ/ *n.* (*pl.* **-ros**) beginner, novice.

tissue /'tɪʃuː/ *n.* any of the coherent substances of which animal or plant bodies are made; tissue-paper; disposable piece of thin absorbent paper for wiping or drying etc.; fine woven esp. gauzy fabric; connected series (*of* lies etc.). **tissue-paper** thin soft unsized paper for wrapping etc.

tit¹ *n.* any of various small birds.

tit² *n.* **tit for tat** blow for blow, retaliation.

tit³ *n. vulg.* woman's breast, nipple.

Titan /'taɪt(ə)n/ *n.* person of superhuman size or intellect or strength etc.

titanic /taɪ'tænɪk/ *a.* gigantic, colossal.

titanium /taɪ'teɪnɪəm/ *n.* dark-grey metallic element.

titbit /'tɪtbɪt/ *n.* choice or delicate morsel or item.

tithe /taɪð/ *hist.* **1** *n.* tenth part of annual produce of land or labour taken as tax for support of clergy and church. **2** *v.t.* subject to tithes.

Titian /'tɪʃ(ə)n/ *a.* (of hair) bright golden auburn.

titillate /'tɪtɪleɪt/ *v.t.* excite pleasantly, tickle. **titillation** *n.*

titivate /'tɪtɪveɪt/ *v.t. colloq.* adorn or smarten (*oneself*); put finishing touches to.

title /'taɪt(ə)l/ *n.* name of book or work of art; heading of chapter etc.; title-page; caption or credit title of film; form of nomenclature denoting person's status or used in addressing or referring to person; championship in sport; legal right to possession of (esp. real) property; just or recognized claim (*to*).

title-deed document constituting evidence of ownership; **title-page** page at beginning of book bearing title and particulars of authorship etc.; **title-role** part in play etc. from which title is taken.

titled /'taɪt(ə)ld/ *a.* having title of nobility or rank.

titmouse /'tɪtmaʊs/ *n.* (*pl.* -**mice**) = **tit**[1].

titrate /taɪ'treɪt/ *v.t.* ascertain quantity of constituent in (solution) by adding measured amounts of reagent. **titration** *n.*

titter /'tɪtə(r)/ 1 *v.i.* laugh covertly, giggle. 2 *n.* such laugh.

tittle /'tɪt(ə)l/ *n.* particle, whit.

tittle-tattle *n.* & *v.i.* gossip, chatter.

tittup /'tɪtəp/ 1 *v.i.* go friskily or jerkily, bob up and down, canter. 2 *n.* such gait or movement.

titular /'tɪtjʊlə(r)/ *a.* held by virtue of title; existing or being such only in name.

tizzy /'tɪzɪ/ *n. sl.* state of nervous agitation.

TNT *abbr.* trinitrotoluene.

to /tu:/ 1 *prep.* in direction of; as far as, not short of; used to introduce indirect obj. of verb etc., to introduce infinitive, to express purpose or consequence etc., and to limit meaning or application of adj. 2 *adv.* to or in normal or required position or condition, esp. to a standstill. 3 **to and fro** backwards and forwards, from place to place; **to-do** *colloq.* bustle, fuss.

toad *n.* froglike amphibian breeding in water but living chiefly on land; repulsive person. **toadflax** a yellow-flowered plant; **toad-in-the-hole** sausages or other meat baked in batter.

toadstool /'təʊdstu:l/ *n.* fungus (usu. poisonous) with round top and slender stalk.

toady /'təʊdɪ/ 1 *n.* sycophant; obsequious hanger-on. 2 *v.* fawn, behave servilely (*to*); fawn upon. 3 **toadyism** *n.*

toast 1 *n.* bread in slices browned on both sides by heat; person or thing in whose honour company is requested to drink; call to drink or instance of drinking thus. 2 *v.* brown by heat, warm at fire etc.; drink to the health or in honour of. 3 **toasting-fork** long-handled fork for toasting bread etc.; **toastmaster** person announcing toasts at public dinner; **toast-rack** rack for holding slices of toast at table.

toaster /'təʊstə(r)/ *n.* electrical device for making toast.

tobacco /tə'bækəʊ/ *n.* (*pl.* -**os**) plant of Amer. origin with leaves used for smoking, chewing, or snuff; its leaves esp. as prepared for smoking etc.

tobacconist /tə'bækənɪst/ *n.* dealer in tobacco.

toboggan /tə'bɒgən/ 1 *n.* long light narrow sledge for going downhill esp. over snow. 2 *v.i.* ride on toboggan.

toby jug /'təʊbɪ/ mug or small jug in shape of seated man in 3-cornered hat.

toccata /tə'kɑːtə/ *n. Mus.* composition for keyboard instrument designed to exhibit performer's touch and technique.

tocsin /'tɒksɪn/ *n.* alarm-signal; bell used to sound alarm.

today /tu'deɪ/ 1 *adv.* on this present day; nowadays, in modern times. 2 *n.* this present day; modern times.

toddle /'tɒd(ə)l/ *v.i.* walk with young child's short unsteady steps; *colloq.* take casual or leisurely walk. 2 *n.* toddling walk.

toddler /'tɒdlə(r)/ *n. colloq.* child just learning to walk.

toddy /'tɒdɪ/ *n.* sweetened drink of spirits and hot water.

toe 1 *n.* any of terminal members of foot; part of footwear that covers toes; lower end or tip of implement etc. 2 *v.t.* touch with toe(s). 3 **on one's toes** alert, eager; **toe-cap** reinforced part of shoe covering toes; **toe-hold** slight foothold, small beginning or advantage; **toe the line** *fig.* conform esp. under pressure.

toff *n. sl.* distinguished or well-dressed person.

toffee /'tɒfiː/ *n.* a kind of firm or hard sweet made of boiled butter and sugar etc. **toffee-apple** toffee-coated apple on stick; **toffee-nosed** snobbish or pretentious.

tog 1 *n.* unit of thermal resistance of quilts etc.; *sl.* in *pl.* clothes. 2 *v.t. sl.* dress (*out*, *up*).

toga /ˈtəʊgə/ n. ancient Roman citizen's loose flowing outer garment.

together /təˈgeðə(r)/ 1 adv. in(to) company or conjunction; simultaneously; one with another; in unbroken succession. 2 a. colloq. well organized or controlled.

toggle /ˈtɒg(ə)l/ n. device for fastening with cross-piece which can pass through hole in one position but not in other; Computers command which alternatively activates and switches off a function etc.

toil 1 v.i. work long or laboriously (at); make slow painful progress. 2 n. labour; drudgery. 3 **toilsome** a.

toilet /ˈtɔɪlət/ n. lavatory; process of washing oneself and dressing etc. (**make one's toilet** do this). **toilet-paper** soft paper for cleaning oneself after using lavatory; **toilet-roll** roll of toilet-paper; **toilet water** scented liquid used after washing.

toiletries /ˈtɔɪlətriːz/ n.pl. articles used in making one's toilet.

toils /tɔɪlz/ n.pl. net, snare.

token /ˈtəʊkən/ n. sign or symbol (of); reminder; keepsake; voucher exchangeable for goods; anything used to represent something else, esp. money. 2 a. perfunctory. 3 **token payment** payment of small proportion of sum due as indication that debt is not repudiated; **token strike** brief strike to demonstrate strength of feeling only.

tokenism /ˈtəʊkənɪz(ə)m/ n. granting minimum concessions.

told past & p.p. of **tell**.

tolerable /ˈtɒlərəb(ə)l/ a. endurable; fairly good.

tolerance /ˈtɒlərəns/ n. willingness or ability to tolerate; permitted variation in dimension or weight etc.

tolerant /ˈtɒlərənt/ a. disposed or accustomed to tolerate others; enduring or patient of.

tolerate /ˈtɒləreɪt/ v.t. allow the existence or occurrence of without authoritative interference; leave unmolested, not be harmed by; find or treat as endurable. **toleration** n.

toll¹ /təʊl/ n. charge payable for permission to pass barrier or use bridge or road etc.; fig. cost or damage caused by disaster or incurred in achievement.

toll-gate barrier preventing passage until toll is paid.

toll² /təʊl/ 1 v. (of bell) ring with slow succession of strokes, cause (bell) to strike thus, esp. for death or funeral; announce or give out thus. 2 n. tolling or stroke of bell.

toluene /ˈtɒljuiːn/ n. colourless liquid hydrocarbon used in manufacture of explosives etc.

tom n. (in full **tom cat**) male cat.

tomboy /ˈtɒmbɔɪ/ n. girl who enjoys rough noisy recreations.

tomfool /tɒmˈfuːl/ 1 n. fool. 2 a. extremely foolish. 3 **tomfoolery** n.

tomtit /tɒmˈtɪt/ n. tit, esp. blue tit.

tomahawk /ˈtɒməhɔːk/ n. war-axe of N. Amer. Indians.

tomato /təˈmɑːtəʊ/ n. (pl. **-toes**) glossy red or yellow fleshy edible fruit; plant bearing this.

tomb /tuːm/ n. grave; burial-vault; sepulchral monument. **tombstone** memorial stone over grave.

tombola /tɒmˈbəʊlə/ n. kind of lottery.

tome n. large book or volume.

Tommy /ˈtɒmɪ/ n. British private soldier.

tommy-gun /ˈtɒmɪgʌn/ n. kind of sub-machine-gun.

tomorrow /təˈmɒrəʊ/ 1 adv. on day after today; in future. 2 n. the day after today; the near future.

tom-tom /ˈtɒmtɒm/ n. kind of drum usu. beaten with hands.

ton /tʌn/ n. measure of weight, 2,240 lb. (**long ton**) or 2,000 lb. (**short ton**) or 1,000 kg. (**metric ton**); unit of measurement for ship's tonnage; colloq. large number or amount; sl. speed of 100 m.p.h., £100.

tonal /ˈtəʊn(ə)l/ a. of or relating to tone or tonality.

tonality /təʊˈnælɪtɪ/ n. relationship between tones of a musical scale or of colour-scheme of a picture; observance of single tonic key as basis of musical composition.

tone 1 n. sound, esp. with reference to pitch, quality, and strength; modulation of voice to express emotion etc., corresponding style in writing; musical note, sound of definite pitch and character; tint or shade of colour; prevailing character of morals and sentiments etc.; proper firmness of bodily organs, state of (good) health. **2** v. give tone or quality to; harmonize; alter tone or colour of. **3 tone-deaf** unable to perceive differences in musical pitch; **tone down** lessen emphasis or vigour of, undergo such lessening; **tone up** provide with or receive higher tone or greater vigour.

toneless /'təʊnlɪs/ a. dull, lifeless; unexpressive.

tongs n.pl. implement consisting of two limbs connected by hinge or pivot etc. for grasping and lifting things.

tongue /tʌŋ/ n. muscular organ in mouth used in tasting, speaking, swallowing, etc.; tongue of ox etc. as food; faculty or manner of speaking; words, language; thing like tongue in shape.**tongue-tied** too shy to speak; **tongue-twister** sequence of words difficult to pronounce quickly and correctly.

tonic /'tɒnɪk/ **1** n. invigorating medicine; anything serving to invigorate; tonic water; *Mus.* keynote. **2** a. serving as a tonic, invigorating; of tones in music, esp. of the keynote. **3 tonic sol-fa** musical notation used esp. in teaching singing; **tonic water** carbonated drink with quinine.

tonight /tə'naɪt/ **1** adv. on present evening or night; on evening or night of today. **2** n. the present evening or night, the evening or night of today.

tonnage /'tʌnɪdʒ/ n. ship's internal cubic capacity or freight-carrying capacity; charge per ton on cargo or freight.

tonne /tʌn/ n. metric ton (1,000 kg.).

tonsil /'tɒnsɪl/ n. either of two small organs on each side of root of tongue.

tonsillectomy /tɒnsɪ'lektəmɪ/ n. surgical removal of tonsils.

tonsillitis /tɒnsɪ'laɪtɪs/ n. inflammation of tonsils.

tonsorial /tɒn'sɔːrɪəl/ a. of barber or his work.

tonsure /'tɒnʃə(r)/ **1** n. shaving of head or of patch on crown as clerical or monastic symbol; bare patch so made. **2** v.t. give tonsure to.

too adv. to a greater extent than is desirable or permissible; in addition, moreover; *colloq.* extremely.

took past of **take**.

tool /tuːl/ **1** n. implement for working

upon something, usu. one held in hand; simple machine e.g. lathe; thing used in activity; person used by another merely for his own purposes. **2** v. dress (stone) with chisel; impress design on (leather book-cover); *sl.* drive or ride (*along*, *around*) esp. in casual or leisurely manner.

toot /tuːt/ **1** n. sound (as) of horn etc. **2** v. sound (horn etc.); give out such sound.

tooth /tuːθ/ n. (pl. **teeth**) each of a set of hard structures in jaws of most vertebrates, used for biting and chewing things; toothlike projection or thing, e.g. cog of gear-wheel, point of saw or comb etc.; sense of taste; in pl. force or effectiveness. **fight tooth and nail** fight fiercely; **get one's teeth into** devote oneself seriously to; **in the teeth of** in spite of, in opposition to, directly against (wind etc.); **show one's teeth** adopt threatening manner. **toothache** pain in teeth; **toothbrush** small brush with long handle, for cleaning teeth; **toothpaste** preparation for cleaning teeth; **toothpick** small sharp instrument for removing food etc. lodged between teeth.

toothsome /'tuːθsəm/ a. (of food) delicious.

toothy /'tuːθɪ/ a. having large or numerous or prominent teeth.

tootle /'tuːt(ə)l/ v. toot gently or continuously.

top[1] **1** n. highest point or part; upper surface, upper part; cover or cap of container etc.; highest rank, foremost place, person holding this; garment for upper part of body; (usu. in pl.) leaves etc. of plant grown chiefly for its root; utmost degree; height; *Naut.* platform round head of lower mast. **2** a. highest in position or degree or importance. **3** v.t. furnish with top or cap; be higher than or superior to; surpass; reach or be at top of; remove top of; hit golf-ball above centre. **4 on top** above, in superior position; **on top of** fig. fully in command of, in addition to; **top brass** colloq. high-ranking officers; **topcoat** overcoat, final coat of paint etc.; **top dog** sl. victor, master; **top drawer** high social position or origin; **top-dress** apply manure or fertilizer on top of (earth) without ploughing it in; **top-**

flight in highest rank of achievement; **top hat** tall silk hat; **top-heavy** overweighted at top; **topknot** bow or tuft or crest etc. worn or growing on top of head; **topmast** smaller mast on top of lower mast; **top-notch** *colloq*. first-rate, excellent; **top secret** most secret, extremely secret; **topside** outer side of round of beef, side of ship above waterline; **topsoil** top layer of soil; **top up** fill up (partly empty container).

top² *n*. toy with sharp point at bottom on which it rotates when set in motion.

topaz /'təʊpæz/ *n*. semi-precious stone of various colours, esp. yellow.

toper /'təʊpə(r)/ *n*. *arch*. person who drinks to excess, esp. habitually.

topi /'təʊpiː/ *n*. (also **topee**) sun hat or helmet.

topiary /'təʊpɪərɪ/ **1** *n*. art of clipping trees etc. into ornamental shapes. **2** *a*. of this art.

topic /'tɒpɪk/ *a*. subject of discourse or argument or discussion etc.

topical /'tɒpɪk(ə)l/ *a*. dealing with esp. current or local topics. **topicality** /-'kæl-/ *n*.

topless /'tɒplɪs/ *a*. without a top; (of woman's garment) leaving breasts bare; (of woman) so clothed.

topmost /'tɒpməʊst/ *a*. uppermost, highest.

topography /tə'pɒɡrəfɪ/ *n*. natural and artificial features of a district; knowledge or description of these. **topographer** *n*.; **topographical** *a*.

topology /tə'pɒlədʒɪ/ *n*. study of geometrical properties unaffected by changes of shape and size. **topological** *a*.; **topologist** *n*.

topper /'tɒpə(r)/ *n*. *colloq*. top hat.

topple /'tɒp(ə)l/ *v*. (cause to) fall from vertical to horizontal position.

topsy-turvy /tɒpsɪ'tɜːvɪ/ *adv*. & *a*. upside down; in utter confusion.

toque /təʊk/ *n*. woman's close-fitting brimless hat.

tor *n*. rocky hill-top.

torch *n*. small portable electric lamp; piece of resinous wood or twisted flax etc. soaked in tallow for carrying lighted in hand; source of inspiration etc. **carry a torch for** have (esp. unreturned) love for.

tore *past* of **tear¹**.

toreador /'tɒrɪədɔː(r)/ *n*. bullfighter, esp. on horseback.

torment 1 /'tɔːment/ *n*. (cause of) severe bodily or mental suffering. **2** /tɔː'ment/ *v.t*. subject to torment, tease or worry excessively. **3 tormentor** *n*.

tornado /tɔː'neɪdəʊ/ *n*. (*pl*. **-does**) violent storm over small area, esp. rotatory one advancing in narrow path.

torpedo /tɔː'piːdəʊ/ **1** *n*. (*pl*. **-does**) cigar-shaped self-propelled underwater or aerial missile that can be aimed at ship. **2** *v.t*. destroy or attack with torpedo(es); *fig*. make ineffective. **3 torpedo-boat** small fast warship armed with torpedoes.

torpid /'tɔːpɪd/ *a*. sluggish; dull; dormant; numb. **torpidity** *n*.

torpor /'tɔːpə(r)/ *n*. apathy; being dormant.

torque /tɔːk/ *n*. twisting or rotary force in mechanism etc.; twisted metal necklace worn by ancient Britons and Gauls etc.

torrent /'tɒrənt/ *n*. rushing stream of water etc.; downpour of rain; violent flow (*of* words etc.). **torrential** /-'ren-/ *a*.

torrid /'tɒrɪd/ *a*. scorched, parched; intensely hot.

torsion /'tɔːʃ(ə)n/ *n*. twisting, twist.

torso /'tɔːsəʊ/ *n*. (*pl*. **-sos**) trunk of human body; statue lacking head and limbs; mutilated or unfinished work.

tort *n*. breach of legal duty (other than under contract) with liability for damages. **tortious** *a*.

tortilla /tɔː'tiːlə/ *n*. Latin Amer. thin flat maize cake eaten hot.

tortoise /'tɔːtəs/ *n*. land or freshwater slow-moving reptile with body enclosed in horny shell. **tortoiseshell** mottled yellowish-brown turtle-shell, cat or butterfly with markings suggesting tortoiseshell.

tortuous /'tɔːtjʊəs/ *a*. winding, indirect, involved. **tortuosity** *n*.

torture /'tɔːtʃə(r)/ **1** *n*. infliction of severe bodily pain e.g. as punishment or means of persuasion; severe physical or mental pain. **2** *v.t*. subject to torture; distort, strain, wrench.

Tory 1 *n*. member of Conservative party. **2** *a*. Conservative. **3 Toryism** *n*.

tosh *n*. *sl*. rubbish, nonsense.

toss 1 *v*. throw or roll about from side to

side, restlessly or with fitful to-and-fro motion; throw, esp. lightly or carelessly or easily; (of bull etc.) fling up with horns; throw back (head), esp. in contempt or impatience; throw (coin) into air to decide choice etc. by way it falls, settle question or dispute with thus. **2** *n.* tossing; sudden jerk, esp. of head; throw from horseback etc. **3 argue the toss** dispute choice already made; **toss off** dispatch (work) rapidly or easily, drink (liquor) off at a draught; **toss up** toss coin; **toss-up** tossing of coin, doubtful matter.

tot¹ *n. colloq.* small child; small quantity of liquor.

tot² *v.* add (*up*), mount *up* (to).

total /'təʊt(ə)l/ **1** *a.* complete; comprising the whole; absolute, unqualified. **2** *n.* sum of all items; total amount. **3** *v.* reckon total of; amount to or *to*. **4 totality** /-'tæl-/ *n.*

totalitarian /təʊtælɪ'teərɪən/ *a.* of regime permitting no rival loyalties or parties. **totalitarianism** *n.*

totalizator /'təʊtəlaɪzeɪtə(r)/ *n.* device showing number and amount of bets staked on race when total will be divided among those betting on winner; this betting system.

totalize /'təʊtəlaɪz/ *v.t.* combine into a total.

tote¹ *n. sl.* totalizator.

tote² *v.t. colloq.* convey, carry. **tote bag** large and capacious bag.

totem /'təʊtəm/ *n.* natural object (esp. animal) adopted among N. Amer. Indians as emblem of family or clan; image of this. **totem-pole** post with carved and painted totem(s).

totter /'tɒtə(r)/ **1** *v.i.* stand or walk unsteadily or feebly; be shaken, be on the point of falling. **2** *n.* unsteady or shaky movement or gait. **3 tottery** *a.*

toucan /'tuːkən/ *n.* tropical Amer. bird with large bill.

touch /tʌtʃ/ **1** *v.* be placed or move so as to meet at one or more points; put one's hand etc. so as to meet thus, cause (two things) to meet thus; strike lightly; reach as far as; approach in excellence; affect slightly, produce slightest effect on; have to do with in slightest degree; affect with tender or painful feelings; (in *p.p.*) slightly crazy. **2** *n.* act or fact of touching; sense of feeling; sensation

conveyed by touching; light stroke with pencil etc.; small amount, tinge or trace; manner of touching keys or strings of esp. keyboard musical instrument, instrument's response to this; artistic skill or style; communication, agreement, sympathy; *Footb.* part of ground outside touchlines; *sl.* act of getting money from person. **3 touch-and-go** of uncertain result, risky; **touch at** *Naut.* call at (port etc.); **touch down** touch ground behind goal with football, (of aircraft) alight; **touchdown** *n.*; **touch-line** side limit of football field; **touch off** explode by touching with match etc., initiate (process) suddenly; **touch on** refer to or mention briefly or casually, verge on; **touch-paper** paper impregnated with nitre to burn slowly and ignite firework; **touchstone** dark schist or jasper for testing alloys by marks they make on it, criterion; **touch-type** use typewriter without looking at keys; **touch up** correct, give finishing touches to; **touch wood** put hand on something wooden to avert ill-luck; **touchwood** readily inflammable rotten wood.

touché /'tuːʃeɪ/ *int.* acknowledging hit by fencing-opponent or justified accusation by another in discussion.

touching /'tʌtʃɪŋ/ **1** *a.* arousing tender feelings. **2** *prep.* concerning.

touchy /'tʌtʃɪ/ *a.* apt to take offence, over-sensitive.

tough /tʌf/ *a.* hard to break or cut or tear or chew; able to endure hardship, hardy, stubborn, difficult; *colloq.* acting sternly or vigorously; *colloq.* (of luck etc.) hard; *US sl.* vicious, ruffianly; (of clay etc.) stiff, tenacious. **2** *n.* tough person, esp. ruffian.

toughen /'tʌf(ə)n/ *v.* make or become tough(er).

toupee /'tuːpeɪ/ *n.* false hair to cover bald part of head.

tour /tʊə(r)/ **1** *n.* expedition or pleasure journey including stops at various places; spell of military or diplomatic duty. **2** *v.* go on a tour; travel through (country etc.). **3 on tour** going from place to place to give performances etc.

tour de force /tʊə də 'fɔːs/ feat of strength or skill. [F]

tourism /'tʊərɪz(ə)m/ *n.* organized

touring or service for tourists, esp. on commercial basis.

tourist /'tʊərɪst/ *n.* holiday traveller. **tourist class** a cheap class of passenger accommodation in ship or aeroplane etc.

tourmaline /'tʊəməliːn/ *n.* mineral with unusual electric properties and used as gem.

tournament /'tʊənəmənt/ *n.* medieval sport of mounted combat with blunted weapons; any contest of skill between number of competitors.

tournedos /'tʊənədəʊ/ *n.* (*pl.* same) small piece of fillet of beef.

tourney /'tʊənɪ/ *hist.* 1 *n.* tournament. 2 *v.i.* take part in tournament.

tourniquet /'tʊənɪkeɪ/ *n.* bandage etc. round limb for stopping flow of blood through artery by compression.

tousle /'taʊz(ə)l/ *v.t.* pull about; make (hair, person) untidy.

tout /taʊt/ 1 *v.* pester possible customers with requests (*for* orders); solicit custom of or for; spy on horses in training. 2 *n.* person who touts.

tow[1] /təʊ/ 1 *v.t.* pull along behind, esp. with rope etc. 2 *n.* towing or being towed. 3 **in tow** being towed, accompanying or in the charge of a person; **on tow** being towed; **tow-path** path beside canal or river orig. for towing.

tow[2] /təʊ/ *n.* fibres of flax etc. ready for spinning. **tow-headed** having head of very light-coloured or tousled hair.

towards /tə'wɔːdz/ *prep.* (also **toward**) in direction of; as regards; in relation to; for the purpose of; near.

towel /'taʊəl/ 1 *n.* absorbent cloth or paper etc. for drying after washing etc. 2 *v.t.* (*past & p.p.* **towelled**) rub or dry with towel.

towelling /'taʊəlɪŋ/ *n.* material for towels.

tower /'taʊə(r)/ 1 *n.* tall structure often forming part of castle or church or other large building; similar structure housing machinery etc.; fortress etc. having tower. 2 *v.i.* reach high (*above*); soar, be poised, aloft. 3 **tower block** tall modern building; **tower of strength** *fig.* person who gives strong and reliable support.

towering /'taʊərɪŋ/ *a.* high, lofty; (of rage etc.) violent.

town /taʊn/ *n.* considerable collection of dwellings, densely populated settlement; London or the chief city or town in one's neighbourhood; central business area of one's neighbourhood. **go to town** act or work with energy and enthusiasm; **on the town** in carefree pursuit of urban pleasure; **town clerk** officer of town corporation, in charge of records etc.; **town gas** manufactured inflammable gas for domestic etc. use; **town hall** building for town's official business and public entertainments etc.; **town house** house in town, esp. one of terrace; **town planning** planning for regulated growth of towns; **township** *US & Canad.* administrative division of county, or district 6 miles square, *Aus. & NZ* small town or settlement; **townspeople** inhabitants of town.

townee /taʊ'niː/ *n.* (also **townie**) *derog.* inhabitant of town.

toxaemia /tɒk'iːmɪə/ *n.* blood-poisoning; condition of abnormally high blood-pressure in pregnancy.

toxic /'tɒksɪk/ *a.* of or caused by or acting as poison.

toxicology /tɒksɪ'kɒlədʒɪ/ *n.* study of poisons. **toxicological** *a.*; **toxicologist** *n.*

toxin /'tɒksɪn/ *n.* poison esp. of animal or vegetable origin; poison secreted by micro-organism and causing particular disease.

toy 1 *n.* thing to play with; trinket or curiosity. 2 *v.i.* play or fiddle or dally *with.* 3 **toy dog** dog of diminutive breed.

trace[1] 1 *n.* mark left behind; indication of existence or occurrence of something; slight amount (*of*). 2 *v.t.* follow track or path of; follow course or line or history etc. of; observe or find traces of; copy (drawing etc.) by marking its lines on superimposed sheet, esp. of tracing-paper etc.; delineate, mark out, write esp. laboriously. 3 **trace element** one occurring or required, esp. in soil, only in minute amounts.

trace[2] *n.* each of two side-straps or chains or ropes by which horse draws vehicle. **kick over the traces** *fig.* become insubordinate or reckless.

tracer /'treɪsə(r)/ *n. Mil.* projectile whose course is made visible by flame etc. emitted; *Med.* artificial radio-isotope whose course in human body etc. can be followed by radiation it produces.

tracery /ˈtreɪsərɪ/ *n.* decorative stone open-work esp. in head of Gothic window; lacelike pattern resembling this.

trachea /trəˈkiːə/ *n. Anat.* windpipe.

tracing /ˈtreɪsɪŋ/ *n.* traced copy of map or drawing etc.; process of making this. **tracing-paper** semi-transparent paper placed over drawing etc. to be traced.

track 1 *n.* mark or series of marks left by person or animal or vehicle etc. in passing along; in *pl.* such marks esp. footprints; path, esp. one beaten by use; course taken; prepared racing-path; continuous railway-line; band round wheels of tank or tractor etc.; particular recorded section on gramophone record or magnetic tape. **2** *v.t.* follow track of; trace (course, development, etc.) from vestiges. **3 in one's tracks** *sl.* where one stands, there and then; **make tracks** *sl.* go or run away; **make tracks for** *sl.* go in pursuit or towards; **track down** reach or capture by tracking; **track events** running-races; **track record** person's past achievements; **track suit** warm outfit worn by athlete etc. when training.

tract¹ *n.* region or area of indefinite extent; *Anat.* bodily organ or system.

tract² *n.* essay or pamphlet esp. on religious subject.

tractable /ˈtræktəb(ə)l/ *a.* easily managed; docile. **tractability** *n.*

traction /ˈtrækʃ(ə)n/ *n.* pulling; hauling; *Med.* therapeutic sustained pull on limb etc. **traction-engine** steam or diesel engine for drawing heavy load.

tractor /ˈtræktə(r)/ *n.* motor vehicle for hauling other vehicles or farm machinery etc.; traction-engine.

trad *colloq.* **1** *a.* traditional. **2** *n.* traditional jazz.

trade 1 *n.* exchange of goods for money or other goods; business carried on as means of livelihood or profit; skilled handicraft; *the* persons engaged in one branch of trade. **2** *v.* buy and sell, engage in trade; have a transaction *with*, exchange (goods) in commerce. **3 trade in** give (used article) in part payment

for another; **trade mark** device or word(s) legally registered to distinguish goods of a particular manufacturer etc.; **trade name** name by which a thing is known in the trade, or given by manufacturer to proprietary article, or under which business is carried on; **trade off** exchange as compromise; **trade on** take (esp. unscrupulous) advantage of; **tradesman** person engaged in trade, esp. shop-keeper; **trade(s) union** organized association of workpeople of a trade or group of allied trades formed to further their common interests; **trade-unionist** member of trade union; **trade wind** constant wind blowing towards equator from NE or SE.

tradescantia /trædɪsˈkænʃə/ *n.* perennial herb with large blue, white, or pink flowers.

trading /ˈtreɪdɪŋ/ *n.* engaging in trade. **trading estate** area occupied by industrial and commercial firms; **trading stamp** token given by tradesman to customer and exchangeable in quantity for various articles.

tradition /trəˈdɪʃ(ə)n/ *n.* opinion or belief or custom handed down from one generation to another esp. orally; handing down of these.

traditional /trəˈdɪʃən(ə)l/ *a.* of or based on or obtained by tradition; (of jazz) based on early style.

traditionalism /trəˈdɪʃənəlɪz(ə)m/ *n.* great or excessive respect for tradition. **traditionalist** *n.*

traduce /trəˈdjuːs/ *v.t.* slander. **traducement** *n.*

traffic /ˈtræfɪk/ **1** *n.* coming and going of persons and vehicles and goods by road, rail, air, sea, etc.; trade, esp. in illicit goods; number or amount of persons or goods conveyed; use of a service. **2** *v.* (*past & p.p.* **trafficked**) trade; engage in traffic (in); deal in. **3 traffic island** paved etc. area in road to direct traffic and provide refuge for pedestrians; **traffic lights** automatic signals for controlling road traffic by coloured lights; **traffic warden** person employed to control movement and parking of road vehicles.

tragacanth /ˈtræɡəkænθ/ *n.* vegetable gum used in pharmacy etc.

tragedian /trə'dʒiːdɪən/ n. author of or actor in tragedies.

tragedienne /trədʒiːdɪ'en/ n. actress in tragedies.

tragedy /'trædʒədɪ/ n. drama of elevated theme and diction and with unhappy ending; sad event, serious accident.

tragic /'trædʒɪk/ a. of or like tragedy; sad, calamitous, distressing. **tragically** adv.

tragicomedy /trædʒɪ'kɒmədɪ/ n. drama of mixed tragic and comic events.

trail 1 v. draw or be drawn along behind; drag along, walk wearily; be losing in contest; hang loosely; (of plant) grow or hang downwards, esp. so as to touch or rest on ground; follow trail of, shadow. **2** n. track or scent or other sign of passage left by moving object; beaten path esp. through wild region; thing that trails or is trailed; long line of people or things following behind something. **3 trailing edge** rear edge of aircraft's wing.

trailer /'treɪlə(r)/ n. cart etc. drawn by vehicle and used to carry load; set of extracts from film etc. shown in advance to advertise it.

train 1 n. series of railway carriages or trucks drawn by a locomotive; succession or series of persons or things; body of followers, retinue; thing drawn along behind or forming hinder part, esp. elongated part of woman's skirt or of official robe. **2** v. bring to desired standard of efficiency or obedience etc. by instruction and practice; undergo this process; teach and accustom (to do etc.); bring or come to physical efficiency by exercise and diet; cause (plant) to grow in desired shape; point, aim. **3 in train** arranged, in preparation; **train-bearer** person holding up train of another's robe.

trainee /treɪ'niː/ n. person being trained esp. for occupation.

trainer /'treɪnə(r)/ n. person who trains horses or athletes etc.; soft shoe worn esp. by athletes in training.

training /'treɪnɪŋ/ n. process of training for sportor contest or occupation.

traipse v.i. colloq. tramp or trudge wearily; go about on errands.

trait /treɪ/ □ See page 665. n. feature, distinguishing quality.

traitor /'treɪtə(r)/ n. person guilty of betrayal, one who acts disloyally. **traitorous** a.

trajectory /trə'dʒektərɪ/ n. path of body (e.g. comet or bullet) moving under given forces.

tram n. (also **tramcar**) passenger vehicle running on rails in public road. **tramlines** rails for tram, colloq. either pair of parallel lines at edge of tennis etc. court.

trammel /'træm(ə)l/ **1** n. kind of fishing-net; (usu. in pl.) impediment, restraint. **2** v.t. hamper.

tramp 1 v. walk with firm heavy tread; walk laboriously across or along; go on walking expedition; live as tramp. **2** n. person who tramps roads esp. as vagrant; sound (as) of person walking or marching; sl. dissolute woman; freight-vessel, esp. steamer, on no regular line.

trample /'træmp(ə)l/ v. tread heavily on or on.

trampoline /'træmpəliːn/ **1** n. canvas sheet connected by springs to horizontal frame, used for acrobatic exercises etc. **2** v.i. use trampoline.

trance /trɑːns/ n. sleeplike state; hypnotic or cataleptic condition; mental abstraction from external things, absorption, ecstasy.

tranny /'trænɪ/ n. sl. transistor radio.

tranquil /'træŋkwɪl/ a. serene, calm, undisturbed. **tranquillity** n.

tranquillize /'træŋkwɪlaɪz/ v.t. make tranquil esp. by drug etc.

tranquillizer n. drug used to diminish anxiety.

trans- in comb. across, beyond, over, to or on farther side of.

transact /træn'zækt/ v.t. do, carry on, (action, business, etc.).

transaction /træn'zækʃ(ə)n/ n. transacting of business; piece of commercial or other dealing; in pl. reports of discussions and lectures at meetings of learned society.

transatlantic /trænzət'læntɪk/ a. crossing or beyond the Atlantic; American; US European.

transceiver /træn'siːvə(r)/ n. combined radio transmitter and receiver.

transcend /træn'send/ v.t. go beyond

or exceed limits of; rise above, surpass, excel.

transcendent /træn'send(ə)nt/ *a.* of supreme merit or quality; (of God) existing apart from, or not subject to limitations of, material universe. **transcendence** *n.*; **transcendency** *n.*

transcendental /trænsən'dent(ə)l/ *a.* a priori, not based on experience; consisting of or dealing in or inspired by abstraction. **Transcendental Meditation** meditation seeking to induce detachment from problems and relief from anxiety.

transcontinental /trænzkontɪ'nent(ə)l/ *a.* extending across a continent.

transcribe /træn'skraɪb/ *v.t.* copy out; reproduce in ordinary writing; *Mus.* adapt for other than original instrument or voice. **transcription** *n.*

transcript /'trænskrɪpt/ *n.* written copy.

transducer /trænz'djuːsə(r)/ *n.* device for changing the variations of a quantity (e.g. pressure) to those of another (e.g. voltage).

transept /'trænsept/ *n.* part of cruciform church at right angles to nave; either arm of this.

transfer 1 /træns'fɜː(r)/ *v.* (*past & p.p.* **transferred**) convey or transmit or hand over etc. from one person or place etc. *to* another; *Law* convey by legal process; convey (design etc.) from one surface to another; move (person) to, or change or be moved to, another group; change from one station or line etc. to another to continue journey. **2** /'trænsfɜː(r)/ *n.* transferring or being transferred; conveyance of property or right, document effecting this; design etc. that is or can be conveyed from one surface to another. **3 transferable** *a.*; **transference** /'træns-/ *n.*

transfigure /træns'fɪgə(r)/ *v.t.* change appearance of, make more spiritual or elevated. **transfiguration** *n.*

transfix /træns'fɪks/ *v.t.* pierce with lance etc.; (of horror etc.) paralyse faculties of (person).

transform /trɒns'fɔːm/ *v.t.* change form or appearance or condition or function etc. of, esp. considerably; *Electr.* change voltage of (current). **transformation** *n.*

transformer *n. Electr.* apparatus for reducing or increasing voltage of alternating current.

transfuse /træns'fjuːz/ *v.t.* cause (fluid, colour, etc.) to permeate *into*; imbue *with*; transfer (blood or other liquid) into blood-vessel to replace that lost. **transfusion** *n.*

transgress /trænz'gres/ *v.* infringe (law etc.); overstep (limit laid down); sin. **transgression** *n.*; **transgressor** *n.*

transient /'trænzɪənt/ *a.* quickly passing away; fleeting. **transience** *n.*

transistor /træn'sɪstə(r)/ *n.* small semi-conductor device capable of replacing thermionic valve; radio set using transistors.

transistorize /træn'sɪstəraɪz/ *v.t.* equip with transistors rather than valves.

transit /'trænsɪt/ *n.* going or conveying or being conveyed across or over or through; passage, route; apparent passage of heavenly body across disc of another or meridian of place.

transition /træn'sɪʒ(ə)n/ *n.* passage or change from one state or subject or set of circumstances etc. to another; period of this. **transitional** *a.*

transitive /'trænsɪtɪv/ *a. Gram.* (of verb) requiring direct object expressed or understood.

transitory /'trænsɪtərɪ/ *a.* not lasting, momentary; brief, fleeting.

translate /trænz'leɪt/ *v.t.* express sense of in another language or in other words or another form of representation; infer or declare or convey significance of; remove (bishop) to another see. **translation** *n.*; **translator** *n.*

transliterate /trænz'lɪtəreɪt/ *v.t.* represent (word etc.) in more or less corresponding characters of another alphabet or language. **transliteration** *n.*

translucent /trænz'luːs(ə)nt/ *a.* allowing light to pass through (esp. without being transparent). **translucence** *n.*

transmigrate /trænzmaɪ'greɪt/ *v.* (of soul) pass into different body.

transmissible /trænz'mɪsəb(ə)l/ *a.* that may be transmitted. **transmissibility** *n.*

transmission /trænz'mɪʃ(ə)n/ *n.* transmitting or being transmitted; broadcast programme; gear transmitting power from engine to axle in motor vehicle etc.

transmit /trænz'mɪt/ *v.t.* send or convey etc. to another person or place or thing; allow to pass through, be medium for, serve to communicate (heat, electricity, emotion, message, etc.).

transmitter *n.* equipment used to transmit message, (esp. broadcast) signal, etc.

transmogrify /trænz'mɒgrɪfaɪ/ *v.t. joc.* transform esp. in magical or surprising manner.

transmutation /trænzmju:'teɪʃ(ə)n/ *n.* transmuting or being transmuted. **transmutation of metals** turning of other metals into gold as alchemists' aim.

transmute /trænz'mju:t/ *v.t.* change form or nature or substance of; convert into different thing. **transmutative** *a.*

transom /'trænsəm/ *n.* cross-beam, esp. horizontal bar above door or in window; window above this.

transparency /træns'pærənsɪ/ *n.* being transparent; picture (esp. photograph) to be viewed by light passing through it.

transparent /træns'pærənt/ *a.* that can be clearly seen through because allowing light to pass through without diffusion; (of disguise, pretext, etc.) easily seen through, obvious; easily understood.

transpire /træns'paɪə(r)/ *v.* (of secret, fact, etc.) come to be known; emit (vapour, moisture) or pass off through pores of skin etc. □ See page 666. **transpiration** *n.*

transplant 1 /træns'plɑ:nt/ *v.t.* remove and replant or establish elsewhere; transfer (living tissue or organ) from one part of body or one person or animal to another. 2 /'trænsplɑ:nt/ *n.* transplanting of tissue or organ; thing transplanted. 3 **transplantation** *n.*

transport 1 /træns'pɔ:t/ *v.t.* take from one place to another; *hist.* deport (criminal) to penal colony; (esp. in *p.p.*) affect with strong emotion. 2 /'trænspɔ:t/ *n.* transporting, means of conveyance; ship or aircraft etc. used

in transporting troops or military stores; vehement emotion.

transportation /trænspɔ:'teɪʃ(ə)n/ *n.* transporting; *hist.* deporting of criminals; *US* transport.

transporter /træns'pɔ:tə(r)/ *n.* vehicle used to transport other vehicles or heavy machinery etc. **transporter bridge** bridge carrying vehicles across water on suspended platform.

transpose /træns'pəʊz/ *v.t.* cause (two or more things) to change places; change position of (thing) in series; *Mus.* write or play in different key. **transposition** *n.*

transsexual /trænz'seksjʊəl/ 1 *a.* having physical characteristics of one sex and psychological characteristics of the other. 2 *n.* transsexual person. 3 **transsexualism** *n.*

trans-ship /træn'ʃɪp/ *v.* transfer from one ship or conveyance to another. **trans-shipment** *n.*

transubstantiation /trænsəbstænʃɪ'eɪʃ(ə)n/ *n.* conversion of Eucharistic elements wholly into body and blood of Christ.

transuranic /trænzjʊ'rænɪk/ *a. Chem.* (of element) having higher atomic number than uranium.

transverse /trænz'vɜ:s/ *a.* situated or arranged or acting in crosswise direction.

transvestism /trænz'vestɪz(ə)m/ *n.* dressing in garments of opposite sex.

transvestite /trænz'vestaɪt/ *n.* person given to transvestism.

trap 1 *n.* device, often baited, for catching animals; arrangement to catch out unsuspecting person; device for releasing clay pigeon to be shot at or greyhound at start of race etc.; curve in drain-pipe etc. serving when filled with liquid to seal it against return of gas; two-wheeled carriage; trapdoor; *sl.* mouth. 2 *v.t.* catch (as) in trap; set traps for game etc.; furnish with traps. 3 **trapdoor** door flush with surface of floor or roof etc.

trapeze /trə'pi:z/ *n.* horizontal crossbar suspended by ropes as swing for acrobatics etc.

trapezium /trə'pi:zɪəm/ *n.* (*pl.* **-zia** or **-ziums**) quadrilateral with only one pair of sides parallel; *US* trapezoid.

trapezoid /'træpɪzɔɪd/ *n.* quadrilateral with no sides parallel; *US* trapezium.

trapper /'træpə(r)/ *n.* person who traps wild animals for their fur etc.

trappings /'træpɪŋz/ *n.pl.* ornamental accessories; ornamental cloth covering for horse.

traps *n. pl. colloq.* portable belongings, baggage.

trash *n.* waste or worthless stuff; rubbish; worthless or disreputable person(s). **trashy** *a.*

trauma /'trɔːmə/ *n.* (*pl.* **-mas**) emotional shock; wound, injury. **traumatic** *a.*

travail /'træveɪl/ 1 *v. literary* laborious effort; *arch.* pangs of childbirth. 2 *v.i. literary* make laborious effort; *arch.* suffer pangs of childbirth.

travel /'træv(ə)l/ 1 *v.* go from one place to another; make journey(s) esp. of some length or abroad; journey through or pass over, traverse; *colloq.* withstand long journey; act as commercial traveller; move or proceed in specified manner etc.; *colloq.* move quickly; pass from point to point; (of machine or part) move or operate in specified way. 2 *n.* travelling; range or rate or mode of motion of part in machinery. 3 **travel agency** agency making arrangements for travellers; **travelling crane** crane moving on esp. overhead support.

travelled /'træv(ə)ld/ *a.* experienced in travelling.

traveller /'trævələ(r)/ *n.* person who travels or is travelling; commercial traveller. **traveller's cheque** cheque for fixed amount, encashable on signature for equivalent in most currencies; **traveller's joy** wild clematis.

travelogue /'trævəlɒg/ *n.* film or illustrated lecture with narrative of travel.

traverse 1 /trə'vɜːs/ *v.* travel or lie across; consider or discuss whole extent of; turn (large gun) horizontally. 2 /'trævəs/ *n.* sideways movement, traversing; thing that crosses another. 3 **traversal** *a.*

travesty /'trævɪstɪ/ 1 *n.* gross parody, ridiculous imitation. 2 *v.t.* make or be travesty of.

trawl 1 *n.* large wide-mouthed fishing-net dragged by boat along bottom of sea

etc. 2 *v.* fish with trawl or in trawler; catch with trawl.

trawler /'trɔːlə(r)/ *n.* boat used in fishing with trawl-net.

tray *n.* flat shallow vessel used for carrying or containing small articles etc.; shallow lidless box or drawer forming compartment of trunk etc.

treacherous /'tretʃərəs/ *a.* violating faith or betraying trust; perfidious; not to be relied on, deceptive. **treachery** *n.*

treacle /'triːk(ə)l/ *n.* syrup produced in refining sugar; molasses. **treacly** *a.*

tread /tred/ 1 *v.* (*past* **trod**; *p.p.* **trodden**) set one's foot down; (of foot) be set down; walk on, press or crush with feet; (of male bird) copulate (with). 2 *n.* manner or sound of walking; top surface of step or stair; part of wheel that touches ground, thick moulded part of vehicle tyre for gripping road, part of sole of boot etc. similarly moulded. 3 **tread-mill** device for producing motion by treading on steps on revolving cylinder, formerly used as prison punishment, *fig.* monotonous routine; **tread water** maintain upright position in water by moving feet and hands.

treadle /'tred(ə)l/ *n.* lever moved by foot and imparting motion to machine.

treason /'triːz(ə)n/ *n.* violation by subject of allegiance to sovereign or State; breach of faith, disloyalty.

treasonable /'triːzənəb(ə)l/ *a.* involving or guilty of treason.

treasonous /'triːzənəs/ *a.* treasonable.

treasure /'treʒə(r)/ 1 *n.* precious metals or gems etc.; hoard of them; thing valued for rarity or associations etc.; accumulated wealth; *colloq.* beloved or highly valued person. 2 *v.t.* store (*up*) as valuable; receive or regard as valuable. 3 **treasure-hunt** search for treasure, game in which players seek hidden object; **treasure trove** treasure of unknown ownership found hidden.

treasurer /'treʒərə(r)/ *n.* person in charge of funds of society or municipality etc.

treasury /'treʒərɪ/ *n.* place where treasure is kept; funds or revenue of State or institution or society etc.; department managing public revenue of a country. **Treasury bench** government front bench in parliament; **treasury**

bill bill of exchange issued by government to raise money for temporary needs.

treat 1 v. act or behave towards in specified way; deal with or apply process to etc.; deal with disease etc. in order to relieve or cure; provide with food or drink or entertainment at one's own expense; negotiate (with); give exposition of. 2 n. thing that gives great pleasure; entertainment designed to do this; treating of others to food etc.

treatise /ˈtriːtɪs/ n. literary composition dealing esp. formally with subject.

treatment /ˈtriːtmənt/ n. process or manner of dealing with or behaving towards person or thing; medical care or attention.

treaty /ˈtriːtɪ/ n. formally concluded and ratified agreement between States; agreement between persons esp. for purchase of property.

treble /ˈtreb(ə)l/ 1 a. threefold, triple; 3 times as much or many; (of voice) high-pitched; Mus. soprano (esp. of boy's voice or of instrument). 2 n. treble quantity or thing; soprano; high-pitched voice. 3 v. multiply or be multiplied by 3.

tree 1 n. perennial plant with single woody self-supporting stem, usu. developing woody branches at some distance from ground; shaped piece of wood for various purposes; chart or diagram like branching tree. 2 v.t. cause to take refuge in tree. 3 **tree-creeper** small creeping bird feeding on insects in tree-bark; **tree-fern** kind of large fern with upright woody stem; **tree surgeon** person who treats decayed trees in order to preserve them.

trefoil /ˈtrefɔɪl/ n. kind of plant with leaves of 3 leaflets; 3-lobed thing esp. ornamentation in tracery etc.

trek 1 v.i. (past & p.p. **trekked**) make arduous journey; travel or migrate, esp. by ox-wagon. 2 n. such journey; each stage of it.

trellis /ˈtrelɪs/ n. lattice or grating of light wooden or metal bars, used as support for climbing plants or as screen etc.

tremble /ˈtremb(ə)l/ 1 v.i. shake involuntarily with fear or cold or excitement etc.; be affected with fear or

suspense etc.; move in quivering manner. 2 n. trembling, quiver, tremor. 3 **trembly** a.

tremendous /trɪˈmendəs/ a. awe-inspiring, overpowering; colloq. remarkable or considerable or excellent.

tremolo /ˈtremələʊ/ n. (pl. -los) Mus. tremulous effect in playing music or singing.

tremor /ˈtremə(r)/ n. shaking; quiver; thrill of fear or other emotion; slight earthquake.

tremulous /ˈtremjʊləs/ a. trembling, quivering.

trench 1 n. deep ditch, esp. one dug by troops as shelter from enemy's fire. 2 v. make trench(es) or ditch(es) in, dig trench(es); make series of trenches so as to bring lower soil to surface. 3 **trench coat** lined or padded waterproof coat, loose belted raincoat.

trenchant /ˈtrentʃ(ə)nt/ a. sharp, keen; incisive, decisive. **trenchancy** n.

trencher /ˈtrentʃə(r)/ n. wooden platter for serving food.

trencherman n. (pl. -men) feeder, eater.

trend 1 v.i. have specified direction or course or general tendency. 2 n. general direction or course or tendency. 3 **trend-setter** person who leads the way in fashion etc.

trendy /ˈtrendɪ/ colloq. usu. derog. 1 a. fashionable. 2 n. fashionable person.

trepan /trɪˈpæn/ n. surgeon's cylindrical saw for making opening in skull. 2 v.t. perforate (skull) with trepan.

trepidation /trepɪˈdeɪʃ(ə)n/ n. agitation, alarm, anxiety.

trespass /ˈtrespəs/ 1 v.i. enter unlawfully on another's land or property etc.; encroach on. 2 n. act of trespassing; arch. sin, offence.

tress n. lock of hair; in pl. hair.

trestle /ˈtres(ə)l/ n. supporting structure for table etc. consisting of bar supported by two divergent pairs of legs or of two frames fixed at an angle or hinged; trestle-work. **trestle-table** table of board(s) laid on trestles; **trestle-work** open braced framework to support bridge etc.

trews n.pl. close-fitting usu. tartan trousers.

TRH abbr. Their Royal Highnesses.

tri- in comb. three (times).

triad /ˈtraɪæd/ n. group of 3 (esp. notes in chord). **triadic** a.

trial /ˈtraɪəl/ n. judicial examination and determination of issues between parties by judge with or without jury; process or mode of testing qualities; experimental treatment, test; trying thing or experience or person.

triangle /ˈtraɪæŋg(ə)l/ n. figure of 3 straight lines each meeting the others at different points; any 3 things not in a straight line, with the imaginary lines joining them; implement etc. of this shape; *Mus.* instrument of steel rod bent into triangle sounded by striking with small steel rod.

triangular /traɪˈæŋgjʊlə(r)/ a. triangle-shaped; (of contest, treaty, etc.) between 3 persons or parties; (of pyramid) having 3-sided base.

triangulate /traɪˈæŋgjʊleɪt/ v.t. divide (area) into triangles for surveying purposes. **triangulation** n.

tribe n. (in some societies) group of families under recognized chief and usu. claiming common ancestor; any similar natural or political division; (usu. *derog.*) set or number of persons esp. of one profession etc. or family. **tribesman** member of tribe. **tribal** a.

tribulation /trɪbjʊˈleɪʃ(ə)n/ n. great affliction.

tribunal /traɪˈbjuːn(ə)l/ n. board appointed to adjudicate on particular question; court of justice, judicial assembly.

tribune[1] /ˈtrɪbjuːn/ n. popular leader, demagogue; *Rom. hist.* officer chosen by the people to protect their liberties.

tribune[2] /ˈtrɪbjuːn/ n. platform, rostrum.

tributary /ˈtrɪbjʊtərɪ/ 1 n. stream etc. that flows into larger stream or lake; person or State paying or subject to tribute. 2 a. that is a tributary.

tribute /ˈtrɪbjuːt/ n. thing done or said or given as mark of respect or affection etc.; periodical payment exacted by one sovereign or State from another; obligation to pay this.

trice n. instant, moment.

triceps /ˈtraɪseps/ n. muscle (esp. in upper arm) with 3 points of attachment.

trichinosis /trɪkɪˈnəʊsɪs/ n. disease caused by hairlike worms in muscles.

trichology /trɪˈkɒlədʒɪ/ n. study of hair. **trichologist** n.

trichromatic /traɪkrəˈmætɪk/ a. 3-coloured.

trick 1 n. thing done to fool or outwit or deceive; optical or other illusion; knack or way of doing something; feat of skill or dexterity; malicious or foolish or stupid act; hoax, joke; characteristic habit; cards played in one round, winning of round. 2 v.t. deceive by trick, cheat; take by surprise.

trickery /ˈtrɪkərɪ/ n. deception, use of tricks.

trickle /ˈtrɪk(ə)l/ 1 v. (cause to) flow drop by drop; come or go slowly or gradually. 2 n. trickling flow. 3 **trickle charger** *Electr.* device for slow continuous charging of accumulator.

trickster /ˈtrɪkstə(r)/ n. deceiver, rogue.

tricky /ˈtrɪkɪ/ a. requiring care and adroitness; crafty, deceitful.

tricolour /ˈtrɪkələ(r)/ n. flag of 3 colours, esp. French national flag.

tricot /ˈtrɪkəʊ/ n. knitted fabric.

tricycle /ˈtraɪsɪk(ə)l/ n. 3-wheeled pedal-driven vehicle; 3-wheeled motor vehicle for disabled driver. **tricyclist** n.

trident /ˈtraɪd(ə)nt/ n. 3-pronged spear.

Tridentine /trɪˈdentaɪn/ a. of traditional RC orthodoxy.

triennial /traɪˈenɪəl/ a. lasting 3 years; recurring every 3 years.

trifle /ˈtraɪf(ə)l/ 1 n. thing of slight value or importance; small amount or article; sweet dish of sponge-cakes with custard and cream etc. 2 v.i. talk or act frivolously.

trifling a. trivial.

trigger /ˈtrɪgə(r)/ n. lever or catch pulled or pressed to release spring or otherwise set mechanism in motion, esp. catch for releasing hammer of firearm. 2 v. set off reaction or process etc. by comparatively small action etc. 3 **trigger-happy** apt to shoot on slight provocation.

trigonometry /trɪgəˈnɒmɪtrɪ/ n. branch of mathematics dealing with measurement of sides and angles of triangles, and with certain functions of angles. **trigonometrical** /-ˈmet-/ a.

trike n. *colloq.* tricycle.

trilateral /traɪˈlætər(ə)l/ a. having 3 sides; existing etc. between 3 parties.

trilby /ˈtrɪlbɪ/ n. soft felt hat with narrow brim and indented crown.

trilingual /traɪˈlɪŋgw(ə)l/ a. of or in or speaking 3 languages.

trill 1 n. quavering or vibratory sound (e.g. quick alternation of notes in singing, bird's warbling, the letter r). **2** v. produce trill; warble (song); pronounce (r etc.) with trill.

trillion /ˈtrɪlɪən/ n. million million millions; US etc. million millions. **trillionth** a. & n.

trilobite /ˈtraɪləbaɪt/ n. kind of fossil crustacean.

trilogy /ˈtrɪlədʒɪ/ n. set of 3 related dramatic or other literary works.

trim 1 v. make neat or tidy; remove irregular or unsightly etc. parts by planing or clipping etc.; ornament; adjust balance of (ship, aircraft) by distribution of weight; arrange (sails etc.) to suit wind. **2** n. state or degree of readiness or fitness or adjustment etc.; good order; ornament or decorative material; trimming of hair etc. **3** a. in good order, neat; not loose or ungainly. **4 trim one's sails** fig. adjust one's policy etc. to changing circumstances.

trimaran /ˈtrɪməræn/ n. vessel like catamaran, with 3 hulls side by side.

trimming /ˈtrɪmɪŋ/ n. ornamental addition to dress or hat etc.; in pl. colloq. accessories, usual accompaniments.

trinitrotoluene /traɪnaɪtrəʊˈtɒljʊiːn/ n. a high explosive.

trinity /ˈtrɪnɪtɪ/ n. being 3; group of 3. **the Trinity** Theol. the 3 persons of the Godhead as conceived in orthodox Christian belief; **Trinity Sunday** Sunday after Whit Sunday.

trinket /ˈtrɪŋkɪt/ n. small or trifling ornament, esp. piece of jewellery.

trio /ˈtriːəʊ/ n. (pl. -os) musical composition for 3 performers; the performers; any group of 3.

trip 1 v. go lightly and quickly along; catch one's foot and stumble; commit blunder or fault; cause (person) to stumble by entangling his feet; release (part of machine) suddenly by knocking aside catch etc. **2** n. journey or excursion esp. for pleasure; stumble, tripping or being tripped up; colloq. visionary experience caused by drug;

contrivance for tripping mechanism etc. **3 trip up** (cause to) stumble, detect in error or inconsistency etc.; **trip-wire** wire stretched close to ground to operate warning device etc. if disturbed.

tripartite /traɪˈpɑːtaɪt/ a. consisting of 3 parts; shared by or involving 3 parties.

tripe n. first or second stomach of ox or other ruminant prepared as food; sl. worthless or trashy thing, rubbish.

triple /ˈtrɪp(ə)l/ **1** a. threefold; of 3 parts or involving 3 parties; 3 times as much or as many. **2** n. number or thing 3 times another; set of 3. **3** v. multiply by 3. **4 triple crown** pope's tiara, winning of 3 important sporting events; **triple time** Mus. tempo of 3 beats to a bar.

triplet /ˈtrɪplɪt/ n. one of 3 children born at one birth; set of 3 things, esp. of notes played in time of two or verses rhyming together.

triplex /ˈtrɪpleks/ a. triple, threefold.

triplicate 1 /ˈtrɪplɪkət/ a. existing in 3 examples; having 3 corresponding parts; tripled. **2** /ˈtrɪplɪkət/ n. state of being triplicate. **3** /ˈtrɪplɪkeɪt/ v.t. make in triplicate; multiply by 3. **4 triplication** n.

tripod /ˈtraɪpɒd/ n. 3-legged or 3-footed stand or support or seat etc.

tripos /ˈtraɪpɒs/ n. honours examination for BA degree at Cambridge University.

tripper /ˈtrɪpə(r)/ n. person who goes on pleasure trip.

triptych /ˈtrɪptɪk/ n. picture etc. with 3 panels hinged vertically together.

trireme /ˈtraɪəriːm/ n. ancient warship, prob. with 3 men at each oar.

trisect /traɪˈsekt/ v.t. divide into 3 (usu. equal) parts. **trisection** n.

trite a. well-worn, hackneyed, commonplace.

tritium /ˈtrɪtɪəm/ n. Chem. radioactive isotope of hydrogen with mass about 3 times that of ordinary hydrogen.

triumph /ˈtraɪəmf/ **1** n. state of being victorious; great success or achievement; joy at success; supreme example of, Rom. hist. processional entry of victorious general into Rome. **2** v.i. gain victory, prevail, be successful; exult (over); Rom. hist. ride in triumph.

triumphal /traɪˈʌmf(ə)l/ a. of or celebrating or used in a triumph or victory.

triumphant /traɪˈʌmf(ə)nt/ a. victorious, successful, exultant.

triumvir /traɪˈʌmvə(r)/ n. (pl. **-viri** /-vɪriː/ or **-virs**) member of a triumvirate.

triumvirate /traɪˈʌmvərət/ n. government or board of 3 men.

trivalent /traɪˈveɪlənt/ a. Chem. having a valence of 3.

trivet /ˈtrɪvɪt/ n. iron tripod or bracket for cooking-pot or kettle to stand on.

trivia /ˈtrɪvɪə/ n.pl. trifles, trivialities.

trivial /ˈtrɪvɪəl/ a. of small value or importance; concerned only with trivial things. **triviality** n.

trod past of **tread**.

trodden p.p. of **tread**.

troglodyte /ˈtrɒglədaɪt/ n. cave-dweller.

troika /ˈtrɔɪkə/ n. Russian vehicle drawn by 3 horses abreast.

Trojan /ˈtrəʊdʒ(ə)n/ 1 a. of ancient Troy. 2 n. inhabitant of ancient Troy. 3 **Trojan Horse** fig. person or device insinuated to bring about enemy's downfall.

troll[1] /trəʊl/ n. supernatural being, giant or dwarf, in Scandinavian mythology.

troll[2] /trəʊl/ v. sing out in carefree manner; fish by drawing bait along in water.

trolley /ˈtrɒlɪ/ n. small table on wheels or castors; small handcart for carrying luggage etc. or for use in supermarket etc.; low truck, esp. running along rails; wheel attached to pole etc. for collecting current from overhead electric wire to drive vehicle. **trolley bus** electric bus using trolley.

trollop /ˈtrɒləp/ n. disreputable girl or woman.

trombone /trɒmˈbəʊn/ n. large brass wind-instrument with sliding tube. **trombonist** n.

troop /truːp/ 1 n. assembled company, assemblage of persons or animals; in pl. soldiers, armed forces; cavalry unit commanded by captain; artillery unit; group of 3 or more Scout patrols. 2 v. come together or move in a troop. 3 **troop the colour** transfer flag ceremonially at mounting of gar-

rison guards; **troop-ship** ship for transporting troops.

trooper /ˈtruːpə(r)/ n. private soldier in cavalry or armoured unit; US & Aus. mounted or motor-borne policeman; troop-ship.

trope n. figure of speech.

trophy /ˈtrəʊfɪ/ n. thing kept as prize or memento of any contest or success; group of things arranged for ornamental display.

tropic /ˈtrɒpɪk/ n. parallel of latitude 23° 27′ N. or S. of equator. **the tropics** region lying between these.

tropical /ˈtrɒpɪk(ə)l/ a. of or peculiar to or suggestive of the tropics.

troposphere /ˈtrɒpəsfɪə(r)/ n. layer of atmosphere extending from earth's surface to stratosphere.

trot 1 v. (of person) run at moderate pace esp. with short strides; (of horse etc.) proceed at steady pace faster than walk; traverse (distance) thus. 2 n. action or exercise of trotting. 3 **on the trot** colloq. continually busy, in succession; **trot out** fig. produce or introduce (as if) for inspection or approval.

troth /trəʊθ/ n. arch. faith, fidelity.

trotter /ˈtrɒtə(r)/ n. horse bred or trained for trotting; animal's foot esp. as food.

troubadour /ˈtruːbədɔː(r)/ n. medieval romantic or amatory poet.

trouble /ˈtrʌb(ə)l/ 1 n. vexation, affliction; inconvenience, unpleasant exertion; cause of annoyance; faulty condition or operation; in pl. public disturbances. 2 v. cause distress to; agitate, disturb; afflict, cause pain etc. to; subject or be subjected to inconvenience or unpleasant exertion. 3 **in trouble** subject to censure or punishment etc.; **trouble-maker** person who habitually causes trouble; **trouble-shooter** person who traces and corrects faults in machinery etc., mediator in dispute.

troublesome /ˈtrʌbəlsəm/ a. causing trouble, annoying.

troublous /ˈtrʌbləs/ a. arch. full of troubles, disturbed.

trough /trɒf/ n. long narrow open receptacle for water or animal feed etc. to stand in; channel or hollow comparable to this; *Meteor.* region of low barometric pressure.

trounce /traʊns/ *v.t.* inflict severe punishment or defeat on.

troupe /truːp/ *n.* company of actors or acrobats etc.

trouper /ˈtruːpə(r)/ *n.* member of theatrical troupe; staunch colleague.

trousers /ˈtraʊzəz/ *n.pl.* two-legged outer garment from waist usu. to ankles. **trouser-suit** woman's suit of trousers and jacket.

trousseau /ˈtruːsəʊ/ *n.* (*pl.* **-eaus**) bride's collection of clothes etc.

trout /traʊt/ *n.* (*pl.* same) kind of fish related to salmon.

trove *n.* treasure-trove.

trow /trəʊ/ *v.t. arch.* think, believe.

trowel /ˈtraʊəl/ *n.* flat-bladed tool for spreading mortar etc.; scoop for lifting small plants or earth.

troy *n.* system of weights used for precious metals etc.

truant /ˈtruːənt/ *n.* child who absents himself from school; person missing from work etc. **play truant** stay away thus. **truancy** *n.*

truce *n.* temporary cessation of hostilities; respite; agreement for this.

truck[1] *n.* strong vehicle for heavy goods; open railway wagon; handcart, barrow for moving luggage etc.

truck[2] *n.* **have no truck** avoid dealing *with*.

truckle /ˈtrʌk(ə)l/ *v.i.* submit obsequiously (*to*). **truckle-bed** low bed on wheels that may be pushed under another.

truculent /ˈtrʌkjʊlənt/ *a.* aggressive, fierce. **truculence** *n.*

trudge 1 *v.i.* walk laboriously or without spirit. 2 *n.* trudging walk.

true 1 *a.* in accordance with fact or reality; genuine, real, correct, proper; accurately placed or fitted or shaped; (of ground etc.) level, smooth, even; loyal, faithful, constant (*to*). 2 *adv.* truly, accurately; without variation.

truffle /ˈtrʌf(ə)l/ *n.* underground fungus with rich flavour; sweet made of soft chocolate mixture.

trug *n.* shallow oblong garden-basket.

truism /ˈtruːɪz(ə)m/ *n.* self-evident or hackneyed truth.

truly /ˈtruːlɪ/ *adv.* with truth; sincerely; loyally; accurately. **yours**

truly formula preceding signature of letter, *joc.* I, me.

trump[1] 1 *n.* playing-card of suit temporarily ranking above others; advantage, esp. involving surprise; *colloq.* helpful or excellent person. 2 *v.* defeat with trump; play trump. 3 **trump card** card turned up to determine trump suit, *fig.* valuable resource; **trump up** fabricate or invent (story, accusation, etc.); **turn up trumps** *colloq.* turn out well or successfully, prove extremely kind or generous etc.

trump[2] *n. arch.* (sound of) trumpet.

trumpery /ˈtrʌmpərɪ/ 1 *a.* showy but worthless, delusive, shallow. 2 *n.* worthless finery.

trumpet /ˈtrʌmpɪt/ 1 *n.* metal tubular or conical wind instrument with flared mouth and bright penetrating tone; trumpet-shaped thing; sound (as) of trumpet, esp. elephant's loud cry. 2 *v.* blow trumpet; (of elephant) make trumpet; proclaim loudly.

trumpeter *n.* player of trumpet.

truncate /trʌŋˈkeɪt/ *v.t.* cut off top or end of; cut short. **truncation** *n.*

truncheon /ˈtrʌntʃ(ə)n/ *n.* short club carried by policeman; staff or baton as sign of authority.

trundle /ˈtrʌnd(ə)l/ *v.* roll or move on wheels, esp. heavily or noisily.

trunk *n.* main stem of tree; person's or animal's body apart from head and limbs; large luggage-box with hinged lid; *US* boot of car; elephant's elongated prehensile nose; in *pl.* men's close-fitting shorts worn for swimming or boxing etc. **trunk-call** telephone call on trunk-line with charges according to distance; **trunk-line** main line of railway or telephone system etc.; **trunk-road** important main road.

truss 1 *n.* supporting framework of roof or bridge etc.; surgical appliance for support in cases of hernia etc.; bundle of hay or straw. 2 *v.t.* tie up (fowl) compactly for cooking; tie person (*up*) with arms to sides; support with truss(es).

trust 1 *n.* firm belief that a person or thing may be relied upon; state of being relied upon; confident expectation; thing or person committed to one's care, resulting obligation; *Law* trusteeship, board of trustees, property committed to trustee(s); association of several companies for purpose of united action to prevent competition. **2** v. place trust in, believe in, rely on; consign *to*; allow credit to; hope earnestly. **3 trustworthy** deserving of trust, reliable. **4 trustful** a.

trustee /trʌs'tiː/ n. person or member of board given possession of property with legal obligation to administer it solely for purposes specified; State made responsible for government of an area. **trusteeship** n.

trusting /'trʌstɪŋ/ a. not given to suspicion or apprehension.

trusty /'trʌstɪ/ **1** a. arch. trustworthy. **2** n. prisoner who is given special privileges for good behaviour.

truth /truːθ/ n. quality or state of being true or truthful; what is true.

truthful /'truːθfʊl/ a. habitually speaking the truth, true.

try 1 v. attempt, endeavour; test (quality), test qualities of (person, thing) by experiment, ascertain by experiment; make severe demands on; examine effectiveness or usefulness of for purpose; investigate and decide (case, issue) judicially, subject (person) to trial (*for* crime). **2** n. attempt; *Rugby footb.* touching-down of ball by player behind goal-line, entitling his side to a kick at goal. **3 try one's hand** have attempt *at*; **try on** put (clothes etc.) on to test fit etc., begin experimentally to see how much will be tolerated; **try-on** colloq. act of trying something on, attempt to deceive; **try out** put to the test, test thoroughly; **try-out** experimental test.

trying a. difficult to bear; exhausting; exasperating.

tryst /trɪst/ n. arch. time and place for meeting esp. of lovers.

tsar n. title of former emperor of Russia.

tsetse /'tsetsɪ/ n. Afr. fly carrying disease to men and animals by biting.

T-shirt, T-square: see **T**.

TT abbr. Tourist Trophy; tuberculin-tested; teetotal(ler).

tub 1 n. open flat-bottomed usu. round vessel; colloq. bath; derog. or joc. clumsy slow boat. **2** v. plant or bathe or wash in tub. **3 tub-thumper** ranting preacher or orator.

tuba /'tjuːbə/ n. low-pitched brass wind instrument.

tubby /'tʌbɪ/ a. tub-shaped; short and fat.

tube 1 n. long hollow cylinder, natural or artificial structure having approximately this shape with open or closed ends and serving for passage of fluid etc. or as receptacle; colloq. underground electric railway; inner tube containing air in pneumatic tyre; cathode-ray tube, esp. in television; *US* thermionic valve. **2** v.t. equip with tubes; enclose in tube. **3 the tube** *US* television.

tuber /'tjuːbə(r)/ n. short thick rounded root or underground stem of plant.

tubercle /'tjuːbək(ə)l/ n. small rounded swelling in part or organ of body, esp. as characteristic of tuberculosis in lungs.

tubercular /tjuː'bɜːkjʊlə(r)/ a. of or affected with tuberculosis.

tuberculin /tjuː'bɜːkjʊlɪn/ n. preparation from cultures of tubercle bacillus used for treatment and diagnosis of tuberculosis. **tuberculin-tested** (of milk) from cows shown by tuberculin test to be free of tuberculosis.

tuberculosis /tjuːbɜːkjʊ'ləʊsɪs/ n. infectious bacterial disease marked by tubercles, esp. in lungs.

tuberculous /tjuː'bɜːkjʊləs/ a. of or having or caused by tubercles or tuberculosis.

tuberose /'tjuːbərəʊz/ n. plant with creamy-white fragrant flowers.

tuberous /'tjuːbərəs/ a. having tubers; of or like a tuber.

tubing /'tjuːbɪŋ/ n. length of tube or quantity of tubes; material for tubes.

tubular /'tjuːbjʊlə(r)/ a. tube-shaped; having or consisting of tubes.

TUC abbr. Trades Union Congress.

tuck 1 v. draw or fold or turn outer or end parts of (cloth or clothes etc.) close together or so as to be held; draw together into small compass; cover snugly and comfortably *in* or *up*; stow (thing) away in specified way; make stitched fold in (material or garment). **2** n. flattened fold sewn in garment etc.; sl. eatables, esp. cakes and sweets. **3 tuck in** sl. eat heartily; **tuck-shop**

shop selling sweets etc. to schoolchildren.

tucker /'tʌkə(r)/ *v.t. US colloq.* tire (*out*), exhaust.

Tudor /'tjuːdə(r)/ *a.* of royal family of England from Henry VII to Elizabeth I; of the architectural style of this period.

Tues. *abbr.* Tuesday.

Tuesday /'tjuːzdeɪ/ *n.* day of week following Monday.

tufa /'tjuːfə/ *n.* porous rock formed round springs of mineral water; tuff.

tuff *n.* rock formed from volcanic ashes.

tuft *n.* number of feathers or threads or hairs or grass-blades etc. growing or joined together in cluster or knot.

tug 1 *v.* pull hard, pull violently *at*; tow (vessel) by means of tugboat. 2 *n.* hard or violent or jerky pull; tugboat. 3 **tugboat** small powerful boat for towing others; **tug of war** trial of strength between two sides pulling opposite ways on a rope.

tuition /tjuː'ɪʃ(ə)n/ *n.* teaching, instruction.

tulip /'tjuːlɪp/ *n.* bulbous spring-flowering plant with showy cup-shaped flowers; its flower. **tulip-tree** tree with tulip-like flowers.

tulle /tjuːl/ *n.* thin soft fine silk net for veils and dresses.

tumble /'tʌmb(ə)l/ 1 *v.* fall suddenly or headlong; fall rapidly in amount etc.; roll, toss; move or rush in headlong or blundering fashion; fling or push roughly or carelessly; perform acrobatic feats esp. somersaults; disarrange, rumple. 2 *n.* fall; somersault or other acrobatic feat. 3 **tumbledown** falling or fallen into ruin, dilapidated; **tumble-drier** machine for drying washed clothes etc. in heated rotating drum; **tumble to** *colloq.* grasp meaning of (idea etc.).

tumbler *n.* drinking-glass without handle or foot; acrobat; part of mechanism of lock.

tumbrel /'tʌmbr(ə)l/ *n.* (also **tumbril**) open cart in which condemned persons were carried to guillotine during French Revolution.

tumescent /tjuː'mes(ə)nt/ *a.* swelling.

tumid /'tjuːmɪd/ *a.* swollen, inflated, pompous. **tumidity** *n.*

tummy /'tʌmɪ/ *n. colloq.* stomach.

tumour /'tjuːmə(r)/ *n.* abnormal or morbid swelling in the body.

tumult /'tjuːmʌlt/ *n.* riot, angry demonstration of a mob; uproar or din; conflict of emotions etc. **tumultuous** *a.*

tumulus /'tjuːmjʊləs/ *n.* (*pl.* **-li** /-laɪ/) ancient burial mound.

tun *n.* large cask or barrel; brewer's fermenting-vat.

tuna /'tjuːnə/ *n.* tunny; (also **tuna-fish**) its flesh as food.

tundra /'tʌndrə/ *n.* vast level treeless Arctic region where subsoil is frozen.

tune 1 *n.* melody with or without harmony; correct pitch or intonation in singing or playing, adjustment of instrument to obtain this. 2 *v.* put (instrument) in tune; adjust (radio receiver) to desired wavelength etc.; adjust (engine etc.) to run smoothly; adjust or adapt (*to* purpose etc.). 3 **change one's tune** change one's manner esp. from insolent to respectful; **in, out of, tune**, in, out of, proper pitch or intonation, or *fig.* proper condition or harmony (*with*); **tune in** set radio receiver to right wavelength to receive signal; **tune up** bring (instrument) up to proper pitch, adjust instruments for playing together; **tuning-fork** two-pronged steel instrument giving particular note when struck.

tuneful /'tjuːnfʊl/ *a.* melodious, musical.

tuner /'tjuːnə(r)/ *n.* person who tunes pianos etc.

tungsten /'tʌŋst(ə)n/ *n.* heavy steel-grey metallic element.

tunic /'tjuːnɪk/ *n.* close-fitting short coat of police or military uniform; loose often sleeveless garment.

tunnel /'tʌn(ə)l/ 1 *n.* artificial underground passage under hill or river or roadway etc.; underground passage dug by burrowing animal. 2 *v.* make tunnel through (hill etc.); make one's way so.

tunny /'tʌnɪ/ *n.* large edible sea-fish.

tuppence, tuppenny, = *twopence, twopenny.*

turban /'tɜːbən/ *n.* man's head-dress of linen or silk wound round cap, worn esp. by Muslims and Sikhs; woman's hat or head-dress resembling this.

turbid /'tɜːbɪd/ *a.* muddy, thick, not

clear; confused, disordered. **turbidity** n.

turbine /'tɜːbaɪn/ n. rotary motor driven by flow of water or gas.

turbo- in comb. turbine.

turbo-jet /'tɜːbəʊdʒet/ n. jet engine in which jet also operates turbine-driven air-compressor; aircraft with this.

turbo-prop /'tɜːbəʊprɒp/ n. jet engine in which turbine is used as in turbo-jet and also to drive propeller; aircraft with this.

turbot /'tɜːbət/ n. large flat-fish valued as food.

turbulent /'tɜːbjʊlənt/ a. disturbed, in commotion; (of flow of air) varying irregularly; insubordinate, riotous. **turbulence** n.

turd n. vulg. ball or lump of excrement.

tureen /tjʊə'riːn/ n. deep covered dish for serving soup.

turf 1 n. (pl. **turves** or **turfs**) short grass with surface earth bound together by its roots; piece of this cut from ground; slab of peat for fuel. 2 v.t. lay (ground) with turf; sl. throw out. 3 **the turf** racecourse, horse-racing; **turf accountant** bookmaker. 4 **turfy** a.

turgid /'tɜːdʒɪd/ a. swollen, inflated; (of language) pompous, bombastic. **turgidity** n.

Turk n. native of Turkey.

turkey /'tɜːkɪ/ n. large orig. Amer. bird bred for food; its flesh. **turkey-cock** male turkey.

Turkey carpet /'tɜːkɪ/ thick-piled woollen carpet with bold design.

Turkish /'tɜːkɪʃ/ 1 a. of Turkey. 2 n. language of Turkey. 3 **Turkish bath** hot-air or steam bath followed by massage etc.; **Turkish delight** kind of gelatinous sweet; **Turkish towel** one made of cotton terry.

turmeric /'tɜːmərɪk/ n. E. Ind. plant of ginger family; its aromatic root powdered as flavouring or dye.

turmoil /'tɜːmɔɪl/ n. din and bustle and confusion.

turn 1 v. move round so as to keep at same distance from a centre; (cause to) receive such motion; change from one side to another, invert, reverse; give new direction to, take new direction, adapt, have recourse to; move to other side of, go round; pass age or time of; cause to go, send, put; change in nature,

form, condition, etc., (cause to) become; shape (object) in lathe; give (esp. elegant) form to. 2 n. act or fact or process of turning; turning of road; point of turning or change; change of tide from ebb to flow or flow to ebb; tendency, formation; short performance on stage, in circus, etc.; opportunity, occasion, privilege, or obligation, that comes successively to each of several persons etc.; service of specified kind; one round in coil of rope etc.; colloq. momentary nervous shock; Mus. ornament of principal note with those above and below it. 3 **do a bad turn** make slightest effort; **in turn** in succession; **on the turn** just changing; **take turns** work etc. alternately; **turn against** make or become hostile to; **turncoat** person who changes sides; **turn down** fold down, place face downwards, reduce (volume of sound, heat, etc.) by turning knob, reduce flame etc. of by turning tap, reject; **turn in** fold or incline inwards, hand in, colloq. go to bed; **turnkey** gaoler; **turn off** enter side-road, stop flow or working of by means of tap, knob, etc., colloq. cause to lose interest; **turn on** start flow or working of by means of tap or knob etc., colloq. arouse interest or emotions of, depend on, face hostilely; **turn out** expel, extinguish (light etc.), fold or incline outwards, equip, dress, produce (manufactured goods etc.), empty of contents or expose thus, colloq. get out of bed, colloq. go out of doors, (cause to) assemble for duty, be found, prove to be the case, result; **turn-out** turning out esp. for duty, number of persons who go to vote etc., equipage; **turn over** (cause to) fall over, expose or bring uppermost the other side of, cause (engine etc.) to revolve, consider thoroughly, transfer conduct of (thing to person); **turnover** turning over, pie or tart made by turning half of pastry over filling, amount of money taken in business, number of persons entering or leaving employment etc.; **turnpike** US road on which toll is collected at gates; **turnstile** admission-gate with arms revolving on post; **turntable** circular revolving platform; **turn to** begin work, apply oneself to, go on to consider next; **turn turtle** capsize;

turn up unearth, make one's appearance, increase (volume of sound, heat, etc.) by turning knob, increase flame etc. of by turning tap, place face up, *colloq.* cause to vomit; **turn-up** thing turned up, lower end of trouser leg, *colloq.* commotion, *colloq.* unexpected event; **turn upon** turn on.

turner /'tɜːnə(r)/ *n.* lathe-worker.

turnery /'tɜːnəri/ *n.* objects made on lathe; work with lathe.

turning /'tɜːnɪŋ/ *n.* place where roads meet, road meeting another; use of lathe; in *pl.* chips or shavings from this. **turning-circle** smallest circle in which vehicle can turn; **turning-point** point at which decisive change occurs.

turnip /'tɜːnɪp/ *n.* plant with globular root used as vegetable and fodder; its root.

turpentine /'tɜːpəntaɪn/ *n.* resin got from terebinth and other trees; (in full **oil of turpentine**) volatile inflammable oil distilled from turpentines and used in mixing paints etc.

turpitude /'tɜːpɪtjuːd/ *n.* baseness, wickedness.

turps *n. colloq.* oil of turpentine.

turquoise /'tɜːkwɔɪz/ *n.* opaque precious stone, usu. greenish-blue; this colour.

turret /'tʌrɪt/ *n.* small tower, esp. decorative addition to building; usu. revolving armoured structure in which guns are mounted or housed; rotating holder for tools in lathe etc.

turtle *n.* sea reptile with horny shell and flippers. **turtle-neck** high close-fitting neck or collar.

turtle dove /'tɜːt(ə)l/ wild dove noted for soft cooing and affection for its mate.

tusk *n.* long pointed tooth esp. projecting beyond mouth as in elephant or walrus or boar.

tussle /'tʌs(ə)l/ *n.* & *v.i.* struggle, scuffle.

tussock /'tʌsək/ *n.* clump of grass etc.

tut *int.*, *n.*, & *v.* = **tut-tut**.

tutelage /'tjuːtɪlɪdʒ/ *n.* guardianship; being under this; instruction, tuition.

tutelary /'tjuːtɪlərɪ/ *a.* serving as protector or patron.

tutor /'tjuːtə(r)/ 1 *n.* private teacher; university teacher supervising studies and welfare of assigned under-

graduates; instruction book. 2 *v.* act as tutor (to); restrain; discipline. 3 **tutorship** *n.*

tutorial /tjuː'tɔːrɪəl/ 1 *a.* of tutor. 2 *n.* period of instruction given to single student or small group.

tut-tut 1 *int.* expr. rebuke or impatience or contempt. 2 *n.* such exclamation. 3 *v.i.* exclaim thus.

tutu /'tuːtuː/ *n.* dancer's short skirt of layers of stiffened frills.

tuxedo /tʌk'siːdəʊ/ *n.* (*pl.* **-dos**) *US* dinner-jacket.

TV *abbr.* television.

twaddle /'twɒd(ə)l/ 1 *n.* useless or dull writing or talk. 2 *v.i.* indulge in this.

twain *n.* & *a.* two.

twang 1 *n.* sound made by plucked string of musical instrument or bow etc.; quality of voice compared to this, esp. nasal intonation. 2 *v.* emit twang, cause to twang.

tweak 1 *v.t.* pinch and twist or jerk. 2 *n.* such action.

twee *a.* affectedly dainty or quaint.

tweed *n.* rough-surfaced woollen cloth freq. of mixed colours; in *pl.* suit of tweed. **tweedy** *a.*

tweet 1 *n.* chirp of small bird. 2 *v.i.* make chirping noise.

tweeter *n.* loudspeaker for high frequencies.

tweezers /'twiːzəz/ *n.pl.* small pair of pincers for picking up small objects or plucking out hairs etc.

twelfth /twelfθ/ 1 *a.* next after eleventh. 2 *n.* one of twelve equal parts. 3 **Twelfth night** eve of Epiphany.

twelve /twelv/ *a.* & *n.* one more than eleven. **twelvemonth** year.

twenty /'twentɪ/ *a.* & *n.* twice ten. **twentieth** *a.* & *n.*

twerp *n. sl.* stupid or objectionable person.

twice *adv.* two times; on two occasions; doubly.

twiddle /'twɪd(ə)l/ 1 *v.t.* twist idly about. 2 *n.* act of twiddling. 3 **twiddle one's thumbs** twirl them idly esp. for lack of anything to do.

twig[1] *n.* small shoot or branch of tree or plant.

twig[2] *v. colloq.* understand, catch meaning (of); observe, notice.

twilight /'twaɪlaɪt/ *n.* light from sky when sun is below horizon, esp. in evening; period of this; state of imperfect understanding; period of decline. **twilight zone** area between others in position and character.

twilit /ˈtwaɪlɪt/ a. dimly illuminated (as) by twilight.

twill n. textile fabric with surface of parallel diagonal ribs.

twilled /twɪld/ a. woven as twill.

twin 1 n. each of two children or animals born at a birth; each of closely related pair; counterpart. 2 a. born as (one of) twins; forming one of a pair. 3 v. join or match closely, pair; bear twins. 4 **twin bed** either of pair of single beds; **twin set** woman's matching jumper and cardigan; **twin towns** two towns, usu. in different countries, establishing special links.

twine 1 n. thread or string of thickness used for tying small parcels or sewing coarse materials etc.; coil, twist. 2 v. twist strands together to form cord; wreathe, clasp; twist, coil, wind.

twinge /twɪndʒ/ 1 n. sharp momentary local pain. 2 v.i. suffer twinge.

twinkle /ˈtwɪŋk(ə)l/ 1 v.i. shine with rapidly intermittent light, sparkle; move rapidly; emit (light) in quick gleams. 2 n. sparkle or gleam of eyes; slight flash of light; short rapid movement.

twirl 1 v.t. spin or swing or twist quickly and lightly round. 2 n. twirling, whirling; thing that twirls.

twist 1 v. change the form of by rotating one end and not the other or the two ends opposite ways; undergo such change; make or become spiral, distort, wrench; wind strands etc. about each other to form rope etc.; take curved course; colloq. cheat. 2 n. twisting, being twisted; thing made by twisting; peculiar tendency of mind or character etc.; distortion; unexpected development etc.

twister /ˈtwɪstə(r)/ n. colloq. swindler.

twit[1] n. sl. foolish person.

twit[2] v.t. reproach, taunt, (with).

twitch 1 v. quiver or jerk spasmodically; pull with light jerk, pull at. 2 n. twitching. 3 **twitchy** a.

twitter /ˈtwɪtə(r)/ 1 v. (of bird, or fig. of person) utter succession of light tremulous sounds; utter or express

thus. 2 n. twittering; colloq. tremulously excited state.

two /tuː/ a. & n. one more than one. **two-dimensional** having or appearing to have length and breadth but no depth; **two-edged** having 2 cutting edges, fig. ambiguous; **two-faced** insincere; **two-handed** used with both hands or by 2 persons; **twopence** /ˈtʌpəns/ sum of 2 pence, thing of little value; **twopenny** /ˈtʌpnɪ/ worth twopence, fig. cheap, worthless; **twopenny-halfpenny** /tʌpnɪˈheɪpnɪ/ fig. contemptible, insignificant; **two-piece** suit of clothes or woman's bathing-suit comprising 2 separate parts; **two-ply** (wool etc.) having 2 strands, (plywood) having 2 layers; **two-step** ballroom dance in march or polka time; **two-stroke** (of internal-combustion engine) having power cycle completed in one up-and-down movement of piston; **two-time** sl. deceive (esp. by infidelity); **two-way** operating in two directions. **twofold** a.

twosome /ˈtuːsəm/ n. pair or couple of persons.

tycoon /taɪˈkuːn/ n. colloq. business magnate.

tying partic. of **tie**.

tyke n. cur; low or objectionable fellow.

tympanum /ˈtɪmpənəm/ n. (pl. **-na**) ear-drum, middle ear; space between lintel and arch above door etc.

type 1 n. class of things having common characteristics; person or thing or event or model serving as illustration or symbol or characteristic specimen etc.; small block with raised letter or figure etc. on upper surface for use in printing; set or supply or kind of these; colloq. person, esp. one of specified character. 2 v. write with typewriter; typify; determine type of, classify according to type. 3 **type-cast** cast (performer) in role appropriate to his nature or previous successful roles; **typeface** set of types in one design, inked surface of types; **type-script** typewritten document; **typesetter** compositor; **typewriter** machine with keys enabling user to produce printlike characters; **typewritten** produced thus.

typhoid /ˈtaɪfɔɪd/ n. (in full **typhoid**

fever) infectious bacterial fever attacking intestines.

typhoon /taɪˈfuːn/ n. violent hurricane in E. Asian seas.

typhus /ˈtaɪfəs/ n. an acute contagious fever.

typical /ˈtɪpɪk(ə)l/ a. serving as characteristic example, distinctive.

typify /ˈtɪpɪfaɪ/ v.t. be representative example of; represent by type. **typification** n.

typist /ˈtaɪpɪst/ n. (esp. professional) user of typewriter.

typography /taɪˈpɒgrəfɪ/ n. printing as an art; style or appearance of printed matter. **typographer** n.; **typographical** a.

tyrannical /tɪˈrænɪk(ə)l/ a. acting like or characteristic of tyrant.

tyrannize /ˈtɪrənaɪz/ v.i. exercise tyranny (*over*); rule despotically.

tyrannous /ˈtɪrənəs/ a. tyrannical.

tyranny /ˈtɪrənɪ/ n. cruel and arbitrary use of authority; rule by tyrant; period of this; State thus ruled.

tyrant /ˈtaɪərənt/ n. oppressive or cruel ruler; person exercising power or authority arbitrarily or cruelly.

tyre n. rubber covering, usu. inflated, placed round wheel to prevent jarring.

tyro var. of **tiro**.

U

ubiquitous /juːˈbɪkwɪtəs/ a. present everywhere or in several places simultaneously; often encountered. **ubiquity** n.

UCCA abbr. Universities Central Council on Admissions.

udder /ˈʌdə(r)/ n. pendulous baggy milk-secreting organ of cow etc.

UDI abbr. unilateral declaration of independence.

UFO abbr. unidentified flying object.

ugh /ʌh or ʊh/ int. expr. disgust etc.

ugli /ˈʌglɪ/ n. mottled green and yellow citrus fruit.

ugly /ˈʌglɪ/ a. unpleasing or repulsive to sight or hearing; unpleasant, threatening, abusive; morally repulsive, vile. **ugly duckling** person who turns out to be more beautiful or talented etc. than was at first expected.

UHF abbr. ultra-high frequency.

UHT abbr. ultra heat treated.

UK abbr. United Kingdom.

ukulele /juːkəˈleɪlɪ/ n. small 4-stringed guitar.

ulcer /ˈʌlsə(r)/ n. open sore on external or internal surface of body; corroding or corrupting influence. **ulcerous** a.

ulcerate /ˈʌlsəreɪt/ v. form ulcer (in or on). **ulceration** n.

ulna /ˈʌlnə/ n. (pl. **-nae** /-niː/) bone of forearm on opp. side to thumb; corresponding bone in animal's foreleg or bird's wing. **ulnar** a.

ulster /ˈʌlstə(r)/ n. long loose overcoat of rough cloth.

ult. abbr. ultimo.

ulterior /ʌlˈtɪərɪə(r)/ a. beyond what is obvious or admitted.

ultimate /ˈʌltɪmət/ a. last, final; fundamental, unanalysable.

ultimatum /ʌltɪˈmeɪtəm/ n. (pl. **-tums**) final statement of terms, rejection of which by opposite party may lead to war or end of co-operation etc.

ultimo /ˈʌltɪməʊ/ adv. of last month.

ultra- in comb. extremely, excessively; beyond.

ultra-high /ˈʌltrəhaɪ/ a. (of frequency) between 300 and 3000 megahertz.

ultramarine /ʌltrəməˈriːn/ 1 n. brilliant deep-blue pigment. 2 a. of this colour.

ultrasonic /ʌltrəˈsɒnɪk/ a. pitched above upper limit of human hearing.

ultrasound /ˈʌltrəsaʊnd/ n. ultrasonic waves.

ultraviolet /ʌltrəˈvaɪələt/ a. of or using invisible rays just beyond violet end of spectrum.

ululate /ˈjuːljʊleɪt/ v.i. howl, wail. **ululation** n.

umbel /ˈʌmb(ə)l/ n. flower-cluster in which stalks of nearly equal length spring from common centre. **umbellate** a.

umbelliferous /ʌmbəˈlɪfərəs/ a. (of plant) belonging to the family including carrots and celery etc.

umber /ˈʌmbə(r)/ 1 n. dark brown earth used as pigment. 2 a. umber-coloured.

umbilical /ʌmˈbɪlɪk(ə)l/ a. of navel. **umbilical cord** flexible cordlike structure attaching foetus to placenta.

umbra /ˈʌmbrə/ n. (pl. **-brae** /-briː/ or **-bras**) shadow cast by moon or earth in eclipse. **umbral** a.

umbrage /ˈʌmbrɪdʒ/ n. offence; sense of slight or injury.

umbrella /ʌmˈbrelə/ n. light portable device for protection against weather, consisting of collapsible usu. circular canopy of cloth mounted on central stick; protection, means of this; co-ordinating agency.

umpire /ˈʌmpaɪə(r)/ 1 n. person chosen to decide between disputants etc. and enforce rules of game or contest etc. 2 v. act as umpire etc.

umpteen /ʌmpˈtiːn/ a. sl. many; an indefinite number of. **umpteenth** a.

un- pref. freely used in comb. with adjs. and nouns to express negation, not, in-, non-; in comb. with verbs, verbal derivatives, etc. to express contrary or reverse action, deprivation or removal of quality or property, etc. The number of words with this prefix being practically unlimited, many of those whose meaning is obvious are not listed here.

UN abbr. United Nations.

unaccountable /ʌnəˈkaʊntəb(ə)l/ a. that cannot be explained, strange; (person) not responsible.

unadopted /ʌnəˈdɒptɪd/ a. (of road) not maintained by local authority.

unaffected /ʌnəˈfektɪd/ a. free from affectation; sincere; not affected (by).

unalloyed /ʌnəˈlɔɪd/ a. unmixed, pure.

unanimous /juːˈnænɪməs/ a. all of one mind; agreeing in opinion; held or given etc. with general agreement or consent. **unanimity** /-ˈnɪm-/ n.

unanswerable /ʌnˈɑːnsərəb(ə)l/ a. that cannot be answered or refuted.

unassailable /ʌnəˈseɪləb(ə)l/ a. that cannot be attacked or questioned.

unassuming /ʌnəˈsjuːmɪŋ/ a. making little of one's own merits or status.

unawares /ʌnəˈweəz/ adv. unexpectedly; unconsciously; by surprise.

unbacked /ʌnˈbækt/ a. not supported, having no backers (esp. in betting); having no back or backing.

unbalanced /ʌnˈbælənst/ a. not balanced; mentally unstable or deranged.

unbeknown /ʌnbɪˈnəʊn/ a. (also **unbeknownst**) not known. **unbeknown to** without the knowledge of.

unbend /ʌnˈbend/ v. (past & p.p. **-bent**) change from bent position, straighten, relax from strain or exertion or severity; become affable.

unbidden /ʌnˈbɪd(ə)n/ a. unasked, uninvited.

unblock /ʌnˈblɒk/ v.t. remove obstruction from.

unblushing /ʌnˈblʌʃɪŋ/ a. shameless.

unbosom /ʌnˈbʊz(ə)m/ v.t. disclose; **unbosom oneself** disclose one's thoughts or feelings etc.

unbridled /ʌnˈbraɪd(ə)ld/ a. unrestrained, uncontrolled.

uncalled-for /ʌnˈkɔːldfɔː(r)/ a. impertinently offered or intruded.

uncanny /ʌnˈkænɪ/ a. mysterious, uncomfortably strange or unfamiliar.

unceremonious /ʌnserɪˈməʊnɪəs/ a. informal; abrupt in manner, lacking courtesy.

uncertain /ʌnˈsɜːt(ə)n/ a. not certain; not to be depended on; changeable. **uncertainty** n.

uncle /ˈʌŋk(ə)l/ n. parent's brother or brother-in-law; sl. pawnbroker. **Uncle Sam** colloq. US government.

unclean /ʌnˈkliːn/ a. not clean, foul; ceremonially impure.

uncommon /ʌnˈkɒmən/ a. unusual, remarkable.

uncompromising /ʌnˈkɒmprəmaɪzɪŋ/ a. refusing compromise; unyielding, inflexible.

unconcern /ʌnkənˈsɜːn/ n. freedom from anxiety; indifference, apathy.

unconscionable /ʌnˈkɒnʃənəb(ə)l/ a. having no conscience; not right or reasonable, excessive.

unconscious /ʌnˈkɒnʃəs/ **1** a. not aware (of); not conscious; done etc. without conscious intention. **2** n. the part of the mind not normally accessible to consciousness.

unconsidered /ʌnkənˈsɪdəd/ a. disregarded; not based on consideration.

uncork /ʌnˈkɔːk/ v.t. draw cork from (bottle); colloq. give vent to (feelings).

uncouple /ʌnˈkʌp(ə)l/ v.t. release from couples or coupling.

uncouth /ʌnˈkuːθ/ a. awkward, clumsy, boorish.

uncover /ʌnˈkʌvə(r)/ v. remove cover or covering from; lay bare, disclose; take off one's hat or cap.

unction /ˈʌŋkʃ(ə)n/ n. anointing with oil as religious rite or symbol; thing used in anointing; fervent or sympathetic quality in words or tone caused by or causing deep emotion; pretence of this.

unctuous /ˈʌŋktjʊəs/ a. full of (esp. simulated) unction; greasy.

uncut /ʌnˈkʌt/ a. not cut; (of book) with leaves not cut open or margins not trimmed; (of film) not censored; (of diamond) not shaped; (of fabric) with loops of pile not cut.

undeceive /ʌndɪˈsiːv/ v.t. free from deception or mistake.

undeniable /ʌndɪˈnaɪəb(ə)l/ a. that cannot be denied or disputed.

under /ˈʌndə(r)/ **1** prep. in or to position lower than, below; inferior to, less than; subjected to, undergoing, liable to; governed, controlled, or bound by; in accordance with; in the time of. **2** adv. in or to lower place or subordinate position. **3** a. lower. **4** undermost a.

underarm /ˈʌndərɑːm/ a. Crick. etc. (of bowling) with arm below shoulder-level.

underbelly /ˈʌndəbelɪ/ n. under surface of animal etc. esp. as vulnerable to attack.

underbid /ʌndəˈbɪd/ v. make lower bid than; bid too little (on).

undercarriage /'ʌndəkærɪdʒ/ n. landing-gear of aircraft; supporting framework of vehicle etc.

undercliff /'ʌndəklɪf/ n. terrace or lower cliff formed by landslip.

underclothes /'ʌndəkləʊðz/ n.pl. (also **underclothing**) clothes worn under others, esp. next to skin.

undercoat /'ʌndəkəʊt/ n. layer of paint under another; (in animals) coat of hair under another.

undercover /ʌndə'kʌvə(r)/ a. surreptitious, spying esp. by working among those observed.

undercroft /'ʌndəkrɒft/ n. crypt.

undercurrent /'ʌndəkʌrənt/ n. current flowing below surface; suppressed or underlying activity or force etc.

undercut /ʌndə'kʌt/ v.t (past & p.p. -cut) sell or work at lower price than; strike (golf etc. ball) to make it rise high. 2 n. under-side of sirloin.

underdog /'ʌndədɒg/ n. loser in fight etc.; person in state of subjection or inferiority.

underdone /ʌndə'dʌn/ a. lightly or insufficiently cooked.

underemployed /ʌndərɪm'plɔɪd/ a. not fully occupied.

underestimate 1 /ʌndə'restɪmeɪt/ v.t. form too low an estimate of. 2 /ʌndə'restɪmət/ n. estimate that is too low.

underfelt /'ʌndəfelt/ n. felt for laying under carpet.

underfoot /ʌndə'fʊt/ adv. under one's feet; into state of subjection or inferiority.

undergarment /'ʌndəgɑːmənt/ n. piece of underclothing.

undergo /ʌndə'gəʊ/ v.t. (past -went; p.p. -gone /-'gɒn/) be subjected to, endure.

undergraduate /ʌndə'grædjʊət/ n. member of university who has not taken first degree.

underground 1 /ʌndə'graʊnd/ adv. below surface of ground; in(to) secrecy or hiding. 2 /'ʌndəgraʊnd/ a. situated underground; secret or hidden. 3 /'ʌndəgraʊnd/ n. underground railway; secret group or activity esp. aiming at subversion.

undergrowth /'ʌndəgrəʊθ/ n. shrubs or small trees growing under large ones.

underhand /ʌndə'hænd/ a. secret, deceptive; *Crick.* etc. underarm.

underlay 1 /ʌndə'leɪ/ v.t. (past & p.p. -laid) lay thing under (another) to support or raise. 2 /'ʌndəleɪ/ n. thing laid under another, esp. carpet.

underlie /ʌndə'laɪ/ v.t. (past -lay; p.p. -lain) lie under (stratum etc.); *fig.* be basis of, exist beneath superficial aspect of.

underline 1 /ʌndə'laɪn/ v.t. draw line under (words etc.); emphasize. 2 /'ʌndəlaɪn/ n. line placed under word or illustration.

underling /'ʌndəlɪŋ/ n. (usu. *derog.*) subordinate.

undermanned /ʌndə'mænd/ a. having too few people as crew or staff.

undermine /ʌndə'maɪn/ v.t. make excavation under; wear away base of; injure or wear out etc. insidiously or secretly or imperceptibly.

underneath /ʌndə'niːθ/ 1 *prep.* at or to lower place than, below. 2 *adv.* at or to lower place; inside. 3 n. lower surface or part.

underpants /'ʌndəpænts/ n.pl. undergarment for lower body and part of legs.

underpass /'ʌndəpɑːs/ n. road etc. passing under another.

underpin /ʌndə'pɪn/ v.t. place masonry etc. support under; support, strengthen.

underprivileged /ʌndə'prɪvɪlɪdʒd/ a. less privileged than others; not enjoying normal living standard or rights.

underrate /ʌndə'reɪt/ v.t. have too low an opinion of.

underseal /'ʌndəsiːl/ v.t. seal underpart of (esp. motor vehicle against rust etc.).

under-secretary /ʌndə'sekrɪtərɪ/ n. subordinate official, esp. junior minister or senior civil servant.

undersell /ʌndə'sel/ v.t. (past & p.p. -sold) sell at lower price than.

undershoot /ʌndə'ʃuːt/ v.i. (past & p.p. -shot) (of aircraft) land short of (runway etc.).

undershot /'ʌndəʃɒt/ a. (of wheel) turned by water flowing under it.

undersigned /ʌndə'saɪnd/ a. whose signature is appended.

undersized /'ʌndəsaɪzd/ a. of less than usual size.

understaffed /ʌndə'stɑːft/ a. having too few staff.

understand /ʌndə'stænd/ v. (past & p.p. **-stood** /-'stʊd/) comprehend, perceive meaning of; know how to deal with; infer, esp. from information received; take for granted.

understanding 1 n. intelligence; ability to understand; agreement, thing agreed upon. 2 a. having understanding or insight; sympathetic.

understate /ʌndə'steɪt/ v.t. express in restrained terms; represent as being less than it really is. **understatement** n.

understudy /'ʌndəstʌdɪ/ 1 n. person who studies another's role or duties so as to act in his absence. 2 v.t. study (role etc.) thus; act as understudy to.

undertake /ʌndə'teɪk/ v.t. (past **-took** /-'tʊk/; p.p. **-taken**) agree to perform; make oneself responsible for; engage in; accept obligation (to do); guarantee, affirm that.

undertaker /'ʌndəteɪkə(r)/ n. person who professionally makes arrangements for funerals.

undertaking /ʌndə'teɪkɪŋ/ n. work etc. undertaken; enterprise; promise; /'ʌn-/ management of funerals.

undertone /'ʌndətəʊn/ n. subdued tone, underlying quality or feeling.

undertow /'ʌndətəʊ/ n. current below sea surface in opposite direction to surface current.

undervalue /ʌndə'væljuː/ v.t. value insufficiently.

underwater /ʌndə'wɔːtə(r)/ 1 a. situated or done under water. 2 adv. under water.

underwear /'ʌndəweə(r)/ n. underclothes.

underweight /ʌndə'weɪt/ a. below normal or suitable weight.

underworld /'ʌndəwɜːld/ n. those who live by organized crime and immorality; *Myth.* abode of the dead.

underwrite /ʌndə'raɪt/ v.t. (past **-wrote**; p.p. **-written**) sign and accept liability under (insurance policy); accept (liability) thus; undertake to finance or support.

underwriter /'ʌndəraɪtə(r)/ n. insurer, esp. of shipping.

undesirable /ʌndɪ'zaɪərəb(ə)l/ 1 a. unpleasant, objectionable. 2 n. undesirable person.

undies /'ʌndiz/ n.pl. colloq. (esp. women's) underclothes.

undo /ʌn'duː/ v.t. (past **-did**; p.p. **-done** /-'dʌn/) unfasten and open; annul; ruin prospects or reputation or morals of.

undone 1 p.p. of **undo**. 2 a. not done.

undoubted /ʌn'daʊtɪd/ a. certain, not questioned.

undress 1 /ʌn'dres/ v. take off one's clothes; take off clothes of. 2 /'ʌndres/ n. ordinary dress opposed to full dress or uniform; casual or informal dress.

undue /ʌn'djuː/ a. excessive, disproportionate; improper. **unduly** adv.

undulate /'ʌndjʊleɪt/ v.i. have wavy motion or look. **undulation** n.; **undulatory** a.

unduly: see **undue**.

undying /ʌn'daɪɪŋ/ a. immortal.

unearth /ʌn'ɜːθ/ v.t. discover by search or in course of digging or rummaging.

unearthly /ʌn'ɜːθlɪ/ a. supernatural; mysterious; colloq. absurdly early.

uneasy /ʌn'iːzɪ/ a. disturbed or uncomfortable in body or mind.

unemployable /ʌnɪm'plɔɪəb(ə)l/ a. unfitted by character etc. for paid employment.

unemployed /ʌnɪm'plɔɪd/ a. temporarily out of work; lacking employment; not used.

unemployment /ʌnɪm'plɔɪmənt/ n. lack of employment. **unemployment benefit** payment made by State to unemployed worker.

unequivocal /ʌnɪ'kwɪvək(ə)l/ a. not ambiguous, plain, unmistakable.

UNESCO /juː'neskəʊ/ abbr. United Nations Educational, Scientific, and Cultural Organization.

unexampled /ʌnɪg'zɑːmp(ə)ld/ a. without precedent.

unexceptionable /ʌnɪk'sepʃənəb(ə)l/ a. with which no fault can be found.

unexceptional /ʌnɪk'sepʃən(ə)l/ a. not out of the ordinary.

unfaithful /ʌn'feɪθfʊl/ a. not faithful, esp. adulterous.

unfeeling /ʌn'fiːlɪŋ/ a. lacking sensitivity, unsympathetic, cruel.

unfit /ʌn'fɪt/ 1 a. not fit, unsuitable; in

poor health. **2** *v.t.* make unsuitable (*for*).

unflappable /ʌnˈflæpəb(ə)l/ *a.* colloq. imperturbable.

unfledged /ʌnˈfledʒd/ *a.* inexperienced; not fledged.

unfold /ʌnˈfəʊld/ *v.* open out; reveal; become opened out; develop.

unfortunate /ʌnˈfɔːtʃʊnət/ **1** *a.* unlucky; unhappy; ill-advised. **2** *n.* unfortunate person.

unfrock /ʌnˈfrɒk/ *v.t.* deprive of ecclesiastical status.

unfurl /ʌnˈfɜːl/ *v.* unroll, spread out.

ungainly /ʌnˈɡeɪnlɪ/ *a.* awkward, clumsy, ungraceful.

unget-at-able /ʌnɡetˈætəb(ə)l/ *a.* colloq. inaccessible.

ungodly /ʌnˈɡɒdlɪ/ *a.* impious, wicked; colloq. outrageous, dreadful.

ungovernable /ʌnˈɡʌvənəb(ə)l/ *a.* uncontrollable, unruly.

ungracious /ʌnˈɡreɪʃəs/ *a.* not kindly or courteous.

unguarded /ʌnˈɡɑːdɪd/ *a.* incautious, thoughtless; not guarded.

unguent /ˈʌŋɡjʊənt/ *n.* ointment.

ungulate /ˈʌŋɡjʊlət/ **1** *a.* hoofed. **2** *n.* hoofed mammal.

unhallowed /ʌnˈhæləʊd/ *a.* unconsecrated; not sacred; wicked.

unhand /ʌnˈhænd/ *v.t.* take one's hands off.

unhappy /ʌnˈhæpɪ/ *n.* not happy; unfortunate; unsuccessful.

unhealthy /ʌnˈhelθɪ/ *a.* not in good health; harmful to health; unwholesome; *sl.* dangerous to life.

unheard-of /ʌnˈhɜːdɒv/ *a.* unprecedented.

unhinge /ʌnˈhɪndʒ/ *v.t.* derange, disorder (mind).

unholy /ʌnˈhəʊlɪ/ *a.* profane, wicked; colloq. awful, dreadful.

uni- *in comb.* having or composed of one.

unicameral /juːnɪˈkæmər(ə)l/ *a.* having one legislative chamber.

UNICEF /ˈjuːnɪsef/ *abbr.* United Nations Children's Fund.

unicellular /juːnɪˈseljʊlə(r)/ *a.* consisting of a single cell.

unicorn /ˈjuːnɪkɔːn/ *n.* mythical animal resembling horse, with single horn projecting from its forehead.

unicycle /ˈjuːnɪsaɪk(ə)l/ *n.* one-wheeled pedal-propelled vehicle.

unification /juːnɪfɪˈkeɪʃ(ə)n/ *n.* unifying or being unified.

uniform /ˈjuːnɪfɔːm/ **1** *a.* unvarying; plain, unbroken; conforming to same standard or rule. **2** *n.* distinctive clothing worn by members of same school or organization etc. **3** *uniformity* *n.*

unify /ˈjuːnɪfaɪ/ *v.t.* reduce to unity or uniformity.

unilateral /juːnɪˈlætər(ə)l/ *a.* done by or affecting one side only.

unimpeachable /ʌnɪmˈpiːtʃəb(ə)l/ *a.* giving no opportunity for censure.

uninviting /ʌnɪnˈvaɪtɪŋ/ *a.* unattractive, repellent.

union /ˈjuːnɪən/ *n.* uniting, being united; whole resulting from combination of parts or members; trade union; marriage; concord, agreement; **Union** general social club and debating society at some universities. **Union Jack** national flag of UK with combined crosses of 3 patron saints.

unionist /ˈjuːnɪənɪst/ *n.* member of trade union, advocate of trade unions or of union, esp. supporter of maintenance of union between Britain and Northern Ireland. **unionism** *n.*

unionize /ˈjuːnɪənaɪz/ *v.t.* bring under trade-union organization or rules.

unique /juːˈniːk/ *a.* being the only one of its kind; having no like or equal or parallel. □ See page 666.

unisex /ˈjuːnɪseks/ *a.* designed in a style suitable for either sex.

unison /ˈjuːnɪs(ə)n/ *n.* coincidence in pitch; combination of voices or instruments at same pitch. **in unison** at same pitch, *fig.* in agreement or harmony.

unit /ˈjuːnɪt/ *n.* individual thing or person or group regarded as complete; quantity chosen as standard for expressing other quantities; smallest share in unit trust; device with specified function in complex mechanism; piece of furniture for fitting with others like it or made of complementary parts; group with special function in an organization. **unit trust** company investing in varied stocks the combined contributions from many persons.

Unitarian /juːnɪˈteərɪən/ *n.* member of religious body maintaining that God is one person not Trinity. **Unitarianism** n.

unitary /' juːnɪtərɪ/ a. of unit(s); marked by unity or uniformity.

unite /juːˈnaɪt/ v. join together; make or become one, combine; consolidate; agree, co-operate (in). **United Kingdom** Great Britain and Northern Ireland; **United Nations** international peace-seeking organization; **United States (of America)** republic in N. America.

unity /'juːnɪtɪ/ n. oneness, being one or single or individual; due interconnection of parts; harmony between persons etc.; thing forming complex whole; Math. the number one.

universal /juːnɪˈvɜːs(ə)l/ a. of or belonging to or used or done by etc. all persons or things in world or in class concerned; applicable to all cases. **universal coupling, joint**, one transmitting power by a shaft at any selected angle. **universality** /-'sæl-/ n.

universe /'juːnɪvɜːs/ n. all existing things; all creation; all mankind.

university /juːnɪˈvɜːsɪtɪ/ n. educational institution instructing or examining students in many branches of advanced learning, and conferring degrees; members of this collectively.

unkempt /ʌnˈkempt/ a. dishevelled, untidy, neglected-looking.

unleash /ʌnˈliːʃ/ v.t. free from leash or restraint; set free in order to pursue or attack etc.

unless /ʌnˈles/ conj. if not; except when.

unlettered /ʌnˈletəd/ a. illiterate.

unlike /ʌnˈlaɪk/ a. & adv. not like, different(ly).

unlikely /ʌnˈlaɪklɪ/ a. improbable; unpromising.

unlisted /ʌnˈlɪstɪd/ a. not included in list, esp. of Stock Exchange prices or of telephone numbers.

unload /ʌnˈləʊd/ v.t. remove cargo or anything carried or conveyed from; remove (cargo); remove charge from (gun); relieve of burden; fig. get rid of.

unlock /ʌnˈlɒk/ v.t. release lock of; fig. disclose (secret etc.).

unlooked-for /ʌnˈlʊktfɔː(r)/ a. unexpected.

unlucky /ʌnˈlʌkɪ/ a. not lucky or fortunate or successful; wretched; bringing bad luck; ill-judged.

unman /ʌnˈmæn/ v.t. deprive of courage or self-control etc.

unmannerly /ʌnˈmænəlɪ/ a. rude; without good manners.

unmask /ʌnˈmɑːsk/ v. remove mask from; expose true character of; take off one's mask.

unmentionable /ʌnˈmenʃənəb(ə)l/ a. not fit to be mentioned; unspeakable.

unmistakable /ʌnmɪˈsteɪkəb(ə)l/ a. that cannot be mistaken or doubted.

unmitigated /ʌnˈmɪtɪgeɪtɪd/ a. not modified; absolute.

unnatural /ʌnˈnætʃər(ə)l/ a. contrary or doing violence to nature; lacking natural feelings; artificial, forced.

unnecessary /ʌnˈnesəserɪ/ a. not necessary; more than necessary.

unnerve /ʌnˈnɜːv/ v.t. deprive of strength or resolution etc.

UNO abbr. United Nations Organization.

unofficial /ʌnəˈfɪʃ(ə)l/ a. not officially authorized or confirmed; (of strike) not formally approved by strikers' trade union.

unparalleled /ʌnˈpærəleld/ a. having no parallel or equal.

unparliamentary /ʌnpɑːləˈmentərɪ/ a. contrary to parliamentary usage. **unparliamentary language** oaths, abuse.

unpick /ʌnˈpɪk/ v.t. undo stitching of.

unplaced /ʌnˈpleɪst/ a. not placed as one of the first three in race etc.

unpleasant /ʌnˈplez(ə)nt/ a. disagreeable.

unpopular /ʌnˈpɒpjʊlə(r)/ a. not in popular favour, disliked.

unpractised /ʌnˈpræktɪst/ a. not experienced or skilled, not put into practice.

unprecedented /ʌnˈpresɪdentɪd/ a. for which there is no precedent, unparalleled, novel.

unprincipled /ʌnˈprɪnsɪp(ə)ld/ a. not having or based on sound or honest principles of conduct.

unprintable /ʌnˈprɪntəb(ə)l/ a. too indecent or libellous etc. to be printed.

unprofessional /ʌnprəˈfeʃən(ə)l/ a. not professional; not worthy of member of profession.

unprofitable /ʌnˈprɒfɪtəb(ə)l/ a. without profit; serving no purpose.

unqualified /ʌnˈkwɒlɪfaɪd/ a. not qualified or competent; not modified or limited.

unquestionable /ʌnˈkwestʃənəb(ə)l/ a. that cannot be questioned or doubted.

unquote /ʌnˈkwəʊt/ v.i. terminate passage that is within quotation-marks.

unravel /ʌnˈræv(ə)l/ v. separate threads of, disentangle; undo, esp. by pulling single thread(s); become or be unravelled.

unreasonable /ʌnˈriːzənəb(ə)l/ a. exceeding the bounds of reason; not guided by or listening to reason.

unrelieved /ʌnrɪˈliːvd/ a. lacking the relief given by contrast or variation.

unremitting /ʌnrɪˈmɪtɪŋ/ a. incessant.

unreservedly /ʌnrɪˈzɜːvɪdlɪ/ adv. without reservation.

unrest /ʌnˈrest/ n. disturbance, turmoil, trouble.

unrivalled /ʌnˈraɪv(ə)ld/ a. having no equal, peerless.

unroll /ʌnˈrəʊl/ v. open out from rolled-up state; display, be displayed.

unruly /ʌnˈruːlɪ/ a. not amenable to rule or discipline; turbulent.

unsaturated /ʌnˈsætʃəreɪtɪd/ a. not saturated; *Chem.* able to combine with hydrogen to form a third substance by joining of molecules.

unsavoury /ʌnˈseɪvərɪ/ a. uninviting; disgusting.

unscathed /ʌnˈskeɪðd/ a. uninjured, unharmed.

unscientific /ʌnsaɪənˈtɪfɪk/ a. not in accordance with scientific principles.

unscrew /ʌnˈskruː/ v.t. unfasten by removing screws, loosen (screw).

unscripted /ʌnˈskrɪptɪd/ a. made or delivered etc. without prepared script.

unscrupulous /ʌnˈskruːpjʊləs/ a. without scruples; unprincipled.

unseat /ʌnˈsiːt/ v.t. remove from seat; dislodge from horseback; depose (MP etc.) from seat.

unseen /ʌnˈsiːn/ **1** a. not seen; invisible; (of translation) to be done without preparation. **2** n. unseen translation.

unselfish /ʌnˈselfɪʃ/ a. not selfish or self-regarding; generous.

unsettled /ʌnˈset(ə)ld/ a. not settled; open to further discussion; liable to change; not paid.

unsex /ʌnˈseks/ v.t. deprive of qualities of one's (esp. female) sex.

unsighted /ʌnˈsaɪtɪd/ a. not yet in sight; prevented from seeing.

unsightly /ʌnˈsaɪtlɪ/ a. unpleasing to look at; ugly.

unsocial /ʌnˈsəʊʃ(ə)l/ a. not social; not suitable for or seeking society.

unsophisticated /ʌnsəˈfɪstɪkeɪtɪd/ a. artless, simple, natural.

unsound /ʌnˈsaʊnd/ a. not sound; unhealthy; rotten; erroneous; unreliable.

unsparing /ʌnˈspeərɪŋ/ a. lavish.

unspeakable /ʌnˈspiːkəb(ə)l/ a. that words cannot express; good or bad beyond description.

unstick /ʌnˈstɪk/ v.t. (past & p.p. -stuck) separate (thing stuck to another). **come unstick** *colloq.* fail.

unstressed /ʌnˈstrest/ a. not subjected to or pronounced with stress.

unstring /ʌnˈstrɪŋ/ v.t. (past & p.p. -strung) remove string(s) of; loosen string(s) of (bow, harp); take (beads etc.) off string.

unstructured /ʌnˈstrʌktʃəd/ a. without structure; informal.

unstudied /ʌnˈstʌdɪd/ a. easy, natural, spontaneous.

unswerving /ʌnˈswɜːvɪŋ/ a. steady, constant.

unthinkable /ʌnˈθɪŋkəb(ə)l/ a. that cannot be imagined or grasped by the mind; *colloq.* highly unlikely or undesirable.

untidy /ʌnˈtaɪdɪ/ a. not tidy, not neat in appearance or habits. **untidiness** n.

until /ʌnˈtɪl/ prep. & conj. = **till¹**.

untimely /ʌnˈtaɪmlɪ/ a. inopportune; premature.

unto /ˈʌntʊ/ prep. arch. to.

untold /ʌnˈtəʊld/ a. not told; not counted; beyond count.

untouchable /ʌnˈtʌtʃəb(ə)l/ n. Hindu of group held to defile higher castes on contact.

untoward /ʌntəˈwɔːd/ a. perverse; awkward; unlucky.

untruth /ʌnˈtruːθ/ n. being untrue; falsehood, lie.

unusual /ʌnˈjuːʒʊəl/ a. not usual; remarkable.

unutterable /ʌnˈʌtərəb(ə)l/ a. above or beyond description.

unvarnished /ʌnˈvɑːnɪʃt/ a. not varnished; plain, direct, simple.

unveil /ʌnˈveɪl/ v.t. withdraw drapery from (new statue etc.) with ceremonies; reveal (secrets etc.).

unwarrantable /ʌnˈwɒrəntəb(ə)l/ a. (also **unwarranted**) unauthorized, unjustified.

unwell /ʌnˈwel/ a. not in good health; indisposed.

unwieldy /ʌnˈwiːldɪ/ a. slow or clumsy of movement; awkward to handle etc. by reason of size or shape or weight.

unwitting /ʌnˈwɪtɪŋ/ a. not knowing, unaware; unintentional.

unworkmanlike /ʌnˈwɜːkmənlaɪk/ a. amateurish.

unworthy /ʌnˈwɜːðɪ/ a. not worthy or befitting the character (of); discreditable; contemptible, base.

unwritten /ʌnˈrɪt(ə)n/ a. not written (down); oral; traditional.

unzip /ʌnˈzɪp/ v. undo zip-fastener of; admit of being unzipped.

up 1 adv. towards or in higher place or state or number; to or in capital or university or place further north or in question etc.; to or in erect or vertical position, out of bed, out of lying or sitting or kneeling posture, in(to) condition of efficiency or activity; (with vbs., usu.) expressing complete or effectual result etc.; colloq. amiss, wrong. 2 prep. upwards along or through or into; at higher part of. 3 a. directed upwards. 4 v. colloq. start (abruptly or unexpectedly) to say or do something; raise, esp. abruptly. 5 **on the up-and-up** colloq. steadily improving, honest(ly); **up against** close to, in(to) contact with, colloq. confronted with; **up against it** colloq. in great difficulties; **up-and-coming** colloq. (of person) making good progress and likely to succeed; **uphill** sloping up, ascending; arduous; **upstairs** up the stairs, to or on or of upper floor of house etc.; **upstream** against flow of stream etc., moving upstream; **up to** until, not more than, equal to, incumbent on, capable of, occupied or

busy with; **uptown** US residential part of town or city; **up with** as int. expr. wish for success of. 6 **upward** a. & adv.; **upwards** adv.

upbeat /ˈʌpbiːt/ 1 n. Mus. unaccented beat. 2 a. optimistic, cheerful.

upbraid /ʌpˈbreɪd/ v.t. chide, reproach.

upbringing /ˈʌpbrɪŋɪŋ/ n. bringing up (of child), education.

up-country /ʌpˈkʌntrɪ/ a. & adv. inland.

update /ʌpˈdeɪt/ v.t. bring up to date.

up-end /ʌpˈend/ v. set or rise up on end.

upgrade /ʌpˈɡreɪd/ v.t. raise in rank etc.

upheaval /ʌpˈhiːv(ə)l/ n. sudden esp. violent change or disturbance.

uphold /ʌpˈhəʊld/ v.t. (past & p.p. **-held**) give support to; maintain, confirm.

upholster /ʌpˈhəʊlstə(r)/ v.t. provide (chair etc.) with textile covering or padding etc. **upholstery** n.

upkeep /ˈʌpkiːp/ n. maintenance in good condition; cost or means of this.

upland /ˈʌplənd/ 1 n. higher part of country. 2 a. of this part.

uplift 1 /ʌpˈlɪft/ v.t. raise. 2 /ˈʌplɪft/ n. colloq. elevating influence.

upon /əˈpɒn/ prep. on.

upper /ˈʌpə(r)/ 1 a. higher in place; situated above; superior in rank or dignity etc. 2 n. upper part of shoe or boot. 3 **on one's uppers** extremely short of money; **upper case** capital letters; **upper crust** colloq. the aristocracy; **upper-cut** hit upwards with arm bent; **the upper hand** mastery, control, advantage; **Upper House** House of Lords or other higher legislative assembly.

uppermost /ˈʌpəməʊst/ 1 a. highest in rank or place. 2 adv. on or to the top.

uppish /ˈʌpɪʃ/ a. colloq. (also **uppity**) self-assertive, arrogant.

upright /ˈʌpraɪt/ 1 a. erect, vertical; (of piano) with vertical frame; strictly honourable or honest. 2 n. post or rod fixed upright, esp. as support to some structure; upright piano.

uprising /ˈʌpraɪzɪŋ/ n. insurrection.

uproar /ˈʌprɔː(r)/ n. tumult, violent disturbance, clamour.

uproarious /ʌpˈrɔːrɪəs/ a. very noisy, with loud laughter.

uproot /ʌpˈruːt/ v.t. pull (plant etc.) up

from ground together with its roots; displace (person) from accustomed location, eradicate.

upset /ʌpˈset/ v. (past & p.p. **-set**) overturn; disturb temper or digestion or composure of. **2** /ˈʌpset/ n. disturbance, surprising result.

upshot /ˈʌpʃɒt/ n. outcome, conclusion.

upside-down /ʌpsaɪdˈdaʊn/ adv. & a. with upper part where lower part should be, inverted; in(to) total disorder.

upstage /ʌpˈsteɪdʒ/ **1** a. & adv. nearer back of theatre stage. **2** v.t. move upstage from (actor) to make him face away from audience; fig. divert attention from (person) to oneself.

upstanding /ʌpˈstændɪŋ/ a. standing up; strong and healthy; honest.

upstart /ˈʌpstɑːt/ **1** n. person who has risen suddenly to prominence or who behaves arrogantly. **2** a. that is an upstart; of upstarts.

upswept /ˈʌpswept/ a. (of hair) combed to top of head.

upswing /ˈʌpswɪŋ/ n. upward movement or trend.

uptake /ˈʌpteɪk/ n. colloq. understanding.

uptight /ʌpˈtaɪt/ a. colloq. nervously tense, angry; rigidly conventional.

upturn 1 /ʌpˈtɜːn/ v.t. turn up or upside-down. **2** /ˈʌptɜːn/ n. upward trend, improvement.

uranium /jʊəˈreɪnɪəm/ n. radioactive heavy grey metallic element capable of nuclear fission and used as source of nuclear energy.

urban /ˈɜːbən/ a. of or living or situated in city or town. **urban guerrilla** terrorist operating in cities etc. by kidnapping etc.

urbane /ɜːˈbeɪn/ a. courteous; suave. **urbanity** /-ˈbæn-/ n.

urbanize /ˈɜːbənaɪz/ v.t. render urban; remove rural quality of (district). **urbanization** n.

urchin /ˈɜːtʃɪn/ n. mischievous child, esp. boy; sea-urchin.

ureter /jʊəˈriːtə(r)/ n. either of two ducts conveying urine into bladder.

urethra /jʊəˈriːθrə/ n. (pl. **-ras**) duct through which urine is discharged from bladder.

urge /ɜːdʒ/ **1** v.t. drive forcibly, impel;

entreat or exhort earnestly or persistently; advocate pressingly. **2** n. urging impulse or tendency; strong desire.

urgent /ˈɜːdʒ(ə)nt/ a. requiring immediate action or attention; importunate. **urgency** n.

uric /ˈjʊərɪk/ a. of urine.

urinal /jʊəˈraɪn(ə)l/ n. place or receptacle for urinating.

urinary /ˈjʊərɪnərɪ/ a. of or relating to urine.

urinate /ˈjʊərɪneɪt/ v.i. discharge urine. **urination** n.

urine /ˈjʊərɪn/ n. fluid secreted by kidneys and discharged from bladder.

urn n. vase with foot, esp. as used for storing ashes of the dead; large vessel with tap in which water is kept hot or tea etc. made.

ursine /ˈɜːsaɪn/ a. of or like a bear.

us pron. obj. case of **we**.

US abbr. United States (of America).

USA abbr. United States of America.

usage /ˈjuːsɪdʒ/ n. manner of using or treating; customary practice, established use (esp. of word).

use 1 /juːz/ v. cause to act or serve for purpose as instrument or material; put into operation, avail oneself of; treat in specified manner; in p.p. second-hand; in past (usu. /juːst/) had as one's or its constant or frequent practice or state (to do, be, etc.); in p.p. (/juːst/) familiar by habit, accustomed, to. **2** /juːs/ n. using, employment; right or power of using; serviceability, utility, purpose for which thing can be used; custom, usage; ritual and liturgy of church or diocese etc. **3 make use of** use, benefit from; **no use** of no value or utility; **use up** consume, find use for (remainder).

useful /ˈjuːsfʊl/ a. of use, serviceable; producing or able to produce good results; colloq. creditable, efficient.

useless /ˈjuːslɪs/ a. serving no purpose, unavailing.

user-friendly /juːzəˈfrendlɪ/ a. (of computer or program etc.) easy for user to understand and operate.

usher /ˈʌʃə(r)/ **1** n. person who shows people to their seats in hall or theatre etc.; door-keeper of court etc.; officer walking before person of rank. **2** v.t. act as usher to; announce or show in etc.

usherette /ʌʃəˈret/ *n.* female usher, esp. in cinema.

USSR *abbr.* Union of Soviet Socialist Republics.

usual /ˈjuːʒʊəl/ *a.* such as commonly occurs, customary; habitual. **as usual** as commonly occurs.

usurer /ˈjuːʒərə(r)/ *n.* person who practises usury.

usurp /juːˈzɜːp/ *v.* seize or assume power or right etc. wrongfully. **usurpation** *n.*

usury /ˈjuːʒərɪ/ *n.* lending of money at interest, esp. at exorbitant or illegal rate. **usurious** /juːˈzjʊərɪəs/ *a.*

utensil /juːˈtens(ə)l/ *n.* implement or vessel, esp. in domestic use.

uterus /ˈjuːtərəs/ *n.* (*pl.* **-ri** /-raɪ/) womb. **uterine** /-raɪn/ *a.*

utilitarian /juːtɪlɪˈteərɪən/ **1** *a.* designed to be useful rather than attractive; of utilitarianism. **2** *n.* adherent of utilitarianism.

utilitarianism *n.* doctrine that actions are justified if they are useful or for benefit of majority.

utility /juːˈtɪlɪtɪ/ **1** *n.* usefulness, profitableness; useful thing. **2** *a.* severely practical and standardized; made or serving for utility. **3** **utility room** room containing large fixed domestic appliances.

utilize /ˈjuːtɪlaɪz/ *v.t.* make use of, turn to account, use. **utilization** *n.*

utmost /ˈʌtməʊst/ **1** *a.* farthest, extreme; that is such in highest degree. **2** *n.* the utmost point or degree etc. **3** **do one's utmost** do all that one can.

Utopia /juːˈtəʊpɪə/ *n.* imaginary perfect social and political system. **Utopian** *a.*

utter[1] /ˈʌtə(r)/ *a.* complete, total, unqualified. **uttermost** *a.*

utter[2] /ˈʌtə(r)/ *v.t.* express in words; emit audibly; put (esp. forged money) into circulation.

utterance /ˈʌtərəns/ *n.* uttering; power or manner of speaking; thing spoken.

U-turn /ˈjuːtɜːn/ *n.* turning a vehicle to face in opposite direction without reversing; reversal of policy.

UV *abbr.* ultraviolet.

uvula /ˈjuːvjʊlə/ *n.* (*pl.* **-lae** /-liː/) fleshy part of soft palate hanging above throat. **uvular** *a.*

uxorious /ʌkˈsɔːrɪəs/ *a.* excessively fond of one's wife.

V

V, v, Roman numeral 5.

V *abbr.* volt(s).

v. *abbr.* verse; versus; very; *vide.*

vac *n. colloq.* vacation.

vacancy /ˈveɪkənsɪ/ *n.* being vacant; unoccupied post or place etc.

vacant /ˈveɪkənt/ *a.* not filled or occupied; not mentally active, showing no interest. **vacant possession** ownership of unoccupied house etc.

vacate /vəˈkeɪt/ *v.t.* leave vacant; cease to occupy.

vacation /vəˈkeɪʃ(ə)n/ *n.* fixed period of cessation from work esp. in lawcourts and universities; *US* holiday; vacating or being vacated.

vaccinate /ˈvæksɪneɪt/ *v.t.* inoculate with vaccine. **vaccination** *n.*

vaccine /ˈvæksiːn/ *n.* preparation used for inoculation, esp. one of cowpox virus giving immunity to smallpox.

vacillate /ˈvæsɪleɪt/ *v.i.* fluctuate in opinion or resolution. **vacillation** *n.*; **vacillator** *n.*

vacuity /vəˈkjuːɪtɪ/ *n.* vacuousness.

vacuous /ˈvækjʊəs/ *a.* vacant, unintelligent.

vacuum /ˈvækjʊəm/ **1** *n.* (*pl.* **-cua** or **-cuums**) space entirely devoid of matter; space or vessel from which air has been completely or partly removed by pump etc.; absence of normal or previous content; *colloq.* (*pl.* **-cuums**) vacuum cleaner. **2** *v. colloq.* use vacuum cleaner (on). **3 vacuum brake** brake worked by exhaustion of air; **vacuum cleaner** apparatus for removing dust etc. by suction; **vacuum flask** vessel with double wall enclosing vacuum so that liquid in inner receptacle retains its temperature; **vacuum-packed** sealed after partial removal of air; **vacuum tube** containing near-vacuum for free passage of electric current.

vagabond /ˈvægəbɒnd/ **1** *n.* wanderer, esp. idle one. **2** *a.* wandering, having no settled habitation or home.

vagary /ˈveɪgərɪ/ *n.* caprice, eccentric act or idea.

vagina /vəˈdʒaɪnə/ *n.* (*pl.* **-nae** /-niː/ or **-nas**) canal joining womb and vulva of female mammal. **vaginal** *a.*

vagrant /ˈveɪgrənt/ **1** *n.* person without settled home or regular work. **2** *a.* wandering, roving. **3 vagrancy** *n.*

vague /veɪg/ *a.* not clearly expressed or perceived, uncertain, ill-defined; not clear-thinking; inexact, indefinite.

vain *a.* conceited, proud (*of*); empty, of no effect, unavailing. **in vain** without result or success.

vainglory /veɪnˈglɔːrɪ/ *n.* extreme vanity; boastfulness. **vainglorious** *a.*

valance /ˈveɪləns/ *n.* short curtain round frame or canopy of bedstead or over window etc.

vale *n.* valley.

valediction /vælɪˈdɪkʃ(ə)n/ *n.* bidding farewell; words used in this. **valedictory** *a.*

valence[1] /ˈveɪləns/ *n. Chem.* combining- or replacing-power of an atom as compared with hydrogen atom.

valence[2] var. of **valance.**

valency /ˈveɪlənsɪ/ *n.* unit of combining-power of an atom; this power.

valentine /ˈvæləntaɪn/ *n.* (usu. anonymous) letter or card sent to person of opposite sex on St. Valentine's day (14 Feb.); sweetheart chosen on that day.

valerian /vəˈlɪərɪən/ *n.* any of various kinds of flowering herb.

valet /ˈvælɪt/ **1** *n.* man's personal servant. **2** *v.* act as valet (to).

valetudinarian /vælɪtjuːdɪˈneərɪən/ **1** *n.* person who is of poor health or unduly anxious about his health. **2** *a.* that is a valetudinarian.

valiant /ˈvælɪənt/ *a.* brave, courageous.

valid /ˈvælɪd/ *a.* sound, defensible; having legal force. **validity** *n.*

validate /ˈvælɪdeɪt/ *v.t.* make valid, ratify. **validation** *n.*

valise /vəˈliːz/ *n.* travelling-bag, suitcase.

valley /ˈvælɪ/ *n.* long depression or hollow between hills; any valley-like hollow.

valour /ˈvælə(r)/ *n.* courage, esp. in battle. **valorous** *a.*

valuable /ˈvæljʊəb(ə)l/ **1** *a.* of great value or price or worth. **2** *n.* (usu. in *pl.*) valuable thing.

valuation /væljʊˈeɪʃ(ə)n/ *n.* estimation (esp. by professional valuer) of thing's worth; estimated value.

value /'vælju:/ 1 *n*. worth, desirability; qualities on which these depend; worth as estimated; amount of money or goods for which thing can be exchanged in open market; equivalent of a thing; what represents or is represented by or may be substituted for a thing; something well worth the money spent; ability of a thing to serve a purpose or cause an effect; in *pl*. one's principles or standards, one's judgement of what is valuable or important in life; *Mus*. duration of sound signified by note; *Math*. amount denoted by algebraical term or expression. 2 *v.t.* estimate value of, appraise; have high or specified opinion of, attach importance to. 3 **value added tax** tax on amount by which value of an article has been increased at each stage of its production; **value judgement** subjective estimate of quality etc.

valuer *n*. person who estimates or assesses values professionally.

valve *n*. automatic or other device for controlling passage of fluid through pipe etc., usu. to allow movement in one direction only; membranous part of organ etc. allowing flow of blood etc. in one direction only; thermionic valve; device to vary length of tube in trumpet etc.; each of two shells of oyster or mussel etc.

valvular /'vælvjʊlə(r)/ *a*. having valve(s); having form or function of valve.

vamoose /və'mu:s/ *v.i. US sl*. depart hurriedly.

vamp¹ 1 *n*. upper front part of boot or shoe. 2 *v*. repair or make *up* or produce (as) by patching or piecing together; improvise musical accompaniment (to).

vamp² *colloq*. 1 *n*. unscrupulous flirt; woman who exploits men. 2 *v*. allure or exploit (man); act as vamp.

vampire /'væmpaɪə(r)/ *n*. ghost or reanimated corpse supposed to suck blood of sleeping persons; person who preys on others; blood-sucking bat.

van¹ *n*. covered vehicle or closed railway-truck for conveyance of goods etc.

van² *n*. vanguard, forefront.

vanadium /və'neɪdɪəm/ *n*. hard grey metallic element used to strengthen steel.

vandal /'vænd(ə)l/ *n*. wilful or ignorant destroyer or damager of works of art or other property. **vandalism** *n*.

vandalize /'vændəlaɪz/ *v.t.* destroy or damage wilfully.

Vandyke /væn'daɪk/ *n*. **Vandyke beard** small neat pointed beard; **Vandyke brown** deep rich brown.

vane *n*. weathercock; blade of windmill or propeller etc.

vanguard /'vænɡɑːd/ *n*. foremost part of army or fleet etc. moving forward or onward; leaders of movement or of opinion etc.

vanilla /və'nɪlə/ *n*. extract obtained from vanilla-pod or synthetically and used to flavour ices and chocolate etc.; tropical climbing orchid with fragrant flowers; fruit of this. **vanilla-pod** fruit of vanilla.

vanish /'vænɪʃ/ *v.i.* disappear; cease to exist. **vanishing-point** point at which receding parallel lines viewed in perspective appear to meet.

vanity /'vænɪtɪ/ *n*. desire for admiration because of one's personal attainments or attractions; futility, unreal thing; ostentatious display. **vanity bag, case,** bag containing small mirror and make-up etc.

vanquish /'væŋkwɪʃ/ *v.t. literary* conquer, overcome.

vantage /'vɑːntɪdʒ/ *n*. advantage, esp. in tennis. **vantage-point** place affording good view.

vapid /'væpɪd/ *a*. insipid, flat. **vapidity** *n*.

vaporize /'veɪpəraɪz/ *v*. convert or be converted into vapour. **vaporization** *n*.

vaporous /'veɪpərəs/ *a*. in the form of or consisting of vapour.

vapour /'veɪpə(r)/ *n*. moisture or other substance diffused or suspended in air; *Phys*. gaseous form of a normally liquid or solid substance. **vapour trail** trail of condensed water from aircraft etc. **vapoury** *a*.

variable /'veərɪəb(ə)l/ 1 *a*. that can be varied or adapted; apt to vary, not constant, unsteady; *Math*. (of quantity) indeterminate, able to assume different numerical values. **2** *n.* variable thing or quantity. **3 variability** *n.*

variance /ˈveərɪəns/ *n.* difference of opinion; dispute; discrepancy.

variant /ˈveərɪənt/ **1** *a.* differing in form or details from that named or considered; differing thus among themselves. **2** *n.* variant form or spelling or type etc.

variation /veərɪˈeɪʃ(ə)n/ *n.* varying; departure from former or normal condition etc. or from standard or type; extent of this; thing that varies from a type; *Mus.* tune or theme repeated in changed or elaborated form.

varicose /ˈværɪkəʊs/ *a.* (of vein etc.) permanently and abnormally dilated.

variegated /ˈveərɪəgeɪtɪd/ *a.* marked with irregular patches of different colours. **variegation** *n.*

variety /vəˈraɪətɪ/ *n.* diversity; absence of monotony or uniformity; collection of different things; class of things differing in some common qualities from the rest of a larger class to which they belong; specimen or member of such class; different form or kind or sort (*of*); *Biol.* grouping within subspecies. **variety entertainment, show,** mixed series of dances and songs and comedy acts etc.

various /ˈveərɪəs/ *a.* of several kinds; diverse; several.

varlet /ˈvɑːlɪt/ *n. arch.* menial, rascal.

varnish /ˈvɑːnɪʃ/ **1** *n.* resinous solution or other preparation applied to surface to produce hard shiny transparent coating. **2** *v.t.* coat with varnish; gloss (over); disguise.

varsity /ˈvɑːsɪtɪ/ *n. colloq.* university.

vary /ˈveərɪ/ *v.* change, make or become different, modify, diversify; be different or of different kinds.

vas deferens /væs ˈdefərenz/ (*pl.* **vasa deferentia** /ˈveɪsə defəˈrentɪə/ sperm duct of testicle.

vascular /ˈvæskjʊlə(r)/ *a.* of or containing vessels for conveying blood or sap etc.

vase /vɑːz/ *n.* vessel, usu. tall and circular, used as ornament or container for flowers etc.

vasectomy /vəˈsektəmɪ/ *n.* removal of part of each vas deferens esp. for sterilization of patient.

Vaseline /ˈvæsəliːn/ *n.* (**P**) type of petroleum jelly used in ointments etc.

vassal /ˈvæs(ə)l/ *n.* humble dependant; *hist.* holder of land by feudal tenure.

vast /vɑːst/ *a.* immense, huge, very great.

vat *n.* large tank or other vessel, esp. for holding liquids or something in liquid in process of brewing or tanning or dyeing etc.

VAT *abbr.* value added tax.

vaudeville /ˈvɔːdəvɪl/ *n.* variety entertainment.

vault **1** *n.* arched roof; vaultlike covering; underground room as place of storage; underground burial-chamber; act of vaulting. **2** *v.* leap or spring, esp. while resting on hand(s) or with help of pole; spring over thus; make in form of vault; furnish with vaults.

vaunt *n.* & *v. arch.* boast.

VC *abbr.* Victoria Cross.

VD *abbr.* venereal disease.

VDT *abbr.* visual display terminal.

VDU *abbr.* visual display unit.

veal *n.* calf's flesh as food.

vector /ˈvektə(r)/ *n. Math.* quantity having both magnitude and direction; carrier of disease. **vectorial** /-ˈtɔːr-/ *a.*

veer *v.* change direction, esp. (of wind) in direction of sun's course; change in opinion or course.

vegan /ˈviːgən/ **1** *a.* eating no animals or animal products. **2** *n.* vegan person.

vegetable /ˈvedʒətəb(ə)l/ **1** *n.* (esp. herbaceous) plant or part of one used for food; person living uneventful and monotonous life; person incapable of normal intellectual activity through injury etc. **2** *a.* of or of the nature of or derived from or concerned with or comprising plants.

vegetarian /vedʒɪˈteərɪən/ **1** *n.* person who eats no animal products or none obtained by destruction of animal life. **2** *a.* of vegetarian(s); living on or consisting of vegetables. **3 vegetarianism** *n.*

vegetate /ˈvedʒɪteɪt/ *v.i.* lead dull monotonous life; grow as plants do.

vegetation /vedʒɪˈteɪʃ(ə)n/ *n.* plants collectively; plant life.

vegetative /ˈvedʒɪtətɪv/ *a.* concerned with growth and development rather than sexual reproduction; of vegetation.

vehement /'vi:əmənt/ a. showing or caused by strong feeling, ardent. **vehemence** n.

vehicle /'vi:ək(ə)l/ n. carriage or conveyance used on land or in space; thing or person used as medium for thought or feeling or action; liquid etc. as medium for suspending pigments or drugs etc. **vehicular** /vɪ'hɪkjʊlə(r)/ a.

veil /veɪl/ 1 n. piece of usu. more or less transparent material attached to woman's hat or otherwise forming part of head-dress, esp. to conceal face or protect against sun or dust etc.; piece of linen etc. as part of nun's head-dress; curtain, esp. that separating sanctuary in Jewish Temple; disguise, pretext. 2 v.t. cover (as) with veil; partially conceal. 3 **beyond the veil** in the unknown state of after death; **draw a veil over** avoid discussing or drawing attention to; **take the veil** become nun.

vein /veɪn/ n. any of the tubes carrying blood from all parts of body back to heart; *pop.* any blood-vessel; rib of leaf or insect's wing; streak or stripe of different colour in wood or marble or cheese etc.; fissure in rock filled with ore; distinctive character or tendency, mood. **veined** a.; **veiny** a.

Velcro /'velkrəʊ/ n. (P) fastener for clothes etc. consisting of 2 strips of nylon fabric which adhere when pressed together.

veld /velt/ n. (also **veldt**) S. *Afr.* open country.

vellum /'veləm/ n. fine parchment orig. from calf's skin; manuscript on this; smooth writing-paper imitating vellum.

velocity /və'lɒsɪtɪ/ n. speed esp. of motion in particular direction.

velour /və'lʊə(r)/ n. (also **velours**) woven fabric with plushlike pile.

velvet /'velvɪt/ 1 n. closely woven fabric with thick short pile on one side; furry skin growing on antler. 2 a. of or like or soft as velvet. 3 **on velvet** in advantageous or prosperous position; **velvet glove** outward gentleness cloaking inflexibility. 4 **velvety** a.

velveteen /velvə'ti:n/ n. cotton fabric with pile like velvet.

Ven. *abbr.* Venerable.

venal /'vi:n(ə)l/ a. that may be bribed; (of action etc.) characteristic of venal person. **venality** n.

vend v. sell; offer (esp. small articles) for sale. **vending-machine** machine for automatic retail of small articles. **vendor** n.

vendetta /ven'detə/ n. blood feud; prolonged bitter hostility.

veneer /və'nɪə(r)/ 1 v.t. cover (wood) with thin layer of finer wood. 2 n. thin coating; superficial disguise.

venerable /'venərəb(ə)l/ a. entitled to veneration on account of age or character etc.; title of archdeacon. **venerability** n.

venerate /'venəreɪt/ v.t. regard with deep respect. **veneration** n.

venereal /və'nɪərɪəl/ a. of sexual desire or intercourse; (of disease) communicated by sexual intercourse with infected person.

Venetian /və'ni:ʃ(ə)n/ 1 a. of Venice. 2 n. native or dialect of Venice. 3 **Venetian blind** window-blind of horizontal slats that may be turned to admit or exclude light.

vengeance /'vendʒ(ə)ns/ n. retribution exacted for wrong to oneself or to person etc. whose cause one supports. **with a vengeance** in extreme degree, thoroughly, violently.

vengeful /'vendʒfʊl/ a. seeking vengeance, vindictive.

venial /'vi:nɪəl/ a. (of sin or fault) pardonable, not mortal. **veniality** n.

venison /'venɪs(ə)n/ n. deer's flesh as food.

Venn diagram *Math.* diagram using overlapping and intersecting circles etc. to show relationships between sets.

venom /'venəm/ n. poisonous fluid of snakes or scorpions etc.; malignity, virulence of feeling or language or conduct. **venomous** a.

venous /'vi:nəs/ a. of or full of or contained in veins.

vent[1] n. small outlet or inlet for air or smoke etc.; anus esp. of lower animals; outlet, free passage, free play. 2 v.t. give vent or free expression to.

vent[2] n. slit in garment, esp. in back of coat.

ventilate /'ventɪleɪt/ v.t. cause air to circulate in (room etc.); make public, discuss freely. **ventilation** n.

ventilator /'ventɪleɪtə(r)/ n. appliance or aperture for ventilating room etc.

ventral /'ventr(ə)l/ a. of or on abdomen.

ventricle /'ventrɪk(ə)l/ n. cavity of body; hollow part of organ, esp. brain or heart.

ventricular /ven'trɪkjulə(r)/ a. of or shaped like ventricle.

ventriloquism /ven'trɪləkwɪz(ə)m/ n. act or art of producing vocal sounds without visible movement of lips. **ventriloquist** n.; **ventriloquize** v.i.

venture /'ventʃə(r)/ 1 n. undertaking of risk, commercial speculation; 2 v. dare, not be afraid; dare to go; take risks, expose to risk, stake. 3 **at a venture** at random, without previous consideration; **Venture Scout** senior Scout.

venturesome /'ventʃəsəm/ a. disposed to take risks.

venue /'venju:/ n. appointed meeting-place, esp. for match; Law district in which case is to be tried.

veracious /və'reɪʃəs/ a. truthful, true. **veracity** /-'ræs-/ n.

veranda /və'rændə/ n. open roofed platform along side of house.

verb n. part of speech which expresses action or occurrence or being.

verbal /'vɜ:b(ə)l/ a. of or concerned with words; oral, not written; Gram. of (the nature of) a verb; (of translation) literal.

verbalism /'vɜ:bəlɪz(ə)m/ n. minute attention to words.

verbalize /'vɜ:bəlaɪz/ v. express in words; be verbose. **verbalization** n.

verbatim /vɜ:'beɪtɪm/ adv. & a. in exactly the same words.

verbena /vɜ:'bi:nə/ n. plant of a genus of herbs and small shrubs.

verbiage /'vɜ:bɪɪdʒ/ n. needless accumulation of words.

verbose /vɜ:'bəʊs/ a. using or expressed in more words than are needed. **verbosity** /-'bɒs-/ n.

verdant /'vɜ:d(ə)nt/ a. abounding in green foliage; green. **verdancy** n.

verdict /'vɜ:dɪkt/ n. decision of jury; decision, judgement.

verdigris /'vɜ:dɪgrɪs/ n. green deposit forming on copper or brass.

verdure /'vɜ:dʒə(r)/ n. green vegetation; greenness of this.

verge[1] n. brink, border; grass edging of path etc.

verge[2] v.i. incline downwards or in specified direction. **verge on** border on, approach closely.

verger /'vɜ:dʒə(r)/ n. caretaker and attendant in church; official carrying rod etc. before dignitaries of cathedral or university etc.

verify /'verɪfaɪ/ v.t. establish truth or correctness of by examination or demonstration; fulfil, bear out. **verification** n.

verily /'verɪlɪ/ adv. arch. in truth, really.

verisimilitude /verɪsɪ'mɪlɪtju:d/ n. appearance of truth or reality.

veritable /'verɪtəb(ə)l/ a. real, properly or correctly so called.

verity /'verɪtɪ/ n. true statement; truth.

vermicelli /vɜ:mɪ'tʃelɪ/ n. pasta made in long slender threads.

vermicide /'vɜ:mɪsaɪd/ n. substance used to kill worms.

vermiform /'vɜ:mɪfɔ:m/ a. worm-shaped. **vermiform appendix** small blind tube extending from caecum in man and some other mammals.

vermilion /və'mɪljən/ 1 n. brilliant scarlet pigment made esp. from cinnabar; colour of this. 2 a. of this colour.

vermin /'vɜ:mɪn/ n. (usu. treated as pl.) mammals and birds injurious to game or crops etc.; noxious or parasitic worms or insects; vile persons.

verminous /'vɜ:mɪnəs/ a. of the nature of or infested with vermin.

vermouth /'vɜ:məθ/ n. wine flavoured with aromatic herbs.

vernacular /və'nækjulə(r)/ 1 n. language or dialect of the country; language of a particular class or group; homely speech. 2 a. (of language) of one's own country, not learned or foreign.

vernal /'vɜ:n(ə)l/ a. of or in or appropriate to season of spring.

vernier /'vɜ:nɪə(r)/ n. small movable graduated scale for obtaining fractional parts of subdivisions on fixed scale of barometer etc.

veronica /və'rɒnɪkə/ n. kind of flowering herb or shrub.

verruca /və'ru:kə/ n. (pl. -**cae** /-si:/ or -**cas**) wart or similar protuberance, esp. on foot.

versatile /'vɜːsətaɪl/ a. turning easily or readily from one subject or occupation etc. to another, showing facility in varied subjects, many-sided. **versatility** /-'tɪl-/ n.

verse n. metrical composition, poetry; stanza of metrical lines; metrical line; numbered subdivision of Bible chapter.

versed /vɜːst/ a. experienced or skilled in.

versicle /'vɜːsɪk(ə)l/ n. short sentence, esp. each of series in liturgy said or sung by minister or priest alternately with response of congregation.

versify /'vɜːsɪfaɪ/ v. turn into or express in verse; compose verses. **versification** n.

version /'vɜːʃ(ə)n/ n. particular form of statement or account etc.; particular rendering of work etc. in another language.

verso /'vɜːsəʊ/ n. (pl. **-sos**) left-hand page of open book, back of leaf.

versus /'vɜːsəs/ prep. against.

vertebra /'vɜːtɪbrə/ n. (pl. **-brae** /-briː/) each segment of backbone. **vertebral** a.

vertebrate /'vɜːtɪbrət/ **1** a. having spinal column. **2** n. vertebrate animal.

vertex /'vɜːteks/ n. (pl. **-tices** /-tɪsiːz/ or **-texes**) highest point, top, apex; meeting-point of lines that form an angle.

vertical /'vɜːtɪk(ə)l/ **1** a. at right angles to plane of horizon; in direction from top to bottom of picture etc.; of or at vertex. **2** n. vertical line or plane. **3 vertical take-off** taking off without needing a long runway.

vertiginous /vɜː'tɪdʒɪnəs/ a. of or causing vertigo.

vertigo /'vɜːtɪgəʊ/ n. dizziness.

vervain /'vɜːveɪn/ n. herbaceous plant of verbena genus, esp. one with small blue or white or purple flowers.

verve n. enthusiasm, energy, vigour.

very /'veri/ **1** adv. in high degree, to great extent, extremely. **2** a. real, true, properly so called etc. **3 very high frequency** in range 30–300 megahertz; **very well** formula of consent or approval.

vesicle /'vesɪk(ə)l/ n. small bladder or blister or bubble.

vespers /'vespəz/ n.pl. evening service.

vessel /'ves(ə)l/ n. hollow receptacle esp. for liquid; ship or boat, esp. large one; duct or canal etc. holding or conveying blood or sap etc.

vest 1 n. knitted or woven undergarment worn on upper part of body; US & Commerc. waistcoat. **2** v.t. furnish (person with powers, property, etc.). **3 vested interests, rights**, etc. interests or rights the possession of which is established by right or by long association; **vest in** (of property, rights, etc.) come into possession of (person); **vest** (property, powers) **in person** confer formally on him an immediate fixed right of present or future possession of; **vest-pocket** of size suitable for the (waistcoat-)pocket.

vestal virgin /'vest(ə)l/ virgin consecrated to Vesta, Roman goddess of hearth and home, and vowed to chastity.

vestibule /'vestɪbjuːl/ n. antechamber, lobby; entrance-hall.

vestige /'vestɪdʒ/ n. trace, evidence; slight amount, particle; Biol. part or organ now degenerate but well developed in ancestors. **vestigial** a.

vestment /'vestmənt/ n. any of official garments worn by priest etc. during divine service etc.; (esp. ceremonial) garment.

vestry /'vestri/ n. room or part of church for keeping of vestments etc.; hist. meeting of parishioners usu. in vestry for parochial business, body of parishioners meeting thus.

vet colloq. **1** n. veterinary surgeon. **2** v.t. submit to careful and critical examination; examine or treat (animal).

vetch n. plant of pea family largely used for fodder.

veteran /'vetərən/ n. person who has grown old in service or occupation, esp. in armed forces; US ex-serviceman. **veteran car** one made before 1916, or before 1905.

veterinarian /ˌvetərɪ'neərɪən/ n. veterinary surgeon.

veterinary /'vetmərɪ/ **1** a. of or for diseases and injuries of domestic and other animals, or their treatment. **2** n. veterinary surgeon. **3 veterinary sur-**

geon person skilled in veterinary treatment.

veto /ˈviːtəʊ/ **1** *n.* (*pl.* **-toes**) constitutional right to prohibit passing or putting in force of enactment or resolution etc.; exercise of this; prohibition. **2** *v.t.* exercise veto against; forbid.

vex *v.t.* anger by slight or petty annoyance, irritate; *arch.* grieve, afflict. **vexed question** question much discussed.

vexation /vekˈseɪʃ(ə)n/ *n.* vexing or being vexed; annoying or distressing thing.

vexatious /vekˈseɪʃəs/ *a.* such as to cause vexation; *Law* not having sufficient grounds for action and seeking only to annoy defendant.

VHF *abbr.* very high frequency.

via /ˈvaɪə/ *prep.* by way of, through.

viable /ˈvaɪəb(ə)l/ *a.* capable of living or surviving; (of plan etc.) feasible, esp. from economic standpoint.

viaduct /ˈvaɪədʌkt/ *n.* bridgelike structure carrying railway or road over valley or river etc.

vial /ˈvaɪəl/ *n.* small glass bottle.

viands /ˈvaɪəndz/ *n.pl.* articles of food.

viaticum /vaɪˈætɪkəm/ *n.* Eucharist given to person dying or in danger of dying.

vibes /vaɪbz/ *n.pl. colloq.* vibraphone, vibrations.

vibrant /ˈvaɪbrənt/ *a.* vibrating, thrilling *with*, resonant. **vibrancy** *n.*

vibraphone /ˈvaɪbrəfəʊn/ *n.* percussion instrument of metal bars with motor-driven resonators and metal tubes giving vibrato effect.

vibrate /vaɪˈbreɪt/ *v.* move unceasingly to and fro, esp. rapidly; (of sound) have quivering or pulsating effect; quiver; (cause to) swing to and fro periodically, oscillate. **vibratory** /ˈvaɪ-/ *a.*

vibration /vaɪˈbreɪʃ(ə)n/ *n.* vibrating; in *pl.* mental (esp. occult) influence.

vibrato /vɪˈbrɑːtəʊ/ *n.* (*pl.* **-tos**) *Mus.* tremulous effect in pitch of singing or of playing stringed or wind instrument.

vibrator /vaɪˈbreɪtə(r)/ *n.* thing that vibrates, esp. *Med.* electric or other instrument used in massage.

vicar /ˈvɪkə(r)/ *n.* incumbent of C. of E. parish where tithes formerly belonged

to chapter or religious house or layman. **Vicar of Christ** the Pope.

vicarage /ˈvɪkərɪdʒ/ *n.* vicar's house.

vicarial /vɪˈkeərɪəl/ *a.* of or serving as vicar.

vicarious /vɪˈkeərɪəs/ *a.* experienced imaginatively through another person; acting or done etc. for another; deputed, delegated.

vice[1] *n.* evil, esp. grossly immoral, habit or conduct; bad habit; particular form of depravity; defect, blemish. **vice squad** police department enforcing laws against prostitution etc.

vice[2] *n.* instrument with two jaws in which things may be gripped and held steady.

vice[3] /ˈvaɪsɪ/ *prep.* in place of, in succession to.

vice- *in comb.* person acting in place of, assistant, person next in rank to.

vice-chancellor /vaɪsˈtʃɑːnsələ(r)/ *n.* deputy chancellor (esp. of university, discharging most administrative duties).

vicegerent /vaɪsˈdʒerənt/ **1** *a.* exercising delegated power, deputy. **2** *n.* deputy.

viceregal /vaɪsˈriːg(ə)l/ *a.* of viceroy.

vicereine /ˈvaɪsreɪn/ *n.* viceroy's wife; woman viceroy.

viceroy /ˈvaɪsrɔɪ/ *n.* ruler on behalf of sovereign in colony or province etc.

vice versa /vaɪsɪˈvɜːsə/ with order of terms changed, the other way round.

Vichy water /ˈviːʃɪ/ effervescent mineral water from Vichy in France.

vicinage /ˈvɪsɪnɪdʒ/ *n.* neighbourhood, surrounding district; relation of neighbours.

vicinity /vɪˈsɪnɪtɪ/ *n.* surrounding district; nearness in place. **in the vicinity (of)** near.

vicious /ˈvɪʃəs/ *a.* of the nature of or addicted to vice; bad-tempered, spiteful. **vicious circle** unbroken sequence of reciprocal cause and effect or action and reaction, fallacious reasoning by which proposition is proved by conclusion drawn from it.

vicissitude /vɪˈsɪsɪtjuːd/ *n.* change of circumstances, esp. of condition or fortune.

victim /ˈvɪktɪm/ *n.* person killed or made to suffer by cruelty or oppression; one who suffers injury or hardship etc.; living creature sacrificed to deity etc.

victimize /ˈvɪktɪmaɪz/ v.t. single out (person) for punishment or unfair treatment; make (person etc.) a victim. **victimization** n.

victor /ˈvɪktə(r)/ n. conqueror; winner of contest.

Victoria Cross /vɪkˈtɔːrɪə/ decoration awarded for conspicuous bravery in armed services.

Victorian /vɪkˈtɔːrɪən/ 1 a. of time of Queen Victoria. 2 n. person of this time.

victorious /vɪkˈtɔːrɪəs/ a. conquering, triumphant; marked by victory.

victory /ˈvɪktərɪ/ n. winning of battle or war or contest.

victual /ˈvɪt(ə)l/ 1 n. (usu. in pl.) food, provisions. 2 v. supply with victuals, lay in supply of victuals; eat victuals.

victualler /ˈvɪtələ(r)/ n. person who furnishes victuals. **licensed victualler** innkeeper licensed to sell alcoholic liquor etc.

vicuña /vɪˈkjuːnə/ n. S. Amer. mammal with fine silky wool; cloth made from its wool; imitation of this.

vide /ˈvɪdeɪ/ v.t. in imper. refer to, consult. [L]

videlicet /vɪˈdeliset/ adv. that is to say; namely.

video /ˈvɪdɪəʊ/ 1 a. relating to recording of images on videotape or playing or broadcasting of these. 2 n. (pl. **-os**) such recording or broadcasting; apparatus for recording or playing videotapes; a videotape.

videotape /ˈvɪdɪəʊteɪp/ 1 n. magnetic tape suitable for recording television pictures and sound. 2 v.t. make recording of (broadcast material) with this.

vie v.i. (partic. **vying**) contend or compete (with) for superiority.

view /vjuː/ 1 n. inspection by eye or mind; what is seen, scene, prospect; picture etc. of view; range of vision; mental survey, mental attitude; opinion. 2 v. survey with eyes or mind; form mental impression or judgement of; watch television. 3 **in view of** having regard to, considering; **on view** open to inspection; **viewdata** news and information service from computer source to which TV screen is connected by telephone link; **viewfinder** part of camera showing extent of picture;

viewpoint point of view, standpoint; **with a view to** with the hope or intention of.

viewer /ˈvjuːə(r)/ n. television-watcher; device for looking at film transparencies etc.

vigil /ˈvɪdʒɪl/ n. keeping awake during time usually given to sleep, watchfulness; eve of festival, esp. eve that is a fast.

vigilance /ˈvɪdʒɪləns/ n. watchfulness; caution. **vigilance committee** US self-appointed committee for maintenance of order. **vigilant** a.

vigilante /vɪdʒɪˈlæntɪ/ n. member of vigilance committee or similar body.

vignette /viːˈnjet/ n. illustration not in definite border; photograph etc. with background gradually shaded off; short description, character sketch.

vigour /ˈvɪɡə(r)/ n. activity and strength of body or mind; healthy growth, animation. **vigorous** a.

Viking /ˈvaɪkɪŋ/ n. Scandinavian trader and pirate of 8th-10th cc.

vile a. disgusting; morally base, depraved; colloq. abominably bad.

vilify /ˈvɪlɪfaɪ/ v.t. speak ill of, defame. **vilification** n.

villa /ˈvɪlə/ n. detached or semi-detached small house in residential district; country residence; house for holiday-makers at seaside etc.

village /ˈvɪlɪdʒ/ n. group of houses etc. in country district, larger than hamlet and smaller than town.

villager /ˈvɪlɪdʒə(r)/ n. inhabitant of village.

villain /ˈvɪlən/ n. person guilty or capable of great wickedness; colloq. criminal.

villainous /ˈvɪlənəs/ a. worthy of a villain; colloq. abominably bad.

villainy /ˈvɪlənɪ/ n. villainous behaviour.

villein /ˈvɪlɪn/ n. hist. feudal tenant entirely subject to lord or attached to manor. **villeinage** n.

vim n. colloq. vigour, energy.

vinaigrette /vɪnɪˈɡret/ n. salad dressing of oil and wine vinegar.

vindicate /ˈvɪndɪkeɪt/ v.t. clear of suspicion; establish existence or merits or justice etc. of. **vindication** n.; **vindicator** n.; **vindicatory** a.

vindictive /vɪn'dɪktɪv/ *a.* tending to seek revenge; punitive.

vine *n.* trailing or climbing woody-stemmed plant bearing grapes; any trailing or climbing plant.

vinegar /'vɪnɪgə(r)/ *n.* sour liquid produced by fermentation of wine or malt liquors etc.; sour behaviour or character. **vinegary** *a.*

vinery /'vaɪnərɪ/ *n.* vine greenhouse.

vineyard /'vɪnjɑːd/ *n.* plantation of grape-vines, esp. for wine-making.

vingt-et-un /væter'ɜ̃/ *n.* pontoon¹. [F]

vinous /'vaɪnəs/ *a.* of or like or due to or addicted to wine.

vintage /'vɪntɪdʒ/ **1** *n.* grape-harvest; season of this; season's produce of grapes; wine made from this; wine of high quality kept separate from others; year etc. when thing was made; thing made etc. in particular year etc. **2** *a.* of high quality; of a past season. **3 vintage car** car made between 1917 and 1930.

vintner /'vɪntnə(r)/ *n.* wine-merchant.

vinyl /'vaɪnɪl/ *n.* any of a group of plastics made by polymerization.

viol /'vaɪəl/ *n.* medieval stringed musical instrument similar in shape to violin.

viola¹ /vɪ'əʊlə/ *n.* kind of large violin.

viola² /'vaɪələ/ *n.* any of group of plants including violet and pansy, esp. a cultivated hybrid.

violate /'vaɪəleɪt/ *v.t.* disregard, fail to comply with; transgress; infringe; break in upon; rape. **violation** *n.*; **violator** *n.*

violence /'vaɪələns/ *n.* being violent; violent conduct or treatment; unlawful exercise of physical force. **do violence to** act contrary to, outrage.

violent /'vaɪələnt/ *a.* involving great physical force; intense, vehement; (of death) resulting from external force or from poison.

violet /'vaɪələt/ **1** *n.* plant with usu. blue, purple, or white flowers; colour at opposite end of spectrum from red, blue with slight admixture of red; violet colour or paint or clothes etc. **2** *a.* of this colour.

violin /vaɪə'lɪn/ *n.* musical instrument with 4 strings of treble pitch played with bow; player of this. **violinist** *n.*

violist¹ /vɪ'əʊlɪst/ *n.* viol-player.

violist² /'vaɪəʊlɪst/ *n.* viola-player.

violoncello /vaɪələn'tʃeləʊ/ *n.* (*pl.* **-os**) cello.

VIP *abbr.* very important person.

viper /'vaɪpə(r)/ *n.* small venomous snake; malignant or treacherous person.

virago /vɪ'rɑːgəʊ/ *n.* (*pl.* **-gos**) fierce or abusive woman.

viral /'vaɪər(ə)l/ *a.* of or caused by a virus.

virgin /'vɜːdʒɪn/ **1** *n.* person, esp. woman, who has had no sexual intercourse. **2** *a.* of or befitting or being a virgin; not previously used etc. **3 the Virgin** Christ's mother, the Blessed Virgin Mary. **4 virginity** *n.*

virginal /'vɜːdʒɪn(ə)l/ **1** *a.* that is or befits a virgin. **2** *n.* (usu. in *pl.*) legless spinet in box.

Virginia creeper /və'dʒɪnɪə/ vine cultivated for ornament.

Virgo /'vɜːgəʊ/ *n.* sixth sign of zodiac.

virile /'vɪraɪl/ *a.* having masculine vigour or strength; of or having procreative power; of man as opp. woman or child. **virility** /-'rɪl-/ *n.*

virtual /'vɜːtjʊəl/ *a.* that is such for practical purposes though not in name or according to strict definition.

virtue /'vɜːtjuː/ *n.* moral goodness; particular moral excellence; chastity, esp. of woman; good quality or influence, efficacy. **by, in, virtue of** on strength or ground of.

virtuoso /vɜːtjʊ'əʊsəʊ/ *n.* (*pl.* **-si** /-siː/ or **-sos**) person skilled in technique of an art, esp. music. **virtuosity** /-'ɒs-/ *n.*

virtuous /'vɜːtjʊəs/ *a.* possessing or showing moral rectitude, chaste.

virulent /'vɪrʊlənt/ *a.* poisonous; malignant, (of disease) extremely violent; bitter. **virulence** *n.*

virus /'vaɪərəs/ *n.* any of numerous kinds of very simple organisms smaller than bacteria, able to cause diseases; *fig.* poison, source of disease.

visa /'viːzə/ *n.* (*pl.* **-sas**) endorsement on passport etc. permitting holder to enter or leave a country. **visaed** /-zəd/ *a.*

visage /'vɪzɪdʒ/ *n. literary* face.

vis-à-vis /viːzɑː'viː/ **1** *prep.* in relation to, opposite to. **2** *adv.* facing one another. **3** *n.* person or thing facing another. [F]

viscera /'vɪsərə/ *n.pl.* internal organs of the body. **visceral** *a.*

viscid /'vɪsɪd/ *a.* glutinous, sticky. **viscidity** *n.*

viscose /'vɪskəʊz/ *n.* viscous solution of cellulose used in making rayon etc.

viscosity /vɪ'skɒsɪtɪ/ *n.* quality or degree of being viscous.

viscount /'vaɪkaʊnt/ *n.* British nobleman ranking between earl and baron. **viscountcy** *n.*

viscountess /'vaɪkaʊntɪs/ *n.* viscount's wife or widow; woman with own rank of viscount.

viscous /'vɪskəs/ *a.* glutinous, sticky; semifluid, not flowing freely.

visibility /vɪzɪ'bɪlɪtɪ/ *n.* being visible; range or possibility of vision as determined by conditions of light and atmosphere.

visible /'vɪzɪb(ə)l/ *a.* capable of being seen, that can be seen; in sight; apparent, open, obvious.

vision /'vɪʒ(ə)n/ *n.* act or faculty of seeing; sight; thing or person etc. seen in dream or trance; thing seen vividly in imagination; imaginative insight; foresight, sagacity in planning; person etc. of unusual beauty; what is seen on TV screen.

visionary /'vɪʒənərɪ/ **1** *a.* given to seeing visions or to indulging in fanciful theories; existing only in vision or in imagination, unpractical. **2** *n.* visionary person.

visit /'vɪzɪt/ **1** *v.* go or come to see (person, place, etc., or also.) socially or on business etc.; reside temporarily with or at; be visitor; (of disease, calamity, etc.) come upon, attack; *Bibl.* punish, inflict punishment for (sin) *upon* person. **2** *n.* act of visiting, temporary residence with person or at place; occasion of going *to* doctor etc., formal or official call.

visitant /'vɪzɪt(ə)nt/ *n.* (supernatural) visitor.

visitation /vɪzɪ'teɪʃ(ə)n/ *n.* official visit of inspection etc.; divine dispensation of punishment or reward.

visitor /'vɪzɪtə(r)/ *n.* person etc. who visits person or place; migratory bird.

visor /'vaɪzə(r)/ *n.* movable part of helmet covering face; shield at top of vehicle windscreen to protect eyes from bright sunshine; *hist.* mask.

vista /'vɪstə/ *n.* view or prospect, esp. through avenue of trees or other long narrow opening; mental view of long succession of events etc.

visual /'vɪzjʊəl/ *a.* of or concerned with or used in seeing; received through sight. **visual display terminal, unit,** device displaying output or input of computer on screen.

visualize /'vɪzjʊəlaɪz/ *v.t.* make visible esp. to one's mind (thing not visible to the eye). **visualization** *n.*

vital /'vaɪt(ə)l/ **1** *a.* of or concerned with or essential to organic life; essential to existence or success etc.; full of life or activity; fatal. **2** *n.* in *pl.* vital parts, e.g. lungs and heart. **3 vital statistics** those relating to births and deaths and health etc., *colloq.* measurements of woman's bust, waist, and hips.

vitality /vaɪ'tælɪtɪ/ *n.* animation, liveliness; ability to sustain life.

vitalize /'vaɪtəlaɪz/ *v.t.* endow with life, infuse with vigour. **vitalization** *n.*

vitamin /'vɪtəmɪn/ *n.* any of a number of substances occurring in certain foodstuffs and essential to health and normal growth etc.

vitaminize /'vɪtəmɪnaɪz/ *v.t.* introduce vitamins into (food).

vitiate /'vɪʃɪeɪt/ *v.t.* impair quality or efficiency of, debase; make invalid or ineffectual. **vitiation** *n.*

viticulture /'vɪtɪkʌltʃə(r)/ *n.* vine-growing.

vitreous /'vɪtrɪəs/ *a.* of or of the nature of glass.

vitrify /'vɪtrɪfaɪ/ *v.* change into glass or glassy substance, esp. by heat. **vitrification** *n.*

vitriol /'vɪtrɪəl/ *n.* sulphuric acid or a sulphate; caustic speech or criticism. **vitriolic** /-'ɒl-/ *a.*

vituperate /vɪ'tjuːpəreɪt/ *v.t.* revile, abuse. **vituperation** *n.*; **vituperative** *a.*

viva[1] /'viːvə/ **1** *int.* 'long live'. **2** *n.* cry of this as salute. [It.]

viva[2] /'vaɪvə/ *n. & v.t.* (*past & p.p.* **vivaed** /-vəd/) *colloq.* viva(-)voce.

vivacious /vɪ'veɪʃəs/ *a.* lively, animated. **vivacity** /vɪ'væsɪtɪ/ *n.*

vivarium /vɪ'veərɪəm/ *n.* (*pl.* **-ria**) place for keeping living animals etc. in natural conditions.

viva voce /'vaɪvə 'vəʊtʃɪ/ oral(ly); oral examination.

viva-voce *v.t.* examine viva voce.

vivid /'vɪvɪd/ *a.* bright; intense; lively; incisive; graphic.

vivify /'vɪvɪfaɪ/ *v.t.* give life to, animate.

viviparous /vɪ'vɪpərəs/ *a.* bringing forth young alive, not egg-laying.

vivisect /'vɪvɪsekt/ *v.t.* perform vivisection on.

vivisection /vɪvɪ'sekʃ(ə)n/ *n.* dissection or other painful treatment of living animals for scientific research.

vivisectionist *n.*

vixen /'vɪks(ə)n/ *n.* she-fox; spiteful woman.

viz. *abbr.* videlicet.

vizier /vɪ'zɪə(r)/ *n.* high administrative official in some Muslim countries.

vocable /'vəʊkəb(ə)l/ *n.* word, esp. with ref. to form not meaning.

vocabulary /və'kæbjʊlərɪ/ *n.* words used by a language or book or branch of science, or author; list of these; person's range of language.

vocal /'vəʊk(ə)l/ *a.* of or concerned with or uttered by the voice; expressing one's feelings freely in speech. **vocal cords** voice-producing part of larynx; **vocal music** music written for or produced by the voice.

vocalic /və'kælɪk/ *a.* of or consisting of vowel(s).

vocalist /'vəʊkəlɪst/ *n.* singer.

vocalize /'vəʊkəlaɪz/ *v.* form (sound) or utter (word) with voice. **vocalization** *n.*

vocation /və'keɪʃ(ə)n/ *n.* divine call to, or sense of fitness for, career or occupation; employment, trade, profession. **vocational** *a.*

vocative /'vɒkətɪv/ **1** *n.* case of noun used in addressing or invoking. **2** *a.* of or in the vocative.

vociferate /və'sɪfəreɪt/ *v.* utter noisily; shout, bawl. **vociferation** *n.*

vociferous /və'sɪfərəs/ *a.* noisy, clamorous; loud and insistent in speech.

vodka /'vɒdkə/ *n.* alcoholic spirit distilled esp. in Russia from rye etc.

vogue /vəʊg/ *n.* prevailing fashion; popular favour. **in vogue** in fashion, generally current; **vogue-word** word currently fashionable.

voice 1 *n.* sound formed in larynx etc.

and uttered by mouth, esp. human utterance in speaking or singing etc.; ability to produce this; use of voice, utterance esp. in spoken words, opinion so expressed; right to express opinion; *Gram.* set of verbal forms showing whether verb is active or passive. **2** *v.t.* give utterance to, express; utter with vibration of vocal cords. **3 voice-over** narration in film not accompanied by picture of speaker.

void 1 *a.* empty, vacant; not valid or binding. **2** *n.* empty space; sense of loss. **3** *v.t.* invalidate; excrete.

voile /vɔɪl/ *n.* thin semi-transparent dress-material.

vol. *abbr.* volume.

volatile /'vɒlətaɪl/ *a.* readily evaporating at ordinary temperature; changeable, flighty, lively; transient.

volatility /-'tɪl-/ *n.*

volatilize /və'lætɪlaɪz/ *v.* turn into vapour. **volatilization** *n.*

vol-au-vent /'vɒləʊvɑ̃/ *n.* (usu. small) round case of puff pastry filled with savoury mixture.

volcanic /vɒl'kænɪk/ *a.* of or like or produced by volcano.

volcano /vɒl'keɪnəʊ/ *n.* (*pl.* -noes) mountain or hill with opening(s) through which ashes and gases and (molten) rocks etc. are or have been periodically ejected.

vole /vəʊl/ *n.* small herbivorous rodent.

volition /və'lɪʃ(ə)n/ *n.* act or faculty of willing. **volitional** *a.*

volley /'vɒlɪ/ **1** *n.* simultaneous discharge of a number of weapons; bullets etc. thus discharged at once; noisy emission (*of* oaths etc.) in quick succession; *Tennis, Footb.,* etc. playing of ball before it touches ground. **2** *v.t.* return or send by volley. **3 volley-ball** game for two teams of 6 sending large ball by hand over net.

volt /vəʊlt/ *n.* unit of electromotive force, difference of potential capable of sending current of one ampere through conductor with resistance of one ohm. **voltmeter** instrument measuring electric potential in volts.

voltage /'vəʊltɪdʒ/ *n.* electromotive force expressed in volts.

volte-face /vɒlt'fɑːs/ *n.* complete change of position in argument or opinion.

voluble /'vɒljʊb(ə)l/ *a.* with vehement or incessant flow of words. **volubility** *n.*

volume /'vɒljuːm/ *n.* set of usu. printed sheets bound together usu. within cover and containing part of a book or one or more books; solid content, bulk; amount or quantity *of*; quantity or power of sound; moving mass *of* water or smoke etc.

volumetric /vɒljʊ'metrɪk/ *a.* of measurement by volume.

voluminous /və'ljuːmɪnəs/ *a.* (of book or writer) running to many volumes or great length; (of drapery etc.) loose or ample.

voluntary /'vɒləntərɪ/ **1** *a.* done or acting or able to act of one's own free will; unpaid; (of institution) supported by voluntary contributions; brought about by voluntary action; controlled by the will. **2** *n.* organ solo played before, during, or after church service.

volunteer /vɒlən'tɪə(r)/ **1** *n.* person who voluntarily offers services or enrols himself for enterprise, esp. for service in any of armed services. **2** *v.* undertake or offer voluntarily; make voluntary offer of one's services.

voluptuary /və'lʌptjʊərɪ/ *n.* person given up to luxury and gratification of senses.

voluptuous /və'lʌptjʊəs/ *a.* of or tending to or occupied with or derived from sensuous or sensual pleasure.

volute /və'ljuːt/ *n.* spiral scroll in stonework as ornament of capital.

vomit /'vɒmɪt/ **1** *v.* eject contents of stomach through mouth; be sick; eject violently; belch forth, spew out. **2** *n.* matter vomited from stomach.

voodoo /'vuːduː/ **1** *n.* use of or belief in religious witchcraft as practised among W. Ind. etc. Blacks. **2** *v.t.* affect by voodoo, bewitch.

voracious /və'reɪʃəs/ *a.* greedy in eating, ravenous. **voracity** /-'ræs-/ *n.*

vortex /'vɔːteks/ *n.* (*pl.* **-tices** /-tɪsiːz/ or **-texes**) whirlpool, whirlwind, whirling motion or mass; thing viewed as swallowing those who approach it. **vortical** *a.*

votary /'vəʊtərɪ/ *n.* person bound by vow(s), esp. to religious life; devotee, ardent follower (*of*). **votaress** *n.*

vote 1 *n.* formal expression of will or opinion in regard to election or passing of law or resolution etc., signified by ballot or show of hands etc.; *the* right to vote; opinion expressed by majority of votes; *the* collective votes given by party etc. **2** *v.* give vote; enact etc. by majority of votes; *colloq.* pronounce by general consent, announce one's proposal (*that*). **3** vote down defeat (proposal) by voting; **vote in** elect by votes.

voter *n.* person entitled to vote.

votive /'vəʊtɪv/ *a.* given or consecrated in fulfilment of vow.

vouch /vaʊtʃ/ *v.i.* answer or be surety *for*.

voucher /'vaʊtʃə(r)/ *n.* document exchangeable for goods or services as token of payment made or promised; document establishing payment of money or truth of accounts.

vouchsafe /vaʊtʃ'seɪf/ *v.t.* condescend to grant or *to do*.

vow /vaʊ/ **1** *n.* solemn promise or engagement, esp. to deity or saint. **2** *v.t.* promise solemnly; *arch.* declare, esp. solemnly.

vowel /'vaʊəl/ *n.* speech-sound produced by vibrations of vocal cords, but without audible friction; letter representing this.

vox populi /vɒks 'pɒpjʊli:/ public opinion, general verdict, popular belief. [L]

voyage /'vɔɪdʒ/ **1** *n.* expedition to a distance by water or air or in space. **2** *v.i.* make voyage.

voyeur /vwɑː'jɜː(r)/ *n.* person who derives sexual gratification from looking at sexual organs or acts of others. **voyeurism** *n.*

vs. *abbr.* versus.

VSO *abbr.* Voluntary Service Overseas.

VTO(L) *abbr.* vertical take-off (and landing).

vulcanite /'vʌlkənaɪt/ *n.* hard black vulcanized rubber.

vulcanize /'vʌlkənaɪz/ *v.t.* make (rubber etc.) stronger and more elastic by treating with sulphur at high temperature. **vulcanization** *n.*

vulgar /'vʌlgə(r)/ *a.* of or characteristic of the common people; coarse; in common use, generally prevalent. **vulgar fraction** fraction expressed by numerator and denominator, not decimally; **the vulgar tongue** native or vernacular language. **vulgarity** /-'gær-/ *n.*

vulgarian /vʌl'geəriən/ *n.* vulgar (esp. rich) person.

vulgarism /'vʌlgərɪz(ə)m/ *n.* word or expression in coarse or uneducated use, instance of coarse or uneducated behaviour.

vulgarize /'vʌlgəraɪz/ *v.t.* affect with vulgarity, spoil by making too common or frequented or well known. **vulgarization** *n.*

Vulgate /'vʌlgeɪt/ *n.* 4th-c. Latin version of Bible.

vulnerable /'vʌlnərəb(ə)l/ *a.* that may be wounded, open to or not proof against attack or injury or criticism etc. **vulnerability** *n.*

vulpine /'vʌlpaɪn/ *a.* of or like fox; crafty, cunning.

vulture /'vʌltʃə(r)/ *n.* large bird of prey feeding chiefly on carrion; rapacious person.

vulva /'vʌlvə/ *n.* external female genitals.

vv. *abbr.* verses.

vying *partic.* of **vie**.

W

W *abbr.* watt(s); west(ern).

w. *abbr.* wicket(s); wide(s); with.

wacky /'wækɪ/ *a. sl.* crazy.

wad /wɒd/ 1 *n.* lump of soft material to keep things apart or in place or to block hole; roll of bank-notes. 2 *v.t.* fix or stuff with wad; stuff or line with wadding.

wadding /'wɒdɪŋ/ *n.* soft material usu. of cotton or wool for stuffing quilts or packing fragile articles in etc.

waddle /'wɒd(ə)l/ 1 *v.i.* walk with short steps and swaying motion. 2 *n.* such walk.

wade 1 *v.* walk through water or other impeding medium; progress slowly or with difficulty (through etc.). 2 *n.* spell of wading.

wader /'weɪdə(r)/ *n.* long-legged water-bird; in *pl.* high waterproof boots.

wadi /'wɒdɪ/ *n.* rocky watercourse in N. Africa etc., dry except in rainy season.

wafer /'weɪfə(r)/ 1 *n.* very thin light crisp biscuit; disc of unleavened bread used in Eucharist; disc of red paper stuck on law papers instead of seal. 2 *v.t.* seal with wafer. 3 **wafer-thin** very thin. 4 **wafery** *a.*

waffle¹ /'wɒf(ə)l/ 1 *n.* aimless verbose talk or writing. 2 *v.i.* indulge in waffle.

waffle² /'wɒf(ə)l/ *n.* small crisp batter-cake. **waffle-iron** utensil for cooking waffles.

waft /wɒft/ 1 *v.* convey or be conveyed smoothly (as) through air or over water. 2 *n.* whiff of perfume etc.

wag 1 *v.* shake or move to and fro. 2 *n.* single wagging motion; facetious person. 3 **wagtail** kind of long-tailed small bird.

wage 1 *n.* in *sing.* or *pl.* employee's regular pay, esp. paid weekly. 2 *v.t.* carry on (war). 3 **wage freeze** ban on wage-increases.

wager /'weɪdʒə(r)/ *n.* & *v.* bet.

waggish /'wægɪʃ/ *a.* playful, facetious.

waggle /'wæg(ə)l/ *v. colloq.* wag.

wagon /'wægən/ *n.* (also **waggon**) 4-wheeled vehicle for heavy loads; open railway truck. **on the wagon** *sl.* abstaining from alcohol.

wagoner /'wægənə(r)/ *n.* (also **waggoner**) driver of wagon.

waif *n.* homeless and helpless person, esp. abandoned child; *Law* object or animal found ownerless.

wail 1 *n.* prolonged plaintive inarticulate cry of pain or grief etc.; sound resembling this. 2 *v.i.* utter wail or persistent lamentations or complaints.

wain *n. poet.* etc. wagon.

wainscot /'weɪnskət/ *n.* wooden panelling or boarding on room-wall.

waist *n.* part of human body between ribs and hips; narrowness marking this; circumference of waist; middle narrower part of anything; part of garment corresponding to waist; bodice, blouse; *Naut.* middle part of (upper deck of) ship. **waistcoat** usu. sleeveless and collarless garment covering upper part of body down to waist and worn under jacket etc.; **waistline** outline or size of waist.

wait 1 *v.* defer action until expected event occurs; pause; await, bide; defer (meal) until someone arrives; act as waiter or attendant. 2 *n.* act or time of waiting; watching for enemy; in *pl.* street singers of Christmas carols. 3 **waiting-list** list of applicants etc. for thing not immediately available; **waiting-room** room for persons to wait in esp. at railway station or surgery; **wait (up)on** await convenience of, be attendant or respectful visitor to.

waiter /'weɪtə(r)/ *n.* man who takes orders and brings food etc. at hotel or restaurant tables. **waitress** *n.*

waive *v.t.* refrain from insisting on or using.

waiver /'weɪvə(r)/ *n. Law* waiving.

wake¹ *v.* (*past* **woke** or **waked**; *p.p.* **woken** or **waked**) cease to sleep, rouse from sleep; *arch.* be awake; disturb with noise; evoke. 2 *n.* (chiefly in Ireland) vigil beside corpse before burial, attendant lamentations and merrymaking; (usu. in *pl.*) annual holiday in (industrial) N. England.

wake² *n.* track left by moving ship etc. on surface of water; turbulent air left by moving aircraft. **in the wake of** following, as result or imitation of.

wakeful /'weɪkfʊl/ *a.* unable to sleep, sleepless, vigilant.

waken /ˈweɪkən/ v. make or become awake.

wale n. weal, ridge on corduroy etc.; *Naut.* broad thick timber along ship's side.

walk /wɔːk/ 1 v. move by lifting and setting down each foot in turn with one foot always on the ground at any time; travel or go on foot, take exercise thus; traverse (distance) in walking; tread floor or surface of; cause to walk with one. 2 n. act of walking; ordinary human gait; slowest gait of animal; person's action in walking; spell or distance of walking; excursion on foot; place or track meant or fit for walking. 3 **walkabout** informal stroll by royal person etc., Aus. Aboriginal's period of wandering; **walking-stick** stick carried or used as support when walking; **walk off with** colloq. steal, win easily; **walk of life** one's occupation; **walk out** depart esp. suddenly or angrily; **walk-out** n.; **walk out on** desert; **walk-over** easy victory; **walk the streets** be prostitute; **walkway** passage or path for walking along.

walker n. person etc. who walks esp. as recreation; framework for person unable to walk unaided.

walkie-talkie /wɔːkɪˈtɔːkɪ/ n. small portable radio transmitting and receiving set.

wall /wɔːl/ 1 n. continuous narrow upright structure of stone or brick etc., enclosing or protecting or separating a house or town or room or field etc.; thing like wall in appearance or effect; outermost layer of animal or plant organ or cell etc. 2 v.t. block *up* with wall; (esp. in *p.p.*) provide or protect with wall, shut *in* or *off* thus. 3 **go to the wall** fare badly in competition; **wall-flower** fragrant garden plant with deep-coloured flowers, colloq. partnerless woman at dance; **wall game** Eton form of football played beside wall; **wallpaper** paper for covering interior walls of rooms.

wallaby /ˈwɒləbɪ/ n. small species of kangaroo.

wallah /ˈwɒlə/ n. Anglo-Ind. person connected with a specified occupation or task; colloq. man, person.

wallet /ˈwɒlɪt/ n. flat case for holding paper money and documents etc.

wall-eye /ˈwɔːlaɪ/ n. eye with iris whitish or streaked etc. or with outward squint. **wall-eyed** a.

wallop /ˈwɒləp/ sl. 1 v.t. thrash, beat. 2 n. whack; beer.

wallow /ˈwɒləʊ/ 1 v.i. roll about in mud or sand or water etc.; take gross delight *in*. 2 n. act of wallowing; place where animals wallow.

wally /ˈwɒlɪ/ n. colloq. foolish or incompetent person.

walnut /ˈwɔːlnʌt/ n. nut with kernel in pair of boat-shaped shells; tree bearing this; its timber used in cabinet-making.

walrus /ˈwɔːlrəs/ n. long-tusked amphibious arctic mammal. **walrus moustache** long thick drooping moustache.

waltz /wɔːlts/ 1 n. dance in triple time performed by couples progressing with smooth sliding steps; music for this. 2 v.i. dance waltz; dance *in* or *out* etc. in joy etc.; move easily or casually.

wampum /ˈwɒmpəm/ n. strings of shell-beads formerly used by N. Amer. Indians for money and ornament etc.

wan /wɒn/ a. pale, colourless, weary-looking.

wand /wɒnd/ n. magician's or music conductor's baton; slender rod or staff carried as sign of office etc.

wander /ˈwɒndə(r)/ v.i. go from place to place without settled route or aim; go aimlessly *in* or *off* etc.; diverge from right way; be unsettled or incoherent in mind or talk etc., be inattentive or delirious, rave. **wanderlust** strong or irresistible desire to travel or wander.

wane 1 v.i. (of moon) decrease in apparent size; decrease in size or splendour, lose power or importance. 2 n. process of waning. 3 **on the wane** declining.

wangle /ˈwæŋg(ə)l/ sl. 1 v.t. obtain or bring about etc. by scheming or contrivance. 2 n. act of wangling.

want /wɒnt/ 1 n. desire for something, thing desired; lack or deficiency *of*; poverty. 2 v. have desire for, wish for possession or presence of; require, need; be without or insufficiently supplied with; be in want (*for*); in *p.p.* suspected of being criminal etc.

wanting /ˈwɒntɪŋ/ a. lacking quality or quantity; unequal to requirements, absent.

wanton /'wɒnt(ə)n/ **1** *a.* licentious, unchaste; unprovoked, reckless, arbitrary; sportive, capricious; luxuriant, wild. **2** *n.* licentious person. **3** *v.i. arch.* be sportive or capricious.

wapiti /'wɒpɪtɪ/ *n.* large N. Amer. deer.

war /wɔ:(r)/ **1** *n.* strife usu. between nations conducted by armed force; hostility between persons; efforts against crime or disease etc. **2** *v.i.* make war, be at war. **3 at war** engaged in war; **be at war. 3 at war** engaged in war; **go to war** begin hostile operations; **war-cry** phrase or name shouted in battle, party catchword; **war-dance** dance performed by primitive peoples before war or after victory; **warhead** explosive head of missile; **war-horse** trooper's horse, *fig.* veteran soldier; **war memorial** monument to those killed in a war; **warmonger** /-mʌŋgə(r)/ person who seeks to cause war; **war-paint** paint put on body esp. by N. Amer. Indians before battle; **war-path** march of N. Amer. Indians to make war (**on the war-path** engaged in conflict, taking hostile attitude); **warship** ship for use in war; **war-widow** woman whose husband has been killed in war.

warble /'wɔ:b(ə)l/ **1** *v.* sing in sweet gentle continuous trilling manner. **2** *n.* warbling sound.

warbler *n.* any of various kinds of small bird.

ward /wɔ:d/ **1** *n.* separate room or division of hospital etc.; administrative division esp. for elections; minor etc. under care of guardian or court; guarding, guardianship; in *pl.* notches and projections in key and lock to prevent opening by wrong key. **2** *v.t.* (usu. with *off*) parry (blow), avert (danger etc.).

wardroom officers' quarters in warship.

warden /'wɔ:d(ə)n/ *n.* president or governor of institution; official with supervisory duties; traffic warden.

warder /'wɔ:də(r)/ *n.* official in charge of prisoners in jail. **wardress** *n.*

wardrobe /'wɔ:drəʊb/ *n.* place, esp. large cupboard, where clothes are kept; room where theatrical costumes and properties are kept; stock of clothes. **wardrobe master, mistress,** person in charge of theatrical wardrobe or costumes.

wardship /'wɔ:dʃɪp/ *n.* tutelage.

ware *n.* articles made for sale, goods, esp. vessels etc. of pottery; in *pl.* things person has for sale.

warehouse /'weəhaʊs/ **1** *n.* building in which goods are stored or shown for sale. **2** *v.t.* store in warehouse.

warfare /'wɔ:feə(r)/ *n.* state of war; campaigning.

warlike /'wɔ:laɪk/ *a.* fond of or skilful in war; military.

warlock /'wɔ:lɒk/ *n. arch.* sorcerer.

warm /wɔ:m/ **1** *a.* of or at fairly high temperature; (of person) at natural temperature or with skin temperature raised by exercise or external heat; (of clothes) serving to keep one warm; hearty, animated, affectionate, passionate; (of reception, welcome, etc.) heartily friendly or vigorously hostile; (of colour) suggesting warmth esp. by presence of red or yellow; (of scent in hunting) fresh and strong. **2** *v.* make or become warm. **3 getting warm** near what is sought; **warm-blooded** (of animals) having blood temperature well above that of environment; **warm-hearted** affectionate, sympathetic; **warming-pan** flat closed vessel holding live coals, formerly used for warming beds; **warm up** make or become warm, reach temperature of efficient working, prepare for performance by exercise or practice.

warmth /wɔ:mθ/ *n.* being warm.

warn /wɔ:n/ *v.t.* put on guard, caution *against*; give timely notice of impending danger or misfortune; give cautionary notice or advice. **warn off** give notice to keep away (from).

warning *n.* what is said or done or occurs to warn person.

warp /wɔ:p/ **1** *v.* make or become crooked or twisted esp. by uneven shrinkage or expansion; distort or pervert (person's mind); suffer such distortion; move (ship etc.) by hauling on rope attached to fixed point. **2** *n.* threads stretched lengthwise in loom to be crossed by weft; contorted state of warped wood etc.; mental perversion or bias; rope used in warping a ship.

warrant /'wɒrənt/ **1** *n.* thing that authorizes an action; written authorization to receive or supply money or goods or services or to carry out arrest or search; certificate of service rank held by warrant-officer. **2** *v.t.* serve as warrant for, justify; guarantee. **warrant-officer** officer of rank between commissioned and non-commissioned officers.

warranty /ˈwɒrəntɪ/ *n.* authority or justification; seller's undertaking that thing sold is his and fit for use etc., often accepting responsibility for repairs needed over a period.

warren /ˈwɒrən/ *n.* piece of land where rabbits breed or abound; densely populated or labyrinthine building or district.

warrior /ˈwɒrɪə(r)/ *n.* person famous or skilled in war; fighting man (esp. of primitive peoples); *attrib.* martial.

wart /wɔːt/ *n.* small round dry growth on skin; protuberance on skin of animal or surface of plant etc. **wart-hog** Afr. wild pig. **warty** *a.*

wary /ˈweərɪ/ *a.* on one's guard; cautious, circumspect.

was: see **be.**

wash /wɒʃ/ **1** *v.* cleanse with liquid; take *away* or *off* or *out* by washing; wash oneself or esp. one's hands (and face); wash clothes; (of fabric or dye) bear washing without damage; *colloq.* bear scrutiny or investigation; moisten, (of water) flow past, beat upon, sweep *over*, surge *against*, carry *along* or *away* etc.; sift (ore) by action of water; brush watery colour over. **2** *n.* washing, being washed; treatment at laundry; quantity of clothes for washing; motion of agitated water or air esp. due to passage of vessel or aircraft; kitchen slops given to pigs; thin or weak or inferior or animals' liquid food; liquid to spread over surface to cleanse or heal or colour. **3** **wash-basin** basin for washing one's hands etc.; **wash down** accompany or follow (food) *with* drink; **washed out** faded by washing, *fig.* limp, enfeebled; **washed up** *sl.* defeated, having failed; **wash one's hands** decline responsibility *of*; **wash out** clean inside of by washing, *colloq.* cancel; **wash-out** breach in railway or road caused by flood, *sl.* complete failure; **wash-stand** piece of furniture for holding wash-basin and soap-dish etc.; **wash up** wash (table

utensils etc., or usu. absol.) after use, (of sea) carry on to shore.

washable /ˈwɒʃəb(ə)l/ *a.* that may be washed without damage.

washer /ˈwɒʃə(r)/ *n.* flattened ring of metal or leather or rubber etc. placed between two surfaces or under plunger of tap or nut etc. to tighten joint; washing machine.

washerwoman /ˈwɒʃəwʊmən/ *n.* (*pl.* **-women** /-wɪmɪn/ laundress.

washing /ˈwɒʃɪŋ/ *n.* clothes to be washed or that have been washed. **washing-machine** machine for washing clothes; **washing-powder** powder of soap or detergent for washing clothes; **washing-up** washing of table utensils after use, dishes etc. for washing.

washy /ˈwɒʃɪ/ *a.* too watery or weak, lacking vigour.

wasp /wɒsp/ *n.* stinging insect with black and yellow stripes. **wasp-waist** very slender waist.

WASP /wɒsp/ *abbr.* US (usu. *derog.*) White Anglo-Saxon Protestant.

waspish /ˈwɒspɪʃ/ *a.* irritable, snappish.

wassail /ˈwɒseɪl/ **1** *n.* festive drinking. **2** *v.i.* make merry.

wastage /ˈweɪstɪdʒ/ *n.* amount wasted; loss by use or wear or decay etc.; loss of employees other than by redundancy.

waste /weɪst/ **1** *a.* superfluous, no longer serving a purpose; not inhabited or cultivated. **2** *v.* use to no purpose or for inadequate result or extravagantly; fail to use; wear away; make or become weak; lay waste. **3** *n.* act of wasting; waste material; waste region; diminution from use or wear; waste-pipe. **4** **lay waste** devastate, ravage; **run to waste** be wasted; **waste land** land not utilized for cultivation or building; **waste paper** paper thrown away as spoiled or useless etc.; **waste-pipe** pipe carrying off superfluous or used water or steam; **waste product** useless byproduct of manufacture or bodily process etc.

wasteful /ˈweɪstfʊl/ *a.* extravagant, causing or showing waste.

waster /ˈweɪstə(r)/ *n.* wasteful person; *sl.* wastrel.

wastrel /ˈweɪstr(ə)l/ *n.* good-for-nothing person.

watch /wɒtʃ/ **1** *n.* small portable time-piece for carrying on person; state of being on the look-out, constant attention; *Naut.* 4-hour spell of duty, part of crew taking it; *hist.* watchman or -men. **2** *v.* be on the watch, be vigilant, look *for* opportunity etc.; exercise protecting care *over*; keep eyes fixed on, keep under observation; follow observantly; look out for, await (opportunity etc.). **3 on the watch** waiting for expected or feared occurrence; **watch-dog** dog kept to guard property, person etc. charged with protecting rights etc.; **watching brief** brief of barrister who follows case for client not directly concerned; **watchman** man employed to look after empty building etc. at night; **watch-night service** religious service on last night of year; **watch out** be on one's guard; **watch-tower** tower for observation of approaching danger; **watchword** phrase summarizing some party principle.

watchful /'wɒtʃful/ *a.* accustomed to watching, on the watch.

water /'wɔːtə(r)/ **1** *n.* transparent colourless tasteless odourless liquid forming seas and rivers etc., and falling as rain etc.; this as supplied for domestic use; tears, saliva, urine, etc.; sheet or body of water; in *pl.* part of sea or river, mineral water at spa, etc.; state of tide; solution of specified substance in water; transparency and lustre of diamond or pearl. **2** *v.* supply (plant or animal) with water; dilute with water; (of mouth, eyes) secrete or run with water; in *p.p.* (of silk fabric etc.) having irregular wavy finish. **3 make water** urinate; **of the first water** of finest or extreme quality; **water-bed** rubber mattress filled with water; **water-biscuit** thin unsweetened biscuit; **water-cannon** device giving powerful water-jet to disperse crowd etc.; **water-closet** lavatory with means of flushing pan with water; **water-colour** pigment diluted with water and not oil, picture painted or art or method of painting with this; **watercourse** stream of water, bed of this; **watercress** kind of cress with pungent leaves growing in springs and clear running streams; **water-diviner** dowser; **water down** dilute, make less

forceful or horrifying; **waterfall** stream or river falling over precipice or down steep hill; **waterfowl** bird(s) frequenting water; **waterfront** part of town adjoining river etc.; **water-hole** shallow depression in which water collects; **water-ice** frozen confection of flavoured water and sugar; **watering-can** portable vessel for watering plants; **watering-place** pool where animals drink, spa or seaside resort; **water-jump** place where horses in steeplechase or show-jumping must jump over water; **water-level** surface of water, height of this, water-table; **water-lily** aquatic plant with broad floating leaves and showy flowers; **water-line** line along which surface of water touches ship's side; **water-logged** filled or saturated with water so as to be unbuoyant, (of ground etc.) made useless by saturation with water; **waterman** boatman plying for hire; **watermark** distinguishing mark or design in paper visible when it is held up to the light; **water-meadow** meadow periodically flooded by stream; **water-melon** elliptical smooth kind with red pulp and watery juice; **water-mill** mill worked by water-wheel; **water-pistol** toy pistol shooting jet of water etc.; **water polo** game played by teams of swimmers with ball like football; **water-power** mechanical force from weight or motion of water; **waterproof** impervious to water, (*n.*) such garment or material, (*v.t.*) make waterproof; **water-rat** water-vole; **water-rate** charge for use of public water-supply; **watershed** line between waters flowing to different river basins, turning-point in events; **waterside** margin of sea or lake or river; **water-ski** one of pair of skis on which person towed by motor boat can skim water-surface; **waterspout** gyrating column of water and spray produced by action of whirlwind on sea and clouds above it; **water-table** plane below which ground is saturated with water; **water-tight** so closely constructed or fitted that water cannot leak through, (of argument etc.) unassailable; **water-tower** tower with elevated tank to give pressure for distributing water; **water-vole** ratlike aquatic kind of vole; **waterway** navigable channel; **water-wheel** wheel rotated by action of water and used for driving machinery or used to raise water; **waterwings** inflated floats used to support person learning to swim; **waterworks** establishment for managing water-supply, *sl.* shedding of tears, *sl.* urinary system.

watery /ˈwɔːtəri/ *a.* of or consisting of water; containing too much water; *fig.* vapid, uninteresting, (of colour) pale.

watt /wɒt/ *n.* unit of electrical power.

wattage /ˈwɒtɪdʒ/ *n.* amount of electrical power expressed in watts.

wattle¹ /ˈwɒt(ə)l/ *n.* Aus. acacia with fragrant golden-yellow flowers; interlaced rods and twigs or branches used for fences etc. **wattle and daub** wickerwork plastered with mud or clay as building-material.

wattle² /ˈwɒt(ə)l/ *n.* fleshy appendage hanging from head or neck of turkey etc.

wave 1 *v.* move (hand etc.) to and fro in greeting or as signal; show sinuous or sweeping motion; give such motion to; wave hand or held thing *to* person as signal or greeting; tell or direct thus, express thus; give undulating form to, have such form. 2 *n.* ridge of water between two depressions; long body of water curling into arched form and breaking on shore; thing compared to this; gesture of waving; waving of hair; temporary heightening of influence or condition; disturbance of particles in fluid medium to form ridges and troughs for propagation of motion or heat or light or sound etc.; single curve in this. 3 **wave aside** dismiss as intrusive or irrelevant; **wave down** wave to (vehicle or driver) as signal to stop; **wavelength** distance between crests of successive waves, this as distinctive feature of radio waves from a transmitter, *fig.* person's way of thinking.

wavelet /ˈweɪvlɪt/ *n.* small wave.

waver /ˈweɪvə(r)/ *v.i.* become unsteady or irresolute; begin to give way.

wavy /ˈweɪvɪ/ *a.* having waves or alternate contrary curves.

wax¹ 1 *n.* sticky plastic yellowish substance secreted by bees as material of honeycomb; this bleached and purified for candles or modelling or as basis of polishes etc.; any similar substance. 2 *v.t.* cover or treat with wax. 3 **waxwork** object esp. lifelike dummy modelled in wax, making of these, in *pl.* exhibition of wax dummies.

wax² *v.i.* (of moon) increase in apparent size; grow larger; *arch.* become.

waxen /ˈwæks(ə)n/ *a.* smooth and pale and translucent like wax; made of wax.

way 1 *n.* road, track, path, street; course, route; method, means; distance (to be) travelled; unimpeded opportunity for passage or advance or progress etc.; (direction of) travel or motion; habitual course or manner of action; normal course of events; state, condition; in *pl.* structure of timber etc. down which new ship is launched. 2 *adv. colloq.* far. 3 **by the way** *fig.* incidentally, in passing; **by way of** by means of, as a form or method of, passing through; **give way** retreat, fail to resist, make concessions, break down, collapse; **give way to** yield to, be superseded by; **lead the way** act as guide or leader; **make one's way** go, prosper; **make way** allow to pass, be superseded by; **out of the way** unusual, not obstructing, remote, disposed of; **pay one's way** pay expenses as they arise, contrive to avoid debt; **under way** in motion or progress; **way back** *colloq.* long ago; **way-bill** list of passengers or goods conveyed; **wayfarer** traveller, esp. on foot; **wayfaring** *n.*; **waylay** lie in wait for, stop to rob or accost; **way-leave** right of way rented to another; **way of life** principles or habits governing one's actions; **way-out** *colloq.* unusual, progressive, excellent; **wayside** side of road, land at side of road.

wayward /ˈweɪwəd/ *a.* childishly self-willed; capricious.

WC *abbr.* water-closet; West Central.

W/Cdr. *abbr.* Wing Commander.

we *pron.* (*obj.* **us**, *poss.* **our** /aʊə(r)/) *pl.* of I² (used also for *I* in royal proclamations etc. and by editorial writer in newspaper).

weak *a.* lacking in strength or power or number; fragile; feeble; unsound. **weak-kneed** lacking resolution; **weak-minded** mentally deficient, lacking resolution; **weak verb** one forming inflexions by suffix, not by vowel-change only.

weaken /'wiːkən/ v. make or become weak(er).

weakling /'wiːklɪŋ/ n. feeble person or animal.

weakly /'wiːklɪ/ a. sickly, not robust.

weakness /'wiːknɪs/ n. being weak; weak point; self-indulgent liking *for*.

weal¹ 1 n. ridge raised on flesh by stroke of lash etc. 2 v.t. raise weals on.

weal² n. *arch.* welfare, well-being.

wealth /welθ/ n. riches; being rich; abundance or a profusion *of*.

wealthy /'welθɪ/ a. having abundance of money.

wean v.t. accustom (infant or other young mammal) to food other than mother's milk; detach, alienate *from*, reconcile gradually to being deprived of something.

weapon /'wepən/ n. thing designed or used or usable for inflicting bodily harm; means employed for getting the better in a conflict.

wear /weə(r)/ 1 v. (*past* wore; *p.p.* worn) be dressed in, have on or as part of one's person; waste or damage or deteriorate gradually by use or attrition; make (hole etc.) by attrition; exhaust, tire or be tired out; endure continued use (*well* etc.), last; (of time) pass esp. tediously. 2 n. wearing or being worn; things worn; fashionable or suitable apparel; (also **wear and tear**) damage from ordinary use. 3 **wear out** use or be used until no longer usable, tire or be tired out.

wearisome /'wɪərɪsəm/ a. causing weariness, monotonous, fatiguing.

weary /'wɪərɪ/ 1 a. tired, worn out, intensely fatigued; sick *of*; tiring, tedious. 2 v. make or become weary.

weasel /'wiːz(ə)l/ n. small ferocious reddish-brown carnivorous animal.

weather /'weðə(r)/ 1 n. atmospheric conditions prevailing at specified time or place with respect to heat or cold and sunshine or fog and strength of wind etc.; *attrib.* windward. 2 v. expose to or affect by atmospheric changes; wear away or discolour etc. by exposure to weather; come safely through (storm etc.); get to windward of. 3 **keep a weather eye open** be watchful; **make heavy weather of** find trying or difficult; **under the weather** *colloq.* indisposed; **weather-beaten** affected by exposure to weather; **weather-board** sloping board attached at bottom of door to keep out rain, one of series of horizontal boards with overlapping edges covering walls etc.; **weather-cock** revolving pointer on church spire etc. to show direction of wind, inconstant person; **weather forecast** prediction of weather for next few hours or longer; **weather-vane** weathercock.

weave¹ 1 v. (*past* wove; *p.p.* woven) form (fabric) by interlacing threads, form fabric out of (threads), esp. in loom; intermingle, form or introduce *into* whole; make (story etc.) thus. 2 n. style of weaving.

weave² v.i. move repeatedly or deviously from side to side.

weaver /'wiːvə(r)/ n. person whose occupation is weaving; kind of tropical bird building elaborately interwoven nest.

web n. woven fabric; amount woven in one piece; complex series; cobweb or similar tissue; membrane connecting toes of aquatic bird or animal; large roll of paper for printing. **web-footed** having toes connected by web.

webbed /webd/ a. (of bird's or animal's foot) having toes connected by web.

webbing /'webɪŋ/ n. strong narrow closely-woven fabric for belts etc.

wed v. (*past* wedded; *p.p.* wedded or wed) marry; unite or join *to* or *with*.

Wed. *abbr.* Wednesday.

wedded /'wedɪd/ a. of marriage; obstinately attached *to* pursuit etc.

wedding /'wedɪŋ/ n. marriage ceremony with its attendant festivities. **wedding breakfast** meal between wedding and departure for honeymoon; **wedding-cake** rich decorated cake distributed to guests at wedding and to absent friends; **wedding-ring** ring used at wedding and worn on finger of married person.

wedge 1 n. piece of wood or metal etc. with sharp edge at one end, used for splitting stone etc. or forcing things apart or fixing them immovably etc.; wedge-shaped thing. 2 v.t. force *open* or *apart* or fix firmly with wedge; drive or push (object) into position where it is held fast; pack or crowd (*together*) in limited space. **3 thin end of the wedge** small beginning that may lead to something greater.

wedlock /'wedlɒk/ *n.* married state. **born in, out of, wedlock** born of married, unmarried, parents.

Wednesday /'wenzdeɪ/ *n.* day of week following Tuesday.

wee *a.* tiny, very small.

weed 1 *n.* wild plant growing where it is not wanted; lanky and weakly horse or person; *colloq.* tobacco. **2** *v.* rid of weeds; remove or destroy weeds; eradicate or remove or clear *out* (faults, inferior individuals, etc.).

weeds *n.pl.* deep mourning worn by widow.

weedy /'wiːdɪ/ *a.* full of weeds; growing freely like a weed; lanky and weak.

week *n.* 7-day period reckoned usu. from Saturday midnight; any 7-day period; the 6 days between Sundays; the 5 days Monday to Friday, period of work then done. **weekday** day other than (Saturday or) Sunday; **weekend** Saturday and Sunday.

weekly /'wiːklɪ/ **1** *a.* done or produced or occurring once every week. **2** *adv.* every week. **3** *n.* weekly newspaper or periodical.

weeny /'wiːnɪ/ *a. colloq.* tiny.

weep 1 *v.* (*past & p.p.* **wept**) shed tears (*over*); lament for; shed moisture in drops, exude. **2** *n.* fit or spell of weeping.

weeping /'wiːpɪŋ/ *a.* (of tree) having drooping branches.

weepy /'wiːpɪ/ *a. colloq.* inclined to weep, tearful.

weevil /'wiːv(ə)l/ *n.* destructive granary-beetle.

weft *n.* threads crossing from side to side of web and interwoven with warp.

weigh /weɪ/ *v.* find weight of; balance in hand (as if) to guess weight of; estimate relative value or importance of, consider, ponder; be of specified weight or importance; have influence (*with*); heave up (anchor) before sailing. **weighbridge** weighing-machine for vehicles on road; **weigh down** bring down by weight, depress, oppress; **weigh in** be weighed (of boxer before contest, or jockey after race); **weigh in with** *colloq.* advance (argument etc.)

confidently; **weigh one's words** choose those words which precisely express one's meaning; **weigh up** *colloq.* form estimate of.

weight /weɪt/ **1** *n.* tendency of bodies to fall to earth; quantitative expression of a body's weight, a scale of such weights; body of known weight for use in weighing; heavy body esp. used in mechanism etc.; load or burden; influence, importance; preponderance (*of* evidence etc.); = **shot²** (in athletics). **2** *v.t.* attach a weight to, hold down with a weight; impede or burden *with*. **3 weight-lifting** sport or exercise of lifting heavy objects.

weighting /'weɪtɪŋ/ *n.* extra pay in special cases.

weighty /'weɪtɪ/ *a.* heavy, momentous; deserving attention or carrying weight; influential, authoritative.

weir /wɪə(r)/ *n.* dam or barrier across river etc. to retain water and regulate its flow.

weird /wɪəd/ *a.* uncanny, supernatural; *colloq.* queer, incomprehensible.

welcome /'welkəm/ **1** *int.* of greeting. **2** *n.* kind or glad reception or entertainment. **3** *v.t.* give welcome to, receive gladly; greet. **4** *a.* gladly received; acceptable as visitor; ungrudgingly permitted or given right *to.* **5 make welcome** receive hospitably.

weld 1 *v.t.* unite (pieces of esp. heated metal etc.) into solid mass by hammering or pressure; form by welding into some article, *fig.* fashion effectually *into* a whole. **2** *n.* welded joint.

welfare /'welfeə(r)/ *n.* good fortune, happiness, or well-being; maintenance of persons in such condition, money given for this purpose. **Welfare State** State with highly-developed social services controlled or financed by government; **welfare work** organized effort for welfare of class or group.

welkin /'welkɪn/ *n. literary* sky.

well¹ 1 *adv.* in right or satisfactory way; in kind way; thoroughly, carefully; with heartiness or approval; probably, reasonably; to considerable extent. **2** *a.* in good health; in satisfactory state or position; advisable. **3** *int.* introducing remark or statement; expr. astonishment or resignation etc. **4 as**

well with equal reason, preferably, in addition, also; **as well as** to the same extent as, in the same degree as, in addition to; **well-advised** prudent; **well and truly** decisively; **well-appointed** properly equipped or fitted out; **well away** having made considerable progress; **well-balanced** sensible, sane, equally matched; **well-being** happy or healthy or prosperous condition, moral or physical welfare; **well-born** of noble family; **well-bred** having or showing good breeding or manners; **well-connected** related to good families; **well-groomed** with carefully tended hair and clothes etc.; **well-heeled** *colloq.* wealthy; **well-informed** having much knowledge or information about subject; **well-intentioned** having or showing good intentions; **well-judged** opportunely or skilfully done; **well-knit** compact; **well-known** known to many; **well-meaning** well-intentioned; **well off** fortunately situated, fairly rich; **well-read** having read (and learnt) much; **well-spoken** ready or refined in speech; **well-to-do** prosperous; **well-tried** often tried or tested with good result; **well-wisher** person who wishes well to another or to a cause etc.; **well-worn** trite, hackneyed.

well² 1 *n.* shaft sunk in ground to obtain water or oil etc.; enclosed space resembling well-shaft, esp. central open space of staircase, lift-shaft, or deep narrow space between surrounding walls of building(s); receptacle for liquid, esp. ink. 2 *v.i.* spring *up* or *out* etc. (as) from fountain. 3 **well-head, -spring**, original or chief source.

wellington /'welıŋt(ə)n/ *n.* waterproof rubber boot usu. reaching knee.

Welsh¹ 1 *a.* of Wales. 2 *n.* language of Wales; *the* Welsh people. 3 **Welshman, Welshwoman**, native of Wales; **Welsh rabbit (or rarebit)** dish of melted cheese on toast.

welsh² *v.i.* (of loser of bet, esp. bookmaker) decamp without paying; break an agreement, esp. avoid paying debts.

welt 1 *n.* leather rim sewn to shoe-upper for sole to be attached to; mark of heavy blow, weal; ribbed or reinforced border of garment. 2 *v.t.* provide with welt; raise weals on, thrash.

welter /'weltə(r)/ 1 *v.i.* roll or lie prostrate, be soaked *in*. 2 *n.* state of turmoil or upheaval; surging or confused mass.

welterweight /'weltəweıt/ *n.* boxing-weight (up to 67 kg.).

wen *n.* benign tumour on skin.

wench *n. joc.* girl or young woman.

wend *v. arch.* **wend one's way** go.

went *past of* **go¹**.

wept *past & p.p.* of **weep**.

were see **be**.

werewolf /'wıəwʊlf/ *n.* (*pl.* **-wolves**) *Myth.* human being who changes into wolf.

Wesleyan /'wezlıən/ *hist.* 1 *a.* of Protestant denomination founded by John Wesley. 2 *n.* member of this denomination.

west 1 *n.* point of horizon where sun sets; western part of world or country or town etc. 2 *a.* towards or at or near or facing west; coming from west. 3 *adv.* towards or at or near west. 4 **go west** *sl.* be killed or wrecked etc.; **West End** fashionable part of London. 5 **westward** *adv., a., & n.*; **westwards** *adv.*

westering /'westərıŋ/ *a.* (of sun) nearing the west.

westerly /'westəlı/ *a.* from or to west.

western /'west(ə)n/ 1 *a.* of or in west. 2 *n.* film or novel about cowboys in western N. Amer. 3 **westernize** *v.*

westerner /'westənə(r)/ *n.* inhabitant of west.

wet 1 *a.* soaked or covered with water or other liquid; (of weather) rainy; (of paint) not yet dried; used with water; *sl.* mistaken, feeble. 2 *v.t.* make wet. 3 *n.* liquid that wets something; rainy weather; *sl.* feeble or spiritless person; *sl.* drink. 4 **wet blanket** person or thing damping or discouraging enthusiasm or cheerfulness etc.; **wet-nurse** woman employed to suckle another's child, (*v.t.*) act as wet-nurse to, *fig.* treat as if helpless.

wether /'weðə(r)/ *n.* castrated ram.

Wg. Cdr. *abbr.* Wing Commander.

whack 1 *v.t. colloq.* hit, esp. with stick; in *p.p.* tired out. 2 *n.* sharp or resounding blow; *sl.* share.

whacking /'wækıŋ/ *colloq.* 1 *a.* large. 2 *adv.* very.

whale 1 *n.* large fishlike marine mammal. 2 *v.i.* hunt whales. 3 **whalebone** elastic horny substance in upper jaw of some whales; **whale-oil** oil obtained from blubber of some whales.

whaler /'weɪlə(r)/ n. whaling ship or seaman.

wham int. expr. forcible impact.

wharf /wɔːf/ 1 n. (pl. **wharfs**) structure at water's edge for loading or unloading of vessels lying alongside. 2 v.t. moor (ship) at wharf; store (goods) on wharf.

what /wɒt/ 1 interrog. a. asking for selection from indefinite number or for specification of amount or number or kind etc. 2 excl. a. how great, how strange, how remarkable! etc. 3 rel. a. the or any...that. 4 interrog. pron. what thing(s)?; what did you say? 5 excl. pron. what thing(s), how much! 6 rel. pron. that or those which; thing(s) that, anything that. 7 adv. to what extent. 8 **know what's what** have good judgement or comprehension, know the matter in hand etc.; **whatever** = what (in relative uses) with emphasis or indefiniteness, though any(thing), (with neg. or interrog.) at all, of any kind; **what for?** for what reason?; **what have you** anything else similar; **what not** other similar things; **whatsoever** = whatever; **what with** because of.

wheat n. a cereal bearing dense 4-sided seed-spikes, from which bread is usu. made; its grain. **wheatmeal** wholemeal.

wheatear /'wiːtɪə(r)/ n. kind of small migratory bird.

wheaten /'wiːt(ə)n/ a. made of wheat.

wheedle /'wiːd(ə)l/ v.t. coax by flattery or endearments; get out of by wheedling.

wheel 1 n. circular frame or disc arranged to revolve on axle and used to facilitate motion of vehicle or for various mechanical purposes; steering-wheel; wheel-like thing; motion as of wheel; movement esp. of line of men etc. with one end as pivot. 2 v. turn on axis or pivot; swing round in line with one end as pivot; (cause to) change direction or face another way; push or pull (wheeled thing); go in circles or curves. 3 **wheel and deal** US engage in political and commercial scheming; **wheelbarrow** shallow open box with shafts and one wheel for carrying small loads on; **wheelbase** distance between axles of vehicle; **wheelchair** invalid's chair on wheels; **wheel-spin** rotation of vehicle's wheels without traction; **wheels within wheels** intricate machinery, fig. indirect or secret agencies; **wheelwright** maker of wheels.

wheelie /'wiːlɪ/ n. manœuvre on two-wheeled vehicle etc. in which front wheel is held off the ground.

wheeze 1 v.i. breathe hard with audible whistling sound. 2 n. sound of wheezing; sl. trick, dodge.

wheezy /'wiːzɪ/ a. wheezing or sounding like a wheeze.

whelk n. spiral-shelled marine mollusc.

whelp 1 n. young dog, puppy; arch. cub; ill-mannered child or youth. 2 v.i. bring forth whelp(s).

when 1 adv. at what time?; on what occasion?, how soon?; (time etc.) at or on which. 2 conj. at the or any time that, as soon as; although; after which, and just then. 3 pron. what time?; which time. 4 n. time, occasion. 5 **whenever**, **whensoever**, at whatever time, on whatever occasion, every time that.

whence 1 adv. from where, from what place or source; (place etc.) from which. 2 conj. to the place from which; and thence.

where /weə(r)/ 1 adv. in or to what place or position?; in what respect, from what source, etc.; in or to which. 2 conj. in or to the or any place or direction or respect in which; and there. 3 pron. what place? 4 n. place, locality. 5 **whereabouts** in or near what place?; (n.) person's or thing's location roughly defined; **whereas** in contrast or comparison with the fact that, taking into consideration the fact that; **whereby** by which, by what; **wherefore** for what reason?; **wherein**, **whereof**, **whereon**, **wherewith**, in, of, on, with, what or which; **whereupon** immediately after which; **wherever** at or to whatever place etc.; **wherewithal** /-wɪðɔːl/ colloq. money etc. needed for a purpose.

wherry /'werɪ/ n. light rowing-boat, usu. for carrying passengers; large light barge.

whet v.t. sharpen; make (more) acute. **whetstone** stone for sharpening cutting-tools.

whether /'weðə(r)/ *conj.* introducing dependent question etc. and expressing doubt or choice etc. between alternatives.

whew /hwju:/ *int.* expr. astonishment or consternation or relief.

whey *n.* watery liquid left after separation of curd from milk.

which 1 *interrog. a.* asking for choice from definite set of alternatives. **2** *rel. a.* being the one just referred to, and this or these. **3** *interrog. pron.* which person(s) or thing(s)? **4** *rel. pron.* which person(s) or thing(s). **5 whichever** any which.

whiff *n.* puff of air or smoke or odour etc.; small cigar.

Whig *n. hist.* member of political party succeeded by Liberals. **Whiggery** *n.*; **Whiggism** *n.*; **Whiggish** *a.*

while 1 *n.* space of time, esp. time spent in doing something. **2** *rel. adv.* (with *time* etc.) during which. **3** *conj.* during the time that; for as long as; although; and at the same time, besides that. **4** *v.t.* pass (time etc.) *away* in leisurely manner or without wearisomeness. **5 for a while** for some time; **in a while** soon; **once in a while** occasionally.

whilst /wailst/ *adv. & conj.* while.

whim *n.* sudden fancy, caprice.

whimper /'wimpə(r)/ **1** *v.i.* cry querulously; whine softly. **2** *n.* feeble whining sound.

whimsical /'wimzik(ə)l/ *a.* capricious; fantastic. **whimsicality** *n.*

whimsy /'wimzi/ *n.* whim.

whin *n.* furze. **whinchat** small song-bird.

whine 1 *n.* long-drawn complaining cry (as) of dog or child; querulous tone; feeble complaint. **2** *v.* utter whine(s); utter whiningly, complain.

whinge /windʒ/ *v.i. colloq.* complain peevishly.

whinny /'wini/ **1** *n.* gentle or joyful neigh. **2** *v.i.* emit whinny.

whip 1 *n.* stick with lash attached, for urging on or for flogging or beating; person appointed to maintain discipline of political party in House of Parliament; whip's written notice requesting member's attendance; food made with whipped cream etc.; whipper-in. **2** *v.* apply whip to; urge *on* thus; make (eggs, cream, etc.) light and

frothy by stirring or beating; move suddenly or briskly; snatch; make *up* quickly or hastily; *sl.* steal, excel, defeat; bind round closely with twine or thread etc.; sew with overcast stitches. **3 whipcord** tightly twisted cord; **whip hand** upper hand, control (of), advantage; **whiplash** lash of whip, similar sudden jerk; **whipper-in** huntsman's assistant who manages hounds; **whipping-boy** scapegoat, *hist.* boy educated with young prince and chastised in his stead; **whipping-top** top kept spinning by strokes of lash; **whip-round** appeal for contributions from group of people; **whip-stock** handle of whip.

whipper-snapper /'wipəsnæpə(r)/ *n.* young and insignificant but impertinent person.

whippet /'wipit/ *n.* small dog of greyhound type, used for racing.

whippoorwill /'wipuəwil/ *n.* N. Amer. nightjar.

whippy /'wipi/ *a.* flexible, springy.

whirl 1 *v.* swing round and round, revolve rapidly; send or travel swiftly in orbit or curve; convey or go rapidly in car etc.; be giddy, seem to spin round. **2** *n.* whirling movement; state of intense activity or confusion. **3 whirlpool** circular eddy in sea or river etc.; **whirlwind** whirling mass or column of air moving over land or water.

whirligig /'wɜ:ligig/ *n.* spinning or whirling toy; merry-go-round; revolving motion.

whirr 1 *n.* continuous buzzing or softly clicking sound. **2** *v.i.* make this sound.

whisk 1 *v.* brush or sweep lightly and rapidly from surface; beat esp. with whisk; convey or go or move with light rapid sweeping motion. **2** *n.* instrument for whipping eggs or cream etc.; bunch of twigs or bristles etc. for brushing or dusting; whisking movement.

whisker /'wiskə(r)/ *n.* hair on cheeks or sides of face of adult man; projecting hair or bristle on upper lip or near mouth of cat etc.; *colloq.* small distance. **whiskery** *a.*

whiskey /'wiski/ *n.* Irish whisky.

whisky /'wiski/ *n.* spirit distilled esp. from malted barley.

whisper /'wispə(r)/ **1** *v.* use breath instead of vocal cords; talk or say in barely audible tone or confidential way; rustle, murmur. **2** *n.* whispering speech or sound; thing whispered.

whist *n.* card game, usu. for two pairs of opponents. **whist drive** whist-party with players moving on from table to table.

whistle /'wɪs(ə)l/ 1 *n.* clear shrill sound made by forcing breath through lips contracted to narrow opening; similar sound made by bird or wind or missile, or produced by pipe etc.; instrument used to produce it, e.g. as signal. **2** *v.* emit whistle; summon or give signal thus; produce or utter or call or send (*away*, *up*, etc.), by whistling. **3** **whistle for** *colloq.* seek or expect in vain; **whistle-stop** *US* small unimportant town on railway, politician's brief pause for electioneering speech on tour.

whit[1] *n.* particle, least possible amount.

Whit[2] *a.* connected with or belonging to or following **Whit Sunday** 7th Sunday after Easter, commemorating Pentecost.

white 1 *a.* of colour produced by reflection or transmission of all light; of colour of snow or milk; pale; **White** of the human racial group having light-coloured skin; *fig.* innocent, unstained. **2** *n.* white colour or paint or clothes etc.; (player using) lighter-coloured pieces in chess etc.; translucent or white part round yolk of egg; visible part of eyeball round iris; **White** White person. **3 white ant** termite; **white-bait** small silvery-white food-fish; **white bread** bread made from fine bolted flour; **white cell** leucocyte; **white Christmas** one with snow; **white coffee** coffee with milk or cream; **white-collar** (of worker) not engaged in manual labour; **white corpuscle** leucocyte; **white elephant** burdensome or useless possession; **white feather** symbol of cowardice; **white flag** plain white flag of truce or surrender; **white heat** degree of heat making metal etc. glow white, *fig.* state of intense anger or passion; **white hope** person expected to achieve much; **white horses** white-crested waves; **white-hot** at white heat; **white lead** lead carbonate as white pigment; **white lie** harmless or trivial untruth;

White Paper Government report giving information; **white pepper** pepper made by grinding husked berry; **white sale** sale of household linen; **white sauce** sauce of flour and melted butter and milk etc.; **white slave** woman entrapped for prostitution; **white spirit** light petroleum as solvent; **white sugar** purified sugar; **white tie** man's white bow-tie worn with full evening dress; **whitewash** liquid composition of lime or whiting and water etc. for whitening walls etc., *fig.* glossing over of faults, (*v.*) apply whitewash (to), *fig.* gloss over, clear of blame etc.; **whitewood** light-coloured wood esp. prepared for staining etc. **4 whitish** *a.*

whiten /'waɪt(ə)n/ *v.* make or become white.

whither /'wɪðə(r)/ *arch.* **1** *interrog. adv.* to what place or state? **2** *rel. adv.* (with *place* etc.) to which. **3** *conj.* to the or any place to which; and thither.

whiting[1] /'waɪtɪŋ/ *n.* small edible sea-fish.

whiting[2] /'waɪtɪŋ/ *n.* chalk prepared for use in whitewashing or plate-cleaning.

whitlow /'wɪtləʊ/ *n.* small abscess esp. under or near nail.

Whitsun /'wɪts(ə)n/ **1** *n.* weekend or week including Whit Sunday. **2** *a.* Whit[2]. **3 Whitsuntide** Whitsun.

whittle /'wɪt(ə)l/ *v.* pare or shape wood by cutting thin slices or shavings from surface; reduce by repeated subtractions.

whizz (also **whiz**) **1** *n.* sound made by body moving through air at great speed. **2** *v.i.* move with or make a whiz. **3 whizz-kid** *colloq.* brilliant or highly successful young person.

who /huː/ *pron.* (*obj.* **whom**, *poss.* **whose** /huːz/) what or which person(s), what sort of person(s); (person or persons) that; and or but he or they etc. **whoever**, **whosoever**, whatever person(s), any (one) who, no matter who.

WHO *abbr.* World Health Organization.

whoa /wəʊ/ *int.* command to horse etc. to stop or stand still.

whodunit /huː'dʌnɪt/ *n. colloq.* murder or detective story.

whole /həʊl/ **1** *a.* in uninjured or unbroken or intact or undiminished or undivided etc. state; all, all of. **2** *n.* full or complete or total amount (*of*); complete thing; organic unity, total made up of parts. **3 on the whole** all things considered, in general, for the most part; **whole foods** foods not artificially processed or refined; **whole-hearted** given or done or acting etc. with all one's heart, sincere; **wholemeal** meal or flour or bread made from whole grain of wheat, not bolted.

wholesale /'həʊlseɪl/ **1** *n.* selling in large quantities, esp. for retail by others. **2** *a.* & *adv.* by wholesale; on a large scale. **3** *v.t.* sell wholesale.

wholesome /'həʊlsəm/ *a.* promoting physical or mental or moral health.

wholly /'həʊllɪ/ *adv.* entirely, without limitation, purely.

whom /huːm/ *pron.*, obj. case of **who**. **whomsoever** obj. case of **whosoever**.

whoop /huːp or wuːp/ **1** *n.* cry expressing excitement etc.; characteristic drawing-in of breath after cough in whooping-cough. **2** *v.i.* utter whoop. **3 whooping-cough** /'huːpɪŋ/ infectious disease esp. of children, with violent convulsive cough.

whoopee /'wʊpiː/ *int.* expr. wild joy or excitement etc. **make whoopee** *colloq.* rejoice noisily or hilariously.

whoops /wʊps/ *int. colloq.* apology for obvious mistake.

whop *v.t. sl.* thrash, defeat.

whopper /'wɒpə(r)/ *n. sl.* big specimen; great lie.

whopping /'wɒpɪŋ/ *a. sl.* very big.

whore /hɔː(r)/*n.* prostitute; sexually immoral woman. **whore-house** brothel.

whorl /wɜːl/ *n.* ring of leaves round stem; one turn of spiral; circle formed by ridges in finger-print.

whortleberry /'wɜːtəlberɪ/ *n.* bilberry.

whose /huːz/ *pron.* poss. case of **who** and occas. of **which**.

why /waɪ/ **1** *interrog. adv.* on what ground?; for what reason or purpose? **2** *rel. adv.* on account of which. **3** *int.* expressing esp. mild or slight surprise or slight protest etc. **4** *n.* reason, explanation.

WI *abbr.* West Indies; Women's Institute.

wick *n.* strip or thread feeding flame with fuel.

wicked /'wɪkɪd/ *a.* sinful, vicious, morally depraved; *colloq.* very bad, malicious, mischievous.

wicker /'wɪkə(r)/ *n.* plaited osiers etc. as material of baskets or chairs etc. **wickerwork** wicker, things made of wicker.

wicket /'wɪkɪt/ *n.* small gate or door, esp. beside or in larger one; *Crick.* set of 3 upright stumps with bails in position defended by batsman, ground between the two wickets, state of this, batsman's avoidance of being out. **wicket-keeper** fielder stationed close behind batsman's wicket.

wide 1 *a.* having sides far apart, broad, not narrow; extending far, not restricted; open to full extent; far from, or not within reasonable distance of, point or mark; (appended to measurement) in width. **2** *adv.* at or to many points; with wide interval or opening; so as to miss mark or way. **3** *n.* wide ball. **4 far and wide** over or through large space or region; **wide awake** fully awake, *colloq.* fully aware of what is going on, alert; **wide ball** *Crick.* ball judged by umpire to be beyond batsman's reach; **wide-eyed** surprised, naïve; **widespread** widely distributed.

widen /'waɪd(ə)n/ *v.* make or become wide or wider.

widgeon /'wɪdʒ(ə)n/ *n.* kind of wild duck.

widow /'wɪdəʊ/ **1** *n.* woman who has lost her husband by death and not married again. **2** *v.t.* make into widow or widower.

widower /'wɪdəʊə(r)/ *n.* man who has lost his wife by death and not married again.

widowhood /'wɪdəʊhʊd/ *n.* being a widow or widower.

width *n.* measurement from side to side; piece of material of full width; large extent. **widthways** *adv.*

wield /wiːld/ *v.t.* hold and use, control, manage.

wife *n.* (*pl.* **wives**) married woman esp. in relation to her husband.

wifely /'waɪflɪ/ *a.* befitting a wife.

wig¹ *n.* artificial head of hair.

wig² *v.t. colloq.* rebuke sharply.

wiggle /'wɪg(ə)l/ *colloq.* **1** *v.* (cause to)

move from side to side. **2** *n.* wiggling movement.

wight /waɪt/ *n. arch.* person.

wigwam /ˈwɪɡwæm/ *n.* N. Amer. Indian's hut or tent.

wilco /ˈwɪlkəʊ/ *int.* expr. compliance or agreement.

wild /waɪld/ **1** *a.* in original natural state; not domesticated or tamed or cultivated; uncivilized; tempestuous; lawless; out of control; violently excited or agitated; passionately desirous (*to* do); elated, enthusiastic; rash, ill-aimed, random. **2** *adv.* in wild manner. **3** *n.* wild or waste place, desert. **4 run wild** grow or stray unchecked or undisciplined; **wildcat** *fig.* hot-tempered or violent person, (*a.*) reckless, financially unsound, (of strike) unofficial; **wildfire** highly inflammable composition used in warfare etc. (**like wildfire** with extraordinary speed); **wild-goose chase** foolish or hopeless quest; **wildlife** wild animals collectively; **wild oat** tall grass resembling oats (**sow one's wild oats** indulge in youthful follies before becoming steady); **Wild West** western US in time of lawlessness.

wildebeest /ˈwɪldəbiːst/ *n.* gnu.

wilderness /ˈwɪldənɪs/ *n.* desert, uncultivated and uninhabited land or tract; confused assemblage *of.* **in the wilderness** (of political party) out of office, (of person) in exile or disgrace, out of favour.

wile **1** *n.* trick, cunning procedure. **2** *v.t.* lure *away*, *into*, etc.

wilful /ˈwɪlfʊl/ *a.* deliberate, intentional; obstinately self-willed; wayward.

will **1** *v.aux.* (*pres.* **will**, *past* **would** /wʊd/) *expr.* future or conditional statement or order or question. □ See page 667. **2** *v.t.* desire or choose to or consent or be persuaded or have constant tendency to be accustomed or likely to; (with regular inflexional forms) intend unconditionally, impel by will-power, bequeath by will. **3** *n.* faculty by which one decides what to do; will-power; fixed desire or intention; arbitrary discretion; disposition towards others; usu. written directions in legal form for disposition of one's property after death. **4 against**

one's will under compulsion; **at will** whenever one wishes; **will-power** control by deliberate purpose over impulse; **with a will** vigorously.

willing /ˈwɪlɪŋ/ **1** *n.* cheerful intention. **2** *a.* ready to consent or undertake; given etc. by willing person.

will-o'-the-wisp /ˌwɪləðəˈwɪsp/ *n.* phosphorescent light seen on marshy ground; elusive or delusive thing or person.

willow /ˈwɪləʊ/ *n.* waterside tree or shrub with pliant branches; **willow-herb** plant with leaves like willow; **willow-pattern** conventional Chinese design of blue on white china etc.

willowy /ˈwɪləʊɪ/ *a.* having willows; lithe and slender.

willy-nilly /ˌwɪlɪˈnɪlɪ/ *adv.* whether one likes it or not.

wilt **1** *v.* (cause to) fade, droop, become limp. **2** *n.* plant-disease causing wilting.

wily /ˈwaɪlɪ/ *a.* crafty, cunning.

wimple /ˈwɪmp(ə)l/ *n.* head-dress covering neck and sides of face, worn by nuns etc.

win *v.* (*past* & *p.p.* **won** /wʌn/) get or gain as result of fight or contest or bet etc.; be victorious in (game, battle, race, etc.), gain victory; make one's way *to* or *through* etc. **2** *n.* victory in game or contest. **3 win the day** be victorious in battle.

wince **1** *n.* start or involuntary shrinking movement of pain etc. **2** *v.i.* give wince.

winceyette /ˌwɪnsɪˈet/ *n.* kind of lightweight napped flannelette used for night-clothes etc.

winch **1** *n.* crank of wheel or axle; windlass. **2** *v.t.* lift with winch.

wind[1] /wɪnd/ **1** *n.* air in natural motion; smell carried by this as indicating presence; artificially-produced air-current esp. for sounding a wind instrument, air (to be) so used; wind instruments in orchestra etc.; breath as needed in exertion or speech, power of breathing without difficulty; point below centre of chest where blow temporarily paralyses breathing; gas generated in bowels; empty talk. **2** *v.* exhaust wind of by exertion or blow; make breath quick and deep by exercise; detect presence of by scent. **3 get wind of** begin to suspect; **get**, **have**, **the wind up** *sl.*

become, be, frightened; **in the wind**
fig. about to happen; **put the wind up**
sl. frighten; **take the wind out of person's sails** frustrate him by anticipation; **windbag** wordy orator;
wind-break thing, esp. row of trees
etc., used to break force of wind; **wind-
cheater** windproof jacket; **windfall**
fruit blown down by wind, piece of unexpected good fortune, esp. receipt of
money; **wind instrument** musical instrument in which sound is produced
by current of air; **wind-jammer** merchant sailing-ship; **windmill** mill
worked by action of wind on sails;
wind-pipe air-passage between throat
and lungs; **windscreen** screen of glass
in front of driver of car etc.; **wind-sock**
canvas cylinder or cone on mast to
show direction of wind; **wind-swept**
exposed to high winds; **wind-tunnel**
enclosed chamber for testing (models
or parts of) aircraft in winds of known
velocities.

wind² /waɪnd/ **1** *v.* (*past* & *p.p.* **wound**
/waʊnd/) go in spiral or crooked or
curved course; make one's way thus;
coil, wrap closely around something or
upon itself, enclose or encircle thus;
tighten *up* coiled spring of (clock etc.).
2 *n.* bend or turn in course. **3 wind
down** unwind, lower by winding;
winding-sheet linen in which corpse
is wrapped for burial; **wind up** coil
whole of, tighten coiling or coiled
spring of or *fig.* tension or intensity of,
bring to a conclusion, end, arrange
affairs of and dissolve (company),
colloq. arrive finally.

windlass /'wɪndləs/ *n.* mechanical device with horizontal axle for hauling or
hoisting.

window /'wɪndəʊ/ *n.* opening, usu.
with glass, in wall etc. to admit light
and air; the glass itself; space behind
window of shop for display of goods
etc.; opening resembling window in
shape or function. **window-box** box
placed outside window for cultivating
plants; **window-dressing** art of
arranging display in shop-window etc.,
adroit presentation of facts etc. to give
falsely favourable impression;
window-seat seat below window;
window-shopping looking at displays

in shop-windows without buying
anything.

windsurfing /'wɪndsɜːfɪŋ/ *n.* sport of
riding on board similar to surf-board
with sail.

windward /'wɪndwəd/ **1** *a.* & *adv.* in
the direction from which wind is blowing. **2** *n.* this direction.

windy /'wɪndɪ/ *a.* exposed to or stormy
with wind; generating or characterized
by flatulence; wordy; *sl.* frightened,
apprehensive.

wine 1 *n.* fermented grape-juice as alcoholic drink; fermented drink resembling it made from other fruits etc.;
colour of red wine. **2** *v.* drink wine, entertain to wine. **3 wine-bibber** tippler;
wine-cellar cellar used for storing
wine, its contents; **wineglass** small
glass for wine, usu. with stem and foot;
winepress press in which grape-juice
is extracted for wine.

wing 1 *n.* one of the limbs or organs by
which flying is effected; winglike supporting part of aircraft; projecting part
of building or organ or structure or battle array; in *pl.* sides of theatre stage;
Footb. etc. player at either end of line,
side part of playing-area; extreme section of political party; mudguard of motor vehicle; air-force unit of several
squadrons. **2** *v.* traverse or travel on
wings; equip with wings, enable to fly;
send in flight; wound in wing or arm. **3
on the wing** flying; **take wing** fly
away; **take under one's wing** treat as
protégé; **wing-case** horny covering of
insect's wing; **wing-chair** chair with
projecting side-pieces at top of high
back; **wing-collar** man's high stiff collar with turned-down corners; **wing
commander** officer of RAF next below
group captain; **wing-nut** nut with projections to turn it by; **wing-span,
-spread**, measurement right across
wings.

winger /'wɪŋə(r)/ *n. Footb.* etc. wing
player.

wink 1 *v.* blink; close eye(s) for a moment; close one eye momentarily;
(cause to) flicker like eyelid, twinkle;
convey signal or hint etc. by winking or
flashing lights etc. **2** *n.* act of winking;
short sleep (**not a wink** no sleep at all).
wink at purposely avoid seeing, pretend not to notice.

winkle /'wɪŋk(ə)l/ **1** n. edible sea snail. **2** v.t. (with out) extract, prise out. **3** **winkle-picker** sl. long pointed shoe.

winning /'wɪnɪŋ/ **1** a. bringing victory; attractive. **2** n. in pl. money won. **3** **winning-post** post marking end of race.

winnow /'wɪnəʊ/ v.t. blow (grain) free of chaff etc.; blow (chaff etc.) away or from; sift, separate (out) from worthless or inferior elements.

winsome /'wɪnsəm/ a. winning, engaging; twee.

winter /'wɪntə(r)/ **1** n. coldest season of year. **2** a. characteristic of or fit for winter. **3** v. spend the winter at or in etc. **4** **winter garden** garden of plants flourishing in winter; **winter-green** kind of plant remaining green all winter; **winter sports** skiing, skating, and other open-air sports practised on snow or ice; **winter wheat** etc. wheat etc. sown in autumn and remaining in ground all winter.

wintry /'wɪntrɪ/ a. characteristic of winter; lacking warmth.

winy /'waɪnɪ/ a. wine-flavoured.

wipe **1** v. clean or dry surface of by rubbing with something soft; get rid of (tears), or clean (vessel) out or make clean etc. by wiping. **2** n. act of wiping. **3** **wipe out** avenge (insult etc.), utterly destroy or defeat.

wiper /'waɪpə(r)/ n. device for keeping windscreen clear of rain etc.

wire **1** n. metal drawn out into slender flexible rod or thread; piece of this; length or line of this used for fencing or as conductor of electric current etc.; colloq. telegram. **2** v.t. provide or support or stiffen or secure with wires; colloq. telegraph. **3** **get one's wires crossed** fig. become confused; **wire-haired** (of dog) having rough hard wiry coat; **wire netting** netting made of wire twisted into meshes; **wire-tapping** tapping of telephone wires; **wire wool** mass of fine wire for cleaning; **wire-worm** destructive larva of a kind of beetle.

wireless /'waɪəlɪs/ n. radio, radio receiving set.

wiring /'waɪərɪŋ/ n. electrical circuits in a building.

wiry /'waɪərɪ/ a. tough and flexible as wire; sinewy; untiring.

wisdom /'wɪzdəm/ n. being wise; soundness of judgement in matters relating to life and conduct; knowledge, experience, learning. **wisdom tooth** hindmost molar tooth on each side of upper and lower jaws, usu. cut at age of about 20.

wise[1] /waɪz/ a. having or showing or dictated by wisdom; having knowledge; suggestive of wisdom; sl. alert, crafty. **wisecrack** colloq. smart remark, witticism; **wise man** wizard, esp. one of the Magi; **wise to** sl. aware or informed of.

wise[2] /waɪz/ n. arch. way, manner, degree.

wiseacre /'waɪzeɪkə(r)/ n. person who affects to be wise.

wish **1** v. have or express desire or aspiration for; want or want (person) to do; request; desire esp. something good for (person etc.). **2** n. desire or request, expression of this; thing desired. **3** **wishbone** forked bone between neck and breast of cooked bird; **wish-fulfilment** tendency of esp. unconscious wishes to be satisfied in fantasy.

wishful /'wɪʃful/ a. desiring (to do). **wishful thinking** belief founded on wishes rather than facts.

wishy-washy /'wɪʃɪwɒʃɪ/ a. feeble or poor in quality or character.

wisp n. small bundle or twist of straw etc.; small separate quantity of smoke or hair etc. **wispy** a.

wistaria /wɪ'steərɪə/ n. (also **wisteria**) climbing shrub with blue or purple or white hanging flowers.

wistful /'wɪstful/ a. yearningly or mournfully expectant or wishful.

wit n. intelligence, understanding; in sing. imaginative and inventive faculty; amusing ingenuity of speech or ideas; person noted for this. **at one's wits' end** utterly at a loss or in despair; **have one's wits about one** be mentally alert; **out of one's wits** mad, distracted; **to wit** that is to say, namely.

witch n. woman supposed to have dealings with devil or evil spirits; old hag; fascinating or bewitching woman. **witchcraft** use of magic, sorcery; **witch-doctor** sorcerer of primitive people; **witch-hunt** searching out and persecution of supposed witches or per-

sons suspected of unpopular or unorthodox political etc. views.

witchery /'wɪtʃərɪ/ *n.* witchcraft; fascination exercised by beauty or eloquence or the like.

with /wɪð/ *prep.* expr. instrumentality
or means, cause, possession, circumstances, manner, material, agreement and disagreement, company and
parting of company, and antagonism.
with it *colloq.* up to date, (capable of)
understanding new ideas etc.; **with
that** thereupon.

withal /wɪˈðɔːl/ *adv. arch.* moreover;
as well.

withdraw /wɪðˈdrɔː/ *v.* (*past* **-drew**;
*p.p.***-drawn**) pull aside or back; take
away, remove; cancel (statement,
promise, etc.); retire or go apart; in *p.p.*
unsociable. **withdrawal** *n.*

withe /wɪθ/ *n.* tough flexible branch or
shoot, esp. of willow.

wither /'wɪðə(r)/ *v.* make or become
dry or shrivelled; deprive of or lose vigour or freshness etc.; blight with scorn
etc.

withers *n.pl.* ridge between shoulder-
blades of horse etc.

withhold /wɪðˈhəʊld/ *v.t.* (*past* & *p.p.*
-held) refuse to give or grant or allow;
hold back, restrain.

within /wɪˈðɪn/ **1** *adv.* inside; indoors.
2 *prep.* inside; not out of or beyond; not
transgressing or exceeding; not further
off than.

without /wɪˈðaʊt/ **1** *prep.* not having
or feeling or showing; in want of; free
from; in absence of; *arch.* outside. **2**
adv. arch. outside, out-of-doors.

withstand /wɪðˈstænd/ *v.t.* (*past* & *p.p.*
-stood /-stʊd/) hold out against,
oppose.

withy /'wɪðɪ/ *n.* withe.

witless /'wɪtlɪs/ *a.* foolish; crazy.

witness /'wɪtnɪs/ **1** *n.* person giving
sworn testimony; person attesting another's signature to document; person
present, spectator; testimony,
evidence, confirmation; person or
thing whose existence or position etc.
is testimony *to* or proof *of*. **2** *v.* sign
(document) as witness; see, be spectator of; serve as evidence or indication
of; bear witness. **3 bear witness (to)**
give or be evidence (of), be confirmation (of); **witness-box** (*US*

-stand) enclosed space in lawcourt
from which witness gives evidence.

witticism /'wɪtɪsɪz(ə)m/ *n.* witty
remark.

wittingly /'wɪtɪŋlɪ/ *adv.* knowingly,
intentionally.

witty /'wɪtɪ/ *a.* showing verbal wit.

wives *pl.* of **wife**.

wizard /'wɪzəd/ **1** *n.* person of extraordinary powers; magician, conjuror. **2**
a. colloq. wonderful. **3 wizardry** *n.*

wizened /'wɪz(ə)nd/ *a.* of shrivelled or
dried-up appearance.

WO *abbr.* Warrant Officer.

woad *n.* plant yielding a blue dye; the
dye.

wobble /'wɒb(ə)l/ **1** *v.i.* move unsteadily or uncertainly from side to
side or backwards and forwards; rock,
quiver, shake; hesitate, waver. **2** *n.*
wobbling motion. **3 wobbly** *a.*

woe *n.* affliction, bitter grief; in *pl.* ca-
lamities, troubles. **woebegone**
dismal-looking.

woeful /'wəʊfʊl/ *a.* feeling affliction;
afflicting; very bad.

wok *n.* bowl-shaped frying-pan used
esp. in Chinese cookery.

woke, woken, *past* & *p.p.* of **wake**[1].

wold /wəʊld/ *n.* high open uncultivated
or moorland tract.

wolf /wʊlf/ **1** *n.* (*pl.* **wolves**) wild animal related to dog; *sl.* man who pursues
women. **2** *v.t.* devour greedily. **3 cry
wolf** raise false alarm; **keep the wolf
from the door** avert starvation; **wolf-
hound** dog of kind used orig. to hunt
wolves; **wolfsbane** aconite; **wolf-
whistle** whistle expressing man's admiration of woman's appearance.

wolfram /'wʊlfrəm/ *n.* tungsten; tungsten ore.

wolverine /'wʊlvəriːn/ *n.* N. Amer.
animal of weasel family.

woman /'wʊmən/ *n.* (*pl.* **women**
/'wɪmɪn/) adult human female; the female sex; *attrib.* female.

womanhood /'wʊmənhʊd/ *n.* state of
being a woman; womanliness;
womankind.

womanish /'wʊmənɪʃ/ *a.* effeminate,
unmanly.

womanize /'wʊmənaɪz/ *v.i.* (of man)
be promiscuous.

womankind /'wʊmənkaɪnd/ *n.*
women in general.

womanly /ˈwʊmənlɪ/ a. having or showing qualities befitting a woman.

womb /wuːm/ n. organ in female mammals in which child or young is conceived and nourished till birth; place where anything is generated or produced.

wombat /ˈwɒmbæt/ n. burrowing herbivorous Austr. marsupial.

women /ˈwɪmɪn/ pl. of **woman**. **Women's Lib, Liberation**, movement for release of women from subservient status; **women's rights** position of legal and social equality with men.

womenfolk /ˈwɪmɪnfəʊk/ n. women in general; women in family.

won past & p.p. of **win**.

wonder /ˈwʌndə(r)/ 1 n. strange or remarkable thing or specimen or event etc.; emotion excited by what is unexpected or unfamiliar or inexplicable. 2 v. marvel, be affected with wonder; feel doubt or curiosity, be desirous to know or learn. 3 **no wonder** this event is quite natural; **wonderland** fairyland, place of surprises or marvels.

wonderful /ˈwʌndəfʊl/ a. very remarkable or admirable.

wonderment /ˈwʌndəmənt/ n. surprise.

wondrous /ˈwʌndrəs/ poet. 1 a. wonderful. 2 adv. wonderfully.

wonky /ˈwɒŋkɪ/ a. sl. shaky, unsteady; unreliable.

wont /wəʊnt/ arch. 1 a. accustomed, used (to do). 2 n. custom; habit.

won't /wəʊnt/ will not.

wonted /ˈwəʊntɪd/ a. habitual, usual.

woo v. court, seek love of; seek to win, invite.

wood /wʊd/ n. hard compact fibrous substance of tree, whether growing or cut for timber or fuel; growing trees occupying piece of ground; wooden cask used for storing wine etc.; bowl in game of bowls, wooden-headed golf-club. **out of the wood** clear of danger or difficulty etc.; **woodbine** honeysuckle; **woodchuck** N. Amer. marmot; **woodcock** game-bird related to snipe; **woodcut** design cut in relief on wood block, print made from this; **woodland** wooded country; **wood-louse** small land crustacean with many legs; **woodman** forester; **woodpecker** kind of bird pecking holes in tree-trunks etc. to find insects etc.; **wood-pigeon** ringdove; **wood-pulp** wood-fibre prepared as material for paper etc.; **woodwind** wind instruments of orchestra made (orig.) of wood; **woodwork** work done in wood, wooden part (of), esp. wooden interior parts of building; **woodworm** beetle larva that bores in wood.

wooded /ˈwʊdɪd/ a. having woods.

wooden /ˈwʊd(ə)n/ a. made of wood; like wood; stiff or clumsy.

woody /ˈwʊdɪ/ a. wooded; of or like wood.

woof¹ /wʊf/ 1 n. gruff bark of dog. 2 v.i. give woof.

woof² /wuːf/ n. arch. weft.

woofer /ˈwʊfə(r)/ n. loudspeaker for low frequencies.

wool /wʊl/ n. fine soft wavy hair forming fleece of sheep etc.; woollen yarn or cloth or garments; wool-like substance. **woolgathering** absent-mindedness; **Woolsack** Lord Chancellor's seat in House of Lords.

woollen /ˈwʊlən/ 1 a. made (partly) of wool. 2 n. woollen fabric; in pl. woollen garments.

woolly /ˈwʊlɪ/ 1 a. bearing or like wool; indistinct; confused. 2 n. colloq. woollen (esp. knitted) garment.

word /wɜːd/ 1 n. meaningful element of speech usu. shown with space on either side of it when written or printed; speech as opp. action; one's promise or assurance; in sing. or pl. thing said, remark, conversation; in pl. text of song or actor's part; in pl. angry talk; news, message; command, password, motto; unit of expression in computer. 2 v.t. put into words, select words to express. 3 **word-blindness** dyslexia; **word for word** in exactly the same words, literally; **the Word of God** the Bible; **word of honour** assurance given on one's honour; **word of mouth** speech (only); **word-perfect** having memorized one's part etc. perfectly; **word-processor** computer programmed for storing text entered from keyboard, incorporating corrections, and producing printout.

wording /ˈwɜːdɪŋ/ n. form of words used, phrasing.

wordy /ˈwɜːdɪ/ a. using (too) many words; consisting of words.

wore *past* of **wear**.

work /wɜːk/ **1** *n*. application of effort to a purpose, use of energy; task to be undertaken, materials to be used in task; thing done or made by work, result of action; employment esp. as means of earning money; literary or musical composition; in *pl.* all such pieces by an author or composer etc.; doings or experiences of specified kind; things made of specified material or with specified tools etc.; in *pl.* operative part of clock etc.; *sl.* in *pl.* all that is available; in *pl.* operations of building or repair; in *pl.* (often treated as *sing.*) place of manufacture; (usu. in *pl.*) defensive structure. **2** *v.* make efforts, engage in work; be in action, do appointed work; be craftsman *in* material; operate or function, esp. effectively; carry on, manage, control; put or keep in operation or at work; cause to toil; produce as result; knead, hammer, bring to desired shape or consistency; do or make by needlework etc.; (cause to) make way or make (way) slowly or with difficulty; gradually become by motion; excite artificially *into* mood etc.; solve (sum) by mathematics; purchase with labour instead of money; be in motion or agitated, ferment; have influence (*on*, *upon*). **3 workaday** ordinary, everyday, practical; **work-basket** basket etc. for holding sewing materials; **workday** day on which work is usu. done. **work-force** workers engaged or available, number of these; **workhouse** *hist.* public institution for maintenance of paupers; **work in** find place for in composition or structure; **work-load** amount of work to be done; **workman** man hired to do manual labour, craftsman, person who works in specified manner; **workmanlike** showing practised skill; **workmanship** degree of skill in workman or of finish in his product; **workmate** person engaged in same work as another; **work off** get rid of by work or activity; **work out** solve (sum) or find (amount) by calculation, be calculated *at*, have result, provide for all details of; **work-out** practice or test or performance of exercises; **work over** examine thoroughly, *colloq.* treat with violence; **workpeople** people engaged in labour for wages; **workshop** room or building in which manufacture is carried on, place for concerted activity, such activity; **work-shy** disinclined for work, lazy; **work to rule** follow rules of one's occupation with pedantic precision to reduce efficiency as form of protest; **work up** bring gradually to efficient state, advance gradually *to*, elaborate or excite by degrees, learn (subject) by study.

workable /'wɜːkəb(ə)l/ *a.* that can be worked or will work or is worth working. **workability** *n*.

worker /'wɜːkə(r)/ *n.* manual or industrial etc. employee; neuter bee or ant.

working /'wɜːkɪŋ/ **1** *a.* engaged in work, esp. in manual or industrial work; functioning, able to function. **2** *n.* activity of work; functioning; mine or quarry. **3 working capital** capital used in conduct of business, not invested in buildings etc.; **working class** class of those employed for wages, esp. in manual or industrial work; **working day** workday, part of day devoted to work; **working knowledge** knowledge adequate to work with; **working order** condition in which machine works; **working party** committee appointed to advise on some question.

world /wɜːld/ *n.* the earth or a heavenly body like it; the universe, all that exists; time or state or scene of human existence; secular interests and affairs; human affairs, active life; average or respectable people or their customs or opinions; all that concerns or all who belong to specified class or sphere of activity; vast amount *of*. **out of this world** *colloq.* incredibly good etc.; **think the world of** have the highest possible regard for; **world-famous** known throughout the world; **world war** one involving many important nations; **world-wide** covering or known in all parts of the world.

worldly /'wɜːldlɪ/ *a.* temporal, earthly; engrossed in temporal affairs, esp. pursuit of wealth and pleasure. **worldly-wise** prudent as regards one's own interests.

worm /wɜːm/ **1** *n.* any of several types of creeping invertebrate animal with long slender body and no limbs; larva of insect; in *pl.* internal parasites; abject or contemptible person; spiral of screw. **2** *v.* move with crawling or wriggling motion; insinuate *oneself* into favour etc.; draw *out* (secret etc.) by craft. **3 worm-cast** convoluted mass of earth voided by earthworm and left on surface of ground; **worm-eaten** full of holes made by burrowing insect larva.

wormwood /'wɜːmwʊd/ *n.* woody herb with bitter aromatic taste; bitter humiliation; source of this.

wormy /'wɜːmɪ/ *a.* full of worms; worm-eaten.

worn 1 *p.p.* of **wear**. **2** *a.* impaired by use or exposure or wear; looking tired and exhausted.

worry /'wʌrɪ/ **1** *v.* make or be anxious and ill at ease; harass, importune; be trouble or anxiety to; shake or pull about with teeth, kill or injure thus. **2** *n.* thing that causes anxiety or disturbs tranquillity; disturbed state of mind, anxiety. **3 worry beads** string of beads manipulated with fingers to occupy or calm oneself.

worse /wɜːs/ **1** *a.* (*compar.* of **bad**) more bad; in or into worse health; in worse condition. **2** *adv.* (*compar.* of **badly**) more badly or ill. **3** *n.* worse thing(s).

worsen /'wɜːs(ə)n/ *v.* make or become worse.

worship /'wɜːʃɪp/ **1** *n.* homage or service paid to deity; acts or rites or ceremonies displaying this; adoration, devotion. **2** *v.* adore as divine; honour with religious rites; idolize; attend public worship. **3 your, his, Worship** title of respect for magistrate or mayor etc.

worshipful /'wɜːʃɪpfʊl/ *a.* honourable or distinguished (esp. in old titles of companies or officers).

worst /wɜːst/ **1** *a.* (*superl.* of **bad**) most bad. **2** *adv.* (*superl.* of **badly**) in worst manner; to worst degree. **3** *n.* that which is worst. **4** *v.t.* get the better of, defeat. **5 at (the) worst** in the worst possible case; **do one's worst** do the utmost harm possible; **get the worst of** be defeated in; **if the worst comes to the worst** if things fall out as badly as possible or conceivable.

worsted /'wʊstɪd/ *n.* fine woollen yarn; fabric made from this.

wort /wɜːt/ *n.* infusion of malt or other grain before it is fermented into beer.

worth /wɜːθ/ **1** *a.* of value of (specified amount, sum, etc.), equivalent to or good return for; deserving or worthy of; possessed of. **2** *n.* value; equivalent (*of*). **3 worth it** *colloq.* worth while; **worth (one's) while** worth the time or effort spent; **worthwhile** that is worth while.

worthless /'wɜːθlɪs/ *a.* without value or merit.

worthy /'wɜːðɪ/ **1** *a.* estimable, deserving respect; deserving *of*; of sufficient worth or desert or merit etc. (to do). **2** *n.* worthy person; person of some distinction in his country or time etc.

would: see page 667 and **will**. **would-be** vainly aspiring to be.

wound[1] /wuːnd/ **1** *n.* injury done by cut or blow to living tissues; injury to reputation, pain inflicted on feelings. **2** *v.* inflict wound (on).

wound[2] *past* & *p.p.* of **wind**[2].

wove, woven, *past* & *p.p.* of **weave**[1].

wow /waʊ/ **1** *int.* expr. astonishment or admiration. **2** *n. sl.* sensational success. **3** *v.t. sl.* have immense success with.

w.p.b. *abbr.* waste-paper basket.

WPC *abbr.* woman police constable.

w.p.m. *abbr.* words per minute.

WRAC *abbr.* Women's Royal Army Corps.

wrack *n.* seaweed cast up or growing on seashore.

WRAF *abbr.* Women's Royal Air Force.

wraith /reɪθ/ *n.* ghost; spectral appearance of living person supposed to portend his death.

wrangle /'ræŋg(ə)l/ **1** *n.* noisy argument or dispute. **2** *v.i.* engage in wrangle.

wrap 1 *v.* envelop in folded or soft encircling material; arrange or draw (pliant covering) *round* or *about* etc. **2** *n.* shawl or scarf or other such addition to clothing. **3 under wraps** *fig.* in secrecy; **wrap up** finish off (matter), protect oneself from cold with wraps, in *p.p.* engrossed or absorbed *in*.

wrapper /'ræpə(r)/ *n.* paper cover for sweet or book or posted newspaper etc.; loose enveloping robe or gown.

wrapping /'ræpɪŋ/ *n.* (esp. in *pl.*) wraps, wrappers, enveloping garments. **wrapping paper** strong or decorative paper for wrapping parcels.

wrasse /ræs/ n. brilliant-coloured edible sea-fish.

wrath /rɒθ/ n. anger, indignation. **wrathful** a.

wreak v.t. give play to (vengeance etc.) (up)on; cause (damage etc.).

wreath /riːθ/ n. (pl. pr. /riːðz/) flowers or leaves wound together into ring esp. as ornament for head or building or for laying on grave etc.; curl or ring of smoke or cloud etc.

wreathe /riːð/ v. encircle as or (as) with wreath; wind (flexible object) round or over something; move in wreathlike shape.

wreck 1 n. destruction or disablement, esp. of ship; ship that has suffered wreck; greatly damaged or disabled building or thing or person. 2 v. cause wreck of (ship, hopes, etc.); suffer wreck; in p.p. involved in wreck.

wreckage /ˈrekɪdʒ/ n. wrecked material; remnants of wreck.

wrecker /ˈrekə(r)/ n. person who tries from shore to bring about shipwreck in order to plunder or profit by wreckage.

wren[1] n. small short-winged usu. brown song-bird.

Wren[2] n. member of WRNS.

wrench 1 n. violent twist or pull or turn; tool for gripping and turning nuts etc.; fig. pain caused by parting etc. 2 v.t. twist, turn; pull (away, off, etc.) violently or with effort; injure or pain by straining or stretching.

wrest v.t. twist, distort, pervert; force or wrench away from person's grasp.

wrestle /ˈres(ə)l/ 1 n. contest in which two opponents grapple and try to throw each other to ground; tussle, hard struggle. 2 v. have wrestling-match (with); struggle with or against; do one's utmost to deal with.

wretched /ˈretʃɪd/ a. unhappy or miserable; of bad quality or no merit; contemptible, unsatisfactory or displeasing.

wriggle /ˈrɪg(ə)l/ 1 v. twist or turn body about with short writhing movements; move or make way etc. with wriggling motion; be slippery, practise evasion. 2 n. wriggling movement.

wring 1 v.t. (past & p.p. **wrung**) press, squeeze or twist, esp. so as to drain or

make dry; distress, rack; extort, get (money, concession) out of or from by exaction or importunity; clasp (person's hand) forcibly or with emotion. 2 n. act of wringing. 3 **wringing wet** so wet that water can be wrung out; **wring one's hands** clasp them as gesture of grief; **wring neck of** (chicken etc.) kill it by twisting head.

wringer /ˈrɪŋə(r)/ n. device for wringing water from washed clothes etc.

wrinkle /ˈrɪŋk(ə)l/ 1 n. crease or furrow of skin or other flexible surface; colloq. useful hint, clever expedient. 2 v. make wrinkles in; form wrinkles. 3 **wrinkly** a.

wrist n. joint connecting hand and forearm; part of garment covering wrist. **wrist-watch** small watch worn on strap etc. round wrist.

wristlet /ˈrɪstlɪt/ n. band or ring worn on wrist to strengthen it or as ornament or to hold watch etc.

writ n. formal written court order to do or refrain from doing specified act.

write v. (past **wrote**; p.p. **written**) mark paper or other surface with symbols, letters, or words; form or mark (such symbols etc.); form or mark symbols of (word or document etc.); fill or complete with writing; put (data) into computer store; engage in writing or authorship; produce writing; convey (message etc.) by letter. **write down** set down in writing, write in disparagement or depreciation of, reduce to lower amount; **write off** cancel (debt etc.), reckon as lost; **write-off** vehicle etc. so damaged as not to be worth repair; **write up** write full account of, praise in writing; **write-up** laudatory description in newspaper etc.

writer /ˈraɪtə(r)/ n. person who writes, esp. author. **writer's cramp** muscular spasm due to excessive writing.

writhe /raɪð/ v. twist or roll oneself about (as) in acute pain; suffer mental torture.

writing /ˈraɪtɪŋ/ n. handwriting; written document; in pl. writer's works. **in writing** in written form.

written p.p. of **write**.

WRNS abbr. Women's Royal Naval Service.

wrong 1 a. mistaken; not true; in error; unsuitable, less or least desirable; contrary to law or morality; amiss, out of order. **2** *adv.* in wrong direction or manner, with incorrect result. **3** *n.* what is morally wrong; wrong or unjust action. **4** *v.t.* treat unjustly; mistakenly attribute bad motives to. **5 go wrong** take wrong path, get out of working order, cease virtuous behaviour; **in the wrong** responsible for quarrel or mistake or offence; **wrongdoer** person guilty of breach of law or morality; **wrong-doing** *n.*; **wrong-headed** perverse and obstinate; **wrong side** worse or undesirable or unusable side; **wrong way round**, in opposite of normal orientation.

wrongful /ˈrɒŋfʊl/ *a.* unwarranted, unjustified.

wrote *past* of **write**.

wroth /rəʊθ/ *a. arch.* angry.

wrought /rɔːt/ *arch. past* & *p.p.* of **work**. **wrought iron** tough malleable form of iron suitable for forging or rolling, not cast.

wrung *past* & *p.p.* of **wring**.

WRVS *abbr.* Women's Royal Voluntary Service.

wry /raɪ/ *a.* distorted, turned to one side; contorted in disgust or disappointment or mockery; (of humour) dry and mocking. **wryneck** small bird able to turn head over shoulder.

wt. *abbr.* weight.

wych- /wɪtʃ/ *pref.* in names of trees etc. with pliant branches. **wych-hazel** N. Amer. shrub, astringent extract of its bark.

X

X, x, *n.* Roman numeral 10; first unknown quantity in algebra; cross-shaped symbol esp. used to indicate position or incorrectness, or to symbolize kiss or vote, or as signature of person who cannot write.

xenophobia /zenəˈfəʊbɪə/ *n.* morbid dislike of foreigners.

Xerox /ˈzɪərɒks/ 1 *n.* (**P**) a dry copying process; copy so made. **2** *v.t.* **xerox** reproduce by this process.

Xmas *abbr.* Christmas.

X-ray /ˈeksreɪ/ 1 *n.* in *pl.* electromagnetic radiation of short wavelength, able to pass through opaque bodies; in *sing.* photograph made by X-rays. **2** *v.t.* photograph or examine or treat with X-rays.

xylophone /ˈzaɪləfəʊn/ *n.* musical instrument of graduated wooden bars struck with hammer(s).

Y

Y, y, *n.* second unknown quantity in algebra; Y-shaped thing.

yacht /jɒt/ 1 *n.* light sailing-vessel; larger usu. power-driven vessel used for private pleasure excursions and cruising etc. **2** *v.i.* race or cruise in yacht. **3 yacht-club** club for yacht-racing; **yachtsman** person who yachts.

yah *int.* of derision, defiance, etc.

yahoo /jəˈhuː/ *n.* bestial person.

yak *n.* long-haired Tibetan ox.

yam *n.* tropical or subtropical climbing plant; edible starchy tuberous root of this; sweet potato.

yank[1] *n. & v.* pull with a jerk.

Yank[2] *n. colloq.* (also **Yankee**) inhabitant of US, American; *US* inhabitant of New England or of northern States of USA.

yap 1 *v.i.* bark shrilly or fussily; *colloq.* talk noisily or foolishly. **2** *n.* sound of yapping.

yapp *n.* limp-leather book-binding with overlapping edges or flaps.

yard[1] *n.* linear measure of 3 ft. (0.9144 m.); this length of material; square or cubic yard; spar slung across mast for sail to hang from. **yard-arm** either end of ship's yard; **yardstick** rod a yard long usu. divided into inches etc., standard of comparison.

yard[2] *n.* piece of enclosed ground, esp. surrounded by or attached to build-

ing(s) or used for particular purpose;
US garden of house.

yardage /ˈjɑːdɪdʒ/ *n.* number of yards
of material etc.

yarmulka /ˈjɑːmʌlkə/ *n.* skull-cap
worn by Jewish man.

yarn 1 *n.* fibre spun and prepared for
weaving or knitting etc.; *colloq.* story,
tale. 2 *v.i. colloq.* tell yarns.

yarrow /ˈjærəʊ/ *n.* kind of perennial
herb, esp. milfoil.

yashmak /ˈjæʃmæk/ *n.* veil concealing face except eyes, worn by some
Muslim women.

yaw 1 *v.i.* (of ship, aircraft, spacecraft)
fail to hold straight course, go unsteadily. 2 *n.* yawing of ship etc. from course.

yawl *n.* kind of ship's boat or sailing- or
fishing-boat.

yawn 1 *v.i.* open the mouth wide and
inhale esp. in sleepiness or boredom;
(of chasm etc.) gape, be wide open. 2 *n.*
act of yawning.

yaws *n.pl.* (usu. treated as *sing.*) contagious tropical skin-disease.

yd(s). *abbr.* yard(s).

ye *pron. arch. & of* **thou**.

yea /jeɪ/ *adv. & n. arch.* yes.

yeah /jeə/ *adv. colloq.* yes.

year *n.* time occupied by one revolution
of earth round sun (about 365¼ days);
period from 1 Jan. to 31 Dec. inclusive,
any period of 12 calendar months; in *pl.*
age, old age; (usu. in *pl.*) period, times,
a very long time. **year-book** annual
publication bringing information on
some subject up to date.

yearling /ˈjɪəlɪŋ/ *n.* animal between 1
and 2 years old.

yearly /ˈjɪəlɪ/ 1 *a.* done or produced or
occurring once every year; of or for or
lasting a year. 2 *adv.* once every year.

yearn /jɜːn/ *v.i.* be filled with longing
or compassion or tenderness.

yeast *n.* greyish-yellow fungous substance, got esp. from fermenting malt
liquors and used as fermenting agent
and in raising bread etc.

yeasty /ˈjiːstɪ/ *a.* frothy; in a ferment;
working like yeast.

yell 1 *n.* sharp loud outcry of strong and
sudden emotion; shout of pain or anger
or laughter etc. 2 *v.* make or utter with
yell.

yellow /ˈjeləʊ/ 1 *a.* of the colour of gold
or lemons or buttercups etc.; having

yellow skin or complexion; *colloq.* cowardly. 2 *n.* yellow colour or paint or
clothes etc. 3 *v.* turn yellow. 4 **yellow
fever** tropical fever with jaundice etc.;
yellowhammer bunting with bright-
yellow head and throat etc.; **yellow
pages** section of telephone directory on
yellow paper and listing business subscribers according to goods or services
they offer; **yellow streak** trace of
cowardice.

yelp 1 *n.* sharp shrill bark or cry (as) of
dog in excitement or pain etc. 2 *v.i.* utter yelp.

yen[1] *n.* (*pl.* same) Japanese monetary
unit.

yen[1] 1 *n.* intense desire or longing. 2 *v.i.*
feel longing.

yeoman /ˈjəʊmən/ *n.* (*pl.* -men) man
owning and farming small estate; member of yeomanry force. **Yeoman of the
Guard** member of bodyguard of English sovereign, now acting chiefly as
warders of Tower of London; **yeoman
service** efficient or useful help in need.

yeomanry /ˈjəʊmənrɪ/ *n.* body of yeo-
men; *hist.* volunteer cavalry force in
British army.

yes /jes/ *adv.* expr. affirmative reply to
question or command etc. 2 *n.* the word
yes. 3 **yes-man** *colloq.* person who en-
dorses or supports all opinions or pro-
posals of a superior.

yesterday /ˈjestədeɪ/ 1 *adv.* on the day
before today. 2 *n.* the day before today.

yet 1 *adv.* up to this or that time; (with
neg. or interrog.) as soon as or by now
or then; again, in addition; in the time
that remains before the matter ends;
(with compar.) even; nevertheless, and
or but in spite of that. 2 *conj.* but nevertheless. 3 **as yet** hitherto; **not yet** still
not, not by this or that time.

yeti /ˈjetɪ/ *n.* unidentified anthropoid or
ursine animal in Himalayas.

yew *n.* dark-leaved evergreen coniferous tree; its wood.

Yiddish /ˈjɪdɪʃ/ 1 *n.* language used by
Jews in or from Europe. 2 *a.* of this
language.

yield /jiːld/ 1 *v.* produce or return as
fruit or profit or result; surrender or
make submission (*to*); concede; give
way *to* persuasion or entreaty etc., give
consent; give right of way (*to*). 2 *n.*
amount yielded or produced.

yippee /'jɪpiː/ *int.* expr. delight or excitement.

YMCA *abbr.* Young Men's Christian Association.

yob *n.* (also **yobbo**, *pl.* **-os**) *sl.* lout, hooligan.

yodel /'jəʊd(ə)l/ 1 *v.* sing with melodious inarticulate sounds and frequent changes between falsetto and normal voice, in manner of Swiss mountain-dwellers. 2 *n.* yodelling cry.

yoga /'jəʊgə/ *n.* Hindu system of meditation and asceticism etc.; system of physical exercises and breathing control used in yoga.

yoghurt /'jɒgət/ *n.* semi-solid sourish food made from milk fermented by added bacteria.

yogi /'jəʊgɪ/ *n.* devotee of yoga.

yoicks *int.* used in foxhunting to urge on hounds.

yoke 1 *n.* wooden cross-piece fastened over necks of two oxen etc. and attached to plough or wagon to be drawn; pair *of* oxen etc.; object like yoke in form or function, e.g. wooden shoulder-piece for carrying pair of pails; top part of dress or skirt etc., from which the rest hangs; sway or dominion or servitude; bond of union esp. of marriage. 2 *v.* put yoke on; couple or unite (pair); link (one *to* another); match or work together.

yokel /'jəʊk(ə)l/ *n.* country bumpkin.

yolk /jəʊk/ *n.* yellow internal part of egg.

yon *arch.* 1 *a.* & *adv.* yonder. 2 *pron.* yonder person or thing.

yonder /'jɒndə(r)/ 1 *adv.* over there; at some distance (but within sight). 2 *a.* situated yonder.

yore *n. literary* **of yore** in or of time long past.

york *v.t. Crick.* bowl out with yorker.

yorker /'jɔːkə(r)/ *n. Crick.* ball that pitches immediately under the bat.

Yorkist /'jɔːkɪst/ 1 *a.* of House of York or its supporters in Wars of the Roses. 2 *n.* Yorkist person.

Yorkshire /'jɔːkʃə(r)/ *n.* **Yorkshire pudding** light baked batter pudding usu. eaten with or before roast meat; **Yorkshire terrier** small long-haired terrier.

you *pron.* (*obj.* same, *poss.* **your**) 2nd pers. sing. and pl. pronoun; the person(s) or thing(s) addressed; (in general statements) one, a person.

young /jʌŋ/ 1 *a.* not far advanced in life or development or existence; not yet old; immature, inexperienced; characteristic of youth. 2 *n. collect.* offspring esp. of animals before or soon after birth.

youngster /'jʌŋstə(r)/ *n.* child, young person.

your /jɔː(r)/ *pron. poss.* case of **you**, with absol. form **yours**.

yourself /jɔː'self/ *pron.* (*pl.* **-selves**) *emphat.* & *refl.* form of **you**.

youth /juːθ/ *n.* (*pl. pr.* /juːðz/) being young; early part of life, esp. adolescence; the young; young man; quality or condition characteristic of the young. **youth club** place for young people's leisure activities; **youth hostel** place where (esp. young) holiday-makers etc. can put up cheaply for the night.

youthful /'juːθfʊl/ *a.* young or having characteristics of youth.

yowl /jaʊl/ 1 *n.* loud wailing cry (as) of cat or dog in distress. 2 *v.i.* utter yowl.

Yo-yo /'jəʊjəʊ/ *n.*(P) (*pl.* **-yos**) toy consisting of pair of discs with deep groove between them in which string is attached and wound, and which can be made to fall and rise.

yr. *abbr.* year(s); younger; your.

yrs. *abbr.* years; yours.

yucca /'jʌkə/ *n.* white-flowered garden plant.

Yugoslav /'juːgəslɑːv/ 1 *a.* of Yugoslavia. 2 *n.* native or inhabitant of Yugoslavia.

yule *n.* festival of Christmas. **yule-log** large log burnt at Christmas; **yule-tide** period of yule.

yummy /'jʌmɪ/ *a. colloq.* tasty, delicious.

YWCA *abbr.* Young Women's Christian Association.

Z

zabaglione /zɑːbɑːlɪˈəʊnɪ/ n. Italian sweet of whipped and heated egg yolks and sugar and wine.

zany /ˈzeɪnɪ/ 1 a. comically idiotic; crazily ridiculous. 2 n. buffoon, simpleton.

zap v.t. sl. hit, attack, kill.

zeal n. ardour or eagerness in pursuit of end or in favour of person or cause. **zealous** /ˈzeləs/ a.

zealot /ˈzelət/ n. extreme partisan, fanatic.

zebra /ˈzebrə or ˈziː-/ n. African striped horselike animal. **zebra crossing** striped street-crossing where pedestrians have precedence.

zebu /ˈziːbuː/ n. humped ox domesticated in India etc.

Zen n. form of Buddhism emphasizing value of meditation and intuition.

zenana /zɪˈnɑːnə/ n. part of house for seclusion of women of high-caste families in India and Iran.

zenith /ˈzenɪθ/ n. point of heavens directly overhead; highest point or state, culmination.

zephyr /ˈzefə(r)/ n. soft mild gentle wind or breeze.

zero /ˈzɪərəʊ/ 1 n. (pl. -os) figure 0, nought, nil; point marked 0 on graduated scale, esp. in thermometer etc.; lowest point, bottom of scale; (in full **zero-hour**) hour at which planned (esp. military) operation is timed to begin, crucial or decisive moment. 2 v.i. **zero in on** take aim at, focus attention on.

zest n. piquancy; keen interest or enjoyment, relish, gusto; orange or lemon peel.

zigzag /ˈzɪɡzæɡ/ 1 n. succession of straight lines with abrupt alternate right and left turns. 2 a. with abrupt alternate right and left turns. 3 adv. in zigzag manner or course. 4 v.i. move in zigzag course.

zillion /ˈzɪlɪən/ n. colloq. indefinite large number.

zinc n. hard bluish-white metallic element.

zing colloq. 1 n. vigour, energy. 2 v.i. move swiftly or shrilly.

zinnia /ˈzɪnɪə/ n. garden plant with showy flowers.

zip 1 n. colloq. light sharp sound; energy, force, impetus; zip-fastener. 2 v. close or fasten (up) with zip-fastener; move or go with sound of zip or with great rapidity or force. 3 **zip-fastener** fastening device of two flexible strips with interlocking projections closed and opened by sliding clip pulled along them.

zipper /ˈzɪpə(r)/ n. zip-fastener.

zircon /ˈzɜːkən/ n. translucent crystalline native silicate of zirconium used as gem.

zirconium /zɜːˈkəʊnɪəm/ n. grey metallic element.

zither /ˈzɪðə(r)/ n. musical instrument with flat sound-box and many strings, held horizontally and played by plucking.

zodiac /ˈzəʊdɪæk/ n. belt of the heavens including all apparent positions of sun and planets as known to ancient astronomers, and divided into 12 equal parts called **signs of the zodiac**. **zodiacal** /zəʊˈdaɪək(ə)l/ a.

zombie /ˈzɒmbɪ/ n. corpse said to be revived by witchcraft; colloq. dull or apathetic person.

zone 1 n. area having particular features or properties or purpose or use; any well-defined region of more or less beltlike form; area between two concentric circles; encircling band of colour etc.; arch. girdle or belt. 2 v.t. encircle as or with zone; arrange or distribute by zones; assign to specific area. 3 **zonal** a.

zoo n. zoological garden.

zoological /zəʊəˈlɒdʒɪk(ə)l or zuː-/ a. of zoology. **zoological garden(s)** public garden or park with collection of animals for exhibition and study.

zoology /zəʊˈɒlədʒɪ or zuː-/ n. scientific study of animals. **zoologist** n.

zoom /zuːm/ 1 v.i. move quickly, esp. with buzzing sound; cause aeroplane to mount at high speed and steep angle;

(of camera) change (esp. quickly) from long shot to close-up. **2** *n.* aeroplane's steep climb. **3 zoom lens** lens allowing camera to zoom by varying focus.

zoophyte /ˈzəʊəfaɪt/ *n.* animal resembling plant or flower in form.

zucchini /zuːˈkiːnɪ/ *n.* (*pl.* same or **-nis**) courgette.

zygote /ˈzaɪɡəʊt/ *n.* cell formed by union of two gametes.

APPENDICES

Some points of English usage

What follows is intended as guidance on a number of uses that, although widely found, are the subject of adverse comment by informed users. They should be avoided, especially in formal speech or writing. For further information see *The Oxford Guide* or *Miniguide to English Usage*.

1 Pronunciation

The following words are often mispronounced:

comparable	/ˈkɒmpərəb(ə)l/	not /kəmˈpær-/
contribute	/kənˈtrɪbjuːt/	not /ˈkɒn-/
controversy	/ˈkɒntrəvɜːsɪ/	is preferable to /kənˈtrɒv-/
deity	/ˈdiːɪtɪ/	not /ˈdeɪ-/
dispute	/dɪˈspjuːt/	not /ˈdɪs-/
distribute	/dɪˈstrɪbjuːt/	not /ˈdɪs-/
exquisite	/ˈekskwɪzɪt/	not /ɪksˈkwɪz-/
formidable	/ˈfɔːmɪdəb(ə)l/	not /fəˈmɪd-/
harass(ment)	/ˈhærəs/	not /həˈræs/
irreparable	/ɪˈrepərəb(ə)l/	not /ɪrɪˈpær-/
irrevocable	/ɪˈrevəkəb(ə)l/	not /ɪrɪˈvəʊk-/
kilometre	/ˈkɪləmiːtə/	not /kɪˈlɒm-/
lamentable	/ˈlæmɪntəb(ə)l/	not /ləˈment-/
necessarily	/ˈnesɪsərɪlɪ/	not /nesɪˈse-/
preferable	/ˈprefərəb(ə)l/	not /prɪˈfɜːrəb(ə)l/
primarily	/ˈpraɪmərɪlɪ/	not /praɪˈmer-/
reputable	/ˈrepjʊtəb(ə)l/	not /rɪˈpjuːt-/
surveillance	/sɜːˈveɪləns/	not /səˈveɪjəns/
temporarily	/ˈtempərərɪlɪ/	not /tempəˈre-/
trait	/treɪ/	not /treɪt/

2 Spellings

Avoid these common misspellings:

alright the correct form is **all right**,
barbeque the correct form is **barbecue**,
onto the correct form is **on to**,
'til the correct form is **till**, (it is not a contraction of **until**).

3 Meanings

The following words are often misused:

alibi is not a synonym for 'excuse'.

anticipate is not a synonymn for 'expect'.

decimate means 'destroy or kill one tenth of' and should not be used as if it meant 'destroy or kill most of'.

dilemma is not a synonym for 'problem'.

disinterested does not mean 'uninterested'.

enormity does not mean 'large size'.

fulsome is not a synonym for 'full' or 'copious'.

parameter does not mean 'limit'.

pristine does not mean 'pure' or 'fresh'.

protagonist does not mean 'advocate' or 'champion'.

refute is not a synonym for 'repudiate' or 'deny'.

transpire does not mean 'happen'.

The following words have strong meanings and should not be used when a weaker word is meant:

crucial should not be used if 'important' will do.

unique does not just mean 'unusual', and a thing cannot be 'more unique' than another.

3.1 *Pairs.* Do not confuse:

> alternate *and* alternative
> comprise *and* compose
> deprecate *and* depreciate
> derisive *and* derisory
> flaunt *and* flount
> infer *and* imply
> militate *and* mitigate
> practice *and* practise
> seasonable *and* seasonal

4 Plurals

Aborigines is a plural noun but there is no singular *Aborigine*; use **Aboriginal**.

bacteria is the plural of **bacterium**.

criteria is the plural of **criterion**.

data is the plural of **datum**.

graffiti is the plural of **graffito**.

media is the plural of **medium**.

referendums is the recommended plural of **referendum**, not *referenda*.

strata is the plural of **stratum**.

None of these should be used with a singular verb.

5 Grammar

The following points often cause confusion:

less means 'a smaller amount or quantity of' and is used with mass nouns such as *money* or *porridge*, whereas

fewer means 'a smaller number of' and is used with plural, countable nouns such as *people* or *buttons*.

shall and **will** should be used in the following way:

To express the simple future use

> I/we **shall**
> you **will**
> he/she/it/they **will**
> as in 'I shall be at home tomorrow'; 'he will arrive later'.

To express an intention or determination use

> I/we **will**
> you **shall**
> he/she/it/they **shall**
> as in 'I will be heard'; 'you shall go to the ball'.

The same rule applies to **should** and **would**.

like should not be used as a conjunction, as in *do like I say*, *not like I do*; use **as**.

APPENDIX II

Countries of the world and related adjectives

Afghanistan /æf'gænɪstɑːn/, Afghan /'æfgæn/
Albania /æl'beɪnɪə/, Albanian
Algeria /æl'dʒɪərɪə/, Algerian
American: see United States of America
Andorra /æn'dɒrə/, Andorran
Angola /æŋ'gəʊlə/, Angolan
Antigua and Barbuda /æn'tiːgə, bɑːˈbuːdə/, Antiguan /æn'tiːgən/, Barbudan
Argentina /ɑːdʒənˈtiːnə/, Argentine /'ɑːdʒəntaɪn/ or Argentinian /ɑːdʒənˈtɪnɪən/
Australia /ɔːˈstreɪlɪə/, Australian
Austria /'ɔːstrɪə/, Austrian
Bahamas, the /bə'hɑːməz/, Bahamian /bə'heɪmɪən/
Bahrein /bɑːˈreɪn/, Bahreini
Bangladesh /bæŋgləˈdeʃ/, Bangladeshi
Barbados /bɑːˈbeɪdəs/, Barbadian
Belgium /'beldʒ(ə)m/, Belgian
Belize /be'liːz/, Belizean
Benin /be'niːn/, Beninese /benɪ'niːz/
Bhutan /buːˈtɑːn/, Bhutanese /buːtə'niːz/
Bolivia /bə'lɪvɪə/, Bolivian
Botswana /bɒt'swɑːnə/
Brazil /brə'zɪl/, Brazilian
British: see United Kingdom
Brunei /'bruːnaɪ/, Bruneian /bruːˈnaɪən/
Bulgaria /bʌl'geərɪə/, Bulgarian
Burkina /bɜːˈkiːnə/, Burkinan
Burma /'bɜːmə/, Burmese /bɜːˈmiːz/
Burundi /bʊ'rʌndɪ/, Burundian
Cambodia /kæm'bəʊdɪə/, Cambodian
Cameroon /kæmə'ruːn/, Cameroonian
Canada /'kænədə/, Canadian /kə'neɪdɪən/
Cape Verde /keɪp vɜːd/, Cape Verdean
Central African Republic

Chad /'tʃæd/, Chadian /'tʃædɪən/
Chile /'tʃɪlɪ/, Chilean
China /'tʃaɪnə/, Chinese /tʃaɪ'ni:z/
Colombia /kə'lʌmbɪə/, Colombian
Comoros /kə'mɔ:rəʊz/, Comoran
Congo /'kɒŋgəʊ/, Congolese /kɒŋgə'li:z/
Costa Rica /'kɒstə 'ri:kə/, Costa Rican
Cuba /'kju:bə/, Cuban
Cyprus /'saɪprəs/, Cypriot /'sɪprɪət/
Czechoslovakia /tʃekəʊslə'vækɪə/, Czech /tʃek/ or **Czechoslovak**
    /tʃekə'sləʊvæk/ or Czechoslovakian
Denmark /'denmɑ:k/, Danish /'deɪnɪʃ/
Djibouti /dʒɪ'bu:tɪ/
Dominica /dɒmɪ'ni:kə/, Dominican /dɒmɪ'ni:kən/
Dominican Republic /də'mɪnɪkən/, Dominican /də'mɪnɪkən/
Dutch: see Netherlands, the
Ecuador /'ekwədɔ:(r)/, Ecuadorean /ekwə'dɔ:rɪən/
Egypt /'i:dʒɪpt/, Egyptian /ɪ'dʒɪpʃ(ə)n/
El Salvador /el 'sælvədɔ:(r)/, Salvadorean /sælvə'dɔ:rɪən/
England /'ɪŋglənd/, English /'ɪŋglɪʃ/
Equatorial Guinea /'gɪnɪ/
Ethiopia /'i:θɪ'əʊpɪə/, Ethiopian
Fiji /'fi:dʒi:/, Fijian
Filipino: see Philippines, the
Finland /'fɪnlənd/, Finnish /'fɪnɪʃ/
France /'frɑ:ns/, French /frentʃ/
Gabon /gæ'bɒn/, Gabonese /gæbə'ni:z/
Gambia /'gæmbɪə/, Gambian
German Democratic Republic /'dʒɜ:mən/, East German
Germany, Federal Republic of /'dʒɜ:mənɪ/, West German
Ghana /'gɑ:nə/, Ghanaian /gɑ:'neɪən/
Greece /gri:s/, Greek
Grenada /grə'neɪdə/, Grenadian
Guatemala /gwætɪ'mɑ:lə/, Guatemalan
Guinea /'gɪnɪ/, Guinean /'gɪnɪən/
Guinea-Bissau /gɪnɪ'bɪsaʊ/
Guyana /gaɪ'ɑ:nə/, Guyanese /gaɪə'ni:z/
Haiti /'haɪtɪ/, Haitian /'haɪʃ(ə)n/
Honduras /hɒn'djʊərəs/, Honduran
Hungary /'hʌŋgərɪ/, Hungarian /hʌŋ'geərɪən/

Iceland /'aɪslənd/, Icelandic /aɪs'lændɪk/
India /'ɪndɪə/, Indian
Indonesia /ɪndə'niːʒə/, Indonesian
Iran /ɪ'rɑːn/, Iranian /ɪ'reɪnɪən/
Iraq /ɪ'rɑːk/, Iraqi /ɪ'rɑːkɪ/
Irish Republic /'aɪərɪʃ/, Irish
Israel /'ɪzreɪl/, Israeli /ɪz'reɪlɪ/
Italy /'ɪtəlɪ/, Italian /ɪ'tælɪən/
Ivory Coast /'aɪvərɪ kəʊst/
Jamaica /dʒə'meɪkə/, Jamaican
Japan /dʒə'pæn/, Japanese /dʒæpə'niːz/
Jordan /'dʒɔːd(ə)n/, Jordanian /dʒɔː'deɪnɪən/
Kenya /'kenjə/, Kenyan
Kiribati /'kɪrɪbæs/, i-Kiribati
Korea /kə'rɪə/, Korean
Kuwait /kʊ'weɪt/, Kuweiti
Laos /'lɑːɒs/, Laotian /lɑː'əʊʃ(ə)n/
Lebanon /'lebənən/, Lebanese /lebə'niːz/
Lesotho /lə'səʊtəʊ/
Liberia /laɪ'bɪərɪə/, Liberian
Libya /'lɪbɪə/, Libyan
Liechtenstein /'lɪktənstaɪn/
Luxembourg /'lʌksəmbɜːg/
Madagascar /mædə'gæskə(r)/, Malagasy /mælə'gæsɪ/
Malawi /mə'lɑːwɪ/, Malawian
Malaysia /mə'leɪzɪə/, Malaysian
Maldives, the /'mɔːldɪvz/, Maldivian
Mali /'mɑːlɪ/, Malian
Malta /'mɔːltə/, Maltese /mɔːl'tiːz/
Mauritania /mɒrɪ'teɪnɪə/, Mauritanian
Mauritius /mə'rɪʃəs/, Mauritian
Mexico /'meksɪkəʊ/, Mexican
Monaco /'mɒnəkəʊ/, Monegasque /mɒnɪ'gæsk/
Mongolia /mɒŋ'gəʊlɪə/, Mongolian
Morocco /mə'rɒkəʊ/, Moroccan
Mozambique /məʊzæm'biːk/, Mozambican /məʊzəm'biːkən/
Nauru /nɑː'ʊruː/, Nauruan
Nepal /nə'pɔːl/, Nepalese /nepə'liːz/
Netherlands, the /'neðələndz/, Dutch
New Zealand /'ziːlənd/